History *of* Fayette County Alabama

Compiled & Edited
by:
Herbert Moses Newell, Jr. and
Mrs. H.M. (Jeanie Patterson) Newell, Jr.

Southern Historical Press, Inc.
Greenville, S.C. 29601

This volume was reproduced from
an 1960 edition located in the
Publisher's private library
Greenville, South Carolina

Please direct all correspondence and book orders to:
**Southern Historical Press, Inc.
PO Box 1267
375 West Broad Street
Greenville, S.C. 29602-1267**

Originally printed & ©: Fayette, AL. 1960
Reprinted with permission by:
    Southern Historical Press, Inc.
    Greenville, S.C. 29601
ISBN #0-89308-811-0
Printed in the United States of America

Publishers Note

Due to the nature of the original printing, we have made every effort to reproduce this book in the highest quality as possible. There are a few light spots/pages that we have given extra effort to make legible for the reader but several will remain light or faint. Thank you for your understanding and happy reading.

LOVINGLY DEDICATED

To Our Parents

Mr. & Mrs. Victor Samuel Patterson, Sr.

Mr. & Mrs. Herbert Moses Newell, Sr.

and

Our Son

Herbert Moses Newell, III

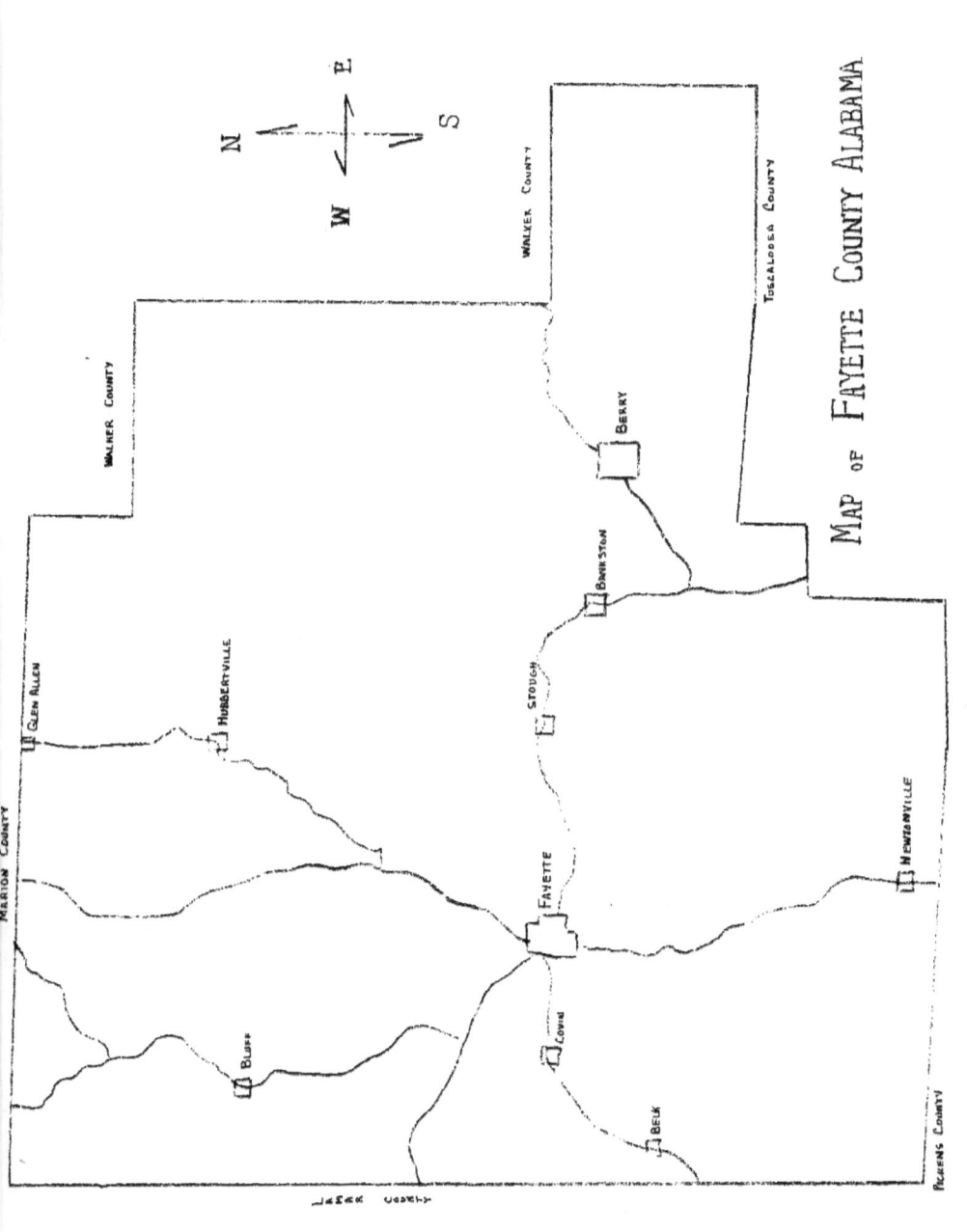

PREFACE

This volume is published in the hope that it will fix in the reader's memory those of Fayette County, both living and dead, who have contributed to the development and growth of Fayette County, Alabama. Much valuable material has, of necessity, from lack of space, had to be deleted. We have tried to preserve the most vital facts and information. The compilers and editors, in presenting this volume to the public, realize there may be errors, typographically and from material that was contributed, but we have tried to check all data as thoroughly as possible to eliminate the errors. (If the readers find errors, please bear in mind that this work has been "free gratis" so far as our months and years of labor is concerned and we welcome anyone to the task of doing better.)

We have labored to collect the material matter and data recorded herein, most of which, in the course of time, would have been lost in tradition. This material has been collected over a period of many years and we sincerely hope that it will be a heritage to our younger generations. If our effort along this line meet with the approval of a generous public, we will feel more than gratified.

We are most grateful to Mrs. Roy (Frankie Nuckols) Martin, daughter of Mr. & Mrs. Frank Arthur Nuckols, for reading our material and for the data she contributed. Mrs. Martin made many helpful suggestions. She is to be admired ofr her inspiration to others in preserving family records.

For the many favors and courtesies, which we have received in the preparation of this volume, we extend our grateful thanks, with special appreciation to: Mrs. Peggy England, Mrs. Jessie Peters, Mrs. A. M. Nix (deceased) Mrs. J. E. Hooker, Mrs. David Wright, Mrs. G. W. Wages, Mrs. Joe Gibson, Mrs. Willie Mayfield, Mrs. Roy Renfroe, Mrs. Blanche Roberts, Mrs. John D. Hassell, Mr. Wiley Hollingsworth, Mrs. Snow Hamner, Mrs. Dorothy Traweek, The Family of Mr. M. L. Coons, Mrs. Floy Collins, Mrs. J. T. Hurst, Hon. Carl Elliott, Mr. Douglas Barbour for radio publicity, Mr. Lewis Mitchell for newspaper publicity, Mr. Peter A. Brannon, for State Archives Permission, Mrs. Ruby Alexander, Mrs. Maggie Davis, Mrs. A. K. Callahan, Mrs. Lucy Crutcher, Mrs. Frankie Martin's high school students, Miss Irene White, Mr. Roy Martin, Mr. Lloyd Humber, Mr. Charlie Jones, Mr. Marcellus Doughty, Mrs. Jeff R. Robertson, Mrs. Theron Cannon, and the many other, too numerous to name, who responded with personal, business and civic material.

Our deepest gratitude to Herbie Newell, III, for his patience and sweet disposition while his parents spent at least 3 of his 3½ years, to date, in research and typing, and to Allen Grocholski for giving his 1959 summer vacation time to entertain Herbie.

Herbert and Jeanie Patterson Newell

TABLE OF CONTENTS

MAP OF FAYETTE COUNTY -- i

PREFACE --- ii

CHAPTER I - EARLY HISTORY AND PIONEER SETTLEMENT ---------------------- 1
Rivers, Soil, Resources, Early Homes, Heads of Household
(1830 - 1840 Federal Census Index)

CHAPTER II - TOWNS AND COMMUNITIES ----------------------------------- 12

CHAPTER III - ECONOMIC DEVELOPMENTS ---------------------------------- 34
Rivers and Canals, Roads, Frontier Trade, Railroads, Mail
Service and Post Offices, Private Business, Industry,
Banking, Public Services, etc.

CHAPTER IV - GOVERNMENT -- 68
Court Houses, Circuit Clerks, Circuit Courts, County
Court and Probate Judges, Clerks of County Court, Clerks
of Commissioner's Court, Tax Assessors, Tax Collectors,
Sheriffs, Precincts of Fayette County, Senators and
Representatives.

CHAPTER V - WARS -- 75
Indian Seminole, Fayette County War Pensioners - War of
1812, Civil War, Civil War Census of 1907, C.S.A. Cemetery Records, and Other C.S.A. Data.

CHAPTER VI - NEWSPAPERS, LIBRARY AND RADIO --------------------------100

CHAPTER VII - EDUCATION ---103
Superintendent of Education, Schools of Fayette County.

CHAPTER VIII - RELIGION ---149
Early Religious Life, Assembly of God, Baptist (Freewill),
Baptist (Missionary), Baptist (Primitive), Catholic, Church
of Christ, Methodists, Nazerene and Presbyterian.

CHAPTER IX - FRATERNAL ORGANIZATIONS --------------------------------183

CHAPTER X - FAMILY GENEALOGIES --------------------------------------196

BIBLIOGRAPHY ---426

INDEX --427

CHAPTER I

EARLY HISTORY AND PIONEER SETTLEMENT

Before 1819 the entire country, now within the boundaries of Alabama suffered from land speculation. Individuals or groups would buy large tracts of land for a very small sum and later sell it in much smaller tracts for much higher prices. In 1819 the land law was amended and small tracts could be purchased for one dollar and twenty-five cents per acre.

A great host of settlers thronged the roads of Alabama seeking lands and as a suitable region was reached by these homeseekers, they stopped. Among these migrants there were represented all classes and all degrees of the social scale, from the entourage of a wealthy planter with his many slaves in wagons, to those who came with all their possessions packed in a single wagon, or to those who could afford only pack horses to transport their goods. Others, who were even poorer, carried their few belongings on their backs.

The pioneer's first cabin was erected with the crude implements brought along. A single-room cabin, with just one door and one window for light was the usual type home. Ventilation was supplied by the cracks in the walls and the floor. A shutter was put on both the window and the door; the door was made of rough clapboards fastened together with wooden pegs driven into auger holes. Glass windows were unknown. The clumsy old shutters swung and creaked on wooden hinges for steel hinges were not known.

Later when wealth was accumulated and trade developed, dwellings began to improve; newn logs were used instead of round logs; the cabins were more carefully and more neatly plastered with mud; and instead of the rough clapboards, they used high grade boards and shingles, sawed with an old hand whipsaw before the establishment of sawmills.

With axe, saw, knife, plane, augers and chisels, all very crude, the master of the household made his chairs, stools, bedsteads, benches and cradles from the timber that grew around his cabin. A cradle was common to every household and it was simply half of a hollow log with a bit of rocker-shaped board fastened on each end. In such cradles the young ones were lulled to sleep.

Kitchen furnishings were both crude and scanty. There were no cooking stoves and the utensils of the best equipped homes consisted of a skillet, an oven and a pot. Plates, bowls and spoons were made of pewter and knives of material almost as soft. Tin cups, gourds and squash rinds completed the furnishings. As the pewter utensils were hard to replace, every disabled piece was carefully saved until the "tinker" came around to repair it.

Clothes were hung on wooden pegs driven into the walls. A water shelf and a bucket, a churn and dasher, a brush broom, a spinning wheel, a reel and a pair of cards and a loom usually completed the household equipment.

Until the first crop was made, food was quite scarce. Fowls were available at the cost of hours of hunting and an accurate shot; but bread was scarce and the luxury items of sugar, tea, coffee, salt and pepper were almost unobtainable. When salt could be bought, it was for a price far too high for the average, selling as it did for as much as ten dollars a bushel.

The pioneers brought corn along from the old settlements, when possible, on their pack horses; but the supply was very limited. As long as the corn lasted, "ash cake" and "johnny cake" were very popular.

After the settler had built his cabin, he busied himself with clearing and fencing fields. Trees were hacked down with dull and clumsy axes and the rails for the fences were split with mauls made of dogwood or hickory. Everything was rushed as much as possible to get the land ready for the first crop to be planted. This first crop usually was corn, various vegetables, tobacco, cotton and sometimes flax.

Until the first cotton crop came in, the clothing of the pioneer was mostly made from skins and furs of the wild animals.

If the pioneers became sick, they usually doctored themselves. An illness had to be unusually severe to have the doctor called. An older woman of the family was the doctor as well as the druggist. She learned to make her own medicines of bark, roots, leaves and berries of the herbs, and she knew how to "dose" these medicines, for the different illnesses.

The grandmothers and the doctors were helpless before the epidemics of pneumonia and the various fevers, and at times the mortality rate was alarmingly high.

There was no remedy for a decaying tooth as dentistry was unknown. When a tooth became troublesome the only thing to do was to have it pulled by a professional tooth-puller who used rough iron or steel pinchers which had been made in the black-smith shop, or by the non-professional tooth-puller who jerked the tooth out with a piece of cord or knocked it out by placing a nail or spike against the tooth and hitting it with a hammer.

This section of Alabama where these early pioneers settled later became Fayette County, Alabama. The most important streams in this section are the Luxapallila, popularly referred to as "Floating Turtle", which is the Indian name for "Creek where the terrapin crawls", an indication of original occupancy by the Indians as the territory was undoubtedly a common hunting ground of the Creeks, Choctaws and Chickasaws; but the territory was off the early trails and there are no references to Indian towns within the limits of Fayette County, although potsherds, arrow and spear points and broken pipes were found at different locations in the county. Besides the Luxapallila, there are the Sipsey and the North Rivers: Lost, Cane, Wolf, Yellow and Hell's Creeks that flow through the county. These, through their tributaries, reach every portion of Fayette County.

The soils of Fayette County are much above the average in fertility. The prevailing and most important soil of Fayette is a brown loam with red clay sub-soil. There are other lands which are thinner and less fertile, but the valley lands, which follow along the many streams that flow through the county, are generally very rich. There are several noted valley regions in the county, including the Sipsey Valley, which is about 30 miles long, and two to three miles wide; the Luxapallila Valley, which is very much like the Sipsey in area and fertility; and the North River Valley, which is about 20 miles in length and one mile wide.

These lands produce a wide variety of crops, including cotton, corn, wheat, oats, rye, cane, peas, peanuts, tobacco, pumpkins, and almost every kind of vegetable and many fruits.

The county's contour varies from lowlands to hilly sections and as a whole affords splendid farmlands. The drainage system of Fayette County is divided by a ridge running north and south and is known as the Byler Ridge, all west of this ridge is through the Luxapallila and Sipsey Rivers into the Tombigbee; while the drainage on the east of the Byler Ridge is through North River into the Warrior. The eastern section of the county is drained by Lost, Cane and Wolf Creeks.

Fayette County has a very favorable climatic condition with an annual rainfall precipitation of about 53 inches. Its altitude above sea level is 359 feet and the average mean temperature is about 61 degrees.

The timber is one of the county's best resources as it grows post, red, and blackjack oaks, chestnut, short leaf pine and along the streams - cypress, beech, gum and maples. In the wild-life family there are to be found most of the common birds, fox, possums, wild-cats, rabbits and, in the earliest days, the black bears roamed the forests of Fayette County.

Rich in natural resources, Fayette County, Alabama, was the thirty-third county to be organized in Alabama after the state was admitted to the Union on November 14, 1819. This county was created by an act of Legislature on December 20, 1824. (The territory in which Fayette County was formerly included was within the boundaries of Tuscaloosa County.)

Fayette County is located in the northwest section of Alabama and is bounded by Marion, Walker, Tuscaloosa, Pickens and Lamar Counties. It has an area of 643 square miles, equivalent to 411,520 acres. Fayette County was named in honor of the famous French Patriot, General Lafayette, who gained renown in the United States for the part he played in the American Revolution.

Until 1867, Fayette County included that part cut off to form Lamar, (Jones, Sanford) County. At that time its area was 1,264 square miles with a population of only 3,547. There was an average of 226 acres of land for each man, woman and child in the county, which was divided into 14 precincts as follows: Town, Berry, Betts, Collins, Coles, Gilpin, Holly Springs, Hico, Lawrence, Loftis, Milloort, North River, Steens, and Trulls.

Soon after Lamar County was organized, the commissioners began to divide the remainder of Fayette County into precincts and beats. On January 10, 1876, Fayette County was divided into four commissioners' districts.

Since Fayette County was originally organized it has shown a slow, steady population increase.

In the 1830 Returns of the Fifth Federal Census there were 3,035 white persons and 512 slaves, making a total population of 3,547 listed.

One of the many natural resources in Fayette County consists of the boundless coal and iron ore that lie within its limits, so far unmolested. Acres of coal are almost naked in certain places in the county. The bed of Dry Creek in the northeastern part of the county is a mass of unknown thickness. About the year 1838 a drift of logs in the channel of this creek was set on fire and the coal caught from it. It burned for several weeks, causing uneasiness in the vicinity and when extinguished by the rain that made the creek flow, a huge cavity had been burned in the creek bed.

In some places in the county the farmers mine their coal from the bed of the creeks, when they are low in water in the summer, also from the banks of these small streams and sometimes even from the side of the bank of the road side.

The largest mining comonay in the county has been the Moss-McCormick Mining Company at Howard in the eastern section of the county. This company has, in days gone by, mined a great deal of coal, employing several hundred men for a period of ten years or more. However, at the present time this mine has been closed and much of the machinery moved away.

Many strip mines have been operated over the county. In these mines the coal is found near the top of the ground. The top of the ground is stripped off by a steam shovel or by a slip scrape. Then the coal is dug out of the ground.

In the northeastern part of Fayette County, we still have undiscovered fields of nature's "black-diamonds".

The development of oil and gas in Fayette County has been centered around the gas field just southeast of Fayette, in the valley of the Sipsey River.

In 1909, a diamond drill hole (Brennen Diamond Well) was put down at this point in search for coal. This hole reached a depth of 475 feet, encountering two sandstones with slight shows of oil. Encouraged by these indications, a company was formed and two deep tests were made in the vicinity of the diamond drill hole. On December 20, 1909, one of these wells, located southeast of the diamond drill well, began producing at an estimated rate of 1,600,000 cubic feet of gas a day at a closed pressure of 630 pounds to the square inch.

This well was drilled by the Providence Oil and Gas Company. They drilled 37 wells but none of them produced as the first one did. There were 3 gas producing wells at one time, two south of the railroad and one on the north side. The gas came in abundance for a while and then began to slow up, not so much from a failure of the flow from the wells as that the pipes got sand in them and it was more from lack of proper equipment and lack of capital than nature's fault that the service was suspended.

During the time that these wells were producing the whole town of Fayette was lighted and heated, primarily by the gas from these wells.

There seems to be little doubt of Fayette County having oil as well as gas fields which one day may be worth much to the County and its people.

The first lumber manufactured in Fayette County was done with what was called a whip-saw. This saw was set in a frame for dividing timber into boards and was operated by two persons. The log from which the lumber was made was elevated on a scaffold made for the purpose, and one man was placed on top of the log and the other on the ground, working the saw up and down through the log end-wise. Two men could saw three or four plank for a days work.

An improvement was developed when the water power of the different streams was utilized for power to turn wheels and sash saw mills were built and operated. The saws of these mills consisted of a single straight piece of metal with hawkbill teeth placed in a frame and inserted between two upright posts with the lower end of the frames attached to a crank made secure to a horizontal, revolving water wheel. The lumber was cut with the down stroke and one of these mills properly constructed would cut four or five hundred feet of lumber each day.

Some times the man at the saw would be gone from his work as a sawyer for a considerable time, attending to other duties, for these water mills had, in addition to the saw, cotton gins for separating the lint from the seed of the cotton plant and grist mills for grinding corn into meal or wheat into flour. These water mills were a pleasant place of meeting for the people of the surrounding country.

The barefoot boys of Fayette County looked forward to their weekly trips to the mill astride a mule or horse with a sack of corn or wheat. These days would pass too rapidly for the boys who spent the day at the mill playing games, wrestling, boxing, fishing and during warm weather, using the great pond of water for a swimming pool.

The men of these mills congregated themselves into groups, chewed home grown tobacco, told yarns, swapped horses, discussed politics and crops and occasionally engaged in fist fights. When two stalwart, square-jawed combatants of this past generation, decided to settle their personal difficulties, they never resorted to the use of a knife, a stick or a pistol, but always sized up, fought with their bare fists and when one was over-powered and ready to quit, they sat down and as soon as they could catch their breath they arose, shook hands and nothing more was ever heard of the trouble.

These old water mills were erected on most of the small streams and it was not unusual for a customer of one of these mills to carry a sack of corn or wheat on his back and travel a distance of many miles and be gone from home for several days.

Some of Fayette County's early water mills were Lindsey's Mill below Fayette on the Sipsey River, Newton's Mill east of Fayette on the Sipsey River, and Thornton's Mill and Jones' Mill below Ashcraft Corner.

The next improvement in the manufacture of lumber was the turbine water wheel. These mills were equipped with circular saws. The turbine wheel was a horizontal wheel with a vertical axis, or shaft, extending above the floor level of the millhouse. On the upper end of this shaft was placed a pulley on which a belt for turning the machinery was attached. These mills could cut four or five thousand board feet of lumber for a day's work.

Another wonderful stride in lumber manufacturing was when the steam engine was brought into use together with the circular saw. The largest of this type mill ever to operate in Fayette County was the W. P. Brown & Sons Lumber Co. This company had four band saws, four dry kilns and their plant covered about 20 acres of land. The capacity of band saws and steam was more than 200,000 board feet of lumber per day.

Compared with today's modern machinery we can better understand the struggles of our forefathers.

To better understand our forefather's dwellings we include the following: "AN EARLY FAYETTE COUNTY HOME" — One of these first homes in Fayette County, according to E. A. Powell in his history, Fifty-five Years in West Alabama, was built by Henry Moore, on what is now the James V. Tarwater farm. This farm is located on the old Winfield Road and is five miles from the town of Fayette.

It is thought that this old home was built in the early 1820s. Mr. Powell says there were very few people living there at that time. In what is today a beautiful setting on a level rise of ground and near a spring of water, this home was built of riven logs. The bricks used in building the chimneys were hand made. After it fell into dis-uses timbers and bricks from this old house place were carried away for other uses. Nothing but two piles of brick now mark the location of this early dwelling.

A home and over four hundred acres of land must have been a fulfillment of the hopes and dreams of the Irish emigrant, Henry Moore, who was born in Ireland about the year 1789. What someone has said of our ancestors might be said of Henry Moore. He most likely looked toward America with an empty pocket but a heart full of hope.

Old records tell us that he first entered land from the government on November 26, 1820. Fayette County was established December 20, 1824. Other lands were added to this by entry from the government and by purchase. These lands were known as the Henry Moore Plantation.

According to the census records of 1850 the wife of Henry Moore was named Rachel. She was born in North Carolina. In the early 1850's Henry Moore died at the age of sixty-one or two. On January 13, 1853, Letters of Administration were granted to James H. Moore, his son, who was administrator of the estate.

Some years later a petition to sell the real estate lists the following heirs: John C. Moore, Nancy Collins, wife of A. M. Collins, Jane E. Powell, James H. Moore, Mary L. Stewart, wife of R. C. Stewart, all of Fayette County. Others were F. M. (Martin) Moore of Missouri, M. A. J. Moore, deceased, M. F. (Francis) Moore and D. W. (Daniel) Moore deceased. No mention is made of Rachel, the wife, so it is assumed that she had died.

The son, James H. Moore, bought a part of these lands at a sale and final settlement of this estate. All the property and lands of James H. Moore were willed to his only child, Zora I. Moore, who became the wife of L. L. Cochran. In 1916 she sold three hundred and twenty acres of this land to James V. Tarwater, whose family remain in possession.

On the site of this early home are a great many beautiful trees. Many of them are cedars and live oaks, but one which attracts the attention and arouses the curiosity of all who see it, is an old, old pear tree. The trunk of this tree is about two feet in diameter and according to the recollections of Mrs. Melissa McClure Appling, who remembered when it was planted, is nearly seventy years old. Throughout the years people from that community have helped themselves to pears from this tree. Like our ancestors in the old country, they have enjoyed the privilege of the "right of common".

From "Fifty-Five Years in West Alabama" by Hon. E. A. Powell, as published in the Alabama Historical Quarterly, Winter Issue, 1942. (The Tuskaloosa Gazette, October 28, 1886.)

"There are several old primitive buildings in the county (Fayette), and although they are of modest pretensions, still their antiquity entitles them to notice. One of these is the house in which Mrs. Downs now lives -- thirteen miles south of the Court House. I think it is almost certain that it is the oldest frame building between the Warrior and Bigby Rivers. It stands on the divide between the waters of these two rivers, and rain falling on one side of the road goes to the Bigby, and that falling on the other goes into the Warrior. The old house looked well weather beaten in 1831. It was built by Mr. James Richards, a man of considerable note in the early days of the county. There was a large family of the Richards, but most of them have passed away. I suppose the next two frame houses in point of age are in the town of Fayette. One is a part of what is now known as Phillips Hotel, and the other is part of what is Walters old store immediately west of the Court House. The first was built by Samuel B. Henry, and the second by Henry P. Leonard, each being built for store-houses. There is a cabin on the place known as the Aunt Polly Murray place which is deserving of notice. It is a hewd-log house, and was built somewhere in the high up twenties, -- covered with shingles at the time, and it has the same roof today that was originally put on it, and I am told that it does not leak but little as yet. Passing through the country, you will now and then find one of the original tenements, but they are very rare, indeed. From Tuskaloosa to Fayette Court House there are but four to be seen: One on Mrs. Caraway's place, six miles from North Port; one at Binion's Creek, sixteen miles from North Port; the next the Down's place, already noticed, and last, the Old Rob't Nicholas place, three miles south of Fayette C. H. There were two others until within this year, to-wit; the John Moore, or old Jenkins place, which was burned in the spring, -- and the other the present residence of Captain Cowdon. The old house has given way to a very handsome country residence now in process of construction.

I know of no house now standing between the rivers running on either side of Fayette C. H. that was standing when I went to the country, except the cabin heretofore mentioned on the Aunt Polly Murray place, and one or two miles above the Court House, -- known to the old settlers as the Bingham place, and the George Thompson place, about six miles from Fayette. -- If there are others, I am not apprised of it. On the west side of Luxapallila there are but two that I am aware of. One is the residence of Col. John W. Collins, which was built by 'old Uncle Joe Smith' as we boys were wont to call him; the other by Henry Moore. I do not know who lives at the place now. These were two of the primitive settlers of that neighborhood. They were good neighbors -- but death has long since called them away. I might here mention a number of good citizens living in that neighborhood at that time, -- few of them leaving even a representative of their families. There was Richard I. Murray, John McClure, John M. Moore -- names that I will never forget. These, with 'Uncle Joe Smith' and Henry Moore, and a great many others living there at the time, showed a kindness to my mother in her distressed condition at the death of my father, that had made an impression upon my mind that will last while memory asserts its prerogative. Three of the families named are today represented in the persons of Esquire R. Allen Smith, Judge John C. and Capt. James H. Moore, and Mr. B. F. McCane (McClure). I could notice many other of the old settlers, but it would spin out these sketches too long."

The majority of Fayette County's earliest settlers migrated south and west from South Carolina and Georgia. Others were from Tennessee, North Carolina, Virginia and a small per-centage from the other states then in existence.

An alphabetical list of the heads of the household, taken from the Federal Census of 1830 and 1840 for Fayette County, Alabama follows, giving an accurate record of who our earliest settlers were.

ABBOT, William; ABEL, Joseph, William; ADAMS, John M., Margret M.; ADKINS, Joseph; ALBERSON, Henderson; ALDRIDGE, David, Isom, James and Wm.; ALDRIGE, Arkly, Isom, Joseph, and Wm.; ALLEN, Joseph, and Moses; ALLEY, Nicholas; ALLY, Nicholas; AMERSON, Phebe, Young; ANDERSON, James, Wm.; ANDREWS, David, Roland, Rollin; APLIN, Sami.; APPLERY, Henry; ARMSTRONG, Absolem, John, Mathew; ARNOLD, Asbury; ASHCRAFT, J. M., John, Thomas; ATKINS, J. C., Jos., Lewis, Mastin, Spencer, Wyatt; AUSTIN, Robt.: AYRES, Abraham.

BABB, Joseph; BAGWELL, Fredk., Littleton; BAKER, Anthony, Bethel, Elijah, Joel, John, Nicholas, Obed, Vasser, William; BALEY, Moses; BALL, John; BANAS?, Edwin; BARKER, Isaac, John; BARNES, Jesse, Jethro, Walker; BARNS, Jesse; BARRON, Hannah, James, Joseph; BARTON, David; BASWELL, Gus; BATES, C. F.; BAYLES, Eldridge; BEAL, John; BEAN, J. W., John; BEASLEY, Gabriel, Jesse; BEASLY, Elijah; BEATY, Thos.; BELK, Wm.; BELL, John; BENNETT, Joel; BERRY, David, George, Henry, John, Robt., Thompson, Wm., Wm. C., Z. F., Ro. C.; BETTS, Charles; BEVILL, James; BICKERS, John; BICKERSTAFF, Johnson; BILLIONS, L.; BIRDWELL, John; BISHOP, Charles; BLACK, David, Jacob; BLACKBURN, Augustin, J., John; BLACKWELL, Davidson, Jas. M.; BLAKENY, Thos.; BLANCANBAKER, C.; BLANKENSHIP, C., Augustine, Cul., Sampson; BLANTON, Aaron; BLYTHE, Constantine, James; BOBET, Wm.; BOBETT, Wm.; BOEN?, Sarah; BOSWELL, David; BOUNCHER, Elisha; BOWLES, James; BOX, John, Jos. T., Lisles, Josiah, Lyle, Marmaduke, Masen, Michael, Wm.; BOYD, Levi, Wm.; BRADSHAW, Henry, Wm. K.; BRAND, Gale; BRANDON, N.; BRASHER, John; BRASIER, Lawrence; BRASIRE, John; BRAZEL, John; BRENT, Thos.; BREWER, J. H., John, Ransom, Thos., Wm.; BROCK, Alfred, James, John S.; BROGDEN, Jas., Jorden; BROOKS, Zacheriah; BROWN, Burrel, James, John M., N. J., Warren, Washington, Wm.; BRUTON, Enoch, J. G.; BRYAN, Wiliis; BRYANT, J. H., Jacinth H.,

Willis; BULL, Wm.; BULLIN, Wm.; BURNAM, Wm. T.; BURNS, James; BURTON, James G.;

CALDWALD, Wm.; CAMPBELL, Lemuel; CAPLE, Litleton, Sam'l., Wm.; CAPLES, CARAWAY, A. D., W. J.; CARRINGTON, Eliz.; CARROLL, Heneretta; CATLAGE, Alson; CHAPEL, Miles; CHAPPELL, Miles; CHATENE?, Alex; CHEEK, Valentine; CHILDERS, G. J.; CHRISMAN, Jacob, Samuel; CHRISTMAN, George, G. H., Michael, Micnel; CISM, Susannah; CLARE, E. J.; CLARK, Benj., James, Squire; CLARY, Aquerel L.; CLEMENTS, Wm.; CLIFTON, G. D., Wm.; CLURE, E. J.; COAPLIN, Wm.; COATS, Abner; COBB, Jas. S., Wilson; COCHRAN, John, Pinkney; COCK, Charles; COCKERHAM, Elijah, J. N.; COCKRAN, John; COKER, Wm.; COLE, John B., Josiah W., Little, Richr., W. B., Wm. B., Wm.; COLLIER, Barnet, Wm.; COLLINGS, George; COLLINS, A. M., D. A., George, J. L., J. M., COLLUMS, Demni, Dewrie; COOK, L. S., Reuben, Thomas; COOPER, James, Martin, Mary; CORDIN, Vincent; COTLEGE, Alson; COTTON, Joseph; COW, John E.; COX, A. J.; CRANFORD, Abner; CRAWFORD, Abner; CRISTMAN, G. H., Jacob; CROKER, John; CROLEY, Francis; CROW, James, Lewis; CROWLEY, Saml.; CRUMP, Simeon V., S. V.; CURTIS, Solomon; CURTON?, Bolin; CVENTON, James.

DAVIS, A., Benj., Burges., Charles A., James, John, John H., Isum, Matthew, Reuben, Robt., Sherwood, Sherwood, Shurwood, Thomas, William; DAWSON, Hiram; DEAS, Jesse; DEBORAH, Alfred; DELK, Mathew; DENNIS, Benj; DICK, Mathew; DICKERSON, Joseph; DIXON, Martha; DOBBINS, J. C., Joseph C.; DODSON, Enoch, Wesley; DOLLAR, Jesse; DOWDALL, Allen; DOWNS, Wm; DUKE, B. S., Richd.; DULANEY, David; DUMAS, E. W.; DUNCAN, James; DUNHAM, Jonathan; DUNMORE, Clarissa; DUNN, Andrew, John.

EAKER, Alfred; EARNEST, Jas., Wm. P.; EDNEY, Wm. B.; ELLIS, Neal; ELLISON, John; EMORY, A. H.; ENIS, W. B., Wm.; ERWIN, Wm.; ESTELL, James;

FAGGOTT, J. T.; FARQUEHAR, A.; FARQUHAR, Anderson, James; FELTMAN, Jacob, Jas. B.; FIELDS, Joel, Nathl., Obed; FILES, Abner, Sr., Abner, Manly, Manly, Jr.; FISH, Christer, Wm.; FISK, Robt.; FORD, Daniel, W. B., Wm. B.; FORT, Martha; FOSTER, Edwd., Jeremiah, Levi, M. D., Thos.; FOWLER, A. J., Dan'l., Eliz., James, James B., Joshua, Nimrod; FRANKLIN, David, Gillis; FREEMAN, David, Nicholas, Burgess, James, Jesse, John, Wm.; FREMAN, Wm.; FRESHOURS, Geo.; FULLERTON, R.; FURGERSON, H. A.; FURGUSSON, Jas.

GARBOT, Thos. M.; GAINES, E. T., GALLOWAY, Thos; GAMES, E. T., H. P.; GANES, H. P.; GARDINER, Lewis; GARDNER, Jas., John, Lewis, GEE, John H.; GENTRY, Youngblood; GEORGE, Asa, Thos.; GESIN, Isaac; GILBERT, Jno. T.; GILL, Thos. M.; GILLUM, Howell; GILMORE, John; GILPIN, Richmond; GIVEN, John, Miles; GLAZE, Thos.; GOFFIN, Wm.; GOODWIN, Isaiah; GORDEN, Henry; GORDON, Henry; GOUTON, James; GRACY, John, Joseph, P. D.; GRAHAM, Miles; GRAM, Miles; GRAMMAR, Joseph; GRAVES, Asa, Benj., Thos.; GRAY, R. N., Richd., Wm.; GREAR, H. M.; GREEN, Ezekiel, John, Levi, Jesse, Miles, Morris, Thos.; GREENLEE, Hugh; GREGORY, James; GRIFFIN, Thornton, Troy; GRIMES, Morris; GROSS, John; GRUEN, Morris; GUESS, Saml.; GUIN, Coder, Gilbert, Isaac; GUIRE, Coder; GUTRY, Hanah, Isom.

HALE, Ezekiel; HALL, James; HALMACH (see Halmark; Geo.; HAM, Bright, Henry, John, Spious, W.; HAMBRIC, Sandy; HAMBRICK, John; HAMBY, John, Saml.; HANKINS, John, Richd., Stephen, John M.; HARBIN, James, John, Lewis; HARBISON, Lydia; HARDIN, J. A., Y. O.; HARDINTON, Young J.; HARKINS, Andrew, Stephen, Walter, Wm. T., W. S.; HARKIS, Andrew; HARLIN, Lewis; HARMAN, James; HARPELL, James W.; HARRINGTON, Jas. H.; HARRIS, Adlai, Adley, Edwin, James, Thos. Williamson; HARTIN, Amy, Green, H. W., John, L. L.; HARVEY, Nehemiah; HARVY, David, James W., Thos., Zephaniah; HATFIELD, Champion, Henry, Moses; HAUL, Jess, HAWKINS, D. G., Henry, John, John M., Richd., Stephen, HAWL, (or Haul or Hall)

8

Davio, Davis, John, Sam., E.J. HAYES, Lazarus; HAYS, John; HEARD, W. H., Wm. H.; HELLUMS. Heowood, Jacob, John; HEMPHILL, Nathl., HENDERSON, Hugh G.; HENRY, James,H, John, Margaret; HERNDON, **Geo**., James; HERRINGTON, J. H.; HESTER, Robt.; HICKMAN, John, Mary, Wm.; HIPPE, John; HIPPER, John; HODGE, Wm.; HOLLAND, Henry; HOLLEY, Richd; HOLLINGER, Jas.; HOLLINGSWORTH, John, Saml.; HOLLINSWORTH, John; HOLLOMAN, Elijah, V.; HOLLOWAY, James, Mary; HOLLY, Richd; HOLMARK. George; HOPKINS, John; HOPSON, Edmund; HORN, Jesse; HOUTON, Abraham, Abram; HOWARD, Isaac, James, Jesse, John; HOWELL, Tillman; HOWELL, Elijah,L., Mansfield; HOWTON, Jonathan; HUBBERT, George, James, Nathaw; HUBERT, B. A.; HUCHERSON, T. J.; HUDSON, Dan'l; HUGHES, James M., Jesse; HUMPHRIES, Jas. W.; HUTCHERSON, A. J.; HUTCHINSON, Henry; HYSON,Jas.
    IRELAND, Shederick; IRVIN. Wm., ISBELL, G. I.
    JACKSON, Right; JAMASON, R. w.; JAMBKINS, Lockhart; JENKINS, Edney, Lewis; JENNINGS, Joshua, Wm.; JOHNSON, Anderson, **Andrew**, B., Benj., D. M., Fredk., George, Grief, George T., Hesekiah, John, Jno. G., James, Margaret, Mathew, Price M., Prier M., Fleasant, R. G., Saml., Thos., Wm., Wm. H.; JONES, Benjr., Fletcher, Isaac, Jas. W., Jesse, John, Mary, Reuben, Seaborn, Thos., S. D., Wm.; JORDAN, Allen, Nathan; JORDEN, Allen; JUSTUS,Moses.
    KEATH, M.; KEARD, W. H.; KELLEY, Edmond, J. D.; KENEDY, Stevison; KENNY, Ira; KILGORE, George; KIRKLAND, A., D. G., John, John R., W. W.; KISIAH, Manuel.
    LACY, James; LAMBKINS, Astin. Lockhart, Wm.; LAMKIN, Wm.; LAMPKINS, Lockhart; LANE, Uriah, Joseph; LANGHAM, Solomon; LANGSTON, Ezekiel, Haywood, Jesse, John, Penelope; LANSDALE, Isaac; LASTER, John; LAWRENCE, Alex'r., Martin, Richd.; LEE, Jeptha, Wm.; LEISHMAN, James; LEONARD, H. P.; LESTER, J.B.; LILES, George; LILLY, Fred; LINDLEY, Jacob; LINDSAY, Levi; LINDSEY, Levi, Wm. I.; LISLES, George; LITTLE, Anderson, Mary; LIVINGSTON, Moses; LOFTIS, David, Lemuel; LOGAN, Ro.; LONG, Wm.; LONGMIER, George; LONGMIRE, George; LOVITT, John; LOWE, Wm.; LOWREMORE, John; LOWRYMORE, John, Wm.; LOWRY, Benj., Christopher, Edwd., Issac F., James T., Peter; LOYD, F. M.; LUCAS, James, Thomas; LUSK, Davidson; LYON, John; LYRD, Jesse.
    MAGAHA, Wm.; MALONE, Drury, Isaac; MALORY, Danl.; MALOY, Danl.; MANASCO, Joseph; MANN, Warham; MANSFIELD, Isaac; **MARCHBANKS**, Elijah; MARK, Balsom; MARSHALL, Lewelen or Leirien; MARSHBANKS, A. R., Elijah; MASSAY?, Job, Joseph, Saml.; MASSEY, Wm.; MATTON, John; MATTOX, John, Steandin?; MAY, Geo., Hampton, J. T., John, Phillip, Robt.; MAY, Thos., Wm.; MAYS, John; MEACK?, John S.; MEEKS, Mark; MELTON, Ell H.; MERRAY, James; MERRITT, Allen, John; MITCHELL, Banister; MICHISON, Zemri, Zemry; MICKIE, J. M.; MIDDLETON, Benj., James; MIERS, Loranso D.; MILES, Thos; MILLER, Henry, Isom, Isaac, James. **John**; MIRES, Noel; MITCHEL, Aquilla, Banister, Ira J.; MITCHELL, Aquilla, G. M. W.?; MIXON, Alex; McCALEB, Briten, Ichabod, Joseph, Wm.; MIZE, S. W.; MONASCO, David; MONCHET, J. G.; MONTGOMERY, Madison, P. P., Wm. W.; MOORE, Elijah. Henry, James A., John M., John P., John, Jas. E., Lewellen, Moses, R. N., Robt., Thos., W.O., Wm.; MORDICA, Isaac; MORGAN, James, James L., Thomas, Wm.; MORRIS, Andrew, D. S., J. B., John G., Reubin; MORROW, Alex, David, James M., John D., John; MORTON, A. P., Isabella, Jas. P., John, Wm.; MOSLEY, John, Wm.; MOUCHET, J.G.; MUCHELBURY, Reuben; MURRAY, James, Mary, Richd.; MURRY. R. J.; McADAMS, Hannah, James, Margaret N.; McANEAR, Alex; McCAIN, Hance, John, Wm ; McCALEB, Andrew, Hugh; McCAY, Hiram; McCLUNG, Francis, Jonas, N. E.; McCLURE, John; McCOLLOUGH, Saml.; McCOLLUM, George, Jas., James R., Joseph, Wm.; McCONNELL, John; McCOOL, B. A., Andrew, John; McCRAY, Ivy, Joel, Saml.; McCRAY, John; McCREW, Ivy; McDANIEL, Briton, Charles; McGILL, Thos. M.; McGUIRE, H. W.; McKINNEY, Hugh, Wm.; McKNIGHT, Jno. F.; McMAHAN, Phereby; McMILON, Asa, Jas.; McNEESE, Mary, Wm.;

McNIGHT, Andrew, John; McVAY, John.

NALL, Jacob, Nathan; NASH, J. C., James; NATION, Richd.; NEAL, Edison, George M., Gram?.; NICHOL, Wm.; NICHOLES, Wm.; NICHOLS, Jas., Osburn, Ransom, Root., Wm.; NICKS, Elijah; NIGHT, Barbary; NOLTON, Elihu; NORMAN, Thos.: NORRIS, Jas. A., Lewellen, Reubin; NORSWORTHY, Truston.

OAR, Samole; OATS, Wm.; ODEN, C. B.; ODOM, Wm., Jordan; ODUM, Aaron, Ferdinand; OGDEN, Francis; OLIVER, Jas.; ORR, Howel, Piron, Sample; OSBURN, Wm.; OSTEN, Phebe; OWEN, Daniel; OWENS, Daniel; OWINTON, James.

PAGE, James; PAMPLIN, R. J.; PAPERSON, Walter; PARKER, Richd., Saml., Wm.; PARKERSON, Thos. J., Walter; PATE, Jacob; PATTERSON, George W., James, John, Robt.A., Saml., Walter, Wm. B.; PATTON, Andrew, Dorron, Dosson; PAYNE, Archelaus, Ephriam, John, Nicholas, Zechariah; PEARSON, Henry; PEDEN, James, John, Saml., Wm. T.; PEEDEN, Margaret; PEEPLES, Jesse; PENINGTON, Benj., Wm.; PENNINGTON, Alfred, Benj., H., James, Jesse, John, Jas., Martin, Solomon, Wm; PERKINS, John, Moses, Saml., Wm.; PEYDEN, Losen P.; PEYTON, Daniel; PHILLIPS, Aaron, James, Jane; PHILLIPS, Aaron, John, Lewis; PHILPOT, Jesse R.; PICKLE, Henry, Jas., Jacob, Robt.; PIKE, Joseph, Phillip P., Phillip, Wm.; PILGRIM, Ezekiel, Sarah; PINKERTON, Mathew; PIRON, Thos.; POE, Alfred, George, H. B., James, John, Phebe, R. H., Simeon, Simon, Stephen, Thos.; POKE, Phillip P.; POLLARD, Benjn.; POOL, Fieldin; PORTER, Jesse, John, Saml.; POTTER, John; POWEL, Benj., Ezekiel, James, John; POWELL, B. B., Ezekiel, James, Sarah; PRESBRIDGE, Joel; PRESTRIDGE, Joel; PREWET, A. M.; PREWIT, Lucretia; PRICE, David; PRIOR, John; PRUIT, Robt.; PYRANT, Thos.

QUIN, Benj., Benj. C.; QUINTON, James.

RALLY, Thos.; RAMSEY, A. R.; RAMSY, Alexr., Susanna; RAY, John H.; Alexr., Catherine, David, Duncan, J. H., James, John, Michael, Patterson, Thos., Wm. G.; RECTOR, Jeremiah; REDUS, H. M.; REED, Jonas, Joseph, Moses, Wm.! REPIAH, Manuel; REYNOLDS, Alvah M., B. C., J. W., John; RICE, Hesikieh, James, Jeptha; RICHARDS, George, Green N. John J., Martin; RIDGEWAY, Jonas; RIEVES, Allen; RIGGS, George; RION, Michael; ROBERSON, A., Eli, John, Ratio; ROBERTS, J.(I) W., John, O. C., Step., Wm.; ROBERTSON, Daniel; ROBINSON, Horatio; ROBY, Rachel, Thos., Wm. W.; RODGER, Thos., Wm.; ROGERS, Richd., Thos., Wm.; ROLLINS, John; ROSE, Drury; ROSS, Frances, John; ROSWELL, John; RUSH, Wm.; RUSSELL, Wm. O.; RUSSEL, Wm. O.;

SANDERS, Elijah; SAVAGE, Benj., John; SELF, Elijah, Jackson, Wm.; SERRET, Saml.; SHARKS, Nath'l.; SHARP, Andrew, E. G., John, Wm.; SHAW, Joseph; SHELTON, George A.; SHEPHERD, Isaac, Laburn; SHIELD, Obadiah; SHIP, John, O. N.; SHIRLEY, Joshua, Nath'l., Robt.; SHOEMAKE, Joseph; SHOEMAKER, Henry, Jesse; SHORTRIDGE, Hiram; SHUFFIELD, A. B.; SISM, John, Thos., Wm.; SKATES, Geo.; SKILES, Wm.; SKINNER, Augustine C.; SLOAN, John, Matthew, Wm.; SMITH, Amos, Brackston, Daniel, David, Gilbert, Hiram, James, John, Joseph, Joel, Lemuel, Moses, R. G.,Roddy, Sarah, Stephen, W. R.; SORSBEY, Alex.; SPARKS, Jno., Wm.; SPEARS, Nathan, S. B.; SPERLIN, Green; SPRINGER, Jos.; SPROUSE, John; SPURGEON, John; STANTON, James; STARK, Wm. J.; STEARN, James, John, Wm.; STEEN, James, John, W. H., Wm.; STEWART, John, Joseph, Larkin, Mary, Reuben, Robin; STILLMAN, Saml., Thos.; STOK, Resolve; STOKES, F. W.: STONE, Susannah; STORY, Wm. M.; STRAWBRIDGE, Jas., Wm.; STREET, B. N.; STRICKLIN, B. P.; STRONG, Elijah, Eliz., Johnson, W. M., Wm.; STUDYVANT, John; SUGG, Harbard; SUMMERS, Moses; SWAN, Jas.; SYRD?, Jesse;

TACKETT, John, Lancaster; TACKETTE, Lancaster; TAGET, Wm.; TAGGART, Wm.; TAGGETT, Jo. T.; TANKESLY, Z. T.; TAYLOR, C. N., Charles,M., Geo. R., Levi, Levy, Mary A., S. J., Saml. B., Wm., Wm. S., Wm T?.; TEREY, Jesse; THOMAS, Solomon: THOMASON, John: THOMPSON, Alex., C. C., F. T., James, John, Jonathon,

Nath'l., S. J., Sarah, Thos., Wm.; THOMSON, Flemming; THORNLEE, T. B.; THORN-
TON, David, Thos., Richd., W.; THREET?, E. B.; TIDWELL, Benj., Henry, Jemi-
ma, John; TIREY, Jesse; TODD, E. B.; TOMLIN, D. S.; TOWNLEY, Henry; TRACEY,
Wm.; TRAWEEK, George, James. Spencer: TRAYWEAK, D. W., Spencer; TRAYWEEK, Geo.,
Hugh; TRIM, Elener; TRIMM, John; TRULL, J. A.; TUCKER, B. F., Daniel, Lewis,
Sanders, Simon, Spious, Thos.,; TYNER, Wm. C.

USSELTON, James G.

VAIL, Joshua; VALL, Nathan; VAN HOOSE or (VANHOOSE), Isaiah, Jesse, John;
VAN HORN, Jesse; VANZANT, Sarah; VASH, J. C.; VERTER, Thos.; VEST, W. H.;
VICE, John R., Morgan.

WADE, Drury; WADLE, Margaret; WAITS, James; WALDEN, James, John; WALKER,
Wm.; WALLIS, Allen; WALTERS, Moses; WARBINGTON, Horatio, John, Wm.; WARD, Al-
cany, Coleman, Eleanor, James, Jonathon, Stephen, Wm.; WARE, George; WARREN,
Alderman, John; WATERS, John, Micajah; WATKINS, J. D.; WATSON, Isreal, Mark,
Solomon, Willis, Wyatt; WEATHERS, Jas. E., Jesse; WEDGWORTH, Jn. D.; WELCH,
Eli; WEST, Berry, Jesse, John, Thos., W.; WHEELER, A. J.; WHITE, Abel, Asahel,
Asahel, A. W., Fredk., G. W., Isaac N., Jeptha, John, M. N., Mary, Patrick,
Saml.; WHITLEY, Jonas; WHITLY, Wm. T.; WHITTEN, Elijah; WIDEMAN, John; WIDMAM,
Wm.; WILCOX, James; WILKES, Asa; WILKS, Asa; WILLIAMS, Alfred E., Henry F?,
John, John H., J. D., Jas. W., Wm.; WILLINGHAM, Beverly, C. B., Isaac; WIL-
LIS, Mel, Wm.; WILSON, B. W., Graim, Harvey, Jacob, James, John, Wm., Wm. B.;
WIMBERLEY, Thos; WIMBLE, Thos, J.; WINGATE, T. V.; WINSTEAD, Saml.; WINSTED,
Saml.; WINTER, Joseph; WINTERS, Joseph; WOODS, Alcany, John, Phillip R. or
N?.; WOODWARD, A.; WORLEY, Geo.; WRIGHT, Francis, Henry, Isaac, Jas., Jesse,
John, Jos., Lazarus, Moses, Rebecca, Richd., Wm. L.

YANDELL, W. B. F.; YANZY, Ely; YERBY, Hogan; YORK, James, John, Thos.;
YORRIC, Jas.; YOUNG, Alexr., E. W., Wm.; YOUTON, James; ____, Valentine.

CHAPTER II

TOWNS AND COMMUNITIES

BANKSTON -- In 1942 Mrs. Ruby Alexander and her ninth grade students collected data concerning Bankston and that general area of Fayette County. They interviewed some of the older citizens, Mrs. Queen Willingham, Mr. Tom Waldon and Mr. George Freeman, all of whom are deceased now. Following are some of the facts gathered during that project.

Bankston was first settled by William M. Strong, who entered land from the government in 1831 and again in 1836; Littleton Cole entered land in 1834; Joseph McClure, who entered land in 1855; Ruben Gams, who entered land in 1855 and Joseph Townsend, who entered land in 1859. After this time others came steadily to build up a community and homestead the land.

There was no post office in Bankston from 1866 through 1880 and the mail was brought by horseback once a week from Tuscaloosa. The people would go to Mr. Jim Mell's house, located about one and one-half miles north of Bankston on the Byler Road, to pick up their mail. Dr. Woods, a medical doctor who also sold goods, was the first postmaster.

Since the land was very low and wet, most of the houses were built on the side of the hill overlooking the present site of Bankston.

The present town of Bankston actually started when the water tank for the railroad was built near Mr. Lorenzo' Micheal's place in 1883. The first engineer on the train was a Charlie Hankins. The second was a Mr. Banks (the town is supposed to have been named for him); he was a very cheerful type person. When the trains came through and stopped for water, the citizens would go to the tank to chat with Mr. Banks and the water tank was named Banks Tank. About 1889 this was changed to the name of Bankston.

Dr. Woods, the first postmaster, bought land from William Strong in 1880 and built the first gin and sawmill and later a cannery. Dr. Smith moved to the community before the turn of the century and operated a store along with his medical practice. He was the father of Mrs. Mollie Taylor. Dr. Weathers came to Bankston about 1906. He was a devout member of the Church of Christ and was the father of Lomax Weathers. Dr. Weathers died in 1917.

"Doc" Hollingsworth owned and operater a livery stable from about 1908 to 1915, but the advent of the automobile ruined his horse and buggy business. By the end of the nineteenth century other general stores, with their cracker barrels had been added. In the early 1900's three churches were organized; the Baptist; the Church of Christ and the Methodist. The only hotel ever built in Bankston was built by M. L. Parks about 1887. About 1904 he sold it to Jack Smith who owned and operated it until 1924 when T. C. Smith, Sr. bought it. Mr. Smith used it for a while as a hotel and boarding house but later the old building was torn down and Mr. Smith, a grandson of the Mrs. Parks, built a lovely brick dwelling for his family on the old hotel site.

In the earlier days the Masonic Hall was upstairs over the old Baptist Church. The Odd Fellows Hall was over a store. In 1909 an oil company from

Texas drilled for oil in Bankston and struck gas which was "harnessed" and piped to several homes for lights and heat. Mr. Murry Fowler operated a blacksmith shop for several years and this shop was operated in later years by Willie Hammack.

At least three storms have caused considerable damage to property in Bankston. The last one doing a great bit of damage was about 1950 when the post-office and Joe Williamson's store was destroyed.

Bankston's peak of prosperity was from about 1910 to 1930. There was at one time a large warehouse, a barber shop operated by Dave Johnson, a grist mill, a gin, a sawmill, a railroad section with two sections of houses and about fifteen or twenty houses in the immediate vicinity of Bankston.

Following are some of the stores that have operated in Bankston through the years; J. H. Willingham, Dick Collins, M. L. Parks, T. H. Parks, J. M. Traweek, P. N. Fortenberry, Fenton & Silas Berry "Berry Brothers, Jesse Smith, Dr. J. G. Smith, H. T. Taylor, Felix Newton, Zac Sanders, T. C. Smith, T. C. Smith, Jr., R. S. Smith, Jack Smith, T. A. Willingham, Dr. Woods, J. L. Williamson, Jep Woods, L. B. Deavours, Deavours Store and Jesse Sands.

Some of the gins that have operated in Bankston have been; J. H. Willingham Gin, J. T. Willingham Gin, & J. I. Awtrey Gin.

The Railway Depot Agents were: Tildon Walker, E. C. White, Lee Bagwell, Mr. Odom, Mr. Weatherly, Robert Wilson, Lands Mitchell and Mr. Williams.

Doctors who served the people of Bankston through the years have been; Dr. William R. Willingham, Dr. Woods, Dr. J. G. Smith, Dr. J. H. Weathers, Dr. Coleman and Dr. Stanley Johns.

BELK -- The first post office in Belk was named B. B. and was located at Mack Smith's dwelling. Later it was moved to Mulberry Tank Junction to the A. J. Taylor Store. The name was changed to Belk about 1904 or 1905. Mr. A. J. Taylor was the postmaster in Belk and the position was passed on to his son J. G. Taylor, who served as postmaster until 1944 when his daughter-in-law was appointed postmistress and still holds the position.

One of the first businesses located in Belk was a water mill run by Jobe Williams, where meal and flour were ground and cotton was ginned, with the water power supplied by the Luxapallila River. A. J. Taylor operated a general merchandise store which was later sold to his son J. G. Taylor. In 1946, grandsons of the original owner, John D. Taylor and Aubery Belk purchased the store and in 1948 Jonas Crowley bought the business and still operates the store.

A modern gin and grist mill have taken the place of the water mill and it is owned by Roy Gilreath. There are four stores at present, also a modern sawmill and lumber business operated by the Newman Lumber Co., owned by Grady Newman and Sons.

A franchise for a railroad from Birmingham to the Mississippi State line and thence to Columbus was secured in 1870 by the Elyton and Aberdeen Railroad Company. The original right-of-way through Belk was graded by Jobe Williams in 1884 and the track was laid from Columbus, Mississippi to Day's Gap (later changed to Oakman). The track was finished to Birmingham, Alabama in 1887, and Belk (first known as Mulberry Tank) was a regular scheduled stop until 1933.

The first depot agent was John Coleman, who served from 1908 until 1911 when E. R. Williams was appointed agent and remained agent until 1933. The agency was discontinued in 1933 and the depot building was removed in 1935. During the steam engine's day there was a water pump, operated by Jefferson

Richards and later by Buddy Richards, a nephew. The old water tank and pump remained by the track until the depot was removed in 1935.

BERRY -- Construction was started on the section of the Georgia-Pacific Railroad that passes through the present site of Berry, Alabama in 1882 and reached completion in 1883. A depot was located at the present site of Berry through an arrangement made by Mrs. Ben Jeffries and Mrs. Eliza Harvey with a man who had obtained a right from the railroad to set the location of the depot. The depot was named Berry for Thompson Berry, the father of Mrs. Jeffries and Mrs. Harvey. Mr. Berry was the first man to live within the present boundaries of the town.

Soon after the tracks were laid as far as Berry, Ab. Seay had his boxcar, which he used as a combined store and post office, brought to that location. Jake Rich erected Berry's second store a short time afterward.

Sometime during 1883, the exact date is lost, Berry was incorporated so that saloons could be legally operated. The town limits were set by measuring one-half mile in all directions from a public well dug near the present site of Barnes Variety Store. Birks Bagwell was the first mayor and John Kirkland was the first town marshall. The first aldermen are not known.

Immediately following the incorporation of Berry, Jack Clements opened a saloon. Other saloons were operated in Berry by Dall Logan, Bill Ferguson, and Hort Stanley. All were out of business by 1886 because of lack of customers. This fact is explained by a lack of money and the fact that anyone wanting whiskey generally had a barrel of his own brew. There has not been a saloon in Berry since 1886.

School was first taught in 1884 in an old store by Mrs. Lulu Stanley. School continued to be taught in old store and saloon buildings and churches until 1891 when the first school house was built on the site of the present grammar school. John Windham was the first principal.

The first school building burned in January of 1895 and was replaced that same year by the Tuscaloosa District High School on the same site. This school was supported by the Methodist Church and continued until it burned in April, 1913. At that time the support of the school was assumed by the state and Berry Grammar School was built, again on the same spot.

The Methodists established the first church at Berry in 1884 or 1885 when the Church known as Tabernacle was moved to Berry. The first Methodist church was burned and replaced in 1898.

The Methodists were closely followed by the Baptists who organized a Church in Berry in 1886. The other two Churches of Berry were founded at much later dates, approximately 1911 for the Christian Church and the Nazarene Church in 1935. Raymond Frost was the first Nazerene pastor. Services for that church were held in the Masonic Hall until 1941 when the church building was put into use.

The Alabama Christian College was founded in Berry in 1912 by members of the Christian Church. Classes were taught in the Christian Church until the college building was completed in 1913. The college lasted until 1922 when the building was bought for use as the Berry High School.

In 1891 the first general merchandise store still in business was started by N. F. Cannon who moved from the Old Town of Fayette. Capp Shepherd sold fertilizer prior to that date but the Shepherds did not have a general store until 1897.

Berry suffered its first major fire on the night of January 2, 1902. A Mr. Popwell's store caught about 2 o'clock in the morning and the fire spread to destroy W. R. Willingham's store, Dr. Seay's drug store and several vacant buildings that were located in the neighborhood of where Dr. Scrivner's office was later built.

Berry's second fire occured in early 1913. The fire started in Ed Newman's store and was not stopped until it had destroyed the central office, D. W. Johnson's store, Wood's drug store, the post office, Dr. Patterson's house and several vacant buildings composing the block now occupied by the drug store and postoffice.

The Bank of Berry, now in operation, was founded January 13, 1915, by J. C. Shepherd, Sr. The directors were G. W. Johns, A. M. Grimsley and Fred W. Johnson. The bank was robbed once in 1931 and again in 1933. A small bank was established in Berry in 1910 by Alabama Trust and Saving Co., but went bankrupt the following year.

No records were found of the mayors of Berry between 1883 and 1926, but it is known that mayors during that period included Birks Bagwell, Frank Freeman, S. L. Dobbs, Sam South, J. T. McCracken and Cooch Boone.

In 1926 and 1927 J. C. Shepherd, Sr. was Mayor. The aldermen were R. B. Jones, S. L. Dobbs, J. B. Johnson, J. B. Griffin and D. W. Johnson. On February 28, 1927, this group passed forty-one town ordinances including laws on taxes, public drunkeness, bad checks, weeds around houses, regulations for hog pens and speed limits which were set at 15 miles per hour. All of these laws were drawn up by R. B. Jones and S. L. Dobbs.

The mayors after 1927 were: 1928 - 1932 Mack Karrah; 1932 - 1936 Fred W. Johnson; 1936 - 1940 M. L. Chism; 1940 - 1944 J. D. Scrivner; 1944 - 1946 L. C. Christian; (L. C. Christian resigned 1946); 1946 - 1948 Fred "Sox" Johnson (Mr. Johnson was appointed to fill 1946 resignation.); 1948 - 1950 Fred J. "Sox" Johnson - resigned Aug. 1950; 1950 - 1955 Fred W. Johnson - Died May 1955; 1955 - 1955 D. C. Studdard - Took office May 1955, resigned June 1955 due to wife's illness; 1955 - 1956 J. U. Walker - pro tem tenure; 1956 - 1956 D. C. Studdard - Took office April 1956, resigned October 1956; 1956 to present time Garland Barnes who was elected for four years September 1956, took office October 1956 and is presently serving.

Modern conveniences first appeared around the turn of the century when Dr. Collins installed the first "Delco" electrical system. A Methodist minister, Rev. E. L. Roy owned the first car in Berry in 1910.

The present electrical system was installed by the Alabama Power Co., in 1925. A water system was put in Berry in 1933. The City Hall was also built in that year. The highway was paved in 1938 - 1939. One mile through town was paved in 1937 and one other block of the town street was paved in 1938. The Miss-Ala Stages Bus Line was established through Berry in early 1938. The remaining unpaved portions of the business section of Berry were paved in 1949.

In 1932 the old Christian College building burned and was replaced by the present high school in 1934. The old grammar school building was torn down in 1929 and the building to replace it was erected the same year. The vocational building was constructed in 1936. The gymnasium was completed in 1948 as was the athletic field.

In 1936 the old Baptist Church was replaced by the present church building. The present Christian Church replaced the frame building in 1928. The old Methodist Church was torn down in the fall of 1945 and the new church was put in use in 1948.

Berry's last major fire occured November 1, 1941, when the film in the picture show caught. The theatre, a shooting gallery, V. G. Hall's store, and a building owned by John Freeman that contained some cars and trucks, were destroyed.

Berry's first gin since the town was incorporated was owned by Newt Olive. Since that time Berry has had several gins and small saw mills, but none employed a large number of men until H. C. Newton located a saw mill in Berry in early 1941. Mr. Newton's mill was followed by the Carpenter Brothers Mill in August of 1941. The Berry Box and Crate Co., was established in 1945.

Following is a partial list of the business houses operating in Berry in 1959: Barnes Store, Baker Sales & Service, Bank of Berry, Berry Feed Mills, Theron Cannon & Co. (Berry's largest merchandise house is one of the oldest business firms in Fayette County, having been founded by the late Melville Fortescue Cannon at old Fayette Court House many years before the railroad was built in 1883. After the railroad came through Fayette County, M. F. Cannon moved the business to Berry and operated it until his death on May 2, 1921. The business is now operated by the founder's son, Theron Cannon. The company's slogan is "We handle most everything from a cradle to a coffin."), Dobbs' Radio Shop, Griffin Drug Store, Harbin's Flower Shop, Honeycutt Drug Store, Hudson's Garage, Hudson's Cafe, Jitney Jungle Grocery Co., J. C. Jones' Store, Pendley Store, Shepherd Mercantile Co., Thornton Grocery, West's Cafe and the Yellow Front Store.

BLUFF -- In about 1902, a small Post Office was built near the head of Hell's Creek about twelve miles northwest of Fayette. Mrs. Mollie Holliman named it Bluff, from the large rocks on what is now called Bluff Mountain. In 1904, the post office was moved about a half mile from where it was originally built In the same year a grist mill and cotton gin were erected. About a year later two more stores were built. After a few years two of the stores went out of business and were torn down. The other store remained in business about twenty years.

In 1907 a school house was built at Bluff. Only seven grades were taught there. In 1927 the people around Bluff School and four other schools, Center, Shady Grove, Bethel and Bethabra consolidated and built a larger school which they called Kirkland. It was named for Mr. B. D. Kirkland.

During the time the old school was being used there was a large storage house at Bluff. The freight merchandise was hauled there from Winfield in wagons and stored.

In about 1931 another store was built, and is still in use. A few years after this store was built several warehouses were built by two Jones Brothers. Bluff now consists of a store, a grist mill, a gin, four warehouses and a planer. This is one of the most fertile of the agricultural areas in the county.

COVIN -- The little town of Covin was named for an early settler of that section of the county, Mr. L. E. Covin who had land that was needed for the railroad, gave the land needed and the depot was named "Covin".

A store was built by P. C. Guin, who lived at Hell's Creek and came back and forth to run his store. Later the first post office was built and Mr. P. C. Guin was the first post master. Later, after the railroad was under construction, a saloon was opened by Foster Bobo. The people working on the right-of-way for the railroad settled near the place and created the need for the stores and business houses that were built. The first Doctor of Covin was Dr. Harris, who had his office in Covin. At one time a hotel was built and today there are several stores, two churches, Baptist and Methodist, and quite a number of houses. Dr. Arlington Bobo made Covin his home from the time of his retirement from active medical practice until his death.

Some of the businesses in Covin in 1959 are: H. M. Brock Store, Comer Bobo Store, Richards Store, a Garage and two or three service stations.

FAYETTE -- The people who early came to settle what is now called "Old Town", located on an elevated area, overlooking many miles of the course of the nearby Sipsey River, with its beautiful mountainous regions on the eastern side.

In those days Fayette had its pioneer preachers and educators who, without highways, blazed the trees for those who followed.

The first merchant of this town was J. C. Robertson whose descendants operated the same mercantile establishment until December 31, 1958, when the old store was closed. The second merchant was Thomas Cannon who also operated a mercantile business and his descendants continued to operate the store until the mid 1950's.

The early history of these pioneers is closely interwoven with the present history of Fayette County, and reflects, at every step, the early struggle they made to secure what we have today. As they departed, they left footprints in the sands of time.

The present City of Fayette has been known by various names at different times and has occupied different territory in its history, and to give the names consecutively, we find that it had been called, LaFayette, Fayette Court House, Fayetteville, Fayette Depot Town or Frog Level, Latona and just plain Fayette as it is known at the present time.

If the town ever bore the name of LaFayette, it must have been for a very short time; however it is probable that a settlement, which occupied the same territory as Fayette Court House later on, was known by that name to give honor to General LaFayette, the patriotic Frenchman, who was on a visit to this country at about the time the settlement was made.

According to the history of Alabama by different writers, Fayette Court House was incorporated as a town on January 15, 1821. It is recorded that Fayette County was created by act of the legislature on December 20, 1824.

There is reasonable doubt as to whether Fayette was incorporated on the date mentioned. The main reason for this doubt, is the fact that there was no Fayette County until almost four years later.

The town must have been known as Fayette Court House for nearly sixty years. The descendants of the pioneers remembered the fact that all mileboards directing to the town were marked F. C. H. even after the incorporation of the town as Fayetteville in 1880.

Fayetteville, the third name by which the town was known was incorporated on the 8th day of December 1880, and the following are the provisions of the Code under which the town was incorporated as adopted by the corporate authorities by proceedings authorized by the Revised Code of Alabama and by virtue of an election held on the 8th day of December, 1880; "The boundary lines of the corporation are circular, with the Court House in said town as a center, including a district of county one-half mile from said court house in every direction." Fayetteville was the first town in the county to incorporate themselves into a municipality.

When the Richmond and Danville Extension Company built the Georgia Pacific Railroad into Fayette County in 1883, the county seat was located at Fayetteville, one mile north of the railroad. A short time after the railroad was built the people began to move nearer the depot. This new town was called Fayette Depot Town, or "Frog Level".

A great many who had property and stores and had spent their lives in the old town objected to the move; however they continued to abandon Fayetteville until nearly all of the business houses were located near the depot. The principal objection to the new location was that a considerable portion of the territory was covered with water in the winter and spring.

When the weather began to warm up in the early spring, the frogs would burst forth each night with their constant mournful croaking. A citizen of that day humorously named the community "Frog Level". The name stuck and a post office was established bearing that name. The first postmaster of Frog Level was Joe Mason with G. W. Howton assistant. Mason was succeeded by Dr. Kilby Newton. The third postmaster at this office was A. J. Renfro.

This new town was not incorporated under the name Fayette Depot Town or "Frog Level" but some of the citizens desired a change of name and incorporated themselves into a municipality calling the town, Latona.

On June 29, 1891, James J. Ray filed a petition with the probate judge with the necessary number of adult inhabitants of the town of Fayette Depot, stating in the petition that they desired to become a body cooperate and to form a municipal corporation under the name of Latona.

Holland M. Bell, Judge of Probate of Fayette County directed that an election be held at the school house near Fayette Depot on the Georgia Pacific Railroad on Saturday the 11th day of July, 1891. The inspectors for this election were L. P. Humber, F. M. Caine and James S. Williams.

On July 13, 1891, the town of Latona was incorporated with the following boundary lines, one-half mile distance in every direction from a stake set up at the place of Fayette Depot where it stood before being burned down, provided the line north shall only extend to the corporation line of the town of Fayetteville in said county, and provided the line south east shall not extend further than within fifty yards of the Stough bridge on the Tuscaloosa Road. The sheriff was ordered to call an election for Mayor and Councilmen. These men, who will be listed later were elected and qualified on August 3, 1891.

One of the outstanding acts of this administration, which stands today as a monument to the forethought of those men, was the planting of the water oak trees along Temple Avenue and along other streets in the town.

The change of the name of Latona to Fayette did not legally take place until November 12, 1898, but before this last named date the town was called Fayette.

On October 12, 1898, H. B. Propst filed a petition with T. B. Morton, Judge of Probate of Fayette County, signed by the required number of legal voters of the town of Latona in Fayette County, stating in the petition that they desired an alteration or change of the name of said town from Latona to that of Fayette, with the boundary lines to remain unchanged.

On November 8, 1898, there was an election held, the object being to change the name of Latona to Fayette. Forty-seven votes were cast, four were colored and forty-three were white. Following is a list of the voters and the affidavit of the inspectors holding the election as it appeared in the County Newspaper, November, 1898.

"J. Fenton Caine, A. J. Renfro, J. B. Mace, J. P. Robertson, Thomas E. Goodwin, R. F. Peters, R. P. Caine, W. T. Naugher, B. J. Ingram, W. L. Stephens, D. W. Morton, R. T. Hamner, Dr. Ed. VanDiver, G. W. Coggin, Arthur Gentry, Belton H. Propst, Lee Lenderman, W. M. Glenn, L. M. Dodds, J. S. VanDiver, T. J. Mace, Lewis Burris, J. A. Cook, J. H. Hyde, Bob Jones, Sanford Fleming, Billie Smith, Calvin McDowell, Frank Jeffries, George Howton, Gaither VanDiver, Dr. W. A. Graham, A. N. Harris, T. B. Morton, J. W. Price, B. W. Tarwater, J. A. Smith, J. B. Kemp, Walter Phillips, Raymon Harris, Simp Lindsey, J. P. Dickinson, Banks Hyde, W. B. Melton, Ed Goodwin, J. T. Sanford.

We hereby certify that the above is a correct list of those who voted in said election on the 8th day of November, 1898. --- A. J. Renfro, J. B. Mace, and J. R. Robertson." (From the original newspaper article, only 46 are listed, as above.)

The corporation lines of the new town of Fayette remained the same as the corporate limits of Latona until the 9th day of January 1911, when a resolution was adopted by the mayor and board of aldermen of the town of Fayette, extending the limits.

The last extension of the City Limits was made in the late summer of 1959 taking in a large area in several directions.

Following is a list of Mayors and aldermen who have served the town of Fayette under its various names, until the present:

The officers of the town of Fayetteville were the first elected men to serve. 1880 - 1884 - Mayor, J. N. Black, Aldermen, H. D. Phillips, Dr. Henry Shelton, R. J. Smith, W. W. Harkins, and Dr. William McCay. 1884 - 1887 Mayor, John B. Sanford, Aldermen, John W. Blackburn, L. B. Shelton, John N. Edney, John W. Miles, and Richard J. Smith. 1887 - 1889 - Mayor, John B. Sanford, Aldermen, J. A. Cook, J. A. Sudduth, J. C. Moore, G. W. Coggins and H. B. Propst. 1889 - 1891 - Mayor, John B. Sanford, Aldermen, A. M. Nuckols, Henry Shelton, John C. Moore, Dr. J. H. Duncan and Wm. A. Ayres. 1891 - until the corporation was killed by act of legislature - Mayor, J. S. Williams, Aldermen, J. A. Sudduth, D. F. Propst, G. W. Coggins, J. A. Hancock and R. F. Peters.

The officers of the town of Latona:

1891 - Mayor, J. S. Williams, Councilmen, L. P. Humber, Mathew Howton, Levi Lindsey, James Yerby and W. F. Smith.

1892 - Mayor, J. S. Williams, Councilmen, G. W. Howton, Joe Lindsey, A. J. Renfro, L. P. Humber, and D. F. Propst.

1893 - J. S. Williams, Councilmen, G. W. Howton, D. F. Propst, W. F. Smith, T. M. Peters and Joe Lindsey.

1894 - Mayor, A. S. Preston, Councilmen, G. W. Howton, D. F. Propst, W. F. Smith, T. M. Peters and Joe Lindsey.

On October 4, 1894, A. S. Preston resigned as mayor and on October 16, R. F. Peters was elected by the board of Aldermen to fill the unexpired term.

1895 - Mayor, R. F. Peters, Councilmen, H. B. Propst, D. W. Morton, Max Harkins, W. M. Glenn and Simp Lindsey.

1896 - 1897 - Mayor, R. F. Peters, Councilmen, J. A. Cook, D. V. Morton, S. N. Lindsey, E. M. Harkins and J. M. Glenn.

Following is a list of the Mayors who have served the new town of Fayette since incorporation in 1898:

1898 - Mayor, R. F. Peters, Councilmen, G. W. Howton, B. J. Ingram, T. J. Mace, E. M. Harkins and John Kemp.

1899 - Mayor, J. R. Robertson, Councilmen, G. W. Howton, J. A. Cook, T. J. Mace, E. M. Harkins and John Kemp.

1900 - 1902 - Mayor, J. R. Robertson, Councilmen, G. W. Howton, J. B. Mace, E. M. Harkins, W. R. Enis, and E. P. Goodwin.

1902 - 1904 - Mayor, J. R. Robertson, Councilmen, G. W. Howton, J. B. Mace, E. M. Harkins, A. N. Harris and W. R. Enis.

1904 - 1906 - Mayor, J. R. Robertson, Councilmen, R. J. Robertson, A. N. Harris, E. Rose, G. W. Howton, R. P. Caine.

1906 - to October 1, 1908 - Mayor, W. S. McNeil, Councilmen, Dr. C. B. Blackburn, W. R. Enis, B. D. Williams, R. C. Robertson and E. Rose.

The Legislature changed the date of election on municipal officers from January 1st. to October 1st. and elections to be held every two years.

The McNeil administration held office for two years and nine months, or to the first Monday in October, 1908 to comply with the act of legislature.

1908 - 1910 - Mayor, T. M. Peters, Councilmen, W. T. Naugher, E. Rose, O. L. Ekwursel, C. B. Blackburn, and U. E. Walker.

1910 - 1912 - Mayor, J. E. Chandler, Councilmen, E. Rose, J. E. Caine, O. L. Ekwursel, U. E. Walker and S. J. Sanders.

1912 - 1914 - Mayor, J. E. Chandler, Councilmen, J. E. Caine, G. C. Propst, J. A. Oswalt, S. J. Sanders and E. R. Van Diver.

1914 - 1916 - Mayor, W. B. Atkins, Councilmen, D. D. Arnold, M. L. Coons, C. M. Dodson, Victor Hyde and E. R. Taylor.

1916 - 1918 - Mayor, T. M. Peters, Sr., Councilmen, D. D. Arnold, M. L. Coons, J. H. Basket, Victor Hyde and E. R. Taylor.

1918 - 1920 - Mayor, E. Rose, Councilmen, T. A. Wilson, D. D. Arnold, E. M. Kelly, Thomas McCool and Golden Brown.

1920 - 1922 - Mayor, M. C. Dobbs, Councilmen, W. A. Dodson, J. P. Daniel, T. A. McCool, E. A. Bagwell and Cleon Enis.

1922 - 1924 - Mayor, M. C. Dobbs, Councilmen, E. M. Grimsley, W. A. Dodson, J. D. Dickson, C. B. Isbell and T. H. Robertson.

On April 7, 1924, M. C. Dobbs resigned as mayor and the board of aldermen appointed J. H. Yuckley to fill the unexpired term from April 7 to October, 1924.

1924 - 1926 - Mayor, L. M. Dodds, Councilmen, E. M. Grimsley, W. M. Cannon, B. E. Thornton, J. D. Dickson and C. B. Isbell.

1926 - 1928 - Mayor, M. L. Coons, Councilmen, W. H. Humber, T. L. Lindsey, C. M. Dodson, C. N. Pollard and C. B. Isbell.

1928 - 1930 - Mayor, M. L. Coons, Councilmen, J. A. Richards, C. M. Dodson, T. L. Lindsey, W. H. Humber and C. B. Isbell.

1930 - 1932 - Mayor, C. B. Isbell, Councilmen, J. A. Richards, T. L. Lindsey, W. H. Humber, J. C. Bragg and J. W. Newman.

In 1932 the term was changed from two years to four years.

1932 - 1936 - Mayor, Joe R. Robertson, Councilmen, W. C. Bragg, M. C. Dobbs, T. L. Lindsey, W. H. Humber and Malcolm Jeffries.

1936 - 1940 - Mayor, W. A. Dodson, Councilmen, W. C. Bragg, J. D. Coward, C. E. Smith, T. L. Lindsey and M. C. Dobbs.

1940 - 1944 - Mayor, W. A. Dodson, Councilmen, J. D. Coward, George H. Gullett, Joe Goodwin, N. T. Mothershed and T. L. Lindsey.

1944 - 1948 - Mayor, W. A. Dodson, Councilmen, N. T. Mothershed, F. M. Fowler, Max Branyon, and E. A. Bagwell.

1948 - 1952 - Mayor, C. M. Holder, Councilmen, Joe E. Caine, G. C. Propst, Wightman Cannon, Sr., Nonus C. Hubbert and Guthrie J. Smith.

1952 - 1956 - Mayor, Joe E. Caine, Councilmen, Guthrie J. Smith, E. A. Bagwell, Fuller Kimbrell, Grover C. Propst, James C. Haughton and as replacements Carey Pollard (appointed) and Claude Patterson (appointed). Mr. Caine died in October, 1955, and the board of aldermen appointed Guthrie J. Smith to serve the unexpired term, as Mayor. Pollard and Patterson replaced Bagwell, who died and Kimbrell who was elected to a State Office.

1956 - 1960 - Mayor, Guthrie J. Smith, Councilmen, Willard Nichols, Snow Hamner, Carey Pollard, Gus Woodard and W. Clyde Freeman.

(The following article gives a vivid description of the business section of "Old Town", "Fayette Court House" or "Fayetteville", when the county seat of Fayette County was located one mile north of modern day Fayette. This account was given by Mr. Leon Dodds, told to Fred McEachin in 1949.)

"First, let me tell you how old I am, so you'll know how long I've been around Fayette. I was born on a farm four miles north of Fayette Court House, August 10, 1873, and have lived in this county all of my life with the exception of one year down in Lamar County.

"During my life-time I've seen some marvelous changes take place in Fayette. I can remember when the present-day Fayette was known as Frog Level and ox wagons used to haul merchandise from the depot where it is now, to the business houses up in Old Town. I've plowed many a long row behind a mule where houses now stand, out on North Temple Avenue. I worked from "Can 'til Can't" for 25¢ a day.

"I went to school up at Old Town at a place called The Academy which was just west of the Baptist Church next to the cemetery. We kids walked anywhere from a mile to four and five miles to school and carried our lunches in a tin gallon pail. We'd put our lunch pails out on a limb to keep the ants out of them and our milk bottles would be put in the spring to keep the milk from souring. Those were the days that you've heard about the teachers teaching reading, writing and 'rithmetic to the tune of a hickory stick. Teachers in those days didn't put up with any foolishness.

When I was 18 years old I went to work for F. M. Robertson at Robertson's Store in Old Twon at $15.00 per month. That was in 1891 and the railroad had been coming to Depot Town or Frog Level for only eight years then.

Fayette Court House, the official name of Old Town at that time was an entirely different sight from what it is today with its wide paved streets and beautiful homes with well kept lawns.

Bob Robertson who came to the United States a few years after his brother John C. Robertson came from Scotland, had a harness and saddle shop on the lot where William Humber's home now stands. (West Elyton Road.) Behind this was Tom Oliver's saloon and on the east side of that street which led to the depot a mile away, was Naugher Brothers saloon. Blackburn & Coggins store was across the dirt road from the Humber residence of today.

And across on the corner was the frame Phillips Hotel. East of the hotel and next door to it was S. J. Cannon's Drug Store and next to that was Propst Brothers livery stables. On the opposite side of the road was the U. S. Post Office which was operated by Miss Leona Moore.

I can't say who did it, but one Christmas Eve, a bunch of the boys climbed up on top of the building that housed the post office and dropped a bunch of geese down the chimney. You never saw such a mess in all of your life as those geese made as they fluttered down the chimney bringing plenty of soot and racket with them. It took Miss Leona quite a time to clean up after this unexpected visit from the unwelcome geese.

East of the post office was the two-story Jim Moore Hotel and north of the Phillips Hotel was Dr. Agnew's Drug Store and next to him was Harkins and Shelton's General Merchandise Store; then Dr. Henry Shelton's two-story home. The court house faced south and behind it was a two-story wood jail. When I was a little boy my father was jailer and I'll never forget the night that a gang of torch-bearing, gun-toting men from an adjoining county came to free one of their pals who was being held in the jail. Those angry men had the biggest pistols I have ever seen, before or since.

Across from the court house and next door to the Humber's present-day residence was Harkins & Burris General Merchandise Store and next to that was F. M. Robertson's warehouse and his store was located where the Paul Nuckols house stands today across the street from the big vacant lot where the court house used to be. (Roy Couch's property today - 1959.)

West of F. M. Robertson's Store was the J. B. Jones Store and upstairs was the newspaper office. I don't recall the name of the paper but the Editor was George Gullett, father of George Gullet, Jr. who,(with his mother and his brother, Jimmy Gullett) operates a mercantile house in Fayette now. Across the ally from this building was M. F. Cannon's Store which was later moved to Berry, Ala.

On the same side of the street as the court house was the two-story Tom Cannon Store. Then there was a vacant lot and then J. B. Sanford's law office. On the northwest corner opposite the two-story brick court house was Collier & McGuire's law office, two of the prominent attorneys of the day. Mr. McGuire was the father of Mrs. W. B. Bankhead.

On up the dirt road, which was either dusty or muddy, was the Methodist Church on the side of the cemetery. Of course, today's cemetery is where it was in those days, only it's larger. Upstairs over the church was the Odd Fellows meeting hall. The Baptist Church was on the other side of the cemetery near the school house and the Masonic Order held their meetings upstairs.

Mr. Bob Robertson's home was located on the site where Jimmie Branyon's home is today and the John C. Robertson home was where it now is. I never did know Mr. John C. because he died in 1877 when I was only four years old.

That ought to give you a pretty good picture of what Old Town looked like before it was moved to what is now Fayette. Of course in those days we didn't have automobiles, electric lights, radio or any of the so-called modern conveniences that we now have, but we didn't miss them, because we didn't know what they were. Those were the good old days, all right, but as for me, give me these modern times!"

EARLY HOMES IN FAYETTE, "OLD TOWN" (See Map No. 1, page 23)
(1) William Worth Harkins married Lula Burgess. (2) Judge Holland Middleton Bell married: Margarette Miles. (3) "Joe" Joseph H. McGuire married: Mrs. Seleta J. (Anderson) Windham. (4) Felix McConnell Robertson married: Lucy Belle Wilson. (5) John H. Bankhead, Sr. married: Tallulah James Brockman. (6) Grandmother Bankhead's home. (7) Elliott Priest Jones married: L. J. Page. (8) Rev. Vincent Hubbard married: Mrs. Elizabeth (Murray) Hamm. (9) Old Hotel, once owned by Benjamin Giles Jones. (10) John Crichton Robertson married: Mary Fletcher Alley. (11) Miss Jennie Harris and Mrs. Etta McKay.

EARLY BUSINESS HOUSES IN "OLD TOWN" (See Map No. 2, page 23)
(1) William Worth Harkins and John H. Bankhead. (2) Phillips' Hotel - Walter Phillip's father. (3) John Jones - Hotel upstairs. (4) James H. Hyde and Yerby Brothers' (Inge, John and Jimmy Yerby) Store. (5) John Blackburn and George Coggins. (6) William M. "Bud" and Jim Cannon. (7) John Miles' Saloon. (8) Thomas C. Olive's Saloon. (9) Robert J. "Long Bob" Robertson. (10) John C. Robertson and Sons. (11) James B. Jones. (12) Mel F. Cannon. (Described by Basil Manly Richards, Jr.)

Some of the early businesses named by Paul Nuckols as remembered in his early life were as follows: 1 - John C. Robertson and Sons. 2 - Burr Dodd's Store. 3 - A. B. Legg's Candy Store. 4 - Felix Robertson. 5 - Thomas Robertson. 6 - Melvin Cannon. 7 - Jimmie Jones. 8 - Joe R. Robertson. 9 - Spencer Carpenter. 10 - A. M. Nuckols' Cotton Warehouse. 11 - Dr. Shelton.

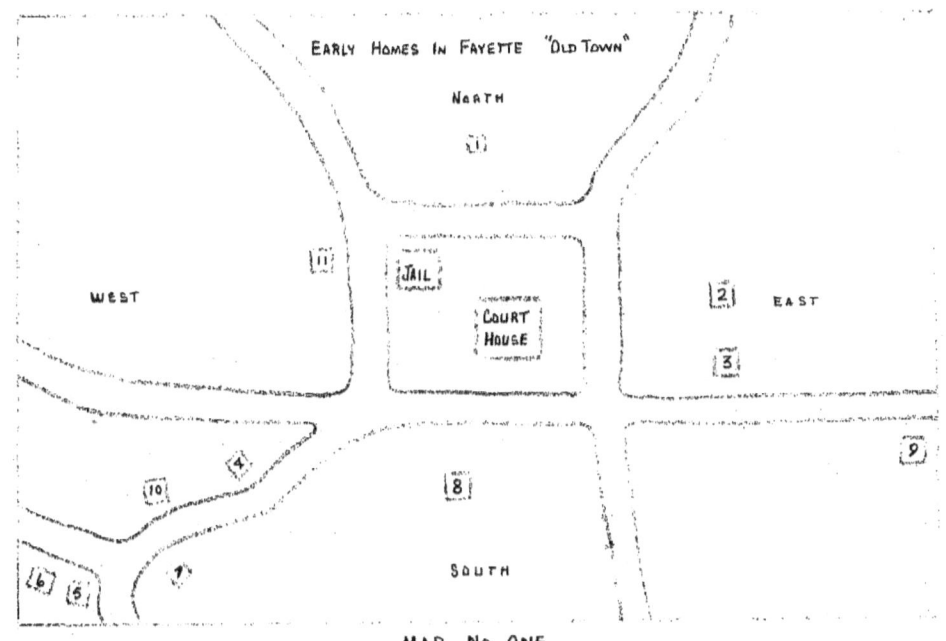

Mr. S. G. James was in charge of the railroad work and told the people of Fayetteville that he would extend the railroad through the "old town" of Fayetteville for a $1,000 dollars. The land around old town was rough and hilly, up grade most of the way, however the citizen's thought the railroad would come through Fayetteville, anyway and did not pay the $1,000 dollars. Engineer James surveyed the track to cut through from Boxes Creek to the overhead bridge and by the trestle along the low level land.

Afterwards, Mr. James told the people that he would survey the land next to the railroad and stake it off in lots for half of the lots surveyed. This was done and the lots were sold by his attorney.

When Fayette Depot Town first moved to Fayette's present location there were no houses on the south side of the railroad, it was just an open field. At the railroad where Hamby's store was built later, there was a black-smith shop owned by Mr. Howton.

When the town moved to its present location some of the stores in the new town were; Cannon's, Robertsons, Harkins, Propst, Nuckols, Rose & Phillips and Sudduths. The first store was built by Mr. Sudduth in January 1892. The second business was by Rose and Phillips in May, 1892. Propst, Cannon and Robertsons built the block from the present corner on James Street, across from Hodges to Cannon Drug Store. The first post-office was located between Yellow Front Store and Anhalt's 5¢ and 10¢ Store on Temple Avenue.

The 1911 fire destroyed the complete town from the present Masonic Temple Building to the depot. Box cars were pulled up to save the depot and were pulled away as they caught fire. The Whitney House and main residences were not burned.

To finish the description of the town before the fire of 1911, Harkins store was located in the section where the present hotel is located. Cannon' where Hodges Store is today, Propst in the location of the present Hodges Bargain Dept. adjoining the main Hodges Store.

The streets were dirt. Mr. Propst owned a livery stable and hauled people about for hire. The store buildings were constructed of wood.

There was a well in the middle of the street in front of the Tom Robertson Store. This well was where the people got their drinking water and also watered their horses. There was a cotton yard near the depot where the people camped when they came to town. There was plenty of room to "hitch" their horses.

Fayette then had three saloons, one located where George H. Gullett's Department Store is today, this being the largest of the three.

The first automobiles in Fayette were of some service but a great source of fear for the mules and horses. Mr. W. D. Putman brought the first automobile to Fayette. Due to a small difficulty, Mr. Putman put the car under a shed and never used it.

(Under date of Thursday, March 30, 1911, The Fayette Banner carried complete news coverage of the most sensational happening to occur in Fayette to that time --- the disastrous fire which completely wiped out the business district early on the morning of Friday, March 24, 1911.)

The complete story reprinted from the files of the Fayette Banner follows:
DISASTROUS FIRE SWEEPS FAYETTE -- ENTIRE BUSINESS DISTRICT IS CONSUMED IN ONE HOUR AND FORTY MINUTES.

Will rebuild Town at once - The total loss, from best information obtainable, is $383,350.00 with insurance of about $43,850.

The entire business district of Fayette, Ala. including the $40,000 court house and four residences was destroyed by fire on last Friday morning, March 24.

The origin of the fire is unknown, the blaze being first discovered by Mr. Thornton, of the Fayette Mill and Fertilizer Company, at 6:15 o'clock in the drug store of Dr. J. D. Young, situated on the east side of Temple Avenue.

The fire spread very rapidly. Having started near the northern limit of the business district, and the wind blowing in a strong gale in a southeasterly direction, it could easily be seen that the entire street was doomed.

The entire population of the town turned out and formed themselves into a bucket brigade to fight the flames, and to their efforts is due the fact that the greater section of the residence section of the town was not also destroyed.

The town had only recently invested in a small chemical engine which did good service in saving the home of Zed Graham, and thereby preventing the spread of the confragration to the eastern residence section.

The depot of the Southern Railway was saved, after having caught fire several times. This building and the county jail were all of any consequence left in the region of the fire.

There were no lives lost, nor were there any serious accidents, though many were caught in close quarters and had narrow escapes.

The buildings in every instance were totally lost, and but few of the merchants saved stock of much value.

The heaviest losers were Robertson & Dodds and Propst Brothers, which firms owned their own buildings and carried very large stocks of merchandise.

A number of the firms have already resumed business with the small amount of goods saved. Some have improvised small structures on their former lots, while others have secured places on the outskirts of the town, one firm securing temporary quarters in the rear of a blacksmith shop.

The town council will immediately pass an ordinance fixing a fire limit, in which only buildings constructed of brick, stone or concrete will be permitted. The entire population of the town seems of one sentiment in regard to this matter, and will demand the enforcement of the ordinance when passed.

One contract was let on last Saturday, the day following the fire, for the erection of three two-story brick stores. This contract was let by Dr. T. M. Peters, Smith-Dodson & Co., and W. D. Putnam. A contractor of Columbus, Mississippi is to do the work.

The records of the probate judge's office are thought to be all safe, but this cannot be determined until the vault is opened.

The chancery records were consumed, as were those of the tax assessor. The circuit clerk, sheriff and tax collector saved their records. Unable to learn whether the county superintendent of education saved the records of his office.

The plant of the Fayette Banner, the only newspaper in the county was totally destroyed, but the paper will be issued as usual, the work being done by the Western Newspaper Union until a new plant can be installed.

The same spirit prevails with every merchant and business man in the town.

Among those who have already begun business with goods saved from the fire are Robertson & Dodds, Propst Brothers, J. R. Robertson, Berry Brothers, B. J. Bogard, Jones Brothers, Graham & Mallory, W. M. Cannon, City Meat Market and the two livery stables, both of which saved all of their livestock, but little else. - - - - - - - - -

That a handsomer and more enduring town will arise from this fire-swept city is the determination of the merchants who suffered in the conflagration that swept out the entire business district.

The people, with true American grit, are determined to begin anew on firmer foundations. While the ruins were smoldering there were plans being made for new structures and the rebuilding of the city.

The lack of proper fire fighting facilities has been brought home in an expensive but effective manner. The fire that began at six in the morning had every business house in its grip in less than an hour and a half, and the county court house was doomed.

Losses fall the more heavily on the city from the fact that so little insurance was carried. This is a serious feature of the diaster that is due to the confidence of the citizen's in the immunity of the city from fire.

There was no suffering here from lack of food or shelter, despite the fact that every store in town is in ashes.

Heav, as the blow has been to the town, there is no abatement of confidence in the future of Fayette among the citizens, and new structures will be erected on the ruin of the old as soon as the ground is cooled and the debris cleared away. - - - Following is a list of the businesses destroyed and estimated loss: Robertson & Dodds, $100,000; Proost Brothers, $75,000; W. M. Cannon, $30,000; Smith, Dodson & Co., $12,000; Walker Brothers & Co., $10,000; Courthouse, $40,000; S. J. Cannon, $10,000; Mrs. Kate Turner, $7,500; Fayette County Bank, $5,000; F. A. Nuckols & Co., $6,000; Beasley & Wright, $4,500; C. A. Beasley, $1,500; Fayette Telephone Co., $3,500; Masonic Lodge, $4,500; Odd Fellows Lodge, $3,000; Dr. J. A. Branyon, $7,000; Dr. J. D. Young, $5,000; E. P. Goodwin, $2,500; G. T. Hassell & Co., $2,500; Berry Brothers, $2,000; W. A. Anderson, $2,000; R. T. Hamner, $4,000; Miss E. Shepherd, $5,000; Dr. T. M. Peters, $1,250; ___Thornton, $1,500; J. W. Blackburn, $1,000; Dr. C. B. Blackburn, $800; J. B. Mace, $1,000; Southern Railway, Co., $2,000; W. L. Sykes, $1,000; Dr. N. W. Stallworth, $1,000; The Fayette Banner, $2,000; J. M. Stewart, $2,500; W. O. Wallcae, $1,500; Dr. W. A. Graham, $1,250; Postoffice, $1,000; Jones Brothers, $6,500; R. F. Peters, $2,500; Graham & Malloy, $2,500; E. Rose, $2,500; C. W. Sanders, $1,000; B. J. Bogard, $2,000; B. J. McClure, $1,000; W. D. Putnam, $1,000; Fayette L. & F. Co., $500; Sidney LeBlanc, $600; W. S. McNeil, $350; J. R. Robertson, $700; Dr. Claude Bell, $750; Jeffries Stables, $500; W. A. Tipton, $250; S. T. Lowery, $500; S. J. Sanders, $300; S. E. Jones, $400; Marvin McCaine, $200; City Meat Market, $500; -- Total Loss $ 383,350.

- - - - - On Monday, March 27, 1911, Mayor J. E. Chandler called a meeting of the town council and immediately passed an ordinance fixing the fire limits of Fayette and prohibiting the erecting of any wooden structures within this zone."

In 1926, the people of Fayette and Fayette County decided that it was necessary to pave the main street of Fayette north to the intersection beyond the First Baptist Church. At this time the roads and streets were not good enough for the heavy travel that took place since the town was becoming more thickly settled. In June the State Engineers under a local law passed, began paving on Temple Avenue, but this work was not complete until 1927. It was a period of at least ten years before another street was paved. During this time the roads had been improved with gravel. In 1927 James Street; South side of Temple Avenue; Columbus Street; McGuire Street; Blackburn Street; and the High School Street were completed. Curb and gutter and sewer lines were laid along with this project. The City Park Street was paved in 1938, a project of the W.P.A. The man in charge of this paving was Mr. Charles Inman, who resided in Fayette County at the time. In 1948 Walker Street was paved and work was started on opening Aylette Street. Aylette was completed in 1949 and 1950.

Through the years as these other streets have been paved, concrete sidewalks have been laid on many streets and sewer, water and gas lines have been expanded to form a city-wide network. Telephone and electric power lines have been installed and a modern system of traffic signals control the city's automotive traffic.

During the years since World War II the city has enjoyed a building boom which has resulted in the construction of many new residences and commercial buildings. Today the extended City limits reach approximately 3 miles from the courthouse.

The Northwest Gas District came to Fayette in the year 1955. The homes of Fayette are heated today with Natural Gas, Butane Gas, Electricity and Coal.

A new $65,000 City Hall was constructed in 1955 and moved into early in 1956. The Citizen's Bank (new building) was constructed in 1956 and opened August 8, 1956. The Faaette County Hospital was completed and put into use in October, 1958.

Just as the pioneer settlers of this community had faith in the future growth and progress of their little village, so have the modern progressive citizens of Fayette a firm faith in the city's future expansion and development. "Faith in Fayette", is our slogan.

GLEN ALLEN -- When the Frisco Railroad was built through the northern part of Fayette County in the 1880's a water tank was located at the present site of Glen Allen and from that beginning, the little settlement of Glen Allen came to be.

First appearing on the records in 1888, Glen Allen is located in Fayette County, Beat 11, on the Frisco Railroad and Highway 78. There are two stores, a post office, the Frisco Depot and three coal processing plants. The only church is a Methodist Church, where all of the citizens attend and the children attend the schools in Winfield and Hubbertville, as the Glen Allen School burned in 1945.

Glen Allen was incorporated July 18, 1959, after 75 years from its beginning and the following men, elected on July 11, to serve the new town, were sworn into office on July 18, 1959, by Judge Clyde C. Cargile, Fayette County Probate Judge: Mayor, J. P. Gilstrap, Aldermen, W. H. Stewart, Ray F. Aldridge, J. W. Dozier, W. M. Logan and John D. Franks.

GUMBUD COMMUNITY -- In 1896 the Gumbud or Macedonia Baptist Church was established with 12 charter members. The building was used as the church and as the school. This was a common practice in those days.

Gumbud is about four miles south of Fayette on the Concord Road. The community is mostly agricultural and very fertile as it lies in the Sipsey Valley.

HOWARD MINES -- For many years the town of Howard Mines was a busy community. The Moss-McCormick Mining Company opened their mine here and for ten years or more, employed several hundred men to work in the Coal Mines.

At this time (1959) the Mine is closed and has been for several years. After a tragic explosion this section gradually grew less active in the mining industry.

HUBBERTVILLE -- This community is located in the north central part of Fayette County and one of the three high schools of Fayette County is located here. There are several churches in the area, the largest number being of the denomination of Church of Christ. There are several stores in and around Hubbertville.

The community received its name from the Hubbert Family, some of the earliest settlers of this section. Being in the Sipsey Valley, this is one of the richest agricultural areas in the county.

The following poem by one of Hubbertville High School's beloved teachers, Ruth Ezell McCaleb, tells in a beautiful manner the story of a scene familiar to many Fayette Countians, and especially those citizen's who live near Hubbertville. This old Mill is known as "McCaleb's Mill" and has truly been a spot of beauty in our Fayette County, with the covered bridge and the winding stream.

RESURRECTION -- (Nearby flows a winding lovely river -)
Which is fed by gurgling streamlets many. -- One, The Old Mill Creek, that nurses on its bank -- The Old Water Mill and turns the giant wheel -- To which the ever curious public comes -- To view with admiration and commercial pride -- This ancient land mark as it now abides, -- Strong in its ageless sinews through all seasons -- Sunshine, rain, storms, famine and prosperity. -- The silver spray, running from the race -- Touched with regerberation the age worn wheel -- To set it moving and vibrating with the trembling -- Pulse of its people's need.

Twas here lovers plighted their vows - one the Master's son -- Knowing that the soft rapt acceptance was drowned -- From outside world by the stream's happy laughter -- Joining in bliss too sweet to share, yet as old as creation -- Nature gave her blessing in the low murmur of the water -- And the silent nodding of the pines, oaks, maples and ferns -- the dogwood, the crabs and the judas trees were aware -- That they must lend their loveliness as fare -- To mix with rhododendron and honeysuckles sweet -- And send Spring's sweetest perfumed breath of air -- To bless these lovers, who without premeditation, -- Were so ignorantly unaware of -- What life ere long would demand - taking the one -- Leaving the other to grope her way in aching pain -- To the cross of re-adjustment. -- Now they walked blissfully happy their way in fair Eden's garden.

When life is full and fair and gay -- We take no time to ponder immortality. -- When doubts and darkness surround us -- We then question why human souls must surpass -- A streamlet in the limitless earth - assigned its task to do. -- Here, amid the beauty of love's first young dream, -- The lone one came to wistfully tarry and fathom, if possible, -- The reason of life and the greater riddle of death. -- The streamlet seemed to leap in glad greeting, as if -- It could forever play and loiter on its way almost -- Bursting from the many glad happy things it had to say -- About now and the happenings of yesteryear. -- Memories crowded thick and fast; pain grew more -- Acute and hard to bear because it had been -- Kept buried in the recesses of a deader self.

Laboriously she moved on, until she came to deeper -- Pools, where the water moved in quiet sad reveries, -- As if it knew all the pain and sorrow which had flown -- From the kindred band who lived within its glow. -- Then, as if, suddenly seeming to realize its mighty task -- The waters gleamed and flashed o'er its rock ribbed -- Changing course as if Duty is the word that -- Destiny has appointed us all to follow. --

Then the dreamer remembered other years when -- The mighty river had

reached flood stage and -- Its waters spread like a flaming silver fire to --
Destroy the crops and corn. -- The streamlet contributed its share in this
sorrow stricken work -- Only later to have its course washed clean and --
Clear of all debris; the soft rich sediment settled -- On the fields by its
side to give richer soils for more -- Abundant crops to its laboring people,
-- For a time, the old wheel was still and the bell -- Sent no merry challenging ring, until the Master -- Spent through hours of darkness and anxiety, --
Found a way to supply these hungry sinews of this -- All demanding temple and
never ceasing stream.

    Now the Master is gone - the Master's son is gone; -- Other hands open the
door through which in -- Other days, far more fair, many a neighbor had --
Paused to enter there to exchange friendly greetings -- And to inquire concerning the planting of the fields, -- Or the impending weather, which might bring
to bear -- Bountiful crops or devastation rare. -- The wooden bridge which
spanned the creek -- Was still there, and the old road, which circled -- The
crest of the hill, was unchanged. -- Many lovely trees had fallen to man's
prey,- leaving -- An open gaping vale of white sand and more -- Sickly looking cornstalks. The old blacksmith -- Shop nestled in the arms of the rising
cliff -- And the lovely tree, on which the sweet muscadines -- Grew to yield
the year's supply of jelly, was gone. -- Yet, through all the pain of change
and growth, -- The mill had not ceased to serve the intention of its purpose.
-- The jolly flowing, versatile-mooded creek had never -- Failed to water in
abundance. Nothing had ceased -- To do its work; neither could they cease,
because to be -- Idle is but to die.

    Thus in the dreamer's sad reverie she knew the -- Purpose of sorrow is to
lend enrichment to the -- Purpose of life. She knew that in each life there
-- Can be a ressurection. There must be a resurrection -- When we cheerfully
bury our own dead sorrows and -- Busily arise to a renewed work of spiritual
and -- Moral revolution to duty in the hearts and minds -- Of all mankind.
She drained her cup of -- Crucifixion and put it quietly aside. -- She had
found the Holy Grail; she turned -- Her face to the sun; she took up the purpose of -- Life through change of growth and incessant pain -- Is ever on and
on! -- She could not fathom the riddle of death. -- She was content to wait
until we reach Home -- And the Eternal Stream where the purpose of -- Immortality will be revealed in the day of all -- Resurrections. Our lives will then
be free of -- All devastating floodstage and choking debris.

LAWRENCE'S MILL COMMUNITY. -- In years gone by, there was a large mill pond at
the location of the Lawrence's Mill. The old dam with the little stream
trickling away was a beautiful scene and in the little creek below the dam
many good people were baptized into several of the churches in the neighborhood.

    In the early days the post office located at this place was known as
Hugent. It was and still is a bee-hive of activity.

    Today, the Lawrence Brothers have a modern cotton gin, a lumber mill and
a general merchandise store to serve the people of this section of the county.
About a mile over on the Winfield Highway is the general merchandise store
and lumber mill operated by Linwood Smith. Besides the lumber mill and the
cotton gin, this section is very productive in agriculture and there are many
fertile fish ponds. The church nearest this settlement is the Hopewell Primitive Baptist Church, one of the oldest churches in Fayette County. Another
very old church standing nearby is the Bethlehem Methodist Church.

MT. VERNON COMMUNITY -- Mt. Vernon is located in the Collin's Beat. Its first settlers were: McClures, Moores, Powells, Abarnathys, Smiths, Cargiles, Harkins, and Collins. The Collins family came from South Carolina and settled at Mt. Vernon January 1, 1839. At that time the church was named Horn Church and had only one grave in the cemetery. The name of the Beat was at first, Hesters Beat. The voting for Collins, Thompsons and probably other Beats was at Aron Howton's place. There was a post office at Mr. Hosea Collins home and it was called the Machine Post Office.

Hell's Creek received its name from a family who lived near it. The name of the family was Heralds, but the creek's name was shortened to Hell's. Sometime between 1825 and 1835, two Moore brothers were camping near a creek. When night fell, they made some corn bread dough and cooked it in the hot ashes and coals of their campfire. The next morning when they were getting the bread out of the ashes the "pone" rolled down the bank into the creek and since that time the little stream has been called Ash Pone Creek.

Mr. Ab. Powell, newspaper editor, once lived at Mt. Vernon and in 1863 wrote a history of the section around Mt. Vernon, as well as other parts of Fayette County and published it in the newspaper. The article was "Fifty-five Years In West Alabama". When Mr. Ab. Powell first settled at Mt. Vernon in 1838, there were only two houses in the community.

In the earlier days, schools were taught in log churches at Mt. Vernon. One of these churches burned about 1913, but was rebuilt. The first Mt. Vernon School House was built in 1904, this school being taught by Mr. Smith. Later, in 1918 the church house and the school house were blown down by a cyclone. The church replacing this was built in 1919 and the present brick church was completed in 1954. The present Junior High School was constructed in 1935. The Fayette-Vernon Highway was made a highway in 1928 and improved and paved in 1938.

In the early days od our county, almost all families had private family graveyards around their homes. After many years the present custom of public cemeteries started and a walk through the Mt. Vernon Cemetery gives an idea as to the age of the community and the families who have lived there for several generations.

NEWTONVILLE -- Newtonville is thought to be the oldest settlement in Fayette County. The first settlers came by horseback from the Carolinas, the date is unknown. It is known, however that the first three men in the area were - a Mr. Poe, Hogan Yerby and a Mr. Blakeney. (Even though Newtonville is believed to be the oldest settlement, the oldest land grant in Fayette County was issued to Adley Harris - signed by John Q. Adams - location on Ford's Mountain)

The first foot of road in Fayette County was built from Newtonville across Sipsey bottoms of white oak, split logs, by the settlers of the community.

Some of the families coming to this section before, during and shortly after the Civil War, were - Blakeneys, Nalls, Brents and Savages. Most of these families were slave owners of a peaceful nature and content until the renegades came along and killed the Nalls slaves and drove them from their homes. After this killing, the land was sold off to other families as the Gravlees, Sudduths and others.

The Savage family raised sheep and made wool in a factory owned by the family. The Savages also owned a gin and a grist mill, at one time. They were the last to have slaves in the Newtonville Community. Dr. William Welburn's family started the cemetery in Newtonville when a child of theirs died there.

Before the coming of the railroad through Fayette County, Newtonville was the largest community in the county, having at one time, four two-story buildings. There was also, a very active Masonic Lodge.

The present highway through Newtonville was surveyed in 1942 and is one of today's better roads.

RENFROE VALLEY or APPLING COMMUNITY -- About five miles west of Fayette on what is known as the Vernon Highway, is the community sometimes called "Renfroe Valley". The main attraction of this settlement was the fertile farm land. Some of the early settlers were the Tate, Renfroe, Hassell, Pinkerton and Appling families. The Renfroes settled in the lower part of the valley, the Hassel family settled farther west and the Applings settled north of them. Since the Appling family was the first to settle here it was sometimes referred to as the Appling Community.

As late as 1937 old farming methods were still being used but today, modern equipment has replaced the old bone plow and the small fields have been put together making larger fields. From 1937 to 1940 the roads were improved and the Vernon Highway was paved. The "pike" road to Winfield was surveyed for pavement. In 1938 the Alabama Power Company started the rural electrification and today most homes and farms are modern in every respect.

Renfro's Store and the County Building and Supply Company are located in the Renfro Valley. This section is thickly settled.

ROSALIND CITY -- Rosalind City is a scattered agricultural community. It came into being when the railroad was completed and a water tank was located there for the trains. There are two churches, the Baptist and Methodist and a grist mill to serve the community. In the early days, Rosalind City and Stough were joining communities and at one time the children from both communities attended a joint school.

The settlement was first called Legg, (Mr. Legg operated a small store and kept the depot). Later the name was changed to Sipsey and finally the name Rosalind City was decided on for the permanent name of this community.

STEWART SETTLEMENT -- The first settlement in what is now Russell's Beat was made in 1818 or 1819 by Ruben Stewart and his brother William Stewart, and was known as the Stewart Settlement. The land, some two or three sections, was purchased from the United States Government before Alabama was admitted as a State.

Reuben Stewart married Elizabeth McConnell, an aunt of Mr. Posey McConnell, whose descendants live just north of Fayette and whose ancestors came to Alabama with the Stewarts.

Their route from North Carolina extended southwest through Tennessee and on through the sections of Alabama that is now Birmingham; south to the present Taylorsville, in Tuscaloosa County, Ala. Here they left their families and some servants as guards, for those were the days of Indians and wild beasts. The men and negro slaves started on the journey northward, through, in part, an unbroken forest. Family history records that the route was along or near what is now the Moore's Bridge Road. Since the McConnell's made a settlement just south of Moore's Bridge, this tradition is likely correct.

After the McConnells stopped, the Stewarts, William and Reuben and a cousin George, traveled on, cutting their own road through the dense forest to ten miles north of the present town of Fayette, Alabama, and here they cleared the forest, built cabins and left a few trusted servants in charge while they returned to Taylorsville for their families. These men and their families proudly established the Stewart Settlement.

The Stewarts sold land to the other settlers as they joined them in the new settlement. Some of these early settlers were the Musgroves, the Hodges, the Websters, Dodsons and Hams.

By 1840 large tracts of land had been cleared for corn and wheat, rice and some cotton were being grown. The nearest markets for their products and the only place they could buy supplies were Tuscaloosa, Alabama, and Columbus, Mississippi. (Transportation was by ox-drawn wagons and as late as 1880 the men were hauling cotton to Columbus and driving cattle on foot to New Orleans, La.)

When the Civil War was looming, many land owners saw the uncertainty of the future. Mr. William Musgrove and others of the community were brave soldiers during the war. Russell's Beat was well represented at the front. The old Muster Ground, where the young men were trained for conflict was on Mr. Mark Russell's place, just southeast of the present Bobo School. The Military Prison was on the hill near the present Musgrove Chapel Church, just east of the church.

Shortly after the Civil War the U. S. Government established a Post Office, named "Mont Calm", with Mr. William Musgrove as the first postmaster. Mr. Charles C. Stewart was the first justice of the Peace and at his death in 1878, Mr. William Musgrove became the justice and later Mr. Larkin Stewart was appointed to the position.

Farming tools were scarce, but it is said that the first crop was corn and was made without a plow. Every family soon established its own brick yard. The houses were built of logs, but the chimneys were constructed of home pressed bricks.

For a long period of time there were no public schools so the Stewart families joined in the effort to provide a tutor for their children and school was held in the different homes. A Mr. Lovey was one of those teachers, also a Mr. Martin Harkins. As the community grew, private schools were taught in the Mt. Joy Church house, located on the hill just south of Stewart Creek. These schools were for only 3 months duration in the summer, and some of the earlier teachers were Miss Minnie Stewart, Roscoe and Nando Wheeler, and Prof. Vaughn Windham. Later a school house was built at Pine Grove and these school sessions were taught by Jesse Couch, Chelses ___, Thomas Lucas, Mabel Stewart and others. By this time the schools were beginning to be graded and rapid improvement was made. Later Bobo High School was organized and the new building is on the original tract deeded by President Monroe to the first settlers.

STOUGH -- Shortly after the close of the Civil War, Jacob Henderson Stough moved from Pike County, Ala. and settled in Fayette County at a place later to be known as Sardis, Alabama. When Mr. Stough settled here, there were no railroads. The mail was carried from Fayette to Birmingham by horseback. Jacob H. Stough had the contract for carrying the mail to Birmingham and back, once a week.

The first school was a church known as Old Boxes, which stood down near Rosalind City Community. The children who lived in this section had to walk there to school. Later, there were churches built that were named Oak Grove and Bethel. After these were built the children attended schools held in the churches. Later these schools were consolidated into one large school which is now located in Stough and is a fine Junior High School. In those early years the children went to school only five months each year. There was only one teacher to each school to teach about one hundred or more pupils of all ages ranging from seven to twenty-one years.

The ways of travel were by ox-team and horses and by foot. In the 1880's when the railroad was built there was a post office established, known as Sardis. During the construction of the railroad a large water tank was erected for the trains and Mr. J. H. Stough kept the post office while he and his sons worked in building the railroad. The building of the railroad caused other families to come and settle here.

About 1890, the name of this community was changed from Sardis to Stough, being named for Mr. J. H. Stough. As other families moved in and bought land in the settlement and built their homes the small village began to grow. The chief occupation has always been farming. Later there were sawmills, the first being owned and operated by Mr. Whitley and Mr. Farquhar who later sold out to the Gardner Brothers. The Gardner Brothers operated a gin, a grist mill and a small store for a number of years. Other stores in operation at that time were operated by Mr. Powers and Mr. Honeycutt.

The churches in Stough today are Oak Grove Methodist Church, Bethel Church, Stough Church and The Prophecy of God Church.

WAYSIDE -- The community of Wayside was named in an unusual way. The people living in that section of the county were trying to get a post office established and needed a name for it. Mr. T. M. Reese was one of the leaders in seeking to get the new post office, so he turned to his wife, Margaret Agnes (Harris) Reese one day and asked if she had any suggestion for a name. She looked out the window and after some thought replied, "Since we are here by the way side of this road (the pike to Guin), why not name it Wayside?"

According to the records of the Post Office Department in Washington, D. C. a post office was established at Wayside on September 16, 1878, with Terrell Reese appointed to serve as the only postmaster. It was discontinued on September 30, 1905.

A site location report of May 2, 1899, from the postmaster at Wayside shows that the office was located one mile west of Luxapallila River, one-half mile west of Dodson Creek, 13 and one-half miles from Fayette, four miles south of Galilee, six miles north of Cane and two and one-half miles west of Mont Calm.

After the post office was established the Wayside Methodist Church was built with the Odd Fellow Lodge meeting in the same building. Later the school Wayside was built and a few stores were added to make a little community that is still very active today.

CHAPTER III

ECONOMIC DEVELOPMENTS

Sipsey River is a tributary of the Tombigbee River and necessarily a part of the Sipsey and Tombigbee drainage system. The length of the Sipsey River proper is estimated to be about 140 miles. It rises in Winston County, runs through the southeast corner of Marion County until it reaches Fayette County where it becomes Sipsey River, and then its course for ninety miles is almost due south, and from that point it flows southwestward and empties into the little Tombigbee about one mile south of the old Viena Village site, which is estimated to be 343 miles by river from Mobile.

Transportation was quite a problem for the farmers and miners of Fayette County, before the railroad was built. Before the drainage of the Sipsey River a barge was built by some of the farmers for the purpose of transporting their cotton to Mobile, Ala. In the fall, the barge was loaded with bales of cotton and when the rains started and there was a rise in the river the barge started on its journey down the Sipsey River. The crew guided the barge with poles and oars and their equipment also included saws and axes that were used to cut the fallen logs and brush out of the way. This trip ended abruptly at Newtonville, Alabama, still in Fayette County when the barge broke in half. Teams of Oxen were carried to the river to haul the cotton away from the ill-fated barge and the old barge sank in the river.

The question of the drainage and opening of Sipsey River was first started in the early 1870's when Woodard Moore, commonly called "Commodore Moore" who then resided in the northeastern part of Fayette County, along with several others, formed what was known as the "Sipsey River Navigation Company", the purpose of which was to open up and drain the Sipsey River and provide navigation so that barges or boats could transfer the products of this county direct to Mobile, especially coal and cotton, and in furtherance of this project barges were built for conveying coal down the Sipsey River, the destination being Mobile, Ala.

The last barge to make the trip down the river was owned by Mr. Moore. This last trip was made in 1875 and carried coal and other commodities down the river. This barge was being brought back up the river, laden with merchandise and was landed six miles below Fayette on the boundary of McCracken Farm, where the remainder of its cargo being brought from southern Alabama, was sold from the barge. Soon after this time, the death of "Commodore Moore" occurred, and the business of the Sipsey River Navigation Co. was discontinued and since that time the old barge remained stationary. It was still visible in the water in 1938.

Prior to 1859, there were no bridges across the larger streams of Fayette County and in time of floods the local travel was confined to the territory between the streams. On February 28, 1859, James Ford was granted a franchise permit to build and operate a toll bridge across New River or Sipsey River on the Jasper road in Fayette County and the rates he was allowed to charge under the permit for each horse wagon, "four bits", for each two horse wagon, "two bits", for one horse and vehicle, twenty cents, for a man and horse, one dime and for a foot man, five cents.

A similar permit, on the same day, was granted to William Farquhar to build and operate a toll bridge across New River or Sipsey River on the Elyton road (this road was from Fayette to Elyton, the county seat of Jefferson County, at that time) and the charges to be the same as that allowed to James Ford. The bridge built by Mr. Farquhar was later known as Newton's Bridge and was not far from the old Newton's Mill.

At the time these permits were granted, the Sipsey River was from seventy-five to one hundred feet wide with perpendicular banks from ten to twenty feet to the water in normal times. The present day Sipsey River is greatly changed as a result of the clearing up and cultivation of the original forest and the erosion of the hills along the valley. It is changed from a stream with deep banks to a stream that floods the entire surface between the hills at every unusual rainfall and overflows thousands of acres of very rich bottom land.

The success of any pioneer settlement depends in a large measure upon the means of transportation -- for the settler to get into the country and transportation for him to get his products to market.

There were no roads prior to 1820 other than the Indian trails and those that were built by the settlers themselves. Those built by the settlers were little more than wide paths cut through the forest.

The best roads in the state were constructed by private corporations as turnpikes or toll roads and were operated as commercial enterprises, many of the companies also, operating stages on their roads.

One such road was of extreme importance to Fayette County. On December 16, 1819, an act was passed authorizing John Byler and Association to construct a turnpike from Big Shoal Creek in Lauderdale County to Tuscaloosa, coming through the eastern side of Fayette County. By 1822 this road was completed. The act authorizing the road also stipulated the toll rates to be charged, as follows: "On four wheel carriage and team, seventy-five cents; on a two wheel carriage, fifty cents; on a man and horse, twelve and a half cents; on each pack horse, six and a fourth cents; for each head of cattle, one cent; for each head of hogs or sheep, half a cent." Postmen, express messengers, Federal and state troops, footmen, persons going to and from Church and laborers on their way to or from their fields were exempted from tolls.

"Byler Road" as it is still known today, entered Fayette County on the north side three or four miles southwest of the present town of Eldridge, in Walker County, and left the county on the south side of the present town of Berry at the county line. This road gave the early settler a highway over which to haul his products to Tuscaloosa, which was to be the main trading center for Fayette County until the advent of the railroads, almost seventy years later. In wagons, drawn, usually by oxen, the people hauled their corn and cotton and staves and other products to town, and their supplies, particularly salt, back home. The round trip frequently took a week and the people often went in parties of two or more, camped out along the road at night and tried to make a picnic of the journey.

(From - "Fifty-Five Years in West Alabama", by: E. A. Powell, as written in The Tuscaloosa Gazette, December 2, 1886.)

"What a Calico Dress Cost" -- From 1828 to 1833 the times were stringent. The price of cotton ranged from 6 to 8 cents, and money was scarce - while most of the articles of necessity were high. Coffee from 4 to 5 pounds to the dollar; very common sugar 6 to 8 pounds, salt $3 to $4 dollars per sack. I remember very well when salt got down to $2 dollars in the winter of 1834 - 1835. A prominent farmer in Fayette County came to Tuskaloosa and bought two or three hundred sacks on speculation, - with a view to holding it until it would rise. In June following the man died and his administrators sold the salt before there was any material rise. Brown domestice from 35 to 37½ cents a yard; Calico from 50 to 75 cents. I remember on one occasion being with my father in North Port, where he was laying in his year's supplies. The merchant proposed to sell him a calico dress for my sisters, who were growing up to womanhood. Father plead his inability and fears about making his bill too large, etc. The merchant replied, "I will sell it to you so cheap that you can't resist it." At the same time showing him some, and said, "I will sell you that at the low price of 43-3/4 cents a yard," and the dresses were bought. This, however, was after the rise in cotton. In the fall of 1833 the price of cotton began to advance and ran from 11 to 13 cents and continued to rise until it culminated in 1835-6, at 17 to 20 cents. I remember my father sold his little crop at 18½ cents. In the fall of 1836 the price opened at 14 to 15 and stood at about these figures until 1837, when there came a tremendous crash. Down went cotton in a short time to 10 cents. From the fall of 1833 to the latter part of 1837, began and ended what has since been characterized as "The Flush Times". -----"

After the advent of the "T-Model" the people still had their problems in travel. If the weather was dry the dust rolled in great clouds when these vehicles came down the road and in some cases, where the road was sandy it was quite common to get "stuck" in the deep sand. And on the other hand if the weather was wet, there was mud everywhere and the driver of a "T-Model" spent much of his travel time in walking to get some good farmer to bring his horses to pull the auto out of the mud. And in those days, when the gas ran out there were not many gas stations and that called for another long walk, sometimes miles were involved, to get a small can of gas to get on with the trip. And another snare was the "flat-tire" of days gone by. It presented quite a problem to improvise some kind of "jack" to get the car off the ground and then to set about with the old patching kit to get the patch to "stick".

Today with our modern roads and fast automobiles it is sometimes hard to realize the wonderful advancement of our world. In the old days when the automobile was very young, fifteen miles per hour was a great speed.

The Byler Road, already mentioned was improved and paved in 1958. Other important roads in Fayette County have played a great part in making Fayette County the successful county that it is.

In 1914 several of the counties were working to get the legislature to establish a highway from Florence to Tuscaloosa as nearly as practical along the old Andrew Jackson military road. This highway would connect the Tennessee River and the Gulf of Mexico. Fayette was fortunate that it came through Fayette County instead of going through Walker County -- this would have left Fayette County completely off this great route of today. This highway was completely hardsurfaced in the 1930's, completing it from Fayette to Winfield and the section between Fayette and Tuscaloosa was completely hard surfaced in the 1940's.

The Fayette-Vernon Highway was paved in 1938. Newtonville Road was surveyed in 1942 and completely hard surfaced to the Tuscaloosa County Line. The Concord Road was hard surfaced in the early 1950's. State Lake Road was completed in 1957. The Bluff - Guin Road was hard surfaced and completed in the late 1940's. Townley Road was hard surfaced to the county line in the 1940's. The Carbon Hill road was completed and paved in the 1950's and the Hubbertville - Glen Allen Road was finished in the 1950's.

Since modern travel goes to our farms as well as our cities we have numerous "farm-to-market" roads paved all over the county.

Fayette's first passenger train arrived at the depot in May, 1883. According to old records it was a memorable event and attracted a large crowd of curious spectators from miles around to get their first glimpse of an "Iron Horse".

The city's first railroad line was the Georgia Pacific Railway Company. It was organized in Georgia in 1881 and the actual construction for the railroad was done by the Richmond and Danville Extension Company.

The road was completed between Atlanta and Columbus, Miss. in 1887 and on July 1, 1889 it was finished to Greenville, Miss. In 1883 the Georgia Pacific Railway Company leased the road to the Richmond and Danville Extension Company for a period of 20 years. The railroad was later sold to the Southern Railway System.

Before the advent of the railroad to Fayette County, cotton and other agricultural products grown in this section was transported by ox wagon to Tuscaloosa or Columbus. All of the provisions to stock the shelves of the merchants of Fayette Court House or Fayetteville were brought in on wagons, also.

The second railroad to be built in Fayette County was the Mobile and Gulf. The original purpose of this road was for the transportation of logs to the sawmill built by the Basket Lumber Company, which was organized in April, 1912, with Lee Basket of Kentucky as president. This company built its line of railroad from Fayette to Moore's Bridge and finally extended it to connect with the Mobile & Ohio at Buhl in Tuscaloosa County.

The only other railroad through Fayette County is the Frisco Railroad that crosses the northern part of the county.

POST OFFICES OF FAYETTE COUNTY -- By an act of Congress of March 3, 1819, a mail route was authorized from Tuscaloosa by Marion County to Columbus, Miss., this route seems to have served the territory which was afterwards Fayette County.

On July 2, 1836, ten years after the post office was located in the town of Fayette (called at that time Fayette Court House) a mail route was established from Fayette Court House, by Millport to Columbus, Miss. and on March 3, 1845, Congress established a route from Tuscaloosa by Fayette to Russellville.

In the absence of any records it is a well known fact from people who lived in the county in earlier years, that routes in later years were established direct between Fayette Court House and Columbus, Miss., and also between Fayette Court House and Elyton (county seat of Jefferson County, at that time) besides other routes. It was not until after 1882 when the Georgia Pacific Railway (now Southern) passed through Fayette County that the mail was brought in or carried out except over routes carried by a single horse and rider.

TOWN OF FAYETTE POST OFFICE -- The first postmaster to hold office in the town of Fayette Court House was Jessie VanHoose, who was appointed on February 14, 1826. He continued as postmaster from 1826 to March 30, 1841, and the total amount of money received by him for this fifteen years service as postmaster was $324.02, and in the meantime he was the first representative from Fayette County to the State Senate.

After the formation of Fayette County on December 20, 1824, the postal facilities for Fayette County were entirely different from what they are now. There was perhaps one mail each week or less, when at the present time and since the establishment of rural routes with carriers, there is hardly a citizen but that is served daily mail.

As stated, the first post office in Fayette County was established at Fayette Court House February 14, 1826. The name of the office was changed from Fayette Court House to Fayette on May 26, 1892. On January 1, 1907 the office was made presidential with a salary of $1,100 a year.

In 1925 a village delivery service was inaugerated to deliver the mail to local residents and at that time there were seven rural routes which were served by horse and buggy vehicles. Several years later some of the rural routes were consolidated.

The Fayette Post Office Building was completed and occupied on March 10, 1937. In 1949 the Fayette Post Office served five rural routes six days a week with fast automobile delivery. During the time around 1949 the longest rural route in Alabama was Fayette Route 3 which covered a distance of 83 miles. In this same period the rural routes covered a distance of 325 miles per day and the city routes two deliveries totaled 14 miles. Today the distance is even greater in the city delivery. In April, 1957, routes 6 and 7 were reestablished.

Following is a list of postmasters for the town of Fayette from its establishment to the present time with the date of their appointments:

Jesse Vanhoose appointed February 14, 1826; Azor Vanhoose appointed March 30, 1841; Elliott P. Jones appointed August 29, 1845; Henry P. Leonard appointed April 10, 1850; James H. Moore appointed December 15, 1851; Richard A. Smith appointed February 20, 1852; John L. Walton appointed June 19, 1856; R. Allen Smith appointed January 10, 1859; Vincent Hubbard appointed October 19, 1865; William C. Norris appointed November 13, 1866; Kisiah C. Zinniz appointed September 30, 1867; John C. Moore appointed January 16, 1874; William R. Smith, Sr. appointed July 30, 1885; James S. Williams appointed October 1, 1885; Thomas B. Morton appointed June 25, 1889;

Name of Office changed to Fayette on May 26, 1892 - Thomas B. Morton reappointed May 26, 1892; Daniel W. Norton appointed November 30, 1892; Robert P. Caine appointed October 30, 1893; Edward Rose appointed October 22, 1896; Daniel W. Morton appointed January 13, 1898; Andrew J. Treadway appointed January 25, 1902; Walter W. Harkins appointed January 31, 1905;

Office made presidential on January 1, 1907 - Walter W. Harkins reappointed January 13, 1908 with salary of $1,200.00; Walter W. Harkins appointed July 18, 1912 with salary of $1,400.00; Walter W. Harkins appointed August 2, 1916 with salary $1,700.00; Joe E. Caine (Acting Postmaster) August 1, 1919 with salary of $1,900.00; Thomas L. Lindsey appointed May 28, 1920 with salary of $1,900.00; Perry W. Caraway (Acting Postmaster) October 16, 1924; Perry W. Caraway appointed January 28, 1925 with salary of $2,400.00; John R. Fowler (Acting Postmaster) January 31, 1929; John R. Fowler appointed March 2, 1929 with salary of $2,500.00; S. J. Sanders appointed March 2, 1930 with salary of $2,500.00; Joe E. Caine (Acting Postmaster) January 1, 1945; Arcaster Kimbrell appointed August 19, 1948 with salary of $3,750.00.

RURAL ROUTE AND CARRIERS -- The first mail route established in Fayette County was at Fayette, service having been authorized on rural route No. 1 effective April 15, 1905, nearly nine years after the first route established in the State.

The following statements show the official dates of establishment of the rural routes in Fayette County with the carriers first appointed, the carriers as of July, 1930 and the present 1959 carriers.

Route No. 1 established April 5, 1905 with G. H. Young as first carrier appointed; U. J. Hankins as carrier in 1930 and Aaron Gibson as carrier in 1959.

Route No. 2 established June 15, 1905 with G. B. Vandiver as first carrier appointed; Homer Campbell as carrier in 1930 and James Dodson as carrier in 1959. (Rayburn Humber as substitute.)

Route No. 3 established June 15, 1905 with J. E. Caine as first carrier appointed; R. L. Chandler as carrier in 1930 (retired in 1957) and Dale Blackburn as carrier in 1959.

Route No. 4 established August 15, 1905 with W. H. Humber as first carrier appointed; J. A. Ayres as carrier in 1930 (retired in 1957) and Bradley Yerby as carrier in 1959.

Route No. 5 established August 15, 1905 with R. L. Chandler as first Carrier appointed; W. L. Jones as carrier in 1930 and David Galloway as carrier in 1959.

Route No. 6 established January 2, 1914 with J. C. Black as first carrier appointed; J. F. Long as carrier in 1930. Route No. 6 was discontinued at one time and re-established April 1957 with Willie Loftis as the carrier in 1959.

Route No. 7 established April, 1957 with Clarence Smith as carrier in 1959.

According to records Mr. R. L. Chandler was the Route No. 3 carrier from June 19, 1906 until his retirement November 1957. His record of serving one route is longer than that of any other.

Other Post Offices that have been active at one time or another in Fayette County are as follows:

ANTIOCH POST OFFICE -- A post office was established at Antioch on May 12, 1900, with John H. Howton appointed as the only postmaster. It was discontinued on September 15, 1906.

A site location report of March 22, 1900, from the proposed postmaster at Antioch shows that the office was to be located in the middle of Section 27, Township 15, Range 12 West.

ASBURY POST OFFICE -- A post office was established on October 12, 1839, at Asbury, Fayette County, Ala. It was discontinued on July 18, 1866. Names of postmasters at Asbury and dates of their appointment were as follows: John Hamby, October 12, 1839; Timothy Ekes, March 19, 1850; Philip A. Otts, February 24, 1851; Joshua Vail, June 25, 1852; James M. Smith, February 4, 1853; William Owens, September 17, 1855; Manly J. Smith, November 11, 1856; Frederick Vernon, December 5, 1856; Samuel Estes, May 26, 1858; Johiel Dyer, June 30, 1859; and John R. Cooper, September 17, 1860.

BIG POND POST OFFICE -- A post office was established at Big Pond on November 12, 1849. It was discontinued on July 18, 1866, reestablished on October 15, 1866, and discontinued on June 17, 1874. Names of postmasters who served at Big Pond and dates of their appointment were as follows: David Loftis, November 12, 1849; Benjamin R. Hopkins, October 15, 1866; and Samuel F. Cline, May 4, 1868.

BUCK SNORT POST OFFICE -- A post office was established at Buck Snort on October 20, 1873 with Jacob Miller appointed as the only postmaster. It was discontinued on April 21, 1894.

A site location report of December 9, 1873 shows that the office was located in the northwest quarter of the southwest quarter of Section 1, Township 16, Range 11 West.

CANE POST OFFICE -- A post office was established at Cane, Fayette County, Alabama on July 12, 1878. It was discontinued on June 15, 1905. Names of postmasters who served at Cane and dates of their appointment were as follows: Jonas B. Mason, July 12, 1878; Edmond Vernon, January 21, 1880; and Reuben H. Corbett, May 3, 1897.

A site location report of July 1, 1878, from the proposed postmaster at Cane shows that the office was to be situated in the Southeast quarter of Section 2, Township 15, Range 13. The directions of the township and range are not shown.

CAVE SPRINGS POST OFFICE -- A post office was established at Cave Springs, Fayette County, Ala. on September 11, 1856. It was discontinued on July 25, 1866, reestablished on June 12, 1871, discontinued on October 24, 1887, reestablished on April 24, 1888, and discontinued on January 17, 1894. Names of postmasters who served at Cave Springs and dates of their appointment were: as follows: Samuel Richardson, September 11, 1856; Simeon Hamil, February 22, 1861; Joel Ashcraft, June 12, 1871; Isaac N. Ashcraft, February 18, 1873; George W. Ashcraft, April 24, 1888; and William H. Brown, June 9, 1893.

The earliest site location report among the postal records in the National Archives shows that on April 10, 1871, the office was located in the northwest quarter of Section 33, Township 17, Range 13, West. The direction of the township is not shown.

CORDOVA POST OFFICE -- A post office was established at Cordova, Fayette County, Ala. on May 10, 1858, with Raymond D. Redden appointed as the only postmaster. It was discontinued on January 28, 1867.

COVIN POST OFFICE -- (or BROCKTON or TALLULA) -- The post office at Covin was established as Brockton on February 4, 1884. The name was changed to Tallula on March 4, 1890, and to Covin on March 1, 1892. Names of postmasters who served at this office and dates of their appointment were as follows: Reuben J. Brock, February 4, 1884; Perry C. Guin, November 19, 1886; Jasper G. Harper, November 3, 1902; and John W. Dodson, January 16, 1905 (still serving in 1929).

Similar records of the other postmasters are on record in the Post Office Department in Washington, D. C.

The site location report of March 21, 1890, shows that Tallula (later Covin) was located in the southwest quarter of Section 3, Township 16, Range 13, West.

CROSSVILLE POST OFFICE (or MILITARY SPRING) -- A post office was established at Crossville, Fayette County, Ala. on December 28, 1846. Its name was changed to Military Springs on December 10, 1840. Names of postmasters who served at Crossville and dates of their appointment were as follows: Hugh McGaughey, December 28, 1846; and Joseph Pennington, February 10, 1849.

DAVIS CREEK POST OFFICE -- A post office was established at Davis Creek, Fayette County, Ala. on September 7, 1847. It was discontinued on February 14, 1870; reestablished on June 12, 1871; discontinued on September 25, 1872; reestablished on June 11, 1873; discontinued on February 1, 1875; reestablished on July 27, 1875; discontinued on December 29, 1897; reestablished on March 1, 1898; and discontinued on September 15, 1906. Names of postmasters who served at Davis Creek and dates of their appointment were as follows: William R. Smith, September 7, 1847; Green M. Richards, October 7, 1847; G. W. Richards, June 13, 1866; Robert Black, October 17, 1866; Elihu Willingham, June 12, 1871; Ellis Logan, June 11, 1873; John W. Blackburn, March 1, 1898; and Robert T. Beard, November 8, 1905.

A site location report of July 24, 1871, shows that the office was situated in the northwest quarter of Section No. 1, Township 17 south, Range 12 west.

GALILEE POST OFFICE -- A post office was established at Galilee on June 8, 1892. It was discontinued on September 30, 1905. Names of postmasters who served and dates of their appointments were as follows: Virgil A. Taylor, June 8, 1892 and George S. Malloy, May 1, 1896.

A site location report of April 28, 1892, from the proposed postmaster at Galilee shows that the office was to be situated in the Southeast quarter of Section 28, Township 13, Range 13, west.

HICO POST OFFICE -- A post office was established at Hico on January 14, 1892. It was discontinued on December 31, 1913. Names of postmasters who served at Hico and dates of their appointment were as follows: Wilbur J. Johnson, January 14, 1892; Arthur A. Gentry, October 5, 1895; Thomas J. Wright, March 27, 1896; Clyde B. Brotherton, December 24, 1897; James M. Holliman, December 10, 1903; Arthur Savage, November 1, 1904; Bell Sullivan, November 27, 1905; and Effie Savage, November 3, 1910.

A site location report of December 7, 1891, from the proposed postmaster at Hico, shows that the office was to be situated in the Northeast quarter of Section 13, Township 17, south, Range 13, west.

HILL POST OFFICE -- A post office was established at Hill, Fayette County, Ala. on November 21, 1853. It was discontinued on July 25, 1866, reestablished on March 27, 1873 and discontinued on July 27, 1874. Names of postmasters who served at Hill and dates of their appointments were as follows: Lewis Bobo, November 21, 1853; and Joseph B. Dennis, March 27, 1873.

HUGENT POST OFFICE -- A post office was established at Hugent on March 14, 1892. It was discontinued on October 16, 1907. Names of the postmasters who served at Hugent and dates of their appointments were as follows: James P. Dickinson, March 14, 1892; John J. Jones, December 24, 1897; George W. White, December 9, 1898; Joseph N. Jones, February 14, 1900; and James J. Jones, January 16, 1902.

A site location report of July 22, 1904, shows that the office was situated in the Northwest quarter of Section 16, Township 15 south, Range 12 west.

MONT CALM POST OFFICE -- A post office was established at Mont Calm, Fayette County, Ala. on September 17, 1873. It was discontinued on September 30, 1905. The names of the following are the postmasters who served at Mont Calm and dates of their appointments: William A. Musgrave, September 17, 1873;

L. E. Jones, June 7, 1876; William A. Musgrave, July 10, 1876; and Mary G. Musgrave, June 7, 1902.

NEW RIVER POST OFFICE -- A post office was established at New River, in Fayette County, Ala. on August 11, 1853. The first postmaster's salary for the year 1855 was $5.83. The office was discontinued on January 7, 1867. On August 19, 1869, the office was reestablished. It continued to function until September 30, 1911, when it was discontinued. Those who served as postmasters for the New River Post Office were as follows: Hugh W. McCaleb, August 11, 1853; John R. Yerby, April 16, 1855; Preston B. Phillips, December 30, 1856; Simeon Randolph, August 19, 1869; Andrew McCaleb, December 28, 1870; and John T. McCaleb, July 17, 1899 to September 30, 1911.

New River Post Office was located in the southeast quarter of Section 1, Township 14, Range 12, according to a site location report on August 9, 1869. The same location is known in 1959 as Hubbertville, about fifteen miles northeast of Fayette.

NEWTONVILLE POST OFFICE -- A post office was established at Newtonville on February 24, 1851. It was discontinued on July 22, 1852, reestablished on July 14, 1853, discontinued on January 7, 1867, reestablished on October 3, 1867, discontinued on December 2, 1868, and reestablished on December 12, 1871. Names of postmasters who served at Newtonville and dates of their appointments were as follows: George A. Skelton, February 24, 1851; Richmond M. Shepherd, July 14, 1853; Stephen E. Bell, February 15, 1859; Alexander F. Yerby, Feburary 11, 1860; William M. Ward, November 8, 1860; David A. Gray, October 3, 1867; Jacob Shepherd, December 12, 1871; William W. Jones, April 23, 1877; and John M. Sullivan, November 27, 1903 (still serving in 1929).

Similar information about this office after 1929 is retained by the Post Office Department, Washington, D. C.

A site location report of May 1, 1899, shows that Newtonville was situated in the Northeast quarter of the Southwest quarter of Section 28, Township 17 south, Range 12 west.

The following information gives the only data available regarding the annual compensation of the postmasters at Newtonville, Ala.: 1903, compensation $ 89.62; 1905, compensation $ 105.78; 1907, compensation $204.00; and 1909, compensation $ 217.00.

SHEFFIELD POST OFFICE - (CLEAR CREEK and HARVEY'S CROSS ROADS) -- The post office as Sheffield was established as Clear Creek on December 11, 1835. Its name was changed to Harvey's Cross Roads on December 23, 1839, and to Sheffield on November 30, 1841. The office was discontinued on January 2, 1845, reestablished on March 20, 1846, discontinued on October 9, 1866, reestablished on December 28, 1868, discontinued on January 13, 1871, reestablished on January 27, 1872 and discontinued on June 17, 1880. The following are names of postmasters who served at Sheffield and dates of their appointment: Green H. Strong, December 11, 1835; Edward Gray Sharp, January 7, 1837; Calvin York, June 3, 1839; Henry P. Leonard, October 28, 1839; Robert Clayton, July 7, 1843; Henry P. Leonard, May 30, 1844; James W. Johnson, March 20, 1846; Josiah H. Freeman, March 8, 1847; Green H. Strong, March 19, 1850; William Griffin, September 8, 1851; Henry W. Cole, July 13, 1855; James H. Freeman, October 22, 1855; Owen Wood, January 4, 1856; Henry W. Cole, March 25, 1856; Littleton Cole, November 9, 1857; Sarah Stephenson, December 28, 1868; Adaline Griffin, February 22, 1869; Nancy T. Willingham, January 22, 1872; William R. Willingham, April 28, 1874; and Susan A. Willingham, September 14, 1875.

The earliest site location report among the postal records in the National Archives shows that on May 10, 1872, the office was located in the Northeast quarter of Section 22, Township 16, Range 11, west. The direction of the township is not shown.

WAYSIDE POST OFFICE -- A post office was established at Wayside, Fayette County, Ala. on September 16, 1878, with Terrell Reese appointed to serve as the only postmaster. It was discontinued on September 30, 1905.

A site location report of May 2, 1899, from the postmaster at Wayside shows that the office was located one mile west of Luxapallila River, one-half mile west of Dodson Creek, 13 and one-half miles from Fayette, four miles south of Galilee, six miles north of Cane and two and one-half miles west of Mont Calm.

PRIVATE BUISNESS, INDUSTRY, BANKING, PUBLIC SERVICES, ETC. -- Following is listed the businesses of earlier days and the present time with a brief factual sketch, where material was made available, about each.

PRIVATE BUSINESSES:

A. & M. LAUNDRY AND DRY CLEANERS -- A. & M. Laundry and Dry Cleaners made its advent into the commercial life of Fayette on January 1, 1949. The original owners were Robert T. McWhorter and Ralph Agee. The A. & M. plant is located on South Temple Avenue just south of the City swimming pool.

A. & P. (THE GREAT ATLANTIC AND PACIFIC TEA COMPANY) -- The A. & P. Tea Co. came to Fayette about 1932 and the store was first located in the building just east of the Terry Drug Store on Columbus Street. In September 1939, Mr. W. B. Scott came to Fayette as Manager of the store and is still serving in that position. The new store, that is presently occupied by the A. & P. Tea Co. was completed and moved into in 1947. The store was remodeled and air-conditioned in 1958 and 1959.

ANDERSON HARDWARE COMPANY -- Mr. E. E. Anderson bought the Haughton Hardware Co. from Mr. Curt Haughton in 1950 and started operating the business as Anderson Hardware Co. on April 1, 1950. The store was formerly located just east of the Terry Drug Store on Columbus Street. In the early months of 1958, the Andersons remodeled and moved into the present location on Temple Avenue, just north of Central Drug Store.

ANDERSON SERVICE COMPANY -- Owner and Operator, C. D. "Bluie" Anderson.

ATLANTIC OIL COMPANY, INC. -- Offices of the Atlantic Oil Company, Inc. are in the Water Works Building on East Columbus Street. The operation of the business covers wholesale and retail petroleum products. Mr. Felix Grimsley and Mr. Eric Grimsley are the owners and managers of this firm.

AYRES, WADE H. ASSOCIATES -- Electrical Service. Wade H. Ayres Manager.

AYRES & WAGES BLACKSMITH SHOP -- Owners are Otis Ayres and G. W. Wages.

BAGWELL REAL ESTATE RENTALS --

BARNES INSURANCE AGENCY -- In 1944, Mr. Zack N. Sanders opened the State Farm Insurance Agency in Fayette. Mr. Leborn Barnes became the agent for State Farm on January 1, 1955, and is presently the owner and manager of Barnes Insurance Agency.

BERRY DRY CLEANERS -- Owners, Mr. & Mrs. Cecil Berry.

BERRY, DR. H. E. -- Dentist.

BEVAN TIN SHOP -- Owner, Calvin Bevan.

BLACK, JAMES H. - WRECKING CO. -- Located on Winfield Highway.

BOBO'S PAINT & BODY SHOP -- Owner, Thais Bobo, located on the Covin Highway.

BOBO, J. T. GROCERY -- Owned by Mr. & Mrs. J. Thomas Bobo, on Winfield Highwy.

BOBO, COMER - GULF SERVICE STATION -- Located on Covin Highway.

BOBO PLUMBING -- Proprietor, Claude Bobo.

BOOTH JEWELRY COMPANY -- Mr. Waldo Booth opened his present jewelry business on October 1, 1958. About three years before this time he operated a Jewelry Store on Temple Avenue, but closed this store and moved away, coming back to Fayette in October, 1958.

BROWN MACHINE SHOP -- Owner, Charles Brown.

BUS STATION CAFE -- Owner, Dean Hyder.

BUTLER GRAIN COMPANY -- Manager, Jack Butler. Specialize in seeds.

BUTLER TRACTOR & IMPLEMENT CO. -- Owner, Albert B. Butler.

BYARS SERVICE STATION -- Owner, J. B. "Red" Byars. Gulf Products.

BYNUM GARAGE -- Owner and Manager, J. C. Bynum.

BYNUM TRACTOR SALES -- Manager, James Bynum.

C. & L. POULTRY --

CAMERON TILE COMPANY --

CAMPBELL JEWELRY COMPANY -- Mr. Joe Campbell opened for business in 1945 in a small building on the site of Scotty's Cafe and moved to a new location next door to the Temple Garden Drug Store in 1947. In 1956 the new building was completed and he moved a few doors to the present location. Mr. Harry Mc-Cutcheon works with Mr. Campbell as a competent watch repairman.

CANNON, DR. C. C. -- Dentist.

CANNON DRUG STORE -- Sidney J. Cannon, Sr. bought the Phillip's Drug Store, believed to be the first drug store in the town of Fayette. S. J. Cannon, Jr. operated this store until his death in 1945. His brother, Thomas Harvey Cannon, took over the drug business in 1945 and continued to operate the Cannon Drug Store until his death in August, 1952. The widow of T. H. Cannon and his sons are presently the owners and operators of the Cannon Drug Store.

CARDINAL MOTEL -- The Cardinal Motel was officially opened on August 29, 1952, under the ownership of Mr. Robert L. Smith and Mr. Guthrie J. Smith. It is the first motel to be operated in Fayette.

CATHERINE'S BEAUTY BAR -- Miss Catherine White opened Catherine's Beauty Bar in 1957 and the shop is located on West James Street. Miss Ozell Sanders and Miss Jean Bozeman are presently affiliated with Catherine, as beauty operators.

CENTRAL DRUG STORE -- Central Drug, located on Temple Avenue, directly across from Richard's Theatre is one of the most progressive and modern drug establishments in this section of Alabama. Central has a long record of satisfactory business dealings with the citizens of the Fayette Area and has been depended upon for many years to accurately compound prescriptions. Before becoming Central Drug Store it was at one time owned and operated by Mr. Rube Barnett and went under the name of Barnett's Drug Store. After his death, Mrs. Pearl Freeman Walton, bought it and operated it for several years before selling it to the present owners, who gave the name Central Drug Store to this business that had served the people for many years. In addition to their prescription department, Central Drug Store also carries a complete stock of drug sundries, cosmetics, candies, toilet goods, gift ware, and has an excellent soda fountain.

CHEF CAFE -- Located on Winfield Highway.

CHEF'S AMOCO (PAN-AM) SERVICE STATION -- Located on Winfield Highway.

CHRISTINE's BEAUTY BAR -- Operator, Mrs. Christine Bannister.

CITY CURB MARKET -- Owners Willis and Paul Christian, located on Temple Ave.

COBB MOTOR COMPANY -- Lee B. Lollar founded Lollar Motor Company in 1936, to sell Dodge and Plymouth cars as well as Dodge trucks. The business was closed from 1940 to 1946 because of World War II and the shortage of cars for sale. The business was located at 315 Fouracre Street in Fayette and was reopened in 1946 with Lee B. Lollar and William Connell as partners. In 1948 the Connell interest was purchased by Lee B. Lollar, who was then sole owner. Upon Mr. Lollar's death, in April, 1950, the business was purchased by Paris H. Black, Mrs. Lee B. Lollar and Guthrie J. Smith.
On April 1, 1952, Lollar Motor Company was sold to R. C. Cobb, who sold an interest in the business to A. C. Thomas. This partnership has since operated as Cobb Motor Company and on December 29, 1956, Arthur Motor Co., Inc. was purchased from Richard Arthur and Mr. & Mrs. Louis (Jane Arthur) Moore and the business consolidated with Cobb Motor Co.
The Company sells and services Chrysler, Dodge and Plymouth cars and in addition Dodge trucks and Simca cars imported from France by Chrysler Corp. The company employs the following personell: Salesmen, E. E. Hindman and S.

Y. Shelton; Service Manager, H. D. McCoy; Mechanics, James Cantrell, Thurman Cargile and Doyce Sprinkles; Body Shop, Bruce Adams; Parts Manager, Wayne Hubbert; Upholstery Dept. P. H. Black; Lubrication Dept., Johnny Gray; Bookkeeper, Mrs. Blanch Bobo and Manager, A. C. Thomas.

COOPER T. V. SERVICE -- Edgar Cooper, Jr. - Television and Electrical repair.

COUCH, ROY D., FEED STORE AND HATCHERY -- In 1933, Mr. Roy D. Couch opened a cotton and trucking concern in Fayette and later went into the Farm Feed business. In connection with his feed business he also started a chicken hatchery which has grown into one of the largest in this section of Alabama. The hatchery and retail departments of his business are located just north of the Southern Railroad. The brooders and chicken farm is located just north of Fayette.

COUNTY BUILDING SUPPLY -- Owners, Sam J. Renfroe, Jr. and Sam J. Renfroe, Sr. All types of building supplies and materials.

CRAWLEY, JONAS D., GROCERY -- Located at Belk, Ala. - General Merchandise.

CREDIT BUREAU OF FAYETTE -- Owner, Mrs. Corrine Fulmer of Tuscaloosa, Ala. Former owners of the Credit Bureau of Fayette have been V. W. Poe and Ted Carmack; Herbert M. Newell; Billy Joe Jenkins; and Jake Garrison.

D. & H. AUTO PARTS STORE -- In the summer of 1958, Mr. Linton Dobbs and Mr. Snow Hamner opened the D. & H. Auto Parts Store on Columbus Street. Mr. Dobbs was earlier connected with the Gas Service Station business and Mr. Hamner was at one time affiliated with M. & M. Chevrolet Co. and before going into the Auto Parts business was owner of the Fayette Cattle Sale Barn on the Winfield Highway.

DAVIS, MARION PUBLISHING CO. -- This modern, progressive printing establishment has been operating as a publishing house since 1938 and has shipped thousands of song books to various sections of the United States, Canada and England. Mr. Davis publishes two widely circulated religious publications, "Truth In Love" and "The Gospel Digest". Mr. Davis also does job printing of all types. Mr. Davis was the first firm in the state of Alabama to publish song books.

DEAL, DR. C. E. -- Veterinarian.

DOBBS BROTHERS WOOD DEALER -- M. C. Dobbs, Jr. and Buford Dobbs, owners.

DOBBS FURNITURE CO., - Owners, M. C. Dobbs, Sr., M. C. Dobbs, Jr. and Buford Dobbs.

DRUID BUTANE GAS COMPANY -- Branch of Druid Butane Gas Co., Tuscaloosa, Ala.

DUNCAN'S BEAUTY SHOP -- Mrs. Maggie Duncan, owner since 1948. Former owners have been; Mrs. Marion McCaleb and Mrs. Eddie Dobbs.

ELLIS, DR. B. R. -- Chiropractor.

V. J. ELMORE 5¢, 10¢, $1.00 STORES, INC. -- The local V. J. Elmore Store was opened in Fayette in the early 1940's with Miss Pauline Shipman as the first manager. The present manager is Mr. J. P. Boyles. The V. J. Elmore Co., was organized November, 1925 at Clanton, Alabama. The main office is located in Birmingham, Alabama, at this time, and there are 66 stores in Alabama, Mississippi and Georgia. Each store operates on a local level, selling variety store merchandise, which is a wide selection of the most used goods in the community.

ENSLEN, DAVID McKAY -- Attorney.

THE FABRIC SHOP -- On September 4, 1957, Mrs. Frank Jeffries opened The Fabric Shop on Columbus Street. It was first located next door to the Fayette Motor Company but in 1959 moved to a new location, still on Columbus Street, but more centrally located.

THE FAIR STORE -- Manager, Mrs. Gus Woodard.

FAIRVIEW FARM & SEED COMPANY -- Manager, Jack Butler. Located on Winfield Rd.

FARMER'S MARKETING & EXCHANGE ASSN. -- Manager, Willie B. Bobo.

FAYCO METAL CULVERT CO. -- Branch of Fayette Concrete Pipe Co.

FAYETTE AUTO PARTS -- Fayette Auto Parts came to Fayette as a branch of the N.A.P.A. Warehouse on September 1, 1945 and was managed by Mr. Ralph D. King. On December 1, 1945, Mr. King purchased the business, a wholesale and retail automotive parts store. The store operated under his ownership until August 15, 1954 when it was sold to Sam McConnell Jones and John Tinsley "Scotty" Young. In 1945 the business employed three. In 1954 it employed six and today, with branches in Sulligent and Winfield, it employs nine.

FAYETTE BONDED WAREHOUSE - Owner, Perry W. Caraway.

FAYETTE CHAIN SAW COMPANY -

FAYETTE 5¢ & 10¢ STORE -- The Fayette 5¢ & 10¢ Store is a variety store handling all kinds of merchandise, including hardware, housewares, cosmetics, notions, dry goods, costume jewelry, etc. from 5¢ to $5.00. This firm was opened in August 1940, and is located on Temple Avenue. Mr. Milton L. Anhalt was the original founder and still operates the store.

FAYETTE GRAIN & FEED COMPANY -- Owner, Sam Collins. Grinds and mixes all kinds of farm feeds.

FAYETTE ICE & COAL COMPANY --

FAYETTE'S INSURANCE FIRMS -- The oldest Insurance Firm in Fayette at this time (1959) is E. E. Thomason Agency. Others who have been very active in the insurance field through the years have been: Mr. G. L. Smith, Mr. Paul Nuckols, Mr. Zack Sanders, Mr. Dick Poe, Mr. Bill Sanders, Mr. Bob Sanders, Mr. J. L. Barnes, Mr. E. C. Herren and countless other men connected with the numerous companies, especially the various burial and life insurance companies.

FAYETTE INSURANCE AGENCY -- Owner, V. W. "Dick" Poe.

FAYETTE MATTRESS COMPANY -- Owner, Miss Jimmie Lee Hallman.

FAYETTE MEMORIAL COMPANY --

FAYETTE MOTOR COMPANY -- Fayette County's oldest automobile agency was established here when the Fayette Motor Company was organized in 1916 to supply this territory with its first Ford automobiles. Two years later, in 1918, this pioneer automobile concern was incorporated by Orville Pope and G. H. Brown. In 1918, a new Ford automobile could be purchased for approximately $375 as compared to approximately $3,500, today in 1959. This Company has grown and prospered and now occupies one of the up-to-date buildings in Fayette.
    The Fayette Motor Company has been operated for several years by F. H. and T. M. Jeffries. At one time, earlier the company was operated by Mr. V. E. Butler and at another time by Mr. L. B. Lollar.
    Fayette Motor Co. repair shop offers complete service for motorists of this section. Mr. T. M. Jeffries has been connected with the company since 1918.

FAYETTE PROCESSING PLANT -- Meat Processor.

FAYETTE RADIATOR SERVICE --

FAYETTE RECAPPING COMPANY -- Sixteen years ago Fayette Tire Recapping Co. was organized as a part of Fayette Motor Company, affording motorists and commercial truck owners a complete and up-to-date recapping service. In 1947, Mr. Chester Hallman became the owner of this establishment and served a large number of customers until 1957 when Mr. Hayne, from Aliceville, Ala. became the owner. On September 1, 1959, Mr. Chester Hallman purchased the business and is presently the owner and operator.

FAYETTE USED PARTS --

FAYETTE SHOE SHOP -- The Fayette Shoe Shop was established in 1919 by Mr. Nathan Michael and is the oldest shoe shop in Fayette.

FAYETTE STOCK YARD, INC. -- Cattle are brought in and sold to the highest bidders at the livestock commission sale barn which was originally owned by F. M. Fowler from 1947 to September 15, 1949. Snow Hamner operated the barn from September 15, 1949 to February 1, 1957, leasing it, at times to Phelan Parrish and Mc McCaleb. In February 1957, B. W. Kimbrell, W. R. Bobo and K. D. Galloway bought the business and are still operating it.

FLYNN's (L. G.) STORE -- Located at Bluff - General Merchandise.

FOWLER OIL COMPANY -- A wholesale distributing station for Pan-Am Petroleum Products was organized in Fayette in the year 1926. Today the gasoline products are known as Amoco Oil and Gasoline. There are many retail stations over Fayette County today.
    The first owner of this distributing plant was Thomas Chambless in 1926. Second owner was Mr. G. L. Smith in 1927. The third owner and manager was Mr. Fletcher M. Fowler who bought the business in 1936 and continued to operate

it until his death in December, 1949. In January, 1950, Mr. Fowler's son, W. A. "Bill" Fowler became the fourth owner and manager. The modern office of the Amoco Products is located on the Winfield Highway.

FREEMAN MOTOR COMPANY -- Owner, Isaac Freeman.

FREEMAN BARBER SHOP -- Owner, Isaac Freeman.

FROSTY-LAND DRIVE-IN CAFE -- Owner and Manager, Mr. & Mrs. Merle Holliman.

GARRISON APPLIANCE & FURNITURE CO. -- Owner, Jake Garrison.

GARRISON, HERMAN T., STORE -- Owner, H. T. Garrison - General Merchandise.

GIBSON DAIRY BAR -- Owner, Fred Gibson.

GIBSON SELF-SERVICE LAUNDRY - Owner, Fred Gibson.

GOODWIN, JOE, SERVICE STATION -- Standard Oil Products, Joe Goodwin, Mgr.

R. C. GORDON ACCOUNTING OFFICE -- Raymond C. Gordon has engaged in accounting work since 1937. For several years he was affiliated with a large accounting firm in Decatur, Ala. He left the Decatur Firm in 1942 for three years service in the United States Army, serving twenty-five months in the European Theatre. In 1945 he opened his own offices in Huntsville, with a branch in Scottsboro. This business was sold to the Decatur Firm in 1947 and Mr. Gordon returned to Fayette. He opened his local accounting office on Fouracre Street in January, 1953.

GRAVLEE'S -- Gravlee's is located next to the First National Bank on Temple Ave. and was the first business concern in Fayette to install air-conditioning equipment and install a modernistic front. Under the able management of Mr. M. W. Gravlee, this popular store has grown steadily since it was established on September 23, 1932. Gravlee's stocks a large variety of merchandise for the shoppers of the Fayette Trade Territory. At the present time, Mr. Horace Berry, Jr. is co-manager of the store.

GROCHOLSKI UPHOLSTERY SHOP -- On August 1, 1958, Mr. & Mrs. Roman A. (Mary Bobo) Grocholski opened the Grocholski Upholstery Shop just south of the railroad in the old Hamby Warehouse building. They specialize in all types of upholstery. Mr. Grocholski is a native of Milwaukee, Wisconsin, coming to Fayette after the close of World War II. His parents were born near Warsaw, Poland, and came to the United States before 1900.

GULF OIL CORPORATION -- Distributor, James A. Branyon.

GULLETT'S -- Gullett's Department Store was originally organized in 1923 and was known as Rose and Gullett. In the early years the store was located in the present location of the Yellow Front Store and Mr. George Gullett, Sr. and Mr. T. A. Rose were partners. The store operated under the Rose and Gullett name until 1933. From 1933 until January 1952, George Gullett, Sr. was sole owner and operated the store until 1945 as a general merchandise firm. In 1937 Gullett's moved to their present location and in 1945 remodeled and changed the store to Men's Apparel, Women's Apparel, Giftware and Interior Decorating. After the death of Mr. Gullett, Sr. a partnership was formed consisting of Mrs. George Gullett, Sr., George H. Gullett, Jr. and James H. Gullett. Today, Gullett's is one of the most beautiful and modern department stores in this section of Alabama.

HAUGHTON REALTY COMPANY -- Owner, Curt Haughton.

HERREN, E. C., INSURANCE AGENCY --

HERREN, HOYT, ANTIQUE SHOP --

HODGES DEPARTMENT STORE -- The history of Hodges Department Store dates back to August, 1911, when the formal opening of The Star Store was announced by Harry Hodges, just a few months after the devastating fire of March 24, 1911. The name was changed to Hodges Department Store several years later and it has now grown to be Fayette's largest retail establishment. Under the guidance and able management of Mr. Harry Hodges, this business institution has grown to be a credit to this county and stocks a large assortment of quality merchandise for the entire family.

After Mr. Harry Hodges death, the duties of management were taken over by his twin sons, Morris and Jacob and his brother Louis Hodges, who is a partner in the business. The store was completely remodeled in the fall of 1959.

HOLDER, C. M. -- Attorney.

HOLLIS RADIO & T. V. SERVICE - Owner, Britt Hollis.

HOTEL FAYETTE -- Located on Temple Avenue.

HOWELL'S FLOWER SHOP -- In 1951, Mr. & Mrs. Arnie V. Howell opened the Howell Flower Shop. The business was originally located in the building presently occupied by the Radio Station on Temple Avenue. During the month of August, 1957, the flower shop was moved to its present location.

THE HUB -- Sinclair Service Station, Owner, C. H. "Hub" Dodson.

IDEAL MARKET AND GROCERY -- Owner, Tyrus Williamson.

I. G. A. GROCERY STORE -- Mr. T. A. McCool came to Fayette in 1904 and after completing his schooling went to work in the mercantile business with Mr. E. Rose in 1905. He then worked for Mr. J. R. Robertson and later with Walker, Nuckols & Co. In 1927 he opened the I. G. A. Grocery Store on the corner across from Hodges and next door to the old Cannon Building on the east side of Temple Avenue. It was one of the busiest firms of its kind until 1932.

INDEPENDENCE CONSTRUCTION COMPANY --

JACKSON, E. C., INSURANCE AGENCY --

JAKE'S PLACE -- Grocery owned by Mr. & Mrs. Jake Hollingsworth. A favorite trading spot with the youngsters in the elementary school. Located on North Aylette Street and Walker St., just east of the Grammar School.

JITNEY JUNGLE SUPER MARKET -- The Jitney Jungle Store was opened in Fayette, on June 6, 1947. The original founders and owners of the Jitney Jungle were J. C. Wiggins, Dorsey Young and Bill Freeman. The first location of the store was on Temple Ave. next to the Masonic Building. On March 5, 1959, Jitney Jungle opened for business in their new location Fouracre and Frierson Streets, with Mr. J. C. Wiggins as manager and owner.

JOE'S RECORD BAR -- Seeing a need for a music and record store, Mr. Joe Campbell established Joe's Record Bar in 1957 and this store has proved to be one of the most popular, with record collectors, in Fayette. Items sold are records of all types, record players, radios, etc.

KEMP & BARBOUR GENERAL MERCHANDISE STORE -- On October 13, 1945, Mr. Jesse R. Kemp and Mr. Douglas A. Barbour entered into a partnership and opened the Kemp and Barbour General Merchandise Store located on the Winfield Highway at 1351 North Temple Ave. They offer a complete line of merchandise and their store is a favorite stopping place for the people of Fayette and Fayette County. Mr. Kemp is Commissioner of District No. 1. He is out with the county work most of the time. Mr. Barbour is welcomed into most of the homes of Fayette County daily with his program "Out of the Night"-each morning. This program originates in Mr. Barbour's office in his store and is broadcast Monday through Saturday over Radio Station W.W.W.F. This program was first broadcast in June 1956 and has grown to be anticipated by the citizens. Mr. Barbour gives local news items, sports, birth announcements, birthday greetings, funeral announcements, hospital news and numerous civic announcements. His ad libbing and announcements for his sponsors are a source of delight to all who hear him. His name for his "agency" is - "The Big Wind Productions" and his favorite phrase for closing his program is - "W.W.W.F. the thousand watter with a million squatters".

KILGORE & WHEAT -- Dentists

KILLINGSWORTH GIN -- Many years ago in the Killingsworth community in the north eastern part of Fayette County, Jim Killingsworth started the Killingsworth Gin and Grist Mill. Since 1899 this old firm has been operated by J. C. Killingsworth, son of the founder. The present location of the Gin is at Five Points in the northern section of the City of Fayette, where their Deisel gin operates at top capacity. The Killingsworth Gin and Grist Mill has been located at Five Points since 1928. Mr. Killingsworth operates a general merchandise store in connection with the mill and gin.

LAWRENCE, J. G. & SONS -- Gin and Grist Mill and General Merchandise Store - Owned and operated by Clayton Lawrence and Malcolm Lawrence.

LAWRENCE & JONES GARAGE -- Since 1946, Lawrence & Jones Garage located in Fayette and specialized in all types of automobile repair and work on heavy equipment, graders and tractors. This firm was first located at the N. Y. A. Center, but is presently located on Tuscaloosa Street, and owned and operated by Mr. A. H. Lawrence and Mr. Claude Jones.

LIBERTY NATIONAL LIFE INSURANCE CO. --

LOFTIS ELECTRIC SHOP -- Owned and operated by Bill Loftis.

LOFTIS CAFE -- Manager, Glenn Loftis.

LOFTIS SEWING CENTER -- Mr. J. D. Myers first came to Fayette with the Singer Sewing Machine Co., in 1935. He hired Mr. T. G. Loftis in 1936 and they both worked with the Singer Company until World War II. Mr. Loftis continued in the sewing machine business and became a partner with his son, Jake Loftis in the Loftis Sewing Machine and Electric Shop. On January 1, 1952, Mr. J. D. Myers bought the Sewing Machine business from Mr. T. G. Loftis and has continued to operate the business at 105 Luxapallila St. The business still operates under the name of Loftis Sewing Center. Mr. Myers sells sewing machines, services machines in need of repair and his wife, Mrs. Annie Ruth (Loftis) Myers, teaches sewing lessons.

LOWREY TRUCKING SERVICE -- Owner and Manager, Dewey Lowrey, Jr.

LUCILLE'S BEAUTY SHOP -- Owner and Operator, Mrs. Lucille Canterberry.

M. & M. CHEVROLET CO. -- Owner and Manager, N. T. Mothershed.

MADDOX SERVICE STATION -- Manager, Joe Maddox.

MADDOX MOTORS, INC. -- Maddox Motors, Inc. in the local dealer for Cadillacs, Oldsmobiles and G. M. C. trucks and was originally the Dobbs Motor Co. Mr. James F. "Jimmy" Maddox purchased the company and operated it until his death in 1955, at which time his widow, Mrs. Maddox and her son-in-law, M. C. "Hap" Dobbs, Jr. assumed managership. The business is located on Fouracre Street.

McCALEB'S MILL END SHOP -- Mr. & Mrs. Joe McCaleb opened their mill end shop in the early spring of 1959. They specialize in all materials that are necessary for sewing, including a wide variety of fabrics.

McCLUSKEY SHOE SHOP -- Mr. C. McCluskey owns and operates this firm.

McCRACKEN HEATING AND ROOFING CO., INC. -- The Fayette Sheet Metal Works was established in March, 1948, and was first owned and operated by Mr. G. L. Goodwin. The next owner and operator was Mr. Sam J. Renfro, Jr. of the Renfro Construction Co. Thomas McCracken bought the firm and is presently operating it. The firm had been moved to the old T. H. Robertson & Sons building and the name is now - McCracken Heating and Roofing Co.

MODERN RETREADING CO. --

MOORE'S FLOWERS -- Moore's Flower Shop was originally established in 1940 by Mrs. Elizabeth Dunn and was located on the ground floor of the Wright Building. This was the first flower shop to be operated in Fayette. In 1946 a modern brick building was erected on Temple Avenue to house the operations of the growing concern which specializes in flowers for all occasions. In October, 1947, the company was purchased from Mrs. Dunn by the present owners, Mrs. Stella P. Moore, widow of the late Judge J. M. Moore and her son, James M. Moore, Jr. The name was changed from Dunn's Flower Shop to Moore's Flowers at this time. This floral concern has continued to grow and keep pace with Fayette's progress. Moore's Flowers also specializes in landscaping under the direction and supervision of James M. Moore, Jr. who received his training in this field of work at A. P. I., Auburn, Ala.

NATIONAL FARM LOAN ASSOCIATION --

NICHOLS STUDIO -- Some of the earlier photographers of Fayette have been Mr. George Gullett, Sr., Mr. Fred Jones and Mr. Max Jones. In 1942, Cullen Griffin opened the Griffin Studio on Columbus Street and continued to operate the studio until July 24, 1949 when Mr. Ulys Nichols bought the studio and changed the name of the firm to Nichols Studio. "Nic" continued to operate the studio at the Columbus Street address until early in 1956 when he moved to the location on Temple Avenue.

NOLEN, CHARLES -- Attorney.

OSWALT DRY CLEANERS -- One of the earliest dry cleaning establishments in Fayette was the Oswalt Dry Cleaners owned and operated by Mr. Bedford Oswalt. He sold the business in the early 1950's and it is no longer in operation. The plant was originally owned and operated by Mr. E. C. Goodson and in late 1925 the dry cleaning plant was purchased by Mr. V. S. Patterson, Sr. and he and his wife owned and operated the firm, with the assistance of Cecil Berry and Curt Nichols, until Mr. Oswalt bought the business and equipment in 1927. The first plant was located where "Scotty's Restaurant" now stands. In 1935, Mr. Oswalt bought out the interest of Mr. Ned Jeffries and remained in the dry cleaning business until the time that he sold the establishment to Mr. Wm. C. Stokes in the early 1950's.

PALACE BEAUTY & GIFT SHOP -- Owned and Operated by Mrs. Sarah Nell Lawrence.

PALMER'S PLUMBING & HEATING --

PAN AM CAFE or BROTHERTON'S CAFE -- The first cafe, beginning a long public service, that today is the Pan-Am Cafe located on West Columbus Street, was founded in 1923 and operated until 1934 - the name of this establishment is not known. In 1934, the business was operated under the name of DeWitt's Cafe and used this name until 1937 when the name was changed to Freeman's Cafe. Then in 1940 the name was changed again to Brown's Cafe and in 1944 when the new building was completed the cafe was renamed Pan-Am Cafe. Mr. F. D. Brotherton operated the cafe until 1951 and at that time his wife, Mrs. F. D. Brotherton, and sons took over the management and today with the added, private dining room the Pan Am is one of the favorite eating places in Fayette.

PAN-AM SERVICE STATION or AMOCO SERVICE CENTER -- Mgr. Bob Maddox.

PATTERSON, CLARENCE, -- Monument Agent.

PATTERSON, G. H., -- Monument Agent.

PATTERSON SHOE SHOP -- During World War II, Mr. Claude Patterson began his career in the shoe repair business. He operates a "Bait Shop" along with the shoe repair business.

PERRY, DR. B. E. -- Chiropractor.

POE'S CONSTRUCTION CO. -- Organized 1956 - Owners M. L. & V. W. "Dick" Poe.

THE QUALITY STORE -- The Quality Shop, which is a ladies' specialty shop carrying nationally famous brands, was opened August 25, 1939, by Mrs. Snow Hamner. Mrs. Hamner was owner and manager until April, 1957. During her ownership of the store, it also had both an infant and men's department in addition to handling all ladies' apparel, except shoes. Mrs. J. B. McClendon, wife of the Fayette High School coach, bought the store in April, 1957, selling it in July, 1958, when her husband was transferred to Dothan High School. The store was purchased then by Mrs. Elizabeth E. Jones. Quality merchandise was continued in all departments but the men's department, which was discontinued. All three owners of the store have endeavored to carry only high-grade merchandise and to make it possible for the people of Fayette to trade at home.

RENFROE CONSTRUCTION CO. -- Organized 1950 - Owner, Sam J. "Bo" Renfroe, Jr.

RICHARDS THEATRE -- The Richards Theatre is the results of Mr. J. A. Richards successful career as one of Fayette's business men. On December 20, 1924, Mr. J. A. "Jeff" Richards bought the "first" Richards Theatre from Mr. W. D. Putnam and Mrs. Lee Putnam. The first "movie house" in Fayette was located on Columbus Street in the building where the Fayette County Times is presently located. This early theatre was the scene of many "quiet" movies and ushered in the "Talkies" in Fayette. After twelve successful years in the theatre business, Mr. Richards purchased the property where Dobbs Furniture Store is presently located and built the first "modern" theatre. On November 28, 1936, the Roxy Theatre was opened and served the City of Fayette for many years before the advent of T. V. in every home. This property was bought from Mr. R. T. & Mrs. Jesse R. Hamner. During the time of the Roxy Theatre, there was another theatre in Fayette for a short while, The Temple Theatre, located on Temple Avenue in the southern part of the Hodges building. One of the popular children's movies at the Roxy was "Snow White and The Seven Dwarfs" when first released. The present Richards Theatre was opened on November 5, 1947, by Mrs. Lucille Richards Cobb and her son R. C. Cobb -- daughter and grandson of Mr. J. A. Richards. This building was formerly the old Smith & Dodson Building, and is located on the corner of Temple Ave. and Columbus, St. just south of the Fayette County Court House. In September, 1950, the Dixie-land Drive-In Theatre, located on the Winfield Highway was opened by Mrs. Lucille Richards Cobb and her son R. C. Cobb. All of these theatres have played an interesting part in the quiet entertainment of Fayette.

ROBBIE'S CHILDREN'S WEAR -- In August, 1957, Mrs. Robbie (B. E.) Perry opened the Robbie's Children's Wear Shop on Temple Ave. located on the first floor of the Masonic Building.

ROBERTS MOTOR COMPANY -- In August, 1948, the Roberts Motor Company was formed and the location of the Sales Shop and Repair Shop was on north Temple Ave. across from the postoffice. They were the General Motors Dealer for Buick Automobiles, also dealers in new and used cars and service. In May, 1959 the company moved to a new location at Fouracre Street.

ROBERTS - NICHOLS HARDWARE COMPANY -- On September 1, 1954, Mr. Valford Roberts and Mr. Neal Nichols formed a partnership and started into business as the Roberts - Nichols Hardware Company. This firm sells a general and complete line of hardware. The store was first opened on south Temple Ave. across the street from Hodges, but within a few months it had grown so much that more space was needed and they moved into their present location on No. Temple Ave. across the street from the Post Office. The store was enlarged in the summer and fall of 1959 and reaches from Temple Avenue back to Four-acre Street.

T. H. ROBERTSON & SONS GENERAL MERCHANDISE. -- In February, 1844, a thrifty and ambitious Scotsman named John C. Robertson walked down the gang-plank of a trans-Atlantic boat which had just docked at the wharf in New Orleans, La. With little money in his pocket and big ambitions in his heart, the Scot tailor left New Orleans and headed toward Alabama. After some time he arrived in a little village of Fayette Court House and spent the night with intentions of traveling on the next day, but through some twist of fate he decided to remain in Fayette and accepted a job in a small tailor shop. After a short while he bought the controlling interest in the little shop and launched into his career as a merchant. A receipt dated 1847 is proof that John C. Robertson was a merchant as early as that year.

When John C. Robertson died in 1877 the business was operated for a while by two of his sons, Felix and Fenton, who later sold it to their brother Thomas H. Robertson who managed the big store for a number of years at "Old Town" before it was moved to Fayette on the site of Temple Avenue and James Street on the northwest corner. Mr. L. M. Dodds went to work at Robertson's Store in 1892 and several years later bought an interest in the business when the name of the firm was changed to Robertson & Dodds. When the big fire destroyed the business district of Fayette in 1911, the concern was completely wiped out and suffered a loss of $100,000. In 1914, Mr. Dodds bought out the interest of Mr. Thomas Robertson and operated the store in his name until 1924 when he sold the business back to Mr. Robertson.

When Mr. T. H. Robertson, Sr. died in 1936, the operation of the store passed on into the hands of his two sons, T. H., Jr. and John C. Robertson who successfully operated Fayette County's oldest business house until the death of Mr. T. H. Robertson, Jr. in 1955. The business continued until the close of 1958 when the doors were closed.

ROSE MARKET -- This grocery and meat market was purchased from Mr. Fletcher Bogard, by Mr. & Mrs. T. A. Rose on October 1, 1934 and has continued to serve Fayette with the finest merchandies and free delivery service within the city limits. In 1922, Mr. T. A. Rose and Mr. George Gullett, Sr. formed a partnership and operated the Rose and Gullett General Store until it was disbanded in 1932. This store was located where the present Yellow Front Store is today. Mr. Alfred (T. A.) Rose came into the store business naturally as his father came to Fayette and followed the trade of carpentry for two years and then went into the general merchandise business. His store was moved from the "Old Town" and was one of the first in the new Fayette. This store continued to serve the people of Fayette County until about 1917 when Mr. Edward Rose retired.

ROSEMORE, DR. FREDERICK M. -- Optomitrist.

THE SANDERS AGENCY -- The Sanders Agency is a general insurance firm, writing general insurance, fire, casualty, bonds and life. The business was started January 17, 1946, by William E. Sanders. At that time the Agency was known as the William E. Sanders, Agency. Robert P. Sanders, brother of W. E., began working with the firm on August 16, 1952. He became a partner on July 1, 1953. The new building located at 306 Caine Street, was constructed in 1955. The name of the business was changed to The Sanders Agency and formally opened in the new building on December 22, 1955. Companies represented are New Amsterdam Casulaty Co., St. Paul Fire and Marine Insurance Co., Niagara Fire Insurance Co., The Pacific Insurance Co., National Surety Corp., American Insurance Co., and the Prudential Insurance Co. of America.

SCOTTY'S RESTAURANT -- Scotty's was opened for business on Temple Avenue in December, 1946, by Mr. J. T. "Scotty" Young. The business started in a small shop serving only donuts, coffee and soft drinks. In 1948 the wooden building was enlarged and the new brick building was erected in 1952. Scotty's is a favorite place with the teen-agers and with the adults, as well. In 1957, Mr. Leslie Nichols bought the business and is the present owner. The business still goes by the original name.

SEWING BASKET -- Mrs. A. N. Wallace opened the Sewing Basket in February, 1959 and she specializes in all types of sewing. This business is located on Columbus Street.

SEXTON'S BEAUTY & BARBER SHOP - Owners, Mr. & Mrs. Clyde Sexton.

SHEPHERD'S STYLE SHOP -- On September 12, 1903, Miss Emma Shepherd opened the doors of Shepherd's Style shop, on Temple Avenue directly across the street from the present (1959) location of the First National Bank. According to the most accurate information obtainable, Miss Emma Shepherd is the oldest merchant, from a standpoint of continous service in the same business. Since the opening date of Shepherd's Style Shop in 1903, this ladies store has kept pace with the growth and progress of Fayette. Miss Emma was born at Newtonville in the southern part of Fayette County. She taught school for three or four years and then went to work for Propst Brothers as manager of the millinery department before opening her own store. She remained in the Temple Ave. location for 14 years and has been in her present location on Columbus Street since 1917.

SINCLAIR REFINING CO. -- C. H. DODSON, MARKETER -- On August 28, 1946, Mr. C. H. "Hub" Dodson became the manager of the Sinclair Wholesale Petroleum Product Plant in Fayette. There are numerous Sinclair stations over the county and Mr. Dodson has one of the largest and most modern stations, "The Hub" (at the same location of his wholesale office at 314 Sipsey Street on the southside.)

SINCLAIR SERVICE STATION -- Manager, Bert Hollingshead.

SMITH, BRUCE, - STORE -- Located on Concord Road.

SMITH CHICKEN FARM -- Mr. Guthrie I. Smith owns a large chicken farm just south of Fayette. The primary function of this farm is raising chickens for the broiler market and fresh eggs for the egg market.

LINWOOD S. SMITH GENERAL STORE -- Located on the Winfield Highway, this business was organized under the name of J. D. Smith and Sons. Owners were John

Smith and sons, Orrin and Linwood. The store is about five miles north of Fayette. In 1942, Linwood S. Smith bought the business and it has been called the Linwood Smith Store since that time. This is a general store and there is a sawmill located near by that is also operated by Mr. Linwood Smith. Smith's store became the distributor for Lombard Chain Saws in 1954.

SOUTHERN UNITED LIFE INSURANCE CO. --

STANDARD OIL COMPANY BULK PLANT -- Manager, Wm. Hammond Humber.

STANDARD FURNITURE CO., -- Opened 1959 - Manager, Arnie V. Howell.

STERMAN'S STORE -- Owner, Al Sterman

TANNER BROTHERS WHOLESALE PRODUCE COMPANY -- In 1930, Mr. Preston B. Smith founded the Smith Produce Company and the company has been serving a large number of retail outlets in the Fayette trade territory with their produce, fruit and vegetable requirements since that time. P. B. Smith operated the business as sole owner until 1940 when his son Robert L. Smith became a partner. This partnership continued from 1940 to 1943, when Robert L. Smith bought controlling interest. In 1946, Robert L. and his brother, Guthrie J. Smith formed a partnership and this partnership operated Smith Produce Co. until September 1952 when the business was sold to Tanner Brothers of Tuscaloosa, Ala. Tanner's operates a large fleet of trucks which regularly supply the merchants of Fayette, Marion, Lamar and Pickens counties. Bananas, potatoes, seasonal fruits and vegetables are the chief commodities sold by this firm. The main office and plant of Tanner Produce is located on North Temple Avenue in a modern fireproof building, which is equipped with the latest and most up-to-date cold storage vaults for the storing of perishable commodities.

TERRY DRUG STORE -- The Terry Drug Store was originally the Jones Drug Store, established on November 11, 1918, by Mr. T. Marion Jones of Fayette. The store was operated by Mr. Jones and his son Tom for many years before it was sold. At one time it was known as the Freeman Drug Store and it is presently owned and operated by the Terry family.

THOMASON, E. E., INSURANCE AGENCY --

THOMSON IMPLEMENT CO., INC. -- Owner, Richard Thomson.

TIM'S MODERN CLEANERS -- Mr. "Shine" Hill originally established this cleaning business and it was known as Hill's Dry Cleaners and was located for many years on Luxapallila Street just across from the Post Office. Mr. T. L. "Tim" Bobo purchased the shop from Mr. Hill and operated it for some time before he went away to World War II. After the war, Tim bought the business and has continued to operate it. In July, 1959, the plant was moved to Columbus St. into a larger building with the most modern and up-to-date machinery in the State.

TUCKER HARDWARE COMPANY -- Tucker Hardware Company was originally Madden Hardware Co. in the earlier days of the new Fayette. Mr. A. C. Madden went into the hardware business in the 1920's and the store was then located on Temple Avenue. In the 1940's Mr. F. M. Fowler and Mr. E. E. Anderson bought the

Madden Hardware Co. and changed the name of the firm to Fowler and Anderson Hardware Co. This partnership continued until Mr. Fowler's death in December, 1949. In 1950 Mr. Anderson sold his interest to the Fowler Estate. In 1957 Mr. F. N. Fowler's daughter and her husband, Paul Tucker moved the business to its present location and changed the name of the firm to Tucker Hardware Company.

VAUDEVILLE THEATRE -- In the early 1900's Tol Long and Tom Piper owned a Vaudeville Theatre, operating their business in a wooden building located where the back entrance of the Fayette County Times is today. About 1913 Mr. Thomas A. McCool bought the interest in the business, of Mr. Tom Piper and the establishment continued to operate as the main amusement of the Town of Fayette, until about 1915 when the old wooden building burned and all of the equipment, including the theatre's piano, was lost. Mr. Putnam built a brick structure to replace the ruins and operated a silent movie there until Mr. J. A. Richards bought the business. (See Richards Theatres.)

VICK BROTHERS STORE -- Owner, Z. D. Vick.

VICK IMPLEMENT COMPANY -- Owner, Charley Vick and W. C. Davis. Dealers in Pontiac automobiles and International Harvester trucks and tractors.

VICK OIL COMPANY --

VOGUE BEAUTY SHOP -- Owned and operated by Mrs. L. C. Hall.

WEEMS FURNITURE COMPANY -- Owner, W. L. "Bill" Weems, Manager, D. L. Collins.

WESTERN AUTO ASSOCIATE STORE -- Manager, L. K. Gay.

WILLIAMS MOTOR COMPANY --

WILLIAMSON JEWELRY COMPANY -- The Williamson Jewelry Company is the oldest jewelry firm in Fayette. It was established before 1915. Mr. Marion Williamson received his training in watch repair and then purchased the Jewelry Company from Mr. Mace in 1915, and has continued in business to the present time.

WOODARD, GUS, GROCERY STORE -- Located on the Winfield Highway.

WRIGHT'S T. V. SHOP -- Owner and operator, Harry Wright.

YELLOW FRONT STORE (DEPT. & GROCERY) -- Manager, T. W. Karrh.

YOUNG'S DRUG SUNDRIES -- Established in 1927 by Dorsey Young. Presently operated by Mr. & Mrs. Billy Joe Shelton.

INDUSTRIES:

ARTHUR LUMBER COMPANY -- One of Fayette's oldest and largest industrial concerns is the Arthur Lumber Company which was established here in 1896 by the late Grover C. Arthur. Following Mr. Arthur's death in 1947 this progressive concern has been managed and directed by Richard Arthur, son of Mr. G. C. Arthur, the founder. Arthur Lumber Co. is engaged in an extensive saw-milling program which includes seven mills located in this section of West Alabama. Their modern plant and concentration yard is located on Tuscaloosa Street. In addition to shipping lumber in carload lots to various wholesale outlets throughout the United States, this establishment carries a complete line of building materials.

COURINGTON, R. L., SAWMILL -- Located off the Winfield Highway.

DAN RIVER MILLS, INC., -- The textile mill organization, Alabama Mills Inc. formed the first textile mill in Fayette County, located in Fayette in September, 1928. This was an organization that owned several other textile mills located in different parts of the State of Alabama. In the 1940's an annex was added to the original building and warehouses have been added through the years until this unit of Alabama Mills was one of the largest.

On August 11, 1956, after the stockholders voted to sell the company, Dan River Mills, Inc. bought the Fayette unit of Alabama Mills, Inc. and is engaged in making all types of cotton textiles. Some of the items being manufactured today are; (all good in the grey) drapery, toweling, hopsacking, and other textiles. This plant uses about 350 bales of cotton a week and has the largest payroll of any industry located in Fayette County.

In September 1959, the Dan River Plant was sold to the Union Underwear Co., and will weave white broadcloth for use in the company's other plants.

FAYETTE COCA-COLA BOTTLING PLANT -- In 1924, Mr. L. M. Dodds purchased the local Coca Cola Plant from Mr. B. J. Bogard and was owner until his death in 1955 when his son-in-law, Mr. Alex Smith, Jr. became the president of the company. When Mr. Dodds assumed ownership of the local Coca Cola Franchise, the bottling plant was located in a one-story frame building on Columbus St. across from the T. H. Robertson & Sons Store. In those days the popular soft drink was bottled with hand and foot operated machines and its daily capacity was just a fraction of today's mechanized output with the very best of modern sanitary bottling equipment. Today the company is housed in a modern two-story brick building and is up-to-date in every respect.

FAYETTE CONCRETE PIPE CO. -- Fayette Concrete Pipe Co. was organized by Mr. E. A. Bagwell. He was engaged in the machine shop business and was a dealer in automobiles prior to establishing the concrete pipe business. At Mr. Bagwell's death his estate took over the management and in 1958 Fuller Kimbrell bought a part interest in the business and a new department of metal pipe for heavy construction was added to the different types of products previously manufactured by the firm.

FAYETTE MANUFACTURING CO. -- The City of Fayette sold bonds and erected the building to house the Fayette Manufacturing Co., in 1955. The Company manufactures children's wear. A. Jack Newell is the manager. The addition to the plant building was constructed in the fall of 1959 and the spring of 1960.

FAYETTE MILL, GIN & ICE CO. -- Fayette Mill, Gin & Ice Company, one of Fayette's oldest business establishments was originally organized by a group of Fayette County citizens about 1904. When this concern was first established it was known as the Sipsey Valley Oil & Fertilizer Company and was owned and controlled by a group of local stockholders. After the company had been operated for several years the mill and light plant which furnished Fayette with its first electric lights, was purchased by T. H. Robertson. The cotton oil mill department was destroyed by fire in 1917. Mr. Robertson continued to operate the company until he sold his interests to J. A. Richards in 1918. It was continued under the Richards management until 1923 when he sold the electric light plant to the Alabama Power Company and the remainder of the company's holdings to J. C. Grimsley, E. M. Grimsley and C. V. Matthews. In 1925 Mr. Matthews sold out his part of the business to J. C. and E. M. Grimsley when it was incorporated January 1, 1925, as Fayette Mill, Gin & Ice Company. Under the direction and management of the Grimsleys, the concern continued to grow and expand; and as the farmers of this section began to show an interest in dairying and cattle raising, they added a mixed feed mill. A creamery was also built and at one time furnished ice cream to retail outlets throughout West Alabama. The company also operated a large cotton gin and in 1945 added a wholesale grocery department. The property was sold to another firm of the city of Fayette in 1958, for the purpose of erecting a new manufacturing business and at the close of the business in January, 1959, the following were the officers: President, Mrs. A. M. Grimsley; Vice President, A. M. Grimsley, Jr.; Secretary & Treasurer, Mr. J. J. Taylor - Mr. Taylor had been with the company since June 1, 1922.

DAIRIES -- In the past few years many farmers have built Grade A barns and sell their daily output to the local milk processing plants. In order to meet the requirements for a grade A. barn, a dairy farmer must build a barn with concrete floors that can be easily washed and scrubbed. The milk must be immediately cooled to 40 degrees after milking and taken to a milk processing plant within two hours. The milk and containers must be handled in a room separate from the milking and hot water for sterilizing all equipment and utensils must be available at all times. The cows must be free of disease and insects must be kept away from the barns.

FAYETTE PURE MILK COMPANY or "FLAV-O-RICH" DAIRY -- The Flav-O-Rich Dairy of Fayette was organized June 10, 1946, under the name of "Fayette Pure Milk Co." to process and bottle milk. The name was changed July 1, 1956, to "Flav-O-Rich Dairy". Mr. A. J. Huffman organized the business and operates the plant with a sister plant located in Florence, Ala. The local farmers sell their milk to Mr. Huffman for processing and bottling into the delicious products that are found in the dairy case of all local grocers, including homogenized milk, buttermilk, skimmed milk, cream cheese and other products.

DEEP SOUTH DAIRY -- In January, 1959, Mr. N. V. Varnes changed his dairy from the Barnes Dairy to "Deep South Dairy". This dairy also sells the many dairy products that are found in every home. Mr. Barnes had been in the dairy business for several years before changing to "Deep South".

GOLDEN EAGLE TABLE SYRUP MANUFACTURERS -- In October, 1928, V. S. Patterson had a vision for the establishment of a syrup plant in Fayette. The formula for Golden Eagle Table Syrup was compounded by Mr. & Mrs. Patterson in their home and has resulted in one of the largest concerns of its kind in the South. Golden Eagle Syrup has been made continuously, in Fayette, since 1928 and today is being supplied to wholesale jobbers and distributors in several states. In 1944, Mr. Patterson purchased a large brick building, formerly owned by Tyler Wholesale Grocery Company and remodeled it into a modern factory. The location is on Fouracre and James Streets. Besides Mr. & Mrs. Patterson, their son Victor Patterson, Jr., their son-in-law Herbert M. Newell, and Joe H. Coons are connected with the management.

HABCO SOUTHERN TEXTILE CO. -- Manager, Robert Burt.

HARKINS LUMBER COMPANY -- Owner, Bruce F. Harkins.

LAWRENCE LUMBER COMPANY -- Owner, Clayton Lawrence.

LOPER LUMBER COMPANY -- In April 1912, the Basket Lumber Co. was organized with Mr. Lee Basket of Kentucky as the president. Shortly afterwards a sawmill was built. In a few years Mr. W. P. Brown bought the lumber mill from the Basket Brothers. He did not use the original mill, but built a new one. In 1926, the Mobile and Gulf railroad was chartered. This line was built for the lumber company, ran from Fayette to Buhl, and was used as a log road. When the mill first began operation, it consisted of a planer, a re-saw and three band saws. One of these bandsaws was used to cut hardwood. Later the hardwood saw was removed. At the peak of the company's operation, approximately 230,000 feet of lumber was cut daily. The Brown Lumber Co. was the main industry for many years for Fayette. After the timber supply began to get low, another of the band saws was discarded, leaving only one which remained in use until the mill burned in October, 1944. After the mill burned its output was never restored to the original capacity and now the Fayette Division is an office for handling the shipping sales of the Company. Mr. Ray E. Loper, the present owner, lived in Fayette for several years until the mill discontinued the mill operations. Mr. J. B. Houston is the manager of the Fayette office.

NEWMAN LUMBER COMPANY -- Located at Belk, Ala. Owner, Grady Newman.

NEWTON LUMBER COMPANY --

PARKS LUMBER COMPANY -- The Parks Lumber Company was originally organized in 1944 as the Benton-Fowler Lumber Co. Mr. John D. Parks purchased the plant and lumber yard in 1946 and has operated it continuously since that time. The company specializes in pine and hardwood and ships several million board feet yearly to all parts of the United States.

PULPWOOD -- During the was (World War II), when paper was scarce and the prices were high on everything, the pulpwood industry began to boom in Fayette County. Much of the timber of the county was cut and hauled to Holt, Alabama, to the paper mill. Since the war the pulpwood business has continued to grow and several million feet of pulpwood is shipped from Fayette each week. Some of the local dealers in pulpwood in Fayette County are: Dobbs Brothers, Pulpwood Dealers; T. C. Smith, Jr., Pulpwood Dealer; and Mrs. Sam Willingham, Pulpwood Dealer.

SOUTHERN LUMBER COMPANY -- The Southern Lumber Company was organized in 1918 and is presently operated by Mr. Felix Grimsley and Mr. Eric Grimsley. Their office is located in the Water Works Building on East Columbus Street. They have two hardwood mills in South Alabama. Other operations of the company include wholesale and commission sales of lumber.

WHITTIMORE BROTHERS CORPORATION -- The Whittimore Brothers Corporation was founded in 1840 in Cambridge, Mass. and moved the manufacturing plant to Fayette, Ala. in 1951. This company manufactures a complete line of Whittimore's Shoe Polishes and Dressings. The plant is located in the old N.Y.A.

section.

WOOL FACTORY -- In the early days of Fayette County, there was a Wool Factory located at the Joe Reeves Mill eleven miles north west of Fayette on the Luxapallila River. (This mill was later known as the Matt Sims Mill.) When Fayette County was young, large flocks of sheep were raised in the county and this old wool factory carded the wool and made it into rolls. In those days they did the work on shares, for part of the finished wool. After the wool was made into rolls at the factory, the farm women spun the rolls into thread. Sometimes they would take cotton and card it and spin it into thread and then mix the yarns. In weaving the material used for dresses, pants and shirts for the family, they would put the cotton thread in the warp and the wool thread in the filling on the looms. These looms (a must in every home) had foot peddles near the floor and as the foot peddles were pressed the thread would cross and then the shuttle with the filling was passed through the warp and the process repeated of pressing the foot peddles. Some of the yarn was used for knitting socks and stockings for the entire family and in the early days of Fayette County, most of the families of the county were dressed in these homespun creations.

BANKING:

CITIZEN'S BANK OF FAYETTE -- From an humble beginning on June 7, 1913, the Citizen's Bank of Fayette has grown to be one of the strongest and largest financial institutions in this section of Alabama. On opening day in 1913 this little bank's total resources were only $27,148.38. Its total resources of today are proof of its sound financial condition. Its original name was Alabama State Bank & Trust Company and its first officers were T. H. Robertson, president; E. P. Goodwin, vice-president; and H. M. Williams, cashier. The first directors were T. H. Robertson, E. P. Goodwin and C. A. Beasley. On December 10, 1919, its state charter was amended and its name changed to The Citizen's Bank. The present (1959) officers are J. C. Robertson, president; T. L. Lindsey, vice-president & cashier; and T. L. Lindsey, Jr. and Wm. B. Riley, assistant cashiers. The following advertisement which appeared in The Fayette Banner in 1913, shortly after the bank was organized, typifies its friendly policy; "We will appreciate your account, whether large or small, and solicit the business of farmers, wage-earners, and all persons desiring the assistance and accomodations of a bank." A new $125,000 building was erected on the corner of Temple Avenue and Columbus Street and open house was held on August 8, 1956.

FIRST NATIONAL BANK -- On the morning of August 1, 1900, the doors of the Fayette County Bank were opened for business. This was a private bank, organized, owned and operated by W. H. Terry, formerly of Prescott, Arkansas. The location was the same as the First National Bank today, just north of the Court House but was situated in a one story frame building. The capital stock was $15,000.00. E. P. Goodwin worked in the bank until the death, in 1907 of his father, Thomas Goodwin, at which time he was appointed Probate Judge of Fayette County to fill his father's unexpired term. The banking hours were from daylight until the day's work was finished. Mr. Terry sold, in 1908, his interest to some Birmingham investors who in turn retained the control and sold some stock locally. During this period of ownership, R. P. Caine served as President and E. P. Cox as Cashier. In 1909, the control of stock was bought by A. M., E. M. and J. C. Grimsley who closed out their Naval store operations in South Alabama and moved to Fayette. In the re-organization, A. M. Grimsley was elected president, E. E. Thomason, cashier and R. P. Caine, assistant cashier, and plans were made for the erection of a one story brick building which was completed at an early date. When the town burned March 24, 1911, the bank building was completely destroyed and the front part of the present building erected. Later, it was extended twice the size. The Fayette County Bank was converted into the First National Bank of Fayette in 1913 and the capital stock was increased from $25,000.00 to $50,000.00. One of the first acts of the new national Bank was to issue currency. The shipment arrived and A. M. Grimsley, president and E. E. Thomason, cashier, spent an entire day signing greenbacks which were put into circulation the following morning. Mr. Grimsley remained president until his death February 23, 1948, a period of 39 years. A. M. Grimsley, Jr. was then elected president. The present officers are Mrs. A. M. Grimsley, chairman of the Board of Directors; A. M. Grimsley, Jr., president; G. L. Smith, vice-president; and Morris Roberts, cashier. The oldest employee, Mr. Smith, having been connected with the institution since 1917, has served for 42 years.

PUBLIC SERVICES:

ALABAMA POWER COMPANY -- In 1929, when Alabama Power Company purchased the Fayette Light Plant from J. A. Richards, the local generating plant here supplied current through a 75-kilowatt and 100-kilowatt generator to serve about 500 customers. Very few residents beyond the city limits enjoyed the convenience of electrical power. Alabama Power Company now serves several thousand customers in Fayette County through tie-ins with its general transmission system. Electric service is now available to most of the farms in the county and future construction will make it available to every section and mile of Fayette County. Alabama Power Company's general transmission system is fed by six large hydro-electric plants on the Coosa and Tallapoosa Rivers and major steam plants at Gorgas, Gadsden and Chickasaw, Alabama, with a generating capacity nearly five times greater than the company's plants had in 1923 when its service was first extended to Fayette.

ALABAMA TELEPHONE COMPANY -- Fayette's first telephone company was organized sometime prior to 1912 by T. G. Johnson and was located near the location of the present Gullett's Store. Mr. Johnson sold his interest in the exchange to a group of stockholders composed of Al Cannon, A. J. Wright, J. Z. Bradley, W. W. Stallworth and M. Brotherton in 1912. A year later Mr. Brotherton purchased the company and moved the entire exchange which had 32 telephones to a new location above the present (1959) Loftis Cafe (once the P. B. Smith Produce Store) on the east side of Temple Avenue (across the street from the Court House). By the time that he sold the exchange to J. D. and C. P. Shannon, of New Albany, Miss. in 1928, the number of local subscribers had increased to 285 and the number of telephones in service in the rural area was 269. The Shannons operated the exchange for a while and then sold it to an organization known as the South Central Telephone Company. The Alabama Telephone Company, which operates the telephone service in this part of the state at the present, was organized May 1, 1938, after purchase by H. W. Vaughn and James N. Cox. The property had first been purchased by a Chicago Company and survived some five years in consolidation, but had been thrown into the hands of a receiver about 1933, and was subsequently sold to Mr. Cox and Mr. Vaughn.

When the present Alabama Telephone Company was organized in 1938, the facilities were in a very rundown condition and had only 800 stations. The new owners immediately began the task of overhauling and reconstructing the outmoded plant. They issued $75,000 in bonds and paid a debt of $35,000 to the R.F.C. After this bond issue, installation of new equipment was begun. The Alabama Telephone Company now has several thousand stations in their 14 exchanges, a large per-cent of these are dial. The dial service for Fayette was put into use January, 1959.

FAYETTE COUNTY FARM AGENT (ALABAMA EXTENSION SERVICE) -- The County Farm Agents office was first established in Fayette County on July 1, 1914. This office is connected with the Alabama Extension Service and its duties consist of giving instructions and practical demonstrations in agriculture and home economics to persons not attending colleges in communities through field demonstrations, publications and otherwise. Following is a list of the County Agents who have served Fayette County since the office was established here: Mr. R. G. Arnold, no dates available because of fire; Mr. J. C. Ford, October 21, 1927 to June 30, 1938; Mr. P. R. Pettis, July 1, 1938 to June 4, 1955 (death); Mr. S. L. Davis, July 1, 1955 to June 30, 1958; and Mr. Albert Pitts, Jr., July 1, 1958 and presently serving.

FAYETTE COUNTY DEPARTMENT OF PENSIONS AND SECURITY (FORMERLY, WELFARE DEPT.)
The Fayette County Department of Pensions and Security was organized September 5, 1935, as the Fayette County Welfare Department and is located in the Court House Annex. This Department was changed from the Fayette County Department of Public Welfare to the present name October, 1955. The Department of Pensions and Security administers all public assistance, including old age pensions, child welfare program and cooperates with all local and state agencies. Following are the directors who have served the Fayette County Department since its organization in 1935; Miss Bennie Walton; Miss Maude Smyley; Miss Christine Downing; Miss Nolen Meroney; Miss Mildred Jenkins; Mrs. Betty Coons (Acting); and Miss Bess Savage, January 1, 1948 to present time.

FAYETTE COUNTY HEALTH DEPARTMENT -- The Fayette County Health Department was set up in Fayette County, April 5, 1937, with a basic unit consisting of a health office, a public nurse, a sanitation officer and a secretary. County medical associations elect five of their members to serve as county boards of health, whose duty is to set local policies and elect county health officers subject to confirmation by the state health officer. County governing bodies appropriate local funds for the operation of county health departments. County departments also receive state and federal funds which are allocated to them through the State Health Department on a per capita basis. The program of the health department is largely a preventive one, accomplished through immunization against various forms of communicable diseases. The health department investigates and reports the occurence of communicable and other selective diseases to the U. S. Public Health Service. The health department maintains a register of all known cases of tuberculosis; supervises the home care of active cases, find cases by conducting surveys and follows up persons known to have been in contact with a case. The local health department keeps a register of known cancer cases and administers home care and educational programs. Also under the direction of the health department is a maternal and child care program and a dental hygiene schedule with a weekly clinic conducted by a local dentist. The health department reviews and approves **plans** for the installation of sanitary facilities, such as sewer connections, septice tanks and pit privies. The department engages in programs for the control of rats, mosquitoes and flies. The public health is further protected through the inspection of all types of food-handling establishments, such as restaurants, dairies, milk pasteurization and bottling plants, school lunch rooms and bakeries. All such establishments to do business must have a permit which is issued on the basis of the inspection by the health department. At the time of organization of the local health department, Dr. R. V. Taylor served as health officer from April 5, 1937 to September 12, 1938. Assisting him were Mrs. Nina L. Newton, Public Health Nurse from April 5, 1937 to April 4, 1942; Mr. J. R. Spence, Sanitation Officer, from July 1, 1937 to July 1, 1938, and Mrs. Nell Hamilton Stovall who began work with the health department April 5, 1937, as Secretary, a position she continues to hold. Other personnel who have served in the various positions are as follows: Health Officer, Dr. H. D. Barber; Dr. J. H. Ashcraft; Dr. W. J. Donald; Dr. Ralph McBurney and Dr. J. Banks Robertson, who is the present health officer. Public Health Nurse: Misses Kathryn Collier and Maron Aylin; Mrs. Faye M. Boone and Mrs. Thelma Humber, who is presently employed in this position. Sanitation Officers: L. G. Prentice; William P. Moss; Paul W. Frederick; and L. H. Collier, the present officer.

FAYETTE COUNTY HOME DEMONSTRATION AGENT -- The Fayette County Home Demonstration Agent became a vital part of the county in July 1939, and its growth and expansion seem almost phenomenal. Through the medium of the Home Demonstration Clubs, almost every problem confronting the homemaker is discussed and helpful suggestions offered. Through the years, vast stores of canned goods have been the result of the many canning centers over the county; handcrafts have added beauty and brightness to many homes; and numerous homes have been remodeled and re-decorated the "Do-It-Yourself" way. Following is a list of the Home Agents who have served Fayette County since the office was established here: Miss Evelyn Peyton, July 1, 1939 to April 30, 1948; Miss Kathleen Thompson, May 1, 1948 to September 13, 1952; Miss Sarah Hickman, September 13, 1952 to December 18, 1953; Miss Anita Helms, January 1, 1954 to April 30, 1956; and Miss Annie Mary Hester, May 1, 1956 and still serving.

FAYETTE COUNTY HOSPITAL -- The Fayette County Hospital is the result of many months and years of planning and working. It is a general hospital equipped with the most modern hospital equipment. An open house for public inspection was held on Sunday afternoon, September 21, 1958, and the first patients were admitted on Wednesday, September 24, 1958. Mr. Robert Boone is the administrator of the Fayette County Hospital and the following are members of the Fayette County Hospital Board. Herbert Matthews, Chairman; Corbett Langston, C. S. Campbell, B. W. McNease, M. D., G. S. Logan, J. D. Scrivner, M. D., J. D. Crawley, Marvin Smith, H. M. Studdard and Robert H. Boone, Administrator. Following are the Fayette County Commissioners, clerk and attorney, whose untiring efforts helped to make this fine hospital a reality for the people of Fayette County: Fleetwood Watkins, Clerk; C. M. Holder, Attorney; and County Commissioners J. R. Kemp, E. W. Moss, Mrs. Sula Walker and A. T. Stovall.

FAYETTE COUNTY IN TOMBIGBEE-WARRIOR CONSERVATION DISTRICT -- Fayette County is one of seven counties included in the Tombigbee-Warrior Soil Conservation District, being organized October 3, 1939. O. H. Frederick was the first member of the board of supervisors from Fayette County of the Tombigbee-Warrior

District. Mr. Frederick, as chairman signed the memorandum between the U. S. Department of Agriculture and the District, October 3, 1939. It was the signing of this document that started the program to work in Fayette County. The objectives of the district program is to furnish on the farm, in the field, assistance to farmers in planning and putting into practice soil and water conserving measures. The Soil Conservation Service had two men assigned to give this assistance to any and all farmers within this county that want the help. The service is free, being rendered by Mr. Henry J. Young and his assistant, Mr. Dexter Clark. Mr. Luther S. Bobo was the first farmer in Fayette County to be assisted in making a soil conservation plan. Mr. Bobo's plan was made on November 22, 1939.

FAYETTE SWIMMING POOL -- The Fayette Swimming Pool was completed and first used in 1939. It was built at the site of the old "City Springs". Before the swimming pool was built there was a spring house built around the fine springs with ample space for picnics and parties. It was used quite frequently for birthday parties for the youngsters of Fayette. In building the swimming pool, Mr. Clyde Lawley was the engineer and Mr. Grady Hallman supervised the actual construction.

FAYETTE WATER WORKS BOARD -- The Water Works Board was created in 1946. Up until that time the Water Works was not a separate unit. The new Water Plant located on the Tuscaloosa Highway was put into operation in 1947 with Mr. Ulys Meherg as the superintendent of the system. The water supply for Fayette is pumped from the Sipsey River and filtered through the plant, with chemicals added to safeguard the health of the citizens of Fayette. In 1955 a large water tank was installed on the Southside to better serve that section of the town of Fayette.

THE GAS BOARD OF THE CITY OF FAYETTE -- An agreement dated December 12, 1953, was signed between the Northwest Alabama Gas District and the City of Fayette. The Gas Board of the City of Fayette was incorporated July 1, 1954, and the contract with the Northwest Alabama Gas District signed. On July 6, 1954, at 4:00 P.M. the members of the board of directors met and elected the following: R. C. Cobb, Chairman of the Board of Directors; A. J. Huffman, Vice-Chairman of the Board of Directors; V. W. Poe, Secretary & Treasurer of the Corporation; and Alex J. Smith, Jr. was appointed attorney for the board of directors. The low bid for the laying of the pipes was awarded Hendrix & Mayes, Inc. Mr. R. C. Cobb resigned his position on the board of directors in September, 1954, and T. L. Lindsey, Jr. was appointed by the City Council to fill the vacancy. Mr. Lindsey was nominated to be the chairman of the board of directors. Those having served as Superintendent of Operations of the Gas Board have been Mr. R. E. Patterson from February, 1955 to January 1, 1956. Mr. John J. Quinn became the second superintendent and the present superintendent is Mr. Willard Livingston.

McNEASE AND ROBERTSON CLINIC AND HOSPITAL -- In March, 1936, Dr. B. W. McNease moved into his new clinic building and started one of the finest medical clinics in this section of Alabama. In July, 1936, Dr. J. Banks Robertson came to Fayette as a co-worker with Dr. McNease. The great need for a hospital to serve this part of Alabama was felt by these men and in 1937 the hospital section had been built and the McNease and Robertson Hospital officially opened to the public with Dr. Robertson as the surgeon. Through the years many young doctors have been affiliated with this fine clinic. Some came for their intern work, others came to settle with us and become a part of our lives. Some who have served in the clinic have been: Dr. Richard Carter, Dr. Thomas Wiley, Dr. John Anderson, Dr. Pitts, Dr. Clarke Gravlee, Dr. Inez Fowler and others. Shortly after World War II, Dr. Henry G. Hodo, Jr., who was reared in Millport, Ala. came to the McNease and Robertson Hospital as surgeon. Dr. Robertson retired at this time because of his health. In 1954 Dr. Richard O. Rutland came to Fayette and joined the staff at the clinic. Dr. Inez Fowler left the clinic early in 1959 to further her studies in a specialized field and in July, 1959, Dr. James Lee Davis, III joined the staff. The latest member to join the clinic staff is Dr. Britling, who came in the fall of 1959. In 1950 an additional section was completed for use of the hospital and the McNease and Robertson Hospital continued to operate as one of the finest institutions available until the completion of the new Fayette County Hospital, a larger plant. The patients who were in the McNease and Robertson Hospital on September 24, 1958, were moved by ambulance to the new Fayette County Hospital and thus came the closing chapter of the McNease and Robertson Hospital. The Clinic has expanded greatly since the hospital closed and serves a wide section of north Alabama.

SELECTIVE SERVICE SYSTEM - LOCAL BOARD NO. 29 -- The Local Board No. 29 is an agency of the Federal Government and the office is located in the First National Bank Building. This board is a three member board of approximately 3,250 registrants. The board is comprised of Mr. James E. Moore, Chairman; Mr. Joe O. Campbell and Mr. Max H. Branyon, members. Mr. Miles C. Dobbs is Appeal Agent; Dr. B. W. McNease is Medical Advisor and Mrs. Bill Jeffries is Clerk. The local board office has been housed in its present location since 1950. During World War II the office was located in the Courthouse. During operation under the 1948 Act it was located in the Fayette Motor Co. Bldg. and from 1949 to 1950 it was again in the Court House. Serving as first clerk of this local board was William A. Parrish, with Mrs. Lorena Jeffries and Lizzie Robertson as assistants. Past clerks in addition to Mr. Parrish are Mrs. Johnny Cannon, Mrs. Jesse Peters, Hosea D. McArthur, Lloyd C. Adams, Willie B. Mosley, Miss Frances Daniel, Mrs. Carolyn Rudicell and Mrs. Doris Jeffries. Former board members include: N. T. Mothershed, Virgil Gray, B. F. Jeffries, L. H. Parrish, Bert Hollingshead, O. H. Cline, Billie Guin, Delmer Hocutt, E. F. Frederick, B. B. Gardner, John Morgan Brown, Troy Loftis, Dr. B. W. McNease and Hobson Watkins.

VEAZEY'S MORTUARY -- Veazey's Mortuary was bought by Thomas Veazey in January, 1949, from Carl Griffin, and the firm's name was changed from Griffin Funeral Home to Veazey's Mortuary. In April of 1955 Thomas Veazey bought the Short Funeral Home in Fayette, Ala. and the two funeral homes were consolidated and the business is now operated as Veazey's at 851 North Temple Ave., Fayette, Ala. In October, 1959, Thomas Veazey and James M. Moore, Jr. opened the new Oakwood Memorial Cemetery adjoining the McConnell Cemetery north of Fayette.

CHAPTER IV

GOVERNMENT

FAYETTE COUNTY COURT HOUSES -- Fayette County has dispensed justice in seven different court houses since its creation in 1824. The first house used for the court was a hatter's shop located on the Fayette and Winfield Highway, just north of the little creek near D. O. McConnell's farm and on the left side of the pike on top of the hill. This is according to tradition but is no doubt authenic. How long court convened at that place is unknown; however we know that when the town of Fayetteville was located, some kind of courthouse was built, perhaps out of logs and seated with crude, rough benches. We find from the records that this building served as a courthouse until 1854 when it was destroyed by fire.

On May 30, 1854, a contract was awarded to John J. Spain and Ira D. Farmer by the county commissioners of Fayette County to erect a new courthouse to take the place and to occupy the same ground as the old building.

Another fire, on the 14th of April 1866 again destroyed the Fayette County Court House together with most of the records of the court and on June 11, 1866, John C. Robertson was paid the sum of $200.00 for rent of a tavern in the town of Fayetteville for use as a court house.

After the burning of the court house, the commissioners undertook to build a new meeting place for the court, beginning in the autumn of 1866 to bake brick for the new building. John C. Robertson furnished, from his store, supplies for the hands working at the brick yard, and also loaned the county the money to pay for a new supply of blank books for the office of the probate judge.

A contract to build a new courthouse was awarded to John C. Robertson for the sum of $4,000. According to the records this building was in use until 1892 when Fayette was moved to its present site. At that time, however, Fayette was known as Latona.

The town was gradually being moved near the depot to the new town. The question of the removal of the court house, or the construction of a new and more modern building on the original site, became a very live issue. Some of the citizens wanted to move to the new location, while others desired that the old site be retained.

The agitation for the removal became so insistent that under an act of the Legislature approved December 8, 1890, William A. Musgrove, Willis B. Newton, Terrell M. Reese, William F. Baker, Phillip M. Newton, John F. Ashcraft and John Tyler McCaleb were appointed commissioners to select the most suitable location for the erection of the court house. They were given authority to purchase or receive donation, the title to land on which to build the new courthouse.

The people of the county were very much wrought up over the question of the removal of the court house from the old town to the new, and divided themselves into three opposing groups; one for the retention of the court house in the old town, one for the location at Fayette Depot Town and the third for the place called "Center".

Finally the citizens of Fayette County were given the right to express their choice in the matter and were given three places from which to make their selection. These porposed locations were the site of the court house at Fayetteville; Fayette Depot Town; or "Center", a place supposed to be the geographical center of the county, about one mile north of Stough, a small station on the Georgia Pacific Railroad.

After the three places had been selected by the commissioners, an election was held and as neither of the places received a majority, a second election was called to be held in July, 1891. This election resulted in the selection of the site in Depot Town, of Fayette as it is now known.

This particular parcel of land was entered by John McConnell, who received his patent on March 20, 1826, it then passed into the ownership of Levi Lindsey, who conveyed it to Harkins & Bankhead on March 14, 1891, who in turn sold it to Fayette County on July 15, 1891.

Although no official records exist to show the exact date the court house was moved to its present site, it is stated by old-time residents that the records of the county were moved to the new court house in March, 1892, and the fall term of the circuit court was held there. Some time after the completion and use of this building an annex was added.

This court house remained the temple of justice from 1892, to March 24, 1911, when the most disastrous fire in the history of the town occured, destroying not only the court house, with a great many valuable court records, but the entire business section of the town. The circuit court was in session at the time of the fire.

On April 17, 1911, the commissioners met and after all preleminaries were over, the contract for the construction of the new building was awarded to the Little Cleckler Construction Co. of Anniston, Alabama, for the sum of $58,347.21.

The court of county commissioners at the time of the fire were E. P. Goodwin, Judge of Probate; N. H. Harbin, Felix Howton, Jno. W. Porter, and S. L. South.

The Fall term of court was held in some old shacks west of the court house property, but the Spring term of the court was convened in the finished, new building, and this building stands today as a monument to the thrift, energy and progress of the people of Fayette County.

One year after the fire that destroyed the entire town, the citizens of Fayette and Fayette County gave a big barbecue celebrating the first anniversary of the burning of the town and the court house.

CIRCUIT COURT OF FAYETTE COUNTY -- The constitution of 1819 provided that the State be divided into circuits to contain not less than three nor more than six counties, and these courts had original jurisdiction in all criminal matters; and in all civil cases where the amount involved was more than fifty dollars.

The circuits in those early days covered a large territory and the holding of courts in each county was a semi-annual event. Nearly all of the citizens of the county attended these affairs to hear the charge of the judge to the juries, to swap horses, to patronize the corner saloon and imbibe freely of the cup that cursed their lives.

It was not uncommon of the early states that the circuit court of any particular county be held at the home of some citizen, and be seated on the crude log porches, or gathered at a convenient place in the yard where the judge, juries, attorneys and clients were administering the greatest system of law in all the world.

There is an old (and pretty well authenticated) legend that has been handed down from generation to generation about the first court ever held in Fayette County, and from facts gathered from the older citizens of the earlier days, there must be a certain amount of truth, as well as fiction, that has been mixed in with all of these legends and recollections of these pioneers.

It is said that the first court ever held in the county was convened in an old hatter's shop just across the little creek on the Fayette and Winfield Highway north of the D. O. McConnell farm.

The seats for the judges and jurors were made from blocks of wood sawed to the right height. When the court was called and the jury empanneled, the first case to be tried was between two old women, who had some time in the preceding days become involved in a misunderstanding or dispute as to which one had the legal title to a wash pot. They had tried as neighbors, to settle the question as to ownership without resorting to the court for a verdict, but had failed to come to a satisfactory agreement to both, so the case was tried and argued before the jury by eminent council on both sides and a verdict of some kind was rendered by the jury. It is not known for sure who the judge for this court was. Mark Meeks was the sheriff at the holding of the first term of court.

Following is a list of the clerks of the circuit court: Azor VanHoose, May 25, 1825; B. A. Lindsey, August 13, 1829; Robert J. Moore, August 22, 1833; Daniel Peyton, August 30, 1837; Daniel Peyton, September 10, 1841; Daniel Peyton, August 11, 1845; James B. Morton, October 6, 1845; Alexander Cobb, March 1, 1846; Murray Williams, October 13, 1849; Mark Russell, August 12, 1850; Mark Russell, August 11, 1856; John Earp, August 9, 1862; John C. Moore, November 5, 1866; John B. Burris, August 17, 1868; H. M. Bell, November 14, 1874; Thomas H. Davis, August 16, 1880; Thomas H. Davis, May 28, 1884; John W. Miles, November 12, 1885; John N. Black, August 9, 1886; Robert F. Peters, October 25, 1887; Robert F. Peters, July 20, 1888; Thomas E. Goodwin, August 9, 1892; Thomas E. Goodwin, August 2, 1896; D. P. McConnell, August 1, 1898; D. O. McConnell, November 6, 1904; D. O. McConnell, November 8, 1910; and A. C. Nichols, November 7, 1916.

By an act of the legislature, approved August 22, 1919, the Clerk of the Circuit Court was made Clerk of the County Court.

COUNTY COURT AND PROBATE JUDGES -- There was a very early law establishing county courts in the territorial period of the State. The Governor of the State was empowered to appoint and commission five persons in each county, one of whom was designated to be chief justice of the orphans' court. The law required the court to be held twice each year and restricted the time of holding the court to not more than six days. The court was given power of attorney to probate wills, to take conveyances and place them on records and to issue letters of administration; they were further empowered to take notice of all action of a civil nature where the value of the matter in controversey was not more than $1,000. The marked change in the law was the act under which only one judge of the county court, in each county, in the State was elected by vote of both houses of the general assembly. This method of appointment of the county court judges, by general assembly continued in force until a constitutional amendment was adopted in 1850. This amendment placed in the hands of the qualified voters of each county the election of a probate judge, and their duties and manner of election remains about the same to the present time. Various other duties have been added to the office of probate judges during the years. Following is a list of County Court Judges and Judges of the Probate Court of Fayette County from 1824 to 1959:

COUNTY COURT JUDGES -- 1824 - Jesse Van Hoose, resigned November 15, 1824; 1825 - John Ship, resigned November 28, 1827; 1827 - John McConnell; 1829 - Roddy Smith; 1830 - Burr W. Wilson; 1834 - Fleming Thompson; 1838 - Walter Harper; 1847 - James B. Morton; 1848 - Elliott P. Jones, served to the first Monday in May after which it seems the County Court was made the Probate Court.

JUDGES OF THE PROBATE COURT -- 1850 - John C. Moore; 1856 - Wm. P. Harvey; 1859 - R. Allen Smith (Wm. P. Harvey deceased); 1860 - B. H. Williams; 1864 - B. H. Williams; 1866 - B. H. Williams; 1868 - B. W. Wilson; 1874 - B. H. Williams; 1880 - Holland M. Bell; 1886 - Holland M. Bell; 1892 - Thomas B. Morton; 1898 - T. E. Goodwin; 1904 - T. E. Goodwin, died in 1908 leaving an unexpired term of two years plus; 1908 - E. P. Goodwin; 1916 - J. Alex Smith, Sr.; 1922 - J. Newton Collins; 1928 - J. Alexander Smith, Sr.; 1934 - J. M. Moore; 1940 - J. M. Moore, died in 1942 leaving an unexpired term; 1942 - W. P. Lawrence, appointed; 1942 - J. C. McGough; 1948 - J. C. McGough; 1954 - Clyde C. Cargile, still serving in 1959.

Following is listed the Clerks of the County Courts: 1825 - Daniel Thornton; 1829 - Daniel Peyton; 1833 - James B. Morton; 1837 - James B. Morton; 1845 - John C. Moore; 1849 - John C. Moore; 1858 - A. A. Summers.

All records available show that after 1858, the Probate Judges were the Clerks of the County Courts; 1868 - B. W. Wilson; 1874 - T. G. Williams; 1880 - Holland M. Bell; 1886 - Holland M. Bell; 1892 - Thomas B. Morton; 1898 - T. E. Goodwin; 1904 - T. E. Goodwin; 1908 - E. P. Goodwin, filled unexpired term of T. E. Goodwin; 1910 - E. P. Goodwin; 1916 - John Alexander Smith, Sr.

By an act of the Legislature approved August 22, 1919, the Clerk of the Circuit Court was made Clerk of the County Court. 1919 - A. C. Nichols; 1922 - A. B. Corbett; 1928 - A. B. Corbett; 1934 - R. L. Mosley; 1959 - W. S. Cooper.

CLERKS OF COMMISSIONER'S COURT SINCE 1935 -- 1935 - J. C. McGough; 1942 - Mrs. Bernice Rutledge Hankins; 1943 - W. Roy Martin; 1948 - Fleetwood Watkins;

The employee with the longest term of service in the Fayette County Court House in 1959 is Mrs. William (Ruth Collins) Riley. She has been a Clerk in the Probate Judge's Office since 1919.

TAX ASSESSORS -- From existing records we find the following serving in the office of Tax Assessor: 1844 - James M. Morrow; 1845 - C. D. Childreth; 1846 - Alexander Cobb; 1846 - Benjamin Reynolds; 1854 - James M. Smith; 1865 - Thomas A. Monroe; 1867 - George M. Neal; 1868 - John M. McCaleb; 1869 - George M. Neal; 1871 - P. E. Thornton; 1874 - William N. Edmons; 1878 - J. B. McClung; 1880 - J. B. McClung; 1884 - J. B. McClung; 1888 - J. B. McClung; 1892 - W. T. Baker; 1896 - George W. Coggins; 1900 - George W. Coggins; 1904 - George W. Coggins; 1908 - George W. Coggins; 1912 - George W. Coggins; 1916 - H. Willis May; 1920 - A. E. Patterson; 1924 - J. O. McCluskey, appointed to fill the unexpired term of A. E. Patterson, deceased, on June 21, 1924 and by an act of the Legislature the term was extended to 1926; S. E. Jones; 1935 - P. G. Lawley; 1954 - Aubrine A. Nichols; 1959 - Aubrine A. Nichols.

TAX COLLECTORS -- From 1891 to 1959 the following have served as Tax Collectors of Fayette County. 1891 - 1895 - Mr. ___ McCollum; 1896 - 1900 - W. A. Hyde; 1901 - 1909 - Robert Perry Caine; 1909 - 1921 - W. S. Bobo; 1921 - 1927 - J. R. Fowler; 1927 - 1935 - R. D. Newton; 1935 - 1943 - H. Matt Brock; 1943 - 1959 - P. D. Berry, still serving.

SHERIFFS OF FAYETTE COUNTY -- The office of sheriff, no doubt, dates back to the very beginning of civilization, when the inhabitants of the earth began to formulate laws for their own government and protection. The powers of the sheriff in the United States are almost exclusively ministerial, that is, he can, in his own person, or by deputy execute civil and criminal processes, throughout his own county, but has no authority to try cases or act in a judicial capacity.

There is in his charge the keeping of the jail and prisoners, he must attend the courts, and is also the main conservator of the peace for his entire county. In the territorial period of Alabama the sheriff was appointed by the governor and his term of office is not mentioned in the first constitution of the State of Alabama in 1819. All indications are that the terms were the same as when the State was a part of the Mississippi Territory, that being probably two years. This term remained the same until the constitution of 1865, which declares, "A Sheriff shall be elected in each county by the qualified electors thereof and shall hold his office for three years unless sooner removed ....."

This law of a three year term for sheriffs remained the same until 1875 when the constitution changed it to four years. This four year term for the office of sheriff went into effect in 1880.

One of the most grewsome duties the sheriff was called on to perform was the hanging of criminals sentenced to the death penalty. This unpleasant duty has been taken away from the sheriffs and hanging has been replaced by the electric chair, and the warden of Kilby Prison has become the executioner. This law was passed by act of the Legislature, approved September 29, 1923, but did not go into effect until 1927.

Following is a list of sheriffs serving Fayette County from 1825 to the present time: 1825 - Mark Meeks; 1828 - Daswell C. Thompson; 1832 - Mark Meeks; 1837 - George Hubbard; 1840 - Rosa H. Poe; 1846 - James Morrow; 1849 - Moses Summers; 1851 - Green T. Harton; 1854 - A. A. Summers; 1857 - James H. Harton; 1860 - Thomas D. Enis; 1863 - L. W. Worford; 1865 - Samuel Morrow; 1866 - Thomas D. Enis; 1868 - F. M. Treadaway; 1871 - Joseph Henry; 1874 - A. A. Walden; 1877 - P. W. Thornton; 1880 - Thomas E. Goodwin; 1884 - M. F. Caine; 1888 - Robert P. Caine; 1892 - W. R. Enis; 1896 - Robert P. Caine; 1900 - W. R. Enis (The constitution of 1901 extended the terms of all sheriffs in the State for an extra term of two years, thus extending the time of W. R. Enis to 1906); 1906 - James H. Oswalt; 1910 - W. R. Enis; 1914 - James H. Oswalt; 1918 - R. A. Burrow; 1922 - J. T. Chambless; 1926 - W. F. Berry; 1930 - Joe McConnell; 1934 - Grady Mitchell; 1938 - Will P. Jordon; 1942 - Travis Lawrence; 1944 - Luther V. Key, served while Travis Lawrence was away in World War II; 1946 - Travis Lawrence, died February, 1953; 1953 - Oscar Pinkerton, appointed; 1954 - Oscar Pinkerton; 1959 - Travis McKinney began serving January 1959, still serving.

PRECINCTS OF FAYETTE COUNTY, ALABAMA -- Until 1867 Fayette County had, including that part cut off to form Lamar County, an area of 1,264 square miles on 302,752 acres, with a population of only 3,547 to occupy this large territory. The entire county was divided into fourteen precincts as follows: Town, Berry, Betts, Collins, Cole, Gilpin, Hollysprings, Hico, Lawrence, Loftis, Millport, North River, Steens and Trulls.

Soon after Jones, now Lamar County, was created, the commissioners began to divide the remainder of Fayette County into precincts and beats. The first new precinct was formed on March 18, 1868, and was called Russell Beat and several other precincts were formed during that year. On December 28th the commissioners proceeded to lay the county off into election precincts and named the place of voting. Following is a list of these voting precincts and the places of voting, as designated: Town Beat, with voting at Fayette Court House; Hico Beat with voting at Mose Perkins; Collins Beat with voting at Wyley Miles; Webster Beat with voting at Mt. Pleasant Church; Russell Beat with no place named; Lincoln Beat with voting at Jame's Mill; Gilpin Beat with voting at Reynold's Mill; North River Beat with voting at David Sudduths; Coles Beat with voting at B. Phillips; Berry Beat at Samuel J. Patterson's; Hollysprings Beat with voting at Berry's Shop; Boley Springs Beat with voting at Boley Springs; Lee Beat with voting at New Bethel.

On January 10, 1876, Fayette County was divided into four commissioner's districts. The First District was composed of Town, Hico, Lee, Collins and Thompson's beats. The Second District was composed of Webster, Russell, Lincoln and Gilpin. The Third District was composed of Coles, Clear Creek, North River and Boley Springs, and the Fourth District was composed of Holly Springs, Ridge, Stonewall, and Berry beats. The lines of these beats have been changed from time to time and other beats have been added.

Following are the beats as listed in 1931 -- Town Beat No. 1; Ridge No. 2; North River No. 3; Berry No. 4; Russell No. 5; Cole No. 6; Hico No. 7; Collins No. 8; Holly Springs No. 9; Lee No. 10; Brown No. 11; Webster No. 12; Boley No. 13; Gilpin No. 14; Clear Creek No. 15; Thompson No. 16; Stonewall No. 17; Byler No. 18; Ford No. 19; George's Creek No. 20; Hankins No. 21 and Sugar Creek No. 22.

The above list is given to give an idea as to the different sections of the county and to show the number of beats in 1931.

SENATORS REPRESENTING FAYETTE COUNTY -- 1826 - 1826 - Jesse Van Hoose; 1827 - 1828 - James Moore; 1829 - 1832 - Rufus K. Anderson; 1834 - 1835 - Henry Burrough; 1837 - 1841 - Burr W. Wilson; 1843 - 1844 - Elijah Marchbanks; 1847 - 1848 - Daniel Coggin; 1851 - 1858 - Elliott P. Jones; 1861 - 1862 - A. J. Coleman; 1863 - J. F. Morton; 1865 - 1866 - Elliott P. Jones; 1871 - 1872 - J. De F. Richards and J. M. Martin; 1872 - 1876 - J. M. Martin; 1876 - 1877 - J. H. Bankhead; 1878 - 1881 - W. A. Musgrove; 1882 - 1883 - A. L. Moorman; 1884 - 1885 - A. C. Moorman; 1886 - 1887 - George C. Almon; 1888 - 1889 - G. A. Almon; 1890 - 1893 - R. L. Bradley; 1894 - 1895 J. L. Hollis; 1896 - 1897 - J. S. Hollis; 1898 - 1899 - T. L. Sowell; 1900 - 1901 - J. J. Ray; 1903 - Christopher Columbus NeSmith; 1907 - 1909 - M. L. Leith; 1911 - Cecil Ackmond Beasley; 1915 - J. C. Milner; 1919 - M. L. Leith; 1923 - Walter Scott McNeil; 1935 - Walter Scott McNeil, died December 24, 1934; 1935 - John Almond Kuykendall; 1947 - Fuller Asberry Kimbrell; 1959 - Woodrow Wilson Roberts.

REPRESENTATIVES FROM DISTRICT REPRESENTING FAYETTE COUNTY -- 1828 - 1829 - Samuel J. Parker; 1829 - 1830 - John Shipp; 1830 - 1832 - James K. McCollum; 1832 - 1833 - Caswell C. Thompson; 1833 - 1834 - Wm. S. Taylor; 1834 - 1835 Wm. S. Taylor and Caswell C. Thompson; 1835 - 1836 - Wm. S. Taylor and Burr W. Wilson; 1836 - 1837 - Wm. S. Taylor and C. Boyd; 1837 - 1838 - Lawrence Brasher and Wm. S. Taylor; 1838 - 1839 - Wm. S. Taylor and R. J. Morrow; 1839 - 1840 - Wm. S. Taylor and Wilson Cobb; 1840 - 1841 - Wilson Cobb and Elijah Marchbanks; 1841 - 1842 - Wm. S. Taylor and Elijah Marchbanks; 1842 - 1843 - James M. Morris and Elijah Marchbanks; 1843 - 1844 - James M. Morris and Allen Harris; 1844 - 1845 - Alvis Davis and Wm. W. Bell; 1845 - 1846 - Alvis Davis and Elzer Williams; 1847 - 1848 - Alvis Davis and J. R. Kirkland; 1849 - 1850 - A. J. Coleman and J. K. McCollum; 1851 - 1852 - A. J. Coleman and J. K. McCollum; 1853 - 1854 - E. W. Lawrence and A. M. Reynolds; 1855 - 1856 - J. C. Kirkland and T. P. McConnell; 1857 - 1858 - A. J. Coleman and James Brock; 1859 - 1861 - A. J. Coleman and James Seay; 1861 - 1863 - James Middleton and Alexander Cobb; 1863 - 1865 - James Seay and Alexander Cobb; 1865 - 1866 - Thomas Malloy and Alexander Cobb; 1866 - 1867 - Thomas Malloy and E. W. Lawrence; 1868 - _____; 1869 - 1870 - _____ ; 1870 - 1872 - W. H. Kennedy; 1872 - 1873 - W. A. Musgrove; 1874 - 1877 - J. C. Kirkland; 1878 - 1879 - Gustavus Legg; 1880 - 1881 - J. C. Kirkland; 1882 - 1883 - J. B. Sanford; 1884 - 1885 - R. W. Wood; 1886 - 1889 - James M. Files; 1890 - 1891 - John M. Davis; 1892 - 1893 - J. S. Hollis; 1894 - 1895 - Zach Savage; 1896 - 1897 - W. B. McCollum; 1898 - 1899 - J. S. Hollis; 1899 - 1901 - J. S. Hollis; 1903 - Robert Frierson Peters; 1907 - 1909 - W. M. Cannon; 1911 - Sim T. Wright; 1915 - J. M. Moore; 1919 - Robert F. Peters; 1923 - John Franklin Ashcraft; 1927 - William Morrow Cannon; 1931 - John Glass Hamby; 1935 - Harry Hodges; 1939 - Max H. Branyon; 1943 - Miles C. Dobbs; 1947 - Miles C. Dobbs; 1951 - Truman A. Simpson, died August 12, 1951; 1951 - James A. Branyon, II; 1955 - James A. Branyon, II; 1959 - James A. Branyon, II, still serving.

CHAPTER V

WARS

<u>FAYETTE COUNTY PENSIONERS - WAR OF 1812</u> -- List of Pensioners on the Roll, January 1, 1883, giving the name of each pensioner, the cause for which pensioned, the Post-Office address, the rate of pension per month, and the date of original allowance, as called for by Senate Resolution of December 8, 1882. Volume V. Washington Government Printing Office. - 1883. Page 227.

No. of Certificate	Name of Pensioner	Post Office Address	Cause for which pensioned	Monthly Rate	Date of original allowance.
24,259	Cook, Charity	Buck Snort	Widow 1812	$8.00	May 1879
21,790	Black, Mary	Davis Creek	Widow	8.00	March 1879
12,606	Logan, Julia A.	Davis Creek	Widow 1812	8.00	Dec. 1878
12,475	Blackburn, Susannah	Davis Creek	Widow 1812	8.00	Nov. 1878
10,439	Crow, Catharine	Fayette C. H.	Widow 1812	8.00	Oct. 1878
6,174	Smith, Temoerance	Fayette C. H.	Widow 1812	8.00	June 1874
21,564	Harris, Malinda	Fayette C. H.	Widow 1812	8.00	March 1879
25,554	Ward, Mary	Fayette C. H.	Widow 1812	8.00	July 1879
14,477	Chapell, Milo (Miles)	Fayette C. H.	Survivor '12	8.00	March 1872
21,164	Hollingsworth, John	Fayette C. H.	Survivor '12	8.00	Nov. 1873
5,940	Walters, William	Fayette C. H.	Survivor '12	8.00	Oct. 1871
11,334	Wolf, William	Fayette C. H.	Survivor '12	8.00	Jan. 1872
82,688	Cook, Nancy A.	Handy	Widow	8.00	March 1872
30,725	Pulliam, Nancy R.	Handy	Widow 1812	8.00	Nov. 1880
153,508	Taylor, Jonathan	Mont Calm	Rheum. & curv. spine	6.00	June 1878
19,501	Dickinson, Rachel	Mont Calm	Widoe 1812	8.00	March 1879
31,478	Hollingsworth, Silpha	New River	Widow 1812	8.00	March 1881
27,222	Davis, Hannah	New River	Widow 1812	8.00	Oct. 1879
25,650	Mat, Hannah	Palo	Widow 1812	8.00	July 1879
25,653	May, Martha	Palo	Widow 1812	8.00	July 1879
16,746	Deavours, Abigail	Spencer	Widow 1812	9.00	Feb. 1879
20,254	Stoddard, Samuel	Spencer	Survivor '12	8.00	Feb. 1873
28,598	Reed, Sytha	Wayside	Widow 1812	8.00	Jan. 1880
30,425	Holloman, Elizabeth	Webster	Widow 1812	8.00	Sept. 1880

<u>INDIAN SEMINOLE WAR</u> -- Following are the names of a few from Fayette County Volunteers in the Indian Seminole War: Daniel G. Kirkland, Thomas P. McConnell, Richard P. Olive, father of Ira Griffin, and father of E. C. Willingham.

There are others, but records are not available to give a more complete list.

CIVIL WAR -- By 1859 the war clouds were looming, and shortly thereafter the able-bodied men were off to war.

Although there were many hardships of life imposed upon her people, Fayette County was free of hostile invasion until a few months before the close of the war. Early in 1865, General J. H. Wilson, with a force of 13,500 Federal Cavalry set out from Lauderdale County upon a raid into Central Alabama, which finally ended at Selma. A part of this force came through Fayette County the latter part of March or the first part of April, 1865, and burned several buildings and destroyed any food supplies that they could not carry with them. Many depredations were committed. The soldiers robbed the people of anything that happened to strike their fancy. Fortunately, the column was moving fast, and their stay was short, yet in that short stay, Wilson's Raiders left behind them a path of desolation.

In giving Civil War records we feel the service of the men will prove more interesting at this point and in the following pages we are giving the Census or Enumeration of Confederate Soldiers Residing in Alabama - 1907 - Fayette, County, Alabama - on file in the Fayette County Court House, Fayette, Alabama.

No. 1 - AKINS, JAMES W., Glen Allen, Ala. was born on Oct. 31, 1831 in the County of Greene, Ga. First entered service as 3rd Sargent on 1 April 1862 at Rockford, Coosa County, Ala. in the 3rd Ala. Bat. Co. B. and continued until March 1863. Consolidated and re-enlisted as Private, March 1863 at Cumberland Gap, Tenn. in the 59 Ala. Regt. Inf. Co. K. and continued until 25 March 1865. Captured at Petersburg, Va. and remained in prison at Point Lookout Mtn. until May 16, 1865 and paroled.

No. 2 - AMERSON, HUGH G., Toleda, Ala. was born on Oct. 22, 1837 at Fayette County Alabama. First entered the service as Private on March 9, 1862 at Fayette Co., Ala. in the 32 Ala. Regt. Inf. Co. I. and continued until Oct. 1862. Captured at ____, Tenn. - Parolled Oct. 11, 1862. Exchanged and re-enlisted as Private on March 1863 at Fayette County, Ala. in the 10 Ala. Regt. Col. Gutery Co. and continued until May 1865. Discharged in North Ala. and returned home.

No. 3 - AMERSON, RILEY J., Corrona, R.F.D. No. 2 was born on June 30, 1841 at Fayette County, Ala. First entered the service as Private on April 1862 at Fayette County, Ala. in the 32 Ala. Regt. Inf. Co. I. and continued until Sept. 1864. Transferred as Private on Sept. 1864 at Jackson, Miss. in the Co. K. Hewett Bat. and continued until May 1865. Discharged near Jasper, Ala. and returned home.

No. 4 - ASHCRAFT, WILLIAM M., Loco, R.F.D. No. 1 was born on 3 Aug. 1845 at Fayette County, Ala. First entered service as Private on Oct. 1862 at Monroe County, Miss. in the 9 Miss. Regt. Col. Co. C. and continued until May 1865. Discharged and taken oath of allegiance at Okalona, Miss.

No. 5 - ALLRIDGE, JAMES J., Glen Allen, Ala. was born on 17 Sept. 1845 at Fayette County, Ala. First entered service as Private on April 1862 at Tuskaloosa, Ala. in the Picketts Regt. Co. K. and continued until April 1865. Discharged and returned home.

No. 6 - ADAMS, WILLIAM R., Berry, Ala. was born 19 Oct. 1832 at Pendleton Dist. in the state of S. C. First entered service as Private on 9 May 1862 at Fayette County, Ala. in the 38 Ala. Regt. Inf. Co. H. and continued until 13 Dec. 1864. Returned home from the service and never paroled.

No. 7 - BAKER, WILLIAM G., Bankston, Ala. was born on 28 Dec. 1839 at Fayette County, Ala. First entered service as Private on 17 Sept. 1861 at Fayette Co. Ala. in the 26 Ala. Regt. Inf. Co. A. and continued until discharged from wounds received Jan. 1864 at Orange Court House, Va.

No. 8 - BAGWELL, WILLIAM D., Fayette, Ala. was born on 11 Sept. 1842 at Jefferson County, Ala. First entered the service as Private on Sept. 1863 at Jasper, Ala. in the 13 Ala. Regt. Col. Co. A. and continued until May 1865 - Disbanded.

No. 9 - BELL, HOLLAND M., Fayette, Ala. was born on 25 June 1839 at Tuskaloosa Co., Ala. First entered service as Private on 14 April 1862 at Fayette, Ala. in the 41 Ala. Regt. Inf. Co. U. and continued until captured at Hatcher Run south of Petersburg, Va. March 29, 1865 and remained in prison at Johnson Island, Lake Erie until June 16, 1865 and paroled.

No. 10 - BEARD, AUGUSTUS, Bankston, Ala. was born on 2 Sept. 1841 at Fayette County, Ala. First entered the service as Private on Aug. 1861 at Fayette Co., Ala. in the 26 Ala. Regt. Inf. Co. I. and continued until Nov. 1864. Captured at Nashville, Tenn. and remained in prison at Camp Darylop, Ill., until June 1865 and parolled.

No. 11 - BEARD, CHARLEY M., Fayette, Ala. R.F.D. No. 4 was born on 16 May 1832 at Lincoln County, Tenn. First entered service as Private on March 1, 1861 at Fayetteville, Tenn. in the 1st Tenn. Regt. Inf. Co. G. and continued until Feb. 1864. Captured at Chatanouga, Tenn and remained in prison at Rock Island, Ill. until close of war and parolled.

No. 12 - BERRY, ALFORD W., Fayette, Ala. was born on 14 Oct. 1833 at Fayette Co., Ala. First entered the service as Private on 14 April 1862 at Fayette Co., Ala. in the 41 Ala. Regt. Inf. Co. U. and continued until captured near Nashville, Tenn. Remained in prison 15 days and taken oath and parole of honor.

No. 13 - BERRY, JOHN T., Stough, Ala. was born on 26 July 1838 at Fayette Co., Ala. First entered service as Private on 17 Sept. 1861 at Fayette Co., Ala. in the 26 Ala. Regt. Inf. Co. A. and continued until May 1865. Discharged at Tupelo, Miss.

No. 14 - BELK, ALEXANDER, Belk, Ala. was born on 30 Jan. 1844 at Union Co., N. C. First entered the service as Private on May 1862 at Fayette Co., Ala. in the 26 Ala. Regt. Inf. Co. C. and continued until Feb. 1865 and discharged.

No. 15 - BLACKBURN, WILLIAM A., Bankston, Ala. was born at Fayette Co., Ala. First entered service as 1st Orderly Sargent on 14 April 1862 at Fayette Co., Ala. in the 41 Ala. Regt. Inf. Co. H. and continued until Dec. 1863. Captured near Nashville, Tenn. and remained in prison 15 days, taken oath and parole of honor.

No. 16 - BLACK, ENOCH, Fayette, Ala. R.F.D. 2 was born on 5th Feb. 1845 at York Dist. S. C. First entered the servie as Private on July 1, 1862 at Fayette Co., Ala. in the 5th Ala. Regt. Cal. Co. D. and continued until April 1865. Disbanded near Selma, Ala. and taken oath of allegiance at Columbus, Miss.

No. 17 - BLANKSHIP, WILLIAM J., Winfield, Ala. R.F.D. 1-was born on 20 Jan. 1840 in Coosa Co., Ala. First entered the service as Private on July 1861 at Coosa Co., Ala. in the 13 Ala. Regt. Inf. Co. 26 and continued until May 1865. Disbanded and taken oath of allegiance at Montgomery, Ala.

No. 18 - BOBO, BARRAM F., Covin, Ala. R.F.D. 1-was born in Spartanburg District, S. C. First entered service as Private on 16 May 1862 at Fayette Co., Ala. in the 56 Ala. Regt. Co. I. and continued until Nov. 1864. Discharged on account of eyes and now blind.

No. 19 - BOBO, WILLIS, Covin, Ala. R.F.D. 1-was born on 7 Aug. 1842 at Spartanburg District, S. C. First entered service as Private on 16 May 1862 at Fayette County, Ala. in the 56 Ala. Regt. Cal. Co. I. and continued until

Nov. 1864 - Eyes and now blind.

No. 20 - BOBO, JAMES, Fayette, Ala. R.F.D. 2 was born on Jan. 9, 1837 at Spartanburg Dist., S. C. First entered the service as Private on 16 Oct. 1861 at Piker County, La. in the 10 La. Regt. 9th Co. A. and continued until Oct. 1864. Wounded and sent home on furlough. Re-enlisted as Private Jan. 1864 (1865?) at Fayette Co., Ala. in Regt. Cal. Co. I. and continued until May 1, 1865. Discharged and taken oath of allegience at Columbus, Miss.

No. 21 - BOBO, DAVID P., Covin, Ala. R.F.D. 1-was born on 4 March 1848 at Fayette, Fayette County, Ala. First entered service as Private on June 1864 at Fayette Co., Ala. in the Capt. Cerington Co. Home Guard and continued until April 1865. Discharged and taken oath of allegiance at Columbus, Miss. The above Co. operated in Fayette and Walker Counties as Home Guard.

No. 22 - BOSS, JAMES W., Fayette, Ala. R.F.D. 3, was born on 23 Oct. 1829 at Cabarros Co., N. C. First entered the service as Private on April 1861 at Blunt Co., Ala. in the 19 Ala. Regt. Inf. Co. K. and continued until wounded 25 Dec. 1863 - furloughed. Was disabled from service and taken oath of allegience at Guntersville, Ala., April 1865.

No. 23 - BROCK, REUBIN J., Covin, Ala. was born on 24 Dec. 1846 at Fayette County, Ala. First entered service as Private on 8 May 1864 at Fayette Co., Ala. in the 8 Ala. Regt. Cal. Co. I. and continued until captured at Columbus, Ga. 16 April 1865. Paroled at Macon, Ga. April 26, 1865.

No. 24 - BROTHERTON, FRANK A., Hico, Ala. was born on 18 Mar. 1840 at Lincoln Co., N. C. First entered the service as Private on 19 June 1861 at Fayette County, Ala. in the 11 Ala. Regt. Inf. Co. I. and continued until 9 April 1865. Surrendered in Virginia and paroled.

No. 25 - BRASHER, HENDERSON, Bankston, Ala., was born on 11 July 1828 at Greenville District, S. C. First entered service as Private on 17 Sept. 1861 at Fayette Co., Ala. in the 26 Ala. Regt. Inf. Co. A. and continued until discharged at Richmond, Va. April 1863.

No. 26 - BARNARD, ASBURY F., Dry Creek, Ala. was born on 24 July 1824 at Herd Co., Ga. First entered the service as Private on May 1862 at Valley Head, DeCalb Co., Ala. in the 3rd Regt. Confederate Cal. Co. B. and continued until May 1865. Surrendered and paroled at Greensboro, N. C.

No. 27 - BLACK, GEORGE W., Fayette, Ala. R.F.D. 4, was born on 25 Oct. 1845 at Fayette Co., Ala. First entered service as Private on Sept. 1863 at Fayette Co., Ala. in the 8th Ala. Regt. Cal. Co. I. and continued until 1 April 1865. Captured at Selma, Ala. and paroled at Montgomery, Ala., April 13, 1865.

No. 28 - CAMPBELL, JOSEPH H., Fayette, Ala., R.F.D. , was born 14 June 1823 at N. C. First entered service as Private on Oct. 1863 at Talladega, Ala. in the 32nd. 58 Ala. Reg. Inf. Co. G., and continued until May 1, 1865 and disbanded at Meridan, Miss. and taken oath of allegiance.

No. 29 - CHAMBLESS, MASTEN E., Fayette, Ala., R.F.D. 5, was born on 4 Feb. 1836 in Ala. First entered service as Private on Sept. 15, 1861 at Fayette Co., Ala. in the 10 Ala. Regt. Cal. C. A. and continued until May 1865 - Disbanded

No. 30 - CHRISTIAN, PRESTON M., Toleda, Ala. was born on 6 Mar. 1846 at Tuskaloosa Co., Ala. First entered the service as Private on April 1865 at Fayette Co., Ala. in the 10 Ala. Regt. Cal. C. Whitley, and continued until May 1865. Furloughed and at home at the surrender.

No. 31 - CHAFFIN, CALVIN C., Guin, Ala. R.F.D. 2, was born on 11 Aug. 1835 at Cherokee Co., Ga. First entered service as Private on Feb. 1862 at Stones Cross Roads, Miss. in the 28 Miss. Regt. Cal. Co. 26 and continued

78

until May 27, 1865. Disbanded and taken oath at Columbus, Miss.

No. 32 - COUCH, MARIDA, Winfield, Ala. R.F.D. 2, was born on Nov. 14, 1840 at Lawrence Co., Ala. First entered service as Private on Mar. 1862 at Marion Co., Ala. in the 5 Ala. Regt. Col. Co. A, and continued until 1863. Regt. changed number and became 10 Ala. Regt. Col. and continued until Battle Selma, Ala. 1865 - disbanded and sent home.

No. 33 - COLLINS, JAMES B., Covin, Ala. R.F.D. 2, was born on June 27, 1831 at Spartanburg Dist. S. C. First entered service as Private in the 8 Ala. Regt. Col. Co. A. and continued until 7th day of May 1865 and taken oath of allegiance at Fayette, Ala. Was on detach service at Tensun Station near Mobile County stock and disbanded.

No. 34 - COOK, ELIZA, Winfield, Ala. R.F.D. 2, was born on 19 Aug. 1842 at Henry Co., Ga. First entered service as Private on May 1862 at Henry Co., Ga. in the 44 Ga. Regt. Inf. Co. I. and continued until captured 10 May 1864. Remained in prison at Ft. Delamore, released from prison Mar. 10, 1865. Extensive furlough and at home at time of surrender.

No. 35 - COCKRAN, HYRUM, Covin, Ala. R.F.D. 1, was born on 23 Sept. 1845, at Fayette Co., Ala. First entered service as Private on 1 Aug. 1863 at Fayette Co., Ala. in the 8 Ala. Regt. Col. Co. A. and continued until disbanded in April 1865 near Marion,Ala. and taken oath of allegiance at Fayette, Ala. May 1865.

No. 36 - CAPLES, WILLIAM D., Fayette, Ala. was born on 29 Nov. 1829 at Fayette Co., Ala. First entered service as Private on Mar. 1861 at Fayette Co., Ala. in the 17 Ala. Regt. Inf. Co. C. and continued until March 1862. Consolidated as Private on Mar. 1862 at Mobile Ala. in 58 Ala. Regt. Inf. Co. E. at Greensboro, N. C. and paroled.

No. 37 - DAILEY, TINSLEY M., Fayette, Ala. R.F.D. 5 was born on 5 Dec. 1845 at Jackson Co., Ga. First entered service as Private on Sept. 1863 at Fayette Co., Ala. in the 8 Ala. Regt. Col. Co. I. and continued until 16 May 1865. Disbanded and taken oath of allegiance at Columbus, Miss.

No. 38 - DANIEL, GUS, Fayette, Ala. R.F.D. 1, was born 16 May 1840 at Todd Co., Ky. First entered service as Private on April 1861 at Hopkinsville, Ky. in the 1 Ky. Regt. Col. Co. I. and continued until disbanded in Ga. April 1865 and taken oath of allegiance at Hopkinsville, Ky. April 1865.

No. 39 - DAVIS, THOMAS J., Berry, Ala. was born on 10 Mar. 1845 at Fayette Co., Ala. First entered service as Private on April 1862 at Fayette Co.,Ala. in the 41 Ala. Regt. Inf. Co. F. and continued until captured at Petersburg, Va. July 1864 remained in prison at Elmira, N. Y. until 2 Mar. 1865 and paroled

No. 40 - DAVIS, DOCK W., Berry, Ala. R. 1,was born on 7 Sept. 1847 at Tuscaloosa Co., Ala. First entered service as Private on May 1864 at Tuscaloosa, Ala. in the 51 Ala. Regt. Col. Co. G. and continued until May 1865, discharged at Saulsberry, N. C.

No. 41 - DAVIS, SAMUEL K., Toledo, Ala. was born on 11 July 1826 at Morgan Co., Ala. First entered service as Private on Sept. 1864 at Fayette Co. Ala. in the Capt. Reed Company Home Guards, and continued until - operated in Fayette and adjoining counties until May 1865, and discharged.

No. 42 - DODD, ALFRED P., Fayette, Ala. was born on 23 May 1841 at Cherokee Co., Ga. First entered service as Private on 17 Sept. 1861 at Fayette, Co., Ala. in the 26 Ala., Regt. Inf. Co. A. and continued until April 1865. Surrendered at Appomatax Court House, Va. and parolled.

No. 43 - DOBBS, ALBERT, Dry Creek, Ala. was born on June 1861 at Readford Co., Tenn. First entered as Private on May 1862 at Fayette Co., Ala. in the 41 Ala. Regt. Inf. Co. I. and continued until captured in Va. Dec.

1864. Remained in prison until close of the war and paroled.

No. 44 - DODSON, WESLEY J., Fayette, Ala. R. 2 was born on 11 Feb. 1841 at Fayette Co., Ala. First entered service as Private on Mar. 1862 at Fayette Co., Ala. in the 36 Ala. Regt. Inf. Co. K. and continued until Jan. 1865. Re-enlisted as Private on Feb. 1, 1865 in the Stewarts Bat. Co. H, and continued until April 1865 and disbanded.

No. 45 - DODSON, GEORGE W., Fayette, Ala. R. 2, was born on 3 Aug. 1839 at Fayette Co., Ala. First entered service as Private and drummer on June 1, 1861 at Fayette Co., Ala. in the 26 Ala. Regt. Inf. Co. Reeds, and continued until July 1, 1861. Re-enlisted as Private on 1 July 1861 at Fayette Co., Ala. in the 5th Ala. Bat. Co. B. and continued until Battle of Shilo 1862. Re-enlisted as Private on June 1862 at Corinth, Miss. in the 17 Ala. Regt. Inf. Co. C. and continued until June 1863 and then joined 10 Ala. Regt. Col. Co. D. and continued until spring of 1865, taken oath at Columbus, Miss.

No. 46 - DODSON, REUBIN A. J., Winfield, Ala. R. 2, was born on 22 June 1830 at Fayette Co., Ala. First entered service as Private in the 5 Ala. Regt. Col. Co. H. and continued until Sept. 1863 and discharged. Re-enlisted as Private on Oct. 1863 at Fayette Co., Ala. in the Capt. Reed Co. Home Guards, and continued until June 1864 and discharged.

No. 47 - DAVIS, REUBIN, Berry, Ala. was born on 4 Dec. 1840 at Fayette Co., Ala. First entered service as Private on Sept. 1862 at Fayette Co., Ala. in the 26 Ala. Regt. Inf. Co. I. and continued until Feb. 1865. Discharged at Guina Station, Va.

No. 48 - EARNEST, MANUEL, Corona, Ala. R. 2, was born on 31 Mar. 1840 at Walker Co., Ala. First entered service as Private on July 1862 at Tuscaloosa, Ala. in the 51 Ala. Regt. Col. Co. G. and continued until Nov. 1862. Transferred as Private on Nov. 1862 in State of Ga. in the 43 Ala. Regt. Inf. Co. K. and continued until July 1864. Furloughed, came home and never served any longer.

No. 49 - EASON, MOSES, Dublin, Ala. was born on 21 Jan. 1832 at Noonaur, Corvites Co., Ga. First entered service as Private on 15 May 1862 at Fayette Co., Ala. in the 41 Ala. Regt. Inf. Co. I. and continued until surrendered at Appomatox Court House, Va. April 1865 and paroled.

No. 50 - EDWARDS, THOMAS R., Fayette, Ala. was born on 12 Mar. 1835 at Montgomery Co., Ala. First entered service as Private on 1 July 1861 at Wetumpka, Ala. in the 13 Ala. Regt. Inf. Co. C. and continued until April 1865. Surrendered and paroled at Appomotox Court House, Va.

No. 51 - ELLIS, WILLIAM A., Bankston, Ala. R. 1, was born on 24 Mar. 1835 at Jasper Co., Ga. First entered service as Private on Jan. 1862 at Fayette Co., Ala. and continued until Aug. 1, 1863 and discahrged.

No. 52 - ENIS, WILLIAM M., Spencer, Ala. was born on 27 Mar. 1830 at Fayette Co., Ala. First entered service as 3 Lt. on Sept. 1862 at Fayette Co., Ala. in the 10 Ala. Regt. Col. Co. K. and continued until May 1865. Paroled at Decatur, Ala.

No. 53 - FOWLER, COLEMAN G., Fayette, Ala. R. 5, was born on 24 Oct. 1829 at Greenville Dist. S. C. First entered service as Private on 7 May 1862 at Fayette Co., Ala. in the 8 Ala. Regt. Col. Co. A. and continued until April 1865 - Disbanded and paroled at Decatur, Ala.

No. 54 - FREEMAN, ISHAM, Newtonville, Ala. was born on 1 Sept. 1843 at Newton Co., Ga. First entered service as Private on 2 April 1861 at Pickens Co., Ala. and continued until 14th Aug. 1864. Captured at New Hope, Ga. and remained in prison camp Chase .... until 18 day may 1865 and paroled.

No. 55 - FULLERTON, THOMAS J., Stough, Ala. was born on 29 Sept. 1846 at Fayette Co., Ala. First entered service as 1 Corpl. on Sept. 1863 at Fayette

Co., Ala. in the 8 Ala. Regt. Col. Co. I. and continued until April 1865. Surrendered at Greenville, Ala. and paroled.

No. 56 - GARDNER, TILLEY G., Stocks, Ala. was born on 15 May 1843 at Fayette County, Ala. First entered service as Private on 14 April 1862, at Fayette Co., Ala. in the 41 Ala. Regt. Inf. Co. H. and continued until captured March 1865 at Farmsville, Va. and remained in prison at New Port News until June 1865 and released on parole.

No. 57 - GARDNER, JOHN B., Stocks, Ala. was born on 14 Oct. 1834 at Fayette Co., Ala. First entered service as Private on 14 April 1862 at Fayette Co., Ala. in the 41 Ala. Regt. Inf. Co. H. and continued until captured March 1865 at Farmsville, Va. and remained in prison at New Port News until June 1865, and released from prison on parole.

No. 58 - GARRISON, THOMAS J., Bankston, Ala. R. 1, was born on 9 July 1839 at Coweten Co., Ga. First entered the service as Private on Aug. 1861 at Fayette Co., Ala. in the 26 Ala. Regt. Inf. Co. C. and continued until Aug. 1864. Disabled and came home after battle of Franklin, Tenn.

No. 59 - GOOLSBY, CHARLES D., Winfield, Ala. R. 2, was born on 24 June 1843 at Jefferson Co., Ala. First entered service as Private on 1 Mar. 1861 at Jonesboro, Ala. in the 28 Ala. Regt. Inf. Co. D. and continued until May 1865 and paroled.

No. 60 - GOODE, HENRY H., Corona, Ala. R. 2, was born on 29 Mar. 1837 at Covington, (Burnt Corn Co.?) Tenn. First entered service as Private on April 1862 at Tuskaloosa, Ala. in the 43 Ala. Regt. Inf. Co. D. and continued until captured 5 Feb. 1865 and paroled on the banks of the James River. Return Richmond, Va.

No. 61 - GOSA, WELSEY W., Guin, Ala. R. 2, was born on 24 June 1832 at Marion Co., Ala. First entered service as Private on 7 April 1862 at Marion Co., Ala. in the 36 Ala. Regt. Inf. Co. K. and continued until captured at Missionary Ridge, Tenn. 9 Dec. 1863. - remained in prison at Rock Island, Ill. until June 20, 1865 and paroled.

No. 62 - GOODWIN, THOMAS E., Fayette, Ala. was born on 8 June 1848 at Cumberland Co., N. C. First entered service as Private on 14 Sept. 1864 at Fayette Co., Ala. and continued until April 1865. Paroled at Tuskaloosa, Ala.

No. 63 - HAMMACK, JAMES W., Bankston, Ala. R. 1, was born on 23 April 1845 at Murry Co., Ga. First entered service as Private on June 1861 at Murry Co., Ga. in the 22 Ga. Regt. Inf. Co. D. and continued until 9 April 1865. Surrendered at Appomotox Court House, Va. and paroled.

No. 64 - HARBIN, JOHN W., Winfield, Ala, R. 1, was born on 21 May 1845 at Cobb Co., Ga. First entered service as Private on 16 May 1863 at Kelleyton, Ala. in the 5 Ala. Bat. Col. Co. B. and continued until 16 Feb. 1864. Consolidated as Private on Feb. 1864 in 10 Ala. Regt. Col. and continued until April 1865. Disbanded and returned home.

No. 65 - HARBIN, LEWIS B., Bankston, Ala. was born on 11 July 1846 at Fayette Co., Ala. First entered service as Private on Jan. 1863 at Fayette Co., Ala. in the 8 Ala. Regt. Col. Co. K. and continued until April 1865. Surrendered at Selma, Ala. and paroled.

No. 66 - HARBIN, JEFFERSON J., Winfield, Ala. R. 1, 2as born on 28 Feb. 1830 at Elbert Co., Ga. First entered the service as Marine on Sept. 1862 at Fayette Co., Ala. in the Gun Boat Tennessee and continued until 4 Aug. 1864. Captured and released on parole May 1865.

No. 67 - Harkins, William B., Covin, Ala. was born on 19 Sept. 1840 at Fayette Co., Ala. First entered service as Private on April 1862 at Fayette Co., Ala. in the 41 Ala. Regt. Inf. Co. I. and continued until April 1865. Surrendered at Appomotox Court House, Va. and paroled Apr. 12, 1865.

No. 68 - HARKNESS, ELIAS S., Glen Allen, Ala. was born on 27 Feb. 1843 at Lincoln Co., Tenn. First entered service as Private on 10 Aug. 1861 at Blunt Co., Ala. in the 19 Ala. Regt. Inf. Co. K. and continued until July 1862. Re-enlisted as Private on July 1862 at Tupelo, Miss in the 1 Ala. Bat. Sharp Shooters and continued until Aoril 14, 1864 - wounded and furloughed. Re-enlisted as Private on Sept. 1864 at Blue Minter, Ala. in the Lewis Squadron Co. B. and continued until May 1865. Disbanded and returned home.

No. 69 - HASSELL, WILLIAM J., Fayette, Ala. R. 3, was born 27 May 1841 at Tuskaloosa Co., Ala. First entered service as Private on 13 Sept. 1861 at Tuskaloosa Co., Ala. in the 20 Ala. Regt. Inf. Co. K. and continued until May 1865. Surrendered at Saulsberry, N. C. and paroled.

No. 70 - HAMILTON, JOHN N., Fayette, Ala. R. 4 was born on 1 Mar. 1844 at Shelby Co., Ala. First entered service as Private on 15 June 1862 at Columbiana, Ala. in the 25 Ala. Regt. Inf. Co. B. and continued until captured at Petersburg, Va. April 1865. Remained in prison until 5 Aug. and paroled.

No. 71 - HARRIS, GEORGE S., Winfield, Ala. R. 1, was born on 23 July 1837 at Marion Co., Ala. First entered service as 1 Corpl. on 1 Sept. 1863 at Marion Co., Ala. in the 1 Ala. Bat. Col. Co. A. and continued until Feb. 1863. Consolidated as Private on Feb. 1, 1864 at Tuscumbia, Ala. in the 5th Ala. Regt. Col. Co. D. and continued until April 1865. Disbanded after the battle of Selma, Ala., returned home and taken oath and paroled at Columbus, Miss.

No. 72 - HENDERSON, BEN, Winfield, Ala., R. 1, was born on 12 May 1839 at Newton Co., Ga. First entered service as Private on Sept. 1862 at Fayette Co., Ala. in the 5 (mone's?) Bat. Co. A. and continued until -.... Consolidated as Private in the 10 Ala. Regt. Col. Co. A. and continued until May 1865, disbanded and come home.

No. 73 - HOLLIMAN, JAMES F., Fayette, Ala. R. 2, was born on Jan. 28, 1839 at Tuskaloosa Co., Ala. First entered service as Private on Sept. 1861 at Fayette Co., Ala. in the 9th Ala. Bat. Co. B. and continued until after the battle of Shilo, 1862. Consolidated as Lt. Sept. 1862 in the 17 Ala. Regt. Inf. Co. B. and continued until Nov. 3, 1863. Captured and remained in prison Johnson Island, Ohio until 13 June 1865 and paroled.

No. 74 - HOMES?, THOMAS, Stocks, Ala. was born on 16 Feb. 1822 at Edgefield Dist. S. C. First entered service as Private on Apr. 1862 at Coosa Co. Ala. in the Halls Bat. Co. K. and continued until Dec. 1862. Consolidated as Private on Dec. 1862 at Cumberland Gap in the 59 Ala. Regt. Col. Co. K. and continued until 6 April 1865 - Captured and remained in orison New Port News, Va. Paroled 18 July 1865.

No. 75 - HOCUTT, LEUCIOUS T., Fayette, Ala. R. 4, was born on 23 Oct. 1843 at Tuskaloosa Co., Ala. First entered service as Private on Mar. 1863 at Tuscaloosa, Co., Ala. in the Picketts Regt. Co. G. Rody Cal. and continued until May 1865. Disbanded at Decatur, Ala.

No. 76 - HOCUTT, RUFUS E., New Lexington, Ala. was born on 6 April 1840 at Tuscaloosa Co., Ala. First entered service as Private on 1 Apr. 1862 at Meekingmill, Ala. in the 32 Ala. Regt. Inf. Co. I. and continued until June 1864. Captured and remained in prison at Rock Island, Va. and paroled at close of war.

No. 77 - HOBBS, THOMAS J., Fayette, Ala. R. 5, was born on 11 July 1844 at Lauderdale Co., Miss. First entered service as Private on Sept. 1861 at Lauderdale Co., Miss. in the 2 Miss. Regt. Inf. Co. H. and continued until Dec. 1864. Captured near Richmond, Va. and remained in prison at Point Lookout, Md. until close of the war and paroled and returned home.

No. 78 - HOLLINGSWORTH, WILEY J., Glen Allen, Ala. R. 1, was born on 27 June 1845 at Fayette Co., Ala. First entered service as Private on 12 May

1864 at Fayette Co., Ala. in the 5 Ala. Regt. Cal. Co. A. and continued until Jan. 1, 1865. Consolidated on Jan. 1, 1865 at Pond Springs, Ala. in the 10 Ala. Regt. Cal. Co. A. and continued until May 1. Disbanded and paroled at Columbus, Miss.

No. 79 - HOLLINGSWORTH, JOHN P., New River, Ala. was born on 15 Nov. 1837 at Fayette Co., Ala. First entered service as Private on 15 May 1862 at Tuscaloosa, Ala. in the 41 Ala. Regt. Inf. Co. I. and continued until one month put in substituted and discharged.

No. 80 - HOLLINGSWORTH, JACOB, New River, Ala. was born on 5 June 1832 at Fayette Co., Ala. First entered service as Private on 14 Aug. 1862 at Fayette Co., Ala. in the 41 Ala. Regt. Inf. Co. I. and continued until July 1964. Transferred 1st July in 2 Eng. Regt. Howards Co. and continued until 5 April 1865. Captured and paroled at New Port News, Va. July 2, 1865.

No. 81 - HUDSON, ASBERY, Fayette, Ala., R. 1. was born on 22 March 1844 at Tippa Co., Miss. First entered service as Private on Oct. 1862 at Columbus, Miss. in the Capt. Throlls Battery No. 4 and continued until Oct. 1863 and discharged.

No. 82 - HUTTON, WILLIAM H., Eldridge, Ala., R. 1, was born on 19 July 1842 at Jefferson Co., Ala. First entered service as Private on Aug. 1862 at Jefferson Co., Ala. in the 39 Ala. Regt. Inf. Co. D. and continued until Dec. 1862. Transferred as Private on Dec. 1862 at Mobile, Ala. in the 18 Ala. Regt. Inf. Co. D. and continued until Aug. 1864 left Atlanta, Ga. and joined United States Army.

No. 83 - JINKINS, JAMES A., Fayette, Ala. R. 3, was born on 15 Dec. 1842 at Coffee Co., Ala. First entered service as Private on 16 May 1862 at Fayette Co., Ala. in the 41 Ala. Regt. Inf. Co. I. and continued until 9 April and paroled in Virginia.

No. 84 - JINKINS, FREEMAN S., Bankston, Ala. R. 1, was born on 9 Sept. 1847 at Fayette Co., Ala. First entered service as Private on 17 Sept. 1864 at Fayette Co., Ala. in the 10 Ala. Regt. Cal. Co. K. and continued until May 29, 1865 and paroled North Alabama.

No. 85 - JINKINS, JOHN S., Fayette, Ala. R. 1, was born on 20 Oct. 1829 at Montgomery Co., N. C. First entered service as Private on March 1862 at Fayette County, Ala. in the 58 Ala. Bat. Co. D. and continued until Mar. 1863. Consolidated as Private on Mar, 1863 at North Miss. in the 32 - 58 Ala. Regt. Co. B. and continued until May 1865 - disbanded and taken oath of allegiance at Columbus, Miss.

No. 86 - JONES, EARLES, Glen Allen, Ala. R. 1. was born on 1 Mar. 1844 at Chester Dist. S. C. First entered service as Private on 11 July 1861 at Rockford, Ala. in the 13 Ala. Inf. Co. H. and continued until captured 3 July 1863 at Getlesburg, Va. and remained in prison at Ft. Delaware 15 June 1865 and paroled.

No. 87 - JONES, ELIZA N., Newtonville, Ala. Rt. 1, was born on 2 Aug. 1822 at Jasper Co., Ga. First entered service as Home Guard on Sept. 1862? at Tallapoosa Co., Ala. in the William Wagner Co. and continued until May 1865 and disbanded.

No. 88 - JONES, ELIZA S., Fayette, Ala. R. 1, was born on 17 June _____ at Fayette Co., Ala. First entered service as Private on 5 June 1863 at Fayette Co., Ala. in the 10 Ala. Regt. Cal. Co. D. and continued until May 1865, paroled in North Alabama.

No. 89 - JONES, ROBERT G., Berry, Ala. was born on 27 March 1834 at New Moulton, Luverne County, Ala. First entered service as Private on 11 May 1862 at Fayette Co., Ala. in the 43' Ala. Regt. Inf. Co. I. and continued until 25 Mar. 1865. Captured and paroled at Point Lookout, Md. June 14, 1865.

No. 90 - JOHNSON, FRED, Berry, Ala. was born on 10 Aug. 1836 at Fayette Co., Ala. First entered service as Private on Sept. 1862 at Tuscaloosa Co., Ala. in the 51 Ala. Regt. Cal. Co. G. and continued until April 1865. Disbanded in S. C. and returned home.

No. 91 - JOHNSON, GEORGE W., Berry, Ala. was born on 14 April 1832 at Fayette Co., Ala. First entered service on April 1862 at Fayette County, Ala. in the 38 Ala. Regt. Inf. Co. F. and continued until Feb. 1863. Furloughed and furlough continued to close of war on account of eyes.

No. 92 - JOHNSON, WILLIAM R., Spencer, Ala. was born on 10 Oct. 1836. First entered service as Private on Oct. 1862 at Fayette Co., Ala. in the Hewitt Bat. Cal. Co. A. and continued until May 1863. Quit the service, came home and remained.

No. 93 - JOHNSON, PLEASANT C., Spencer, Ala. was born on 4 _____ 1835 at Fayette Co., Ala. First entered service as Private on April 1862 at Fayette Co., Ala. in the 43 Ala. Regt. Inf. Co. H. and continued until Oct. 1864 and went to the United States Army.

No. 94 - JULION, GEORGE W., Berry, Ala. was born on 24 Sept. 1824 in Lawrence Co., Ala. First entered service as Private on 13 Feb. 1862 at Fayette Co., Ala. in the State Militia and continued until sworn in camp 6 days and discharged.

No. 95 - KELLEY, JOHN H., Winfield, Ala. was born on 6 April 1840 at Franklin Co., Ala. First entered service as Private on 17 June 1861 at Fayette Co., Ala. in the 26 Ala. Regt. Inf. Co. A. and continued until 24 Dec. Lost a leg and discharged.

No. 96 - KEMP, JOHN B., Fayette, Ala. was born on 21 Nov. 1842 in Tuscaloosa Co., Ala. First entered service as Private on Oct. 1861 at Tuscaloosa, Ala. in the 10 Ala. Regt. Cal. Co. and continued until May 1865. Disbanded near Selma, Alabama.

No. 97 - KIMBRELL, WILLIAM N., Corona, Ala. R. 1, was born on 26 Oct. 1842 at Jasper Co., Ga. First entered service as Private on April 1862 at Fayette Co., Ala. in the 32 Ala. Regt. Inf. Co. I. and continued until Oct. 1863. Transferred on Oct. 1863 in 10 Ala. Regt. Cal. Co. K. and continued until May 29, 1865, disbanded and paroled.

No. 98 - KIMBRELL, PEYTON G., Berry, Ala. R. 1, was born on 24 Nov. 1823 in Autoga Co., Ala. First entered service as Private on 1 Nov. 1864 at Coosa Co., Ala. in the 6 Ala. Regt. Cal. Co. Mitchell, and continued until May 1865. Surrendered and paroled at Montgomery, Alabama.

No. 99 - KIMBRELL, JOHN J., Bankston, Ala. was born on 20 May 1844 in Bibb Co., Ala. First entered service as Private on 28 No. 1862 in the 2 Ala. Engr. Cor. Co. B. and continued until May 1865 - Surrendered and paroled at Meridan, Miss.

No. 100 - KIMBRELL, GEORGE W., Corona, Ala. R., was born at Garnatt Co., Ga. First entered service as Private in 1863 in the 10 Ala. Regt. Cal. Co. K. and continued until spring 1865 and disbanded.

No. 101 - KIZZIRE, LINARD, Fayette, Ala. R. 4, was born on 20 April 1846 at Tuscaloosa Co., Ala. First entered service as Private on May 1863 at Fayette Co., Ala. in the 41 Ala. Regt. Inf. Co. and continued until wounded March 1865 at Petersburg, Va. Sent to hospital at Richmond - furloughed and arrived home 3 March 1865.

No. 102 - KIZZIRE, ENOCK, Stough, Ala. was born on 18 March 1838 in Tuscaloosa Co., Ala. First entered service as Private on 1 Aug. 1862 at Fayette Co., Ala. in the 41 Ala. Regt. Inf. Co. H. and continued until Dec. 1863.

Captured at Knoxville, Tenn. Remained in prison 15 days and paroled.

No. 103 - KILLINGSWORTH, WILLIAM J., Dry Creek, Ala. was born on 11 July 1840 in Tuscaloosa Co., Ala. First entered service as Private on 16 April 1862 at Fayette Co., Ala. in the 41 Ala. Regt. Inf. Co. I. and continued until April 1865. Surrendered and paroled at Appomotox Court House, Va.

No. 104 - **KILLINGSWORTH**, MORRIS D., Winfield, Ala. R. 1, was born on 14 Dec. 1842 in Tuscaloosa Co., Ala. First entered service as 1st. Col. on June 1861 at Fayette Co., Ala. in the 26 Ala. Regt. Inf. Co. A. and continued until June 1862. Captured at Ft. Henry, remained in prison until Feb. 1863 - Exchanged. Re-enlisted as Private on Feb. or Mar. 1863 in the 26 Ala. Regt. Inf. Co. I. and continued until wounded at Gettysburg, Va. = furloughed. Re-enlisted as Private on Jan. 1864 in the 8 Ala. Regt. Cal. and continued until May 1865 and disbanded.

No. 105 - LANE, JOSEPH A., Stough, Ala. was born on 25 Dec. 1840 at Fayette Co., Ala. First entered service as Private on Sept. 1861 at Fayette Co., Ala. in the 26 Ala. Regt. Inf. Co. A. and continued until 8 May 1865 and paroled at Fayette, Ala.

No. 106 - LANGSTON, SAMUEL R., Covin, Ala. R. **2**. was born on 21 March 1842 at Fayette Co., Ala. First entered service as Private on 1 Nov. 1861 at Columbus, Miss. in the 8 Confederate Cal. Co. G. and continued until May 1865. Paroled at Columbus, **Miss.**

No. 107 - LEWIS, COLUMBUS W., Fayette, Ala. R. 6, was born on June 6, 1846 at Coosa Co., Ala. First entered service as Private on 25 July 1861 at Coosa Co., Ala. in the 18 Ala. Regt. Inf. Co. D., and continued until May 10, 1865. Surrendered and paroled at Meridan, Miss.

No. 108 - LONG, ANDREW J., Fayette, Ala. was born on 29 April 1844 at Greenville Court House, Greenville District, S. C. First entered service as Private on April 1862 at Fayette Co., Ala. in the 41 Ala. Regt. Inf. Co. H. and continued until Oct. 1864. Furloughed and at home at surrender.

No. 109 - LOVE, DAVID G., Winfield, Ala. R. 2, was born on 31 March 1836 at Clarkesville, Habersham Co., Ga. First entered the service as Private on May 1861 at Clarksville, Ga. in Phillip's Geiger Defences Co. C. and continued until May 1865 and paroled.

No. 110 - MARTIN, JESSEY, Covin, Ala. R. 1, was born on 1837 at Fayetteville, Chambers Co., Ala. First entered service as Private on 1 April 1861 at Choctaw in the W. T. Carnes Battery Arty. and continued until captured April 1865 at Saulisberry, N. C. and remained in prison at Camp Chase, Ohio until 18 June 1865 and paroled.

No. 111 - MANASCO, WILLIAM C., Fayette, Ala. was born on 23 Mar. ____ in Fayette Co., Ala. First entered service as Private on May 1862 at Fayette Co., Ala. in the 41 Ala. Regt. Inf. Co. H. and continued until April 3, 1865. Captured near Danville, Va. and paroled.

No. 112 - MARTIN, HYRUM, Fayette, Ala. was born on Feb. 1827 in Bibb Co., Ala. First entered service as Private on Aug. 1862 at Coosa Co., Ala. in the 12 Ala. Regt. Inf. Co. B. and continued until April 1865. Surrendered at Appomotox Court House, Va. and paroled.

No. 113 - MEADERS, HYRUM, Bankston, Ala. was born on 26 Feb. 1831 at Greenville District, S. C. First entered service as Private on Oct. 1863 at Manchester, Tenn. in the 41 Ala. Regt. Inf. Co. H. and continued until Mar. 1865 at Petersburg, Va. - Crossed the lines and went north and went to work.

No. 114 - MELTON, JOHN W., Winfield, Ala. was born on 6 May 1833 at Macon, Co., Ga. First entered service as Private on Aug. 1862 at Columbus, Miss. in the 42 Ala. Regt. Inf. Co. D. and continued until discharged Dec. 1862 from effects of wounds received.

No. 115 - MUSGROVE, HENRY F., Winfield, Ala. R. 1, was born on 10 Nov. 1833 at Fayette Co., Ala. First entered service as 2nd Sgt. on Oct. 1861 at Mont Calm, Ala. in the 5th Ala. Regt. Cal. Co. D. and continued until Oct. 1862. Consolidated as Private on Oct. 1862 in the 10 Ala. Regt. Cal. Co. A. and continued until May 1865 and disbanded.

No. 116 - MUSGROVE, WASHINGTON T., Winfield, Ala. R. 1, was born on 24 Dec. 1831 at Marion Co., Ala. First entered service as 1st. Lt. on Dec. 1861 at Fayette Co., Ala. in the 5th Ala. Regt. Inf. Co. B. and continued until May 1862. Re-enlisted as Orderly Sgt. on May 1862 at Morgan Co., Ala. in the 10 Ala. Regt. Cal. Co. D. and continued until May 1865 and paroled.

No. 117 - MILLS, JAMES V., Glen Allen, Ala. R. 1, was born on 7 Mar. 1841 at Marion Co., Ala. First entered service as Private on Aug. 1861 at Marion Co., Ala. in the 26 Ala. Regt. Inf. Co. H. and continued until Aug. 1863 and discharged.

No. 118 - MILLS, LAWSON F., Glen Allen, R.1, was born on Sept. 1838 at Marion Co., Ala. entered service as Private on Oct. 1862 at Mobile, Ala. in the 38 Ala. Regt. Inf. Co. D. and continued until Aug. 1863 and discharged.

No. 119 - MILES, WILBUR F., Covin, Ala. R. 2, was born on 9 Aug. 1841 at Spartanburg, Spartanburg District, S. C. First entered service as 3rd Sgt. on 1 May 1862 at Fayette Co., Ala. in the 41 Ala. Regt. Inf. Co. H. and continued until Nov. 29, 1863 - wounded and transferred. Re-enlisted as 2nd Sgt. on 1 March 1864 at Fayette Co., Ala. in the Stewart Bat. Co. F. and continued until April 1865 and disbanded.

No. 120 - MILES, LANDON, Fayette, Ala. R. 2, was born 22 Oct. 1845 at Spartanburg Dist., S. C. First entered service as 1st Cpl. on Aug. 1863 at Fayette Co., Ala. in the 8 Ala. Regt. Cal. Co. A. and continued until April - Captured and paroled in south Alabama near Selma.

No. 121 - MOZINGO, JACK, Glen Allen, R. 1, was born on 28 Dec. 1841 at Bibb Co., Ala. First entered service as Private on March 1862 at Tuscaloosa Co., Ala. in the Fowler's Battery and continued until May 1865 and paroled.

No. 122 - MOORE, GEORGE H., Fayette, Ala. R.F.D. 6, was born on 4 June 1827 at Perry Co., Ala. First entered service as Private on Nov. 1862 at Fayette Co., Ala. in the 5 Ala. Regt. Cal. Co. B. and continued until May 1865 at home on furlough at close of war.

No. 123 - MOORE, DAVID, Belk, Ala. was born 23 March 1835 at Gwinnett Co., Ga. First entered service as Private on Mar. 1, 1862 at Fayette Co., Ala. in the 26 Ala. Regt. Inf. Co. C. and continued until April 1865 at home on furlough at time of surrender.

No. 124 - MONTGOMERY, JAMES V., Bankston, Ala. was born on 24 Aug. 1838 at Conecuh Co., Ala. First entered service as Private on Sept. 1861 at Columbus, Miss. in the 8 Confederate Regt. Cal. Co. G. and continued until furloughed Mar. 1865 - At home at time of surrender.

No. 125 - McCARVER, GEORGE W., Corona, Ala. was born on 3 Aug. 1832 at Franklin Co., Ala. First entered service as Private on March at Fayette Co., Ala. in the 5th Ala. Bat. Inf. Co. and continued until after the Battle of Shilo. Consolidated at North Miss. in the 17 Ala. Regt. Inf. Co. K. and continued until Nov. 1864. Captured and remained in prison at Johnson Island, Volunteered and went on the Mintier.

No. 126 - McCOLLOUGH, WILLIAM H., Glen Allen, Ala. was born on 31 Aug. 1840 at Chambers Co., Ala. First entered service as Private on 4 July 1861 at Fayette Co., Ala. in the 26 Ala. Regt. Inf. Co. G. and continued until Feb. 1865 and paroled.

No. 127 - McCLUSKEY, WILLIAM N. J., Winfield, Ala. was born on 9 July 1845 at Lawrence Co., Ala. First entered service as Private on 1 Jan. 1863 at Winston Co., Ala. in the 56 Ala. Regt. Co. K. and continued until April 1865 and paroled.

No. 128 - McCALEB, WILLIAM F., Glen Allen, Ala. was born on 1825 at Fayette Co., Ala. First entered service as Private on April 1864 at Fayette Co., Ala. in the 3 Ala. Regt. Co. D. and continued until May 1865. Paroled at Johnson Island.

No. 129 - McDONALD, ANDREW J., Winfield, Ala. was born on 28 April 1821 at Walton Co., Ga. First entered service as Private on 28 June 1861 at Walton Co., Ga. in the 9 Ga. Regt. Inf. Co. C. and continued until 3 July 1863. Captured and remained in prison Davis Island, N. Y. until 1865 and paroled and returned home.

No. 130 - McDONALD, ANGUS N., Fayette, Ala. R. 1, was born on 2 April 1839 at Elba, Coffee Co., Ala. First entered service as Private on July 1861 at Marion, Ala. in the 20 Ala. Regt. Inf. Co. H. and continued until surrendered and paroled near Atlanta, Ga. April 1865.

No. 131 - McFARLAND, DANIEL M., Bankston, Ala. R. 1. was born on 14 Dec. 1847 at Perry Co., Ala. First entered service as Private on 1 Jan. 1863 in the 8 Ala. Regt. Cal. Co. F. and continued until May 1865. Surrendered and paroled near Greensboro, Ala.

No. 132 - Not listed.

No. 133 - NORTHCUTT, GID J., Fayette, Ala. R. s. was born on 30 Aug. 1846 in Marion Co., Ala. First entered service as Private on July 1863 at Marion Co., Ala. in the 5 Ala. Regt. Ca. Co. D. and continued until April 1865. Disbanded near Selma, Ala., taken oath Fayette, Ala.

No. 134 - NEWMAN, ART, Covin, Ala., R. 2, was born on 25 July 1840 in Spartanburg, Dist. S. C. First entered service as Private on May 1863 at Fayette Co., Ala. in the 41 Ala. Regt. Inf. Co. I. and continued until captured at Battle Murfersboro. Remained in prison until April 1863 - Exchanged. Re-enlisted as Private on Sept. 1863 at Fayette, Ala. in Rody's Calv. and continued until on furlough at time of surrender.

No. 135 - OWEN, WILLIAM B., Fayette, Ala. R. 1, was born on 10 June 1845 at Hart Co., Ga. First entered service as Private on Sept. 1863 at Fayette Co., Ala. in the 8 Ala. Regt. Cal. Co. I. and continued until May 1865 and paroled in south Alabama.

No. 136 - PANE, ISAAC M., Fayette, Ala. R. 5, was born on 29 June 1835 at Greenville District, S. C. First entered service as Private on Aug. 1862 at Fayette Co., Ala. in the 26 Ala. Regt. Inf. Co. I. and continued until captured at Nashville, Tenn. and remained in prison until June 12, 1865.

No. 137 - PAPAZAN, THOMAS J., New Lexington, Ala. R. 1, was born on 18 Feb. 1846 at Fayette Co., Ala. First entered service as Private on 1 May 1864 at Fayette Co., Ala. in the 26 Ala. Regt. Inf. Co. I. and continued until Jan. 1865. Discharged at Tuscaloosa, Ala.

No. 138 - PATTERSON, JOSEPH J., New Lexington, Ala. R.F.D. 1, was born on 22 Sept. 1842 in Fayette Co., Ala. First entered service as Private on 17 Sept. 1861 at Fayette Co., Ala. in the 26 Ala. Regt. Inf. Co. I. and continued until Feb. 1, 1865. At home on furlough at close of war.

No. 139 - PERKINS, THOMAS A. (or William A.), Belk, Ala. was born on July 1837 at Fayette Co., Ala. First entered service as Private on July 1861 at Fayette Co., Ala. in the 26 Ala. Regt. Inf. Co. I. and continued until Feb. 1865. Regiment disbanded in No. Miss. for 10 days to recruit up and never entered the service anymore.

No. 140 - PERRY, ISAAC, Glen Allen, Ala. R. 1, was born on 18 Jan. 1835 at Jasper Co., Ga. First entered service as Private on Oct. 1862 at Fayette Co., Ala. in the 5 Ala. Regt. Cal. Co. A. and continued until Oct. 1863.

Transferred as Private on Oct. 1863 at No. Alabama in the 10 Ala. Regt. Cal. Co. D. and continued until March 1865 and came home.

No. 141 - PENDLEY, WASHINGTON A., Corona, Ala. R. 1, was born on 9 Jan. 1843 at Gwinnett Co., Ga. First entered service as Private at Mobile, Ala. in the 32 Ala. Regt. Inf. Co. I. and continued until Oct. 1862. Captured at Lauen, Tenn. and came home. Re-enlisted as Private on 1863 at Tulahoma, Tenn. in the 32 Ala. Regt. Co. I. and continued until Battle Missionary Ridge and wounded. Re-enlisted as Private at Moulton, Ala. in the 42 Regt. Whatley Co. and continued until Spring or close of the war - paroled in Walker Co. Ala.

No. 142 - PHILLIPS, JAMES R., Dry Creek, Ala. was born on 27 Nov. 1845 at Fayette Co., Ala. First entered service as Private on Dec. 1, 1863 at Fayette Co., Ala. in the 4 Ala. Regt. Co. K. and continued until May 1865 and disbanded.

No. 143 - PICKEL, JOHN T., Bankston, Ala. R. 1, was born on 1 Sept. 1841 at Fayette Co., Ala. First entered service as Private on 4 July 1862 at Spencer, Ala. in the 26 Ala. Regt. Inf. Co. A. and continued until Jan. 1, 1864. Crossed the Federal lines, but never aided the Federal Army in any way.

No. 144 - PINION, JAMES O., Berry, Ala. R. 1, was born on 4 May 1837 at Tuscaloosa Co., Ala. First entered service as Private on Sept. 1862 at Fayette Co., Ala. in the Garlidy Bat. Co. K. and continued until Sept. 1863. Consolidated as Private on Sept. 1863, at near Memphis, Tenn. in the 50 Ala. Regt. Inf. Co. K. and continued until March 1865. Captured at Munfordsville, Ky. and remained in prison until paroled 1865.

No. 145 - PINION, ABNER W., Berry, Ala. was born on 28 July 1845 at Tuscaloosa Co., Ala. First entered service as Private on Sept. 1863 at Fayette Co., Ala. in the 9 Ala. Cal. Co. I. and continued until April 1865 at home on furlough at close of war.

No. 146 - POE, JAMES J., Fayette, Ala., R. 4, was born on 16 Feb. 1835 at Tuscaloosa Co., Ala. First entered service as Private on April 1861 at Tuscaloosa Co., Ala. in the 33 Ala. Regt. Inf. Co., I. and continued until captured Oct. 1863 at Lurvene, Tenn. Paroled and came home. Re-enlisted as Private on Mar. 1864 at Moulton, Ala. in the 10 Ala. Regt. Cal. Co. B. and Continued until March 1865. Furloughed and at home at time of surrender. Taken oath at Monroeville? May 1865.

No. 147 - POE, WILLIAM S., Corona, Ala. R. 1, was born on 26 April 1837 at Fayette Co., Ala. First entered service as Private on April 1862 at Fayette Co., Ala. in the 32 Ala. Regt. Inf. Co. I. and continued until captured at Missionary Ridge, Tenn. Released from prison June 12, 1865 on parole.

No. 148 - PRICE, BENJAMIN F., Fayette, Ala. R.,3, was born on 27 March 1842 in Jackson Co., Ala. First entered service as Private on June 1861 at Hanover, Coosa County, Ala. in the 18 Ala. Regt. Inf. Co. D. and continued until wounded at Chickamauga and discharged. Was never able for service any more - taken oath at Talladega, Ala.

No. 149 - RAY, ALEXANDER, Berry, Ala. was born on 24 April 1843 at Fayette Co., Ala. First entered service as Private on 1 May 1862 at Fayette Co., Ala. in the 38 Ala. Regt. Inf. Co. F. and continued until Oct. 1863. Furloughed at home from hospital at Marietta, Ga. Re-enlisted as Private on Jan. 1, 1864 at Fayette Co., Ala. in the Frank Woodrow Co. Home Guards, and continued until April 1865 and disbanded, by his captain.

No. 150 - RAY, THOMAS J., Winfield, Ala. R. 2, was born on 17 Sept. 1839 at Edgefield Dist. S. C. First entered service as Private on 16 May 1862 at

Fayette Co., Ala. in the 41 Ala. Regt. Inf. Co. I. and continued until May 1855. Paroled in Virginia.

No. 151 - REESE, HENRY A., Fayette, Ala. R. 2, was born on 6 Jan. 1840 in Marion Co., Ala. First entered service as Private on July 1861 at Fayette Co., Ala. in the 26 Ala. Regt. Inf. Co. E. and continued until Nov. 1863. Re-enlisted as Private on Jan. 1, 1864 at Courtland, Ala. in the Pickett Regt. Rody Col. and continued until spring 1865 and disbanded, and paroled at Millville, Ala.

No. 152 - REEVES, CHARLES H., Fayette, Ala. R. 3, was born on 5 Dec. 1834 in Walton Co., Ga. First entered service as Private on 12 May 1862 at Monroe, Ga. in the 2 Ga. Cal. Co. D. and continued until Nov. 1, 1864. Furloughed and at home at surrender.

No. 153 - ROBINSON, WILLIAM M., Corona, Ala. was born on 22 Nov. 1844 in Benton Co., Ala. First entered service as Private on 1 Sept. 1863 at Fayette Co., Ala. in t e 8 Ala. Regt. Cal. Co. I., and continued until May 1865. Discharged from hospital at Macon, Ga. - paroled at Macon, Ga.

No. 154 - ROBERTS, JAMES C., Winfield, Ala. R. 1, was born on 1 March 1833 in Pickens Dist. in the State of S. C. First entered service as Private on Aug. 1862 at Pickens District, S. C. in the 4. So. Caro. Cal. Co. C. and continued until 1 Dec. 1864. Captured and remained in prison until July 1865 and paroled.

No. 155 - ROBERTS, JACOB H., Corona, Ala. was born on 18 Nov. 1840 in Bedford Co., Tenn. First entered service as Private on May 1862 at Fayette Co., Ala. in the 41 Ala. Regt. Inf. Co. H. and continued until April 1865. Surrendered at Appomotox Court House, Va. and paroled.

No. 156 - ROBERTS, ROBERT M., Fayette, Ala. R. 4, was born on 3 Jan. 1842 in Fayette Co., A a. First entered service as Private on April 1863, at Fayette Co., Ala. in the 8 Ala. Regt. Cal. Co. A. and continued until discharged March 1865.

No. 157 - RICHARDSON, NATHAN P., Kennedy, Ala. R. 2, was born on 21 Dec. 1843 in Anderson District, S. C. First entered service as 1st Cpl. on 22 March 1862 at Fayette Co., Ala. in the 41 Ala. Regt. Cal. Co. B. and continued until May 1865 and paroled.

No. 158 - RICHARDSON, SAMUEL J., Kennedy, Ala. was born on 25 Oct. 1845 in Franklin Co., Ga. First entered service as Private on Oct. 15, 1863 at Fayette Co., Ala. in the 6 Miss. Regt. Cal. Co. H. and continued until May 12, 1865, and paroled.

No. 159 - RUSSELL, JOHN W., Winfield, Ala. was born on 13 Sept. 1838 in Fayette Co., Ala. First entered service as 3rd Lt. on Nov. 1861 at Fayette Co., Ala. in the 5 Ala. Bat. Inf. Co. B. and continued until April 27, 1862 and discharged.

No. 160 - SAVAGE, ZACK, Hico, Ala. was born on 12 Nov. 1847 in Fayette Co., Ala. First entered service as 1st Sgt. on 2 Feb. 1864 at Fayette Co., Ala. in the 8 Ala. Regt. Cal. Co. I. and continued until 26 April. Surrendered at Gainsville, Ala. and paroled.

No. 161 - SIZEMORE, JOSOELL H., Guin, Ala. R. 2, was born on 16 April 1829 in Marion Co., Ala. First entered service as Private on Oct. 1863 at Fayette Co., Ala. in the 10 Ala. Regt. Cal. Co. H. and continued until May 1865 and discharged.

No. 162 - SHERER, J. D., Dry Creek, Ala. was born on 6 Sept. 1842 in York Dist., S. C. First entered service as Private on 31 July 1861 at Jasper, Ala. in the 16 Ala. Regt. Volunteers Co., B. and continued until captured at Franklin, Tenn. Nov. 30, 1864. Remained in prison at Camp Douglas, Ill.

Released on parole June 18, 1865.

No. 163 - SELLMAN, BENJAMIN K., Bankston, Ala. R. 1, was born on 23 Aug. 1844 in Talladega Co., Ala. First entered service as Private on 17 Sept. 1864 at Fayette Co., Ala. in the 10 Ala. Regt. Cal. Co. K. on May 29, 1865 - Disbanded and discharged.

No. 164 - SHILTMAN, JOHN B., Covin, Ala. was born on 3 May 1845 in Fayette Co., Ala. First entered service as Private on 18 May at Fayette, Ala. in the 56 Ala. Regt. Cal. Co. I. and continued until April 1865. Was at home on furlough when war closed.

No. 165 - SHEPHERD, ROBERT A., Fayette, Ala. was born on 6 Aug. 1830 at Jasper Co., Ga. First entered service as Private on Feb. 1863 at Aberdeen, Miss. in the 28 Miss. Regt. Cal. Co. H. and continued until April 1865. Surrendered and paroled at Columbus, Miss.

No. 166 - SHEPHERD, JAMES M., Newtonville, Ala. was born on 1 April 1847 in Fayette Co., Ala. First entered service as 3rd Sgt. on Mar. 1863 at Fayette Co., Ala. in the 10 Ala. Regt. Cal. Co. A. and continued until April 4, 1865. Disbanded at Selma, Ala. and paroled at Columbus, Miss.

No. 167 - SHEPHERD, GEORGE W., Fayette, Ala. R. 1, was born on 23 Nov. 1844 at Monroe Co., N. C. First entered service as Private on Oct. 1862 at Fayette Co., Ala. in the 26 Ala. Regt. Inf. Co. C. on April 1865. Surrendered and paroled in Ga.

No. 168 - STANLEY, BENJAMIN D., Fayette, Ala. was born on 14 April 1829 in Bedford Co., Tenn. First entered service as Private on Aug. 1862 at Walker Co., Ala. in the Camp of Instruction at Taladega. Hired substitute and returned home ...?? ... on 1863 and worked in salt works at Village Creek, Ala. until close of war and disbanded.

No. 169 - STANLEY, FRANK M., Berry, Ala. R. 1, was born on 28 April 1845 in Tuscaloosa Co., Ala. First entered service as Private on 3 Oct. 1863 at Fayette Co., Ala. in the 56 Ala. Regt. Cal. Co. I. and continued until Dec. 1864. At home on furlough at close of war. Paroled at Windham Springs, Ala.

No. 170 - SPILLER, JAMES A., Bankston, Ala. was born on 7 May 1842 in Randolph Co., Ala. First entered service as Private on 1 Jan. 1864 at Shelby Co., Ala. in the William Basket Co. Horne, and continued until April 1865 and disbanded by Capt.

No. 171 - SOUTH, JOHN A. (or U.) Fayette, Ala. R. 4, was born 15 Dec. 1830 in Tuscaloosa Co., Ala. First entered service as Private on April 1861 at Fayette Co., Ala. in the 41 Ala. Regt. Inf. Co. H. and continued until about two months before the surrender and crossed the lines, but never aided the Federal Army.

No. 172 - SOUTH, LEVY W., Fayette, Ala. R. 4, was born on 8 May 1836 in Tuscaloosa Co., Ala. First entered service as Private on Sept. 1861 at Fayette, Co., Ala. in the Banks Co. Sharp Shooters, and continued until Sept. 1862. Consolidated on Sept. 1862 at Mobile, Ala. in the 43 Miss. Regt. Inf. Co. K. and continued until captured at Vicksburg, Miss. and paroled. Exchanged as Private on 1864 at Fayette, Ala. in the 10 Ala. Regt. Cal. Co. K. and continued until May 1865 and discharged.

No. 173 - SPARKS, JOHN, Fayette, Ala. R. 5, was born on 5 May 1831 at Fayette Co., Ala. First entered service as Private at Columbus, Miss. in the Baskerville? Miss. Bat. Cal. Co. G. and continued until April 1864. Captured near Louden, Tenn. and remained in prison at Rock Island, Ill. until June 1865 and paroled.

No. 174 - SKIPPER, LEVY R., Fayette, Ala. R. 1, was born on 27 May 1842 at McKinney, Maringo Co., Ala. First entered service as Private on Aug. 1861 at Maringo Co., Ala. in the 2 Ala. Bat. Artillery Co. D. and continued until April 19, 1865. Surrendered at Augusta, Ga. and paroled at Atlanta, Ga.

No. 175 - SMITH, WILLIAM D., Carbon Hill, Ala. R. 1, was born on 12 Nov. 1845 at Madison Co., Ga. First entered service as Private on 7 Nov. 1863 at Sweet Water, Tenn. and continued until wounded at Rice Station, Ga.? April 1865 and paroled at Sharlotte, N. C. April 1865.

No. 176 - SMITH, JAMES R., Covin, Ala. R. 1, was born on 29 May 1846 at Jackson Co., Ga. First entered service as Private on May 1864 at Fayette Co., Ala. in the 8 Ala. Regt. Cal. Co. A. and continued until May 1865. Paroled in South Alabama.

No. 177 - SMITH, JAMES M., Fayette, Ala. R. 3, was born on 2 Dec. 1844 at Walton Co., Ga. First entered service as Private on Nov. 1862 at Monroe, Ga. in the 11 Ga. Regt. Inf. Co. H. and continued until April 9, 1865. Surrendered at Aopomotox Court House, Va. and paroled.

No. 178 - STOCKS, EFHRUM, Dankston, Ala., R. 1, was born on 10 April 1833 in Cambell Co., Ga. First entered service as Private on Jan. 1862 at Shelby Co., Ala. in the 21 Ala. Regt. Inf. Co. H. and continued until May 1865. Surrendered and paroled at Meridan, Miss.

No. 179 - STRONG, ROBERT J., Fayette, Ala. was born on 6 March 1844 at Fayette Co., Ala. First entered service as Private on 5 Aug. 1861 at Franklin Co., Ala. in the 16 Ala. Regt. Inf. Co. E. and continued until disbanded April 1865 and paroled at Pond Springs, Ala.

No. 180 - STRONG, WILLIAM E., Covin, Ala. R. 2, was born on 26 June 1845 at Fayette Co., Ala. First entered service as Private on May 1863 at Burleson, Ala. in the Capt. Newton Co. Rody Cal. and continued until Spring 1865. Disbanded and paroled at Pond Srpings, Ala.

No. 181 - STEWART, CHARLES J., Winfield, Ala. R. 1, was born on 28 Feb. 1844 at Marion Co., Ala. First entered service as Private on Aug. 1862 at Fayette Co., Ala. in the 5 Ala. Regt. Cal. Co. D. Consolidated as Private in the 10 Ala. Regt. Cal. Co. D. and continued until Spring 1865 and disbanded.

No. 182 - STEWART, REUBIN J., Covin, Ala. was born on 26 May 1831 in Fayette Co., Ala. First entered service as Private on 18 June 1861 at Fayette, Ala. in the 11 Ala. Regt. Inf. Co. I. and continued until wounded June 3, Battle 7 days near Richmond. Furloughed, returned to Richmond 1862 and transferred. Re-enlisted as 1st. Lt. on Dec. 1862 at Richmond, Va. in the 10 Ala. Regt. Cal. Co. I. and continued until April 1865 and paroled at Columbus, Miss.

No. 183 - STEWART, JOHN M., Fayette, Ala. was born on 11 June 1844 at Fayette Co., Ala. First entered service as Private on Aug. 1861 at Fayette Co., Ala. in the 26 Ala. Regt. Inf. Co. B. and continued until Oct. 1861. Re-enlisted as Private on Dec. 1861 at Newburn, Ga. in the 9 Ala. Bat. Co. B. and continued until June 1862. Consolidated as Private on June 1862 at Tenn. in 58 Ala. Regt. Inf. Co. B. and continued until Sept. 20, 1863 - Wounded and lost right leg at Battle Chickamauga - Furloughed from hospital and came home.

No. 184 - TAYLOR, LITTLEBERRY G., Kennedy, Ala., Rt. 1, was born on 5 May 1845 in Fayette Co., Ala. First entered service as Private on Nov. 1863 at Fayette Co., Ala. in the 56 Ala. Regt. Cal. Co. I. and continued until May 1865. Disbanded about 30 miles south of Tupelo, Miss. and paroled at Columbus, Miss.

No. 185 - TAYLOR, CHARLES R., Covin, Ala. was born on 13 July 1845 in Cherokee Co, Ala. First entered service as Private on 20 Dec. 1862 at Fayette Ala. in the 17 Ala. Regt. Inf. Co. A. and continued until July 1863 and discharged. Re-enlisted as Private on Aug. 1864 at Fayette Co., Ala. in the 8 Ala. Regt. Cal. Co. A. and continued until May 1865 and paroled at Columbus, Miss.

No. 186 - TAYLOR, JOSEPH W., Bankston, Ala. R. 1, was born 20 Feb. 1840 at Montgomery, Montgomery Co., Ala. First entered service as Private on April 1861 at Jackson, Ala. in the 7 Ala. Bat. Co. H. and continued until Aug. 1861. Consolidated on Aug. 1861 at Chattanooga, Tenn. in the 7 Ala. Regt. Cal. Co. H. and continued until Spring 1865 and paroled.

No. 187 - TOWNSEND, JAMES S., Fayette, Ala. R. 6, was born on 14 Feb. 1847 in Tuscaloosa, Co., Ala. First entered service as Private on July 1864 at Fayette Co., Ala. in 1 Ala. Reserves Co. C. and continued until furloughed from hospital, Lauderdale Springs, Miss. and never able for service anymore.

No. 188 - TIDWELL, EATEN, New River, Ala. was born on Jan. 1837 in Fayette Co., Ala. First entered service as Private on Jan. 1864 at Fayette Co., Ala. in the 10 Ala. Regt. Cal. Co. Whatley and continued until April 1865. At home on furlough at time of surrender.

No. 189 - TUCKER, ISAAC J., Glen Allen, Ala. was born 12 Jan. 1825 in Marion Co., Ala. First entered service as Private on Dec. 1862 at Dry Sorings, Tenn. in the 4 Ala. Regt. Cal. Co. K. and continued until Dec. 1863. Re-enlisted as Private on Dec. 1863 in the 10 Ala. Regt. Cal. Co. B. and continued until May 1865 and disbanded.

No. 190 - TUCKER, THOMAS F., Glen Allen, Ala. was born on 10 Dec. 1828 in Marion Co., Ala. First entered service as Private on Sept. 1862 at Near Courtland, Ala. in the 4 Ala. Regt. Cal. Co. B. and continued until Sept. 1864. Transferred as Private on 1864 in 10 Ala. Regt. Cal. Co. B. and continued until Spring 1865 and disbanded.

No. 191 - TYNER, GEORGE R., Berry, Ala. R. 1, was born on 10 Feb. 1844 at Fayette Co., Ala. First entered service as Private on 2 Apr. 1863 at Tuscaloosa, Ala. in the 26 Ala. Regt. Inf. Co. A. and continued until April 1865. Surrendered at Greensboro, N. C. and paroled at Saulisberry, N. C.

No. 192 - WARD, JAMES N., Fayette, Ala. R. 2, was born on 2 June 1839 at Fayette Co., Ala. First entered service as Private on Oct. 1861 at Fayette Co., Ala. in 5 Ala. Bat. Inf. Co. C. and continued until Aug. 1862. Consolidated as Private on Aug. 1862 at Mobile, Ala. in the 17 Ala. Regt. Inf. Co. B. and continued until April 1863. Consolidated as Private on April 1863 in Tenn. in the 58 Ala. Regt. Inf. Co. B. and continued until 1865 May - Surrendered near Mobile, Ala. and paroled.

No. 193 - WATKINS, JOHN D., Lexington, Ala. was born on Dec. 1, 1846 in Tuscaloosa, Co., Ala. First entered service as Private on 4 July 1863 at Fayette Co., Ala. in the 10 Ala. Regt. Co. and continued until disbanded near Columbus, Miss. and paroled at Columbus, Miss.

No. 194 - WAYERS, (or WYERS), JOHN A., Carbon Hill, Ala. R. 1, was born on 16 March 1844 in Bibb Co., Ala. First entered service as Private on Sept. 1862 in Walker Co., Ala. in the 56 Ala. Regt. Cal. Co. G. and continued until 1864 - Furloughed and went home and never went back to service.

No. 195 - WHISENANT, THOMAS M., Winfield, Ala. R. 1, was born on 23 Mar. 1845 in Walker Co., Ga. First entered service as Private at Hall Co., Ga. in Capt. Smith Co. Home Guards and continued until May 1865 and disbanded by Capt.

No. 196 - WHITE, WILLIAM L. J., Fayette, Ala. R. 4, was born on 15 Dec. 1845 in Coosa Co., Ala. First entered service on 1 Oct. 1864 at Coosa Co., Ala. in the 18 Ala. Regt. Cal. Co. B. and continued until May 1865. Surrendered at Selma, Ala and Paroled at Taladega, Ala.

No. 197 - WHITE, ANDREW J., Fayette, Ala. R. 2, was born on 5 April 1833 in Blunt Co., Ala. First entered service as Private on 2 May 1862 in Fayette Co., Ala. in the 32 Ala. Regt. Inf. Co. I. and continued until Nov. 24, 1863. Captured at Missionary Ridge, Tenn. and remained in prison at Rock Island, Ill. until June 22, 1865 and paroled.

No. 198 - WHITE, JAMES S., Lexington, Ala. was born on 25 Jan. 1830 in Merryweather Co., Ga. First entered service as Private on Oct. 1861 at Tuscaloosa Co., Ala. in the 50 Ala. Regt. Inf. Co. A. on Dec. 15, 1864. Captured and remained in prison at Camp Douglas until June 20, 1865 and paroled.

No. 199 - WILSON, JOWELL (?), Kennedy, Ala. R. 2, was born on 5 Sept. 1838 in Fayette Co., Ala. First entered service as Private on Mar. 22, 1862 at Fayette Co., Ala. in the 41 Ala. Regt. Inf. Co. B. and continued until May 1865. Paroled and taken oath.

No. 200 - WILKES, MODICA D., Fayette, Ala. R. 3, was born on 13 Dec. 1836 in Fayette Co., Ala. First entered service as 1st Cpl. on Mar. 1, 1862 at Fayette Co., Ala. in the 41 Ala. Regt. Inf. Co. I. and continued until 20 Sept. 1863 - Wounded at Chickamauga and disabled. Re-enlisted as Private on July 1, 1864 at Eldridge, Ala. in the 5 Ala. Regt. Cal. Co. ?...? and continued until April 1865. Disbanded and taken oath at Tuscaloosa, Ala.

No. 201 - WIMBERLEY, JAMES R., Winfield, Ala. R. 4, was born on 18 April 1846 in Fayette Co,, Ala. First entered service as Private on Feb. 1864 at Fayette Co., Ala. in the 10 Ala. Regt. Cal. Co. A. and continued until 10 Apr. 1865. Disbanded near Selma, Ala. and paroled.

No. 202 - WILLINGHAM, JAMES H., Bankston, Ala. was born 16 Sept. 1841 at Fayette Co., Ala. First entered service as Private on Sept. 1861 at Columbus, Miss. in the 8 Confederate Cal. G. and continued until captured at Danville, Ky. Oct. 1863. Paroled at Peryville, Ky. 20 Oct. 1863. Re-enlisted as Private on Feb. 1864 at Fayette Co., Ala. in the 5 Ala. Regt. Cal. Co. B. and continued until Jan. 1865. Consolidated as 3rd Lt. on Jan. 1865 at Tuscumbia, Ala. in the 10 Ala. Regt. Cal. Co. A. and continued until disbanded and paroled at Decatur, Ala., 1865.

No. 203 - WILLCUTT, ELIZA, Corona, Ala. R. 1, was born on 9 May 1843 in Fayette Co., Ala. First entered service as Private on April 1864 at Tuscaloosa, Ala. in the 1 ?....? Regt. Inf. Co. C. and continued until Nov. 1864. Left the army near Jacksonville, Ga. sick and not able for service and came home.

No. 204 - WOODS, JAMES C., Fayette, Ala. R. 3, was born on 10 Oct. 1843 in Tenn. First entered service as Private on May 1864 at Fayette Co., Ala. in the Stewart Bat. Cal. Co. F. and continued until May 27, 1865 and disbanded and paroled at Columbus, Miss.

No. 205 - WOODWARD, STEPHEN, Dry Creek, Ala. was born on 21 May 1835 in Johnson Co., N. C. First entered service as Private on March 1862 at Taladega, Ala. in the Capt. Trus. Home Guard and continued until four months and discharged.

No. 206 - YERBY, ISAAC S., Fayette, Ala. R. 4, was born on 27 Feb. 1838 at Newtonville, Fayette Co., Ala. First entered service as Private on 17 Sept. 1861 at Fayette Co., Ala. in the 26 Ala. Regt. Inf. Co. A. and continued until Sept. 1864. Furloughed 18 days - at home and cutt off from word. Re-enlisted as Private on Oct. 1, 1864 near Jasper, Ala. in the 10 Ala. Regt. Cal. Co. Whatly and continued until April 1865 - disbanded and came home and taken oath of allegiance at Fayette, Ala.

No. 207 - YERBY, JAMES C., Fayette, Ala. was born on 18 May 1839 in Fayette Co., Ala. First entered service as Private on 18 Sept. 1861 at

Fayette Co., Ala. in the 26 Ala. Regt. Inf. Co. A. and continued until Dec. 1864 - Captured at Nashville, Tenn. and remained in prison at Camp Chase, Ohio until June 1865 and paroled.

No. 208 - YERBY, JOHN T., Hico, Ala. was born on 4 Feb. 1833 at Fayette Co., Ala. First entered service as Private on May 1862 at Fayette Co., Ala. in the 41 Ala. Regt. Inf. Co. G. and continued until wounded at Petersburg, Va. 17 June 1864. Furloughed from hospital and sent home and never able for service.

No. 209 - YOUNG, JOHN A., Fayette, Ala. was born on 10 April 1833 in Chester District, . C. First entered service as Private on May 1863 in Lamar Co., Ala. in the 43 Miss. Regt. Inf. Co. H. and continued until June 1864. Transferred as Private at Lamar Co., Ala. in the 10 Ala. Regt. Cal. Co. I. and continued until April 1865. Furloughed and at home at time of surrender.

(This Census Record was copied at Fayette County Court House by Herbert M. and Jeanie P. Newell in July and August, 1958.)

<u>CONFEDERATE VETERANS BURIED IN FAYETTE COUNTY, ALABAMA</u> -- This following list is from a survey made of all known cemeteries in Fayette County and it gives the name and dates for all the Confederate Soldiers buried in Fayette County, Ala. There may be others whose tombstones were not marked that served in the Confederate States Army and occasionally there is a veteran listed whose relatives gave the information stating that they served in the C.S.A.

HOPEWELL PRIMITIVE BAPTIST CHURCH CEMETERY (North of Fayette, east of U. S. Highway 43) --Henry N. Reeves - Co. K. Ga. Inf. C.S.A. - B. Feb. 2, 1823 D. July 27, 1897; Corp. H. D. Roycroft - Palmers Co. Ala. Res. C.S.A. - B. Nov. 2, 1819 - D. March 18, 1898; Charles H. Reeves - Co. D. Georgia C.S.A.; William M. Riley - Pvt. Co. E. 9 Regt. Ala. Inf. C.S.A. - Service May 29, 1863 - B. Oct. 21, 1817 - D. July 26, 1890; David R. Watson - Co. B. 4 Ala. Cav. C.S.A.; Peyton I. Dickinson - Pvt. 56 Regt. Ala. Partisan Rangers C.S.A. B. Dec. 16, 1826 - D. Sept. 5, 1880; Killingsworth, Corpl. M. D. - Co. I. 26 Ala. Inf. C.S.A.; E. S. Jones - B. June 17, 1846 - D. Aug. 11, 1927 - C. S.A.;

CAINES RIDGE BAPTIST CHURCH (South of Fayette on Gordo Road) -- J. T. Holliman - Co. H. 41 Ala. Inf. C.S.A.

WHITLEY OR WHITSON FAMILY CEMETERY (West of Fayette north of U.S. 43) Thomas W. Hamner, - Co. G. 11 Ala. Inf. C.S.A.

OLD ROCKY MOUNT BAPTIST CHURCH CEMETERY (Near Covin) -- M. C. Weathers Co. K. 36 Ala. Inf. C.S.A.

OLD MT. LEBNON BAPTIST CHURCH CEMETERY (West of Bluff Road) -- Miles Bobo - Co. H. 41 Ala. Inf. C.S.A.

PROVIDENCE METHODIST CHURCH CEMETERY (West of Bluff) -- John K. Miller, 23 S. C. Inf. Co. F. C.S.A. - B. Mar. 12, 1841 - D. April 11, 1932.

HOLLIMAN OR STEWART FAMILY CEMETERY (West of Bluff Road) -- 1st. Lt. James F. Holliman - 58 Ala. Inf. Co. B. C.S.A.

CONCORD BAPTIST CHURCH CEMETERY (On Concord Road) -- John Thomas Poe 41 Ala. Inf. Co. G. C.S.A.

PATTERSON FAMILY CEMETERY (South of Concord Road) Rev. J. J. Patterson, B. Sept. 22, 1842 - D. May 12, 1918 - C.S.A.

BETHLEHEM METHODIST CHURCH CEMETERY (East of Winfield Road, U.S. 43) -- Sgt. James A. Jenkins - 41 Ala. Inf. Co. I. C.S.A.; John S. Jenkins - 58 Ala. Inf. Co. B. C.S.A.; Benjamin F. Price - 18 Ala. Inf. Co. D. C.S.A.; J. A. Porter - 10 Ala. Cav. Co. K. C.S.A.

NEW LIBERTY FREEWILL BAPTIST CHURCH CEMETERY or Possum Trot (North of Townley Road) -- 2 Lt. Joseph W. Taylor - Co. H. 7 Regt. Cav. C.S.A.

MT. VERNON METHODIST CHURCH CEMETERY (On Vernon Highway) -- R. J. Brock Co. I. 8 Ala. Cav. C.S.A. - B. Dec. 24, 1846 - D. Apr. 6, 1937; James R. Thomas - Co. D. 2 N. C. Inf. C.S.A.; Landon Miles - Co. a. 9 Ala. Av. C.S.A. B. Oct. 22, 1845 - D. Oct. 20, 1930; Valentine Prater - Co. L. 41 Ala. Inf. C.S.A.; Corpl. Jesse F. Ellis - 41 Ala. Inf. Co. I. C.S.A.; Enoch Brock - Co. D. 10 Ala. Cav. C.S.A.

WESLEY CHAPEL METHODIST CHURCH CEMETERY (West & North of Covin) -- Wesley J. Dodson - Co. K. 36 Ala. Inf. C.S.A.; Robert Waldrop - Co. F. 9 Ga. Cav. C.S.A.

CITY OF FAYETTE, ALABAMA PUBLIC CEMETERY (In Fayette) -- Rev. J. O. A. Pace - B. 1845 - D. 1924 - C.S.A.; Joseph Patrick Smith - Co. D. 9 Texas Cavalry - B. 1845 - D. Aug. 3, 1920 - C.S.A.; Col. Holland M. Bell - Co. H. 41st Ala. Inf. C.S.A. 1861 - 1865 - B. 1839 - D. 1943; Dr. Leroy F. Shelton B. Aug. 27, 1836 - D. July 2, 1892 - C.S.A.; B. W. Tarwater - Co. K. 16 Ala. Inf. C.S.A.; J. V. Neal - D. Jan. 11, 1894 - Age 52 Yrs. - C.S.A.; *No Name - C.S.A. Soldier; Capt. Richard A. Smith - Co. B. 5 Ala. Inf. C.S.A.; J. C. Yerby - B. May 18, 1839 - D. Dec. 5, 1912 - C.S.A.; R. H. Jennings - B. Dec. 27, 1828 - D. Oct. 31, 1914 - C.S.A.; *No Name - C.S.A. Soldier; Capt. James H. Moore - B. July 18, 1824 - D. March 21, 1894 - C.S.A.; John M. Edney - B. Oct. 20, 1832 - D. March 8, 1896 - C.S.A.; S. V. Hinton - B. Feb. 8, 1834 - D. Apr. 9, 1913 - C.S.A.; *No Name - C.S.A. Soldier; Judge John C. Moore - B. Elbert Co., Ga. Aug. 17, 1818 - D. Fayette Court House, Ala. Aug. 21, 1889 - C.S.A.; Augustine Melville Nuckols - B. Oct. 26, 1823 in Barren Co., Ky. - D. Dec. 13, 1896 - C.S.A.; Capt. A. L. White - B. Huntsville, Ala. May 13, 1843 - D. Mar. 14, 1906 - C.S.A.

PILGRIM'S REST BAPTIST CHURCH CEMETERY (South of Fayette on Gordo Road) -- Allen H. Freeman - Co. H. 41 Ala. Inf. C.S.A.; Thomas Ray - Co. B. 41 Ala. Inf. C.S.A. - D. Aug. 4, 1935 - 92 Yrs.

MUSGROVE CHAPEL METHODIST CHURCH CEMETERY (South of Winfield, west of U. S. Highway 43) -- Sgt. William H. Curl - Co. C. 55 Regt. Ala. Inf. C.S.A. - B. Mar. 11, 1823 - D. Nov. 25, 1884.

SHEPHERD BAPTIST CHURCH (Newtonville) -- James Martin Shepherd - B. 1847 D. 1921 - C.S.A.

SAND SPRINGS or FRIENDSHIP BAPTIST CHURCH CEMETERY (East of Winfield Rd. U.S. 43) -- Columbus W. Lewis - Co. D. 18 Ala. Inf. C.S.A.; William J. Akins Co. K. 59 Ala. Inf. C.S.A.; William C. Manasco - Co. H. 41 Ala. Inf. C.S.A.

ZION METHODIST CHURCH CEMETERY (On New Byler Road) -- John Keller Co. C. 18 Ill. Inf. C.S.A.; J. W. Hammack - Co. D. 22 Ga. Inf. C.S.A.

ANTIOCH FREEWILL BAPTIST CHURCH or BELK BAPTIST CHURCH CEMETERY (Near Belk) D. Cook - B. Mar. 12, 1842 - D. May 18, 1915 - C.U.V. - 1861 - 1865; B. T. Terry - Co. C. 35 Miss. Inf. C.S.A.; Daniel L. Carmack - Co. F. 33 Tenn. Inf. C.S.A.

OAK GROVE METHODIST CHURCH CEMETERY (South of U.S. 43 near Stough) -- Joseph A. Lane - Co. 26 Ala. Inf. C.S.A.; James Amos Spiller - Burkette Ala. G.D.S. - C.S.A.; Enoch Kizzire - Co. H. 41 Ala. Inf. - C.S.A.

SHADY GROVE BAPTIST CHURCH CEMETERY (West of U.S. 43 just south of Berry Turnoff) -- Mus G. R. Tyner - Freeman's Co. Ala. Prison Guard - C.S.A.

SHADY GROVE NAZARENE CHURCH CEMETERY (East of Bluff Road) -- Thomas C. Roberts - Co. H. 5 Ala. Cav. C.S.A.; Henry A. Reese - Co. E. 26 Ala. Inf. C.S.A.

BERRY CITY PUBLIC CEMETERY (In Berry) -- A. J. Hocutt - Haskin's Btry.

Miss. L. Arty. - C.S.A; William P. Earnest - Co. T. 32 Ala. Inf. - C.S.A.; J. R. Stephens - B. June 8, 1845 - D. Oct. 26, 1928 - C.S.A.

OLD TABERNACLE CHURCH CEMETERY (Near Berry) -- Ord. Sgt. Joseph Fondren Co. A. 9 Ala. Cav. - C.S.A.

PANTER FAMILY CEMETERY (Near Pea Ridge) -- Jasper Whitley - Co. A. 1st Ala. Cav. C.S.A.

ENIS FAMILY CEMETERY (South of Townley Road) -- James H. Sawyer - Co. A. 26 Regt. Ala. Inf. C.S.A. - B. 1830 - D. 1904; Andrew J. Hendon - Co. D. 4 Regt. Ala. Cav. - C.S.A. - B. 1829 - D. 1889.

STUDDARD'S CROSS ROADS BAPTIST CHURCH CEMETERY (At Studdard's Cross Roads) Nah'l Studard - Co. A. 1st Ala. Cav. C.S.A.; Noah Parris - Co. L. 1st Ala. Cav. C.S.A.; Solomon Castleberry - Co. E. 1st Ala. Cav. C.S.A.

PLEASANT GROVE BAPTIST CHURCH CEMETERY (Near Howard Mines on Carbon Hill Road) -- P. C. Johnson - Co. A. 1 Battn. Miss. M.T.D. Rifles - C.S.A.; M. L. Johnson - Co. L. 1 Ala. Cav. - C.S.A.; John A. Myers - Co. G. 1 Ala. Cav. C.S.A.

CEDAR GROVE COMMUNITY CHURCH CEMETERY (South of Townley Road) -- Henry Brasher - Co. A. 26 Ala. Inf. - C.S.A. - B. Apr. 24, 1831 - D. Apr. 6, 1903; Robert Taylor - Co. L. 28 Ala. Inf. - B. Dec. 15, 1840 - D. Jan. 11, 1915.

OLD UNION PRIMITIVE BAPTIST CHURCH CEMETERY (On Bluff & Guin Road) -- Elijah Cook - Co. I. 44 Ga. Inf. C.S.A.

STEWART FAMILY CEMETERY (Off Winfield HiWay U.S. 43) --W. F. M. Harbin - Co. I. 8 Ala. Cav. C.S.A.; Corpl. J. A. Harbin - Co. B. 10 Ala. Cav. C.S.A.

ROBERTSON FAMILY CEMETERY (In Fayette) -- John B. Sanford - B. Feb. 19, 1844 - D. Oct. 29, 1898 - C.S.A.

CHAPEL HILL BAPTIST CHURCH CEMETERY (Off west side of Gordo Road near Ashcraft Corner) -- James H. Howard - Co. A. 19 Ala. Inf. C.S.A.; T. C. Robinson - Co. G. 41 Ala. Inf. C.S.A.; John L. Smith - Co. A. 41 Ala. Inf. C.S.A.; Gus Daniels - Co. I. Ky. Cav. C.S.A.; S. J. Richardson - Co. H. 6 Miss. Cav. C.S.A.

OWENS FAMILY CEMETERY (Near Oak Ridge Baptist Church - off Gordo Road) -- John Shade Owens - Co. I. 8 Ala. Cal. C.S.A.

OLD NEW BETHEL BAPTIST CHURCH CEMETERY (Near Belk) -- Robert Moore - Co. C. 26 Ala. Inf. C.S.A.; Louis Williams - Co. B. 41 Ala. Inf. C.S.A.

MT. PLEASANT BAPTIST CHURCH CEMETERY (West off State Lake Road) -- Leonard Kizzire - Co. H. 41 Ala. Inf. C.S.A.; Daniel Gray - Co. D. 36 Ala. Inf. C.S.A.; Mark E. Stillman - Co. K. 26 Ala. Inf. C.S.A.; John Anders South - Co. H. 41 Ala. Inf. C.S.A.; John R. Sanford - Co. H. 41 Ala. Inf. C.S.A.; Wly White - Co. B. 18 Ala. Inf. C.S.A.; Alexander Kizziah - Co. E. 13 Ala. Partisan Rangers - C.S.A.; James J. Farquhar - Co. H. 41 Ala. Inf. C.S.A. - B. Oct. 9, 1844 - D. ___ 21, 1864; A. J. Farquhar - Co. A. 26 Ala. Inf. C.S.A. B. Apr. 25, 1838 - D. Dec. 23, 1860; Thomas J. Griffin - Co. F. 41 Ala. Inf. C.S.A.; John B. Gardner - Co. H. 41 Ala. Inf. C.S.A.; Jesse G. Gardner - Co. H. 41 Ala. Inf. C.S.A.; Charley M. Beard - Co. C. 41 Tenn. Inf. C.S.A.

WHITE SPRINGS CHURCH CEMETERY (East of Winfield Road U.S. 43) -- J. V. Mills - Co. H. 26 Ala. Inf. C.S.A.

BROTHERTON FAMILY CEMETERY (West of Newtonville Road) -- Frank A. Brotherton - B. 1840 - D. 1908 - C.S.A.

SAVAGE FAMILY CEMETERY (West of Newtonville Road) -- Zack Savage - B. Nov. 12, 1847 - D. June 1, 1910 - C.S.A.

NEW RIVER CHURCH OF CHRIST CEMETERY (On Carbon Hill Road) -- Hiram Hyde Co. F. 38 Ala. Inf. C.S.A.

NEW RIVER BAPTIST CHURCH CEMETERY (On Carbon Hill Road) -- J. M. Wake-

field - Co. K, 4 Ala. Cav. C.S.A. - B. Apr. 12, 1846 - D. Aug. 8, 1920.
   JOHNSON FAMILY CEMETERY (Between Carbon Hill Road & Townley Road) -- Corpal R. G. Johnson - Co. L. 12t Ala. Cav. C.S.A.
   MORRIS FAMILY CEMETERY (Between Carbon Hill Road & Marion Co. Line) -- Wm. H. McCollough - Co. I. 26 Ala. Inf. C.S.A. - B. Aug. 31, 1840 - D. Aug. 25, 1911.
   HOPEWELL BAPTIST or ROSEHILL or HEGGARD CEMETERY (North of Concord and Ettica Road) Peter Vick - Killed in the C.S.A. at Dalton, Ga. Feb. 25, 1864 - 30 Yrs.
   MONTGOMERY or KIMBRELL or WILLIAMSON FAMILY CEMETERY (West of U.S. 43 below Berry Turnoff) James V. Montgomery - Co. G. 8 Cav. - C.S.A.
   PLEASANT HILL METHODIST CHURCH CEMETERY (North of Berry Highway) -- R. W. Pinion - Co. I. 8 Ala. Cav. - C.S.A.; Thomas J. Davis - Co. F. 41 Ala. Inf. C.S.A.; David H. Stanley - Co. F. 38 Ala. Inf. C.S.A.; William P. Berry - Co. F. 38 Ala. Inf. C.S.A.; Reuben Davis - Co. I. 26 Ala. Inf. C.S.A.
   JINKINS FAMILY CEMETERY (Near Pea Ridge) -- L. W. Jinkins - B. Sept. 16, 1822 - D. Jan. 20, 1863 - C.S.A.
   PEA RIDGE METHODIST CHURCH CEMETERY (In Pea Ridge) -- David Mitchell - Tarrant's Batry. Ala. Lt. Arty. - C.S.A.; George W. Bowen - Co. K. 36 Ala. Inf. C.S.A.
   MT. WILLIAM CHURCH CEMETERY (Northern part of county - off Bluff Road) -- Elisha D. Warren - Co. H. 5 Ala. Cav. - C.S.A.
   BRANYON FAMILY CEMETERY (North of Belk) -- John J. Branyon - Co. B. 41 Ala. Inf. C.S.A.
   MOORE FAMILY CEMETERY (Edge of Lamar Co., near Belk) -- Wm. H. Moore - B. May 15, 1840 - D. Nov. 11, 1922 - 82 Yrs. 5 Mo. 26 Days. - C.S.A.
   HARMONY GROVE BAPTIST CHURCH CEMETERY (South of Winfield just in Fayette County) -- J. W. Maddox - 27 Ga. Inf. C.S.A. - B. Dec. 22, 1841 - D. Jan. 5, 1910; Henry W. Weeks - B. Dec. 17, 1847 - D. Mar. 17, 1927 - C.S.A.
   OLD SHEPHERD CHURCH CEMETERY (Near Newtonville) -- William M. Johnson - Co. G. 41 Ala. Inf. - C.S.A.; LaFayette McCool - Co. B. 41 Ala. Inf. C.S.A.
   WESLEY CHAPEL METHODIST CHURCH CEMETERY (Near Picken's Co. Line) -- N.P. Richardson - B. Dec. 21, 1843 - D. Jan. 10, 1929 - C.S.A.
   OLD WESLEY CHAPEL METHODIST CHURCH CEMETERY (Near Picken's Co. Line) -- Joel Wilson - B. Sept. 5, 1838 - D. May 2, 1919 - Co. B. 41 Inf. Ala. C.S.A.
   SANDERS FAMILY CEMETERY (West off Gordo Road) -- Harvey M. Sanders - Co. G. 41 Ala. Inf. C.S.A.; John T. Sanders - Co. B. Ala. Cav. C.S.A.
   (This cemetery record is the result of checking 129 cemeteries in Fayette County, Ala. Checked between July 1958 and April 1959 by Herbert M. & Jeanie Patterson Newell)

   To conclude the data pertaining to the Civil War and how it affected Fayette County, we include the following article taken from the "Northwest Alabamian", the Thursday edition, December 15, 1932 -- "More About the War Between The States" - by M. L. Coons ...
   " A list of Muster Roll of Company A. 26th Alabama Regiment, Infantry - from Fayette County in the War Between the States, 1861 - 1865. As remembered by Enoch M. Van Diver, Capt. Wm. Berry, 1st. Sgt. James H. Hyde, 2nd Sgt. Joseph A. Lane, Sr., Sgt. James C. Yerby and A. P. Dodds.
   James H. Moore, Capt. resigned July 1862 and afterwards became Capt. of Cavalry Company. Enoch M. Van Diver, 1st. Lt. promoted to Capt. July 1862; wounded May 3rd at Battle of Chancellorsville, Va.; permanently retired and assigned to light duty. Samuel P. Morrow, 2nd Lt. resigned and joined Caval-

ry Co. James A. Lindsey, 3rd. Lt. wounded, captured and taken prisoner on Johnson's Island and kept until surrender.

William Berry, 1st. Sgt.; J. H. Hyde, 2nd Sgt.; Wiley Enis, 3rd Sgt.; Harvey Stewart, 4th Sgt.; George W. Lane, 5th Sgt.; Ed Ayers, 1st. Cpl.; and Harvey Stewart, 2nd Cpl.

List alphabetically arranged: Isaac N. Autrey, promoted to teamster. Joel Appling, died of smallpox in 1863. Joe Anthony. Ed Ayers, wounded in battle. Marion Black. William Berry, 1st. Sgt., wounded May 3rd 1863 in Battle at Chancellorsville, Va. William G. Baker, wounded in Battle at Sharpsburg, Md. J. Newton Baker. J. H. Brasher, discharged in 1862. Henry Brasher, wounded. John T. Berry. Robert Crowley. William Caraway, died July 1862 at Richmond, Va., Castleberry. Thomas Carter, killed at Malvern Hill, July 1st, 1862. George W. Cotton. Rufus Durrett, promoted to 3rd Lt. in Va. Lost his arm in Nashville Battle. Elisha Dyer, died in Virginia. Bud Dyer, died in Virginia. A. P. Dodds, detailed for teamster in A. P. Hill's for capturing wagon and team. John Dodds. Benjamin Dennis. Asburry, Dodds. Robert Dodds, died in Abbington, Va. John Edmons, lost in battle of Gettysburg. Alva Ellis, lost in battle of Gettysburg. Viley Enis, wounded near Atlanta, Ga. Charles Fortenberry, killed in Battle of South Mountain, Md. William Fullerton, died at Yorktown in 1862, was Sgt. Robert Fullerton, honorably discharged on account of old age. Bud Farquhar. Stephen Farquhar. Thomas Gladden, wounded in Battle of Malvern Hill, Va. and never heard of anymore. James Going, killed at Kennisaw Mountain, Ga. James Gurley, died in Va. in June or July 1862. W. A. Hyde, 1st. Lt. Aug. 1862. J. H. Hyde, 2nd. Lt. wounded in Battle of Malvern Hill, July 1862, honorably discharged. J. L. Harbin. George Harbin, died in Va. during Yorktown seige. John Harbin. Wilmington Hill, killed in Battle of South Mountain, Md. Matt Howton, served during the war, unhurt. David Howton. George Howton, died in Yorktown siege. Willis Howton. Elijah Howton. Samuel Jones, captured and died in prison. William Johnson, died with measles in Va. John Kelley, lost his leg in Battle of Peachtree Creek, Atlanta, Ga. Absolom Kelley, killed in Battle of So. Mountain, Md. William Lindsey, promoted to Capt. Co. I. Lost his arm in Battle of Franklin, Tenn. and died. John Lane, wounded in Battle of Malvern Hill, died in Atlanta, Ga. Simeon Lane, shot through the breast, ball coming out his back, returned and served remainder of war. Joe A. Lane, wounded by explosion of shell at Atlanta, Ga., recovered and served during remainder of war. Cpl. George W. Lane. D. T. Miles, died in Richmond, Va. Carson Moore, killed in Battle of So. Mountain, Md. Jeff Melton, died in Richmond, Va. Stephen McGuinnes, wounded in Battle and honorably discharged. Joe Nelmus. Murray Norman, died in Tuscaloosa, Ala. William Nelson, detailed guard for quartermaster and died in Va. William Owing, wounded. Lewis Olive. Joe Pryor. John Pickle. Alfred Peters, shot in arm at Sharpsburg, Md. and permanently discharged. John Palmer. Alexander Ray, died in Va. Ben F. Stillman, arm shot off in June, 1862 in Seven Day Battle and permanently discharged. Sid. B. Smith, promoted to Capt. Co. E. Joe Stewart. James Sawyer. Harvey Stewart, wounded near Atlanta, Ga. Nathan Threat. G. R. Tyner. Ben Townsend, died in Va. Abe Vick, died with measles in Tuscumbia, Ala. in 1861. Wilson Vansant. James S. Van Diver, Sgt. Major, honorably discharged on account physical disability. E. M. Van Diver, 1st. Lt. promoted to Capt. July 1862, wounded May 3, at Chancellorsville, Va., permanently retired and assigned to light duty. Chris Wright, killed in Tennessee Battle. Thomas Welch, wounded in Battle of Malvern Hill, in hand and thigh. Stephen Wright killed in battle of Tennessee. John Wheeler, killed in Battle of Fredericksburg, Va. Samuel Walters, killed at Chancellorsville, Va. May 2, 1862. John A. Welch, wounded in Battle of Chancellorsville, Va. May 3, 1863 and transferred to cavalry. J. W. White. John Wiley. J. C. Yerby, slightly wounded at Gettysburg, Pa. and served to end of war. I. S. Yerby, slightly wounded at Gettysburg, Pa. and served to end of ear. ____ Yerby, killed in Battle of Seven Pines.

There are listed above, 97 men of Co. A. 26th Ala. Regiment (Infantry) out of a possible 100, the number constituting a full company. Out of this number 11 were killed in battle - 23 died from wounds and diseases, 14 seriously wounded, together with 3 missing and never heard from.

Of the several hundred leaving Fayette County which included Lamar County at that time, to engage in the war between the states, only 12 are alive at this time (Dec. 6, 1932) in the two counties; 7 i. Lamar County and 5 in Fayette County.

The 7 in Lamar County are: Daniel Greer, Sulligent, Rt.; John W. Ward, Vernon, Rt. 1; R. M. Baird, Melbourne, Rt. 1; B. F. Duncan, Millport; E. Holliman, Millport; T. J. Spruill, Millport, Rt. 1; and F. M. Varnon, Millport.

The 5 in Fayette County are: W. M. Bell; H. T. Berry; Enoch Kizzire; Thomas Ray and V. D. Smith." . . . .

In a later edition -- Mr. Coons writes: "Mr. I. W. White sends me the following names of war veterans whom he says had not been listed as engaging in the war between the states.

J. W. White, Co. A. 26th Ala.; Hiram Meadows; Alexander Downs; Avery Kidd; Jeptha Hollingsworth; John Hollingsworth; Henry Hollingsworth; James Hollingsworth; Newton Ford; Jid Smith; George Reynolds; Matthew Roberts; Virgil Wimberley; Louis Winberlye; Daniel Arnold; Joe Arnold; and William Arnold.

One among many of the bloody battles fought by Fayette County soldiers was the 7 day's fight at Frazier's Farm. Company I. 11th Ala. Regiment being the first Company to leave the county was in that battle.

This particular battle, which proved so disastrous to the Company was fought on the 30th day of June 1862 in which 11 Fayette County soldiers were killed and many wounded. Among the killed were: Capt. Stephen E. Bell; and John Bell, brothers of Judge H. M. Bell.

CHAPTER VI

NEWSPAPERS, LIBRARY AND RADIO

NEWSPAPERS OF FAYETTE COUNTY -- Sometime in the Fall of 1849 in the little village of Fayette Court House, the seat of justice, known as "Old Town" the first newspaper on Fayette County soil had its birth. It was in the form of one sheet printed from a font of battered type, on a crude wooden press, of the flat bottom variety operated by muscular power. Emblazoned over its columns were the words, "The Fayette Banner". It was edited by Messers. Thomas and Hill. A copy of the Fayette Journal, dated July, 1887, traces its date back to the year 1849 through its volume numbers.

Three years after its establishment, R. Allen Smith, Esq. purchased the Banner from Messers. Thomas and Hill and changed the name of the publication to The Fayette Democrat, under which name it went out to the public, until after the Civil War.

Having various owners and editors, and suffering many different degrees of misfortune the Democrat was succeeded by "The Fayette Watchman", "The Fayette Journal", respectively retaining the name of "The Journal" until 1881.

Succeeding The Journal, in 1881, The Fayette Sentinel was established, continuing its publication in Old Town of Fayette Court House as it was then, until a very short time after the removal of the Court House to its present site. After the removal of the plant from Fayette Court House to Fayette, the paper continued under the name of "The Sentinel", until Jan. 7, 1899, at which time the name was changed to "The Fayette Tribune".

In 1900, S. H. Morris, publisher of the Berry paper, "Berry Recorder" moved to Fayette Courthouse and renamed his publication the Fayette Banner. This was the first real newspaper opposition and on Oct. 3, 1900, "The Tribune" disposed of its plant, good-will and subscription list to The Banner and ceased to operate.

M. Brotherton, T. A. Wilson and Wallace P. Pruitt became the publishers in 1906. The paper was purchased by J. W. Ayres, Sr. in 1925 and kept by him until 1941 when he sold it to Mr. G. Gunter. A few weeks later Gunter sold the paper to Paul Corwin who was at that time, publishing The Northwest Alabamian.

The Northwest Alabamian was established in 1925, when T. M. Peters, Jr. of Covin, Dr. T. M. Peters and Eugene Wilson began its publication. Five years later it was sold to Robert F. Peters and Bill Ford. Sometime after this, Paul Corwin, Jimmy Faulkner and Thurston Faulkner bought the Northwest Alabamian.

The Northwest Alabamian and The Banner consolidated when Jay Thornton of Haleyville, purchased the papers in 1942. O. C. Morgan was the editor of the paper until November 1953 when the Warrior Printing Co. began publishing it, as The Fayette County Times.

The Warrior Printing Co. owned by O. C. Anders, Cullen Morgan, Ed Pierce

and Ec. Bounds began publishing the paper Nov. 1, 1953. In Sept. 1958, Lewis
Mitchell bought the paper and is the present editor and publisher. (1959)

FAYETTE COUNTY MEMORIAL LIBRARY -- From a small room in the courthouse to a
modern brick building and a bookmobile is a long step, but that is the story
of the Fayette Library.

The Progress Club, first a literary organization, was formed by a group
of Fayette Women in 1921 with the establishment of a library as one of their
first objectives. It was 1922, however, before the library came into existence in the courthouse. It was made up largely of donations and club members
voluntarily kept it in operation.

Steady work by the club soon produced a small frame building that was
moved to the lot behind the Presbyterian Church and a small income allowing
them to employ a woman to keep the library open two days a week. The building was redecorated and the city paid the cost of its lights. After the
frame building became too dilapidated to use any longer, the books were moved to several different locations before finally being placed in the Wright-
Smith Building. First they went to the basement of the Welfare Building, but
it was too damp there so they were placed in two rooms on the second floor of
the First National Bank Building where they stayed until being moved to the
Wright-Smith Building in February 1946.

Library service was increased to include the entire county in 1942, when
the project was turned over to the county and to the Works Progress Administration. The W.P.A. paid the salary of a trained librarian and the nine
assistants who classified and catalogued the books and stations were put into
operation in the various sections of the county with the additional help of
the Public Library Service, which furnished more books.

When the Library Project was closed in May, 1943, the librarian's salary
was assumed by the county with the city still responsible for heat, lights,
and rent of the quarters.

The county service was increased and put on a much more efficient basis
in 1944, when the club purchased a World War I Army Ambulance and the County
Board of Education converted it into a rolling library or bookmobile. The
bookmobile went into operation in Sept. 1945, servicing the 18 schools and
volunteer stations, in homes exchanging their books every three weeks. During the summer months small communities were visited regularly by the bookmobile and people could borrow books by meeting it.

The bookmobile was wrecked in April, 1948, and this service was discontinued until January, 1949. when the Board of Education converted a discarded
schoolbus and began regular service again.

After the library was moved into the Wright-Smith Building in 1946, it
grew steadily

The lovely Fayette County Memorial Library Building on Temple Avenue was
completed and dedicated in 1956. Many new and rare books are being added to
the fine collection regularly.

RADIO STATION W. W. W. F. - FAYETTE -- On September 3, 1949, Fayette's Radio
Station W. W. W. F. became a reality and the air-waves hummed with the music
and voices originating in the studio on the Tuscaloosa Highway just beyond
the Sipsey River.

The Bankhead Broadcasting Company began building the studio and the transmitter for Radio Station W.W.W.F. in the spring of 1949. This station broad-
casts in the daytime only with a frequency of 990.

The Studios were moved from the first location on Highway 43 to 505 No. Temple Avenue, in the City of Fayette on November 16, 1956. The transmitter is still located on the Tuscaloosa Highway No. 43.

Mr. Jack Black came here in 1949 as the manager of the station and he has helped to make the station a great asset to Fayette County.

CHAPTER VII

EDUCATION

FAYETTE COUNTY'S EARLY EDUCATION -- Prior to the year 1854, Alabama had no superintendent of education, not only none in the different counties, but none in the State. The rural schools before that time, and for many years after, were private and taught in private homes, or in rough hewn log houses built for school purposes. The houses were equipped with seats of split logs, with the flat side up, these seats had four peg legs and were built so high that the feet of the smaller pupils dangled several inches above the floor. The floors for the building were made from split timbers with the top side hewn smooth and flat. The house had only one door and the windows were small holes cut in the walls with solid shutters that were made to slide for either opening or closing.

For heat, a large stick and dirt chimney was built in one end of the one room school house, so wide and deep that a great many of the children could stand in the jams of the fire-place. The fuel for these huge fire-places was furnished from the near-by forest, by the patrons, and it was the duty of the larger boys to cut the wood into the proper length and keep the fire burning.

The school house was usually located near some spring, regardless of its convenience to the roads and paths were cut from the homes of the patrons, radiating in every direction from the school house, these paths frequently reaching a distance of three or four miles.

There was a hole bored in the wall, usually on the right hand side of the door, and in that auger hole was kept a forked stick about eight inches long, so that when a child wished to "go out" between recess and play time he did not ask permission of the teacher, but carried the stick out and on his return placed it back in the hole.

These schools were usually taught during the winter and continued for two or three months, and at times one or two months in the summer after the crops were "laid-by". The teachers of these schools were sometimes referred to as "old field teachers" and their equipment consisted mostly of a big hickory stick which was used to beat on the door to call the pupils to "books" and in a convenient place there was a good supply of seasoned switches which were used on occasions of the least infraction of the rules of the teacher.

The teacher rarely had a definite place to board, but divided his time among the patrons, stopping a week with each one. The patrons and the children were always happy when it came their turn to entertain the teacher for a whole week.

In these schools of long ago the boys had as their sport and past time, a game of "townball" from which evolved the modern, national game of baseball. Other games were "skinning the cat", shinning the pole, foot races, wrestling and marble playing. The amusements for the girls were jumping the rope, playing base, hide and seek, and "Pharoah's horses". The Friday afternoons were spent in "spelling bees" and speech making.

The teacher in those old time schools, for the last lesson for the day, had the entire school lined up before him for reciting the multiplication table in a song, to the tune of "Yankee Doodle" with the fifth line for the chorus, beginning with "five times five are twenty-five and five times six are thirty", on to the last to five times twelve are sixty, then back to the second line until the entire multiplication table was gone over.

Special schools in which grammar, geography, arithmetic, writing and other subjects were taught in each respective school were not an uncommon thing. The students in geography became so efficient that they could, in a sing-song voice, repeat the names of every river, mountain, lake, sea, ocean and the names of all the states in the United States.

These early teachers took pride in teaching their pupils how to spell correctly, and the word given from the dictionary not only had to be spelled correctly, but the definition of the word given had to be stated, otherwise the one who missed was "turned down". Pride was also taken in teaching the pupil to write, and some of the records on file in the court houses of the State show writing that is as beautiful as script, and can be read as easily as the typewritten page of today.

This brief description of the school of the progenitors of this middle-age and young generation, who are housed in buildings better than those occupied by the kings of old, with every convenience to make the acquisition of an education pleasant, makes it hard to realize that these are facts from the lives of the older people of Fayette County in the years gone by.

FAYETTE COUNTY'S SUPERINTENDENTS OF EDUCATION -- The first County Superintendent of Education for Fayette County was selected in 1856, two years after the State's first Superintendent took charge of the funds appropriated by the general assembly for public school purposes. A list of the names of all the County Superintendents of Education who have served the county from that time to the present follows:

1856 - James Middleton; 1862 - N. A Suggs; 1867 - James S. Van Diver; 1868 - T. W Dodson; 1871 - B. F. Peters; 1877 - B. F. Peters; 1881 - A. M. Nuckols; 1883 - A. M. Nuckols; 1884 - A. M. Nuckols; 1886 - A. M. Nuckols; 1888 - A. M Nuckols; 1890 - Chelcy M. South; 1892 - J. N. Collins; 1894 - J. N. Collins; 1896 - J. N Collins; 1898 - Andrew J. Treadaway; 1900 - Andrew J. Treadaway; 1902 - Ben E. Jones (Appointed); 1902 - J. T. Lucas; 1904 - J. W. Barnard; 1908 - J. Alexander Smith, Sr.; 1912 - J. Alexander Smith, Sr.; 1916 - Dan W. Berry; 1918 - R. L. Reaves; 1919 - R. L. Reaves; 1921 - Z. D. Vick; 1923 - J. A. Kuykendall; 1925 - J. A. Kuykendall; 1927 - J. A. Kuykendall; 1928 - B. L. Balch; 1930 - B. L. Balch; 1938 - B. F. Harkins; 1945 - Clyde C. Cargile; 1953 - Paul W. Colburn; and 1959 - Paul W. Colburn.

SCHOOLS OF FAYETTE COUNTY -- There are three high schools in the county, Fayette, Berry and Hubbertville. Transportation in the steel-bodied buses, owned and operated by the county, is furnished for all children in the rural districts. Transportation and all other facilities of the schools are equal for the colored children as well as for the white children.

There are cafeterias in most of the schools in the county giving all the children in these schools access to a hot lunch every day.

To give a glance at the number of rural schools before they were consolidated, we give the following census taken by the Superintendent of Education's office in the year 1924. We are listing the names as they were copied from that office.

Shady Grove, Malloy, Glen Allen, Chapel Hill, Morris Hill, Mallet Hill, Gumbud, Bankston, Covin, Center Point, Wesley Chapel, Pea Ridge, Unity, Bethel, Concord, Hankins, Eldridge, Gravie Hill, Blue Wanter, Fayette, Sizemore, Pilgrim, Olive, Mt. Pleasant, Union, Hubbertville, Sipsey Valley, Smith, New River, Boley, Fowler, Cedargrove, Center #20, Pleasant Grove, Oppossomtrot, Studdard's Cross Roads, Johnsons, Newtonville, Bluff Springs, Bluff, Sulphur Springs, Flat Too, Ashcraft, New Chapel, Spring Hill, Berry Grammar, Pleasant Hill, Siloam, Fayette Grammar, Oak Ridge, Salem, Bethlehem, Pine Grove, Bethabara, Oak Grove, Rocky Hill, Clover Hill, Alta, Deavours, Collins, Belk, Yellow Jacket, and Mulberry Hollow.

Others listed in 1917 (not listed above) are as follows: Wayside - Holt, Providence, Wilson's, Ballard, Hickory Rock, Boxes Creek, Mars Hill, Simmons and Wolf Creek.

Schools that have existed and some still in operation are given with a sketch of the school. These sketches are arranged in alphabetical order.

ALABAMA CHRISTIAN COLLEGE, BERRY, ALABAMA -- (The following is quoted from an article by Mr. Hal P. McDonald.)

"The original and first Alabama Christian College was promoted, founded and opened for work in 1912. This school was conceived, financed and built by members of the Churches of Christ and friends of Christian education in this section of Alabama that the Bible might have prime place in the educational and practical life of the school.

This school was located on a choice eight acre campus in the very heart of the little town of Berry, the Beautiful. Berry is midway between Birmingham and Columbus, Miss., about sixty miles from either, on the Southern Railway, at which time there were four passengers trains daily. Berry is the highest point between these two fine cities, flanked by the foothills of the Great Appalachian Mountain System, overlooking the greatest mineral and mining region of the great and beautiful Southland. Near the center of this eight acre campus stood the two story, brick veneer college building with its unique, sweet tolling bell of some 2,300 pounds weight, the gift of Grandma Shepherd."

The teachers for Alabama Christian College are listed through 1921, when the school was taken over by the Berry High School.

1912 - 1913 - G. A. Dunn, Sr., Pres., Addie Bailey, Robert Snow. 1913 - 1914 - G. A. Dunn, Sr., Pres., Mrs. J. B. Nelson, S. I. Jones, Minnie Hammon, J. B. Nelson and Louise Dasher. 1914 - 1915 - G. A. Dunn, Sr., Pres., Miss Phillips, S. I. Jones, J. B. Nelson, Miss Smith, Mrs. J. B. Nelson. 1915 - 1916 - Paul Hanlin, Pres., Ruth Jordon, Mrs. Paul Hanlin, S. I. Jones, Emilie Burleson, Alice Ezzell. 1916 - 1917 - Hal P. McDonald, Pres., Miss Ruth Hawk, R. B. Clements, Mrs. Hal. P. McDonald, A. M. Scott and Miss Dorothy Plunk, Librarian. Teachers for 1917 through 1921 - an average of six per year were -- Hal P. McDonald, Pres., Cecil L. Simpson, Haley Rainwater, Elbert Deason, Jane Head, Virgie Johnson, Edna Alsop, Dovie Johnson, Ira Underwood, Lois Johnson (music teacher), Ella Smith, Addie Bailey, Kate Terry, Melva Deason, Florence Underwood, Dorothy Plunk, Bessie Reeves, Sister Aberdeen (librarian), Annie Mae Holliday and Cathern Logan (librarian).

Trustees of the Alabama Christian College were -- J. C. Shepherd, John Tomlin, Mose P. Bailey, and C. C. Dobbs.

BANKSTON SCHOOL -- The first school was built on the hill overlooking Bank-

ston about 1900. It was a two teacher school with a Mr. Adkins and a Miss Swinwood as the first teachers. Later a larger building was needed and a four room school building was erected neat the present site of Bankston.
   In 1937 the P. W. A. labor built the present ten room building and in 1940 the lunch program was started. To begin with, the cooking was done in a small coal house behind the main school building, and in 1941 the kitchen and dining rooms were added.
   From 1943 to 1949, Bankston employed ten teachers, but presently there are only six teachers. Following is a list of some of those who have taught at the Bankston school: ____ Windham, ____ Norton, Ada Mae White, T. L. Harbin, Beulah Vick, J. O. Belk, A. B. Moore, Willis May, Morris Lewis, Zora Prater, Mollie Smith, Georgia Nunn, ____ Phillips, J. D. Turner, and Charles J. Alexander, and his wife, Mrs. Alexander.
   Mr. Charles J. Alexander has been the principal of Bankston School since 1941.

BERRY HIGH SCHOOL and ELEMENTARY SCHOOL -- In the spring of 1923, ten students received the first diplomas issued from Berry High School. These students attended school in the old Christian College Building. In the fall of 1933 the old Christian College burned. The school year was finished in the Masonic Hall and the Churches. By the fall of 1935 the new building was ready for use. Later additions to the building were made in 1936 and 1942. In 1936 the Vocational Building was completed and in early 1937 the Teacherage was finished.
   The Berry Elementary School burned in 1954 and a new building was completed in 1956.
   While still known as Alabama Christian College the teachers were -- 1918 - 1919 - Mr. Clardy, Principal, Miss Amanda Moore, Mrs. Mattie Griffin, Mrs. Hester McCracken, and Mrs. Emilie Cannon. 1919 - 1920 - Mr. Steeley, Prin., Floyd Johnson, Mrs. Emilie Cannon and Miss Hester McCracken.
   Following is listed the faculty and the graduating class for each year since 1923, including the faculty of the Elementary School:
1922 - 1923 High School Faculty: C. R. Weldon, Prin., Mr. Scofield, Prin. (replaced Mr. Weldon), Miss Blake Barfield, Mr. R. C. Christopher (coach), Miss Nell Miller, and Miss Vera Ray. Graduating Class; Eunice Ausbon, Jessie Belle Boone, Charlie Cole, Fletcher Cornelius, John Griffin, Sarah Griffin, Valzie Hudson, Lucille Jenkins, Evie Johns, and Clifton Jones. Elementary Teachers: Miss Ada Griffin, Miss Ann Martin, Mrs. Mary Peterson, and Miss Beulah Vick.
1923 - 1924 - High School Faculty: W. S. McLeod, Prin., Hugh Barfield, Miss Lilly Burleson, R. C. Christopher, Neil Miller, and Tom Treadaway. Graduating Class: Frederic Carl Collins, Vera Dunn, Para Lee Evans, Melvin Hall, George Hardwick, Maxwell Johnson, Attie Belle Kimbrell, Gordon Kimbrell, William Floyd Nelson, Julian Shepherd, Sarah Beatrice Simpson, Olin Traweek, and Florence Yerby. Elementary Teachers: Mrs. W. S McLeod, Prin., Mrs. Emilie Cannon, Miss Para Lee Evans, Miss Estelle Farris and Miss Ann Jones.
1924 - 1925 - High School Faculty: G. W. Yarbrough, Prin., Hugh Barfield, Miss Lilly Burleson, Miss Eleanor Chandler, R. C. Christopher, and Neil Miller. Graduating Class: Wilford Berry, Henry Christopher, Robert Corry, Dolphus Cotton, Murrial Crowley, Otha Garrard, Gladys Gibson, Meryl Hall, Bill Holder, Lena Jones, Logan Madison, Clyde Patton, Essie Pendley, Leon Studdard, and Velma Traweek. Elementary Teachers: J. D. Dendy, Prin.,

Mrs. Emilie Cannon, Miss Para Lee Evans, Miss Mabel Mayfield, and Miss Eunice Osborn.

1925 - 1926 - High School Faculty: G. W. Yarbrough, Prin., Hugh Barfield, Miss Lily Burleson, Miss Eleanor Chandler, Herbert Ford, and Mrs. Thelma Yarbrough. Graduating Class: Sherman Bolton, Miriam Cannon, Harold Clardy, Estelle Cole, Mary Davis, Leland Dobbs, Barna Dunn, Ester Earnest, Ora Fowler, Floyd Handley, Delmer Hocutt, Myra Johns, Nina Loyal Johns, Lester Key, Bruce Lint, Treavour Shook, Cecil Studdard, Kermit Studdard, Oscar Tearce, Kolan L. Vick, and Leo Williams. Elementary Teachers: J. S. Bobo, Prin., Miss Brown, Mrs. Emilie Cannon, Miss Para Lee Evans and Miss Eunice Osburn.

1926 - 1927 - High School Faculty: George W. Yarbrough, Prin., Miss Lily Burleson, Hugh Barfield, Herbert Ford, Miss Ruby Little, Miss Marie Turner, and Mrs. Thelma Yarbrough. Graduating Class: Richard Cornelius, Trilla Davis, Spurgeon Deavours, Gwendolyn Hall, Eula Hudson, Fred Johnson, Travis Kimbrell, Mildred LaGrone, Daniel McCain, Joe Moore, Howard D. Patton, Floyd Rutledge, Raymond Shook, Kermit Strickland, Houston Studdard, Jim Studdard, Cleophus Taggart and Nell Tucker. Elementary Teachers: J. S. Bobo, Prin., Mrs. Emilie Cannon, Miss Para Lee Evans, Miss Ora Hollingsworth, and Miss Velma Traweek.

1927 - 1928 - High School Faculty: G. W. Yarbrough, Prin., Miss Lily Burleson, Miss Bess Christian, Miss Mary Howard, Fred McNat, and Miss Frances Parks. Graduating Class - Abilene Berry, Alonzo Clements, Virlia Earnest, Vela Hudson, Paul Johns, Loyd Jones, David Key, Hustis LaGrone, Annette Olive, Burnett Patton, Thurston Shepherd. Elementary Teachers: J. S. Bobo-Prin., Mrs. Emilie Cannon, Miss Para Lee Evans, Miss Ora Hollingsworth, and Miss Velma Traweek.

1928 - 1929 - High School Faculty: George W. Yarbrough, Prin., Hugh Barfield, Miss Mimian Gregg, Fred McNat and Miss Mary Trammell. Graduating Class: Oleta Lois Bagwell, Lowell Austin Barnes, Brack Augustus Cornelius, Susie Louise Cowart, Thelma Dean Crowell, John Boyd Deavours, Paul Conrad Dobbs, Vera Eirline Gilliam, James Woods Griffin, Lylia Mae Hall, Ruby Gordon Hall, Hobson Eugene Hudson, Delma Key, Wyman Otto Kimbrell, Carra Mae Kidd, Rosilie Killingsworth, William Orville McCaleb, Mary Catherine Miller, Lizamae Mouchette, Mildred Ann Moore, Inez Violet Moore, Reba Ethel Shook, Ned Augustus Strickland, Hattie Lou Traweek, George Elton Traweek, and William Theron Vick. Elementary Teachers: J. S. Bobo, Prin., Mrs. Emilie Cannon, Miss Para Lee Evans, Miss Velma Traweek and Mrs. Thelma Yarbrough.

1929 - 1930 - High School Faculty: George W. Yarbrough, Prin., Fred McNat, George Newton, Miss Czarina Peterson, and Mary Trammel. Graduating Class: Ozella Brady, Olon Bagwell, Wyman Crowell, Laura Mae Cannon, Pauline Clements, Blonnie Deavours, Loyal Dunn, Joe Everett, Aulene Falls, Arcaster Kimbrell, Gertrude Kimbrell, Fuller A. Kimbrell, Harold McNees, Willard Sawyer, Mary Bill Studdard, Norman Shook and Oscar West. Elementary Teachers: J. S. Bobo, Prin., Mrs. Emilie Cannon, Miss Para Lee Evans, Miss Rubye Hall, and Miss Annie Bell Doughty.

1930 - 1931 - High School Faculty: George W. Yarbrough, Prin., Fred McNat, George Newton, Miss Czarina Peterson, Mary Trammel and Mrs. Thelma Yarbrough. Graduating Class: William Taft Aldridge, Martha Lou Barnes, Hortense Bagwell, Solon Brady, Nora Blackburn, Cole Berlene, Verna Marie Dobbs, Woodrow William Doughty, Johnnie Major Garrison, Fred Bendie Gibson, Kermit W. Hudson, Raymond Coleman Johnson, Mary Key, Trannie Myrtle Kimbrell, Myrtie Ola Lowry, Aaron Nelson, Lucille Panter, Recia Louise Pinion, Susan Bess Poe, Annie Ray Boyd, Olen Y. Taylor, Maggie Lena Tyner, Ola Rea Williamson, and Christine Willingham. Elementary Teachers: Joe Dearing, Prin., Mrs. Emily Cannon, Miss Annie Belle Doughty, Miss Para Lee Evans and Miss Velma Traweek.

1931 - 1932 - High School Faculty: George W. Yarbrough, Prin., P. M. Barlow, Bill Green, Helen Mitchell and Mrs. G. W. Yarbrough. Graduating Class: Margaret Cole, Emily Cornelius, Jessie Cornelius, Aller Mae Crowell, Audra Davis, Allen Fowler, Vessie Gilliam, Myrtie Gillion, Olen Jones, Thurmon Jones, Wilmer Lowry, Carrie Moore, Sula Moore, Albert Lee Oden, Ormond Simpson, Aline Smith, Lorene Smith, Oline Smith, Gertrude Stewart, Lois Taylor, Avis Traweek, Hermon Westbrook, Bura Whitson and Edith Yerby. Elementary Teachers: Mrs. Emilie Cannon, Prin., Annie Belle Doughty, Para Lee Evans, Vera Gilliam, Inez Hankins and Velma Traweek.

1932 - 1933 - High School Faculty: G. W. Yarbrough, Prin., R. M. Barlow, Bess Christian, Charlie Cole and Mary Lebrons. Graduating Class: Ralph Barnes, Maynell Berry, Melbourne Cannon, Willard Cannon, Aubrey Christian, Wilma Agnas Collins, Mary Davis, Edith Dobbs, Solon Earnest, Johnny Hall, Mayfred Holt, Maynard Holt, Carmen Lollar, Truman McCaleb, Maxine Milliner, Elmer Louise Oline, Truman A. Simpson, Olen Smith, T. C. Smith, Jr., Edith Westbrook, Wimbreth Wright and Phillio Yerby. Elementary Teachers: Mrs. Emilie Cannon, Prin., Miss Martha Lou Barnes, Miss Pauline Clements, Miss Burline Cole, Miss Para Lee Evans, Miss Vera Gilliam, and Miss Velma Traweek.

1933 - 1934 - High School Faculty: George W. Yarbrough, Prin., R. M. Barlow, Miss Grace Bentley, Charlie Cole. Graduating Class: W. S. Able, Florence Adams, Agnes Lorene Bagwell, Percy S. Davis, Eva Lucile Fowler, Hazel Jean Gregg, Millard Key, Felix M. Key, Mamie Zora Kimbrell, Howard H. Lowery, Gladys Moore, Dorthula Moore, Paul Aden Johnson, Clell H. Ray, Jr. George T. Simpson, Alva Dell Simpson, Travis Auldon Smith, Mary Ellen Smith, Edythe Strickland, Myrtle Isabella Tucker, Thomas Millard Woods, and Aster Lee Williamson. Elementary Teachers: Mrs. Emilie Cannon, Martha Lou Barnes, Pauline Clements, Para Lee Evans, Vera Gilliam, Lyla Mae Hall, Mildred LaGrone, Velma Traweek.

1934 - 1935 - High School Faculty: C. P. Vick, Prin., R. M. Barlow, Grace Bentley, Edith Crew, O. P. Richardson. Graduating Class: Jimmie Nell Bagwell, Pansy Berry, John Blackburn, Clara Belle Cole, Duoree Deavours, Lee Davis, Mae Jewell Hocutt, Thelma Griffin, Clara Frances Kimbrell, Carmen Lollar, Gertrude Moore, Jimmy C. Moore, Lehman Nelson, Shelton Pinion, Arnold Poe, Nell Ray, Floyd Shook, Era Smith, Derthia Whitson and Tolbert Yerby. Elementary Teachers: Mrs. Emilie Cannon, Prin., Para Lee Evans, Trannie Kimbrell, Hester McCracken, Loudelle Newton, Velma Traweek, Mrs. C. P. Vick and Theron Vick.

1935 - 1936 - High School Faculty: C. P. Vick, Prin., R. M. Barlow, Miss Edith Crew, Alma Green, and O. P. Richardson. Graduating Class: Shirley Alexander, Verna Mae Bagwell, Willie Frank Boone, Buena Bonner, Ann Carter, Harold Clements, Audra Dorough, Pauline Gibson, Vada Gilliam, R. L. Hamner, Rosalynd Karrh, Wilfred Key, Jeannette Key, Paunelle Lee, Mary Lou Lollar, Ulys Rutledge, James Scrivner, W. T. Simpson, Frank Stiff, Bert Leon Traweek, Eulene Vick, La Gatha Westbrook, and Opal Williamson. Elementary Teachers: Mrs. Emilie Cannon, Prin., Para Lee Evans, Trannie Kimbrell, Hester McCracken, Thela Terry, Mrs. Sam Thornton, Velma Traweek, Mrs. C. P. Vick and Theron Vick.

1936 - 1937 - Ford Watson, Prin., Kathleen Armbrester, Lylia Mae Dobbs, W.

B. Hicks, Elizabeth Horn, J. W. Gullate, Emma Roper, Johnie K. Smith, Thela Terry. Graduating Class: Cornelius Alexander, Leon Brady, James Campbell, Charles Cannon, Lanelle Deavours, Mack Griffin, Lecile Hall, Vergie Hudson, John Paul Jones, Oventin Kemp, John Kimbrell, Beatrice Neal, Goldwyn Olive, Elizabeth Scrivner, Georgia Studdard, and John U. Walker. Elementary Teachers: Mrs. Emilie Cannon, Asst. Prin., Ralph Barnes, Mae Nell Berry, Para Lee Evans, Vesie Gilliam, Mary Key, Trannie Kimbrell, Hester McCracken, Minta Robinson, Velma Traweek, Cora Lou White and Edith Yerby.

1937 - 1938 - High School Faculty: W. T. Tiller, Prin., Cecilia Burchfield, Lylia Mae Dobbs, J. W. Gullatte, J. B. Hicks, R. C. Lipscomb, Elizabeth McCain, Thela Terry, and Sara Williams. Graduating Class: Willie Mae Aldridge, Travis Bonner, Alta Brown, Richard Cannon, Ruby Nell Chism, Hazel Cole, Rayford Deavours, Mary Nell Francis, Henry Oscar Garrard, Gladys Hall, Doris Hocutt, Loyal Jenkins, Signa Jones, Venita Jones, Auanelle Key, Madylin La Grone, Feltman Lawrence, Avis McDonald, Eunice Neal, Donald Poe, Dean Rainey, Marjorie Ray, Bryan Simpson, Felix Tidwell, John David Walton, Maxine Walton, and John L. Yerby. Elementary Teachers: Mrs. Emilie Cannon, Prin., Ralph Barnes, Louise Bonner, Trannie Kimbrell Crownover, Para Lee Evans, Vessie Gilliam, Hester McCracken, Mrs. Annie Thornton, and Velma Traweek.

1938 - 1939 - W. T. Tiller, Prin., Cecilia Burchfield, Emilie Cannon, Lylia Mae Dobbs, E. E. Eubank, J. W. Gullatte, E. C. Merritt, Mrs. Irma Plott and Thela Terry. Graduating Class: Cladius Alexander, Eulene Baird, Odessa Bonner, Earl Cannon, J. D. Davis, Carrie Mae Deavours, Ruby Nell Edmondson, S. C. Edmonson, Allene Gant, Lois Galloway, Alta Merle Jones, Opal Johnson, Edwin C. Keller, S. T. Key, Ena Kitchens, Frances Moore, Herbert Moore, Paul Nabors, Ruth Raynes, Hubert Sanford, Louise Sawyer, John Boyd Studdard, Louise Taylor, Lois Taylor, Loyd Williamson, and Lenox Willingham. Elementary Teachers: Ralph Barnes, Asst. Prin., H. L. Bonner, Trannie Crownover, Para Lee Evans, Vesie Gilliam, Hester McCracken, Annie Thornton, Velma Traweek and Edith Yerby.

1939 - 1940 - High School Faculty: J. W. Tiller, Prin., Mrs. Emilie Cannon, Mrs. Lilla Mae Dobbs, Margaret Edge, G. H. Ellis, E. E. Eubank, J. W. Gullette, Elizabeth Ann Humphrey, Mrs. Maggie Lee Kerr, E. C. Merritt, Mrs. Erma Plott, and S. L. Taylor. Graduating Class: Lucy Belle Bowen, Bertha Clark, Janis Clark, Gene Crowell, Buford Deavours, Bonnie Deavours, Beaufort Dobbs, Dugan Durrough, Fleetwood Gilliam, S. L. Hall, Curtis Handley, Linnell Hocutt, Vernon Hudson, Felix Kitchens, Karl La Grone, Ruby Nell Lollar, Andoe Lollar, J. W. Moore, Maynard Pless, Sarah Hill Ray, Blanch Simpson, Bud Sparks, Verna Smith, Janaka South, Pete Walker, William Whitson and Mauline Williamson. Elementary Teachers: H. L. Bonner, Prin., Vessie Gilliam Crownover, Para Lee Evans, Mrs. Pauline Hocutt, Hester McCracken, Ruby Hall Skinner, Annie Thornton, Velma Traweek and Edith Yerby.

1940 - 1941 - High School Faculty: C. C. Cargile, Prin., Emilie Cannon, James Dean, Jr., Lylia Mae Dobbs, J. W. Gullotte, Alva Hilbish, Marilyn Mottey, Wm. E. Robinson, Czarina Shepherd, Bess Studdard, and Earl Thomas. Graduating Class: Guy Ables, Tommye Nell Adcox, James Wesley Baker, Charles Wyatt Boone, Jewell Courington, Kate Covin, Voncile David, Paul Ellison, Jr., Mary Ruth Fowler, Rhuelma Gant, Thomas C. Henry, L. M. Hunnicutte, Jr., Jewell Johnson, George Kilgore, Jr., Hildridge Lollar, Meryl Lollar, Theron Louis Miller, Jesse Moore, Lois Moore, Norman Pendley, Donald Scrivner, J. T. Thompson, Fleetwood Watkins, Eugene Williamson, Irene Williamson and Thomas Hollis Williamson. Elementary Teachers: H. L. Bonner, Asst. Prin., Mrs. Clyde Cargile, Vesie G. Crowell, Para Lee Evans, Pauline Hocutt, Hester McCracken, Annie Thornton, Velma Traweek and Edith Yerby.

1941 - 1942 - High School Faculty: C. C. Cargile, Prin., Minta Amerson, Emilie Cannon, Trannie Crownover, Lylia Mae Dobbs, Para Lee Evans, Elizabeth Alyne Gardner, Arnold Moore, Mabeth Skelton, Bess Studdard, and Earle Thomas. Graduating Class: Charles Ray Adcox, Mildred Atkins, Garland Barnes, Dale Blackburn, Edgar Blanton, Herman Bowles, Ivory Bruner, Ted Campbell, Joan Cannon, Edna Courington, Willie Nell Crowell, Thomas Deavours, Myrtie Dunn, Loudelle Edmonson, Grady Esary, Charles Freeman, Otto Fulmer, Sam Gay, Jr., Hiram Griffin, Robert Hammock, Erma Ruth Hocutt, Carolyn Johns, Herman La Grone, Vaughn Miller, Ruby Nell Moore, Myra Lee Neal, Willie Pendley, Thais Ray, W. C. Reed, Ruth Rowland, Kathleen Scrivner, George T. Simpson, Malcom Simpson, Sudie Strickland, Jessie Gara Taylor, Golda Tidwell, Julius Tirey, Emogene Tittle, Albert Walton, Elizabeth Ward, Louise Watkins, Mary Frances Walborn, Leon Williamson, Hazel Willingham, Willard Woods and Granvielle Yerby. Elementary Teachers: H. L. Bonner, Asst. Prin., Mrs. Clyde Cargile, Vessie G. Crowell, Pauline Hocutt, Hester McCracken, Mrs. Sam Thornton, Velma Traweek, and Eidth Yerby.

1942 - 1943 - High School Faculty: Clyde C. Cargile, Prin., Mrs. Minta Amerson, Miss Merle Chapman, Miss Para Lee Evans, Miss Lois Johnson, J. S. Pearce, Mrs. Czarina Shepherd, Mrs. Bess C. Studdard, Earl Thomas, Miss Alice Turner, and Miss Edith Yerby. Graduating Class: Mildred Ausbon, Nadene Blanton, Archie Bonner, Laura Mae Brasfield, Wilford Christian, Lester Cole, Jr., Wanda Cornelius, Ann Davis, Emily Dunn, Vernell Dunn, Stanley Files, Mary Jane Freeman, John Wesley Gant, Jociafean Gant, Julia Gay, Stancel Gilliam, Marvine Hocutt, Victorine James, Dorothy Johnson, Doris Lollar, Ostra Morgan, Marcell Moore, Sue Osborn, James Sawyer, June Shirley, Dorothy Sims, Louise Smith, Ruth Smith, Mildred Stewart, Raymond Studdard, Reita Thomas, Marie Thornton, Golda Tidwell, Harris Wellburn, Imogene Wellburn, Othelia Whitley, Wilahueete Williamson, Eugene Williamson, Hazel Willingham, Billy Wright, Mildred Yerby and Montelle Zeanah. Elementary Teachers: Mrs. Emilie Cannon, Asst. Prin., Mrs. Trannie Crownover, Pauline Hocutt, Mrs. Annie Belle Johnson, Miss Hester McCracken, Mrs. Lenora Miller, Mrs. Mildred Simpson, Mrs. Annie Thornton, and Miss Velma Traweek.

1943 - 1944 - High School Faculty: Clyde C. Cargile, Prin., Mrs. Minta Amerson, Mrs. Vessie Crowell, Miss Ruby Nell Chism, Mrs. Gwendolyn Dobbs, Miss Para Lee Evans, Miss Elizabeth Gravlee, Mrs. Alice Going, Miss Lois Johnson, Mrs. Nash Nelson, Mrs. Czarina Shepherd and Mrs. Bess Christian Studdard. Graduating Class: Eleanor Ruth Barnes, Lonell Best, Lureda Blanton, Ewell Bonner, Robe Christian, V. C. Courington, Eloise Deavours, Gertrude Dobbs, Helen Dunn, Thomas Dunn, Margaret Ellis, Alice Gibson, Verna Mae Handley, J. V. Harbin, Ruby Johnson, Mary Ruth Moore, Frances Osborn, Kathleen Poe, Billie Jo Ray, A. M. Shirley, Jacqueline Studdard, Garland Taylor, George Thompson and Catherine White. Summer School Graduates: Nell Cannon, Agnes Patton & Leonard Patton. Elementary Teachers: Mrs. Emilie Cannon, Asst. Prin., Mrs. Trannie Crownover, Mrs. Pauline Hocutt, Mrs. Annie Belle Johnson, Miss Hester McCracken, Mrs. Lenora Miller, Mrs. Lucy Nelson, Mrs. Mildren Simpson, Mrs. Annie Thornton, and Miss Velma Traweek.

1944 - 1945 - High School Faculty: Clyde C. Cargile, Prin., Mrs. Lola Berry, Miss Nell Chism, Mrs. Vessie Crowell, Mrs. Ella Everett, Miss Elizabeth Gravlee, Miss Lois Johnson, Mrs. Elizabeth Lott, Mrs. Louise McGraw, Mrs. Jeff Roberts and Mrs. Czarina Shepherd. Graduating Class: Carleson Bowen, Lucy Campbell, Avelene Davis, Roberta Deavours, Catherine Edmonson, Edelene Fulmer, Austin Gray, Maxine Hendon, Marjorie Honeycutt, Corine James, J. C. Kemp, Arthur Kimbrell, Margene Kimbrell, Olene Oakley, Ruby Nell Stewart, Adelene Thornton, Jennie Roxy Vick, Sue Watkins, Madge Williamson, Charlton Whitson and Lindy Watkins. Elementary Teachers: Mrs. Emilie Cannon, Asst. Prin., Mrs. Minta Amerson, Mrs. Trannie Crowell, Mrs. Gwen Dobbs, Mrs. Annie Johnson, Miss Hester McCracken, Mrs. Lucy Nelson, Mrs. Annie Thornton, Mrs. Dorothy Traweek, and Miss Velma Traweek.

1945 - 1946 - High School Faculty: James P. Floyd, Prin., Miss Nell Chism, Miss Para Lee Evans, Mrs. Ella Everett, Miss Elizabeth Gravlee, Mrs. Pauline Hocutt, Miss Lois Johnson, Arlie May, Miss Hester McCracken, L. L. Perry, Mrs. Czarina Shepherd and Mrs. Ruby Skinner. Graduating Class: Hugh Bailey, Galera Blanton, Gladys Bonner, Lois Bonner, Vera Nell Bowen, Ray Bowles, Lou Emma Cameron, Jimmie Campbell, Olive Christian, Billie D. Crowell, Dortha N. Crownover, Louise Deavours, Milford Deavours, Cleo Dunn, Frank Earnest, Jr., Vera Nell Earnest, David Ellis, Richdean Ellis, Freeda Freeman, Elvie Mae Fulmer, Billie Joe Griffin, Nadine Gurganus, Lorene Handley, Eleanor Honeycutt, Joyce Honeycutt, Nellie Boyd Howton, Alice Hyde, Pearl Johnson, Harold Key, Herbert Kitchens, Melba Lollar, Carolyn Moore, Nellie Mae Neal, Nellie Gene Pinion, Pearlene Sanford, Gwendolyn Studdard, Blanch Thacker, Walter Gene Tyner, Eloise Williamson, and Inez Watkins. Summer School Graduates: Hal Beard, Kathlene Esary, Billy Jones, Jamelle Moore and Joe James Williamson. Elementary Teachers: Mrs. Emilie Cannon, Asst. Prin., Mrs. Minta Amerson, Mrs. Trannie Crownover, Mrs. Era Lee Dobbs, Mrs. James Floyd, Mrs. Lucy Nelson, Mrs. Annie Thornton, Mrs. Dorothy Traweek and Miss Velma Traweek.

1946 - 1947 - High School Faculty: J. D. Turner, Prin., L. H. Collier, Mrs. Ella Everett, Miss Maxine Hendon, Miss Lois Johnson, Mrs. Perry Nell Little, Arlie May, Mrs. Czarina Shepherd, Miss Marjorie Simmons, Mrs. Jessie D. Studdard, Mrs. Mary Turner. Graduating Class: Eve Adams, Wallace Baker, Perthadean Best, Bathil Bonner, Leon Courington, Billy Cunningham, Gayla Deavours, David Dunn, Voncille Ellis, Faye Files, Carlean Frost, Herbert Deavours, Edith Fulton, Alfred Hammack, Marvine Harbin, Ralph Hendon, Therisia Ann Hocutt, George Honeycutt, George Key, Emogene Killian, Dewey Lowrey, Justine Lowrey, George H. Martens, Fairy Moore, Lillie Mae Morris, James Nelson, Rayburn Nelson, Mary Ruth Osburn, Kathleen Pinion, Hope Rutledge, Frances Stewart, Frances Stocks, Mary Tidwell, Alfred Vick, Albert Watkins, Howell Whitson, Wilma Willis and Jean Yerby. Elementary Teachers: Mrs. Emilie Cannon, Asst. Prin., Mrs. Trannie Crownover, Mrs. Pauline Hocutt, Miss Hester McCracken, Mrs. Nora Moore Miller, Mrs. Lucy Nelson, Mrs. Mary Stough, Mrs. Annie Thornton, Mrs. Dorothy Traweek and Miss Velma Traweek.

1947 - 1948 - High School Faculty: J. D. Turner, Prin., Mrs. Minta Amerson, Leon Brock, Mrs. Marilyn Cannon, Mrs. Nell Chism, Morris Davis, Mrs. Ella Everett, Miss Lois Johnson, Mrs. Gertrude McLemore, Arnold Poe, Mrs. Czarina Shepherd and Mrs. Jessie D. Studdard. Graduating Class: Charles Alexander, Donald Best, Linette Blanton, Marion Brasfield, Ruth Campbell, Paul Christian, Guy Deavours, Clera Dunn, Bobby Fields, Helen Files, Leon Frost, Guy Fulmer, Robert Fulmer, Jackie Fay James, Jim Jennings,

Donald Jones, Irene Kimbrell, Loyce Kimbrell, Thurston Kimbrell, Dionnie Fay Lowery, Nola Harris Milner, Roy Morris, Loudell Nelson, Evelyn Oakley, Dewey Pendley, Lorene Pinion, Nellie Rea Pinion, John Phillips, Harold Rainwater, Mary Ette Rainwater, Ruby Lois Sanford, J. C. Shepherd, Homer Gene Simpson, Jimmie Rose Strickland, Alfred Taylor, Frances Taylor, Sam Thornton, Jr., Cecil Tingle, Tom Tyner, Sue Vick, Ilene Wilcutt, and Inez Young. Elementary Teachers: Mrs. Emilie Cannon, Asst. Prin., Miss Velma Traweek, Mrs. Dorothy Traweek, Mrs. Trannie Crownover, Mrs. Lucy Nelson, Mrs. Annie Thornton, Mrs. Annie Belle Johnson, Mrs. Janet Williams, Mrs. Mary Stough, Miss Hester McCracken and Mrs. Pauline Hocutt.

1948 - 1949 - High School Faculty: J. D. Turner, Prin., Mrs. Minta Amerson, Mrs. Essie Barrentine, Leon Brock, Mrs. Emilie Cannon, Mrs. Marilyn Cannon, Mrs. Daisy Conrad, Mrs. Ella Everett, Miss Lois Johnson, Arnold Poe, Mrs. Jessie D. Studdard, Miss Marie Thornton, Mrs. Mary M. Turner and Ernest Williamson. Graduating Class: Jimmy Austin Barnes, Ted Deavours, Vernon Deavours, Clifford Edmonson, D. L. Esary, George Fields, Juanita Forrester, Paul Fulmer, Carol Gann, Annette Gray, Bob Grizzell, Pauline Gurganus, Jimmy Hammack, Eloise Hendon, Rayford Hocutt, Robert Holley, Thomas Honeycutt, Lee Olan Killian, Lynn Kimbrell, Owen Kilgore, Jonnie Lollar, Betty Martens, Inez Moore, Octavia Nairemore, Carlos Nelson, Jr., Inez Nelson, Mary Nelson, Jimmy Osborn, Rachel Pendley, Betty Jane Smith, Harold Stovall, Eddie Walker & J. C. Williams. Elementary Teachers: Mrs. Emilie Cannon, Asst. Prin., Mrs. Trannie Crownover, Mrs. Pauline Hocutt, Miss Hester McCracken, Mrs. Lucy Nelson, Mrs. Mary Stough, Mrs. Mary Studdard, Mrs. Annie Thornton, Mrs. Dorothy Traweek and Miss Velma Traweek.

1949 - 1950 - High School Faculty: J. D. Turner, Prin., Mrs. Minta Amerson, T. L. Brock, Mrs. Emilie Cannon, Mrs. Marilyn Cannon, Mrs. Ella Everett, Miss Lois Johnson, Arnold Poe, Mrs. Czarina Shepherd, Mrs. Jessie Studdard, Miss Marie Thornton, Mrs. Mary Turner and Ernest Williamson. Graduating Class: Charles Adams, Betty Barnes, Hilda Blanton, Mamie Morris Cole, Lomax Dunham, Gilford Fowler, Ozella Freeman, Wilford Gray, Mabel Gurganus, Inez Bonner Handley, Howard Holley, Earl Johnston, Opal Kelley, Joe Kimbrell, J. T. Laboone, Llewellyn Loe, Walter McAlpin, Bill Moore, Bob Moore, Ewell Mullinax, Biven Nelson, Jayne Nelson, Lorene Pendley, Dorene Pinion, Barney Rutledge, Leonard Simmons, Lewis Skinner, Curry Smith, Louise Smith, Ronald Sparks, Alfred Trimm, Robert Tyner, Dot Vick, Vernell Wilcutt, Wallace Winters and Nedra Yerby. Elementary Teachers: Mrs. Emilie Cannon, Asst. Prin., Mrs. Trannie Crownover, Mrs. Pauline Hocutt, Mrs. Annie Belle Johnson, Miss Hester McCracken, Mrs. Lucy Nelson, Mrs. Mary Studdard, Mrs. Annie Thornton, Mrs. Dorothy Traweek and Miss Velma Traweek.

1950 - 1951 - High School Faculty: J. D. Turner, Prin., Mrs. Minta Amerson, Leon Brock, Mrs. Emilie Cannon, Mrs. Marilyn Cannon, Mrs. Ella Everett, Miss Lois Johnson, Mrs. Czarina Shepherd, Miss Marie Thornton, Mrs. Mary Turner, Arnold Poe and Raymond Yarbrough. Graduating Class: Franklin Alexander, Billy Wayne Ary, Erston Bonner, Deloyd Bowen, Lucille Bowles, Charles Wayne Campbell, Rayford Davis, Barnell Dunn, Lora Dunn, Boyd Fowler, Martha Gant, Wayne Garner, Ruby Gay, Sue Gibson, Hoyt Griffin, Zelma Gurganus, Lorez Kilgore, Doris Kimbrell, Carolyn Lowery, Ruby Pasley, Huey Phillips, Della Ruth Pinion, Abner Potts, T. A. Simpson, Jr., L. C. Stines, Wynes Stripling, Tony Stough, Nira Sue Studdard, Jackie Lou West, Orene Willcutt, Jo Ann Willingham and Joyce Yerby. Elementary Teachers: Mrs. Jessie D. Studdard, Asst. Prin., Mrs. Trannie Crownover,

Mrs. Pauline Hocutt, Mrs. Annie Belle Johnson, Miss Hester McCracken, Mrs. Lucy Nelson, Mrs. Mary Stough, Mrs. Mary Studdard, Mrs. Annie Thornton, Mrs. Dorothy Traweek and Miss Velma Traweek.

1951 - 1952 - High School Faculty: Mrs. Jessie D. Studdard, Prin., Mrs. Minta Amerson, Leon Brock, Mrs. Kathleen Campbell, Mrs. Marilyn Cannon, Mrs. Emilie Cannon, Miss Lois Johnson, Mrs. Madelle Kyser, Mrs. Clara Moore, Arnold Poe, Mrs. Czarina Shepherd, Mrs. Mary Turner and Kolan Vick. Graduating Class: Faye Alexander, Rayford Atkins, Naomi Barrentine, Olivia Barrentine, Maxine Berry, Norma Lee Beacours, Freida Dunn, George Feltman, Helen Fulmer, Gail Gibson, Eleanor Hamilton, Herbert Handley, Raymond Handley, Jewell Kelley, Doyle Kimbrell, Ola Faye Lemons, Billy Lollar, Thurman Lollar, Theron Minor, Joyce Mullinax, Betty Joyce Nelson, Devoughn Patton, Virginia Sawyer, Beverly Shepherd, Ernestine Simmons, Zora Nell Sims, Harold Dean Simpson, Titus Stovall, Gracie Swartz, Willard Tyner, Marie Utley and Bessie Nell Myers. Elementary Teachers: Mrs. Trannie Crownover, Mrs. Pauline Hocutt, Miss Delma Key, Miss Hester McCracken, Mrs. Lucy Nelson, Mrs. Mary Studdard, Mrs. Annie Thornton, Mrs. Dorothy Traweek, and Miss Velma Traweek.

1952 - 1953 - High School Faculty: Mrs. Jessie D. Studdard, Prin., Mrs. Minta Amerson, Mrs. Dixie Brock, T. L. Brock, Mrs. Kathleen Campbell, Mrs. Emilie Cannon, Mrs. Marilyn Cannon, Miss Lois Johnson, Mrs. Nell Chism May, Arnold Poe, Mrs. Czarina Shepherd, Mrs. Jessie Vick and Kolan Vick. Graduating Class: Delois Alexander, Betty Lou Arey, Velma Bevan, Arnold Blanton, Adelle Bonner, Alton Bonner, Ollie Brown, Bill Cannon, Virginia Carpenter, Dan Cunningham, Emma Jean Davis, Hansel Dobbs, James Dunn, Thomas Dunn, Glenn Gann, Bennie Gant, Billy Ray Gurganus, Barbara Hammonds, Betty Lou Hocutt, Gladys James, Jo Ann Jones, Sue Killian, Jimmie Nell Kimbrell, Raburne Kimbrell, Naomi Latham, James Lollar, Betty Jean Lowery, Virginia Moore, Myra Jean Nichols, Doyle Pendley, Irene Bailey Pendley, Joe Perkins, Gladys Pinion, Carol Rutledge, Holley Shepherd, Carl Taylor, Betty Ruth Wallace, Sandra Woods, and Gail Yerby. Elementary Teachers: Mrs. Trannie Crownover, Mrs. Delma Fowler, Mrs. Pauline Hocutt, Miss Hester McCracken, Mrs. Lucy Nelson, Mrs. Mary Stough, Mrs. Mary Studdard, Mrs. Annie Thornton, Mrs. Dorothy Traweek and Miss Velma Traweek.

1953 - 1954 - High School Faculty: Mrs. Jessie D. Studdard, Prin., Mrs. Minta Amerson, Marcus Beck, Mrs. Dixie Brock, Leon Brock, Mrs. Emilie Cannon, Mrs. Marilyn Cannon, Miss Lois Johnson, Mrs. Nell C. May, Herbert Moore, Arnold Poe, Mrs. Czarina Shepherd and Freeman Smith. Graduating Class: Dorothy Nell Ary, Gail Barrentine, Margaret Beck, Kathleen Bowles, Delloyd Drasher, Gwen Brown, Leolin Brown, Billy Butts, Barbara Ann Cooke, James Walter Doughty, Eadrell Dunn, James Earnest, Bettye Jean Files, Nelson Francis, Johnny Gay, Billy Gibson, Milton Gurganus, Neta Jean Hocutt, Rutha Johnston, Ann Kelley, Gaynell Laye, Leon Leitch, Rachel Norris Madison, Bobbie Sue Campbell Madison, LaBatha McCaleb, Faye Nelson, Davis Ray Nichols, Lu Creaty Nichols, Helen Jean Olive, Doyle Pendley, Hazel Ruth Pendley, Mary Angeline Peterson, Carrol Smith, Betty Jo Sparks, Rayford Studdard, Reba Tucker, Mary Lee Uptain, and Annie Belle Watkins. Elementary Teachers: Herbert Moore, Asst. Prin., Trannie Crownover, Delma Fowler, Pauline Hocutt, Hester McCracken, Lucy Nelson, Mary Stough, Mary Studdard, Annie Thornton, Dorothy Traweek and Velma Traweek.

1954 - 1955 - High School Faculty: Mrs. Jessie D. Studdard, Prin., Mrs. Minta Amerson, T. L. Brock, Mrs. Emilie Cannon, Mrs. Marilyn Cannon, Mrs. Lois Johnson, Herbert Moore, Arnold Poe, Miss Mina Propst, Mrs. Czarina

Shepherd, Freeman Smith and W. S. Thompson. Graduating Class: Johnnie Ruth Aldridge, Robbie Jack Amerson, Ruby Lois Ary, Melba Barrentine, Shelba Barrentine, Billie Sue Bircheat, Ellis Bowens, Carol Jean Bowles, James Bowles, Eugene Crowell, Evelyn Crowell, Georgie Lou Davis, Thelma Dunn, Robert Ellis, Wilford Files, Fayree Gurganus, LaDew Hall, Edwin Hammonds, Christine Handley, Hermiel Handley, Ralph Lollar, Nell Lowery, Shelby Lowery, Kenneth Mason, Margurite Nichols, James Paul Patton, Cecil Pendley, Sidney Pendley, Ray Pinion, Syble Pinion, James Raynes, Charles Rosser, Marilyn Rutledge, Dorothy Pendley Sands, Mary Pauline Smith, Carolyn Strickland, Vera Nell Tidwell, Annie Laura Thompson, Dale Tyner, Wilma Lou Vice, Jeanie Rose Watkins and Paul Yerby. Elementary Teachers: Mrs. Trannie Crownover, Mrs. Delma Fowler, Mrs. Pauline Hocutt, Miss Hester McCracken, Mrs. Lucy Nelson, Mrs. Mary Stough, Mrs. Mary Studdard, Mrs. Annie Thornton, Mrs. Dorothy Traweek and Miss Velma Traweek.

1955 - 1956 - High School Faculty: Felix Smallwood, Prin., Mrs. Dixie Brock, Leon Brock, Mrs. Emilie Cannon, Mrs. Marilyn Cannon, Miss Lois Johnson, Jeffie Lawrence, Arnold Poe, Mrs. Czarina Shepherd, Mrs. Betty Smallwood and Freeman Smith. Graduating Class: Betty Baker, Major Bailey, Martha Berry, Victor Bonner, Jr., Raymond Brown, Ricky Christian, Mary Lou Davis, Norma Fondren, Jimmy Fowler, Rhoda Fulmer, Woodrow Garrison, Bobby Gurganus, Lyman Harbin, Glenn Johnston, Baldwin Key, Shelby Kimbrell, Roy Kimbrell, Pat Kirkland, R. L. Madison, Annette Moore, Dorothy Nelson, Rex Nelson, Bobby Odom, Barney Olive, Lula Belle Panter, Julian Parker, Ralph Patton, Charles Pendley, Edna Mae Pendley, Ted Simmons, Clara Faye Simpson, George Simpson, La Nell Taylor, Lettie Stough, Julia Uptain, Ray Westbrook and Mildren Willcutt. Elementary Teachers: Freeman Smith, Asst. Prin., Mrs. Trannie Crownover, Mrs. Delma Fowler, Mrs. Pauline Hocutt, Miss Hester McCracken, Mrs. Lucy Nelson, Mrs. Mary Stough, Mrs. Mary Studdard, Mrs. Dorothy Traweek and Miss Velma Traweek.

1956 - 1957 - High School Faculty: Fred Webster, Prin., Mrs. Minta Amerson, Mrs. Dixie Brock, Leon Brock, Mrs. Emilie Cannon, Mrs. Marilyn Cannon, Wm. Green, Lois Johnson, Herbert Potter, Mrs. Czarina Shepherd and Mrs. Carrie Nell Webster. Graduating Class: Roy Gene Aldridge, Jerry Barrentine, Susie Bonner, Lynn Fowler, Thelon Fowler, Wayne Gant, Bobby Griffin, Merle Garner, Carolyn Gurganus, Jo Ann Lollar, Ann Lowery, Delois Lowery, Jerry Olive, Johnnie Rae Panter, Armond Pendley, James Pendley, Lorene Pendley, Ralph Pinion, James Poe, Ted Sands, Betty Simmons, Fayet Stoker, Donald Strickland, Hoyt Studdard, Buddy Swartz, Fay Uptain and Ray Williamson. Elementary Teachers: T. L. Brock, Asst. Prin., Mrs. Essie Barrentine, Mrs. Trannis Crownover, Mrs. Delma Fowler, Mrs. Pauline Hocutt, Miss Hester McCracken, Mrs. Lucy Nelson, Mrs. Mary Stough, Mrs. Mary Studdard, Mrs. Annie Thornton, Mrs. Dorothy Traweek and Miss Velma Traweek.

1957 - 1958 - High School Faculty: Fred Webster, Prin., Mrs. Minta Amerson, Mrs. Dixie Brock, Leon Brock, Mrs. Emilie Cannon, Mrs. Marilyn Cannon, William Green, Miss Lois Johnson, Herbert Potter, Mrs. Czarina Shepherd and Mrs. Carrie Nell Webster. Graduating Class: J. T. Aldridge, James Ary, Aaron Bailey, Peggy Anne Baker, Randall Barnes, Charles Bowles, John Brown, Jerry Crownover, Geraldean Davis, J. C. Dunn, Loretta Dunn, Lynwood Edmondson, Jimmy Ellis, Marianne McCaleb Ellis, Alli Mae Fowler, Barbara Fulmer, Dancon Gray, Dorothy Griffin, Carolyn Honeycutt, Jo Ann Knight, Clifton LaBoone, R. L. Madison, Geraldine Moore, Doris Mullinax, Hoyette Odom, Ralph Olive, Bette Pendley, Clyde Pendley, Eva Mae Pendley, Rayford Simmons, Joan Simpson, Martha Smith, Johnny Sparks, Martha Lou

Strickland, Richard Studdard, David Tyner, Billy Fred Webster, Jerry Don Whitson and Carolyn Yerby. Elementary Teachers: Mrs. Essie Barrentine, Mrs. Trannie Crownover, Mrs. Era Lee Dobbs, Mrs. Delma Fowler, Mrs. Pauline Hocutt, Miss Hester McCracken, Mrs. Mary Stough, Mrs. Mary Studdard, Mrs. Annie Thornton, Mrs. Dorothy Traweek and Miss Velma Traweek.

1958 - 1959 - High School Faculty: Fred Webster, Prin., Mrs. Minta Amerson, Mrs. Dixie Brock, Leon Brock, Mrs. Marilyn Cannon, William Green, Miss Lois Johnson, William C. Jones, Mrs. Nell C. May, Herbert Potter, Mrs. Czarina Shepherd, and Mrs. Carrie Nell Webster. Graduating Class: Johnny Barrentine, Mavis Barrentine, Maurice Bonner, Ray Clark, Ronald Crownover, Betty Cunningham, Ralph Feltman, Vera Nell Feltman, Kenneth Godsey, Lavon Gray, Jim Tom Handley, Ted Harbin, Kenneth Johnston, Rosemary Kimbrell, Francia Knight, Kenneth Lollar, Terry Lollar, Sonny (William Fred) Nelson, Bobby Pendley, Greta Pendley, Earl Pendley, Jimmy Pendley, Lehman Pendley, Annie Sue Pinion, Sherry Poe, Frances Rosser, Shirley Seaborn, Macon Shepherd, Billie June Simpson, Hoyt Stough, Tallulah Studdard, Joan Watkins, Shirley Watkins, Linda Webster and Joy Ann Woods. Elementary Teachers: T. L. Brock, Asst. Prin., Mrs. Essie Barrentine, Mrs. Trannie Crownover, Mrs. Era Lee Dobbs, Mrs. Delma Fowler, Mrs. Pauline Hocutt, Mrs. Mary Stough, Mrs. Mary Studdard, Mrs. Annie Thornton, Mrs. Dorothy Traweek and Miss Velma Traweek.

Berry, originally a very small school, has grown greatly through the years, both in enrollment and in activities. The first clubs were the glee clubs, organized soon after the beginning of the high school. This was followed by the 4-H Club, the F.F.A. and F.H.A. organized in the early 1930's. In 1940 the first issues of the Bee Hi-Buzz were published. The following year, in 1941, the first band was organized and in 1942 the first "Spotlight" was printed. It was in the early 1940's that the student government was first practiced and the junior Red Cross was organized. The later additions to the school cirriculum have been the Tespian Club in 1944 and the Beta Club in 1945. Berry High School has had a proud past and with the future improvements it will have an even prouder future.

BELK SCHOOL -- The first school was a community school held in the church and after a school building was erected and moved into the school was known as Antioch. Several years later the school was moved into the dwelling known as the Grover Arthur House, located in Belk and classes were held here until it was moved to the present location.

The first building on the present site was of wood construction and served the community for several years. In the early 1950's the building burned and was immediately replaced with a fire-proof, masonry building. (Se Fay. Co. Jr. High Schools for list of principals.)

BETHELEHEM SCHOOL -- This school was organized in 1902 and served the community for many years. For the term of 1901 to 1902 the school was held in the Hopewell Primitive Baptist Church Building and moved the next year to the Bethlehem Church and School where it remained until it desolved.

Following are some of the teachers who once taught in this fine old school: W. F. Gibson, W. W. Dyer, John Phagan, Bill Chism, Lonnie Smith, T. L. Harbin, N. V. Burleson, Miss Robertson, Russell Jones, W. L. Jones, Miss Susie Howton, R. T. Brock, Miss Emma Thompson and others.

BLUFF SRPINGS SCHOOL -- Bluff Springs School was located near the present

Auburn Experimental Forest during the years 1899 - 1904. Some of the teachers of this old school were as follows: Miss Ada Stanley, Mr. Harvey Ward, John Ward, Wash Smith, Mr. Little, Mr. Hillwright Howell, Miss Florence Dodson and Miss Florence Musgrove.

CENTER SCHOOL -- Center School was located on the old Fayette-Guin Pike seven and one-half miles northwest of Fayette. The first building was built about 1890 to 1894 by the men of the community. Some of these men were J. H. Ballinger, D. J. Ballinger, A. P. Turner, R. L. White, Robert McCarver, J. F. Villis and others.

The first school was a one-teacher school taught by Mr. Robert McCarver. The next year another room was added with an old style stage. The teachers were Mr. McCarver and Miss Huey.

The following teachers have taught there at various times; Mr. Joe Couch, Mr. Albert Reese, Miss Della Roe, Mr. Howell, Mr. Alexander Smith and Mr. John Branyon.

After several years the building burned. A new building was built by the same citizen's. It was still a two-teacher school. The following teachers taught in the new school: Mr. Felix Sizemore, Mr. Emit Sizemore, Mr. Garland Smith, Dr. Horace Berry, Miss Mattie Smith and Mr. Shelton Welch.

In 1911 the building was again destroyed by fire and this term of school was completed in a nearby church building. Mr. Houston Robertson deeded the land for the new building to be built near the road and the school remained a two-teacher school. The following teachers taught in this last school building of Center: Mr. & Mrs. R. L. Mosley, Miss Julia Coggins, Mr. Linton Smith, Miss Connie Ballinger, Miss Lottie Collins and Mrs. Jala May White taught the last school there in 1936. After this the county schools were consolidated.

*CENTER SCHOOL -- Located northeast of Fayette on the present Hubbertville Road is the site of the old Center School for the surrounding community. There are not many available sources for this school and we find that at one time Mr. Lonie Smith and Miss Effie Yerby were teachers for this school. As many of the county schools, this one, too, was consolidated in the early 1930's and the pupils were then carried in buses to the schools in the town of Fayette. Before the county bought buses the children rode on buses owned by individuals and some of these were very small for the group of children they carried. Most of the earliest buses had cloth curtains on each side to keep the rain and the wind out in the coldest weather and then they were raised and tied up for the warmer months. There were numerous fights on these buses among the youngsters. One would want to sit in a certain place and if another child "beat" him to the place this usually provoked a fist fight. Of course, there were countless other reasons for these young folks to wrestle. These buses were equipped with a long seat down each side by the windows and if the bus was large enough there was a long bench-like seat down the middle of the ilse. The early days of transporting the children to the larger schools had their problems, also.

COLLINS SCHOOL -- The Collin's School was established about 1900 and was active through the 1920's. Some of the teachers who taught in this school were as follows: Belle Tomlin, Luther Knight, Lycargus Morris, Lee Stewart, Leonard Fowler, Mary Jones, Thomas Berry, Jim Simpson, Glen Gurley, Ando Simoson, John Thad Duckett, George B. Cotton, Leonard Harbin, Arthur Fowler, Eunice McCaleb, Alice Hamner and Edna Fowler.

This school was located about four miles northeast of Bankston. It was consolidated with Oakley School about 1925.

CONCORD SCHOOL -- The school derived its name from the Concord Church as the school was held in the Concord Baptist Church for years since there was no school house.

It is not known how long this school was in existence before 1882, but it was already an established school at this time. School was taught in the old church until a new church was built in 1901 and school continued in the new church until a school house was built in 1912. The school house was built near the Concord Church and later a storm destroyed both the church and the school. Both buildings were rebuilt and the school continued to function until the schools were consolidated in the 1930's when it was closed and the children were transported on buses to other schools.

Some of the teachers of the Concord School were as follows: W. B. Melton, Hugh Harton, A. W. Tate, A E. Patterson, Boss Henry, G. C. Oswalt, W. W. Dyer, Miss Fannie Kirkpatrick, Tom Black, Mrs. Della V. Barnett, J. Leonard Barnett, Miss Velma Hollis, Miss Ethel Ayres, Miss Maud Mitchum and Miss Edna Kirk.

FAYETTE MALE AND FEMALE INSTITUTE -- Prior to 1860, before the schools were graded, there was established an institution of higher learning in the town of Fayette Court House, known as "The Fayette Male and Female Institute" which was supported largely by individual contributions. This school was probably the inspiring link that established the more advanced and graded school by the same name that was incorporated in 1884.

Following is a copy of the "Honor Roll" for the month of February 1888, of the Fayette Male and Female Institut

"Honor Roll" - Of the Fayette Male and Female Institute. Report for the Month ending February 24th, 1888. Subjoined is the roll of honor, 100 is perfect, 90 is the lowest a scholar can have and appear on the roll. (In the following roll, R will represent Recitation and D. will represent Deportment.) Willie Bankhead, Recitation, 100, Department, 100; Willie Cannon, R. 98, D. 100; John Sanford, R. 97, D. 100; Willie Lea, R. 100, D. 100; Willie Grey Bell, R. 99, D. 100; Leon Dodds, R. 98½, D. 100; N. Hollingsworth, R. 100, D. 100; Felix McConnell, R. 100, D. 100; Thos. E. Newton, R. 100, D. 100; Sherman McCaleb, R. 97½, D. 100; Henry Sudduth, R. 96½, D. 100; Murray Cannon, R. 96 - D. 99; Arthur Gentry, R. 97, D. 99; Jacob McCaleb, R. 98½, D. 100; John Jordan, R. 100, D. 100; Clyde Harkins, R. 94, D. 98; Snow Cannon, R. 97, D. 100; Claude Bell, R. 97½, D. 99; Henry Bankhead, R. 97½, D. 98; Bruce Robertson, R. 100, D. 100; Miss C. Cannon, R. 100, D. 100; Miss Sallie Pope, R. 100, D. 100; Miss Virgie Wilks, R. 100, D. 100; Miss Eva Smith, R. 100, D. 100; Miss Ella Berry, R. 100, D. 100; Miss Lula Berry, R. 100, D. 100 ; Miss Mary Harvey, R. 94, D. 100; Miss Emma Newton, R. 100, D. 100; Miss Musa Harkins R- 98, D. 100; Miss Essie Cannon, R. 99, D. 100; Miss Susie Hyde, R. 95½, D. 100; Miss Lena Jones, R. 100, D. 100; Miss Gertie Jones, R. 96½, D. 100; Miss D. Connerly, R. 99½, D. 100; Miss Julia Edney, R. 97½, D. 100; Miss Lillie Connerly, R. 98½, D. 100; Miss Julia Ponder, R. 96, D. 100; Miss Luna Ponder, R. 91, D. 100; Miss W. M. Little, R. 97, D. 100; Miss Susie Sanford, R. 97, D. 98; Miss Mary Sanford, R. 97½, D. 99; Miss Blanch Williams, R. 98, D. 99; Lola Sudduth, R. 97½, D. 98; Miss Alma Sudduth, R. 96½, D. 99; Jennie Black, R. 98, D. 99; Miss Sallie Newton, R. 99, D. 99; Miss Lula Cannon, R. 100, D. 98; Mary Cannon, R. 100,

D. 98; Miss Everette McGuire, R. 96 - D. 100; Miss Lucy Bell, R. 96, D. 99; Miss V. Shelton, R. 98, D. 100; Miss Ruby Shelton, R. 100, D. 98; Miss Olevia Smith, R. 98½, D. 100; Miss Vashtie Jones, R. 100, D. 99; Miss Mattie May Pope, R. 100, D. 100; Bun Dodds, R. 100, D. 98; Fletcher Hyde, R. 98, D. 100; A. Chism (3 weeks) R. 100 - D. 100; Miss I. Guin (2 weeks) R. 100, D. 100; Lee Cane, R. 98, D. 100; L. Williams (2Weeks) R. 98, D. 100; Hill Shelton (2 weeks) R. 100, D. 100; Mirt Shelton, R. 100, D. 100; R. Harris (1 week) R. 100, D. 100; and P. Wakefield, (2 weeks) R. 100, D. 100.

The above report is correct as to lessons. We never taught a Month with as few bad recitations. The name of every scholar has been in school during the Month appears on the roll. But we confess that good lessons cover a multitude of sins for a few of the scholars so far as deportment is concerned.

M. B. DuBose, Principal
Miss Susie C. Doby, Assistant.

(Following is a sketch of "School in Fayette" in 1887 as written by Mrs. Lula Berry McCaleb, who will be 88 in October, 1959.)

"In 1887, my father, William Berry decided to send Ella (my oldest sister) and me to Fayette to school one year. We went to school in what is called "Old Town" as there was no new town then. The place consisted of a few residents which was composed of Rays, Yerbys, Edneys, Seymores and others. At that time we only had two teacher schools. Our teachers were Professor Dubose, Principal, and Miss Susie Doby, Assistant. They were really fine teachers, and students sure did study in those days. I was only sixteen then, but a few of us could spell every word in the "blue-back" speller. Some of my classmates were -- Will Cannon, Leon Dodds, Will Barkhead, Virgie Wilks, Carrie Cannon, Helen Jones, Ida Guin, Emma Newton, and there are many more whose memory is still sweet to me, but everyone I know has "crossed over the river" except my sister Ella and me." (Sister Ella is Mrs. Ella Berry Patterson, age 90, January, 1960.)

The Honor Roll for the class that Mrs. McCaleb wrote about precedes this sketch to give a glance of the grades of the pupils of earlier days, also, giving the names of most of those attending school in Fayette in that period.

THE FAYETTE GRAMMAR SCHOOL -- In tracing the history of the Fayette Grammar School, we find it has operated under different names at different times and has been sponsored by some of the best citizens of the town and county. A detailed history of this school from its inception to the present cannot be given, but such material as is possible to get has been collected and it is noted that sometime in the month of May, 1884, a stock company was formed for the purpose of building and maintaining a graded school in the town of Fayette. The original incorporators were: J. H. McGuire, Daniel Collier, John B. Sanford, Thomas P. McConnell, John W. Miles, Henry Shelton and W. B. Harkins and more than fifty of the citizens of the town and county subscribed for the stock of the incorporation. This school was to bear the name of "The Fayette County Male and Female Institute" and a minute description of the building appeared in the "Fayette Journal" under date of 1884, written by R. F. Peters, as follows:

"Although, as we have often heard, there is not much in a name, yet, we trust, the above long-drawn name under which High School (graded) has been incorporated, is at least not at all commensurate with the long and prosperous career of usefulness which we anticipate is to characterize this laudable enterprise. Our people are justly proud of this institution of learning, which promises in the near future to add so much to our material prosperity, to the education and character of our children, and the building up of good society in our midst.

The building itself, which is rapidly advancing toward completion, will be an ornament to our town, and is such as would reflect credit upon any town or community. The main body of the house, we learn, is 50 feet long by 25 feet wide, and two full stories high, and by means of patent rolling partitions may be converted into four large rooms 25 feet square, or into two large halls of dimensions as above. Back of this, and forming a sort of T with the main body of the house are added three recitation rooms 12 x 15 feet each, two below and one above, being approached from the large rooms above and below through doors opening into each and every room respectively, all of which are well ventilated and lighted by quite a number of large and beautifully ornamented windows. The approach to the main building is through two large doors opening into a beautiful vestibule 12 x 24 feet, with movable partitions, from which, leading to the upper story, are constructed two stairways finished in modern style opening upon the upper floor of the vestibule, opposite the upper doors of the main building, or body of the house; the vestibule, however, being left open above and without partition. The bell tower and steeple, also, which have been framed but not finished, will add greatly to the appearance and character of the building. The rooms are to be ceiled - not plastered - with beaded stuff, and all to be overlaid with heavy coats of white lead, inside and out.

The building is under contract to be finished by the first day of October next, when it is expected the school will open with a full corps of teachers and at least 100 scholars, to begin with." —

(The original building of the Fayetteville Male & Female Institute was moved to Latona or Fayette and rebuilt about the year 1893.)

In 1902, an advertisement in a local newspaper carried advertising for the Fayette Academy which is now called the Fayette Grammar School.

The principal and other officers of the school were - John B. Ziegler, Prin.; V. H. Terry, Pres.; E. P. Goodwin, Sec. & Treas.; H. B. Proost, W. M. Cannon, E. B. Newton, John Renfro, Joseph Morgan, W. A. Graham, and W. H. Brown, board of trustees.

. . "Closing Exercises of Fayette Academy - On Friday Evening at 7:30 in the Academy Hall, the closing exercises of the school began. An outline of the program is appended herewith: 1. Song by Choir. 2. Salutatory - Misses Susie Caraway and Mattie Robertson. 3. Come Play With Me, pantomine - Primary Class. 4. Extracting a Tooth - Thos. Propst, A. Rose, Geo. Gullett and Murray Rector. 5. Doll Drill and Burlesque - Primer Class. 6. A Christmas Gale, concert recitation - Senior Class. 7. Moonlight Music & Love, duet - Misses Lucy Bell and Erdeal Caine. 8 Scarf Drill - Intermediate Class. 9. Advertising For A Cook, dialogue - Girls of the Senior Class. 10. Palm Branches, solo - by Annie Sanders. 11. On The Rappahammack, recitation - by Sallie Robertson. 12. My Two Sweethearts, solo - by Loudelle Smith. 13. A "Cullud" Debatin" Sassiety, a debate - by Boys of Senior Class. 14. Taking the Census, dialogue - by Loudelle Smith and Archie Caraway. 15. A Photographer's Studio Farce - by Murray Rector, Arthur Glenn, and Robert Caine. 16. Valedictory, - by Nellie Ziegler. 17 Closing Address - by Rev. R. A. Timmons. 18. Song - by the Choir. . . . .

The next we find of the Grammar School is on July 4th, 1916 when the Town Council of the Town of Fayette called an election to submit to the qualified voters of the Town of Fayette a proposition to issue the bonds of said town to the amount of ten thousand dollars for the purpose of erecting a public school house in the town of Fayette. This election was held on August 7th, 1916, and the vote was 115 for the bond issue and 3 votes against the bond issue. Bids for partial construction of the public school building were received and it was found that the bid of Walker Brothers & Co. of Fayette, Ala. was the lowest and best bid, and a building committee was appointed, consisting of D. D. Arnold, M. L. Coons, of the board of Aldermen, and one citizen of the town, this member of the committee to be appointed by the town committee.

The old original building that was moved and rebuilt in 1893 was demolished to give place for the construction of the $65,000 Grammar School erected in its stead. This building and equipment was destroyed by fire on the morning of January 29, 1930, leaving more than 450 children in the grammar school age without a place in which to finish the 1929 and 1930 term.

Arrangements were made with the Methodist, Baptist and the Christians, for the use of their churches to finish the term ending in May, 1930.

When the time came to rebuild the Grammar School Building several citizens were of the opinion that a more desirable location from off Temple Avenue should be secured. To that end efforts were made to secure a building site adjacent to the present high school ground but satisfactory arrangements could not be made.

In all matters pertaining to the rebuilding of the Grammar School the County Board of Education appointed a committee consisting of the local district trustees, namely; L. B. Lollar, W. H. Humber and R. D. Dobbs and the County Superintendent of Education B. L. Balch. This Committee employed Chas. F. McCauley of Birmingham to draw the plans of the building. When the bids were opened to erect the building it was seen the M. L. Waddell Company of Tuscaloosa was the low bidder at a figure of $30,288.00. This bid was considerably less than the amount of the insurance collected because of the burning of the old building.

About 1938 a wooden building was built behind the brick building to house the lower grades. This was torn down in 1955 and several rooms of mason construction were added to the back of the original building. The Fayette Grammar School is a modern arrangement in all respects with a very fine cafeteria.

The faculty of the Fayette Grammar School is listed as follows: (As records are not available, the first portion of this list is approximately dated) - 1890's - James S. Van Diver. 1895 - 1896 Miss Luabbie Chambless and Miss Puckett, who stayed with the Rose family and taught first grade. Before 1900 (And other early teachers.) Mr. Davis, Mamie Gravlee, Walter Turner, R. T. Anderson, Mr. Koon, Mr. Moore (Mrs. A. C. Madden's father.), Mr. A. M. Nuckols, and Mr. Frank Arthur Nuckols. 1900 - 1901 J. W. Monroe. 1901 - 1902 John D. Ziegler, Prin. 1902 - 1903 Shelton Welch. 1903 - 1904 Mr. Cahoon, J. S. Van Diver, Mr. Crump, Sue Morton and Miss Luabbie Chandler. 1904 - 1905 Not available. 1905 - 1906 Not Available. 1906 - 1907 Mr. C. J. Usury, Prin.

1907 - 1908 Ben Lowery, Prin., John F. Huffstutler, C. J. Usury, and Bessis Lollar. 1908 - 1909 John F. Huffstutler, Prin.

1909 - 1910 J. S. Thorne, Prin., J. Alex Smith, Miss Lenora Cowan, Miss Edna Pace, Miss Bessie Robertson - Music (started term), and Miss Pinkey Sanford - Music (finished term.) 1910 - 1911 _____ Bonner, Prin.

1911 - 1913 _____ Kelley, Prin., Annie Lou Chambless, Miss Florence Rogers, Willis Mays, Ruth Brown, Josie Walker and Sallie Robertson. 1913 - 1914 Willis Mays, Prin., Miss Florence Rogers, Ruth Brown, Josie Walker, Miss Sallie Robertson and Miss Bessie Robertson.

1914 - 1915 Mittie Burge, and Miss Fronie Connell. 1915 - 1916 Mr. N.

F. Greenhill, Prin., Mrs. Sallie (Robertson) Frazier, Mrs. J. A. (Edna Pace) Branyon and Miss Corinne Nichols. 1916 - 1917 Mr. E. R. Harris, Prin., Miss Emma Lee Ledbetter, and Miss Ruth Foreman.

1917 - 1918 Miss Maggie Berry, Prin. 1918 - 1919 Mr. Wilson, Prin., Miss Wilma Kirkley, Prin. (Mr. Wilson died during the school term and Miss Kirkley replaced him.)

1919 - 1920 Mr. Willis May, Prin., Mrs. Bess Cook, Mrs. W. H. Terry, Mrs. Maude (Shepherd) Carter, Miss Lizzie Mae Jones, Mrs. J. A. Branyon, Miss Wilma Kirkland and Miss Marguerite Brotherton.

1920 - 1921 Mr. R. L. Reaves, Prin., Mrs. Inez (Reeves) Shirley, Miss Lizzie Mae Jones, and Mrs. Bess Cook.

(Records were available from here for the first through eight grades.)

1921 - 1922 Mr. R. L. Reaves, Prin., Beuma Nichols, Mrs. Bess Cook, Miss Era Smith, Mrs. J. D. Irene White) Wright, Mrs. Inez Shirley, and Miss Biddie Guin.

1922 - 1923 Mr. C. L. Chambers, Prin., Mrs. Inez Shirley, Mrs. Bess Cook, Miss Wilkie Brown, Miss Julia Coggin, Mrs. J. D. (Irene) Wright, Miss Velma Robertson, Miss Biddie Smith and Miss Ozella Smith.

1923 - 1924 Miss Sara Stone, Prin., Miss Eula Mae Barley, Miss Julia Coggins, Miss Velma Robertson, Mrs. Irene Wright, Miss Ella Reaves, Miss Wilkie Brown, and Miss Era Smith.

1924 - 1925 Miss Sara Stone, Prin., Miss Eula Mae Barley, Miss Lucyle Barnett, Miss Julia Coggin, Miss Annie Mae Allison, Miss Eunice McCaleb, Miss Ella Reaves, Miss Leone Hagwood, and Miss Mabel Daniel - Music.

1925 - 1926 Miss Sara Stone, Prin., Mrs. Locke (Floy Waldrop) Collins, Miss Lucyle Arnold, Miss Julia Coggin, Miss Hazel Hill, Mrs. Irene Wright, Miss Ella Reaves, Miss Eunice Cunningham, and Miss Mabel Daniels - Music.

1926 - 1927 Miss Sara Stone, Prin., Mrs. Locke Collins, Miss Ruby Marle, Miss Lucyle Arnold, Miss Julia Coggin, Mrs. Irene Wright, Miss Katie Sumerall, Miss Carrie Daniel and Miss Mabel Daniel.

1927 - 1928 Miss Sara Stone, Prin., Mrs. Locke Collins, Miss Evelyn Walker, Miss Jasmine Gilmore, Miss Sallie Branyon, Miss Julia Coggin, Miss Virgie Waldrop, Mrs. Irene Wright, Mrs. Lillian Hay, Miss Carrie Daniel, and Mrs. J. M. Brown.

1928 - 1929 Miss Sara Stone, Prin., Mrs. Locke Collins, Miss Pauline Ward, Miss Lucille Farquhar, Miss Julia Coggin, Miss Martha Reaves, Mrs. Irene Wright, Mrs. Lillian Hay, Miss Virgie Waldrop and Miss Carrie Daniel.

1929 - 1930 Mrs. Locke Collins, Prin., Louise Caraway, Wilkie Newman, Mrs. Irene Wright, Artie McCool, Julia Coggin, Lucille Farquhar, Martha Reaves, Mrs. Lillian Hay, Miss Virgie Waldrop, Mrs. M. H. (Jeannette) Sherer, and Carrie B. Daniel.

1930 - 1931 (First through sixth grades.) Mrs. Locke Collins, Prin., Louise Caraway, Wilkie Newman, Artie McCool, Julia Coggin, Lucille Farquhar, Everette McCluskey, Mrs. Irene Wright, Miss Virgie Waldrop, Mrs. Lillian Hay, Mrs. Jeannette Sherer, Miss Willene Hyde, Miss Elizabeth Humber - Music.

1931 - 1932 Mrs. Locke Collins, Prin., Louise Caraway, Wilkie Newman, Artie McCool, Julia Coggin, Lucille Farquhar, Mrs. Irene Wright, Everette McCluskey, Miss Virgie Waldrop, Carrie Daniel, Willene Hyde and Mrs. M. H. Sherer.

1932 - 1933 Mrs. Locke Collins, Prin., Louise Caraway, Wilkie Newman, Artie McCool, Lucille Farquhar, Julia Coggin, Mrs. Irene Wright, Everette McCluskey, Carrie Daniel, Virgie Waldrop, Willene Hyde, and Mrs. M. H. Sherer.

1933 - 1934 Mrs. Locke Collins, Prin., Louise Caraway, Artie McCool, Julia Coggin, Mrs. Irene Wright, Everette McCluskey, Carrie Daniel, Mrs. M. H.

Sherer, and Willene Hyde.

1934 - 1935 Mrs. Locke Collins, Prin., Mrs. Louise (Caraway) Moore, Miss Lucyle Arnold, Mary Holliman, Julia Coggin, Mrs. Irene Wright, Miss Everette McCluskey, Carrie Daniel, Hazel Terry, Miss Robbie Lee Lollar, Mrs. M. W. Sherer and Miss Mabel Daniel - Music.

1935 - 1936 Mrs. Locke Collins, Prin., Mrs. Louise Moore, Mrs. Lucyle (Arnold) Barnett, Mrs. Louise Vick, Julia Coggin, Miss Carrie Daniel, Everette McCluskey, Mrs. Irene Wright, Hazel Terry, Robbie Lee Lollar, Willie Jane Maddox, and Mabel Daniel.

1936 - 1937 Mrs. Floy (Locke) Collins, Supervising Prin., Mrs. Louise Vick, Mrs. J. D. (Mary Holliman) Turner, Mrs. Louise Moore, Miss Julia Coggin, Mrs. Irene Wright, Miss Everette McCluskey, Miss Carrie Daniel, Miss Robbie Lee Lollar, Miss Hazel Terry, Miss Willie Jane Maddox, Miss Carolyn Collins, Mrs. Eron Gibson, Mrs. C. P. Vick and Miss Ora Hollingsworth.

1937 - 1938 Mrs. Floy Collins, S. Prin., Mrs. Clyde C. (Lottie Collins) Cargile, Miss Julia Coggin, Miss Carrie Daniel, Mrs. Eron Gibson, Miss Robbie Lee Lollar, Miss Willie Jane Maddox, Miss Everette McCluskey, Mrs. Herman (Louise Caraway) Moore, Miss Hazel Terry, Mrs. Mary Turner, Mrs. C. P. Vick, Mrs. Lois Williams, and Mrs. Irene Wright.

1938 - 1939 Mrs. Floy Collins, S. Prin., Mrs. Clyde Cargile, Miss Julia Coggin, Miss Carrie Daniel, Mrs. Eron Gibson, Willie Jane Maddox, Everette McCluskey, Mrs. Herman Moore, Hazel Terry, Mrs. Mary Turner, Mrs. C. P. Vick, Mrs. Theron (Louise) Vick, Mrs. Lois Williams, Mrs. Irene Wright, Miss Mary Gibson, and Miss Ora Hollingsworth.

1939 - 1940 Mrs. Floy W. Collins, S. Prin., Mrs. Clyde Cargile, Miss Julia Coggin, Mrs. Eron Gibson, Miss Mary Gibson, Miss Willie Jane Maddox, Miss Everette McCluskey, Miss Gwendolyn Stewart, Miss Hazel Terry, Mrs. Mary Turner, Mrs. C. P. Vick, Mrs. Louise Vick, Mrs. Inez Webster, Mrs. Lois Williams, and Mrs. Irene Wright.

1940 - 1941 Mrs. Floy W. Collins, S. Prin., Mrs. Mary Turner, Miss Julia Coggin, Mrs. C. P. Vick, Mrs. Louise Vick, Mrs. Inez (Webster) Hankins, Mrs. Eron Gibson, Miss Gwendolyn Stewart, Miss Mary Elizabeth Thompson, Miss Everette McCluskey, Mizz Hazel Terry, Miss Carrie Daniel, Mrs. Lois Williams, Miss Mary Gibson, Miss Willie Jane Maddox, and Miss Chloe Spann.

1941 - 1942 Mrs. Floy W. Collins, S. Prin., Mrs. Mary Turner, Miss Julia Coggin, Mrs. C. P. Vick, Mrs. Louise Vick, Mrs. Inez Webster, Mrs. Eron Gibson, Miss Gwendolyn Stewart, Miss Mary Louise Thompson, Miss Everette McCluskey, Miss Hazel Terry, Miss Carrie Daniel, Mrs. Lois Williams, Miss Mary Gibson, Miss Willie Jane Maddox and Mrs. Buster (Chloe Spann) South.

1942 - 1943 Mrs. Floy W. Collins, S. Prin., Mrs. Mary Turner, Miss Julia Coggin, Mrs. C. P. Vick, Mrs. Claude (Ora Hollingsworth) Patterson, Mrs. Inez Webster, Mrs. Eron Gibson, Miss Gwendolyn Stewart, Miss Everette McCluskey, Miss Hazel Terry, Miss Carrie Daniel, Mrs. Lois Williams, Miss Mary Gibson, Miss Willie Jane Maddox, Mrs. Chloe S. South, and Mrs. Mabel (Daniel) Jeffries.

1943 - 1944 Mrs. Floy W. Collins, S. Prin., Mrs. Mary Turner, Miss Julia Coggin, Mrs. C. P. Vick, Mrs. Ora Patterson, Mrs. Inez Webster, Mrs. Eron Gibson, Miss Gwendolyn Stewart, Miss Everette McCluskey, Miss Hazel Terry, Miss Carrie Daniel, Mrs. Lois Williams, Miss Mary Gibson, Miss Willie Jane Maddox, Mrs. Chloe S. South, Mrs. J. A. (Edna Pace) Branyon, and Mrs. Mabel Jeffries.

1944 - 1945 Mrs. Floy W. Collins, S. Prin., Mrs. Mary Turner, Miss Julia Coggin, Mrs. C. P. Vick, Mrs. Ora Patterson, Mrs. Inez Webster, Mrs. Eron Gibson, Miss Everette McCluskey, Miss Hazel Terry, Miss Carrie Daniel, Mrs. Lois Williams, Miss Mary Gibson, Mrs. Chloe S. Spann, Mrs. Edna Branyon, Miss

Beatrice Ray, Mrs. Bruce (Willielary) Stewart, Mrs. Mabel Jeffries.

1945 - 1946 Mrs. Floy Collins, S. Prin. Mrs. Mary Turner, Miss Julia Coggin, Mrs. C. P. (Lillian) Vick, Mrs. Ora Patterson, Mrs. Inez Webster, Mrs. Eron Gibson, Miss Everette McCluskey, Miss Hazel Terry, Miss Carrie Daniel, Miss Mary Gibson, Mrs. Chloe S. South, Mrs. Edna Branyon, Miss Beatrice Ray, Mrs. Williary Stewart, Mrs. Hazel (Waldrop) Olive, and Mrs. Mabel Jeffries.

1946 - 1947 Mrs. Floy Collins, S. Prin., Miss Julia Coggins, Mrs. Lillian Vick, Mrs. Ora Patterson, Mrs. Inez Webster, Miss Everette McCluskey, Miss Hazel Terry, Miss Carrie Daniel, Miss Mary Gibson, Mrs. Chloe S. South, Mrs. Edna Branyon, Mrs. Willielary Stewart, Mrs. Pauline Chandler, Mrs. Kara (Crock) Robertson, Mrs. Mabel Jeffries - Piano, and Mrs. Ruby Jo. Dobbs, Public School Music.

1947 - 1948 Mrs. Floy W. Collins, S. Prin., Miss Julia Coggin, Mrs. Lillian Vick, Mrs. Ora Patterson, Mrs. Inez Webster, Mrs. Eron Gibson, Mrs. Guthrie J. (Robbie Lee Lollar) Smith, Miss Hazel Terry, Miss Carrie Daniel, Miss Mary Gibson, Mrs. Chloe S. South, Mrs. Edna Branyon, Mrs. Willielary Stewart, Mrs. Pauline Chandler, Mrs. Kara Robertson, Mrs. Ruby Jo Dobbs - Public School Music, Mrs. Hazel Olive, Mrs. Era (Smith) Hankins, and Mrs. Mabel Jeffries - Piano.

1948 - 1949 Mrs. Floy W. Collins, S. Prin., Miss Julia Coggin, Mrs. Lillian Vick, Mrs. Ora Patterson, Mrs. Inez Webster, Mrs. Eron Gibson, Mrs. Era Hankins, Miss Hazel Terry, Miss Carrie Daniel, Mrs. French (Mary Gibson) Maxwell, Mrs. Chloe South, Mrs. Edna Branyon, Mrs. Willielary Stewart, Mrs. Pauline Chandler, Mrs. Kara Robertson, Mrs. Ruby Jo Dobbs, Mrs. Robbie Smith, Miss Betty Hazel Galloway, and Mrs. Mabel Jeffries.

1949 - 1950 Mrs. Floy V. Collins, S. Prin., Miss Julia Coggin, Mrs. Lillian Vick, Mrs. Ora Patterson, Mrs. Inez Webster, Mrs. Eron Gibson, Miss Hazel Terry, Miss Carrie Daniel, Mrs. Mary Maxwell, Mrs. Chloe South, Mrs. Edna Branyon, Mrs. Willielary Stewart, Mrs. Pauline Chandler, Mrs. Kara Robertson, Mrs. Robbie Smith, Mrs. Fanny S. Nunnally, Mrs. Doris (Newton) Merritt, Mrs. Thelma (McCaleb) Caraway, Mrs. Elsie M. Doughty, Mrs. Henry Davis and Mrs. Mabel Jeffries.

1950 - 1951 Mrs. Floy W. Collins - S. Prin. Miss Julia Coggin, Mrs. C. P. Vick, Mrs. Ora Patterson, Mrs. Inez Webster, Mrs. Eron Gibson, Miss Hazel Terry, Miss Carrie Daniel, Mrs. Mary Maxwell, Mrs. Chloe South, Mrs. Edna Branyon, Mrs. Willielary Stewart, Mrs. Pauline Chandler, Mrs. Kara Robertson, Mrs. Robbie Smith, Mrs. Fannie S. Nunnally, Mrs. Doris Merritt, Mrs. Thelma Caraway, Mrs. Phyllis Davis and Mrs. Mabel Jeffries.

1951 - 1952 Mrs. Floy W. Collins - S. Prin., Miss Julia Coggin, Mrs. C. P. Vick, Mrs. Ora Patterson, Mrs. Mary Maxwell, Mrs. Thelma Caraway, Mrs. Inez Webster, Mrs. Eron Gibson, Miss Carrie Daniel, Mrs. Edna Branyon, Mrs. Chloe South, Mrs. Willielary Stewart, Miss Hazel Terry, Mrs. Pauline Chandler, Mrs. Doris Merritt, Mrs. Herbert (Fannie) Nunnally, Mrs. P. W. Colburn, Mrs. Kara Robertson, Mrs. Robbie Smith and Mrs. Mabel Jeffries.

1952 - 1953 Mrs. Floy V. Collins - S. Prin., Miss Julia Coggin, Mrs. Lillian Vick, Mrs. Ora Patterson, Mrs. Mary Maxwell, Mrs. Thelma Caraway, Mrs. Inez Webster, Mrs. Eron Gibson, Miss Carrie Daniel, Mrs. Willielary Stewart, Mrs. Chloe South, Miss Hazel Terry, Mrs. Pauline Chandler, Mrs. Doris Merritt, Mrs. Fannie S. Nunnally, Mrs. P. W. Colburn, Mrs. Kara Robertson, Mrs. Robbie Smith, Mrs. Wilma Killingsworth and Mrs. Mabel Jeffries.

1953 - 1954 Mrs. Floy V. Collins - S. Prin., Miss Julia Coggin, Mrs. C. P. Vick, Mrs. Ora Patterson, Mrs. Mary Maxwell, Mrs. Thelma Caraway, Mrs.

Inez Webster, Mrs. Eron Gibson, Miss Carrie Daniel, Mrs. Edna Branyon, Mrs. Willielary Stewart, Mrs. Chloe South, Miss Hazel Terry, Mrs. Pauline Chandler, Mrs. Gene (Carolyn Sue Robertson) Logan, Mrs. Fannie S. Nunnally, Mrs. Flora Lee Newton, Mrs. Kara Robertson, Mrs. Robbie Smith, Miss Malinda Robertson, and Mrs. Mabel Jeffries.

1954 - 1955 Mrs. Floy W. Collins - S. Prin., Mrs. Edna P. Branyon, Miss Julia Coggin, Miss Carrie B. Daniel, Mrs. Eron Gibson, Mrs. Carolyn Sue Logan, Mrs. Mary Gibson Maxwell, Mrs. Flora Lee Newton, Mrs. Mattie (Harbin) Newton, Mrs. Ora H. Patterson, Mrs. Kara B. Robertson, Mrs. Malcolm (Malinda Jane Robertson) Daniel, Mrs. Robbie Lee L. Smith, Mrs. Chloe S. South, Mrs. Willielary Stewart, Mrs. Lillian B. Vick, Mrs. Inez H. Webster, Mrs. Wilma L. Yerby, Miss Hazel Terry and Mrs. Mabel Jeffries.

1955 - 1956 Mrs. Floy W. Collins - S. Prin., Mrs. J. A. Branyon, Mrs. Flora Lee Newton, Mrs. C. P. Vick, Mrs. Pauline Chandler, Miss Julia Coggin, Miss Carrie Daniel, Mrs. Robbie Lee Smith, Mrs. Hazel Olive, Mrs. J. E. Webster, Mrs. Willielary Stewart, Mrs. Wilma Yerby, Mrs. Sue Logan, Miss Hazel Terry, Mrs. Eron Gibson, Mrs. Kara Robertson, Mrs. Ora Patterson, Mrs. Mary Gibson, Mrs. Mattie Newton, and Mrs. Mabel Jeffries.

1956 - 1957 Mrs. Floy W. Collins - S. Prin., Mrs. J. A. Branyon, Mrs. Flora Lee Newton, Mrs. C. P. Vick, Mrs. J. E. Webster, Mrs. Pauline Chandler, Miss Julia Coggin, Miss Carrie Daniel, Mrs. Robbie Lee Smith, Mrs. Florence Smith, Mrs. Doris Merritt, Mrs. Willielary Stewart, Mrs. Wilma Yerby, Mrs. Chloe South, Miss Hazel Terry, Mrs. Eron Gibson, Mrs. Kara Robertson, Mrs. Ora Patterson, Mrs. Mary Maxwell, Mrs. Mattie Newton, Mrs. Artie (McCool) Hallman, and Mrs. Mabel Jeffries.

1957 - 1958 Mrs. Floy W. Collins - S. Prin., Mrs. Betty Ferguson, Mrs. Flora Lee Newton, Mrs. C. P. Vick, Mrs. J. E. Webster, Mrs. Pauline Chandler, Mrs. Grady H. (Artie McCool) Hallman, Mrs. Anice (Williamson) Benton, Miss Julia Coggin, Miss Carrie Daniel, Miss Louise Waldrop, Mrs. Doris Merritt, Mrs. Willielary Stewart, Mrs. Wilma Yerby, Mrs. Chloe South, Miss Hazel Terry, Mrs. Eron Gibson, Mrs. Kara Robertson, Mrs. Ora Patterson, Mrs. Mary Maxwell, Mrs. Mattie Newton, Mrs. Marguerite (Peters) England, and Mrs. Mabel Jeffries.

1958 - 1959 Mrs. Floy W. Collins - S. Prin., Nolen Robertson, Mrs. Flora Lee Newton, Mrs. C. P. Vick, Mrs. Anice P. Benton, Mrs. J. E. Webster, Mrs. Pauline Chandler, Mrs. Artie Hallman, Miss Julia Coggin, Mrs. Willie Grey Dubose, Miss Louise Waldrop, Mrs. Doris Merritt, Mrs. Willielary Stewart, Mrs. Ozella Stough, Mrs. Chloe South, Miss Hazel Terry, Mrs. Eron Gibson, Mrs. Kara Robertson, Mrs. Ora Patterson, Mrs. Mary Maxwell, Mrs. Mattie Newton, Mrs. Ruby (Marie) Houston, Mrs. Carrie Robertson, and Mrs. Mabel Jeffries.

1959 - 1960 Mrs. Floy W. Collins - S. Prin., Nolen Robertson, Mrs. Flora Lee Newton, Mrs. C. P. Vick, Mrs. Inez Webster, Mrs. Pauline Chandler, Mrs. Artie Hallman, Miss Julia Coggin, Miss Louise Waldroo, Mrs. Willielary Stewart, Mrs. Mattie Newton, Mrs. Ozella Stough, Mrs. Chloe South, Miss Hazel Terry, Mrs. Eron Gibson, Mrs. Kara Robertson, Mrs. Ora Patterson, Mrs. Mary Maxwell, Mrs. Wilma Yerby, Mrs. Willie Grey Dubose, Mrs. Ruby Houston, Mrs. Annie Lee Franks, Mrs. Carrie Robertson, Mrs. James (Mabel) Jeffries - Piano, and Mrs. !. M. Brown - Public School Music.

FAYETTE COUNTY JUNIOR HIGH SCHOOLS -- Following is listed the Junior High Schools, 1959, in the county giving the names of the principals and the years served by each:

BANKSTON JUNIOR HIGH SCHOOL -- 1929 - 1931 E. C. Herren. 1931 - 1932 John H. Holliman. 1932 - 1933 L. C. Tucker. 1933 - 1941 J. D. Turner. 1941 - 1942 Grady Dillard. 1942 - present 1959 Charles Alexander.

BELK JUNIOR HIGH SCHOOL -- 1929 - 1931 W. C. Kirk. 1931 - 1933 Clyde C. Cargile. 1933 - 1935 Floy Ham. 1935 - 1936 Mrs. Janet Williams. 1936 - 1942 Claude S. Campbell. 1942 - 1947 Mrs. Pauline Chandler. 1947 - 1953 Berta W. Smith. 1953 - 1954 E. C. Herren. 1954 - 1958 Berta V. Smith. 1959 - present John B. White.

BOBO JUNIOR HIGH SCHOOL -- 1929 - 1931 Elmer Burnett. 1931 - 1937 J. E. Webster. 1937 - 1947 Earnest Moss. 1947 - 1948 J. E. Webster. 1948 - 1956 Fred Webster. 1956 - 1959 James Lavaughn Ballinger.

KIRKLAND JUNIOR HIGH SCHOOL -- 1929 - 1932 Terrell Cannon. 1932 - 1934 John H. Holliman. 1934 - 1935 Clyde C. Cargile. 1935 - 1937 Arlie May. 1937 - 1938 Dwight Kirk. 1938 - 1941 Oveat Earnest. 1941 - 1942 J. D. McCarver. 1942 - 1947 Berta V. Smith. 1947 - 1959 present, Arlie May.

MT. VERNON JUNIOR HIGH SCHOOL -- 1929 - 1931 R. D. Buckner. 1931 - 1933 Lee Watkins. 1933 - 1934 Clyde C. Cargile. 1934 - 1951 Paul W. Colburn. 1951 - present 1959 Loyd F. Fowler.

STOUGH JUNIOR HIGH SCHOOL -- 1929 - 1932 Fred Morris. 1932 - 1936 Wilburn Smith. 1936 - 1937 E. C. Herren. 1937 - 1941 J. E. Webster. 1941 - 1952 E. C. Herren. 1952 - 1953 Mrs. Flora Lee Newton. 1953 - 1954 Riley McGee. 1954 - 1955 Mrs. Ozella G. Stough. 1955 - 1956 Herbert Moore. 1956 - 1958 John B. White. 1958 - present 1959, Mrs. Georgie L. Sanford.

WAYSIDE JUNIOR HIGH SCHOOL -- 1929 - 1932 Paul W Colburn. 1933 - 1934 E. Grady Cook. 1934 - 1936 C. R. Allen. 1936 - 1948 Fred M. Webster. 1948 - 1950 H. S. Chaffin. 1950 - 1955 Fred P. Colburn. 1955 - present 1959, Harold McDonald.

FAYETTE HIGH SCHOOL -- The question of the education of the children in the rural districts and in the small towns engaged the serious attention of the educators of the State for many years, and as the population increased the "little red school house on the hill" became inadequate to meet the demands of an advanced civilization, as the authorities of the State of Alabama, with the cooperation of the cities and towns, set themselves the task of bettering conditions and in 1907, the legislature passed an act providing for the establishment of high schools in the State and to make appropriations for such schools.

The Fayette County High School was located June 11th, 1914, on a five acre tract of land donated by W. T. Naugher.

The next step in securing the school was up to the citizens of the town, and the money for the erection of the building had to be raised by public subscription and by bond issue of the town of Fayette.

An election was called to be held on Monday the 7th day of August, 1915, and the bond issue carried by a vote of 115 for and 2 against. The High School Building was completed in time for the beginning of the fall term of 1916.

In the years of the duration of the Fayette County High School, it has sent out into the world a large number of young men and women who are proving their worth in the various vocations of life.

The building burned in 1933 and the present, modern building was erected in 1934. After a few years the Agricultural and Home Economics Building was erected (in late 1930's). About 1940 additional class rooms and a cafeteria were added. The Athletic Stadium was constructed in the mid 1940's and is one of the nicest in this section of Alabama. The new gymnasium and auditorium were completed in 1950's.

The extra-curricula activities of Fayette County High School consist of the Beta Club, Ushers Club, F.F.A., F.H.A., F. Club, 4 H Club, Glee Club, Future Teachers Club and Spanish Club.

The first high school newspaper for the Fayette County High School was named "The Reflector". Later the name of the school newspaper was changed to "The Tiger Rag".

The first year book or annual of the school was compiled for the graduating class of 1937. The pictures for the book were made in numbers sufficient to use in the number of books made and were pasted in by hand. The 1938 yearbook, "The Echo" was the first to have the pictures professionally done.

Following is a list of the faculty and the members of the graduating class for each year of the Fayette County High School since it was organized. The list begins with the class of 1916 and goes through the forty-fifth year.

1915 - 1916 Faculty: R. L. Reaves - Prin., Metar Chapman, A. D. Roberts and Earnest White. Graduating Class: Ola Barnes, Maggie Berry, Culberson Brown, Eloise Caine, Randolph Caine, Lewis Cannon, Julia Coggin, Jimmie Collins, Lottie Collins, Eunice Grimsley, Felix Grimsley, Susie Howton, Carlos Nelson, Lillian Newton, Charles Odom, Dorothy Osborne, Sara Nell Proost, Ora Reese, Willette Smith, Lurline Stewart, Sidney Tarwater and Milner Young.

1916 - 1917 Faculty: R. L. Reaves - Prin., J. R. Clements, Ruth Lee Long, and Corrine Nichols. Graduating Class: Ethel Ayers, Maye Arnold, Ruth Berry, Harvey Cannon, Lizzie Caraway, Lester Davis, Lois Dodd, Lucille Gentry, Mildren Graham, Rosalie Mathes, Broadus Pace, Hester Patterson, Mina Putnam, Inez Reaves, Walker Reaves, Dicie Richards, Helen Sanders, Joe Shelton, Klein Sims, Ovella Smith, Matilea Stokes, Beechal White and Irene White.

1917 - 1918 Faculty: F. M. Nelson, - Prin., C. C. Bush, Miss Crew, Miss Ruth Long and Miss Christine Robbins. Graduating Class: Lizzie Davis, Zula Gibson, Howard Griffin, Beuma Nichols, Eunice Richards, Thomas Robertson, Arthur Shafer and Fletcher Stamps.

1918 - 1919 Faculty: J. J. Moore - Prin., Miss Elizabeth Cross, Miss Brazzie Price, and Miss Sarah Stone. Graduating Class: Victor Chambless, Ollie Chism, Floyd Curl, Christine Dodson, Velma Dodson, Lucille Dorroh, Estelle Gibson, Irene Higgins, Cecil Holliman, Walter Holliman, James Jeffries, Lizzie Mae Jones, Lucille Richards, Emilie Scharnagel, Roberts Scharnagel, Vera Smith, Sallie Mae Spear, Floy Waldrop and Lillian Willingham.

1919 - 1920 Faculty: F. D. Graves - Prin., Adelaide Bell, James B. Boone, Cathline Carr and Miss Sarah Stone. Graduating Class: Ulysses Akins, Lee Barns, Cecil Blakney, Ruth Collins, Roy Doughty, Lawrence Higgins, Cella Beryl Johns, Lee Legg, Hazel Mathes, Eunice McCaleb, Othela Nichols, Charley Proost, Mary Bell Roberts, Augusta Robertson, Clarence Smith, Herschel Smith, Mary Lee Thompson, Charley Vick, Susie Vick, Annie Waldrop and Eardeal Walters.

1920 - 1921 Faculty: R. A. Pegues - Prin., Cathline Carr, Miss Mildred Harris Mr. Johnson and Mrs. (Adelaide Bell) Van Diver. Graduating Class: Ida Ayers, Eula Mae Barley, Jiminell Branyon, Bessie Dodson, Burdett Mayfield, Roberta Peters, Theron Poe, Ella Reaves, Delton Smith, Curruth Smith, and Evelyn Walker.

1921 - 1922 Faculty: R. L. Reaves - Prin., Cathaline Carr, Festis Eubank, Ann Hoffman and Mrs. Van Diver. Graduating Class: Max Branyon, Miriam Cannon, Charlie Dodson, Ben Enis, Leroy Hallman, Eardeal Hassel, Elette

Henry, Rymon Hollis, Ruth Johnson, Banard Killingsworth, Mae McCluskey, William Monroe, Katherine Nuckols, Noland Propst, Martha Reaves, Geraldine Studdard, Gladys Sumrall, Katie Sumrall, Lee Vick, Oliver Wilkerson and Marilee Wilson.

1922 - 1923 Faculty: B. L. Balch - Prin., Ann Hoffman, Lotta Spear, N. C. Thompson, Mrs. Van Diver and J. E. Wright. Graduating Class: Lucille Arnold, Robert Buckner, Louise Caraway, Malcolm Couch, Kathleen Goodwin, Terry Griffin, Grady Hallman, Hobson Hankins, Mae Hankins, Samilee Hankins, Isadore Hodges, Ora Hollingsworth, Eva Howell, Clarence Hubbert, Frank Jeffries, Earline Johnson, Floyd Lawrence, Vilma Lawrence, Posey McConnell, Nora Moore, Alfred Newman, Lennie Newman, Wilkie Newman, Grace Newton, William Newton, Gertie Patterson, Louise Proost, Charley Rowland, Kate South, B. O. Stanley, Lydia Strother, Marjorie Tarwater, Drazzie Waldrop, V. B. Wheeler, and Mrs. V. B. Wheeler.

1923 - 1924 Faculty: B. L. Balch - Prin., Ruth Burdick, Ann Hoffman, Charles Scott, Mrs. Charles Scott, Lotta Spear and J. E. Wright. Graduating Class: Guy Allen, Nora Lee Austin, Ray Belk, Ruth Berry, Eldon Blackburn, Hattie Bobo, Wilma Bobo, James Branyon, Adine Brazil, Bradley Brock, Kora Brock, Musa Brock, Claudia Campbell, Ray Cargile, Verna Cargile, Lucille Chambers, Villena Collins, Mary Coons, Belton Dodson, Johnny Dodson, Clara Foote, Mamie Lou Gibson, Annie Graham, Robert Hamner, Edward Hankins, Bruce Harkins, Dutchie Harkins, Pansy Higgins, Exie Hollingsworth, Thomas Hollingsworth, Loudell Kemp, Mae Killingsworth, Kathleen Kimball, Harley Langston, May Mayfield, Wilburn Mayfield, George Newton, Newton Morris, Frankie Nuckols, Floy Patterson, Jimmie Phillips, Alice Putnam, O. P. Richardson, Dixie Rowland, Adelle Smith, Claude Smith, Mamie Mae Smith, Milton Smith, Wilma Stephens, Earman Thornton, Lydia Vick, Lucille Valdrop, Willie Webster, Victor West, Lois Wilson and Inge Yerby.

1924 - 1925 Faculty: B. L. Balch - Prin., Ruth Burdick, Savanah Hillis, Charles Scott, Mrs. Scott, Lotta Spears, & J. E. Wright. Graduating Class: Cecil Berry, Fulmer Bobo, Lewis Bohanon, May Brock, Knowlton Brown, Joe Neal Butler, Lucille Cannon, Elsie Cargile, Voncile Cargile, Dean Collins, Iva Connor, Mabry Lee Couch, Agnes Dodds, Leon Dyer, Alice Freeman, Jessie Freeman, Henry Grady Goodson, Ed Penn Goodwin, Clara B. Graham, Rebecca Gravlee, J. T. Griffin, James Guyton, Isabel Ham, Gwyn Harkins, Mary Holliman, Floyd Hunt, Jack Jeffries, Grady Killingsworth, Hugh Kemp, Audrey Lawrence, Raburn Lawrence, Aubrey Lee, Artie McCool, Motie McCool, Mary Moore, Morgan Moseley, Daniel Newman, James Newton, Loudelle Newton, Curt Nichols, Olene Patterson, Minnie Lee Pruett, Charles Savage, Cora Lee Sims, Lucy Sims, Ruby Sims, Theron South, Curt Waldrop, Eunice Waldrop, Edwyna Walker, J. C. Watson, Susie Wilks, Levert Wilson, and Frances Wright.

1925 - 1926 Faculty: B. L. Balch - Prin., Ruth Burdick, Irene Magee, Matsie McKeel, Charles Scott, Mrs. Scott, Maud Sutton and J. E. Wright. Graduating Class: Lois Allen, Ola Barnard, Festus Barnes, Jane Berry, Powell Berry, Ernest Bobo, Fletcher Bogard, Aaron Branyon, William Branyon, Harold Cain, Louise Cantrell, Addine Collins, Baxter Collins, Minnie L. Collins, Ora Collins, Johnnie Corbett, Jobe Couch, William Dodson, Cleburne Doughty, Gertie Doughty, Lavous Dubose, Cecil Dyer, Lucille Farquhar, Lei Guyton, Inez (Blackhead) Hankins, Inez (Redhead) Hankins, Obeal Harkins, Roland Hankins, Bert Harkins, Bertha Hodges, Iva Hubbert, Merie Hyde, Mae Hyder, Claudia Kemp, Marguerite Kimbrell, Clyde Lawley, Annie L. Lee, Fletcher Legg, Ethel Lindsey, Leo Lockart, Katherine Loftis, Dewey Michael, Elie Moseley, Nina Parks, Drewery Parrish, Lillie Patterson, Vashti Patterson, Charles Patton, Ruby

Reaves, Mary Rigell, Latilou Robertson, Ruby Lee Savage, Julia Sawyer, Eli Sims, John Sims, Dalcus Smith, Ausburn South, Susie South, Woodruff South, Carrie Spiller, Addie Stamos, Ranzie Stamos, Howard Stanley, Carribel Stewart, George Lee Thompson, Kalie Bell Turner, Lucy Mae Wallace, Dean Webster and Gladys Windham.

1926 - 1927 Faculty: D. L. Balch - Prin., J. M. Brown, Ruth Burdick, Claud Clayton, Aatsie McKell, Robbie Sawyer, and J. E. Wright. Graduating Class: Burlin Barnes, Onnie Rae Belk, Mamie Berry, Elva Blackburn, Clara Mae Bobo, Vera Nell Boone, Bedsie Brock, Mary Lou Cannon, Loena Cantrell, Susie Caraway, Clyde Cargile, Lottie Collins, Mary Lou Crowe, Clayton Dodson, Ralph Dodson, Lola Foote, Nancy Foote, Bertha Fowler, Elbert Fowler, Lorraine Fowler, Lake Freeman, Richard Freeman, Ruby Gaddis, Ozelle Gardner, Cephas Gladden, Elizabeth Humber, Marjorie Hunt, Gaines Jeffries, Ned Jeffries, Louise Jones, Cecil Killingsworth, Ora Langston, Clyde Lawley, Helen Lea, Robert E. Lee, Fenton Long, Edna Madden, May Mayfield, Everette McCluskey, Mary McCool, Dewey Michael, Emma Morrison, Ora Moseley, Elsie Newman, Isabel Nuckols, Ollie Oswalt, John D. Parks, Verna Patterson, Vista Patterson, Zora Patterson, Beulah Patton, Marguerite Peters, Annie Sue Propst, Mary Lou Propst, Leland Sanford, Wilma Sides, Ethel Smith, James Alexander Smith, Jr., James Harris Smith, Guy Strother, Bruce Tarwater, Marguerite Tarwater, Eron Taylor, Denver Turner, Bessie Waldrop, Jim Weathers, Leroy Wiggins, and Andrew Wright.

1927 - 1928 Faculty: R. L. Balch - Prin., J. M. Brown, Ruth Burdick, Claud Clayton, Ben Hudson, Mrs. T. A. Peters, and Robbie Sawyer. Graduating Class: Eva Mae Auston, Leslie Berry, Ruby Dell Bobo, Theodore Bobo, Rena Brock, Chester Cargile, William B. Curl, Herbert Dodson, Robert Gibson, Robert Graham, Zora Hill Hankins, Austin Hendrix, Erline Howton, Clinton Hubbert, Charlie Hyde, Willene Hyde, Loyl Hyder, Clinton Jackson, Elizabeth Humber,(irregular), Thomas Johnson, Edith Jones, Auburn Lawrence, Robbie Lee, Howard Miles, Jenia Mitchell, Exie McCluskey, Sam Morris, Mary Lou Oswalt, Audrey Patterson, Pauline Powell, Theoma Powell, Madelion Powers, Rachel Powers, Theron Raley, Cecil Rasberry, Lucille Renfroe, Leora Roberts, James Rowland, Fred Schaill, Wilma Smith, Wilma Stephens, Guy Strother, Lucy Tarwater, Clyde Waldrop, Lomax Weathers, Ruth Welch, Willie Nell Wheeler, Ruth Wiggins, Gertrude Williamson.

1928 - 1929 Faculty: A. S. Scott - Prin., Verna Brasher, Cliff Brown, Janelle Brown, Lois Kaylor and Altie McGahey. Graduating Class: Willie Barnett, Theodore Bobo, Burt Bogard, Irene Bradley, Curt Branyon, Lawrence Branyon, Magdaline Campbell, William Campbell, Ray Chambless, Mayople Collins, Lillian Cook, Marion Coons, Robert Gibson, Dale Griffin, Nellie G. Fulford, Mattie Harbin, Thomas Harbin, Euline Harton, Dan Henry, Ed Howell Hyde, Max Jones, Burnice Little, Cecil Maddox, Nellie Jane Maddox, O'Connell McConnell, Lillie McGehee, Mary Blanche Mitchell, Elaine Oswalt, Wayne Pinion, Edward Propst, Sara Renfro, James Roberts, Sally Roberts, Bill Sanders, Oleta Smith, Frank Stallworth, Talmadge Suddeth, Irene Taylor, Hazel Terry, Lula Thompson, Murray Thompson, Grace Tigett, Lois Waldrop, Homer Watkins, Lindsey Watkins, Etma Welch, Cara Lou White and Morris White.

1929 - 1930 Faculty: A. S. Scott - Prin., Verna Brasher, Nellie Brown, C. E. Green, Mrs. C. E. Green, Rebecca Huff, Alice Lowrey, Paul Meigs, and N. H. "Tex" Sherer. Graduating Class: Bernice Arthur, Bama Lynn Ayres, Elizabeth Blalock, Chris Buckner, Albert Butler, Shannon Coleman, Roy Couch, Clyde Freeman, Percy Freeman, Sara Nell Freeman, Herman Garrison, Mary Nell Gentry, Aaron Gibson, Kate Gibson, Louise Gibson, Mabel Gibson, Joe Goodwin,

Raymond Gordon, Jewel Griffin, Floyd Ham, Sadie Humber, L. C. Joiner, Eunice Lindsay, Solon Lindsay, Lucy Maddox, Lena McDonald, Ossie McGehee, Lorene Meherg, Bruce Musgrove, Thad Odum, Laura Patterson, Irene Randolph, Bernice Rowland, Sam J. Sanders, Hugh Sims, Whit Stokes, Celesta Sudduth, Thela Terry, Eula Mae Walker, Edith West, Wayne West, Avadale Wilson, Estelle Windham and Katherine Wright.

1930 - 1931 Faculty: A. S. Scott - Prin., Theresa Bosworth, Verna Brasher, Nell Brown, J. D. Gibson, Rebecca Huff, Alice Lowrey, Paul Meigs, Roberta Parker, and M. H. Sherer. Graduating Class: Jimmie Lou Ayres, Gladys Belk, Emmett Bobo, Talmadge Bobo, Graham Brock, Ruby Nell Butler, Delbert Cargile, Edith Cargile, Loudell Cargile, Robert Cargile, Leon Crowley, Naomi Dodson, Purvy Doughty, Vivian Ford, Kittie Foster, Edward Fulford, Nell Gibson, Pat Gladden, Raymond Gordon, J. M. Guin, Floy Ham, Doyle Hannah, Desserie Harbin, Alline Hodges, Lois Kimbrell, Clayton Lawrence, Evelyn Lawrence, Robbie Lee Lollar, Marcene Madden, Sydney Maddox, James A. McCool, Ossie McGehee, Talton Newman, Donald Newton, Zoe Pinion, Grady Randolph, Beatrice Ray, Jeffie Richards, Lillie Mae Roach, Linnie Lee Shelton, Mary Lee Sims, Guthrie Smith, Cecil Spiller, Larkin Stanley, Anne Thompson, Wayne West, Sara Wilkes and Alexander Williams.

1931 - 1932 Faculty: J. M. Brown - Prin., Virginia Bishop, Nell Brown, J. D. Gibson, Lorene Hankins, Rebecca Huff, Jeraldine McKenzie, Paul Meigs, Evelyn Pearson, Melba Selman and M. H. Sherer. Graduating Class: Virginia Ary, Crawford Balch, Susie Blackburn, Katherine Blackburn, Emmett Bobo, Howard Bobo, Mary Lee Brock, Katherine Burson, Edith Cargile, Eunice Cargile, Ruby Lee Cargile, Minnie Pearl Cargile, Leonard Cotton, Rebecca Davis, Buford Dobbs, Maytle Files, Etoile Hannah, Euline Harbin, Erdeal Howard, Dean Hyder, Margaret Isbell, Lorena Jones, Jessie Lea, Jeeis B. Lockart, Sula Lee Logan, Nocie McArthur, Joe Ed McConnell, C. McCluskey, Adelle Mitchell, Lizzie Nuckols, Gene Pinion, Savada Powers, Wallace Rasberry, Kathleen Richards, Denzil Rowland, Lynnie May Sharpe, Floyd Smith, Nola Stanley, Pauline Tarwater, John Ed. Thompson, Cecil Waldrop, Delta Walden, Garion Williams, Thomas Alexander Williams, and Mary Etta Yerby.

1932 - 1933 Faculty: J. M. Brown - Prin., Mary Sue Aldridge, Virginia Bishop, Travis Black, Nelle Brown, Lorene Hankins, Rebecca Huff, Jeraldine McKenzie, Paul Meigs, and Melba Selman. Graduating Class: Floyd Barnard, Flavie Barnes, Mae Nell Berry, Howard Bobo, Terry Bobo, Cyrus Brock, Myrtle Brock, Ross Burns, Margie Cargile, Alice Chandler, Carolyn Collins, Irene Fowler, Irene Garrison, Rube Greer, Taft Johnson, Wiley Johnston, Tom Jones, Jewell Killingsworth, Leland Langston, Clifford Lawrence, Brownie Lollar, Fronie Maddox, Marvin McCain, Jr., McCluskey, C., Sally McConnell, Frank Moore, Lois Newman, Neal Nichols, Frances Posnack, Dicie Lee Rasberry, Wallace Rasberry, Denzil Rowland, Mildred Sanford, Linnie May Sharpe, Christine Sudduth, Roston White, Thurston White, and Rachel Williams.

1933 - 1934 Faculty: J. M. Brown - Prin., Travis Black, Bess Christian, Lorene Hankins, Rebecca Huff, Jeraldine McKenzie, Melba Selman and Edwyna Walker. Graduating Class: Buford Arnold, Virginia Bogard, Rayford Brasher, Andrew Campbell, Joe Campbell, Virginia Coons, Etta Neal Dodson, Johnnie Dubose, Elise Nichols Faulkner, Frances Fowler, Bessie Freeman, Eulene Gilliland, Lillian Cathleen Gurley, Lois Henley, William Humber, Mary R. Hunnicutt, Virginia Hyde, Ruby Jones, Robert Killingsworth, Elizabeth McCain, Evelyn McConnell, Loree McClung, Doris Newton, Neal Nichols, Paul Oden, Hilda Proost, Muriel Mildred Rainey, Ernestine Seymore, Lorena Shepherd, Naufleet Shirley, Addie South, John South, Bob Tarwater, Mary E. Thompson, Mary Wilks, and Odell Yerby.

    1934 - 1935 Faculty: J. M. Brown - Prin., Travis Black, D. B. Borden, Bess Christian, Lorene Hankins, Rebecca Huff, Jeraldine McKenzie, Melba Selman, Anna Thames, and Edwyna Walker. Graduating Class: Inez Abernathy, J. V. Ayres, Braxton Bates, Hazel Bates, Ruby Nell Belk, Leon Brock, A. J. Brown, Andrew Campbell, Jewell Corbett, Marguerite Cowart, Hugh Green Ford, V. K. Fowler, Steve Frazier, Bessie Freeman, Irene Gardner, Fred Gibson, Eulene Gilland, Wilburn Gilpin, Huston Gravlee, Gayle Greer, Jack Hamner, Bill Tom Hutton, Nelle Jones, Gladys Killingsworth, Robert Killingsworth, Herbert Matthews, Dorothy McCracken, Christine Mothershed, Lewallen Newton, Willard Nichols, Bessie Taylor, Everett Taylor, Thelma Terry, T. J. Thompson, Wayne Walters, Essie Webster, and Willard Yerby.

    1935 - 1936 Faculty: J. M. Brown - Prin., D. B. Borden, Jr., Sara Bradford, Mrs. Edwyna Walker Branyon, Mrs. Melba Caldwell, Guy Carmichael, Bess Christian, Lorene Hankins, Odel Hartley, Jeraldine McKenzie, and Jewel Strickland. Graduating Class: Zebedee Abernathy, Richard Arthur, Kathleen Ayres, Docia Brock, Nellie Brock, Helen Brown, Hazel Burns, Charlotte Butler, Marjorie Butler, Clyde Caraway, Barney Cargile, Eleanor Chandler, Grady Chism, Jr., Clara Belle Deavours, Vivian Doughty, Louis Eidson, Everette Gardner, Mary Gibson, Annie Lee Gilliland, Alice Green, Mary Bell Griffin, Leo Harbin, Robert Harris, Mary Agnes Hilton, Henry Loal Hobbs, Jewel Hobbs, Jacob Hodges, Maurice Hodges, Charlie Isbell, Billie Jeffries, Sam Jones, Malcolm Lawrence, Russell Lawrence, Fred McCaleb, Edna McGee, Frances Moore, Woodrow Newman, Audra Oswalt, Isadore Palmer, Molly Jo Peterson, Mary F. Robertson, Irene Starnes, Charles Swanson, Gene Tarwater, Everett Taylor, Octavia Taylor, Ozella Taylor, Wynelle Taylor, Charlie Thompson, Dorothy Vick, Wymon Vick, Z. D. Vick, Hazel Waldrop, Lula Dean Walters, Oscar Watkins and Velma Williamson.

    1936 - 1937 Faculty: J. M. Brown - Prin., D. B. Borden, Mrs. D. B. Borden, Mrs. James A. Branyon, II, Mrs. Bradford Caldwell, Guy Carmichael, Miss Mary Loftin, Miss Jeraldine McKenzie, Miss Elizabeth Pritchett, Miss Jewel Strickland, Mrs. Lynn "Bess" Studdard, and Miss Ruby Jo Watson. Graduating Class: Elsie Ayres, Ector Lane Bagwell, Helen Hope Balch, Virginia Barnard, Joe Frank Barnett, Baughn Brasher, Jewell Banks Brown, Julia Bell Burson, Sara Catherine Caine, Glyn Cameron, Mary Chandler, Marguerite Clark, Fred Cook, Evaline Corbett, Lois Couch, Roesle Davis, Johnnie Duke, Albert Estes, Jr., Merle Fowler, Reeves Gaddis, Elizabeth Gibson, A. M. "Buster" Grimsley, Jr., Emily Grimsley, Mary Nell Hamby, Leo Harbin, Raymond Holcomb, Catherine Horn, Pauline Hughes, Carey Humber, Wynell Hurnicutt, B. J. Johnson, Virginia Jones, Pearl Killingsworth, Stacia Lawrence, Densie Maddox, Eloise Maxwell, Oleta McCool, James McGee, Leon Mosley, Eugene Norris, W. D. Olive, Elred Oswalt, Vaudie Lou Otts, Maburn Perkins, Lucy Railey, Dessiree Rainey, Chester Lee Robertson, Dorothy Rowland, James H. Shirley, Marie Sims, Virginia Thompson, Frances Trammell, Milton Turner, Tim Vick, Louise Waldrop, Lanier Walker, Guy Watkins, Virginia West, Augie Lee White, Carrie Lou White, Franklin White, Freddie White, Frank Whitney and V. Ella Yerby.

    1937 - 1938 Faculty: John Morgan Brown - Prin., Mrs. Edwyna Branyon, Mrs. Melba Caldwell, Mrs. Elizabeth Carlton, Miss Susie DeMent, T. L. Faulkner, Mrs. Clarice Holder, E. S. Jenkins, Miss Jerry McKenzie, Lamar Moye, Mrs. Mary Proost, Mrs. Bess Studdard, Mrs. Jewel Tarwater, Theron Vick and Miss Ruby Jo Watson. Graduating Class: Mae Agerton, Richard Arthur, James Daniel Berry, Murray Barnes, Elizabeth Beaty, Rose Lee Brasher, Bill Brotherton, Jack Butler, Clanton Cargile, Joe Palmer Chandler, Roy Chandler, Joe H. Coons, Bernice Corbett, Mary Dockery, George Floyd, Inez Fowler, Joe Arnold Fulford, Garland Gardner, A. J. Gibson, Jr., Howard Harbin, Katherine Harris, Frances Hay, Jane Henderson, Vella Mae Holliman, Mildred Hood, Louis Inman, Kathleen Jones, Omer Kizzire, Helva Lawley, F. P. Lea, Woodrow McCarver, Bob McConnell, A. C. McKnight, Tla Dean Maddox, Bruce Maddox, Ira Matthews, Juanita Miles, Brownie Mitchell, Louise Moore, Eunice Morris, Buren Mosley, Mogene Newman, Aubrine Nichols, Hazie Nichols, Wilson Nichols, Macon Oswalt, Paul Oswalt, Victor Patterson, Jr., Raiford Ray, Mildred Roberts, Dewitte Shirley, James Shirley, Adrelle Smith, Thelma South, Audra Taylor, Elwood Waldrop, Inez Waldrop, Alfred Wallace, Ottis Walters, Lorene Watkins, Jimmie Lee White, Phynes Williamson, Ruth Williamson, Abbie Kate Windham, and Dessie Ree Woods.

1938 - 1939 Faculty: J. M. Brown - Prin., John Bloodworth, Mrs. Edwyna Branyon, Mrs. Melba Caldwell, Miss Susie DeMent, T. L. Faulkner, Mrs. Sadie Goodwin, Mrs. Mary Hinson, Mrs. Clarice Holder, W. E. Jackson, Miss Jerry McKenzie, Mrs. Mary Pronst, Mrs. Bess Studdard, Mrs. Bob Tarwater and Theron Vick. Graduating Class: Adolph Blakeney, Virginia Blackburn, Augusta Bobo, Lowrey Brock, Kenneth Belk, Raymond Best, Hilary Brandon, Eardeal Byars, Richard Campbell, Inez Shepherd Campbell, Edith Chism, Bobby Cobb, Bobbie Couch, Audrey Davidson, M. C. "Hap" Dobbs, Jr. Dorsey Doughty, Sara Drury, Carey Dyer, Burt Eidson, Barney Ray Estes, Clyde Gibson, Mary Gibson, Postelle Gibson, Dorothy Gravlee, Elizabeth Gravlee, Jimmy Gunter, Danylu Herren, Troy Gilpin, Sarah Hollingshead, Martha L. Hollis, Rebon Howton, Bob Jones, Holly Lawrence, Jr., Lecial Lockart, Frances Lowrey, Junior Maddox, Louise McKnight, Dorothy McDaniel, Neal McGough, Eubeeman Newman, Lucille Oswalt, Floy Lee Otts, Catherine Patterson, Frances Renfroe, Ruth Rowland, Myron Sterman, George Y. Shirley, Joe William Stewart, Benjamin Swann, J. G. Wallace, Raymond Waldrop, Lanier Williamson, Lindsey Wright, Mary Lou Wright and Kilby Lee Yerby.

1939 - 1940 J. M. Brown, - Prin., John Bloodworth, Mrs. Burleson, Clyde C. Cargile, Miss Cunningham, Miss Susie DeMent, T. L. Faulkner, Mrs. Sadie Goodwin, Mr. Dick Hamner, Mrs. Mary Henson, Mrs. C. M. Holder, Miss Jerry McKenzie, Miss Thelma McKenzie, Mrs. Bob Tarwater, Miss Rosalie Tutwiler, Theron Vick and Mrs. Irene Wright. Graduating Class: Hoyet Abbott, Mildred Akins, Jack Alford, Jane Arthur, Gaynell Ayres, Boston Beard, Derrell Barnett, Robert T. Black, Eugene Brasher, Eddie Rene Bohannon, Carlton Brock, Lowrey Brock, Naomi Brock, Frank Brown, Robert Brown, Lee Cargile, Jean Daniels, Odesle Davis, Eloise Davidson, James Dockery, Euline Dodson, Connie Bea Estes, Julia Bell Forsythe, Bernard Fowler, William Frederick, Stella Frye, Dorothy Galloway, Helen Galloway, Duward Gardner, Virginia Garrison, Alvin Griffin, E. J. Hobbs, Theo Hobbs, Brett Hollis, Dorothy Hubert, N. T. Hubbert, Doris Ann Humber, James Johnson, Christine Jones, Bernice King, Leroy Lawrence, Mary Frances Madden, Dorothy Maddox, James Maddox, Martha Matthews, Evelyn Moore, James Moore, Clancy McCaleb, Eloise McCarthy, Dorothy Newman, Oliver Newman, Daisy Nichols, Maurice Pastuer, Buell Raley, Dora Bea Sanders, Nella Mae Sexton, Juanita Smith, Purless Stoker, Vaudine Stough, Jeane Trammell, John Trimm, Lorene Turner, Emma Jean Vick, J. D. White, Lonell White, Margie Sue White, Sybil Whitney, Bernice Woods, William Woods, and Arthur Wright.

1940 - 1941 Faculty: J. M. Brown - Prin., Edwyna Branyon, Margaret Debardeleben, Susie DeMent, Lucille Garlington, Mary Henson, Clarice Holder, T. L. Faulkner, Amanda Keelyn, Maggie Kerr, Lee Kimball, Bruce Little, Jeraldine McKenzie, Elizabeth Noblin, C. E. Ray, Jamie Thomas, Prentice Thomas, Rosalie Tutwiler, Theron Vick and Irene Wright. Graduating Class: Jack Alexander, Iris Alford, Hubert Anthony, Gladys Berry, Grady Black, Violet Blackburn,

Wallace Ray Bobo, Martha Bragg, Mildred Butler, Elizabeth Butts, Neal Byars, Wilkie Byars, Motie Campbell, Joe Cannon, Charleen Cargile, Frankie Cargile, Gertrude Cargile, Virginia Chambless, Laura Ann Cobb, Jimmy Cook, Mildred Coons, Lomax Davis, Grace Duke, Leon Estes, Bob Frances, Dalton Giloin, Mildred Gray, Dick Gunter, Borden Haney, Mary Ellen Hinton, Nina Henson, Virginia Hollingshead, Blanton Hood, Avie Lou Howard, Lloyd Humber, Bonneal Hyndman, Millard Johnson, Billy Jones, Stella Loe, Martha Loftis, Beatrice Maddox, A. G. McGough, Mildred McGough, Gay Miles, Lou Gene Muse, Earlene Nabors, Ernestine Nabors, Bernice Newman, Jesse Nichols, Eulene Norris, George Owens, Nell Matthews Patterson, Evelyn Pickett, W. E. Poe, Vera Nell Pollard, Eurice Potter, Justine Rainwater, Harold Rainwater, Buddy Ranfroe, Dorothy Roberts, John Roberts, Florence Rowland, Lois Sanford, Van Vure Sanford, Vera Nell Savage, Edral Sims, Kathleen Smallwood, Bessie South, Mary Virginia Taber, Jeannette Taylor, William Turner, Virginia Unger, Frances Vick, Annie Ruth Walters, Robert Walters, Roselyn Weaver, Nora White, Virginia Williams, Mary Elizabeth Williams and Muriel Wright.

1941 - 1942 Faculty: J. M. Brown - Prin., Lucille Barnett, Margaret Debardeleben, Susie DeMent, Emma Evins, Mary Harkins, Clarice Holder, Leigh Kimball, Bruce Little, Jerry McKenzie, Elizabeth Noblin, Fred Payne, Frances Ray, Woodall Rogers, Margaret Stallworth, Jamie Thomas, Prentice Thomas, Rosalie Tutwiler, Theron Vick, Alva Wade and Irene Wright. Graduating Class: Catherine Abbott, Jimmie Allen, Maxine Ayres, Mary Grace Bailey, Reble Barnes, Morgan Barnett, Marjorie Beard, Louise Howard Best, Wilma Blackburn, Billy Bragg, Jo Ann Caine, Della Jane Cannon, Kathleen Cannon, Betty Couch, Mildred Davidson, Norma Davis, Jack Dyer, Dorothy Ellis, Thomas Etheridge, Nell Fowler, Howard Frederick, Kenneth Galloway, Harold Gibson, Eula Guin, Yeuell Herren, Edwin Hocutt, Leonard Hodges, Dewey Holliman, Lanette Holliman, Eva Hollingsworth, Frances Hollis, Ella Fair Hunnicutt, Horace Jay, Sarah Maude Johnson, Bobby Jones, Luther V. Key, Jr. Jeffie Lawrence, Johnnye Lou Lee, Bill Lollar, Mary Lee Madison, Edwin McClure, Ethel Shirley McGuff, L. E. Mitchell, Wynelle Mitchell, Louis Poe Moore, Christine Nelson, Russell Newman, Kathleen Newton, Gaylon Northan, Geraldine Otts, Gladys Otts, Hazel Otts, Kathleen Otts, Othelia Otts, Leona Pate, Hazel Patterson, Jean Patterson, Erdeal Pennington, Willow Mae Phillips, Annie Mae Potter, Ruth Rasberry, Leathy Roberts, Emily Dean Rose, Eloise Sanders, Voncile Sanders, Olene Sanford, Hoyt Sims, Mavalene Smith, Milton Sterman, Martha Stewart, Shelton Vick, Shivers Vick, Irene Williams, Pauline Williams, Kathleen Williamson, Louise Wilson, Ruby Lee Woods, Marshall Woods and Doyle Yerby.

1942 - 1943 Faculty: J. M. Brown - Prin., Mrs. L. B. Allen, Mrs. Lucyle Barnett, Miss Nellie Brock, Miss Margaret DeBardeleben, Miss Susie DeMent, Miss Emma Evins, Mrs. Bruce Harkins, Mrs. C. M. Holder, Mr. Leigh Kimball, Mrs. Roy Martin, Miss Jerry McKenzie, Miss Elisabeth Prater, Miss Ouida Ray, Mr. R. P. Robbins Mr. W. W. Rogers, Miss Margaret Stallworth, Miss Zelma Tankersley, Miss Thelma Terry, Mrs. Delmar Wright, and Miss Minnie Watt Fite. Graduating Class: Margaret Alexander, William Ayres, Pauline Bailey, Harry Barnett, Ruth Bobo, Vaudene Bobo, Perry Nell Caraway, Frances Chambless, Peggy Cobb, Buna Colley, Elizabeth Cooper, Hilda Falls, Helen Faulkner, Aline Fowler, Fillsmore Fowler, Eva Nell Freeman, Anita Galloway, Billie Jo Gammon, L. E. Gilliland, Drowss Gilpin, George Gullett, Jr. Earl Golson, Gaston Golson, Frank Hamby, Bobby Hamilton, Lula Gager Harkins, Hoyt Herren, Mary Glenn Herren, Marion Howton, Elizabeth Jones, Edwin Lawrence, Tommy Lindsey, James Ethel Little, W. M. Maddox, Jr. Azilee Martin, Martha Montgomery, Charlotte Muse, Carol McCool, Lewis Nelson, Maxine Nix, Lottie Pate, Gracia Ponds,

Louise Reeves, Charles Renfroe, Sam J. "Do" Renfroe, Jr., Bob Sanders, Veleria Shelton, Beatrice Spiller, Carol Swanson, Alice Striegel, Bobby Taylor, Carol Thomason, Eloise Tilley, Ernestine Traweek, Harry Unger, Charles Walker, Inez White, Blanche Whitley, Olene Williamson, and Sarah Alice Wright.

1943 - 1944 Faculty: J. M. Brown - Prin., Vida Allen, Lucyle Barnett, Nellie Gray Brock, Alma Cannon, Margaret DeBardeleben, Sara DeBardeleben, Susie DeMent, Emma Evins, Sadie Goodwin, Clarice Holder, Frankie Martin, Jerry McKenzie, Elizabeth Prater, W. W. Rodgers, R. P. Robbin, Zelma Tankersley, Thelma Terry and Irene Wright. Graduating Class: Nina Ayres, Carolyn Chandler Perry, Amaryllis Berryhill, Roquemore Beard, Eloise Black, Joy Blackburn, Kenneth Bragg, Wylodean Brandon, Sara Kate Branyon, Mary Nell Brock, Joe Allen Brown, Eleanor Jean Buckner, Bryce Cargile, Fred Colburn, Almeda Cooper, Araline Davidson, James Dodson, Jolene Francis, Warren Loftis Freeman, Bryan (f) Fullerton, Obera Fullerton, Dan Galloway, Nades Gibson, Selma Gray, Louise Hinton, Orlene Hobbs, Clara Lee Hollis, Elizabeth Hollis, Hamilton Humber, Edith Jordan, Alexander Kizzire, Thelma **Lambert**, Ivyree Lambert, Mildred Lawrence, Thomas Lawrence, Billy Loftis, James Maddox, Rachel Martinolich, Margie Mathis, Mary Alice Matthews, Hazel McConnell, Marthellon Otts, Camille Randolph, Dorothy Renfroe, David Sanford, Irene Stough, Billy Tabor, Doris Thomas, Lavene White, Avis Whitley, Ida Key Whitley, Betty Lou Willis, Earlene Wilson, and James Woods.

1944 - 1945 Faculty: J. M. Brown - Prin., Mrs. L. B. Allen, Mrs. Lucyle Barnett, Miss Nellie Brock, Mrs. Alma Cannon, Paul Darnell, Miss Margaret DeBardeleben, Mrs. Sadie Goodwin, Mrs. C. M. Holder, Miss Estelle Jones, Mrs. Frankie Martin, Fred Payne, Mrs. Ruth Page, W. W. Rodgers, Miss Gwendolyn, Mrs. Laura Ann Stubbs, Miss Thelma Terry, Mrs. Marie Williams, Mrs. Irene Wright, and Miss Susie DeMent. Graduating Class: Joe Alexander, Doris Jean Alvis, Eloise Atkinson, Dorothy Ayres, Kathleen Brazil, Jewel Bridges, Betty Ann Cannon, Tom Cannon, Harry D. Cargile, Bertha Lee Champion, Sarah Champion, Mary Nell Cooper, Marguerite Connell, A. B. Corbett, Audrey Davis, Cohen Davis, Don Dockery, Ima Lou Edwards, Ivalene Edwards, Louelle Freeman, Betty Hazel Galloway, Bobby Galloway, Wynell Galloway, Jeweldean Gardner, Jimmy Gullett, Ema Dell Hobbs, Jeaneva Holt, Iva Johnson, Mary Kate Kemp, Jaqueline Loftis, Nocal Madison, James Moore, Aileen Morris, Ermine Muse, Eloise Nelson, Jack Newman, Maxine Newman, Mary Nell Nichols, Paul Nichols, Roy Curtis Oswalt, Elois Pinkerton, Ruby Nell Pritchett, Mary Rasberry, Billy Ray, Mary Reynolds, Thomas Alfred Rose, Jr., Orell Shepherd, Bessie Nell Sims, Katherine Smith, Sara Speed, Gloria Sterman, Clarence Stewart, Albert Taylor, Ann Ethel Thompson, Jack Thornton, Ray Walters, Eloise Watkins, Estelle Weeks, Catherine White and Dewitt Williams, Jr.

1945 - 1946 Faculty: J. M. Brown - Prin., Miss Nellie Gray Brock, Mrs. Terrell Cannon, Mrs. Clyde Cargile, Miss Susie DeMent, Mrs. James Dockery, Mrs. C. M. Holder, Mrs. J. B. Houston, Miss Estelle Jone, Mrs. L. B. Lollar, Mrs. Frankie Martin, Mrs. W. W. (E.J.Vick) Norden, Fred Payne, W. Woodall Rodgers, Mrs. Guthrie Smith, Mrs. Helen Stevenson, Miss Gwen Stewart, Miss Thelma Terry, Miss Frances Vick, Mrs. Z. D. Vick, Jr. and Mrs. Delmar Wright. Graduating Class: Lavaughn Ballinger, Grafton Belk, Polly Black, Bette Jo Burdette, Ned Butler, Dessie Mae Cagle, Christine Caraway, Grace Cargile, Billie Hocutt Daniel, Lawrence Ellii, Kathleen Fowler, Fayet Gilpin, Clark Gravlee, Joe Gunter, Ina Banks Hankins, Mary Evelyn Harkins, Dorothy Hollingsworth, Kathleen Hollingworth, Rex Hollis, Mary Frances Horn, H. J. Howard, Alene Hubbert, Hershel Johnson, Bernice Kizzire, Peggy Lindsey, Sara Joy Maddox, Marcelle Miles, Helen Montgomery, Ruth Montgomery, Mary Angelyn McNease,

Betty Jo Newton, Syble Oswalt, Marcheta Otts, Vivian Pastuer, Manley Phillips, Wynell Porter, Ivy Potter, J. W. Pritchett, Betty Rasberry, W. F. Richards, Joyce Roberts, Elizabeth Rowland, Betty Sharpe, George Hassell Shepherd, Mary Lee Smith, Murry Gae Smith, Mary Lee Spiller, Betty Striegel, Ruby Salurin, Helda Van Hook, Earlene Watkins, James Howard Watkins, Susie Gray Weeks, Betty White, Jewel Dean Brazil White, Eloise White, Mary Spain Wiggins, Betty Lindsey Williams and Frances Young.

1946 - 1947 Faculty: J. M. Brown - Prin., Hoyt Brewer, Miss Nellie Brock, Mrs. Terrell Cannon, Mrs. Clyde Cargile, Mrs. M. C. (F.Vick) Davis, Mrs. James Dockery, Mrs. J. P. (E.Jones) Garrison, Mrs. J. B. Houston, Mrs. W. H. Humber, Sr., Mrs. Roy Martin, Mrs. Earl McDonald, Fred Payne, W. W. Rodgers, Mrs. S. J. (Gwen Stewart) Sanders, Jr., Miss Marion Scrivner, Miss Geraldine Sherman, Wayne Shoemaker, Mrs. Malcolm (M.McGough) Smith, Miss Thelma Terry and Mrs. Delmar Wright. Graduating Class: Howard Anderson, William Barnes, Harold Berry, Johnny Boyd, Jack Branyon, Curt Branyon, Ozella Brasher, Ruby Grey Brown, J. D. Burson, Otheal Burson, Doulton Butler, Joe Neal Butler, Jr., Bob Cannon, Elna Lou Caraway, Betty Cargile, Kathleen Waldrop Clark, Wightman Cannon, Cratie Cargile, Ray Crowe, Polly Darnell, Evanal Davis, Flora Maye Dodson, Lora Faye Dodson, Emogene Doughty, Billy Dan Dyer, John R. Estes, Bill Falls, Amy Lou Fullerton, Bill Galloway, Denna Maye Gartman, Elsie Dean Gilpin, Alma Jean Gladden, Mary Sue Harbin, Benny Hindman, Vilma Hollingshead, Barnes Houston, Betty Houston, James Cecil Jackson, Fred Johnson, Fred C. Jones, Willette Kemp, Mildred Kizzire, Howard Lawrence, Gene Logan, Iva Lee Logan, Norma Madison, Bernice McCool, Dewitt McCracken, Louise Godfrey Maddox, Chester R. Moore, Donald Nelson, Max Newman, Bill Nichols, Agnes Pinkerton, Margaret E. Propst, Sue Propst, Beachel Rainey, Faye Rice, Lloyd Richards, Joyce Rowland, Collen Spiller, Imogene Stoker, Edward Stough, Louise Stough, Olene Stough, Annie Gay Striegel, Martha Taylor, Evelyn Wallace, Aline Walden, Evelyn White, Katie Lee Williamson, Thomas Loyd Williamson, Adella Woods and Jimmy Young.

1947 - 1948 Faculty: J. M. Brown - Prin., Hoyt Brewer, Miss Nellie Brock, Mrs. Cora Lee Brown, Mrs. Alma Cannon, Mrs. Lottie Cargile, Mrs. Estelle Garrison, Miss Dorothy Gravlee, Mrs. Clarice Holder, Miss Martha Holley, Mrs. Ruby Houston, Mrs. Frankie Martin, Fred Payne, Miss Helen Peterson, W. W. Rodgers, Mrs. Gwen Sanders, Buell M. Scott, Miss Marguerite Shirley, Mrs. Virginia Garrison Spivey, Miss Thelma Terry, Mrs. Irene Wright. Graduating Class: June Carolyn Alexander, Ethel Ayres, Leon Ballinger, Tommy Branyon, Joy Beard, Ted Brasher, Flossie Brock, Norma Jean Byars, Noel Bynum, Kelcy Cargile, Warren G. Cargile, Catherine Carmack, Jeff Cobb, Bette Jo Collins, Joe Dobbs, Wallace Dodson, Dottie Estes, Helen Estes, Kenneth Farquhar, L. A. Fowler, Billy Frances, Sue Lee Gardner, Dorothy Gartman, Colleen Godfrey, Vaudene Gregg, Fell; Grimsley, Jr., Maggie Mae Hallman, Sam Hill, Tommie Hinton, Maxine Holliman, Gay Wista Howton, Ed Gaines Jeffries, D. H. Kizzire, Billy Gene Maddox, James Maddox, Jimmy Mason, Willie Gray Miles, Hillard Milligan, Norma Thomas Milligan, Sammy Moore, Eugene McCool, Mary Faye McCraw, Pete Newton, Carroll Otts, Sue Carol Pinkerton, Melba Lee Rainey, Malinda Robertson, Sue Robertson, Sara Alice Rosborough, Billy Rowland, Ozell Sanders, Betty Jo Sexton, Rayford Shepherd, Audrey Smallwood, Clarence Smith, James Smith, Janeene Smith, Billy Stewart, Aline Whitley, Albert Wise, Frank West, Martha Woods, and Sara Alice Yerby.

1948 - 1949 Faculty: John Morgan Brown - Prin., Miss Margaret Alexander, Mrs. Maxine Ashcraft, Mrs. Dixie Brock, Miss Nellie Gray Brock, Mrs. Cora Lee, Brown, Mrs. Alma Cannon, Mrs. Lottie Cargile, Mrs. Frances Moore deVilton,

Mrs. Estelle Garrison, Robert Harwell, Mrs. Ruby Houston, Miss Eugenia Hughes, Mrs. Frankie Martin, S. F. Payne, Miss Helen Peterson, Mrs. Gwen Sanders, Mrs. Mary Glenn Herren Smith - Office, and Miss Thelma Terry. Graduating Class: Anita Ayres, Haskell Barnes, Erbie Lee Boyd, Max Branyon, Dora Brock, Johnny Mack Brown, Buddy Cannon, J. C. Christian, Myra Connell, John Corbett, Bill Dennis, Wylodene Dobbs, Lorene Estes, Hulon Fowler, Frank Gravlee, Betty Renfroe Griffin, Kenneth Hallmark, Lee Brooks Hankins, Bobbie Jean Harbin, Jackie Harkins, Braxton Hocutt, Carolyn Hollis, Frank Horne, Bobby Jackson, Eugene Jenkins, Maudene Johnson, Gila Rae Key, Terry Kirkley, Sue Lindsey, Jimmy Mason, Pat McNease, Bobby Meherg, John Wesley Muse, Lyndall Nelson, Edward Newman, Edwin Newman, Rose Ann Newton, Nancy Otts, Blanche Rainey, Janette Rasberry, Mary Ellen Rushing, Ozell Sanders, Buddy Shelton, Janie Shepherd, Betty Lou Sims, L. C. Smith, Maxine South, Lloyd Stephens, Lorene Swindle, Floyce Ann Vaughn, Carolyn Wiggins, Billie Angelyn Wilson and Jasper Nell Woods.

   1949 - 1950 Faculty: John Morgan Brown - Prin., Miss Margaret Alexander, Thomas Bailey, Miss Nellie Gray Brock, Mrs. Cora Lee Brown, Mrs. Alma Cannon, Mrs. Lottie Cargile, Henry Davis, Mrs. Estelle Garrison, Mrs. Sadie Goodwin, Robert Harwell, Mrs. Voncile Kelly, Mrs. Frankie Martin, S. F. Payne, Miss Helen Peterson, Mrs. Gwen Sanders, Miss Thelma Terry, J. E. Webster, Bill Williamson, and Miss Frances Yates. Graduating Class: Martha Alexander, Jimmie Lou Ballinger, Joe Barnes, Louise Barnes, Bobby Belk, Samuel Benton, Fulton Branyon, Myra Jo Branyon, Betty Brasher, Dale Brasher, Evelyn Brock, Hubert Brock, Bobby Burdette, Eula Burkett, Mary Eunice Bynum, John Morrow Cannon, William A. Cannon, Maynard Colburn, Verden Davis, Clark Dodson, Walter Hugh Ferguson, Dorothy Nell Fisher, Della Gartman, Ina Gilpin, Dean Gray, Lemmie Gray, Patsy Griffin, Wilma Hallman, Buddy Hallmark, Ray Hassell, Kenneth Herren, Gayle Houston, Irene Hughes, Mary Fletcher Jenkins, Bobbie Sue Sanford Kelly, Mildren Kuykendall, Gaines Lawrence, Jeffie Lawrence, Betty Louise Loe, Lionell Loftis, Ann Lowe, Eugene Lowe, Eulene Lowery, Sue McCaleb, Riley McGee, Kathleen Madison, Macon Madison, John Montgomery, J. V. Morgan, Mary Ellen Nelson, William Nelson, Jeneil Nichols, L. B. Northam, Tom Peters, Harlan Philips, Betty Pinkerton, Inez Pritchett, Mina Propst, Robert Earl Roby, Billie Rowland, Mary Agnes Sanders, James Allen Shepherd, Billy Jean Smith, Eunnell Smith, William C. Stokes, Jewel Stough, Betty Jon Sullivan, Charles Valden, Doris Watkins, Katherine Wallace, Billy Roy Williamson, Betty Ruth Winsted, Jean Wright, Murray Wright, Myrtle Wright, and Millie Young.

   1950 - 1951 Faculty: John Morgan Brown - Prin., Miss Margaret Alexander, Miss Nellie Gray Brock, Mrs. Cora Lee Brown, Mrs. Alma Cannon, Mrs. Lottie Cargile, Mr. Rube Courington, Mr. Henry Davis, Mrs. Margaret Enslen, Mrs. Estelle Garrison, Mrs. Frankie Martin, Mr. J. B. McClendon, Miss Ann Norwood, Mr. W. E. Pendergrass, Miss Helen Peterson, Mr. J. V. Raines, Mrs. Gwen Sanders, Mr. Ewell Scott, Miss Thelma Terry and Mr. J. E. Webster. Graduating Class: Dorothy Lee Barclay, Bobbie Beard, Bobby Black, Johnny Brasher, Hubert Brock, Romona Lee Brock, Joe Stanley Brown, Thomas Campbell, James Lohrone Cannon, Wayne Cargile, Frances Chism, Hosea Collins, Sara Davis, Jimmie Dunagan, David Fullerton, Sara Nell Fulmer, Eddie Hammons, Edgar Harkness, Mary Carol Hendrix, Aaron Herron, Bertha Jo Jenkins, Bobby Jo Kemp, Leroy McCaleb, Larry McConnell, Barbara Gayle McDaniel, John Arthur Martin, Joe Earl Meherg, Polly Mitchell, J. C. Moore, Grady Nelson, Vaudie Mae Nelson, Arlie Madison, Donna Newton, Eleanor Jane Newton, Robert Norris, Melva Phillips, Catherine Rainey, Peggy Randolph, Alby Rice, Mary Rowland, Billie Rowland, Bobbie Jean Sanders, Maurice Sanford, Milford Smith, Vauda Ann Smith, Nelda

Jeune Stanley, Joe Taylor, Gresham Waldrop, Novilene Waldrop, Sue Watkins, John Billy White, Ted Whitley, Anice Williamson, Douglas Wright, Jane Wright, Joyce Yerby and Rhetta Yerby.

1951 - 1952 Faculty: J. M. Brown - Prin., Miss Margaret Alexander, Miss Nellie Brock, Mrs. Cora Lee Brown, Mrs. Alma Cannon, Mrs. Lottie Cargile, P. W. Colburn, Mrs. Margaret Enslen, Mrs. Estelle Garrison, Mrs. Sadie Goodwin, Robert Harwell, Mrs. Frankie Martin, J. B. McClendon, Miss Helen Peterson, Mrs. Gwen Sanders, Ewell Scott, Miss Janeene Smith, Miss Thelma Terry and J. E. Webster. Graduating Class: Ann Anders, Linton Ballinger, Nelda Ann Bircheat, Betty Ann Black, Maylene Black, Bobbie Bobo, Dean (f) Bohannon, N. S. Burns, Ned Cargile, Sue Christian, Elreta Dodson, Rebecca Dodson, Calvin Foster, John A Fowler, John Ed. Fowler, Jerry Galloway, Helen Gartman, Eleanor Gray, Martha Griffin, Betty Grimsley, Christine Shepherd Grizzell, Gayle Herren, Everette Hocutt, Leland Holliman, Carol McCaleb Howell, Eugene Howell, Gayle Jemison, Olean Jenkins, Mavis Johnson, Doris Kizzire, Duddy Lawley, Betty Lou Lawrence, Helen Norris Lawrence, Joe Alfred, Duddy Lindsey, Janice McCool, Beulah Madison, Caroly Newton, Leon Pettis, Connie Rainey, Jimmie Riley, Norma Roberts, Nolan Robertson, Bernice Shelton, Margie Shelton, Jo Nell Spiller, John Stamps, Betty Barton Stephens, Ted Stephens, Guy Stough, Betty Webster, Linda Williamson, Autie Bell Woods and Billy Jane Younghance.

1952 - 1953 Faculty: J. M. Brown - Prin., Mrs. Loudelle Berry, Mrs. Margaret Alexander Black, Miss Nellie Brock, Mrs. Cora Lee Brown, Mrs. Alma Cannon, Mrs. Lottie Cargile, Mrs. Margaret Enslen, Mrs. Estelle Garrison, Robert Harwell, Mrs. Frankie Martin, J. B. McClendon, Paul McCully, Miss Helen Peterson, Mrs. Gwen Sanders, Miss Janeene Smith, Miss Thelma Terry, Miss Betty Tinsley and J. E. Webster. Graduating Class: Betty Andrews, Dean Bagwell, George Bagwell, Max Belk, Myrtle Berry, Betty Black, Jerry Bobo, Branyon Boyd, Sula Brasher, Doris Ann Brock, Jane Brock, Barbara Clark, Frances Daniel, Marie Davis, Sylvia Davis, Tom Davis, Yvonne Davis, Jeanie Jo Dobbs, Lynwood Duncan, Gloria Ann Etheridge, Frank Ferguson, Janis Fowler, Sara Katherine Franks, Ralph Gibson, Eloise Gilpin, Bette Graham, Mary Griffin, Bryce Allen Hall, Joe Hallman, Valoris Hallman, Hershel Ham, Kenneth Hankins, Rosalyn Jaughton, Elaine Hindman, Roy Howard, Virginia Knight, Ben Logan, Gary Maddox, Maxine Maddox, Lynn Madison, Helen Miles, Billy Morrison, Dorothy Newton, Chester Pauline, Patsy Roberts, Thomas Roberts, Jerry Robinson, Billy Jack Sharpe, Jannette Shuford, Jane Smith, Martha Stewart, Lorraine Tucker, Etelene White, June White, Cornelia Williams, Sue Wilson, Janet Wright and Jimmy Young.

1953 - 1954 Faculty: J. M. Brown - Prin., Mrs. Loudelle Berry, Miss Nellie Brock, Mrs. Cora Lee Brown, Mrs. Alma Cannon, Mrs. Lottie Cargile, Mrs. Cora Lee Colburn, Mrs. Margaret Enslen, Mrs. Estelle Garrison, Robert Harwell, Clarence Kirkley, Mrs. L. B. Lollar, Mrs. Frankie Martin, J. B. McClendon, Paul McCully, Mrs. Gwen Sanders, Miss Thelma Terry, Miss Bette Tinsley, and J. E. Webster. Graduating Class: Martha Jane Andrews, Robert Bagwell, Jennie Beasley, Caroline Benton, Aileene Blackwell, Thomas Bobo, Martha Branyon, Max Brasher, Noel Brock, Mary Joyce Brown, Lounell Buckner, Charles Burns, Joe Cargile, Jimmie Sue Chastain, Patircia Chastain, Mary Cockrell, Bent Collins, Billy Gene Colston, Carlton Davis, Donald Estes, Linton Fowler, Gaylon Fowler, Jo Ann Fowler, Joe Fowler, Louellen Fowler, John D. Freeman, Jo Frances Gibson, George Griffin, Jr., Sylvia Hallman, Paula Harbin, Alton Harkins, Doris Ann Hayes, James Hendrix, Joe Edd Hocutt, Lanelle Holliman, Johnnie Humber, Suzanne Jackson, Billy Ray Jenkins, Shelby Jean Killingsworth, Rachel Kizzire, Carolyn Lawrence, Armon Loe, Bill Musgrove, Ira Musgrove,

Glenn Newton, Gary Newton, Franklin Nichols, Callie Porter, Ted Randolph, Betty Rowell, Benny Rushing, Kenneth Seaborn, Clayton Sims, Doyle Simmons, Mildred Smith, Mary Stewart, Shirley Richards Stokes, Sudie Stoker, J. B. Taylor, Rita Gayle Waldrop, Dorothy Wallace, Harold Wilson, Kenneth White, Betty Williamson, Jack Yielding and Maury Anne Young.

1954 - 1955 Faculty: J. M. Brown - Prin., Miss Carol Beck, Mrs. Loudelle Berry, Miss Nellie Brock, Mrs. Cora Lee Brown, Mrs. Alma Cannon, Mrs. Lottie Cargile, Mrs. Cora Lee Colburn, Mrs. Margaret Enslen, Mrs. Estelle Garrison, Robert Harwell, N. K. Jenkins, Clarence Kirkley, Mrs. L. B. Lollar, Mrs. Frankie Martin, J. B. McClendon, Paul McCully, Mrs. Sue Propst McCully, Mrs. Gwen Sanders, Miss Thelma Terry, Miss Bettie Tinsley, J. E. Webster, and Mrs. Helen Peterson Yeargen. Graduating Class: Lomax Ballinger, Mamie Black, Billy Joe Bobo, Evelyn Bobo, James Bohannon, Perry Branyon, Mary Frances Brasher, Sue Prasher, Nell Cannon, Caines Clark, Tommy Collins, Johnny Davis, Louise Duckworth, Peggy Elmore, Jerry Fowler, Teddy Garrison, Mona Fay Gary, Dean Gilliam, Shelby Jean Gray, Edith Sue Hallman, Herrie Harbin, Kay Frances Howell, Helen Humber, Erma Jean Jenkins, Jimmie Carl Jones, Jimmy Ray Jones, Rayburn Key, Ted Kilgore, Bonnie Sue Kizzire, Rena Mae Loftis, Ada Sue Loftis, Calvin Madison, Clyde McCaleb, Frank Wade McCutheon, Judy McNease, Dorothy Miles, Patsy Newton, May Otts, Ray Pierce, Bobby Jean Price, Malinda Rasberry, Gordon Robinson, Dale Sanford, Charles Sims, Marilyn Smith, Teresa Smith, Martha Ann South, Max South, Reuben Stewart, Sara Sularin, Joe Dear Taylor, Kelly Rae Taylor, Phillip Taylor, Faye Thomas, Betty Jo Wallace, David White, James White, Etheleen Williams, Joy Wilson and Peggy Yerby.

1955 - 1956 Faculty: J. M. Brown - Prin., Mrs. Loudelle Berry, Miss Nellie Brock, Mrs. Cora Lee Brown, Mrs. Lottie Cargile, Mrs. Cora Lee Colburn, Fred Colburn, Mrs. Margaret Enslen, Mrs. Estelle Garrison, Mrs. Joe Goodwin, Miss Mary Alice Gross, Robert Harwell, N. K. Jenkins, Clarence Kirkley, Mrs. L. B. Lollar, Mrs. Frankie Martin, J. B. McClendon, Paul McCully, Mrs. Sue McCully, Mrs. Frances Moore, Mrs. Gwen Sanders, Miss Thelma Terry, Miss Bettie Tinsley and J. E. Webster. Graduating Class: Joel Barnes, Noel Barnes, Ronnie Barton, Cecil Belk, Margaret Ann Benton, J. W. Berry, Max Bohannon, Charles M. Buckner, Melva Lee Bynum, Bobby Christian, Joy Clanton, Gwendolyn Cooper, Joe Corbett, Kathleen Dobbs, Wayne Dubose, Shirley Elmore, Bob Finley, Laxene Fowler, Patsy Franks, Linda Freeman, Barbara Gibson, Sarah Hall, Jerry Hamby, Judith Ann Hankins, Hugh Harkins, Preston Harkins, Barbara Heath, Jane Henderson, Myra Hill, Clara Belle Hocutt, Rayburn Howard, James Hubbert, Jerrie Sue Jeffries, Louise Jenkins, Edward Key, Charles Lawley, Levert Lawrence, Bobbie McCool, Joe Maddox, Suzanne Mansfield, Walter Lee Mathews, Paul Moore, Lauranne Musgrove, Charlotte Nichols, James Otts, Joe Dale Perkins, Malinda Renfroe, Martha Sue Godfrey, Janice Shook, Patsie Sisson, Charles Sisson, J. W. Smith, Ross Lee Smith, Lula Rose Smith, Ruby Stocks, Charles Terry, Lander Waid, Wayne Waldrop, Denzil Wallace, Elizabeth Ann Watkins, Billy Watkins, Joan White, E. C. Whitley, Patsy Williams, Linda Wilson, Josephine Young, Mary Young and M. C. Younghance.

1956 - 1957 Faculty: John M. Brown - Prin., Mrs. Loudelle Berry, Mrs. Margaret Black, Jerry Bobo, Miss Nellie Brock, Mrs. Cora Lee Brown, Mrs. Maxine Butler, Mrs. Clyde Cargile, Fred Colburn, Mrs. Paul Colburn, Mrs. Malcolm (Malinda Robertson) Daniel, Dan Galloway, Mrs. Joe Goodwin, Mrs. Sara Davis Gullett, Robert Harwell, Mrs. Robert Harwell, N. K. Jenkins, Clarence Kirkley, J. B. McClendon, Paul McCully, Mrs. Sue McCully, Mrs. Gwen Sanders, Miss Thelma Terry, and J. E. Webster. Graduating Class: John Douglas Andrews, Melvyn Anhalt, Carl Ballinger, Lola Hope Barnes, Stella Belk, Jane Bobo, Jeff

Bogard, Ruthie Mansfield Bone, Ellon Branyon, Hugh Stanley Branyon, Marilyn Branyon, Wanda Brock, Martha Harriette Brown, Rhetta Burns, Kay Calton, Betty Ruth Chastain, Ila Dean Chastain, Doris Janeene Colston, Darrell Clark, Norma Cook, John Crutcher, Sarah Elizabeth Elmore, Jane Fowler, Gene Fulmer, J. C. Gary, Jr., Martha Sue Gilpin, Geraldine Gladdin, Jack Godfrey, Millie Hocutt Griffin, Carolyn Hallman, Mary Frances Harbin, Rayburn Hayes, Johnny Hendrix, Calvin Larry Howton, Carol Hughes, Shirley Jenkins, Charlie Dale Keeton, Harold Kelley, Sonia Gale Kizzire, Eugene Knight, Ronny Lawrence, Sarah Lemons, Sarah Mathes, Bobbie Reed Medlock, Martha McCutheon, Martha McIntosh, Allen Meherg, Eloise Morrison, Amelia Brown Musgrove, Martha Nelson, Barbara Newton, Elizabeth Otts, Iris Otts, Jerrie Palmer, Dwight Phillips, Alvadale Porter, William Porter, Curtis Rainey, Juanita Roberts, Martha June Dobbs Robinson, Margene Rushing, Dale Simmons, Lynn Smith, Murl Smith, Rhonda Stamps, Willie Max Stoker, Sarah Stough Sexton, Bobby Joe Watkins, Donald Watkins, Tommy Webster, Betty White, Linda Ann White, Kay Patrick Wiggins and Dessiree Wright.

1957 - 1958 Faculty: John Morgan Brown - Prin., Mrs. Loudelle Berry, Mrs. Margaret Black, Jerry Bobo, Miss Nellie Brock, Mrs. Cora Lee Brown, Mrs. Maxine Butler, Mrs. Willie Nell Ashcraft, Mrs. Cora Lee Colburn, Fred Colburn, Mrs. Frances Davis, Mrs. Estelle Garrison, Mrs. Sadie Goodwin, Mrs. Sara Gullett, Robert L. Harwell, N. K. Jenkins, Clarence Kirkley, Mrs. L. B. Lollar, J. B. McClendon, Mrs. Frances Moore, Mrs. Gwen Sanders, James R. Saxton, Miss Thelma Terry, Miss Lula Dean Walters and J. E. Webster. Graduating Class: Virginia Abernathy, Bill Andrews, Alice Ayres, James Beasley, Linda Brasher, Joe Young Campbell, Cynthia Ann Carroll, Edrena Caudle, Davis O'Connell Couch, Adean Crowlen, Janice Dickinson, Ralph Dobbs, Peggy Jean Dodson, Sue Dudley, Wayne Edwards, Derrell Estes, Frances Finley, Bud Gardner, Harold Fowler, Judy Freeman, James Edwin Godfrey, Garland Gray, Lomax Greene, Kenneth Hallman, Charles Hendrix, Orman Howton, Thelma Ann Howton, Melvin Howard, Jimmy Hubbert, LaNelle Johnson, Frances Yvonne Kelley, Charlotte Kemp, Jerry D. Killingsworth, Judy Langston, Cecil Kimbrell, Barbara Lathum, Gayle Loftis, Mary Alice Loftis, Louie Maddox, Curtis Madison, Nathan Madison, James Meherg, Robert Merritt, Breland McCool, Ronald Morrison, Ned Newton, Danny Propst, Mary Edith Reese, Woody Roberts, Betty Sue Robertson, Bill Robertson, Judy Rushing, Frances Sims, Mary Lee Smith, Ned Smith, Stephen Smith, Dorothy Stephens, Patricia Ann Stripling, Dorothy Taylor, Ralph Thornton, Ted Taylor, Richard Tucker, Len G. Waldrop, Ollie Waldrop, Shannon Waldrop, Johnny Wallace, John Williamson and Jewel Dean Wright.

1958 - 1959 Faculty: John M. Brown - Prin., Mrs. Willie Nell Ashcraft, Mrs. Lucille Barnett, Mrs. Loudelle Berry, Mrs. Margaret Black, Jerry Bobo, Miss Nellie Brock, Mrs. Cora Lee Brown, Mrs. Maxine Butler, Mrs. Cora Lee Colburn, Fred Colburn, Mrs. Frances Davis, Mrs. Estelle Garrison, Mrs. Sara Davis Gullett, Mrs. Erma Harwell, Robert Lee Harwell, Clarence Kirkley, Jr., Mrs. Frankie Martin, John Raper, Nolen Robertson, Mrs. Gwen Sanders, Miss Thelma Terry, J. E. Webster and Mrs. Frances Moore. Granduating Class: Linda Jean Crowley Ballinger, Joan Barnes, Sylvia Barton, Carlton Benton, Derry Joe Benton, Henry Benton, Johnny Bess, Tony Bobo, Betty Bone, Mattie Lou Brock, Phyllis Brown, Marie Bynum, June Calton, Dwain Campbell, James Campbell, Patsy Cannon, Cecil Canterberry, Jimmy Cargile, Jerry Clark, William A. Cook, William E. Cook, Butch Coons, Anita Davis, Robert Dollar, Gwen Duncan, Lenny Fulmer, Luellen Gault, Sarah Gay, Arron Franklin Gibson, Jr., Sarah Gladden, Linda Graves, Sandra Holliman, Kenny Housh, Morris Ann Hyde, Sandra Jeffries, Peggy Johnson, George Anne Kirksey, Jerry Lawrence, Rebecca

Lindsey, E. J. Lowery, Terry Maddox, J. L. Madison, Faye Marlowe, Nancy McCutheon, Mary Miles, Laymon Mitchell, Lymon Mitchell, Lounell Moore, Robert L. Musgrove, Wanda Nichols, Diane Peritz, Robert Pritchett, Jewel Roberts, Barbara Sanders, John Sanders, Gerald Stanley, Frances Stewart, Jennie V. Stoker, Betty Tilly, Jane Trimm, William Watkins, O'Neal White, Anne Woods, and Johnny Banks Young.

1959 - 1960 Faculty: John Morgan Brown - Prin., J. E. Webster, Mrs. Estelle Jones Garrison, Robert Lee Harwell, Fred Paul Colburn, Jerry Bobo, Mrs. Margaret Alexander Black, Clarence Kirkley, Miss Nellie Gray Brock, Mrs. Cora Lee Colburn, Miss Thelma Terry, John Loyd Raper, Mrs. Gwen Stewart Sanders, Mrs. Loudell Newton Berry, Mrs. Cora Lee Brown, Mrs. Willie Nell Hollingsworth Ashcraft, Mrs. Frances Vick Davis, Mrs. Maxine Butler, Mrs. Frankie Nuckols Martin, Jeffie Lawrence, Mrs. Erma Harwell, Mrs. Frances Moore, Mrs. Margaret Enslen, and Miss Carol McCool. Graduating Class: Mary Abernathy, Sandra Anthony, Carey Ayres, John C. Bagwell, Elaine Ballinger, James Beasley, Ted Bobo, Jim Walker Branyon, Bill Brasher, Billy Butler, Mary Cannon, Delbert Cargile, Jr., Jimmy Cargile, Lottie Chambless, Juanita Chandler, Barry Cunningham, Gene Deal, Elna Jane Dobbs, Sharon Duckworth, Jerry Dyer, Lorna Ellis, Jim Finley, Jim Floyd, Wayne Gilliam, James Gladden, Joe Gladden, Jody Goodwin, Faye Gosa, Macon Graviee, Jerry Griffin, Danny Hallman, Annette, Harbin, Ronald Howard, Carolyn Humber, Wayne Jenkins, Patricia Jones, Patricia Kelly, Marlec Kitchens, Mary M. Lawrence, Joyce Lowery, Barbara Mabury, Robert Melvin, John Merritt, Mickey Moss, Herbert Mullally, William Newman, Evelyn Nichols, Judith Oswalt, Douglas Otts, Betty Patterson, Dean Perkins, Winston Plyler, Ann Campbell Porter, Thelma Rainwater, Sara Jo Smith, Patsy Sparks, Wynell Stephenson, Beatrice Still, Franklin Taylor, Jimmy Taylor, Marsha Turner, Ann Webster, Martha Webster, Richard Whipple, Carolyn Benton White, Margaret Williamson and Helen Wright.

FAYETTE COUNTY TRAINING SCHOOL -- The Fayette County School for Negroes is located at Fayette, having been moved to the county seat from Newtonville in 1937 and given its present name. Constructed of brick and concrete blocks, the building is modern.

Severne Frazier was the first principal and at the present time (1959) James Beatty is serving as the head of the school.

FLAT TOP SCHOOL -- The Flat Top School was taught in the old Daniel's Chapel Church, located north of Fayette and west of highway No. 43. Three of those who taught at Flat Top were - Miss Julia Coggin 1919 - 1920, Miss Wilma Patterson and the last to teach there was Miss Sarah Renfroe. The little school was closed when the county consolidated many of the smaller schools.

HALEY CREEK SCHOOL -- Possibly one of the oldest schools in Fayette County was the school located on the hill just beyond Haley Creek, near where the first court house of Fayette County stood. This old school served a large part of the county as it was not uncommon for the pupils to walk five to ten miles to get an education in those days.

Some of the teachers of that old school in the later days were - Miss Florence Huey, Dr. Van Diver's father, Miss Jimmie Watts and W. F. Gibson.

HOPEWELL SCHOOL -- This was one of the older schools of the county and there are very few details about it, except that it was established about 1850. One of the teachers was Rev. L. M. Wimberley.

The school was taught in the Hopewell Primitive Baptist Church building, north of Fayette.

HUBBERTVILLE HIGH SCHOOL -- Hubbertville High School came into being in 1922 when the New River, the John Hubbert, and the Jones Schools consolidated into one school. The communities came together and built a three room building. Mr. Cantrell was principal the first year. He was followed by Mr. Clifton Kuykendall, Mr. E. C. Herren, Mr. John Holliman and Mr. Wiley Hollingsworth. This school continued to grow and in 1935 it became an accredited high school with the State Department of Education.

The first building burned in the spring of 1934 when the roof caught fire from the burning woods, nearby. The community worked together as one, in building a new, twelve room building, completely with free labor from the people of the community, except the foreman, who was paid $5 per day for fifty-three days. This building went up in smoke on the morning of October 6, 1939, just as the teachers and the pupils were arriving for school.

The present building stands as the result of the cooperation of the P.W.A., Fayette County Department of Education, and the community's families.

Mr. Wiley Hollingsworth became principal of the school in 1930. The list of teachers from its beginning to 1934 is not available.

Following is listed the faculty and the graduating class members since Hubbertville became an accredited high school in 1935:

1935 - 1936 High School Faculty: Wiley Hollingsworth - Prin., Annie Mae Holliman, L. E. Hutcheson, Frankie N. Martin, Ruth E. McCaleb and Essie Patterson. Graduating Class: Ernestine Anderson, Berta Lee Anthony, Louie Eason, Henry Cortez Ehl, Lowell Haley, Wiley Johnston, J. C. McCaleb, Ruth Perry, Ezra Smith, Frances Stovall and Ruby Worth. Elementary Teachers: John Holliman, John Wakefield, Vester Hollingsworth, Mary Morris, Vera Parris and Louise Harris.

1936 - 1937 High School Faculty: Wiley Hollingsworth - Prin., Annie Mae Holliman, John Holliman, L. E. Hutcheson, Frankie Martin, Ruth E. McCaleb and vera Ray. Graduating Class: Evacile Davis, Garvin Dodd, Evelyn Guyton, Lloyd Hallmark, Elene Hiten, Earlene Hollingsworth, Irene Grace Howell, Virgie Hubbert, Wyman Jones, Annie Lou McCaleb, Carlos McCaleb, Ophelia Martin, Mary Sexton, John Stovall, Hershell Whitson, Arnold Woodard and Robbie Rae Woodard. Elementary Teachers: John Wakefield, Vester Hollingsworth, Mary Morris, Vera Parris and Louise Harris.

1937 - 1938 High School Faculty: Wiley Hollingsworth, Prin., Elizabeth Stokes, Annie Mae Holliman, L. E. Hutcheson, Frankie Martin, Ruth E. McCaleb, and G. V. Williams. Graduating Class: Troy Aultman, Estelle Bly, Albert Box, Ola Box, Leon Campbell, Newbern Fowler, Rosa Lee Fowler, T. D. Hubbert, Inez Marshall, Clarence Perry, Grady Tucker and Lester Webster. Elementary Teachers for 1937 - 1938 not available.

1938 - 1939 High School Faculty: Wiley Hollingsworth - Prin., L. E. Hutcheson, Ruth E. McCaleb, Annie Mae Holliman, Gladys F. Caddell, Frankie Martin, M. E. Smalley, Bess Studdard, G. V. Williams, and Ruby Jo Dobbs. Graduating Class: Robert Willis Anthony, Cullen Baker, Lois Baker, Sam Campbell, Allison Chambless, Audrey Chambless, Buford Colley, Lewis Cunningham, Connie Deavours, Mary Belle Cunningham, Ethlene Fowler, J. Edmond Guyton, Green Marion Haley, Clifton Hallmark, Velma Hubbert, Howard Hunt, Louella Hunt, Estelle Jones, J. T. Jones, Fred Killingsworth, Lora Lee Little, Bessie Lee McAlpin, Ray McCaleb, Rudie Mitchell, Hill Moss, Clayton O'Mary, Erdil Perry, Virginia Rollins, Orman Sims, Grapple Smith, Paul Smith, Walter

Sullens, Lawrence Tucker, Ezzie Whitson and Iris Woodard. Elementary Teacher List not available.

1939 - 1940 High School Faculty: Wiley Hollingsworth - Prin., Gladys F. Caddell, M. E. Smalley, Ruth E. McCaleb, Frankie Martin, Bess Studdard, G. V. Williams and Ruby Jo Dobbs. Graduating Class: Mildred Box, Elaine Cunningham, Edith Hiten, Wynelle Hiten, Haley Hollingsworth, Villa Hubbert, Albert Kizzire, Tracy Lee, Billy Poer, Nell Randolph, Leon Stough, Floy Mae Webster and Orman Whitehead. Elementary Teachers: Coy Gann, Wilma Haney, John Wakefield, Alma Cannon, Neva Lee Lawrence, and Mary Belle Whitehead.

1940 - 1941 High School Faculty: Wiley Hollingsworth - Prin., Ruth Perry, Ruth E. McCaleb, Thelma Terry, Gladys F. Caddell, Frankie Martin, M. E. Smalley, R. S. Johnson and G. V. Williams. Graduating Class: Evelyn Anderson, Jessie Lee Anthony, Reedie Ballard, Edith Bly, Donald Cunningham, Cecil Davis, Emerald Davis, Clara Hallmark, Howard Hollingsworth, Marie Hollingsworth, Sam Lee, Jr., Cordie Lowery, Fred McArthur, Eloise McCaleb, Huie Lee McCaleb, Willard McCaleb, Robbie Faye McCaleb, Raymond O'Mary, Edith Smith, Erna Mae Sims, Robertes Spann, Bernice Sims, and Roland Sullivan. Elementary Teachers: Coy Gann, John Wakefield, Alma Cannon, Wilma Haney, Neva Lee Lawrence, Mary Belle Whitehead and Ruby Kimbrell.

1941 - 1942 High School Faculty: Wiley Hollingsworth - Prin., Bealon Smith, M. E. Smalley, Thelma Terry, Gladys F. Caddell, R. S. Johnson, Frankie Martin, Ruth E. McCaleb, J. E. Webster and Ruby Jo Dobbs. Graduating Class: Leland Anderson, Joyce Anthony, Janie Baker, Glenn Ballard, John Eddie Bishop, Lois Brady, Foy Campbell, Vaudell Campbell, Kathleen Cannon, James Fowler, Melba Guthrie, Clancie Hubbert, Donice Lee, Maelean Lee, Brownie Mitchell, Willie Mae Sims, J. M. Smith, Jr., Mae Doris Sprinkle, Eldon Stovall, and Lois Whitson. Elementary Teachers: Coy Gann, John Wakefield, Alma Cannon, Neva Lee Lawrence, Ruby Kimbrell, Mary Belle Whitehead and Eula Mae Poer.

1942 - 1943 High School Faculty: Wiley Hollingsworth - Prin., Coy Gann, Ruth Perry, C. S. Campbell, Ruth E. McCaleb, Gladys F. Caddell, O. J. Hawkins, Sue Hawkins, and Bealon Smith. Graduating Class: Gerald Ballard, Willie Mae Bly, Ila Mae Everett, Cullen Hollingsworth, Willa Johnson, Agnes Johnston, Elene McCaleb, Minnie Lee Manley, Dezzie Moore, Evie Moore, L. R. Perry, Wm. I. Perry, Clayton Randolph, Rue Nell Sims, Elsie Stough, Sarah Faye Stewart, Wilburn Tucker and Loyd White. Elementary Teachers: Lucille Campbell, Neva Lee Lawrence, Mrs. L. B. Lollar, Ruby Kimbrell, Hazel Olive, Eula Poer, Ola H. Woodard and Ruby Jo Dobbs.

1943 - 1944 High School Faculty: Wiley Hollingsworth - Prin., Sue Hawkins, Alma Cannon, C. S. Campbell, Ruth E. McCaleb, Elizabeth Cranford, Ruth Perry, Bealon Smith, Mabry Lee Bauer, Gladys F. Caddell and O. J. Hawkins. Graduating Class: Kathleen Avery, Mary Nell Box, Junior Cunningham, Roland Davis, Tessie Hallmark, Laura Little, Marcile McCaleb, Robert Miles, Mary Kate Mitchell, Louise Mills, Howard Perry, Gladys Sims, Edith Sherer, Louise Spann, Beatrice Smith, Cecil Stough, Billy Tucker, Hilda Webster, Lucille Webster, Fred D. Whitehead and Cephas Whitson. Elementary Teachers: Lucille Campbell, J. R. Hiten, Mrs. L. B. Lollar, Vera Parris, Catherine Patterson, Ola H. Woodard and Thelian McDonald.

1944 - 1945 High School Faculty: Wiley Hollingsworth - Prin., O. J. Hawkins, Sue Hawkins, Elizabeth Cranford, Ruth E. McCaleb, Coy Gann, Bealon Smith, Ruth Perry and C. S. Campbell. Graduating Class: Clara Mae Avery, Jessie Mae Baker, Hazel Gladys Dodd, Elease Ehl, Ronald B. Harper, Mattie Sue Hollingsworth, Thelma Hubbert, Mary Lee Hunt, Jack B. Jones, Imogene Jordan, Gerthal Dean McIntosh, Lester Poer, Jr., Virginia Tidwell, J. C. White, Jemima Woodard, and Melvina Woodard. Elementary Teachers: Lucille Campbell, J.

R. Hiten, Mrs. L. B. Lollar, Vera Parris, Ola H. Woodard, Marion McCaleb, Audrey Brasher and Thelia McDonald.

1945 - 1946 High School Faculty: Wiley Hollingsworth - Prin., Coy Gann, Ruth E. McCaleb, Elizabeth Cranford, C. S. Campbell, Marie Hollingsworth, Ruth Perry, Bealon Smith and N. S. Nelson. Graduating Class: Mary Nell Aldridge, Joe Beasley, Helen Box, Juanita Davis, Dellaree Dozier, Loudell Ehl, Wilburn Joe Haley, Ida Sue Hollingsworth, Fay Howell, Wylean Little, Cassie Lowery, _____ McAlpin, Clarence McCaleb, Olus McCaleb, Inez McDonald, Edna Earl McIntosh, Wynelle McIntosh, Wynelle Moore, Dorothy Nichols, Dorothy O'Mary, Bessie Poer, Robert Walker, Myrl Webb, O. C. Whitehead, Mary Ruth Whitley, and J. C. Winters. Elementary Teachers: Lucille Campbell, J. R. Hiten, Vera Parris, Mattie Sue Hollingsworth, Hazel Sims, Pauline Hollingsworth, Evelyn Perry, Earline Dyer and Lama McCartney.

1946 - 1947 High School Faculty: Wiley Hollingsworth - Prin., Marie Hollingsworth, Elizabeth Cranford, Ruth Perry, Grace Wakefield, C. S. Campbell, Janie Irwin, Ruth E. McCaleb, N. S. Nelson, and Bealon S. Nelson. Graduating Class: Eva Nell Aldridge, Lillian Anthony, Lawrence Bishop, Coleen Bowen, Tom Cunningham, Clarence Dozier, Lizzie Dozier, James Duke, Rayford, Jack Galloway, Harold Gaut, Harry Gene Guyton, James Hallmark, Helen Hollingsworth, Louise Hollingsworth, Theodore Hubbert, Jimmie Nell Jones, Ruth Jones, James Lee, Omega Leonard, Harold Luallen Eulan McCaleb, James F. Miles, R. L. Patton, Maymie Pennington, Florence Perry, Cecil Poer, Rex Porter, Robbie Lee Sprinkle, Earl Stovall, Kenneth Tucker, Lucille Webb and Ray Webster. Elementary Teachers: Lucille Campbell, J. R. Hiten, Vera Parris, Mattie Sue Hollingsworth, Pauline Hollingsworth, Evelyn Perry, Lama McCartney and Faye Stewart.

1947 - 1948 High School Faculty: Wiley Hollingsworth - Prin., Ruth E. McCaleb, Myrtle Aldridge, Kathleen Cannon, Delia Hiten, J. H. Hollingsworth, Imaell Kornegay, N. S. Nelson, Bealon Nelson and John Wakefield. Graduating Class: Ellis Aldridge, John Lewis Avery, Roland Bishop, Avalee Chambless, Charlie Chambless, Hassie Chambless, Maxine Cunningham, Solon Cunningham, Kathleen Dozier, Rosa Lee Dozier, Paul Eads, Opal Earley, Joe Ed Earnest, Vaudine Galloway, Josie Jean Hallmark, Charles Holcomb, Billy Hollingsworth, Wynelle Jones, Doyle Lee, Edward Lee, Abe Leonard, Felix McCaleb, Jr., Joe D. McCaleb, Thomas W. McCaleb, Junior McCluskey, Kathryn McIntosh, Roy J. Mills, Katie Moore, Floyd Norris, Robbie Norris, Ronald Sims, Hazel Smith, Balsie Stovall, Ernest Vaughn, Charlene Whitehead, Wilma Dean Whitehead, Johnie Willis, R. L. Williams, Emma Lou Woodard, Bobby Jim Woodard, Jane Woodard and Mary Woodard. Elementary Teachers: Beatrice Aldridge, Junia Perry, Lucille Campbell, Marrie Sue Hollingsworth, Pauline Hollingsworth, J. R. Hiten, Lama McCartney, Vera Parris, Evelyn Perry, and Fay S. Perry.

1948 - 1949 High School Faculty: Wiley Hollingsworth - Prin., Delia Hiten, John Wakefield, N. S. Nelson, Hoyt Brewer, Bealon S. Nelson, Dorothy Gravlee Henry, C. S. Campbell, J. H. Hollingsworth, Ruth E. McCaleb. Graduating Class: James Aultman, Betty Joy Bobo, Jo Nell Bobo, Billy Gene Dodd, Thomas Dunnavant, Johnnie Nell Estes, Mattie Dew Everett, M. L. Farris, Billy Haley, Caldwell Hollingsworth, James Herbert Hollingsworth, Ruby Nell Hollingsworth, Junior Howell, Jewel Dean Hubbert, Tessie Hubbert, Judge Jones, Horace Kendrick, Betty Sue McCaleb, Charles McCaleb, James McCluskey, Oneida McCaleb, Ray McCollum, Charlie Marshall, Charles Maxwell, Junior Oneal Mayfield, Leon Mayfield, Wallace Poer, Tolbert Randolph, Ray Roby, Arvil Smith, Clyde Smith, Harold Smith, Winnie Jo Stewart, Juanita White, Mary Elizabeth Whitehead, Nadeen Whitehead, Loyd Whitley and Valerine Youngblood.

Elementary Teachers: Myrtle Aldridge, Junia Bowen, Sallie Branyon, Lucille Campbell, Thelma Carraway, Mary Gravlee, J. R. Hiten, Lama McCartney, Evelyn Perry and Mary Belle Whitehead.

1949 - 1950 High School Faculty: Wiley Hollingsworth - Prin., Hoyt Brewer, J. H. Hollingsworth, Bealon S. Nelson, Clara Albreast, C. S. Campbell, Delia Hiten, Ruth E. McCaleb, N. S. Nelson and John Wakefield. Graduating Class: Foy Anthony, Clovia Armstrong, Charles E. Avery, Betty BaumGartner, Faye Beasley, Betty Jo Campbell, Harold Dozier, Ralph Duke, R. V. Gosa, Perry Gene Harris, Loree Harrison, Clarence E. Herren, Carlton Johnston, Claudia Gene Livingston, Jimmie Lou McCaleb, Marceil McCaleb, Virginia Marshall, Billy Newt Mills, Ray Lee Mills, Carlos Moore, Jimmie Lou Morris, Evelyn Patton, Sara Joyce Smith, Lynette Sprinkle, Billy Gene Stovall, Kenneth Whitley, Willie B. Willis. Elementary Teachers: Beatrice Aldridge, Myrtle Aldridge, Junia Bowen, Sallie Branyon, Lucille Campbell, Mary Gravlee, Lama McCartney, Evelyn Perry, Jennie Vick and Mary Belle Whitehead.

1950 - 1951 High School Faculty: Wiley Hollingsworth - Prin., Ruth E. McCaleb, Bealon S. Nelson, Delia Hiten, J. H. Hollingsworth, Ida Catherine Smith, R. L. Lott, C. S. Campbell, N. S. Nelson and Marian McCaleb. Graduating Class: Joyce Atkins, Bobbie Lee Aultman, C. W. Box, Lewis Craft, Joe Neil Davis, Christine Dodd, James Dewey Dodson, Ray Lee Dozier, Hugh Ellis, James Curtis Fowler, Frank Ned Haley, Ray Harris, Robert Jones, Euna Jordan, Colphus Lee, Claudell Luallen, Betty Ann McCaleb, M. V. McCaleb, Jr., Raymond McCollum, Deloyd Moore, J. R. McMickin, Opal O'Mary, Ruth Palmer, Louise Perry, Dale Riley, Roy Gene Roby and Maurice Sanford. Elementary Teachers: Beatrice Aldridge, Myrtle Aldridge, Junia Bowen, Sallie Branyon, Lucille Campbell, Mary Gravlee, Wilma Killingsworth, Lama McCartney, Evelyn Perry, Jennie Vick and Mary Belle Whitehead.

1951 - 1952 High School Faculty: Wiley Hollingsworth - Prin., I. L. Davis, C. S. Campbell, Delia Hiten, J. H. Hollingsworth, R. L. Lott, Ruth E. McCaleb, Bealon S. Nelson, N. S. Nelson and Ida Catherine Smith. Graduating Class: Imogene Aldridge, Charles Boner, Donald Boner, Clovia Lee Box, Leon Burkett, Betty Jean Dodd, Jessie Lee Dodd, Deanie Dozier, Billy Gunter, Ray Haley, Jurl Dean Herren, Johnny Hickman, Charlene Hollingsworth, Virginis Key, Lucy McCaleb, Jerry Maxwell, Christine Meherg, Donald Pierce, Ronel Pierce, Woodrow Poer, Cardie Stocks, Bernice Stovall, Bobby Tucker, Eulan Tucker, Jo Ann Willis and J. D. Weeks. Elementary Teachers: Beatrice Aldridge, Myrtle Aldridge, Junia Bowen, Sallie Branyon, Lucille Campbell, Mary Gravlee, Wilma Killingsworth, Lama McCartney, Jennie Vick and Mary Belle Whitehead.

1952 - 1953 High School Faculty: Wiley Hollingsworth - Prin., C. S. Campbell, J. H. Hollingsworth, Bealon S. Nelson, Mary Gravlee, Delia Hiten, R. L. Lott, Ruth E. McCaleb, N. S. Nelson and Fay F. Winborne. Graduating Class: Carolyn Aldridge, Estelle Aldridge, Edward Bowen, Eva Lou Craft, Pervis Dunnavant, Homer Farris, Tommy Galloway, William Earl Garrison, Mary Ellen Holcomb, Mary Joyce Hollingsworth, George Hubbert, Joe Dexter Hubbert, Ernest Ray Jordan, McCoy Keeton, Beulah Dean Lowery, Faye Lowery, Nita McCaleb, Mary McCollum, A. B. McCluskey, Billy Earl McCollum, Winnie Jo McDonald, Randall Moore, Alton Norris, Hollis O'Mary, Bobbie Ann Stewart, Arnold Tidwell, Charles Tittle, Jimmy Tucker, Sarah Catherine Tucker, Jack Turner, Irene Whitehead, Samuel Whitson, Jimmie Sue Willis and Jewel Ann Woodard. Elementary Teachers: Beatrice Aldridge, Myrtle Aldridge, Junia Bowen Sallie Branyon, Lucille Campbell, Evelyn P. Maddox, Lama McCartney, Mary Turner, Jennie Vick, and Mary Belle Whitehead.

1953 - 1954 High School Faculty: Wiley Hollingsworth - Prin., Delia Hiten, N. S. Nelson, C. S. Campbell, Jo Nell Hollingsworth, Sue Sanders, J. H. Hollingsworth, Bealon S. Nelson, Ruth E. McCaleb, and R. L. Lott. Graduating Class: Herman Aultman, Lester Cunningham, Bessie Dodd, Betty Jane Dodd, Landon Farris, A. B. Fowler, James Robert Herren, Ila Jean Hollingsworth, Rosa Lee Hollingsworth, Bobbie Hubbert, Paul Ray Hubbert, Tom Hubbert, Huie Hollingsworth, Dwain Johnson, Patsy Nell Long, Billy Ray McCaleb, Billy Ray Mills, Grant Morris, Bernice Norris, Billy Joe Price, Billy Joe Sims, Catherine Stewart, Jeannette Tucker, Jerry Tucker, Gaylon Whitehead and Raymond Youngblood. Elementary Teachers: Myrtle Aldridge, Sallie Branyon, Lucille Campbell, Mary Gravlee, Evelyn Maddox, Lama McCartney, Mary Turner, Jennie Vick and Mary Belle Whitehead.

1954 - 1955 High School Faculty: Wiley Hollingsworth - Prin., R. L. Lott, Maxine Butler, C. S. Campbell, George Courington, Delia Hiten, J. H. Hollingsworth, J. Nell Hollingsworth, Bealon S. Nelson and N. S. Nelson. Graduating Class: Oneal Burkett, Bobby Dodd, James Flynn, David Fowler, Wardell Gann, Joe Galloway, Ted Hallmark, Ann Henderson, Hancie Henderson, Mary Grace Hollingsworth, Betty Lou Hollingsworth, Hoyt Lowery, Bertha Miles, Rayford Moore, Edd Morgan, Basil Robison, Sally Riley, Dale Smith, Dorothy Nell Tucker, Louise Tucker, Edwin Turner, Pollard Wakefield, Jack Willis and Sonny Wyers. Elementary Teachers: Myrtle Aldridge, Sallie Branyon, Lucille Campbell, Mary Gravlee, Myrtle E. Herren, Evelyn Maddox, Mary Turner, Jennie Vick and Mary Belle Whitehead.

1955 - 1956 High School Faculty: Wiley Hollingsworth - Prin., Maxine Butler, C. S. Campbell, Caldwell Hollingsworth, Delia Hiten, J. H. Hollingsworth, Jo Nell Hollingsworth, R. L. Lott, Bealon S. Nelson, N. S. Nelson and Mary Turner. Graduating Class: Cecil Bobo, Florence Box, Jim Farris, Lenora Henderson, Mary Jo Hollingsworth, Frank Hubbert, David Lowery, Carol McCaleb, Nelda McCaleb, Jerry McCluskey, Horace Randolph, Kalos Sims, James Stewart, A. J. Stovall, Shirley Sullens, Eugene Tidwell, James Webster, Martha Webster, Charles Whitley, Joe Whitley, Betty Jo Woodard, Doria Woodard, Agnes Worthy and Roy Youngblood. Elementary Teachers: Myrtle Aldridge, Sallie Branyon, Lucille Campbell, Mary Gravlee, Myrtle Herren, Pauline C. Hollingsworth, Evelyn Maddox, Mary Belle Whitehead.

1956 - 1957 High School Faculty: Wiley Hollingsworth, - Prin., C. S. Campbell, Olan Cunningham, Delia Hiten, Caldwell Hollingsworth, Jo Nell Hollingsworth, Lou Etta Knight and Bealon S. Nelson. Graduating Class: James Aldridge, Gwyn M. Allred, Kenneth C. Anthony, Peggy J. Clark, Faye Lois Cook, Genine Cook, J. C. Files, Ruthie Jane Fowler, Garland Guyton, Anna Pearl Hollingsworth, Billy J. Hollingsworth, Margaret Hollingsworth, Thealon C. Hubbert, Wayne Hubbert, Ralph B. Johnson, J. Dale Johnston, Robert Little, Sarah McCaleb, Peggy Jane McCluskey, Earl McDonald, Harold McDonald, Neal Moore, Johnny Mansfield, Barbara Alice Norris, Norma F. Porter, Edna Mae Shaw, Rufus Smith, Ted Sprinkle, Robbie Stewart, Harold F. Stovall, Gay Nell Stripling, B. Jean Tidwell, Wayne B. Wright, Dale Wright and Martha Sue Box. Elementary Teachers: Myrtle Aldridge, Sallie Branyon, Lucille Campbell, Mary Gravlee, Myrtle Herren, Pauline C. Hollingsworth, Evelyn Maddox, and Mary Belle Whitehead.

1957 - 1958 High School Faculty: Wiley Hollingsworth - Prin., C. S. Campbell, Olan Cunningham, Delia Hiten, Caldwell Hollingsworth, J. H. Hollingsworth, Jo Nell Hollingsworth, Lou Etta Knight, Bealon S. Nelson and N. S. Nelson. Graduating Class: Glen Dale Anthony, Betty E. Box, Kenneth Dodd, Gene Flynn, Jack Gann, Mary Sue Harrison, Billy Herren, Sidney Herren, Milton Hollingsworth, Larue Hollingsworth, Judy Hubbert, Jane Hubbert, Scott

Key, Wanda Herren, Shirley Luallen, Arlene Morris, Bradford Perry, Yonice Perry, Louise Smith, Henry Stewart, Imogene Tidwell, David Tucker, Estalene Tucker, Randy Wakefield, William Whitehead, Ethelene Whitson, Dorothy Woodard, Dale Wright, Lloyd Wright, Dorothy Youngblood and James Dunavant. Elementary Teachers: Myrtle Aldridge, Sallie Branyon, Lucille Campbell, Mary Gravlee, Myrtle Herren, Pauline C. Hollingsworth, Evelyn Maddox, and Paul Ray Hubbert.

1958 - 1959 High School Faculty: Wiley Hollingsworth - Prin., Sallie Branyon, C. S. Campbell, Hugh Harrison, Delia Hiten, Caldwell Hollingsworth, J. H. Hollingsworth, Jo Nell Hollingsworth, Lou Etta Knight and N. S. Nelson. Graduating Class: Charles W. Aldridge, Jerrel Aldridge, Shirley Baker, Tony Besaley, William Edwin Birmingham, James Brasher, Hillman Clark, Delynn Dodd, James Flynn, James Fowler, Bobby Lee Hollingsworth, Gloria Jean Hollingsworth, James Howell, Nelda Dean Howell, Wallace Hubbert, Warren Hubbert, Johnny Jordan, Ann Kirkley, Dorothy Little, Paul Marcum, Jimmy McCaleb, Kenneth McCaleb, Robert McCaleb, Steve McCaleb, Ralph Moore, Betty Norris, Joy Fay Norris, Eddie Rutledge, Gay Sawyer, Roy Hill Sims, Tex Sparks, Jimmy Tate, John Rex Tucker, Loveta Tucker, Barbara Ann Whitley, Conrad Whitson and Betty Lou Wright. Elementary Teachers: Pauline C. Hollingsworth, Mary Gravlee, Mamie Barnes, Lucille Campbell, Myrtle Herren, Myrtle Aldridge, Evelyn Maddox and Jeannette Herren.

MARS HILL SCHOOL -- In 1910 A. J. McCaleb deeded land to the State for the Mars Hill Grammar and Junior High School and gave the lumber for the building. Some of the teachers were the following: Thomas Ary, George B. Cotton, Mitchell White, Ando Simpson, Leonard Harbin, Walton Key, Cleborn McCaleb, Minda Miller, Eunice McCaleb, Georgia Nunn, Annie Grace Waldrop, Mrs. ____Everett, Logan Madison and Charlie Cole.

A. J. McCaleb was a trustee from the beginning of the school in 1910 until 1926.

MONT CALM SCHOOL -- Mont Calm School was one of the older schools in the county and we have no records of this school except the following letter that was written by one of the teachers to her Uncle Thomas Anderson who resided in another state:

Mont Calm, Fayette County, Ala.
December 16, 1873

My dear Uncle,

Sometime having elapsed since I wrote to you. I've thought perhaps a few lines might not be amiss now; especially as I have some few news items to write this time, for instance I have gotten some employment at last.

I am teaching a small school about three miles from Sisters. I thought I would try it in the winter session, perhaps the confinement would not prove injurious if I could avoid exposure, and come out very well. This is the third week for me. Yet we have had no very disagreeable weather. The children are not very far advanced consequently I thought I might be doing some good to others as well as be making something for myself. It is true it will not be very remunerative but I considered it would not be better to desoise the day of small things. It is some satisfaction to know that I can earn my board at least.

I have some pretty rude boys, I somewhat fear that I may have trouble, but I pray for strength and wisdom to guide them and patience too, for it is exhaustive on patience. I have had no serious trouble as yet.

It is a considerable wonder to me how parents can quiet their consciences, when they consider how they raise their children, it comes very near being spontaneous growth. It makes a teacher's path somewhat rugged to take a number of children, some of whom are allowed to curse and fight at home, and to whom obliging manners are never mentioned and politeness considered a stuck up mess. I know that there is reason in all things. I have considerable dislike for the person who thinks politeness and good apparel go to make up the sum total of a gentleman or lady, but I do know it is elegant on a brown visaged and plain dressed person just as well. I involuntarily pay homage to the sturdy blunt looking fellow, when I discover he is courteous. Somehow I feel as if all his actions might bear close inspection. True politeness is very essential to earthly happiness, as little as it is practiced, its absence is felt.

We did have some of the strangest weather in November, I ever witnessed. One Sabbath night, the 16th there came a considerable wind with but a few minutes warning, which would have swept everything before it, had it only been a little lower. It did no damage in this immediate section, but we hear that it was quite disastrous some sixty miles from here. The wind has blown very hard every since until this week. I could not help thinking of the sailors and the 29th Psalm. I one time read a geographical description of the Storm described in that Psalm, it was a great deal more sublime when we could nearly put ourselves in the writer's place, and then look about and see the storm as he described it. It is said that one portion indicates that they retreated into Solomon's porch. If David is the author, it is strange how they should retreat into Solomon's porch, when as I understand it, Solomon did not build any until after David's decease. Yet for all that, that description makes that Psalm much more interesting to me.

I am not unnecessarily afraid of storms or lightning, it is true it makes me feel solemn, and brings forcibly before me my entire dependence upon my Creator. Yet, there is something grand as well as terrible to me in a war in the elements. Although not being scary myself, I can sympathize with those who are easily frightened, for there is nothing amusing to me connected with the fright or painful emotions of another. A great many have been very much frightened, thinking our time had come for us to be taken off in a tornado as there was a dreadful tornado passed through the counties below this some four years since. I think their fears are not unreasonable. It is my earnest desire to be ready, let my departure be by flame or flood, by storm or disease, I crave a convoy of angels, of those whom I loved here on earth to bear me company to my home in glory.

Our conference year has closed and we are all anxiously awaiting the arrival of our new Preacher. We did have a most excellent preacher this year, yet he failed to please the people. A better preacher has not been on this work since I've been here, yet nearly all have succeeded in gaining the affections of the people more than he. He is somewhat fastidious. I make it a rule to act out my methodist principles enough to try to like my preacher. I will not run him down simply because he, like other men, proves to be human, even if he does not come up to my standards of Methodist Preachers. I am a full Methodist in all but two things, viz, I haven't religion enough and I don't like Sabbath collections.

Uncle Thomas, I am at the Schoolhouse, a little log hut built in an old pine field for a "cropper", some two hundred yards from Uncle Henry Horn's residence (with whom I am boarding). He and his wife (Aunt Nancy, as I call them) his son and family all live together. They are all Methodists and exceptional ones at that. I do love Aunt Nancy and Uncle Henry. I (and every other one, too) have great faith in their religion. There are few Uncle Henry's and Aunt Nancy's in my estimation. They are ripening for the Harvest, and I think it will be a joyful time to both.

It is twilight now, I began to write since I dismissed. Two of the little boys have come back trying to chop because I am here. They were very inquisitive about my letter. I showed them the state you lived in and satisfied them. They seem to think a great deal of me. Hoping to hear from you soon that you are all well and I will close by assuring you of my esteem and affection for you, my mother's only Brother. Pray for me, Uncle Thomas, as I often pray for you. Give my love to Aunt Annie,

Yours truly,
Maggie

We have a new P. O. named Mont Calm. It is located at the store in the lane at Sister's. Mr. Musgrove is at Montgomery. Sister's health has not improved any.

M.A.H. (Margaret Agnes Harris)

(This letter was written by Margaret Agnes Harris (later Mrs. T. M. Reese) to her Uncle - and copied by her daughter, Mrs. R. E. Moore, Sr. (Jennie Lee Reese) of Winfield, Ala.)

MT. VERNON SCHOOL -- To begin with the schools in the Mt. Vernon Community were taught in log churches. The first school building was erected in 1904 and the school for this year was taught by a Mr. Smith.

The building burned in 1913 and was rebuilt. Later in 1918 the church and the school house were blown down by a cyclone. The community rebuilt these in 1919 and the present building of the Mt. Vernon Junior High School was completed in 1935.

Following are several of the principals - others are listed with dates under Junior High Schools -- Mr. Russell, Mr. Phillips, Mr. Lee Watkins, Mr. Clyde C. Cargile, Mr. Paul Colburn and Mr. Loyd Fowler.

Some of the teachers who have molded the young lives of the community are listed as follows: Miss Newell, Miss Dickey, Miss Connie Ballinger, Miss Verna Cargile, Mrs. Elva (Newt) Norris, Mrs. Lee Hollis, Mrs. Lee Moseley, and Mrs. Johnson.

NEWTONVILLE SCHOOL -- The first Newtonville School was a one-room, one-teacher school until it burned in 1918. It was located one and one-half miles west of Newtonville. A new building was erected at Newtonville in 1920 or 1921 and for several years the school employed three and four teachers. Through the years the school decreased in size until it was a one teacher school again with Mrs. Estell Davis being the last teacher when the school was abandoned and the children transported to other schools. The land and building were sold in 1951 for $950.00.

Following are listed some of the teachers of the old Newtonville School, beginning with the year 1884: Prof. John Dag Thomas, Mrs. Flora (J.D.) Thomas, Prof. Tom Alexander, Prof. A. M. Nuckols, Prof. Charlie Geer (from Kennedy), Prof. Joseph J. "Boss" Henry, Prof. W. A. Graham (Later became Dr. W. A. Graham of Fayette.), Prof. Mathews (from Florence), Prof. Peabody Peguise Mayfield, Miss Mamie Bridges, Miss Lula Deason (from Tuscaloosa), Miss Clarice Barnes, Miss Bessie Davis, Miss Amelia Perry, Prof. Thomas Ary, Mrs. Mary Peterson, Mr. Tom Black, Mr. Hugh White, Mr. Wiley Gravlee, Miss Ada Stanley, Miss Nettie Ashcraft, and Miss Little.

When the new building was erected in 1920 or 1921 there were three rooms and two more were added later. Some of the teachers from 1920-1921 were as follows: First year 1920-1921 - Mrs. Mary Peterson; others - Miss Carie Manning, Miss Mary Wright, Miss Beatrice Grace, Mrs. Estelle Gibson Davis, Miss Christine Dodson, Miss Katherine Gravlee, Miss Geraldine Studdard, Mrs. Gene (nee Holliman) Harris, Miss Janet Holliman, Mary Holliman, Essie Patterson, Miss Price, Pauline Barkley, Miss Mattie Oswalt, Mr. Terrell Cannon, Mr. John Holliman, Mr. Spence Bobo, Max Branyon, William Monroe, Vester Hollingsworth, Theron Vick, Ruben Newton, Floy Ham, Mr. Berta Smith, Miss Louise Jones, Miss Eron Taylor, Miss Artie McCool, Miss Poore, Miss Marguerite Tarwater, Miss Louise Gibson, Miss Mabel Mayfield, Miss Doris Newton, Miss Lucy Mae Wallace.

OLD HICKORY SCHOOL -- The Old Hickory School was taught in the church. This school served a section of the north central part of the county. In later years the community built a new church which is the Sandsprings Baptist Church, west of the Hubbertville Highway and east of the Winfield Highway.

SPRING HILL SCHOOL -- This school was established about 1912, possibly before this date and was located west of the Winfield Highway No. 43 near the farm of W. T. Bobo.

Some of those who taught in this school were as follows: John Garrison, Lucille Leatherwood, Vera Stewart, Miss Floy Waldrop, Miss Cross, Mrs. Green, Mrs. Lula Rushing Smith, Carl Patterson, Delia Hiten, Iler Livingston, Mary D. Stough, Verna Sizemore, Clara Bobo, Virginia Holliman, Mattie Harbin Newton, and Wilkie Newman.

When the schools were consolidated this small school was closed and the building was later sold to Mr. Easby Jones, who moved it to his property.

PUBLIC SCHOOL NO. I AT UNION CHURCH -- Following is a copy of a teacher's contract of 1861, giving a very good description of what was expected of our early teachers, their pay and such.

"It is agreed between T. M. Reese and H. H. Reed, School Trustees in T. 14 R-13 and Fayette County and T. M. Reese, a school teacher in the same county, that the said T. M. Reese will take charge of public school no. 1 located at Union Church House for the term of nine scholastic months commencing about the 18th day of March, 1861 and ending about the 20th day of December, 1861 and that he will use all his energy to improve the minds of the pupils that may attend said school, keep a true record of the pupils in attendance and report the same to the trustees and to conform to all the law regulating free public school in the State of Alabama and for such services properly rendered we the said T. M. Reese and H. H. Reed, trustees promise to pay to the said T. M. Reese as follows: Out of the public fund for the three first months sixty-three dollars and 80 cents. The remainder of the session that amount of the fund to which said school may be found to be entitled according to the average daily attendance at the rate of one dollar per scholar, per month.

Given under our hands the 9th day of March 1861."

H. H. Reed - Trustee   T. M. Reese, Teacher
T. M. Reese - Trustee

CHAPTER VIII

RELIGION

We know that with the earliest settlers came the itinerant preacher, calling the sinners to repentance. These preachers followed their usual vocation on week days; farming, milling, etc. as the case may be; but on Sundays they devoted their time and efforts to their work for the church, for which they received no pay whatever. Preaching services were first held in the homes of settlers where small groups would come, or occasionally to larger assemblages under the boughs of trees. In this way churches were founded, and in the course of time secured regular pastors. The Primitive Baptist, Methodist and Baptist religions were the predominating ones in those early days.

(Ezekiel Abner Powell, author of "Fifty-five Years in West Alabama", published in the Tuskaloosa Gazette in 1886-1889, was born in Laurens District, S. C., May 27, 1817, and died in Northport, Alabama, September 1, 1892. He was married December 22, 1846, in Northport, to Amanda Melvina Lee, born March 27, 1824, and died March 9, 1872, in Northport. The author was the son of Reuben Powell, born August 27, 1784 in Culpepper County, Va. and died July 23, 1836, in Fayette County, Alabama. He married about 1808, in Laurens District, S. C., his first cousin, Sarah Powell. For a glimpse of the religions of his day we include the following from E. A. Powell's writings.)

"Fayette County was then (1831) a newly-settled country, but few of the settlers having lived there more than eight years. They were for the most part, an energetic people, suited to frontier life, - kind and neighborly. Many of them would occasionally get drunk and fight; but in few instances did the combatants leave the ground without "making friends", as the term was then used. But notwithstanding this peculier characteristic of many of the people of that period, the reader must not suppose that there was no exception to the rule. The fact is, the characters named constituted the exception and not the rule. The churches were very well represented even at that day and time: the denominations being Primitive Baptist, Methodist and the two branches of Presbyterian, - the Old Side and the Cumberland - at least that was the term then used to distinguish the two bodies. There may have been, now and then, a member of some other denomination in the county, but if so, the fact was not generally known.

The Baptists had one leading church, called Hopewell, - its membership was scattered over an area of from twenty to thirty miles. The Church was supplied by Elder Luellen Moore, or as he was famililarly known as "Uncle Lewis" or "Father Moore". He was a man without any education, yet his influence was very great with his people. He raised a large family, all of whom were men and women of high respectability. Some few of his descendants remain in the county, but his only living children are west of the Mississippi River. The old church organization still exists, and they still hold to the old Primitive faith and practice.

The Missionary Baptists have taken most of the territory in the county, – that is, so far as Baptist influence is concerned. They have a number of churches in the county, and have accomplished a great deal of good in spreading moral and religious influence.

The Methodists had also penetrated that part of the country, and had established churches in many of the neighborhoods. The Circuit Rider as the people generally called the Pastor, was looked for at his periodical rounds; and whether on Sunday or week-day, they generally had fair congregations considering the strength of the settlement. There was another practice, at that day, that has almost grown into disuetude, – whether for good or evil I will not say. It was this, – when the "Circuit Rider" came round to his week-day appointments, he was always invited to the house of some brother to dine and spend the night. That invitation carried with it the request, if not the demand, that the preacher should pay for the entertainment given to him by preaching to the neighbors that night. This draft on the preacher was very rarely, if ever, dishonored, and the preaching sometime formed the nucleus around which a very respectable society would cluster, and very soon become one of the regular appointments on the Circuit, and would be returned on the plan for the next year's work. Then would come the Quarterly Meeting, at which the Presiding Elder was expected, and it was always expected that he would give the people a good sermon; and in most cases they were not disappointed.

But at the time the leading instrumentality in building up the Methodist Church, and as far that matter assisting all other denominations, was THE CAMP MEETINGS -- At these meetings large crowds would gather, the preaching would generally be plain pointed and powerful, and the effects produced would cause the beholder to almost think that he was witnessing the re-enactment of the scenes of the day of Pentecost. Could almost hear the cry of the startled multitude; "Men and brethren what shall we do?" and then the answer coming as if from one of the sons of thunder, "Repent!" At these meetings would occur many things which some people would call extravagant, still looking back now and following the subsequent life of great numbers of the subjects of these exciting occasions, when I can remember that I have seen the saloon keeper of long years standing, transferred from the saloon to the Pulpit; the unfortunate inebriate taken out of the mire of the slough and made a sober man for life, the man whose habit of profanity had become so closely interwoven with his every day life that people regarded it as a part of his nature, at once and forever break off from the habit, Yes: when I can go back in thought and remember all these and many, very many more, of similar character, all the results of these if you please, extravagant meetings, I am almost ready to say would to God that these days of religious excitement or if you prefer it extravagance, would return.

Speaking of camp meetings, I remember one place deserving particular notice -- "Old Bethlehem". Oh! what are the memories clustering around thy sacred precincts; how many hundreds have I known to go there in the "gaul of bitterness and in the bonds of iniquity" - return rejoicing in hope, and who have long since left the walks of men, but leaving behind them a bright evidence that all was well, blessing God that they ever attended a camp meeting at that place. And then, too, I remember so many of the old, and elderly men of that day under whose auspices the meetings were held. In imagination I can see old Father McCraw, James Murry, Mathew Davis, and scores of others giving their time and influence to the success of the meeting, and all for the good of others. The preachers - and where are they? There was Kennon, a Hearn, a Caloway, a Levert, a Neir, a Shanks, and a Murrah who filled the office of Presiding Elder, all of whom have long since gone to their reward except Murrah, he is still in the field, blowing the trumpet, though not in the effective work.

Then there were many of the Circuit Riders who were men worthy of notice, Austin Gore, a man of fine preaching talent, pleasant in address, a sweet singer, and above and better than all, a man of deep piety. His influence was great, he labored zealously and faithfully for a few years, and was called to his reward. S. B. Sawyer, who, that ever listened to the sweet, persuasive words, that fell from his lips, can forget the influence he exercises? He, too, after filling many appointments, finished his work, falling at his post.

William B. Neal, was a man of more than average power in the pulpit, whose deportment was such as to command the respect of all. Well do I remember on one occasion when he was called back to the old camp ground (at camp meeting) to preach the funeral of James Murry - seeing him stand up in the stand, and sing a then popular hymn, commencing – "In evil long I took delight." He sang it alone, no one joined him, it seemed that the congregation regarded the occasion as being too solemn for any other; the effect on the congregation was simply powerful. He still lives and is an effective worker in the Alabama Conference.

William G. Flemming was one of the giants of those days. As a preacher the equal of almost any, but few years ended his course, and he was called home. Many other preachers on that work might be named, but 'space' says, "Thus far shalt thou go and no farther." But who that lived in those times, if he or she should happen to read this - would consider the narrative incomplete without a reference to one, whose faith, zeal and energy are only commensurate with his deep toned piety. Who that ever witnessed one of his camp, or protracted meetings, will or can forget his never tiring energy, his plain, practical and yet forcible sermons and exhertations, his sweet and melodious notes in song! his prayers and then the faith he exercised in the results! forty-nine years, have utterly failed to efface these scenes from memory. What, forget scenes at old Bethlehem, October, 1838. No! they are not to be forgotten. George Scheaffer lingered in the camp; beloved of all who knew him, until last January when the Master said, "It is enough, come up higher." And no doubt thousands will rejoice in Heaven that they ever knew him. I think there was held at that place twenty-seven or twenty-eight camp meetings. But the days of its glory have departed, no sign of its original splendor is to be seen. One or two old shade trees remain and thus the tale is told. But before leaving the old ground, I must recur to one other camp meeting occasion, 1833; Rev. E. V. Levert was conducting a meeting, at first the prospect did not seem encouraging, (as I then understood not being at it.) But on Sunday night a deep interest sprung up, which grew in intensity until the whole country for miles around was so leavened by its influence, that for several days the topic of conversation every where was the meetings, and if you met a neighbor in the road, the first inquiry was the news from the meetings. Fifty-three years have passed: nearly all who participated in the results of that meeting have gone to the far off land, but here and there I meet with one who waits for the word, "Come home."

The Cumberland Presbyterians also had a church and camp ground in the county. They were a good people, many of them would tent at the Methodist meeting, and many of the Methodists at theirs, so that each meeting would be well supported. Among their preachers were several that ranked deservedly high. There was Shook, Stevenson, Wilson, Oden and others. They preached and labored faithfully; many of them sang almost seraphically. Of the old side Presbyterians I know but little, they had no church organizations in the country, I only knew a few of their members, who were very excellent people. Since that day of Campbellite, or Christian church has grown to considerable proportions and to day they have several churches, and quite a large membership. They are generally a very good people, their preachers are rather fond of debate, and proselyting. Some of them would transpose the declaration of Paul where he thanked God that he was sent not to Baptize, but to preach the Gospel. At this day the Methodists and Missionary Baptist are the leading denominations in point of numbers. But I must leave the religious aspect of the narative and return to other matters."

(The above was taken from Chapter I, as written and published in The Tuskaloosa Gazette, August 12, 1886.)

To cover the religious aspects of Fayette County today (1959) we list the following churches, alphabetically, according to the denomination.

ASSEMBLY OF GOD CHURCH - FAYETTE - The Assembly of God Church is located on the corner of Pinion Street and Harding Ave. This church was organized Aug. 1, 1952 with the following charter members: R. L. Stough, Mrs. R. L. Stough, Mrs. O. M. Dykes, Ira Perkins, Mrs. Verna Lowery, Mrs. Rosie Hayes, W. F. Jenkins, Mrs. W. F. Jenkins, Howard Poe, Mrs. Howard Poe, Mrs. F. E. McCraw, and Mrs. Charles Hayes.

Pastors serving the church, in the order they served have been - Rev. O. M. Dykes, Rev. M. R. Pipkin, Rev. L. E. Ward, Rev. C. J. Wilkes and Rev. Bill Schultz.

This is the only Assembly of God Church in Fayette County at this time.

FREEWILL BAPTIST CHURCH - BELK - The Belk Freewill Baptist Church, originally named Antioch, was organized in 1894 and was located one mile from the little town of Belk. The present Belk or Antioch Cemetery is located at the first site of the church. This cemetery is one of the largest rural cemeteries in the county.

The church was organized by J. R. Robertson. Some of the charter members were as follows: Bud Williams, John Williams, Jim Foster, John Wallace, Rachel Harton, Mary Williams and Joe Abbott.

Bud Williams and John Williams served the church as deacons until their deaths. The church was moved to the present location on the Highway in 1916. The building was originally wood and was brick veneered in 1933. The Sunday School rooms and new pews were added in 1947. The present membership is 158.

Those who have served as pastor of the church since 1894 are the following: J. D. Byars - three times, J. M. Pinkerton - two times, J. W. Brown, G. W. Hollis, J. R. Robertson, J. E. Mathis, V. E. Harbin, T. L. Walker, O. C. Weaver, N. L. Hollis, L. O. Larwood, A. L. Warren, W. O. Knight, M. E. Carpenter, Charles Craddock, Leander McAdams, O. Z. Johnson and J. L. Lavender.

The present pastor is Rev. R. L. Warren and the church clerk is Mr. R. H. Yerby.

FREEWILL BAPTIST CHURCH - FAYETTE - Located on Aylette Street.

FAYETTE COUNTY MISSIONARY BAPTIST ASSOCIATION -- The first Missionary Baptist Association in the territory covering Fayette County was organized sometime near 1825 and was called the Buttahatchee Association. The entire northern end of the State of Alabama at that time was in two associations, the Buttahatchee and the Cahaba, which extended from the Georgia State line on the east and included a part of Mississippi on the west.

From a portion of the Buttahatchee was formed the North River Missionary Baptist Association in the year 1834, and in October, 1871, several churches in the first district of the North River Association obtained letters of dismission for the purpose of organizing the "New River Association", and met at Fayetteville to effect the organization; the following churches composed the New River Association organized in October, 1871; these bringing letters from the North River Association - Fayetteville, Mt. Joy, Mt. Olive, Mt. Pleasant, New Bethel, Pilgrim's Rest, Rocky Mount (Later Covin), Shady Grove, Shepherd and Union. Three newly constituted churches were also enrolled - Chapel Hill, Mt. Zion and Philadelphia.

At the 49th session of the New River Association held with Pleasant Hill Church on October 16 - 17, 1919, the name of the association was changed to the "Fayette County Missionary Baptist Association". There were 18 churches represented at the 49th session of the association.

The North River Association, started in 1834, had six churches and 150 members with only two ordained ministers. Elder D. W. Andrews was called the father of the North River Association. In 1824 the Rev. Andrews was licensed to preach and in 1831 was ordained to the full functions of the gospel ministry. He came to Alabama in 1832 and joined the Bethel Church, near Tuscaloosa and in July, 1832, he carried on a protracted meeting at Salem, the first Baptist Church organized in Fayette County and at this meeting 97 converts were baptized into the fellowship of the Salem Church. The results of this meeting was said to be the germ of the North River Missionary Baptist Association's beginning. It is a historical fact that at that meeting was the beginning of the agitation of the question of missions or no missions which finally culminated in a split in the Baptist Church.

Out of the North River Association four other associations have been made. The Yellow Creek Association was formed in 1861, the New River Association was formed in 1871, the Fayette County Association was formed in 1919 and also, the Clear Creek Association was formed from the North River Association. This shows that the North River Association covered a very large territory at its formation.

In the early days of the church the white folks and the slaves attended church together, the slaves taking their places on their designated benches and the white folks on their benches. The white land owners and the slaves joined the same church and were even baptized together. Shortly after the Civil War, letters of dismission were granted to the former slaves and they went out and formed churches for their own race.

Another interesting fact about the early church life in Fayette County, was that a church member would be excluded from the fellowship of the church for any of the following reasons: having a misunderstanding with a relative or friend, drunkenness, unbecoming speech, failure to attend services regularly and for any number of other similar reasons. The only way to be received back into the full fellowship of the church and brethren was to come before the church and make a public acknowledgement of their sin and make the matter right again, to the satisfaction of a committee of the brethren appointed for that one purpose.

The first Sunday Schools were started in Fayette County in 1880. The other number of organizations were not organized until many years later. The **Ladies Aid Society** (today's W.M.U.) was first organized in Fayette First

Baptis Church in 1900.

The following is taken from the Minutes of the Fiftieth Session held at the Fayette Baptist Church, Fayette, Alabama - October 13-14, 1920:

"Whereas, it was thought expedient to divide the North River Association, several churches of the First District obtained letters of dismission for the purpose of organizing a new association. With a view to this end the delegates from aforesaid churches met at the Fayetteville Baptist meeting house, Saturday before the fifth Sabbath in October 1871." - Quotation from the minutes of the first session.

In the earlier years, especially, it seems there were many misunderstandings. Councils and committees were being appointed often to untangle dissensions and advise harmony. Peace was much sought after, but oftentimes hard to find. Prejudices and opinions were contended for and on many occasions fellowship was withdrawn from churches which seemed in disorder.

In these earlier years the Association lasted for two or three days and the visiting delegates went and spent the nights in the homes of those in the neighborhood of the host church. In the more recent years this has been changed to keep pace with the fast rate everything moves in. Now, the association is for one day and until about 9:00 P.M. that same night with the host church furnishing the lunch and supper for the visiting delegates.

Following is a historical table of the New River (later) Fayette County Baptist Association:

Date	Church	Moderator	Date	Church	Moderator
1871	Fayetteville	D. V. Shirley	1872	Pilgrim Rest	D. V. Shirley
1873	Union	D. V. Shirley	1874	Shady Grove	D. V. Shirley
1875	Macedonia	D. V. Shirley	1876	Shepherd	J. D. Huckabee
1877	Mt. Olive	J. B. Huckabee	1878	Mt. Pleasant	J. B. Huckabee
1879	Mt. Lebanon	J. B. Huckabee	1880	Concord	J. B. Huckabee
1881	Harmony Grove	J. B. Huckabee	1882	Pilgrims Rest	J. B. Ferguson
1883	Philadelphia	J. B. Ferguson	1884	Shady Grove	J. B. Ferguson
1885	Union	J. B. Ferguson	1886	Fayetteville	J. B. Ferguson
1887	Friendship	W. G. Baker	1888	Concord	V. G. Baker
1889	Oak Grove	J. B. Ferguson	1890	Mt. Pleasant	J. B. Ferguson
1891	Pleasant Hill	G. W. Gravlee	1892	Pilgrims Rest	G. W. Gravlee
1893	Unity	W. G. Baker	1894	Salem	J. F. Willis
1895	Macedonia	G. W. Gravlee	1896	Fayetteville	G. W. Gravlee
1897	Bankston	G. W. Gravlee	1898	Shepherd	G. W. Gravlee
1899	Mt. Pleasant	G. W. Gravlee	1900	Unity	G. W. Gravlee
1901	Concord	G. W. Gravlee	1902	Fayette	G. W. Gravlee
1903	Philadelphia	G. W. Gravlee	1904	Pilgrims Rest	G. W. Gravlee
1905	Bankston	G. H. White	1906	Friendship	G. W. Gravlee
1907	Pleasant Hill	G. W. Gravlee	1908	Shepherd	G. W. Gravlee
1909	Concord	G. W. Gravlee	1910	Fayette	G. W. Gravlee
1911	Rehobeth	G. W. Gravlee	1912	Pilgrim Rest	G. W. Gravlee
1913	Mt. Pleasant	G. W. Gravlee	1914	Friendship	G. W. Gravlee
1915	Bankston	G. W. Gravlee	1916	Fayette	G. W. Gravlee
1917	Bethabara	G. W. Gravlee	1918	Shepherd	G. W. Gravlee
1919	Pleasant Hill	G. W. Gravlee	1920	Fayette	F. Wilson
1921	Mtn. Home	F. Wilson	1922	Unity	F. Wilson
1923	Macedonia	F. Wilson	1924	Bankston	F. Wilson
1925	Shepherd	F. Wilson	1926	Concord	F. Wilson
1927	Rehobeth	S. W. Clements	1928	Bethabara	S. W. Clements
1929	Salem	S. W. Clements	1930	Pleasant Hill	W. W. Monroe

Date	Church	Moderator	Date	Church	Moderator
1931	Unity	W. W. Monroe	1932	Philadelphia	W. W. Monroe
1933	Mt. Joy	J. L. Clements	1934	Macedonia	J. L. Clements
1935	Shady Grove	J. L. Clements	1936	Shepherd	J. L. Clements
1937	Pleasant Grove	J. L. Clements	1938	Berry	J. L. Clements
1939	Concord	J. L. Clements	1940	Salem	J. L. Clements
1941	New River	J. L. Clements	1942	Mt. Pleasant	A. M. Nix
1943	Fayette	A. M. Nix	1944	Belk	A. M. Nix
1945	Rehobeth	A. M. Nix	1946	Fayette??	A. M. Nix
1947	Macedonia	A. M. Nix	1948	Fayette,	A. M. Nix
1949	Friendship	A. M. Nix	1950	Fayette	A. M. Nix
1951	Fayette	A. M. Nix	1952	Fayette	A. M. Nix
1953	Fayette	A. M. Nix	1954	Fayette	A. M. Nix
1955	Fayette	A. M. Nix	1956	Fayette	A. M. Nix
1957	Fayette	A. M. Nix	1958	Fayette	A. M. Nix
1959	Bethel	A. M. Nix			

(The following minutes are given for the purpose of recording the actions of the religious groups of our county at the turn of the century.)
MINUTES OF THE THIRTIETH ANNUAL SESSION OF THE NEW RIVER BAPTIST ASSOCIATION.

"The thirtieth session of the New River Baptist Association was held with Unity Baptist Church, October 13, 14, 15 and 16, 1900, with G. W. Gravlee of Newtonville, Ala. as Moderator; J. E. Cox, Fayette, as Clerk; W. B. Melton, Fayette, as Treasurer and S. W. Clements, New Lexington, Ala. as Corresponding Secretary.

"The next session of this association will be held at Concord Church, commencing on Saturday before the second Sunday in October, 1901.

"On Saturday, October 13, 1900, the New River Baptist Association was called to order for permanent reorganization by G. W. Gravlee, former Moderator, with Rev. J. S. Shirley and Bro. S. W. Clements acting as reading clerks. The letters from the churches were placed on the table as the names were called. Absentees were marked thus: *
SALEM: S. W. Clements, Tom Kelley*, W. B. Davis. FRIENDSHIP: Elder W. J. Blankenship, J. M. Mehard, and R. R. White*. PHILADELPHIA: Elder J. S. Townsend, T. J. Garrison and W. B. Dobbs*. SHEPHERD: Elder G. W. Gravlee, P. P. Mayfield*, and R. L. Sudduth*. ROCKY MOUNT: J. R. Agerton*, W. S. Bobo and C. P. Taylor. PILGRIM REST: J. A. Freeman, W. J. Nelson and G. W. Freeman*. CONCORD: J. C. Poe, G. W. Black, and J. M. Doughty. REHOBETH: Elder B. T. Selman*, W. F. Nichols, and W. F. Meadows. PLEASANT GROVE: J. R. Palmer, A. M. Lowery*, and J. Henderson. MT. LEBANON: J. F. Willis, J. F. Holliman and D. J. Ballinger. PLEASANT HILL: J. H. Newton*, M. E. Chambliss, and D. I. Chambliss*. BANKSTON: J. H. Willingham, L. B. Harbin, T. C. Griffin*. EL BETHEL: Elder W. F. Gilpin, J. W. May and W. J. Hassell. LIBERTY: W. R. Gardner, L. A. Gardner*, and T. B. Gardner*. MOUNT PLEASANT: Elder G. H. White, R. M. Olive, and I. W. White. UNITY: Elders J. S. Shirley and A. N. Reeves, and Bro. J. M. Keenum. MACEDONIA: Elder J. E. Cox, S. N. Lindsey, and John A. South*. FAYETTE FIRST CHURCH: J. M. Stewart, W. B. Melton and Ed P. Goodwin. (Organized 1900, petitioned for admittance to New River Body, presented by E. P. Goodwin and J. M. Stewart.) FAYETTEVILLE: not represented. SHADY GROVE: Not represented.

"The following committees were appointed:
On Documents: A. N. Reeves, W. F. Nichols, W. J. Blankenship, I. W. White and J. M. Doughty. On Arrangements: J. S. Shirley, S. L. Raney, and W. J. Has-

sell. On Nominations: J. M. Stewart, C. P. Taylor, and J. P. Meharg. On Literature: A. N. Reeves, W. D. Melton, and J. W. Willingham. On Education: J. S. Townsend, E. P. Goodwin and Sam W. Clements. On Orphan's Home: W. F. Gilpin, R. B. White and S. M. Lindsey. On Finance: John A. Freeman, J. C. Poe and J. M. Keenum.

"Correspondents from sister Associations were called for and the following responded: Yellow Creek - Elders Silas N. Waldrop and W. J. Cunningham were welcomed by the moderator. Returned correspondence to Yellow Creek: Elders A. N. Reeves, J. S. Shirley, W. F. Gilpin and Bro. J. G. Jones.

"The Committee report on Sunday School was read by W. F. Nichols, chairman, and the following committee members appointed: Shepherd - P. P. Mayfield; Pleasant Hill - J. H. Newton; Concord - J. S. White; Fayette - John M. Stewart; Fayetteville - Frank Arthur Nuckols; Macedonia - W. D. White; Shady Grove - Samuel South; El Bethel - J. G. Jones; Rehobeth - W. F. Nichols; Rocky Mount - W. F. Shackelford; Friendship - J. H. Meharg; Unity - H. T. Shirley; Salem - S. W. Clements; Pleasant Grove - J. R. Palmer; Pilgrim Rest - J. A. Freeman; Mt. Pleasant - R. T. Beard; Liberty - W. A. Gardner; Bankston - J. T. Willingham; and Philadelphia - G. W. McGinnis.

"The New River Baptist Association recommended these brethren and sisters as worthy the confidence and christian fellowship of any of our churches, and advise any Baptist church to which they may apply for admittance into fellowship, to receive them without letters, or that they may be organized into a local church, provided the cause of Christ demands such organization: J. E. Kirkland, Kate Kirkland, J. N. Collins, E. E. Collins, E. G. Morris, M. J. Morris, A. P. Stanley, Davis Collins, Laura Blakeney, Jane Collins, H. D. Collins; all of whom are worthy, zealous Christian men and women.

"District Meetings:

First District met with Liberty Church on Friday before the first Sunday in September, 1900. Participants: Elder W. G. Baker, Elder J. J. Patterson, J. H. Newton, J. D. Thomas, J. S. Townsend, Moderator; J. R. Gladden, Clerk.

Second District met with Friendship Church on Friday before the second Sunday in September, 1900. Participants: W. F. Gilpin, S. L. Raney, J. H. Davis, A. M. Reeves, W. M. Olive, J. S. Shirley Moderator; and G. W. Freeman, Clerk.

"W. B. Morrow, representing the Sipsey Association brought correspondence from Oak Ridge Church. Returned Correspondence: Elders G. W. Gravlee, Frank Wilson and W. J. Nelson.

"Nominations Committee Report: Elder J. S. Townsend to preach the opening sermon, next session of this body, G. H. White, Alternate; W. J. Akin to preach at 11 o'clock on Sunday, W. F. Gilpin, Alternate.

"Mission Board: W. H. Terry, chairman, W. F. Nichols, J. R. Agerton, W. J. Hassell, J. S. Shirley, J. A. Freeman and J. R. Gladden.

"Ministerial Education: A. N. Reeves, W. F. Gilpin and G. H. White - J. M. Stewart, chairman.

"Returned correspondence: To Sipsey Association: Elders F. Wilson, G. W. Gravlee and Brethren W. D. Melton and W. J. Nelson. To Harmony Grove Association: Elders W. J. Blankenship, A. N. Reeves. Messengers elected to State Convention: J. E. Cox and A. N. Reeves. To Southern Baptist Convention: G. W. Gravlee, J. P. Dickinson, Alternate.

List of Ordained Ministers:

G. W. Gravlee, Newtonville, Ala.; Frank Wilson, Hico; A. N. Reeves, Ballard; J. S. Shirley, Hugent; B. T. Sellman, Hugent; G. H. White, Davis

Creek; W. G. Baker, Bankston; S. L. Raney, Hico; G. W. Freeman, Fayette; W. F. Gilpin, Hugent; J. F. Willis, Fayette; J. E. Cox, Fayette; J. P. Dickinson, Fayette; J. M. Olive, Machine; W. J. Akins, Ballard; W. J. Blankenship, Ballard; J. S. Townsend, Ballard; J. J. Patterson, Ridge; J. S. White, Ridge; J. V. Hosmer, Fayette.

Churches	Pastors	Clerks	Post Office
Bankston	A. N. Reeves	J. T. Willingham	Bankston
Concord	I. R. Collins	T. J. Black	Ridge
El Bethel	W. F. Gilpin	G. T. Hassell	Hugent
Fayetteville	not represented	Frank Arthur Nuckols	Fayette
Fayette	J. P. Dickinson	W. B. Melton	Fayette
Friendship	J. S. Townsend	J. H. Akins	Ballard
Liberty	J. J. Patterson	J. V. Montgomery	Bankston
Macedonia	J. E. Cox	S. N. Lindsey	Fayette
Mt. Pleasant	G. W. Gravlee	J. D. Lokey	Davis Creek
Pleasant Hill	W. G. Baker	E. B. Newton	Fayette
Pleasant Grove	S. L. Raney	J. Henderson	
Philadelphia	W. G. Baker	I. B. Deavours	Handy
Pilgrim Rest	J. M. Olive	J. A. Freeman	Hico
Rocky Mount	F. Wilson	W. S. Bobo	Fayette
Rehobeth	B. T. Selman	W. F. Nichols	Hugent
Salem	J. B. Ferguson	W. F. Dawson	New Lexington
Shepherd	G. W. Gravlee	P. P. Mayfield	Newtonville
Shady Grove	Not represented	--- ---	Bankston
Unity	A. N. Reeves	H. T. Shirley	Ballard

19 Churches in the Association.
Sunday Meetings: 8 churches met every Sunday. 2 churches met 3 times a month. 3 churches met twice a month. 4 churches met once a month. 2 churches not reported.

Baptized	31	Associational Fund	$ 9.25
Received by letter	26	State Missions	1.15
Restored	7	Home Missions	9.52
Excluded	13	Foreign Missions	10.75
Died	16	Association Missions	20.00
Dismissed by letter.	14	Orphan's Home	11.93
		Minute Fund	16.35

The following churches have at one time been active in the "North River", "New River", of the "Fayette County Baptist Associations". Many are still active, others have very few records, if any, but the information is from official minutes of the association or of the individual churches.

Where records were available the date of organization, charter members, pastors served and any outstanding data is included for each church listed.

ARBOR SPRINGS BAPTIST CHURCH -- This church was constituted before 1883 and from the minutes we find the following ministers who have served this church. J. B. Ferguson, 1883; A. M. King, 1884; W. J. Hosmer, 1888; N. O. Dobbs, 1891.

ASHCRAFT CORNER BAPTIST CHURCH -- Constituted 1889. Pastors as follows: W. E. Robertson, 1945; Ira Patterson, 1948 - 1949; Rosco Hollman, 1950; Amon Foster, 1951; Leon Brown, 1953; Erskine Stripling, 1954 - 1955; E. E. Davis, 1956 - 1958.

BANKSTON BAPTIST CHURCH -- Constituted 1888. Pastors as follows: J. W. Hosmer, 1889 - 1890; G. W. Baker, 1891 - 1893; J. I. McCollum, 1895; J. E. Cox, 1896; J. I. McCollum, 1897; A. N. Reeves, 1898 - 1900; G. T. Gravlee, 1901 - 1903; A. B. Batson, 1904 - 1905; W. W. Dyer, 1907; L. A. Connell, 1908 - 1909; A. B. Batson, 1911- 1912; J. A. Huggins, 1913 - 1915; H. C. Curtis, 1916; A. N. Reeves, 1917; J. A. Huggins, 1918 - 1919; P. B. Head, 1919, also; Newbern Patterson, 1920; A. B. Batson, 1920 - 1921; J. P. Jages, 1922 - 1924; J. L. Dobbs, 1925 - 1926; J. A. Huggins, 1927; L. M. Spencer, 1928 - 1929; B. P. Burks, 1930; J. L. Clements, 1931 - 1945; A. C. Nichols, 1948 - 1949; J. L. Clements, 1950 - 1958.

BELK MISSIONARY BAPTIST CHURCH -- The Missionary Baptist Church was organized July 20, 1908, by Rev. W. K. Pennington and Rev. B. E. Cunningham, with Rev. Pennington as moderator and G. M. Estes as clerk.
   Charter members were the following: George J. Belk, Martha Belk, Oscar C. Belk, Ollie Moore, G. M. Estes, Lillie Estes, Jenny Smith, Mack Smith, Alpha Branyon and Bud Brazil.
   The following men have served the church as pastor: Rev. W. K. Pennington; Rev. B. E. Cunningham; O. J. Moore; George Vaughn; J. L. Soann, 1930 - 1934; W. C. Kirk, 1935; J. L. Clements, 1937; S. E. Walker, 1938 - 1940; A. C. Nichols, 1941 - 1945; W. A. Johnson, 1948 - 1951; A. N. Reeves, 1952; T. L. Griffin, 1953 - 1956; Jerry Robinson, 1957; G. W. Pitts, 1958.
   In the fall of 1950, the Baptist Church built a new building of masonry construction with four Sunday School rooms; and at present they are adding four more Sunday School rooms. The present membership is 125; the Sunday School Superintendent is W. O. Porter and the church clerk is Mrs. C. O. Belk.

BERRY BAPTIST CHURCH -- Organized 1886. Brick building was erected in 1936. Pastors who have served are as follows: Audie L. Mays, 1933; J. L. Clements, 1934 - 1939; W. E. Robinson, 1940; J. F. Goree, 1941 - 1942; Adolph Blakeney, 1945; Clyde Latham, 1948 - 1952; Marcus Beck, 1953; R. H. Parrish, 1955; R. H. Parrish, 1958.

BETHABARA BAPTIST CHURCH -- Organized 1865. Received into Association 1912. Pastors who have served are as follows: J. S. Townsend, 1910; L. A. Connell, 1911; J. P. Hallman, 1912- 1913; W. W. Dyer, 1914 - 1916; S. W. Clements, 1917; R. M. Mills, 1918 - 1919; W. W. Dyer, 1920 - 1922; Jeff Ellis, 1923; J. L. Dobbs, 1924 - 1926; J. O. Dearing, 1927; J. N. Black, 1928 - 1932; A. N. Reeves, 1933; S. E. Walker, 1935; Willie Roberts, 1936; J. E. Horton, 1938; J. Floyd Goree, 1940 - 1941; J. C. Boyd, 1945; W. M. Bevan, 1948; Clyde Latham, 1949 - 1950; J. P. Dobbs, 1951 - 1952; Frank M. Bobo, 1954 - 1959.

BETHABRA BAPTIST CHURCH -- Organized 1925. Pastors who have served are as follows: A. C. Nichols, 1948 - 1953; T. L. Griffin, 1955; Jim Windle, 1956 - 1957; and John Thompson, 1958.

BETHANY BAPTIST CHURCH -- Originally organized 1865 -- re-organized 1908. Pastors who have served are as follows: Claud J. Files, 1931 - 1932; W. A. Kimbrell, 1933; J. S. Clark, 1934 - 1939; F. M. Hyatte, 1940; R. B. Kilgore, 1941 - 1942; Houston Brand, 1945; H. V. Hallman, 1948 - 1949; W. G. Smith 1950.

BETHLEHEM BAPTIST CHURCH -- Organized 1873 or 1886 - records vary. Pastors are as follows: S. E. Walker, 1935 - 1936; Ike B. Cannon, 1937 - 1939; Wm. B. Smith, 1940; Ike B. Cannon, 1941 - 1949; Wiley Bevans, 1950; H. L. Hammons, 1951; Ike B. Cannon, 1952; Pete Koster, 1953.

BETHEL BAPTIST CHURCH -- The Bethel Baptist Church was organized about 1893 and was in the Yellow Creek Baptist Association for many years. The charter members list is not available but the following is a list of the pastors who have served this church since 1891, as listed in the Yellow Creek Minutes and the Fayette County Baptist Association Minutes.
 J. P. Dickinson, 1891; J. F. Willis, 1895; J. F. Willis, 1903 - 1905; W. K. Pennington, 1905 - 1906; C. D. Stewart, 1906 - 1912; W. F. Gilpin, 1925 - 1926; W. H. Hamilton, 1926 - 1927; A. M. Nix, 1927 - 1959.
 Rev. A. M. Nix is serving his thirty-second year as pastor of Bethel Baptist Church, one of the larger churches in the county.

CAINES RIDGE BAPTIST CHURCH -- Organized 1901 (records vary). Pastors - F. Wilson, 1901 - 1903; J. H. Gardner, 1904; S. W. Clements, 1905; F. Wilson, 1906 - 1910; W. W. Dyer, 1911 - 1913; F. Wilson, 1914 - 1915; W. W. Dyer, 1917 - 1920; W. M. Kizziah, 1921 - 1923; Frank Wilson, 1924; S. E. Walker, 1928; W. M. Kizziah, 1931 - 1933; J. W. Johnson, 1934; T. C. Conaway, 1935; W. M. Kizziah, 1938; Neal Kizzich, 1939; J. E. Horton, 1941; Houston Strickland, 1942 - 1945; Leon Brown, 1948; Albert Johnson, 1949; W. A. Johnson, 1950; R. R. Holliman, 1951 - 1952; E. E. Davis, 1953 - 1957.

CALVARY BAPTIST CHURCH -- Organized 1933. Pastors - V. B. Tigett, 1933 - 1934; J. V. Johnson, 1935; L. A. Hayes, 1936 - 1938; C. C. Holliman, 1939; J. E. Horton, 1940 - 1941; L. A. Hayes, 1945; Burt Johnson, 1949; Frank A. Bobo, 1950 - 1951; E. E. Davis, 1954 - 1955.

CHAPEL HILL BAPTIST CHURCH -- Organized 1866. Pastors - J. M. Chism, 1883 - 1898; J. B. White, 1899; (No records on minutes until 1930; S. E. Walker, 1930 - 1931; Wm. T. Roberts, 1932 - 1933; J. Neil Kizzire, 1934 - 1937; J. R. Sweedenburg, 1938 - 1942; W. A. Johnson, 1945 - 1948; Amon Foster, 1949 - 1950; Albert A. Coats, 1951; R. R. Holliman, 1952 - 1955; J. J. Crowe, 1956 - 1958.

CONCORD BAPTIST CHURCH -- The following people met at the old Fellowship Meeting House on June 29, 1839, and became the charter members of the Concord Baptist Church: Tilmon Howell, Mary Howell, Thomas Brent, Amelia Brent, Elihu Melton, Sally B. Melton, Elijah Alawine, Daniel Traweek, John Cates, Celia Cates, Sarah McGuire, Nancy Winter, Celian Turnbow, Mary Brent - Slave of Thomas Brent, Henrietta Taylor, Rhoda Traweek and Martha Traweek.
 Following are the pastors who have served the Concord Church from its beginning: Tilmon Howell, 1839 - 1844; B. B. Smith, 1844 - 3 mos.; R. R. Strawn, 1844 - 1845; John Walters, 1845 - 1853; J. R. Arnold, 1853 - 1859; Calvin Poe, 1859 - 1860; Joe Rushing, 1860 - 1861; Levi Coleman, 1861 - 1862; W. L. Jones, 1862 - 1866; J. J. Watts, 1866 - 1867; W. L. Jones, 1867 - 1868; M. J. Dyer, 1868 - 1870; W. L. Jones, 1870 - 1871; L. B. Harbin, 1871 - 1872; J. M. Chism, 1872 - 1894; Ira L. Collins, 1894 - 1907; J. J. Patterson, 1907 - 1908; W. W. Dyer, 1908 - 1911; G. W. Gravlee, 1911 - 1912; L. R. Spencer, 1912 - 1913; J. E. Bell, 1913 - 1914; J. R. Hallman, 1914 - 1915; Frank Wilson, 1915 - 1920; S. E. Walker, 1920 - 1926; S. W. Clements, 1926 - 1930; J. L. Clements, 1930 - 1931; R. S. Marler, 1931 - 1932; L. A. Connell, 1932 - 1935; Fred Kitchens,

1939 - 1945; Houston Strickland, 1945 - 1946; Adolph Plakney, 1946 - 2 mos.; Loyd Griffin, 1946 - 1949; John Thompson, 1949 - 1951; Hollie Patterson, 1951-1959.

COVIN BAPTIST CHURCH -- (See Rocky Mount Baptist Church) This church was organized or renamed Covin Baptist Church from Rocky Mount Church in 1914. After the church was revived in 1952 under the leadership of Rev. Frank M. Bobo, a beautiful masonry building was erected and the mortgage paid in full during his ministry with the church.

Pastors who have served this church are as follows: J. E. Bell, 1914 - 1917; L. A. Weathers, 1917 - 1919; J. J. Milford, 1919 - 1920; S. A. Clements, 1920 - 1922; Frank Wilson, 1924 - 1927; G. H. Vaughn, 1927 - 1928; V. R. Seymore, 1930 - 1934; D. W. Griffin, 1935 - 1940; A. M. Reeves, 1940 - 1942; L. A. Weathers, 1942 - 1943; J. E. Horton, 1945 - 1946; Frank M. Bobo, 1952 - 1958; Dan Cargile, 1958 - 1959.

DOUBLE BRANCHES BAPTIST CHURCH -- There are no available records on this church. It was listed among those churches belonging, at one time, to the Association.

EL BETHEL BAPTIST CHURCH -- Organized and Constituted August 18, 1887.

Elders J. N. Dyer and J. S. Shirley met at Jones School House and organized El Bethel Baptist Church. The following presented their letters and became the charter members of El Bethel: W. F. Jones, E. J. Jones, W. L. Caple, M. B. Hassel, O. Canterberry, E. J. Canterbery, A. F. Gilpin, K. A. Gilpin, G. A. Caple, M. A. Caple, J. G. Jones, P. F. Jones, E. D. Gilpin, and L. L. Gilpin.

The members adopted the second Sabbath and the Saturday before as regular meeting days. They chose Bro. J. P. Dickinson as first pastor and asked Mt. Olive Church to set Bro. Dickinson apart to the ministry .... Voted to take Communion in May and September .... 1888 - Building Committee appointed .... April 4, 1891 - paid balance for land amount $2.00 .... Nov. 30, 1894 - Started Bible Class in connection with Prayer Meeting .... April 30, 1898 - Gave Bro. A. N. Reeves the sum of $3.65 to pay expenses as a delegate to Southern Baptist Convention to be held at Norfolk, Virginia.... (The above was taken from the original minutes.)

Pastors who served El Bethel Baptist Church from organization to date the Church was dissolved were as follows: J. P. Dickinson, 1887 - 1894; A. N. Reeves, 1893 - 1899; A. F. Gilpin, 1899 - 1902; A. N. Reeves, 1902; J. W. Akins, 1903 - 1904; A. F. Gilpin, 1904 - 1906; O. L. Corbett, 1906 - 1907; A. F. Gilpin, 1907 - 1912; J. L. Spann, 1912 - 1913; A. F. Gilpin, 1913 - 1917; B. E. Cunningham, 1917 - 1918; A. F. Gilpin, 1918 - 1919; R. L. Berry, 1919 - 1920; A. F. Gilpin, 1920 - 1927; Dissolved July 13, 1927.....

FAYETTE FIRST BAPTIST CHURCH -- The first Baptist Church to be organized in the town of Fayetteville was in 1850 and was in the North River Baptist Association.

The church known as the Fayetteville Baptist Church was a two story wooden building located in Old Town near the entrance of the Fayette City Cemetery. It held that name until the organization of the church in the town of Fayette. This new church was named the Fayette Baptist Church. Sixteen members of the original church organized the new church and moved from its old site to the present location on Temple Avenue.

On January 20, 1898, a deed was made to E. C. Lawless, J. H. Olive and J. M. Stewart, deacons of the Missionary Baptist Church of Fayette, by C. J. Wilkes and wife Mrs. M. D. Wilkes and J. P. Dickinson and wife Mrs. M. F. Dickinson, for a consideration of $40.00. This property is situated on Tempa Avenue on Lot 4 - Block 31.

For about two years after the purchase of the lot the members of the Missionary Baptist Church held their meetings in the old Grammar School Building.

Fayette Missionary Baptist Church was constituted July 22, 1900, under the ministry of Rev. J. P. Dickinson, who was at that time pastor of the Fayetteville Missionary Baptist Church. The Charter Members who came out of the Fayetteville Church and presented their letters on July 22, 1900, were as follows: E. P. Goodwin, Dr. W. A. Graham, Mrs. W. A. (Dora) Graham, Mrs. Kate Harton, Mrs. Lula Kidd, Mrs. M. H. Poe, John N. Stewart, Mrs. J. N. Stewart, John Young Stewart, Mr. W. H. Terry, Mrs. W. H. Terry, Mr. J. C. Yerby, Mrs. J. C. Yerby, Miss Effie Yerby, Miss Tosie Yerby and Miss Lula Lee Yerby. (The above names were taken from the original church records in the office of the Fayette Baptist Church. For more about charter members, see end of this sketch.)

After the Fayette Church purchased their lot a building committee was selected, composed of Dr. W. A. Graham, E. P. Goodwin, W. B. Melton, F. N. Caine, F. A. Bentley, and the pastor Rev. J. P. Dickinson. Within a few months a wooden structure was erected on the lot. In October of 1900 the first Ladies Aid Society (W.M.S.) was organized at the Fayette Baptist Church.

In 1923 the members decided to build a new brick building and the following men were selected as the building committee: B. E. Kinney, Chm., Edgar Walker, B. J. Bogard, J. C. Grimsley, and J. E. Carter.

The brick building was erected and dedicated late in 1924. This beautiful building stands today as a monument of the efforts of the various people who have at one time or another belonged to this church.

In 1941 the Hammond Organ was installed; the church also built a brick pastorium on the lot behind the church.

The Educational Building was completed and occupied in the summer of 1955. The main building was completely air-conditioned this same year.

Rev. A. M. Nix delivered his last sermon as pastor of the church on December 28, 1958. He resigned after a long and fruitful ministry and the church paid all indebtedness on his last day of service to the Fayette Baptist Church.

Following are the pastors who served the original Fayetteville Baptist Church from 1850 to 1871; (these names are listed without reference to the time served by each.) Louis B. Harbin, William Jones, J. J. Watts, E. T. Akins, Robert Adams and Nimrod Dodson.

The pastors serving the Fayetteville Baptist Church from 1871 until it was disbanded in 1905 were as follows: J. C. Jones, 1871; J. E. Bell, 1874 - 1878; J. B. Huckabee, 1880; J. W. Rogers, 1883; J. E. Cox, 1884; G. W. Gravlee, 1885; S. F. White, 1886; N. L. Gideon, 1887 - 1888; J. W. Rogers, 1890; S. W. Gravlee, 1892 - 1893; J. I. McCollum, 1895; J. P. Dickinson, 1896; A. M. Reeves, 1897; J. P. Dickinson, 1898 - 1905; Disbanded - 1905.

Pastors serving the Fayette Baptist Church from date of organization, July 22, 1900, to the present time have been as follows: J. P. Dickinson, 1900; W. G. Baker, 1902; M. M. Wood, 1903 - 1904; A. B. Metcalf, 1906 - 1908; D. M. Morgan, 1909 - 1911; J. M. McCord, 1911 - 1913; I. W. Martin, 1914 - 1915; J. J. Milford, 1917 - 1919; Spencer B. King, 1919 - 1921; W. M. Murray,

1922; M. R. Stone, 1923; Dr. J. A. Blackwelder, 1925 - 1929; Dr. M. R. Seymore, 1930 - 1934; Roy Chandler, 1935 - 1939; A. M. Nix, 1941 - 1958 (Resigned effective Dec. 28, 1958); B. F. Atkins, 1959 - 4 mos. - Supply; June 1, 1959, B. H. Atkins.

(In compiling the data collected for this volume we give the following list of charter members "as remembered", by Mrs. Motie McCool and submitted by her, in conjunction to the list taken from the church records. Mr. & Mrs. Melton (2 daughters), Miss Lena Melton, Miss Clara Melton, Mr. & Mrs. Y. M. Olive and daughter, Miss Pearl Olive, Mrs. Mary Poe and daughter, Miss Della Poe, Mr. & Mrs. John Stewart and son, John Young Stewart, Mr. & Mrs. J. C. Yerby and three daughters, Miss Effie Yerby, Miss Tosie Yerby, Miss Lula Lee Yerby, Dr. & Mrs. W. A. Graham, Mr. Arthur Nuckols - Clerk, Mr. E. P. Goodwin, Rev. & Mrs. J. P. Dickinson and daughter, Motie Dickinson, Mr. & Mrs. Henry Bentley, Mr. Frank Bentley, Miss Kizzie Walters, and Miss Vina Walters.

Mrs. McCool states that she was the youngest member, having joined in the last revival held before the formation of the new church. Rev. Dickinson was the pastor and the visiting evangelist was Rev. G. W. Gravlee.)

FLATWOODS BAPTIST CHURCH -- Organized 1940. Pastors - W. M. Fowler, 1945; Houston Brand, 1949 - 1951.

FRIENDSHIP BAPTIST CHURCH -- (Or Sandsprings Baptist Church) Organized 1876, (dates vary). Pastors serving this church were as follows: J. S. Shirley, 1884 - 1887; W. J. Blankenship, 1888 - 1891; A. N. Reeves, 1895 - 1896; W. J. Akins, 1896 - 1897; A. N. Reeves, 1897 - 1898; J. S. Townsend, 1899 - 1902; J. H. Akin, 1903 - 1904; S. L. Rainey, 1904 - 1908; J. A. Trim, 1909 - 1914; W. F. Gilpin, 1914 - 1915; O. L. Corbett, 1916 - 1917; ... Records not available until 1930 ... J. S. Clark, 1930 - 1935; S. E. Walker, 1935 - 1937; J. E. Horton, 1937 - 1938; L. A. Hayes, 1938 - 1940; C. C. Polliman, 1940 - 1946; Amon Foster, 1948 - 1950; E. E. Davis, 1950 - 1957; Hollie Patterson, 1957 - 1959.

FRIENDSHIP BAPTIST CHURCH -- (Tuscaloosa County) -- Date of organization not available. Pastors serving this church as far as records are available, while in the Association were as follows: R. J. Mayfield, 1883 - 1889; J. W. Colow, 1889.

GOODWATER BAPTIST CHURCH -- Organized 1911. During the ministry of Bro. Glen V. Moulditch this church erected a brick building following a fire that destroyed the former building.

The following are pastors for which records are available: J. L. Spann, 1930; A. N. Reeves, 1931 - 1933; F. M. Holley, 1933 - 1935; A. L. Mays, 1935 - 1936; A. N. Reeves, 1936 - 1937; J. E. Horton, 1938 - 1941; Fred Kitchens, 1942 - 1946; Rev. Hayes, 1948 - 1949; Fred Bedenbough, 1949 - 1952; Glen V. Houlditch, 1953 to Sept. 1959.

GRACE ARBOR BAPTIST CHURCH -- Constituted - 1919. Pastors - W. M. Dyer, 1919 - 1920. No other records available.

GRACE BAPTIST CHURCH -- On May 6, 1959, at 7:00 P.M. a group of Baptist met at the old Presbyterian Church Building in Fayette for the purpose of organizing a new Baptist Church. After a short devotional, the resolution was read by Rev. A. M. Nix, Moderator of the Fayette County Baptist Association and pastor of the Bethel Baptist Church. Mr. Paul W. Colburn read the Church Covenant.

The following people are those having their letters and desiring to become the charter members of the newly organized Grace Baptist Church: E. E. Anderson, Mrs. E. E. Anderson, Bill Anderson, Bob Anderson, John A. Ayres, Miss Kathleen Ayres, G. Homer Campbell, Mrs. G. Homer Campbell, Dwain Campbell, Raymond C. Gordon, Mrs. Raymond C. Gordon, J. C. Holliday, Mrs. J. C. Holliday, Claude W. Langston, W. Malcolm Lawrence, Mrs. W. Malcolm Lawrence, Mary Mitchell Lawrence, Lingee Mitchell, Mrs. Lingee Mitchell, Jerry Wayne Mitchell, Laymon Mitchell, Lymon Mitchell, Willie Ray Mitchell, Herbert M. Newell, Mrs. Herbert M. Newell, Miss Vivian Pastuer, Victor S. Patterson, Jr., Mrs. Victor S. Patterson, Jr., V. S. Patterson, Sr., Mrs. V. S. Patterson, Sr., W. B. Scott, Mrs. W. B. Scott, Paul M. Tucker, Mrs. Paul M. Tucker, Harry O. Unger, Mrs. Harry O. Unger and Miss Ruth Williamson.

Those serving the church as pastor from its beginning have been as follows: Bro. Glen Houlditch - Morning Supply - April 22, 1959 to Oct. 1, 1959; Bro. Frank M. Bobo - Evening Supply - April 22, 1959 to Oct. 1, 1959; Bro. Glen Houlditch - Full Time - Oct. 1, 1959.

HARMONY GROVE BAPTIST CHURCH -- (Now - 1959 - in the Marion Association). Date of organization not available. Pastors - J. C. Hendon, 1883 - 1884; J. N. Dickinson, 1884 - 1887; J. S. Shirley, 1887 - 1888; J. P. Dickinson, 1888 - 1891 .... Records not available from 1891... Glen V. Houlditch, 1955 - 1959.

HICKORY GROVE BAPTIST CHURCH -- Organized 1939. Pastors - L. A. Hayes, 1939 - 1940; R. R. Holliman, 1940 - 1943; T. L. Griffin, 1945; E. E. Davis, 1948 - 1949; Amon Foster, 1950 - 1951; J. J. Crowe, 1951.

HOPEWELL BAPTIST CHURCH -- Original date of organization not available; reorganized 1906. Pastors - J. N. Dickinson, 1883 - 1884; E. T. Akins, 1884 - 1887; R. Colburn, 1887 - 1889; J. W. McGaha, 1889 - 1890 ..... Louis Hays, 1931.

HOWARD BAPTIST CHURCH -- Organized 1936. Pastors - David Dodd, 1936 - 1938; J. E. Horton, 1938 - 1940; David Dodd, 1940 - 1942.

LEBANON BAPTIST CHURCH -- The only record found for this church: 1933 - Thomas Moncrief served as pastor.

LIBERTY BAPTIST CHURCH -- Constituted 1892 or 1898 - records vary. Pastors - G. W. Gardner, 1897 - 1899; J. J. Patterson, 1899 - 1901; J. S. Townsend, 1901 - 1904; J. J. Patterson, 1904 - 1905; H. W. Little, 1905 - 1907; G. H. White, 1907 - 1911; L. R. Hallman, 1911 - 1912; J. G. White, 1911 - 1912; G. H. White, 1912 - 1914; L. A. Weathers, 1915 - 1917; L. R. Hallman, 1917 - 1918; R. L. Berry, 1918 - 1920; Wilburn W. Rice, 1920 - 1924; J. S. Clark, 1924 - 1927; J. G. White, 1927 - 1929; A. V. Skelton, 1930 - 1931; L. C. Lockart, 1932 - 1933; W. W. Rice, 1934 - 1935; H. V. Hallman, 1935; Quitt Ingram, 1939; Ernest Best, 1942; Gib Carmack, 1945; Ira Patterson, 1948; H. V. Hallman, 1949 - 1951; John Thompson, 1951 - 1952; W. M. Bevans, 1952 - 1953; H. L. Hammonds, 1953 - 1954; Fred Bowles, 1954 - 1955 ... Inactive 1955.

MACEDONIA or GUMBUD BAPTIST CHURCH -- Date of organization not available - received into Association in 1895.

Pastors serving this church have been as follows: G. W. Gravlee, 1883 - 1885; J. B. Ferguson, 1885 - 1886; W. J. Akin, 1886 - 1888; G. W. Gravlee, 1888; Frank Wilson, 1895 - 1900; J. E. Cox, 1900 - 1902; G. H. White, 1902 - 1906; W. G. Baker, 1906 - 1909; S. L. Rainey, 1909 - 1912; G. H. White, 1912 - 1913; J. R. Hallman, 1913 - 1916; F. Wilson, 1916 - 1918; L. A. Weathers, 1918 - 1922; J. S. Clark, 1922 - 1923; S. E. Walker, 1923 - 1926; W. M. Skelton, R. L. Berry, 1927 - 1928; L. M. Spencer, 1928 - 1930; J. S. Clark, 1930 - 1932; Herman Brown, 1932 - 1933; W. R. Seymore, 1933 - 1935; R. L. Berry, 1935 - 1937; A. C. Nichols, 1938 - 1941; J. E. Horton, 1941 - 1942; A. C. Nichols, 1942 - 1943; S. E. Walker, 1945 - 1949; Burt Johnson, 1949 - 1950; W. A. Johnson, 1950 - 1952; Fred Kitchens, 1952 - 1955; W. A. Johnson, 1955 - 1958.

<u>MEADOW BRANCH BAPTIST CHURCH</u> -- The date of organization for this church is not available. Meadow Branch Baptist Church is located in the edge of Lamar County and in the early years belonged to the New River Association but left this association later and joined one more centrally located. Pastors who served this church, as recorded in the New River Association Minutes are as follows: J. M. Chism, 1883 - 1885; N. J. Dyer, 1887 - 1890; S. M. Waldrop, 1891.

<u>MOUNTAIN HOME BAPTIST CHURCH</u> -- Constituted 1914. Pastors - J. S. Townsend, 1914 - 1915; R. L. Berry, 1915 - 1916; G. H. White, 1916 - 1917; S. E. Walker, 1917 - 1918; R. L. Berry, 1918 - 1919; S. E. Walker, 1919 - 1922; S. W. Clements, 1922 - 1923; W. W. Dyer, 1924 - 1925; A. M. Skelton, 1925 - 1926; A. Sweat, 1928 - 1929; S. W. Clements, 1929; S. E. Walker, 1935 - 1937; J. E. Horton, 1937 - 1938; L. C. Lockart, 1938 - 1941; L. A. Hayes, 1941 - 1943; G. M. Fowler, 1945 - 1949; C. C. Holliman, 1949 - 1951; J. J. Crowe, 1951 - 1952; Avery Tilley, 1952 - 1953; Marvin Fowler, 1953 - 1954; Joe Jack Crowe, 1954 - 1955; Dewey Hendrix, 1955 - 1958; M. D. Hubbert, 1958.

<u>MT. JOY BAPTIST CHURCH</u> -- (Or Alta) -- Organized possibly 1844. Records of pastors are as follows: N. J. Dyer, 1883; W. L. Jones, 1884; W. J. Blankenship, 1887 - 1888; N. J. Dyer, 1889; ..... J. H. Black, 1931 - 1932; Tillman Kimbrell, 1933 - 1934; J. L. Clements, 1935 - 1940; R. B. Kilgore, 1941 - 1942; Clay Kimbrell, 1949 - 1950; T. L. Griffin, 1951 - 1953; Frank W. Dobo, 1955 - 1959.

<u>MT. LEBANON MISSIONARY BAPTIST CHURCH</u> -- A group met at the Henry Moore School House and the Mt. Lebanon Baptist Church was constituted on March 20, 1942. The constitution was signed by Samuel McCullough and Wm. W. Nash.

Old records show that the church was located at the old cemetery approximately five and one-half miles northwest of Fayette, Ala. and approximately one mile west of the old Fayette and Guin Road. (This road is now paved.)

Some of the first members were as follows: George W. Richards, (wife) Lucinda Richards, Wm. F. Collins, Marinda Moore, Judy Willis and a Bro. Lewis.

Sometime later a church building was built approximately two and one-half miles northwest of this site just off the old cotton gin road near the spring. Later the church was moved back near the original cemetery. Several years later, (the exact date is not known) Mt. Lebanon was moved to its present location eight miles northwest of Fayette, about one-half mile east of the old Fayette and Guin Highway.

Some of the pastors who have served the church are as follows: Reuben R.

Strawn; John Walters; J. R. Arnold; Enoch Dodson; B. V. Shirley; J. Watson; A. F. Atkins; J. E. Bell; J. B. Huckabee; G. W. Gravlee; 1883 - 1884; J. M. Chism, 1887 - 1888; N. J. Dyer; J. F. Willis, (W.F.) 1888 - 1898; S. M. Waldrop, 1898 - 1900; A. J. Cunningham; A. K. Pennington, W. F. Gilpin; and J. T. Johnson.

MT. OLIVE BAPTIST CHURCH -- Date of organization not available. Pastors - N. J. Dyer, 1883 - 1888; J. P. Dickinson, 1888 - 1889; W. J. Blankenship, 1889.

MT. PISGAH BAPTIST CHURCH -- Date organized not available. Pastors - J. B. Ferguson, 1883 - 1885; W. G. Baker, 1887 - 1889; W. G. Baker, 1889 - 1892.

MT. PLEASANT BAPTIST CHURCH -- Organized 1855. Pastors have been as follows: J. E. Bell, 1871 - 1873; J. B. Ferguson, 1874; G. W. Gravlee, 1879 - 1885; E. J. Akin, 1887 - 1888; G. W. Gravlee, 1888 - 1892; J. W. Hosmer, 1892 - 1894; A. N. Reeves, 1895 - 1896; W. J. Akin, 1896 - 1898; G. W. Gravlee, 1899 - 1902; G. H. White, 1902 - 1906; L. A. Connell, 1906 - 1907; W. G. Baker, 1907 - 1908; W. W. Dyer, 1908 - 1911; L. A. Connell, 1911 - 1913; J. E. Bell, 1913 - 1914; S. W. Clements, 1914 - 1920; L. R. Spencer, 1920 - 1922; S. E. Walker, 1923 - 1925; R. L. Berry, 1925 - 1930; J. L. Clements, 1930 - 1931; A. N. Reeves, 1931 - 1935; L. C. Lockart, 1935 - 1936; J. V. Johnson, 1937 - 1938; W. N. Kizzire, 1938 - 1940; J. Allen Kyser, 1940 - 1943; C. C. Holliman, 1943 - 1946; Leon A. Brown, 1948 - 1951; John Thompson, 1951 - 1952; Cephus Fowler, 1952 - 1953; Avery Tilley, 1954 - 1955; Hubert Hammons, 1955 - 1956; M. A. Tilley, 1956 - 1957; Marvin Fowler, 1957 - 1959.

NEW HOPE BAPTIST CHURCH (Fayette County) -- Only available record shows - 1889 - Q. D. Haney as pastor.

NEW HOPE BAPTIST CHURCH (Just in Tuscaloosa County) -- Minutes show pastors as follows; J. B. Ferguson, 1889 - 1890; J. W. Peters, 1891 - 1892.

NEW RIVER BAPTIST CHURCH -- Organized 1881. Pastors have been as follows: J. L. Soann, 1930 - 1933; O. M. Fox, 1933 - 1934; R. L. Berry, 1934 - 1935; David Dodd, 1935 - 1937; Fred Kitchens, 1937 - 1940; David Dodd, 1940 - 1941; Louis Hayes, 1941 - 1946; Earl M. Hall, 1948 - 1950; Jas. A. Lyles, 1950 - 1951; T. L. Griffin, 1952 - 1953; W. D. McConnell, 1954 - 1956; Billy G. Colston, 1956 - 1957; R. E. Pate, 1957 - 1958.

NORTH HIGHLAND BAPTIST CHURCH -- Organized in 1936. Those serving this church as pastor have been as follows: L. A. Weathers, 1936 - 1939; C. C. Holliman, 1939 - 1951; John Thompson, 1951 - 1955; M. A. Tilley, 1955 - 1957; Marvin Smith, 1957 - 1958; M. A. Tilley, 1958 - 1959.

OAK GROVE BAPTIST CHURCH -- Date of organization not available. Pastors have been as follows: W. J. Kirk, 1883 - 1887; Jonathan Taylor, 1884 - 1887; A. W. Green, 1888, 1892.

OAK RIDGE BAPTIST CHURCH -- Date of organization not available. Pastors have been as follows: Elijah Howell, 1883 - 1884; E. Hocutt, 1884 - 1885; Silas Waldrop, 1887 - 1890; ..... S. E. Walker, 1930 - 1934; J. V. Johnson, 1934 - 1937; L. R. Stokes, 1937 - 1940; W. O. Prisson, 1940 - 1942; R. R. Holliman,

1942; Ira Patterson, 1945 - 1948; E. E. Davis, 1949 - 1954; W. A. Johnson, 1954 - 1959.

PHILADELPHIA BAPTIST CHURCH -- The date of organization is not available; records show that this church was received into the Association in 1871. Pastors who have served this church have been as follows: J. B. Ferguson, 1871 - 1879; P. M. Newton, 1880 - 1881; D. W. Andrews, 1883 - 1884; E. Howell, 1884 - 1885; G. W. Gravlee, 1886 - 1889; W. G. Baker, 1889 - 1901; A. B. Batson, 1901 - 1907; J. A. Trim, 1907 - 1910; A. B. Batson, 1910; W. G. Baker, 1911; G. H. White, 1912 - 1913; J. S. Townsend, 1913 - 1914; J. W. Dyer, 1914 - 1916; L. A. Weathers, 1916 - 1918; J. W. Dyer, 1918 - 1919; S. E. Walker, 1919 - 1920; P. L. Berry, 1921 - 1923; J. S. Clark, 1923 - 1924; A. W. Skelton, 1924 - 1927; B. B. Burks, 1927 - 1929; J. M. Black, 1929 - 1934; Nelson Crow, 1934 - 1935; J. L. Clements, 1935 - 1936; D. W. Holiday, 1936 - 1937; J. E. Horton, 1937 - 1940; Fred Kitchens, 1940 - 1942; C. C. Holliman, 1948 - 1951; John Thompson, 1951 - 1952; T. L. Griffin, 1952 - 1955; Jack Branyon, 1955 - 1955; R. R. Holliman, 1957;

PILGRIM'S REST BAPTIST CHURCH -- Organized in 1841. Pastors serving this church have been as follows: J. C. Jones, 1871 - 1873; D. V. Shirley, 1874 - 1875; G. W. Gravlee, 1879, 1881; N. J. Dyer, 1883 - 1884; A. A. Smith, 1884 - 1885; J. E. Cox, 1885 - 1887; J. W. Hosmer - Supply?, 1885 - 1887; J. B. Huckabee, 1887 - 1888; J. W. Hosmer - Supply?, 1887 - 1888; W. G. Baker, 1888 1889; J. P. Dickinson - Supply? 1888 - 1889; F. Wilson, 1889 - 1898; G. W. Freeman, 1898 - 1899; F. Wilson, 1899 - 1900; F. M. Olive, 1900 - 1901; F. Wilson, 1901 - 1904; J. S. Townsend, 1904 - 1905; F. Wilson, 1905 - 1927; S. E. Walker, 1927 - 1929; John Cobb, 1929 - 1930; O. H. Vaughn, 1930 - 1932; J. Victor Johnson, 1932 - 1937; L. R. Stokes, 1938 - 1943; A. C. Nichols, 1945; Ira Patterson, 1948 - 1949; W. A. Johnson, 1949 - 1955; T. L. Griffin, 1955 - 1957; W. A. Johnson, 1957 - 1959.

PISGAH BAPTIST CHURCH -- Organized 1934. Pastors have been as follows: J. M. Mills, 1935 - 1936; A. C. Nichols, 1938 - 1956; Jerry Robinson, 1956 - 1958; Dan Cargile, 1958 - 1959.

PLEASANT GROVE BAPTIST CHURCH -- Organized in 1877. Pastors have been as follows: W. J. Akin, 1889 - 1892; J. P. Dickinson, 1895 - 1896; W. J. Akin, 1896 - 1898; J. S. Townsend, 1899 - 1900; S. L. Raney, 1900 - 1901; W. J. Akin, 1901 - 1902; J. S. Townsend, 1902 - 1904; A. B. Batson, 1904 - 1905; W. G. Baker, 1905 - 1906; S. L. Rainey, 1906 - 1907; G. H. White, 1910 - 1913; J. M. McCord, 1913 - 1914; .... O. M. Fox, 1933 - 1940; Fred Kitchens, 1940 - 1941; David Dodd, 1941 - 1942; Fred Kitchens, 1945 - 1946; J. E. Horton, 1948 - 1951; R. E. Pate, 1951 - 1958; L. W. Simmons, 1958 - 1959.

PLEASANT HILL BAPTIST CHURCH -- The Pleasant Hill Baptist Church was organized December 22, 1878, by Rev. J. B. Huckabee. The charter members were as follows: E. D. Newton, G. W. Lawrence, D. A. Nichols, Jane Farquhar, Frances E. Berry, Sara Lawrence, M. E. Townson, Lucinda Gardner, Leona Gardner and Julia A. Nichols.

Pastors serving this church have been the following: J. B. Huckabee, 1879; W. G. Baker, 1889 - 1891; J. E. Cox, 1891 - 1894; J. W. Hosmer, 1895 - 1898; J. P. Dickinson, 1898 - 1900; W. G. Baker, 1900 - 1909; J. S. Townsend, 1909 1910; W. G. Baker, 1910 - 1911; J. S. Townsend, also 1910 - 1911; J. M. Mc-

Cord, 1912 - 1913; J. C. Bell, 1914 - 1915; L. W. Dyer, 1915 - 1925; John Lollar, 1926 - 1928; L. R. Spencer, 1928 - 1930; J. H. Black, 1931 - 1934; A. N. Reeves, 1934 - 1936; A. C. Nichols, 1936 - 1954; Jack Branyon, 1955 to Nov. 1955; Billy G. Colston, 1955 - 1957; Clarence Grammar, 1957   A. J. Goodin, Jr., 1957 - 1959.

Under the pastorate and guidance of Rev. A. C. Nichols, a brick church was built. Shortly after the building was completed, he resigned, and the church elected him honorary Pastor for life.

The present church officers are as follows: Pastor - Rev. A. J. Goodin, Jr.; Sunday School Superintendent - David Chambles ; Training Union Director - Grady Esary; Deacons - Morgan Spiller, J. E. Newton, Jack Beiley and Grover Propst.

PLEASANT RIDGE BAPTIST CHURCH --- Organized in 1839. Pastors have been as follows: J. V. Johnson, 1935 - 1938; J. N. Kizziah, 1938 - 1939; Floyd Goree, 1940 - 1941; James Sweedenburg, 1941 - 1942; W. E. Robertson, 1942 - 1943.

REHOBETH -- Organized before 1883. Pastors serving this church as follows: J. B. Ferguson, 1883 - 1886; W. J. Akin, 1886 - 1888; A. J. Hosmer, 1888 - 1889; ... E. T. Selman, 1896 - 1901; J. S. Townsend, 1902 - 1904; S. L. Rainey, 1904 - 1908; J. A. Trim, 1908 - 1915; Frank Wilson, 1915 - 1918; R. L. Berry, 1918, 1919; S. E. Walker, also 1918 - 1919; Frank Wilson, 1919 - 1922; R. L. Berry, 1922 - 1929; J. C. Deering, 1929 - 1931; Paul Meigs, 1931 - 1933; Ralph Fields, 1934 - 1935; J. E. Horton, 1935   1937; J. V. Johnson, 1937 - 1938; A. C. Nichols, 1938 - 1939; C. C. Holliman, 1939 - 1942; A. M. Mix, 1942 - 1953; A. C. Nichols, 1954 - 1955; J. P. Ables, 1956 - 1957; Sam Wolfe, 1957 - 1958; Wayne Watts, 1958 - 1959.

ROCKY MOUNT BAPTIST CHURCH -- (See Covin Baptist Church.) This church was organized in 1871 or earlier. Pastors serving Rocky Mount have been as follows: N. J. Dyer, 1871 - 1875; S. Covin, 1879 - 1880; D. W. Andrews, 1880 - 1886; N. J. Dyer, 1886 - 1888; D. W. Andrews, 1888 - 1889; S. P. Waldrop, 1889 - 1891; D. W. Andrews, 1891 - 1892; J. F. Willis, 1892; A. Pennington, 1892 - 1894; D. W. Andrews, 1894 - 1895; A. Pennington, 1895 - 1896; F. Wilson, 1896 1903; W. J. Godfrey, 1903 - 1904; L. A. Connell, 1904 - 1906; J. S. Townsend, 1907 - 1908; L. A. Connell, 1908 - 1909; F. Wilson, 1910 - 1912; -- According to Minute Records Rocky Mount became Covin Baptist Church in 1914.

SALEM BAPTIST CHURCH --- Organized in 1824. According to available records the Salem Baptist Church is the oldest Baptist Church in the Fayette County territory. Pastors who have served this church have been as follows: J. W. Rogers, 1887 - 1888; J. B. Ferguson, 1888 - 1889; J. W. Rogers, 1889 - 1890; Wm. Ashcraft, 1891; I. L. Collins, 1895 - 1900; J. B. Ferguson, 1900 - 1905; ... J. L. Dobbs, 1923 - 1929; J. L. Clements, 1929 - 1933; L. C. Lockart, 1933 - 1934; J. L. Clements, 1934 - 1935; I. Vester Hallman, 1935 - 1937; J. L. Watson, 1937 - 1938; J. L. Clements, 1938 - 1939; W. C. Kirkley, 1939 - 1941; J. E. Horton, 1941 - 1942; C. H. Bobo, 1945; Adolph Blakeney, 1948 - 1949; Wesley Tatum, 1949 - 1950; John M. Tatum, 1950 - 1951; J. L. Clements, 1951 - 1959.

SANDSPRINGS BAPTIST CHURCH -- (See Friendship Baptist Church - Fayette County.)

SHADY GROVE BAPTIST CHURCH -- This church was organized in 1864 or 1871 - the records vary. Pastors serving this church have been as follows: J. E. Bell, 1871 - 1879; J. B. Ferguson, 1880 - 1881; J. M. Chism, 1883 - 1885; G. W. Gravlee, 1886 - 1889; J. J. Patterson, 1890 - 1893; W. G. Baker, 1893 1894; M. W. Olive, 1895 - 1896; G. H. White, 1896 - 1897; I. B. Davis, 1897 1898; J. S. Townsend, 1899 - 1900; G. H. White, 1901 - 1904; J. J. Patterson, 1904 - 1905; G. H. White, 1906 - 1908; J. R. Hallman, 1908 - 1913; G. H. White, 1913 - 1915; J. D. Cobbs, 1915 - 1918; S. E. Walker, 1918 - 1919; L. A. Weathers, 1919 - 1921; W. W. Rice, 1921 - 1928; Hollie G. Patterson, 1928 1931; J. L. Clements, 1933 - 1938; W. N. Kizziah, 1938 - 1939; J. H. Cole, 1939 - 1940; G. M. Fowler, 1940 - 1946; Charston Whitson, 1949 - 1951; A. C. Nichols, 1952 - 1953; J. L. Clements, 1953 - 1959.

SHEPHERD BAPTIST CHURCH - NEWTONVILLE -- Shepherd Baptist Church was organized in 1834. One of the founders was Mr. Jacob Shepherd but the old church books have been lost and there is no record of the charter members.

Following are some of the pastors who have served this church: N. J. Dyer, 1871 - 1873; B. V. Shirley, 1874; G. W. Gravlee, 1878 - 1882; J. M. Chism, 1883 - 1886; G. W. Gravlee, 1887 - 1890; H. T. Wright, 1890 - 1891; S. W. Waldron 1891 - 1894; Frank Wilson, 1894 - 1895; Ira Collins, 1895 - 1896; J. M. Chism, 1896 - 1897; G. W. Gravlee, 1897 - 1902; J. B. Ferguson, 1902 - 1903; J. H.? Gardner, 1903 - 1904; I. L. Collins, 1905 - 1906; G. W. Gravlee, 1906 - 1908; S. W. Clements, 1908 - 1914; Frank Wilson, 1914 - 1916; G. W. Gravlee, 1916 - 1917; W. W. Dyer, 1917 - 1918; J. A. Trim, 1918 - 1919; S. W. Clements, 1919 - 1921; W. N. Kizziah, 1921 - 1922; S. E. Walker, 1923 - 1932; Victor Johnson, 1933 - 1934; L. A. Connell, 1934 - 1937; D. W. Griffin, 1937 1938; James Sweedenburg, 1938 - 1940; W. E. Robertson, 1941 - 1943; Ira Patterson, 1945 - 1949; A. M. Nix, 1949 - 1950; J. E. Horton, 1950 - 1953; W. A. Johnson, 1953 - 1959.

SILOAM BAPTIST CHURCH -- The Siloam Baptist Church was organized in 1884 and the brick building was erected in 1956. Following are the pastors who have served this church, as they are listed in the Associational Minutes; Jonathan Taylor, 1884 - 1890; J. E. Bernard, 1891. No other records were available.

SILVERTOWN BAPTIST CHURCH -- Organized in 1944. Pastors who served were as follows: S. V. Hallman, 1945; Early Davis, 1948 - 1950; W. A. Johnson, 1950 1952; T. L. Griffin, 1952; ... The church became inactive in 1955.

SIPSEY VALLEY BAPTIST CHURCH -- The date of organization is not available. Pastors listed in the records were as follows: Silas White, 1887 - 1888; J. W. White, 1888 - 1889; J. S. White, 1889 - 1890; W. J. Akin, 1891; J. S. White, 1895 - 1896; J. W. Hosmer, 1896 - 1898.

SOUTHSIDE BAPTIST CHURCH -- The Southside Baptist Church of Fayette was organized into a church on November 28, 1957. This church had its beginning a few weeks prior to this date as a mission being fostered by the Fayette First Baptist Church. The charter members were as follows: Rev. B. G. Colston, Mrs. B. G. Colston, Mr. J. C. Gary, Mrs. J. C. Gary, Mr. Aaron Branyon, Mrs. Aaron Branyon, Mr. E. M. Boling, Mrs. E. M. Boling, Mr. Fred Wilkerson, Mrs. Fred Wilkerson, Mr. M. L. Smith, Mrs. M. L. Smith, Mrs. Burt Terry and Mrs. E. J. Phillips.

The pastors who have served the Southside Baptist Church have been Rev. Billy Gene Colston from November, 1957 to August, 1959 - and Rev. J. P. Ables from September, 1959.

STUDDARD'S CROSS ROADS -- There are no records on this church in the Minutes except that this church was a member of the association at one time.

UNION BAPTIST CHURCH -- Organization date not available. Pastors who have served this church are as follows: W. G. Baker, 1883 - 1888; James J. McCollum, 1889 - 1890; J. S. Shirley, 1891.

UNION BAPTIST CHURCH - (Marion County) --Organization date is not available. This church belonged to the New River Association, but was not listed in the later years. Following are the pastors who were listed as serving this church: C. J. Kirk, 1883 - 1884; Joseph Baldwin, 1884; J. Taylor, 1887 - 1888; A. L. Green, 1888 - 1889; Q. D. Haney, 1889 - 1890; J. W. Peters, 1891 - 1892.

UNION GROVE BAPTIST CHURCH -- Organized in 1886. Pastors serving this church were as follows: J. S. Clark, 1931 - 1934; L. C. Lockert, 1934 - 1936; J. S. Clark, 1936 - 1938; G. M. Fowler, 1938 - 1941; Houston Brand, 1945 - 1946; Paul Blanton, 1948 - 1949; Clyde Latham, 1949 - 1950; H. V. Hallman, 1950 - 1952; W. B. Glover, 1952 - 1953; Houston Brand, 1953 - 1956; Fletcher Kimbrell, 1956 - 1959.

UNITY BAPTIST CHURCH -- Faced by financial and other problems the members of a little country church, about six and one-half miles north of Fayette, were considering the possibility of dissolving their church.

When the situation was at its lowest ebb, fire almost completely destroyed the building, leaving only a few chairs and an old-fashioned organ.

Not far from the site of the burned church stood another proud little frame building known as the Mt. Olive Baptist Church. The small group of people from Mt. Olive had a suggestion - "Why not move the few possessions belonging to the former church into the Mt. Olive building?" and be considered as one church.

After accepting the generous offer the members raised the question about the renaming of the church. When all suggested names were considered and one by one eliminated, only one very appropriate name remained. Due to the fact that two little churches were united into one, the church was given the name "Unity".

Through the years, though there have been new buildings to replace the old ones, the little church still bears the original name, "Unity". Unity was received into the New River Baptist Association in 1890. The known pastors have been as follows: N. J. Dyer, 1890; J. S. Shirley, 1892; A. N. Reeves, 1893 - 1895 - 1896 - 1897 - 1900; J. S. Townsend, 1899 - 1901 - 1902 1903; L. A. Connell, 1904 - 1905 - 1908 - 1911; S. L. Rainey, 1907; J. A. Trim, 1912 - 1917; R. L. Berry, 1918 - 1919 - 1920; R. L. Berry, 1920 - 1928; A. M. Nix, 1929 - 1936; Luther Tucker, 1938; A. M. Nix, 1939 - 1946; S. E. Walker, 1948; Earl Hall, 1949 - Supply; Marvin Palmer, 1950; J. E. Horton, 1951 - 1955; Theron Holliman, 1955 - 1956; Dan Cargile, 1957 - 1958.

WINFIELD BAPTIST CHURCH -- This church was found in the records as belonging to the New River Association and in the year 1891 had Rev. J. W. McGaha as pastor. No other records appear.

PRIMITIVE BAPTIST CHURCHES OF FAYETTE COUNTY
The Primitive Baptist Church is the oldest denomination for which we have any record in Fayette County and many of our other churches were formed by original members of the Primitive Baptist. The following Primitive Churches are listed (when records were available to give this information) with those who served the churches as Elders.

CONCORD PRIMITIVE BAPTIST CHURCH -- It is not known what year this church was constituted, but in 1871 the Pastor was Elder L. M. Wimberley. Other records are not available for other ministers or the charter members.

DOUBLE SPRINGS PRIMITIVE BAPTIST CHURCH -- Organized possibly in 1837. The Minutes list the following as delegates: ___ McCollum and B. Pruett.

EMMAUS PRIMITIVE BAPTIST CHURCH -- Date of organization is not known, but in 1871 the pastor was Elder J. S. Bolton. There are no other records showing others who served as minister of this church.

FRIENDSHIP PRIMITIVE BAPTIST CHURCH -- The date of organization is not known for this church but the following are listed as delegates in the Minutes of the Buttahatchee Association in 1833: E. Thompson, Sanders Mills, and Wm. Stinson.

HARMONY PRIMITVE BAPTIST CHURCH -- The Primitive Baptist Church at Harmony was constituted into a church on Saturday the 4th day of August, 1860.
Charter Members who presented Letters on August 4, 1860 were as follows: David Duncan, Luca Duncan, John W. Moore, Nancy Moore, Wm. L. Caples, Obadiah Strickland, James A. Caples, Jasper Duncan, Cassinder Duncan, Myna Caples, Grisham Tailor, and William Malone.
Following are some of the ministers who have served this church: Elder David Duncan, Elder L. M. Wimberley, Elder J. A. Smith, Elder C. H. Davis, Elder G. W. Berry, Elder W. M. Dorris, Elder William Haney, Elder A. B. Dyer, Elder E. Z. McCool, Elder J. W. McCool, Elder E. D. Griffin and Elder H. M. Brock (Presently serving -- 1959.)

HOPEWELL PRIMITIVE BAPTIST CHURCH -- The Hopewell Primitive Baptist Church is one of the oldest landmarks in the county. Available records give the date of organization as 1818. This church is located just east off the Winfield Highway about six miles north of Fayette.
Following are listed the names of the men who have preached at this church through the many years: Elder J. S. Bolton, Elder Jessie Jones, Elder Alvy (A. M.) Reynolds, Elder J. M. Thompson, Elder T. J. Norris, Elder J. W. Roby, Elder L. M. Wimberley, Elder W. W. Barton, Elder G. W. Norris, Elder J. M. Smith, Elder C. H. Davis, Elder J. W. Brock, Elder G. W. Berry, Elder W. D. Griffin - 1900 - 1931, Elder W. L. Norris and Elder Louis Moore.

LITTLE HOPE PRIMITIVE BAPTIST CHURCH -- It is believed that this church was organized in 1860, but this date is not positive. Following are the ministers who have served this church to the present date: Elder G. W. Norris, Elder J. W. Brock, Elder L. M. Wimberley, Elder C. H. Davis, Elder E. Z. McCool, Elder G. W. Berry, Elder Wilson Brock and Elder H. M. Brock (present).

MACEDONIA PRIMITIVE BAPTIST CHURCH -- The Macedonia Primitive Baptist Church was organized in 1823. Following are those who have served this church as ministers: Elder William E. Cook, Elder John Burnette, Elder Sanders B. Mills, Elder Guyton, Elder Amon Taylor, Elder Johnson, Elder Jeffries, Elder L. Maze, Elder William Moore, Elder A. J. Eggar, Elder George Nolen, Elder L. M. Wimberley, Elder E. T. Sorrels, Elder M. L. Vandiver, Elder W. J. Otts, Elder J. R. Pennington, Elder C. H. Davis, Elder J. T. Randolph, Elder W. D. Griffin, and Elder E. G. McGough (present - 1959).

MT. CARMEL PRIMITIVE BAPTIST CHURCH -- The original records of this church were burned and the date it was organized is not known. Following are listed some of the ministers who have served this church: Elder C. H. Davis, Elder J. B. Dean, Elder L. M. Wimberley, Elder W. M. Dorris, Elder E. Z. McCool, Elder W. D. Griffin, Elder J. R. Pennington, and Elder H. M. Brock (Present).

NEW PROSPECT PRIMITIVE BAPTIST CHURCH -- Organization date is unknown, but in 1873 Elder I. Watson was the minister. The present minister (1959) is Elder H. M. Brock.

NEW RIVER PRIMITIVE BAPTIST CHURCH -- The New River Primitive Baptist Church was organized in 1826 and following are the ministers whose names were found in the old records: Elder John Canterberry, Elder Nathan Roberts, Elder James Barnes, Elder A. M. Reynolds, Elder L. M. Wimberley, and Elder J. M. Smith.

NORTH RIVER PRIMITIVE BAPTIST CHURCH -- The following names, listed as delegates from this church, were found in the 1833 Minutes of Buttahatchee Association: Grief Johnson, Z. Tanksley, and H. R. Williams.

PLEASANT HILL PRIMITIVE BAPTIST CHURCH -- Constituted Saturday before the fourth Sunday in October, 1895. Presbytery: Elder R. G. Guthree, Elder Heram Barton and Elder I. N. Roberts.
    Names of members composing this church at that time are as follows: Noah Pyris, P. C. Johnson, Frances Johnson, Nancy Tidwell, David Rutledge, Martha Rutledge, J. V. Aldridge, J. W. Johnson, Sidney Johnson, Martha Ann Nelson, and J. B. McGowan. The only pastor that was listed in this record was A. T. Randolph.

POPLAR SPRINGS PRIMITIVE BAPTIST CHURCH -- The Poplar Springs Baptist Church was organized in 1834 and the following ministers have served the church to the present time: Elder Robert Portwood, Elder William Halbert, Elder Alvy Reynolds, Elder Edman Thompson, Elder W. West, Elder A. J. Coleman, Elder William C. Hunter, Elder Jonah Vail, Elder A. J. Egger, Elder T. J. Norris, Elder L. M. Wimberley, Elder J. B. Dean, Elder C. H. Davis, Elder W. M. Dorris, Elder J. F. Sanders, Elder G. V. Berry, Elder H. M. Brock, Elder E. Z. McCool, Elder W. D. Griffin, and Elder H. C. Moon (present - 1959).

PROVIDENCE PRIMITIVE BAPTIST CHURCH -- The date of organization is not known for this church, but the Minutes of Buttahatchee Association in 1833 listed the following as delegates from this church: Elder Robert Portwood, James Sorewell, and Ben H. Stribling.

SALEM PRIMITIVE BAPTIST CHURCH -- The Salem Primitive Baptist Church was constituted on Sunday the 20th day of September, 1874, by the Elder Hiram Barton and Elder A. J. Gibson. The following members were present: N. N. Gibson,

Nancy Gibson, James Poe, Mary Poe, Apsoner Poe, A. T. Poe and Nancy Ann Jones.

Constitution of Salem Church: We the undersigned being called on as a presbytery, met at Sulphur Springs Church in Tuscaloosa County on the third Sunday in September 1874 and the following brethren and sisters were examined in the faith of the Gospel and found to be orthodox in principle to wit: W. N. Gibson, Nancy Gibson, James Poe, Mary Poe, Apsonance Poe, A. T. Poe and Nancey An Jones.

We therefore proceeded to constitute them into a Primitive Baptist Church on the abstracts of faith on the Lost Creek Baptist Association of the Primitive Order on the day and date above named. .... Hiram Barton, A. J. Gibson.

Met at Salem Church on Saturday before the 4th Sunday in September 1874 and the church called Elder A. J. Gibson as pastor and elected Brother W. N. Gibson Church Clerk for the next year. These served until 1877 when Elder A. J. Gibson was reelected pastor and A. T. Poe Church Clerk.

Elders who have served the church are as follows: Elder A. Raburn, Elder J. S. Kitchens, Elder W. R. Brown, Elder A. T. Randolph and Elder W. R. Utley. G. W. Poe served as Church Clerk from 1891 until his death in 1953. The early list of membership includes the following names: W. N. Gibson, Nancy Gibson, James Poe, Mary Poe, Apsoner Poe, A. T. Poe, Nancy An Jones, Mary E. Patton, W. S. Poe, Rhoda Poe, Mary An Kimbrell, William Maries, John M. Thacker, W. D. Earnest, Nancy Earnest, James Patton, Susan J. Kimbrell, Benjimen Pendley, Ann Pendley, A. J. Gibson, Mary Gibson, G. W. Poe, Lovie Poe, M. W. Robson, Mary Jane Robson, A. R. Poe, W. T. Randolph, Roxie Randolph, and Ellen Sexton.

SMYRNA PRIMITIVE BAPTIST CHURCH -- The date of organization for this church is not known but in the Minutes of Buttahatchee Association in 1831 the following names were found listed as delegates representing Smyrna Church: Nicholas Baker, Miles Chappel, and George Longmire. This is all that appeared in the records concerning this church in Fayette County.

UNION PRIMITIVE BAPTIST CHURCH -- The Union Primitive Baptist Church was organized in 1826 and the following men have served the church as ministers: Elder Holly, Elder Hiram Roberts, Elder A. M. Reynolds, Elder Jonathan Holcombe Elder S. J. Norris, Elder Horace Dodson, Elder James S. Bolton, Elder Jesse Jones, Elder L. M. Wimberley, Elder C. H. Davis, Elder J. C. Huddleson, Elder G. W. Berry, Elder J. W. McCool, Elder E. Z. McCool and Elder H. M. Brock (present - 1959).

The records vary slightly as to the exact date of organization. An article giving a list of the charter members (which follows) states that the church was organized May 21, 1825.

Charter members were as follows: George Poe, Elizabeth Poe, Hiram Robertson, John Cast, Levi Taylor, A. Armstrong, Sarah Armstrong, Mary Vanshan, Susanah Vanshan, John J. Sharp, Leach Allen, and Nancy Mather.

The presbytery for the organization were Elders Nathan Roberts and Jannis Baines.

STS. JAMES & JOHN ROMAN CATHOLIC MISSION - FAYETTE -- The Sts. James & John Roman Catholic Mission was established November, 1957, and the first place of worship is located on Aylette Street. The first and present pastor is Rev. Father Joseph Corradine. Parishoners are as follows: Mr. & Mrs. Alexander & Family (Guin), Mr. Paul Cawthorn (Hamilton), Mrs. Robert Cunningham & Family (Fayette), Mr. & Mrs. Charles Greene (Hamilton), Mrs. George Dickerson

(Brilliant), Mrs. Robert Jones & Family (Fayette), Mrs. Rayford Pritchett & Family (Fayette), Mrs. Henry Reisweig (Fayette), Mr. James Stokes (Guin), and Mrs John Waggoner (Fayette).

This mission was organized in the home of Mrs. Rayford Pritchett and met there for a short while before the mission was located.

BANKSTON CHURCH OF CHRIST -- The Bankston Church of Christ was built in 1914 on property adjoining the Bankston Cemetery. R. S. "Ned" Smith and Dr. J. T. Weathers were the elders of this early church. In May 1914 the first series of meetings was conducted, by Bro. C. T. Cannon of Rocky, Okla.

The annual Easter Singing had its beginning at that church in 1916. The church building was destroyed by a storm in the spring of 1932 and the new building was erected at the present site on the Southern Railroad near the old water tank. Mrs. Lorenzo Michael selected the first song, "We'll Work 'Til Jesus Comes" that was sung after the new building was completed.

Some of the early elders of the church were Doc Hollingsworth, Bus Hollingsworth, Ed Spiller, R. S. Smith and Dr. J. T. Weathers.

Among the ministers who have served are the following: Wiley Hollingsworth, Bro. Baker, S. W. Thompson, C. V. Duncan, J. D. Jones, C. T. Cannon, Chester Honeycutt, Bob Gray, C. W. Lewis, Charles Wheeler, Bro. Guance, Bro. Crowder, Bro. Gossett, Bro. Fite, Bro. McCluskey, Bro. Price, Bro. Freeman, and Bro. Wagner.

BEREA CHURCH OF CHRIST -- This church was organized in 1845. Minister John Taylor held the first meeting on the Thornton Farm (now the Wiley Perry Farm). Jeremiah Randolph, another pioneer preacher, worked with John Taylor to establish Churches in Fayette, Walker, Lamar and other nearby counties and also, West Tennessee during the 1840's.

Berea is the first and only Church of Christ in the county of Fayette, organized before the Civil War. Later, Berea was moved to a school building on the McCollum or McCaleb Farm (partially on both farms) as four acres were later deeded to the church by W. T. McCaleb and H. C. McCollum.

A partial list of the charter members follows: W. P. Anthony, H. C. McCollum, Andrew McCaleb, and W. T. McCaleb. Other families among the charter members were the Thorntons, Logans, McArthurs, and several others.

Some of the preachers have been as follows: 1. John Taylor, 2. Jeremiah Randolph, 3. John McCaleb, Jimmy Woods, E. C. Fuqua, James Wade, O. C. Dobbs, Gus Dunn, Sr., Gus Nichols, Houston Haney, Wiley Hollingsworth.

BERRY CHURCH OF CHRIST -- The Berry Church of Christ started meeting in the store of Mrs. Oliver C. "Granny" Dobbs in the early 1900's. The Church was officially organized in 1911 and some of the charter members were Mrs. Oliver Dobbs, J. R. Dobbs, O. C. Dobbs, J. D. Dobbs, Sam Dobbs, Mr. & Mrs. Cap Shepherd, Mrs. C. H. Pinion, Mr. & Mrs. Cager Shepherd, Mrs. Cardie Stewart, Mr. & Mrs. Mose Bailey, Mr Lump Smith, Mr. & Mrs. Joe B. Johnson and Mr. & Mrs. Fenton Anthony.

A partial list of the preachers gives the following men: Charlie Wheeler, Frank Baker, O. C. Dobbs, G. A. Dunn, J. B. Nelson and Gus Nichols.

CLEVELAND CHURCH OF CHRIST -- Cleveland Church was organized in the early part of the 1890's. Cleveland Hyde gave the land for the church, therefore the church was named for him.

Jeremiah Randolph held a "Brush Arbor" meeting at the location of the present church two and one-half miles north of Bankston on the "Old Byler Road". Among the members helping to build the old log house about 1890 were Alexander Brannenbery, W. A. Hyde, Bill Ellis and sons, Jim, Joe and Walter, Mose Bailey, Jim Lowery and others.

The present building was erected in 1926 by the members, with the aid of funds solicited by Mrs. Walter Ellis and Mrs. A. J. McCaleb.

The oldest members were as follows: Mr. & Mrs Alexander Brannenbery, Mr. & Mrs. Jasper Smith, Mr. & Mrs. Cleveland Hyde, Mr. & Mrs. W. A. Hyde, Mr. & Mrs. Bailey and Mr. & Mrs. Bill Ellis.

Ministers through the years have been the following: Jeremiah Randolph, Virgil Randolph, T. F. Srygley, C. A. Wheeler, W. A. Tipton, Jimmie Woods, Gus Dunn, Sr., O. C. Dobbs, Hal P. McDonald, Gus Nichols, Charlie Nichols, V. R. Willcutt, Houston Haney, D. C. Salter, W. A. Black, Chester Estes, John McCleskey, F. Freeman Crowder, Bob Gray, Chester Honeycutt, A. C. Plylar, Hamond Horton, Edward J. Craddock, Wiley Hollingsworth, Pervie Nichols, Pat Kirkland and Bryce Ellis.

Elders of the church since 1890 have been Hiram Hyde, Mose P. Bailey, A. J. Tucker, Sr. Walter Ellis, J. H. Walton, A. J. McCaleb, M. V. Deavours, J. R. Sanford, V. H. Sawyer, and Willie Bobo.

FAYETTE CHURCH OF CHRIST -- The congregation of the Church of Christ was begun earlier than the year 1923. By this year there were about 15 members who were meeting in the Fayette County Court House for worship. John R. Fowler was the leader of the group.

In the latter part of 1923, C. R. Nichol from Clifton, Texas, conducted a revival meeting which resulted in two additions. Soon after this meeting a movement was started to raise funds to erect a suitable building in which to meet to worship. After many business meetings were held the work was finally started which resulted in the present building on Temple Avenue.

Not long after the completion of the building H. P. Hardeman of Henderson, Tenn., was engaged to hold a meeting and this effort resulted in several additions.

Among the preachers who have served the Fayette Church of Christ are the following: C. R. Brewer, G. C. Brewer, Gus Dunn, Jr., Gus Dunn, Sr., John T. Hinds, Foy Wallace, Jr., Jack Hackworth, LeRoy Brownlow, H. A. Dixon, Willis Jernigan, G. K. Wallace, Chester Estes, Flavil Nichols, J. G. Pounds, J. C. Davidson, G. L. Mann, Bobby Cheetom, and Curtis V. Posey (1958 - to present).

In the early 1950's the church added an educational building, joining the back of the main church building and in 1957 they completed a lovely brick pastorium.

HOUSH'S CHAPEL CHURCH OF CHRIST -- Housh's Chapel Church of Christ was begun in 1945 with the following active and inactive members: Mr. & Mrs. John Sims, Miss Bernice Sims, Mr. & Mrs. Ormand Sims, Mr. & Mrs. Whitson, Miss Clara Whitson, Mr. Ceohas Whitson, Mr. Deward Whitson, Mr. Jason Whitson, Miss Ola Whitson, Mr. & Mrs. Dalton Hubbert, and Mrs. Morgan Kirkley.

Mr. Belton Whitson and son Deward were the leaders in the church's activities but in 1946, both were killed in a well cave-in. After this tragedy Mr. Cogar Hubbert of Hubbertville and Mr. Clarence Ehl and family of New River began meeting with the church to help with the various activities. The membership is approximately 40, with only seven of the charter members meeting there; the average attendance is approximately sixty.

Some of the ministers who have assisted this church follow: Bro. Pervie

Nichols, Bro. Marshall Wyers, Bro. Wiley Hollingsworth, Bro. Wiley Herren, Bro. Aaron Herren, Bro. Charlie Dunn, Bro. Ray Duncan, Bro. Curtis W. Posey, Bro. Dale Buckley, Bro. Randy Jernigan, Bro. Wayne Jackson, Bro. Charles W. Brown, and Bro. Windell Fikes.

HOWARD CHURCH OF CHRIST -- In 1929, the Howard Church of Christ was organized and the present building was erected in 1931.

The charter members were as follows: Mr. & Mrs. Austin Sawyers, Mr. & Mrs. P. B. Hendon, Mr. & Mrs. L. W. Herron, Mr. & Mrs. Hollie Studdard, Mr. & Mrs. Frank Herron, Mr. & Mrs. Otto Alexander, Mr. & Mrs. Grady Latham, and Mr. & Mrs. Ulys Latham.

The following ministers have served the church: C. A. Wheeler, C. M. Geer, Sam Gant, Gus Nichols, G. A. Dunn, Chester Estes, J. G. Pounds, W. R. Willcutt, A. M. Plyler, C. V. Alexander, and Aaron Herron.

HUBBERTVILLE CHURCH OF CHRIST -- This church was first organized in 1926 with the following as charter members: John M. Hubbert, Wiley Perry, John A. Hollingsworth, Curvey Anderson, Fenton Anthony, Tom McArthur, S. N. Lawrence, A. J. Hubbert, Henry McDonald, and V. H. Aldridge.

Those serving as Elders have been Wiley Perry, John M. Hubbert, and Curvey Anderson.

A new building was erected in 1952 and the charter members for this reorganization were as follows: W. H. Aldridge, Thomas McArthur, G. E. Hubbert, Verdo Johnson, W. Orville McCaleb, Clyde Hubbert, Monroe Stough, Cleburn Hubbert, E. L. Hubbert, Floyd Tucker, and Vester Anderson.

The preachers from 1926 to the present time (1959) have been the following: Bro. C. F. Cannon, Bro. Gus Nichols, Bro. Charlie Nichols, Bro. C. C. Nichols, Bro. G. A. Dunn, Bro. Jack Hackworth, Bro. John Kelly, Bro. Charlie Wheeler, Bro. Houston Haney, Bro. Jim Wade, Bro. Chester Estes, Bro. W. A. Black, Bro. J. D. Jones, Bro. L. A. Fowler, Bro. Winfred Clark, Bro. C. W. Posey, Bro. Vandervilt, Bro. Plato Black, Bro. E. L. Hubbert, Bro. Johnnie Payne, Bro. Garland Cross, Bro. G. L. Mann, Bro. Carlos Killingsworth, Bro. Oneal Smelser, Bro. Wiley Herren, Bro. Bryce Ellis, Bro. Bobby Cheatem, Bro. Jimmie Tolle, Bro. Windell Fikes, Bro. Frank Farriss, Bro. Wiley Hollingsworth, Bro. Hal P. McDonald, Bro. Marshall Wyers, and Bro. Edward Craddock.

MT. OLIVE CHURCH OF CHRIST -- This church was begun before 1900 by Bert Barnes who invited preachers to preach to his neighbors in the yard of his home. Later they held meetings under "Brush Arbors". The old Mt. Olive Church Building was built about 1900 and the first Elders of the church were Bert Barnes and Taylor Fowler.

The charter members were as follows: Mr. & Mrs. Bert Barnes, Mr. & Mrs. Jim Mobley, Mr. & Mrs. Jimmie Collins, Mr. & Mrs. Doc Hyder, Mr. & Mrs. Hardy Housh, Mr. & Mrs. Taylor Fowler, A Harper Family, A Dobbs Family and Mr. & Mrs. Murry V. Stewart.

Some of the older preachers of this church were Jeremiah Randolph, Joe Holbrooks, R. L. Taylor, Jimmie Woods, Preacher Stansberry, and others.

The present building is a brick structure located on highway 107. The first meeting held in the new church house began July 4, 1947. The Elders in 1959 are C. C. Nichols who also preaches and L. A. Fowler, a preacher, who is the son of one of the first Elders, Taylor Fowler.

NEW RIVER CHURCH OF CHRIST -- The New River Church of Christ was organized in

1886. Some of the charter members were as follows: Mr. & Mrs. Jerry Randolph, Mr. & Mrs. Virgil Randolph, Mr. & Mrs. John Tyler McCaleb, Mr. & Mrs. Joe Holbrooks, Mr. & Mrs. John Hollingsworth, and Mr. & Mrs. Jim Davis.

The Church was built by Mr. John Tyler McCaleb except for $18.00 that was given by Mr. Jim Wade.

The following ministers have served the church: Jeremiah Randolph, Virgil Randolph, Green Haley, Joe Holbrooks, C. A. Wheeler, W. A. Tipton, Sammie Carson, Howell Taylor, Willie Loyd, Gus Nichols, Cephas Cannon, O. C. Dobbs, Houston Haney, Willett Black, Vanderbilt Black, Wiley Hollingsworth, Edsel Burleson, Marshall Myers and Paul D. Murphy.

Mr. John Tyler McCaleb was an Elder of the Church as long as he lived, from 1886 until 1918. John Hubbert was an Elder from 1918 until 1929.

PEA RIDGE CHURCH OF CHRIST -- The Pea Ridge Church of Christ was established in 1911 with the following charter members: Mr. & Mrs. Ben Panter, Mr. & Mrs. Woodard Panter, Mr. & Mrs. Charlie Panter, Mr. & Mrs. Richard Panter, Mr. Doc Panter, Mr. & Mrs. Tom Key, Miss Roxey Panter, Miss Della Panter, Mr. Ben Panter and Mr. Jim Madison.

Some who have served the church as preachers are as follows: O. C. Dobbs, Gus Nichols, Charles Nichols, Sid Cannon, R. L. Willcutt, Corey Nichols, Bobby Gray, Avery Fike, John McCluskey, Edsel Burleson, Carlos Killingsworth and Bryce Ellis.

The Elders of the Church are Mr. Richard Panter and Mr. Tom Key, who has served continously from 1918 to 1959.

WHITE'S CHAPEL CHURCH OF CHRIST -- This church was established in 1927 with the following charter members: Mr. & Mrs. Bob Herron, Mr. & Mrs. Jerry White, Mr. & Mrs. Oscar Dobb, Mr. & Mrs. Boss Tucker, Mr. & Mrs. Henry Hollingsworth, Mr. & Mrs. White Howell, Mr. & Mrs. Anderson Howell, Mr. & Mrs. Tom Hollingsworth.

Ministers who have served this church have been the following: C. A. Wheeler, Gus Nichols, A. D. Diaz, Chester Estes, W. A. Black, Edsel Burleson, and V. P. Black.

METHODISTS -- The New River Circuit first appeared in the list of the appointments for 1824. It was organized just one year before the county of Fayette, Alabama, was established, and the principal part of the Circuit lay in what constituted that county when it was first established, though the Circuit extended somewhat into the counties adjoining to Fayette County, and the Circuit possibly had a few appointments in the State of Mississippi. The Territory occupied by the New River Circuit had formerly been in the Marion Circuit.

The preachers on the New River Circuit were as follows: 1824 - John G. Lee and Daniel H. Williams; 1825 - John Collier and Thomas S. Abernathy; 1826 - Eugene V. Levert and Henry J. Brown; 1827 - Thomas Burpo; 1828 - Thomas E. Ledbetter, and John Collier; 1829 - Henry J. Brown; 1830 - Nathan Hopkins and Benjamin D. Smith; 1831 - Mark Westmoreland; and 1832 - Griffin R. Christopher and Sidney S. Squires.

At the Annual Conference in December 1833, Walker Mission was made and put in the list of appointments ... The Walker Mission at that time (1833) occupied the eastern half of Walker County, and was sometimes associated with Blount Counties. The pastoral charge called Jasper, and then called New Lexington lay along and on either side of Byler's Road and extended from Northport on the Warrior River to the northern boundary of Walker County, parts of

Fayette, Marion, Tuskaloosa and Walker were included in that charge. No doubt some of the preaching places on that work had previously belonged to other circuits. The preaching places mentioned in that Circuit in 1842 were as follows: Bethel, Bethlehem, Blanton's, Cole's, Jasper, New Lexington, North Port, Pleasant Hill, Pryor's, Rock Springs, Shiloh, Snow's, ZION, Tubb's, Turner's, Williams, and Yellow Creek.

The Whitsons, Freemans and Coles had their membership at ZION in the south-eastern part of Fayette County. Rev. Anthony Dickinson was one of the preachers in the early days of the Walker Circuit.

The early history of the Methodists would not be complete without a brief description of a camp meeting of the 1830's and 1840's. Of course these meetings continued until the turn of the century, but the following is a description of those early camp meetings:

"..A Camp meeting in the 1830's and 1840's would reveal people pouring into the encampment by the hundreds. They came from far and near. They came in style and without style, and by all modes of travel. They came to hear the great preacher. One who never saw the atire of the wealthy and the poor in the days of the camp-meetings cannot have a clear idea of the peculiar mingle and parade of such an occasion. The carriage of the wealthy family in Alabama in the days of slavery was of special model. It was a four-wheeled vehicle fitted to double harness and the use of a pair of horses. The body of that carriage was of rather massive proportions. It was delicately lined and trimmed within with linen, silk and satin and furnished with two double seats softly cushioned. On the outside, it was ornamented with finely polished metals and in front was a high-mounted seat. The body of the carriage was hung on mammoth springs. The mother and daughters of the family usually rode in these fine carriages. On the high seat in front sat the driver, a well-dressed Negro man who was trusted with the reins, and with him sat the waiting maid, who was a Negro woman, well-dressed, neat and clean. The driver and the waiting-maid seated on front of the carriage were the badge of the large wealth and superior elegance of the family to which the outfit belonged. The Negro who drove the family carriage in Alabama in that day had a sacred trust and a distinguished position of which he was sufficiently proud. A Negro in Congress today is not more important.

"The line-up for a wealthy family on their way to camp-meeting would usually consist of the family carriage containing mother, daughters, driver and waiting-maid in front; next a fine buggy, drawn by a fine horse, with the father or head of the family and his Negro attendant seated in it; next two elegant saddle horses each trapped with saddle, bridle and martingale, and mounted by the sons of the household, and last but not least, two mules, each wearing an old saddle and an inferior bridle - one mule carrying "Peter", the oldest Negro man belonging to the place, and the other carrying "Jane", the oldest Negro woman on the premises, who had a cloth as white as snow tied about her head, which completed the group.

"In contrast, a poor family starting out on a beautiful Sunday morning to the Great Camp-meeting looked quite different but equally as happy. Many of the poor had no outfit of any kind; some had only the ox and cart by which the grist was conveyed to and from the mill; others had only horses which pulled the plow. Several horses and several saddles in the possession of a family was the most extensive outfit and the best equipage to which the poor aspired. With or without outfits, the poor were there. They would come out from the hills and woods. Men, women and children would go. They would go; on foot, on ox-carts, on ox-wagons, on horse-back, some in the saddle, some in the lap and some behind; in that day a horse which would not carry double and thribble was not by any means a choice animal. It took all these, the rich and the poor, to make a Camp-meeting in the thirties and forties of this century.

"As the dusty crowds from the hills and woods swelled the throng and as the numerous groups of the rich, with the roar and clatter of wheels and hoofs, the glare and glitter of trappings and fixtures, approached the outskirts and rolled through the encampment the interest became intense. The scene was really impressive. Sometimes these meetings continued for as long as two weeks and often more than 100 joined the church. The shed, the stand, the altar with its straw and the group of tents, were common to every camp ground and were usually made of rough materials, in most instances the shed being built of the brush and boughs of the forests. Tents were made of coarse cloth. There was preaching four times a day." *
*(Source, "A History of Methodism in Alabama" - by Rev. Anson West, D.D.)

BERRY METHODIST CHURCH -- Tuscaloosa District - North Alabama Conference -- From Rev. Anson West's "History of Alabama Methodism", covering the first half of the nineteenth century, we learned that within a radius of four miles of the present church, there lived in 1839, a few staunch Methodist families. Men worthy of mention as exhorters who did good in divine cause were: William Crump, Benjamin Jones, Jonathan Shirley, and Jessee Freeman. This community was included in the Jasper Charge (for ten years called the New Lexington Charge) and this Charge extended from Northport to the northern part of Walker County which, at that time, included the present county of Winston. The first Methodist Sunday School in this locality was organized at Pleasant Hill Meeting House (less than two miles from the present town of Berry) in 1838. For a short while before 1850 a small group of Methodists worshipped in a one room log house on the Benjamin Jones (father of Mrs. Theron Cannon) farm two miles east of Berry.

About 1850, a Dr. John Pendleton Thomas moved from Blount County, Alabama, to Fayette County, locating about three miles north of where the town of Berry is now located. Through his efforts a Methodist Episcopal Church South was organized one and one-half miles north of Berry just off the present Alabama Highway 18. A small cemetery now marks the spot. This church was named Tabernacle. The principal families composing the new church were: Thomas, Jones, Rogers, Jacksons and Fondrens. R. G. Jones, the last charter member, died March 14, 1922 thirteen days before his eighty-eight birthday.

The land where the Tabernacle Church was located is within a 40 acre plot. Originally, there were 4 acres, but on March 14, 1905, Dr. A. R. Seay, acting for Berry Church, sold 3 acres to G. W. Julian. The Tabernacle Cemetery is on the remaining acre.

In 1886, soon after the Southern Railroad was built from Columbus, Miss. to Birmingham, Alabama, a church conference voted to move Tabernacle Church to the new town of Berry. The transaction of moving the church was done under the pastorate of the Rev. W. J. Reid. As late as 1894 the church was called Tabernacle, later Berry-Tabernacle, and finally, Berry Methodist Church.

The church and parsonage lots were deeded to the trustees of the Methodist Episcopal Church South of the Sheffield Circuit by P. J. Jeffries and his wife, P. P. Jeffries, Eliza Harvey, J. S. James and wife. M. E. A. James of Douglas County, Ga. The trustees were as follows: G. W. Julian, Joe Henry, A. Legg, R. C. J. Olive, R. G. Jones, B. F. West, Andrew Cline, V. R.

Tierce, and William Berry. The first church, a one room frame structure, burned in March, 1897. A large frame building with sanctuary and two Sunday School rooms was erected in 1897-98 under the pastorate of the late Rev. R. M. Archibald. This building was demolished in the fall of 1945 for the purpose of erecting the present building.

In 1946, the pastor, Rev. O. D. Thomas, appointed the following committees: Building Committee: James Scrivner, Chm., Arch Pulliam, Ralph Barnes and M. L. Chism, and Rev. O. D. Thomas, co-chm. Finance Committee: Dr. D. H. Wright, Chm., W. A. Barnes, Julian Shepherd, Theron Cannon, Frank Jones, Dr. J. D. Scrivner with Rev. O. D. Thomas, co-chm. Furnishings Committee: Mrs. Theron Cannon, chm., Mrs. Pearl Shepherd, Mrs. D. H. Wright, with Mrs. O. D. Thomas, co-chm.

Construction of the present building was begun in 1946-47 under the pastorate of Rev. Hewlett Aldridge. Services were first held in this building in 1947 by Rev. Aldridge. This building was completed in March, 1956, during Rev. Freeman Smith's fourth year as pastor and Dr. P. D. Wilson, District Superintendent. It was dedicated by Bishop Clare Purcell, Easter Sunday afternoon, April 1, 1956.

This church has participated in the various church organizations. As early as 1883 when the church was still at Tabernacle there was an active Sunday School. In June of that year, Benjamin Elliott Jones, a young man just returned home from a boarding school, was elected Sunday School superintendent succeeding his father, R. G. Jones. B. E. Jones served this church as Sunday School Superintendent for fifty-three years.

The first woman's organization was a Ladies Aid Society organized by the pastor, G. W. Alley, in the spring of 1910. During the pastorate of the late Rev. J. F. T. Brown, in 1922, the Ladies Aid Society became the Woman's Missionary Society and this name was changed to the Woman's Society of Christian Service in keeping with the change made by the churches throughout Methodism in 1940.

An Epworth League was organized under the leadership of Rev. J. F. T. Brown in 1921. Later, this organization, in keeping with the church at large, became the Methodist Youth Fellowship.

From this church Rev. J. C. Persinger, Dr. M. R. Seay, Rev. W. T. Daniel, and Rev. J. P. Cornelius (all deceased) were licensed to preach. Also licensed were G. W. O. Tierce and John W. Zeanah, Jr.

BETHLEHEM METHODIST CHURCH -- The first known record of Bethlehem Church was in 1881. The Church was a small log building located on the old mill race, southeast of where Morris Roberts' present home is standing. The property was owned then by a Mr. Porter and later was known as the Frank Thompson Place and is presently owned by Morris Roberts. The roof of this first building fell in from a big snow in the year of 1883 and all of the building that could be used was hauled in an ox wagon to where the present church stands.

The second Bethelehm was a small building of 18 X 20 feet and was used as a church and a school building. In checking through the records it is noted that the church was well organized and the first pastor was Bro. Olin W. Samples, who received $62.50 as his salary. The records also show that the male members were assessed $5.00 and the women $2.50 and the single people .25¢.

Some of the charter members were the following: T. P. McConnell, Daniel O'Connell McConnell, Frank Thompson, Lee Thompson, Bob Murray, Cass Thompson, W. F. Gibson, J. D. Musgrove, Felix Dickinson, Mrs. D. O. McConnell, Mrs. Frank Thompson, Mrs. N. A. Dickinson, Mrs. L. A. Thompson, Mrs. Willie White, and Mrs. Mary Roycroft.

The third Bethlehem Church building was constructed in 1886, being a much larger building that was used until 1923 when the present building was erected. The cemetery was deeded to the church by Frank Thompson, who owned the ground adjoining the church. The first grave in the cemetery was that of Mr. Thompson's sister, Mrs. Lula Thompson Appling.

The fourth building of the church, built in 1923, was built while S. V. Lemonds was pastor of the church. Bro. Lemonds was a great inspiration in getting the building under way. Viley Farquhar was chairman and with the help of all the people the building was ready for use in March of 1923. Bro. Lemonds built the pews and did the choir rails and painted them. Mr. Tom McConnell gave the Pastor's chair and Mary Lee Thompson gave the Bible stand.

In 1946 W. H. Roberts gave the florescent light fixtures in memory of his wife, Mrs. Sudie Roberts. Four of the eldest members in the church at the present time are Mrs. J. M. Taylor, Mrs. Florence Musgrove, Mrs. D. A. Kemp, and Mrs. Lon Eva Smith.

The five Sunday School rooms were added to the church in January, 1947. This addition was a great help to the program of the church.

While Rev. J. H. Moore was the pastor in 1953, Bethlehem was changed from a half-time to a full-time station.

With the assistance of the Pastor and his wife a complete kitchen was added in 1958. Bethlehem has been blessed through the years with good workers and leaders. The present officers of the church are the following: Pastor - Rev. S. D. Lankford; Sunday School Superintendent - Herbert Matthews; Ass't. S. S. Supt., - Jack Butler; and Pianist - Mrs. Morris (Martha Matthews) Roberts.

COVIN METHODIST CHURCH -- The Covin Methodist Church was organized in 1902. Following is a list of some of the men who have served the church as preacher: Rev. Rice, Rev. E. L. Roy, Rev. Bob Wilson, Rev. Slosser, Rev. Bennett, Rev. Jones, Rev. Wilson, and Rev. Osborne.

DANIEL'S CHAPEL METHODIST CHURCH -- At one time this little church was active and was usually supplied a minister from the Bethlehem Methodist Church. Daniel's Chapel was located west of Bethlehem and the Flat Top School was taught in the same building. Besides the ministers from Bethlehem who served this little church, Rev. John Frank Dickinson was pastor at one time.

There are no available records for the charter members, date of organization or a list of those who served the church as minister.

FIRST METHODIST CHURCH - FAYETTE -- The Fayette Methodist Church has an illustrous history dating back to 1830 when it was organized as one of the first churches in the North Alabama Conference.

The First Methodist Church building was erected near the entrance of the present cemetery site in old Fayette Court House, six years after Fayette County was organized, in 1824. There were forty charter members.

Many years later, it was moved to the new Fayette as the town began to grow up after the railroad came here in 1883. When the church was moved from its first location, it was built on the property now occupied by the Pan-Am Cafe on Columbus Street. Some years later the present property on Temple Avenue was purchased and a wooden frame church building was erected on the site of the present-day house of worship.

Some of the ministers serving this charge were as follows: Shoemaker Fulmer, T. A. Timmons, W. K. Simpson, J. E. Morris, R. H. Jones, W. H. Mansfield, L. M. Harris, M. R. Heflin, J. I. Williams, E. M. Barnes, Sr., U. S. Pitts, S. M. Robinson, W. H. Abernathy, J. S. Blackburn, W. F. Price, E. H. Clark, P. L. Clem, Paul Cook, John Perkins and O. G. Wald.

In 1923, during the pastorate of the Rev. J. I. Williams, the present sanctuary was erected. Following is the newspaper article giving the account of the laying of the cornerstone: "October 4, 1923 - Laying Cornerstone of The Fayette Methodist Church Last October 4. -- The Methodist Congregation at Fayette, Ala., is erecting a new church to cost, when completed, approximately $65,000.

T. L. Brodie is the architect, Charles W. Hall the contractor. L. M. Dodds, E. M. Grimsley, S. J. Sanders and B. E. Thornton compose the building committee .... The plan provides comfortably for a congregation of 500 with separate departments for beginners, primaries, juniors, intermediates and seniors. The young people and adults will use the auditorium for assembly and then repair to adjacent class rooms for class work. ....

The auditorium is 47 X 50 feet in size and has a seating capacity, including the gallery and choir of approximately 500 people....

The ceremonies at the laying of the corner stone, while simple, were impressive. Rev. W. W. Scott, the presiding elder, opened with a fervent prayer and read impressively the service used by the Methodists on such occasions. The local choir sang ...

An address was given by Dr. Frank Willis Barnett, of Birmingham ....

The deposits were made, first by Ivan J. Williams, lovely young daughter of the sick pastor, she placing in it a Holy Bible; then records were put in by the board of trustees, the Sunday School, the Missionary Society and the Epworth League. Copies of the Alabama Christian Advocate and other church papers were deposited, as was also a copy of the Fayette Banner." ...

In 1949, under the pastorate of the Rev. Paul L. Clem, the new church school annex was completed.

MT. VERNON METHODIST CHURCH -- The Mt. Vernon Methodist Church is located six miles west of Fayette on the Vernon Highway and was organized in or about 1850.

There have been four church buildings on the present property (not exact location). One church was destroyed by fire and one was destroyed by a tornado. The present brick building was erected in 1948.

It is told that the first church had no way to heat the small log building, so the congregation would stand around a log fire on the outside until time for the worship services, and then go into the log house for their services.

A camp meeting was organized in 1898 and a large arbor was built for the services. The people built small shelters to live in for the ten days of revival services. They carried their food and clothing for the meeting and sent someone home each day to do the chores and bring fresh perishable food for the family at the camp meeting. This was the custom until the days of the automobile.

Some of the charter members were the families of Miles, Harkins, Smiths, Cargiles, Hankins, Newmans, McClures and many others.

Some of the former pastors, since 1880 were as follows: Rev. Roberts, Rev. Tierce, Rev. Miller, Rev. H. B. Ralls, Rev. G. W. Alley, Rev. W. E. Guthrie, Rev. J. W. Curl, Rev. R. L. Baker, Rev. A. S. Osborn, Rev. J. C. Draper, Rev. T. H. Wilson, Rev. J. M. Clark, Rev. L. L. Jones and many others.

The present pastor (1959) is Rev. M. C. Bridges. The church has a membership of 302.

ZION METHODIST CHURCH -- Zion and two other Methodist Churches, Pleasant Hill southwest of Berry and McConnell Chapel were established in the 1830's. Zion was at one time, before and after the Civil War, a very large church. Many old time camp meetings were held there. It seemed to be an active church after the turn of the 19th century; probably until about 1915.

At or near where the present Zion Cemetery now is, was a camping ground where the stage coaches and travelers could spend the night and rest their horses.

On March 1, 1861, Samuel D. Blankenship deeded three acres to seven trustees: William L. Harvey, E. Cole, J. W. Ellis, Charles Palmer, J. W. Whitson, Daniel Fowler, and Thomas J. Johnson.

In August, 1941, the Zion Church and Cemetery Association was organized with the following trustees: George B. Cotton, Curtis M. Simpson, Fannie Welburn, E. H. Sawyers, S. C. Edmondson, Robert Lowery, and T. C. Johnson. The purpose of this organization was to care for the property and cemetery.

When the church ceased to function as an active church the last members whose names have been submitted were the following: George H. Cotton, J. L. Davis, Dan Ary, Jane Cotton, Maggie Davis, Millie Ary and Fannie Welburn.

WESLEY CHAPEL METHODIST CHURCH -- Located northwest of Covin, Ala.

WESLEY CHAPEL METHODIST CHURCH -- Located near the Pickens County line.

MUSGROVE CHAPEL METHODIST CHURCH -- Located south of Winfield.

(We were unable to secure a complete list of the Methodist Churches in Fayette County.

NAZARENE CHURCH OF BERRY -- The Nazerene Church of Berry was organized in 1935 with Raymond Frost as the first pastor.

SALEM NAZERENE CHURCH -- Located northeast of Berry.

SHADY GROVE NAZERENE CHURCH -- Located east of the Bluff Road.

FAYETTE PRESBYTERIAN CHURCH -- The Presbyterian Church of Fayette was organized and built in 1906. Complete records are not available, but the following are known to have been charter members: Mr. & Mrs. Edward Rose, Dr. & Mrs. T. M. Peters, Mr. R. F. Peters.

Following are listed some of the pastors who served the church while it was active: Dr. Rev. Ponder, Rev. McWright, Rev. Paul Darnell.

The church became inactive in 1946 and following are those who were active members at that time: Mr. & Mrs. Alfred Rose, Mrs. Augusta Robertson, Mr. & Mrs. Grady Mitchell, Mr. Frank Arnold, Mrs. May Galloway and Mrs. Lucille Barnett.

CHAPTER IX

FRATERNAL ORGANIZATIONS

ALPHA DELTA RHO CHAPTER OF ALABAMA -- In the spring of 1957 Epsilon Chapter of Alpha Delta Kappa, Tuscaloosa, Ala. extended an invitation to a group of Fayette County Teachers to affiliate with Alpha Delta Kappa, a National Sorority. On April 20, 1957, twenty-three teachers were initiated as the Alabama RHO Chapter of Alpha Delta Kappa. Following is a list of those charter members: Myrtle Aldridge, Glen Allen; Villanell Ashcraft, Fayette; Loudell Berry, Fayette; Edna Branyon, Fayette; Sallie Branyon, Fayette; Pauline Chandler, Fayette; Julia Coggins, Fayette; Carrie Daniels, Fayette; Eron Gibson, Fayette; Myrtle Herren, Fayette; Vistas May, Fayette Rt. 2; Mary Maxwell, Fayette; Doris Merritt, Fayette; Dealon Nelson, Glen Allen; Flora Lee Newton, Fayette; Ora Patterson, Fayette; Villalory Stewart, Fayette; Ozella Stough, Fayette; Hazel Terry, Fayette; Thelma Terry, Fayette; Inez Webster, Fayette; Mary Bell Whitehead, Winfield; and Wilma Yerby, Fayette. New members added since that time are Estelle Garrison, Fayette; and Julia Fowler, Fayette.

The ground-work for the National Organization was laid in the two years before August 14, 1947, when the State of Missouri issued a Charter to Alpha Delta Kappa, incorporating it as a National Sorority. Later permission was granted to organize chapters in other parts of the world making it an Internationational Organization.

In August of 1957, Mrs. Ora Patterson, Mrs. Eron Gibson and Misses Hazel and Thelma Terry attended the second National Convention in Kansas City, Mo.

In 1958 the third National Convention was held in Miami, Florida and members of the Fayette organization attending were Mrs. Eron Gibson, Mrs. Ora Patterson, Mrs. Inez Webster, Misses Hazel and Thelma Terry, Mrs. Flora Lee Newton, Mrs. Mary Maxwell and little Miss Frenchie Maxwell as a guest of her mother.

The poem by Thelma Ireland illustrates the spirit of dedication of these teachers......

"THE ANSWER" -- by Thelma Ireland

I sometimes wonder why I teach; .... My day is never through ....
With plans to make and tests to grade, ... There's always work to do ..
It doesn't pay like other jobs, ... And it demands so much --- ....
Good conduct, education, health, ... Great patience, love and such. ...
But when some grubby little hand .... Grabs my hand like a leech ....
And clings to me with love and trust, ... Then I know why I teach.

AMERICAN LEGION -- FAYETTE POST NO. 127 -- The Fayette County American Legion Post No. 127 has a history dating back to about 1922.

When the local American Legion Post No. 127 was organized, its first commander was Mr. W. C. Cragg and its first adjutant was W. D. Harkins. The total Membership that first year was 110 and since that time it has continued to grow.

In 1944 the Post was successful in an effort to provide a Service Commissioner for Fayette County to serve veterans of all wars. This phase of veteran's affairs has been in continous operation since November 1, 1944. In 1949 the Post erected the American Legion Building -- being joined in this project by the V.F.W. Post 5406. This building is located on Bagwell Street. A list of charter members and of the Commanders is not available.

BUSINESS & PROFESSIONAL WOMEN'S CLUB - FAYETTE -- The Fayette Business and Professional Women's Club was organized and Federated in 1941. The Tuscaloosa B.P.W. Club were sponsors in helping to organize our Fayette Club. The first meeting was held in the Fayette County Court House. There were fourteen charter members, as follows: Miss Bennie Walton, Mrs Nell Hamilton Stovall, Mrs. Jessie Peters, Mrs. Eunice Hamner, Mrs. Annie W. Gunter, Miss Carrie Daniels, Mrs. C. P. Vick, Miss Evelyn Peyton, Mrs. James Jeffries, Mrs. Alice Proost, Mrs. Lucy W. Golson, Miss Everette McCluskey, Mrs. Frankie N. Martin and Mrs. Estella Oswalt.

Following are those who have served as BPW Club President to the present: Miss Evelyn Peyton, Mrs. C. P. Vick, Mrs. Annie W. Gunter, Mrs. Jessie Peters, Miss Maron Aylin, Miss Pauline Shipman, Mrs. J. A. Branyon, Mrs. B. F. Harkins, Miss Cathleen Thompson, Mrs. Cathleen McClure, Mrs. Laura Poe Haupt, Mrs. Stella Poe Moore, Mrs. Frankie N. Martin, Mrs. Lula Holladay, Mrs. Nell H. Stovall, Mrs. Martha M. Roberts, Mrs. Doris M. Dodson, Mrs. Susie Harris, Mrs. Lucy W. Golson and Mrs. Aline F. Tucker (1959).

CHAMBER OF COMMERCE -- In 1922 the business men of Fayette organized the first Chamber of Commerce. This group apparently was not active for several years as the present Chamber of Commerce was organized in 1947 and has done much to promote the civic and industrial welfare of the city and county.

The first president of the Chamber of Commerce in 1947 was Dr. J. B. Robertson. Others who have served as president since the organization began are the following: Fuller Kimbrell, William Sanders, Carey Pollard, L. B. Lollar, W. A. Fowler, R. C. Cobb, and Sam Jones.

CIVITAN CLUB - FAYETTE -- The Fayette Civitan Club was organized on February 7, 1957, with the following charter members: J. W. Ayres, Jr., J. L. Barnes, Cecil Berry, James P. Boyles, Albert Butler, Delbert Cargile, Aubrey Chambless, Roy L. Chandler, Frank G. Childress, Raymond W. Cobb, W. A. Cook, Jr., D. L. Collins, W. S. Cooper, A. B. Corbett, Linton Dobbs, James B. Dodson, R. O. Finley, Jr., Ran D. Franks, Dan R. Galloway, David L. Galloway, J. P. Garrison, Jr., L. K. Gay, Robert P. Gibson, L. C. Hall, Arnie Howell, Dave Killingsworth, Arcaster Kimbrell, Clyde Lnagston, Cullen Morgan, Charles W. Nolen, Dr. Percy Nolen, Claude Patterson, R. O. Prater, Edwin Redden, Earl Robertson, Dr. F. M. Rosemore, R. R. Thomson, Paul Tucker, J. Thomas Veazey, E. B. Watkins, Hobson Watkins, J. E. Webster, J. C. Wiggins, Fred J. Wilkerson, and Gus Woodard.

Since the organization of the club, the following members have been added: Robert Atkins, T. A. Bobo, R. M. Colburn, Johnny DuBose, Bennie Hammonds, Jack Newell, John Raper, Bobby Roberts, J. V. Roberts, B. B. Yerby and Raphael Yerby.

The following members have served as president and secretary to the present time: Pres. Arcaster Kimbrell, Sec. L. C. Hall; Pres. J. E. Webster, Sec. L. C. Hall; Pres. Frank Childress, Sec. Arnie Howell; Pres. L. C. Hall, and Sec. Clyde Langston.

D. A. R. - LUXAPALLILA CHAPTER - FAYETTE COUNTY, ALABAMA -- The Luxapallila Chapter of the Daughters of the American Revolution was organized on the 30th of October, 1952 at the home of Mrs. A. M. Grimsley. The Chapter was organized with 30 charter members, listed as follows: Mrs. E. Hoyt (Edna McGee) Abbott, Mrs. Carey L. (Lucyle Arnold) Barnett, Mrs. T. L. (Martha Loftis) Bobo, Mrs. F. D. (Sue Bell Green) Brotherton, Miss Kathleen Cannon, Mrs. C. C. (Rosalie Mathes) Cannon, Mrs. C. M. (Maude Shepherd) Carter, Mrs. M. B. (Catherine Reeves) Cox, Mrs. T. L. (E. Jane Mathes) Davis, Mrs. R. C. (Roberta Mathes) Densler, Mrs. Newbern (Betty Newton) Fowler, Mrs. John W. (Lillian Newton) Gilliam, Mrs. A. M. (Adylisse Sherrod) Grimsley, Mrs. Walter F. (Frances Berry) Hall, Mrs. W. J. (Lula Pope) Holladay, Mrs. B. F. (Annie Gibson) Jeffries, Mrs. T. E. (Ada Griffin) Jennings, Mrs. W. M. (Gabriella G. Green) Loftis, Mrs. Wm. Roy (Frankie Nuckols) Martin, Mrs. R. E. (Virginia Lee Reese) Moore, Mrs. W. G. (Carleton Carter) Moseley, Mrs. Wm. (Miriam Sherrod) Moseley, Mrs. J. W. (Mary Guin) Newman, Mrs. R. B. (Kate Whitley) Newton, Mrs. Paul (Dorothy Murphy) Nuckols, Mrs. T. A. (Nellie Clare Arnold) Rose, Mrs. J. F. (Emma Blanche Arnold) Sharpe, Miss Emma Frances Shepherd, and Mrs. F. F. (Florence Moss) Smith.

Any woman is eligible for membership in the National Society of the Daughters of the American Revolution who is not less than eighteen years of age, and who is descended from a man or woman who, with unfailing loyalty to the cause of American independence, served as a sailor or as a soldier or a civil officer in one of the several colonies or States, or in the United Colonies or States, or as a recognized patriot, or rendered material aid thereto; provided the applicant is personally acceptable to the Society.

The following are the Regents who have served since the organization of this chapter: 1952 - 1954 - Mrs. A. M. Grimsley; 1955 - 1956 - Mrs. W. J. Holladay; 1957 - 1958 - Mrs. J. T. Shepherd; and 1959 - Mrs. R. G. Owen.

Following is a list of the present membership of the Luxapallila Chapter of D.A.R.:

Nat'l. No.	Name	Ancestor
410273	Mrs. E.H. (Edna McGee) Abbott	Matthew Davis
410263	Mrs. Milton (Kathleen Cannon) Anderson	Robert Ord
441968	Mrs. Richard (Leila Dickson) Arthur	Moses Powell
410259	Mrs. C.L. (Lucyle Arnold) Barnett	Robert Ord
410265	Mrs. F.D. (Sue Bell Green) Brotherton	Blackman Moseley
410262	Mrs. C.C. (Rosalie Mathes) Cannon	Robert Ord
415345	Mrs. R.C. (Alice McMillan) Cobb	George Dent, Jr.
424602	Mrs. V.W. (Fannie Cleveland) Cotney	William Armistead
410278	Mrs. T.L. (Elnor Jane Mathes) Davis	Robert Ord
422090	Mrs. J.D. (Edwina Tarlton) Denton	Capt. Nathaniel Abney
410270	Mrs. N.L. (Bettie Newton) Fowler	Matthew Davis
402161	Mrs. C.T. (Nancy H.) Frazier	Col. Ralph Humphrey
410267	Mrs. J.W. (Lillian Newton) Gilliam	Matthew Davis
266422	Mrs. A.M. (Adylisse Sherrod) Grimsley	John Foster
"	" " " " "	Gideon Morgan, II
422091	Mrs. J.E. (Nettie Ollie McCleskey) Hooker	James McCleskey
257606	Mrs. W.J. (Lula Pope) Holladay	Capt. John Snoddy
424603	Mrs. J.T. (Lillian Willingham) Hurst	William Hall
410254	Mrs. T.E. (Ada Griffin) Jennings	
440244	Mrs. Terry (Mina L. Proost) Kirkley	Major Thomas Hubbard
410257	Mrs. W.M. (Gabriella G. Green) Loftis	Col. Wynn Dickson
410275	Mrs. W.R. (Frankie Nuckols) Martin	Major Thomas Hubbard

Nat'l. No.	Name	Ancestor
257918	Mrs. R.E. (Virginia Lee Reese) Moore	John Owens
410258	Mrs. W.G. (Miriam Sherrod) Mosley, Jr.	John Foster
410256	Mrs. W.G. (Carleston Carter) Mosley	Matthew Davis
410264	Mrs. W.M. (Martha Louise Loftis Bobo) Murphy	Col. Wynn Dickson
457636	Mrs. Herbert M. (Jean Patterson) Newell	Matthew Davis
410272	Mrs. J.W. (Mary Guin) Newman	Matthew Davis
410269	Mrs. R.B. (Kate Whitley) Newton	Matthew Davis
457635	Mrs. V.S. (Lucy Bobo) Patterson	Matthew Davis
456095	Mrs. R.G. (Vida -- Allen) Owen	George Darden
447939	Mrs. Charles (Ellen Carolyn Driskell) Odom	Moses Stephens
410260	Mrs. T.A. (Nellie Clare Arnold) Rose	Robert Ord
410261	Mrs. J.H. (Emma Blanche Arnold) Sharpe	Robert Ord
410271	Miss Emma Francis Shepherd	Matthew Davis
408805	Mrs. J.T. (Mabel Jennings) Shepherd	John Jennings
422092	Mrs. F.A. (Katherine Nuckols) Sieverman	John Cleveland
	Mrs. Elton (Dorothy Galloway) Traweek	Robert Ord
462470	Mrs. J.T. (Suzanne Jackson) Yeager	Devereux Jarrett

JULIA SHELTON CHAPTER NO. 13, ORDER OF THE EASTERN STAR -- The Julia Shelton Chapter No. 13, Order of the Eastern Star, Fayette, Fayette County, Alabama, was organized August 24, 1900, by Mr. Daniel J. Gibson, who later became the first Worthy Grand Patron of the Grand Chapter in Alabama. Julia Shelton Chapter No. 13 was one of the Chapters that helped to organize the Grand Chapter of Alabama on March 6, 1901, in Birmingham, Ala.

Mrs. Julia Shelton was the first Worthy Matron of Julia Shelton Chapter No. 13. Mr. Robert C. Robertson was the first Worthy Patron and Mrs. Susie Propst was the first Associate Matron.

The following were the 34 charter members: Mrs. Julia Shelton, Mrs. A. J. Renfro, Miss Lou Renfro, Mrs. Annie Propst, Mrs. Belle Sanders, Mrs. Carrie Propst, Mrs. Josie Humber, Mrs. Fannie Hyde, Mrs. Carrie Coggins, Mrs. Susie Propst, Mrs. Kate Turner, Mrs. Bessie Gullett, Mrs. Orphia Treadway, Mrs. Martha Harris, Mrs. Della Enis, Mrs. Wilma Goodwin, Mr. H. B. Propst, Mr. J. M. Collins, Mr. D. F. Propst, Mr. George A. Coggins, Mr. J. P. Dickinson, Mr. J. A. Sudduth, Mr. R. W. Harris, Mr. John T. Sanford, Mr. R. F. Peters, Mr. Thomas E Goodwin, Mr. A. B. Stewart, Mr. W. R. Enis, Mr. Andrew Treadway, Mr. H. C. Enis, Mr. Robert C. Robertson, Mr. E. P. Goodwin, Mr. A. J. Renfro and Mr. Sidney J. Cannon.

One new member came into the chapter making a total of 35 members, the new member being, Mrs. Lena Peters.

Officers for the year 1901 were the following: Worthy Matron, Mrs. Carrie Coggins; Worthy Patron, Mr. A. J. Renfro; and Secretary, Mrs. Lena Peters. There was no increase or decrease in membership.

On March 6, 1901, at Birmingham, Ala., the Grand Chapter of Alabama was organized and the Worthy Grand Matron, Mrs. Elizabeth Salter, appointed Mr. R. C. Robertson from Julia Shelton Chapter No. 13 to serve on the Committee on Credentials.

Regular accredited delegates entitled to seats and to take part in the deliberations of the Convention from Julia Shelton Chapter No. 13 were Mr. D. F. Propst, Mrs. W. A. Graham, Mr. R. C. Robertson and Mrs. Bessie Gullett. At this session of Grand Chapter, Mrs. Susie Propst was elected Associate Grand Matron; Mrs. W. A. (Dora Jones) Graham, Grand Esther; and Mr. Robert C. Robertson, Grand Sentinel of the Grand Chapter for the ensuing year.

On November 7 and 8, 1901, the first session of Grand Chapter, (the first session after the organization) was held at Fayette, Ala. with Mrs. Elizabeth Salter, Grand Matron presiding, pro tem officers selected from Julia Shelton Chapter were as follows: Mrs. Carrie Coggin, Grand Matron; and Mrs. Lena Peters, Grand Martha. The welcome address was given by Mr. Robert F. Peters of the Julia Shelton Chapter. Members present who were entitled to vote were Mrs. Carrie Coggins, Mrs. Lou Robertson, and Mr. A. J. Renfro.

The following officers were chosen from Julia Shelton Chapter to serve as Grand Officers for the ensuing year: Mrs. Susie Propst, Associate Grand Matron; Mrs. Carrie Coggins, Grand Martha and Mrs. Dora Graham, Grand Ruth.

The organization became inactive for a few years but was re-organized on December 8, 1921 and the charter was granted November 22, 1922. The following were the 28 charter members for this re-organization: Mrs. Julia Shelton Bell, Mrs. Susie Proost, Mrs. Bessie Gullett Van Diver, Mrs. Della Enis, Mrs. Josephine Harriet (Moore) Humber, Mrs. Effie Young, Mrs. Dora Jones Graham, Mrs. Carrie Coggins, Mrs. Annie Jones, Mrs. Marguerite Brotherton, Mrs. Mildred Dodd, Mrs. Loudelle Sanders, Mrs. Heartha Tarwater, Mrs. Sarah Posnick, Mrs. Bessie Arthur, Mrs. Sadie Hodges, Mrs. Theresa Morris, Mrs. Otis Branyon, Mrs. Maude Carter, Mrs. Bess Cook, Mrs. Motie McCool, Miss Lois Dodd, Mrs. Alice May, Mr. Robert F. Peters, Mr. Daniel F. Propst, Mr. Toney Posnick, Mr. Sam Sanders, and Dr. James D. Young.

The charter was signed by Mrs. Louise Reed, Worthy Grand Matron and Mr. Horace J. Salter, Worthy Grand Patron of Alabama.

The following is a list of the worthy matrons and worthy patrons, who have served since the Chapter was re-organized in 1921: 1921 - 1923, Mrs. Julia Shelton Bell and Mr. R. F. Peters; 1923 - Mrs. Marguerite Brotherton and Mr. J. T. Tarwater; 1923 - 1924, Mrs. Essie Grimsley and Mr. J. T. Tarwater; 1924 - 1925, Mrs. Bessie Arthur and Dr. J. D. Young; 1925 - 1926, Mrs. Heartha Tarwater and Mr. Edward Pirtle; 1926 - 1927, Mrs. Grace Chambers and Mr. James T. Tarwater; 1927 - 1928, Mrs. Lucy Monroe and Mr. Alex Smith; 1928 - 1929, Mrs. Carrie Coggins and Mr. Alex Smith; 1929 - 1930, Mrs. Bessie Arthur and Mr. Alex Smith; 1930 - 1931, Mrs. Belle Cameron and Mr. Albert Scott; 1931 - 1932, Mrs. Arie Scott and Mr. Alex Smith; 1932 - 1933, Mrs. Irene Wright and Mr. Albert Scott; 1933 - 1934, Mrs. Nettie Sterman and Mr. Alex Smith; 1934 - 1935, Mrs. Maude Jones and Mr. Alex Smith; 1935 - 1936, Mrs. Kate Newton and Mr. R. B. Newton; 1936 - 1937, Mrs. Bessie Arthur, and Mr. Frank Patterson; 1937 - 1938, Mrs. Nettie Sterman and Mr. Frank Patterson; 1938 - 1939, Mrs. Etta Tigett and Mr. Frank Patterson; 1939 - 1940, Mrs. Lillian Hay and Mr. Frank Patterson; 1940 - 1941, Mrs. Sadie Hodges and Mr. Taylor Hurst; 1941 - 1942, Mrs. Willa McGough and Mr. Troy Bobo; 1942 - 1943, Mrs. Mamie Williamson and Mr. Troy Bobo; 1943 - 1944, Mrs. Flora Lee Newton and Mr. Taylor Hurst; 1944 - 1945, Mrs. Flora Lee Newton and Mr. Taylor Hurst; 1945 - 1946, Mrs. Bessie Arthur and Mr. Troy Bobo; 1946 - 1947, Mrs. Bessie Arthur and Mr. J. W. Ayres; 1947 - 1948, Mrs Irene Wright and Mr. J. W. Ayres; 1948 - 1949, Mrs. Margarite Hall and Mr. Trevor D. Shook; 1949 - 1950, Mrs. Emma Campbell and M: Trevor D. Shook; 1950 - 1951, Mrs. Ruby Lawrence, and Mr. Everette Taylor; 1951 - 1952, Mrs. Bessie Arthur and Mr. Everette Taylor; 1952 - 1953, Mrs. Geneva Taylor and Mr. Everette Taylor; 1953 - 1954, Miss Ophelia Whitley and Mr. Everette Taylor; 1954 - 1955, Mrs. Margaret Lawrence and Mr. Joe Campbell; 1955 - 1956, Mrs. Gladys Thompson and Mr. J. B. Porter; 1956 - 1957, Miss Maurene Berryhill and Mr. Allen Whitley; 1957 - 1958, Miss Irene White and Mr. Everette Taylor; 1958 - 1959, Miss Irene White and Mr. Everette Taylor; and 1959 - 1960, Mrs. Juanite Taylor and Mr. Everette

Taylor.

In 1937, Mrs. Leila Holladay appointed Mrs. Nettie Mae Sterman of Julia Shelton Chapter to serve as Grand Esther for that year.

In 1947, Mr. Albert Scott, a former member of Julia Shelton Chapter was elected Associate Grand Patron for the State of Alabama and in 1948 he was elected Worthy Grand Patron.

On December 16, 1954, Mrs. Bessie Arthur was appointed Grand Representative for the State of Nevada in Alabama by Mrs. Lillian Gilliland the Worthy Grand Matron of Alabama. She was elected for a term of three years, but the term ended in October, 1957 due to Mrs. Arthur's death.

THE EXCHANGE CLUB OF FAYETTE -- The Fayette Exchange Club was chartered September 22, 1936 with the following charter members: Rev. N. H. Abernathy, James Vasser Adams, Max H. Branyon, John Morgan Brown, Joseph E. Caine, George E. Doughty, William B. Ford, Jr., Carl M. Griffin, Harry Hodges, Curtis M. Holder, Bert Hollingshead, R. E. Hook, Henry M. Jordan, Jonas C. McGough, Dr. B. N. McNease, Judge James M. Moore, C. E. Smith, James Harris Smith, Dr. G. E. Stewart, Leon Studdard and Roy C. Ward.

Presidents and date of term served are as follows: Preliminary, Judge J. M. Moore; Permanent, Judge J. M. Moore; Jan. 1937, Prof. John Morgan Brown; July 1937, Prof. B. L. Balch; Dec. 1937, Joseph E. Caine; July 1938, Max H. Branyon; Dec. 1938, Alex Smith, Jr.; July 1939, Joe P. Robertson, Dec 1939, James A. Branyon; July 1940, W. H. Humber, Sr. Dec. 1940, Harry Hodges; July 1941, C. M. Holder; Dec. 1941, James Harris Smith; June 1942, Clifford Graham; Jan. 1943, B. F. Harkins; June 1943, P. R. Pettis; Dec. 1943, J. C. McGough; July 1944, L. R. Harris; Jan. 1945, John Morgan Brown; June 1945, Clifford Graham; Jan. 1946, Joseph E. Caine; July 1946, Grover C. Propst; Jan. 1947, W. E. Sanders; July 1947, Guthrie J. Smith; Dec. 1947, Liston C. Hall; July 1948, Robert L. Smith; July 1949, William W. Monroe; Jan. 1950, James Moore; June 1950, Jack Black; Dec. 1950, Jack Black; June 1951, James A. Branyon; Jan. 1952, Ralph Agee; June 1952, T. L. Lindsey, Jr.; Dec. 1952, Joe Palmer Chandler; July 1953, William B. Cox; Jan. 1954, Paul W. Colburn; June 1954, Robert P. Sanders; Dec. 1954, Dr. Henry G. Hodo; Sept. 1955, Sam J. Renfroe; Jan. 1956, J. Thomas Veazey; July 1956, J. Thomas Veazey; Jan. 1957, Rev. John D. Perkins; Oct. 1957, Rev. John D. Perkins; Dec. 1957, Jack Black; July 1958, Jack Black; Dec. 1958, Dr. R. O. Rutland, Jr.; and July 1959, Dr. R. O. Rutland, Jr.

FAYETTE GARDEN CLUB -- The Fayette Garden Club was organized Feb. 28, 1953. The charter members were as follows: Mrs. Robert Burt, Mrs. Fuller Kimbrell, Mrs. Roy D. Couch, Mrs. J. E. Webster, Mrs. Mae Caraway, Mrs. Lona Walters, Mrs. W. E. Savage, Mrs. Thomas Savage, Mrs. J. B. McClendon, Mrs. C. H. Dodson, Mrs. N. L. Weems, Mrs. Arnie Howell, Mrs. W. G. Warmack, and Mrs. Linton Dobbs.

Those who have served as president are as follows: 1953 - 1954, Mrs. Robert S. Burt; 1955, Mrs. J. B. McClendon; 1956 - 1957, Mrs. J. E. Webster; 1958 (first half) Mrs. Bruce Harkins; 1958 (second half) Mrs. Paul Colburn; and 1959, Mrs. Robert S. Burt.

The current members are listed as follows: Mrs. Robert S. Burt, Mrs. Milton Anhalt, Mrs. Harry Hodges, Mrs. J. E. Webster, Mrs. Sam Johnson, Mrs. Bobbie Roberts, Mrs. Paul W. Colburn, Mrs. Cecil Berry, Mrs. Sim T. Wright, Jr., Mrs. C. H. Dodson, Mrs. Thomas Lawrence, Mrs. Ray Pritchett, Mrs. Louie Dockery, Mrs Linwood Smith, Mrs. B. E. Perry, Mrs. Clayton Lawrence, Miss

Mattie Ruth Branyon and Miss Sallie Branyon.

FAYETTE JUNIOR CHAMBER OF COMMERCE - "JAYCEES" -- On July 28, 1959, the Fayette Junior Chamber of Commerce "Jaycees" was organized with Thomas L. Lindsey, Jr. as President and Herbert M. Newell as Secretary.

Charter Night was August 14, and the following were the charter members: Melvin Bailey, Douglas D. Berry, Jack Black, William W. Bobo, Robert H. Boone, James F. Cannon, William B. Colburn, Jack Cooley, Edgar Cooper, Jr., David McKay Enslen, William A. Fowler, Elliott P. Gray, Robert Grizzell, H. Hoyt Herren, Howard R. Jones, T. L. Lindsey, Jr., A. Dewey Lowrey, Jr., Richard D. McCracken, James D. Moore, Louis P. Moore, William C. Musgrove, Herbert M. Newell, Jr., Bobby G. Roberts, Horace C. Sims, Joe M. Taylor, Richard Thomson, Harry O. Unger, Chandler S. White, Jr., Macon Madison, Elwood Oswalt, Thomas Roberts, Dr. Richard O. Rutland, Jr., and Clinton Vice.

LION'S CLUB - BERRY -- March 18, 1944, was Charter Night for the Berry Lion's Club. There was a banquet at the Berry High School with 38 charter members.

The following men were selected to serve the club in the various positions: Pres., Julian Shepherd; 1st. V. Pres., Ralph Barnes; 2nd. V. Pres., Thomas L. Brock; 3rd. V. Pres., J. C. Shepherd; Sec. & Treas., K. W. Hudson; Lion Tamer, Orlis Lunsford; Tail Twister, B. D. Hudson; Directors, John U. Walker, Arnold Poe, Phelan Shepherd, and Garland Barnes.

This club did not function and was disbanded.

LION'S CLUB - FAYETTE -- Unable to obtain information.

CHARLES BASKERVILLE LODGE NO. 281 - LODGE OF ANCIENT FREE MASONS -- A petition to the Most Worshipful R. H. Ervin, Grand Master of the Grand Lodge of Ancient Free Masons of the State of Alabama from: William Owens, C. G. Story, Elkanah Bazallel Newton, R. C. Mizell, John C. Moore, James H. Moore, I. L. Walters, and Joseph Smith, from Fayetteville, in the county of Fayette, Ala., was recommended by John Payne Lodge No. 245. This document was dispensed on September 21st, 1860, to the above names and signed by R. H. Ervin, Grand Master, and Daniel Sayre, Grand Secretary.

The Charles Baskerville Lodge No. 281 was organized on October 5, 1860. The Charter to the above named, was issued Dec. 6, 1860 and signed by S. F. Hale, Grand Master; Wm. H. Norris, Deputy Grand Master; L. B. Thornton, Grand Senior Warden; R. I. Dudley, Grand Junior Warden; and Daniel Sayre, Grand Secretary.

Following are listed those who have served as Worthy Master and Secretary with the date they served: (W.M. designates Worthy Master and Sec. designates Secretary) 1860, William Owens, W.M., and John C. Moore, Sec.; 1861, William Owens, W.M., and John C. Moore, Sec.; 1862, William Owens, W.M., and John C. Moore, Sec.; 1863, C. G. Story, W.M., and John C. Moore, Sec.; 1864, C. G. Story, W.M., and John C. Moore, Sec.; 1865, James S. Vandiver, W.M., and John C. Moore, Sec.; 1866, R. C. Mizell, W.M., and Elkanah Bazellel Newton, Sec.; 1867, Elkanah Bazellel Newton, W.M. and Benjamin Frierson Peters, Sec.; 1868, E. B. Newton, W.M. and B.F. Peters, Sec.; 1869, Terrel M. Reese, W.M., and John C. Moore, Sec.; 1871, E. B. Newton, W.M., and Gustavus Legg, Sec.; 1872, Terrel M. Reese, W.M., and Gustavus Legg, Sec.; 1873, Terrel M. Reese, W.M., and Gustavus Legg, Sec.; 1874, Terrell M. Reese, W.M., and Gustavus Legg, Sec.; 1875, Terrell M. Reese, W.M., and Gustavus Legg, Sec.; 1876, Absalam J. Renfro, W.M., and Gustavus Legg, Sec.; 1877, Absalam J. Renfro, W.M., and Gustavus Legg, Sec.; 1878, George W. Julian, W.M., and Gustavus Legg, Sec.; 1879, Elliott P. Jones, W.M., and Gustavus Legg, Sec.; 1880, Absalam J. Renfro, W.M. and Gustavus Legg, Sec.; 1881, E. B. Newton, W.M. and John C. Moore, Sec.; 1882, E. B. Newton W.M., and John C. Moore, Sec.; 1883, E. B. Newton, W.M., and John C. Moore, Sec.; 1884, E. B. Newton, W.M., and John C. Moore, Sec.; 1885, Zack Savage, W.M., and John C. Moore, Sec.; 1887, Zack Savage, W.M., and John C. Moore, Sec.; 1888, Terrell M. Reese, W.M., and John C. Moore, Sec; 1889, Terrell M. Reese, W.M., and Robert F. Peters, Sec.; 1890, Terrell M. Reese, W.M., and Robert F. Peters, Sec.; 1891, Terrell M. Reese, W.M., and Robert F. Peters, Sec.; 1892, Terrell M. Reese, W.M., and R. F. Peters, Sec.; 1893, T. M. Reese, W.M. and Thomas C. Norton, Sec.; 1894, T. M. Reese, W.M., and John R. Collins, Sec.; 1895, T. M. Reese, W.M. and John R. Collins, Sec.; 1896, Thomas C. Norton, W.M. and William Miller, Sec.; 1897, George W. Coggins, W.M., and Wm. Miller, Sec.; 1898, G. W. Coggins, W.M. and Edward Penn Goodwin, Sec.; 1899, G. W. Coggin, W.M., and E.P. Goodwin, Sec.; 1900, G. W. Coggins, W.M., and E.P.Goodwin, Sec.; 1901, G. W. Coggin, W.M., and Benjamin Giles Jones, Sec.; 1902, Robert F. Peters, W.M., and G. W. Coggins, Sec.; 1903, G. W. Coggins, W.M., and Lewis Porter Humber, Sec.; 1904, G. W. Coggin, W.M., and James W. Barnard, Sec.; 1905, G. W. Coggin, W.M., and J. W. Barnard, Sec.; 1906, Geo. W. Coggin, W.M., and John F. Huffstutler, Sec.; 1907, Geo. W. Coggin, W.M., and Daniel O'Connell McConnell, Sec.; 1908, Edwin P. Goodwin, W.M., and Geo. W. Coggin, Sec.; 1909, D. O. McConnell, W.M., and G. W. Coggin, Sec.; 1910, D. O. McConnell, W.M., and G. W. Coggin, Sec.; 1911, D. O. McConnell, W.M., and G. W. Coggin, Sec.; 1912, D. O. McConnell, W.M. and G. W. Coggin, Sec.; 1913, G. W. Coggin, W.M. and E. M. Kelley, Sec.; 1914, Frank Bennett, W.M., and E. M. Kelley, Sec.; 1915, E. R. Taylor, W.M., and E. M. Kelley, Sec.; 1916, E. M. Kelley, W.M., and R. L. Reaves, Sec.; 1917, E. M. Kelley, W.M., and J. Alex Smith, Sec.; 1918, J. H. Collins, W.M., and Sam J. Sanders, Sec.; 1919, J. H. Collins, W.M., and Sam J. Sanders, Sec.; 1920, J. Alex Smith, W.M., and Sam J. Sanders, Sec.; 1921, W. C. Enis, W.M., and Sam J. Sanders, Sec.; 1922, J. T. Tarwater, W.M., and Sam J. Sanders, Sec; 1923, J. T. Tarwater, W.M., and J. O. McCluskey, Sec.; 1924, H. Willis Mays, W.M., and James D. Dickson, Sec.; 1925, J. T. Tarwater, W.M., and H. Willis Mays, Sec.; 1926, S. E. Jones, W.M., and B. W. Brock, Sec.; 1927, J. O. McCluskey, W.M., and B. W. Brock, Sec.; 1928, J. Alex Smith, W.M., and B. W. Brock, Sec.; 1929, J. Alex Smith, W.M., and B. W. Brock, Sec.; 1930, J. Alex Smith, W.M., and B. W. Brock, Sec.; 1931, R. B. Newton, W.M., and J. O. McCluskey, Sec.; 1932, J. D. Young, W.M., and J. O. McCluskey, Sec.; 1933, J. T. Tarwater, W.M., and J. O. McCluskey, Sec.; 1934, J. Alex Smith, W.M., and J. C. McCluskey, Sec.; 1935, R. B. Newton, W.M., and J. O. McCluskey, Sec.; 1936, Henry M. Jordon, W.M., and J. O .McCluskey, Sec.; 1937, J. D. Young, W.M., and J. O. McCluskey, Sec.; 1938, J. T. Tarwater, W.M., and J. O. McCluskey, Sec.; 1939, Vadie Collins, W.M., and J. O. McCluskey, Sec.; 1940, G. C. Propst, W.M., and J. O. McCluskey, Sec.; 1941, Alex H. Sterman, W.M., and J. O. McCluskey, Sec.; 1942, J. W. Ayres, W.M., and J. O. McCluskey, Sec.; 1943, W. R. Martin, W.M., and J. C. McCluskey, Sec.; 1944, J. T. Tarwater, W.M., and L. C. Hall, Sec.; 1945, W. R. Martin, W.M., and L. C. Hall, Sec.; 1946, Cliff Graham, W.M., and L. C. Hall, Sec.; 1947, J. W. Ayres, W.M., and R. L. Smith, Sec.; 1948, Alex H. Sterman, W.M., and E. T. Fowler, Sec.; 1949, Allen Whitley, W.M., and E. T. Fowler, Sec.; 1950, W. R. Martin, W.M., and E. T. Fowler, Sec.; 1951, W. R. Martin, W.M., and E. T. Fowler, Sec.; 1952, M. E. Taylor, W.M., and E. T. Fowler, Sec.; 1953, M. E. Taylor, W.M., and E. T.

Fowler, Sec.; 1954, Allen Whitley, W.M., and E. T. Fowler, Sec.; 1955, Joe O. Campbell, W.M., and E. T. Fowler, Sec.; 1956, Edwin Redden, W.M., and E. T. Fowler, Sec.; 1957, Myron Sterman, W.M., and E. T. Fowler, Sec.; 1958, L. H. Collier, W.M., and E. T. Fowler, Sec., and 1959, H. G. Howard, W.M., and E. T. Fowler.

The present members of the Charles Baskerville Masonic Lodge of Fayette are as follows: James W. Ayres, Milton L. Anhalt, Howard Milton Anderson, Elton E. Anderson, Bennie Bruce Adams, Felix Colon Black, Troy Lee Bobo, Geo. B. Branyon, Franklin P. Barnett, Ernest M. Barnes, James A. Branyon, Lucion C. Brown, Samuel A. Barson, Murry L. Boone, Thomas Pearson Berry, Cary L. Barnett, Richard Loyd Bobo, James Leburn Barnes, William Thomas Benton, Buren Edward Bryant, Geo. Garland Barnes, Jefferson Davis Burson, Jack Bailey, Vadie Collins, Roy D. Couch, William J. Clifton, Geo. B. Cotton, Willard Duncan Cannon, Wilrey H. Caraway, Terrell Fenton Cannon, Clyde Chandler Cargile, Joe Oliver Campbell, Cecil Valler Carpenter, Lawson Henry Collier, John Thomas Cannon, William Otto Cargile, Harry D. Cargile, Robert Newton Caraway, C. A. Cox, James Thelon Cook, Andrew Benton Corbett, Marsellis F. Doughty, Barna Dunn, James Byron Dickinson, J. Cleon Enis, Raymond Ellis, Clifton Forsyth, Howard Thomas Fowler, Elmer Fowler, Bernard Fowler, E. T. Fowler, Wm. Alfred Freeman, Ural Howard Floyd, James Troy Fowler, David L. Galloway, Thomas C. Graham, Stephen E. Garrison, J. Virgil Garrison, Brice Basil Gardner, Wm. C. Garrison, James Woods Griffin, Theodore Gray, Bradley Jefferson Gaddy, Jr., Louis Hodges, Sam. M. Hood, LeRoy Hallman, Charles A. Hocutt, Marlon Snow Hamner, James Taylor Hurst, Liston Clyde Hall, Cleon Carlyle Holliman, Thos. Wiley Hollingsworth, Jacob Thomas Hodges, Maurice Hodges, Ealon Aubrey Hubbert, Harvey Gayron Howard, Arnie V. Howell, Wm. Joseph Holladay, James McConnell Henry, Albert Hudson, Oliver Columbus Handley, Johnnie C. Holliday, Rex Reginald Hollis, Charles B. Isbell, Sameul E. Jones, Clifton Jones, Wm. Luther Jones, Wiley Johnston, Dewey Camon Johnson, Troy Lee Johnson, Murry D. Kizzire, Marion Grady Killingsworth, Arcaster Kimbrell, Geo. Depew King, J.A. Kuykendall, Thomas Maxwell Karrah, Ernest A. Kelley, Fuller Asbery Kimbrell, Dave Wm. Killingsworth, Wm. W. Loftis, S. U. Lemond, James Clayton Lawrence, J. C. Latham, Wm. Banks Lowrey, Raymond Malton Lowrey, John Thomas Lawrence, A. Dewey Lowrey, Jr., Jeffie James Lawrence, Wm. L. Maddox, Wm. Harry Moore, James W. Maddox, N. T. Mothershed, Wm. Roy Martin, Geo. Dewey Moore, Robert Leon Maddox, Nolan C. Morgan, John Dixon Mullally, Arvil Delaws Mullally, Robert Lee Musgrove, James Douglas Myers, Hessie Hayes Moore, Ben W. McNease, Jonas C. McGough, Joe McConnell, T. A. McCool, Harry Emmett McCutheon, Ramon Dempsey McGough, Charles Baird McGahey, Jr., Wm. B. Newton, John F. Neville, Willard Dalton Nichols, Charles Wm. Nolen, Jack Nevill Nolen, Bedford W. Oswalt, Richard A. Olive, Elwood Oswalt, Max C. Oswalt, Robert Hollis Oswalt, Victor S. Patterson, Sr., U. S. Pitts, Grover C. Propst, Geo. H. Patterson, C. D. Propst, Victor Winford Poe, Denver D. Porter, James Billie Porter, Wm. A. Parrish, Oliver Lee Parker, Burla Elkilston Perry, Harlan Hollis Phillips, Joe P. Robertson, Wm. Festus Richards, Edwin L. Redden, Walter L. Roberts, Troy Dick Roberts, Frederick M. Rosemore, Sam Renfro, Edwin Frank Rechtman, James Woffard Richards, Jr., James Clayton Randolph, Mercer Harrison Sherrer, John Alex Smith, Jr., Alex H. Sterman, Phelon Shepherd, Belton H. Smith, Holly G. Smith, Trevor Dorsey Shook, Robert Lee Smith, Myron J. Sterman, Selma Sanford, James R. Sumrall, Geo. Young Shirley, Larkin Everett Sanford, Roy Edwin Sutherland, Alva Stough, Victor D. Strother, Jesse Curry Smith, Jr., Paul Seaborn, Floyd Calvin Springer, James Festus Stoker, John Denver Turner, Gilreath Todd, Millard Everett Taylor, Albert Taylor, Ermon Francis Thornton,

Paul Tucker, Geo. Lee Thompson, Jr., Floyd Taylor, Robert Earl Tolbert, Alison Mack Taylor, Carl Edwin Taylor, Zebedee D. Vick, Kolon L. Vick, Euell I. Vick, J. Thomas Veazey, Elbert C. Williams, Henry Attee Wilson, Robert Lee Watkins, William Allen Whitley, John Williams, Jess Harris Welborn, Jr., Woodrow Thomas Wiggins, Howard Collis Wright, Aaron Curt Whitley, James Eccla Webster, J. C. Wheat, Fletcher Monroe Williams, Gus Woodard, and John Tinsley Young.

FAYETTE PROGRESS CLUB -- On a rainy afternoon, March 23, 1921, a group of ladies met at the home of Mrs. E. P. Goodwin for the purpose of forming a literary and civic club.

Following is a partial list of that group who became charter members of the Fayette Progress Club: Mrs. E. P. Goodwin, Mrs. T. H. Robertson, Sr., Mrs. W. W. Monroe, Mrs. Julia Bell, Mrs. A. M. Grimsley, Sr., Miss Bessie Robertson, and Mrs. R. F. Peters.

The name of the club was suggested by Miss Bessie Robertson and in 1922 the club started on its first project - the Library. On March 16, 1922, a library committee was named, consisting of Mrs. T. A. Wilson, Mrs. J. A. Branyon and Mrs. H. K. Donaldson. The first library opened with only 68 books.

Following is a list of those who have served as president of the Progress Club: First Pres., Mrs. T. H. Robertson, Sr., Mrs. J. A. Branyon, Mrs. T.M. Peters, Mrs. W. W. Monroe, Mrs. J. A. Smith, Mrs. R. A. Hinson, Mrs. A. C. Branyon, Mrs. T. H. Robertson, Mrs. C. K. Donaldson, Mrs. H. E. Berry, Mrs. Lee Lollar, Mrs. G. E. Stewart, Mrs. C. M. Holder, Mrs. J. B. Houston, Mrs. W. F. Price, Mrs. John D. Parks, Mrs. Richard Arthur, and Mrs. B. F. Harkins.

U. D. C. - FAYETTE CHAPTER NO. 1672 -- The Fayette Chapter was organized March 7, 1917, with fourteen charter members, as follows: Mrs. W. H. Terry, Mrs. T. H. Robertson, Mrs. N. F. Greenhill, Mrs. R. A. Hinson, Miss Minnie Hogue, Mrs. W. W. (Lucy) Monroe, Mrs. Julia Bell, Mrs. A. M. Grimsley, Mrs. C. A. Lewis, Mrs. W. D. Putnam, Mrs. E. R. Van Diver, Mrs. Joe E. Caine, Mrs. Ruby Milan Yuckley, and Miss Emma Shepherd.

The organization's flower is the jasmine and the motto: "The South's Dearest Memory Is Her Heroes". Meetings are held the third Thursday in each month. Following is a list of the presidents and the term served: 1917-1918, Mrs. W. H. Terry; 1918-1921, Mrs. T. H. Robertson; 1921-1923, Mrs. W. W. Monroe; 1923-1926, Mrs. A. M. Grimsley; 1928-1930, Mrs. T. A. Wilson; 1930-1932, Mrs. J. A. Branyon; 1932-1934, Mrs. J. A. Smith; 1934-1935, Mrs. F. D. Hyde, 1935-1936, Mrs. W. W. Monroe; 1936-1937, Miss Emma Shepherd; (From 1937 to 1950 the dates were not available.) Mrs. H. E. Berry; Mrs. J. M. Moore; Mrs. W. W. Monroe; Mrs. A. M. Grimsley; Mrs. N. T. Mothershed; Miss Clarice Barnes; Mrs. A. M. Grimsley; 1950, Mrs. J. A. Branyon; 1950-1951, (not available); 1951-1952, Mrs. P. L. Henderson; 1952-1953, Mrs. P. L. Henderson; 1953-1954, (not available); 1954-1956, Mrs. W. J. Holladay; 1956-1958, Mrs. Lee B. Lollar; and 1958-1960, Mrs. A. M. Grimsley, Sr.

Following is a list of the present membership of U. D. C. Chapter No. 1672: (Member's name is listed with the ancestor following the member's name.) Mrs. Joe (Margaret Brewer) Alexander, I. A. Brewer - Co. B. 5th Ala.; Miss Letitia Clarice Barnes, Reuben Carroll Stewart - Co. A. 8th Cal. Ala.; Mrs. W. E. (Velma Branyon) Berry, W. P. Rowland - Co. H. 50th Ala.; Mrs. B. J. (Pauline Lackey) Bogard, Jr., Andrew Jack Russell - Co. K. 3rd Cal.; Mrs. E. M. (Jewel Winefred) Boling, Erastus Porter Bell - 45th. Tenn.; Miss Sallie Branyon, John Jasper Branyon - Co. B. 41st. Ala.; Mrs. Max (Madge Davidson)

Branyon, Wm. Alex. Curtis -- Co. E. - 4th Miss.; Miss Mattie Ruth Branyon, John Jasper Branyon - Co. B. 41st. Ala.; Mrs. J. A. (Edna Pace) Branyon, J. O. A. Pace -- Co. A. Stewart's Batn. Patterson Brigade; Mrs. J. A. (Edwyna Walker) Branyon, II, Thos. Jefferson White - Co. A. Regt. 9, Ala.; Mrs. E. C. (Maytie Files) Butler, Robert M. Roberts - Co. A. 8th Cal. Ala.; Mrs. Joe E. (Annie Robertson) Caine, Thos. P. McConnell -- Capt. Palmer State Res.; Mrs. Theron (Mary Jones) Cannon, R. G. Jones -- Co. I. 43rd Ala.; Mrs. L. H. (Loring Henderson) Cates, Luther Hamilton Wells - Co. C. 8th Reg. Ky.; Mrs. W. A. (Mae Anderson) Caraway, T. J. Davis - Co. F. 41st Ala.; Mrs. J. D. (Lorene Basinger) Coward, Richard Baird - Co. I. 7th Ala.; Mrs. C. A. (Mable Howton) Fisher, G. W. Howton - 56th Cal. Ala.; Mrs. A. N. (Adylisse Sherrod) Grimsley, Wm. Crawford Sherrod - Patterson Com. 5th Reg. Ala.; Mrs. A. N. (Etta Neal Dodson) Grimsley, Jr., James Henry Hyde - Co. A. 26th Ala.; Mrs. J. J. (Ruth Mayfield) Gibson, James J. Mayfield -- Co. G. 38th Inf. Ala.; Mrs. Snow (Eunice McCaleb) Hamner, W. M. Berry - Co. A. 26th Ala. Inf.; Mrs. J. Q. (Susie South) Harris, Levi Woodruff South - Co. K. 10th Cal. Ala.; Mrs. Wm. (Majoria Forrester) Harris, Jr., Wm. Jones Frazier - Co. B. 51st Cal.; Mrs. P. L. (De Ila Brotherton) Henderson, Franklin A. Brotherton -- Co. I. 10th Ala.; Mrs. V. J. (Lula Pope) Holladay, Leondas Napolean Pope - Co. F. Asbys 2nd. Tenn. Cal., and Dibrell's 8th Tenn. Cal.; Mrs. Bert (Mary Drew) Hollingshead, John Haston - Home Guard; Mrs. (Ruth Howton) Hillhouse, G. W. Howton - 56th Cal. Ala.; Mrs. J. T. (Lillian Willingham) Hurst, Jas. Hugh Willingham - Co. G. 8th Calvary; Mrs. C. B. (Pearl Propst) Hyde, W. W. Propst - Co. B. 41st. Ala.; Mrs. T. E. (Ada Griffin) Jennings, F. M. Stanley - Co. I. 56th Ala.; Mrs. Lee B. (Lodessa Brown) Lollar, Samuel H. Hankins -- Co. I. 43rd. Ala.; Mrs. Lewis H. (Luna Bobo) McAdams, Hiram Y. Bobo - Co. H. 41st Ala.; Mrs. J. C. (Willa Treadaway) McGough, W. M. Berry - Co. A. 26th Ala. Inf.; Mrs. R. N. (Brownie Lollar) Mitchell, Samuel H. Hankins - Co. I. 43rd. Ala.; Mrs. R. L. (Delia Waldrop) Mosley, W. W. Waldrop - Co. I. 8th Ala.; Mrs. Herbert M. (Jean Patterson) Newell, P. I. Dickinson - Partisan Rangers 56th Ala. Regt.; Mrs. Walker (Mary Guin) Newman, J. M. Shepherd -- Co. A. 10th Ala.; Mrs. Chas. (Ellen Driskell) Odom, Jas. Thos. Harris - Co. C. 63rd Ala.; Mrs. V. S. (Lucy Bobo) Patterson, P. I. Dickinson - Partisan Rangers 56th. Ala. Regt.; Mrs. P. T. (Nettie Virginia Cravey) Pettis, Cornelius C. Cravey - Co. F. 36th Ala.; Mrs. H. D. (Mary Gravlee) Peterson, G. W. Gravlee - Co. F. 56th Inf. Ala.; Mrs. D. D. (Ina Rebecca Glover) Prater, E. J. Daffin - Co. I. 32nd Ala.; Mrs. D. F. (Alice Putnam) Propst, A. M. Nuckols - Co. F. 41st Ala.; Mrs. R. D. (Pauline Bobo) Renfroe, James M. Bobo - Co. E. 56th Inf.; Mrs. T. H. (Evelyn Walker) Robertson, Jr., Thomas Jefferson White - Co. A. 9th Ala. Cal.; Mrs. Z. D. (Dora Waldrop) Rowland, W. W. Waldrop - Co. I. 8th Cal. Ala.; Miss Emma Shepherd, J. Mark Shepherd - Co. A. 10th Ala. Cal.; Mrs. G. E. (Clyde Grider) Stewart, Francis Marion Grider - Co. L. 3rd Ala. Inf.; Mrs. J. J. (Mamie Moore) Taylor, David Moore - Co. C. 26th Ala.; Mrs. J. T. (Lockie Hertha --) Tarwater, Luther Hamilton Wells - Co. C. 8th Cal. Ky.; Mrs. J. V. (Ida Miles) Tarwater, Wilbur Fisk Miles - Co. H. 41st. Inf. Ala.; Mrs. L. B. (Emma Thompson) Thomas, Geo. Washington Thompson - Co. D. Reg. 5, Ala.; Mrs. Charles (Ruby Whitney) Trammell, Isian Marion Whitney - Co. A. 22nd Ala. Regt; Mrs. J. D. (Lona Anderson) Walters, T. J. Davis - Co. F. 41st. Ala.; Mrs. (Susie Howton) Wilson, G. W. Howton - 56 Calvary Ala.; Mrs. W. P. (Mamie Collins) Williamson, Wm. W. Maddox - 26th Ala. Inf.; and Mrs. D. H. (Carrie Newton) Wright, Maston E. Chambless - Co. A. 10th. Ala.

STARS AND BARS U. D. C. CHAPTER - FAYETTE -- On March 24, 1959, the Stars and Bars Chapter of the U.D.C. was organized with the following charter members: Mrs. (Nell Hamilton) Stovall, Mrs. (Hazel McConnell) Waldron, Mrs. Grady (Artie McCool) Hallman, Mrs. (Lucy Waldrop) Golson, Mrs. Robert (Virginia Bernard) Burt, Mrs. Paul (Aline Fowler) Tucker, Mrs. (Lucille Cannon) Crowe, Miss Miriam Nichols, Mrs. J. M. (Stella Poe) Moore, Mrs. Homer (Emma Jones) Campbell, Mrs. J. P. (Lucy Tarwater) Crutcher, Jr., Miss Virginia Coons, Mrs. Joe (Betty Gordon) Coons, and Mrs. Morris (Martha Matthews) Roberts.

The first president of the club is (1959) Mrs. Nell Stovall.

V. F. W. - JAMES BLACK - NICHOLS BROTHERS POST NO. 5406 -- Between World War I and World War II there was an active Veterans of Foreign Wars organization in Fayette, but its life was short and records are not available for other data.

The Fayette - James Black - Nichols Brothers V.F.W. Post No. 5406 was re-organized on February 20, 1946, and is recognized to be one of the most active and patriotic organizations in the county.

The Veterans of Foreign Wars Post No. 5406 was named in honor of the following Fayette County World War II Heroes who gave their lives in the service of their country: James Theron Black, U.S.M.C., killed at Pearl Harbor, Dec. 7, 1941, and Louis Duffie Nichols, U.S.N. and Alfred Rose Nichols, U.S.N., killed Dec. 7, 1941, at Pearl Harbor; all three of whom were serving on the U.S.S. Arizona.

At the present time the local V.F.W. Post holds its monthly meetings each second Tuesday night at the National Guard Building - meeting jointly with the newly organized Ladies Auxiliary.

Following is a list of the charter members of the re-organization in 1946: Clyde T. Alexander, Howard Anderson, Jesse A. Ayres, Wade H. Ayres, Richard L. Bobo, Charles L. Brown, Daniel L. Collins, V. A. Collins, James W. Cannon, Garland G. Gardner, William T. Forsyth, Earnest R. Francis, Duward M. Gardner, Edward P. Goodwin, James W. Griffin, Curtis M. Holder, Earl D. Housh, Hosa D. Hyder, Thomas M. Johnston, Howard R. Jones, William F. Lawley, Jeffie G. Lawrence, William T. Lawrence, Cornelius F. Long, George N. Mathis, French L. Maxwell, Jacob C. McCraw, Landon F. McCraw, Wylie B. McDonald, James B. Mosley, Mogene D. Newman, Woodrow W. Newman, Walter F. O'Dell, James E. Oswalt, Max C. Oswalt, Howard K. Parker, Victor S. Patterson, Jr., (V. S. Patterson, Sr. was a charter member of the first organization), Walter E. Porter, Robert R. Renfroe, William E. Sanders, David H. Sanford, Leo B. Sharp, George Y. Shirley, James H. Shirley, Loyd K. Sims, John A. Smith, Jr., Floyd Taylor, Albert L. Walton, Marion Williamson, Jr., Thomas L. Williamson, Fred D. Whitehead, James M. Woods, Simeon T. Wright, Jr., Raphael H. Yerby.

Those who have served as the Post Commander and Quartermaster are listed, as follows: (C designates Commander and QM designates Quartermaster.)
1946 - Wade H. Ayres, C. and Lloyd K. Sims, QM; 1947 - Alex Smith, Jr., C. and Wade H. Ayres, QM; 1948 - V. A. Collins, C. and David O. Jones, QM; 1949 Sim T. Wright, C. and Victor S. Patterson, Jr., QM; 1950 - French L. Maxwell, C. and Victor S. Patterson, Jr., QM; 1951 - Joe Q. Harris, C. and Herbert M. Newell, QM; 1952 - Joe Q. Harris, C. and Herbert M. Newell, QM; 1953 - C. not available, and Joe Q. Harris, QM; 1954 - V. W. "Dick" Poe, C. and Wm. C. Stokes, QM; 1955 - D. L. Collins, C. and Wm. E. Poe, QM; 1956 - Aaron Nelson, C. and Herbert M. Newell, QM; 1957 - B. E. Perry, C. and Herbert M. Newell, QM; 1958 - W. Grady Esary, C. and D. L. Collins, QM; 1959 - W. T. "Buster"

South, C. and Arcaster Kimbrell, QM; and 1960 - Willard Livingston, C. and Lewis Mitchell, QM.

LADIES AUXILIARY TO THE JAMES BLACK - NICHOLS BROTHERS VETERANS OF FOREIGN WARS OF THE UNITED STATES, POST NO. 5406 -- The Ladies Auxiliary to the V.F.W. was instituted October 1, 1958, at Fayette, Ala., with the following charter members: Era Bailey, Evelyn Bobo, Evelyn W. Bobo, Atha Christian, Jewell Edna Clark, Mary Grace Colburn, Hazel Collins, Kittie Lee Crowley, Pauline Esary, Bernice Geer, Ann Griffin, Susie Harris, Montelle Kimbrell, Aline R. Lindsey, Jean Livingston, Ollie McGuire, Ila M. Mitchell, Jeanie P. Newell, Lillian Newell, Vista Newman, Bernice Nolan, Della Jane Oswalt, Lovie Oswalt, Robbie C. Perry, Lona Poe, Margaret Pritchett, Bobbie Shelton, Robbie Smith, Chloe South, Dale Stokes, Mary C. Williams, and Kattie Wright.
    Those who have served as president are the following: 1958 - Mrs. Grady Esary and 1959 - Mrs. Eugene Colburn.

WOODMEN OF THE WORLD --- The local Woodmen of the World - Boone Camp No. 63 was organized in the late 1800's nearing the turn of the century.
    Records are not available for securing a list of the earlier members or the officers. Mr. T. A. Rose has been the secretary since 1922 and is still serving in that post.

CHAPTER X

FAMILY GENEALOGIES

This section contains the family records of many of the families of Fayette County from the eraliest known ancestors on to the first settlers of Fayette County and the present generations. It was our hope to include the family records of all those who were interested in this section of the book. We made continous announcements with the radio and newspaper to advise the people of this project and we hope that all who were interested have been included.
This section is arranged alphabetically, according to the family surname and to avoid repetition of the various families who are connected, each family unit is listed only once. It will be quite simple to trace one's family by referring to the surnames.
To conserve space the following abbreviations are used: b. - born (date & place); m. - married (date & place); d. - died (date & place); months of the year; titles, etc. that appear occasionally. The immediate children in each unit are numbered - 1, 2, 3 etc. since some of the children will have a brief note concerning them especially those who do not appear as a seperate family unit. The surname of each unit is capitalized at the beginning of that description.

ABBOTT, Lonnie Bascom, b. Aug. 20, 1899,- son of Wm. Jackson & Lucinda Callie (Miles) Abbott,- m. Oct. 9, 1921, Wilma T. Dodson, b. June 26, 1905, Fayette Co.,Ala. - dau. of James Henry & Sara Lewis (Wimberley) Dodson. Children: 1. Emma Jean Abbott. 2. Sarah Pauline Abbott. 3. Bruce Abbott. 4. Margie Abbott. 5. Betty June Abbott. 6. Thomas Grafton Abbott. 7. Wiloise Abbott.

ABBOTT, William Jackson, b. Sept. 16, 1866, Fayette Co.,Ala., d. May 1, 1951, - son of Willis & Frances (Smith) Abbott - m. Oct. 20, 1887, Lucinda Callie Miles, b. May 30, 1868, d. Feb. 26, 1932, - dau. of Wiley & Mary Eliz. Floyd Yancy Miles. Children: 1. Merti Abbott, b. Aug. 22, 1889. 2. Ellie Abbott, b. May 1, 1891. 3. Thomas Abbott, b. Nov. 2, 1893. 4. Nellie Abbott, b. Oct. 16, 1895. 5. Mourning Abbott, b. Dec. 24, 1897. 6. Lonnie Abbott, b. Aug. 20, 1889, Fay. Co., Ala., m. Oct. 9, 1921, Wilma Dodson. 7. Eardeal Abbott, b Oct. 10, 1901. 8. Mable Abbott, b. Jan. 9, 1903. 9. Miles Abbott, b. Oct. 1, 1906. 10. Euail Abbott, b. Aug. 7, 1909.

ABELE, Elmer Franklin, b. Mar. 1, 1901, Allentown, Penn., - son of Wm. J. & Emma (Kemmerer) Abele. - m. April, 1922, Nellie Gray Durham, b. Jan. 26, 1906, Jemison, Ala., - dau. of Robert Dixon & Mary Eliz. (McDonaldson) Durham.
E. F. Abele came to Birmingham, Ala. with his parents at the age of 11 yrs. He and Nellie G. Durham were married at Birmingham, Ala. Children: 1. Bettye Nell Abele, b. April 12, 1924, Birmingham, Ala.,m. May 16, 1947, Joe Palmer Chandler, b. May 31, 1920, Fayette Co., Ala.

ABELE, William J., b. Feb. 5, 1866, Penn., d. June 12, 1939, Birmingham, Ala. - m. Emma Kemmerer, b. Aug. 3, 1865, Iowa, d. June 23, 1931, Birmingham, Ala. Wm. J. Abele came from Allentown, Tenn. to Birmingham, Ala. in 1912. Children: 1. William Arthur Abele, b. Penn. 2. Irene Abele, b. Penn., m. Harve C. Tunnell, d. 1953, Birmingham, Ala. 3. Earl Abele, b. Penn. 4. Elmer Franklin Abele, b. Mar. 1, 1901, Allentown, Penn., m. April 1922, Nellie Gray Durham, b. Jan. 26, 1906, Jemison, Ala.

ABERNATHY, Curt, b. Sept. 14, 1901, Fayette Co., Ala. m. Sept. 7, 1922, Lucy Johnson, b. Feb. 14, 1906, Fayette Co., Ala. Children: 1. Erma Abernathy, b. May 11, 1942, Jefferson Co., Ala.
Curt Abernathy's parents - Miles J. Abernathy, b. Nov. 1872, Fayette Co., Ala., m. Aug. 5, 1900, Ellen Plyler, b. Dec. 16, 1879, Fayette Co., Ala. Grandparents - Joseph Abernathy, b. Mar. 1, 1856, Rome, Ga., m. Jan. 11, 1868, Lizzie Holiman, b. April 19, 1856, Fayette Co., Ala. and O. F. Plyler, b. 1853, Fayette Co., Ala. m. Nancy Moore, b. Dec. 6, 1862, Fayette Co., Ala. Great Grandparents - Miles Abernathy, b. 1832, Ga. m. Linda Lukes, b. 1834, Rome, Ga.; Warren Holiman, b. Feb. 7, 1833, Rome, Ga., m. Polly Blakney, b. Jan. 6, 1835, Fayette Co., Ala.; Felt Plyler, b. 1830, Fayette Co., Ala., m. Nancy Belk, b. Nov. 11, 1836, Columbus, Ga.; and David Moore, b. Jan. 1832, Athens, Ga., m. Mary Brown, b. 1837, Athens, Ga. 2-Great Grandparents - Tom Blakeney, b. July, 1800, m. Mary Kemp, b. 1802; John Williams Moore, b. 1784; and Jesse Brown, m. Miss Powell.
Lucy Johnson Abernathy's parents - Curtis Johnson, b. 1879, Fayette Co., Ala., m. Erma Nelson, b. 1881, Fayette Co., Ala. Grandparents - James Johnson, b. 1846, Fayette Co., Ala., m. Ann Wright, b. April 3, 1848, Fayette Co., Ala.; and Jeff Nelson, b. 1846, Fayette Co., Ala., m. Telitha Ray, b. 1851, Fayette Co., Ala. Great-Grandparents - Starley Johnson, b. June 1836, White Co., Ga., m. Becky Crow, b. 1837, White Co., Ga.; Henry Wright, b. 1834, Fayette Co., Ala., m. Susan Ann Ashcraft, b. 1832, Fayette Co., Ala.; __ Ray, m. Lucy Ann Wright. 2 Great-grandparents - Jessie Wright.

ABERNATHY, Samuel B., b. 1809, S. C., d. Mar. 1859, Fayette Co., Ala., m. name unknown but she died enroute from S. C. to Ala. Deeds show he owned land and lived in what is now the City of Fayette. Deeds were dated 1848. Children: 1. Lilly Abernathy, b. 1841, d. 1914, m. Richard J. Smith.

ALDRIDGE, D. E., b. May 7, 1894, - son of John & Mary Eliz. (Berryhill) Aldridge, - m. Essie Lee Hawkins, b. Dec. 17, 1893, - dau. of Bud & Molly (Haney) Hawkins. Children: 1. Herman Aldridge, b. Nov. 4, 1915. 2. Coy Aldridge, b. Sept. 27, 1917. 3. Thelma Aldridge, b. Dec. 28, 1919, m. Vester Madison, b. Feb. 10, 1916, Fayette, Ala. 4. Ilene Aldridge, B. Mar. 13, 1922. 5. Christine Aldridge, b. Oct. 19, 1924. 6. Everette Aldridge, b. Sept. 10, 1926. 7. Eva Nell Aldridge, b. Jan. 13, 1929. 8. Edrel Mae Aldridge, b. May 11, 1934.

ALDRIDGE, John, - son of Manasco Aldridge, - m. Mary Eliz. Berryhill. Children: 1. D. E. Aldridge, b. May 7, 1894, m. Essie Lee Hawkins. 2. W. A. Aldridge. 3. Philex Aldridge. 4. Mary Aldridge. 5. Susin Aldridge.

ALEXANDER, Asa, b. abt. 1805, Ga., d. 1858, m. July 10, 1824, Rebekah Ledbetter, b. abt. 1810, Ga. or Tenn. Asa was the son of Asa C. & Faitha (Wooten) Alexander. She was the dau. of Isaac Ledbetter? They were married in Abbeville, Henry Co., Ala. by Wm. Harper, J.P Asa was a farmer and was elected county clerk of Dale Co., Ala. on Sept. 6, 1827. Children: 1. Calli Donia Alexander, b. 1830, Coffee or Dale Co., Ala. d. Mar. 1912, (age 83). m. bef. 1850, W. J. Newell, b. 1822, N. C. 2. Mary F. Alexander, b. 1832, Ala. d. Feb. 1902, Ala., m. bef. 1849 (1st.) Dr. Nathan Sylvan, b. 1814, Va., (2nd) Jacob Stephens. 3. John Alexander, b. 1835, Ala. 4. Georgia A. Alexander, b. 1837, Ala., 5. Falbia "Sug" Alexander, b. 1840, Ala. d. Apr. 1912, Ala., m. Charles Austin. 6. Alabama "Allie" Alexander, b. 1842, Ala., d. April, 1912, Ala. 7. Columbus Asa Alexander, b. 1846, Ala. m. Jan. 22, 1875, Florida Virginia Berry, d. Mar. 11, 1927.

ALEXANDER, Asa Castellaw, b. July 21, 1760, Ga., d. 1847, - son of Capt. Samuel & Olivia (Wooten) Alexander. Children: 1. Benjamin Alexander (Twin) b. Dec. 28, 1787. 2. David Alexander (Twin) b. Dec. 28, 1787. 3. Simeon L. Alexander, b. July 7, 1791, d. Aug. 7, 1795. 4. Samuel Alexander, b. Oct. 24, 1793, d. 1870, m. Widow Rich. 5. Falba Alexander, b. Aug. 18, 1789, m. Robertus Love. 6. Cullen Wootten Alexander, b. Mar. 11, 1797, d. 1865, m. (1st) Mary Mathews, (2nd) Edaline Dawson. 7. James Albert B. Alexander, b. Jan. 7, 1801. 8. Ezekiel Alexander, b. Mar. 3, 1803, d. 1879, m. 1824, Edaline Dawson? 9. Asa Alexander, b. Jan. 1805, Wilkes Co., Ga., d. 1858, Clayhatchee, Dale Co., Ala. , m. 1827, Rebekah Ledbetter, b. 1810, Ga. or Tenn. 10. Pheriba Alexnader, b. July 18, 1807, d. 1898, m. 1824, David Williams Dawson.

Asa C. Alexander was a private in the service of the United States in the American Revolution. He was drafted to go against St. Augustine under the command of Gov. Houston in the year 1778 and left the service in Aug. 1781. He was later a volunteer under Col. Elijah Clark and was in the first and the last battles of the seige of Augusta. Col. Elijah Clark Commanded the Georgia Militia. Asa was granted a pension for his service on June 11, 1833, while he was a resident of Dale Co., Ala. He is buried at Clayhatchee, Dale Co., Ala.

ALEXANDER, Elmer S., b. Oct. 8, 1905, d. Aug. 25, 1933, m. Vister Lydia Patterson, b. Jan. 11, 1909, Fayette Co., Ala., d. Mar. 21, 1949 - dau. of Tom and Viola (Williamson) Patterson. Children: 1. June Carolyn Alexander, b. Jan. 20, 1932, m. John H. Lair.

ALEXANDER, Rev. John, b. 1703, Mecklenburg, N.C., m. 1728, Bethia Castellaw, b. 1710, - dau. of James & Sarah (Williams) Castellaw. Children: 1. Capt. John Alexander. 2. Capt. Samuel Alexander, b. 1733, Mecklenburg, N.C., d. 1823, Twiggs Co., Ga., m. 1752, Olivia Wootten. 3. Capt. James Alexander, m. Tabitha ___. 4. Capt. Steven Alexander, m. Miss Wilson. 5. Capt. Ezekiel Alexander, m. Mary Neil. 6. Moses Alexander. 7. Sarah Alexander, m. Robert Smith. Martha Alexander, m. Hugh Irwin (Parents of Gov. Irwin of Ga.). 9. Bethiah Alexander, m. Thomas Grier?. 10. Emeline Alexander, m. Cullen Wooten.

Rev. John Alexander was a Presbyterian Missionary to St. George Parish, Ga. There is an order on file from the general assembly to the Sec. or Treas. to pay to John Alexander, in 1767, so many pounds for six months salary as Missionary.

(From "Hero of Hornet's Nest" page 102)-- "The father of Captains Samuel and James Alexander, in his seventy-eighth year, was arrested by particular order of Col. Grierson. He was chained and dragged behind a cart forty miles in two days and when he attempted to lean his feeble limbs against the cart, he was scourged by the driver."

(page 137) "As soon as it was safe for the American soldiers to enter the Fort (Augusta) Captains James and Samuel Alexander went to look for their father, John Alexander, now eighty years of age. (1781) He and the other old men had been held hostages for the neutrality of the up-country men for two years and had been subjected to every indignity, culminating in being placed in the front of the firing line by Col. Grierson." ....

The Alexanders were from Scotland, from the Earl of Stirling Scotland - came over in 1677 and settled, first in Virginia. Came from there to North Carolina and on to Georgia.

ALEXANDER, Capt. Samuel, b. 1733, Mecklinburg, N.C., d. 1823, Twiggs Co., Ga., m. Olivia Wootten. He was the son of Rev. John & Bethia (Castellaw) Alexander. Children: 1. Samuel Alexander, Jr., b. Nov. 8, 1754. 2. James Wootten Alexander, b. May 2, 1758, m. Miss Childers. 3. Asaneth Alexander (Twin), b. July 21, 1760, m. Dr. Willis Roberts. 4. Asa Castellaw Alexander (Twin), b. July 21, 1760, Wilkes Co., Ga., d. Oct. 1, 1847, Clayhatchee, Dale Co., Ala., m. Faitha Wootten. 5. John Lester Alexander, b. Feb. 27, 1763. 6. Ezekiel Alexander, b. May 5, 1765, m. Miss McNeill?. 7. M. Sarah Alexander, b. Aug. 16, 1767, m. Robert Smith?. 8. Mary Alexander, b. May 4, 1773. 9. Moses Alexander, b. Mar. 31, 1776, (Went to Early Co., Ga. in 1843 and left a legacy to the Presbyterian Church.)

Capt. Samuel Alexander commanded a company of Georgia Militia under Col. Elijah Clark. Capt. Samaul Alexander's youngest son, Asa Castellaw Alexander served under him as private, during the war. Capt. Sam'l. Alexander's company under Col. Elijah Clark, who was under Merryweather, were with Wayne when Ft. Corn Wallace was captured. Capt. Alexander and his Company, under Col. Elijah Clark took part in the battles of Long Cane Creek; King's Mountain, Blackstock, S.C.; Seige of Augusta, and many others. He was paid grants of land as a bounty for his services in 1787.

ALLEN, George Washington, b. May 4, 1820, Ga., d. Feb. 6, 1916, m. Winnie Minerva Loftis, b. Jan. 10, 1841, Ga., d. Jan. 5, 1894. He was the son of Thomas & Nancy (Foster) Allen. Children: 1. Alfred J. Allen, b. Lamar Co., Ala. d. Jan. 1960, m. Annie Rowland. 2. David T. Allen, b. Jan. 20, 1861, Lamar County, Ala., d. Dec. 30, 1938, m. Sarah J.___, b. Jan. 8, 1861, d. Jan. 11, 1931. 3. Nettie Pearl Allen, b. Lamar Co., Ala., m. Wilson Brock. 4. Sarah Frances "Fannie" Allen, b. Sept. 3, 1863, Lamar Co., Ala., d. 1943, m. Miles Rainwater, Jr., d. 1857, Covin, Fayette Co.,Ala. d. July 21, 1911. 5. Walter Nathaniel Allen, b. Dec. 6, 1878, Lamar Co., Ala., m. Sophia Ryan, b. Aug. 12, 1884, DeKalb Co., Ala. 6. Nancy Allen, b. Lamar Co., Ala. m. Mr. Robertson. 7. Milford Allen, b. Lamar Co., Ala. , m. Samantha Brock. 8. Richard D. Allen, b. Lamar Co., Ala. 9. Jimmy Allen, b. Lamar Co., Ala., m. Ella Rowland. 10. Bell Allen, b. Lamar Co., Ala. m. Mr. Riley.

ALLEN, Thomas "Tommy", b. abt. 1792, N.C., m. Nancy Foster, b. Sept. 8, 1794, N.C., d. Jan. 18, 1883. They came to Fayette County, Ala. from Georgia between 1850 and 1860. She is buried at the Meadow Branch Baptist Church Cemetery in Lamar Co., Ala. Children: 1. George Washington Allen, b. May 4, 1826, Ga. or N.C., d. Feb. 6, 1916, m. Winnie Minerva Loftis, b. Jan. 10, 1841, Ga., d. Jan. 5, 1894. 2. Nathaniel F. Allen, b. N. C., d. Bef. Jan. 6, 1869 (Estate Settlement), m. Priscilla C. ___. 3. Joseph Allen, B. N.C. 4. H. T. Allen, b. N.C. 5. Sarah Allen, b. N.C., m. Mr. Gravin (Lived in Miss.) 6. Martha C. Allen, b. N.C., m. Mr. Mitchell. 7. Lucy Ann Allen, b. April 17, 1838, N.C., d. May 9, 1888, Fayette Co., Ala.. m. Miles Starling Bobo, b. 1832, S.C., d. Dec. 24, 1902, Fayette Co., Ala.

ALLEY, Nicholas, m. wife unknown. Children: 1. Delitha Douglas Alley, b. Jan. 24, 1823, Ala., d. Aug. 26, 1899, m. Levi Lindsey, b. Sept. 18, 1819, Ala., d. April 4, 1894. 2. Mary Fletcher Alley, b. Sept. 7, 1831, d. July 13, 1915, Fayette Co., Ala., m. Sept. 10, 1846, John Crichton Robertson, b. July 7, 1822, Alyth, Scotland, d. June 9, 1877, Fayette Co., Ala.

ANDERSON, Milton De Witt, Jr., - son of Milton D. & Frances (Hopper) Anderson, m. at Fayette, Ala., Kathleen Jane Cannon, b. July 13, 1924, Fayette, Ala. - dau. of Dr. C. C. & Rosalie (Mathes) Cannon. Children: 1. Kathleen Claudia Anderson, b. Mar. 29, 1957, Huntsville, Ala. 2. Milton DeWitt Anderson, III, b. July 20, 1959, Huntsville, Ala.

ANTHONY, Albert Lee, b. Fayette Co., Ala., m. Dec. 13, 1915, Amanda Emeline "Emma" Watkins, b. Dec. 12, 1896, Fayette Co., Ala. He is the son of Bob Anthony, and she is the dau. of Burl Malcolm Watkins. Children: 1. Robert Lee Anthony, b. Oct. 4, 1916, Fayette Co., Ala. m. Dec. 29, 1937, Ann Dalene Bobo, b. Dec. 31, 1914, Fayette Co., Ala. 2. Brownie Lorene Anthony, b. Dec. 19, 1921, Fayette Co., Ala., m. Robert Benton.

ANTHONY, Bob, m. Miss Goosby. Children: 1. Sam Anthony, b. Fayette Co.,Ala. m. July 19, 1911, Luna Hester Watkins, b. Feb. 24, 1894, Fayette Co., Ala. 2. Sister Anthony. 3. Albert L. Anthony, b. Fayette Co., Ala., m. Dec. 13, 1915, Amanda Emeline "Emma" Watkins, b. Dec. 12, 1896, Fayette Co., Ala. 4. Maude Anthony.

ANTHONY, Robert Lee, b. Oct. 4, 1916, Fayette Co., Ala. - son of Albert & Emma (Watkins) Anthony, m. Dec. 29, 1937, Ann Dalene Bobo, b. Dec. 31, 1914, Fayette Co., Ala. - dau. of Wm. T. & Lula V. (Dickinson) Bobo. They were married at Fayette, Ala. by Rev. Victor Johnson. Robert is a farmer and a truck driver. Children: 1. Sandra Lee Anthony, b. Feb. 12, 1942, Fayette Co., Ala. 2. Robert Terry Anthony, b. Nov. 28, 1947, Fayette Co., Ala.

APLIN, Joe, b. Chapman, Ala., m. Aug. 1957, Mary Nell Branyon, b. 1925, Albertville, Ala. - dau. of E. W. Branyon. They were married at the Baptist Church in Hamilton, Ala., by Rev. Franklin. She is a Home Economist and he is an electrical engineer.

APPLING, Jesse T., b. Aug. 2, 1858, New Lexington, Ala. d. Dec. 31, 1939, Fayette Co., Ala., m. Jan. 2, 1870, Melissa McClure, b. Dec. 14, 1861, Mt. Vernon, Fayette Co., Ala., d. April 28, 1943, Fayette Co., Ala. He is the son of Samuel & Rebecca Appling. She is the dau. of Ben F. McClure. Jesse Appling was an Inspector for the Southern Railway. Both are buried at the Mt. Vernon Methodist Church Cemetery. Children: 1. Lula Tierce Appling, b. Jan. 1, 1880, Mt. Vernon, Fayette Co.,Ala., m. Walter Ben Hutto, b. Oakman, Ala., d. Sept. 7, 1935, Fayette Co., Ala. 2. Maude Ben Appling, b. Dec. 5, 1889, Mt. Vernon, Fayette Co., Ala., m. June 4, 1913, Charles J. Swanson, b. Jan. 13, 1883, Hamburg, N. Y.

APPLING, Samuel, b. Oct. 24, 1823, d. April 16, 1901, - son of Wm. & Eliz. Appling, - m. Oct. 17, 1844, Rebecca M. Willingham, b. Oct. 8, 1825, d. Jan. 30, 1860, - dau. of Isaac & Lura Willingham. Children: 1. Laura A. E. Appling, b. Oct. 12, 1845, d. Mar. 7, 1915, Fayette Co., Ala., m. J. T. Blakney, b. Nov. 15, 1845, d. June 16, 1922, Fayette, Ala. 2. Susan M. Appling,

b. Nov. 16, 1847, d. Jan. 1, 1923, Fayette Co., Ala., m. Dec. 17, 1873, George Thomas Hassell, b. Jan. 25, 1853, d. Jan. 5, 1910, Fayette Co., Ala. 3. Vilious C. Appling, b. June 27, 1850. 4. Louisa M. Appling, b. April 26, 1852, d. Arkansas, m. Mr. Baker. 5. Isaac W. Appling, b. May 2, 1854, d. May 27, 1897, Fayette, Ala., m. (1st) Tannie Stanley, (2nd) Cleon Propst, d. 1930, Fayette, Ala. 6. William T. Appling, b. May 4, 1856, d. Texas. 7. Jesse T. Appling, b. Aug. 2, 1858, New Lexington, Ala. d. Dec. 31, 1939, Fayette Co., Ala., m. 1879, Malissa McClure, b. Dec. 14, 1861, Mt. Vernon, Fayette County, Ala.

APPLINE, William, m. Lula E. Thompson, b. Sept. 10, 1859, d. Mar. 14, 1892, - dau. of Geo. W. Thompson. Children: 1. Minie Appline, m. Andy Homes, 2. Eliza Appline, m. France Murt Haughton. 3. Willie Mae Appline, m. William M, Garett.

ARNOLD, Daniel David, b. Nov. 25, 1867, Limestone Co., Tenn., m. April 17, 1887, Effie Dean Mathes, b. Oct. 20, 1867, Greenville, Tenn. - dau. of John Woodville & Eliza Jane Casandra (Jordon) Mathes. Children: 1. Roma Lee Arnold, b. Nov. 21, 1889, m. (1st) Edward C. Fulford, (2nd) Grady Mitchell. 2. Nellie Clare Arnold, b. Oct. 8, 1890, Limestone Co., Tenn., m. Thomas Alfred Rose. 3. Frank Buford Arnold, b. Sept. 12, 1892, m. Mar. 12, 1915, Lizzie Aycock. 4. Joe Mull Arnold, b. June 1, 1894, (Served in World War I). 5. Bessie Rhea Arnold, b. Oct. 24, 1896, d. Oct. 30, 1896. 6. Mae Rita Arnold, b. May 20, 1898, m. Jesse Galloway. 7. Emma Blanche Arnold, b. Sept. 4, 1900, Rome, Ga., m. J. Holley Sharp. 8. Julia Lucille Arnold, b. Dec. 6, 1905, m. Carey Barnett.

ARNOLD, Frank Buford, b. Sept. 12, 1892, - son of Daniel David & Effie Dean (Mathes) Arnold, - m. Mar. 12, 1915, Lizzie Aycock. Children: 1. Frank Buford Arnold, Jr., b. Dec. 31, 1915, m. Grace Bobo, dau. of Wm. Allen & Vinie Ellen (Young) Bobo.

ARNOLD, Joe Mull, b. June 1, 1895, Rome, Ga., m. at Berry, Ala., Leona Garrard, b. Mar. 2, ___, Ark. Children: 1. Billy Rhea Arnold, b. Jan. 22, 1920, Berry, Ala., m. Velma Evans. 2. Bessie Jo Arnold, b. April 12, 1922, Corona, Ala., m. John Hixson.

ARNOLD, Solomon, m. Mary Jane Armentrout. Children: 1. Daniel David Arnold, b. Nov. 25, 1867, Tenn., m. Effie Dean Mathes. 2. Dr. John Arnold. 3. Joseph Emmanuel Arnold. 4. Molly Arnold. 5. Julia Arnold. 6. Ella or Emma Arnold.

ARTHUR, Grover Cleveland, b. Dec. 13, 1886, d. June 8, 1947, m. June 8, 1910, Bessie Jane Richards, b. Feb. 26, 1891, Belk, Ala., d. Oct. 16, 1957 - dau. of J. A., Jr. & Retta (Taylor) Richards. Children: 1. Bernice Melba Richards, b. April 21, 1912, Belk, Ala., m. Sept. 29, 1933, m. Harlan Irby Prater, Jr., b. Oct. 25, 1910, Millport, Ala. 2. Richard Hiram Arthur, b. Oct. 9, 1916, Belk, Ala., m. Nov. 26, 1941, Leila Dickson, b. Sept. 28, 1917, Lowndsboro, Ala. 3. Retta Jane Arthur, b. Aug. 20, 1922, Fayette, Ala., m. Jan. 29, 1949, Louis Poe Moore, b. Mar. 29, 1924, Montgomery, Ala.

ARTHUR, Richard Hiram, b. Oct. 9, 1916, Belk, Ala., m. Nov. 26, 1941 at Lowndesboro, Ala., Leila Dickson, b. Sept. 28, 1917, Ala. Children: 1. Richard David Arthur, Jr., b. Mar. 6, 1945, Montgomery, Ala. 2. John Grover

Arthur, b. Sept. 9, 1949, Fayette, Ala.

ASTON, Andrew Milligan, m. Minerva Jane Morton. Andrew Milligan Aston was the son of Robert Aston. A. M. Aston served during the Civil War as a Capt. in Co. K. Ala. Volunteers. He was killed in action during the war. Children: 1. John Aston, m. Miss Moss. 2. Fertine Aston, m. Hezekiah Caddell. 3. Martha Aston, m. Tom Smith. 4. Billy Aston (Twin), m. Sarah Smith. 5. Mary Aston (Twin), m. George Smith. 6. Henry Walter Aston, b. Jan. 26, 1860, Ala., d. Aug. 3, 1923, Winfield, Ala., m. Dora Wilmerth McDonald, b. Mar. 1, 1875.

ASTON, Henry Walter, b. Jan. 26, 1860, Ala., d. Aug. 3, 1923, buried Winfield, Ala., m. Nov. 10, 1892, Dora Wilmerth McDonald, b. Mar. 1, 1875. Henry is the son of Andrew Milligan & Minerva Jane (Morton) Aston. Dora is the dau. of Wm. Byrd & Mary Ann (Bishop) McDonald. Children: 1. Andrew Moody Aston, b. Aug. 18, 1893. 2. William Vilburn Aston, b. Sept. 24, 1895. 3. Grace Mae Aston, b. July 16, 1897. 4. Emmit Robie Aston, b. Mar. 11, 1900. 5. Bertie Louise Aston, b. Mar. 24, 1902. 6. Robert Pearson Aston, b. June 18, 1904, d. Mar. 29, 1957, Omak, Wash. 7. John Marvin Aston, b. Dec. 18, 1906. 8. Rubye Lee Aston, b. Dec. 21, 1909, m. Ned M. Jeffries. 9. James Walter Aston, b. May 20, 1912, d. Aug. 18, 1958, Omak, Wash. 10. Joseph Lakeland Aston, b. Aug. 25, 1915, d. Feb. 13, 1918, Winfield, Ala.

ATKINS, Robert Hilton, b. Jan. 3, 1927, Carbon Hill, Ala. - son of Rev. B. F. Atkins, - m. June 7, 1947, Betty Folsom, b. June 16, 1927, Jacksonville, Fla. - dau. of C. L. Folsom. Children: 1. Robert Michael Atkins, b. Dec. 1, 1948, Tuscaloosa, Ala. 2. Gary Hilton Atkins, b. Feb. 4, 1951, Tuscaloosa, Ala. 3. Ginger Lynn Atkins, b. May 4, 1955, Louisville, Ky.

They were married at Northport, Ala. by Rev. B. F. Atkins. Rev. R. H. Atkins became the pastor of the Fayette First Baptist Church on June 1, 1959. They moved to Fayette from Indiana.

AVANT, William M., b. April 27, __, Birmingham, Ala., m. Nov. 27, 1952, Sarah Adeline South, b. Aug. 2, 1916, Fayette Co., Ala. - dau. of Martin D. South. Children: 1. Mart Anderson Avant, b. April 16, 1955, Birmingham, Ala.

AYRES, Elbert, b. Sept. 24, 1888, Fayette Co., Ala., m. Dec. 24, 1936 (2nd) Ruth G. Barnett, b. Sept. 9, 1909, Fayette, Ala. - dau. of Morgan I. & Della V. (Shirley) Barnett. Children: 1. James Edward Ayres, b. Nov. 25, 1937, Fayette, Ala., d. Nov. 25, 1937. 2. Virginia Alice Ayres, b. July 23, 1940, Fayette, Ala. 3. Elbert Carey Ayres, b. May 14, 1942, Fayette, Ala.

AYRES, Ottis, b. Belk, Ala., m. May 18, 1921, Gertrude Belk, b. Lamar Co., Ala. Ottis is the son of Andrew Ayres. Gertrude is the dau. of R. D. Belk. They were married at Belk, Ala. by Bill Sudduth. Mr. Ayres operates the local Ayres and Wages Blacksmith Shop. Children: 1. Maxine Ayres, b. Fayette, Ala., m. Mar. 14, 1942, George W. Wages, b. Blue Mountain, Miss.

BAGWELL, William Willy, m. Lucy Grace Anderson, b. April 30, 1895, Texas. W. W. Bagwell's parents - Willy Dyer Bagwell, b. Sept. 11, 1842, Fayette Co., Ala., & Mary Eliz. (Edmond), born Mar. 18, 1852, Fayette Co., Ala. Lucy Grace (Anderson) Bagwell's parents - Wm. Ledell Anderson, b. Feb. 5, 1869, Texas, & Alice Bell, b. Oct. 8, 1872, Texas. Grandparents - Jim Thomas & Many Cheatman. Children: Robert Bagwell, b. Sept. 20, 1934.

BAILEY, Jack, b. May 7, 1899, m. Sept. 15, 1921, at Talladega, Ala., Era Odessa Phipps, b. Sept. 2, 1900. Children: 1. Mary Grace Bailey, b. Sept. 9, 1922, Fayette Co., Ala., m. July 9, 1943, Eugene A. Colburn. 2. Era Pauline Bailey, b. June 16, 1924, Fayette Co., Ala. m. 1945, Wm. Grady Esary. 3. Raymond Eugene Bailey, b. April 23, 1929, Fayette Co., Ala. d. June 1950, killed in Korea. Entered Army in 1947 with 21st Inf. Reg. 24th Division. 4. Sylvan Fred Bailey, b. Jan. 23, 1932, Fayette Co., Ala. m. 1951, Jimmie Nell Smitherman.

BAINES, George, d. 1797, Chowan Co., N.C., m. July 30, 1789, Sarah Charlton, d. 1804, Chowan Co., N.C. George is son of John Colson Baines, Sr. Children:1. Levinia Baines, b. abt. 1784, N. C., d. 1858, m. April 8, 1805, Miles Hasell, d. 1819, N.C. 2. Ann Baines, d. 1803. 3. Rebecca Baines, m. May 11, 1801, Harrison McCabe. 4. John C. Baines, m. April 6, 1815, Nancy Everett. 5. Lemuel C. Baines, m. April 24, 1817, Mary Everett. 6. Samuel Baines, m. Nov. 8, 1804, Christian Lassiter. 7. Catherine Baines, m. John Powell.

BAINES, John Colson, d. bef. July 19, 1772, Chowan Co., N.C., m. May 29, 1757 at Chowan Co., N.C., Catherine Wilkins - dau. of John Wilkins. Children: 1. George ? Baines, d. 1797, Chowan Co., N.C., m. July 30, 1789, Sarah Charlton, d. 1804, Chowan Co., N.C. 2. John Colson Baines, Jr., d. 1781. 3. A dau. m. William Boyd. 4. Ann Baines.

BAKER, Alfred Walker, m. Etta White - dau. of S. L. White. Children: 1. Starling Walker Baker, m. Louise Orr. 2. Carolyn Baker, m. Carl Edfeldt (Children: Edith, Amelia and Susan Edfeldt.)

BALLINGER, David Jasper, b. Mar. 10, 1861, Fayette Co., Ala., d. Aug. 18, 1930, m. Dec. 30, 1888, Judy Della Bobo - dau. of Miles S. & Lucy (Allen) Bobo, b. May 22, 1870, Fayette Co., Ala. d. Oct. 18, 1950. Children: Bell Ballinger, b. Sept. 24, 1890, Fayette Co., Ala., d. 1891 at 9 mos. 2. Hassie Ballinger, b. Mar. 19, 1893, Fayette Co., Ala., m. Wilmot Woods. 3. Miles Hamilton Ballinger, b. Feb. 24, 1896, Fayette Co., Ala., d. Mar. 1896 at Imo.

BALLINGER, Homer Leon, b. Oct. 12, 1929, Fayette Co., Ala. - son of J.H. & Artie (White) Ballinger - m. 1951, Mary Norton, b. July 6, 1931, San Antonio, Texas. Children: 1. Ronny Norton Ballinger, b. July 11, 1954, Calif. 2. Judy Marie Ballinger, b. Nov. 18, 1955, Tuscaloosa, Ala.

BALLINGER, James Hamilton, b. S.C., m. Sarah Caroline "Eady" Willis, b. Fayette Co., Ala. Children: 1. James W. "Jim" Ballinger, b. Jan. 8, 1860, Fayette Co., Ala. d. Mar. 28, 1946, Fayette Co., Ala., m. Sally Bobo. 2. Jasper Ballinger, b. Mar. 10, 1861, Fayette Co., Ala. d. Aug. 18, 1930, Fayette Co., Ala., m. Della Bobo.

BALLINGER, James Hamilton, b. Feb. 13, 1903, Fayette Co., Ala. - son of J.W. & Sally (Bobo) Ballinger - m. Jan. 22, 1925, Artie White, b. Oct. 12, 1907, Fayette Co., Ala. - dau. of Terrah White. Children: 1. James Lavaughn Ballinger, b. Jan. 25, 1928, Fayette Co., Ala., m. May 29, 1948, Virginia Clardy, b. April 25, 1930, Fayette Co., Ala. 2. Homer Leon Ballinger, b. Oct. 12, 1929, Fayette Co., Ala., m. 1951, Mary Norton, b. July 6, 1931, Texas. 3. Jimmie Lou Ballinger, b. Dec. 31, 1931, Fayette Co., Ala., m. Dec. 23, 1954, Wm. Ernest Thompson, b. April 15, 1935, Fay. Co., Ala. 4. Conley Linton

Ballinger, b. July 12, 1934, Fayette Co., Ala., m. Mar. 27, 1955, Ethelene Williams. 5. Robert Lomax Ballinger, b. Aug. 11, 1937, Fayette Co., Ala. 6. Earl Riley Ballinger, b. Aug. 26, 1939, Fayette Co., Ala., m. Dec. 1958, Linda Jean Crowley, b. July 23, 1941. 7. Sara Elaine Ballinger, b. Mar. 16, 1942, Fayette Co., Ala. 8. Larry Ballinger, b. June 29, 1944, Fayette Co., Ala. 9. Grady Linden "Buddy" Ballinger, b. Nov. 24, 1946, Fayette Co., Ala. 10. Edwin Ballinger, b. Feb. 26, 1950, Fayette Co., Ala. 11. Gravis Leslie Ballinger, b. July 22, 1955, Fayette Co., Ala.

BALLINGER, James Lavaughn, b. Jan. 25, 1928, Fayette Co., Ala., m. May 29, 1948, Virginia Clardy, b. April 25, 1930, Fayette, Co., Ala. He is the son od J.H. & Artie (White) Ballinger and is a schoolteacher. Children: 1. Johnny Hamilton Ballinger, b. Feb. 14, 1949, Fayette Co., Ala. d. Mar. 16, 1949. 2. Dianne Ballinger, b. July 21, 1950, York, Ala. 3. Barbara Ballinger, b. Sept. 2, 1951, York, Ala. 4. Jimmy Ballinger, b. June 8, 1953, York, Ala. 5. Michael Ray Ballinger, b. Dec. 28, 1954, Fayette, Ala. 6. Phillip Anthony Ballinger, b. April 10, 1958, Fayette, Ala.

BALLINGER, James Wm."Jim", b. Jan. 8, 1860, Fayette Co., Ala., d. Mar. 25, 1946, m. Jan. 6, 1884, Sally Thoohosie Bobo, b. July 9, or 19, 1860, Fayette Co., Ala., d. July 4, 1936. He is son of J.H. & Sarah C. (Willis) Ballinger and Sally is the dau. of Miles & Lucy (Allen) Bobo. Children: (all born in Fayette Co., Ala.) 1. Tory Ballinger, (Invalid last years of life) b. May 13, 1885, d. Mar. 6, 1953. 2. Mary Eliz. Ballinger, b. Dec. 12, 1886, m. Nov. 14, 1906, Thomas Bailey Humber, b. May 19, 1879, Ala., d. Aug. 14, 1947. 3. Lucy Ann Ballinger, b. Dec. 29, 1888, m. J. Winston White, b. April 25, 1885, Fayette Co., Ala. d. Oct. 4, 1951. 4. Eadie Ballinger, b. Oct. 3, 1891. 5. Connie Ballinger, b. Jan. 10, 1895, m. 1957, Jesse Ellis Welch. 6. Carrie Ballinger, b. Oct. 7, 1899, m. Thornton White, b. Oct. 19, 1891, Fayette Co., Ala. 7. Hamilton Ballinger, b. Feb. 13, 1903, m. Artie White, b. Oct. 12, 1907, Fayette Co., Ala.

BARBOUR, Alvin (N.M.N.), b. Cincinnati, Ohio, d. Nov. 12, 1948, Memphis, Tenn. - son of Robert & Mary Barbour - m. July 26, 1882, Lula Spaulding, b. Cincinnati, Ohio, d. Aug. 13, 1945, Memphis, Tenn. They were married in Cincinnati, Ohio and were Baptists in belief. Children: 1. William Ernest Barbour, b. Dec. 8, 1883, Cincinnati, Ohio, d. July 31, 1952, at 5:10 P.M. Memphis, Tenn., m. Cora Bertha Jordon, b. Feb. 2, 1885, Halls, Tenn. 2. Charles Oliver Barbour, b. July 31, 1889, m. Oct. 19, 1907, Very Hathaway, b. Tenn.

BARBOUR, Robert, b. W. Va., d. Cincinnati, Ohio, m. at Cincinnati, Mary Hollenbach, b. & d. Cincinnati, Ohio. Children: 1, Alvin Barbour, b. Cincinnati, Ohio, d. Nov. 12, 1948, Memphis, Tenn., m. July 26, 1882, Lula Spaulding, b. Cincinnati, Ohio, d. Aug. 13, 1945, Memohis, Tenn. 2. George Barbour. 3. Cora Barbour, lives in Cincinnati, Ohio. 4. Bertha Barbour, lives in Cincinnati, Ohio.

BARBOUR, William Ernest, b. Dec. 8, 1883, Cincinnati, Ohio, d. July 31, 1952, Memphis, Tenn. - son of Alvin & Lula Barbour, m. Dec. 26, 1904, Cora Bertha Jordan, b. Feb. 2, 1885, Halls, Tenn. - dau. of Robert & Fannie Jordan. Wm. Ernest and Cora Bertha Jordan were married in Ripley, Tenn. by the Justice of Peace. Wm. E. was a Traffic Expert. He is buried in Memorial

Park, Memphis, Tenn. Children: 1. Douglas Alexander Barbour, b. Oct. 19, 1905, Memphis, Tenn., m. Oct. 27, 1939, Claudia Belle Kemp, b. Sept. 6, __ Fayette, Ala. 2. William Edward Barbour, b. June 20, 1907, Halls, Tenn. 3. Robert Galen Barbour, b. Feb. 26, 1911, Memphis, Tenn., m. June 6, 1937, Clorine Christian, b. Denison, Texas. 4. Joy Lea Barbour, b. Mar. 10, 1922, Memphis, Tenn., m. Aug. 22, 1953, Bill McLean, b. Miss. 5. Gene Lewis Barbour, b. Jan. 14, 1924, Memphis, Tenn., m. May 10, 1949, Jackson, Miss., Ann Eliz. Lea, b. Charlottesville, Va. 6. Cora Jane Barbour, b. Oct. 9, 1926, Memphis, Tenn., m. July 23, 1949, Adam A. Rother, b. Memphis, Tenn.

BARNARD, James Hiram, b. June 29, 1884, Fayette, Ala., d. Jan. 16, 1954, Fayette, Ala. - son of James Walter & Mary (Brannan) Barnard - m. Dec. 27, 1911, Cora Williamson, b. Sept. 27, 1893, Tuscaloosa Co., Ala. - dau. of Joseph Cowan & Rosa (Hall) Williamson. They were married at Fayette, Ala. by Judge E. P. Goodwin. J. H. Barnard was a farmer. He is buried in the City Cemetery, Fayette, Ala. Children: 1. James Floyd Barnard, b. Oct. 31, 1914, Fayette, Ala. d. May 20, 1940, Buried at Fayette City Cemetery. 2. Virginia Kathryne Barnard, b. Jan. 2, 1919, Fayette, Ala., m. Robert Stephen Burt, b. Sept. 14, 1918, Birmingham, Ala.

BARNARD, James Walter, b. Nov. 1, 1860, Center, Ala., d. Jan. 22, 1938 - son of Wm. Marion & Amanda C. (Whorton) Barnard - m. Mary Brannan, b. May 5, 1860, Carbon Hill, Ala., d. Feb. 26, 1899 - dau. of Franklin & Susan (Wakefield) Brannan. They were married at Carbon Hill, Ala. James Walter Barnard was a farmer, teacher and at one time, Superintendent of Education. Both are buried at Mt. Pleasant Cemetery, Fayette Co., Ala. Children: 1. William Franklin Barnard, b. Mar. 8, 1882, (he and all bros. & sisters born in Fayette Co.) m. Lizzie Walker, b. June 17, 1886, Pickens Co., Ala. d. May 21, 1958, Gordo, Ala. 2. James Hiram Barnard, b. June 29, 1884, d. Jan. 16, 1954, Fayette, Ala., m. Cora Williamson, b. Sept. 27, 1893. 3. Homer Boyd Barnard, b. Aug. 11, 1886, d. Sept. 23, 1948, Birmingham, Ala., m. Fronia Connell, b. Nov. 28, 1891, Jefferson, Co., Ala. 4. John Leonduros Barnard, b. Oct. 16, 1888, d. Sept. 20, 1902, Fayette Co., Ala. 5. Marion Eugene Barnard, b. Nov. 26, 1890, d. June 9, 1934, Birmingham, Ala., m. Edna Walker, d. Birmingham, Ala. 6. Eula Eleanor Barnard, b. Mar. 5, 1893, m. S. C. White, b. Fayette Co., Ala. 7. Agnes Amanda Barnard, b. Mar. 28, 1895, m., J. W. Bell, buried Elmwood Cem. Birmingham, Ala. 8. Susan Ida Barnard, b. Jan. 5, 1898, d. July 14, 1931, buried Mt. Pleasant Cem., Fayette Co., Ala.

BARNARD, James Walter, m. (2nd) Lula Tesney Leith, b. July 23, 1867, Carbon Hill, Ala. d. Feb. 12, 1936. Children: 1. Rosa Belzora Barnard, b. Jan. 21, 1901, Fayette Co., Ala. 2. Fannie Helen Barnard, b. Feb. 11, 1903, Fayette Co., Ala., m. Charles S. Sanford, b. Fayette Co., Ala. 3. Ola Anice Barnard, b. Aug. 1, 1905, Fayette Co., Ala., m. Hollie G. Smith.

BARNARD, Jesse, b. 1799, Franklin Co., Ga., m., Malissa Williams, b. 1802, Eatonton, Ga. His father was Jesse Barnard, Sr. Jesse, Jr. was a farmer and served as Captain in the Army from 1827 to 1831. Children: 1. William Marion Barnard, b. Mar. 10, 1830, Cherokee Co., Ala., m. Amanda Caroline Whorton, b. Aug. 3, 1834, Whorton's Bend, near Gadsden, Ala., d. Feb. 28, 1907, (Wm. M. d. July 20, 1877, buried at Hebron Cem.) 2. A. Franklin Barnard, b. July 24, 1824, Cherokee Co., Ala., d. Jan. 7, 1909, Nettleton, Miss. 3. James A. Barnard, b. Cherokee Co., Ala. d. - buried at Barnard Cem., Cherokee

Co., Ala. 4. John Barnard, b. Cherokee Co., Ala. d. - buried at Valley Head, Ala. 5. Leemon Barnard, b. Cherokee Co., Ala. 6. Jesse Barnard, b. Cherokee Co., Ala. 7. Mary Barnard, b. Cherokee, Co., Ala. 8. Martha Barnard, b. Cherokee Co., Ala.

BARNARD, William Marion, b. Mar. 10, 1830, Key,(Cherokee), Ala., d. July 20, 1877, m. June 10, 1852, Amanda Caroline Whorton, b. Aug. 3, 1834, Whorton's Bend near Gadsden, Ala., d. Feb. 28, 1907. They were married at Forney, Ala. Wm. M. Barnard was a farmer. He was a Confederate Soldier. He was the son of Jesse & Malissa (Williams) Barnard. She was the dau. of Jacob & Nancy (Lott) Whorton. Both are buried at the Hebron Methodist Church Cemetery at Center, Ala. Children: 1. Jesse Leondius Barnard, b. April 27, 1856, Cherokee Co., Ala., d. - buried at Fayette City Cem., m. Nancy Wakefield. 2. Eugenia Ellen Barnard, b. May 13, 1853, Cherokee Co., Ala., m. M. A. Sutherlin. 3. Jacob Marcue Barnard, b. May 17, 1859, Cherokee Co., Ala., d. 1927, Center, Ala. 4. James Walter Barnard, b. Nov. 1, 1860, Cherokee Co., Ala. d. Jan. 22 1938, Fayette Co., Ala., m. Mary Brannan, b. May 5, 1860, Carbon Hill, Ala. d. Feb. 26, 1899, Fayette Co., Ala. 5. William Harrison Barnard, b. Mar. 22, 1864, Cherokee Co., Ala., d. - Buried at Birmingham, Ala., m. Lula Turner. 6. John Elliott Barnard, b. Oct. 11, 1866, Cherokee Co., Ala. 7. Franklin Barnard, b. Feb. 27, 1866 or 1868, Cherokee Co., Ala., d. Jan. 15, 1943, buried Birmingham, Ala. 8. Lula Jane Barnard, b. Aug. 27, 1872, Cherokee Co., Ala., m. William Stubblefield. 9. George Marion Barnard, b. Mar. 29, 1876, Cherokee Co., Ala.

BARNES, Noel, b. Fayette Co., Ala., m. June 15, 1956, Alice Ann Jeffries, b. Jan. 17, 1938, Fayette, Ala. He is son of W. B. Barnes. She is dau. of Kenneth Jackson Jeffries. Children: Noel Jackson Barnes, b. June 15, 1957, Marion, Ala.

BARNES, Ralph, m. Alice Henry, b. 1917 - dau. of Jim R. Henry. Children: 1. Mary Ruth Barnes, m. J. C. Shepherd. 2. Randall Barnes. 3. Leland Barnes.

BARNETT, J. Leonard, b. Feb. 6, 1897, Fayette Co., Ala., m. Aug. 27, 1922, Lonia Walker. He joined the navy in 1918 and was discharged when the Armistice was signed. Children: A Son, b. Nov. 18, 1923.

BARNETT, Morgan C., b. Oct. 31, 1898, m., Oct. 30, 1919, Icy Oswalt. Children: 1. Morgan C. Barnett, Jr., b. May 26, 1921. 2. Harry W. Barnett, b. July 15, 1925.

BARNETT, Morgan Issac, b. Jan. 29, 1871, Tusca. Co., Ala. m. Mar. 21, 1894, Della Virginia Shirley, b. Oct. 27, 1876, Fayette Co., Ala. - dau. of Leonard C. & Martilia (Ford) Shirley. Morgan I. Barnett was the son of Joseph Riley Barnett, d. Oct. 28, 1898 & Priscilla Logan, d. 1876: grandson of Wm. Riley & Susan (Wally) Barnett: and great-grandson of Uriah Barnett and Joseph Wally. Morgan & Della's children: (all born in Fayette Co., Ala.) 1. Lillie G. Barnett, b. May 13, 1895, d. Oct. 26, 1921, m. Sept. 26, 1917, J. H. Gilbert. 2. J. Leonard Barnett, b. Feb. 6, 1897, m. Aug. 27, 1922, Lonia Walker. 3. Morgan Clifford Barnett, b. Oct. 31, 1898, m. Oct. 31, 1919, Icy Oswalt. 4. Carey L. Barnett, b. May 12, 1901, m. Lucyle Arnold - Carey is a retired Navy Chief, retired after World War II. Served 21 years and 4 months. 5. Willie V. Barnett, b. Feb. 19, 1904, d. July 17, 1930. 6. Ruth Gertrude

Barnett, b. Sept. 22, 1909, m. 1st. Aug. 12, 1928 - Phillip Robinson - 2nd. Dec. 24, 1936 - Elbert Ayres.

BARNETT, William Monroe, b. Tenn., d. 1907, Shelby Co., Ala., m. Martha Ann ?Merrell? b. Shelby, Ala., d. 1917, Shelby Co., Ala. Children: 1. Suzie Bell Barnett, b. Shelby, Ala., m. John Guy. 2. Mark Edward Barnett, b. Shelby Co., Ala., d. July 19, 1959, Caleria, Ala., m. Minnie Weldon, b. Shelby, Ala. 3. Julia Ann Barnett, b. Sept. 9, 1883, Talladega, Ala., m. Dec. 1902, Martin V. Forsyth, b. 1881, Talladega, Ala., d. April 30, 1941, Fayette, Ala. 4. Jeanie Frances Barnett, b. 1885, Talladega, Ala., d. 1910, Shelby, Ala., m. Tom Robertson, b. Talladega, Ala. 5. Ellen Barnett, b. 1889, Talladega, Ala., d. 1914, Shelby, Ala., m. Ed Robertson. 6. Dasey Barnett, b. 1894, Talladega, Ala., d. 1919, Shelby, Ala., m. Sam Kelly, b. Shelby, Ala., d. Texas.

BATSON, Charlie, m. Mar. 14, 1894, Essie Cannon, b. Oct. 30, 1873, Fayette Co., Ala., d. June 8, 1934 - dau. of M.F.Cannon. Children: Vera Nell Batson.

BEASLEY, Luther, b. June 30, 1901, Fayette Co., Ala., m. Oct. 16, 1929, Bertie Morgan, b. Jan. 10, 1908, Fayette Co., Ala. Luther's parents - Sarah Beasley, born Jan. 25, 1871, Miss. - Grandparents, James Beasley, b. 1837, Ga., m. Emily Simms, b. 1845, Ga. - Great-grandparents - Wm. Beasley, m. Lisa Miles: and John Simms, m. Lucille Lucas. Bertie (Morgan) Beasley's parents - Willie Morgan, b. July 11, 1853, Tusca. Co., Ala., m. Ella Porter, b. Nov. 21, 1868, Fayette Co., Ala. - Grandparents - Willis Morgan m. Hazey Clark; and Jessie Porter, m. Elizabeth Straugher. Great-grandparents - Willis Morgan; Sam Clark, b. 1844, Lamar Co., Ala. (then Fayette), m. Sarah Rodgers, b. 1846, Tusca. Co., Ala.: and George Straugher, m. Duciend ___. 2-Great grandparents - Samuel Clark, b. 1802, Eng., m. Nancy Green Appling. 3-Great grandparents - Thomas Appling, m. Nancy Baker. 4-Great Grandparents - Joel Appling; and Odiaiah Baker, m. Rachel ___. Luther & Bertie Morgan's children: 1. Jennie Beasley. 2. James L. Beasley, b. Aug. 9, 1942, Fayette Co., Ala.

BELK, George Washington, b. Oct. 30, 1848, N. C., d. Sept. 29, 1926, m. Martha Bell Hull, b. Mar. 24, 1850, Miss., d. Feb. 17, 1919. Children: 1. Darling J. Belk, b. Sept. 21, 1872, (all children born Fayette Co.), m. 1st. Icy Lindsey, 2nd. Neely Sanders. 2. M. Jennie Belk, b. Nov. 2, 1874, m. Mae Smith. 3. C. Oscar Belk, b. Nov. 18, 1876, m. 1st. Lovie Alexander, 2nd. Mary Seay (Horton). 4. Dora Belk, b. Jan. 27, 1881, m. Jesse Newman. 5. John H. Belk, b. Nov. 22, 1878, m. Evie Williams. 6. Lonnia Belk, b. Jan. 25, 1883, m. Earl Alexander. 7. Sam Washington Belk, b. Jan. 28, 1886, m. Susan Essie Taylor. 8. Effie Belk, b. Dec. 29, 1888, not married. 9. Ealbert Belk, b. Oct. 24, 1890, not married.

BELK, ___, m. Elizabeth ___, b. Mar. 27, 1812, N.C. Children: 1. John E. Belk, b. Apr. 16, 1839, N.C., d. Dec. 3, 1923, 2. Elizabeth J. Belk, b. Dec. 15, 1840, N.C. 3. Alex Belk, b. Jan. 30, 1843, N.C., d. Jan. 2, 1925. 4. Britton Belk, b. Feb. 22, 1845, N.C., d. July 5, 1900. 5. George Washington Belk, b. Oct. 30, 1848, d. Sept. 29, 1926, m. Martha Bell Hull. 6. Fred Belk, b. Jan. 25, 1850, N.C. 7. Marget Belk, b. Nov. 19, 1852, N.C.

BELK, John G., buried at Antioch Cem., Belk, Ala., m. Minnie Mae Freeman, b. Feb. 22, 1879, Chickasaw Co., Miss. - dau. of G.W. & Julia Ann (Bobo) Freeman. Children: 1. Naomi Lee "Oma" Belk, b. Oct. 22, 1898, Fayette Co., Ala., m.

David Abernathy -- (One child: Joe Neal Abernathy, m., Margie Nell ___). 2. Alpha Belk, b. Oct. 14, 1900, Fayette Co., Ala. m., Ervin Moore - (Children: Pauline: Maurine and John Gilbert Moore.) 3.Hattie Belk, b. April 5, 1904, Fayette Co., Ala., m. Elbert Wallace - (Children: Jewel: Nancy Mae and Walter Lee Wallace.) 4. Selena Leona Belk, b. April 24, 1911, Fayette Co., Ala., m. Clyde Smith - (Children: Marilyn Joyce: Yvonne and Douglas Smith).

BELK, Rainey, b. July 21, 1904, Fayette Co., Ala., m. Aug. 14, 1927, Estelle Hamm, b. Sept. 22, 1910, Fayette Co., Ala. Rainey Belk's parents - G.W. Belk, b. May 15, 1870, m. Doshie Lindsey, b. Dec. 19, 1872. Grandparents - Britt Belk, m. Mandy Moore; and Jim Lindsey. Estelle (Hamm) Belk's parents - J. A. Hamm, b. Mar. 23, 1880, m. Jan. 12, 1902, Tabitha Housh, b. Dec. 30, 1885. Grandparents - Bright Hamm, m. Pinina Reese; and Hardy Housh, m. Jane Perry. Great-grandparents - Johnny Reese, m. Ruth ___; and Johnny Perry. Rainey Belk's Children: Stella Fay Belk, b. Aug. 12, 1939, Fayette Co., Ala. and others.

BELL, Dr. ___, m. Elizabeth Jane Wommack. Child: 1. Ada Bell, b. Aug. 31, 1860, d. Oct. 31, 1880.

BELL, _____, Originally the Bells came from Normandy. They were the retainers to the DeBrus. They left Normandy with Robert DeBrus back in 1066 when David I, king of Scotland, invited the Debruses to the island. In 1124 King David gave a grant at Annandale to Robert DeBrus. Here the Bells settled. The Bells held together until the wave of emigration struck Europe. Then the following two brothers migrated to America. Children: 1. Matthew Bell, b. Scotland - He left Ireland and sailed for New York in 1710. From N.Y. he went to Penn. and settled in Cumberland District, Chester Co., Pa. 2. John Bell, b. Scotland - He came nine years after his brother, Matthew, about 1719 and settled in Londonderry, N. H.

BELL, Anthony Fortad, b. June 29, 1808, S.C., d. April 3, 1883, m. Dec. 17, 1829 Elizabeth Middleton, b. Mar. 21, 1810. A. F. Bell was the son of John of Penn. & Amelia (Heard) Bell, b. S.C. Elizabeth M. was the dau. of Zachariah Middleton. A. F. Bell came to Fayette County, Ala. about 1816. He was a tanner - served as County Commissioner several times. He was the county treasurer in 1874. Elizabeth Middleton was a direct descendant of Arthur Middleton, signer of the Declaration of Independence. Children: 1. Marion Francis Bell, b. Nov. 4, 1830, d. Oct. 1925, Calif., m. May 19, 1853 Ann O. H. Maddox. 2. Helen Bell, b. Oct. 6, 1832, m. Nov. 20, 1851 James Smart Sudduth. 3. Montgomery Heard Bell, b. Oct. 10, 1834, d. Texas, m. June 15, 1859 Virginia A. Cochrane. He was a preacher, lawyer and a college professor. 4. John Fortad Bell, b. Mar. 10, 1837, d. June 30, 1862 - Killed in the Chickahomina Battle in the Civil War. 5. Holland Middleton Bell, b. June 25, 1839, Tusca. Co., Ala., d. 1943 - age 104 yrs., m. Jan. 10, 1866 Margaret Miles, b. Jan. 10, 1839, d. July 19, 1917. 6. James Edward Bell, b. Aug. 23, 1842, d. Nov. 2, 1916, m. Dec. 14, 1865 - 1st. Josephine Shelton, 2nd. Mrs. Julia (Props?) Shelton. 7. Elizabeth Amelia Bell, b. Mar. 21, 1845, m. Nov. 19, 1866 John B. Abernathy. 8. Charlotte Elemna Bell, b. Aug. 7, 1847, d. July 22, 1866. 9. Serena Monica Bell, b. Sept. 15, 1849, m. Nov. 19, 1866 Robert Miles. 10. Margrona Vacharias Bell, b. Aug. 13, 1852, m. Feb. 1, 1871 James C. Yerby.

BELL, Holland Middleton, b. June 25, 1839, Tusca. Co., Ala., d. 1943 - age 104 years, Fayette, Ala., m. Jan. 10, 1866 Maggie Miles, b. Jan. 10, 1839, d. July 19, 1917. Judge Holland M. Bell, son of Anthony F. & Elizabeth (Middleton) Bell, was educated in public and private schools until his twenty-first year, when he entered LaGrange Military Academy, Franklin Co., Ala., where he remained fifteen months. He then enlisted - Apr. 14, 1862, in Co. H. 41 Ala. Inf. Regt. as a private, was promoted to Captain in 1864, and served until his capture, Mar. 29, 1865, at Hatcher's Run. His wife Maggie Miles was the dau. of Robert P. Miles of Georgia.

Judge H. M. Bell was elected Circuit Clerk, Fayette County in 1874; Probate Judge, Fayette Co., Ala. 1880 - 1892; Served as Probate Clerk in Fayette Co., for thirty years. He worked in the probate office for forty-two years. He was a Democrat and a Baptist. He often came by the F. A. Nuckol's Store (after 5 P.M.) and bought apples, peppermint stick candy, and salt crackers of which he ate as he walked home. He walked to and from work each day (approximately three miles) and ate no lunch. Children: (There were seven children - we have the record of only three.) 1. Ernest Bell. 2. Claud Bell, M. D.,,b. 1876, d. 1940, m. June 29, ___, Sallie Shepherd - dau. of J.M. Shepherd. 3. Lucy Bell, b. Aug. 17, 1878, d. April 7, 1942, m. William Wright Monroe, b. Oct. 24, 1876.

BELL, John, b. abt. 1712, Chester Co., Pa. - possibly son of Matthew Bell. Children: 1. Samuel Bell. 2. Andrew Bell. 3. James Bell. 4. Robert Bell.

BELL, John, b. Pa. - son of Samuel Bell, b. Pa., - m. wife unknown. John Bell settled nead Charleston. Children:1.Anthony Fortad Bell, b. June 29, 1808, S.C., d. Apr. 12, 1886, m. Dec. 17, 1829, Elizabeth Middleton, b. Mar. 21, 1810. 2. James D. Bell. 3. Hugh L. Bell. 4. Stephen E. Bell. 5. Charlott Bell. 6. Amelia Bell. 7. Monica Bell.

BELL, Samuel, b. Penn., m. wife unknown. Samuel was the son of John Bell, b. 1712, Chester Co., Pa. Children: 1. Hugh Bell - Served as a private in the militia in the Pennsylvanian war records of 1780. 2. John Bell. 3. Samuel Bell. (These three brothers are said to have gone Southwest from Pittsburg at the close of the Revolution.)

BELL, Dr. William Stillman, b. May 6, 1874, d. May 12, 1929, Fla., m. Mabel Tabitha Davis, b. Aug. 21, 1886 - dau. of Charles Hurt Davis. Children: Mary Edna Bell, b. April 5, 1909, Gordo, Ala., m. June 17, 1940, Robert Wood D. Walker, b. Va. (Child: Mary Daily Walker, b. Sept. 1, 1946). 2. William Stillman Bell, Jr., b. Nov. 19, 1912, m. Oct. 21, 1938, Alice Dyle, (children: Martha Joe, b. Mar. 23, 1945 and Wm. Davis Bell, b. Mar. 5, 1949). 3. John Lewis M. Bell, b. Aug. 8, 1914, m. Nov. 5, 1938, Anna Bell Graves, (Children: John Lewis, Jr., b. June 30, 1940 and Mary Jane Bell, b. Sept. 17, 1943). 4. Mabel Bell, b. Feb. 18, 1920, m. Mar. 1, 1943, Lewis Gregory, (children: Mary Hall, b. Jan. 30, 1944; Linda Gaile, b. June 25, 1948; and Jay Bell Gregory, b. Sept. 17, 1953).

BENNETT, Henry H. b. Feb. 9, 1841, Ala. d. Oct. 29, 1905, Bankston, Ala. - his parents b. S.C. - m. Nancy Frances Houston, b. May 8, 1841, Ala., d. May 1, 1914, Bankston - dau. of John & Nancy Houston. Both are buried at Mt. Pleasant Cem., Fayette Co., Ala. H. H. Bennett served in Co. G. Regt. 11 during the Civil War. He entered service in April 1861 and was wounded in Yorktown, Va. in 1862.

Children: 1. William Bennett. 2. Eppie Bennett. 3. Joann I. Bennett, b. Sept. 30, 1867, d. Sept. 15, 1884. 4. Sallie L. Bennett, b. Mar. 12, 1870, d. July 19, 1909, m. Mar. 11, 1906, John G. Kyzer. 5. Julia Ella Bennett, b. May 10, 1873, d. Aug. 17, 1907, m. Mar. 9, 1902, David McIntosh Hallman, b. Dec. 5, 1862, d. April 9, 1933. 6. James W. S. Bennett, b. Feb. 7, 1876, d. Oct. 23, 1901. 7. Nancy Melessia Bennett, d. in infancy.

BERRY, George W., b. Feb. 16, 1858, Fayette Co., Ala., d. June 25, 1940, m. Nancy Newton, b. Feb. 16, 1852, Fayette Co., Ala., d. Jan. 30, 1934 - dau. of Elkanah B. Newton. George W. Berry was a preacher and a farmer. Both are buried at Hopewell Primitive Baptist Church Cem., Fayette Co., Ala. Children: (All born near Fayette in Fayette Co., Ala.) 1. Mae Berry, b. Aug. 10, 1882, m. April 2, 1902, George Thompson, b. April 6, 1880, Fayette Co., Ala., d. - buried in Birmingham, Ala. 2. Sidney Aaron Berry, b. April 11, 1884, d. Nov. 12, 1946, buried at Hopewell Cem., m. Louise Keith. 3. Thomas B. Berry, b. Oct. 25, 1885; m. June 7, 1914, Vivian Hall, b. Aug. 4, 1895, near Gordo, Ala. 4. Horace E. Berry, b. Aug. 2, 1887, m. Sept. 3, 1915, Velma Branyon, b. Dec. 29, 1892, near Belk, Ala. 5. Dan W. Berry, b. Dec. 20, 1888, d. Oct. 16, 1918, buried at Hopewell Cem. Daniel W. Berry served in World War I in Co. G. - 324th Inf. 81st Div. U. S. He died in France. On Sept. 12, 1918, he crossed "No Man's Land", which was the first battle that he fought in. He became ill from exposure and lack of food and died Oct. 16, 1918. He was buried in France and after hostilities ceased his body was returned home and laid to rest in Hopewell Cemetery, Fayette Co., Ala. 6. John Berry, b. Oct. 20, 1891. 7. Maggie Berry, b. Jan. 11, 1894, m. Felix H. Treadway, b. Feb. 25, 1891, Studdards Cross Roads or Spencer, Fayette Co., Ala. 8. Ruth Berry, b. Dec. 18, 1896, m. Dec. 26, 1921, Dr. C. Linton Smith, b. April 3, 1891, near Fayette, Ala. They were married at the home of her parents in Fayette, by Judge H. M. Bell.

BERRY, Horace E., Jr., b. May 19, 1925, Fayette, Ala., m. July 10, 1943 at Columbus, Miss. by Rev. Franks, Carolyn Chandler, b. June 18, 1926, Fayette, Ala. He is the son of Dr. H. E. and Velma Berry. She is the dau. of Roy L. & Florence Chandler. Horace E. Berry, Jr. served three years in World War II in the Navy as Pharmacist Mate 2nd Class. He is presently the manager of Graylee's Dept. Store in Fayette. Children: 1. James Horace Berry, b. Dec. 5, 1950, Fayette, Ala. 2. Barbara Carolyn Berry, b. Feb. 12, 1953, Fayette, Ala.

BERRY, Horace E., Dr., b. Aug. 2, 1887, near Fayette, Ala. - son of Rev. Geo. Berry - m. Sept. 3, 1915 at home on Temple Ave. in Fayette, by Rev. I. W. Martin, Velma Branyon, b. Dec. 29, 1892, near Belk, Ala. - dau. of Dr. James A. Branyon. Dr. Berry has a long established dentistry practice in Fayette. Children: 1. Dr. James Daniel Berry, b. Feb. 17, 1920, m. May 31, 1958, Laura Collins, b. San Francisco, Calif. 2. Horace E. Berry, Jr., b. May 19, 1925, Fayette, Ala., m. July 10, 1943, Carolyn Chandler, b. June 18, 1926, Fayette, Ala. 3. George Harold Berry, b. Aug. 1, 1929, Fayette, Ala., m. May 26, 1956, Ann Hollida, b. Oct. 31, 1934, Sylvania, Ga. (George Harold Berry entered the Korean Conflict from R.O.T.C. as 1st. Lt. Served in Korea, was 1st. Lt. when discharged.)

BERRY, Dr. James Daniel, b. Feb. 17, 1920, Fayette, Ala. - son of Dr. H. E. Berry - m. May 31, 1958, Laura Collins, b. April 14, 1932, San Francisco,

Calif. - dau. of Forrest Collins. Dr. James D. Berry saw military duty as a Neuro-Therapy Officer in the U. S. Army, in New York, during World War II. His rank was Capt. He was stationed on Governor's Island, N. Y. They were married in the Chapel of Grace Cathedral in San Francisco, Calif. by Dean Bartlett. Dr. Berry is presently a Doctor of Medicine and a Surgeon. Children: 1. Alison Maclean Berry, b. Mar. 2, 1959, San Francisco, Calif.

BERRY, Jeff, m. Mattie Gardner - dau. of Jesse Gardner. Children: 1. Jonas Berry. 2. Talmadge Berry. 3. Victor Berry.

BERRY, John, b. Sept. 26, 1823, d. Aug. 12, 1877, m. Eliza Moore, d. Apr. 26, 1908. Children: 1. Sara Berry, b. Nov. 20, 1844, d. Apr. 6, 1931, m. John Stamps, b. Mar. 17, 1831, d. April 29, 1887.

BERRY, Thompson, b. 1801, N.C., m. Rosanna Gutman, b. 1803, S.C. Thompson Berry was a farmer. Children: 1. John Berry, b. 1825, Ala. 2. Caroline Berry, b. 1828, Ala. 3. Henry B. Berry, b. 1829, m. Malissa Jane Jeffries. 4. Eliza Berry, b. 1832, m. Josiah Pierce. 5. Elizabeth Berry, b. 1834. 6. Frances Berry, b. 1832. 7. Mary Berry, b. 1838. 8. Paletine Berry, b. 1841, m. Pleasant Jackson Jeffries.

BERTRAM, Francis Eugene, b. Sept. 30, 1903, Muscatine, Iowa - son of F. P. & Maude Bertram - m. June 29, 1931, Lottie Charlcie Collins, b. Dec. 22, 1897, Fayette Co., Ala. - dau. of John N. & Allia (Buckner) Collins. Francis Eugene Bertram is affiliated with the Agriculture Extension Service. Children: 1. Sarah Frances Bertram, b. June 11, 1932, Fayette, Ala., m. Sept. 5, 1953, Ermar Lamar Evans. 2. Carolyn Bertram, b. Apr. 13, 1935, Montgomery, Ala.

BIRDWELL, George, b. abt. 1721, probably Stafford Co., Va., d. 1781, away from home, in Bedford Co., Va., - son of Benjamin Birdwell who came from England - m. 1st. wife's name not known. 2nd. Mary ___. He acquired land in the bend of the James River in Botetourt Co., Va. in 1751 and lived there until 1780 when he moved with his family to the Hoston River which was then in N. C. but later became Sullivan Co., Tenn. All of his children were born at the Birdwell Homestead in the bend of James River, except the first which was probably before reaching James River and the last child who was born after George's arrival on the Holston. Children: (by first wife.) 1. Robert Birdwell, b. bef. 1751, fought in the American Revolution. 2. Sarah Birdwell, b. 1751 or 1752. 3. Ann Birdwell, b. 1752 or 1753. Children: (by second wife.) 1. George Birdwell, b. Oct. 18, 1760, m. Jane Russell. 2. Elizabeth Birdwell, b. June 1, 1764. 3. Benjamin Birdwell, b. Dec. 21, 1765, d. Oct. 17, 1840 (Revolutionary War Soldier), m. Mar. 3, 1791, Mary Perry. 4. Joseph Birdwell, b. Feb. 19, 1767, d. Aug. 1, 1801, m. Rachel Russell. 5. Moses Birdwell, b. Oct. 15, 1769 (Fought in War of 1812.) 6. John Birdwell, b. Sept. 24, 1770, d. bet. Mar. 27, 1854 & April 24, 1854 in Rusk Co., Texas, m. Mary Allen. 7. William Birdwell, b. Feb. 10, 1772. 8. James Birdwell, b. Aug. 29, 1775. 9. Joshua Birdwell, b. Nov. 4, 1777. 10. Mary Birdwell, b. July 24, 1779. 11. Jane Birdwell, b. Mar. 17, 1781.

BIRDWELL, John, b. Sept. 24, 1770, Va., m. Mary Allen. John is the son of Geo. Birdwell. Children: 1. Allen Birdwell. 2. Lucinda Birdwell, b. 1811, d. Rusk Co., Texas, m. Mr. Vaught. 3. Ann Birdwell, m. James B. Fowler, (Cass Co., Texas.) 4. Sally Birdwell, m. Levi Isbell, (Walker Co., Ala.) 5.

Tabitha Birdwell, b. 1821, m. Smiley Wright (Walker Co., Ala.) 6. John Birdwell, m. Elizabeth ___.

BLACK, Edward, m. Clara White, b. Fayette Co., Ala. - dau. of J. Winston White. Children: 1. Maylene Black, b. Fayette Co., Ala., m. Hulon Hindman. 2. Mamie Lou Black, b. Fayette Co., Ala. 3. Roger Black, b. Feb. 8, 1951, Fayette Co., Ala. d. Feb. 8, 1951, Fayette Co., Ala.

BLACK, Ellis, b. Mar. 2, 1899, Lamar Co., Ala. - son of W.B. Black - m. Apr. 23, 1916, Cora Geneva Bynum, b. May 18, 1901, Fayette Co., Ala. - dau. of J. A. Bynum. They were married at the home of T. H. Woods, by him, in Fayette Co., Ala. Ellis Black is a farmer. Children: 1. Grady Lee Black, b. Oct. 22, 1918, (all children b. in Fayette Co., Ala.), m. Oct. 25, 1942, Lou Edith Crews, b. Mar. 29, 1918, Fayette Co., Ala. 2. James Theron Black, b. May 31, 1921, d. Dec. 7, 1941, Pearl Harbor, Hawaii. (James Theron Black was in the United States Marines, serving on the Battle Ship, Arizona. He was killed December 7, 1941 when the Japanese bombed Pearl Harbor and was buried in the Arizona when it went down.) 3. Roy Hollis Black, b. June 29, 1923, m. July 14, 1945, Palestine "Teen" Warren, b. Jan. 21, 1928, Walker Co., Ala. 4. Arlene Black, b. June 4, 1926, m. Jan. 26, 1946, Thomas Lloyd Humber, b. Sept. 29, 1922, Fayette Co., Ala. 5. Orville E. Black, b. April 14, 1931, m. Aug. 1951, Mary Elizabeth Carlyle, b. Nov. 15, 1933, N.C. 6. Lula Mae Black, b. Feb. 21, 1934, m. May 21, 1954 Harold Grey Burns, b. Mar. 1932, Fayette, Co., Ala. 7. Robert C. Black, b. June 7, 1936.

BLACK, Jack, b. Oct. 21, 1925, Cordova, Walker Co., Ala., m. Aug. 3, 1952, Margaret Alexander, b. Aug. 12, 1925, Fayette, Ala. Jack Black came to Fayette, Aug. 18, 1949, as manager of Radio Station W.W.W.F., which went on the air, Sept. 3, 1949. Children: 1. Claire Alexander Black, b. May 11, 1953, Fayette Co., Ala.
 Jack Black's Parents - James Spencer Black, m. Ruth Sides. Grandparents - Elbert Spencer Black, b. Lee Co., Miss., m. Sarah Calpernia Hyche - dau. of Jackson Eli & Loudinda (Kirkpatrick) Hyche; and George Washington Sides, m. Evaline Sides. Great Grandparents - John Black, m. Frances Barton - dau. of John More Barton. (John Black moved from N.C. to Walker Co., Ala. bef. 1845.); Henry Clay Sides, m. Sarah Pike. 2 Great Grandparents - Andrew Allen Sides, m. Mary Malone Staggs. 3 Great Grandparents - William Sides, m. Cerepta Dill. 4 Great grandparents - Henry Sides, who came from Holland.
 Margaret (Alexander) Black's parents - Joe Alexander, m. Margaret Brewer. (Joe Alexander was born near Millport, Ala., moved to Fayette in 1923. Margaret Brewer is a native of Franklin Co., Ala.) Grandparents - Drew Alexander m. Amanda Eudora Woolbright; and James Anderson Brewer, m. Anna Laura McRight. (James A. Brewer was born 1872, Franklin Co., Ala.) 2 Great grandparents - Thomas Houston Alexander, m. Caroline Fielder. (T. H. Alexander moved from Ky. to Pickens Co., Ala. about 1832.); Samuel Admarine Brewer, m. Sarah Elizabeth Thompson. 3. Great grandparents - James Brewer, m. Elizabeth Holloway. (Jas. Brewer was born in Georgia.)

BLACKBURN, Augustus, b. Ireland, m. wife unknown. Children: 1. John W. Blackburn, b. Aug. 20, 1848, Davis Creek, Ala., d. Feb. 18, 1923, m. 1st. Feb. 19, 1874, Mary Hassell. 2nd. July 1, 1888, Lena Hassell. 2. James Belton Blackburn, b. Jan. 6, 1852, Fayette Co., Ala., d. July 7, 1911, m. Dec. 20, 1877, Vandalia F. Spencer, b. April 14, 1858, d. Oct. 9, 1893.

BLACKBURN, Carl Belton, b. June 2, 1875, Davis Creek, Fayette Co., Ala., d. Mar. 30, 1919, Fayette Co., Ala., m. Dec. 28, 1904, Monnie Weeks, b. May 16, 1885, Texarkana, Ark. Dr. C. B. Blackburn - son of John W. Blackburn - rereived his M. D. from Nashville, Tenn. He practiced medicine in Fayette for many years. When George Cannon was shot in the leg, Dr. Blackburn amputated the leg while working at an ordinary table - time would not permit better conditions. Children: 1. Mary Blackburn, b. July 16, 1906, Fayette, Ala.

BLACKBURN, James Belton, b. Jan. 6, 1852, Fayette Co., Ala., d. July 7, 1911, son of Augustus Blackburn - m. Dec. 20, 1877, Vandalia F. Spencer, b. April 14, 1858, d. Oct. 9, 1893. Children: 1. Earnest Blackburn, b. Dec. 20, 1878, d. July 2, 1959. 2. Diendonie Blackburn, b. May 28, 1881, d. Mar. 16, 1943, m. Ira Lee Griffin, b. Nov. 26, 1872, d. Sept. 29, 1927, Bankston, Ala. 3. Richard Belton Blackburn, b. April 23, 1883, d. Aug. 9, 1883. 4. Walter Dale Blackburn, b. Aug. 27, 1884, d. Mar. 12, 1932. 5. James Chester Blackburn, b. June 22, 1886, d. Apr. 3, 1953. 6. Clyde Elmore Blackburn, b. July 28, 1888. 7. Eula Grace Blackburn, b. May 9, 1890, m. Mr. Griffin. 8. Aster Blackburn, b. July 21, 1892.

BLACKBURN, John W., b. Aug. 20, 1848, Davis Creek, Fayette Co., Ala., d. Feb. 18, 1923, Fayette Co., Ala., m. July 1, 1888, 2nd. Aileen Hassell, b. June 18, 1861, Tusca. Co., Ala., d. May 5, 1932, Fayette Co., Ala. He was the son of Guston Blackburn. She was the dau. of George Washington Hassell. John W. Blackburn was a farmer and owned and operated a gin. Children: (by 1st wife, all born Fayette Co., Ala.) 1. Susan Vista Blackburn, b. July 13, 1878, m. Jan. 20, 1901, Samuel Houston Henry b. Aug. 30, 1876, Fayette Co., Ala. d. Oct. 7, 1951 - son of Joe Henry. 2. Carl Belton Blackburn, b. June 2, 1875, d. Mar. 30, 1919, m. Dec. 28, 1904, Monnie Weeks, b. May 16, 1885, Texarkana, Ark.

BLACKWELL, Willie Gerome, b. Jan. 1, 1905, Miss., m. Eula Mae Hubbert, b. May 23, 1905, Fayette Co., Ala. W. G. Blackwell's parents - Reuben & Pearl (Poe) Blackwell. Grandparents - Westley Blackwell, m. Martha Poe; and Bud T., m. Sally Elmore. Eula Mae (Hubbert) Blackwell's parents - Robert Lee Hubbert, b. 1874, Fayette Co., Ala., m. Mary Ette Bailey, b. Apr. 27, 1885, Fayette Co., Ala. Grandparents - George Washington Hubbert, m. Frances Porter; and Jim Bailey, m. Hannah Brazil. Great Grandparents - George Hubbert, m. Lizzie Bess Stewart; Isaac Bailey, m. Nancy __; and George Brazil, m. Nancy __. W. G. Blackwell's children: 1. Aileene Blackwell, b. Sept. 10, 1936, Fayette Co., Ala.

BLAKELEY, William, d. May 30, 1736, James City Co., m. Sept. 11, 1718 Catherine Kalydee, b. 1698, d. Oct. 25, 1771. Wm. Blakeley's Will proved in York Co., Va. Court, June 1736. Both are buried at Bruton Church. Children: 1. William Blakeley, b. 1731 (Enlisted Sept. 11, 1755 in Capt. Robert Spotswood's Co. French and Indian Wars. Age 24 yrs. - 6 ft. 9 in. - planter from Va.) 2. Janet Carson Blakeley, m. Thompson Swann. 3. Elizabeth Blakeley, m. Robert McLaurine. 4. Mary Blakeley, m. Griffin Stith? (Smith?)

BOBO, Dr. Arlington H., M.D., b. Jan. 28, 1885, Fayette Co., Ala., d. Sept. 1, 1953, Fayette Co., Ala. m. 1911 May Elizabeth Walker, b. Springville, St. Clair Co., Ala. Children: Elizabeth Bobo, b. Feb. 20, 1915, m. S. M. Sayers. 2. Arlington H. Bobo, Jr., b. Dec. 17, 1925, m. Alice Trappe - from

Australia. 3. William Walker Bobo, b. Dec. 17, 1925, m. Bobbie Bobo - dau. of Thias Bobo.

BOBO, Arlie Urvin, b. April 5, 1909, Covin, Ala., m. Lucille Eva Schroeder, b. Mar. 12, 1916. A. U. Bobo is a Methodist Minister and the son of Ira & Catherine (Collins) Bobo. Children: 1. & 2. Female Twins, b. & d. May 18, 1941, Mulga, Ala. 3. Lewis Douglas Bobo, b. Nov. 6, 1942, Mulga, Ala. 4. Suzanne Bobo, b. May 13, 1946, Mulga, Ala. 5. Richard Kindred Bobo, b. Mar. 1, 1954, Mulga, Ala.

BOBO, Barm Spencer, b. Fayette Co., Ala., m. Addie Eggerton, b. S.C. Children: 1. Foster Lee Bobo, b. Aug. 8, 1876, Lamar Co., Ala., m. Oct. 27, 1901 Sheila B. Harris.

BOBO, Comer Tierce, b. Jan. 20, 1907, Lamar Co., Ala. - son of Foster Lee & Shelia B. (Harris) Bobo - m. Nov. 2, 1940 Julia Lois Newman, b. Aug. 19, 1915, Fayette Co., Ala. - dau. of David Andrew & Francis Biddie Newman. Children: Comer Keith Bobo, b. May 11, 1951, Fayette, Ala. 2. Julia Marie Bobo, b. July 7, 1956, Fayette, Ala.

BOBO, Foster Lee, b. Aug. 8, 1876, Lamar Co., Ala., m. Oct. 27, 1901 Shella B. Harris. b. Jan. 3, 1888, Lamar Co., Ala. Foster L. Bobo is the son of Barm Spencer & Addie (Eggerton) Bobo. Shella is the dau. of John Wm. & Eliz. (McDonald) Harris. Children: 1. Archie Bobo, b. Aug. 24, 1902, d. 1908,- 6 yrs. 2. Addie Lee Bobo, b. Dec. 2, 1903. 3. Annie Lou Bobo, b. May 6, 1905. 4. Comer Tierce Bobo, b. Jan. 20, 1907, m. Nov. 2, 1940 Julia Lois Newman. 5. Amos "Jubie" Bobo, b. Jan. 21, 1909, d. 1913 - 4 yrs. 6. Lucy Mae Bobo, b. Jan. 18, 1911, d. 1937 - 26 yrs. 7. Raymond Bobo, b. Oct. 11, 1913, d. 1915 - 2 yrs. 8. J. B. Bobo, b. July 15, 1915. 9. Infant Son, b. Nov. 3, 1918. 10. Bonnie Bobo, b. Sept. 19, 1919, d. 1920 - 4 mos. 11. Bonzell Bobo, b. Aug. 14, 1921. 12. Ruel Bobo, b. April 17, 1924. 13. Wyndall Bobo, b. Nov. 14, 1926.

BOBO, Francis Spencer, came from England, m. ? Mary Mason. Children: 1.Lewis Bobo. 2. Sampson Bobo. 3. Absalom Bobo. 4. Simpson Bobo. 5. Spencer Bobo, Jr. Francis Spencer Bobo came from England in the early 1700's with Ambrose Yarbrough and they married cousins, settling first in Va. and later in S.C.

BOBO, Franklin Miles, b. May 24, 1899, Fayette Co., Ala. - son of Wm. T. & Lula V. (Dickinson) Bobo - m. June 5, 1921 Eula Mae South, b. April 3, 1903, Fayette Co., Ala. - dau. of Carlos & Amanda (Byars) South. Frank M. Bobo is an ordained Missionary Baptist Minister and a farmer. Children: 1. Carrie Nell Bobo, b. Feb. 8, 1922, Fayette, Ala., m. Dec. 18, 1944 Ray Bryant, b. Mar. 18, 1924. Lamar Co., Ala. 2. Lula Irene Bobo, b. Sept. 11, 1925, Fayette Co., Ala., m. Dec. 21, 1944, Silas Calvin Waldrop, b. Sept. 19, 1925, Fayette Co., Ala. 3. Mary Louise Bobo, b. Dec. 17, 1928, Fayette Co., Ala., m. Dec. 29, 1945, Albert Lamar Wise, b. Jan. 27, 1927, Tenn. 4. Dorothy Ann Bobo, b. Aug. 24, 1929, Fayette Co., Ala., m. Mar. 13, 1948, Fred Hayes, b. May 10, 1928, Fayette Co., Ala. 5. Amanda Evelyn Bobo, b. Sept. 26, 1936, Fayette Co., Ala., m. June 5, 1955, Thurman L. "Tim" Bobo, b. Nov. 21, 1918, Fayette Co., Ala.

BOBO, James Holland, b. Aug. 19, 1872, Fayette Co., Ala., d. Oct. 19, 1939, - son of Miles & Lucy A. (Allen) Bobo - m. Jan. 5, 1895, Lula Bell Strong, b.

Oct. 13, 1876, Ala., d. June 27, 1954. Children: 1. W. Ernest Bobo, b. June 17, 1897, (all children born Fayette Co., Ala.) m. Lucy Welch. 2. Eunice Bobo, b. Oct. 18, 1899, m. July 21, 1933, Jeff Griffin, b. Dec. 28, 1899. 3. Arlie B. Bobo, b. Mar. 17, 1906, m. Dec. 27, 1935, Lois Rice. 4. Infant, b. Dec. 25, 1908, d. Dec. 27, 1908. 5. R. Curtis Bobo, b. Jan. 26, 1913, m. Joyce __. 6. R. Lloyd Bobo, b. April 10, 1916, m. Nov. 21, 1943, Christine Maddox.

BOBO, James Maddox, b. June 8, 1837, S.C., d. 1923, Fayette Co., Ala. - son of Spencer & Betsy (Rainwater) Bobo - m. Pauline Moore, b. Jan. 2, 1845, Fayette Co., Ala., d. 1925, Fayette Co., Ala. - dau. of Wm. Owens & Mary A. D. (Kirkland) Moore. James Maddox Bobo was a farmer and a veteran of the Civil War, having served in the Confederate Army. Both are buried at Mt. Vernon Methodist Church. Cem. Children: 1. Mollie Bobo, b. (all children born in Fayette Co., Ala.) d. Ennis Texas, m. Tom Rickman, b. Lamar Co., Ala. d. Ennis, Texas. 2. Wm. Brown Bobo, b. June 25, 1871, d. Jan. 1959, Bessemer, Ala., m. Belle Newman, b. Fayette Co., Ala. d. Bessemer, Ala. 3. Nellie Bobo, b. Mar. 5, __, d. June, 1958, Fayette Co., Ala., m. Ira C. Buckner, d. Fayette Co., Ala. 4. Frank Bobo, d. Texas, m. Lula Woods, b. Fayette Co., Ala. 5. Pervy Bobo, d. Texas, m. Sallie Wade, b. Little Rock, Ark. 6. Luther Spencer Bobo, b. Mar. 8, 1878, m. Dena Irene Ward, b. Mar. 1, 1889, Fayette Co., Ala., d. May 8, 1952, Fayette Co., Ala. 7. Oliver Lee Bobo, b. Fayette, Ala., d. Fayette, Ala. m. Minnie Dodson, b. Fayette, Ala. 8. Clyde H. Bobo, m. Eula Pinkerton, b. Fayette Co., Ala. 9. Mertie Bobo, m. Alfred McCarver.

BOBO, LeVander Walston, b. June 2, 1866, Fayette Co., Ala., d. Jan. 14, 1951, - son of Miles & Lucy A. (Allen) Bobo - m. Alice Robertson, b. May 31, 1868, Ala., d. Aug. 11, 1914. Moved to Miss. abt. 1900. Children: 1. Lilly Bobo, d. age 2 - buried near Crowley's Ridge, Ark. 2. Curtis Claude Bobo, b. May 16, 1895, Ala., m. Belle Miller. 3. Alfred Ernest Bobo, b. April 1, 1897, Ala., m. Gurtha Melton. 4. Autie Bell Bobo, b. Dec. 10, 1899, Ala., m. A. B. Perry. 5. William Pervy Bobo, b. Dec. 15, 1902, Miss., m. Doris Thompson.

BOBO, Lewis, b. Nov. 8, 1804, S.C., d. Jan. 8, 1892, Fayette Co., Ala. m. Nancy Yarbrough, b. Nov. 6, 1805, S.C., d. Feb. 7, 1884, Fayette Co., Ala. Children: 1. L. S. Bobo (Fought in Battle of Gettysburg.) 2. Elizabeth Bobo, b. 1836, S.C. 3. Lewis Bobo, b. 1838, S.C. 4. Murray Bobo, b. 1840, S.C. 5. Victoria Bobo, b. 1844, S.C. 6. George Bobo, b. 1848, Ala. 7. Josephine Bobo, b. 1853, Ala.

BOBO, Levingston, b. Feb. 26, 1806, Spartanburg, S.C., d. Mar. 27, 1883, Fay. Co., Ala., m. Sarah "Sally" Rainwater, b. April 22, 1808, Spartanburg, S.C., d. Jan. 19, 1881, Fayette, Co., Ala. "Lev" was the son of Tillman & Bulah Bobo. "Sally" was the dau. of Miles & Sally (Hutchinson) Rainwater. "Lev" was a farmer, and came with his brothers to Fayette County, Ala. about 1844. They came by wagon train from Spartanburg, S.C. and settled in Fayette County, Ala. northwest of Covin, on the west side of the Luxapillila River. Both are buried at the Wesley Chapel Methodist Church Cemetery. Children: 1. Tillman S. Bobo, b. Dec. 5, 1828, Spartanburg, S.C., d. Oct. 29, 1867, m. Susan Malissa Gwyn, b. Dec. 26, 1834, d. May 12, 1912. 2. Miles Starling Bobo, b. 1832, S. C., d. Dec. 24, 1902, Fayette Co., Ala., m. Lucy Ann Allen, b. Apr. 17, 1838, N.C., d. May 9, 1888. 3. Seberon ? Bobo, b. 1837, S.C., m. ?

Mrs. Nelson. 4. Elizabeth Jane Bobo, b. 1839, S.C., m. Miles Prater. 5. Viney Bobo?, b. 1841, S.C., m. Cumming Gilreath. 6. Absalom Bobo, b. 1841, S. C., d. In Confederate States Army. Buried at Bigles Mill, Va.

BOBO, Luther Spencer, b. Mar. 8, 1878, Fayette Co.,Ala., - son of Jas. M. & Pauline (Moore) Bobo - m. Dena Irene Ward, b. Mar. 1, 1889, Fayette Co., Ala. d. May 8, 1952, Fayette, Ala. - dau. of John W. & Emily (Ham) Ward. Luther Spencer Bobo is a farmer. His wife is buried at Musgrove Chapel Church Cem. in the northern part of the county. Children: (all born in Fayette Co.) 1. Myra Pauline Bobo, b. Oct. 5, 1906, m. Mar. 3, 1923, Roy S. Renfroe, b. Nov. 3, 1895, Fayette Co., Ala. 2. Johnnie Lee (female) Bobo, b. July 3, 1909, m. Emmit LeRoy Rogers. 3. Jimmie Lou Bobo, d. 1922. 4. Mary Imogene Bobo, b. April 13, ___, m. Edgar Vickery, b. Marion Co., Ala. 5. Jala Dean Bobo, b. Nov. 30, 1926, m. Clyde S. Greene, b. Marion Co., Ala.

BOBO, Miles Absolom "Abs", b. Dec. 29, 1862, Fayette Co., Ala., d. Nov. 8, 1954, Fayette Co., Ala. - son of Miles & Lucy A. (Allen) Bobo - m. Sept. 14, 1890, Eppie P. McCarver, b. June 11, 1867, d. Sept. 19, 1942. Children: 1. Dean Bobo, b. Mar. 10, 1892 (all children born Fayette Co.,) d. 1904. 2. Docia L. Bobo, b. Jan. 2, 1894, m. Apr. 5, 1924, Robbie Buckner. 3. Johnny Lois Bobo, b. Jan. 10, 1986, m. Nov. 7, 1915, Mertie Kirkley. 4. Troy Lee Bobo, b. Oct. 31, 1897, m. Feb. 13, 1921, Alice Pearl Meadders, b. June 22, 1898, Fayette Co., Ala. 5. Stella B. Bobo, b. Sept. 17, 1899, m. Nov. 24, 1920, Victor White. 6. Infant, b. 1901, d. Nov. 16, 1901. 7. Zeb L. Bobo, b. Mar. 13, 1902 or 1903, m. 1921, Lois Duckworth. 8. Pauline Bobo, b. Jan. 7, 1905, d. 1905. Ruby Dell Bobo, b. Apr. 30, 1906. 10. Dwight Miles Bobo, b. Mar. 25, 1908, d. Oct. 31, 1944, (Wounded in World War II on Oct. 20, 1944.) 11. Cora Bobo, b. Mar. 11, 1910, m. Dec. 19, 1929, Carlos Faulkner. 12. Infant, b. Nov. 15, 1912, d. 1912.

BOBO, Miles Starling, b. abt. 1834, S.C., d. abt. Dec. 24, 1902, Fayette Co., Ala. - son of Livingston & Sally (Rainwater) Bobo - m. Lucy Ann Allen, b. Apr. 17, 1838, Ga. or N.C., d. May 9, 1888, Fayette Co., Ala. - dau. of Thomas & Nancy (Foster) Allen. Miles Bobo served in the Confederate Army, enlisting April 14, 1862, at Fayette Court House, Ala. He was enlisted by Capt. Kirkland for a period of 3 years or the duration of war. He was a Priv. in Co. H. Reg't. 41, Ala. Inf. He was promoted to Corpl. Apr. 30, 1863 and to Sgt. in Dec. 1863. He was wounded in the side by gunshot and had two fingers shot off during the conflicts of war. He was a farmer. Children: 1. Elizabeth Ann Bobo, b. Oct. 26, 1859, (all children born Fayette Co.) d. Feb. 1954, Columbus, Miss., m. Nov. 26, 1876, Will McReynolds. 2. Sally Trophenie Bobo, b. July 9, 1860, d. July 4, 1936, Fayette Co., Ala., m. Jan. 6, 1884, James William Ballinger, b. Jan. 8, 1860, Fayette Co., Ala., d. Mar. 25, 1946, Fay. Co., Ala. 3. Miles Absolom Bobo, b. Dec. 29, 1862, d. Nov. 8 or 9, 1954, m. Sept. 14, 1890, Eppie L. McCarver, b. June 11, 1867, d. Sept. 19, 1942. 4. LeVander "Van" Walston Bobo, b. June 2, 1866, d. Jan. 14, 1951, m. Alice Robertson, b. May 31, 1868, d. Aug. 14, 1914. 5. William Theoderic Bobo, b. May 3, 1868, d. Nov. 26, 1954, Fayette Co., Ala., m. Jan. 28, 1894, Lula Victoria Dickinson, b. April 1, 1875, Fayette Co., Ala., d. Mar. 17, 1939, Fayette Co., Ala. 6. Judy Della Bobo, b. May 22, 1870, d. Oct. 19, 1950, Fay. Co., Ala., m. Dec. 30, 1888, David Jasper Ballinger, b. Mar. 10, 1861, Fayette Co., Ala., d. Aug. 18, 1930, Fayette Co., Ala. 7. Dean Bobo, b. 1871, d.1871. 8. James Holland Bobo, b. Aug. 19, 1872, d. Oct. 19, 1939, Fayette Co., Ala.

m. Jan. 5, 1895, Lula Bell Strong, b. Oct. 13, 1876, Ala., d. June 27, 1954. 9. Alice Bobo, b. 1875, d. April 18, 1918, buried in Ark., m. July 26, 1891, William Clinton Woods, b. 1872, d. June 1935, Ark.

BOBO, Spencer, b. abt. 1808, Spartanburg, S.C. - son of Tillman & Bulah Bobo - m. Mary "Polly" Rainwater - dau. of Miles & Sally (Hutchinson) Rainwater. Children: 1. Levingston Bobo, b. abt. 1830, S.C. 2. Martha Ann Bobo, b. Apr. 10, 1832, S.C., d. Nov. 1, 1899, Fayette Co., Ala., m. Feb. 8, 1852, George Washington Howton, b. Apr. 16, 1824, d. Jan. 16, 1902, Fayette Co., Ala. 3. Mary Ann Bobo, b. abt. 1836, S.C., m. Mr. Nichols. 4. James Maddox Bobo, b. June 8, 1837, S.C., d. 1923, Fayette Co., Ala., m. Narcissa Pauline "Pearl" Moore, b. Jan. 2, 1845, d. 1925, Fayette Co., Ala. 5. Foster Bobo, b. abt. 1841, S.C. 6. Julia Ann Bobo, b. May 6, 1942, S.C., m. George Washington Freeman, b. Nov. 23, 1845. 7. Baram "Bud" Bobo, b. abt. 1845, Ga. 8. Doctor Bobo, b. abt. 1847, Ala. 9. "Elisa" or Harriet Frances Bobo, m. Matt Brock, (Minister).

Spencer Bobo's 2nd marriage - Miss Barnes, Children: 1. Mandy Bobo, m. Henry Wiggins (Child: Pervy Wiggins). 2. Lou Bobo, m. Landon Miles. 3. Charlie Bobo, m. Jennie Brock (Children: 1 or 2 deceased young and Terry W. Bobo, b. May 16, 1915, m. Helen__.) 4. Florida Bobo, b. Aug. 8, 1862, d. Mar. 17, 1941. 5. Fannie Bobo. 6. Levi Bobo.

BOBO, Spencer, Jr., - son of Spencer (of Eng.) & Mary (Mason) Bobo, - m. Nancy Berry. Children:?? 1. Absalom Bobo (Revo. Soldier) b. 1764. Albermarle Co., Va. 2. Tillman Bobo, b. 1766, Union or Spartanburg Co., S.C., d. 1844, Cross Keys, S.C., m. Bulah __. 3. Sampson Bobo. 4. John T. Bobo, d. Dec. 5, 1841, Cross Keys, S.C. 5. ? Isabel Bobo, m. Walter Stewart. 6. ? Lida Bobo, m. James Stewart (son of Walter by 1st marriage). 7. Dau., m. Mr. Campbell.

BOBO, Thurman L. "Tim", b. Nov. 21, 1918, Fayette Co., Ala. - son of Virgil Bobo - m. 1st. Martha Loftis - dau. of Wm. & Gabreilla (Green) Loftis. Child by 1st marriage, James Timothy Bobo, b. Oct. 13, 1944, Fayette Co., Ala.

Tim Bobo's 2nd marriage, June 5, 1955, Amanda Evelyn Bobo, b. Sept. 26, 1936, Fayette Co., Ala. - dau. of Frank M. & Eula M. (South) Bobo. Children: 1. Pamela Lorraine Bobo, b. Oct. 13, 1958, Fayette, Ala. (Tim served in the United States Army during World War II.) 2. Trena Bobo, b. Feb. 20, 1960.

BOBO, Tillman, b. Mar. 13, 1766, S.C., d. Feb. 23, 1844, Union, S.C. - son of ? Spencer Bobo, Jr. - m. Beulah or Buley __, b. Feb. 29, 1781, Spartanburg, S.C., d. Nov. 10, 1840, Union, S.C. Both are buried in the New Hope Cemetery near Cross Keys, Union, S.C. Children: 1. Loucinda Bobo, b. Aug. 20, 1802, S.C., m. Ambrose Yarbrough, b. Oct. 4, 1800, S.C., d. Aug. 17, 1870. 2. Lewis Bobo, b. Nov. 8, 1804, d. Jan. 8, 1892, Fayette Co., Ala., m. Nancy Yarbrough, b. Nov. 6, 1805, d. Feb. 7, 1884, Fayette Co., Ala. 3. Levingston "Leve" Bobo, Feb. 26, 1806, S.C., d. Mar. 27, 1883, Fayette Co., Ala., m. Sally (Sarah) Rainwater, b. May 22, 1808, S.C., d. Jan. 9, 1881, Fayette Co., Ala. 4. Spencer Bobo, b. abt. 1808, Spartanburg, S.C., m. Mary "Polly" Rainwater, b. abt. 1818, S.C. 5. Charlot Bobo, b. 1810, S.C., d. July 18, 1876, m. George Edwards, b. 1805, S.C., d. July 9, 1876. 6. Rebecca Bobo, b. Sept. 16, 1813, Spartanburg, S.C., d. April 6, 1895, Fayette Co., Ala., m. 183_, Wiley Miles, b. May 7, 1811, Spartanburg, S.C., d. Nov. 5, 1879, Fayette Co., Ala. 7. Absalom Bobo, b. Jan. 3, 1816, Union, S.C., d. Feb. 20, 1900, Florence, Texas, m. Jan. 24, 1839, Elizabeth Fowler, b. Sept. 15, 1821, Spartanburg, S.C., d. June 27, 1901, Florence, Texas. 8. Maria Bobo. 9. Elizabeth Bobo.

BOBO, Tilmon (Sebron?), b. Dec. 5, 1828, Spartanburg, S.C., d. Oct. 29, 1867 - son of Levingston Bobo - m. 1850, Susan Malissa Gwynn, b. Dec. 26, 1834, d. May 12, 1912, Fayette Co., Ala. - dau. of Morris & Rhoda (Williams) Gwynn. Tilmon S. Bobo joined the Confederate States Army May, 1862 - 43rd Ala. Volunteers, Graces Regt. Co. I. He fought in the Battle of Petersburg, Va. After the children were grown, Susan married Dr. Anthony Bell, who died in 1883. During the was Mary Tanzy came to live with Susan and the children and was considered one of the family from that day on. Children: 1. Malissa Jane Bobo, b. Nov. 18, 1852, d. Dec. 25, 1918, Fayette Co., Ala., m. July 5, 1871 Melville Fortescue Cannon, b. 1851, d. May 2, 1920. 2. Harriett Bobo, m. Mr. Caraway. 3. William Seborn "Buddy" Bobo, b. Jan. 14, 1856, Fayette Co., Ala. d. Dec. 26, 1924, Fayette Co., Ala., m. Elizabeth "Lizzie" Sudduth, b. July 15, 1860, Fayette Co., Ala., d. Mar. 27, 1936, Fayette Co., Ala. 4. Eppie Elizabeth Bobo, m. Mr. Walters. 5. Rhoda Abigail Bobo, b. during Civil War.

BOBO, Troy Lee, b. Oct. 31, 1897, Fayette Co., Ala. - son of M."Abs" & E.P. (McCarver) Bobo - m. Feb. 13, 1921, Alice Pearl Meadders, b. June 22, 1898, Fayette Co., Ala. - dau. of S.F. & M.M.(Oswalt) Meadders. Children: 1. Laura Augusta Bobo, b. Nov. 12, 1921, Fayette Co., Ala., m. Oct. 8, 1948, George R. Poe.

BOBO, William Allen, b. Mar. 25, 1867, Fayette Co., Ala., b. Mar. 25, 1867, Fayette Co., (Later Lamar Co.), d. Aug. 11, 1929, m. Vinie Ellen Young, b. Apr. 2, 1876, Fayette Co., Ala. Children: (All born in Fayette Co.) 1. Virgil Bobo, b. Feb. 12, 1892, m. Janie Harton. 2. Hattie Bobo, b. Apr. 19, 1895, d. Dec. 15, 1956, m. Felix Cargile. 3. Albert Bobo, b. Sept. 9, 1897, m. Edith Terrill. 4. Kelsey Bobo, b. May 3, 1900, m. Loe Crosley. 5. Wilma Bobo, b. Feb. 12, 1903, m. Burey Wilson. 6. Eva Bobo, b. Sept. 27, 1905, m. Hugh Richards. 7. Theodore Bobo, b. May 27, 1908, m. Birdie Lee Thompson. 8. Talmadge Bobo, b. Mar. 26, 1911, m. Johanna Bruner. 9. Ormond Bobo, b. Aug. 5, 1913, m. Mary Doyle. 10. Grace Bobo, b. Apr. 10, 1919, m. Buford Arnold.

BOBO, William Seborn "Buddy", b. Jan. 14, 1856, Fayette Co., d. Dec. 26, 1924, Fayette Co., Ala. - son of Tilmon S. & Susan Malissa (Gwynn) Bobo - m. Elizabeth "Lizzie" Sudduth, b. July 15, 1860, Fayette Co., Ala., d. Mar. 27, 1936, Fayette Co., Ala. Children: 1. Abbie Bobo, d. Mar. 13, 1952, Fayette, Ala, m. Fletcher Hyde, b. Fayette Co., Ala., d. Fayette, Ala. 2. Arlington H. Bobo, M.D., b. Jan. 28, 1885, Fayette Co., Ala., d. Sept. 1, 1953, Fayette Co. Ala., m. 1911, May Elizabeth Walker, b. Springville, St. Clair Co., Ala.

BOBO, William T. "Billy", b. May 3, 1868, Fayette Co., Ala., d. Nov. 26, 1954, son of Miles & Lucy Ann (Allen) Bobo - m. Jan. 28, 1894, Lula Victoria Dickinson, b. April 1, 1875, Fayette Co., Ala., d. Mar. 17, 1939 - dau. of J. Frank & M. Evelyn (Dickinson) Dickinson. Wm. T. Bobo was a framer and a storeclerk. He was also an ordained Deacon of the Missionary Baptist Church. Children: 1. Lucy Evelyn Bobo, b. Nov. 5, 1895, Fayette, Ala., m. June 24, 1919, Victor Samuel Patterson, b. Jan. 11, 1895, Fayette, Ala. 2. Charles William Bobo, b. Jan. 10, 1897, Fayette Co., Ala., m. Mar. 6, 1922, Verna Clair Patterson, b. Jan. 25, 1902, Fayette Co., Ala. (Had no children.) 3.

Franklin Miles Bobo, b. May 24, 1899, Fayette Co., Ala., m. June 5, 1921, Eula Mae South, b. Apr. 3, 1903, Fayette Co., Ala. 4. John Thomas Bobo, b. July 3, 1902, Fayette Co., Ala., m. 1st. Feb. 24, 1927, Rachel Pace, 2nd. Mar. 24, 1941, Lou Annie (Cardin) Wise. (No children either marriage.) 5. George Allen Bobo, b. Mar. 17, 1905, Fayette Co., Ala., m. Jan. 16, 1930, Nell Smith, b. Oct. 23, 1905, Hueytown, Ala. (Had one infant son, b. & d. 1930.) 6. Barto Lee "Dick" Bobo, b. Aug. 1, 1907, Fayette Co., Ala., m. Feb. 25, 1933, Lucille Scott, b. June 5, 19__, Birmingham, Ala. 7. Mary Edith Bobo, b. April 21, 1911, Fayette Co., Ala., m. Feb. 17, 1945, Roman Andrew Grocholski, b. Dec. 6, 1907, Milwaukee, Wis. 8. Ann Dalene Bobo, b. Dec. 31, 1914, Fayette Co., Ala., m. Dec. 29, 1937, Robert Lee Anthony, b. Oct. 4, 1916, Fayette Co.

BOLAND, John b. abt. 1753, Germany, d. 1832, m. 1st. Widow Counts, 2nd. Miss Feltman. John Boland immigrated to the United States from Hesse-Cassel, Germany. He settled in S.C. prior to the American Revolution and took part in that struggle. Child: (First marriage) 1. Abraham Boland, b. May 20, 1784, d. Jan. 12, 1837, m. Ever Christine Sease. Children: (Second marriage) 1. John Boland, b. Mar. 26, 1813, d. May 24, 1884. 2. Henry Boland. 3. Adam Boland. 4. George Boland. 5. William Boland. 6. David Boland, b. S.C. (moved to Ga. in 1827) m. Mary Jones, b. S.C. 7. Jacob Boland. 8. Barbara Boland. 9. Mary Boland. (One of these daughters was the wife of Jesse McCartha.)

BOOZER, Andrew, b. 1806, S.C., d. abt. 1883, m. Jane "Jennie" __, b. 1806, Ind. Andrew came from South Carolina with his wife and several children in a covered wagon. Children: 1. Martha A. Boozer, b. 1832, S.C. 2. Pressa C. Boozer, b. 1834, S.C., m. James Poe. 3. Rebecca or Nancy Boozer, b. 1836 S.C., m. Sol Renfroe. 4. Louisa A. "Laura" Boozer, b. 1838, S.C., m. 1st. Mr. Tierce, 2nd. Pink Williamson. 5. Margarette E. or Harriett Boozer, b. 1841, S.C., m. Sam Canterbury. 6. Rachel L. A. Boozer, b. May 17, 1845, Ala. d. Oct. 1, 1876, m. Joseph Franklin Doughty, b. Jan. 15, 1844, d. Feb. 13, 1889. 7. Sarah or Sally Boozer (Twin), b. 1849, Ala., m. Bill Brown. 8. Keziah Clarintine Boozer (Twin) b. 1849, Ala., m. Sam Shirley. 9. Infant Son.

BOOZER, Henry (Rev. Soldier), d. abt. 1837 (Will made 1828), m. Elizabeth __ d. 1845. Henry settled in Newberry Co., S. C. Children: 1. David Boozer, 2. Henry Boozer, (Sr.), m. ?Rebecca __. 3. Frederick Boozer. 4. John Boozer. 5. Sarah Boozer, m. Jacob Cappleman. 6. Daniel Boozer, 7. George Boozer. 8. Elizabeth Boozer, m. Daniel Senn. 9. Adam Boozer, d. 1840, m. Mary. 10. Rebecca Boozer, m. Mr. Hendrix.

BOOZER, Henry, d. Feb. 22, 1859, Newberry Co., S.C. - son of Henry & Eliz. Boozer - Children: 1. Samuel Boozer. 2. Timothy Boozer. 3. Rebecca Boozer. 4. Henry Boozer, (Jr.). 5. John A. Boozer. 6. Daniel Boozer. 7. Wm. A. Boozer. 8. Frederick Boozer. 9. David W. Boozer. 10. Andrew Boozer, b. abt. 1806, S.C., m. Jane __, b. abt. 1806, Ind. 11. Adam P. Boozer. 12, Matthias Pinckney Boozer. 13. George Boozer. 14. Elizabeth Boozer, m. Mr. Lester. 15. Edward Boozer.

BOOZER, Ulrich, b. Europe. Children: (First wife - unknown) 1. George Boozer. 2. Catherine Boozer. Children: (Second wife - unknown) 1. Jacob Boozer. 2. John Boozer. 3. Frederick Boozer, m. Barbara Gray. 4. Henry Boozer, Amer. Rev. Soldier - m. Elizabeth. 5. Ulrich Boozer, Jr.. 6. Gasper Boozer.

7. Rudolph Boozer.
   The pioneer of the Boozer family was Ulrich, Sr., who first settled in the lower section of old Camden District; later some of his sons moved into Lexington Co. and other into Newberry Co., S.C. Numbers of the grandsons of Ulrich Boozer moved into Alabama. Tradition says that three came, one settling in Northeast, Ala. one in South Ala., and one going to Texas.

BOYD, Erbie Lee, b. Oct. 12, 1920, Lamar Co., Ala. - son of Roy & Nancy Evelyn (Evie) Boyd - m., Nov. 5, 1945, Nocal Elizabeth Madison, b. Jan. 14, 1927, Fayette Co., Ala. - dau. of Henry H. & Villa E. Madison. They were married at the Baptist Parsonage in Fayette, Ala. by Rev. A. M. Nix. E. L. Boyd is an Insurance Agent and Mrs. Boyd is a Bank Loan Teller at the Citizen's Bank of Fayette. Children: 1. Infant Son, b. & d. April 20, 1954, Fayette, Ala., buried at Oak Grove Cem. 2. Kerry Lee Boyd, b. July 8, 1958, Fayette, Ala.

BOYD, Roy, b. Nov. 3, 1891, Lamar Co., Ala., d. Mar. 1951 - son of Elzie Levi & Mary Boyd - m. in Miss., Nancy Evelyn "Evie" Perkins, b. Oct. 19, 1892, Lamar Co., Ala., d. Aug. 8, 1951 - dau. of Samuel D. & Mary E. Perkins. Roy was a farmer. Both are buried at Oak Grove Cemetery. Children: 1. Robert Lee Boyd, b. 1912, d. 1912, buried at Nebo Cem., Lamar Co., Ala. 2. Ruby Mae Boyd, b. Dec. 21, 1913, Lamar Co., Ala., m. Olen Richard Stoker, Sr., b. Fay. Co. 3. Cecil Boyd, b. Lamar Co., d. buried in Lamar Co., Ala. 4. Shirley Ray Boyd, b. Oct. 18, 1919, Lamar Co., Ala., m. Claude Dean Duckworth. 5. Erbie Lee Boyd, b. Oct. 12, 1920, Lamar Co., Ala., m. Nov. 5, 1945, Nocal Elizabeth Madison, b. Jan. 14, 1927, Fayette Co., Ala. 6. Johnnie B. Boyd, b. Aug. 7, 1922, Lamar Co., Ala., m. April 5, 1946, Maxine Estes. 7. Rammie Lillian Boyd, b. Lamar Co., d. buried at Nebo Cem., Lamar Co., Ala. 8. Clifton Eugene Boyd, b. May 3, 1927, Fayette Co., Ala., m. Virginia Watkins. 9. Roy Boyd, Jr., b. Mar. 23, 1933, Fayette Co., Ala., m. Mildred Ann Watkins, b. Mar. 24, ___. 10. James Branyon Boyd, b. May 16, 1936.

BRAGG, Wilbur Clark, Jr., "Bill", b. Dec. 18, 1923, Moulton, Ala. - son of W. C. Bragg, Sr. - m. Nov. 12, 1954, Beverly Smith, b. April 3, 1932, Montgomery, Ala. - dau. of Arnold Smith. They were married in Montgomery. Bill is Sales Manager for "Flav-O-Rich" Dairy in Fayette. Children: 1. Dabney Elizabeth Bragg, b. Sept. 30, 1955, Florence, Ala. 2. Martha Clark Bragg, b. Sept. 8, 1957, Florence, Ala.

BRANYON, Arthur Curtis, M.D., b. Dec. 8, 1882, Fayette Co., Ala., d. Aug. 24, 1949, Fayette, Ala. - son of John J. & Kezia Branyon - m. 1st. Martha Savanah Wilkerson, b. Oct. 1, 1884, d. Oct. 24, 1918. Children: (First marriage) 1. Max Hammond Branyon, b. July 25, 1905, Kingsville, Ala., m. June 18, 1928, Madge Davidson, b. June 2, 1906, Detroit, Ala. 2. James A. Branyon, II, b. Pinson, Ala., m. Aug. 17, 1935, Edwyna Walker. 3. Claude Hugh Branyon, b. Aug. 17, 1909, d. June 30, 1910.
   Dr. A. C. Branyon married second, May 1, 1919, Otis Ware, b. April 21, 1886, Pinson, Ala. No children by this marriage. Dr. Branyon served Fayette Countians as physician for many years. His wife, Otis Branyon served as Vice President of Alabama Medical Society of Women's Auxiliary - also, Director of Children of Confederacy to the United Daughters of Confederacy for ten years. She is a retired school teacher.

Another son of Dr. A. C. Branyon and his 1st. wife, (Left off of above list through error) is Arthur Curtis Branyon, II, b. April 15, 1910, Jefferson Co., Ala., m. Oct. 10, 1932, Bernice Rowland, b. June 28, 1912, Lamar Co. Ala. - dau. of Zeb A. & "Dora" (Waldrop) Rowland. Curt was the fourth child of Dr. A. C. Branyon.

BRANYON, Arthur Curtis, II, b. April 15, 1910, Jefferson Co., Ala. - son of Dr. A. C. Branyon - m. Oct. 10, 1932, Bernice Rowland, b. June 28, 1912, Lamar Co., Ala, dau. of Zeb & Dora Rowland. Children: 1. Martha Elizabeth Branyon, b. July 25, 1936, Fayette, Ala. 2. Marilyn Branyon, b. Aug. 18, 1939, Fayette, Ala., m. Jimmy Lowell Burleson, b. June 15, 1937, Winfield, Marion Co., Ala.

BRANYON, Dr. Edgar Waterson, b. May 25, 1923, Albertville, Ala. - son of E. W. Branyon, m. Mary Leyden, b. Anniston, Ala. - dau. of Dr. G. H. Leyden. Children: 1. David Watterson Branyon, b. June 16, 1949, Birmingham, Ala. 2. William Leyden Branyon, b. Mar. 12, 1955, Nashville, Tenn. 3. Laura Beth Branyon, b. July 28, 1958, Birmingham, Ala.

BRANYON, Edgar Waterson, b. Sept. 28, 1890, near Belk, Ala. - son of John S. Branyon - m. Oct. 19, 1919, Emily Nell Walker, b. Carthage, Miss. They were married at Jackson, Miss. He is a high school teacher and has served as the Superintendent of Education. Children: 1. Dr. E. W. Branyon, Jr., b. May 25, 1923, Albertville, Ala.. m. Mary Leyden. 2. Mary Nell Branyon, b. 1925, Albertville, Ala., m. Joe Aplin, b. Chapman, Ala.

BRANYON, James A., II, b. Pinson, Ala. - son of Dr. A. C. Branyon - m. Aug. 17, 1935, Edwyna Walker, b. Fayette, Ala. - dau. of Edgar Walker. They were married at Fayette, Ala. by Rev. Roy Chandler, in the First Baptist Church. J. A. Branyon II, is a Representative from Fayette County. Children: 1. & 2. Twin Infant Daughters. 3. James Walker Branyon, b. Mar. 15, 1942, Fayette, Ala.

BRANYON, Dr. James A., b. Nov. 27, 1868, Fayette Co., Ala., d. Aug. 19, 1942, Fayette, Ala. - son of John Jasper & Kizia Branyon - m. Mar. 10, 1892, Eva Lela Rowland, b. Mar. 26, 1873, near Belk, Ala., d. Feb. 12, 1908, near Belk, Ala. - dau. of Wiley & Priscilla Rowland. They were married at her mother's home. He served the people of Fayette County as a Physician for fifty-two years. Children: 1. Velma Branyon, b. Dec. 29, 1892, near Belk, Ala., m. Sept. 3, 1915, Dr. Horace E. Berry, b. Aug. 2, 1887, near Fayette, Ala. 2. Elmer Branyon (Twin), b. Dec. 15, 1894, near Belk, d. Mar. 14, 1895. 3. Delmer Branyon (Twin), b. Dec. 15, 1894, near Belk, d. Dec. 15, 1894. 4. Jimmie Nell Branyon, b. Oct. 22, 1904, Kingsville, Ala., m. June 14, 1932 Macon W. Gravlee, b. July 5, 1888, Newtonville, Ala.

Dr. James Alexander Branyon married second - Edna Pace, b. Aug. 19, 1886, Russellville, Ala. - dau. of J. O. A. Pace. Mrs. Branyon is a school teacher. There were no children by this marriage.

BRANYON, James Curtis, b. June 14, 1929, Jasper, Ala. - son of Max H. & Madge (Davidson) Branyon - m. June 21, 1953, Myra Linda Connell, b. Oct. 26, 1930, Fayette, Ala. - dau. of Bill & Betty Connell. Children: 1. Linda Ann Branyon, b. May 9, 1954, Tulsa, Okla. 2. Mary Suzanne Branyon, b. Sept. 21, 1955, Norfolk, Va. 3. James Curtis Branyon, Jr., b. Sept. 5, 1957, Tuscaloosa, Ala.

BRANYON, Jeptha Sareptha, b. Mar. 18, 1892, Kennedy, Ala. - son of John S. Branyon - m. Dec. 25, 1920, Lovie Edna Martin, b. Equality, Ala. - dau. of Rev. & Mrs. Martin. They were married in Equality, Ala. by her father, Rev. Martin. Jeptha Branyon is a teacher, High School Principal and Mrs. Branyon is also a teacher. Children: 1. Jean Martin Branyon, b. Oct. 30, 1923, Jasper, Ala., m. at Uniontown, Ala., John William McGaw, b. Nashville, Tenn. d. Mar. 1957, Nashville, Tenn.

BRANYON, John J., b. Jan. 1, 1833, Newtonville, Ala., d. Dec. 3, 1891, Belk, Ala., m. in the 1860's, Kezia Blakeney, b. Feb. 16, 1838, Ala., d. Oct. 21, 1895, Belk, Ala. He was the son of James A. & __ (Ellis) Branyon. She was the dau. of Thomas Blakeney. John J. Branyon served in the Confederate Army. He was wounded at Chickamauga. His sons, James Alexander and Arthur Curtis Branyon were physicians. They had a half brother, Darius Branyon, also a doctor, who lived and died in Texas. Dr. J. A. Branyon left a grandson, Dr. James Daniel Berry, who is a physician and surgeon in San Francisco, Calif. Kiziah was formerly married to a Mr. Lowery. Children: 1. James Alexander Branyon, b. Nov. 27, 1868, Newtonville, Ala., d. Aug. 19, 1942, Fayette, Ala. m. 1893, 1st. Lela Rowland, b. May 26, 1873, Belk, Ala., d. Feb. 12, 1908, Belk, Ala. - m. 2nd. June 2, 1910, Edna Pace, b. Aug. 19, 1886, Russellville, Ala. 2. Kate Branyon, b. April 9, 1870, Fayette Co., Ala., d. Oct. 8, 1941, Fayette, Ala., m. 1892, John Harton, b. Aug. 20, 1853, Fayette Co., Ala., d. Jan. 3, 1924, Fayette, Ala. 3. Lizzie Branyon, b. Mar. 4, 1872, Fayette Co., Ala., d. May 11, 1950, Lamar Co., Ala., m. Henry Rowland, b. Oct. 28, 1867, Fayette Co., Ala., d. July 23, 1945, Lamar Co., Ala. 4. Ella Branyon, b. Nov. 16, 1880, Fayette Co., Ala., d. Feb. 25, 1957, Fayette, Ala., m. 1st. Robert Smith, b. July 21, 1874, Fayette Co., Ala., d. Jan. 1, 1900, Fayette Co., Ala. m. 2nd. 1903, Young Shirley, b. Mar. 14, 1858, Ala., d. Aug. 26, 1913, Fay. Co., Ala. 5. Arthur Curtis Branyon, b. Dec. 8, 1882, Fayette Co., Ala., d. Aug. 24, 1949, Fayette, Ala., m. 1st. 1904, Mattie Wilkerson, b. Lamar Co., Ala., m. 2nd. 1919, Otis Ware, b. Apr. 21, 1886, Jefferson Co., Ala.

BRANYON, John Jasper, b. Jan. 1833, Newtonville, Ala., d. Dec. 3, 1891, Fay. Co., Ala., m. 1859, Sallie Perkins, b. 1837, Southern Miss., d. 1866, Fayette Co., Ala. He was the son of James Alexander Branyon. She was the dau. of Mose Perkins. John Jasper Branyon was a farmer. He is buried in the Branyon Cem. near Belk, Ala. and she is buried in the Wilson Cemetery. Children: 1. John Simpson Branyon, b. Jan. 14, 1861, Chapel Hill, Fayette Co., Ala., d. Nov. 21, 1936, Fayette Co., Ala., m. Alpha Susan Smith, b. Jan. 27, 1869, Conway, Lamar Co., Ala., d. Mar. 22, 1952, Fayette, Ala. 2. Sarah Alice Branyon, b. 1863, Fayette, Ala., d. 1931, Texas, m. Dr. J. P. Collins, b. Kennedy, Ala. d. 1933, Texas. 3. Dr. William Darin Branyon, b. 1864, Fayette Co., Ala., d. 1909, Texas., m. Lizzie Davis, b. Fayette Co., Ala. d. buried in Fayette Cem.

BRANYON, John Simpson, b. Jan. 14, 1861, Fayette Co., Ala., d. Nov. 21, 1936, Fayette Co., Ala., m. Oct. 6, 1889 Susan Anna Alpha Smith, b. Jan. 27, 1869, Conway, Ala., d. Mar. 22, 1952, Fayette, Ala. He was the son of John Jasper Branyon. She was the dau. of Sarepta Smith. John Simpson Branyon was a teacher and a farmer. They were married at Sarepta Smith's home by Rev. Elijah Howell. Both are buried at Wesley Chapel Cem. in Fayette Co., Ala. Children: 1. Edgar Waterson Branyon, b. Sept. 28, 1890, near Belk, m. Oct. 19, 1919, Emily Nell Walker, b. Carthage, Miss. 2. Jeptha Sareotha Branyon, b. Mar. 18, 1892, Kennedy, Ala., m. Dec. 25, 1920, Lovie Edna Martin, b. Equality, Ala. 3. Mattie Ruth Branyon, b. Feb. 14, 1894, Kennedy, Ala. (Teacher). 4. Sallie Era Branyon, b. Mar. 30, 1896, Kennedy, Ala., (Teacher).

BRANYON, Max H., Jr., b. Mar. 31, 1931, Fayette, Ala. - son of Max H. & Madge (Davidson) Branyon - m. Aug. 1956, Sherrie Garrison, b. June 3, 1939, Texas. Children: 1. Michael Steven Branyon, b. June 2, 1957, Pryor, Okla.

BRANYON, Max Hammond, Sr., b. July 25, 1905, Kingsville, Ala., m. June 18, 1928, Madge Davidson, b. June 2, 1906, Detroit, Ala. He is the son of A. C. and Martha Branyon. She is the dau. of J. A. Davidson. They were married at Brimingham, Ala. by Rev. W. I. Daniel. Max H. Branyon is affiliated with the State of Alabama, Education Veteran Department. Children: 1. James Curtis Branyon, b. June 14, 1929, Jasper, Ala., m. June 21, 1953, Myra Linda Connell, b. Oct. 26, 1930, Fayette, Ala. 2. Max H. Branyon, Jr., b. Mar. 31, 1931, Fayette, Ala., m. Aug. 1956, Sherrie Garrison, b. June 3, 1938, Texas. 3. William Monroe Branyon, b. Oct. 14, 1933, Fayette, Ala., m. July 12, 1958, Betty Gage, b. Sept. 26, 1933, Tulsa, Okla. 4. Hugh Stanley Branyon, b. Mar. 9, 1939, Fayette, Ala.

BRANYON, Royce R., b. Dec. 30, 1911. Fayette Co., Ala., m. Oct. 13, 1935, Loueng Howard, b. Dec. 1, 1919, Fayette Co., Ala. Children: 1. Ellon Branyon, b. Mar. 10, 1940, Fayette Co., Ala. 2. Gaile Branyon.
  Royce R. Branyon's parents - Tollie H. Branyon, b. July 14, 1887, Fayette Co., m. Oct. 6, 1909, Purl Richardson. Grandparents - James A. Branyon, b. Nov. 20, 1858, Fayette Co., Ala., m. Oct. 5, 1882, Valutia Kelley, b. June 7, 1857; and William P. Richardson, b. Oct. 9, 1876, m. Margaret A. Cook, b. Dec. 15, 1872. Great-grandparents - John Richardson, m. Clarisa Wilson; and John Cook, m. Martha Bennett.
  Loueng (Howard) Branyon's parents - Victor L. Howard, b. Dec. 28, 1894, Pickens Co., Ala., m. Dec. 25, 1918, Ila Sanders, b. Feb. 10, 1894, Fayette Co., Ala. Grandparents - Thomas J. Howard, m. Rhoda McCluskey; and John M. Sanders, b. Oct. 31, 1871, Fayette Co., Ala., m. Martha Davis, b. Feb. 2, 1874, Fayette Co., Ala. Great grandparents - Jim Howard, m. Jane Duckworth; Harvey Sanders, m. Matilda Parker; and Valzy Davis, m. Mary Bobo. 2 Great grandparents - James & Rose Sanders; Billy & Rebecca Parker; Cannon & Sally (Strioland) Davis; and Acie & Harriett (Skelton) Bobo.

BRASHER, Clinton, b. Sept. 28, 1900, Fayette Co., Ala., m. Oct. 17, 1929, Eunice Hubbert, b. Mar. 27, 1911, Fayette Co., Ala. Clinton Brasher's parents - Thomas Brasher, b. Oct. 4, 1878, Fayette Co., Ala., m. Stella Fowler, b. Feb. 21, 1884, Fayette Co., Ala. Grandparents - T. A. Brasher, m. Lira L. Dobbs; and Jine C. Fowler, m. Martha Frances Lowery. Great grandparents - J. Henderson Brasher, m. Rebecca Dyer; Larry & Milisa Dobbs; C. Green & Ziloha (Hollingsworth) Fowler; and F. M. & Mary L. (Laney) Lowery. 2. Great grandparents - Daniel Fowler; John & Mittie (White) Hollingsworth.
  Eunice (Hubbert) Brasher's parents - Belton Hubbert, b. Oct. 28, 1878, m. Dora McCaleb, b. Oct. 8, 18__. Grandparents - Hugh & Bash (Hollingsworth) McCaleb; and Pierce & Julia (Woods) Hubbert. Great Grandparents - George & Lizzie (Stewart) Hubbert; Alf & Mary Ann (McDonald) McCaleb; and Wiley & Janie (McCaleb) Hollingsworth. 2 Great grandparents - John & Mittie (White) Hollingsworth; and Larie & Annie (McCaleb) McCollum. 3 Great grandparents - Jeotha & Phebe White and Jim & Sally McCollum.

Clinton Brasher's children: 1. Max C. Brasher, b. July 20, 1934, Fayette Co., Ala.

BRASHER, Max C., b. July 20, 1934, Fayette Co., Ala., m. Dec. 28, 1953, Patricia Nell Roberts, b. May 13, 1935, - dau. of Joe M. & Sally (McConnell) Roberts. Children: 1. Joseph Max Brasher, b. Aug. 1, 1954.

BRASHER, ___, m. full-blooded Cherokee Indian. Children: 1, Betsy Brasher, m. 1st. Mr. Henderson, 2nd. Mr. Gurley. (Her children by second marriage: Mary Ann; George and Dave Gurley.) 2. Mirendy Brasher, m. 1st. Mr. Garrison, 2nd. Mr. Martin. (Children: Jim and Alice Garrison.) 3. Armendy Brasher, m. Mr. Smith. 4. Polly Brasher, m. Mr. Henderson. (Children: Ora and Huldah Henderson.) 4. Wiley Ann Brasher, m. Mr. Ayers. (Children: Henry; Buck; Tol; Fanny and Orlenia Ayers.) 6. Harriett Brasher, m. Mr. Edmondson. (Children: John; Ellen; Babe; Nancy; and Necty Edmonson.) 7. Huldah Brasher, m. "Jim" James Hilliard Sawyer. 8. "Duck" McCoy Brasher. (Children: Sally and Boyd Brasher) 9. Henry Brasher. (Children: "Big" John; Davey; Jimmy; and Alice Brasher.) 10. William Brasher. (Children: Tack; Drucilla and Caroline Brasher.) 11. Henderson Brasher. (Children: Martha; Babe and Tissue Brasher; "Little" John; Henry and Quill Brasher.)

BROCK, Alfred, m. Mary "Polly" Dodson, b. June 5, 1820, d. Oct. 28, 1908. Children: 1. John W. Brock, d. Jan. 1929. 2. M. M. Brock. 3. James W. Brock. 4. Reuben J. Brock, m. Martha S. Thomas, b. Oct. 15, 1848, Blountsville, Ala., d. Aug. 16, 1922. 5. Horace Brock. 6. Mary Ann Brock, m. 1st. Mr. Nichols, 2nd. P. C. Guin. 7. Lillie Brock, m. Foster Bobo. 8. Americus Hasseltine Brock, m. Tom Lollar. 9. Jane Brock, m. 1st. Mr. Hankins. 2nd. Mr. Corbett.

BROCK, Jackson, b. Dec. 5, 1870, d. May 27, 1947 - son of John W. & Violet V. (Moore) Brock - m. Nov. 17, 1893, Missouri Byrd. Children: 1. Exie Brock. 2. Connie Isadore Brock, b. Oct. 26, 1894, m. July 25, 1915, Felix Austin Brown, b. Jan. 7, 1895, d. Sept. 14, 1958, Fayette, Ala. 3. Charlie Brock, m. Lola Mae Allen. 4. Ila B. Brock, b. Mar. 31, 1908, m. Jan. 1, 1930, Edward C. Mills, b. July 16, 1910. 5. Banks Brock. 6. Vera Brock, m. Parnell Varnon. 7. Edward Brock. 8. Gertrude Brock, m. Joe Norton.

BROCK, John W., b. Oct. 17, 1845, d. Jan. 10, 1929, m. Violet Virginia Moore, dau. of Carson H. & Sarah E. (Davis) Moore. Children: Sarah Alice Brock, b. Nov. 12, 1868, d. Sept. 11, 1874. 2. Jackson Brock, b. Dec. 5, 1870, d. May 27, 1947, m. Nov. 17, 1893, Missouri Lee Byrd

BROCK, Matt, m. Harriet Frances Bobo, b. abt. 1849, Ala. - dau. of Spencer & Polly Bobo. Matt Brock is a merchant and a Primitive Baptist Minister. Children: 1. Mollie Brock, m. Jim Rowland. (Children: Melvin; Sadie and Hattie Brock Rowland.) 2. Luther Brock, m. Donnie Harkins. (Children: Musa Brock, m. Mr. McGee; - Musa has 1 son; - Kara Brock, m. Selma Robertson - Kara has 1 son, Nolan Robertson, m. Betty ___; and 1 dau. Sue Robertson, m. Gene Logan.) 3. Rosa Brock, m. Talmadge Sudduth. (Children: One)

BROCK, R. Toxie, b. April 13, 1884, m. Jan. 14, 1912, Lillie McConnell, b. July 4, 1885, Fayette Co., Ala. - dau. of D.O. & Alice (Smith) McConnell. Children: 1. Mary Brock, b. Mar. 4, 1913, m. Earl Stewart.

BROCK, T. Wilson, b. Feb. 28, 1879, Fayette Co., Ala., d. May 15, 1938, Fay. Co., Ala., m. Nettie Pearl Allen, b. July 15, 1881, Lamar Co., Ala. d. Dec. 3, 1943, Fayette, Ala. - dau. of Geo. W. Allen. Children: 1. Bradley Brock, b. Sept. 15, 1901, d. Feb. 2, 1938. 2. Mae Brock, m. Mr. Dunn. 3. Effie Brock, m. Leslie Berry. 4. Rena Brock. 5. Mary Lee Brock. 6. Leon Brock, m. Dixie ___. 7. Nellie Gray Brock. 8. Naomi Brock, m. Dr. Henry G. Hodo, Jr. 9. Larry Brock, m. Maxine Nix.

BROTHERTON, Frank A., b. Mar. 18, 1840, N.C. (or 1842), d. Feb. 13, 1908 - son of John Brotherton - m. Feb. 19, 1865, Mary Adyline Brent, b. Sept. 2, 1843, Fayette Co., d. Nov. 4, 1925 - dau. of Thomas A. Brent. Mr. Brotherton settled at Hico in Fayette County, near Newtonville, Ala. He served in the Confederate Army of America in Co. I. 1st. Cavalry. Mary A.'s mother was Amelia Bell, a cousin to Holland M. Bell.
    Children of F. A. Brotherton: (All born in Fayette Co.) 1. Ethel Ada Brotherton, b. Dec. 17, 1865, d. Jan. 5, 1905, m. Mar. 14, 1885 Dr. Julious Shelton. 2. J. F. A. "Manie" Brotherton, b. Dec. 29, 1866, m. Edna Johnson. 3. Clyde B. Brotherton, b. May 8, 1868, m. Lula Patterson. 4. Amelia Irma Brotherton, b. Oct. 10, 1870, d. Feb. 23, 1946, m. Harrison Ion Lawley. 5. Monica Adelane "Lovie" Brotherton, b. June 23, 1879, m. Peter Gunter Lawley.

BROTHERTON, J. F. D. "Manie", b. Dec. 29, 1866, Fayette Co., Ala. - son of F. A. Brotherton - m. Edna Johnson. Children: 1. Frank Dewitt Brotherton, b. July 23, 1892, Fayette Co., Ala., d. Mar. 21, 1951, m. Apr. 24, 1917, Sue Bell Green. 2. William Deroy Brotherton, b. Sept. 21, 1893, Kennedy, Ala., m. Mar. 21, 1920, Elizabeth Gross. 3. Adyline De Ila Brotherton, b. Mar. 25, 1895, Fayette, Ala., m. June 16, 1918, Phillip L. Henderson. 4. Clyde Golen Brotherton, b. Jan. 10, 1899, Hico, Fayette Co., Ala., m. May 22, 1920, Marguerite Sheppard, (m. 2nd. Thelma Taylor). 5. Ethel Irma Brotherton, b. Nov. 8, 1900, Hico, Fayette Co., Ala., m. 1st., June 25, 1917, Sherman Hawkins, m. 2nd. Robert Moorefield.

BROWN, Alexander Johnathan, b. Mar. 28, 1861, d. Dec. 5, 1941, m. April 1, 1886, Nancy Angeline "Bunch" Hankins, b. Nov. 30, 1866, d. Mar. 12, 1914. They were married at Vernon, Ala. by A. A. Cobb. Children: (by this first marriage) 1. Golden Hollis Brown, b. Oct. 1, 1887. 2. Sarah Jaridia Caroline "Callie" Brown, b. Oct. 7, 1889, d. Aug. 17, 1952. 3. Mary Lodessa Elizabeth Brown, b. July 25, 1892, m. L. B. Lollar. 4. William Culberson Brown, b. Oct. 10, 1894. 5. Girley Washington Brown, b. June 20, 1897. 6. Charles Alexander Brown, b. June 11, 1900, d. Aug. 21, 1901. 7. Wilkie Lucile Brown, b. Sept. 19, 1902. 8. Knolton Rias Brown, b. Jan. 20, 1906. 9. Choyce Fairchilds Brown, b. Mar. 27, 1909.
    John Alexander Brown's second marriage - Connie (Rasoberry) Brock, b. Jan. 5, 1879 or 1880, d. Dec. 1935. Children: (by second marraige) 1. Jessie Anderson Brown, b. Oct. 20, 1915. 2. Dorothy Mildred Brown, b. Mar. 24, 1917. 3. Infant Son, b. & d. Sept. 1918.

BROWN, Burl, b. 1800, m. Charlotte Langston, b. 1800. Burl Brown came to Fayette County, Ala. from South Carolina. He was a farmer and a trader. Children: 1. John Anderson Brown, b. Sept. 13, 1841, d. July 1916, Fayette Co., Ala., m. June 12, 1860, 1st. Lydia Caroline Barnes, b. Sept. 7, 1841, d. July, 1905, - 2nd. Frances Duckworth, 3rd. Paralee Harris. 2. Rias or Rice Brown, b. Mar. 1832, d. Dec. 19, 1909, m. Feb. 20, 1851, Mary Ann Hawkins, b. Lamar Co., Ala.

BROWN, Felix Auston, b. Jan. 7, 1895, d. Sept. 14, 1958, Fayette, Ala., m. July 25, 1915, Connie Isadore Brock, b. Oct. 26, 1894 - dau. of Jackson & Missouri (Byrd) Brock. Children: 1. Leslie Burleson Brown, b. July 26, 1916, m. Nov. 27, 1936, Mildred Lorene Scroggins. 2. Jewel Banks Brown, b. May 26, 1919, m. Mar. 12, 1939, John Tinsley "Scotty" Young.

BROWN, James M., m. 1853, in Fayette Co., Ala. 1st. Lydia Lansdale, b. 1831, Montgomery Co., Ala., d. 1863, Attala Co., Miss. - dau. of Isaac & Sarah (Gentry-McCool) Lansdale. They were early settlers of Fayette County. Children: 1. William Thomas Brown. 2. Otis Milton Brown, and two daughters.

BROWN, John Anderson, b. Sept. 23, 1841, d. July 1916, m. June 12, 1860, Lydia Caroline Barnes, b. Sept. 7, 1841, d. July, 1905. He was a Freewill Baptist Minister and also served as a C.S.A. Soldier. Children: 1. Alexander Johnathan Brown, b. Mar. 28, 1861, d. Dec. 5, 1941, m. 1st. Nancy Angeline Hankins, b. Nov. 30, 1866, d. Mar. 14, 1914, - 2nd. Connie (Rasberry) Brock. 2. Litha Ann Brown, b. Mar. 10, 1863. 3. Rhoda Charlotte Brown, b. Jan. 4, 1866. 4. William Jasper Brown, b. Dec. 25, 1869, d. 1917. 5. Mary Harriett "Dooner" Brown, b. Feb. 14, 1874. 6. James Rias Brown, b. Nov. 10, 1877. 7. Amanda Bell Brown, b. April 23, 1880, d. 1918. 8. Eliza Catherine Brown, b. Aug. 29, 1882, d. 1955.

John Anderson Brown married - 2nd. 1906, Frances Duckworth - no children. 3rd. 1907 (or 1909), Paralee Harris - children: 1. Nellie Brown. 2. Banks Brown.

BROWN, Rice or Rias, b. Mar. 1832, d. Dec. 19, 1909, - son of Burl & Charlote (Langston) Brown - m. Feb. 20, 1851, Mary Ann Hankins, b. Lamar Co., Ala. - dau. of Richard Hankins. Children: 1. Mary Catherine Brown, b. Mar. 15, 18_, Lamar Co., Ala., d. Oct. 3, 1904, Lamar Co., Ala., m. John Robertson, b. 1854, d. July 13, 1919, Maud, Okla. 2. John W. Brown. 3. Jesse Brown. 4. Burl Brown. 5. Sara Brown. 6. Jane Brown. 7. Angeline Brown. 8. Georgiana Brown. 9. Martha Brown. 10. Dovie Ann Brown.

BRYANT, Ray, b. Mar. 18, 1924, Lamar Co., Ala., m. Dec. 18, 1944, Carrie Nell Bobo, b. Feb. 8, 1922, Fayette Co., Ala. - dau. of F.M. & Eula M. (South) Bobo. Children: 1. Donnis Faye Bryant, b. Feb. 14, 1948, Fayette Co., Ala. 2. Steve Bryant, b. Jan. 25, 1949. 3. Linda Jean Bryant, b. Nov. 26, 1950. 4. Elizabeth Bryant, b. Nov. 15, 1952. 5. Sherry Lee Bryant, b. July 25, 1955. 6. Thomas Ray Bryant, b. July 4, 1958, Fayette, Ala.

BUCKNER, Chris Howard, b. July 19, 1910, Fayette, Ala., m. Mar. 28, 1937, Gwendolyn Lynett Moore, b. Feb. 10, 1917, Kimberly, Ala. Chris H. Buckner's parents - Charlie Marvin Buckner, b. Nov. 27, 1878, St. Clair Co., Ala., m. Malissa Pinkerton, b. May 1, 1882, Covin, Ala. Grandparents - Thomas & Nancy (McClendon) Buckner; and James William Pinkerton, b. Mar. 13, 1855, S.C. m. Francie Narcisses Newman, b. Jan. 4, 1852, Fayette Co., Ala. Great Grandparents - John B. & Mary (Childress) Buckner; Moman & Mariam (Pearson) McLendon; John G. Pinkerton, b. Jan. 16, 1828, m. May Taylor; and Fanton & Julis Cassie (Wilson) Newman.

Gwendolyn Lynett (Moore) Buckner's parents - Coleman Andrew Moore, b. Nov. 29, 1887, Madison, Co., Ala., m. 1914, Gustava Esco, b. Oct. 10, 1898, Shelby Co., Ala. Grandparents - William & Emily Moore; and Willian Sanford Esco, b. Feb. 23, 1865, Oglethorpe Co., Ga., m. Mary Magdalene White, b. Dec. 20,

1863, Prattville, Ala. Great grandparents - James and Mary Ann Esco.

Chris Buckner's Children: 1. Charles Howard Buckner, b. Mar. 13, 1938, Fayette Co., Ala., m. Kathleen Dobbs.

BUCKNER, Thomas R., m. Nancy Ann McClendon. Children: 1. Minerva Jane Buckner, b. Nov. 24, 1858, Blount Co., Ala., d. Sept. 25, 1878. 2. Mattie Chestney Buckner, b. Blount Co., Ala., m. Jan. 6, 1898, by Reb. G. W. Atley, Elijah A. Edwards. 3. Charlie Marvin Buckner, d. 1934, m. July 3, 1901, by Rev. W. L. Rice, Malissa P. Pinkerton. 4. Mamie Evelyn Buckner, b. Nov. 12, 1872, d. Oct. 7, 1950, m. Early W. Wiggins. Both are buried at Mt. Vernon Cem. 5. Ira C. Buckner, d. 1951, m. Nellie Bobo, d. 1958. 6. Allia Itallia Buckner, b. April 19, 1870, Blount Co., Ala., d. June 1, 1956, Fayette, Ala., m. Sept. 29, 1892, John Newton Collins, b. May 2, 1863, Fayette Co., Ala., d. Sept. 25, 1949, Fayette, Ala. 7. Julia Wilson Buckner, m. Jessie Crumley.

BURCH, Allen, m. Stella Gardner - dau. of Jesse Gardner. Children: 1. Edward Gardner Burch. 2. Charles Burch.

BURCHFIELD, (or Birchfield), Elijah, b. 1792, Tenn., m. ?Duntha __, b. 1810, S.C. He was a planter. Children: (Had abt. 13 boys and 2 or 3 girls - 1st 3 listed are known - others from census record.) 1. Lynn Birchfield. 2. Elizabeth Birchfield, b. Aug. 29, 1827, Tenn. d. July 8, 1920, Sulligent, Ala., m. Dec. 1847, Reuben Jackson Comer, b. Sept. 17, 1818, Tenn. d. 1887 Calhoun Co., Ala. 3. Liza Birchfield, m. Mr. Gilchrist. 4. Joseph Birchfield, b. 1840, Ala. 5. Sarah R. Birchfield, b. 1842, Ala. 6. Elijah L. Birchfield, b. 1844, Ala. 7. Hansford Birchfield, b. 1838, Ala. 8. J. B. Birchfield, b. 1825, Ala. 9. Eliza M. Birchfield, b. 1845, Ala. And others.

BURNS, Clester D., b. Feb. 10, 1906, Jefferson Co., Ala., m. Oct. 30, 1930, Amy C. Willis, b. June 10, 1907, Fayette Co., Ala. Clester D. Burns parents - Charlie S. & Bell Zore (Hughes) Burns. Grandparents - Rufus & _(Sweat) Burns.

Amy C. (Willis) Burn's parents - John W. Willis, b. Feb. 1, 1878, Fay. Co. Ala., m. Apr. 25, 1901, Maggie B. Willis, b. Aug. 13, 1885. Grandparents - John F. & Mary J. (Collins) Willis; and William F. & Kitty (Watson) Gilpin. Great grandparents - Jabez & __(Buckner) Willis; Peter F. Gilpin, b. 1830, Ark., m. Essie D. Jones, b. May 23, 1833, Ark; and David R. Watson, b. Sept. 2, 1830, m. Caroline Nation, b. Oct. 29, 1832.

Clester D. Burn's Children: 1. Charles Burns, b. Nov. 21, 1935, Fayette Co., Ala.

BURT, Robert Stephen, b. Sept. 14, 1918, Birmingham, Ala. - son of Stephen Joseph & Lillie (Farr) Burt - m. July 26, 1941, Virginia Barnard, b. Jan. 2, 1919, Fayette, Ala. - dau. of James Hiram & Cora (Williamson) Barnard. They were married at Siluria, Ala., by Rev. W. I. McCarty. Robert Burt is Plant Superintendent of the Habco Southern Textile Co., in Fayette, Ala. Children: 1. Robert Stephen Burt, b. May 8, 1949, Birmingham, Ala. 2. Richard Floyd Burt, b. Aug. 21, 1950, Birmingham, Ala.

BYNUM, James Andrew Strider, m. Arvezenia Roberts. Children: 1. James Chesley Bynum, b. April 28, 1909, Fayette Co., Ala., m. Jan. 13, 1929, Myrtle Humber, b. Sept. 24, 1907, Fayette Co., Ala.

Arvezenia (Roberts) Bynum's parents - Thomas Roberts, b. 1836, Fayette Co., Ala. m. Feb. 26, 1865, Katherine Reese, b. 1837, Fayette Co., Ala. Grandparents - John Roberts, b. S.C., m. Cynthis Chandler, b. S.C.; and John Reese, b. 1806, m. Ruth Woods.

BYNUM, James Chesley, b. Apr. 28, 1909, Fayette Co., Ala. - son of James Andrew Strider & Arvezenia (Roberts) Bynum - m. Jan. 13, 1929, Carrie Myrtle Humber, b. Sept. 24, 1907, Fayette Co., Ala. - dau. of Thos. Bailey & Mary Eliz. (Ballinger) Humber. They were married at the home of J. W. Shelton in Fayette Co., Ala. by Rev. T. W. Shelton. James Chesley Bynum is an automobile mechanic. Children: 1. James Noel Bynum, b. Nov. 16, 1929, Fayette Co., m. Aug. 8, 1953, Martha Stone Clearman, b. Oct. 16, 1929, Lamar Co., Ala. 2. Mary Eunice Bynum, b. April 4, 1932, Fayette Co. 3. Thomas Homer Bynum, b. Apr. 12, 1934, Fayette Co., m. Sept. 6, 1958, Geraldine Moore, b. July 30, 1940, Tusca, Co., Ala. 4. Melva Lee Bynum, b. Feb. 16, 1938, Marion Co., Ala. 5. Carrie Marie Bynum, b. July 10, 1941, Jefferson Co., Ala. 6. Margaret Ann Bynum, b. Jan. 2, 1944, Fayette Co. 7. Martha Elizabeth Bynum, b. Feb. 8, 1946, Fayette, Co. 8. Andrew Bailey Bynum, b. May 16, 1949, Fay. Co., Ala.

BYNUM, James Noel, b. Nov. 16, 1929, Fayette Co., Ala. - son of James Chesley Bynum - m. Aug. 8, 1953, Martha Stone Clearman, b. Oct. 16, 1929, Lamar Co., Ala. - dau. of Wm. Harvey Clearman. They were married at the Union Chapel Church, in Lamar Co., Ala. by Rev. Wm. Clyde Clearman. James Noel is a Farm Implement Dealer. Children: 1. Martha Karen Bynum, b. Mar. 27, 1955, Fayette, Ala. 2. Jimmy Allen Bynum, b. May 20, 1958, Fayette, Ala.

BYNUM, Thomas Homer, b. Apr. 12, 1934, m. Sept. 6, 1958, Geraldine Moore, b. July 30, 1940, Tusca., Co., Ala. Children: 1. Thomas Tyrone Bynum, b. Sept. 8, 1959, Fayette, Ala.

CAINE, Francis Marion, b. Dec. 10, 1833, d. May 26, 1902, m. Susan Maagaret Savage, b. Oct. 6, 1835, Fayette Co., Ala., d. Sept. 7, 1910. Both are buried in the Savage Family Cem. south of Fayette. Children: 1. Margaret M. Caine, b. Nov. 30, 1867, d. Dec. 11, 1880. 2. A. B. Caine, b. Dec. 18, 1871, d. Jan. 1876. 3. Nolia Caine, m. Mr. Williams. 4. Purvey Caine, d. young. 5. Lee Caine, d. young.

CAINE, Joseph Ezra, b. Sept. 20, 1884, Fayette, Ala., d. Oct. 15, 1955, Fayette, Ala. - son of Robert Perry & Sallie (Lindsey) Caine - m. Jan. 18, 1916, Annie Leila Robertson, b. May 12, 1883, Fayette, Ala. - dau. of Joe R. & Malinda (McConnell) Robertson. They were married at the Joe R. Robertson home, by Rev. W. H. Mansfield. Joe E. Caine served as Acting Postmaster, also as a postal clerk in the Fayette Post Office and was Mayor of the City of Fayette at the time of his death. Children: 1. Sarah Katherine Caine, b. Jan. 6, 1918, Fayette, Ala. 2. Jo Ann Caine, b. June 14, 1924, Fayette, Ala., m. Nov. 9, 1946, James Matson Greer, b. Apr. 1, 1923, Anniston, Ala.

CAINE, Robert P., b. Feb. 13, 1850, Walker Co., Ala., d. Nov. 22, 1925 - son of Robert P. Caine - m. Sallie Lindsey - dau. of Levi & Delitha (Douglas) Lindsey. Robert P. Caine moved from Walker Co. to Fayette County, Ala., when he was 18 years of age. He served as chairman of the Democratic Executive Committee of Fayette County at one time. Also, Sheriff of Fayette County -- Postmaster of Fayette, Ala. (1893) - Tax Collector of Fayette County for two terms. Also belonged to Odd Fellows Lodge, Fayette, Ala. Children: 1. Pearl

Caine, b. Dec. 1878, m. May 20, 1884, Arthur A. Gentry, b. Feb. 1871, Texas. 2. Erdeal Caine, m. Raymond Wm. Harris. 3. Robert Ed Caine, b. 1890, d. 1947. 4. J. Fenton Caine, b. 1876, d. 1942. 5. Joe E. Caine, b. Sept. 20, 1884, m. 1916, Annie Robertson. 6. Randolph Caine. 7. Eloise Caine, m. Wm. Al. Parrish.

CALLAHAN, Artemas Killian, b. May 18, 1904, Tuscaloosa, Co., Ala., m. Jan. 10, 1942, Marguerite Tarwater, b. Apr. 19, 1910, Corona, Walker Co., Ala. - dau. of J. T. & Ida (Miles) Tarwater. Mr. Callahan is a lawyer and has served four terms as a Member of the Legislature of Tuscaloosa County, Ala. Mrs. Tarwater is a former teacher. Children: 1. Nancy Miles Callahan, b. Dec. 1, 1946, Tuscaloosa, Ala. 2. Artemas Killian Callahan, Jr., b. Aug. 13, 1949, Tusca., Co., Ala.

CAMERON, Lonnie Gold, b. Sept. 21, 1877, Union Co., Ark., d. Fayette, Ala., m. Feb. 22, 1914, Nancy Belle Hall, b. Feb. 4, 1879, Etta, Ark. He was the son of Robert & Mary Frances (Griffin) Cameron. Nancy Bell Hall was the dau. of J. K. & Emma (Ledsinger) Hall. Children: 1. Emma Jean Cameron, b. Oct. 23, 1914, m. Frank Hubert Jeffries, b. Feb. 14, 1905. 2. Lonnie Glyn Cameron b. July 29, 1919, Rapides Parrish, Long Leaf, La. Glyn served in the United States Air Force from July 1941 until Sept. 1945. 3. James Edward Cameron, b. Oct. 14, 1922, Etta, Ark.

CAMP, Gus L., b. South Alabama, m. Corene Farrow, b. South Alabama. Gus was son of Marion & Sadie(Watson) Camp. Corene was dau. of "Billy" & Amelia (Harris) Farrow. Children: 1. Horace B. Camp, m. Sue McHam. 2. Elaine Camp, m. Guy M. Thompson. 3. Marion Camp, b. June 7, 1921, Franklin Co.,Ala. m. Joe C. McCaleb, Jr., b. Apr. 27, 1919, Fayette Co., Ala.

CAMPBELL, Homer, b. Oct. 23, 1889, Fayette Co., Ala., d. Dec. 24, 1942, Fay. Ala. - son of A. J. & Susan (Kitchens) Campbell - m. Feb. 2, 1911, Emma Jones, b. Aug. 14, 1891, Fayette Co., Ala. - dau. of Jas. Wm. Rily & Mary Ella (Stacks) Jones. Children: 1. William Homer Campbell, b. Oct. 23, 1912, Fay. Ala., m. Sept. 9, 1934, Grace Tigett. 2. Joe Oliver Campbell, b. Jan. 31, 1915, Fayette, Ala., m. May 12, 1939, Jewel Young. 3. Richard Holmes Campbell, b. June 14, 1920, Fayette, Ala., m. June 12, 1938, Inez Shepherd.

CAMPBELL, Joe Oliver, b. Jan. 31, 1915, Fayette, Ala. - son of Homer & Emma (Jones) Campbell - m. May 12 or 15, 1939, Jewel Adele Young, b. Aug. 17, 1915, Fayette, Ala. - dau. of Dr. Jas. D. & Effie (Humber) Young. They were married at Fayette, Ala. Joe is a jeweler and a merchant. Children: 1. Joe Young Campbell, b. Apr. 20, 1940, Fayette, Ala. 2. James Alan Campbell, b. July 15, 1945, Fayette, Ala.

CAMPBELL, Walter W., b. Feb. 2, 1886, Fayette Co., Ala. - son of Harmon & Rebecca Jane (Watkins) Campbell - m. 1906, Julia Powell, b. April 26, 1891, Fayette Co., Ala. - dau. of Joseph & Elizabeth (Hawkins) Powell. (Elizabeth Hawkins was b. 1859.) Children: 1. Flora Edna Campbell, b. Feb. 29, 1908, Fayette, Ala., m. May 13, 1933, Wm. Ausborn Younghance, b. June 5, 1912, Lamar Co., Ala. There were several other children in the family of Walter W. Campbell.

    Walter Campbell's grandparent's were - Joseph & Suzie (Abernathy) Campbell and John Pinkney & Carline (Novis) Watkins.

CANNON, Alby Wayne, b. Jan. 21, 1872, Tusca. Co., Ala. - son of Joseph Cannon - m. Feb. 5, 1902, Kate Savage, b. Dec. 13, 1881, Fayette Co., Ala. - dau. of Thomas Dudley Savage. Children: 1. George Lorron Cannon, b. Jan. 9, 1903, m. Lois Williamson. 2. Rissie Lucile Cannon, b. June 22, 1904, m. Clarence C. Crowe (A son - Ray Crowe.) 3. Frankine Cannon, b. Feb. 14, 1906, m. Claud Taylor. 4. "Ted" Joseph Roosevelt Cannon, b. Dec. 10, 1907, d. Feb. 8, 19__. 4. Lula Delilah Cannon, m. Burton Rice. (Had 4 children.) 5. Percy Quinton "Bud" Cannon, b. Aug. 20, 1913, Fayette Co., Ala., d. 1959, Fayette, Ala., m. Victoria Lorene Williamson, b. 1916, Berry, Ala. (Had 6 children. His death May 13.) 6. Thomas Fay "Tim" Cannon, b. Feb. 26, 1916, m. Leota Hollman. (1 child - Doria Fay Cannon, m. George Bagwell and has 2 sons.)

CANNON, Dr. Claude Clenton, b. April 11, 1890, Fayette Co., Ala., m. Aug. 19, 1920, Rosalie Mathes, b. Nov. 19, 1898, Portsmouth, Va. - dau. of Samuel Rhea & Kathleen (Hozier) Mathes.. They were married at Birmingham, Ala. by Rev. Bryan. Dr. Cannon is a Dentist. Children: 1. Claude C. Cannon, Jr., b. Oct. 26, 1921, Fayette, Ala., d. June 29, 1923, Fayette, Ala. 2. Kathleen Jane Cannon, b. July 13, 1924, Fayette, Ala., m. Milton Dewitt Anderson, Jr.

CANNON, Curtis - son of M. F. Cannon - m. Fannie Cole. Children: 1. Willard D. Cannon, m. Marlyn Motley. (Children: June & Billie Cannon.) 2. Charles C. Cannon, m. Charline Smith. (Child: Charles Cannon.) 3. Nell Cannon, m. 1st. Sam Gay, 2nd. John Cranford. (Children: 1st. Husband - 1. Sammie Nell Gay - by 2nd husband - 1. Michael & 2. Elisia Cranford.) 4. Earl Cannon, m. Shirley Garner. (Child: Charlotte Cannon.)

CANNON, Isaac, b. Apr. 19, 1792, d. Feb. 12, 1885, m. Oct. 10, 1816, Sarah Barbee, b. Oct. 14, 1799, d. Feb. 5, 1860 - dau. of James & Sarah Martin Barbee. According to articles in the Birmingham News (Mar. 29, 1953) and Birmingham Age-Herald (April 6, 1941) Isaac Cannon and John Wilson, in 1815 established the first white settlement in what in now Tuscaloosa County. They selected the site near the old Indian field at Seminole Fort, near the present site of Tuscaloosa. Isaac and John came on horseback from Sedula, No. Caro. (12 miles from Hendersonville) and soon other pioneers were coming from Georgia, the Carolinas, Virginia and Kentucky. Isaac Cannon's wife, Sarah Barbee is believed to have come to Tuscaloosa with her parents, James and Sarah Martin Barbee, in 1816, from South Carolina. Barbee School and Barbee Creek (near New Lexington) were named for the family. Isaac Cannon was one of the founders of the New River Baptist Association - the first church group in the area. He received a land grant, was a planter and owned Negro slaves. Both Isaac and Sarah Cannon are buried in the Boone Cemetery, New Lexington, Ala. Children: 1. Keziah Cannon, b. Sept. 12, 1817, m. Mr. Waters. 2. Rebecca Cannon, b. Dec. 29, 1819, m. Mr. Mead. 3. Thomas Sidney Cannon, b. June 15, 1821, Tuscaloosa Co., Ala., d. Jan. 4, 1890, Fayette Co., Ala., m. Mary Elon Morrow, b. June 12, 1836, d. June 26, 1903, Fayette Co., Ala. 4. Lucinda Cannon, b. Nov. 1, 1823, m. Mr. Gilliam. 5. Matilda Cannon, b. Mar. 20, 1825. 6. Nancy Cannon, b. Dec. 19, 1826, m. Jackson Olive. 7. Susan Cannon, b. June 1, 1829. 8. Sarah Cannon, b. Oct. 20, 1830. 9. Newton Cannon, b. Dec. 25, 1832. 10. Mary Cannon, b. Dec. 21, 1834. 11. Elijah Wiley Barbee Cannon, b. April 9, 1838, m. Sallie Morris. 12. Catherine Cannon, b. June 12, 1840, m. Lou Rice. 13. Joseph Cannon, b. April 4, 1842, m. Eliza Kelley.

CANNON, James Leonadis, b. 1857, Fayette Co., Ala., d. 1922, Fayette, Ala. - son of Thos. Sidney & Mary Elon (Morrow) Cannon - m. Ida Talitha Eason, b. 1861, Fayette Co., Ala., d. 1932, Fayette, Ala. - dau. of Harrison Eason. James L. Cannon was a merchant. He and his wife are buried in Fayette, Ala. Children: 1. Mary Elon Cannon, b. 1880, Fayette Co., Ala., m. Gather Van Diver. 2. Sam Cannon, b. 1883, Fayette Co., Ala., m. Wilda Coggins. 3. Annie Cannon, b. 1885, Fayette Co. 4. Joe Norman Cannon, b. 1888, Fayette Co. d. 1924, Fayette, Ala., m. Vernette Young. 5. Claude Clenton Cannon, b. Apr. 11, 1890, Fayette Co., m. Rosalie Mathes. 6. John Bankhead Cannon, b. 1898, Fayette Co., d. Fayette, Ala., m. Hollie Hearn. 7. James Ethel Cannon, b. 1901, Fayette Co., m. Morris Sumrall. 8. Miriam Cannon, b. 1904, Fayette Co. m. James H. Banks.

CANNON, Melville Fortescue, b. Oct. 2, 1851, Fayette, Co., Ala., d. May 2, 1921, Berry, Ala. - son of Thos. Sidney Cannon - m. July 5, 1871, Melissa Bobo, b. Nov. 18, 1852, Fayette Co., Ala. d. Dec. 25, 1918, Berry, Ala. Melville Cannon established one of the first mercantile businesses in Berry, Ala. soon after the first railroad came through Fayette County in the early 1880's. Both M. F. & Melissa are buried at the City Cemetery, Fayette, Ala. Children: 1. Willie Cannon, b. June 24, 1872, Fayette Co., Ala., d. Jan. 23, 1915, m. Oct. 4, 1899, Ada Howell. 2. Essie Cannon, b. Oct. 30, 1873, d. June 8, 1934, m. Mar. 14, 1894, Charlie Batson. 3. Murray Cannon, b. Dec. 28, 1874, Fayette Co., Ala., d. Dec. 24, 1939, m. June 20, 1900, 1st. - Leila Lindsey, d. May 20, 1917 - 2nd. Birdie Smith. 4. Snow Cannon, d. July 8, 1927, Berry, Ala., m. Dec. 19, 1906, May Davis. 5. Dean Cannon, b. April 15, 1879, d. Aug. 10, 1880. 6. Lula Cannon, m. John H. Shepherd. 7. Theron Cannon, b. Mar. 2, 1883, Fayette Co., Ala., m. Nov. 28, 1911, Mary Narcissa Jones, b. Dec. 20, 1894, Berry, Ala. 8. Vera Cannon, m. 1st. Marvin Jones, 2nd. Dean Collins. 9. Curtis Cannon, m. Fannie Cole. 10. Henry Cannon, m. Emily Burleson.

CANNON, Murray, b. Dec. 28, 1874, d. Dec. 24, 1938, Birmingham, Ala. - son of M. F. Cannon - m. June 20, 1900, Lila Lindsey, b. May 20, 1917. Children: 1. Melville Cannon. 2. Wilmer Cannon. 3. Katheryn Cannon, m. in New York, Bert Cabral - (Child: Calby Cabral).

CANNON, Sidney Jefferson, b. Nov. 25, 1861, Ala., d. June 10, 1924, Fayette Co., Ala. - son of Thomas Sidney & Mary Elon (Morrow) Cannon - m. Oct. 9, 1889, Lula Ann Harvey, b. Jan. 24, 1868, d. May 2, 1940, Fayette Co., Ala. - dau. of Dr. Lewis Clay & Virginia Carline (Kidd) Harvey. They were married at Weaver Station, Ala. by Rev. John Spence. Sidney Jefferson Cannon entered the business of his father (Cannon & Co.) at an early age. In 1883, he sold his interest in the store back to his family, and ourchased the Philip's Drug Store (Fayette's first Drug Store). Sidney Jefferson operated the S. J. Cannon Drug Co. for forty years, retiring at 62 years of age.

Lula Alma Harvey, wife of Sidney Jefferson Cannon, was educated at the Mississippi State College for Women, Columbus, Miss. She was a member of the Fayette Chapter of the U. D. C. Virginia Caroline Kidd (mother of Lula Harvey Cannon and wife of Dr. Lewis Clay Harvey) was the dau. of John B. Kidd & Narcissus Ward Kidd. John B. Kidd was the son of William & Zilpa (Kimbrough) Kidd. Before coming to Columbus, Miss. the Kidd family resided in Tenn.

Dr. Lewis Clay Harvey, father of Lula Harvey Cannon, served in the 10th Miss. Regt. during the Civil War. Dr. Harvey was educated at the Tulane

University School of Medicine. Dr. Lewis Clay Harvey was the son of Joseph Anderson and Ann (England) Harvey. Joseph Anderson Harvey (son of an American Revolutionary War Soldier from Oglethorpe, Ga.) received an original land grant on the Tombigbee River and erected a home near Forreston, Miss. The home is now owned by Ann Sourlock, a descendant. Children of S. J. Cannon -. 1. Infant Son, b. Aug. 29, 1891, Fayette Co., Ala., d. Aug. 29, 1891, Fayette Ala. 2. Sidney Jefferson Cannon, Jr., b. Dec. 27, 1896, Fayette, Ala., d. Nov. 10, 1945, Fayette, Ala. 3. Thomas Harvey Cannon, b. Aug. 17, 1898, Fayette, Ala., d. Aug. 11, 1952, Fayette, Ala., m Oct. 25, 1922, Margaret Irene Higgins, b. Oct. 29, 1901, Booneville, Ind. 4. Elmer Morrow Cannon, b. Dec. 12, 1900, Fayette, Ala., d. Feb. 10, 1940, Fayette, Ala., m. June 19, 1930, Johnnye Dodson. b. Fayette, Ala.

CANNON, Snow, b. Fayette Co., Ala., d. July 8, 1927, Berry, Ala., m. Dec. 19, 1906, May Davis. He was the son of M. F. Cannon. Children: 1. Mirian Cannon, m. Gus Anders. 2. Emma Snow Cannon. 3. Frank Cannon, m. Pat__. 4. Bill Cannon, m. Helen ___.

CANNON, Terrell F., b. Jan. 21, 1900, Fayette Co., Ala. - son of John & Matilda (Davis) Cannon - m. Jan. 1, 1927, Alma Sherer, b. Sept. 6, 1901, Fayette Co., Ala. - dau. of Ira E. & Lillian (Matthews) Sherer. Children: 1. Albert S. Kizzire (Son of Alma Cannon) b. Aug. 2, 1921, Fayette, Co., Ala. m. Lila Roberson, b. Mar. 19, 1925, Eldridge, Ala. 2. Kathleen Sherer Cannon, b. Oct. 23, 1927, Fayette, Ala., m. Dec. 5, 1953, Richard Randolph Thomson, b. Jan. 9, 1928, Brownville, Ala. 3. Terrell Fenton Cannon, Jr., b. Aug. 26, 1929, Fayette Co., Ala., d. June 12, 1942, Drowned at Tuscaloosa, Ala.

CANNON, Theron, b. Mar. 2, 1883, Fayette Co., Ala., m. Nov. 28, 1911, Mary Narcissa Jones, b. Dec 20, 1884, Berry, Ala. - dau. of B. E. & Mollie Ann (Thompson) Jones. Children: 1. Laura Mae Cannon, b. Oct. 26, __, m. Dec. 22, 1941, Arch Pulliam, b. Oct. 10, ___, Ky. 2. Melbourne Fortescue Cannon, b. Aug. 7, 1916, Berry, Ala., d. May 16, 1943, Ft. Worth, Texas. (Second Lt. in World War II - was chief of the inspection department of the quarter-master division.) 3. Rosemary Cannon, b. Aug. 15, 1918, Berry, Ala., d. June 27, 1922, Berry, Ala. 4. Bennie Jones Cannon, b. Jan. 29, 1929, Berry, Ala., m. Aug. 31, 1949, Jack Merrill Nolen, b. Feb. 20, 1925, Ashland, Ala.

CANNON, Thomas Harvey, b. Aug. 17, 1898, Fayette, Ala., d. Aug. 11, 1952, Fayette, Ala. - son of Sidney Jefferson & Lula Alma (Harvey) Cannon - m. Oct. 25, 1922, Margaret Irene Higgins, b. Oct. 29, 1901, Booneville, Ind. - dau. of Samuel Patrick & Rosa Lillian (Rice) Higgins. Thomas Harvey Cannon, son of Sidney Jefferson and Lula Harvey Cannon, attended the Univ. of Ala. and served in the U. S. Army near the end of World War I. In 1922 Thomas Harvey Cannon opened a general mercantile business in Fayette. He operated the Thomas H. Cannon Store until the death of his brother, Sidney J. Cannon, Jr. in 1945, at which time he became the owner of Cannon Drug Co. Thomas Harvey Cannon ran the Cannon Drug Co. until his death in Aug. 1952. The Thomas Harvey Cannons were married at Fayette, Ala. by Rev. Joe I. Williams. Children: 1. Thomas Harvey Cannon, Jr., b. July 1, 1927, Fayette, Ala. 2. Robert Higgins Cannon, b. June 9, 1929, Fayette, Ala.

CANNON, Thomas Sidney, b. June 15, 1821, Tuscaloosa Co., Ala., d. Jan. 4, 1890, Fayette Co., Ala. - son of Isaac & Sarah (Barbee) Cannon - m. Mary Elon

Morrow, b. June 12, 1836, d. June 26, 1903, Fayette Co., Ala. - dau. of James Morton & Catherine White Peden Morrow. Thomas Sidney Cannon, oldest son of Isaac and Sarah Barbee Cannon, moved to Fayette from Tuscaloosa and opened a mercantile business, known as Cannon and Company in "Old Town". As each of his sons was old enough he took them as partners. Melville F. Cannon sold his interest back to the business and moved to Berry, Ala. where he opened a mercantile business (now know as Theron Cannon & Co.). Sidney J. Cannon sold his interest and bought the Philips Drug Co. (Fayette's first Drug Store). James L. and William Morrow Cannon purchased Cannon and Company from the other stock holders and operated as a partnership until James L. sold out to William Morrow Cannon. Thomas Sidney Cannon was a confederate soldier. Children: 1. Melville Fortescue Cannon, b. Oct. 2, 1851, d. May 2, 1920, Fayette Co., Ala, m. July 5, 1871, Melissa Bobo, b. Nov. 18, 1852, d. Dec. 25, 1918, Fayette Co., Ala. 2. John M. Cannon, b. May 3, 1854, d. Oct. 9, 1856, Fayette, Ala. 3. James Leonadus Cannon, b. 1857, Fayette Co., Ala., d. 1922, Fayette, Ala., m. Ida Talitha Eason, b. 1861, Fayette Co., Ala., d. 1932, Fayette, Ala. 4. Samuel I. Cannon, b. Feb. 17, 1859, d. Nov. 13, 1883, Fayette Co., Ala., 5. Sidney Jefferson Cannon, b. Nov. 25, 1861, d. June 10, 1924, Fayette Co., Ala. m. Oct. 9, 1889, Lula Alma Harvey, b. Jan. 24, 1868, d. May 2, 1940, Fayette Co., Ala. 6. William Morrow Cannon, b. Mar. 15, 1865, d. May 8, 1933, Fayette Co., Ala., m. Mary Jane Humber, b. Nov. 29, 1874, d. Aug. 16, 1932, Fayette Co., Ala. William Morrow Cannon served as a state representative from Fayette Co., Ala. His uncle Robert Jefferson Morrow represented Fayette County from 1838 - 1839. 7. Carrie Waters Cannon, b. April 22, 1870, Fayette Co., Ala., d. Aug. 22, 1938, Fayette Co., Ala., m. Oct. 16, 1889, Henry Belton Propst, b. May 13, 1854, Pickens Co., Ala., d. Aug. 3, 1931, Fayette Co., Ala. 8. Jennie M. Cannon, b. Dec. 22, 1872, d. Oct. 7, 1883, Fayette Co., Ala. 9. Sarah Catherine Cannon, d. San Benito, Texas, m. Richard Collins, d. San Benito, Texas.

CANNON, William Louis, b. Mar. 1, 1898, Fayette, Ala., d. Oct. 25, 1953, m. Aug. 12, 1920, Ruby Jeffries, b. Oct. 19, 1897, Fayette, Ala. He was the son of Wm. Morrow & Mary Jane (Humber) Cannon. She was the dau. of Francis M. & Mary Idelia (Morton) Jeffries. They were married in Fayette, Ala. by Judge H. M. Bell. Children: 1. Della Jane Cannon, b. Oct. 19, 1923, Fayette, Ala. m. Max Clellon Oswalt, b. July 12, 1922, Fayette Co., Ala. 2. Betty Ann Cannon, b. Sept. 5, 1927, Fayette, Ala., m. Carey Norman Pollard, b. Aug. 6, 1927, Fayette, Ala.

CANNON, William Morrow, b. Mar. 15, 1865, d. May 8, 1933, Fayette Co., Ala. son of Thos. Sidney & Mary Elon Morrow Cannon - m. Mary Jane Humber, b. Nov. 29, 1874, d. Aug. 16, 1932, Fayette Co., Ala. Children: 1. William Louis Cannon, b. Mar. 1, 1898, Fayette, Ala., d. Oct. 25, 1953, m. Aug. 12, 1920, Ruby Jeffries, b. Oct. 19, 1897, Fayette, Ala. 2. Wightman Cannon, m. Isabel Nuckols.

CANNON, Willie, b. June 24, 1872, Fayette Co., Ala., d, Jan. 23, 1915, m. Oct. 4, 1899, Ada Howell. Willie was the son of Melville Cannon. Children: 1. Marguerite Cannon, m. Joe Hankins. (Children: June Ann Hankins, m. Morris Hayes.) 2. Anna Jane Cannon, m. Alton Hamrick. (Children: Alton Hamrick, Jr., and Russell Cannon Hamrick.)

CARGILE, Alfred, wife's name unknown, came to Fayette County, Ala. from Spartanburg, S. C. during the childhood of their sons. Children: 1. George Cargile. 2. Ruben Cargile. 3. William Cargile.

CARGILE, Clyde Chandler, b. Dec. 16, 1908, Fayette Co., Ala., - son of T.C. & L.J. (Brock) Cargile - married April 23, 1932, Lottie Mavis Collins, b. July 31, 1909, Fayette Co., Ala. - dau. of H. D. & M. O. (Harkins) Collins. Judge and Mrs. Cargile were married at the Mt. Vernon Methodist Parsonage, Fayette, Ala., by Rev. A. S. Osborn. Both are teachers. Judge Cargile served as the Supt. of Education prior to becoming Judge of Probate of Fayette County in 1954. Children: 1. Wayne Chandler Cargile, b. Jan. 16, 1933, Fayette Co., Ala. 2. Ned Collins Cargile, b. Aug. 22, 1934, Fayette Co., Ala. 3. Lucy Mavis Cargile, b. Feb. 20, 1944, Fayette Co., Ala. 4. Barney Ray Cargile, b. Feb. 10, 1945, Fayette County, Ala.

CARGILE, Delbert, b. July 24, 1911, Fayette Co., Ala., m. May 25, 1940, Buell Raley. Children: 1. Delbert Cargile, Jr. b. Dec. 27, 1941. 2. Jimmie Cargile, b. Aug. 3, 1945. 3. Nancy Cargile, b. Nov. 5, 1948.

CARGILE, George, - son of Alfred Cargile - m. Julia Miles, b. July 16, 1852, - dau. of Wiley M. & Rebecca Miles. Children: 1. Wiley Cargile, b. Feb. 28, 1875, Fayette Co., Ala., d. Mar. 29, 1945, m. Dec. 20, 1900, Cora Collins, b. Mar. 14, 1881, Fayette Co., Ala. 2. Tolliver C. Cargile, b. June 6, 1878, Fayette Co., Ala., m. Nov. 23, 1902, Lucy Jane Brock, b. Nov. 8, 1884, Lamar Co., Ala. 3. Stacy Cargile. 4. Rachel Cargile. 5. Frank Cargile. 6. Ottis Cargile. 7. Climmie Cargile.

CARGILE, Leland, b. Dec. 6, 1906, Fayette Co., Ala. m. Nov. 14, 1937, Virginia Jones. Children: 1. Terry Cargile, b. May 10, 1941. 2. Betty Cargile, b. Jan. 29, 1946.

CARGILE, Tolliver C., b. June 6, 1878, Fayette Co., Ala., m. Nov. 23, 1902, Lucy Jane Brock, b. Nov. 8, 1884, Lamar Co., Ala. Mr. & Mrs. T. C. Cargile were married at Covin, Ala. by Rev. M. M. Brock, Methodist Minister. Children. 1. Roy Clifton Cargile, b. June 3, 1904, Lamar Co., Ala. 2. Mary Elvie Cargile, b. July 29, 1906, Fayette, Co., Ala. 3. Clyde Chandler Cargile, b. Dec. 16, 1908, Fayette Co., Ala., m. April 23, 1932, Lottie Mavis Collins, b. July 31, 1909, Fayette Co., Ala. 4. Robert Matison Cargile, b. July 14, 1911, Fayette Co., Ala. 5. Eunice Pearl Cargile, b. Dec. 11, 1913, Fayette Co., Ala. d. Nov. 14, 1942, m. Edward Hankins. 6. Barney C. Cargile, b. Aug. 27, 1916, Fayette Co., Ala., d. Feb. 20, 1944, Anzio, Italy. Barney C. Cargile was a Lt. in the U. S. Navy and was killed in battle at Anzio, Italy. 7. Horace Lee Cargile, b. May 15, 1919, Fayette Co., Ala. 8. Annie Gertrude Cargile, b. June 24, 1923, Fayette Co., Ala.

CARGILE, Wiley, b. Feb. 28, 1875, Fayette Co., Ala., d. Mar. 29, 1945, Fay. Co., Ala., m. Dec. 20, 1900, Cora Collins, b. Mar. 14, 1881, Fayette Co., Ala. Wiley Cargile was a farmer and a member of the Board of Education of Fayette County for fourteen years. Children: 1. Verna Cargile, b. Feb. 19, 1903, Fayette Co., Ala. (A teacher.) 2. Voncile Cargile, b. Feb. 6, 1905, Fayette Co., Ala., (Teacher) m. April 4, 1931, Ben Hutto. 3. Leland Cargile, b. Dec. 6, 1906, Fayette Co., Ala. (Public Works), m. Nov. 14, 1937, Virginia Jones. 4. Lillian Cargile, b. Aug. 28, 1909, Fayette Co., Ala. (Store Clerk) m. Aug. 14, 1927, Valford Roberts. 5. Delbert Cargile, b. July 24, 1911, Fayette Co.,

Ala., (Public Works) m. May 25, 1940, Buell Raley. 6. Margie Cargile, b. Feb. 17, 1914, Fayette Co., Ala. (Store Clerk). 7. Cecil Cargile, died in infancy.

CARGILE, William Thelma, b. Mar. 7, 1914, Fayette, Ala., m. Jan. 25, 1941 at Columbus, Miss, Sarah Pauline Abbott, b. Mar. 2, 1924, Fayette, Ala. Wm. T. Cargile is the son of Wm. Franklin & Edie (Dudley) Cargile. Sarah Pauline is the dau. of Lonnie B. & Wilma T. (Dodson) Abbott. Children: 1. James Wm. Cargile, b. Feb. 27, 1942, Calidonia, Miss. 2. Jack Taranes Cargile, b. Nov. 9, 1952, Moline, Ill.

CASTELLAW, James, d. abt. 1745, N. C., m. Sarah Williams, dau. of John Williams. Children: 1. William Castellaw. 2. John Castellaw. 3. James Castellaw. 4. Thomas Castellaw. 5. Bethiah Castellaw, b. 1710, m. 1728, Rev. John Alexander, b. 1703, Mecklenburg, N. C. 6. Sarah Castellaw. 7. Katherine Castellaw. James Castellaw of Bertie Precinct was prominent in the early history of North Carolina. His name first appears in the N. C. records in 1718. It was in Bertie that his services to the Colony were rendered.

CHAMBERS, Oscar Lee, b. Feb. 4, 1871, Colbert Co., Ala., d. Sept. 13, 1953, Sheffield, Ala. - son of James Burleson Chambers - m. Mary Lula McRight, b. Franklin Co., Ala., d. Nov. 1913, Franklin Co., Ala. Oscar Lee Chambers was a teacher. Children: 1. Anna Lee Chambers, b. Mar. 31, 1903, Jacksonville, Ala., m. James Dorsey Young, b. Aug. 14, 1902, Fayette, Ala. 2. Lucille Chambers, b. April 15, 1905, Ashville, Ala., d. April 16, 1958, m. Benjamin Franklin Joyce. 3. O. L. Chambers, Jr., b. Dec. 7, 1907, Ashville, Ala., m. Mattie Lott.

CHANDLER, Joe, b. Jan. 7, 1846, Cullman, Ala., d. April 30, 1888, Cullman, Ala. - son of Shade Chandler - m. Catherine Abbott, b. Jan. 10, 1846, Cullman, Ala., d. Nov. 15, 1927, Cullman, Ala. - dau. of Willis & Sis (Davis) Abbott. Children: 1. Dave Chandler, b. Sept. 7, 1881, Cullman, Ala., m. Mar. 6, 19__, Arvie Summerford, b. May 6, 1881, Marion Co., Ala., d. Mar. 6, 1954, Hamilton, Ala. (Arvie Summerford was the dau. of Billy & Sis (Sanderson) Summerford. Dave and Arvie Summerford Chandler's children were - 1. Woodie Chandler, b. Mar. 6, 1920, Marion Co., Ala., m. Annie Bell Kerr, b. May 1, 1919, Itawamba Co., Miss. Woodie and Annie Bell Kerr Chandler had a child - Juanita Chandler, b. Sept. 10, 1942, Marion Co., Ala.)

CHANDLER, Joe Palmer, b. May 31, 1920, Fayette, Ala. - son of Roy Luther & Florence Virginia (Rogers) Chandler - m. May 16, 1947, Bettye Nell Abele, b. April 12, 1924, Birmingham, Ala. - dau. of Elmer Franklin & Nellie Gray (Durham) Abele. They were married at Birmingham, Ala. by Rev. J. H. Chitwood. Joe is affiliated with the Fayette Insurance Agency. Bettye is affiliated with the Dept. of Pensions and Security. Children: 1. Margaret Nell Chandler, b. Oct. 4, 1955, Fayette, Ala.

CHANDLER, Joseph Edward, b. 1857, Carroll Co., Ga., d. 1929, Fayette Co., Ala. m. 1st. Lula Herring, b. Carroll Co., Ga., d. 1888, Carroll Co., Ga. - dau. of Sam & Frances (Chambers) Herring. Children: (by first marriage) 1. Merta Chandler, b. July 1884, Coweta Co., Ga., m. Louis Drake, b. Coweta Co., Ga. 2. Roy Luther Chandler, b. Feb. 12, 1887, Coweta Co., Ga., m. Aug. 14, 1914, Florence Virginia Rogers, b. Mar. 29, 1893, Talladega Co., Ala.

Joseph Edward Chandler married - 2nd. Ora Taylor, b. 1871, Ga., d. 1930. Children: (by second marriage) 1. Stella Chandler, b. 1893, Coweta Co., Ga., d. 1941, Fayette Co., Ala., m. T. C. Long. 2. Joe Edward Chandler, b. July 29, 1890, Coweta Co., Ga., d. Sept. 25, 1957, buried Fayette, Ala., m. Deloris Jatley, b. Walker Co., Ala.

CHANDLER, Roy Luther, b. Feb. 12, 1887, Coweta Co., Ga. - son of Joseph Edward & Lula (Herring) Chandler - m. Aug. 14, 1914, Florence Virginia Rogers, b. Mar. 29, 1893, Talladega, Co., Ala. - dau. of Henry Palmer & Willie Alice (Taliferro) Rogers. They were married at Talladega, Ala. by Rev. Frank Bell Webb. Mr. Roy L. Chandler is a retired rural mail carrier, having served the longest time of any rural carrier in the county. His route was No. 3 and at one time the longest route according to mile, in the state. Children: 1. Alice Chandler, b. Jan. 29, 1915, Talladega, Ala., m. June __, Rogers Tubbs, b. Dec. 24, 1915, Moundville, Ala. 2. Roy L. Chandler, Jr., b. May 15, 1916, Fayette, Ala. 3. Eleanor Chandler, b. Oct. 7, 1918, Fayette, Ala., m. Mar. 13, William Thomas Graves, b. June 1910, Demopolis, Ala. 4. Joe Palmer Chandler, b. May 31, 1920, Fayette, Ala., m. May 16, 1947, Bettye Abele, b. Apr. 12, 1924, Birmingham, Ala. 5. Carolyn Chandler, b. June 18, 1926, Fayette, Ala., m. July 10, 1943, Horace E. Berry, Jr., b. May 19, 1925, Fayette, Ala.

CHAPMAN, John, b. possibly Va., m. Mary T. Dodson. John Chapman was a soldier in the American Revolution and served as a member of Virginia Reg. He received bounty money for service with Capt. Hoggs Co., Virginia Col. Militia (page 118 by Crozier). Both are buried in Spartanburg Co., S. C. and his will is recorded in Spartanburg Co., in Will Book D., Page 456. John Chapman came to South Carolina between 1790 and 1795. Children: Elizabeth Chapman, b. Dec. 23, 1790, Philadelphia, Pa., d. Nov. 15, 1856, m. Moses Richardson, b. June 7, 1780, probably Amelie Co., Va., d. Jan. 25, 1851. (Both are buried in Spartanburg Co., S. A.) 2. Beverly Chapman, m. Sallie Foster.

CHISM, Grady William, b. Dec. 16, 1895, Fayette Co., Ala., d. May 29, 1958, Fayette, Ala., m. Mary "Madie" Moore, b. May 23, 1898, Fayette Co., Ala., d. May 23, 1946, Fayette, Ala. Children: 1. James Daniel Chism, b. Sept. 15, 1916, d. June 10, 1917. 2. Grady William Chism, b. Fayette Co., Ala. 3. Edith Chism, b. Fayette Co., Ala. (Child: Pamela Adams.)

CHISM, J. W. "Bill", d. Paris, Texas, m. Oct. 9, 1890, Lela Isabell Dickinson, b. Nov. 29, 1871, Fayette Co., Ala., d. Mar. 21, 1931, Paris, Texas - dau. of Rev. J.P. & Martha Frances (Hassell) Dickinson. J. W. Chism was a school teacher and a farmer. Children: 1. Floy Chism, b. Aug. 27, 1891, Fayette Co., Ala. 2. Purvy Lee Chism, b. Aug. 27, 1893, Fayette Co., Ala. 3. Grady William Chism, b. Dec. 16, 1895, Fayette Co., Ala., d. May 29, 1958, Fayette, Ala., m. Mary "Madie" Moore, b. May 23, 1898, d. May 23, 1946. (Both are buried at Caines Ridge Cem., Fayette Co., Ala.) 4. Lillie Chism, b. 1897 Fayette Co., Ala., m. Marion Hamrick. 5. Lena Dane Chism (Infant) b. Dec. 8, 1899, Fayette Co., Ala. d. Jan. 29, 1901. 6. Samuel Chism, m. Gladys __. 7. J. Mich Chism, m. Ollie Bell. 8. Thomas Doss Chism, b. May 22, 1906, Fayette Co., Ala., m. July 17, 1930, Mattie Lou Sudduth. 9. Annie Lois Chism, m. C. B. Neely. 10. Ruth Chism, b. Fayette Co., Ala., m. Roy Mack.

CLEARMAN, Worth Burness, m. May 18, 1924, Mamie Beuma Nichols, b. July 23, 1900, Fayette, Ala. - dau. of A. C. Nichols. Children: 1. Ellen Clearman, b. Oct. 8, 1925. 2. Worth Burness "Sonny" Clearman, b. April 17, 1928.

CLEMMONS, Jim, m. Lou Mandie Madison. Children: 1. Catherine Clemmons, b. Mar. 6, 1872, Tenn. m. W. T. Madison, b. Oct. 16, 1871, Walker Co., Ala. 2. Susie Clemmons. 3. Mandie Clemmons. 4. Fayette Clemmons. 5. Tom Clemmons.

CLINE, Lecil Elwin, m. July 5, 1946, Ruth Davis Hayes, b. Aug. 29, 1920, near Ethelsville, Ala. - dau. of W.B. & Maggie (Davis) Hayes. Children: 1. Gene Elwin Cline, b. June 1, 1949, Vernon, Ala.

COBB, Roland Chappell, b. Lamar Co., Ala., m. 1920, Annie Lucille Richards, b. July 23, 1901, Belk, Ala. - dau. of J.A., Jr. & Retta (Taylor) Richards. Children: 1. Roland Chappell "Bobby" Cobb, Jr., b. July 3, 1921, Vernon, Ala. m. Oct. 20, 1943, Alice Hickey McMillian, b. Aug. 2, 1923, Mobile, Ala. 2. Laura Ann Cobb, b. June 23, 1923, Vernon, Ala., m. June 20, 1943, Robert Sherwood Stubbs, II, b. Nov. 11, 1922. 3. Martha Harriet "Peggy" Cobb, b. July 15, 1925, Birmingham, Ala., d. Dec. 7, 1946, in Atlanta, Ga., buried Fayette City Cem. 4. Jefferson Richards "Jeff" Cobb, b. Jan. 3, 1931, Douglas, Ga., d. Dec. 15, 1951, Fayette, Ala.

COBB, Roland Chappell "Bobby", Jr., b. July 3, 1921, Vernon, Ala., m. Oct. 20, 1943, Alice Hickey McMillian, b. Aug. 2, 1923, Mobile, Ala. R. C. Cobb, Jr. served in World War II in the United States Navy in the Atlantic Theatre of War as a Lt. Children: Martha McMillian Cobb, b. Dec. 20, 1946, Fayette, Ala. 2. Robert Martin Cobb, b. May 5, 1949, Fayette, Ala. 3. Jefferson Richards Cobb, b. Aug. 29, 1954, Fayette, Ala. 4. Lucille McMillian Cobb, b. Sept. 28, 1957, Fayette, Ala.

COGGINS, George W., m. Julia ___. Children: 1. Wilda Coggins, m. Sam Cannon. 2. Julia Coggins. 3. Dan Coggins. 4. George Coggins.

COLBURN, Eugene A., b. Feb. 27, 1921, Fayette, Ala. - son of Robert & Effie Lee Colburn - m. July 9, 1943, Mary Grace Bailey, b. Sept. 9, 1922, Fayette Co., Ala. - dau. of Jack & Era O. (Phipps) Bailey. Eugene A. Colburn entered the U. S. Air Force, Aug. 20, 1942 and left for overseas duty on Aug. 9, 1943. Theatre of Operations - European, based in England. Engagements - Flew ten missions over Germany with 351st Bomb Group before being shot down over Germany Feb. 24, 1944. Missing in Action for five months. Escaped through French underground. Returned to States July 20, 1944. Served 39 months. Rank, Technical Sergeant - Discharged at Maxwell Field, Ala., Oct. 27, 1945. Present occupation - Supt. for Renfroe Construction Co., Fayette. Children: 1. Gary Gene Colburn, b. July 2, 1945, Fayette, Ala. 2. Mary Linda Colburn, b. Dec. 24, 1949, Fayette, Ala. 3. Doris Ann Colburn, b. Aug. 18, 1952, Fayette, Ala.

COLLINS, ___, m. Ella Willingham, b. abt. 1875, Bankston, Ala., d. Dallas, Texas. - dau. of Wm. R. "Doc" & Angelyn (Jackson) Willingham. Children: 1. Marion Collins (Twin), m. Hal Winfield Padgett. 2. Mildren Collins (Twin).

COLLINS, Hosea Dean, b. Nov. 28, 1870, Fayette Co., Ala., m. Nov. 2, 1893, Mavis Obera Harkins, b. May 26, 1874, Fayette Co., Ala., d. Apr. 20, 1958. H. D. Collins and Mavis O. Harkins were married at Fayette, Ala. by Judge J. B. Morton. Children: 1. Albert H. Collins, b. Nov. 13, 1894, Fayette Co., Ala., d. June 24, 1945. 2. John Benton Collins, b. Feb. 22, 1896, Fayette Co., Ala., d. Sept. 12, 1918, France. (Killed in World War I in France.) 3.

Beatrice Collins, b. Sept. 9, 1898, Fayette Co., Ala. 4. W. Belton Collins, b. May 25, 1900, Fayette Co., Ala. 5. Ora D. Collins, b. June 29, 1902, Fay. Co. 6. H. Dean Collins, b. Dec. 16, 1903, Fayette Co. 7. Baxter W. Collins, b. May 9, 1905, Fayette Co. 8. Minnie L. Collins, b. April 6, 1907, Fayette Co. 9. Lottie Mavis Collins, b. July 31, 1909, Fayette Co., m. April 23, 1932, Clyde Chandler Cargile, b. Dec. 16, 1908, Fayette Co., Ala. 10. Mayople Collins, b. Mar. 22, 1912, Fayette Co. 11. Virginia Carolyn Collins, b. Aug. 13, 1915, Fayette Co., Ala.

COLLINS, Ira L., m. Melissa Frances Doughty (Twin), b. Aug. 24, 1851, d. July 14, 1916 - dau. of Mordecai F. Doughty. Ira L. Collins was a blind minister. Children: 1. Novella Collins, m. Icay Anthony. 2. LaFoy Collins, m. 1st. __ Waldrop. 3. Hastine Collins, m. Holland Oswalt. 4. Corra Collins, m. William Watson. 5. Gertie Collins, m. Will Waldrop. 6. Claudie Collins, died young.

COLLINS, James Newton, b. Dec. 14, 1895, Fayette Co., Ala., d. Jan. 3, 1959, Indianapolis, Ind. - son of John Newton & Allia (Buckner) Collins, m. June 1930, Josephine Washburn, b. Indiana. James Newton Collins was a radiologist. He is buried in Indianapolis, Ind. Children: 1. Jane Collins, b. Sept. 1931, Indianapolis, Ind., m. Lt. Frank Stanley Wilkerson, Jr. (Child: Bruce Wilkerson, b. 1957, Denver, Colo.) 2. Stephen Washburn Collins, b. Aug. 23, 1936, Indianapolis, Ind.

COLLINS, John L. d. 1958, m. May 14, 1921, Icie May Young, b. Feb. 3, 1900, Lamar Co., Ala. Children: 1. John Evelyn Collins, b. Mar. 28, 1924, Kennedy, Ala., m. Dec. 17, 1941, Floyd J. Jones. 2. Ada Louise Collins, b. Jan. 23, 1927, Kennedy, Ala., m. Feb. 20, ___, Marion P. Mitchell.

COLLINS, John Newton, b. May 2, 1863, Fayette Co., Ala., d. Sept. 25, 1949, Fayette, Ala., m. Sept. 29, 1892, Allia Itallia Buckner, b. April 19, 1870, Blount Co., Ala., d. June 1, 1956, Fayette, Ala. He was the son of John W. & Jane (Wheeler) Collins. She was the dau. of Thos. R. & Nancy (McClendon) Buckner. John Newton Collins was born on a farm seven miles northwest of Fayette, Ala. This farm was established by his grandfather, John or Jack Collins, in 1839, when he came from South Carolina. John W. Collins, father of John Newton Collins procured part of the homestead established by his father. John Newton Collins attended the public schools in Fayette County and assisted his father on the farm until he reached the age of twenty-nine. In 1892 he was elected county superintendent of education in Fayette County and filled that office for three terms (six years). After leaving this county office, he was bookkeeper for Propst Brothers, General Merchants at Fayette, until 1915, and was then with the L. M. Dodds, Mercantile establishment until 1923. He was elected to the office of Judge of Probate Court in Nov. 1922 and served one term (six years). In former years he was a justice of peace. He was a Democrat, a member of the First Baptist Church of Fayette, a past master of Charles Baskerville Lodge No. 281, F. and A. M., a member of H. Clay Armstrong Chapter No. 114, Royal Arch Masons, and was a past grand master of Fayette Lodge No. 39 of the International Order of Odd Fellows. Both he and his wife are buried at the Mt. Vernon Methodist Church Cemetery, in Fayette County. Children: 1. John Thomas Collins, b. Nov. 20, 1893, Fay. Co., d. July 30, 1895, Fayette Co., Ala. 2. James Newton Collins, b. Dec. 14, 1895, Fayette Co., Ala., d. Jan. 3, 1959, Indianapolis, Ind., m. 1930, Joseohine Washburn, b. Indiana. 3. Lottie Charlcie Collins, b. Dec. 22, 1897, Fayette Co., Ala., m. June 29, 1931, Francis Eugene Bertram, b. Sept. 30, 1903, Muscatine, Iowa. 4. Ruth Mildred Collins, b. June 11, 1900, Fayette, Ala., m. Aug. 9, 1932, William Morris Riley, b. Jan. 10, 1905, Fayette Co., Ala.

COLLINS, John W., b. Dec. 1818, S. C., d. 1897, m. Jane Caldwell Wheeler, b. 1830, S. C., d. 1916. They came to Fayette County in 1839 with their families. Children: 1. John Newton Collins, b. May 2, 1863, Fayette Co., Ala., d. Sept. 25, 1949, m. Allia Itallia Buckner, b. April 19, 1870, Blount Co., Ala., d. June 1, 1956. 2. Hosea Dean Collins, m. Mavis Harkins. 3. Eda E. Collins, m. Dec. 27, 1877 at Fayette Co., Ala., D. P. Hassell. 4. Mary Jane Collins, m. Eugene G. Norris.

COLLINS, R. Dean, m. Vera Cannon, dau. of M. F. Cannon. Children: 1. Betty Jane Collins, m. Ross Roberts. (Children: Jane and Ross Roberts.)

COMER, Anderson Burchfield, b. Oct. 15, 1848, Ala., d. April 13, 1911, Lamar Co., Ala. - son of R.J. & Elizabeth (Burchfield) Comer - m. Feb. 7, 1878, Sue Walls, d. June 1882, Calhoun Co., Ala. - dau. of John & Mary Walls. Anderson Burchfield Comer moved to Lamar County, Ala. about 1906 in an ox-drawn wagon. He and several of his brothers moved from Calhoun Co., Ala. Children: (1st. marriage) 1. Mary Elizabeth Comer, b. May 30, 1879, Munford, Ala., d. April 20, 1955, m. 1897, George Washington Fallin, b. Aug. 14, 1869, Upson Co., Ga. d. Nov. 1, 1939. (Both buried Montgomery, Ala.) 2. Mattie Liza Emma Comer, b. Sept. 7, 1880, Calhoun Co., Ala., m. Nov. 11, 1900, Clayborne Noe, b. Nov. 7, 1879, Sulligent, Ala., d. Oct. 22, 1951, Lamar Co., Ala. 3. Robert Elbert Comer, b. May 20, 1882, Calhoun Co., Ala., d. July 1882, Calhoun Co., Ala. ---- A. B. Comer married 2nd. Ann Meadows. Children: (2nd marriage) 1. Effie Comer, b. Mar. 9, 1890, d. July 19, 1954, m. 1911, John H. Harper, d. 1954.

COMER, John, b. Sept. 4, 1782, d. June 1854 - son of Matthew Comer - m. Sallie B. ___, b. April 2, 1787, d. Sept. 12, 1859. Children: 1. Elizabeth "Betsy" Comer, b. Oct. 24, 1805, Va., m. James Bright. 2. Samuel Richardson Comer, b. Aug. 7, 1808. 3. Mary Garrett Comer, b. Aug. 5, 1811, d. Nov. 3, 1822. 4. Stephen E. Comer (Twin) b. Mar. 26, 1815. 5. Thomas W. Comer (Twin) b. Mar. 26, 1815, d. April 1, 1816. 6. Reuben Jackson Comer, b. Sept. 17, 1818, Tenn., d. Calhoun Co., Ala., m. Dec. 1847, Elizabeth Burchfield, b. Aug. 29, 1827, Shelby Co., Ala., d. July 8, 1920, Sulligent, Ala. 7. Susannah Carroll Comer, b. Aug. 8, 1821. 8. William G. W. Comer, b. Dec. 21, 1823, d. 1839. 9. John A. B. Comer, b. Nov. 30, 1828, Tenn., d. 1891, Coldwater, Calhoun Co., Ala., m. Nancy L. Bean, b. 1828, N. C., d. 1909, Calhoun Co., Ala.

COMER, Reuben Jackson, b. Sept. 17, 1818, Tenn., d. June 20, 1878, Calhoun Co., Ala., - son of John & Sallie B. Comer - m. Dec. 1847, Elizabeth Burchfield, b. Aug. 29, 1827, Shelby Co., Ala., d. July 8, 1920, Sulligent, Ala. She was reared by an Uncle living in Elyton, Jefferson Co., Ala. (Father was possibly Elijah Birchfield.) The Comer family came to Alabama from Tenn. in covered wagons. They first settled in Shelby Co., Ala. and later in Calhoun Co., Ala. and the widow of R. J. Comer, with several of her sons, moved to Lamar Co. near Sulligent in the late 1890's. R. J. Comer fought in the 18th Ala. Regt. of the Confederate States Army during the Civil War. Children:

1. Anderson Burchfield Comer, b. Oct. 15, 1848, near Columbiana, Ala., d. d. April 13, 1911, Lamar Co., Ala., m. Feb. 7, 1878, Sue Walls, d. June 1882, Calhoun Co., Ala. 2. Eliza Jane Comer, b. Aug. 12, 1851, Ala., d. Jan. 27, 1913, Lamar Co., Ala. 3. Mary Ann Susan "Polly Ann" Comer, b. June 13, 1852, Ala., m. Sept. 5, 1890, James Clark. 4. Permelia Frances "Kate" Comer, b. May 13, 1854, Ala., d. July 12, 1929, Lamar Co., Ala., 5. Samuel Henderson Comer, b. May 3, 1856, Ala., m. Oct. 4, 1883, Callie Tucker. 6. John Reuben Comer, b. April 22, 1858, Ala., m. Lizzie Ganaway. 7. James Thomas Comer, b. Feb. 15, 1860, Ala., m. Mollie Tidwell of Texas. 8. Oscar Hogan Comer, b. Feb. 16, 1862, Ala. 9. William McCain Comer, b. Mar. 28, 1866, Ala., m. 1st. Mattie Self, 2nd. Mary Lou Clark. 10. Ella Elizabeth Comer, b. April 7, 1870, Ala., m. Nov. 12, 1885, Robert Dickert.

CONNELL, Ulmer, - son of L. A. Connell - m. Lucy Dell Harkins, - dau. of Richard & Laurah Harkins. Children: 1. Marguarite Connell. 2. Kenneth Connell. 3. Laurah Shirley Connell. 4. Luther Gaines Connell. 5. Betty Connell. 6. Lillian Connell.

COOK, Charlie, m. Della Sawyer - dau. of James H. Sawyer. Children: 1. Elsie Cook. 2. Ella Cook. 3. Lonia Cook. 4. Banks Cook. 5. Ed Cook. 6. Tut Cook. 7. Herman Cook. 8. Claburn Cook.

COOK, Spencer, m. Ada Sawyer - dau. of James H. Sawyer. Children: 1. Eva Cook. 2. Lillian Cook. 3. Tot Cook. 4. Mary Cook. 5. Troy Cook. 6. Travis Cook.

COONS, James M. - son of Jacob & Martha (Gunter) Coons, m. Martha Harrington, b. Jan. 20, 1827, d. Jan. 18, 1902 - dau. of Micajah B. & Mary (Robertson) Harrington. Children: 1. Leona C. Coons, b. June 4, 1853, Pickens Co., Ala. d. Dec. 21, 1941, buried Birmingham, Ala., m. Jacob Wilson Propst, b. Oct. 21, 1852, Pickens Co., Ala., d. Nov. 6, 7, 1907, buried Birmingham, Ala. 2. Mattie Coons, m. M. F. Keenun, b. Feb. 20, 1855, d. Aug. 10, 1888. 3. Marion L. Coons, b. Dec. 25, 1858, Lamar Co., Ala., d. Feb. 1935, Fayette, Ala. m. Emma Gourley, b. Mar. 1860, Lamar Co., Ala., d. Oct. 1933, Fayette, Ala. 4. James M. Coons, Jr., m. Jennie Gentry. 5. Jennie Coons, d. Dec. 29, 1958, m. Tom Trapp, b. July 19, 1870, d. April 25, 1942. 6. Kitty Coons, died young at 16 or 17 yrs. 7. Mary Leila Coons, b. Mar. 8, 1855, Lamar Co., Ala. d. Mar. 19, 1913, m. W. Kennedy McAdams, b. Oct. 12, 1854, d. Jan. 7, 1942.

COONS, Joe Harold, b. Nov. 26, 1918, Kennedy, Ala. - son of Leon & Lillie (Propst) Coons - m. Nov. 21, 1945, Betty Gordon, b. June 22, 1923, Healdton, Okla. - dau. of Hugh & Artie (Ward) Gordon. Joe and Betty were married in Byhalia, Miss. by Rev. Milligan. Joe is Plant Supt. of the Golden Eagle Syrup Mfgr. Co., in Fayette, Ala. Betty was formerly affiliated with the Fayette County Welfare Dept. Children: 1. Peggy Jo Coons, b. Nov. 9, 1950, Fayette, Ala. 2. Richard Gordon Coons, b. May 27, 1953, Fayette, Ala. 3. Nancy Virginia Coons, b. Jan. 11, 1956, Fayette, Ala.

COONS, Leon, b. July 20, 1883, Kennedy, Ala., d. Dec. 13, 1958, Fayette, Ala. son of Marion L. & Emma (Gourley) Coons - m. Lillie Propst, b. Jan. 24, 1884, Palmetto, Pickens Co., Ala. - dau. of Samuel A. & Mary (Ellis) Propst. They were married in Kennedy, Ala. by Rev. James Jennings. Mr. Coons was a cabinet maker. Children: 1. Mary Coons, b. Dec. 10, 1907, Kennedy, Ala., d.

Sept. 14, 1957, Fayette, Ala., m. April 23, 1935, R. R. Pitts. 2. Samuel Marion Coons, b. Mar. 4, 1912, Kennedy, Ala., m. Oct. 1935, Clara Moore. 3. Virginia Coons, b. Oct. 5, 1915, Kennedy, Ala. 4. Joe Harold Coons, b. Nov. 26, 1918, Kennedy, Ala., m. Nov. 21, 1945, Betty Gordon, b. June 22, 1925, Healdton, Okla. 5. Mildred Rebecca Coons, m. June 7, 1947, Harold Emory Parkham.

COONS, Marion L., b. Dec. 25, 1858, Lamar Co., Ala., d. Feb. 1935, Fayette, Ala. - son of James M. & Martha (Harrington) Coons - m. Mary Emma Gourley, b. Mar. 1860, Lamar Co., Ala., d. Oct. 1933, Fayette, Ala. - dau. of Hugh & Mary (Cooper) Gourley. Marion L. Coons was the Mayor of Fayette in the 1920's and Fayette County is grateful to him for the many records and other data that he collected prior to the year 1931. Had it not been for his forethought and his unselfish efforts many of the records in this book would have been lost to posterity forever. Children: 1. Leon Coons, b. July 20, 1883, Kennedy, Ala., d. Dec. 13, 1958, Fayette, Ala., m. Sept. 22, 1905, Lillie Propst, b. Jan. 24, 1884, Palmetto, Pickens Co., Ala. 2. Kittie Coons, b. Kennedy, Ala. m. John Graham. 3. Hal Coons, b. Kennedy, Ala., d. April 1956, Jasper, Ala. m. Isabel McClean. 4. Jessie Mae Coons, b. Kennedy, Ala., m. George Floyd. 5. Lois Coons, b. Kennedy, Ala., m. H. Webb Mitchell.

CORBETT, Hugh H., m. Sept. 26, 1940, Mildred Musgrove, b. July 2, 1917, Fay. Co., - dau. of Fant & Ida (Dickinson) Musgrove. Children: 1. David Corbett b. Feb. 26, 1949, Fayette Co., Ala.

COTTON, Jesse Jackson, b. April 2, 1879, Fayette Co., Ala. - son of George H. Cotton - m. July 6, 1902, Naomi Ethel White, b. Mar. 9, 1875, Fayette Co., Ala.- dau. of George Harrison White. Mr. & Mrs. Cotton were married in Fayette, Ala. by Judge Tom Goodwin. Mr. Cotton is a farmer. Children: 1. Juanita Cotton, b. Oct. 2, 1903, Birmingham, Ala., d. July 3, 1905, Fayette, Ala. 2. Infant Son, b. & d. July 28, 1905, Fayette Co., Ala. 3. Bessie Nell Cotton, b. Aug. 27, 1907, Fayette Co., Ala., m. Dec. 26, 1923, Floyd Newman Lawrence, b. Oct. 29, 1901, Fayette Co., Ala. 4. George Willard Cotton, b. Mar. 12, 1910, Fayette Co., Ala., d. Aug. 20, 1915, Fayette Co. 5. Jesse Leonard Cotton, b. Mar. 16, 1912, Fayette Co., Ala., m. Jan. 15, 1934, Lena Christene South, b. Jan. 27, 1911, Fayette Co., Ala. 6. Naomi Desiree Cotton, b. Feb. 15, 1915, Fayette Co., Ala., m. Mar. 19, 1938, David M. McCown, b. Oct. 23, ___.

COTTON, Jessie Leonard, b. Mar. 16, 1912, Fayette Co., Ala., - son of Jesse J. Cotton - m. Jan. 15, 1934, Lena Christene South, b. Jan. 27, 1911, Fayette Co., Ala. - dau. of Martin D. South. Children: 1. Johnny Leonard Cotton, b. April 23, 1948, Parrish, Walker Co., Ala.

COUCH, Christopher Columbus, b. Oct. 15, 1887, d. Feb. 10, 1950, m. Nov. 10, 1910, Nancy Adeline Dodson, b. Nov. 15, 1890, - dau. of John William Dodson - Children: 1. Mildred Couch, b. Aug. 29, 1911, m. Moody B. Roberts. (Child: Jerrill Moody Roberts.) 2. Josie Willean Couch, b. Nov. 10, 1912, d. April 10, 1914. 3. Lanette Couch, b. April 2, 1916, m. Dec. 23, 1934, Richard Earl White. (Child: 1. Nancy Ann White.) 4. John M. Couch, b. Nov. 21, 1918, d. Aug. 21, 1919. 5. Dodson Christopher Couch, b. April 4, 1922, m. Iva May Loden. (Child: Christopher Couch.) 6. Mary Jo Couch, b. Mar. 14, 1925, m. T. T. Stanley. (Child: Terry Richard Stanley.)

COUCH, Roy D. - son of George W. Couch - m. 1935, Evelyn McConnell, b. 1914, Fayette Co., Ala. - dau. of Joseph & Virgie McConnell. Children: 1. Joseph Terrell "Skipper" Couch. 2. Davis McConnell Couch.

COWART, Allen W., b. abt. 1830 to 1833, Pickens Co., Ala., d. in hospital at Dalton, Ga., from wounds received in Civil War, m. abt. 1853 in Pickens Co., Ala., Dorcus Johnson, b. May 18, 1832, Tenn., d. Mar. 2, 1882, buried at Old Mt. Zion Primitive Baptist Church in Pickens Co., Ala. She came to Alabama with parents in early life. Children: 1. Irebell Cowart, b. June 3, 1854, d. Jan. 20, 1894, m. Nov. 3, 1871 in Pickens Co., Ala., W. W. Sanders. 2. John Z. Cowart, b. June 8, 1855, Pickens Co., Ala., d. Abt. 1897, Amory, Miss. 3. Mary Elizabeth Cowart, b. Feb. 22, 1857, Pickens Co., Ala., d. Mar. 27, 1942, Fayette Co., Ala., m. Dec. 13, 1881 in Pickens Co., Ala., James Russell McCool. 4. M. B. Cowart, b. Oct. 17, 1860, Pickens Co., Ala., d. Apr. 20, 1937, Pickens Co., Ala., m. Arminta Jane Autry. 5. Wm. J. Cowart, b. Aug. 11, 1865, Pickens Co., Ala., d. at Amory, Miss.

CROLEY, Sam, m. Tanney Strong, b. Jan. 26, 1780, d. Aug. 6, 1823 - dau. of Johnson Strong. Children: 1. John Croley, b. Dec. 13, 1796. 2. Polley Croley, b. June 3, 1798. 3. Sarah Croley, b. May 13, 1800. 4. Benjamin Croley, b. __ 13, 1802. 5. Elijah Croley, b. April 1804. 6. Elizabeth Croley, b. Dec. 21, 1807.

CROWE, Josiah S., b. 1848, Miss. d. Nov. 6, 1919, Fayette, Ala. - son of Riley & Mandy Crowe - m. April 21, 1867, Mary Jane Hudson, b. Nov. 7, 1842, Miss., d. Jan. 4, 1929, Fayette, Ala. Children: 1. Georgia Ann Ada Crowe, b. Feb. 17, 1862, Lamar Co., Ala., d. Nov. 2, 1871, Lamar Co., Ala. 2. Sarah Frances Elizabeth Crowe, b. Feb. 2, 1870, Lamar Co., Ala., d. Sept. 27, 1912, Fayette, Ala., m. Thomas Edwards. 3. James Jefferson Crowe, b. April 19, 1872, Lamar Co., Ala., m. Emma Thomas, b. Ga. 4. Mary Lucinda Catherine Crowe, b. Oct. 30, 1874, Lamar Co., Ala., m. in Fayette Co., Ala., Elbie S. Washam, b. Coosa Co., Ala. d. Akron, Ohio. 5. Rebecca Isabella Crowe, b. Feb. 27, 1877, Lamar Co., Ala., m. Dec. 14, 1900, D. A. Kemp, b. Sept. 30, 1975, Chilton Co., Ala., d. Feb. 17, 1935, Fayette, Ala. 6. Julia Etta Crowe, b. April 27, 1880, Fayette Co., Ala., d. April 23, 1932, Fayette Co., Ala., m. Henry Freeman, d. Fayette Co., Ala. 7. Joseph Earl Crowe, b. Dec. 17, 1883, Fayette Co., Ala., m. Lizzie Taylor, d. Fayette, Ala. 8. Arlie Walter Fleetwood Crowe, b. June 25, 1888, Fayette Co., Ala., m. Mellie Abbott, b. Fayette Co., Ala. 9. Alma Lee Crowe, b. Feb. 28, 1887, Fayette Co., Ala., d. April 28, 1887.

CRUTCHER, Absolom P., b. probably in Maury or Marshall Co., Tenn., m. Aug. 6, 1818, Jane P. Childrels or Childress. Children: 1. Mary James Crutcher, b. June 28, 1819, d. Jan. 23, 1821. 2. William Preston Crutcher, b. Feb. 26, 1821, d. Nov. 6, 1822. 3. James Mathes Crutcher, b. Mar. 13, 1823, Tenn.? m. (wife's name not known - had six children - Eliza, Sallie, Ophelia, Jim, Richard & Elba Crutcher.) 4. Lee Harris Crutcher, b. Mar. 31, 1825, m. Ann ___. (Children: Blanche, Mary, Jim, Park and Bascum Crutcher.) 5. Ann Oohelia Crutcher, b. Jan. 1, 1827, m. Charlie Roundtree. (Children: John, Maggie, Betty and Molly Roundtree.) 6. Theophilus Pearce Crutcher, b. May 2, 1829, m. Julia Ann Bidwell. (Children: Charles Parker, John Bell, Theophilus Wilburn, Americus Eugene, Edwin J., Jennie Lee, Minnie V. and Frank Bidwell.) 7. Sarah Elizabeth Crutcher, b. June 4, 1831, m. John Sorott. (Children:

Lillie, Sallie, Absolom, John and Pink.) 8. John Erastus Cruthcer, b. Jan. 29, 1833, d. Battle of Shiloh. 9. Emily Jane Crutcher, b. Oct. 30, 1834, m. Gus Buford. (Children: Maggie, Eunice, Frank, Fred, Joe, Ruth, Ella and Edd.) 10. Henry Lawson Crutcher, b. Oct. 13, 1836, m. Margaret Williamson. (Children: Eula, Novella, Willie Mae, Stella, Preston and Lizzie.) 11. Americus Rayburn Crutcher, b. Jan. 18, 1839, Marshall Co., Tenn. m. Ann Williamson. (Children: Cora, John Parker and Celeste.) 12. William Absolom Parker Crutcher, b. April 26, 1841, m. Josie Williamson. (Children: Carrie, Josie, Earnest and Tom.) 13. Augustus Byard Crutcher, b. Mar. 20, 1843, d. April 6, 1843.)

CRUTCHER, Americus Rayburn, b. Jan. 18, 1839, near Lewisburg, Tenn., m. Ann Williamson, b. Maury Co., Tenn. He was the son of Absolom P. & Jane P. (Chilfrels or Childress) Crutcher. She was the dau. of John J. & Eliza B. (Carr) Williamson. Children: 1. Cora Crutcher, b. Tenn. m. at Lewisburg, Tenn. to Clint Gathings, b. Tenn. 2. John Parker Crutcher, b. June 1, 1871, Lewisburg, Tenn., d. Nov. 11, 1947, Sumter Co., Ala., m. Frances Holmes, b. Sumter Co., Ala., d. Jan. 1942, Cuba, Sumter Co., Ala.

CRUTCHER, John Parker, b. June 1, 1871, Lewisburg, Marshall Co., Tenn., d. Nov. 11, 1947, Cuba, Sumter Co., Ala. - son of Americus Rayburn & Ann (Williamson) Crutcher - m. Frances Holmes, b. Sumter Co., Ala., d. Jan. 1942, Cuba, Sumter Co., Ala. - dau. of James Hall & Frances (Ward) Holmes. Children: 1. James Holmes Crutcher, b. Cuba, Sumter Co., Ala., m. at Birmingham, Ala. to Hettie Sibley. 2. John Parker Crutcher, Jr., b. Coalburg, Jefferson Co., Ala., m. May 1, 1937, Lucy Irick Tarwater, b. Corona, Walker Co., Ala. 3. Harold Crutcher, b. Cuba, Sumter Co., Ala., d. 1946, Meridan, Miss., m. Maurine Wells. 4. Ralph Francis Crutcher, b. Cuba, Sumter Co., Ala., m. at Tuscaloosa, Ala. to Eleanor Henderson.

CRUTCHER, John Parker, Jr., b. Coalburg, Jefferson Co., Ala. - son of John Parker & Frances (Holmes) Crutcher - m. May 1, 1937, Lucy Irick Tarwater, b. April 16, 1912, Corona, Walker Co., Ala. - dau. of James Van Diver & Musa Ida (Miles) Tarwater. (Note: the name Van Diver is also spelled Vandiver.) Children: 1. John Van Diver Crutcher, b. Nov. 10, 1938, Tuscaloosa, Ala., 2. Ida Frances Crutcher, b. July 9, 1955, Fayette, Ala.

DANIEL, Douglas, b. Dec. 25, 1898, Ky., d. buried in Kentucky, m. Jan. 20, 1921, Mildred Jeffries, b. Dec. 29, 1899, Fayette, Ala. He was the son of James P. & Virginia (Pritchett) Daniel. She is the dau. of Francis M. & Mary Idelia (Morton) Jeffries. They were married by Rev. Joe I. Williams at Fayette, Ala. Children: 1. Mary Jean Daniel, b. Dec. 13, 1921, Fayette, Ala., m. Jan. 2, 1949, George Nicholds Hellers, b. Sept. 9, 1921, Jamacia, Long Island. They were married by Rev. Paul Clem at Fayette, Ala. 2. Malcolm Douglas Daniel, b. Jan. 30, 1930, Fayette, Ala., m. Malinda Jane Robertson, b. Sept. 21, 1930, Fayette, Ala. 3. Frances Marion Daniel, b. Feb 24, 1935, Fayette, Ala., m. 1959.

DANIEL, Malcolm Douglas, b. Jan. 30, 1930, Fayette, Ala., - son of Douglas & Mildred (Jeffries) Daniel - m. June 19, 1954, Malinda Jane Robertson, b. Sept. 21, 1930, Fayette, Ala. - dau. of Joe P. & Dorothy (Osborn) Robertson. Malcolm "Bud" Daniel served in the U. S. Air Force from Aug. 22, 1950 until Nov. 16, 1953. They were married by Rev. John D. Perkins at Fayette, Ala. Children: 1. Mary Lauretta Daniel, b. Mar. 10, 1955, Fayette, Ala. 2. Dorothy Jeffries Daniel, b. Feb. 14, 1958, Fayette, Ala.

DARNELL, John, b. Nov. 26, 1900, Tenn., m. July 4, 19___, Lillian Moore, b. July 23, 1907, Tenn. Mr. & Mrs. Darnell were married at Huntsville, Ala. They were affiliated with the Alabama Mills when they first came to Fayette, Ala. Children: 1. James Wilson "JayBug" Darnell, b. Aug. 2, 1923, Tenn., d. Nov. 8, 1943, - J. W. Darnell was killed in World War II while serving with the U. S. Marines on Bougainville, Island. He is buried in the Fayette City Cemetery. 2. Dorothy Darnell, b. Jan. 25, 1925, Colbert Co., Tenn., m. Oct. 8, 1943, James Billy Porter, b. Dec. 9, 1923, Fayette, Co., Ala. 3. Ethel Katherine Darnell, b. Aug. 13, 1927, m. Harold Ferguson, Jr. 4. Hildia June Darnell, b. July 2, 1929, m. Doyle Matthews.

DAVIS, Alvis, b. April 16, 1801, N. C., d. Sept. 12, 1875, Fayette Co., Ala., m. 1822, Elizabeth Gregory, b. Aug. 8, 1804. Alvis was the son of John & Mary (Hawkins) Davis. He was a member of the Legislature from Fayette County, Ala. in the 1840's. Children: 1. Elizabeth Jane Davis, b. April 17, 1827, Fayette Co., Ala., d. Aug. 8, 1895, m. Mar. 10, 1853, William Harvey Whitley, b. Oct. 20, 1822, Fayette Co., Ala., d. Mar. 5, 1885. 2. Sarah Davis, m. Mr. Morrow. 3. Frances Davis, m. Mr. Whitley. 4. Thomas Davis. 5. Emma Davis.

DAVIS, Charles Hurt, b. Dec. 16, 1849, Ala., d. July 23, 1924, m. Aug. 10, 1871, Victoria Hasselltine Wimberley. Charles H. Davis was married first to America Wimberley, a sister of Victoria's, and the daughter of L. M. Wimberley. There were no children by the first marriage. Chas. H. Davis was ordained as a Primitive Baptist Minister in 1895. Children: 1. John Monroe Davis, b. Jan. 1, 1875, d. Mar. 7, 1892, Fayette Co., Ala. 2. Charles Davis, b. Feb. 1, 1876, d. May 18, 1915, Drowned in Yellow Creek near Vernon, Ala. 3. Gilbert Eugene Davis, b. June 28, 1883, m. June 15, 1909, Leona Pugh, b. Aug. 19, 1887 (from Gordo, Ala.) 4. Mabel Tabitha Davis, b. Aug. 21, 1886, m. Dr. Wm. Stillman Bell, b. May 26, 1874, Gordo, Ala. 5. Maggie Lee Davis, b. May 14, 1892, m. July 26, 1912, Wazzie Blaine Hayes, b. Lamar Co., Ala.

DAVIS, Gilbert Eugene, b. June 28, 1883, - son of Charles H. Davis - m. June 15, 1900, Leona Pugh, b. Aug. 19, 1887. Children: 1. Gilbert Eugene Davis, Jr., b. Aug. 1, 1912, m. June 10, 1939, Flozzy Smith. 2. Frances Davis, b. April 10, 1910, m. May 31, 1944, Harold Downing, of Gordo. (Children: George Harold, b. April 17, 1946; Carrol, b. Apr. 30, 1945; and Cathy Downing, b. Dec. 28, 19___.) 3. Charles Willis Davis, b. Feb. 21, 1918, m. Joan Kirk, of Texas. (Children: Carol, b. Dec. 7, 1941, Pearl Harbor, Hawaii; Kirk (Twin) and Rick (Twin), b. Dec. 21, 1945.) 4. Emmett M. Davis, b. Sept. 18, 1921, m. Sept. 5, 1942, Margaret Garman of Montgomery, Ala. (Children: Peggy Jean Davis, b. Jan. 28, 1947.)

DAVIS, Jesse L., b. 1845, Fayette Co., Ala., d. 1930, Bankston, Ala., m. Maggie Cotton, b. 1840, Fayette Co., Ala., d. 1930, Bankston, Ala. - dau. of Cynthia Cotton, b. Dec. 25, 1812, d. July 28, 1916. Children: 1. Tanny Davis, b. Mar. 8, 1874, d. Mar. 23, 1953, Bankston, Ala., m. George J. Welburn, b. Mar. 10, 1869, d. Aug. 9, 1927, Bankston, Ala.

DAVIS, John, b. 1775, N.C., d. 1845, m. in Lexington, Ky, 1796 to Mary Hawkins, b. 1779, N.C. or Ky., d. 1850. Children: 1. Matthew Davis II, b. 1793, m. Jan. 31, 1822, in Jefferson Co., Ala. to Jane Lindsey, b. 1800, d. bef.

1860. 2. Alvis Davis, b. 1795, N. C. (or April 16, 1801), d. Sept. 12, 1875, Fayette Co., Ala., m. Oct. 22, 1822, Elizabeth Gregory, b. Aug. 8, 1804. 3. William Davis, b. 1797, m. 1st. Miss Paden, 2nd. Margaret Cheek. 4. James Davis, b. 1800, Warren Co., Tenn., m. 1st. Nancy Jones, 2nd. Mrs. Lockey Woods. 5. John Davis, Jr., b. Feb. 9, 1802, Warren Co., Tenn., d. May 9, 1875, Fayette Co., Ala., m. Nancy Gore Franklin. 6. Robert Davis, b. 1804, Warren Co., Tenn., m. 1831, Nancy Cheek. 7. Mary "Polly" Davis, b. 1807, Warren Co., Tenn. m. Basil Lindsey. 8. Sarah "Sally" Davis, b. Jan. 2, 1809, Warren Co., Tenn. d. 1891, m. 1828, Holland Lindsey, b. 1807, d. 1893. 9. Thomas Davis, b. 1812, Jiles Co., Tenn. 10. Elizabeth "Betsy" Davis, b. 1816, Jiles Co., Tenn., m. Thomas Norman.

DAVIS, John Hawkins, b. Feb. 9, 1807, Warren Co., Tenn. d. May 9, 1875, Marion Station, Miss., - son of John & Mary (Hawkins) Davis - m. July 29, 1828, Nancy Gore Franklin, b. Aug. 25, 1807, Ky., d. Aug. 24, 1867, Fayette Co., Ala. - her mother was a Gore. John Hawkins Davis was a farmer and a Methodist Minister. He died while in the pulpit. Nancy Gore Franklin Davis, his wife was a licensed physician and had her personal carriage and slave to drive her to the homes of the sick. Children: 1. Thomas L. Davis, b. June 4, 1829, Ala., d. Sept. 11, 1863, m. Sept. 18, 1849, Sarah E. Thompson. (He died of measles while home on furlough from the C.S.Army during the Civil War.) 2. Nancy Ann Davis, b. Feb. 19, 1831, Ala., d. Nov. 3, 1911, Grandview, Texas, m. Oct. 10, 1850, Peyton Ivey Dickinson, b. Dec. 17, 1826, Ga. d. Sept. 5, 1880, Fayette Co., Ala. 3. Mary Elizabeth Davis, b. Aug. 6, 1834, Ala., m. Aug. 27, 1856, Humphrey W. Dickinson. 4. Sarah J. Davis, b. Mar. 7, 1839, Ala., m. July 12, 1860, W. T. "Tom" Holland. 5. Frances H. Davis, b. 1841, d. in childhood. 6. Martha L. Davis, b. Mar. 9, 1836, Ala., m. May 17, 1854, John C. Brogan, who was an ex-Catholic Priest and became a Methodist Minister. 7. John Hawkins Davis, Jr., b. Oct. 16, 1842, Ala., d. Sept. 14, 1862. Died on Battlefield in Maryland in the C. S. Army in Civil War. 8. Margaret C. Davis, b. Mar. 9, 1844, Ala., d. Texas, m. Sept. 7, 1866, Thomas Wimberley. 9. Urilda Taylor Davis, b. Feb. 25, 1846, Ala., m. John Wofford. 10. Charles Hurt Davis, b. Dec. 16, 1849, Ala., d. July 23, 1924, m. 1st. Nov. 29, 1868, America Wimberley, who died. 2nd. Victoria Haseltine Wimberley, (second marriage on Aug. 10, 1871.)

DAVIS, Luther M., b. 1879, Tenn., d. 1933, Franklin, Tenn., m. Anna M. Thornton, b. 1879, Hickman Co., Tenn. d. Sept. 9, 1954, Franklin, Tenn. Children: 1. Marion Davis, b. Feb. 27, 1906, Williamson Co., Tenn., m. Willinel Wheeler, b. Aug. 29, 1910, Lamar Co., Ala. 2. William Davis.

DAVIS, Marion, b. Feb. 27, 1906, Williamson Co., Tenn. - son of Luther M. Davis - m. Willinel Wheeler, b. Aug. 29, 1910, Lamar Co., Ala. - dau. of T. T. Wheeler. Marion Davis came to Fayette County in 1930. The Wheeler Family came to Fayette County from Lamar Co., in 1913. Children: 1. James Melton Davis, b. Fayette, Ala. 2. Sara Frances Davis, b. Aug. 28, 1933, Fayette, Ala., m. June 24, 1956, James Hoffman Gullett, b. Feb. 26, 1927, Fayette, Ala.

DAVIS, Matthew, b. 1736, Halifax Dist. N.C., d. 1790, Halifax Dist. N.C., m. 1762, Elizabeth ___, b. 1740, d. after 1785. Matthew Davis was a soldier of the American Revolution in the North Carolina line and a reference to the settlements of his claims for services rendered by the Commissioners of Halifax, in 1784 - 85 is recorded in the North Carolina State records Vol. 17, p.

204. His son, John Davis, was wounded before the battle of New Orleans (1812) but he was able to serve in that battle also. Matthew Davis was a private in the North Carolina Line. Children: 1.William Davis, b. 1773. 2. John Davis, b. 1775, N. C., d. 1845, m. 1796, Mary Hawkins, b. 1779, d. 1850. 3. Matthew Davis. 4. James Davis. 5. Thomas Davis.

DAVIS, Mathew, II, - son of John & Mary (Hawkins) Davis - m. Jan. 31, 1822, Jane Lindsey, b. Feb 8, 1800. Children: 1. John C. Davis, b. Mar. 9, 1823, 2. Macajah Davis, b. Sept. 10, 1824. 3. Mary Ann Davis, b. May 15, 1826. 4. Sarah Elizabeth Davis, b. April 26, 1828, m. Carson Hunter Moore, killed in Civil War. 5. Minerva Jane Davis, b. Aug. 11, 1830. 6. Kimmon Davis, b. 1832. 7. Basil N. Davis, b. 1834. 8. Thomas H. Davis, b. 1836. 9. W. F. Davis, b. 1839.

DAVIS, Nathaniel, b. abt. 1771, d. 1848 in Fayette or Tuscaloosa Co., Ala., m. Elizabeth ___. Children: 1. Pallatiah "Palli" Davis, b. Oct. 9, 1809, Ga. d. Apr'l 22, 1887, Fayette Co., Ala., m. July 29, 1826, Jeotha Rice, b. June 20, 1804, S. C., d. Oct. 15, 1874, Fayette Co., Ala. 2. Willis Davis, m. Apr. 9, 1829, Martha Willingham. 3. Richard Davis. 4. Oliver P. Davis. 5. Arthur Davis. 6. Eleanor "Nelly" Davis, m. Sept. 11, 1832, Hugh Trawick. 7. Malinda Davis, m. Jan. 17, 1837, Duncan Ray. 8. Margaret Davis, m. Benjamin Middleton. 9. Sarah Davis, m. Daniel Stanley.

DAVIS, Tom J., m. Catherine "Cat" York, b. 1847, d. June 5, 1899. T. J. Davis served during the Civil War with Co. I. 41 Ala. Inf. C. S. A. He is believed to be a brother to Richard Davis, born Oct. 14, 1812. She is a sister of Jim York. Children: 1. Sarah Emma Davis, b. Oct. 10, 1867, d. Nov. 19, 1949, Fayette, Ala., m. Will A. Anderson, b. June 5, 1863, Fayette Co., Ala., d. Feb. 10, 1932, Fayette, Ala.

DAVISON, James Washington, b. Aug. 12, 1859, Miss. d. Itawamba Co., Miss. m. Helen B. Dickinson, b. Mar. 15, 1863, Fayette Co., Ala., d. Oct. 5, 1905, Miss. - dau. of Richard & Mary (Whitley) Dickinson. Children: 1. Fleta Davison, b. April 21, 1885, Itawamba Co., Miss., d. Feb. 6, 1906. 2. Pearl D. Davison, b. Dec. 2, 1886, Miss., d. Oct. 29, 1900. 3. Molora "Lora" Davison, b. Jan. 15, 1889, Miss. d. Aug. 5, 1905. 4. Louie Davison, b. Dec. 17, 1890, Miss., m. William Victor Inzer. 5. Mary Vernor Davison, b. Dec. 8, 1892, Miss., d. May 26, 1895. 6. Eley Nathan Davison, b. Sept. 16, 1894. 7. Felix Guldmer Davison, b. April 12, 1897, Miss. 8. Mozzell Davison, b. Mar. 11, 1903. --- Jas. Wash. Davison married second - Mellie Hyder. Children: by 2nd wife: 1. Hermon Davison, b. May 17, 1908, Miss., d. Dec 4, 1908. 2. Imogene Davison, b. Feb. 4, 1910, Miss. 3. Reva Davison, b. May 4, 1915.

DEATON, Richard Zebbie Dennis O'Dell, b. June 15, 1902, Iuka, Tish. Co., Miss., m. April 25, 1925, 1925, Lessie Pearl Humber, b. Sept. 18, 1905, Midway, Tishimingo Co., Miss. - dau. of Robert John Willis Humber. Children: 1. Margaret "Peggy" O'Delle Deaton, b. Feb. 10, 1926, Tish. Co., Miss., m. July 21, 1947, Rolland "Tuck" Maynard Hoover, b. Mar. 7, 1925, Kentland, Ind. 2. Carolyn Loraine Jean Deaton, b. Sept. 24, 1931, Tishimingo Co., Miss., m. Nov. 11, 1950, Hardy Vardiman Luttrell, b. Dec. 17, 1928, Tish. Co., Miss. 3. Mary Yvonne Deaton, b. May 24, 1935, Tish. Co., Miss., m. Oct. 10, 1953, Edward Starkey, b. June 30, 1929, Tish. Co., Miss. 4. Aaron Zeb Deaton, b. Oct. 11, 1946, Tishimingo Co., Miss.

DELANEY, Ray, b. July 16, 1920, m. Emily Dean Rose, b. June 9, 1924, Fayette, Ala. - dau. of T. A. & Nellie (Arnold) Rose. Children: 1. Rebecca Claire Delaney, b. Aug. 25, 1953. 2. Mary Elizabeth Delaney, b. Mar. 24, 1955.

DEAVOURS, Abraham, d. 1857, m. Abigail Davidson. Abraham and Abigail Davidson Deavours came to North River Beat in 1855, from Cherokee Co., Ga. with their large family of children. They settled on the banks of the upper North River and the place is still known as the Deavour's Place. The original house, consisting of two large rooms and a wide hall between, still stands and is intact and occupied in 1959. It is said that at the house raising, help had to be solicited from as far away as Berry Station, New River, Wolfe Creek and other places of distance due to the sparse settlements. Abraham Deavours was a soldier of the War of 1812, serving in Capt. John Walter's Co. of Ga. Volunteers. He is buried at Pea Ridge. His widow, in 1878, applied for and drew a pension of $8.00 per month until her death. Children: 1. Jim Deavours. 2. George Deavours. 3. John Deavours, m. Martha Ann Berry. 4. Isaac Deavours, m. Caroline Fowler. 5. Nancy Deavours, m. Mel Enis. 6. Cynthia Deavours. 7. Rachel Deavours, m. Phillip Newton. 8. Mary Deavours, m. Jack Hendon. 9. Sarah Deavours.

DEAVOURS, Charles Spurgeon - son of Hershell Deavours - m. Carrie Lillie Sawyer - dau. of Wm. Bedford Sawyer. Children: 1. Ted Deavours, m. Kay Francis. (Children: Dianne, Charles Jeffrey and Jo Allison Deavours.) 2. Norma Deavours, m. Fred B. Nabors. (Children: Fred B., Jr. and Patircia Lynn Nabors.) 3. Wanda Kay Deavours. 4. Bonita Deavours. 5. George Edwin Deavours.

DEAVOURS, Hershell, - son of John & Martha Ann (Berry) Deavours - m. Carrie McCaleb. Children: 1. Lillian Deavours, m. Norton Richards. (Children: Donald Richards, m. Nell __ and their child is Donny Richards.) 2. Ila Deavours, m. Percy Griffin. 3. Spurgeon Deavours, m. Carrie Lillie Sawyer. 4. John Boyd Deavours, m. Ruby Lee Houston. (Children: Charlene and Anita Deavours.) 5. Blonnie Deavours, m. Oris Doughty. (Child: Julian Doughty.) 6. Nell Deavours, m. 1st. Eddie Dobbs, - 2nd. Eddie Mueller. 7. Dupree Deavours, m. Hugh Simpson, (Child: Rhett DeWitt Simpson.) 8. Rayford Deavours, m. Eugenia Bruister. (Child: Jeffrey Deavours.) 9. Buford Deavours, m. Ruby Nell Moore. (Children: Steve, Danny Hershell, and Randy Moore Deavours.) 10. Hubert Deavours, m. Fairy Moore. (Children: Gary, Greg, and Blake Deavours.)

DEAVOURS, Isaac - son of Abraham Deavours - m. Caroline Fowler. Children: 1. Ida Deavours. 2. Linda Deavours. 3. Mel Deavours. 4. Selmer Deavours. 5. Birchen Deavours. 6. Arthur Deavours. 7. Clay Deavours.

DEAVOURS, John, d. June 11, 1897 - son of Abraham Deavours - m. Oct. 11, 1874, Martha Ann Berry, d. Jan. 21, 1937. In the Civil War, John Deavours held the office of Orderly Sergeant, in Capt. James H. Moore's Co. - 56th Cavalry, commanded by Col. Robert Bagley of Mobile. John Deavours was Raised to the Sublime Degree of Master Mason in 1861, and remainded a member in good standing until his death. He died June 11, 1897 at the age of 58. His death resulted from an old wound caused by a "minnie" ball in the Civil War. He is buried at the Enis Graveyard. After his death, his wife married Clem Hamner, who died a few years lated and then she married Jule Davis. She was 82 at the time of her death and is buried in the Hopewell Cemetery north of Fayette. Children: 1. Phillip Deavours, died as a child.

2. Lula Deavours, m. Cullen Stricklin. (Children: Lloyd and Mack Striplin.)
3. Hershell Deavours, m. Carrie McCaleb. 4. Nora Deavours, m. Claud Jackson.
5. Celis Deavours, m. Dr. Sam Lytal. (Children: Parvin, Marvin, Homer and Hobert Lytal.) 6. Altia Deavours, m. Dick Kelley. (Child: Myrtle Kelley.) 7. Lester Deavours, died in youth. 8. Wilbur Deavours, m. Edith Copeland. (Child: Jack Deavours.) 9. Charlie Deavours, died in youth.

DICKINSON, Felix, b. Oct. 24, 1868, Fayette Co., Ala., m. Emma White, d. Oct. 26, 1898. He was the son of Peyton I. Dickinson. Children: 1. James Erastus "Ras" Dickinson, b. Fayette Co., Ala., m. Emmie Moon. (Child: Emma Luvada Dickinson, m. Dan Truman Little - have dau. Dana Lou Little, b. 1952.)

DICKINSON, George, b. 1794, Ga., m. Frances "Fannie" Ivey, b. 1803, Ga. They came to Alabama, north Fayette Co. or Marion Co. about 1835 and possibly came from Cherokee Co., Ga. Children: 1. Peyton Ivey Dickinson, b. Dec. 17, 1826 Ga., d. Sept. 5, 1880, Fayette Co., Ala., m. Oct. 1850, Nancy Ann Davis, b. Feb. 19, 1831, Fayette Co., Ala., d. Nov. 3, 1911, Grandview, Texas. 2. Burrell Dickinson, b. 1831, Ga. 3. William A. Dickinson, b. 1834, Ga. 4. Umohra or Humohrey W. Dickinson, b. 1836, Ala. 5. Jonathan H. Dickinson, b. 1838, Ala. 6. George Wylie Dickinson, b. 1843, Ala. 7. Betsy Dickinson.

DICKINSON, Harve J., b. Mar. 24, 1853, Fayette Co., Ala., m. Lockie C. Dickinson, b. Nov. 26, 1859, Fayette Co., Ala. He was the son of Richard Dickinson. She was the dau. of Peyton I. Dickinson. Children: 1. Dora Dickinson. (All children born in Fayette Co., Ala.) 2. Earl Dickinson. 3. May Lee Dickinson. 4. Olan Dickinson. 5. Belton Dickinson.

DICKINSON, James Byron, b. Oct. 15, 1913 - son of Lester & Bannie (Edwards) Dickinson - m. Jeannette Weaver. Children: 1. Janice Kay Dickinson, b. Oct. 18, 1939. 2. Jim Dickinson (Twin), b. Aug. 25, 1943. 3. Bob Dickinson (Twin) b. Aug. 25, 1943.

DICKINSON, Rev. James Polk, b. July 24, 1851, Fayette Co., Ala., d. Mar. 13, 1906, Fayette, Ala. - son of Peyton I. & Nancy Ann (Davis) Dickinson - m. Oct. 5, 1870, Martha Frances "Fannie" Hassell, b. Jan. 21, 1851, Tuscaloosa Co., Ala., d. Feb. 13, 1941, Fayette, Ala. - dau. of Myles & Martha (Johnson) Hassell. Rev. J. P. Dickinson was ordained by the Mt. Olive Baptist Church in 1887. He was also a farmer and a clerk. They were married in Fayette County by T. M. Scott, J. P. Both are buried in the Fayette City Cemetery. Children: (All born in Fayette Co., Ala.) 1. Lela Isabell Dickinson, b. Nov. 29, 1871, d. Mar. 21, 1931, Paris, Texas, m. Oct. 9, 1890, J. W. "Bill" Chism, d. Paris, Texas. 2. Artie Hasselltine Dickinson, b. Aug. 22, 1878, d. Oct. 18, 1897, Fayette Co., Ala., m. Wilson Kelley. (Child: Infant, died Oct. 18, 1897) 3. Motie Frances Dickinson, b. Jan. 26, 1886, m. June 21, 1906, Thomas Allen McCool, b. May 31, 1883, Tuscaloosa Co., Ala. 4. James Velta Dickinson, b. Mar. 29, 1890, d. May 6, 1890, Fayette Co., Ala. 5. Bertha Lee Dickinson, b. July 27, 1893, d. Dec. 5, 1893, Fayette Co., Ala. (Last two infants both buried at El Bethel Baptist Church Cemetery.)

DICKINSON, John Franklin, b. Mar. 9, 1853, Fayette Co., Ala., d. Sept. 22, 1939 - son of Peyton I. & Nancy Ann (Davis) Dickinson - m. Feb. 18, 1874, Meranda Evelyn Dickinson, b. Mar. 11, 1855, Fayette Co., Ala., d. July 3, 1934, - dau. of Richard & Mary (Whitley) Dickinson. John Frank Dickinson was a Methodist Minister and a farmer. Children: (All born in Fayette Co.) 1. Lula Victoria Dickinson, b. April 1, 1875, d. Mar. 17, 1939, Fayette Co., Ala. m. Jan. 28, 1894, William Theoderic Bobo, b. May 3, 1868, Fayette Co., Ala., d. Nov. 26, 1954. Fayette Co., Ala. 2. Lola A. Dickinson, b. Dec. 29, 1875, d. Sept. 29, 1879, (Died in childhood and buried in Arkansas. The family was in a covered wagon going to Texas when she became sick and died. The family later returned to Fayette Co.) 3. Cora Dickinson, b. April 15, 1880, m. Wm. Yerby. 4. Mary B. Dickinson, b. May 17, 1883, d. Birmingham, Ala., m. Aug. 14, 1913, Charles McLaughlin, d. Birmingham, Ala. 5. Ida Ann Dickinson, b. Dec. 15, 1885, d. May 29, 1941, Fayette Co., Ala., m. Jan. 7, 1906, Fant S. Musgrove, b. Jan. 4, 1870, d. Aug. 22, 1953, Fayette Co., Ala. 6. Sally Dickinson, b. Aug. 14, 1888, d. Dec. 6, 1888, Fayette Co., Ala. 7. Lester R. Dickinson, b. Nov. 23, 1889, m. May 6, 1912, Bannie Edwards. 8. Joseph Frank Dickinson, b. April 13, 1893, d. Feb. 12, 1899, Fayette Co., Ala. 9. Florence Dickinson, b. July 25, 1896, m. Sept. 7, 1916, Claude Musgrove.

DICKINSON, Lester R., b. Nov. 23, 1889, Fayette Co., Ala., - son of J.F. & M.E. (Dickinson) Dickinson, - m. May 6, 1912, Bannie Edwards. Children: 1. James Byron Dickinson, b. Oct. 15, 1913, m. Jeannette Weaver. 2. Joe Mack Dickinson, b. Dec. 13, 1920. 3. Charles Richard Dickinson, b. Oct. 22, 1926.

DICKINSON, Peyton Ivey, b. Dec. 16, 1826, Ga., d. Sept. 5, 1880, Fayette Co., Ala. - son of George & Fannie (Ivey) Dickinson - m. Oct. 1850, Nancy Ann Davis, b. Feb. 19, 1831, Ala., d. Nov. 3, 1911, Grandview, Texas - dau. of John Hawkins & Nancy Gore (Franklin) Davis. Peyton Ivey Dickinson served the Confederate States Army as Private in the 56th Regt. Ala. - Partisan Rangers. He came to Alabama with his parents at the age of 9. Peyton is buried at the Hopewell Cemetery, north of Fayette. Nancy is buried in Grandview, Texas. Children: (All born in Fayette County.) 1. James Polk Dickinson, b. July 1, 1851, d. Mar. 13, 1906, Fayette, Ala., m. Oct. 3, 1870, Martha Frances "Fannie" Hassell, b. Jan. 21, 1851, Tusca. Co., Ala., d. Feb. 13, 1941, Fayette, Ala. 2. John Franklin Dickinson, b. Mar. 9, 1853, d. Sept. 22, 1939, Bessemer, Ala., m. Feb. 18, 1874, Meranda Evelyn Dickinson, b. Mar. 11, 1855, d. July 3, 1934, Bessemer, Ala. Both are buried at Hopewell in Fayette Co. 3. Mary Alice Dickinson, b. July 8, 1855, m. Sol Hinton, b. Feb. 8, 18__. 4. Thomas L. Dickinson, b. June 1858, m. Lizzie Hubbard. 5. Lockie C. Dickinson, b. Nov. 26, 1859, m. Harve J. Dickinson, b. Mar. 24, 1853, Fayette Co., Ala. 6. Frances Bell Dickinson, b. June 7, 1861, m. Frank Allen. 7. Ida Ann Dickinson, b. June 1866, m. Oct. 2, 1881, Jonas Houston Dickinson, b. May 5, Fay. Co., Ala. 8. Felix Dickinson, b. Oct. 24, 1868, m. Emma White, d. Oct. 26, 1898, Fayette Co., Ala. 9. Lee "Joe" Dickinson, b. July 1870, died as young man. 10. Solomon Dickinson, b. Dec. 21, 1872, m. Stella Asher, b. Sept. 7, 1875, Tusca. Co., Ala. 11. Bessie Dickinson, b. June 25, 1875, m. Tom Polsom, b. April 15, 1877, Caroll Co., Texas, d. Sept. 24, 1955, Grandview, Tex.

DICKINSON, Richard, b. Feb. 4, 1827, Ala., d. Mar. 1905, Miss., m. June 19, 1850, Mary S. Whitley, b. May 23, 1831, Ala., d. June 24, 1889, Miss. - dau. of Jonas & Rebecca (Moore) Whitley. They were married in Fayette County, Ala. at the home of Jonas Whitley by Everette Parmer, J.P. Richard had a finger shot off while serving in the Spanish-American War. Both are buried in Itawamba Co., Miss. Children: (All born in Fayette County.) 1. Temperance Roxy Dickinson, b. June 5, 1851, Fayette Co., Ala., m. Mr. Thomas. 2. Harvey B. Dickinson, b. Mar. 24, 1853, m. Lockie Dickinson, b. Nov. 26, 1859, Fay. Co.

3. Meranda Evelyn Dickinson, b. Mar. 11, 1855, d. July 3, 1934, Bessemer, Ala., m. Feb. 18, 1874, John Franklin Dickinson, b. Mar. 9, 1853, Fayette Co. Ala., d. Sept. 22, 1939, Bessemer, Ala. - Both are buried in Fayette Co. 4. Rebecca J. Dickinson, b. Feb. 25, 1857. 5. Jonas Houston Dickinson, b. Mar. 5, 1859, m. Oct. 2, 1881, Ida Ann Dickinson, b. June 1866, Fayette Co. 6. Burt Frank Dickinson, b. Mar. 23, 1861 - (Baptist Minister.) 7. Helin B. Dickinson, b. Mar. 15, 1863, d. Oct. 5, 1905, m. James Washington Davidson, b. Aug. 12, 1859, Amory, Miss. 8. John J. Dickinson, b. Aug. 25, 1865. 9. William McCay Dickinson. b. Oct. 5, 1869.

DICKINSON, Solomon, b. Dec. 21, 1872, Fayette, Co., Ala. - son of P.I. Dickinson - m. Stella Asher, b. Sept. 7, 1875, Tusca. Co., Ala. Children: 1. Ollie Dickinson, b. Fayette Co., Ala., m. A. J. Anthony. 2. "Doc" Dickinson, b. Fayette Co., Ala.

DICKINSON, Thomas, b. June 1858, Fayette Co., Ala., m. Lizzie Hubbard. He was the son of Peyton I. Dickinson. Children: (All born in Fayette County.) 1. Deanna Dickinson, m. Oliver T. Brooks. 2. Fitzhugh Dickinson. 3. Jim Dickinson. 4. Nanny Dickinson. 5. Virgie Dickinson. 6. Buren Dickinson. 7. Max Dickinson.

DOBBS, Eddie, m. Nell Deavours, dau.of Hershell Deavours. Children: 1. Martha June Dobbs, m. "Little Bud" Robinson. 2. Eddie Jo Dobbs, m. Ronnie Barton.

DODSON, John William, m. 1st. - Mary Corbett, 2nd. - Cornelia Thompson. Children: (1st. wife) 1. Arlington Dodson, b. 1886, d. 1959, m. Velma Smith. Children: (2nd. wife) 1. Florence Dodson, m. Sept. 9, 1908, Walter Bruce Musgrove, b. Jan. 3, 1873, d. July 3, 1944. 2. Alice Dodson, m. Willis May. 3. Murphy Dodson, m. 1st. - Gertrude Astin, 2nd. - Alice Lawrence. 4. Nancy Adeline Dodson, b. Nov. 15, 1890, m. Nov. 10, 1910, Christopher Columbus Couch, b. Oct. 15, 1887, d. Feb. 10, 1950. 5. Vandiver Dodson. 6. Dora Belle Dodson, m. George Estes. (Children: George, Jr., Dorothy, and John Estes)

DODSON, Murphy, - son of John William Dodson, - m. 1st. - Gertrude Aston. Children: (1st. wife.) 1. Naomi Dodson. 2. Ralph Dodson. 3. Johnnye Dodson, m. Sid Cannon. (Child: John Morrow Cannon.) 4. Autie Jo Dodson, m. Gene Moore.
    Murphy Dodson married second - Alice Lawrence. (Child: Wallace Porter Dodson.)

DODSON, W. Arlington, b. 1886, d. 1959, - son of John William Dodson - m. Velma Smith. W. A. Dodson served the City of Fayette as Mayor for a term. Children: 1. Christene Dodson, m. Jerry Summerall. 2. William Dodson. 3. Bessie Dodson, m. Walter Gray. 4. Herbert "Hub" Dodson, m. Sara Hollingshead. 5. Etta Neal Dodson, m. A. M. Grimsley, Jr.

DOUGHTY, George Andrew, b. Oct. 19, 1849, Tusca. Co., Ala , d. Aug. 3, 1920, Fayette Co., Ala., - son of Mordecai F. Doughty - m. Dec. 3, 1871, Hasseltine "Hassie" Rice, b. Sept. 29, 1852, d. Nov. 29, 1934, Fayette Co., Ala. - dau. of Jeotha Rice. Children: 1. Jeotha Doughty, b. Feb. 1, 1874, d. July 23, 1901, m. July 12, 1896, Addie Williamson. 2. Earl Doughty, b. July 19, 1879, m. Jan. 16, 1899, Victoria Williamson. 3. Marcellus Lafayette Doughty, b.

June 7, 1883, m. Nov. 6, 1902, Florence Victoria Taylor. 4. Leona Roberta Doughty, b. June 28, 1889, m. Dec. 19, 1912, George Washington Logan.

DOUGHTY, James Mordecai, b. Nov. 3, or 7, 1853, Ala., d. Jan. 27, 1930, m. Nancy Hazeltine Hinton, b. May 22, 1853, Ala., d. Dec. 14, 1928. He was the son of Mordecai F. Doughty. Children: 1. Thomas Burton Doughty, m. Alma Kimbrell. 2. Dr. James Mitchell Doughty, m. "Dippey" Lee Flint. 3. Elizabeth Doughty, d. 1923, m. Chester Monton of Reform, Ala. 4. Floy Maye Doughty. 5. Virgie Lee Doughty, m. Luther L. Norris. 6. Dr. Mordecai Edward "Ed" Doughty, m. Sept. 29, 1904, Blanche Gregory.

DOUGHTY, Jeremiah, b. May 14, 1777, d. April 15, 1833 or 1838, Tusca. Co., Ala. - son of Joseph Doughty, Sr. - m. Elizabeth __, b. abt. 1776, S.C. (or N.C.) d. between 1852 - 1855? Children: 1. Susannah Doughty, m. Sept. 18, 1823, Henry Fox. 2. Nancy M. Doughty, b. abt. 1805, S.C., m. Dec. 24, 1829, John V. Bealle, b. 1791, Ga. 3. Sarah Doughty, b. abt. 1808, S.C., m. Nov. 27, 1834, Travis George. 4. Joseph F. Doughty, b. abt. 1811, S.C., m. Margaret Pryor, b. Feb. 10, 1816, Tenn. 5. Mordecai Fulton Doughty, b. Sept. 16, 1813, S.C., d. Mar. 28, 1871, Fayette Co., Ala., m. Jan. 16, 1834, Rebecca Pryor, b. April 29, 1819, Ala., d. Feb. 10, 1862, Fayette Co., Ala. 6. Jeremiah C. Doughty, b. abt. 1817, S.C. 7. Rhoda Doughty, m. Andrew Caddell. 8. Elizabeth Doughty, m. Nov. 20, 1838, Spencer Griffin.

DOUGHTY, Joseph Franklin, b. Jan. 15, 1844, Tusca. Co., Ala. (Edge of Fayette Co.) d. Feb. 13, 1889, Fayette Co., Ala. - son of Mordecai F. & Rebecca (Pryor) Doughty - m. Rachel L. A. Boozer, b. May 17, 1845, Tusca. Co., Ala., d. Oct. 1, 1876, Fayette Co., Ala. - dau. of Andrew & Jennie (___) Boozer. Children: 1. Jenny Doughty, m. Henry White. 2. Maranda Jane Doughty, b. June 5, 1869, Fayette Co., Ala., d. May 27, 1954, m. Feb. 24, 1889, William Castle Patterson, b. May 26, 1866, Fayette Co., Ala., d. Nov. 11, 1922. 3. H. Addie Doughty, b. June 30, 1871, Fayette Co., Ala., d. Mar. 30, 1950, m. Jim H. Oswalt, b. Mar. 31, 1868, Ala., d. Jan. 26, 1941, Fayette, Ala. 4. Quillie Doughty, b. 1872, Fayette Co., Ala., d. Dec. 22, 1957, New Mexico, m. 1892, 1st. - Lee West, b. 1871, Ala., d. 1934, New Mexico, 2nd. F. N. Caldiron. 5. Infant Son, b. 1876, d. at birth.

DOUGHTY, Joseph, Sr. d. before April 14, 1815, S.C. (His will is probated in Anderson Dist. S.C.) m. Nancy __, b. Mar. 14, 1742, d. Nov. 15, 1834, Tusca. Co., Ala. Children: 1. Jeremiah Doughty, b. May 14, 1777, S.C., d. April 15, 1833, Tusca. Co., Ala., m. Elizabeth __, b. abt. 1776, d. between 1852 - 1855. 2. Joseph Doughty, Jr., b. Oct. 12, 1783, S.C., d. May 4, 1848, Tusca. Co., Ala., m. Elizabeth __, b. 1792, S.C. 3. Daniel Doughty, b. S.C., d. bef. Feb. 21, 1805, S.C., m. Rachel __. 4. Sarah Doughty, m. James or Alexander Kilpatrick. 5. Rhody Doughty, m. John ? Clayton. 6. Nancy Doughty, m. James T. Barrett.

DOUGHTY, Marcellus LaFayette, b. June 7, 1883, Fayette Co., Ala., - son of George Andrew Doughty - m. Nov. 6, 1902, Florence Victoria Taylor, b. Jan. 4, 1886, Fayette Co., Ala. Mr. Doughty is a farmer and a Mason. Children: 1. Lizzie Ludell Doughty, b. Feb. 15, 1904, (All children born in Fayette Co.,) m. Dec. 24, 1922, Thomas Burton Hinton, b. & d. in Fayette Co. 2. Samuel Clebourne Doughty, b. Nov. 4, 1905, Fayette Co., Ala., m. June 7, 1933, Frances Lawrence. 3. Infant Son, b. Feb. 28, 1907. 4. Gertie Mae Doughty,

b. April 10, 1908. 5. Emmett O'Neal Doughty, b. Dec. 24, 1909, m. Dec. 24, 1933, Pearly Lynn. 6. Richard Purvey Doughty, b. Jan. 8, 1912, m. Sept. 20, 1936, Mabel Oswalt. 7. Mildred Mamie Doughty, b. Feb. 22, 1914. 8. Vivian Mary Bell Doughty, b. Sept. 8, 1915. 9. Delma Dorsey Doughty, b. Feb. 16, 1918. 10. Eloise Doughty, b. July 9, 1920, m. Aug. 18, 1940, Aaron Hallman. 11. Warren Gladstone Doughty, b. July 24, 1922, m. Dec. 25, 1947, Louise Watkins. 12. George William Doughty, b. July 20, 1925, m. Hedwig "Heddy" Lotske (Polish). 13. Frances Imogene "Gene" Doughty, b. Dec. 3, 1927.

DOUGHTY, Mordecai Fulton, b. Sept. 16, 1813, N. C., d. Mar. 28, 1871, Fayette Co., Ala., m. Rebecca Pryor, b. April 27, 1819, N.C., d. Feb. 10, 1862, Fay-Co., Ala. Children: 1. John Beall Doughty, b. July 1, 1835, Ala., d. Oct. 22, 1871. 2. Sarah Elizabeth Doughty, b. June 25, 1837, Ala., d. Jan. 1, 1921, m. Jan. 1, 1921, m. John Kemp. 3. Jeremiah Newton Doughty, b. Jan. 10, 1839, Ala., d. in Civil War. 4. Nancy Venoy Doughty, b. Nov. 22, 1840, Ala. d. April 21, 1904, m. Zachery "Zac" Taylor Savage. 5. Mary Ann Doughty, b. Aug. 4, 1842, Ala., d. Dec. 25, 1928, m. Aug. 8, 1865, George W. Black (son of Jacob Black) b. Oct. 24, 1844, Fayette Co., Ala., d. April 5, 1925. 6. Joseph Franklin Doughty, b. Jan. 15, 1844, Ala., d. Feb. 13, 1889, Fayette Co. Ala., m. Rachel L. A. Boozer, b. May 17, 1845, Ala., d. Oct. 1, 1876, Fay. Co. 7. William Diongue Doughty, b. Sept. 23, 1845, Ala., d. Dec. 22, 1905, m. Angeline Patterson, b. Mar. 1, 1845, Ala., d. Jan. 1, 1906. 8. Roda Rebecca Doughty, b. Feb. 6, 1848, Ala., d. Oct. 14, 1915. 9. George Andrew Doughty, b. Oct. 19, 1849, Ala., d. Aug. 3, 1920, Fayette Co., Ala., m. Hasseltine Rice b. Sept. 29, 1852, Ala., d. Nov. 29, 1934, Fayette Co., Ala. 10. Melissa Frances Doughty (Twin), b. Aug. 24, 1851, Ala., d. July 14, 1916, m. Ira L. Collins (blind preacher.) 11. Martha Jane Doughty (Twin), b. Aug. 24, 1851, Ala., d. June 12, 1922, m. abt. 1904, Doc West. 12. James Mordecai Doughty, b. Nov. 7, 1853, Ala., d. Jan. 27, 1930, m. Dec. 14, 1873, Nancy Hasseltine Hinton, b. May 22, 1853, Ala., d. Dec. 14, 1928. 13. Isaac Monroe Doughty, b. Oct. 3, 1855, Ala., d. June 8, 1876. 14. Josephene Doughty, b. Nov. 3, 1857, Ala., d. Dec. 31, 1908, m. Joe Suggs. 15. Lethia Adeline Doughty, b. Dec. 15, 1859, d. Nov. 14, 1910, m. Joe Suggs. 16. Infant Son, b. Nov. 10, 1861, Ala., d. Dec. 1, 1861.

DOUGHTY, William Diongus, b. Sept. 23, 1845, d. Dec. 22, 1905, - son of Mordecai F. Doughty - m. Angeline Patterson, b. Mar. 1, 1845, Tusca. Co., Ala., d. Jan. 1, 1906 - dau. of Samuel J. Patterson. Children: 1. Deanna Doughty, m. Barne Winters. 2. Sallie Doughty, m. Harve Hocutt. 3. Ludie Doughty, m. Will Gibson. 4. Dr. Will Doughty, m. 1st. - Essie Olive (Dec.) 2nd. - Mary Ferguson. 5. Trannie Doughty, m. Will McCollum. 6. Zack Doughty, m. Beulah Olive. 7. Bruce Doughty, m. Hassie Ayres.

DOWNS, Byron, m. Ruth Freeman, b. Fayette Co., Ala., - dau. of Littleton L. & Annie (Smith) Freeman. Children: 1. Larry Ronald Downs, b. Nov. 3, 1937. 2. Gayle Downs, b. April 10, 1939. 3. Sandra Lynn Downs, b. July 9, 1941.

DOWNS, T. Alexander, m. Elizabeth Jane Patterson, b. Dec. 20, 1832, Ala., - dau. of Samuel J. Patterson. Children: 1. Helen E. Downs, b. 1856, Tusca. Co., Ala., d. 1945, Northport, Ala., m. Washington Castle Rice, b. May 13, 1850, Tusca. Co., Ala. d. May 27, 1907. Both are buried in the Patterson Fam. Cem., Fayette Co. 2. Tommy Downs. 3. Another Son Downs.

DURHAM, Mercer Silas, b. N. C., m. Elvina Bowles, d. 1882. They were married in Green County, Ga. Mercer Silas Durham came from North Carolina to Green Co., Ga. in the early 1800's. Children: 1. Susan Durham, m. Mr. Vardaman. 2. Mattie Durham, m. Mr. Lellie. 3. Babe Durham, m. __ Teal. 4. Sallie Durham, m. __ Smith. 5. Berry Durham, died in service in Confederate States Army. 6. Alex Durham, died in service in Confederate States Army. 7. John Durham, died in Service in Confederate States Army. 8. James Durham, died in service in Confederate States Army. 9. William Henry Durham, b. 1828, Ga., d. 1882, Ga., m. 1848, Emily Fleming, b. 1831, Coffee Co., Ala., d. 1907. Wm. Henry Durham died of effects of wound received in Battle of Soottsylvania, Va. May 12, 1864.

DURHAM, Robert Dixon, b. 1867, Chipley, Ga., d. 1917, - son of Wm. Henry & Emily (Fleming) Durham - m. Mary Elizabeth McDonaldson, b. June 22, 1873, Autauga Co., Ala., - dau. of Richard & Lucinda Jane (Hunt) McDonaldson. Children: 1. John B. Durham, b. Mar. 1900, Jemison, Ala., m. Helen Peterson, b. Iowa. 2. Mary Lou Durham. b. Mar. 1900, Jemison, Ala., m. Frank Jackson, b. Livingston, Ala., d. 1926. 3. Robert Dixon Durham, Jr., b. 1903, Jemison, Ala., m. Lillian Erickson. 4. Nellie Gray Durham, b. Jan. 26, 1906, Jemison, Ala., m. April 1922, Elmer Franklin Abele, b. Mar. 1, 1901, Allentown, Penn. 5. Dan Hunt Durham, b. Aug. 1907, Jemison, Ala. 6. Bobby Wilson Durham, b. 1909, Jemison, Ala., m. Alice Nell Wiley, b. 1911, Birmingham, Ala. 7. Mottie Claire Durham, b. 1911, Birmingham, Ala., d. 1917, Birmingham, Ala. 8. Bettie Durham, b. 1913, Birmingham, Ala., d. 1917, Birmingham, Ala.

DURHAM, William Henry, b. 1828, Ga., d. 1882, buried at Chipley, Ga., - son of Mercer Silas & Elvina (Bowles) Durham, - m. 1848, Emily Fleming, b. 1830, Ga., d. 1907. In the Civil War, he fought in the Battle of Spotsylvania, Va. and was wounded on May 12, 1864. Children: 1. Mary E. Durham, b. 1849, d. 1856. 2. John Albert Durham, b. 1851, d. 1930, m. Cordelia Cornett. 3. James Hardy Durham, b. 1853, d. 1913, m. Georgia Arrington, b. 1860, d. 1906. 4. Charles H. Durham, b. 1855, d. 1923, m. Beulah DeRamus, b. 1861, d. 1945. 5. Viola L. Durham, b. 1860, d. 1896, m. Will Rivers, b. 1859, d. 1917. 6. William S. Durham, b. 1862, d. 1943, m. Lucy Kenum, b. 1868, d. 1927. 7. Virginia Lula Durham, b. 1865, d. 1954, m. Allen Thompson, b. 1868, d. 1952. 8. Robert Dixon Durham, b. 1867, Chipley, Ga., d. 1917, Birmingham, Ala., m. Mary Elizabeth McDonaldson, b. June 22, 1873, Autauga Co., Ala. 9. Gena D. Durham, b. 1871, d. 1947, m. W. H. Page, b. 1869, d. 1952.

DYER, James Milton, b. Jan. 28, 1912, Fayette Co., Ala., - son of W.W. & Virgie V. (Farquhar) Dyer, - m. June 23, 1934, Annie Odell Yerby, b. June 23, 1914, Lamar Co., Ala., - dau. of John S. & Malinda A. (Robertson) Yerby. Children: 1. Jerry Milton Dyer, b. Jan. 26, 1942, Fayette, Ala., 2. Malinda Faye Dyer, b. Aug. 4, 1944, Fayette, Ala.

DYER, Martin, b. Oct. 16, 1854, d. Aug. 8, 1944, Fayette Co., Ala., - son of Nick Dyer - m. Mary Jane Stewart, - dau. of Jack Stewart. Children: 1. Willard Washington Dyer, b. Mar. 18, 1884, Fayette Co., Ala., d. July 12, 1936, Bibb Co., Ala., m. Oct. 15, 1903, Virgie Viola Farquhar, b. Sept. 24, 1889, Fayette Co., Ala. 2. Willis Dyer. 3. Sam Dyer. 4. Ruben Dyer.

DYER, Nick, - wife unknown. Children: 1. Martin Dyer, b. Oct. 16, 1854, d. Aug. 8, 1944, Fayette Co., Ala., m. Mary Jane Stewart. 2. Bud Dyer. 3. Charlie Dyer. 4. Mary Dyer, m. ___ Gregory.

DYER, Willard Washington, b. Mar. 18, 1884, Fayette Co., Ala., d. July 12, 1936, Bibb Co., Ala., - son of Martin & Mary J. (Stewart) Dyer - m. Oct. 15, 1903. Virgie Viola Farquhar, b. Sept. 24, 1889, Fayette Co., Ala. - dau. of Eueil C. & Francis M. (Stamps) Farquhar. Children: 1. James Milton Dyer, b. Jan. 28, 1912, Fayette Co., Ala., m. June 23, 1934, Annie Odell Yerby, b. June 23, 1914, Lamar Co., Ala. 2. Leon Dyer. 3. Cecil Dyer. 4. Cary Dyer. 5. Joe Dyer. 6. George Dyer. 7. Jack Dyer. 8. Billy Dan Dyer. 9. Elsie Dyer. 10. Ruby Dyer.

ECHOLS, John Elliott, b. Nov. 11, 1900, - son of T. A. & Susie (Willingham) Echols - m. Nov. 24, or 14, 1924, Creata "Rita" Foreman. They were married at Santa Anna, Calif. by Rev. Rhodes. Children: 1. John Elliott Echols, Jr., m. April 8, 1950, Sara Glen Perry, at Florala, Ala. 2. Don Edward Echols, m. Sept. 8, 1948, Norma Louise West, at Tuscaloosa, Ala. 3. Patricia Echols, m. June 29, 1958, Alex. E. Brown, at Tuscaloosa, Ala.

ECHOLS, T. A., b. 1876, Belton, Ga., d. 1942, Ga., - son of Albert Echols - m. Jan. 1900, Susie Willingham, b. Oct. 11, 1882, Fayette Co., Ala., d. 1952, Bankston, Ala. - dau. of John T. Willingham. Children: 1. John Elliott Echols, b. Nov. 11, 1900, m. Nov. 14, 1924 at Santa Anna, Calif. by Rev. Rhodes to Creata "Rita" Foreman. 2. Thomas Paul Echols. (T. A. Echols was known as "Bub" Echols.)

EDWARDS, George, b. 1805, S.C., d. July 9, 1876, Fayette Co., Ala., m. Charlotte Bobo, b. 1810, S.C., d. July 18, 1876, Fayette Co., Ala. Children: 1. Martha A. Edwards, b. 1830, S.C. 2. Nancy Edwards, b. 1833, S.C. 3. Luisa J. Edwards, b. 1834, S.C. 4. William L. Edwards, b. 1836, S.C. 5. George W. Edwards, b. 1838, S.C. 6. Livingston Edwards, b. 1840, S.C. 7. Thomas F. Edwards, b. 1842, S.C. 8. Cornelious V. Edwards, b. 1843, S.C. 9. Rutha Edwards, b. 1844, Ala. 10. Mary Edwards, b. 1845, Ala. 11. Emeline Edwards, b. 1848, Ala.

ELLIOTT, John, m. Mary ___, who lived in Havana, Hale Co., Ala. Children: 1. Eril Elliott, m. H. A. Elmore. 2. Edd Elliott, m. Annie Farmer. 3. Jim Elliott, m. Annie Lee Spiller. 4. Frank Elliott. 5. Dick Elliott. 6. John Elliott. 7. Hunter Elliott, lawyer - Judge at Brewton, Ala. 8. Chartie Elliott. 9. Adelia Elliott.

ENGLAND, Enos Council, b. Knox Co., Tenn., d. buried at Marion, Ala., m. Cynthia Gayle, b. Sumter Co., S.C., d. buried at Marion, Ala. Children: 1. James A. England. 2. Charles England, m. 1st. - Miss Tripp. 3. Matt M. England, b. Franklin Co., Tenn., d. Dec. 2, 1861, buried at Marion, Ala. Confederate Army, Co. K. 11th Ala. Inf. 4. Mary England, b. July 11, 1839, d. April 19, 1882, m. Aug. 2, 1855, Harrison Henry Hurt. 5. Martha England, m. Peter T. Hurt. 6. Hermione England, m. July 7, 1864 at Perry Co., Ala. to Marten W. Smith. 7. William Gayle England, m. Olivia Norton. 8. Fannie England, m. Jack Brazelton. 9. Robert Durant England, M. D., b. Aug. 14, 1826, d. Feb. 19, 1870, Marion, Ala., m. Mary Elizabeth Hornbuckle.

ENGLAND, Enos Edward, b. Mobile, Ala., d. 1902, - son of Wm. Gayle & Olivia (Norton) England - m. Nov. 1871, Francis Huntington Tillman, b. Feb. 11,

1851, Perry Co., Ala., d. 1921 - dau. of John Miller & Elizabeth (Plummer) Tillman. Children: 1. William Edward England, b. Nov. 1872, d. 1925, m. Sept. 9, 1899, Gertrude Blake. 2. John Tillman England, b. Feb. 10, 1875, Mobile, Ala., d. Feb. 22, 1955, Mobile, Ala., m. April 15, 1902, Nettie Gray Rodgerson, b. Dec. 26, 1877, d. Feb. 8, 1960, Mobile, Ala. 3. Norton England, m. Susan C. Shaw.

ENGLAND, Harry M., m. Mary Fletcher Robertson, - dau. of T. H. & Mary B. (Sorott) Robertson. Children: 1. Martha Brockway England. 2. Harry Michael England.

ENGLAND, Henry Grey, b. Sept. 11, 1905, Oakgrove, Ala., - son of John Tillman & Nettie Grey (Rodgerson) England - m. July 25, 1937, Mary Marguerite "Peggy" Peters, b. Jan. 4, 1911, Fayette, Ala., - dau. of Robert Frierson & Jessie May (Richardson) Peters. Henry Grey England is an Electrical Engineer. They were married in Columbus, Miss. by Rev. T. D. Bateman. Children: 1. Julia Grey England.

ENGLAND, John Tillman, b. Feb. 10, 1875, Mobile, Ala., d. Feb. 22, 1955, Mobile, Ala., - son of Enos Ed. & Frances Huntington (Tillman) England - m. April 15, 1902, Nettie Grey Rodgerson, b. Dec. 26, 1877, Chunchula, Ala., d. Feb. 8, 1960, Mobile, Ala., - dau. of Henry Grey & Alpha Anna (Nash) Rodgerson. Children: 1. John Edward England, b. Mar. 9, 1903, Oakgrove, Ala., m. 1st. - Inez Lane. 2. Henry Gray England, b. Sept. 11, 1905, Oakgrove, Ala., m. July 25, 1937, Marguerite "Peggy" Peters, b. Jan. 4, 1911, Fayette, Ala. 3. Anna Nash England, b. May 19, 1907, Mobile, Ala., m. June 1, 1935, Bruno Stolley, b. New Orleans, La. 4. Dr. Francis Tillman England, b. Feb. 11, 1910, Mobile, Ala., m. Jan. 13, 1940, Helen G. O. Rourke, b. Mobile, Ala. 5. Mary Gladden England, b. Aug. 26, 1914, Mobile, Ala., m. Rev. George Palmer Pardington.

ENGLAND, Norton Edward, b. Dec. 29, 1912, Greensboro, N. C. - son of Norton & Susan C. (Shaw) England - m. Nov. 2, 1935 at New Orleans, La. to Mary Nell Gentry, b. Dec. 31, 1912, Fayette, Ala. - dau. of Arthur A. & Pearl (Caine) Gentry. Children: 1. Norton England, b. Dec. 24, 1936, New Orleans, La. 2. Mary Susan England, b. Sept. 27, 1940, New Orleans, La.

ENGLAND, William Gayle, b. Marion, Ala., - son of Enos Council & Cynthis (Gayle) England - m. Olivia Norton, b. Marion, Ala., - dau. of ___ & ___ (Hart) Norton. Children: 1. Enos Edward England, b. Mobile, Ala., d. Dec. 1902, Mobile, Ala., m. Nov. 1871, Francis Huntington Tillman, b. Feb. 11, 1851, Perry Co., Ala., d. 1921, Mobile, Ala. 2. William Gayle England, M. D. 3. ___ England, m. J. T. Guennette.

ENIS, Mel, m. Nancy Deavours, dau. of Abraham Deavours. Children: William Enis, m. Alabama Della Jeffries, b. Sept. 4, 1869, d. Sept. 1, 1953, Fayette, Ala. (He died April 26, 1936. He served three terms as Republican Sheriff in Fayette County.) 2. Babe Enis. 3. Rutherford Enis. 4. Hernando Enis.

ENLOW, Joy Marieth, b. June 3, 1915, Tishimingo Co., Miss., m. Nov. 2, 1935, Onida Delillia Humber, b. Nov. 2, 1915, Tishimingo Co., Miss. - dau. of Robt. John Willis Humber. They were married at Iuka, Miss. by the Methodist Minister, W. C. McGill. Children: 1. Lowell Marieth Enlow, b. Feb. 21, 1937,

Tishimingo Co., Miss., m. Jan. 24, 1953, Barbara Ann Arnold, b. Oct. 15, 1935. (Child: Deborah Enlow, b. July 30, 1954, Memphis, Tenn.) 2. Charles Willis Enlow, b. Mar. 15, 1944, Oxford, Miss. 3. John Paul Enlow, b. Oct. 18, 1946, Oxford, Miss.

EUBANK, Novin Harris, b. Birmingham, Ala., m. Francis Louise Propst, b. July 14, 1905, Fayette, Ala., d. July 5, 1950 - dau. of Daniel F. & Susie Emily (Hyde) Propst. Children: 1. Novin H. Eubank, Jr., b. April 7, 1935. 2. Francis Louise Eubank, b. Oct. 9, 1936, m. Nat Barker.

EVANS, Erman Lamar, m. Sept. 5, 1953, Sarah Frances Bertram, b. June 11, 1932, Fayette, Ala. - dau. of F.E & Lottie C. (Collins) Bertram. Children: 1. Kenneth Lamar Evans, b. Sept. 5, 1954, Prattville, Ala., 2. Elaine Evans, b. Sept. 27, 1957, Baton Rouge, La.

FALLIN, George Washington, b. Aug. 14, 1868, Thomaston, Upson Co., Ga., d. Nov. 1, 1939, Ala., - son of John E. & Bernettie A. (Lowery) Fallin - m. 1897 Mary Elizabeth "Mittie" Comer, b. May 30, 1879, Munford, Ala., d. April 20, 1955, Birmingham, Ala. - dau. of Anderson B. & Sue (Walls) Comer. He was a metalsmith. Both are buried at Montgomery, Ala. Children: 1. Courtney Ballard Fallin, b. Feb. 2, 1898, Birmingham, Ala., d. World War I, 1918. 2. Fay Varren Fallin, b. Aug. 10, 1900, Birmingham, Ala., m. 1st. Aleen Dudley, 2nd. Betty ___, 3rd. Marguerite Byrnes. 3. Mabel Fallin, b. May 25, 1902, Birmingham, Ala., m. 1st. - Dec. 3, 1919, Herbert Moses Newell, b. June 9, 1898, Geneva Co., Ala., d. April 21, 1940, Clanton, Ala., buried Montgomery, Ala., 2nd. Ryland Duke Woodson, m. June 7, 1946, b. Mar. 19, 1890, Anthony, Fla. 4. Myrtle Fallin, B. Sept. 23, 1903, Birmingham, Ala., m. Sept. 23, 1920, Harry Lee Walker, b. 1900. 5. Iva Fallin, b. Oct. 6, 1905, Birmingham, Ala., m. June 5, 1926, Homer Asbury Watts, b. July 24, 1905, Montgomery, Ala. 6. Maggie Onie Fallin, b. April 6, 1909, Birmingham, Ala., m. Aug. 26, 1920, Joseph Brown Davies, b. June 3, 1908, d. Oct. 13, 1953. 7. Katherine Fallin, b. Feb. 1, 1911, Montgomery, Ala., d. 1912. 8. Earl O. Fallin, b. June 29, 1913, Montgomery, Ala., m. Helen Denison, b. Mar. 15, 1917, Bessemer, Ala. 9. Alice Kate Fallin, b. Dec. 1, 1915, Montgomery, Ala., m. 1st. Prater Freeman, 2nd. Sept. 7, 1957, Bennett John "Butch" English.

FALLIN, Jackson, b. 1815, Ga. - son of Thomas & Sarah Fallin - m. Feb. 2, 1836, Elizabeth Minter, b. 1822, d. abt. 1857. They were married in Upson Co., Ga. by Edward Birdsay, J. P. Jackson was a farmer. Children: 1. Asa Fallin, b. 1842, Ga. 2. Wm. C. Fallin, b. 1845, Ga., m. Aug. 20, 1865, Rhoda A. C. Taylor. 3. John Fallin, b. 1847, Ga., m. Jan. 16, 1868, Bernettie Ann Lowery, b. Jan. 13, 1842, near Dalton, Ga., d. 1896, Rocky Face, Ga. 4. Richard Fallin, b. 1850, Fa., m. Dec. 26, 1867, Mary Louise Thompson, b. 1855, Ga. 5. Caroline Fallin, b. 1853, Ga.

Jackson Fallin second marriage, April 22, 1858, Hulda Jones, a widow. Children: (2nd wife.) 1. Rebecca R. Fallin, b. 1859, Ga., 2. Sarah E. Fallin, b. 1860, Ga.

Jackson Fallin third marriage, Minerva ___, b. 1821. Children; (3rd. wife) 1. Thomas Fallin, b. 1865, Ga.

FALLIN, John E., b. 1847, Thomaston, Upson Co., Ga. - son of Jackson & Eliz. (Minter) Fallin - m. Jan. 16, 1868, Bernettie Ann Lowrey, b. Jan. 13, 1842, near Dalton, Ga., d. Feb. 4, 1893, near Dalton, Ga. - dau. of Elisha & Selenia Jane (Love) **Lowrey**. Children: 1. Leonard Chieverson Fallin, b. Dec. 26, 1868, Upson Co., Ga., m. Feb. 10, 1892, Mary Leila Thornburgh, b. Feb. 25, 1868, Americus, Ga., d. Jan. 16, 1954. 2. George Washington Fallin, b. Aug. 14, 1869, Upson Co., Ga., d. Nov. 1, 1939, buried Montgomery, Ala., m. 1897, Mary Elizabeth Comer, b. May 30, 1879, Munford, Ala., d. April 20, 1955, buried at Montgomery, Ala.

FALLIN, Thomas, m. Sarah ___. Children: 1. Jackson Fallin, b. abt. 1815, Ga. m. Feb. 2, 1836, 1st. Elizabeth Minter, b. abt. 1822. 2. Asa P. Fallin, b. abt. 1823, Ga. 3. William Fallin, b. 1826, Ga.

FARQUHAR, Euell Cummings, b. Aug. 22, 1867, Fayette Co., Ala., d. Aug. 19, 1936, Fayette Co., Ala. - son of Wm. & Mary J. (Henry) Farquhar - m. Francis Missouri Stamps, b. Nov. 27, ___, Fayette Co., Ala., d. July 1957, Fayette Co. - dau. of John & Sara (Berry) Stamps. Children: Virgie Viola Farquhar, b. Sept. 24, 1889, Fayette Co., Ala., m. W. W. Dyer, b. Mar. 18, 1884, Fayette Co., Ala., d. July 12, 1936, Bibb Co., Ala. 2. Wiley Farquhar. 3. Lucille Farquhar. 4. Carrie Farquhar. 5. Lulu Farquhar.

FARQUHAR, James, b. 1820, Tuscaloosa Co., Ala., d. 1892, Fayette Co., m. 1850 Bashey McGuire, b. 1823, Tusca. Co., Ala., d. 1882, Fayette Co. Children: 1. Amanda Saphronia Farquhar, b. July 1855, Fayette Co., Ala., d. Mar. 9, 1941, Fayette Co., m. June 1874, George Harrison White, b. Jan. 28, 1855, Fayette Co., Ala., d. Mar. 26, 1920, Fayette Co., Ala.

FARQUHAR, Wiley W., b. Nov. 4, 1888, Fayette Co., Ala., d. Sept. 8, 1955, Fayette, Ala. - son of Euel & Fannie (Stamps) Farquhar - m. Lucena Jones, b. Nov. 5, 1889, Fayette Co., Ala. - dau. of Jas. Wm. Rily & Mary Ella (Stacks) Jones. Children: 1. James Euel Farquhar, b. (All children b. Fayette Co.) m. Jan. 16, 1944, Kyle Willis. 2. Mary Frances Farquhar, m. Aug. 6, 1949, Jack Latham. 3. Wiley Farquhar, Jr., m. Mary Polous. 4. Kenneth Farquhar, m. Aug. 26, 1955, Frankie Webster.

FARQUHAR, William, b. Sept. 8, 1821, d. Dec. 28, 1876, Fayette Co., Ala., m. Apr. 6, 1845, Mary Jane Henry, b. Aug. 17, 1826, d. Sept. 15, 1913, Fayette Co. - sister of Joe "Boss" Henry. Children: 1. Euell Cummings Farquhar, b. Aug. 22, 1867, Fayette Co., d. Aug. 19, 1936, Fayette Co., m. Francis Missouri Stamps, b. Nov. 27, ___, Fayette Co., d. July 1957, Fayette Co. 2. Judge Farquhar. 3. Oma Farquhar. 4. Ella Farquhar. 5. Ozie Farquhar. 6. Naomi Jane Farquhar, b. May 9, 1860, Fayette Co., d. Oct. 25, 1940, m. Feb. 10, 1887, James Lee Whitley, b. May 10, 1866, Fayette Co., d. May 29, 1952. Five other children died at an early age in an epidemic.

FARROW, John, b. 1727 in Va., d. 1776 in Spartanburg, Dist., S.C., m. 1751 Rosanna Waters, b. 1734 in Va., date of death unknown. Her name appears on the 1790 census record of Spartanburg Co., S.C. Other Revolutionary records say that she removed to Georgia.

In 1765 John and Rosanna Waters Farrow left Virginia and went to Spartanburg Dist. S.C. settling on the Enoree River. Rosanna Farrow is listed among South Carolina Heroines of the Revolution. She arranged an exchange of soldiers with the British whereby her sons, who were being held prisoners of war, were released.

Children: 1. Sarah Farrow, b. Dec. 29, 1752, Va., m. 1780, Thomas Miles.

2. Thomas Farrow, b. 1755, Va., m. 1st. Rebecca Ward, 2nd. Patience Rochelle, 3rd. Patillo Harrison. At the beginning of the Revolutionary War, Thomas Farrow was living in Orange County, N. C. On January 1, 1776, he volunteered in the Militia under Col. James Thaxton, Hillsborough, N. C. He was in the well known encounter at Cross Creek, N.C. in which the Scotch were defeated. Under Allen McDonald twelve or fifteen hundred Scotchmen had sought to join forces with the British. He was engaged in fighting the Indians twice during 1776, and in 1780 was captured by the British and held prisoner at Ninety-Six Court House. At this time he had a Lieutenant's Commission from Col. John Thomas, Sr. On Jan. 17, 1781 he fought under Gen. Daniel Morgan in the famous battle of the Cowpens, in Spartanburg Co., S.C. He was wounded three times the last wound breaking his hip. After his recovery he again joined the army and left the service a captain. -- The above information is from Thomas Farrow's own account of his services during the Revolutionary War. His affidavit signed Aug. 21, 1833, is on file in the Archives and Records Dept. in Washington, D. C. -- In 1840 he was listed as a Revolutionary War Pensioner from Spartanburg, S.C. His age was 85. Thomas Farrow is buried at Cross Anchor, S.C., according to relatives who live there. -- From Stub Intries to Indents for Revolutionary War Claims X Part II S.C. - Issued Aug. 8, 1786 to Thomas Farrow Sterling 163 pounds.7 .10 1/4. Interest 6 pounds .15 .4

3. John Farrow, b. 1756, Va., m. Miss Brown. John Farrow was a Revolutionary War Soldier and with his brothers Capt. Thomas Farrow, Samuel Farrow and Landon Farrow was the last to leave the service, according to an affidavit signed by his nephew, Maj. William H. Miles. The affidavit was signed January 28, 1854, and is on file in the Archives Dept. in Washington. The following is taken from Stub Intries to Indents for Rev. War. Claims X Part II S.C. - No. 3486 - Lib X - Issued Aug. 8, 1786 to Mr. John Farrow for 99 lbs. .5 .8 ¼ Sterling, duty in Roebuck's Regt. Per a/ audited. Principal 99 lbs. .5 .8 ½ Interest 6 lbs. .19 -- John Farrow and family are listed on the Census of 1790 as living in Spartanburg, Dist., S.C.

4. Landon Farrow, b. Jan. 6, 1759, Va.. d. May 18, 1799, m. Jan. 1782, Rachel Walker, d. Apr. 27, 1842. Their marriage ceremony was performed by her brother, the Rev. Hezekiah Walker. Landon was a soldier in the Rev. War, serving under Col. Benjamin Roebuck and Col. Brandon as a Light Horseman or Dragoon. He fought under Gen. Daniel Morgan in the battle at the Cowpens on Jan. 17, 1781. Sometime during the year 1781 he was captured by the British and held prisoner at Ninety-Six Court House, according to the recollections of Maj. Joseph McJunkin, who was held prisoner with him. Later he was held on a British prison ship in Charleston, then exchanged. He was in the battles of Eutaw Springs and Musgroves Mill. At one time he served as guard and escort to members of his family and neighbors who took their negroes into the hills of North Carolina to keep them from being captured by the British and Tories. During the war, Landon and Rachel Farrow were married. This is an experience she related to Wm. H. Miles, a nephew of her husband. It was also told by Capt. Thomas Farrow. At one time the Rev. Hezekiah Walker rode up to the Farrow home to warn them that the Tories were coming. Landon and wife, his brothers and Hezekiah barricaded the doors and windows and a fight took place. One of the assailants was killed and the Tories attempted to burn the house. A truce was made, the terms of which called for the surrender of a pistol which Rachel Farrow was compelled to bring out and hand over to the enemy. -Landon and Rachel Farrow had nine children whose birth dates were recorded in the family Bible, this page being in the file on record in the Archives Dept. in Washington, D.C. They were residents of Spartanburg,

Dist., S.C. - The following is from Stub Intries to Indents for Rev. War Claims X Part II S.C. - No. 3487 - Lib X - Issued Aug. 8, 1786 to Landon Farrow for 118 lbs. .11 .5 Sterling duty in Roebucks Regt. Per a/ audited. Principal 118 lbs. .11 .5 Interest 8 lbs. .6

5. Samuel Farrow, b. June 5, 1762, Va., m. Elizabeth Herndon. - The following is a biographical account of Samuel Farrow taken from "The Biographical Directory of the American Congress", 1774 - 1949. ".... a representative from S. C.; born in Va. in 1759; moved to S.C. with his father's family, who settled in Spartanburg Dist. in 1765; served in the Rev. War and was wounded in the face by a saber; studied law; was admitted to the bar in 1793 and commenced practice in Spartanburg, S.C.; also engaged in agricultural pursuits near Cross Anchor; Lieutenant Gov. of S.C. 1810 - 1812; elected as a War Democrat to the Thirteenth Congress (Mar. 4, 1813); was not a candidate for renomination in 1814; resumed the practice of law; also engaged in agricultural pursuits; Member of the State House of Representatives 1816-1821; Died in Columbia, S.C., Nov. 18, 1824; Interment in the family burial ground on his plantation, near battlefield of Musgrove Mill, Spartanburg Co., S.C." -- According to the Bible record of the Landon Farrow family, Landon was born in 1759 NOT Samuel. -- The following is from Stub Intries to Indents for Rev. War Claims X Part II S.C. - No. 3489 - Lib X - Issued Aug. 8, 1786 to Samuel Farrow for 96 lbs. .14 .3¼ Sterling duty in Roebuck's Regt. Per a/ audited - Principal 96 lbs. .14 .3¼ Interest .15 .4 -- From affidavit made by a nephew, Wm. H. Miles, on Jan. 28, 1854, Samuel Farrow, with his brothers Landon Farrow, Capt. Thomas Farrow and John Farrow was the last to leave the service.

6. William Farrow, b. Apr. 3, 1768, Spartanburg, S. C., m. Rhoda Waters. Some say that William Farrow was also a soldier of the Rev. War, but according to his own affidavit dated Feb. 9, 1848, Marshall Co., Miss, he does not claim to have been a soldier but tells of some of his exploits. - William Farrow says that he warned his brothers at their station, that the Tories were coming, then he laid out in an old field all night and heard guns firing. He was eleven years old at the time. He further stated that he thought it was those same Tories who wounded his brother Capt. Thomas Farrow, the next day. Capt. Farrow was shot and his hip bone broken as he fought on the Tyger River. -In the year 1814 William Farrow was still living in Spartanburg, Co., S.C. He with Burwell Bobo was a voting Precinct manager. This information is from "The History of Spartanburg Co., S.C." by J.B.O.Landrum. - On Feb. 19, 1816, Wm. Farrow signed his name as a witness on the Last Will and Testament of his brother-in-law, Spencer Bobo.

7. Jane Farrow, b. Aug. 1, 1771, Spartanburg, S.C., m. Spencer Bobo. Spencer Bobo died prior to July 5, 1816 and was buried at the New Hope Cem., near Cross Anchor, S.C. Tombstones give the following information: Rev. Spencer Bobo - May 29, 1767 - Feb.20, 1816. Jane Bobo - Aug. 1, 1768 - July 28, 1828.

Information for this family record was obtained from Bible records, census records, tombstone inscriptions, Military records from the National and State Archives Dept. Historical collections and from correspondence with relatives in South Carolina and other places.

FARROW, William, b. Apr. 3, 1771, Spartanburg, S.C., - son of John & Rosanna (Waters) Farrow - m. Rhoda Waters, - dau. of Col. Philemon Waters. Children: 1. Jane "Jennie" Farrow, b. abt. 1800 to 1810, m. Dr. David West, b. abt. 1780 to 1790. 2. Charlotte Farrow, m. Willis Arnold. 3. Richard Farrow, m. Elizabeth Stewart. 4. Rosanna Farrow, m. Zebulon Bragg. 5. Elizabeth Farrow, m. Thomas Murphy. 6. Nancy Farrow, m. Isaac Odear. 7. Robert Farrow. 8. William Farrow, m. ?Mary "Polly"? Bragg.

FARROW, William T., b. 1820, S. C., - son of Wm. & Rhoda (Waters) Farrow - m. Mary _ (?Polly Bragg?), b. 1825, S.C. He was a Methodist Clergyman and lived many years in the Spartanburg District. He boarded students of the college in his home. C. L. McCartha was a student who boarded there and married a daughter, Susan Jane Farrow. Children: 1. Miles M. Farrow, b. 1840, S.C. 2. Nancy E. Farrow, b. 1843, S.C. 3. Susan Jane Farrow, b. Feb. 20, 1844, S.C., d. June 2, 1869, near Eufaula, Ala., m. Dec 5, 1861, Clarence Linden McCartha, b. Mar. 15, 1841, S.C., d. Sept. 29, 1920, Troy, Ala. 4. William W. Farrow, b. 1846, S.C. 5. Many E. Farrow, b. 1848, S.C. 6. Sarah M. Farrow, b. 1851, S.C. 7. Eliza F. Farrow, b. 1854, S.C. 8. Thomas C. Farrow, b. 1857, S.C. 9. Charles C. Farrow, b. 1860, S.C.

FAULKNER, Newton Grant, b. June 5, 1863, Lamar Co., Ala. - son of Berlie & Susan (Cannon) Faulkner - m. Dec. 28, 1893, Sarah M. Draper, - dau. of James Wm. and Deliah Susan (Dunnam) Draper. Children: 1. Maggie Susan Faulkner, b. Dec. 14, 1894, Lamar Co., Ala. 2. Minnie Lee Faulkner, b. April 18, 1896, Lamar Co., m. James Edward J. Pasteur. 3. John Harvie Faulkner, b. Nov. 12, 1897, Lamar Co. 4. Emmet Lawton Faulkner, b. Sept. 3, 1899, Lamar Co. 5. Isaiah Faulkner (Twin), b. Aug. 10, 1901, Lamar Co. 6. Mary Ida Faulkner (Twin), b. Aug. 10, 1901, Lamar Co. 7. James Andrew Faulkner, b. Aug. 28, 1910, Lamar Co. 8. Henry Edward Faulkner, b. Feb. 15, 1908, Lamar Co.

FELTMAN, George, m. Emma Sawyer - dau. of Jas. H. Sawyer. Children: 1. Exie Feltman, m. George Cook. 2. Milliard Feltman.

FINCH, ___, m. Margaret ___, b. 1791, S.C. The widow Finch married a David McGee Aug. 2, 1832, but records do not show any children except by the Finch marriage. Children: (1st. marriage) 1. Elizabeth Finch, b. Feb. 25, 1813, Ala., d. Aug. 22, 1892, Fayette Co., m. Oct. 2, 1831, James Ransom South, b. July 16, 1811, S.C., d. June 10, 1860, Fayette Co. Both are buried in the South Family Cemetery, Fayette Co. 2. Mary Finch, b. 1815, m. Sampson McGee. 3. Masterson Finch, b. 1827, d. May 25, 1890, m. Elizabeth Hendrix, b. 1831, d. May 13, 1908. Both are buried in the Hagar Graveyard. 4. Sarah M. Finch, m. 1839, W. G. Drake.

FINCH, Masterson, b. 1827, d. May 25, 1908, - son of Margaret Finch (2nd. marriage to David McGee) - m. Elizabeth Hendrix, b. 1831, d. May 13, 1908. Both are buried at the Hagar Graveyard (Rose Hill or Hopewell Baptist Church Cemetery). Children: 1. Margaret Frances Finch, b. Dec. 3, 1866, Fayette Co., d. Oct. 16, 1933, Fayette Co., m. 1887, Isaac Michael, b. July 4, 1862, Athens ? Ga., d. Feb. 24, 1938, Fayette Co., Ala. 2. Corrie Finch, b. Fayette Co., d. buried in Pickens Co., Ala., m. John Blake. 3. Hassie Finch, d. buried at Cordova, Ala., m. Jim Rice. 4. Villa Finch. 5. James Finch, d. buried in Miss., m. Sally Willingham.

FINCH, Paul A., b. Vernon, Ala., m. 1945, Mary Ann Jones, b. Sept. 11, 1929, - dau. of Fred & Lona Frances Jones. Children: 1. Mervin C. Finch, b. Nov. 25, 1946, Fayette, Ala.

FORD, James, b. Mar. 24, 1821, d. July 24, 1892, m. Elizabeth West, b. Feb.

18, 1814, d. June 24, 1882. He served in the Civil War. They came to Fay. Co. Ala. several years preceding the Civil War. Children: 1. John Perry Ford, b. June 12, 1844, d. in camp during Civil War. 2. Stephen James Ford, b. Dec. 10, 1848. 3. Sarah Jane Ford, b. April 23, 1850. 4. Martelia Ford, b. Sept. 30, 1852, d. June 2, 1926, m. Jan. 19, 1871, Leonard C. Shirley.

FORSYTH, Martin Van, b. 1881, Talladega, Ala., d. April 30, 1941, Fayette, Ala., m. Dec. 1902, Julia Ann Barnett, b. Sept. 9, 1883, Talladega, Ala. - dau. of Wm. Monroe Barnett. They were married at Shelby, Ala. by Justice of Peace Pearson. M. V. Forsyth was a railroad section foreman. Children: 1. Lillian Lela Forsyth, b. Dec. 3, 1903, Talladega, Ala., m. Garland S. King. 2. Clarence Jackson Forsyth, b. 1905, d. Dec. 1928 (Typhoid Fever). 3. Ezell Forsyth, b. 1907, Shelby, Ala. 4. Grady L. Forsyth, b. Dec. 13, 1910, Shelby, Ala., d. Nov. 10, 1944 (Killed in World War II.) 5. Clifton Forsyth, b. Sept. 6, 1913, Shelby, Ala., d. buried Fayette City Cem., m. O'Bera Fullerton, b. Fayette Co., Ala. 6. Cara Forsyth, b. Sept. 6, 1913, Shelby, Ala., m. Lorene Thompson, b. Nov. 1 __. 7. Julia Bell Forsyth, b. Feb. 8, 1921, Fayette, Ala., m. Feb. 16, 1946, Archie J. Gibson, Jr., b. Nov. 1, 1918, Newtonville, Ala.

FOSTER, Garland, b. April 4, 1798, Spartanburg, Co., S.C., d. May 24, 1858, m. 1825, Nancy Moss, b. Aug. 12, 1806, Spartanburg Dist., S.C. Both are buried in Spartanburg Co., S.C. He was the son of Wm. "Maj. Billy" & Mary Ann (Jones) James Foster. She was the dau. of James & Emily (Harrison) Moss. Children: 1. Emily Foster, b. June 1, 1826, Spartanburg Dist.,S.C., d. July 15, 1894, Pickens Co., Ala., m. Oct. 15, 1850, Wm. Pinckney Richardson, b. Jan. 16, 1818, Spartanburg, S.C., d. Dec. 26, 1860, Pickens Co., Ala. 2. John James Foster, b. Oct. 29, 1824, m. in Australia, Margaret Boyd, b. Ireland. Settled on Williamette River in State of Washington. 3. Sallie Foster, b. Nov. 27, 1827. 4. Calvin Foster, b. July 18, 1829, m. 1853, Elizabeth Dodd. 5. Mary A. Foster, b. April 20, 1831, m. James Foster. 6. Wm. H. Foster, b. Apr. 21, 1833, m. 1st. - Lucy or Mary Dodd, 2nd. - Judith Coons. 7. Robert Benton Foster, b. June 16, 1835. 8. Elijah Foster, b. July 15, 1837, m. Fannie Vingo. 9. Fannie Goodlet Foster, b. Nov. 6, 1839, d. Nov. 13, 1879, Texas, m. Sept. 21, 1869, John James Richardson, b. Aug. 28, 1837, DeKalb Co., Ala., d. Mar. 25, 1909. 10. Julie J. Foster, b. Aug. 16, 1841. 11. Augusta A. Foster, b. Apr. 26, 1844, m. John J. Simpson. 12. Laura T. Foster, b. July 31, 1846, m. William Vingo.

FOSTER, James or Thomas, m. Jane __. Children: 1. Wm. "Maj. Billy" Foster, b. 1753, Amelia Co., Va., m. Mrs. Mary Ann (Jones) James. 2. James Foster. 3. John Foster. 4. Col. Isham Foster (Rev. Soldier.) 5. Madon or Maiden Foster. 6. Sallie Foster. 7. Moses Foster.

FOSTER, Wm. "Maj. Billy", b. 1753, Va., d. Mar. 9, 1818, - son of James or Thomas Foster - m. Mrs. Mary Ann (Jones) James, - dau. of John & Sallie (Hughes) Jones. Major Billy Foster moved from Amelia Co., Va. to South Carolina in 1791 near Mt. Zion Church, Spartanburg Dist., S.C., where he is buried. For reference on his Revolutionary War Service - National D.A.R. No. 100642 - D.A.R. Lineage Book Vol. 101, page 200. Children: 1. Annie Foster, b. April 20, 1783, m. James Young. 2. Jones Foster, b. July 20, 1784, m. Nancy Walker. 3. James Foster, b. July 4, 1786, m. Ann Turner. 4. Moses Foster, b. Oct. 9, 1787, m. Mason Vingo. 5. Maiden or Madon Foster, b. Feb.

14, 1790, m. Collin Smith. 6. Elijah Foster, b. Dec. 23, 1791, m. ___ Hancock, and moved to Tenn. 7. Sallie Foster, b. Oct. 23, 1793, m. Beverly Randolph Chapman. 8. Garland Foster, b. April 4, 1798, d. May 24, 1858, Spartanburg, S.C., m. 1823, Nancy Moss, b. Aug. 12, 1806, d. Spartanburg, S.C. 9. Calvin Foster, b. Mar. 16, 1800.

FOWLER, Andrew M., b. May 7, 1898, Fayette Co., Ala., m. Nov. 16, 1917, Dollie Ree Moore, b. Sept. 1, 1900, Fayette Co. Andrew M. Fowler's parents - Taylor & Francis (Price) Fowler. Grandparents - Dan Fowler.
    Dollie Ree (Moore) Fowler's parents - Wiley & Maggie Dailey (Cargile) Moore. Grandparents - John & Nannie (Miles) Moore; and William & Katheran (Smith) Cargile. Great Grandparents - Carson & Sara (Davis) Moore.
    Andrew M. Fowler's Children: 1. Gaylon Miles Fowler, b. Oct. 6, 1935, Fayette, Ala.

FOWLER, Fletcher M., b. May 22, 1902, Bankston, Ala., d. Dec. 22, 1949, Fay. Ala. - son of Wm. J. & Mary (Rice) Fowler, - m. June 22, 1924, Exie Pearl Hollingsworth, b. Feb. 22, 1905, Fayette Co., Ala. - dau. of John A. & Sara I. Hollingsworth. They were married in Fayette County, Ala. by Posey Johnson. F. M. Fowler was owner and manager of Fowler Hardware Co. and also, distributor of the Pan-American Oil Company Products. Children: 1. Willena Aline Fowler, b. May 15, 1925, Fayette Co, m. 1st. Jimmy Williams, b. Northport, Ala., d. Dec. 21, 1949, Fayette, Ala., 2nd. - Paul M. Tucker, b. May 5, 1922, Fayette, Ala. 2. William Andrew Fowler, b. Dec. 7, 1928, Winfield, Ala., m. Sarah Joy Maddox, b. Jan. 2, 1928, Fayette Co., Ala.

FOWLER, William Andrew, b. Dec. 7, 1928, Winfield, Ala., - son of F.M. & Exie (Hollingsworth) Fowler - m. Oct. 12, 1947, Sarah Joy Maddox, b. Jan. 2, 1928, Fayette, Ala. - dau. of Wm. Y. & Josie (South) Maddox. They were married at Fayette, Ala. by Rev. A. M. Nix. W. A. Fowler is Distributor for the American Oil Company Products. Children: 1. William Andrew Fowler, Jr., b. Aug. 8, 1948, Fayette, Ala. 2. Deborah Joy Fowler, b. Dec. 9, 1950, Fayette, Ala. 3. Stephen Fletcher Fowler, b. Feb. 28, 1957, Fayette, Ala.

FOWLER, William Jacob, b. June 23, 1858, d. July 23, 1932, Fayette Co., Ala. m. Mary Rice, b. Nov. 11, 1858, d. June 2, 1938, Fayette Co., Ala. Both are buried at the Philadelphia Church Cemetery, north of Bankston, Ala. Children: (All born in Fayette Co.) 1. Fletcher M. Fowler, b. May 22, 1902, Bankston, Ala., d. Dec. 22, 1949, Fayette, Ala., m. Exie Pearl Hollingsworth, b. Feb. 22, 1905, Fayette Co. 2. Austin A. Fowler, m. Dorothy Willingham. 3. Arnold B. Fowler, d. buried Elmwood Cem., Birmingham, Ala., m. Seatus Hamilton. 4. Arthur C. Fowler, m. Grace Ellison, b. Sterling Community, Tusca. Co., Ala. 5. Ethel Fowler, m. Charlie Brady. 6. Esther Fowler, m. J. Cleve Smith. 7. Edna Fowler, m. W. Olen Dobbs, Fayette Co., Ala. 8. Eva Fowler, m. Wilson S. Dobbs, b. Fayette Co., Ala., d. Dec. 25, 1957, Fayette, Ala.

FRAZIER, Stephen A., b. Jan. 16, 1887, Pulaski, Tenn. - son of Francis & Margaret Frazier - m. Oct. 25, 1916, Sallie McConnell Robertson, b. Sept. 28, 1885, Fayette, Ala. - dau. of Joseph R. & Malinda (McConnell) Robertson. They were married at the First Methodist Church in Fayette, Ala. by Rev. W. H. Mansfield. S. A. Frazier is a lumberman. She is a teacher. Children: 1. Stephen Robertson Frazier, b. Aug. 20, 1917, Fayette, Ala., m. Sept. 14, 1940 Margaret Heflin Kyle, b. Oct. 2, 1917, Oklahoma City, Okla.

FREEMAN, Allen Hamby, b. 1831, S.C., d. Dec. 13, 1895 - son of Wm. & Delila (Walters) Freeman - m. Mary Evaline Crowe, b. 1832, d. Feb. 18, 1914. He was a farmer. On Feb. 1, 1893, Allen H. Freeman applied for a pension for his Confederate military service. He certified that he had served as a Priv. in Co. H. 41st. Ala. Regt. C.S.A. and that on or about July 1, 1863, he was wounded in the arm at Jackson, Miss. He stated that he was also wounded in the hand at Bean Station, Tenn. Mr. Freeman proved his claim to the satisfaction of the Pension Board and his pension was granted. After his death, his widow, Mrs. M. E. Freeman drew a Confederate widow's pension. Both are buried at the Pilgrim's Rest Baptist Church, Fayette Co., Ala. Children: 1. William L. "Bill" Freeman, b. May 14, 1860, d. June 26, 1929, Fayette Co., m. Mary Ella Lindsey, b. Jan. 3, 1877, d. May 6, 1956, Fayette Co., Ala. 2. John A. Freeman, b. July 12, 1862, d. Aug. 6, 1913, Fayette Co., m. Mollie Abernathy, b. Oct. 6, 1878, d. April 10, 1952, Fayette, Ala. 3. Charles M. "Bud" Freeman, b. 1871, d. 1946, Fayette, m. Lona Lindsey. 4. Jane Freeman. 5. Melvins "Sis" Freeman. 6. Baba Freeman, m. Isom Channell. 7. George Freeman, m. Sis Belk. 8. Fannie Freeman, m. "Hoss" Threet.

FREEMAN, Charles M., b. 1871, d. 1946, Fayette Co., Ala. - son of Allen Hamby & Evaline (Crowe) Freeman - m. Lona Lindsey - dau. of John Lindsey. Chas. M. Freeman was a farmer and a carpenter. Both are buried at Pilgrim's Rest Cemetery, Fayette Co. Children: 1. Gertrude Freeman, b. Mar. 12, 1900, Fayette Co., m. Claude Edwards. (Children: Ivaline Edwards, m. John Cash Walden.) 2. Charlie Freeman, b. Nov. 28, 1902, Fayette Co. 3. Maude Freeman, m. Delbert Belk. (Children: Constance "Connie" Belk.) 4. Mamie Freeman, m. Earnest Walters. (Child: Sharkie Walters.) 5. Bessie Freeman, m. A. O. Rayfield. 6. Lessie Freeman, m. Gardner Cash. 7. Choyce Freeman. 8. Pauline Freeman, m. B. I. Davis. (Child: John Davis.) 9. Bailey Freeman, m. Ruby Handley. 10. Bobbie Freeman, m. Gordon Belk. 11. John Buford Freeman, m. Elizabeth Gosa. 12. Mozell Freeman, m. Venoy Porter. (Children: Jack and Jimmy Porter.)

FREEMAN, Clyde Lee, b. Jan. 3, 1897, Fayette Co., Ala. - son of Wm. L. & Mary Ella (Lindsey) Freeman - m. Velma Nelson, b. Jan. 20, 1899, Fayette Co. Children: 1. Lattie Freeman (Twin), b. May 23, 1920, m. Marion Williamson, Jr. 2. Lottie Freeman (Twin) b. May 23, 1920, m. ___ Cannon. 3. Alfred Wm. Freeman, b. Nov. 13, 1924, m. "Winnie" Maurine Loftis. (Child: Tommy Freeman)

FREEMAN, George David, b. Oct. 21, 1909, Fayette, Ala. - son of Littleton L. & Annie (Smith) Freeman - m. Dessie White, b. Oct. 2, 1909, Fayette Co., Ala. Children: 1. Flora Lee Freeman, b. Mar. 24, 1929, m. Elmer Galen Cargile, b. Jan. 27, 1927. (Child: Cecelia Pauline Cargile, b. Nov. 14, 1952.) 2. John David Freeman, b. Jan. 16, 1935, m. Peggy ___. (Children: David Lamar Freeman, b. Sept. 19, 1956.) 3. Linda Jean Freeman, b. Jan. 18, 1938, m. Aug. 8, 1959 ___ Harris.

FREEMAN, George Washington, b. Nov. 23, 1845, Fayette Co., d. Jan. 6, 1920, Fayette Co., - son of Wm. & Delila Freeman - m. Selena Leona Stillman, b. May 3, 1848, d. May 1871 - dau. of Thomas & Mary (Ward) Stillman. G. W. Freeman was a farmer and an ordained minister of the Missionary Baptist Church. Selena is buried at the Stillman Family Cemetery, Fayette Co., Ala. and he is buried in the Pilgrim's Rest Baptist Church Cemetery, Fayette Co. Children: 1. John Franklin Freeman, b. Sept. 23, 1869, Fayette Co., d. Dec. 7, 1943,

Fayette Co., m. Jan. 1, 1899, Mollie Agnes Howton, b. July 28, 1866, Fayette Co., d. May 3, 1953, Fayette, Ala. 2. William Leander Freeman, b. Oct. 18, 1870, Fayette Co., d. Aug. 18, 1938, Fayette Co., m. Dona Sykes, b. Feb. 5, 1880, d. Oct. 28, 1952, Fayette Co.

G. W. Freeman married second to Julia Ann Bobo, b. May 6, 1842, S.C., d. Nov. 1929, Fayette Co. - dau. of Spencer & Polly Bobo. Children: (by second marriage.) 1. Michael Walters Freeman, b. July 21, 1873, Chickasaw Co., Miss. d. Feb. 22, 1949, Fayette Co., m. Lillie Moore, b. Feb. 7, 1884. 2. Henry Shelton Freeman, b. Aug. 21, 1875, Chickasaw Co., Miss., d. Mar. 24, 1941, Fayette Co., m. Jan. 15, 1899, Etta Crowe. 3. James LaFayette Freeman, b. Aug. 7, 1877, Chickasaw Co., Miss., m. Mrs. Zora (Owens) Lindsey, b. Feb. 18, 1879. 4. Minnie Freeman, b. Feb. 22, 1879, Chickasaw, Co., Miss. m. John Belk. 5. Littleton Leroy Freeman, b. Mar. 11, 1882, Chickasaw Co., Miss., m. 1st. - Mamie Ellis, 2nd. - Annie Smith.

FREEMAN, Gordon (Twin, b. Dec. 6, 1905, Fayette Co., - son of Littleton L. & Mamie (Ellis) Freeman - m. Joy Inez __, b. 1913. Children: 1. Joy Delorice Freeman, b. Aug. 3, 1936, m. Leonard Dale Hoover, b. Jan. 29, 1932. (Children: Charlotte Lynn, b. Jan. 14, 1953 and Linda Gayle Hoover, b. Nov. 1, 1954.)

Gordon Freeman, second marriage to Wilda Pearl Parker, b. Aug. 17, 1922. Children: (2nd. marriage.) 1. James Grady Freeman, b. Aug. 24, 1953.

FREEMAN, Gorman (Twin), b. Dec. 6, 1905, Fayette Co., - son of Littleton L. & Mamie (Ellis) Freeman - m. 1st. - Ruby Nelson. Children: (1st. wife.) 1. Billy Freeman. 2. Kenneth Freeman. 3. Joe Neal Freeman. 4. Infant Dau.

Gorman Freeman second marriage to Lois Henley - dau. of John Henley. Children: (2nd wife.) 1. Mamie Ellis Freeman, d. Nov. 1959. 2. Alice Faith Freeman, b. Jan. 29, 1943. 3. Buddy Freeman.

FREEMAN, Grady, b. May 6, 1911, Fayette Co., d. Sept. 12, 1952, buried at Union Chapel, Lamar Co., Ala., m. Gladys Shelton. Children: 1. Don Freeman, b. July 9, 1935, m. Margaret Foster. (Children: Donna Freeman.) 2. Elizabeth Ann Freeman, b. Jan. 31, 1943. 3. Martha Sue Freeman.

FREEMAN, Henry Shelton, b. Aug. 21, 1875, Chickasaw Co., Miss., d. Mar. 24, 1941, Fayette, Ala. - son of G. W. & Julia Ann (Bobo) Freeman. Children: 1. Dan Freeman, b. Jan. 1, 1900, Fayette Co., d. 1905, Fayette, Ala. 2. Basil Manley Freeman, b. Oct. 16, 1902, Fayette Co., 3. Joe Buron Freeman, b. Dec. 1, 1906, Fayette Co., m. Mertie Nichols. 4. Lorene Freeman, b. Dec. 6, 1914, Fayette Co., m. Marion Martin. (Child: 1. Tony Martin.)

FREEMAN, Jim, brother of William Freeman - m. Sallie Caine. Children: 1. Shackelford "Shack" Freeman, m. Sallie Hayes. (Children: Richard and Emily Freeman, m. a Morgan.) 2. Mattie Freeman, m. Thomas Clifton. 3. Mary Elizabeth "Lizzie" Freeman, m. Marion Johnson. (Children: W. Albert "Bert" Johnson and Buren Johnson, deceased.)

FREEMAN, Joe Buron, b. Dec. 1, 1906, Fayette Co., m. Mertie Nichols. He is a son of Henry Shelton & Etta (Crowe) Freeman. Children: 1. James Henry Freeman, b. Apr. 22, 1926. 2. Joe B. Freeman, b. Apr. 2, 1928. 3. Naomi Freeman, b. Feb. 13, 1930. 4. William Edward Freeman, b. Mar. 26, 1932. 5. Billie Sue Freeman, b. May 11, 1934. 6. Mary Fay Freeman (Twin) b. Apr. 5, 1936.

7. Jimmie Ray Freeman (Twin), b. Apr. 4, 1936, d. Apr. 7, 1936. 8. Dorothy Jane Freeman, b. Aug. 25, 1939. 9. Joe Ed Freeman, b. Sept. 4, 1942. 10. Charles Alfred Freeman, b. Sept. 12, 1943. 11. Barbara Ann Freeman, b. Jan. 8, 1946.

FREEMAN, John A., b. July 12, 1862, d. Aug. 6, 1913, Fayette Co., Ala. - son of Allen Hamby & Evaline (Crowe) Freeman - m. Mollie Abernathy, b. Oct. 6, 1878, d. Apr. 10, 1952, Fayette Co., Ala. - dau. of Joel & Lizzie (Holliman) Abernathy. Both are buried at the Pilgrim's Rest Cemetery, Fayette Co., Ala. Children: 1. Florence Freeman, 2. Flossie Freeman. 3. Mattie Lou Freeman. 4. Eula Freeman. 5. John Sourgeon Freeman.

FREEMAN, John Franklin, b. Sept. 23, 1869, Fayette Co., d. Dec. 7, 1943, Fayette, Ala. - son of Geo. Wash. & Selena L. (Stillman) Freeman - m. Jan. 1, 1899, Mollie Agnes Howton, b. July 28, 1866, Fayette Co., Ala., d. May 15, 1953, Fayette, Ala. - dau. of Geo. Wash. & Martha Ann (Bobo) Howton. They were married at the home of her father, G. W Howton by Rev. Matt Brock, near Covin, Ala. John Franklin Freeman was a farmer, teacher and a justice of the peace. Both are buried at Macedonia Baptist Church Cemetery, Fayette Co., Ala. Children: 1. Jessie Freeman, b. June 15, 1900, Fayette Co., d. July 17, 1951, m. Dec. 22, 1928, Lanthus Theodore Hughes, b. July 29, 1900, Fayette Co., Ala. 2. Alice Freeman, b. April 7, 1903, Fayette Co., Ala. 3. Robert Howard Freeman, b. Sept. 2, 1908, Fayette Co., Ala., m. Dec. 21, 1935, Mary Lee Waldrop, b. Sept. 22, 1914, Tusca. Co., Ala.

FREEMAN, Littleton Leroy, b. Mar. 11, 1882, Chickasaw Co., Miss - son of Geo. W. & Julia Ann (Bobo) Freeman - m. 1st. - Mamie Ellis. Children: (1st wife.) 1. Gordon Freeman (Twin) b. Dec. 6, 1905, Fayette Co., m. 1st. - Joy Inez __, b. 1913, 2nd. - Wilda Pearl Parker, b. Aug. 17, 1922. 2. Gorman Freeman, (Twin) b. Dec. 6, 1905, Fayette Co., m. 1st. - Ruby Nelson, 2nd. - Lois Henley. Littleton Leroy Freeman, second marriage to Annie Smith - dau. of David Smith. Children: (2nd. wife.) 1. George David Freeman, b. Oct. 21, 1909, Fayette, Ala., m. Dessie White, b. Oct. 2, 1909, Fayette Co., Ala. 2. Grady Freeman, b. May 6, 1911, Fayette Co., d. Sept. 12, 1952, Fayette Co., m. Gladys Shelton. 3. Annie Grace Freeman, b. Oct. 22, 1913, Fayette, Co., m. Joe Reid Long. 4. Ruth Freeman, m. Byron Downs. 5. Julia Freeman, b. April 17, 1917, Fayette Co., m. Floyd Irving Guerney, b. Apr. 5, 1917, Michigan.

FREEMAN, Michael Walters, b. 1841 - son of Wm. & Delila (Walters) Freeman - m. Fannie Peters. Children: 1. William Freeman, m. Bell Suggs. 2. Charlie Freeman. 3. Claborne Freeman. 4. Edward Freeman, m. __Cauley. 5. George Freeman. 6. Lillie Freeman, m. Smith Patterson. 7. Myrtle Freeman. 8. Earl Freeman. 9 Elisha Freeman.

FREEMAN, Micahel Walters, b. July 21, 1873, Chickasaw Co., Miss., d. Feb. 22, 1949, Fayette Co., Ala. son of Geo. W. & Julia Ann (Bobo) Freeman - m. Lillie Moore, b. Feb. 7, 1884. Children: 1. Lucille Freeman, b. May 19, 1907, Fayette Co., m. Oct. 30, 1927, Albron Brooks Sullivan. (Children: Billy Brooks, b. Feb. 7, 19___, m. Mary Nell Dunn Feb. 6, 1946; Twin Sons, unnamed, b. & d. Dec. 28, 1930; and Lucille Sullivan, m. Archie L. Montgomery.) 2. Robert E. Lee Freeman, b. Mar. 14, 1904, Fayette Co., m. Pauline Ray. (Children: Mary Evelyn, m. a Reynolds; Billy Gene; Roberta; Virgie Ruth and Annette Freeman.) 3. Louella Freeman, b. Mar. 2, 1925, Fayette Co., m. Oakley

Easley. (Children: Linda Faye Easley.)

FREEMAN, Robert Howard, b. Sept. 2, 1908, Fayette Co., - son of John Franklin & Mollie Agnes (Howton) Freeman - m. Dec. 21, 1935, Mary Lou Waldrop, b. Sept. 22, 1914, Tusca. Co., Ala. - dau. of Geo. Marshall & Mary Isabel (Williamson) Waldron. They were married at the Mt. Vernon Methodist Parsonage in Fayette Co., Ala. He enjoys farming and is affiliated with the Highway Dept. of Tuscaloosa Co., Ala. Children: 1. Mary Agnes Freeman, b. Aug. 26, 1937, Fayette Co., Ala., m. April 12, 1956, Leonard Julius Smith, b. Aug. 30, 1937. 2. Bobbie Sue Freeman, b. Aug. 23, 1940, Fayette Co., Ala. 3. Clelia Ann Freeman, b. Oct. 2, 1941, Fayette Co., Ala.

FREEMAN, William, b. 1810, N.C. - brother of Jim Freeman - m. Delila Walters, b. 1811, N.C. He was a farmer. Both are buried in Fayette Co., Ala. Children: 1. Allen Hamby Freeman, b. 1831, S.C., m. Evaline Crowe, b. 1832. (He served in Co. H. 41 Ala. Inf. C.S.A.) 2. Mary Ann Freeman, b. 1837, m. Simon Lane. 3. Isabella Freeman, b. 1838, m. Angus McDonald. (Both are buried at Pilgrim's Rest Cem.) 4. Michael Walters Freeman, b. 1841, m. Fannie Peters. 5. George Washington Freeman, b. Nov. 23, 1845, m. 1st. - Selena Leona Stillman (died), 2nd. - Julia Ann Bobo, b. May 3, 1848. 6. Delile Jane Freeman (Twin), m. Acie Anthony. (Children: Annie, Bell; Zena; Will; and Oscar Anthony.) 7. Kizzie Mahala Freeman (Twin) m. William Sidney Nichols.

FREEMAN, William Leander, b. Oct. 18, 1870, Fayette Co., d. Aug. 18, 1939, Fayette Co., m. Dona Sykes, b. Feb. 5, 1880, d. Oct. 10, 1952, Fayette Co. He was a farmer. Both are buried at the Macedonis Cemetery, Fayette Co., Ala. Children: 1. Sophia Freeman, b. July 12, 1899, m. "Red" Gables. (Children: Lewis Monroe, b. Feb. 18, 1917; and Wendon Veto Gables, b. Jan. 5, 1919.) 2. Fletcher Freeman, b. Mar. 19, 1898, m. Gracie Anderson. (Children: Vaudine; Jack; and Yvonne Freeman.) 3. Autie Freeman, b. Nov. 14, 1903, m. __Sanford. (Children: Joe Lee; Arval Gray; Beatrice; and Dan Sanford.) 4. Willia Dean Freeman, b. June 20, 1907, m. Marshall Allen Stephens, b. May 30, 1907. See Stephens.

FREEMAN, William Lewis "Bill", b. May 14, 1860, d. June 26, 1929, Fayette Co. Ala. - son of Allen Hamby & Mary E. (Crowe) Freeman - m. Mary Ella Lindsey, b. Jan. 3, 1877, d. May 6, 1956, Fayette Co., Ala. - dau. of John & Judy Catherine (Taylor) Lindsey. He was a farmer. Both are buried at Pilgrim's Rest Cem., Fayette Co., Ala. Children: 1. Clyde Lee Freeman, b. Jan. 3, 1897, Fayette Co., m. Jan. 13, 1918, Velma Nelson, b. Jan. 20, 1899, Fayette Co. 2. Claude Leach Freeman, b. Dec. 22, 1898, Fayette Co., d. Aug. 23, 1949, Fayette Co. 3. Clabe Lindsey Freeman, b. Nov. 12, 1900, Fayette Co., m. Mabel Lucille Baker, b. near Toronto, Canada. 4. Edwyna Freeman, b. May 18, 1904, Fayette Co., d. Nov. 10, 1941, m. Oct. 29, 1921, Mitt Wilson. 5. Wilma Freeman, b. Aug. 22, 1906, Fayette Co., m. Jan. 14, 1939, Henry Grady Holliman, b. Oct. 13, 1900. 6. Commodore L. "Sweet" Freeman, b. Feb. 8, 1903, d. July 9, 1903. 7. Tinie Freeman, b. Nov. 28, 1909, d. Oct. 15, 1915. 8. Etoile Freeman, b. Aug. 27, 1895, d. Apr. 25, 1901.

FRIERSON, Robert, b. 1740, d. 1808 - son of Wm. & Mary Frierson - m. Elizabeth McCauley, b. 1746, d. 1822. Children: 1. William Josiah Frierson. 2. John Frierson, III. 3. Thomas James Frierson. 4. Elijah Frierson. 5. Mary Frierson. 6. Elizabeth Frierson. 7. Jane Frierson. 8. Susannah Frierson.

9. Robert Frierson, Jr., m. 1st. - Mary Witherspoon, 2nd. - Mary C. McCrea or McCray.

FRIERSON, Robert, Jr. - son of Robert & Elizabeth (McCauley) Frierson, - m. 1st. - Mary Witherspoon. Children: (1st wife.) 1. Robert Pinckney Frierson. 2. James Harvey Frierson, b. 1812, d. 1846, m. Mary Frierson, b. 1815, d. 1868. He was a Medical Doctor. 3. Mary Ann Frierson, b. 1796, m. James Blakely Witherspoon, b. 1795, d. 1832. 4. Sarah Amelia Frierson, b. 1819, d. 1841, m. 1828, Robert Josiah Frierson, b. 1808.
    Robert Frierson, Jr. married second, Mary McCrea or McCray - dau. of Thomas McCrea or McCray. Robert Frierson, Jr.'s Will is recorded in Will Bk. 1, 1821 - 1855 in Tuscaloosa, Ala. He was born in Tuscaloosa Co., Ala. Children: (2nd. wife.) 1. Sidney Witherspoon Frierson. 2. Thomas McCray Frierson. 3. Elmira Frierson, m. ___ Norris. 4. Adaline Matilda Frierson, b. Tuscaloosa Co., Ala., d. buried Jasper, Ala., m. Rev. Benjamin F. Peters, b. Sept. 3, 1818, Abbeville Dist., S.C., d. Nov. 3, 1903, Fayette, Ala.

FULFORD, Edward Cleveland, m. Jan. 1, 1911, Roma Lee Arnold, b. Nov. 21, 1889 - dau. of Daniel David & Effie Dean (Mathes) Arnold. Children: 1. Nellie Geneva Fulford, b. Jan. 7, 1912, m. Albert Butler. 2. Edward Cleveland Fulford, Jr., b. Apr. 17, 1914, Ala. 3. Joe Arnold Fulford, b. July 5, 1917, Ala., m. Ruby Lee Cargile.

FULFORD, Edward Cleveland, Jr., b. Apr. 17, 1914 - son of Edward C. & Roma Lee (Arnold) Fulford, - m. Nokel Ann Taylor. Children: 1. Danny Taylor Fulford, b. Feb. 12, 1938. 2. Cassandra Jane Fulford, b. Dec. 29, 1942. 3. Candice Elizabeth Fulford, b. Mar. 7, 1951.

FULFORD, Joe Arnold, b. July 5, 1917 - son of Ed. C. & Roma L. (Arnold) Fulford - m. Ruby Lee Cargile. Children: 1. William Joseph "Jody" Fulford, b. June 13, 1945, Fayette, Ala. 2. Judith Ann Fulford, b. Dec. 16, 1946, Fayette Ala. 3. George Edward "Eddie" Fulford, b. July 3, 1953, Fayette, Ala.

GALLOWAY, Bobby Neil, b. Dec. 29, 1926, Fayette, Ala., - son of Jesse Galloway - m. Mar. 27, 1948, Mildred Kizzire, b. Mar. 29, 1930, Fayette, Ala. - dau. of Murry & Neta Kirzire. Bobby & Mildred were married at Berry, Ala. by Rev. Thomson. Children: 1. Peggy Diane Galloway, b. Apr. 7, 1949, Fayette, Ala. 2. Bobbie Jane Galloway, b. Nov. 13, 1956, Fayette, Ala.

GALLOWAY, David Luther, b. June 5, 1896, Crossville, DeKalb Co., Ala. - son of General Franklin Galloway - m. Sept. 7, 1919, Katie Merle Harkins, b. Aug. 24, 1902, Fayette Co., Ala. - dau. of Wm. Stewart Harkins. They were married at the Bride's Home in Fayette County, Ala. by Rev. R. L. Berry. Children: 1. Helen Louise Galloway, b. Oct. 1, 1922, Fayette Co., Ala., m. David Olious Jones, b. April 27, 1919, Bessemer, Ala. 2. Daniel Roy Galloway, b. Dec. 7, 1925, Fayette Co., Ala., m. Carolyn Valera Moore, b. Feb. 24, ___, Fayette Co., Ala. 3. Betty Hazel Galloway, b. Apr. 7, 1927, Fayette, Ala., m. Leonard Murdock Murchison, b. Jan. 8, 1927, Indianapolis, Ind.

GALLOWAY, General Franklin, b. Jan. 31, 1874, Rome, Ga., d. Jan. 13, 1944, - son of Lawrence Galloway - m. 1895, Roxie Palistine Guest, b. Sept. 2, 1871, Crossville, Ala., d. Mar. 19, 1918 - dau. of John Richard Guest. Children: 1. David Luther Galloway, b. June 15 or 5, 1896, Crossville, DeKalb Co., Ala. m. Sept. 7, 1919, Katie Merle Harkins, b. Aug. 24, 1902, Fayette Co., Ala.

2. Jesse Dupree Galloway, b. Oct. 15, 1899, Albertville, Ala., m. Mar. 20, 1921, Maye Nita Arnold, b. May 20, 1898, Rome, Ga. 3. Lola Mae Galloway, b. Aug. 10, 1901, m. Walter Shady Meherg. 4. William Uly Galloway, b. Aug. 24, 1905, Fayette Co., Ala., d. buried in Shirley Family Cem., m. Gladys Meherg. 5. Ludy Oliver Galloway, b. Feb. 9, 1909, Fayette Co., Ala., m. Oct. 4. ___, Roberta Bates. 6. Dora Belle Galloway, b. June 9, 1913, Fayette Co., Ala., m. May 25, 1935, Harry E. McCutheon.

GALLOWAY, Jessie Dupree, b. Oct. 15, 1899, Albertville, Ala. - son of General Franklin Galloway - m. Mar. 20, 1921, Maye Nita Arnold, b. May 20, 1898, Rome, Ga. - dau. of Dan & Effie Arnold. Jessie & Maye Galloway were married in Jasper, Ala. by Rev. J. P. Ponder. Children: 1. Dorothy Claire Galloway, b. Dec. 6, 1921, Corona, Ala., m. July 12, 1941, George Elton Traweek, b. Aug. 15, 1910, Berry, Ala. 2. Kenneth Dupree Galloway, b. Oct. 8, 1928, Fayette Co., Ala., m. Jan. 30, 1943, Buna Colley, b. May 1, 1923, Fayette, Ala. 3. Mary Anita Galloway, b. Dec. 3, 1924, Fayette, Ala., m. Nov. 25, 1944, Thomas Thomley, b. Sept. 12, 1924, Birmingham, Ala. 4. Bobby Neil Galloway, b. Dec. 29, 1926, Fayette, Ala., m. Mar. 29, 1948, Mildred Kirzire, b. Fay. Co., Ala.

GALLOWAY, Kenneth Dupree, b. Oct. 8, 1923, Fayette Co., Ala. - son of Jesse & Maye Galloway - m. Jan. 30, 1943, Buna Colley, b. May 1, 1923, Fayette, Ala. dau. of Homer Colley. Kenneth and Buna were married in Fayette, Ala. by Rev. J. E. Horton. Children: 1. Kenneth Dupree Galloway, Jr., b. Dec. 24, 1946, Fayette, Ala., 2. Richard Allen Galloway, b. Mar. 9, 1953.

GARDNER, Babe, - son of Jesse Gardner - m. Vinnia Burch. Children: 1. R. D. Gardner. 2. Marcella Gardner. 3. Clyde Gardner.

GARDNER, Elmer, son of Walter E. & M. J. (Vick) Gardner - m. Jan. ___. Children: 1. Verta Gardner. 2. E. Gardner. 3. Jane Gardner. 4. Riley Gardner. 5. Stevie Gardner.

GARDNER, Erbin, - son of Walter & Maude (Vick) Gardner - m. Mallirt Randolph. Erbin Gardner came to Fayette, Ala., in 1946 and opened a Scrap Iron Business. He presently is located on, and owns, the property originally owned by the earlier Gardners. He came to Fayette from Walker Co., Ala. Children: 1. Lois F. Gardner, m. May 8, 1959, Donald Freeman. 2. Foy Gardner, b. Aug. 1944. 3. Ray Gardner, b. 1953. 4. Gary Gardner, b. 1956. 5. Ruf Gardner, b. 1957.

GARDNER, Felix - son of Jesse Gardner - m. Altie Clayton. Children: 1. Allen Gardner. 2. Jewell Gardner. 3. Jean Gardner. 4. Mearline Gardner.

GARDNER, James - son of Wright Gardner. Children: 1. John Gardner. 2. Jesse Gardner. 3. George Gardner. 4. Elizza Gardner.

GARDNER, Jesse - son of James Gardner, - m. 2nd. - Jane Farquhar. Children: (1st wife, name unknown) 1. L. A. Gardner, m. Hassie Montgomery. Children: (2nd. wife) 1. Georgia Gardner, b. 1886. 2. Walter E. Gardner, d. 1952, m. Maude Jane Vick. 3. Felix Gardner, d. 1952, m. Altie Clayton. 4. "Mattie" Martha Gardner, m. Jeff Berry. 5. Rufus Gardner, d. 1909. 6. "Babe" Fralie Young Gardner, m. Vinia Burch. 7. J. Thomas Gardner, m. Minnie ___. 8. Ilia

Stella Gardner, m. Allen Durch. 9. Samuel Harrison Gardner, m. Clara Henderson.

GARDNER, Jesse - son of Wright Gardner - m. Matilda Lawrence. Children: 1. Jesse Gardner, Jr. 2. Montgomery Gardner. 3. Horace Gardner. 4. Sarah Ann Gardner, m. William "Bill" Vick. 5. Leona Gardner. 6. Pernice Gardner. 7. Ellen Gardner, m. Jacobe Sanford. 8. "Dump" Gardner, m. Pinkney Gray.

GARDNER, L. A. - son of Jesse Gardner - m. Hassie Montgomery. Children: 1. Virgie Gardner, m. __Stoker. 2. Samuel J. Gardner. 3. Harris Gardner. 4. Estell Gardner. 5. Flora Gardner, m. __Forsyth.

GARDNER, Sam - son of Jesse Gardner - m. Clara Henderson. Children: 1. Cornelius Gardner. 2. Earline Gardner. 3. Howard Gardner. 4. Swain Gardner. 5. Befford Gardner. 6. Betty Gardner.

GARDNER, Tom - son of Jesse Gardner - m. Minnie __. Children: 1. Ruby Gardner. 2. Clifford Gardner. 3. Lucy Gardner. 4. Dick Gardner. 5. Calvin Gardner. 6. Hubbert Gardner. 7. Connie Gardner. 8. Daisy Gardner. 9. Jack Gardner.

GARDNER, Walter E. - son of Jesse Gardner, m. Maude Jane Vick. Children: 1. Elmer Gardner, m. Jane. 2. Erbin Gardner. 3. Clarice Gardner. 4. Roy Gardner. 5. Chephas Gardner, d. 1941.

GARDNER, Wright. The first Gardners who came to Fayette County, Ala. in 1818, came in a wagon train consisting of about one hundred wagons. Some of the families in the train were: Gardners, Berrys, Strongs, Coles, Kizzires and others. Wright Gardner was in Andrew Jackson's Army when it came through what is now Fayette County. In 1818 Wright came to Fayette County and settled near the site presently known as the old Newton's Mill site. Wright Gardner is a descendant of Aunt Mary E. Gardiner, a widow, who brought seven sons from Scotland in the Colonial Days. She came from near Glasgow, Scotland. She settled in North Carolina. Children: (of Wright Gardner) 1. John Gardner, went to Arkansas - had sons Jehu and Samuel Gardner. 2. Jesse Gardner. (Had eight children.) 3. James Gardner. 4. A daughter who married a Dennis and lived in Miss. She was 105 years old in 1900. 5. A daughter who married a Lewellen and lived in Fayette County.

GAROFALO, Joseph James, b. Sept. 26, 1922, McKees Rocks, Penn. - son of Frank Garofalo - married Nov. 10, 1944, Helen Cordelia McGuire, b. Aug. 10, 1920, Tuscumbia, Ala. - dau. of W. B. McGuire, Sr. They were married at San Diego, Calif. Joe is affiliated with the forestry program in this district of Ala. being located in Fayette. Children: 1. Priscilla Joan Garofalo, b. Dec. 20, 1948, Athens, Ga. 2. Debra Elise Garofalo, b. April 15, 1952, Magnolia, Miss.

GARY, John Clinton, b. Oct. 8, 1911, Newton Co., Miss. m. July 15, 1934, Vrennie Inez Everett, b. Dec. 12, 1907, Newton Co., Miss. John C. Gary's Parents - Arthur Franklin & Nannie (Hall) Gary. Grandparents - Thaddeus & Mary Gary; and William Wesley & Rosie (Hammond) Hall.

Vrennie Inez (Everett) Gary's parents - James Sellers Everett, b. Dec. 29, 1866, Newton Co., Miss., m. Jan. 30, 1896, Minnie Lee Fanning, b. Dec. 13, 1881, Jasper Co., Miss. Grandparents - Samuel Everett, b. Dec. 10, 1821

& Mary Monroe, b. 1826; and James Burton & Annie (Crosby - b. 1848) Fanning. Children: 1. Mona Fay Gary, b. Dec. 7, 1936, Newton Co., Miss. 2. John Clinton Gary, Jr.

GENTRY, Arthur Ashley, b. Feb. 1871, Texas, d. 1932 - son of Merril & Louisa (Propst) Gentry - m. May 20, 1884, Pearl Caine, b. Dec. 17, 1878, Fayette, Ala. Children: 1. Mary Nell Gentry, b. Dec. 31, 1912, Fayette, Ala., m. Norton Edward England, b. Dec. 29, 1912, Greensboro, N. C. 2. Lucille Gentry. 3. Oveat Gentry, m. Stella Dean.

GENTRY, Merril, m. Cynthia Louisa Propst - dau. of Daniel & Annie (Shelton) Propst. Children: 1. Arthur Ashley Gentry, b. 1871, d. 1932, m. Pearl Caine. 2. Oscar Gentry, died in infancy.

GIBSON, Archie J., Jr., b. Nov. 1, 1918, Newtonville, Ala., - son of Archie J. Gibson, Sr., - m. Feb. 16, 1946, Julia Bell Forsyth, b. Feb. 8, 1921, Fayette, Ala. They were married at Fayette, Ala. by Rev. A. M. Nix. A. J. is an Insurance Agent. Children: 1. Teresa Ann Gibson, b. Jan. 16, 1951, Fayette, Ala. 2. Elizabeth Gibson, b. Dec 22, 1959, Fayette, Ala. (Julia Bell is the dau. of Martin Van Forsyth.)

GIBSON, James F., b. Fayette Co., Ala., m. Mary Isabella Whitley, b. Fayette Co., Ala. Children: 1. Clay Gibson. 2. Will Gibson, m. Ludie Doughty.

GIBSON, James Walter, b. May 8, 1884, Newtonville, Ala., d. Aug. 10, 1935, Newtonville, Ala. - son of Joseph James, Sr. & Pinina (Shepherd) Gibson, - m. 1910, Lillie Irene Elliott, b. June 21, 1884, Havana, Hale Co., Ala., d. April 4, 1959 - dau. of John & Mary Elliott. They were married in Columbus, Miss. and he was a farmer. Children: 1. Joseph James Gibson, b. May 31, 1911, Newtonville, Ala., m. June 9, 1940, Ruth Elizabeth Mayfield, b. Oct. 29, 1909, Newtonville, Ala. 2. Nell Gibson, b. Feb. 1, 1913, Newtonville, m. James Daniel Newman, b. Oct. 31, Covin, Fayette Co., Ala. 3. Max Elliott Gibson, b. Aug. 14, 1915, Newtonville, m. Marija Roberts, b. Aug. 8, 1920, Elrod, Tusca. Co., Ala. (Child: Butch Gibson, b. Mar. 19, 1944.) 4. Clyde Nathaniel Gibson, b. Jan. 15, 1917, Newtonville, d. Nov. 1943, India. (Killed in plane crash in India during World War II.) 5. Nina Evelyn Gibson (Twin), b. June 8, 1920, Newtonville, m. 1937, Clyde Newton Caraway, b. Mar. 23, 1916, Newtonville. (Clyde N. Caraway served in World War II. They have one child: David Earl Caraway, born May 18, 1938.) 6. Mary Virginia Gibson (Twin), b. June 8, 1920, Newtonville, m. Carey Sam Dyer, b. Jan. 8, 1915. (Carey S. Dyer served in World War II. They have two children: Dan Ella Dyer, b. Mar. 5, 1952, and Mary Sue Dyer, b. Nov. 13, 1954.) 7. William Victor Gibson, b. Nov. 7, 1924, Newtonville, m. Bessie Efird, b. Aug. 27, 1927, N. C. (Wm. V. served in the United States Navy during World War II.)

GIBSON, Joseph James, b. May 31, 1911, Newtonville, Ala. - son of James W. & Lillie (Elliott) Gibson - m. June 9, 1940, Ruth Elizabeth Mayfield, b. Oct. 29, 1909, Newtonville, Ala. - dau. of Dr. P. B. & Willmetta (Jones) Mayfield. Joseph J. Gibson served in World War II. He is a United States Postal Clerk in the Fayette Post Office.

GIBSON, Joseph James, Sr., b. 1849, d. 1936, Fayette Co., Ala., m. Penniah Shepherd, b. Aug. 22, 1849, Newtonville, Ala., d. Jan. 9, 1934, Fayette Co.,

Ala. - dau. of Jacob Shepherd. Children: 1. Jacob Gibson, b. Nov. 30, 1872, (All children born Newtonville, Ala.) d. Jan. 21, 1950, m. Sudie K. Butler, b. Aug. 17, 1872, d. Jan. 18, 1953, Newtonville, Ala. 2. Arch Gibson, b. Jan. 18, 1875, m. Annie Winn, b. May 18, 1882, Moores Bridge, Ala. 3. Cullen L. Gibson, b. Aug. 4, 1877, d. June 22, 1956, m. Sybee Elliott, b. Leeds, Ala. 4. Claude Gibson, b. Feb. 14, 1880, m. Dora Freeman. 5. James Walker Gibson, b. May 8, 1884, d. Aug. 10, 1935, m. Lillie Irene Elliott, b. June 21, 1884, d. April 4, 1959. 6. Victor Gibson, b. Nov. 10, 1885. 7. Virgil B. Gibson, b. 1888, d. 1950, m. Pearl Baker. b. Mar. 1892.

GLADDEN, Millard, b. 1915, Fayette Co., Ala., m. 1934, Gertrude Thompson, b. 1919, Fayette Co., Ala. Millard's parents - Roscoe Gladden, b. 1898, Fayette Co., m. 1913, Pearl Kizzire, b. 1894, Fayette Co. Grandparents - Bill Gladden, b. 1864, Fayette Co. m. Silphia Stocks, b. 1870, Fayette Co.; and G. R. Kizzire, b. 1868, Fayette Co., m. Nan Roberts, b. 1864, Fayette Co., Ala. Great grandparents - Jim & Nancy (Nichols) Gladden; Jim Jessie & Mandy (Lyon) Stocks; Ene & Mary (Berry) Kizzire; and Haywood & Sarah (Gladden) Roberts. 2-Great grandparents - John Martin Gladden; Mervil Elizabeth Peeples; Bill & Ella (Pool) Kizzire; and William & Massey Berry.

Gertrude's parents - Carl Thompson, b. 1887, Coosa Co., Ala., m. 1912, Etter Dailey, b. 1893, Tusca. Co., Ala. Grandparents - T. A. Thompson, b. 1863, Ga. m. Mary Jane Calloway, b. 1870, Ga.; and George Dailey, b. 1857, Tusca. Co., Ala., m. Rhoda Clark, b. 1870, Tusca. Co., Ala. Great grandparents - Tom T. Thompson, b. 1825, m. Jennie Spear, b. 1830; Joe Calloway, b. 1848, m. Sally Collier, b. 1851; Benson Dailey, b. 1830, m. Sarah White, b. 1834; and Sam Clark, b. 1844, m. Sarah Rodgers, b. 1846. 2-Great grandparents - John & Kitty White; Samuel Clark, b. 1802, Eng., m. Nancy Green (Appling); and William & Martha (Phillips) Rogers. 3-Great grandparents - Thomas & Nancy (Baker) Appling. 4-Great grandparents - Joel Appling; and Obidiah and Rachel Baker.

Millard & Gertrude's children: 1. Geraldine Gladden, b. 1939, Fayette Co., Ala. 2. James Carl Gladden.

GLENN, Allen Turner, b. June 28, 1871, Conger, Ala., d. Feb. 17, 1921, Atlanta, Ga., m. July 17, 1892, Carrie Hamner, b. Sept. 23, 1871, Fayette, Ala. d. Dec. 10, 1945, Atlanta, Ga. Children: 1. Thomas Winfield Glenn, b. Aug. 17, 1894, Fayette, Ala., m. Oct. 14, 1919, Mina Lee Putnam, b. Sept. 3, 1898. 2. John James William Glenn, b. 1896. 3. Sidney Franklin Glenn. 4. Susie Lavona Glenn, b. 1898. 5. Allen Turner Glenn, Jr. b. 1906. 6. Mary Elizabeth Glenn, b. 1904. 7. Vera Glenn, b. 1912. 8. Annie Virginia Glenn, d. at age 2 months. 9. Williard Glenn, d. at age 2 months.

GLENN, John James Winfield, b. June 19, 1832, Washington, Ga., d. Sept. 20, 1922, m. May 25, 1852, Mary Anne Nunnally, b. Lawrenceville, Ga., d. Sept. 3, 1872. Children: 1. Allen Turner Glenn, b. June 28, 1871.

GOBER, A. T., m. Nancy Louella Humber, - dau. of Robert Hayes "Bud" Humber. Children: 1. Elwa Gober, m. ___ Noyle. 2. Edna Gober, b. Feb. 15, 1898, Vina, Ala., m. Aug. 27, 1916, Napolean "Poley" Hardwick, b. Tishimingo Co., Miss. 3. Robert Leland Gober. 4. Cecil Gober. 5. Harvey E. Cleston Gober. 6. Evie Emmaline Gober, b. Feb. 26, 1904, Franklin Co., Ala., m. July 22, 1923, Virgil H. Pate. 7. Eva Gober, b. May, 25, 1907, Tish. Co., Miss. m. Feb. 3, 1929? Mannon Thomas Spradley. 8. Infant Son, b. & d. 1911. 9. Era

Mae Gober, b. June 5, 1915, d. Dec. 24, 1929.

GODFREY, John William, b. Fayette Co., Ala., m. June 4, 1954, Audie Bell Woods, b. Jan. 23, 1934, Fayette Co., Ala. - dau. of Wilmot & Hassie (Ballinger) Woods. Children: 1. Johnny William Godfrey, Jr., b. April, 1957, Cleveland, Ohio.

GOLSAN, Henry Lewis, Jr., b. July 20, 1875, Autaugaville, Ala., d. 1947, buried in Birmingham, Ala. - son of Henry Lewis Golsan - married Fannie Mae Gaston, b. April 5, 1880, Tyler, Texas, d. Feb. 1959, Tyler, Texas - dau. of R. E. & Sadie (Baldwin) Gaston. Children: 1. Gordon Lewis Golsan, b. June 14, 1901, Tyler, Texas, d. 1950, Tuscaloosa, Ala., m. Feb. 14, 1922, Irsa Dyson, b. July 2, 1900. They were married at Camp Hill, Ala. He is buried at Memorial Park, Tuscaloosa, Ala. 2. J. Gaston Golsan, b. Sept. 10, 1903, Tyler, Texas, d. Dec. 28, 1928, Birmingham, Ala., m. Sept. 3, 1924, Lucy Irene Waldrop, b. Sept. 28, 1902, Sulligent, Ala.

GOLSAN, J. Gaston, b. Sept. 10, 1903, Tyler, Texas, d. Dec. 28, 1928, Birmingham, Ala. - son of Henry Lewis & Fannie Mae (Gaston) Golsan - m. Sept. 3, 1924, Lucy Irene Waldrop, b. Sept. 28, 1902, Lamar Co., Ala. - dau. of Starling V. & Roxanna (Godfrey) Waldrop. They were married at Sulligent, Ala. by Reb. Hugh L. Tulley. He is buried in the Forest Hill Cem. in Birmingham, Ala. Children: 1. J. Gaston Golsan, Jr. (Twin), b. June 26, 1925, Sulligent, Ala., m. April 15, 1945, Annie Katheryn Smith. 2. Lewis Earl Golsan (Twin), b. June 26, 1925, m. Mar. 21, 1947, Mary Evelyn Griggs.

GOLSAN, J. Gaston, Jr., b. June 26, 1925, Sulligent, Ala., - son of J.G. & Lucy (Waldrop) Golsan - m. April 15, 1945, Annie Katheryn Smith, b. Sept. 28, 1924, Lineville, Ala. - dau. of C. & Annie (Carpenter) Smith. They were married at the Methodist Church in Lineville, Ala. Children: 1. J. Gaston Golsan, b. Jan. 5, 1951, Atlanta, Ga. 2. Kathan Golsan, b. Nov. 4, 1954, Columbus, Ga. 3. Lewis "Lew" Franklin Golsan, b. July 8, 1959, Columbus, Ga.

GOLSAN, Lewis Earl, b. June 26, 1925, Sulligent, Ala., - son of J.G. & Lucy (Waldrop) Golsan - m. Mar. 21, 1947, Mary Evelyn Griggs, b. Feb. 12, 1927, LaGrange, Ga. - dau. of J. R. & Evelyn (Belisle) Griggs. They were married at the Methodist Church at LaGrange, Ga. Children: 1. Mark Lewis Golsan, b. May 28, 1950, Auburn, Ala. 2. Stephen Earl Golsan, b. Dec. 22, 1952, LaGrange, Ga. 3. Mary Ellen Golsan, b. Mar. 13, 1954, Atlanta, Ga.

GOODWIN, Edward Penn, b. Dec. 19, 1869, Fayette, Ala., d. 1924 - son of Thomas Edward & Lucinda Jane (Lindsey) Goodwin - m. May 20, 1893, Wilma Cora Morton, b. 1872, Fayette, Ala., d. 1925 - dau. of Thomas Benton & Eudocia (McCaleb) Morton. They were married at Fayette, Ala. Edward Penn Goodwin was at one time: Cashier of the Fayette County Bank 1900 - 1908; Member of Board of Aldermen 1900 - 1904; Probate Judge of Fayette County 1908 - 1916; Past Master of Masonry; A Royal Arch Mason; Past Grand Independent Order of Odd Fellows; Past Sachem, Improved Order of Red Men; and Past Chancellor, Knights of Pythias. Children: (All born in Fayette, Ala.) 1. Lillian Goodwin, b. 1899, d. 1919, m. Mr. Place. 2. Mary Goodwin, d. 1959. 3. Kathleen Goodwin, b. Feb. 25, 1905, d. April 8, 1957, Fayette, Ala., m. Edmond Francis Jeffries. 4. Edward Penn Goodwin, Jr., b. 1906. 5. Janie Will Goodwin, m. William Wilson. 6. Thomas Joseph Goodwin, b. Aug. 23, 1912, m. Sadie Humber, b. Fayette.

GOODWIN, Simoson P., b. Nov. 4, 1815, Chatham Co., N.C., d. Sept. 12, 1884 - his father was born in Ireland - m. Elizabeth Green, b. Mar. 2, 1817, Cumberland Co., N.C., d. Mar. 17, 1894 - dau. of Edward Green, Cumberland Co., N.C. Children: 1. Thomas E. Goodwin, d. April 4, 1908, Fayette, Ala., m. Lucinda Jane Lindsey, b. Fayette, Ala.

GOODWIN, Thomas E., b. Cumberland Co., N. C., d. April 4, 1908, Fayette, Ala. - son of Simoson P. & Elizabeth (Green) Goodwin - m. Lucinda Jane Lindsey - dau. of Levi & Delithia (Douglass) Lindsey. Thomas Edward Goodwin entered the 10th Ala. Regt. of Cavalry, C. S. Army, Sept. 12, 1864 and was paroled at Tuscaloosa, Ala., April 1865. He served as Sheriff of Fayette County 1884 - 1888; Clerk of Circuit Court 1890 - 1896; Judge of Probate of Fayette County 1898 - until his death in 1908. He also was a member of Charles Baskerville Lodge, Free and Accepted Masons. Children: 1. Edward Penn Goodwin, b. Dec. 19, 1869, Fayette, Ala., d. 1924, Fayette, Ala. (Judge of Probate) m. May 20, 1893, Wilma Cora Morton, b. 1872, Fayette, Ala., d. 1925, Fayette, Ala.

GOODWIN, Thomas Joseph, b. Aug. 23, 1912, Fayette, Ala., son of E. P. & Wilma C. (Morton) Goodwin - m. Sadie Humber, b. Oct. 23, 1911, Fayette, Ala. - dau. of Wm. Hammond & Annie (Sanders) Humber. Children: 1. Thomas Joseph "Jodie" Goodwin, Jr., b. Feb. 12, 1942, Fayette, Ala. 2. Merribeth Goodwin, b. Jan. 17, 1946, Fayette, Ala.

GRAHAM, Dr. William A., m. April 15, 1891, Ann Dora Jones, b. Jan. 7, 1871, Newtonville, Ala., d. Nov. 16, 1952 - dau. of Dr. W. W. Jones. Dr. Graham and family lived in Fayette. He built the Fayette Hotel. Children: 1. Eulene Graham, b. June 23, 1892, m. __Randolph. (Living in Winfield, Ala.) 2. 2. William Carey Graham, b. July 22, 1894. 3. Bessie Will Graham, b. Nov. 6, 1895, m. Alfred Cook, (Living in Birmingham, Ala.) 4. Mildred Graham, m. Roy Dodd. 5. Sarah Elizabeth Graham, m. __ Caryea. 6. Clara Brooks Graham, m. Motte. (Living in Birmingham, Ala.) 7. Robert Jones Graham, (Living in Wisconsin.)

GRAVLEE, George Washington, b. April 30, 1844, Mulberry River Fork, Walker Co., Ala., d. Jan. 28, 1930 - son of Wm. & Martha C. (Fowler) Gravlee - m. Nov. 7, 1866, Czarina Marissa Nalls, b. July 4, 1847, Newtonville, Ala., d. Dec. 17, 1930 - dau. of Nathan & Elizabeth (Clarke) Nall. George Washington Gravlee joined Major Hewlitt's Cavalry and was a Lt. in Capt. E. J. Rice's Co. G. W. Gravlee was ordained as a Baptist Minister, Oct. 25, 1874 from Walker Co., Ala. Children: 1. Wiley Valter Gravlee, b. Aug. 4, 1867, d. Oct. 7, 1941, m. Mamie Bridgers, b. 1871, d. 1912. 2. Minnie Metta Gravlee, b. July 15, 1869, d. Nov. 20, 1920. 3. Emma Ernestine Gravlee, b. Aug. 12, 1871, d. Aug. 23, 1872. 4. George Jeter Gravlee, b. June 20, 1873, d. Mar. 5, 1957, m. Pearl Barnett. 5. William Nathan Gravlee, b. Mar. 25, 1875, m. Mattie Lou Hodge. 6. Ilar Elizabeth Gravlee, b. April 8, 1877, m. Hugh White. 7. James Bailey Gravlee, b. Feb. 11, 1879, m. Mamie Vasser. 8. Mary Ella Gravlee, b. Feb. 22, 1881, d. Aug. 1921. m. Howard Peterson. 9. Cora Czarina Gravlee, b. Mar. 18, 1883, m. John O. Walker. 10. Bradley Houston Gravlee, b. Nov. 1, 1885, m. Mary E. Newton, b. April 13, 1890, d. June 18, 1941. 11. Macon Washington Gravlee, b. July 5, 1888, m. Jimmy Nell Branyon, b. Oct. 22, 1904, Kingsville, Ala. 12. Infant Daughter, b. & d. Sept. 15, 1891. 13. Leland Clark Gravlee, b. Dec. 18, 1892, m. Mary Annie Wright. (All the Gravlee Children were born at Newtonville, Fayette County, Ala.)

GRAVLEE, Joseph Frank, D.V.M., b. Feb. 20, 1931, Fayette Co., Ala. - son of Leland Clarke & Mary Annie (Wright) Gravlee - m. Carol Elenor Scott - dau. of Hubbert Earl & Gertrude Scott. Dr. Joseph Frank Gravlee received his B. S. Degree in Agricultural Science from A.P.I. at Auburn, Ala. on Dec. 18, 1952 and his Doctor of Veterinary Medicine from A.P.I. at Auburn, on June 2, 1956. He served his internship at Mason-Thomas Veterinary Hospital in Little Rock, Ark. Children: 1. Joseph Frank Gravlee, Jr., b. Feb. 14, 1954, Auburn, Ala. 2. Hubbert Scott Gravlee, b. May 29, 1958.

GRAVLEE, Leban, b. Va. d. April 1814 - son of John & Margaret Gravlee - m. abt. 1804, 1st. - Mary Blythe, b. 1789, d. June 28, 1841 - dau. of Wm. & Sarah (Murphy) Blythe. Children: 1. William Gravlee, b. Feb. 9, 1810, d. 1892, m. Martha Fowler. 2. John Gravlee, b. May 31, 1912, m. 1st. - Rebecca Cornwell, 2nd. - Lizzie Calvert. 3. Sarah Gravlee, m. Manley Stewart. 4. Margaret Gravlee, m. William Burt?.

GRAVLEE, Leland Clarke, b. April 10, 1928, Fayette Co., Ala. - son of Leland Clarke & Mary Annie (Wright) Gravlee - m. Nancy Janeene Smith, b. Fayette, Ala. - dau. of G. L. Smith. Dr. Leland Clarke Gravlee, received his B. S. Degree from A.P.I., Auburn, Ala., in June 1951 and his M. D. Degree from University of Alabama Medical College, Birmingham, Ala., May 29, 1955. He interned and specialized in Gynecology and Obstetrics at University Hospital in Birmingham, Ala. Children: 1. Mary Janeene "Jan" Gravlee, b. Mar. 24, 1955, Birmingham, Ala. 2. Lucy Ann "LuAnn" Gravlee, b. June 17, 1957, Birmingham, Ala.

GRAVLEE, Leland Clarke, Sr., b. Dec. 18, 1892, Newtonville, Ala. - son of Geo. Wash. & Czarina (Nalls) Gravlee - m. Dec. 26, 1923, Mary Annie Wright, b. Miss. - dau. of Joseph Frank & Lucy (Clarke) Wright. Mr. & Mrs. Gravlee were married in Caledonia, Miss. She teaches school and he is a farmer. Children: 1. Leland Clarke Gravlee, Jr., b. April 10, 1928, Fayette Co., Ala., m. Nancy Janeene Smith, b. Fayette, Ala. 2. Joseph Frank Gravlee, b. Feb. 20, 1931, Fayette Co., Ala., m. Carol Elenor Scott.

GRAVLEE, Macon Washington, b. July 5, 1888, Fayette Co., Ala., - son of G.W. & Czarina (Nalls) Gravlee - m. June 14, 1932, Jimmie Nell Branyon, b. Oct. 22, 1904 - dau. of Dr. J. A. Branyon. They were married in Fayette, Ala. by Rev. W. R. Seymour. M. W. Gravlee is a merchant. He belongs to Shrine Zamora Temple, Birmingham, Ala.; Scottish Rite, Birmingham, Ala. and Masonic Chapter, Dora, Ala. Mr. Gravlee opened the Fayette Store of "Gravlees" on Sept. 23, 1932 and the Sumiton store in 1911.

GRAVLEE, William, b. Feb. 9, 1810, d. 1892 - son of Leban & Mary (Blythe) Gravlee - m. Martha Cora Fowler. Children: 1. George Washington Gravlee, b. Apr. 30, 1844, d. Jan. 1. 1929, m. Nov. 7, 1866, Czarina Nalls, b. July 4, 1847, Fayette Co., Ala., d. Dec. 29, 1929. 2. John David Gravlee, b. Dec. 15, 1841, Walker Co., Ala., d. 1855, m. Irville Wharton. 3. William Hardy Gravlee, died at 20 years of age. 4. Lt. Jessie Lafayette Gravlee. (Served in the Civil War as Confederate Soldier in Capt. F. A. Gamble's 28th Regt.) 5. Walter Godfrey Gravlee, b. Mar. 31, 1838, Gravleeton, Walker Co., Ala., m. Sarah Ann Roberts. 6. Harvey Jackson Gravlee, b. Feb. 18, 1847, Walker Co., Ala., m. Nancy Narcissa Gaines. (He was a Confederate Soldier.) 7. Daniel Houston Gravlee. 8. Nancy Matilda Gravlee, m. Thomas P. Lampkin. 9. Mary

Lucintha Gravlee, m. D. E. Mullins. 10. Martha America Gravlee, m. E. J. Rice. 11. Elizabeth Caroline Gravlee, m. 1st. - Martin Roberts, 2nd. - Wm. H. Duffee.

GRAY, Elliott P., Jr., b. Mar. 7, 1927, Tuscaloosa Co., Ala. - son of E.P. & Jeannette Gray, Sr. - m. Dec. 24, 1950, Betty Jean Shirley, b. Aug. 29, 1931 Pickens Co., Ala. Children: 1. Danny Watson Gray, b. Apr. 14, 1952, Tusca. Co., Ala. 2. Kathy Jeannette Gray, b. Feb. 26, 1953, Tusca. Co., Ala. 3. Randy Elliott Gray, b. July 31, 1955, Tusca. Co., Ala.

GRAY, Elliott P., b. Oct. 31, 1901, m. Jeannette, b. Nov. 3, 1901. Children: 1. Elliott P. Gray, Jr., b. Mar. 7, 1927, Tuscaloosa, Ala., m. Dec. 24, 1950 Betty Jean Shirley, b. Aug. 29, 1931, Pickens Co., Ala.

GRAY, William Foster, b. 1804, Va. - son of an Englishman - m. Rachel Lansdale, b. 1807, S. C., d. 1880, Fayette Co., Ala. - dau. of Isaac & Sarah (Gentry) McCool Lansdale. Early settler of Fayette County. Children: 1. William Gray, Jr. 2. Richard V. Gray. 3. Elender Elizabeth Gray. 4. David Gray. 5. James Gray.

GRIFFIN, Ira, b. July 17, 1830, d. Nov. 20, 1895 - son of Troy Griffin - m. Feb. 3, 1856, Susan A. McFarland, b. Jan. 5, 1832, d. Dec. 19, 1900. Children: 1. Emma Griffin, b. Feb. 2, 1856, d. June 9, 1922, Bankston, Ala., m. Frank N. Neal, b. April 22, 1857, d. Feb. 12, 1935, Bankston, Ala. 2. Martha Ella Griffin, b. Feb. 10, 1857, Fayette Co., Ala., d. Sept. 26, 1929, Fayette Co., Ala., m. Joseph Franklin Lindsey, b. Nov. 24, 1861, Fayette Co., Ala., d. Mar. 30, 1900, Fayette Co., Ala. 3. Troy C. Griffin, b. Aug. 26, 1861, d. Feb. 5, 1912, Bankston, Ala., m. Minnie Alice Evans, b. 1872, d. 1959, Bankston, Ala. 4. R. Walker Griffin, b. 1868, d. 1937, m. Martha R. Blackburn, b. 1874, d. 1939. 5. James B. Griffin, b. July 26, 1870, or 1872, d. Mar. 25, 1939, Berry, Ala., m. Emma Woods, b. Oct. 29, 1882, d. Jan. 12, 1959, Berry, Ala. 6. Ira Lee Griffin, b. Nov. 26, 1872, d. Sept. 29, 1927, Bankston, Ala., m. Donnie Blackburn, b. May 26, 1881, d. Mar. 16, 1943, Bankston, Ala.

GRIFFIN, Jeff, b. Dec. 28, 1899, Fayette Co., Ala., m. July 21, 1933, Eunice Bobo, b. Oct. 18, 1899, Fayette Co., Ala. - dau. of J. H. & L. B. (Strong) Bobo. Children: 1. Elna Jo Griffin, b. Jan. 30, 1935, Walker Co., Ala.

GRIFFIN, Percy, m. Ila Deavours - dau. of Hershell Deavours. Children: 1. Marcelle Griffin, m. J. W. Moore. (Children: Glenda; Terry and Mike Moore.) 2. Billie Jo Griffin, m. Bruce Dunn. 3. Hoyt Griffin, m. Laverne __. (Children: Linda and Lynn Griffin.)

GRIFFIN, Thomas J., b. Aug. 14, 1826 - son of Troy Griffin - m. __ Grey. Children: 1. John J. Griffin, m. Mattie Norris. 2. Mandorh M. Griffin, b. Sept. 7, 1873, Fayette Co., Ala., d. Fayette Co., Ala., m. Dec. 15, 1897, Huel South, b. Oct. 25, 1866, Tusca. Co., Ala. d. April 13, 1941, Fayette Co., Ala. 3. James T. Griffin.

GRIFFIN, Thurman I., b. Oct. 6, 1925, m. Betty Sue Renfroe, b. Mar. 30, 1931, Fayette Co., Ala. - dau. of Roy S. Renfroe. Children: 1. James Thurman Griffin, b. Jan. 6, 1951, Fayette, Ala. 2. Janet Sue Griffin, b. June 12, 1953,

Washington, D. C. 3. Linda Jo Griffin, b. Sept. 14, 1956, Washington, D. C.
4. Judith Annette Griffin, b. July 23, 1959, Washington, D. C.

GRIFFIN, Troy, b. July 8, 1801, Ga., d. July 4, 1868, m. Dec. 18, 1823, Martha Willingham, b. Sept. 10, 1794, d, Nov. 2, 1849 - dau. of Wm. Willingham. Children: 1. Martha Griffin, b. Sept. 19, 1824. 2. Thomas J. Griffin. b. Aug. 14, 1826. 3. William Griffin. b. Aug. 12, 1828. 4. Ira Griffin, b. July 16 or 17, 1830, Ala., d. Nov. 20, 1895, Fayette Co., Ala., m. Feb. 3, 1856, Susan A. McFarland, b. Jan. 5, 1832, d. Dec. 19, 1900, Fayette Co., Ala. 5. Elizabeth Griffin, b. April 29, 1833, Ala.
    Troy Griffin married second - Adiline Shepherd. Children: (2nd wife.)
1. Michael S. Griffin, b. July 3, 1856. 2. John B. Griffin, b. July 9, 1854.
3. Laura M. Griffin. b, Nov. 20, 1855. 4. David T. Griffin, b. Feb. 21, 1857.

GRIMSLEY, Alva McGriff, b. Sept. 7, 1874, Crosby, Ala., d. Feb. 23, 1948, -- son of Felix Ashley & Dora (McGriff) Grimsley - m. May 10, 1916 - 2nd. - Adylisse Sherrod, b. July 27, 1891, Moulton, Ala. - dau. of Chas. Morgan & Helen (Gater) Sherrod. Alva M. Grimsley was president of the First National Bank until his death in 1948. He and Mrs. Grimsley were early stock-holders in several of the businesses in Fayette. Mrs. Grimsley and their son, A. M., Jr. are the present owners of the First National Bank. Children: 1. Alva McGriff Grimsley, Jr., b. Nov. 4, 1919, West Point, Miss, m. Etta Neal Dodson.

GRIMSLEY, Alva McGriff, Jr., b. Nov. 4, 1919, West Point, Miss. - son of A. M. & Adylise (Sherrod) Grimsley - m. Aug. 7, 1949, Etta Neal Dodson, b. Nov. 26, 1915, Fayette, Ala. - dau. of W. A. & Velma (Smith) Dodson. Children: 1. Alva McGriff Grimsley, III, b. Jan. 10, 1953, Fayette, Ala. 2. Charles Sherrod Grimsley, b. April 25, 1955, Fayette, Ala.

GROCHOLSKI, Andrew, b. near Warsaw, Poland, m. Josephine Karulak, b. near Warsaw, Poland. They came to the United States in early life and made their home in Milwaukee, Wisconsin. Their son, Roman, came to Fayette, Ala. to make his home in 1946. Children: 1. Roman Andrew Grocholski, b. Dec. 6, 1907, Milwaukee, Wis., m. Feb. 17, 1945, Mary Edith Bobo, b. April 21, 1911, Fayette Co., Ala. 2. Agnes Alice Grocholski, b. Milwaukee, Wis., m. Frank Pavlac. 3. John Frank "Jack" Grocholski, b. Milwaukee, Wis., m. Eleanor __.

GROCHOLSKI, Roman Andrew, b. Dec. 6, 1907, Milwaukee, Wis. - son of Andrew & Josephine (Karulak) Grocholski - m. Feb. 17, 1945, Mary Edith Bobo, April 21, 1911, Fayette Co., Ala. - dau. of Wm. T. & Lula V. (Dickinson) Bobo. He served in the United States Army in World War II in the European Theatre of War and was awarded the Purple Heart. They were married in Fayette, by Rev. A. M. Nix. Children: 1. William Allen Grocholski, b. Sept. 18, 1946, Fayette, Ala.

GROVE, Woodfin Kirk, b. Oct. 23, 1918, Jefferson Co., Ala., m. Feb. 12, 1943, Dorothy Anne Rowland, b. Mar. 6, 1919, Lamar Co., Ala. - dau. of Zeb A. & "Dora" (Waldrop) Rowland. Children: 1. Ruth Anne Grove, b. Dec. 8, 1944, Cullman, Alabama.

GUERNEY, Floyd Irving, b. April 5, 1917, Mich., m. Julia Freeman, b. April 17, 1917, Fayette Co., Ala. - dau. of Littleton L. & Annie (Smith) Freeman. Children: 1. Ruth Ann Guerney, b. Oct. 20, 1941. 2. Judith Gayle Guerney,

b. Aug. 14, 1944. 3. Michael Irving Guerney, b. Aug. 2, 1947.

GULLETT, George Harris, b. July 5, 1889, Fayette, Ala., d. Jan. 24, 1952, Fayette, Ala. - son of Geo. L. & Bessie Gullett - m. Jan. 29, 1923, Ann Hoffman, b. Feb. 14, 1902, Moultrie, Ga., - dau. of James C. Hoffman. George H. Gullett served in the United States Army from April 25, 1918, to July 8, 1919 with the American Expeditionary Force in France and Germany from Sept. 3, 1918 to June 28, 1919. -- G. H. & Ann Gullett established the present Gullett's Dept. Store in Fayette. Children: 1. George Harris Gullett, Jr., b. Jan. 2, 1925, Fayette, Ala. (Military Service: June 8, 1943 to Dec. 9, 1945. Army of the United States, European Theatre - France-Germany from Dec. 9, 1944 to Aug. 21, 1945. 2. James Hoffman Gullett, b. Feb. 26, 1927, Fayette, Ala., m. June 24, 1956, Sara Frances Davis, b. Aug. 28, 1933, Fayette, Ala.

GULLETT, George Lindsey, - son of Geo. M. Gullett - m. Bessie Leigh Harris, b. Sept. 23, 1866, - dau. of Dr. Raymond W. Harris. Moved to Fayette Co., Ala. from Talberton, Ga. Children: 1. Logan Wallace Gullett, b. July 25, 1887, Fayette, Ala., d. Feb. 16, 1908, Fayette, Ala. 2. George Harris Gullett, b. July 5, 1889, Fayette, Ala., d. Jan. 24, 1952, Fayette, Ala., m. Jan. 29, 1923, Ann Hoffman, b. Feb. 14, 1902, Moultrie, Ga.

GULLETT, George Morris, d. Nov. 1835, Talberton, Ga., m. Nancy Townes. Children: 1. Ben Gullett. 2. George Lindsey Gullett, m. Bessie Leigh Harris, b. Sept. 23, 1866, d. Jan. 31, 1926, Fayette, Ala. 3. Mary Gullett.

GULLETT, James Hoffman, b. Feb. 26, 1927, Fayette, Ala., son of G.H.Sr. & Ann (Hoffman) Gullett - m. June 24, 1956, Sara Frances Davis, b. Aug. 28, 1933, Fayette, Ala. - dau. of Marion & Willinel (Wheeler) Davis. Jimmy's Military Service - May 5, 1945 to Dec. 13, 1946 in the United States Army. Asiatic-Pacific Theatre. Japan Nov. 3, 1945 to Oct. 30, 1946. Children: 1. Ann Davis Gullett, b. Sept. 1959.

HALL, Samuel Tobias, b. abt. 1792, S.C., d. abt. 1857 - son of William Hall - m. Nancy Ann Faucett, b. abt. 1795, S.C., d. after 1857. Children: 1. Sarah F. Hall, b. Oct. 18, 1821, S.C., d. Oct. 22, 1869, Tusca. Co., Ala., m. Sept. 21, 1840, George Washington Hassell, b. May 11, 1817, (Or June 12), d. June 12, 1884, Tusca. Co., Ala. 2. John C. Hall, b. 1820, S. C. 3. James Hall, b. 1822, S. C. 4. Elizabeth G. Hall, b. 1825, S.C. 5. Jane Hall, b. 1827, S.C. 6. Lucinda Hall, b. 1832, S. C. 7. Samuel S. Hall, b. 1837, Ala. 8. William Hall. 9. Nancy Hall. 10. Richard Hall. 11. Thomas Hall. 12. Loduska Hall.

HALL, William, b. 1760, S.C., d. after Jan. 20, 1809, Union Co., S.C., m. Susanah Torbert, d. after 1815 - dau. of Samuel Torbert. Children: 1. Samuel Tobias Hall, b. abt. 1792, S.C., d. abt. 1857, m. Nancy Ann Faucett, b. abt. 1795, S.C., d. after 1857.

HALLMAN, David McIntosh, b. Dec. 5, 1862, Bibb Co., Ala., d. April 9, 1933, Bankston, Ala. - son of Rev. Henry J. & Sarah (Langford) Hallman - m. Mar. 9, 1902, Julia Ella Bennett, b. May 10, 1873, Tuscaloosa Co., Ala., d. Aug. 17, 1907, Bankston, Ala. - dau. of H. H. & Nancy Frances (Houston) Bennett. Children: 1. Sula Hallman, b. Feb. 3, 1903, m. 1st. - Frank D. Morris, 2nd. - Oct. 26, 1928, Rev. Duncan Eve White, b. Mar. 17, 1882. 2. Zora Hallman, b. Oct. 28, 1906, m. Feb. 13, 1926, Hubert Alto Dowling, b. Feb. 7, 1907.

3. Minnie Elizabeth Julia Ella Hallman, b. Aug. 15, 1907, d. Aug. 15, 1907.

HALLMAN, Grady Hubert, b. Dec. 19, 1896, Fayette Co., Ala. - son of Jesse Martin & Nancy B. (Papazan) Hallman - m. Oct. 15, 1933, Artie Elizabeth McCool, b. April 7, 1907, Fayette Co., Ala. - dau. of T. A. & Motie F. (Dickinson) McCool. They were married in Columbus, Miss. by a Baptist Minister. Grady is a carpenter and contractor. Artie is a teacher. Children: 1. Joseph Wheeler Hallman, b. Mar. 6, 1936, Lawrence Co., Ala. (Town Creek), m. Oct. 25, 1958, Isolene Edwards, b. Mar. 5, 1935, Miss. 2. Sylvia Nell Hallman, b. Aug. 25, 1936, Pickwick, Tenn, (Hardin Co.) 3. Elizabeth Allen Hallman, b. Jan. 11, 1939, Fayette, Ala. 4. Daniel Martin Hallman, b. Oct. 7, 1941, Fayette, Ala.

HALLMAN, Rev. Henry J., b. Jan. 1, 1812, S. C., d. June 26, 1902, Berry, Ala. - son of Jacob Hallman - m. 1846, 2nd. - Sarah Langford, b. July 18, 1825, d. 1913, Fayette, Ala. Henry J. Hallman first married an Indian woman and they had two children. After her death he married Sarah Langford. They came to Alabama about 1850 and settled in Bibb County. They moved to Tuscaloosa Co. between 1872 and 1880 and sometime between 1880 and 1900 they moved to Fayette County and settled near Berry where they lived until his death. He was a Methodist Minister and a farmer. Children: (1st. marriage) 1. James Henry Hallman, b. April 5, 1839, m. 1864, Rebekah (Garner Lester). 2. Mary Elizabeth Hallman, b. Dec. 8, 1841. Children: (second marriage) 1. William Jackson Hallman, b. Jan. 27, 1848, m. Nancy Fair. 2. Samuel Hallman, b. Jan. 30, 1851, m. Lucindy McGowen, b. 1856, d. July 24, 1941. 3. Jacob Aster Hallman, b. Nov. 13, 1852, m. Elizabeth Fair. 4. Martha Hallman, b. 1854, m. John Sanford. 5. Jessie Martin Hallman, b. Jan. 24, 1856, d. Oct. 25, 1918, m. Mar. 27, 1881, Nancy Belle Papazan, b. Dec. 23, 1858, d. Dec. 19, 1937. 6. Marion Ford Hallman, b. Jan. 25, 1858, m. 1st. - Lottie Colwell, 2nd. - Sarah Ann Poe. 7. Henry Lewellen Hallman, b. Feb. 18, 1860, m. Tina Freeman. 8. David McIntosh Hallman, b. Dec. 5, 1862, d. April 9, 1933, m. Mar. 9, 1902, Julia Ella Bennett, b. May 10, 1873, d. Aug. 17, 1907. 9. Sarah Rebekah Hallman, b. July 10, 1864, m. 1883, William Weaver. 10. Columbus Washington Hallman, b. Oct. 10, 1866, d. Oct. 15, 1956, m. Oct. 28, 1890, Henrietta Cranford, b. Feb. 7, 1874, d. Jan. 4, 1945. 11. Jennie Ann Hallman, b. May 15, 1868, d. Infancy.. 12. Mary Hallman, b. 1870, d. infancy. 13. Julia Joanna Hallman, b. July 28, 1872, d. Dec. 14, 1951, m. Dec. 18, 1902, Leonard Kizzire, b. Apr. 20, 1842.

HALLMAN, Jacob, m. (wife unknown) Children: 1. David Hallman, b. 1807. 2. Henry J. Hallman, b. Jan. 1, 1812, d. June 26, 1902, m. 1846, Sarah Langford, b. July 18, 1825, d. 1913. 3. William "Bill" Hallman, b. June 26, 1818. 4. Joannah Hallman, m. Jacob Oswalt. 5. Jack Hallman.

HALLMAN, Jessie Martin, b. Jan. 24, 1856, Bibb Co., Ala., d. Oct. 25, 1918, Fayette Co., Ala. - son of Henry J. & Sarah (Langford) Hallman - m. Mar. 27, 1881, Nancy Bell Papazan, b. Dec. 23, 1858, Fayette Co., Ala., d. Dec. 19, 1937, Fayette, Ala. - dau. of Leroy Pope & Nancy (Black) Papazan. Children: (All born in Fayette County.) 1. Hattie Hallman, b. June 14, 1882, m. Leroy High. 2. Effie Hallman, b. Sept. 16, 1883, m. John Suggs, buried in Texas. 3. Arrie Hallman, b. Sept. 19, 1884. 4. Lovie Hallman, b. Aug. 28, 1887, d. July 29, 1912, Fayette Co., Ala. 5. Virgil Milo Hallman, b. June 16, 1889, d. Nov. 12, 1953, Ark., m. Ruby Hollis. 6. Ila Elizabeth Hallman, b. June 16,

1891, m. D. Winston Proost, buried at Jasper, Ala. 7. Henry Leroy Hallman, b. Dec. 7, 1892. 8. Iva Nell Hallman, b. April 26, 1895, d. Mar. 1955, Narrows, Va., m. Arthur L. French, b. June 4, 1890. 9. Grady Hubert Hallman, b. Dec. 19, 1896, m. Oct. 15, 1933, Artie E. McCool, b. April 7, 1907, Fayette, Co., Ala. 10. Samuel Martin Hallman, b. April 29, 1899, m. Lola Lowery.

HALLMAN, Joseph Wheeler, b. Mar. 6, 1935, Town Creek, Ala., - son of Grady & Artie (McCool) Hallman - m. Oct. 25, 1958, Isolene Edwards. b. Mar. 5, 1935, - dau. of J. W. Edwards. Joe W. Hallman is a student of aernautical engineering at Mississippi State University. They were married at Starkville, Miss. by the Methodist Minister. She is a school teacher. Children: 1. Phyllis Suzette Hallman, b. June 24, 1959, Tupelo, Miss.

HALLMAN, Samuel, b. Jan. 30, 1851, - son of Henry J. & Sarah (Langford) Hallman - m. Lucindy McGowen, b. 1856, d. July 24, 1941. Children: 1. H. Monroe Hallman. 2. Jodie Hallman, m. J. W. Baggett. 3. Lyde Hallman, m. John C. Brown. 4. Jim M. Hallman. 5. Zula Hallman, m. J. F. Black. 6. Erma Hallman, m. D. M. Golden. 7. George A. Hallman.

HAMBY, Harmon, b. Fayette, Ala. - son of Frank Hamby - m. Thomasine McCool, b. Aug. 10, 1914, - dau. of Thomas A. McCool. Children: 1. Jerry Hamby, b. May, 193_, Fayette, Ala. Jerry was ordained as a Methodist Minister in 1956.

HAMNER, Thomas W., d. 1931 or 1932 - son of Wm. P. & __ (Swindle) Hamner - m. April 20, 18__, Elizabeth Yerby, d. 1925 - dau. of Francis M. & Lydia Ann (Walden) Yerby. Children: 1. Carrie Hamner. 2. Medie Hamner. 3. Manly Holiday Hamner. 4. Elizabeth Hamner. 5. Savannah Hamner. 6. Jenny Hamner. 7. Jim Hamner. 8. Ludie (Luellen) Hamner.

HANKINS, Richard, b. Jan. 8, 1801, d. July 6, 1881 - son of John Hankins - m. July 16, 1829, Sary Dunkin, b. Dec. 20, 1808, d. Sept. 22, 1896. Children: 1. Mary Ann Hankins, b. Feb. 28, 1830, m. Feb. 20, 1851, Rias Brown. 2. Wm. Hankins, d. Jan. 18, 1862. (b. 1831). 3. Bertha Hankins, b. Nov. 13, 1832. 4. Martha Jane Hankins, b. July 7, 1836. 5. Rebecca Hankins, b. Feb. 14, 1840, d. Nov. 9, 1862. 6. James David Hankins, b. Mar. 23, 1842. 7. Jonathan Hankins, b. June 19, 1844, d. Sept. 14, 1880. 8. Susy Hankins, b. Feb. 10, 1846, d. Mar. 23, 1869. 9. Bobby Hankins, b. Aug. 10, 1848.

HANKINS, Samuel Houston, b. April 18, 1843, d. Jan. 19, 1916, m. Sarah Jane Lawrence, b. Jan. 1, 1841, d. Aug. 4, 1882. Samuel Houston Hankins served in Co. I, in the Confederate States Army during the Civil War. Children: 1. Martha Ann Hankins, b. July 25, 1861, m. __Perkins. 2. Mary Frances Hankins, b. 1864, d. Sept. 1901, m. __ South. 3. Nancy Angeline Hankins, b. Nov. 30, 1866, d. Mar. 12, 1914, m. Johnathan Alexander Brown. 4. Cassie Palmelia Hankins, b. Feb. 29, 1868, m. __South. 5. Rebecca Jane Hankins, b. Sept. 27, 1869, d. Oct. 1915, m. __Mosley. 6. Annie Virginia Hankins, b. 1871, m. __ Cunningham. 7. Steven Washington Hankins, b. Oct. 25, 1872, d. May 1945. 8. Sarah Elizabeth Hankins, b. 1874, m. __Walker. 9. George Houston Hankins, b. April 8, 1876, d. 1948. 10. John Franklin Hankins, b. Dec. 29, 1877, d. 1946. 11. William English Hankins, b. 1879, d. Aug. 1881. 12. Thurza Mabel Hankins, b. May 5, 1881, m. __Robertson.

S. H. Hankins second marriage - 1882, Vicey Jeridia Langston. Children: Thomas Jefferson Hankins, b. Aug. 20, 1884.

S. H. Hankins third marriage - Alice "Alcia" Walker, d. 1898. Children: Samuel Walker Hankins, b. abt. 1896.
S. H. Hankins fourth marriage - Betty Maddox. Children: 1. Victor Lee Hankins. 2. Isaac Benton Hankins.

HANKINS, Stephen, b. 1805, d. 1870, m. 1st. - Miss Warren. Children: (1st marriage.) 1. Franklin Hankins, m. ___ Woods. 2. Isom Hankins, m. ___ Marchbanks. 3. David Crockett, m. Martha Ann Woods. 4. Jane Hankins, m. John Barnes. 5. Betsy Hankins, m. Isom Smith. 6. Mary Ann Hankins, m. 1st. - Mr. Taylor, 2nd. - Mr. Pitts. 7. Joseph Hankins, m. Mary Jane Rector.
Stephen Hankins second marriage - Nancy Burrow, b. 1807, d. 1877. Children: (2nd. marriage) 1. Cassie Hankins, m. Madison Oakes. 2. Samuel Houston Hankins, m. 1st. - Sarah Jane Lawrence, 2nd. - Vicey Jaridia Langston, 3rd.- Alice (Alicia) Walker, 4th. - Betty Maddox. 3. Thomas Franklin Hankins, m. Miss Lawrence. 4. Wm. Burton Hankins, m. Elizabeth Collins. 5. Shelby Allen Hankins, m. 1st. - Elizabeth Graves, 2nd. - Emiline Webb, 3rd. - Martha Frances Butler. Shelby Allen Hankins served in the C.S.A.

HANKINS, Uridisa Jess, b. Mar. 21, 1894, Fayette Co., Ala., d. Jan. 24, 1959, - son of Wilson & Lula Bell Hankins - m. April 11, 1925, Era Helen Smith, b. June 18, 1898, Fayette Co., Ala. - dau. of Robert Lee & Ella Francis Smith. U. J. Hankins was a World War I Veteran and was in France for six months after the close of the war. The Hankins were married in Jasper, Ala., by Minister J. J. Tayor, D.D. U. J. Hankins was a Rural Mail Carrier in Fayette County for 38 years. They had no children.

HARBIN, Elbert Marion, b. June 9, 1922, Marion Co., Ala., m. May 9, 1942, Bernice Louise Anderson, b. July 18, 1924, Fayette Co., Ala. Elbert Harbin's parents - Jim Harbin, b. Aug. 2, 1877, Miss., m. Rebecca O'Mary, b. Aug. 10, 1883, Marion Co., Ala. Grandparents - Bill Harbin.
Bernice Louise (Anderson) Harbin's parents - Vester Anderson, b. Oct. 20, 1892, Fayette Co., Ala., m. Nov. 27, 1919, Florence Sexton, b. Apr. 1, 1903, Fayette Co., Ala. Grandparents - Peter Anderson, b. Apr. 16, 1854, m. Mary Jane Manasco, b. Oct. 8, 1855, Lamar Co., Ala.; and Silas Sexton, Jr., b. Oct. 18, 1882, Marion Co., Ala., m. Lener Whitehead, b. 1875, Fayette Co., Ala. Great grandparents - Steve & Sally Anderson; Caroll & Sara (Howton) Manasco; Silas Gaines Sexton, b. Oct. 16, 1849, Tusca. Co., Ala. & Lou Jeanie (Johnston), b. Sept. 18, 1859, N. C.; and Nick & Hassie (McDonald) Whitehead. 2-Great grandparents - Jim & Zadee (Maddox) Sexton; John Johnston, b. May 25, 1800, N. C. & Mary ___, b. Feb. 8, 1807, N. C.
Elbert Harbin's children: 1. Marion Louise Harbin, b. July 15, 1943, Fay. County, Ala.

HARDWICK, Napolean "Poley", m. Aug. 27, 1916, Edna Gober, b. Feb. 15, 1898, Vina, Ala. - dau. of Nancy L. (Humber) Gober. Children: 1. & 2. Infant Daughters, b. Apr. 28, 1917, Tishomingo Co., Miss., d. at birth. 3. Gober Napolean Hardwick, b. Oct. 16, 1918, Tish. Co., Miss. 4. James Barto Hardwick, b. Oct. 30, 1921, McNairy Co., Tenn. 5. W. T. Hardwick, b. Mar. 27, 1924, Alcorn Co., Miss. 6. Milton Cecil Hardwick, b. July 30, 1929, Tish. Co., Miss. 7. David Orlander Hardwick, b. Oct. 12, 1932, Alcorn Co., Miss., d. May 29, 1935.

HARKINS, Richard, m. Laurah Matthews, - dau. of Jerome & Sally (Richards)

Matthews. Children: 1. Sally Harkins, m. Bruce Chambliss. (Children: Ella Virginia and Frances Chambliss.) 2. Lucy Dell Harkins, m. Ulmer Connell. 3. Villa Harkins, m. Barnard Killingsworth. (Child: Richard Killingsworth.) 4. Nannie Lee Harkins, m. Arthur Hallmark. 5. Katie Mae Harkins, m. Boyd Tipper. 6. Annie Laurah Harkins, m. Porter Payton. 7. Helen Harkins, m. George Rockford. 8. Richard Harkins. 9. Ruth Harkins, m. Lucien Boozer. 10. Lillian Harkins, m. Robert Musgrove. 11. Jennie Harkins (adopted).

HARKINS, William Stewart, b. Feb. 21, 1873, Fayette Co., Ala., d. Sept. - son of Wm. Benton Harkins - m. Mar. 1896, Bittie Townsend, b. July 29, 1874, Fay. Co., Ala., d. Dec. 9, 1954 - dau. of Rev. J. S. Townsend. William Stewart Harkins was a farmer and lived all of his life in Fayette Co., Ala. Children: 1. Katie Merle Harkins, b. Aug. 24, 1902, m. Sept. 7, 1919, David Luther Galloway, b. June 5, 1896, Corssville, Ala. 2. Dutchie Harkins, b. Mar. 15, 1904, m. Dwight L. Falls, b. Tusca. Co., Ala. 3. Alice Gwyn Harkins, b. July 12, 1906, m. Lonnie Bobo, b. Jasper, Ala. 4. Robert Lee Harkins, b. June 25, 1908, m. Eulene Oswalt, b. Fayette Co., Ala. 5. Amy Caroline Harkins, b. Aug. 12, 1910, m. Furmon Crowe, b. Fayette Co., Ala. 6. Elijah Daniel Harkins, b. June 12, 1912, m. Mexie Harkins, b. Fayette Co., Ala. 7. Emillie Mahaley Harkins, b. Sept. 15, 1914, m. Cecil Whitley, b. Fayette, Co., Ala. (All Of Wm. S. Harkins children were born in Fayette County.)

HARKNESS, W. E. b. Dec. 21, 1907, Fayette Co., Ala., m. Dec. 6, 1930. Loueve Nichols, b. Sept. 24, 1911, Fayette, Ala. W. E. Harkness's parents - Kennith Lawson Harkness, b. Apr. 22, 1875, m. Apr. 30, 1902, Lula Aldridge, b. July 25, 1888, Fayette Co., Ala. Grandparents - Eli Harkness (son of George Harkness) and Henry & Lila (Tidwell) Aldridge.

Loueve (Nichols) Harkness's parents - J. M. Nichols, b. Aug. 15, 1872, Fayette Co., Ala. m. Nov. 6, 1902, Della Sprinkle, b. May 22, 1887, Fayette Co., Ala. Grandparents - David A. Nichols, b. July 27, 1823, m. Julia Ann Box, b. Nov. 30, 1839, Fayette Co., Ala.; and Bynum Sprinkle, b. Sept. 22, 1852, Ga., m. Nancy Tucker, b. Apr. 20, 1851, Fayette Co., Ala. Great grandparents - Will Nichols; William Arthur Box; Jepth & Elizabeth (Dozier) Sprinkle; and George & Miriam (Woods) Tucker. Children: (W. E. Harkness') Preston Harkness, b. Dec. 12, 1937, Fayette, Ala.

HARRINGTON, Drury - son of Charles & Agnes (Hill) Harrington - m. Rachel Petty. Drury Harrington served in the American Revolutionary War from 1776 to the end of the conflict. He went to South Carolina in 1779 and settled in Union District, near Jonesville, S. C. Children: 1. Jeptha Harrington, b. Feb. 9, 1775, d. April 29, 1865, m. Nancy Darwin.

HARRINGTON, Jeptha, b. Feb. 9, 1775, Chatham, S.C., d. April 29, 1865 - son of Drury & Rachel (Petty) Harrington - m. Nancy Darwin. Children: 1. Micajah B. Harrington, b. Nov. 29, 1800, m. Mary Robertson.

HARRINGTON, Micajah B., b. Nov. 29, 1800 - son of Jeptha & Nancy (Darwin) Harrington - m. Mary Robertson. Children: 1. Martha Harrington, m. James M. Coons. 2. Elizabeth Harrington, m. 1st - Dr. Gibson, 2nd. - Dr. P. T. Gunter. 3. Cynthia Harrington, m. Upton Gore. 4. Abel Lancaster Harrington, m. Elizabeth Guyton.

HARRIS, John William, d. Oct. 30, 1933, m. Elizabeth McDaniel, d. April 11,

1939. Children: Sheila B. Harris, b. Jan. 3, 1888, Lamar Co., Ala., m. Oct. 27, 1901, Foster Lee Bobo.

HARRIS, Dr. Raymond W., d. 1877 in Lowndes Co., Miss., m. Martha Peters. Mrs. Martha Peters Harris moved to Fayette in 1880 with four children, taught School and later started "Turner's Hotel" with her daughter, Kate Harris and son-in-law Gid Turner. (Turner Hotel was destroyed in the 1911 Fire.) Children: 1. Bessie Leigh Harris, b. Sept. 23, 1856, d. Jan. 31, 1926, Fayette, Ala., m. __ Van Diver, who died and she married 2nd. - George Lindsey Gullett. 2. Kate Harris, b. April 8, 1868, d. Oct. 4, 1921, Fayette, Ala., m. Gid Turner. 3. R. W. Harris, Sr., b. Feb. 4, 1876, Lowndes Co., Miss., d. in 1940's in Winfield, Ala. 4. Ben Harris.

HASSELL, George Thomas, b. Jan. 25, 1853, Tuscaloosa Co., Ala., d. Jan. 5, 1919, Fayette, Ala. - son of Myles Baines & Martha (Johnson) Hassel - m. Dec. 17, 1873, Susan M. (Appling) Richards, b. Nov. 16, 1847, Fayette Co., Ala., d. Jan. 1, 1923, Fayette, Ala. - dau. of Samuel Appling. Children: (All born in Fayette Co., Ala.) 1. Susan Aline Hassell, b. Mar. 4, 1875, d. Birmingham, Ala., m. May 19, 1898, B. F. Scott, b. Walker Co., Ala. d. Birmingham, Ala. 2. Myles Samuel Hassell, b. Sept. 10, 1878, m. Aug. 25, 1906, Susie Moore. 3. Martha Alabama Hassell, b. Dec. 30, 1882, m. April 6, 1902, Moses C. Shepherd, b. Walker Co., Ala., d. Nov. 18, 1958, Oakman, Ala. 4. Roxie Lee Hassell, b. Dec. 8, 1886, m. Jan. 12, 1927, Garland G. Shepherd, b. Lamar Co., Ala., d. Oct. 11, 1944, Fayette, Ala.

HASSELL, Marion, b. July 11, 1873, Fayette Co., Ala., d. Mar. 25, 1944, Fay. Co., Ala., m. Lizzie Skipper, b. May 17, 1882. Marion Hassel was the son of W. J. & Guyton (Baker) Hassell. He was a farmer. Both are buried at El Bethel Cemetery. Children: 1. Annie Lou Hassell. 2. Mary Lee Hassel. 3. Infant Son, Floyd Hassell, buried Fayette Co., Ala.

HASSELL, George Washington, b. May 11, 1817, (or June 12,) N.C., d. June 12, 1884, Tusca. Co., Ala. - son of Miles Hassell - m. Sept. 21, 1840, Sarah F. Hall, b. Oct. 18, 1821, S. C., d. Oct. 22, 1869, Tusca. Co., Ala. - dau. of Samuel Tobias Hall. Children: 1. Samuel Lafayette Hassell, b. July 1840, Ala., d. Aug. 15, 1915, m. 1st - Miss Crump, 2nd. - Miss Powell, 3rd. - Nancy Winn. 2. Elizabeth Hassell, b. Ala., m. 1st. - Mr. McGee, 2nd. - Mr Shackleford. 3. Lucy Jane Hassell, b. July 26, 1845, Tusca. Co., Ala., d. Feb. 23, 1886, Fayette Co., Ala., m. June 20, 1865, Levi Woodruff South, b. May 8, 1836, Tusca. Co., Ala., d. July 13, 1918, Fayette Co., Ala. (Both are buried at Mt. Pleasant Cemetery.) 4. Sarah Tanny "Daught" Hassell, m. Mr. Roycroft. 5. Nancy Adeline Hassell, b. Sept. 1851, d. Mar. 5, 1888, Fayette Co., Ala., m. Reuben D. South, b. Aug. 14, 1847, d. Feb. 11, 1898, Fayette Co., Ala. (Both are buried in the South Family Cemetery.) 6. Kate Hassell, b. 1856, d. 1900, Fayette Co., Ala., m. Ham M. Crump. 7. Mary Hassell, b. 1853, m. John W. Blackburn, d. Fayette Co., Ala. 8. Aileen "Lena" Hassell (Twin) b. June 18, 1861, m. John W. Blackburn. (Both buried at Mt. Pleasant Cemetery.) 9. Alabama "Bama" Hassell (Twin) b. June 18, 1861, d. Tusca. Co., Ala., m. Dan McGee. 10. George Hassell.

HASSELL, Miles, d. 1819 - son of Benjamin Hassell - m. April 8, 1805, at Edenton, N.C., Levinia Baines, b. abt. 1784, N. C., d. 1858 - dau. of George? Baines. Children: 1. Ann Gorham Hassell, b. Feb. 13, 1806, d. Jan. 1, 1878,

Prescott, Ark., m. John Yerby. 2. Benjamin Hassell, b. Sept. 22, 1807, d. Jan. 14, 1890, m. Joanah Durrett. 3. Elizabeth Rebecca Baines Hassell, b. July 2, 1810, d. Apr. 13, 1867, m. Feb. 25, 1832, John Deason. 4. Miles Baines Hassell, b. Mar. 18, 1812, Edenton, N.C., d. Mar. 19, Fayette Co., Ala., m. Oct. 27, 1835, Martha Johnson. 5. Katherine Hassell, b. July 27, 1814, d. July 1889, m. Mar. 27, 1859, Alfeus A. Condre. 6. George Washington Hassell, b. May 11, 1817, N. C., d. June 12, 1884, m. Sept. 21, 1840, Sara F. Hall. 7. Lavinia B. Hassell, m. Sept. 11, 1848, Henry H. Hall.

HASSELL, Miles (or Myles) Baines, b. Mar. 25, 1812, Edenton, N. C., d. Mar. 19, 1890, Fayette Co., Ala. - son of Miles & Lavinia (Baines) Hassell - m. Oct. 27, 1835, Martha Johnson, b. Feb. 3, 1818, S. C., d. Dec. 18, 1901, Fayette Co., Ala. The Hassell Family of Fayette County, Ala. date their ancestry back to the 1700's from Benjamin Hassell who came to Chowan County, N.C. from England, with brothers who settled along Albemarle Sound and engaged in fishing and farming. A later descendant was Myles Hassell, who was born in Chowan Co., N. C. and died there in 1819. His widow Lavinia Baines Hassell moved her seven children to Tuscaloosa Co., Ala. in 1821 to be with a brother, Rev. Thomas Baines, a Baptist minister. Myles Baines Hassell, son of Lavinia Baines Hassell was married to Martha Johnson in Tuscaloosa Co., Ala. by Rev. David Andrews and they lived on the Watermelon Road in Tuscaloosa Co., until 1869 when they moved with their twelve children to Fayette County. Only three of these children remained in Fay. Co. They married, reared families and died and are buried here. Descendants of these three families, along with descendants of George Washington Hassell live in Fayette County today. Miles Baines Hassell and his wife, Martha Johnson Hassell are buried at the El Bethel Baptist Church Cemetery, in Fayette County. Children: 1. Samuel Allen Hassell, b. Jan. 10, 1837, Tusca. Co., Ala., d. April 21, 1875. 2. Myles A. Hassell, b. Mar. 4, 1838, Tusca. Co., d. Mar. 17, 1863, Illinois. (Died during Civil War.) 3. Elizabeth A. Hassell, b. April 3, 1839, Tusca. Co., d. buried in Tusca. Co., m. George Sellers. 4. Lavinia Catherine Hassell, b. April 3, 1839, Tusca. Co. 5. William J. Hassell, b. May 27, 1841, Tusca. Co., d. April 13, 1930, Fay. Co., m. Mar. 19, 1866, Guyton Baker, b. May 7, 1852, (or 1849), d. Dec. 13, 1917, Fayette Co., Ala. (Both are buried at El Bethel Cem.) 6. James W. Hassell, b. June 7, 1846, Tusca. Co., m. Melissa __. 7. Mary Jane Hassell, b. July 4, 1848, Tusca. Co., d. Ark., m. Nimrod Jones (Primitive Baptist Preacher.) d. Ark. 8. Martha Frances Hassell, b. Jan. 21, 1851, Tusca. Co., d. Feb. 13, 1941, Fayette, Ala., m. Oct. 3, 1870, Rev. James Polk Dickinson, b. July 24, 1851, Fayette Co., Ala., d. Mar. 13, 1906, Fayette, Ala. 9. George Thomas Hassell, b. Jan. 25, 1853, Tusca. Co., d. Jan. 5, 1919, Fayette, Ala., m. Dec. 17, 1873, Susan Appling Richards, b. Nov. 16, 1847, Fayette Co., Ala., d. Jan. 1, 1923, Fayette, Ala. 10. Benjamin Powell Hassell, b. Jan. 26, 1855, Tusca. Co., d. Walker Co., Ala., m. Vonnie __. 11. Rebecca Alice Hassell, b. Mar. 25, 1857, Tusca. Co., d. Ark., m. Wyle Davis (Methodist Minister.) d. Ark. 12. Sarah (or Sallie) A. Hassell, b. Jan. 1, 1860, Tusca. Co. d. Ark., m. Nanly Roycroft, d. Ark.

HASSELL, Myles Samuel, b. Sept. 10, 1878, Fayette Co., Ala., - son of Geo. T. & Susan Richards Hassell - m. Aug. 25, 1906, Susie Moore. M. S. Hassell is an employee of the Southern Railroad and lives in Birmingham, Ala. Children: 1. Roy Hassell. 2. Jesse Hassell. 3. Marilyn Hassell.

HASSELL, Robert Lee "Zeb", b. Fayette Co., Ala. - son of W.J. & Guyton (Baker) Hassell - m. Mattie Reeves, b. Fay. Co., Ala. Children: 1. Velta Hassell, buried Fayette City Cem., m. Ruth Roberts. 2. Byron Hassell, b. Fay. Co., m. Edna Watkins, b. Feb. 14, 1910, Fayette Co., Ala. 3. Jack Hassell, b. Fayette Co., m. Gladys Markham.

HASSELL, William J., b. May 27, 1841, Tusca., Co., Ala., d. April 13, 1930, Fayette Co., Ala. - son of Myles B. & Martha (Johnson) Hassell - m. Mar. 19, 1866, Guyton Baker, b. May 7, 1852, (Or 1849), d. Dec. 13, 1917, Fayette Co., Ala. - dau. of F. R. & M. A. Baker. Wm. J. Hassell was a farmer. They are both buried at the El Bethel Baptist Church Cemetery. Children: 1. Ada Hassell, m. A. Lanthus Stanley. (Both buried at Fayette, Ala.) 2. Marion Hassell, m. Lizzie Skipper. (Both buried at El Bethel Cem.) 3. Robert Lee "Zeb" Hassell, m. Mattie Reeves.

HAWKINS, Bud, (His mother was a Vickery.) m. Molly Haney (her mother was an Eads.) Children: 1. Essie Lee Hawkins, b. Dec. 17, 1893, m. D. E. Aldridge. 2. Bessie Hawkins.

HAY, Benjamin McFarland Long, b. Nov. 3, 1862, Carrollton, Ga. - son of David Reese Hay - m. Aug. 16, 1891, Lucy Ellen Welburn - dau. of Wm. Harris Welburn. They were married at Cordova, Ala. He was a merchant and is buried at Jasper, Ala. Children: 1. John B. Hay, m. Lila Reese. 2. Robert Hay, m. Margaret -. 3. Mary Hay, m. July 2, 1920, William Rufus Willingham, b. Bankston, Ala. 4. William Harris Hay, b. 1898 or 1899, Jasper, Ala., d. Mar. 21, 1959, Jasper, Ala., m. July 2, 1920, 1st. - Lillian Beatrice Willingham, 2nd. __, 3rd. - Polly __. 5. Lucy Ellen Hay, m. 1st. - Mr. Wolfe. 6. Tom Hay, m. Ina _. 7. Elizabeth Hay. 8. Berta Pope Hay.

HAY, David Reese, m. Isabella Long. Children: 1. Benjamin McFarland Long Hay, b. Nov. 3, 1863, Carrollton, Ga., m. Lucy Ellen Welburn, both are buried at Jasper, Ala.

HAY, William Harris, b. 1899, Jasper, Ala., d. Mar. 21, 1959 - son of Benjamin McFarland Long Hay - m. July 2, 1920, Lillian Beatrice Willingham, b. Nov. 11, 1901, Bankston, Ala. - dau. of James Hugh Willingham. Children: 1. Frances Hugh Hay, b. April 25, 1921, Bankston, Ala., m. April 11, 1943, Wm. Cox Tucker, b. Oct. 29, 1916, Birmingham, Ala.

HAYES, Charles Pierce, b. Sept. 7, 1914, Vernon, Ala. - son of Wazzie & Maggie (Davis) Hayes - m. May 4, 1946, Arva Rae Moore. Children: 1. Mary Beth Hayes, b. April 7, 1951. 2. Benjamin Davis Hayes, b. May 2, 1948.

HAYES, Fred, b. May 19, 1928, Fayette Co., Ala., m. Mar. 13, 1948, Dorothy Ann Bobo, b. Aug. 24, 1929, Fayette Co., Ala. - dau. of F.M. & Eula M. (South) Bobo. Children: 1. Virginia Ann Hayes, b. July 30, 1950, Columbus, Miss. 2. Jimmy Dale Hayes, b. Jan. 3, 1956, Columbus, Miss. 3. George Allen Hayes, b. Sept. 22, 1959, Columbus, Miss.

HAYES, Wazzie Blaine, m. July 26, 1912, Maggie Lee Davis, b. May 14, 1892 - dau. of Chas. Hurt Davis. Children: 1. Charles Pierce Hayes, b. Sept. 7, 1914, Vernon, Ala., m. May 4, 1946, Arva Rae Moore. 2. William Blaine Hayes, b. April 23, 1916, m. June 17, 1939, Emma Rhea Smith, b. April 23, 1916. 3.

Ruth Davis Hayes, b. Aug. 29, 1920, near Ethelville, Ala., m. July 5, 1946, Lecil Elwin Cline.

HAYES, William Blaine, b. April 23, 1916 - son of W.B. & Maggie (Davis) Hayes - m. June 17, 1939, Emma Rhea Smith, b. April 23, 1916. Children: 1. Emily Rhea Hayes, b. Dec. 18, 1954.

HENDERSON, Philip L., b. June 28, 1895, Loudon, Tenn., d. Mar. 16, 1945 - son of Arthur S. Henderson - m. June 16, 1918, De Ila Brotherton, b. Mar. 25, 1895, Fayette Co., - dau. of Manie Brotherton. P. L. Henderson served in World War I. Children: 1. Jane Henderson, b. Nov. 11, 1920, Fayette, Ala., m. Aug. 3, 1941, James L. Phillips, b. May 9, 1920, Sheffield, Ala. 2. Ann Henderson, b. Aug. 15, 1926, Aliceville, Ala., d. Oct. 31, 1940.

HENDON, Andrew Jackson, m. 1st. - Caroline Harris, 2nd. - Mary Deavours - dau. of Abraham & Abigail (Davidson) Deavours. Jack Hendon, at age 33, enlisted in the Confederate Army on July 9, 1862, at Big Spring, Marshall County, Ala., under Capt. William H. Taylor for the duration of the war. He was assigned to Co. D. 4th Cavalry (Russell's) and carried his own horse, valued at $75.00 and horse equipment valued at $15.00. He was taken prisoner at Ft. Donelson, Tenn. and sent to City Point, James River, Va., then to Ft. McHenry, Maryland and then to Fortress Monroe, Va. for exchange. He died about 1890 and is buried at the Enis Graveyard, Fayette Co., Ala. Children; (by 1st. wife.) 1. William Andrew "Dandy" Hendon, b. Feb. 8, 1859. (Children: Viola; Laura; Bervie; Austin; Fernanda; Pearl; Howard; Clyde; and Cora Hendon.) 2. Margaret Hendon, m. William Bedford Sawyer.

HENRY, James McConnell, b. 1912 - son of Jim R. Henry - m. Mayford Holt. Children: 1. James McConnell Henry. 2. Lynn Henry.

HENRY, Jim R., m. Mary E. McConnell, b. Dec. 2, 1878, Fayette Co., Ala., d. May 29, 1922 - dau. of D. O. McConnell. Children: 1. Ellette Henry, b. 1904, m. Harold Cowart. 2. Elizabeth Henry, b. 1906, m. Moody Taylor. 3. Daniel Henry, b. 1910. 4. James McConnell Henry, b. 1912, m. Mayford Holt. 5. Alice Henry, b. 1917, m. Ralph Barnes. 6. Thomas Henry, b. 1920, m. Billy Jo Ray.

HENRY, Thomas, b. 1920, - son of Jim R. Henry, - m. Billy Jo Ray. Children: 1. Richard Allen Henry.

HIGGINS, Samuel Patrick, m. Rosa Lillian Rice. Samuel Patrick Higgins, with his wife and children came to Fayette, Ala., Dec. 29, 1912. They were originally from Indiana. Samuel Patrick Higgins is the son of Samuel C. & Margaret (Callan) Higgins. He is the paternal grandson of Samuel & Rebecca (Warner) Higgins. His maternal grandparents were Patrick & Mary Ann (Sharkey) Callan, who came to Shelby Co., Ind. from Cork, Ireland.
Rosa Lillian Rice, wife of Samuel Patrick Higgins, is the only child of Charles & Julia (Campbell) Rice. Charles Rice was the son of Thomas Jefferson & Louise Rice and the grandson of Alex Rice. Julia (Campbell) Rice, mother of Rosa Lillian Rice Higgins was the dau. of John Biven Campbell and Elizabeth (Hoagland) Campbell. Children: 1. Margaret Irene Higgins, b. Oct. 29, 1901, Booneville, Ind., m. Oct. 25, 1922, Thomas Harvey Cannon. 2. Lawrence Patrick Higgins. 3. Pansy Elizabeth Higgins, m. Curt Haughton.

HINDMAN, Esker, b. 1900, Covin, Ala., m. 1923, Mattie Lou Waldrop, b. 1907, Kennedy, Ala. Esker Hindman's parents - Lewis S. Hindman, b. 1865, m. Nancy Edwards, b. 1865. Grandparents - Hiram Hindman, b. 1833, m. Sarah Bobo, b. 1831; and Pinkney Edwards, b. 1827, m. Mary Parthenia __, b. 1840.
    Mattie Lou (Waldrop) Hindman's parents - Milton Waldrop, b. 1876, m. Alice (Lassiter). Grandparents - S. M. Waldrop, b. 1848, m. Ellen Trimm; and H. Laster, m. Amanda __. Esker Hindman's children: 1. Erskine Hindman, m. Mary Nell Nichols. (Children: Bobby and Larry Hindman.) 2. Ruell Hindman, m. Willa Dean Belk. (Children: Yvonne; Shelia and Hank Hindman.) 3. Eva Nell Hindman, m. Freddie Yerby. (Children: Michael Yerby.) 4. Genevie Hindman, m. L. A. Fowler. (Children: Linda Fowler.) 5. Hulon Hindman, m. Maylene Black. Children: Sammie Hindman.) 6. Clair Dean Hindman, m. Ruben Ary. (Children: Mitchel; Elma Lou; Max; and Gerald Ary.) 7. Louis Hindman, m. Jane Henderson. (Children: Louis "David" Hindman, Jr.) 8. Charlotte Hindman, b. 1938, Fay. Co., Ala. 9. Martha Hindman, b. Fayette, Ala.

HINDMAN, Louis Smith, b. 1865 - son of Hiram Hindman - m. 1st. - Elizabeth Collins. Children: (1st. marriage.) 1. Lockie Hindman, m. Reuben Newman.
    Louis Smith Hindman second marriage - Nancy Charlotte Edward, - dau. of Pinkney Edwards - Children: (2nd. marriage.) 1. Luler Hindman, m. John Wm. Crowley. 2. Katie Hindman, m. Morris Watson. 3. Southie Hindman, m. Bob Speed. 4. Dora Hindman, m. Belton Collins. 5. Mary Hindman. 6. Esker Hindman, m. Mattie Lou Waldrop. 7. Annie Mae Hindman, m. Lonnie Moore. 8. Velma Hindman, m. 1st. - Arly Rasberry, 2nd. - Willie Norris.

HINTON, Sol, b. Feb. 8, __, m. Mary Alice Dickinson, b. July 8, 1855, Fayette Co., Ala. - dau. of Peyton I. Dickinson. Children: 1. Bessie Hinton, m. "Ty" Kizzire. 2. Ivey Hinton, m. "Took" Smith.

HINTON, Thomas Burton, b. 1900, Fayette Co., Ala., d. 1941, Fayette, Ala. - son of J. A. Hinton - m. Dec. 24, 1922, Lizzie Ludell Doughty, b. Feb. 12, 1904, Fayette Co., Ala. Children: 1. Mary Ellen Hinton, b. Nov. 1, 1923, Fayette Co., Ala., m. Robert Ralph Renfroe, b. Fayette Co., Ala. 2. Louise Hinton, b. Jan. 5, 1925, Fayette Co., Ala., m. Jack Porter, b. Fayette Co., Ala. 3. Thomasine "Tommie" Hinton, b. Feb. 6, 1931, Fayette Co., Ala., m. Buddy Shelton, b. Fayette Co., Ala. 4. Jimmy Hinton, b. Aug. 29, 1936, Fayette, Ala., m. Jeannette Smith, b. Hamilton, Ala. (Lizzie Ludell Doughty is the dau. of Marcellus Doughty.)

HOCUTT, Bernard, b. 1915, Fayette Co., Ala. - son of N. Berkeley Hocutt - m. Inell Gray, b. abt. 1928, d. 1943. Children: 1. Millie Jean Hocutt, b. 1939, Ala., m. Sept. 4, 1955, George Griffin, Jr., - m. 2nd. - Aug. 1957, Charles Hugh "Chuck" Isbell, b. Jefferson, Co., Ala. 2. Byron Hocutt, b. 1941, Ala.

HOCUTT, Elmer, b. 1902, Fayette Co., Ala., - son of N. Berkeley Hocutt - m. 1927, Velera Otts, b. Fayette Co., Ala. Children: 1. Billie Hocutt, b. Fay. Co., Ala., m. Murphy Fowler. 2. Bobby Hocutt, b. 1930, d. 1931. 3. Frankie Hocutt, b. 1933, m. Alvan Waldon, b. Fayette Co., Ala. 4. Thomas Hocutt, b. 1936. 5. Johnnie Hocutt, b. 1938. 6. Judy Hocutt, b. 1952. (All children born Fayette Co., Ala.)

HOCUTT, Everette Thomas, b. Aug. 3, 1933, Fayette Co., Ala. - son of Stacy Braxton Hocutt - m. Jan. 1, 1956, Mary Ann Clearman, b. Feb. 8, 1932, Lamar

Co., Ala. - dau. of Wm. Harvey Clearman. They were married at the Union Chapel Church in Lamar Co., Ala. by Rev. J. T. Johnson. Everette is affiliated with the Alabama Telephone Co. Children: 1. Thomas Wayne Hocutt, b. Sept. 28, 1956, Fayette, Ala. 2. Linda Marie Hocutt, b. Oct. 3, 1959, Fayette, Ala.

HOCUTT, Norris Berkeley, b. Mar. 11, 1876, Tuscaloosa Co., Ala., d. Mar. 12, 1943, Fayette, Ala., m. Dec. 8, 1901, Ida Emogene Patterson, b. July 4, 1882, Fayette Co., Ala. - dau. of J. J. & Cenath (Rice) Patterson. Children: 1. Elmer Hocutt, b. 1902, m. Veleria Otts. 2. Dupree Hocutt, b. 1905, d. June 4, 1931, m. Masie Dodson. 3. Leo Hocutt, b. 1911, d. July 27, 1937. 4. Bernard Hocutt, b. 1915, m. Inell Gray, b. 1921, d. 1943. 5. Lillian Hocutt, b. 1917, m. 1937, John Thomas, b. Fayette Co., Ala. 6. Linnie Lee Hocutt, b. 1919, Fayette Co., Ala., m. 1937, Ottis Kuykendall, b. Tusca. Co., Ala. 7. Evelyn Hocutt (Twin) b. July 23, 1924, d. Oct. 1924. 8. Edwin Hocutt (Twin) b. July 23, 1924, m. Carrine Garner, b. Birmingham, Ala. (All these children born in Fayette Co., Ala.)

HOCUTT, Stacy Braxton, b. April 19, 1906, Fayette Co., Ala. - son of P. A. Hocutt - m. Sept. 12, 1928, Minnie Caroline Humber, b. Feb. 21, 1909, Fayette Co., Ala. - dau. of Thos. Bailey Humber. They were married at the Fayette County Court House by Judge J. N. Collins. Stacy is a farmer and a maintenance man. Children: 1. William Braxton Hocutt, b. Mar. 23, 1931, Fayette Co., Ala., m. June 26, 1955, Charlean Trimm, c. Dec. 27, 1933, Fayette Co., Ala. 2. Everette Thomas Hocutt, b. Aug. 3, 1933, Fayette Co., Ala., m. Jan. 1, 1956, Mary Ann Clearman, b. Feb. 8, 1932, Lamar Co., Ala.

HODO, Dr. Henry Gunther, Jr., b. Lamar Co., Ala. - son of H. G. Hodo, Sr., Millport, Ala. - m. Naomi Brock, b. Fayette Co., Ala. - dau. of T. Wilson Brock. Dr. Hodo came to Fayette shortly after World War II. Children: 1. Henry Gunther "Hank" Hodo, III, b. Fayette, Ala. 2. Infant Son, b. 1952, Fayette Co., Ala.

HOFFMAN, James Carson, d. 1959, Dublin, Ga., m. Bobbie Sims, d. 1910, Leslie, Ga. Children: 1. Ann Hoffman, b. Feb. 14, 1902, Moultrie, Ga. (Moved to Fayette from Leslie, Ga. in 1923.) m. Jan. 29, 1923, George Harris Gullett, b. July 5, 1889, Fayette, Ala., d. Jan. 24, 1952.

HOLLADAY, Charles Thomas, b. Feb. 21, 1921, Bledsoe Co., Tenn. - son of W. J. & Lula (Pope) Holladay - m. Oct. 2, 1951, Mildred Ann Gailmard, b. Jan. 30, 1924, Atlanta, Ga. Children: 1. Linda Ann Holladay, b. Oct. 1, 1953, Atlanta, Ga., d. Oct. 3, 1953. 2. Elizabeth Ann Holladay, b. July 12, 1955, Atlanta, Ga. 3. Mary Kathleen Holladay, b. Sept. 30, 1957, Atlanta, Ga.

HOLLADAY, William Joseph, b. Oct. 3, 1890, Putnam Co., Tenn. m. April 9, 1916, Lula Pope, b. Bledsoe Co., Tenn. Mr. Holladay came to Fayette with the Alabama Telephone Company and has made Fayette their home. Children: 1. Charles Thomas Holladay, b. Feb. 21, 1921, Bledsoe Co., Tenn., m. Oct. 2, 1951, Mildred Ann Gailmard, b. Jan. 30, 1924, Atlanta, Ga.

HOLLIMAN, Cornelius, b. 1792, S.C., m. 1813, Elizabeth Plyler (Plyer). Their three sons all settled in Fayette County, Ala. in the early 1830's. Children: 1. Elijah A. Holliman. 2. Uriah Holliman, m. Mary Lucas. dau. of Chas. Daniel & Mary Lucas. 3. Dr. Joshua A. Holliman, later moved to Arkansas.

HOLLIMAN, William Bailey, b. Jan. 19, 1875, d. Aug. 14, 1950, m. Nov. 17, 1901, Sara Bertha Waldrop. Children: 1. William Silas Holliman, m. Lela Bynum. 2. Effie Lucille Holliman, d. Oct. 17, 1923. 3. Alpha Elois Holliman. 4. Bailey Ernest Holliman. 5. Eula Rebecca Holliman, m. Lee Watson. 6. Oreland Holliman, m. Eva White. 7. John Franklin Holliman, m. Robbie Nell White. 8. Vella Mae Holliman.

HOLLINGSWORTH, Jeotha, b. May 28, 1820, d. June 30, 1890, Fayette Co., Ala. m. Martha Ford, b. Nov. 23, 1824, d. May 24, 1899, Fayette Co., Ala. Children: 1. Elizabeth Hollingsworth, b. Feb. 20, 1844, d. July 11, 1937, Fayette Co., Ala., m. Isaac W. Payne, b. Jan. 30, 1834, d. Dec. 9, 1927. 2. John Hollingsworth, b. Sept. 7, 1845, d. May 30, 1906. 3. Matilda Hollingsworth, b. June 20, 1847, d. Nov. 14, 1892. 4. Martha Hollingsworth, b. Dec. 29, 1848, d. Mar. 14, 1917, m. Mr. Shirley. 5. Malinda Hollingsworth, b. Dec. 3, 1851, d. Oct. 22, 1932, m. Mr. Pickle. 6. Mary Hollingsworth, b. May 19, 1853, d. Oct. 2, 1938, m. 1st - not given, 2nd. - Mr. Perry, 3rd. - Mr. Kirkland. 7. Phoebe Hollingsworth, b. May 26, 1855, d. Jan. 2, 1938, m. Mr. White. 8. Jacob Hollingsworth, b. April 18, 1857, d. Jan. 6, 1941. 9. Bell Zoria Hollingsworth, b. Mar. 29, 1859, d. Jan. 19, 1929, m. Mr. Killingsworth. 10. Jennie Hollingsworth, b. Jan. 18, 1861, d. Aug. 11, 1933, m. Mr. Rainey. 11. Sallie Hollingsworth, b. Feb. 2, 1863, m. Mr. Gilpin. 12. Nannie Hollingsworth, b. Feb. 9, 1867, m. Mr. Long. 13. Bashaba Hollingsworth, b. July 4, 1868, d. Oct. 20, 1870.

HOLLINGSWORTH, John A., b. June 13, 1877, Fayette Co., Ala., d. Sept. 2, 1952, Fayette Co., Ala. - son of Wiley & Regina (McCaleb) Hollingsworth - m. Jan. 15, 1900, Sarah Ida Smith, b. June 11, 1879, Marion Co., Ala., d. Mar. 25, 1947, Fayette Co., Ala. - dau. of Thomas & Mary (Aston) Smith. John A. Hollingsworth was a farmer. Both are buried at Berea Church of Christ Cemetery, Fayette Co., Ala. Children: (All born in Fayette Co., Ala.) 1. Exie Pearl Hollingsworth, b. Feb. 22, 1905, m. Fletcher M. Fowler, b. May 22, 1902, Fay. Co., Ala., d. Dec. 22, 1949, Fayette, Ala. 2. Ada Hollingsworth, b. Oct. 23, 1900, m. Lester Jones. 3. Thomas M. Hollingsworth, b. Mar. 25, 1902, m. Hazel Caldwell. 4. Mary Hollingsworth, b. Nov. 27, 1910, m. Fred Morris, b. Fayette Co., Ala.

HOLLINGSWORTH, Wiley J., b. June 27, 1845, d. May 6, 1916, Hubbertville, Ala. m. Regina A. McCaleb, b. Sept. 13, 1844, d. April 8, 1918, Hubbertville, Ala. Children: 1. John A. Hollingsworth, b. June 13, 1877, Fayette Co., Ala., d. Sept. 2, 1952, m. Sarah Ida Smith, b. June 11, 1877, Marion Co., Ala., d. Mar. 25, 1947.

HOOKER, Joseph Earl, m. June 25, 1920, Nettie Ollie McCleskey, b. June 21, 1894, Fayette Co., Ala. - dau. of T. C. McCleskey. Joseph Earl Hooker is a Veteran of World War I. Children: 1. John Kemp Hooker, b. Mar. 24, 1922, Winfield, Ala., m. Sept. 22, 1942, Elsie Kilgore. John Kemp Hooker served in World War II as Flight Officer and Navigator. He and his family live in Huntsvill, Ala., where he is affiliated with the Redstone Arsenal. Their children are - Suzann Rebecca Hooker, b. July 3, 1943, Fayette, Ala. and John Kemp Hooker, II, b. Nov. 23, 1954, Huntsville, Ala. 2. Marjorie Dale Hooker, b. July 29, 1926, Jasper, Ala., m. Sept. 19, 1947, Arthur Conrad Stucki. Arthur and Marjorie Stucki live in Rockville, Maryland and have the following children: Arthur Conrad Stucki, Jr., b. Dec. 5, 1950, Thomas Warren Stucki, b. May 6, 1953, and Allen Stucki, b. Nov. 8, 1956. 3. Mary Rhoda Hooker, b. Feb.

10, 1929, Columbia, S. C.

HOOVER, Rolland "Tuck" Maynord, b. Mar. 7, 1925, Kentland, Ind., m. July 21, 1947, Margaret "Peggy" O'Delle Deaton, b. Feb. 10, 1926, Tishimingo Co., Miss. - dau. of Lessie Pearl (Humber) Deaton. They were married in Iuka, Miss. by Rev. McGill. Children: 1. Mary Ann Hoover, b. Mar. 24, 1948, Watseka, Ill. 2. Carolyn Marie Hoover, b. Mar. 31, 1951, Watseka, Ill, d. April 1, 1951, buried Kentland, Ind. 3. Kathie Jane Hoover, b. July 4, 1955, Watseka, Ill.

HOULDITCH, George Washington, b. July 20, 1888, Ala., d. Mar. 1927, Jasper, Ala. - son of Henry Houlditch - m. Nov. 17, 1907, Lilie May Smith, b. Mar. 24, 1890, Randolph, Bibb Co., Ala. - dau. of George & Virginia (Grey) Smith. Children: 1. Georgia Mae Houlditch. 2. Henry Huey Houlditch. 3. Marie Louise Houlditch. 4. Glen Vance Houlditch. 5. John Howard Houlditch. 6. James Edward Houlditch. 7. Lillian Audoline Houlditch.

HOULDITCH, Glen Vance, b. May 7, 1917, Marvel, Bibb Co., Ala. - son of Geo. Wash. & Lilie Mae (Smith) Houlditch - m. Mar. 30, 1941, Delta Ree Kirkley, b. Aug. 21, 1922, Fayette Co., Ala. - dau. of Marion Jackson & Eliza Jane (Hawkins) Kirkley. They were married at Nauvoo, Ala. Rev. Glen V. Houlditch was ordained as a Missionary Baptist Minister at the Baptist Church in Kansas, Walker Co., Ala. Children: 1. Reata Houlditch, b. Nov. 6, 1943, Kansas, Walker Co., Ala. 2. Glen Rubal Houlditch, b. Aug. 19, 1949, Jasper, Ala. 3. Theron Nathan Houlditch, b. Sept. 26, 1952, Jasper, Ala.

HOWELL, Aubrey Oliver "Duke", b. Tusca. Co., Ala., m. Jasper Nell Woods, b. Sept. 22, 1931, Fayette Co., Ala. - dau. of Wilmot & Hassie (Ballinger) Woods. Children: 1. Kenneth Allen Howell, b. July 12, 1955, Montgomery, Ala.

HOWTON, Abram, - brother of Curtis Howton - m. Dorcas Castleberry. Abram Howton's father came to the United States from Scotland. Abram was a farmer and once owned a large portion of land where the City of Fayette now stands. The family got their water from what was once known as the City Spring, the homeplace being where the present home of Mrs. E. F. Hamby now stands. Children: 1. Betsy Howton. 2. Cassie Howton. 3. Melissa Howton. 4. Sarah Howton. 5. Martha Howton. 6. George Washington Howton, b. April 16, 1824, d. Jan. 16, 1902, Fayette Co., Ala., m. Feb. 8, 1852, Martha Ann Bobo, b. April 19, 1832, Spartanburg, S.C., d. Nov. 1, 1899, Fayette Co., Ala. 7. Duck Howton. 8. Dorcas Howton. 9. Abie Howton. 10. Jimmy Howton. 11. Billy Howton. 12. John Howton. 13. Willis Howton. 14. Matthew Howton. 15. Jonathan Howton. 16. David Howton.

HOWTON, George Washington, b. April 16, 1824, d. Jan. 16, 1902, Fayette Co., Ala. - son of Abram & Dorcas (Castleberry) Howton - m. Feb. 8, 1852, Martha Ann Bobo, b. April 19, 1832, Spartanburg, S.C., d. Nov. 1, 1899, Fayette Co., Ala. - dau. of Spencer & Polly (Rainwater) Bobo. George W. Howton was a farmer. He served in the Civil War in the Confederate States Army - 56th Ala. Cavalry. Children: 1. Marinda Howton, b. Mar. 22, 1853, Fayette Co., Ala. (All the children were born in Fayette Co.) d. Oct. 13, 1860, Miss. 2. Infant Daughter, b. & d. July 9, 1854. 3. George Washington Howton, II, b. Aug. 10, 1855, d. May 26, 1931, Fayette, Ala., m. Jan. 1, 1884, Olivia Louise Smith, b. May 14, 1862, d. Feb. 11, 1949, Fayette, Ala. 4. James Matthew

Howton, b. May 24, 1858, d. Jan. 6, 1922, buried Elmwood Cem. Birmingham, Ala. m. Jan. 13, 1893, Allie Jones, buried Memphis, Tenn. 5. Virginia Emma Howton, b. April 14, 1860, d. Dec. 15, 1930, Fayette Co., Ala. 6. Tilman Foster Howton, b. Aug. 1, 1862, d. June 24, 1864, Fayette, Ala. 7. Noah Howton, b. Oct. 11, 1864, d. Feb. 2, 1865, Fayette, Ala. 8. Mollie Agnes Howton, b. July 28, 1866, d. May 15, 1953, Fayette, Ala., m. Jan. 1, 1899, John Franklin Freeman, b. Sept. 23, 1869, d. Dec. 7, 1943, Fayette, Ala. 9. Silas Melton Howton, b. Feb. 1, 1869, d. Oct. 19, 1933, Fayette Co., Ala. 10. Moses Edgar Howton, b. Aug. 25, 1871, d. Dec. 18, 1904, Fayette Co., Ala. 11. Harriet Elizabeth Howton, b. April 6, 1873, d. Sept. 27, 1874, Fayette, Ala.

HOWTON, George W., II, b. Aug. 10, 1855, Fayette Co., Ala., d. May 26, 1931, Fayette, Ala. - son of Geo. W., I & Martha Ann (Bobo) Howton - m. Jan. 1, 1884, Olivia Louise Smith, b. May 14, 1862, d. Feb. 11, 1949, Fayette, Ala. dau. of Richard J. & Lilly (Abernathy) Smith. Children:(All born in Fayette Co.) 1. Charles Raymond "Cape" Howton, b. Oct. 30, 1884, had one child. 2. Mabel Howton, b. Nov. 20, 1887, m. 1st. - Burnett J. Ritch, died, 2nd. - C. A. "Bud" Fisher. 3. Harry G. Howton, b. May 14, 1890, m. Mattie __. (Had children: Ronnie or Donnie, Richard Alexander and Sharon Howton.) 4. Susie Howton, b. May 11, 1893, m. Eugene Wilson. (No Children.) 5. Mark Howton, b. Sept. 7, 1898. 6. Ruth Howton, b. Mar. 25, 1901, m. Wellman Hillhouse. (Child: Peggy Olivia Hillhouse, m. Samuel Thomas Striegel and had children: Patricia Olivia, b. Dec. 12, 1948, Fayette, Ala. and Samuel Thomas "Buddy" Striegel, Jr., b. Mar. 26, 1950, Fayette, Ala.) 7. George Howton, III, b. Sept. 15, 1903, m. Ruth Jones. (Child: Marion Howton, b. Feb. 18, 1926, Fayette, Ala., m. Sam Reeks and has two children.)

HOWTON, James Matthew, b. May 24, 1858, Fayette Co., Ala., d. Jan. 6, 1922, m. Jan. 13, 1893, Allie Jones. He is buried at Elmwood Cemetery, Birmingham, Ala. and she is buried at Memphis, Tenn. Children: 1. Bruce Jones Howton, b. Dec. 30, 1892, Fayette Co., Ala., d. Sept. 13, 1948, Houston, Texas, m. Ora "Barney" Oldfield. (One son - Bruce J. Howton, Jr., b. Sept. 24, 1917, Jefferson Co., Ala.)

HUBBARD, Thomas - son of Thomas Hubbard - m. abt. 1600, Sarah _. He is buried at Christ Church Parish, Lancaster Co., Va. Children: 1. Thomas Hubbard, m. Mary _. 2. John Hubbard. 3. Mary Hubbard. 4. Elizabeth Hubbard.

HUBBARD, Thomas, d. Will in Lancaster Co., Va. 1745, - son of Thomas & Sarah (_) Hubbard - m. 1717, Mary _. He is buried at Christ Church Parish, Va. Children: 1. Elizabeth Hubbard, b. Feb. 22, 1721, d. Nov. 14, 1789, m. May 18, 1738, William Saunders, b. 1718. 2. Joseph Hubbard, b. 1718, d. 1776, m. Betty __. (Ancestor of the Fosters of Nashville, Tenn.) 3. Ephriam Hubbard, b. 1720, m. July 15, 1749, Hannah? Edwards (Edmonds). (Ancestor of the Fosters of Nashville, Tenn.)

HUBBARD, Thomas, b. Lancaster Co., Va. - son of Thomas & Mary(_) Hubbard - m. Margaret Kirk. There ten children, all names are not known to the descendant. Douglas Register; D.A.R. Papers and Family Bible. All children listed except the first were born in Goochland Co., Va. Children: 1. Thomad Hubbard (third child), b. Nov. 26, 1754, Lancaster Co., Va., d. July 31, 1841, Morgan Co., Ala., m. Oct. 19, 1785, Mary Blekeley Swann. 2. James Hubbard, b. Nov. 17, 1756. 3. William Hubbard, b. Oct. 13, 1758. 4. Ben-

jamin Hubbard, b. July 15, 1760. 5. Christopher Hubbard, b. Aug. 5, 1762.
6. Anne Kirk Hubbard, b. April 18, 1764. 7. Winnifred Hubbard (female) b.
July 15, 1766. 8. Stephen Shilton Hubbard, b. April 24, 1770.

HUBBARD, Thomas, b. Nov. 26, 1754, Lancaster Co., Va., d. July 31, 1841, Morgan Co., Ala. - son of Thomas & Margaret (Kirk) Hubbard - m. Oct. 19, 1785, Molly Blakeley Swann, d. before 1841 - dau. of Thompson & Jannett Carson (Blakeley) Swann. Major Thomas Hubbard was one of George Washington's Staff Officers. (Hertman's "Historical Register of the Officers of the Continental Army".) Children: 1. Green Kirk Hubbard, b. July 7, 1786, m. Sally Robertson Lester. (Senator from Lawrence Co. to Legislature 1822 - Ala. Records, Jones Bol. 66, p. 97. Dict. of Am. Biography, Vol. 9, p. 322. Public Men in Ala., Garrett, p. 297. Brewer's Alabama, p. 307. Palmer's Register of the Univ. of Ala. -- Sally Lester was the dau. of Frederick Lester and Dollie (Robertson) Pollard, widow of Thomas Pollard. Mrs. Virginia (Hubbard) Hudson, 3001 Windsor, Dallas, Texas, is a descendant.) 2. Thomas Hubbard, b. Mar. 13, 1788, m. Elizabeth N. Murry. 3. Vincent Hubbard, b. Feb. 24, 1790, m. 2nd. - Elizabeth (Murray) Hamm. 4. Elizabeth Hubbard, b. Feb. 19, 1792, m. Francis ? Wilson. 5. David Hubbard, b. Mar. 22, 1794, Bedford Co., Va., d. Jan. 20, 1874, La., m. 1st. - Miss Campbell, 2nd. - Miss Studdard. (David Hubbard's granddaughter, Miss Lucy Young, Rt. 3, West Point, Miss. - He was Ala. Representative to Congress; State Senator, 1827, '28, '29, '30, '32, Ala. Records, Jones, Vol. 66; State Representative; Major in War of 1812; First Commissioner of Indian Affairs, C.S.A; Trustee of Univ. of Ala. 1828 - 1835; Built first railroad west of Alleghenies, 1832 - 1834 - "Historical Marker, Tuscumbia, Ala."; and was a cousin to Gen. Sam Houston.) 6. Betsy Hubbard, b. Feb. 23, 1796. 7. Margaret Hubbard, b. July 27, 1798, m. William Hewlett. 8. Stephen Hubbard, b. Sept. 24, 1800. 9. James Hubbard, b. Feb. 15, 1803, m. Eliza DeWoody. 10. Catherine Hubbard, b. June 15, 1805, m. Mar. 12, 1828, John H. Morris.

HUBBARD, Rev. Vincent, b. Feb. 24, 1792, Va. - Probable Bedford Co. d. Dec. 28, 1870, Pickens Co., Ala. - son of Major Thomas & M. B. (Swann) Hubbard - m. Jan. 15, 1829, Mrs. Elizabeth (Murray) Hamm, b. Feb. 18, 1803, Ga., d. Sept. 20, 1883. He was a Presbyterian Minister. They were married in Birmingham, Ala. by Rev. John Williams. Mrs. Elizabeth Hamm, widow of Gideon Hamm, Revolutionary Soldier of Ga. had the following Hamm children: 1. Amanda Hamm, b. 1821, m. Wiley Burgess, b. 1808, Ga. Presbyterian Minister and had - Elizabeth J., b. 1840; Mary E. b. 1842; James W., b. 1843; and Charles W. Burgess, b. 1846. 2. Francis Hamm and Joseph Hamm (Minors at the time of their father's death - "O. Court Records, Madison Co., Ala.")

Mrs. Frankie N. Martin has two pieces of royal ironstone ware brought from Madison Co., Ala. by Mrs. Vincent Hubbard when she came to Elyton as a bride. Vincent Hubbard was a veteran of teh War of 1812. He served as a trumpeter in Capt. Coleman Lock's and _ Pace's Co., Tenn. Militia, Dec. 10, 1812 - April 27, 1815. Both Rev. Vincent Hubbard and his wife are buried in the Fayette Cemetery. Children: 1. Leona Estelle Hubbard. b. Oct. 18, 1829, Elyton, Ala., d. Nov. 18, 1872, Fayette Co., Ala. m. James H. Moore, b. July 18, 1824, d. Mar. 21, 1894, Fayette Co., Ala. (Capt. in C.S.A.) 2. Lizzie Ann Hubbard, b. April 1, 1837, Pickensville, Ala. d. May 16, 1903, Fayette, Ala., m. Jan. 7, 1855, Augustine Melville Nuckols, b. Oct. 26, 1823, Barren Co., Ky., d. Dec. 13, 1896, Fayette, Ala.

HUBBERT, George, b. 1800, Tenn., m. abt. 1827, Elizabeth Stewart, b. 1809, Tenn. Children: 1. William Hubbert, b. 1828, Ala., m. abt. 1847, Elizabeth _. b. 1830, Ala. 2. Joseph Hubbert, b. 1829. 3. Reuben Hubbert, b. 1832. 4. Polly Hubbert, b. 1834. 5. John Hubbert, b. 1836. 6. George Washington Hubbert, b. 1838. 7. Sarah Hubbert, b. 1845. 8. Pierce Hubbert, b. 1853.

HUBBERT, John M., b. 1853 - son of Pierce Hubbert, m. Sept. 11, 1898, Mamie Frances Kimbrell. Children: (Not listed.)

HUBBERT, Mathew, b. Jan. 28, 1810, Tenn., d. 1887, San Luis Rey, Calif., m. April 28, 1833, Elizabeth Stallworth Thornton, b. Mar. 2, 1817, Ga., d. 1902, San Luis Rey, Calif. - dau. of David Thornton. Children: 1. Sarah Hollingsworth Hubbert, b. Feb. 15, 1834, Fayette,Co., Ala., d. 1853, Miss., m. Feb. 15, 1852, Wiley T. Murray. 2. Nancy W. Hubbert, b. Feb. 10, 1835, Fayette Co. Ala., m. 1855, John W. Murray. 3. David Crockett Hubbert, b. June 12, 1836, Fayette Co., Ala., d. Mar. 18, 1907, San Saba, Texas, m. Dec. 31, 1868, Mary William Woods, b. Mar. 13, 1844, Pickens Co., Ala., d. 1921, Texas. 4. Robert Henry Hubbert, b. Dec. 3, 1837, Fayette Co., Ala., d. died in Civil War. 5. Andrew Jackson Hubbert, b. Jan. 19, 1839, Fayette Co., Ala., m. June 13, 1859, Martha A. Davis. 6. George William Hubbert, b. Jan. 19, 1841, Fayette Co., Ala. 7. Martha Ann Hubbert, b. Oct. 22, 1842, Fayette Co., Ala., d. Texas, m. Theodore Martin Rice, b. Oct. 20, 1836, d. Texas. 8. James Monroe Hubbert, b. Feb. 4, 1845, Miss. 9. Presley Thornton Hubbert, b. Nov. 27, 1846. 10. Eppie H. Hubbert, b. Jan. 2, 1848, Miss., m. Ben Warren. 11. Washington Irving Hubbert, b. Jan. 8, 1850, Miss., d. San Saba, Texas. 12. Mary Jane Hubbert, b. Jan. 1, 1852, Miss., d. Calif., m. John McNeil. 13. Elizabeth Hubbert, b. Jan. 19, 1854, Miss., m. John Graves. 14. Susannah Hubbert, b. April 18, 1857, Texas., d. Calif., m. Mr. Hayes. 15. Benjamin Franklin Hubbert, b. June 16, 1860, Texas, d. Calif.

HUBBERT, Vadus, b. Aug. 2, 1923, Fayette, Ala., m. Nov. 22, 1945, James Ethel Little, b. Aug. 17, 1924, Fayette, Ala., - dau. of James N. & Annie (Wiggins) Little. Children: 1. Jane Ethel Hubbert, b. Nov. 27, 1952, Fayette, Fayette Co., Ala.

HUFFMAN, Eulis A., b. Nov. 30, 1906, Caledonia, Miss., m. Nov. 4, 1939, Bertha May Baldwin, b. Oct. 18, 1915. E. A. Huffman's parents - Lester Earnest Huffman, b. Nov. 22, 1872, Green Co., Ala., m. Katherine Glen, b. May 8, 1869, Green Co., Ala. Grandparents - Wm. C. P., b. May 9, 1842, & Rachel J. Thomas, b. Dec. 25, 1840; and Margaret E. S. Johnson, b. Jan. 20, 1833. Great grandparents - James Huffman, b. Jan. 1809 & Jane Curry. 2 Great grandparents - Alexander Huffman, b. Nov. 12, 1782. 3-Great grandparents - Patton Huffman from Germany, whose parents came from Holland to Germany.
Bertha May (Baldwin) Huffman's parents - Benjamin Baldwin, b. Feb. 14, 1888, Texas, & Elizabeth Cowden, b. Nov. 28, 1900, Jefferson Co., Ala. Grandparents - Erwin Baldwin, b. 1838, Winston Co., Ala. & Phebe Whiserhunt, b. 1870, Winston Co., Ala.; and George & Martha (Walters) Cowden. Great grandparents - Joe B. Whiserhunt, b. 1827, & Sarah (Michael), b. 1833; Jack & Nancy (Higgenbottom) Cowden; and Robert Bates & Elizabeth (Simoson) Walters. 2 Great grandparents - Elijah Cowden, b. in Scotland or Ireland; and E. E. L. (Simoson). E. A. Huffman's children: 1. Jo Ann Huffman, b. Nov. 4, 1942, Fayette, Ala. 2. Buster Huffman.

HUGHES, Lanthus Theodore, b. July 29, 1900, Fayette Co., Ala., m. Dec. 22, 1928, Jessie Freeman, b. June 15, 1900, Fayette Co., Ala., d. July 17, 1951. He is a farmer. She is buried at Macedonia Baptist Church Cemetery, Fayette Co., Ala. Children: 1. Carol Howton Hughes, b. July 26, 1939, Fayette Co., Ala., m. June 1, 1957, Aaron Barney Olive.

HUGHES, Mens Emanuel, b. Nov. 6, 1871, Pickens Co., Ala., m. Argie Wright, b. Mar. 16, 1877, Fayette Co., Ala. M. E. Huges parents - James Thomoson Hughes, b. 1828, N.C. & Jane Mitchell, b. June 30, 1834, S.C. Grandparents - Elisha "Lish" Hughes & Miss Wilson; and Acie Mitchell, b. Va. & Cluncy West. Great grandparents - Jimmy Wilson; Jennie (Dorroh) Mithcell - dau. of Jimmy Dorroh.
Argie (Wright) Hughes' parents - Thomas Jefferson Wright, b. 1840, Fayette Co., Ala., & Mary "Molly" Caraway, b. 1844, Fayette, Ala. Grandparents - Archie & Betty (Ray) Wright; and Elijah & Miss (Strickland) Caraway. M. E. Hughes children: 1. Lanthus Hughes, b. July 29, 1905, Fayette, Ala., m. Dec. 22, 1928, Jessie Freeman, b. June 15, 1900, Fayette, Ala., d. July 17, 1951, Fayette, Ala.

HUMBER, Charles Christian, b. May 27, 1781, m. Sept. 17, 1818, Lettice Hammon. Charles C. Humber was the son of John Humber III and Elizabeth (Christian). Charles Christian Humber , the tenth child of John Humber III came to Alabama to visit his brother John, where he met and married Lettice Hammon. The marriage ceremony was performed by John H. Morris. Charles and Lettice then settled in Alabama, near Mud Creek (Little Warrior). Children: (They had a number of children.) Robert Hammon Humber, m. July 12, 1845, Cyntha Jane Noland.

HUMBER, Charles Claude, b. Sept. 23, 1893, d. July 31, 1952 - son of Robert Hayes Humber - m. Apr. 4, 1920, 1st. - Letha Claunch, b. Jan. 8, 1902, d. July, 1922. (Charles Claude was born in Franklin Co., Ala.) Children: (1st. marriage.) 1. Eunice Evelyn Humber, b. Feb. 10, 1921, Tishimingo Co., Miss. m. July 1944, Trevor Lee Anglin, b. Mar. 1923. (Child: Larry Humber Anglin, b. Jan. 10, 1956.)
Charles Claude Humber second marriage - Flora Wynn, b. Dec. 24, 1902. Children: (2nd. marriage.) 1. Edward Thurman Humber, b. Dec. 5, 1926, Tish. Co., Miss., m. Aug. 6, 1945, Francis Ocene Beive, b. Aug. 22, 1926. 2. John David Humber, b. April 10, 1930. 3. Gladys Ruth Humber, b. Mar. 6, 1933, m. July 22, 1950, Charles Tullion Wright, b. Dec. 24, 1929. 4. Claude Denton Humber, b. Nov. 10, 1937, Tish. Co., Miss. 5. Wilmer Loudell Humber, b. Apr. 22, 1943, Tish. Co., Miss.

HUMBER, Edward Thurman, b. Dec. 5, 1926, - son of Charles Claude Humber - m. Aug. 6, 1945, Francis Ocene Beive, b. Aug. 22, 1926. Children: 1. Robert Edward Humber, b. Feb. 10, 1948. 2. Brenda Ann Humber, b. Jan. 6, 1954.

HUMBER, John, b. abt. 1704, England, m. wife unknown. John Humber, ancestor of the Humbers in America, at the age of sixteen, embarked on a sailing vessel from the shores of the Humber River, England, where his family lived and from whom it is said the river Humber derived its name. John reached America about the year 1720, and settled in Hanover, Virginia. Children: 1. John Humber, III, m. 1734, Betty Meeks.

HUMBER, John II - son of John Humber, the English Immigrant - m. 1734, Betty

Meeks. Children: 1. John Humber, III, of Saint Paul Parish, m. Mar. 2, 1757 Elizabeth Christian.

HUMBER, John, III, of Saint Paul Parish - son of John Humber, II, - m. Mar. 2, 1757, Elizabeth Christian - dau. of Charles Christian. Elizabeth's father's Will was probated Feb. 16, 1784, Goochland Co., Va. The Christians were descended from the ancient family of McChristian of the Isle of Man. The name was first written Christian about the year 1600. John Humber III and Elizabeth Christian settled in Goochland Co., Va. thirty-five miles above Richmond, on their estate "Air Hill" where thirteen children were born to them. Children: 1. Charles Humber, b. Jan. 22, 1758, d. Mar. 30, 1758. 2. Christian Humber (Female), b. April 26, 1759, m. Mr. Jarrett. 3. Mary Humber, b. Mar. 31, 1760, d. in infancy. 4. John Humber, b. Jan. 6, 1764, d. June 30, 1765. 5. Elizabeth Humber, b. Jan. 26, 1766, m. Mr. Pleasants. 6. Name not legible -- 7. John Humber, IV, b. Aug. 7, 1772, settled in Ala. 8. Judith Humber, b. June 9, 1775, d. Oct. 2, 1822, m. Edward Cox, Jr. 9. William Humber, b. Feb. 23, 1778, settled in North Carolina. 10. Charles Christian Humber, b. May 27, 1781, settled in Ala., m. Lettice Hammon. 11. Robert Christian Humber, b. June 6, 1783, settled in Monticello, Ga. 12. Mary Christian Humber, b. Feb. 19, 1786. 13. Edward Humber, b. Feb. 14, 1790. One of the sons settled in Crab Orchard, Ky.

HUMBER, John Thomas, b. Oct. 11, 1851, Fayette Co., Ala., d. May 1, 1928 - son of Robert Hammond & Cynthia (Noland) Humber - m. Rebecca Frances South, b. Feb. 12, 1853, Fayette Co., Ala., d. Oct. 28, 1936 - dau. of Ezekial Asbury & Nancy A. (Stewart) South. John Thomas Humber was a farmer and a miller. Children: 1. Cora Humber, b. Oct. 19, 1875, (All children born in Fay. Co., Ala.) d. Jan. 11, 1885. 2. Nancy Jane Humber, b. Oct. 29, 1877. 3. Thomas Bailey Humber, b. May 19, 1879, d. Aug. 14, 1947, m. Nov. 14, 1906, Mary Elizabeth Ballinger, b. Dec. 12, 1886, Fayette Co., Ala. 4. Robert Albert Asbury Humber, b. Aug. 30, 1881, d. Feb. 2, 1932, m. Dec. 25, 1902, Jennie Belle Byars, b. Nov. 26, 1885, Fayette Co., Ala. 5. Sarah Adaline Humber, b. Nov. 21, 1883, m. Moore Sizemore, b. Lamar Co., Ala. 6. Ozie Humber, b. Feb. 20, 1886, d. Nov. 27, 1908. 7. Survilla E. Humber, b. Sept. 1, 1887, d. Jan. 2, 1959, Fayette, Ala., m. Nov. 15, 1906, Andrew Weaterley Cantrell, b. Dec. 8, 1879, Marion Co., Ala., d. Aug. 25, 1951, Fayette, Ala. 8. John Black Humber, b. Oct. 1, 1889, m. June 10, 1914, Minnie Inez Long, b. Oct. 13, 1894, Lee Co., Ala. 9. Fannie Humber, b. Feb. 28, 1891, d. Nov. 8, 1908, Fayette Co., Ala. 10. Carrie Humber, b. Feb. 1, 1893, d. Nov. 21, 1908, Fay. Co., Ala. 11. William Porter Humber, b. May 28, 1895, m. April 28, 1920, Omie Florroa Mobley, b. Jan. 6, 1901. 12. D. Marvin Humber, b. Aug. 9, 1899 d. Mar., 1949, Fayette Co., Ala.

HUMBER, Johnny Rayburn, b. April 19, 1911, Fayette Co., Ala. - son of Thos. Bailey Humber - m. April 20, 1932, Mary Inez Watkins (adopted by Perkins family.), b. April 21, 1911, La. - dau. of John Watkins. They were married at the home of W. F. Gilpin in Fayette Co., Ala. by the Rev. W. F. Gilpin. Rayburn is a farmer. Children: (All born in Fayette County.) 1. Johnny James Humber, b. Feb. 9, 1936, Fayette Co., Ala. 2. Helen Inez Humber, b. Aug. 5, 1937. 3. Betty Carolyn Humber, b. Jan. 6, 1942. 4. Charles Bailey Humber, b. Mar. 29, 1943. 5. Albert Rayburn Humber, b. April 16, 1947. 6. Robert Wilson Humber, b. April 1, 1949.

HUMBER, Lewis Porter, b. Feb. 2, or 12, 1854, Fayette Co., Ala., d. Aug. 2, 1905, Fayette Co., Ala. - son of Robert Hammon & Cyntha Jane (Noland) Humber m. Dec. 18, 1873, Harriett Josephine Moore, b. June 14, 1856, Fayette Co., d. Dec. 27, 1938, Fayette Co., Ala. - dau. of Wm. Owens & Mary Ann D. (Kirkland) Moore. They were married by Rev. A. E. Foster at Fayette, Ala. Witnessed by Dr. W. A. Morton and R. F. Moore. Children: 1. Mary Jane Porter, b. Nov. 29, 1874, d. Aug. 16, 1932. 2. Lula A. Humber, b. Mar. 13, 1876. 3. G. Wilson Humber, b. April 25, 1877, d. Jan. 28, 1932. 4. Nancy Effie Humber, b. July 18, 1879. 5. Lillie Adline Humber, b. Jan. 13, 1881. 6. Jesse Lee Humber, b. April 13, 1883. 7. John Wesley Humber, b. Dec. 7, 1885, d. Sept. 20, 1886. 8. William Hammon Humber, b. Oct. 15, 1887. 9. Lewis Elmer Humber, b. Mar. 25, 1889, d. Mar. 7, 1936. 10. Grover Cleveland Humber, b. June 15, 1892, d. Oct. 12, 1957. 11. Samuel Houston Humber, b. Aug. 27, 1894, d. May 21, 1905.

HUMBER, Robert Hayes "Bud", b. Fayette Co., Ala. - son of Robert Hammond Humber - m. Rebecca Emaline Ward, b. July 31, 1849, Fayette Co., Ala., d. July 31, 1918. Robert Hayes "Bud" Humber served during the Civil War in Co. A. 10 Ala. Cav. C.S.A. He and his wife are buried in the Friendship Church Cem. in Tishimingo Co., Miss. Children: 1. Genera Humber, m. Henry Wilson. 2. Emma Humber, m. Walter Hindman. 3. Mollie Humber. 4. Nancy Louella Humber, m. W. T. Gober. 5. Robert John Willis Humber, b. Aug. 30, 1880, Fayette Co., Ala., d. Sept. 3, 1933, Tish. Co., Miss., m. Dec. 25, 1904, Anna Viola Belve, b. Mar. 10, 1885, Tish. Co., Miss. d. ___ 24, 1932, Paden, Miss. 6. Leora Humber, b. July 2, 1884, d. Nov. 11, 1952, m. John Drew Martin. 7. Charles Claude Humber, b. Sept. 23, 1893, Franklin Co., Ala., d. July 31, Tish. Co., Miss., m. 1st. - April 4, 1920, Letha Claunch, b. Jan. 8, 1902, d. July, 1922, m. 2nd. - Flora Wynn, b. Dec. 24, 1902.

HUMBER, Robert Hammon, - son of Charles Christian & Lettice (Hammon) Humber - m. July 12, 1845, Cyntha Jane Noland. They were married by L. A. Tarrant, J. P. R. H. Humber is buried in Miss. Children: 1. Lettie Humber. 2. John Thomas Humber, b. Oct. 11, 1851, d. May 1, 1928, m. July 12, 1845, Rebecca Frances South, b. Feb. 12, 1853, Fayette Co., Ala., d. Oct. 28, 1936. (John Thos. born Fayette Co.) 3. Mary Jane Humber. 4. Lewis Porter Humber, b. Feb. 12, 1854, Fayette Co., Ala., d. Aug. 2, 1905, Fayette Co., m. Dec. 18, 1873, Harriett Josephine Moore, b. June 14, 1856, Fayette Co., d. Dec. 27, 1938, Fayette Co. 5. Nancy Humber. 6. Charles Christian (or Robert Hayes) Humber, called "Bud", m. Rebecca Emiline Ward, b. July 31, 1849, Fayette Co., Ala., d. July 31, 1918.

HUMBER, Robert John Willis, b. Aug. 30, 1880, Fayette Co., Ala., d. Sept. 3, 1933, Tish. Co., Miss - son of Robert Hayes "Bud" Humber - m. Dec. 25, 1904, Anna Viola Belve, b. Mar. 10, 1885, Tish. Co., Miss. d. 1932, Paden, Miss. Children: 1. Lessie Pearl Humber, b. Sept. 18, 1905, Midway, Tish. Co., Miss. m. April 25, 1925, Richard Zebbie Dennis O'Delle Deaton, b. Iuka, Tish. Co., Miss. 2. Onida Dellilla Humber, b. Nov. 2, 1915, Tish.Co, Miss., m. Nov. 2, 1935, Joy Marieth Enlow, b. June 3, 1915, Tish. Co., Miss.

HUMBER, Thomas Bailey, b. May 19, 1879, Fayette Co., Ala., d. Aug. 14, 1947, Fayette Co., Ala. - son of John Thomas & Rebecca Frances (South) Humber - m. Nov. 14, 1906, Mary Elizabeth Ballinger, b. Dec. 12, 1886, Fayette Co., Ala. dau. of James Wm. & Sallie T. (Bobo) Ballinger. They were married at the home of J. W. Ballinger, Fayette Co., Ala. by Bro. J. Franklin Willis. T. B. Humber was a farmer and is buried at the Mt. Lebanon Church Cem., Fayette Co., Ala. Children: (All born in Fayette County.) 1. Carrie Myrtle Humber, b. Sept. 24, 1907, m. Jan. 13, 1929, James Chesley Bynum, b. April 28, 1909, Fay. Co., Ala. 2. Minnie Carolyn Humber, b. Feb. 21, 1909, m. Sept. 12, 1928, Stacy Braxton Hocutt, b. April 19, 1906, Fayette Co., Ala. 3. Johnnie Rayburn Humber, b. April 19, 1911, Fayette Co., Ala., m. April 20, 1932, Mary Inez Watkins (adopted by Perkins family) b. April 21, 1911, La. 4. Sarah Willene Humber, b. Aug. 16, 1913, m. Feb. 27, 1947, Travis Alden Smith, b. May 13, 1911, Fayette Co., Ala. 5. William Carey Humber, b. July 31, 1917, m. June 15, 1941, Edith Gay Collins, b. Feb. 6, 1922, Lamar Co., Ala. 6. Thomas Lloyd Humber, b. Sept. 29, 1922, Fayette Co., Ala., m. Jan. 26, 1946, Arlene Black, b. June 4, 1926, Fayette Co., Ala. 7. Albert Hamilton Humber, b. Oct. 29, 1925, m. May 18, 1949, Edna Earl Snodgrass, b. Jan. 4, 1923, Bashi, Clarke Co., Ala.

HUMBER, Thomas Lloyd, b. Sept. 29, 1922, Fayette Co., Ala. - son of Thos. Bailey & Mary Eliz. (Ballinger) Humber - m. Jan. 26, 1946, Arlene Black, b. June 4, 1926, Fayette Co., Ala. - dau. of Ellis Black. They were married at the home of T. B. Humber, in Fayette Co., Ala. by Rev. A. M. Nix. Lloyd is an employee of the U. S. Postal Department, and a farmer. Thomas Lloyd Humber entered the U. S. Army Jan. 16, 1943, at Ft. McClellan, Ala. as a Private. On May 12, 1944 he departed for England and arrived there on May 24, 1944. He was a member of the 35 Inf. Div. 137 Inf. Bn. Co. E. in a light machine gun squad. Left England for the Beachhead of France in June 1944, waded ashore at the Normandy Beachhead. He was promoted to Staff Sgt. while on the front line in France, was wounded in France on Sept. 12, 1944, and again in Belgium on Jan. 4, 1945. Decorations and Citations include: Purple Heart and two oak clusters; European-African-Middle Eastern Service Medal with one silver star. He was honorably discharged on Oct. 8, 1945.
Children: (All born in Fayette Co., Ala.) 1. Mary Angela Humber, b. Oct. 25, 1946. 2. Thomas Jerry Humber, b. Sept. 2, 1948 (Twin). 3. James Terry Humber (Twin), b. Sept. 2, 1948. 4. Cora Elizabeth Humber, b. Nov. 13, 1950. 5. Janice Arlene Humber, b. Feb. 15, 1960.

HUMBER, William Carey, b. July 31, 1917, Fayette Co., Ala. - son of Thos. Bailey & Mary Eliz. (Ballinger) Humber - m. June 15, 1941, Edith Gay Collins, b. Feb. 6, 1922, Lamar Co., Ala. - dau. of Murray Collins. They were married at the home of T. B. Humber in Fayette Co. by Rev. J. T. Johnson. He is an electrical worker. Children: 1. Mary Rebecca Humber. b. May 30, 1942, Fay. Co., Ala. 2. Thomas Barry Humber, b. Oct. 29, 1944, Memphis, Tenn. 3. Michael Cary Humber, b. Nov. 26, 1949, Memphis, Tenn. 4. Jeffrie Allan Humber, b. June 29, 1959, Memphis, Tenn.

HUMBER, William Hammond, b. Oct. 15, 1887, Fayette, Ala. - son of Lewis Porter & Harriet Josephine (Moore) Humber - m. July 11, 1909, Annie Sanders, b. Oct. 6, 1888, Fayette, Ala. - dau. of Robert E. & Bell Elizabeth (Propst) Sanders. They were married at Fayette, Ala. by Rev. Robert H. Jones. Mr. Humber was the first wholesale dealer for Standard Oil Company in Fayette. Children: (All born Fayette, Ala.) 1. Elizabeth Humber, b. June 13, 1910, d. Mar. 24, 1956, Fayette, Ala., m. E. Clenton Jackson. 2. Sadie Humber, b. Oct. 23, 1911, m. Thomas Joseph Goodwin, b. Aug. 23, 1912, Fayette, Ala. 3. William Hammond "Bill" Humber, Jr., b. June 2, 1916, m. Thelma Anstead. 4. Doris Ann Humber, b. June 29, 1921, m. Lloyd H. Little.

HUNT, John, b. N. C., d. Autauga Co., Ala., Jane ___. John Hunt came to Autauga Co., Ala. from North Carolina about 1825. Children: 1. Richard Hunt. 2. Bennett Hunt. 3. Jesse Hunt. 4. Narcissus Hunt. 5. William Hunt, b. 1820, d. 1864, Autauga, Co., Ala. m. 1839, Elizabeth Gray, b. 1820, d. 1905, Autauga, Co., Ala.

HUNT, William, b. 1820, d. 1864, Autauga, Co., Ala. - son of John & Jane Hunt -- m. 1839, Elizabeth Gray, b. 1820, d. 1905. William Hunt died in the service of the Confederate States Army at Selma, Ala., while guarding the arsenal. Children: 1. Martha Ann Hunt, b. 1840, d. 1920, m. James A. Butler, b. 1828, d. 1909. 2. John Henry Hunt, b. 1841, d. 1862 -- died in Battle of Seven Pines, Va. 3. Lucinda Jane Hunt, b. 1843, d. 1874, m. Richard McDonaldson. 4. Wm. Thomas Hunt, b. 1845, d. 1862. 5. Mary Virginia Hunt, b. 1846, d. 1917. 6. Francis Marion Hunt, b. 1849, d. 1888. 7. Jesse Hayes Hunt, b. 1851, d. 1912, m. Lula Wells. 8. A. Harvel Hunt, b. 1854, d. 1919, m. Sarah Elizabeth DeRamus, b. 1861, d. 1936. 9. Nathaniel Bennett Hunt, b. 1856, d. 1940. 10. Clarinda Elizabeth Hunt, b. 1859, d. 1927, m. Thomas M. Byrd.

HURST, Dunlap, b. Sept. 14, 1905 - son of James Taylor Hurst - m. Dec. 25, Lake Village, Ark., Virginia Catherine McClung, b. Jan. 3, 1908 - dau. of Wm. Anderson McClung. Children: 1. Dunlap Hurst, Jr., b. Jan. 7, 1938. 2. James Taylor Hurst, b. April 22, 1942. (Son by adoption - Mother Virginia McClung's first marriage to Reynolds. William Reynolds Hurst, b. April 22, 1928, m. Laura Louise (Due) Reynolds. b. Apr. 13, 1932.

HURST, Holmes Peyton, b. Nov. 9, 1911, Morton, Miss - son of James Taylor Hurst - m. May 11, 1942 - Mary Jane Chadderdon, b. Sept. 16, 1914, Mannington, Va. - dau. of L. W. Chadderdon. They were married at San Francisco, Calif. He is presently an Executive on the Social Security Board. Holmes Peyton Hurst entered the service of the U. S. Army (Coast Artillery Corps.) as a reserve officer on Oct. 20, 1941 at Ft. McClellan, Ala. Most of his service was with the Western Defense Command at Presidis of San Francisco, Calif. He was assigned to the Intelligence Section from which he was released at the close of the war with the rank of Lt. Col.

HURST, James Taylor, b. June 13, 1880, Morton, Scott Co., Miss. - son of Philip Asberry Hurst - m. Oct. 26, 1904, Willie Emmie Holmes, b. Mar. 5, 1885, Pulaski, Tenn., d. Aug. 8, 1935, Morton, Miss. - dau. of Sim D. Holmes. They were married at Pulaski, Tenn. by Rev. Moss. J. T. Hurst is a farmer, merchant and has been a postmaster. Children:1. Dunlap Husrt, b. Sept. 14, 1905, Morton, Miss. m. Virginia Catherine McClung, b. Jan. 3, 1908. 2. Holmes Peyton Hurst, b. Nov. 9, 1911, Morton, Miss. m. May 11, 1942, Mary Jane Chadderdon, b. Sept. 16, 1914, Mannington, Va. 3. Robert Taylor Hurst, b. May 15, 1915, Morton, Miss.

James Taylor Hurst second marriage - Feb. 17, 1940, Lillian Beatrice (Willingham) Hay, b. Nov. 11, 1901, Bankston, Ala. - dau. of James Hugh Willingham.

HUTSON, Donald Roy, b. Jan. 31, 1913, Pine Bluff, Ark., m. Dec. 16, 1935, Julia Kathleen "Temp" Richards, b. Oct. 14, 1915, Fayette, Ala. - dau. of J. A., Jr., & Frances (Young) Richards. Mr. & Mrs. Hutson were married in Fayette, Ala. Their present residence is Green Bay, Wisconsin. Children: 1. Julia Clarke Hutson, b. Oct. 3, 1938, Fayette, Ala., m. June 1959, George

Barnes Secor, b. Toledo, Ohio. 2. Martha Young Hutson, b. Feb. 15, 1943, Green Bay, Wisconsin. 3. Jane Roberts Hutson, b. May 15, 1944, Green Bay, Wisconsin.

HUTTO, Ben McClure, b. June 5, 1903, Covin, Ala. - son of Walker & Tiercie Hutto - m. April 4, 1931, Voncile Cargile, b. Feb. 2, 1906, Lamar Co., Ala. dau. of Wiley & Cora Cargile. They were married at Mt. Vernon. Ben is a conductor for the Frisco Railway. Children: 1. Lou Ann Hutto, b. Sept. 16, 1933, Mt. Vernon, Fayette Co., Ala. 2. Joe Osborn Hutto, b. Mar. 15, 1935, Mt. Vernon, d. Sept. 10, 1947, Fayette Co., Ala. 3. Bennie Melissa Hutto, b. June 21, 1941, Mt. Vernon, Fayette Co., Ala.

HUTTO, Walter B., b. April 30, 1879, Oakman, Ala., d. Sept. 7, 1935, Fayette, Ala. - son of W. T. & Millie Hutto - m. Sept. 2, 1899, Lula Tierce Appling, b. Jan. 1, 1880, Mt. Vernon, Ala., d. Feb. 10, 1952, Fayette, Ala. - dau. of Jesse & Melissa Appling. Children: 1. Ben McClure Hutto, b. June 5, 1903, Covin, Ala., m. April 4, 1931, Voncile Cargile, b. Feb. 2, 1906, Lamar Co., Ala. 2. William Thomas Hutto, b. Dec. 22, 1916, Fayette, Ala., m. July 3, 1940, Sara Lou Renfroe, b. April 23, 1917, Mt. Vernon, Fayette Co., Ala.

HUTTO, William Thomas, b. Dec. 22, 1916, Fayette, Ala. - son of Walter B. Hutto - m. July 3, 1940, Sara Lou Renfroe, b. April 23, 1917, Mt. Vernon, Ala. They were married at home by Rev. C. C. Turner. He is a salesman. Children: 1. Tommy Hutto, b. Dec. 5, 1942, Birmingham, Ala.

HYDE, Charles Morris, b. Mar. 25, 1910, Covin, Ala. - son of Fletcher D. & Abbie V. (Bobo) Hyde, - m. Sept. 15, 1940, Mae Jewell Hocutt, b. July 6, 1914, Berry, Ala. - dau. of J. Grover & Lovie Lee (Christian) Hocutt. Children: 1. Morris Ann Hyde, b. Sept. 14, 1941, Fayette, Ala. 2. Charles Fletcher Hyde, b. July 28, 1944, Fayette, Ala.

HYDE, Charlie Banks, b. April 8, 1871, d. May 21, 1919, Fayette, Ala. - son of James H. & Sarah Frances (Willingham) Hyde - m. Daisye Pearl (Propst) Shelton, b. Sept. 22, 1877, Millport, Ala. - dau. of Wesley & Caroline (Garrison) Propst. Children: 1. Charlie Banks Hyde, Jr., b. Mar. 3, 1906, Fayette Co., Ala., d. Mar. 30, 1907, Fayette, Ala. 2. Edd Howell Hyde, b. Fayette, Ala., m. Mary _. 3. Marie Hyde, b. Fayette Co., Ala., m. Ab. Chapman.

HYDE, Fletcher Dyer, b. July 18, 1880, Fayette, Ala. d. Aug. 22, 1929, Fayette Ala. - son of James H. & Francis (Willingham) Hyde - m. Abbie Virginia Bobo, b. Nov. 16, 1882, Covin, Ala., d. Mar. 13, 1952, Fayette, Ala. - dau. of Wm. S. & Elizabeth (Sudduth) Bobo. Children: 1. Charles Morris Hyde, b. Mar. 25, 1910, Covin, Ala., m. Sept. 15, 1940, May Jewell Hocutt. 2. Della Willene Hyde, b. Sept. 20, 1911, Covin, Ala., m. Aug. 3, 1957, E. C. Jackson, b. Aug. 30, 1910 - son of Edmond Clinton & Brockie (Smith) Jackson. 3. Virginia Elizabeth Hude, b. June 9, 1916, Fayette, Ala., m. May 22, 1938, Frank Moore, b. Nov. 26, 1914, - son of Doan C. & Bertha (Allen) Moore.

HYDE, Edd Howell, b. Fayette Co., Ala. - son of Charlie B. & Daisye Pearl (Propst) Hyde - m. Marjorie _. Children: 1. John Banks Hyde. 2. Edd Howell Hyde, Jr.

HYDE, James H., b. Feb. 24, 1843, d. Jan. 10, 1923, Fayette, Ala. - son of

Cleveland Hyde - m. Sarah Frances Willingham, b. Jan. 2, 1848, d. Dec. 6, 1932, Fayette, Ala. - dau. of Thomas Lyon & Susan Ann (Strong) Willingham. Children: 1. Mary Della Hyde, b. Dec. 13, 1868, Fayette Co., Ala., d. May 20, 1891, m. Albin F. Seymour. 2. Susie Emily Hyde, b. Dec. 17, 1874, d. May 2, 1926, m. Daniel Freeman Propst, b. Mar. 2, 1859, d. June 4, 1926, Fayette, Ala. 3. Charles Banks Hyde, b. April 8, 1871, d. May 21, 1919, m. Daisye Pearl (Propst) Shelton, b. Sept. 22, 1877, Millport, Ala. 4. Fletcher Dyer Hyde, b. July 18, 1880, Fayette Co., Ala. d. Aug. 22, 1929, m. Abbie Virginia Bobo, b. Nov. 16, 1882, Covin, Ala., d. Mar. 13, 1952, Fayette, Ala. 5. Victor Hyde, b. Feb. 22, 1883, d. Oct. 29, 1921, m. Lena Fronia Swinwood, b. Jan. 2, 1886, d. July 19, 1956, Fayette, Ala. 6. Johnnie E. Hyde, b. June 5, 1867, d. Oct. 23, 1868. (All Children born in Fayette Co., Ala.)

HYDE, John Thomas, b. Oct. 28, 1846, d. May 6, 1936 - son of Cleveland Hyde - m. Susan Temperance Willingham, b. Mar. 20, 1853, d. Nov. 25, 1883 - dau. of Thomas Lyon Willingham. He was a farmer. Both are buried at the Cleveland Church Cemetery, in Fayette Co. Children: 1. Nina Hyde, b. Feb. 19, 1879, Bankston, Ala., m. Martin D. South, b. Dec. 12, 1878, Fayette Co., Ala., d. Mar. 7, 1957, Fayette, Ala. 2. Tom H. Hyde, b. Nov. 12, 1883, Bankston, Ala. d. Jan. 31, 1936, Fayette Co., Ala., m. Lottie (__) Ketchell.

JACKSON, Claud, m. Nora Deavours, - dau. of John & Martha (Berry) Deavours. Children: 1. Wilma Jackson. 2. Fred Jackson. 3. Richard Jackson. 4. Willie Jackson. 5. Mae Jackson. 6. Paul Jackson. 7. Lucy Belle Jackson. 8. Roy Jackson. 9. Jessie Jackson. 10. Lester Clay Jackson.

JEFFRIES, Benjamin Franklin, b. Dec. 5, 1879, Berry, Fayette Co., Ala. - d. Mar. 21, 1946, Fayette, Ala. - son of Pleasant Jackson Jeffries - m. June 28, 1899, Sarah Annie Gibson, b. May 15, 1876, Corona, Walker Co., Ala., d. Mar. 14, 1955, Fayette, Ala. - dau. of James Daniel Gibson. They were married at Corona, Ala., B. F. Jeffries was a lumberman. Children: 1. James Fenton Jeffries, b. April 6, 1900, Corona, Walker Co., Ala., m. July 8, 1942, Mabel Claire Daniel, b. Sept. 26, 1898, Troy, Ala. 2. Edmond Francis Jeffries, b. April 15, 1902, Corona, Walker Co., Ala., d. July 31, 1956, Fayette, Ala., m. Oct. 24, 1924, Kathleen Goodwin, b. Feb. 25, 1905, Fayette, Ala., d. April 8, 1957, Fayette, Ala. 3. Kenneth Jackson Jeffries, b. Dec. 5, 1904, d. Dec. 5, 1956, Fayette, Ala., m. April 1935, Lorena Jones, b. Feb. 28, 1919 Covington, Ky. (K. J. born Corona.) 4. William Gaines Jeffries, b. Feb. 28, 1909, Fayette, Ala., d. April 24, 1927, Fayette, Ala.

JEFFRIES, Edmond Francis, b. April 15, 1902, Corona, Walker Co., Ala., d. July 31, 1956, Fayette, Ala. - son of Benjamin F. Jeffries, m. Oct. 24, 1924, Kathleen Goodwin, b. Feb. 25, 1905, Fayette, Ala., d. April 8, 1957, Fayette, Ala. - dau. of Ed. P. Goodwin. Children: 1. Edmond Gaines Jeffries, b. Feb. 4, 1930, Fayette, Ala.

JEFFRIES, Francis Marion, b. Mar. 25, 1876, Fayette Co., Ala., d. June 18, 1939, Fayette, Ala. - son of Pleasant Jackson & Paletine (Berry) Jeffries - m. Dec. 23, 1896, Mary Idelia Morton, b. Mar. 9, 1877, Fayette, Ala., d. Dec. 18, 1941, Fayette, Ala. - dau. of Thomas Benton & Eudocia Jane (McCaleb) Morton. They were married at Fayette, Ala. and F. M. Jeffries was a drayman. Children: 1. Rubye Jeffries, b. Oct. 19, 1897, Fayette, Ala., m. Louis Cannon, B. Mar. 1, 1898, Fayette, Ala., d. Oct. 25, 1953, Fayette, Ala. 2. Mildred Jeffries, b. Dec. 29, 1899, Fayette, Ala., m. Douglas Daniel, b. Dec. 25, 1898, Kentucky, d. buried in Kentucky. 3. Thomas Malcolm Jeffries, b. Feb. 1, 1902, Fayette, Ala. 4. Frank Hubert Jeffries, b. Feb. 14, 1905, Fayette, Ala., m. Emma Jean Cameron, b. Oct. 23, 1914, Etta, Ark. 5. Ned Morton Jeffries, b. June 7, 1908, Fayette, Ala., m. Rubye L. Aston, b. Dec. 21, 1909, Winfield, Ala. 6. Kenneth Benton Jeffries, b. Aug. 3, 1911, Fay. Ala., m. Dorothy Chilson, b. Jan. 9, 1917, Birmingham, Ala. 7. William Berry "Bill" Jeffries, b. Jan. 19, 1917, Fayette, Ala., m. Doris Thomas, b. July 21, 1926, Jasper, Ala.

JEFFRIES, Frank Hubert, b. Feb. 14, 1905, Fayette, Ala. - son of Francis M. & Mary Idelia (Morton) Jeffries - m. Mar. 16, 1941, Emma Jean Cameron, b. Oct. 23, 1914, Etta, Ark. - dau of Lonnie Gold & Nancy Bell (Hall) Cameron. Children: 1. Mary Cameron Jeffries, b. July 4, 1943, Fayette, Ala.

JEFFRIES, James Fenton, b. April 6, 1900, Corona, Walker Co., Ala. - son of Benajmin F. Jeffries - m. July 18, 1942, Mabel Claire Daniel, b. Sept. 26, 1898, Troy, Ala. - dau. of Joseph Randolph Daniel. They were married at Fayette, Ala. by Dr. W. F. Price. She teaches piano in the local schools and he is a Postal Employee. No children.

JEFFRIES, Kenneth Benton, b. Aug. 3, 1911, Fayette, Ala. - son of Francis Marion & Mary Idelia (Morton) Jeffries - m. Oct. 10, 1936, Fayette, Ala., Dorothy Chilson, b. Jan. 9, 1917, Birmingham, Ala. - dau. of Raymond Gaine & Clara Mae (Wright) Chilson. Children: 1. Jerry Sue Jeffries, b. Jan. 31, 1938, Fayette, Ala., m. James Albert Lindsey, b. June 13, 1934, Fayette, Ala. 2. Francis Benton Jeffries, b. Nov. 10, 1942, Fayette, Ala.

JEFFRIES, Kenneth Jackson, b. Dec. 5, 1904, Corona, Walker Co., Ala., d. Dec. 5, 1956, Fayette, Ala. - son of Benjamin F. Jeffries - m. April 1, 1935, Lorena Jones, b. Feb. 28, 1919, Covington, Ky. - dau. of Pete Jones. Children: 1. Alice Ann Jeffries, b. Jan. 17, 1938, Fayette, Ala., m. June 15, 1956, Noel Barnes, b. Fayette Co., Ala.

JEFFRIES, Ned Morton, b. June 7, 1908, Fayette, Ala. - son of Francis M. & Mary Idelia (Morton) Jeffries - m. June 22, 1935, Ruby Lee Aston, b. Dec. 21, 1909, Winfield, Ala. - dau. of Henry Walter & Dora Wilmerth (McDonald) Aston. They were married by Rev. C. L. Ellis at Winfield, Ala. Children: 1. Sandra Lee Jeffries, b. May 17, 1941, Fayette, Ala.

JEFFRIES, Pleasant Jackson, b. Aug. 12, 1847, Ga., d. Feb. 25, 1930, m. Palestine Berry, b. April 15, 1841, Fayette Co., Ala., d. Sept. 3, 1917. Pleasant Jackson Jeffries was a farmer. Both are buried in the Pleasant Hill Cemetery, west of Berry, Ala. Children: 1. Alabama Della Jeffries, b. Sept. 4, 1869, d. Sept. 1, 1953, m. William Enis, d. April 26, 1936. Both are buried in Fayette Cemetery. 2. Benjamin Fenton Jeffries, b. Dec. 5, 1879, Berry, Ala., d. Mar. 21, 1946, Fayette, Ala. m. June 28, 1899, Annie Gibson, b. May 15, 1876, Corona, Ala. d. Mar. 14, 1955, Fayette, Ala. 3. Francis Marion Jeffries, b. Mar. 25, 1876, d. June 18, 1939, m. Mary Idelia Morton, b. Mar. 9, 1877, d. Dec. 18, 1941. Both are buried in Fayette Cemetery.

JEFFRIES, William Berry "Bill", b. Jan. 19, 1917, Fayette, Ala. - son of Francis Marion & Mary Idelia (Morton) Jeffries - m. Sept. 28, 1946, Doris

Glynn Thomas, b. July 21, 1926, Jasper, Walker Co., Ala. - dau. of Albert Crutcher & Merle Aline (McLemore) Thomas. "Bill" Jeffries served in the U. S. Air Force from Dec. 6, 1942 to Nov. 19, 1945. They were married in Fayette Ala. by Rev. A. M. Nix. Bill is service mamager at the Fayette Motor Co. in Fayette. Children: 1. William Ned Jeffries, b. Nov. 23, 1955, Fayette, Ala.

JEFFRIES, William Buford, b. Dec. 7, 1815, Ga., d. Oct. 17, 1886, m. Mar. 3, 1836, Adaline Freeman, b. Feb. 22, 1816, Ga., d. June 28, 1899. Wm. B. Jeffries was a farmer. Both are buried at the Pleasant Hill Cemetery west of Berry, Ala. Children: 1. Josiah Pierce Jeffries, b. Sept. 28, 1837, Ga., d. Apr. 2, 1868, m. Eliza Berry, b. 1832, Fayette Co., Ala. - dau. of Thompson Berry. 2. Jessee Jeffries, b. May 19, 1839, d. Killed in Civil War. 3. William Jeffries, b. Feb. 17, 1841. 4. Thomas Lee Jeffries, b. Dec. 22, 1842, d. Sept. 28, 1886, m. Victoria York. 5. Jeremiah Jeffries, b. July 6, 1845, d. Killed in Civil War at Missionary Ridge, Tenn. 6. Pleasant Jackson Jeffries, b. Aug. 12, 1847, d. Feb. 25, 1930, m. Paletine Berry, b. April 15, 1841, d. Sept. 3; 1917, - dau. of Thompson Berry. Both are buried at Pleasant Hill Cem. 7. Catherine Elizabeth Jeffries, b. Nov. 12, 1849, d. Nov. 24, 1861. 8. Malissa Jane Jeffries, b. Nov. 6, 1851, d. Oct. 6, 1921, m. Henry B. Berry b. Dec. 6, 1829, d. Apr. 22, 1895, - son of Thompson Berry. Both are buried at Pleasant Hill Cem. 9. Amarintha Sultana Jeffries, b. Mar. 6, 1854, d. Mar. 9, 1863.

JOHNSON, Starling, m. 1st. - Catherine Crowe, 2nd. - Miss Wilson. Children: (1st. marriage.) 1. Jim Johnson, m. Ann Wright. 2. John Johnson, died in Army. 3. Seville Johnson, m. Bloomer Griffin. 4. Mary Catherine Johnson, b. Oct. 15, 1849, Fayette Co., Ala., d. Jan. 2, 1929, m. William Banister Owens, b. June 10, 1845, Fayette Co., Ala., d. Jan. 19, 1923. Children: (2nd. marriage.) 1. Julus Johnson. 2. Bascom Johnson.

JOHNSON, W. Albert "Bert", b. May 31, 1907, Fayette Co., Ala., m. Mary Lee McCool. W. A. Johnson is a Missionary Baptist Minister. Children: 1. Avis Johnson, m. Douglas Yielding. (Child: Sharon Yielding.) 2. Mavis Johnson, m. Bob Black, (Children: Scott and Dana Black.)

JOINER, David, died 1884, Tupelo, Miss., m. Rachael __, died 1888, Tupelo, Miss. Children: 1. Louise Walker Joiner, b. Feb. 2, 1853, d. Mar. 4, 1931, Fayette Co., Ala., m. 1874, William Franklin Nichols, b. Oct. 27, 1852, d. Mar. 4, 1912, Fayette, Ala.

JONES, Benjamin Elliott, b. Aug. 31, 1860, d. Oct. 20, 1939, Berry, Ala. (b. near Berry, Ala.) m. Dec. 24, 1883, Mollie Ann Thompson, b. July 8, 1860, d. July 31, 1932, Berry, Ala. Children: 1. Mary Narcissa Jones, b. Dec. 20, 1884, Berry, Ala., m. Nov. 28, 1911, Theron Cannon, b. Mar. 2, 1883, Fayette, Ala. 2. Thomas Robert Jones, b. Dec. 20, 1884, Berry, Ala., d. Sept. 18, 1929, New Orleans, La., m. Sept. 16, 1913, Gertrude Conaway. (Had two sons: Olen Thomas and John Elliott Jones.) 3. Evamae Jones. 4. Lena Jones, m. Nov. 28, 1911, J. F. Webb. 5. Lela Jones, m. Preston Cranford. 6. John Frank Jones, b. Mar. 9, 1891, Berry, Ala., m. Mar. 7, 1927, Dovie Jones. (Had a dau. Jo Ann Jones.) 7. Olen Fletcher Jones, b. Nov. 30, 1894, Berry, Ala., d. Aug. 2, 1914. 8. Alice Virginia Jones.

JONES, Benjamin Giles, b. Nov. 23, 1858, d. 1938, m. Jan. 29, 1880, Minerva

Whitney. Moved to Texas about 1918. Children: 1. Dr. Oscar O. Jones, (An X-Ray Specialist in Shreveport, La.) 2. Wyman Jones, d. Marion Texas. 3. Roxey Jones, died young at Fayette, Ala. 4. Florence Jones, d. 1954, San Benito, Texas. 5. Hillard Hillman Jones. 6. Mary Lee Jones.

JONES, Charlie, b. Aug. 14, 1883, Fayette Co., Ala. - son of Eliga S. & Flora (White) Jones - m. Dora _, b. Feb. 11, 1884, d. Apr. 20, 1953. Children: 1. Tranie Jones, b. July 8, 1904, Fayette Co., Ala., m. Rod Beasley.

JONES, Elbert L. - son of H. Russell Jones - m. Frances Lawrence. Children: 1. Marion Jones, m. Mary McCulough. 2. Ola Jones, m. Jake Stough. 3. Ashur Jones.

JONES. Eliga Samuel, b. June 17, 1846, Fayette Co., Ala., d. Aug. 11, 1927, - son of Jesse & Elizabeth (Dodson) Jones - m. Oct. 18, 1867, Flora White, b. Mar. 4, 1850, Ga., d. May 22, 1923 - dau. of T. F. & Martha C. (Sanders) White. Flora came to Fayette Co., Ala. with her parents about 1857 from near Rome, Ga. Children: 1. Eckford Jones, b. Jan. 6, 1873, Fayette Co., Ala., d. May 22, 1903. 2. Adron Jones, b. Aug. 22, 1877, Fayette Co., Ala. d. Aug. 16, 1891. 3. John Jones, b. Dec. 26, 1879, Fayette Co., Ala., d. Nov. 30, 1947. 4. Charlie Jones, b. Aug. 14, 1883, Fayette Co., Ala., m. Dora __. 5. Lucy Jones, b. Oct. 12, 1887, Fayette Co., Ala., d. Jan. 29, 1936.

JONES, Elliott Priest, b. Oct. 21, 1819, Moulton, Lawrence Co., Ala., d. Apr. 18, 1880 - son of Benjamin & Viney (Wallace) Jones, - m. Lucinda J. Page, b. Feb. 9, 1828, d. July 26, 1921 - dau. of Mrs. Jane (Brooks) Page, native of Virginia. E. P. Jones received a common school education in his native county and began his career by teaching school. He read law in the office of Ligon and Walker, Moulton, and began the practice at Fayette in 1844. He was judge of the county court, 1848 - 1850; member of State Senate, 1850 - 1850; member of the constitutional conventions of 1861 and 1865 and during the latter decade, 1853 - 1855 - 1857, was again elected to the senate and served three times. He voted against the adoption of the Secession ordinance and refused to sign it. Upon the creation of a new county, made up of territory he represented, the Legislature gave it the name of Jones in his honor. Later the name was changed to Sanford and finally to Lamar. E. P. Jones was a Methodist; Mason and Odd Fellow. His father, Benjamin Jones was a captain in the Mexican War and was a native of Kentucky. His ancestry was of Irish origin. Children: 1. John W. Jones, (All children born Fayette Co., Ala.) a Confederate Soldier. 2. James B. Jones, b. 1850, d. 1921, m. 1868, Martha Annie Byars, b. 1851, Tusca. Co., Ala., d. 1933. 3. Lucious E. Jones, m. Viola Wimberley. 4. Mattie O. Jones. 5. R. S. Jones. 6. Mary Alice Jones, b. Feb. 4, 1858, d. Nov. 3, 1861. 7. Sylvester F. Jones. 8. Frances I. Jones, m. G. F. Brown of Columbus, Miss. 9. C. S. Jones, m. Angelo Fern, Steens, Miss.

JONES, Fred, b. Mar. 20, 1884, Fayette, Ala., d. April 22, 1952, - son of James B. & Martha Annie (Byars) Jones - m. Nov. 15, 1922, Lona Frances Jones, b. Nov. 19, 1906, Lamar Co., Ala. - dau. of W. J. & Mary Jane (Maddox) Jones. They were married at Vernon, Ala. by Rev. J. I. Williams. Fred Jones was a professional photographer. Children: 1. Fred Curtis Jones, b. Feb. 19, 1925, Fayette, Ala., 2. Mary Ann Jones, b. Sept. 11, 1929, Fayette, Ala., m. 1950, Robert Crump.

JONES, Giles G., b. 1799, Walker Co., Ala., d. Jasper, Ala. - son of Wallace & Susan (Beauert) Jones - m. Mary Ann Brooks, b. 1809, Marshall Co., Ala., d. June 1880, Newtonville, Ala. Dr. Giles G. Jones, was born in Walker Co., in 1799, twenty years before Alabama was admitted to the Union. Reared in a wild and unsettled country, he somehow managed to secure a very good educatin and became a physician and surgeon. He practiced his profession in Jasper and that vicinity, all of his life. He was one of the organizers of York Lodge No. 211 of the Masonic Fraternity in 1854, and served as its first Worshipful Master. Dr. Jones died in Jasper. Children: 1. William W. Jones. 2. Tobias Jones. 3. Warren Jones. 4. Henry Jones. 5. Ras Jones. 6. Marion Jones. 7. Minerva Jones, m. Mr. Compton or Lollar. 8. Elizabeth Jones, m. Mr. Lollar or Compton. 9. Susan Jones, m. Jessie Cantrell.

JONES, Howard Roberts "Bob", b. Aug. 13, 1924, Tuskegee, Ala. - son of Wm. Leech Jones, Sr. - m. Dec. 31, 1948, Mary Jane Vance, b. Feb. 4, 1930, Birmingham, Ala. - dau. of N. R. Vance. They were married at Birmingham, Ala. by the Rev. Walter J. Tobin. Bob is a pharmacist at the Central Drug Store. Children: 1. Robert Alan Jones, b. April 26, 1950, Birmingham, Ala. 2. Nickie Vance Jones, b. Jan. 2, 1953, Fayette, Ala. 3. Nina Dulion Jones, b. June 22, 1955, Fayette, Ala. 4. Michael Anthony Jones, b. Aug. 11, 1957, Fayette, Alabama.

JONES, H. Russell, d. Oct. 1872, m. Mary Virginia Yerby, dau. of Amon & Rachael Yerby. Children: 1. W. F. "Billie" Jones, m. Essie Jones. 2. Drucilla Jones, m. 1885, J. David Musgrove. 3. Columbus (C.C.) Jones, lived and died in Oklahoma. 4. Elbert L. Jones, m. Frances Lawrence. 5. Mary Virginia Jones, m. S. L. White.

JONES, Jack B., b. May 9, 1919, Birmingham, Ala. - son of Wm. & Eva Jones - m. Aug. 1946, Carol Swanson, b. Nov. 13, 1921, Mt. Vernon, Fayette Co., Ala.- dau. of Chas. & Maude Swanson. They were married at Birmingham, Ala. by Dr. S. O. Kimborough. Jack is manager of Street Printing Co. Children: 1. James Tillman Jones, b. Sept. 2, 1947, Birmingham, Ala. 2. Jacqueline Jones, b. June 12, 1950, Birmingham, Ala. 3. Charles William Jones, b. Dec. 25, 1952.

JONES, James B., b. 1850, Fayette Co., Ala., d. 1921 - son of Elliott P. & Lucinda J. Jones - m. 1868, Martha Annie Byars, b. 1851, Tusca. Co., Ala., d. 1933. James B. Jones was a merchant and at one time the editor of Fayette County Journal. He was also listed in the American Newspaper Directory in 1887. Children: 1. Lula Jones, (All children born Fayette Co.) m. Felix G. McConnell. 2. Helen Jones, m. Sidney Preston. 3. Lena Jones, b. 1875, d. May 6, 1909, Fayette, Ala., m. June 2, 1891, Robert F. Peters, b. Oct. 11, 1862, Tusca. Co., Ala., d. Jan. 5, 1941, Fayette, Ala. 4. Will Jones, m. Mattie Ruth _. 5. Fred Jones, b. Mar. 20, 1884, d. April 22, 1952, m. Nov. 15, 1922, Lona Frances Jones, b. Nov. 19, 1906, Lamar Co., Ala. 6. Eugene P. Jones, b. July 17, 1893, m. Katherine Snow, b. Nov. 17, 1899, Birmingham, Ala. 7. Vashtie Jones, b. 1878, d. 1896. 8. Eva Jane Jones, b. 1880, d. 1896.

JONES, James William Rily, b. Dec. 23, 1861, Fayette Co., Ala., d. Mar. 31, 1931, Fayette Co., Ala. - son of Wm. R. & Mary Frances (Parker) Jones - m. Dec. 29, 1881, Ella C. Stacks, b. May 3, 1862, Fayette Co., Ala., d. Aug. 22, 1901, Fayette Co., Ala. - dau. of Samuel Hudson & Susan (Hand) Stacks. Children: 1. Thomas M. Jones. 2. William L. Jones. 3. Samuel Erastus Jones, b.

Sept. 27, 1886, Fayette Co., Ala., m. May 11, 1910, Maude McConnell, b. Oct. 22, 1887, Fayette Co., Ala. 4. Arthur Judson Jones. 5. Charlie Maxwell Jones. 6. James Victor Jones. 7. Lucina Jones, b. Nov. 5, 1889, Fayette Co. Ala., m. Wiley W. Farquhar, b. Nov. 4, 1888, Fayette Co., Ala., d. Sept. 8, 1955, Fayette, Ala. 8. Susan Emma Jones, b. Aug. 14, 1891, Fayette Co., Ala. m. Feb. 2, 1911, Homer Campbell, b. Oct. 23, 1889, Fayette Co., Ala. 9. Mary Etta Jones.

JONES, Jesse, b. Aug. 9, 1809, d. 1875 - son of John & Sarah (Dodson) Jones - m. July 25, 1833, Elizabeth Dodson, b. Oct. 20, 1813, d. 1889, - dau. of Wm. Dodson, d. Mar. 23, 1870. Children: 1. Eliga Samuel Jones, b. June 17, 1846, d. Aug. 11, 1927, m. Oct. 18, 1867, Flora White, b. Mar. 4, 1850, d. May 22, 1923.

JONES, John, m. Sallie Hughes. Her mother's maiden name was Ann Truman and she came from Wales. John Jones owned farm on James River called Jones Landing. Children: 1. Mary Ann Jones, m. 1st. - Mr. James, 2nd. - Wm. "Major Billy" Foster, b. 1753, Amelia Co., Va., d. Mar. 9, 1818. 2. Harrison Jones. 3. Reuben Jones. 4. John Jones. 5. Elijah Jones. 6. Annie Jones. 7. Sallie Jones. 8. Lucy Jones.

JONES, John, d. May 4, 1841, m. Sarah Dodson, d. Feb. 4, 1839. Children: 1. Jesse Jones, b. Aug. 9, 1809, d. 1875, m. July 25, 1833, Elizabeth Dodson, b. Oct. 20, 1813, d. 1889.

JONES, Marvin, m. Vera Cannon - dau. of M. F. Cannon. Children: 1. Marvin Cannon Jones, m. Helen Brown. (Children: Cannon and Melissa Jones.)

JONES, Samuel Erastus, b. Sept. 27, 1886 -son of James Wm. Rily & Ella (Stacks) Jones - m. May 11, 1910, Maude McConnell, b. Oct. 22, 1887, Fayette Co., Ala. - dau. of Daniel O. & Alice (Smith) McConnell. Children: 1. Edith Jones, b. 1910, Fayette Co., Ala., m. Carl Smith. 2. Grace Jones, b. 1916, Fayette Co. Ala., m. Joe Roberts. 3. Samuel McConnell, b. Dec. 17, 1918, Fayette Co., Ala., m. Mar. 12, 1939, Doris Eloise Maxwell, b. Aug. 26, 1918, Walker Co., Ala. 4. Murray Jones, b. Sept. 8, 1921, Fayette Co., Ala. d. July 3, 1923.

JONES, Sameul McConnell, b. Dec. 17, 1918, Fayette Co., Ala. - son of S.E. & Maude (McConnell) Jones - m. Mar. 12, 1939, Doris Eloise Maxwell, b. Aug. 26, 1918, Walker Co., Ala. - dau. of Oscar Lee & Ethel (Beckham) Maxwell. Children: 1. Patricia Ann Jones, b. Oct. 14, 1941, Fayette, Ala. 2. Shirley Lea Jones, b. April 27, 1956, Fayette, Ala.

JONES, Wallace, b. abt. 1775, England, d. 1856, Walker Co., Ala., m. Susan Beauert, b. abt. 1780, England, d. 1870, Walker Co., Ala. Wallace Jones, according to family tradition settled along the Warrior River in Walker Co., Ala. prior to 1800. He was born in England where he learned the trade of millwright and copper. He was a suitor for the hand of Susan Beavert and upon meeting parental objections, the couple eloped from an English Tavern at night and boarded a ship for America. They made their home in North Carolina for a short time before coming to Walker Co., Ala., where he died in 1856. After settling in Walker Co., Susan (Beauert) Jones made two trips, alone and on horseback, to North Carolina to secure her bounty from the government. At that time the country through which she passed was Indian Territory, but they aided her on her way. She died in Walker Co., at the age of ninety. Children: 1. Giles G. Jones, b. 1799, Walker Co., Ala. d. 1859, Jasper, Ala. m. Mary Ann Brooks, b. 1809, Marshall Co., Ala., d. June 1880, Fayette Co., Ala. 2. William Wallace Jone. 3. James Ausborn Jones. 4. Minerva Jones, m. 1st. - Mr. Whitley, 2nd. - Thomas Reed.

JONES, W. F. "Billie" - son of H. Russell Jones, m. Essie Jones - dau. of Wm. & Mary Jones. Children: 1. Joseph Jones, Knoxville, Tenn. 2. Virgil Jones. 3. May Jones, Wetumpka, Ala. 4. Russell Jones. 5. Alice Jones, Walker Co. 6. Burris Jones, Marion Co. 7. Worth Jones, Birmingham, Ala. 8. Vella Jones, drowned in youth in Texas. 9. Dalton Jones, Winfield, Ala. 10. Leila Jones, Franklin, Tenn.

JONES, William, b. Aug. 5, 1773, m. Bashabe Coffee, b. Aug. 21, 1800. Children: (Fifteen in all) 1. Malinda Jones, b. Jan. 20, 1818, d. June 1854, m. June 2, 1839, Beverly V. Shirley, b. Feb. 14, 1820, d. 1877.

JONES, William J., b. Oct. 17, 1868, Lamar Co., Ala., m. Mary Jane Maddox, b. Jan. 25, 1873, Lamar Co., Ala., d. Mar. 7, 1957. Children: 1. Lona Frances Jones, b. Nov. 19, 1906, Lamar Co., Ala., m. Nov. 15, 1922, Fred Jones, b. Mar. 20, 1884.

JONES, William Leech, Jr., b. Feb. 14, 1923, Camden, Ala. - son of Wm. Leech Jones, Sr. - m. May 18, 1948, Evelyn Lenora Reed, b. May, Birmingham, Ala. - dau. of A. Otto Reed. They were married in Birmingham, Ala. by Dr. Herman Cobb. He is affiliated with T.C.I. in Birmingham, Ala. Children: 1. Barbara Jane Jones, b. Feb. 27, 1950, Birmingham, Ala. 2. Howard Leech Jones, b. Nov. 28, 1953, Birmingham, Ala. 3. Murray Paul Jones, b. Sept. 28, 1957, Birmingham, Ala.

JONES, William Leech, b. Dec. 15, 1891. Fayette Co., Ala., d. May 25, 1929, - son of James John Jones - m. Oct. 17, 1915, Maude Lenora "Daisy" South, b. April 4, 1892, Davis Creek, Fayette Co., Ala. - dau. of Levi Woodruff South. Children: 1. William Leech Jones, Jr., b. Feb. 14, 1923, Camden, Wilcox Co., Ala., m. May 18, 1948, Evelyn Lenora Reed, b. May, Birmingham, Ala. 2. Howard Roberts "Bob" Jones, b. Aug. 13, 1924, Tuskegee, Ala., m. Dec. 31, 1948, Mary Jane Vance, b. Feb. 4, 1930, Birmingham, Ala.

JONES, William R., b. 1838, Tusca. Co., Ala. d. Sept. 20, 1863, died in Battle of Missionary Ridge, Tenn., m. Mary Frances Parker, b. Oct. 16, 1837, Murphysboro, Tenn., d. May 17, 1930, Fayette Co., Ala. Children: 1. James Wm. Rily Jones, b. Dec. 23, 1861, Fayette Co., Ala., d. Mar. 31, 1931, Fayette Co., Ala., m. Dec. 29, 1881, Ella C. Stacks, b. May 3, 1862, Fayette Co., Ala., d. Aug. 22, 1901, Fayette Co., Ala.

JONES, Dr. William Wilburn, b. Aug. 1, 1827, Walker Co., Ala., d. Aug. 2, 1910 - son of Dr. G.G. & M.B. (Brooks) Jones - m. Dec. 28, 1851, Minerva J. Stovall, b. Jan. 1827, Walker Co., Ala., d. Nov. 23, 1862, Jasper, Ala. Dr. William Wilburn Jones was reared in Walker County, Ala. He attended the Old Memphis Medical College at Memphis, Tenn. where he graduated with the degree of Doctor of Medicine. From 1856 to 1866 he practiced medicine in Jasper, Ala. During the period of the Civil War he was stationed at Jasper, Ala. as a Confederate surgeon. The yankees burned his office with all his medical supplies and rode off with his saddle horse that he used in his traveling to practice medicine. He came to Newtonville, Fayette Co., Ala. in 1866 and continued his general practice in medicine as long as he was physically able. He also operated a store and the post office for a number of years. He died at Fayette at the home of his son-in-law, and daughter, Dr. & Mrs. William Graham. Children: 1. Mary Belinda Jones, b. Oct. 31, 1852, Jasper, Ala., d. 1865. 2. Dr. James J. Jones, b. May 1, 1854, d. Dec. 1, 1884, m. June 15, 1884, Margaret Scharnagle. 3. Benjamin Giles Jones, b. Nov. 23, 1858, d. 1938, m. Jan. 29, 1880, Minerva Whitney.

Dr. Wm. Wilburn Jones second marriage - Dec. 27, 1863, Elizabeth Jane (Wommack) Bell, (wife of Dr. Bell, who was killed in Civil War.) Children: (2nd. marriage.) 1. William Warren Jones, b. Nov. 2, 1864, d. Nov. 15, 1880. 2. Iza Ida Jones, b. Oct. 10, 1866, d. Aug. 31, 1887, Newtonville, Ala., m. Oct. 14, 1884, Judge James Ray, b. Jasper, Ala. 3. Charlie Jones, b. June 5, 1869, Newtonville, Ala., d. Sept. 9, 1873, Newtonville. 4. Ann Dora Jones, b. Jan. 7, 1877, Newtonville, Ala., d. Nov. 16, 1952, Winfield, Ala., m. Apr. 15, 1891, Dr. William A. Graham. 5. LaFlora Jones, b. Jan. 7, 1871, Newtonville, Ala., d. Aug. 26, 1873. 6. Dr. Tarley Wilburn Jones, b. April 30, 1875, d. April 16, 1926, Fayette Co., Ala. (Finished Vanderbilt Medical School, April, 1900 and was physician in Fayette, Kennedy and Newtonville.)

JONES, Wyman Wilborn, - son of Benjamin Giles & Minerva (Whitney) Jones, - m. at Newtonville, Ala., Minnie Maude Smith, b. Jan. 6, 1891, Carroll Co., Miss., d. May 1936, Fayette, Ala. - dau. of Joseph Patrick & Hassie Kirk (Mothershead) Smith. Children: 1. Mildred Jones, b. 1911, San Benito, Texas, m. at Harlingen, Texas, Harley Cherry. 2. Katherine Jones, b. Birmingham, Ala., m. W. Wayne Parker. 3. Wymon Wilborn Jones, Jr., b. San Benito, Texas.

JORDAN, Robert Caruthers, b. May 13, 1856, d. Oct. 16, 1894, Halls, Tenn. - m. Fannie Newton, b. May 13, 1858, d. Dec. 3, 1951, Halls, Tenn. Robert C. Jordan was a farmer. Children: 1. Robert Horace Jordan, b. Nov. 6, 1879, (All children born Halls, Tenn.) d. Feb. 28, 1957, Halls, Tenn., m. June 26, 1907, Pearl Trabue, of Alton, Ill. b. Alton, Ill. 2. Guy Newton Jordan, b. July 28, 1881, d. April 4, 1950, Halls, Tenn., m. Dec. 10, 1921, Lucy Rawls, b. Halls, Tenn. 3. Fannie Cecile Jordan, b. Mar. 23, 1883, m. Jan. 23, 1918, Marshall Goodwin Pearce, b. RoEllen, Dyer Co., Tenn, d. April 17, 1957, Halls, Tenn. 4. Cora Bertha Jordan, b. Feb. 2, 1885, m. Dec. 26, 1904, William Ernest Barbour, b. Dec. 8, 1883, Cincinnati, Ohio, d. July 31, 1952, Memphis, Tenn. 5. Mary Irma Jordan, b. Aug. 4, 1887, m. June 24, 1908, Noble Grover Parrish, b. Martin, Tenn. 6. Martha Eula Jordan, b. Mar. 18, 1889, m. June 27, 1911, Hubert Andrew Townsend, b. Rutherford, Tenn. 7. Glynn Irl Jordan, b. Mar. 25, 1893, d. July 17, 1922, Halls, Tenn. 8. Robert Caruthers Jordan, Jr., b. June 2, 1895, d. Feb. 3, 1955, Halls, Tenn., m. Feb. 4, 1918, Nell Lawrence, b. Gates, Tenn.

KAIDYEE, William, of York Co., Va., d. 1718, m. Martha ? (Carson), of York Co., Va. Children: 1. Catherine Kaidyee, b. 1698.

KELLEY, Henry D., b. July 31, 1882, Ga., d. June 5, 1957, m. 1st. - Zula Pate, 2nd. - Retta Corra Johnson, b. Oct. 15, 1882, Fayette Co., Ala. Children: (1st. marriage.) 1. Jasper "Jack" Kelley. 2. Henry Kelley. 3. Pearlie Mae Kelley, m. Albert Wallace. 4. Roberta Kelley, m. Henley Medders. Children: (2nd. marriage.) 1. Wilson Kelley, d. 1931. 2. Arlie Kelley, m. Beatrice Foster. 3. Ruby Lee Kelley, m. Rev. Vernon B. Pate. 4. Lancy R. Kelley, b. Oct. 6, 1920, m. 1st. - 1940, Edwin Moiler, 2nd. - Feb. 19, 1946, O'Neal Plyler, b. Dec. 11, 1918, Fayette Co., Ala. 5. Henry D. Kelley, Jr., m. Gladys Wilson.

KEMP, David Alphonso, b. Sept. 30, 1875, Chilton Co., Ala., d. Feb. 17, 1935, Fayette Co., Ala. - son of George W. & Jane Poole Kemp - m. Dec. 14, 1900, Rebecca Isabell Crowe, b. Feb. 27, 1877, Lamar Co., Ala. - dau. of Josiah & Mary Jane Crowe. They were married at Fayette, Ala. He was a farmer and a millright. Children: 1. Jesse Richard Kemp, b. Jan. 16, 1901, Fayette Co., Ala., m. in Fayette Co. Carrie Elizabeth Farquhar, b. Fayette Co., Ala. 2. Vera Edna Kemp, b. June 6, 1903, Fayette Co., Ala., d. Oct. 8, 1904. 3. Mary Loudell Kemp, b. Mar. 1, 1905, Fayette Co., m. Jan. 27, 1926, J. Bascom Henry, b. Fayette Co. 4. Claudia Belle Kemp, b. Sept. 6, 1908, Fayette, Ala. m. Oct. 27, 1939, Douglas A. Barbour, b. Oct. 19, 1905, Memphis, Tenn.

KERR, Rufus, b. May 3, 1855, Itawamba, Miss, d. Mar. 4, 1935, Marion Co., Ala. m. Oct. 12, 1873, Cynthia Hollaway, b. Oct. 9, 1856, Itawambe, Miss., d. June 8, 1947, Marion Co., Ala. Children: 1. Wm. Bailey Kerr, b. Aug. 10, 1890, Marion Co., Ala., m. Mar. 9, 1912, Viola Satterwhite, b. July 11, 1894, Itawamba, Miss. Viola's parents - Johnny Satterwhite, b. Apr. 21, 1871, Ga. d. Sept. 6, 1949, Itawamba, Miss, m. Ellen Pearce, b. Dec. 15, 1875, Marion Co., Ala. (Married April 9, 1893.) Grandparents - Mat D. Pearce, b. Jan. 10, 1855, Itawamba, Miss, d. Sept. 5, 1932, Miss., m. Malinda Jeffries, b. July 17, 1859, Itawamba, Miss, d. April 21, 1945, Miss.
    Wm. Bailey & Viola Kerr's children: Annie Belle Kerr, b. May 1, 1919, Itawamba, Miss., m. Sept. 12, 1937, Woodie Chandler.

KEY, John, b. 1765, Amherst Co., Va., d. 1861, Walker Co., Ala., m. July 15, 1797, Belinda Milstead (Mil Stewart). They moved from Virginia to North Carolina in 1797. Moved to Walker Co., Ala. in 1816. John Key was a pioneer in the Methodist Church in Walker Co., and was a farmer. He died at 96 yrs. of age and is buried near Sipsey, Ala. in Walker County. Children: 1. Washington Key, b. 1802, Va. or N. C. m. Malinda Abbott, died at age of abt. 102 yrs. 2. Lindsey Key, m. Rebecca Winters. 3. Joseph Garland Key, m. Rachel Cole (dau. of Byrd Cole.) 4. John Martin Key, b. 1805, d. 1854, Coal Valley, Walker Co., Ala., m. 1st. - Mary Snow, 2nd. - 1841, Lucy Ann Allen, b. Feb. 23, 1827, Walker Co., Ala. 5. Nancy Key, m. Richard L. "Dick" Chilton. 6. Elizabeth Key, m. William Busby. 7. James Hezekiah Key, m. Elizabeth Herrig. 8. Dock Clifton Key, b. 1825, d. 1865, m. 1845, Nancy Louise Cole, b. 1828, d. 1908, buried at Zion Cem., Walker Co., Ala. 9. Charles Rice Key, m. Dorcia Cole. 10. William S. Key, m. Cynthia Aseneth Abbott. 11. Jane Mills Key, m. Hill Abbott.

KEY, John, b. Mar. 13, 1836, Pleasant Hill, Walker Co., Ala., d. May 29, 1900, Walker Co., Ala. - son of John Martin & Mary (Snow) Key - m. Charity Elizabeth Wood, b. Dec. 31, 1839, d. Mar. 9, 1890, Walker Co., Ala. - dau. of Edward & Minerva Wood. He is buried at the Pleasant Hill (Lawson Place) Cemetery and she is buried at the Davis Graveyard, Coal Valley, Walker Co., Ala. Children: 1. Mary Key, b. May 29, 1858, Coal Valley, Walker Co., Ala., d. May 4, 1929, m. W. H. McClain. 2. Robert Powers Key, b. Sept. 26, 1859, Coal Valley, Ala. d. Dec. 28, 1949, Walker Co., Ala., m. Jan. 12, 1882, Mary Ann Rutledge, b.

Dec. 21, 1861, Walker Co., Ala., d. Oct. 30, 1946, Walker Co., Ala. 3. Minerva Key, b. Mar. 22, 1861, Walker Co., m. A. A. Rutledge. 4. Samuel G. Key, b. Oct. 1, 1862, Walker Co., m. Berthina Nelson. 5. Eliza Key, b. Aug. 24, 1866, Walker Co., m. George H. Myers. 6. Edward Thomas Key, b. Mar. 29, 1868, Walker Co., m. Minnie Sides. 7. Prudy Key, b. Feb. 2, 1870, Walker Co., m. Rufus Bell. 8. John Martin Key, II, b. Jan. 30, 1872, Walker Co., m. 1st. - Minter Swindle, 2nd. - Ida Kilgore. 9. Susan Key, m. 1st. - Mud Ferguson, 2nd. - J. M. Files. 10. Sarah E. Key, b. July 10, 1875, Walker Co., d. Nov. 3, 1877. 11. W. S. Key, b. April 18, 1877, Walker Co. 12. Carroll Rice Key, b. Oct. 25, 1879, Walker Co., d. Oct. 15, 1880. 13. Meda Key, b. May 16, 1882, Walker Co., m. John McDonald.

KEY, John Martin, b. 1805, d. 1854, Coal Valley, Walker Co., Ala. - son of John & Belinda (Milstead) Key - m. 1st - Mary Snow. He was a farmer and is buried at the Lawrence Place at Coal Valley, Walker Co., Ala. Children: (1st. wife.) 1. John Key, b. Mar. 13, 1836, Pleasant Hill, Walker Co., d. May 29, 1900, Walker Co., m. Charity Elizabeth Wood, b. Dec. 31, 1839, d. Mar. 9, 1890 Walker Co. 2. Thomas Key, m. 1st. - Miss Kilgore. 2nd. - Miss Logan, 3rd. Miss Burton. 3. Mary "Polly" Key, m. 1st. - Mr. Kilgore, 2nd. - (her cousin) Wm. Key, son of Wash. Key.
John Martin Key second marriage, 1841 Lucy Allen Woods. Children: (2nd. wife.) 1. Samuel Key, m. 1st. - Miss Courington, 2nd. - Miss Bevill. 2. Rice Key, died during Civil War. 3. Lucy Key, m. 1865, Jasoer Voyles. 4. Bertha Kay, m. Mr. Voyles. 5. Lindy Key, m. Mr. Voyles. 6. Zelphia Key, m. Hugh Lollar. 7. Nancy J. Key, m. Mr. Hamilton.

KEY, Robert Powers, b. Sept. 26, 1859, Coal Valley, Walker Co., Ala., d. Dec. 28, 1949, Walker Co., - son of John & Charity Key - m. Jan. 12, 1882, Mary Ann Rutledge, b. Dec. 21, 1861, Pleasant Grove, Walker Co., Ala., d. Oct. 30, 1946, Walker Co., Ala. - dau. of James & Elizabeth Rutledge. He was a lifelong farmer and they are both buried at the Pleasant Hill Cem. Walker Co. Children: (All born Walker Co.) 1. John R. Key, b. Oct. 18, 1882, d. Feb. 14, 1948, m. Carrie Shannon. 2. James D. Key, b. Aug. 4, 1884, d. Aug. 6, 1946, m. Meta Blanton. 3. Talmadge D. Key, b. Aug. 6, 1886, m. Jeanie Nelson. 4. Henry Grady Key, b. Mar. 11, 1888, d. Nov. 24, 1955, m. Mae Inman. 5. Ada Key, b. July 22, 1890, m. Houston Guthrie. 6. Bedford Thomas Key, b. Sept. 30, 1893, m. Ada Davis. 7. Jenrings D. Key, b. Sept. 26, 1896, d. June 28, 1953, m. Lula Blanton. 8. Annie Key, b. May 9, 1898, m. Ed Guthrie. 9. Bessie Key, b. May 6, 1900, Townley, Ala., m. Mar. 29, 1918, Buren Millard Wright, b. Sept. 18, 1894, Walker Co., Ala. 10. Aubrey Key, b. Sept. 13, 1902, m. Ruby Martin.

KING, James Gordon, b. Dec. 3, 1925, Fayette, Ala. - son of W. Emmett & Milner A. (Young) King - m. Helen Coral Bright. Children: 1. James Gordon King, II. 2. Mary Helen King. 3. Elizabeth King. 4. Rosanne King.

KING, W. Emmett, m. Oct. 19, 1918, Milner Adine Young, b. July 6, 1898, Fay. Co., Ala. - dau. of James D. & Effie (Humber) Young. Children: 1. William Young King, b. Oct. 6, 1919, Fayette, Ala. 2. James Gordon King, b. Dec. 3, 1925, Fayette, Ala.

KING, William Young, b. Oct. 6, 1919, Fayette, Ala. - son of Emmett & Milner A. (Young) King - m. Agnes Maurin. Children: 1. Mary Ellen King, b. Feb.

13, 1947. 2. Dianne King. 3. John William King. 4. Peter Gerard King, b. July 1, 1959.

KIRK, Jessie L, b. May 6, 1791, Mecklinburg, N.C., d. Oct. 11, 1876, Franklin Co., Ala. - son of Patrick Kirk - m. Mary _. Jessie L. Kirk was a saddle maker. He moved from North Carolina to Haywood Co., Tenn. He was in the War of 1812 - came further south and was in the battle of New Orleans. He and his brother James settled in Franklin Co., Ala. at the close of this war. James Kirk was a lawyer in Tuscumbia, Ala. for many years. Jessie L, Kirk was a land owner and a Mason. Children: 1. Matilda Kirk, b. 1815, Miss., d. 1890, Ala., m. Wyatt Pace, b. Carroll Co., Miss, d. 1850, Miss.

KIRK, Patrick, b. 1750, Ireland, m. wife unknown. Children: 1. Jessie L. Kirk, b. May 6, 1791, Mecklinburg, N.C., d. Oct. 1876, Franklin Co., Ala. m. Mary _. 2. James Kirk, b. 1746, N. C. d. Colbert Co., Ala.

KIRKLAND, Archibald, b. 1780, or before, S. C., d. 1848, Fayette, Ala., m. on or before 1802, Mary Chaney, b. 1780 or before, S.C., d. Bef. husband in 1848, Fayette, Ala. The Archibald Kirkland Family lived in Morgan Co., Ala. before moving to Fayette County, Ala. They were listed in the first census of 1830 of Fayette County. Some of the family are said to have remained in Morgan Co. while the other branch of the family went on to Henry Co. and are listed in the 1830 census of that county. The Fayette Co., Kirklands settled at Sipsey. Those children who were married before 1830 were - Jane Kirkland Manasco; Elizabeth Kirkland Moore; John R. Kirkland and Lavenia Kirkland Farquhar. Children: 1. Jane Kirkland, b. abt. 1803, Tenn., d. bef. 1850, m. abt. 1825, David Manasco, b. abt. 1800. 2. Elizabeth Kirkland, b. 1805, Tenn. m. Oct. 19, 1826, John P. Moore, b. July 6, 1805, Tenn. 3. John R. Kirkland, b. 1808, S. C., m. Olie ___, b. 1810. 4. Lavenie Kirkland, b. 1809, Tenn., d. in Texas, m. abt. 1828, Anderson Farquhar, b. 1809, d. in Texas. 5. Jehu Chaney Kirkland, b. April 4, 1812, Tenn., d. Nov. 12, 1888, m. 1831, Permelia Chappell, b. Feb. 6, 1817, Tenn. d. Oct. 26, 1903. 6. Daniel G. Kirkland, b. 1813, Tenn., d. 1897, in Osage, Texas, m. Nov. 15, 1839, Temperance Lindsey, d. May 1843. 7. William W. Kirkland, b. 1815. 8. Mary Ann D. Kirkland, b. 1816, Tenn. d. bef. 1878 in Garvin, Texas, m. Sept. 12, 1833, William Owens Moore, b. May 11, 1816, Tenn. d. bef. 1878, in Garvin, Texas. 9. Robert Kirkland.

KIRKLAND, Daniel G., b. 1813, Tenn. d. 1897, in Osage, Texas - son of Archibald & Mary (Chaney) Kirkland - m. Nov. 15, 1839, Temperance Lindsey, d. May 1843. Daniel G. Kirkland volunteered for service in the Florida Indian War of 1836 at which time he was 22 years of age. He was with the first Alabama Inf. Regt. under Gen. W. S. Taylor. For this service he received land warrants in Fayette Co., Ala. In 1839 he married Temperance Lindsey, who died in 1843. His next wife was Tabiatha Yerby, dau. of Amon & Rachel Yerby. She died before 1870 at which time he was married to Mrs. Sarah Morrow. After her death he married Mrs. Pricilla A. Chambless Ruching, Jan. 27, 1881. They moved to Texas where he died before Mar. 6, 1897. She applied for a widow's pension.

KIRKLAND, Jehu Chaney, b. April 4, 1812, Tenn., d. Nov. 12, 1888, m. abt. 1831, Permelia Chappell, b. Feb. 6, 1817, d. Oct. 26, 1903. Both are buried at Siloam Missionary Baptist Church about four miles south of Winfield, Ala.

on Highway 17. Jehu Chaney lived some years, with his parents, Archibald & Mary (Chaney) Kirkland in the state of Tenn, before coming to Morgan Co., Ala. From there the family moved to Fayette Co., Ala. and settled at Sipsey, near the town of Fayette. The earliest record of the family other than Bible records, is the 1830 census record. One branch of the family is said to have moved on to South Alabama. Permelia was the dau. of Miles & Priscilla Chappell, early settlers of Fayette County. They were the parents of twelve daughters and two sons. Miles Chappell died in 1880 at the age of ninety years. Jehu Chaney Kirkland was in Fayette County as early as 1840 as he is listed in the 1840 Census as head of a family. He was a Democrat and first represented Fayette County in the General Assembly of Ala. in the year of 1855. E. A. Powell, in his "Fifty Five Years in West Ala." describes him as follows: "Jehu C. Kirkland was a farmer of strong native sense, and fine physical appearance; and courteous but quick to show his resentment of anything he thought to be offensive. He was not a candidate again until a few years past, when he twice represented the county in the Lower House. Mr. Kirkland still lives in Fayette County, a highly respected citizen." Jehu C. Kirkland served in the Confederate Army during the War Between the States with Co. B. 41st. Ala. Inf. Reg. enlisting on May 19, 1862. He was a Major at the time of his resignation from the service on April 2, 1863, having resigned because of the fact that all his sons, who were of age, and his sons-in-law had been taken into the army. After the war he served the following terms in the Alabama Legislature from Fayette County; 1874-5; 1875-6; 1876-7; and 1880-1. He was a farmer, lawyer and Kirkland Post Office was named in his honor. Children: 1. Sarah Ann Kirkland, b. 1834, m. James Guin. 2. John Kirkland, b. 1836, d. at age of nineteen. 3. James Kirkland, b. 1837, Killed during the Civil War in the Battle of Seven Pines. He enlisted June 11, 1861, with Co. I. 11th. Ala. Inf. Regt. and was killed May 31, 1862. 4. William F. Kirkland, b. 1839, m. Nov. 7, 1866, Mary A. Poe, 2nd. - Mary Hollingsworth. Served in the Confederate Army. He enlisted on June 11, 1861 and was wounded several times during the war. 5. Missouri Catherine Kirkland. b. 1840, m. John Blakney, 2nd. - Joseph McGaha. 6. Laura Virginia Kirkland, b. 1842, m. Joseph Trull. 7. Anderson Dalles Kirkland, b. 1845, died from wounds received at Appomattox during the Civil War, where he was serving as flag bearer. He is thought to have been with Co., I. 11th Ala. Inf. Regt. His brother William F. stayed with him until he died. 8. Robert Kirkland, b. 1848. 9. Margaret Cardelia Kirkland, b. 1851, m. Monroe Ward. 10. Miles Wilburn Kirkland, b. 1853, m. Mary Jane Ward. 11. Susan Ellen Kirkland, b. 1855, m. Jan. 2, 1873, W. A. May. 12. George Portis Kirkland, b. 1857, m. Nannie Couch. 13. Beaureguard Davis Kirkland, b. 1861, m. Mary Cordelia Ward. There were sixteen children, three having died in infancy.

KIRKLAND, John R., b. 1807, or 8, S. C., m. Olie ___. He lived some years in the state of Tennessee with his parents, Archibald & Mary (Chaney) Kirkland and before coming to Morgan Co., Ala. From there the family moved to Fayette Co. The name of his wife other than Olie is unknown. John R. Kirkland was a Democrat and represented Fayette Co. in the General Assembly of Ala. in 1847. The following is his family as listed in the 1850 census record of Fayette Co: John R. Kirkland, age 42, farmer, b. S.C., Olie, age 40, b. S.C., Elizabeth J. age 19, b. Ala., Virginia, age 18, b. Ala., Constantine, age 16, b. Ala., Robert, age 15, b. Ala., Clark, age 14, b. Ala., John, age 11, b. Ala., Jehu, age 9, b. Ala., Perry, age 7, b. Ala., Ann, age 6, b. Ala., Elliott, age 3, b. Ala. The John R. Kirkland family, according to E. A. Powell in his Fifty Five Years in West Ala., moved to the Northwest sometime after 1850. He was a brother of Jehu C. Kirkland and also a brother of Daniel Kirkland who served in the Florida Indian War of 1836 in the 1st. Ala. Regt. of Volunteers commanded by Wm. Chisolm.

KIRKLEY, Marion Jackson, b. Jan. 30, 1864, d. June 21, 1944, Carbon Hill, Ala., - son of Wm. ' Nancy (Mazingo) Kirkley - m. Nov. 14, 1895, Eliza Jane Hawkins, b. Oct. 6, 1880, Fayette Co., near Bluff, - dau. of Daniel Burgess & Minta Ann (Northam) Hawkins. Children: 1. Mertie Kirkley, m. Lois (m) Bobo. 2. Lloyd Denver Kirkley. 3. Audie Mae Kirkley. 4. Floy Ernest Kirkley. 5. Jackson Dalver Kirkley. 6. Delta Ree Kirkley, m. Glf V. Houlditch.

KIRKLEY, Terry Allen, b. Fayette Co., Ala. - son of B. F. Kirkley - m. June 3, 1955, Mina Louise Propst, b. July 28, 1932, Fayette, Ala. - dau. of Dan F. & Alice (Putnam) Propst. Children: 1. Terry Allen Kirkley, Jr., b. Mar. 29, 1958, Baton Rouge, La.

KIZZIRE, Allen, b. April 20, 1905, Fayette Co., Ala. - son of Leonard & Julia J. (Hallman) Kizzire - m. Mittie Christeen McCraw, b. Oct. 1, 1911. Children: (All born in Fayette County.) 1. Julia Juanita Kizzire, m. Verdo Terry. 2. Travis O'Neal Kizzire. 3. Y. C. Kizzire, b. 1934, d. May 26, 1955, Fayette, Ala. 4. Martha Lou Kizzire, m. Robert Estes, Jr. 5. Edward Allen Kizzire. 6. Amanda Jean Kizzire. 7. Sandra Gayle Kizzire. 8. Dorothy Ann Kizzire.

KIZZIRE, Leonard, b. April 20, 1842 or 46, Tusca. Co., Ala., d. Fayette Co., Ala., m. Dec. 18, 1902, 2nd. - Julia Joanna Hallman, b. July 28, 1872, Bibb Co., Ala., d. Dec. 14, 1951, Fayette, Ala. - dau. of Henry J. & Sarah (Langford) Hallman. Leonard Kizzire, entered the service during the Civil War, as Private, May 1862. He was in the 41st. Ala. Regt. Inf. Co. H, and was wounded Mar. 1865 at Petersburg, Va. and was sent to hospital at Richmond. He arrived home May 3, 1865. Children: Flora Bell Kizzire, b. Oct. 13,1903, (All children born Fayette Co.) m. Feb. 25, 1933, Allie B. Nelson. 2. Allen Kizzire, b. April 20, 1905, m. Mittie Christeen McCraw. 3. Carrah Kizzire, b. Sept. 11, 1907, m. Sept. 27, 1925, Thomas Ervin Price. 4. Irene Kizzire, b. April 20, 1909, m. Oct. 14, 1928, Richmond Pearson Hobson South. 5. Leonard Alfred Kizzire, b. Jan. 26, 1911, m. Jan. 9, 1932, Avery Jo Johnson.

KIZZIRE, Leonard Alfred, b. Jan. 26, 1911, Fayette, Ala. -son of Leonard & Julia J. (Hallman) Kizzire - m. Jan. 9, 1932, Avery Jo Johnson. Children: 1. Doris Kizzire, b. Jan. 12, __, Fayette Co., Ala., m. Joe Stanley Brown. 2. Bonnie Sue Kizzire, b. Fayette Co., Ala., m. Kenneth Dudley. 3. Sonja Gayle Kizzire, m. Jimmy Trull. 4. Jerry Glenda Kizzire. 5. Judy Kay Kizzire.

KUYKENDALL, Ottis, b. Tusca. Co., Ala., m. 1937, Linnie Lee Hocutt, b. 1919, Fayette Co., Ala. - dau. of N. B. & Ida (Patterson) Hocutt. Children: 1. Carol Ann Kuykendall, b. Nov. 30, 1956, Fayette, Ala.

LAIR, John H., m. June Carolyn Alexander, b. Jan. 20, 1932, Fayette, Ala. - dau. of Elmer & Vista (Patterson) Alexander. Children: 1. Patricia Dian Lair, b. Aug. 1953. 2. John Thomas "Dee" Lair, b. Nov. 1954. 3. Dau. b. Mar. 1956. 4. Son, b. Aug. 6, 1958.

LAMBERT, __, m. Ella Willingham, b. Bankston, Ala. d. Dallas, Texas - dau. of

Wm. R. "Doc" Willingham. Children: 1. Clyde Lambert, b. May 30, 1892, d. Aug. 3, 1918, buried at Pleasant Hill Cemetery.

LANSDALE, George, b. 1829, Montgomery Co., Ala. - son of Isaac & Sarah (Gentry McCool) Lansdale - m. 1847 in Fayette Co., Sarah C. Ray, sister of Samuel B. Ray. They were early settlers of Fayette County. Children: (Had large family including -) 1. George Lansdale, Jr. 2. Isaac Lansdale, II.

LANSDALE, Isaac, b. 1760, Newcastle, Delaware, d. 1844, Fayette Co., Ala., m. 1st. and 2nd. unknown. He fought five years in the American Revolution, most of the time in S. C. with the Delaware Continental Line. In the 1830's the Lansdale, McCool, Gray and Ray families came into Fayette County, Ala. from Montgomery Co., Ala. The Lansdale and McCool families had come into Ala. from South Carolina. These families settled in the southern part of the county near Newtonville. Children: (by first two marriages are not fully known but believed to have been -) 1. Isaac Lansdale, Jr. 2. John Lansdale. 3. Abraham Lansdale. 4. William Lansdale. 5. Sarah Lansdale (and possible others not known.

Isaac Lansdales third marriage - abt. 1822, in Montgomery Co., Ala. Widow Sarah McCool (nee Gentry). Children: (Shown in Bible by 3rd wife.) 1. Rachel Lansdale, b. 1807, S. C. d. 1880, Fayette Co., Ala. m. Wm. Foster Gray. 2. Matilda Lansdale, b. 1823, Montgomery, Co., Ala. d. possibly bet. 1860 - 1870, m. Mr. Tidwell, d. abt. 1856 to 1858. Moved to Attala Co., Miss. after her husband's death. 3. Nanay Lansdale, b. 1827, Montgomery Co., Ala., d. 1917, Kosciusko, Miss, (D.A.R. Grave Marker) m. abt. 1853, Samuel B. Ray. 4. George Lansdale, b. 1829, Montgomery, Co., Ala. d. 1878, Attala Co., Miss. m. 1847, Fayette Co., Sarah C. Ray. 5. Lydia Lansdale, b. 1831, Montgomery Co., Ala. d. 1863, Attala Co., Miss. m. 1853, Fayette Co., James M. Brown.

LANGSTON, John, m. wife unknown. John Langston came to South Carolina from North Carolina about 1808. Children: 1. Charlotte Langston, m. Burl Brown. They were married at home near Camden, Richmond Co., S. C.

LAWLEY, Harrison C., b. April 30, 1821, d. June 14, 1862, m. Dec. 2, 1846, Monica Bell, b. Dec. 2, 1827, d. June 6, 1909, dau. of John & Amelia Bell. Children: 1. William Franklin Lawley, b. Sept. 9, 1847, m. Mary Frances Gunter. 2. Mary A. Lawley, b. April 12, 1853.

LAWLEY, Peter Gunter, b. Nov. 17, 1883, Davis Creek, Fayette Co., Ala., d. Aug. 4, 1954, buried in Brotherton Family Cem. - son of Wm. & Frances (Gunter) Lawley, m. Dec. 3, 1902, Lovie Brotherton, b. June 23, 1879, Newtonville, Ala. Children: 1. Clyde Lawley, b. Feb. 23, 1908, Fayette Co., Ala. 2. Edwin Lawley, b. May 9, 1915, Fayette Co. 3. Nelva Lawley, b. Aug. 12, 1918, Fayette Co., m. James Connell.

LAWLEY, William Franklin, b. Sept. 9, 1847 - son of Harrison C. & Monica (Bell) Lawley - m. Mary Frances Gunter, - dau. of Dr. Peter & Elizabeth (Harrington) Gunter. Children: 1. Lonnie Lawley, b. Oct. 23, 1870, (All children born at Davis Creek, Fayette Co., Ala.) 2. James Lawley. 3. Wm. Lawley. 4. John Lawley. 5. Peter Gunter Lawley, b. Nov. 17, 1883, d. Aug. 4, 1954, m. Dec. 3, 1902, Lovie Brotherton, b. June 23, 1879, Newtonville, Ala.

LAWRENCE, Floyd N., b. Oct. 29, 1901, Fayette Co., Ala. - son of J. G. Lawrence - m. Dec. 26, 1923, Bessie Nell Cotton, b. Aug. 27, 1907, Fayette Co., Ala. - dau. of J. J. Cotton. Mr. & Mrs. Lawrence were married in Columbus, Miss. by E. E. Grout, J. P. Mr. Lawrence is a Postal Clerk in the Fayette Post Office. Children: (All born in Fayette Co.) 1. Floyd Edwin Lawrence, b. Feb. 23, 1925, m. Oct. 21, 1944, Dorothy Mae Stinson, b. Oct. 18, 1927, Thomasville, N. C. 2. Howard Newman Lawrence, b. April 21, 1928, m. Dec. 25, 1947, Betty Joyce Sharpe, b. Sept. 30, 1928, Fayette Co., Ala. 3. Richard Gaines Lawrence, b. June 9, 1932, m. Sept. 3, 1950, Helen Marie Norris, b. Oct. 21, 1933, Fayette Co., Ala. 4. George Levert Lawrence, b. Aug. 27, 1938.

LAWRENCE, George, b. July 2, 1807, d. Dec. 30, 1884, m. 1835, Sarah Green, b. Oct. 30, 1807, d. April 8, 1886 - dau. of Abednego & Winnie (Grizzle) Green. Children: 1. Winnie O. Lawrence, b. Sept. 7, 1835, Fayette Co., d. Dec. 4, 1888, Fayette, Co., m. 1853, James W. White, b. April 23, 1826, Fay. Co., d. Feb. 12, 1891, Fayette Co. 2. James Green Lawrence, b. Mar. 14, 1837, Fayette Co., d. Feb. 5, 1907, Fayette Co., Ala., m. 1865, Martha Ann Shirley, b. Mar. 17, 1840, Fayette Co., d. Mar. 10, 1914, Fayette Co. 3. Joel Lawrence. 4. Hannah Lawrence, m. Mr. Grey. 5. Sarah Lawrence, m. Daniel Grey.

LAWRENCE, Howard Newman, b. April 21, 1928, Fayette Co., Ala. - son of Floyd & Bessie Nell (Cotton) Lawrence - m. Dec. 25, 1947, Betty Joyce Sharpe, b. Sept. 30, 1928, Fayette, Ala. - dau. of J. Holley & Emma Blanche (Arnold) Sharpe. Children: 1. Elizabeth Ann Lawrence, b. Jan. 15, 1957, ElPaso, Texas. 2. Dau. , b. Oct. 1959, Texas.

LAWRENCE, James Green, b. Mar. 14, 1837, Fayette Co., Ala., d. Feb. 5, 1907, Fayette Co. - son of George & Sarah (Green) Lawrence, m. 1865, 2nd. - Martha Ann Shirley, b. Mar. 17, 1840, Fayette Co., d. Mar. 10, 1914, Fayette Co., Ala. Children: (2nd. wife.) 1. Jeffie Garrett Lawrence, b. Oct. 29, 1879, Fayette Co., d. Feb. 6, 1942, Fayette Co., m. Dec. 27, 1900, Leether Jane Nichols, b. Dec. 24, 1883, Fayette Co. 2. Willie Lawrence. 3. Hollie Lawrence, m. Mae Fowler. 4. Seth Lawrence, m. Mattie McCarthy.
James Green Lawrence first marriage - Miss Moore. Children: (1st. wife.) 1. Washie Lawrence. 2. Jennie Lawrence, m. Arthur Reeves. 3. Beason Lawrence, m. Jim Marshall. 4. Thomas Lawrence, m. Docie McCarthy. 5. Frankie Lawrence, m. Ebb Jones. 6. Sidney Lawrence.

LAWRENCE, Jeffie Garrett, b. Oct. 29, 1879, Fayette Co., d. Feb. 6, 1942, Fayette Co. - son of James Green Lawrence - m. Dec. 27, 1900, Leether Jane Nichols, b. Dec. 24, 1883, Fayette Co., dau. of Wm. F. Nichols. Children: (All born in Fayette Co.) 1. Floyd Newman Lawrence, b. Oct. 29, 1901, m. Dec. 26, 1923, Bessie Nell Cotton, b. Aug. 27, 1907, Fayette Co. 2. Vera Velma Lawrence, b. Aug. 17, 1903, m. John A. Ayres, b. Aug. 24, 1886, Fayette Co. 3. Wilma Ann Lawrence, b. Mar. 8, 1905, m. Dec. 28, 1929, John Cecil Fowler, b. July 12, 1904, Fayette Co. 4. Rayburn L. Lawrence, b. Jan. 28, 1907, d. April 23, 1954, Fayette, Ala., m. July 6, 1938, Julia Margaret Ayres, b. Nov. 24, 1911. 5. Auburn Hill Lawrence, b. Mar. 7, 1909, m. Dec. 5, 1931, Gustavia Irene Taylor, b. Dec. 4, 1912. 6. Evelyn Walker Lawrence, b. Dec. 25, 1910, m. Dec. 18, 1931, William Claud Jones, b. Nov. 22, 1907. 7. James Clayton Lawrence, b. May 5, 1913, m. Dec. 22, 1934, Ruby Elizabeth Jones, b. July 8, 1914, Fayette Co. 8. William Malcolm Lawrence, b. July 14, 1916,

m. June 18, 1939, Brownie Mitchell, b. Feb. 27, 1919, Fayette Co. 9. Jeffie Garrett Lawrence, Jr., b. Sept. 11, 1922, m. Dec. 24, 1942, Merle Lillian Fowler, b. Sept. 4, 1921, Fayette Co. 10. John Thomas Lawrence, b. Oct. 3, 1925, m. Mar. 2, 1946, Dorothy Virginia Renfro, b. Sept. 13, 1924, Fayette Co.

LAWRENCE, Thomas, b. Oct. 3, 1925, Fayette Co., - son of J. G. Lawrence - m. Mar. 2, 1946, Dorothy Virginia Renfroe, b. Sept. 13, 1924, Fayette Co., dau. of Roy S. Renfroe. Children: 1. Gwyndeline Lawrence, b. Jan. 25, 1947, Fay. Ala. 2. Myra Jo Lawrence, b. Nov. 1, 1951, Fayette, Ala. 3. Brenda Lawrence, b. May 1, 1952, Fayette, Ala.

LAWRENCE, T. L. - son of Martin Lawrence - m. Ella Louise Long - dau. of James Fulton Long. Ella was married first to Erantta Carina. Children: 1. Laura Pamela Lawrence, b. Mar. 22, 1948.

LAWRENCE, Wallace Porter, b. June 11, 1895, Frankfort, Ky, d. Oct. 6, 1952, buried Fayette, Ala. - son of Martin Luther & Lorena (Steele) Lawrence - m. Sarah Nell Propst, b Feb. 5, 1899, Fayette, Ala. - dau. of H. Belton & Carrie Waters (Cannon) Propst. Children: 1. Stacia Elizabeth Lawrence, b. Fay. Ala., m. April 13, 1957, Vernon Louis Kasten, b. Jackson, Missouri. (Son b. Jan. 1960, Mo.)

LAYTON, James, m. Mary Williamson. Several of their children settled in Fay. Co., Ala. in the mid 1800's. Children: 1. Susan Layton, b. June 7, 1811, S. C., d. Mar. 7, 1901, m. Stephen Yarbrough, b. S. C. 2. Martha Layton, b. June 5, 1839, S. C. d. June 28, 1882, m. Hiram Yarbrough (nephew of Stephen Yarbrough.) 3. Willis Layton, b. S.C., m. Miss Wofford, b. S.C. 4. Coleman Layton, b. S.C., m. 1st. - Miss Wofford (Sister to Willis' Layton's wife.) 5. Nancy Layton, b. S.C., m. Riley Fowler (bro. of Nancy Fowler, wife of John Layton.) 6. John Layton, b. S.C., m. Nancy Fowler, b. S.C. 7. Thomas Layton, b. S.C. 8. Frances Layton, b. S.C. 9. Mary Layton, b. S.C. 10. George Layton. 11. Benjamin Layton, b. S.C., d. young.

LEE, __ m. Mary __. Mrs. Mary Lee, a widow, moved to Berry from Tuscaloosa Co., in 1911. She had five children - Clarence Doss (when grown moved to Tuscaloosa.); Clista Doss, m. J. D. Walton - 1890 - 1938. (They had the following children: Jack Walton - died in England, 1944 -- Olen Walton, U.S. N. -- Albert Walton of Tusca. -- Jean Walton Swanson of Mobile.); Clara Doss, m. John Clements - 1881 - 1956. (They had the following children: Alonzo Clements, 1910 - 1928 -- Mary Edna Clements, 1912 - 1914 -- Pauline Clements who married Delmer Hocutt and has two children (Betty Hocutt Dove of Little Rock, Ark. and Kenneth Hocutt). -- Harold Clements of Mobile; Ethel Lee Appling of Birmingham; Effie Lee Travis of Birmingham.

LINDSEY, Joseph Franklin, b. Nov. 24, 1861, Fayette Co., Ala., d. Mar. 30, 1900, Fayette, Ala. - son of Levi & Delitha Douglas (Alley) Lindsey - m. Ella Griffin, b. Feb. 10, 1857, Fayette Co., Ala., d. Sept. 26, 1929, Fayette, Ala. - dau. of Ira & Susan A. (McFarland) Griffin. Children: 1. Thomas Levi Lindsey, b. May 14, 1887, Fayette Co., Ala., m. June 24, 1922, Aline Robertson, b. Oct. 9, 1890, Fayette, Ala.

LINDSEY, Levi, b. Sept. 18, 1819, Ala., d. April 4, 1894, m. Delitha Douglas Alley, b. Jan. 24, 1823, Ala., d. Aug. 26, 1899 - dau. of Nicholas Alley.

Children: 1. Jane L. Lindsey, b. 1850, m. Thomas E. Goodwin, b. Cumberland Co., N. C., d. April 4, 1908. 2. Sallie Lindsey, b. 1855, m. Robert Perry Caine. 3. Joseph Franklin Lindsey, b. Nov. 24, 1861, Fayette Co., Ala., d. Mar. 30, 1900, Fayette, Ala., m. Ella Griffin, b. Feb. 10, 1857, Fayette Co. Ala., d. Sept. 26, 1929, Fayette, Ala. 4. Susan Lindsey, b. 1847, m. Mr Jones. 5. William Lindsey. 6. Simpson Lindsey, b. 1859. 7. Babe Lindsey. 8. Leona Lindsey.

LINDSEY, Thomas Levi, Jr., b. May 31, 1925, Fayette, Ala. - son of T. L., Sr. & Aline (Robertson) Lindsey - m. Mar. 2, 1951, Lillian Norris, b. Sept. 8, West Point, Miss. - dau. of Bennie Watson & Clara (Timbs) Norris. T. L. Lindsey, Jr. is affiliated with the Citizen's Bank of Fayette. They were married at West Point, Miss. Children: 1. Thomas Levi Lindsey, III, b. Aug. 5, 1952 Fayette, Ala. 2. Martha Lillian Lindsey, b. July 1, 1959, Fayette, Ala.

LINDSEY, Thomas Levi, Sr., b. May 14, 1887, Fayette, Ala. - son of Joseph Franklin & Ella (Griffin) Lindsey - m. June 24, 1922, Lucy Aline Robertson, b. Oct. 9, 1890, Fayette, Ala. - dau. of Joseph R. & Malinda (McConnell) Robertson. They were married at the home of J. R. Robertson in Fayette, Ala. by Rev. J. I. Williams. T. L. Lindsey, Sr. is affiliated with the Citizen's Bank of Fayette. Children: 1. Thomas Levi Lindsey, Jr., b. May 31, 1925, Fayette, Ala., m. Mar. 2, 1951, Lillian Norris, b. Sept. 8, West Point, Miss.

LITTLE, Cecil Burnice, b. Nov. 19, 1908, Fayette Co., Ala. - son of James Newton & Annie (Wiggins) Little - m. April 25, 1938, Ruby Nell Newman. Children: 1. Jerry Nolan Little, b. Feb. 10, 1943, Fayette Co., Ala.

LITTLE, James Newton, b. Jan. 15, 1875, Vernon, Lamar Co., Ala., m. Aug. 24, 1907, Annie Wiggins, b. Mar. 4, 1888, Fayette, Ala. Children: 1. Cecil Burnice Little, b. Nov. 19, 1908, Fayette Co., Ala., m. April 25, 1938, Ruby Nell Newman. 2. Jewel Chesney Little, b. May 28, 1914, Fayette Co., Ala., m. May 20, 1935, Eugene Sullivan. 3. James Ethel Little, b. Aug. 17, 1924, Fay. Co., Ala., m. Nov. 22, 1945, Vadus Hubbert, b. Aug. 2, 1923, Fayette Co., Ala.

LIVINGSTON, Willard, b. Dec. 16, 1916, Lamar Co., Ala., m. Oct. 30, 1936, Imogene Herren, b. Feb. 17, 1920. Children: 1. Sheila Jean Livingston, b. Jan. 4, 1949, Jefferson Co., Ala. 2. Sherry Lynn Livingston, b. Sept. 18, 1951, Jefferson Co., Ala.

LOGAN, Alexander, - son of Bob Logan - m. Nancy Beasley, b. Tenn., d. Dec. 19, 1914. Children: 1. Mary Jane Logan, b. Oct. 30, 1854, d. Dec. 17, 1944, buried at Mt. Pleasant Cem., m. 1st. - Therman Henderson, 2nd. - Dec. 19, 1886, Levi Woodruff South, b. May 8, 1836, Tusca. Co., Ala. 2. Tom Logan, b. Dec. 14, 1855, Berea Community, Fayette Co., d. Mar. 31, 1941, m. Dora McCarthy. 3. Andrew "Drew" Logan, b. June 30, 1857, Berea, Fayette Co., Ala., d. Feb. 13, 1918, m. Mary Ann Adair. 4. Josephine Logan, b. Nov. 11, 1862, Berea, d. Nov. 19, 1908, m. Rial May.

LOGAN, Bob, m. Jennie McCaleb. Both are buried at Yamper Town, near Winfield, Ala. They had eight sons in the Confederate Service at the same time. Children: 1. Henry Logan, d. 1904, Marion Co., Ala., m. Mary Matthews. 2. White Logan, d. 1925, m. Narcissoris Norris. 3. Andy Logan, m. Kathryn Cathrum. 4. John "Jack" Logan, m. Margariete Pate. 5. David Logan, m. Betty Pratt. 6.

Lansey Logan, m. 1st. - Polly Moss, 2nd. - Martha Musgrove. 7. Alexander Logan, b. Feb. 1829, d. During Civil War, buried in Soldier's Cemetery, Corinth, Miss. 8. Jim Logan, killed in Battle of Vicksburg, Miss. 9. Polly Logan, m. Bill Anthony. 10. Elizabeth "Bet" Logan, m. Jerry Hunt. 11. Jane Logan, m. Sam Atkins. 12. Vernetta Logan, m. Joe Green. 13. Martha Logan, m. Jim King. 14. Sarah "Sally" Logan, died at age of 50 years.

LOGAN, Freeland E., b. Jan. 15, 1909, Fayette Co., Ala., m. Sept. 25, 1927, Susie Temperance South, b. Oct. 11, 1908, Fayette Co., Ala. - dau. of Martin D. South. Susie's second marriage was to Joseph Quinton Harris - no children by second marriage. Child: (1st. Logan) 1. Gene South Logan, b. May 25, 1928, Fayette Co., Ala.

LOGAN, Freeman, d. Feb. 14, 1874, m. Rhoda Cornelia _, b. Nov. 20, 1844, d. April 15, 1875, N.C. Children: 1. Priscilla Logan.

LOLLAR, Bill Brooks, b. April 23, 1923, Fayette, Ala. - son of L. B. & Lodessa Lollar - m. April 1, 1945, Lanell Wade, b. Oct. 18, 1926, Wetumoka, Ala. Mr. Lollar is a medical technician and Mrs. Lollar is a bookkeeper. Children: 1. James Lee Lollar (Twin), b. Mar. 2, 1946, Montgomery, Ala. 2. Jerry Wade Lollar (Twin), b. Mar. 2, 1946, Montgomery, Ala.

LOLLAR, Lee Brown, b. Nov. 18, 1889, d. April 18, 1950, m. Oct. 5, 1913, Mary Lodessa Elizabeth Brown, b. July 25, 1892. Lee B. Lollar was a teacher and an automobile dealer. Mrs. Lollar is a teacher. Children: 1. Robbie Lee Lollar, b. Aug. 14, 1914, Lamar Co., Ala., m. June 12, 1938, Guthrie J. Smith, b. Fayette, Ala. They were married at the First Methodist Church in Fayette, Ala. by Rev. Hearshell Hamner. 2. Brownie Lollar, b. July 5, 1916, Lamar Co., Ala., m. Mar. 8, 1941, Raymond Nelson Mitchell. 3. Bill Brooks Lollar, b. April 23, 1923, Fayette, Ala., m. April 1, 1945, Lanell Wade.

LOLLAR, Thomas Marshall, b. April 29, 1852, d. Nov. 8, 1941, m. Americus Hasseltine Brock, b. Aug. 28, 1856, d. Oct. 31, 1939. He was a Freewill Baptist Minister. Children: 1. Eudora Lollar, b. Dec. 12, 1878, d. Nov. 30, 1905, m. Mr. Hankins. 2. Marcy Margaret Lollar, b. June 4, 1881, m. Mr. Bobo. 3. William Alfred Lollar, b. Sept. 9, 1883, d. 1892. 4. Murray Cincler Lollar, b. Oct. 17, 1885. 5. Felix Elmore Lollar, b. Jan. 5, 1888. 6. Lee Brown Lollar, b. Nov. 18, 1889, d. April 18, 1950. 7. Thomas Shelton Lollar, b. Dec. 27, 1891, d. Aug. 4, 1949. 8. Samuel LaFayette Lollar, b. Nov. 16, 1893. 9. Clara Ann Lollar, b. Oct. 9, 1896, m. Mr. Johnson.

LOLLAR, William, m. Margaret Fox. Children: 1. Thomas M. Lollar, b. April 29, 1852, d. Nov. 8, 1941, m. Americus Hasseltine Brock, b. Aug. 28, 1856, d. Oct. 31, 1939.

LONG, James Fulton, b. Feb. 18, 1890, Ochlochnee, Ga. - son of James Harrison Long - m. Nov. 16, 1910, Maggie Beulah South, b. Dec. 29, 1894, Davis Creek, Fayette Co., Ala. - dau. of Levi Woodruff South. J. F. Long is a rural mail carrier. Children: 1. Ella Louise Long, b. Aug. 26, 1922, m. 1st. - Erantta Corina, 2nd. - F. L. Lawrence. 2. Laura Mozella Long, b. Mar. 22, 1925, m. Nov. 16, 1944, Wilburn A. Ridgeway.

LONG, Joe Reid, m. Annie Grace Freeman, b. Oct. 22, 1913, Fayette Co., Ala. -

dau. of Littleton L. & Annie (Smith) Freeman. Children: 1. John Reid Long, 2. Mary Ann Long, m. Murphy Ezelle. 3. Valter Long.

LONG, Ritchard H. d. Jan. 22, 1851, m. Jan. 9, 1840, Francis E. Henderson. Children: 1. Mary L. Long, b. Jan. 5, 1841. 2. Hariet E. Long, b. Aug. 29, 1842. 3. Andrew J. Long, b. April 29, 1844. 4. William L. Long, b. April 15, 1846. 5. Ritchard A. F. H. Long, b. Jan. 8, 1848.

LONGCRIER, Henry Leslie, m. Blanche White, dau. of S. L. White. Children: 1. Henry Leslie Longcrier, Jr., m. Jane Cason - had Henry Leslie III; Stephen; and Michael Cason Longcrier.

LOONEY, Bill, m. Ellen Penn. Children: 1. Mary Angeline Looney, m. Wm. Harris Welburn.

LOVE, ___ m. wife unknown. Children: 1. Uriah or Hugh Love. 2. Selenia Jane Love, b. Jan. 15, 1821, Rutherford Co., N.C., d. Feb. 4, 1894, near Dalton, Ga., m. Elisha Lowery, b. May 27, 1817, Habersham Co., N. C. d. Oct. 2, 1899, near Dalton, Ga. 3. Pheriby Love, m. Hugh McBrayer. 4. John Martin Love, m. Samantha _. 5. Dau. Love, m. Mr. McBrayer. 6. Dau. Love, m. Mr. Scoggins.

LOWERY, ___, m. wife unknown. The wife and mother died when the son Elisha, born 1817, was nine days old and his older sister cared for him until he was grown. The older sister, Annie Bowen, lived near Fairmont, Ga. on Villanow Creek. Children: Annie Lowery, m. Mr. Bowen. 2. Meshach Lowery, buried near Arab, Ala. 3. Elisha Lowery, b. May 27, 1817, d. Oct. 2, 1899, m. Selenia Jane Love, b. Jan. 15, 1821, d. Feb. 4, 1894.

LOWERY, Charlie, m. May Sawyer, dau. of Wm. Bedford Sawyer. Children: 1. Harold Lowery, m. Evelyn Oakley (Children: Billy Mitchell and David Lowery.) 2. Blonnie Fay Lowery, m. Frank Gibson (Children: Barbara and Frankie Gibson.)

LOWERY, Elisha, b. May 27, 1817, Habersham Co., N.C. (or Ga?) d. Oct. 2, 1899, Whitfield Co., Ga., m. Sept. 26, 1839, Selenia Jane Love, b. Jan. 15, 1821, Rutherford Co., N.C., d. Feb. 4, 1894, Whitfield Co., Ga. She moved, with her parents to Georgia at the age of 16. A Battle of the Civil War was fought on their farm near Sugar Valley, Ga. Both are buried at the Rocky Face Cem. Rocky Face, Whitfield Co., Ga. Children: 1. James M. Lowery, b. Sept. 28, 1840, (All children born Whitfield Co., Ga.) d. Oct. 30, 1861, died of typhoid fever in Army during the Civil War. 2. Bernettie Ann Lowery, b. Jan. 13, 1842, d. abt. 1896. buried Rocky Face, Ga., m. Jan. 16, 1868, John Fallin b. 1847, Upson Co., Ga. 3. Mary Adaline Lowery, b. Sept. 1, 1844, d. Aug. 1', 1847, Miss. Died as young child while parents and family were on a trip to Mississippi. Buried beside the road in Miss. 4. William A. Lowery, b. Mar. 6, 1846, m. Jennie Fritz. 5. John P. Mosley, b. April 8, 1848. 6. Erlington Lowery, b. Ga. 7. Adolphus E. Lowery, b. Aug. 1, 1850. 8. Elizabeth A. Lowery, b. Dec. 12, 1853, d. buried Rome, Ga., m. May 11, 1871, Gary B. Phillips, b. 1838, Ireland, d. Jan. 28, 1881, Dalton, Ga.

LOWERY, Jiles, b. 1841, Ga., m. Mizella ___, b. 1848, Ala. Children: 1. Martha S. Lowery, b. 1866, Ala. 2. Milly C. Lowery, b. 1868, Ala. 3. Mary C. Lowery, b. 1872, Ala. 4. Termealley F. Lowery, b. 1875, Ala. 5. Jacob A.

Lowery, b. 1877, Ala. 6. Theodosia Lowery, b. 1879, Ala.

LOWRY, A. M., b. Aug. 5, 1878, Fayette Co., Ala. - son of Frank Lowry - m. Feb. 28, 1899, Alice Cockrell, b. Aug. 27, 1877, Randolph Co., Ala. Alice came to Fayette Co. as a young girl. Mr. Lowry is a farmer. Children: 1. A. Dewey Lowry, b. Jan. 25, 1900, (All children born in Fayette Co.) 2. Infant Lowry, b. & d. Sept. 23, 1903. 3. Ruby Lowry, b. Feb. 27, 1905, m. Mr. Brasher - had son Thurman Brasher, b. Apr. 22, 1922. 4. Myrtie Lowry, b. June 13, 1907, m. June 14, 1940. 5. Howard Lowry, b. Oct 14, 1909. 6. Wilma Lowry, b. April 14, 1912. 7. Manilla Lowry, b. Sept. 10, 1915. 8. Leon Lowry, b. May 21, 1921.

LOWRY, Benjamin Franklin, b. Jan. 20, 1812, Ga., m. Mary C. Henderson, b. Oct. 22, 1815. Moved to Fayette County in 1850's and built a log house in 1856 which is still standing 103 years later. B. F. Lowry was wounded in the Battle of Chickamauga, in the Civil War. Children: 1. Frank Lowry, b. Dec. 7, 1836. 2. George Lowry. 3. Ben Lowry. 4. Bill Lowry. 5. Tom Lowry, d. 1862, killed in Civil War.

LUTTRELL, Hardy Vardiman, b. Dec. 17, 1928, Tishimingo, Co., Miss. m. Nov. 11, 1950, Carolyn Loraine Jean Deaton, b. Sept. 24, 1931, Tish. Co., Miss. - dau. of Lessie Pearl (Humber) Deaton. They were married at Tishimingo, Miss. by Rev. W. C. Hamilton. Children: 1. David Louis Luttrell, b. Sept. 17, 1953, Memphis, Tenn. 2. Susan Jean Luttrell, b. Jan. 14, 1957, Memphis, Tenn.

McCALEB, Andrew, b. Feb. 3, 1813, N.C., d. July 2, 1899, Fayette Co., Ala., m. Leah McCollum. Andrew was the son of Hughie McCaleb. Andrew owned several slaves and was called "Boss Andy" by them. He insisted that his son, John Tyler go north during the Civil War because he believed the slaves should be freed. Andrew's wife was of the McCollum family for whom the cemetery at Hubbertville is named. Andrew lived north of Hubbertville where the present Houston Haney farm is located. Children: (All born in Fayette Co.) 1. John Tyler McCaleb, b. Sept. 27, 1840, d. Aug. 13, 1918, m. Oct. 5, 1865, Elizabeth Susan McDonald, b. Fayette Co., Ala. 2. A. J. McCaleb, b. July 6, 1856, d. May 4, 1935, m. Virginia C. ___, b. Oct. 18, 1856, s. Jan. 24, 1928. 3. Bill McCaleb, b. 1859, d. 1928, m. Emma ___, b. 1861, d. 1938.

McCALEB, Andrew Jackson, b. Mar. 14, 1870, New River, Fayette Co., Ala., d. July 4, 1953, New River - son of John Tyler McCaleb - m. Mar. 15, 1893, Lula Frances Berry, b. Oct. 27, 1872, Fayette Co., Ala. A. J. McCaleb and Lula Frances Berry were married by Minister James S. Woods and the marriage license was issued by Judge Thomas Benton Morton. Children: 1. Cleburn McCaleb, b. Mar. 5, 1894, New River, Fayette Co., m. 1916, Eula Jaquess, b. June 25, 1894, Jackson, Tenn. 2. Pluma McCaleb, b. May 6, 1896, New River, d. May 17, 1897, New River. 3. Eunice Larimore McCaleb, b. Feb. 17, 1898, New River, m. Mar. 1, 1925, Snow Hamner, b. Mar. 9, 189_, Fayette Co., Ala. 4. Verna McCaleb, b. July 27, 1901, New River, m. Mar. 7 ___, Harvey Wilson, b. Jasper, Ala. 5. Thelma McCaleb, b. July 15, 1904, New River, m. June 22, 1948, Perry Wyman Caraway, b. Fayette Co., Ala. 6. Orville McCaleb, b. May 6, 1910, Bankston, Ala., m. 1930, Era Hubbert, b. July 25, 1909, Fayette Co., Ala. 7. Truman, McCaleb, b. June 8, 1913, Bankston, Ala., m. Annie Lee Fowler, b. Dec. Hubbertville, Fayette County, Ala.

McCALEB, Arch, b. Scotland, m. wife's name unknown. Arch McCaleb came from Scotland and settled in North Carolina. Children: 1. Hughie McCaleb, b. N. C., d. Fayette Co., Ala., m. Miss Holbrooks.

McCALEB, Hughie, b. North Carolina, d. Fayette County, Ala., m. Miss Holbrooks. Hughie McCaleb came from North Carolina to Tennessee, to Lauderdale Co., Ala. about 1815, then on to Fayette Co., Ala. about 1820. All the McCalebs in Fayette County are descended from him. Hughie McCaleb's wife was a kinsman of Joe H. Holbrooks, who came to Fayette Co. from Lewis County, Tenn. He was a Church of Christ preacher (See "Larimore and His Boys", Chap. XVII) and settled in the New River Community. Hughie McCaleb lived near the present Billy Perry farm near Turkey Creek. Children: 1. Jim McCaleb. 2. Andrew McCaleb, b. Feb. 3, 1813, N.C., d. July 1899, buried in McCollum Cem. - Leah McCollum, b. Fayette Co., Ala., d. buried in McCollum Cem. 3. Wm. "Bill" McCaleb, stayed in Fayette Co., Ala. 4. Alf McCaleb, stayed in Fay. Co. 5. White McCaleb, settled in Texas. 6. John McCaleb, settled in Texas. John became a Church of Christ preacher and a teacher and is the John McKaleb spoken of in "Larrimore and His Boys" Chap. IV. He and his brother White went to Texas and settled. 7. Virginia McCaleb, stayed in Fayette Co.

McCALEB, Joe Campbell, Jr., b. April 27, 1919, Fayette Co., Ala. - son of J. C., Sr. & Ruth (Ezzell) McCaleb - m. July 6, 1941, Marion Camp, b. June 7, 1921, Arab, Marshall Co., Ala. - dau. of Gus L. & Corena (Farrow) Camp. Joe and Marion were married in Fayette Co., Ala. by Houston Haney. They own and operate the McCaleb Mill End Shop, in Fayette. Children: (All born in Fay. Co., Ala.) 1. Joe Camp McCaleb, b. Jan. 29, 1943. 2. John Franklin McCaleb, b. July 22, 1948. 3. Elizabeth Ann McCaleb, b. Aug. 3, 1952. 4. Mary Dona McCaleb, b. July 12, 1956.

McCALEB, Joe Campbell, Sr., b. Aug. 28, 1891, Fayette Co., Ala., d. Dec. 30, 1944, - son of John Tyler McCaleb - m. Ruth Ezzell, b. May 30, 1898, Franklin Co., Ala. - d. Feb. 16, 1954 - dau. of Wm. G. Ezzell. Children: 1. Joe C. McCaleb, Jr., b. April 27, 1919, Fayette Co., Ala., m. Marian Camp, b. June 7, 1921, Arab, Marshall Co., Ala.

McCALEB, John Tyler, b. Sept. 27, 1840, Fayette Co., Ala., d. Aug. 13, 1918 - son of Andrew McCaleb - m. Oct. 5, 1865, 1st. - Elizabeth Susan McDonald, b. Fayette Co., Ala. John Tyler McCaleb served in the Union Army during the Civil War as the McCaleb family was Republican. Children: (1st. wife.) 1. Nadora Savannah McCaleb, b. Oct. 20, 1866, d. Mar. 18, 1890, m. Mr. Haley. 2. Sarah Hassie McCaleb, b. June 15, 1868, d. Oct. 13, 1888. m. J. Walter Reed. 3. Andrew Jackson McCaleb, b. Mar. 14, 1870, New River, Fayette Co., c. July 4, 1953, m. Mar. 15, 1893, Lula Frances Berry, b. Oct. 27, 1872, Fay. Co. 4. Leah McCaleb, b. 1875, d. 1957, age 82, m. George Enis. 5."Bill" Wm. Harrison McCaleb, b. July 7, 1872, d. Dec. 14, 1942, m. Lucy Hyde. 6. Susie McCaleb, b. 1879, d. 1930, m. O. C. Dobbs. 7. Carrie McCaleb, m. Hershell Deavours. 8. Lona McCaleb, d. June 1956, m. Bascom Lee. 9. Dora McCaleb, b. 1886, d. 1919, m. Bazil Johnson. 10. Joe C. McCaleb, b. Aug. 28, 1891, d. Dec. 30, 1944, m. Ruth Ezzell, b. May 30, 1898, d. Feb. 16, 1954.
John Tyler McCaleb second marriage - about 1895, Martha Drucilla Lee. Children: (2nd. wife.) 1. Cora McCaleb, m. Rastus D. Dobbs. Martha D. Lee b. April 26, 1860, d. Dec. 5, 1940. John Tyler McCaleb was the post master of the New River Post Office, the office being located in his home. He was

the original owner of the old water mill near Hubbertville.

McCARTHA, Clarence Linden, b. May 15, 1841, Fairfield Co., S.C., d. Sept. 29, 1920, Troy, Ala. - son of Jeremiah & Emily B. (Worthington) McCartha - m. Dec. 5, 1861, Susan Jane Farrow, b. Feb. 20, 1844, S. C., d. June 2, 1869, near Eufaula, Ala. - dau. of Wm. T. & Mary (_) Farrow of Spartanburg, S.C. Clarence Linden McCartha was a Methodist Minister and a College Professor at Troy State College, Troy, Ala. at the time of his death. He taught schools in South Carolina before coming to Alabama. Children: (1st. wife.) 1. William Emory McCartha, b. Oct. 8, 1862, S.C. 2. Sally Marion McCartha, b. Mar. 29, 1864, S. C., d. Mar. 19, 1898, N.M., buried at Troy, Ala., m. Dr. David Horatio Vaughn. 3. Mamie Warren McCartha, b. Sept. 25, 1865, S.C., d. Feb. 21, 1950, Geneva, Ala., m. Nov. 16, 1884, William Malone Newell, b. Aug. 3, 1856, Ala., d. May 19, 1932, Geneva Co., Ala. 4. Lillie Janie McCartha, b. Oct. 2, 1868, Ala., d. April 9, 1869, near Eufaula, Ala.
    Clarence Linden McCartha second marriage, July 7, 1870, Loula Louise Culver, dau. of Col. G. W. Culver. Children: (2nd. wife.) 1. Lou Ella "Dollie" McCartha, b. May 27, 1872, Ala., d. Sept. 1, 1873, Ala. 2. Clarence Linden McCartha, Jr., b. May 16, 1879, Ala., d. Feb. 21, 1950, Troy, Ala., m. June 6, 1907, Mabel McSwain. 3. Emily Chicora McCartha, b. Nov. 24, 1882, Ala., m. Major Cephas Kendall Knox.

McCARTHA, Jeremiah, b. Jan. 2, 1814, S.C. d, Nov. 18, 1885 - son of Jesse McCartha - m. 1839, Emily Britian Worthington, b. April 2, 1821, S. C., d. June 10, 1890 - dau. of Thomas & Tabitha (Summers) Worthington. He was a school teacher. Children: (All born in S.C.) 1. Clarence Linden McCartha, b. Mar. 15, 1841, Fairfield Co., S. C., d. Sept. 29, 1920, Troy, Ala., m. Dec. 5, 1861, Susan Jane Farrow, b. Feb. 20, 1844, S.C., d. June 2, 1869, near Eufaula, Ala. 2. Willie McCartha, b. 1844, d. 1845. 3. Walter McCartha, b. 1845. 4. Frank McCartah, b. 1851. 5. Mary McCartha.

McCARTHA, Jesse, b. abt. 1780, S.C.? (Scotland or Ireland?) m. Miss Mary or Barbara Boland, b. Lexington Co., S.C. - dau. of John Boland, Soldier in the American Revolution. Jesse McCartha was pure Scotch and a Lutheran. He married and buried five wives in his lifetime and died at the age of 86 years. His first wife, Miss Boland's father came from Hesse-Cassel Germany shortly before the American Revolution. Children: (by 1st. marriage.) 1. Jeremiah McCartha, b. Jan. 2, 1814, S. C., d. Nov. 18, 1885, m. 1839, Emily Britian Worthington, b. April 2, 1821, S. C., d. June 10, 1890.

McCLESKEY, Thomas Columbus, b. July 7, 1859, North Georgia, d. June 9, 1940, Marion Co., Ala., m. Jan. 8, 1882, Rhoda M. Kemp, b. Nov. 16, 1860, Cobb Co., Ga., d. May 22, 1928, Winfield, Ala. T. C. McCleskey was the oldest son of Thomas Smith and Georgia Ann (Babb) McCleskey. He married Rhoda M. Kemp in Cobb Co., Ga. Rhoda M. Kemp was the daughter of John Washington and Mary Ann (Brooks) Kemp. Her father was a Confederate Soldier. T. C. McCleskey and family moved to Fayette Co., Ala. about the year 1888. He bought a farm located on what is now a part of the Auburn Experimental Forest. After Rhoda's death, T. C. Married her sister, Ola (Kemp) Johnson on June 17, 1931, in Center, Ala. He and both of his wives are buried in the Winfield Cem., Marion Co., Ala. Ola died Feb. 13, 1946. Children: 1. Mary Lou McCleskey, b. Feb. 18, 1883, Belleville, Ark., m. Sept. 19, 1923, Oscar L. Haynes, d. Mar. 3, 1940. They had no children. She is a retired school teacher and lives in

Winfield, Ala. 2. John Clifton McCleskey, b. May 15, 1885, Belleville, Ark. He is a painter and carpenter and lives in Birmingham, Ala. 3. Annie Leota McCleskey, b. May 31, 1889, Fayette Co., Ala., m. June 30, 1914, Reuben Alfred Franks, died Nov. 11, 1947. (They had one son, Alfred Franks, Jr., b. April 9, 1915, Winfield, Ala., m. Dec. 23, 1943, Patricia Hadlock in Oklahoma and they have one son, Michael Wayne Franks, b. July 27, 1946, Okla.) Annie Leota is a retired school teacher. She taught Navajo Indians for many years and lives in Tuscon, Ariz. 4. Thomas Mace McCleskey, b. Feb. 21, 1891, Fayette Co., m. 1913, Ida Mae Smith of Washington, Ga. (They had one son, T. M. McCleskey, Jr.) Thomas Mace McCleskey married a second time Elizabeth Shumake (a classmate of Margaret Mitchell who wrote "Gone With The Wind"). Date of 2nd. marriage was Dec. 16, 1938. Thomas Mace, Sr. graduated from Southern College of Pharmacy, Atlanta, Ga. in 1913. (Dr. Desidera Arnaz, of Coral Gables, Fla., father of "Desi Arnaz" of T.V. fame was a member of T. M. McCleskey, Sr.'s graduating class.) T. M. McCleskey is past president of State Board of Pharmacy and former president of Atlanta Retail Druggist Assn. He and his wife live in Atlanta, Ga. 5. Nettie Ollie McCleskey, b. June 21, 1894, Fayette, Co., Ala., m. June 25, 1920, Joseph Earl Hooker. (For children, see Hooker.) 6. Chessie Ann McCleskey, b. Jan. 1, 1897, Fayette Co., m. July 5, 1928, Charles C. Anderson. (They have four children: Charles Kenneth Anderson, b. Oct. 25, 1930, m. June 28, 1958, Ruth Jean Moore and live in Sidney, Neb. where he is employed with International Harvester Co. Chas. served in the Air Corp in World War II; Helen Francis Anderson, b. Mar. 9, 1933, d. June 1934; Curtis M. Anderson, b. Jan. 14, 1936, m. Aug. 16, 1958, Loraine Hodges, have one child, Barney Kenneth Anderson, b. June 29, 1959 and live in Los Angeles, Calif; Dorothy Anderson, b. Oct. 30, 1937. Dorothy graduates from a School of Nursing in Spokane, Wash. in 1959, having attended on a scholarship.) 7. Esker Olen McCleskey, b. Oct. 15, 1902, Fayette Co., Ala. m. April 5, 1933, Grace Light, d. May 29, 1951. (They had two children: Gayle Light McCleskey, b. Dec. 22, 1933, m. Nov. 23, 1958, Marianna Mangum. Gayle graduated from Pharmacy College and is presently a Medic in the Armed Forces, stationed at Ft. McClellan, Ala.; Doris Kathleen McCleskey, b. Oct. 2, 1941.) Esker McCleskey married Mrs. Cleva Puckett Corley, Oct. 8, 1955 and the family resides in Atlanta, Ga.

Thomas Columbus McCleskey, father of these children was a great, great, great grand son of James McCleskey, who was born Jan. 20, 1751, in Penn. James fought in the American Revolutionary War under General George Washington. Thomas Columbus McCleskey taught school and farmed when he moved from Georgia to Alabama. He was the first farmer in Fayette Co. to sell watermelons commercially. One of his largest melons was shipped to William Jennings Bryan when he was a candidate for the presidency of the United States. In connection with his farm he purchased a store from George White and sold general merchandise. It was the only store between Winfield and Fayette at the time and following is listed some of the prices paid for merchandise and prices charged for merchandise in the store as taken from his ledger between 1892 and 1896: Prices paid for merchandise - Eggs, 10¢ per doz.; fryers, .07 to .12½¢ ea.; peas, .50¢ per Bu.; Syrup, .25¢ gal.; Corn, .50¢ per bu.; Cotton Seed, .10¢ per bu.; 4,000 shingles, $10.00; lumber, .80¢ per hundred; wool, .20¢ per lb.; butter,.10¢ lb.; chufus, .50¢ gal.; feathers, .40¢ lb. - Prices charged Customers - Coffee, .25¢ lb.; flour, $5.50 per barrel; 8 lbs. sugar, .50¢; sulphur, .05¢ lb.; plug tobacco, .06¢; kerosene, .20¢ per gal.; lawn, .07¢ per yard; calico, .05¢ per yard; coffee pot,.10¢ each.

McCLESKEY, Thomas Mace, Jr., b. Nov. 17, 1917 - son of T.M.McCleskey, Sr. - m. 1938, Vilma Ferguson. T. M. McCleskey, Jr. served as Medic in World War II. He is a graduate in Pharmacy. Children: (1st. marriage.) 1. Shirley McCleskey, b. Jan. 17, 1943.
   T. M. McCleskey, Jr. second marriage, Feb. 15, 1947, Edna Allen. Children: (2nd. marriage.) 1. Thomas Mace McCleskey, III, b. Oct. 7, 1953. 2. Mala Leigh McCleskey, b. May 1, 1958.

McCLUSKEY, Robert J., b. Sept. 18, 1868, d. Dec. 26, 1956, m. Decinie Reese, b. Jan. 24, 1873, d. Mar. 3, 1943 - dau. of T. M. & Rhoda F. (Dodson) Reese. Children: 1. Ceaborn McCluskey. 2. Eugene McCluskey. 3. Pervy McCluskey. 4. Haskel McCluskey, b. Oct. 12, 1898, d. Mar. 10, 1899. 5. Albert McCluskey (Twin), d. Infancy, 1902. 6. Elbert McCluskey (Twin), d. at 19 yrs. 7. Murphy McCluskey. 8. Murry McCluskey, b. Mar. 27, 1900, Fayette Co., m. Madie Shirley, b. Vicksburg, Miss. 9. Lillian McCluskey. 10. Carl McCluskey. 11. Clyde McCluskey. 12. Era McCluskey. 13. Robert McCluskey.

McCLURE, Ben F., b. June 7, 1839, Mt. Vernon, Ala., d. Nov. 11, 1911, Fay. Co., Ala., - son of John & Ellen McClure - m. Mar. 5, 1861, Josephine Miles, b. June 14, 1839, Mt. Vernon, Ala., d. July 26, 1863, Fayette Co. - dau. of Wiley & Elizabeth Miles. They were married at home by Rev. Wiley Miles. Ben was a farmer. Children: 1. Melissa McClure, b. Dec. 14, 1861, Mt. Vernon, d. April 28, 1943, Fayette Co., m. Jan. 2, 1879, Jesse T. Apling, b. Aug. 2, 1858, New Lexington, Ala., d. Dec. 31, 1939, Fayette Co., Ala.

McCONNELL, Daniel O'Connell, b. Dec. 23, 1856, Fayette Co., Ala., d. April 26, 1936, Fayette Co., Ala. - son of Thomas Posey & Martha (Murray) McConnell - m. Jan. 15, 1878, Alice Elizabeth Smith, b. Nov. 8, 1858, Fayette Co., Ala., d. June 22, 1947, Fayette Co., Ala. - dau. of Richard & Lilly (Abernathy) Smith. Children: (All born Fayette Co., Ala.) 1. Mary E. McConnell, b. Dec. 2, 1878, d. May 29, 1922, m. Jim R. Henry. 2. Thomas Oscar McConnell, b. June 20, 1881, d. June 29, 1955, Fayette Co., m. April 15, 1903, Villa Matthews, b. Nov. 20, 1883, d. Oct. 17, 1957, Fayette Co. 3. Richard Posey McConnell, b. June 20, 1881, m. Verrie Welch, b. 1886, d. 1957. 4. Joseph McConnell, b. July 4, 1885, m. Virgie Roberts, b. 1888, d. 1938. 5. Lillie McConnell, b. July 4, 1885, m. Jan. 14, 1912, R. Toxie Brock, b. Apr. 13, 1884. 6. Earline McConnell, b. Mar. 10, 1891, m. June 12, 1916, Mercer Matthews, b. April 6, 1889, d. Feb. 21, 1929. 7. Maude McConnell, b. Oct. 22, 1887, m. Samuel Erastus Jones. 8. William Murray McConnell, b. July 13, 1894, d. June 9, 1939, m. 1917, Pauline Jones. 9. Alice Lucretia "Brownie" McConnell, b. Jan. 9, 1899, m. Simon Tankersley Wright, Sr., b. June 29, 1874, d. July 11, 1952.

McCONNELL, John W., b. 1786, S. C., d. 1867, Tusca. Co., Ala., m. Mary ___, b. 1791, Ga., d. 1860, Tusca. Co., Ala. Certificate No. 4745 dated Aug. 9, 1825, shows grant from United States of America to John W. McConnell. Land now a part of the City of Fayette. Both are buried in the McGee Cemetery, Tusca. Co., Ala. Children: 1. Thomas Posey McConnell, b. 1815, d. 1903. 2. Joseph A. McConnell, b. 1825, d. 1858. 3. John W. McConnell, b. 1828. 4. Genubath James McConnell, b. 1830, d. 1835. 5. Mary Fletcher McConnell, b. 1824, d. 1862.

McCONNELL, Joseph, b. July 4, 1885, Fayette Co., Ala. - son of D. O. & Alice

(Smith) McConnell - m. Virgie Roberts, b. 1888, d. 1938. Children: I. Evelyn McConnell, b. 1914, Fayette Co., Ala., m. 1935, Roy D. Couch. 2. O'-Connell McConnell, b. 1906, Fayette Co., Ala., m. Marie Perry (Children: Barbara and Billie Zoe McConnell.) 3. Joe Edd McConnell, b. 1913, Fay. Co. m. Georgia May. 4. George Robert "Bob" McConnell, b. Mar. 25, 1917, Fayette Co., m. 1952, Mildred Butler. (Children: George Robert, Jr., b. 1955, and Rebecca Jane, b. 1958, Fayette.)

McCONNELL. Richard Posey, b. June 20, 1881, Fayette Co. - son of D. O. McConnell, m. Verrie Welch, b. 1886, d. 1957. Children: I. Rayburn McConnell, m. Elizabeth Milam. (Children: Rayburn, Jr. and Sally McConnell.)

McCONNELL, Thomas Oscar, b. June 20, 1881, d. June 29, 1955, Fayette Co., Ala. - son of D. O. McConnell - m. Villa Matthews, b. Nov. 20, 1883, Fayette Co., d. Oct. 17, 1957 - dau. of Jerome Matthews. Children: I. Thomas Posey McConnell, b. June 18, 1904, Fayette Co. (All born Fay. Co.) d. Sept. 18, 1940, m. 1928, Ina Mae Killingsworth, b. Nov. 20, 1903. 2. Sally Elizabeth McConnell, b. May 5, 1914, m. Nov. 1933, Joe Murphy Roberts, b. April 14, 1910. 3. Lula Annette McConnell, b. Mar. 21, 1917, m. Jan. 21, 1933, William Bruce Musgrove, Jr., b. April 3, 1912. 4. Hazel McConnell, b. Mar. 7, 1926, m. Dec. 26, 1946, Raymond Chester Waldrop, b. Sept. 7, 1919, d. Oct. 23, 1956, m. 2nd. Dec. 1959, Charles Walker.

McCONNELL, Thomas Posey, b. Mar. 31, 1815, Tusca. Co., Ala., d. May 7, 1903, Fayette Co., Ala. - son of John W. & Mary McConnell - m. Dec. 14, 1841, Martha Ann Murray, b. June 22, 1824, Fayette Co., d. June 1, 1890, Fayette Co., dau. of James & Polly (Ivy? Wood) Murray. They were plantation owners. Both are buried in the McConnell Family Cemetery, Fayette Co., Ala. Children: I. Daniel O'Connell McConnell, b. Dec. 23, 1856, d. April 25, 1936, Fay. Co., m. Jan. 15, 1876, Alice Elizabeth Smith, b. Nov. 8, 1858, d. June 1947, Fayette. 2. Malinda K. McConnell, b. Aug. 6, 1859, d. Jan. 1930, Fayette, m. Joseph Randall Robertson. 3. J. W. Robertson, (Children: James & Blanche Robertson). 4. Joshua Murray McConnell. 5. Felix Grundy McConnell, b. Mar. 29, 1867, d. April 21, 1937, m. Lula Jones, b. May 13, 1869, d. Sept. 22, 1953. (Children: Thomas McConnell, m. Mabelle Naugher.) 6. Joe McConnell. 7. Sallie McConnell. 8. Lucretia McConnell. 9. Mary McConnell.

McCONNELL, Thomas Posey, b. June 18, 1904, Fayette Co., d. Sept. 18, 1940, Fayette, Ala. - son of Thos. O. & Villa (Matthews) McConnell - m. 1928, Ina Mae Killingsworth, b. Nov. 20, 1903. Children: I. James Larry McConnell, m. Aug. 25, 1952, Jimmie Nell Dunagan.

McCOOL, Benjamin Allen, b. Oct. 10, 1810, Montgomery Co., Ala., d. Sept. 23, 1893, Attala Co., Miss. - son of Thos.? & Sarah (Gentry) McCool - m. Jan. 8, 1829, Jane Tatum, b. 1811, Montgomery Co., Ala., d. 1894, Attala Co., Miss. Came to Fayette County, Ala. in the 1830's. Children: I. Lafayette McCool, b. Nov. 20, 1829, Montgomery Co., Ala., d. June 1862, in Tusca. Co., in C.S.A. m. 1850, Elender Elizabeth Gray, b. abt. 1832, Montgomery Co., Ala., d. Oct. 1869, Fayette Co. 2. Sarah Elizabeth McCool, b. July 30, 1832, d. Sept. 3, 1891, m. Tom Ward. 3. Mary Jane McCool, b. May 3, 1835, d. July 15, 1889, m. John Ward. 4. Thomas P. McCool, b. June 22, 1837, Fayette Co., d. killed in war., m. Catherine __. 5. Alecy Ann McCool, b. Oct. 22, 1840, Fayette Co. 6. James H. McCool, b. June 30, 1842, Fayette Co. 7. Martha S. McCool, b. June 15, 1844, Fayette Co., d. Oct. 13, 1911, m. Wm. Joseph Ward. 8. George Cassel McCool, b. Sept. 17, 1846, Fayette Co., d. Oct. 13, 1941, Attala Co., Miss., m. M. E. "Bessie" Ward. 9. Malissa Elender McCool, b. April 16, 1850, Fayette Co., d. Dec. 7, 1878, Calhoun Co., Miss., m. Marion Ward. 10. Andrew Jackson McCool, b. April 11, 1852, Fayette Co., d. Jan. 21, 1884, Calhoun Co. Miss. 11. Benjamin Newton "Curly Newt" McCool, b. Oct. 6, 1854, Pickens Co., Ala., d. Oct. 22, 1911, Attala Co., Miss., m. Nannie Catherine White.

McCOOL, James Allen, b. June 17, 1912, Fayette Co., - son of Thos. A. McCool - m. 1942, Rosalie Tutwiler. Children: 1. Rosalie Tutwiler McCool, b. July 4, 1943. 2. James Allen McCool, Jr., b. Nov. 1, 1949.

McCOOL, James Russell, b. Jan. 1, 1857, Tusca. Co., Ala., d. July 22, 1915, Moore's Bridge, Ala. - son of Thomas Benton & Elizabeth Jane McCool - m. Mary Elizabeth Cowart, b. Feb. 22, 1857, Pickens Co., Ala., d. Mar. 27, 1942, Fay. Co., Ala. Children: 1. Thomas Allen McCool, b. May 31, 1883, Tusca. Co., m. June 21, 1906, Motie Frances Dickinson, b. Jan. 26, 1885, Fayette Co., Ala. 2. Leona Bell McCool, b. June 14, 1885, Moore's Bridge, Ala., m. 1st. - Mose Sudduth, 2nd. - Earle Vinn. 3. Ona O. McCool, b. Aug. 5, 1887, Moore's Bridge, Ala., d. abt. 1948, Northport, Ala., m. Curtis Rambsey. 4. Ethel Lou McCool, b. Mar. 6, 1889, Moore's Bridge, m. Victor Connell. 5. Dollie Dorcus McCool, b. Nov. 23, 1891, Moore's Bridge, d. abt. 1920, m. Ranon Brazeal. 6. James Early McCool, b. Mar. 20, 1893, Moore's Bridge, m. Maggie Sudduth. 7. Mattie Lee McCool, b. May 25, 1896, Moore's Bridge, m. Grover C. Sudduth. 8. Dessie Lee McCool, b. Dec. 26, 1899, Moore's Bridge, m. 1st. - Charles Guin, 2nd. - R. Hackett.

McCOOL, John, b. abt. 1815, Montgomery Co., Ala., d. 1888, Attala Co., Miss. son of Thomas? & Sarah (Gentry) McCool - m. 1st. - Elizabeth Ray, 2nd. - Martha __. Children: 1. Sarah McCool, b. 1836. 2. Rufus McCool, b. 1837. 3. Gastern McCool. 4. Harvey McCool, b. 1841. 5. Catherine McCool, b. 1842, m. Mr. Lucas. 6. Guincy McCool, b. 1846. 7. Berry Alexander McCool, b. 1847, d. 1928, m. 1st. - Rosella Burney, 2nd. - Missouri C.__, 3rd. - Widow Shumaker. 8. Chesley McCool. b. 1849. 9. Tabitha Ann (or Talitha) McCool, b. 1851. 10. Jasper McCool, b. 1856, m. Anna __. 11. John McCool, b. 1864, m. Florence White, (descendants now in Texas.) 12. William McCool, m. Una Reynolds. 13. George McCool, m. Miss Davis (moved to Texas). 14. Mattie Jane McCool, m. Lonnie Oliver.

McCOOL, Lafayette, b. Nov. 20, 1829, Montgomery, Co., Ala., d. 1862, Tusca. Ala. in C.S.A., m. 1850, Elender Elizabeth Gray, b. abt. 1832, Montgomery Co., Ala., d. Oct. 1869, Fayette Co., Ala. Children: (All born in Fayette Co.) 1. Henry McCool, b. 1851, d. Infancy. 2. Wm. Benjamin Columbus Draper McCool, b. Jan. 1851, d. 1896, Attala Co., Miss. m. Rena Tims. 3. James Franklin McCool, b. Feb. 24, 1853, d. Mar. 2, 1919, Kosciusko, Miss., m. Jan. 20, 1881, Mary Niles. 4. Richard Miles McCool, b. 1856, d. Feb. 11, Madison Co., Ala. m. Malvina Cauthen. 5. George W. McCool, b. 1859, d. 1940, Attala Co., Miss. m. Nov. 10,1878., Georgianna Ray. (Had 12 Children.)

McCOOL, Thomas ?, b. 1782, Fairfield Co., S. C., m. Sarah Gentry. Living in Montgomery Co., Ala. in 1810. Children moved to Fayette County, Ala. in 1830's Children: (All born Montgomery Co.) 1. Benjamin Allen McCool, b. Oct. 10, 1810, d. Sept. 23, 1893, Attala Co., Miss., m. Jan. 8, 1829 in Montgomery Co., Jane Tatum. b. 1811, Montgomery Co., d. 1894, Attala Co., Miss. 2. John McCool

b. 1815, d. 1888, Attala Co., Miss. m. 1st. - Elizabeth Ray, 2nd. - Martha _. 3. Thomas C. McCool, b. Aug. 15, 1820, d. Feb. 1, 1909, Winston Co., Miss., m. Renie Carroll, b. 1819, d. June 1, 1901

McCOOL, Thomas Allen, b. May 31, 1883, Tusca. Co., m. June 21, 1906, Motie Frances Dickinson. b. Jan. 26, 1885, Fayette Co. He is the son of James Russell & Elizabeth McCool. She is the dau. of J. P. & Frances (Hassell) Dickinson. Mr. McCool came to Fayette from Moore's Bridge, in Tuscaloosa Co., Ala. in the latter part of Oct. 1904. He has engaged in the mercantile business for many years. In 1927 he operated the I.G.A. Grocery Store in Fayette. In 1918, he was elected to the City Board as Councilman. He has been with the Robert Tailoring Co. since 1935 and he is a Baptist Deacon. Children: (All born in Fayette Co.,Ala.) 1. Artie Elizabeth McCool, b. April 7, 1907, m. Grady H. Hallman. 2. Mary Frances McCool, b. Dec. 23, 1909, m. Wm. Guy Walker. 3. James Allen McCool, b. June 17, 1912, m. Rosalie Tutwiler. 4. Thomasine McCool, b. Aug. 10, 1914, m. Harmon W. Hamby. 5. Nina Oleta McCool, b. June 15, 1919, m. Thomas Coy Scroggins. 6. Carol Anne McCool, b. Aug. 27, 1923.

McCOOL, Thomas Benton, b. abt. 1833 or 1834 in Ala. or S.C., d. Killed in Civil War at Battle of Chickamauga, m. May 27, 1854, Elizabeth Jane Sullivan, b. abt. 1833, Ala. or S.C., d. 1905, age 75 yrs. in Paris, Texas - dau. of Russell & Isabella Sullivan. Thomas Benton McCool shown as Thomas McCool on original Muster Roll, dated May 29, 1862, at Tuscaloosa, Ala. on file in the Ala. State Dept. of Archives and History, Montgomery, Ala. - Co. G. 41st. Ala. Inf. Regt. C.S.A. Also, Confederate Veterans Book, Court House, Tusca. Ala., shows that he transferred to Co. B. 41st. April 13, 1863. Children: 1. Rebecca Isabell McCool, b. June 27, 1855, Tusca. Co., d. 1941, Parris, Texas, m. John Brazeal. 2. James Russell McCool, b. Jan. 1, 1857, Tuscaloosa Co., Ala., d. July 22, 1915, Moore's Bridge, Ala., m. Mary Elizabeth Cowart. 3. W. Burton McCool, b. Jan. 15, 1859, Tusca. Co., m. 1st. - Mary Sanders, 2nd. - Dealy Reese. 4. John Duncan McCool, b. Sept. 15, 1860, Tusca. Co., d. Parris, Texas, m. Lula Smith. 5. Thomas Benton McCool, Jr., b. Oct. 23, 1862 Tusca. Co., d. abt. 1929, Fayette Co., m. Lela Wallace.

McCOOL, Thomas C. (Rev.) b. Aug. 15, 1820, Montgomery Co., Ala., d. Feb. 1, 1909, Winston Co., Miss. - son of Thomas? & Sarah (Gentry) McCool - m. Renie Carroll, b. 1819, d. June 1, 1901. Children: 1. Ben McCool, b. 1846, m. Susan Hughes. 2. George McCool, b. 1848, m. Julia Glover Hughes. 3. John McCool, m. Liza Kelly. 4. Newton McCool, b. Oct. 10, 1859, d. Oct. 6, 1937 m. 1st. - Nancy Hansboro, 2nd. - Lucinda Cummins. 5. Hollie McCool, m. Nannie Belk (Plyler) 6. Martha Jane McCool, m. Wm. James McGee. 7. Elizabeth McCool, m. Bill Guynes.

McCULLY, Nathan Paul, m. April 19, 1954, Lenora Sue Propst, b. Dec. 5, 1929, Fayette, Ala. - dau. of Dan F. & Alice (Putnam) Propst. Children: 1. Stephen Paul McCully, b. April 19, 1956, Fayette, Ala. 2. William Daniel McCully, b. Jan. 30, 1960.

McCRAW, Madison, d. in Civil War, m. Mary Perkins. Children: 1. Sarah Ann McCraw, b. Jan. 6, 1860, Walker Co., Ala., d. April 28, 1935, Lamar Co., Ala. m. Richard Newton Yerby, b. July 24, 1854, Lamar Co., Ala., d. June 30, 1942 Lamar Co., Ala. 2. John McCraw. 3. Jacob McCraw. 4. Malissa McCraw.

McDONALDSON, Richard, m. Lucinda Jane Hunt, b. 1843, d. 1874 - dau. of William & Elizabeth (Gray) Hunt. Children: 1. Mary Elizabeth McDonaldson, b. June 22, 1873, Autauga Co., Ala., m. Robert Dixon Durham, b. 1867, d. 1917, Birmingham, Ala.

McGAW, John William, Jr., b. Nashville, Tenn. d. Mar. 1958, Nashville, m. Dec. 2, 1948, Jean Martin Branyon, b. Oct. 30, 1923, Jasper, Ala. - dau. of Jeptha S. Branyon. They were married at Uniontown, Ala. by Rev. Judson Martin. J. W. McGaw, Jr. was a Building Contractor and died of a heart attack as a young man. Jean is a dietician at Vanderbilt Hospital in Nashville, Tenn. Children: 1. Patricia Branyon McGaw, b. 1950, Nashville, Tenn. 2. John William McGaw, III, b. Dec. 6, 1953, Nashville, Ala.

McGOUGH, Jonas C., b. May 22, 1895, Marion Co., Ala. - son of Richard L. & Susan (O'Mary) McGough - m. July 7, 1918, Willa Alberta Treadaway - dau. of Richard C. & Alice (Berry) Treadaway. J. C. McGough is a Veteran of World War I. He has also served as Probate Judge of Fayette County, Ala. from 1942 to 1952. Children; 1. Herbert Neal McGough, b. Oct. 30, 1921, m. Doris _, H. N. McGough graduated from Annapolis in 1943. He has two children. Marilyn and Mike McGough. 2. Mildred Alice McGough, b. Nov. 13, 1923, m. Aug. 1946, Malcolm Smith, b. Ohio. Mildred graduated from Auburn in 1945, and has two daughters.

McREYNOLDS, Will, b. Dec. 10, _, m. Nov. 26, 1876, Elizabeth A. Bobo, b. Oct. 26, 1859, Fayette Co., Ala., d. Feb. 1954, Columbus, Miss. - dau. of Miles & Lucy A. (Allen) Bobo. He was a blacksmith and a farmer. Children: 1. Lillie McReynolds (Twin), m. Billy Ferguson. 2. Will McReynolds, (Twin) died in infancy. 3. Jess McReynolds, m. Frankie Chatam. 4. Jim McReynolds. 5. Charley McReynolds, m. Sally Gee. 6. Dean McReynolds, m. Ellen Nolan.

MADDOX, James Hill, m. April 1947, Mary Alice Matthews, b. Sept. 19, 1926, dau. of Mercer & Earline (McConnell) Matthews. Children: 1. James Stephen Maddox. 2. William McConnell Maddox.

MADDOX, Walter William, b. Feb. 14, 1889, Tusca. Co., Ala. - son of John Wiley Maddox - m. April 6, 1911, Nancy Josephine South, b. Nov. 29, 1887, Davis Creek, Fayette Co., Ala. - dau. of Levi Woodruff South. They were married by George White at his home. Children: 1. Mary William Maddox, b. July 16, 1912, Davis Creek, Ala. (All children born at Davis Creek, Fayette Co.) m. April 24, 1937, Aaron Nelson, b. 1912, Berry, Ala. 2. Lucy Cara Maddox, b. Sept. 10, 1913, m. Nov. 24, 1933, Ellis Hope, b. Mar. 1900, La. 3. Kenneth Bruce Maddox, b. Aug. 16, 1916, m. Nov. 22, 1952, Fay Barton, b. Nov. 17, 1918, Ill. 4. Robert Leon "Bob" Maddox, b. Sept. 20, 1919, m. Winnie Callie Bobo, b. July 13, 1924. 5. Dorothy Mozelle Maddox, b. April 12, 1921, m. Nov. 14, 1942, James Cannon, b. Oct. 30, 1916, New Lexingtin, Ala. 6. James Levi Maddox, b. Sept. 9, 1924, d. Dec. 1, 1951, m. Evelyn Perry. 7. Sara Joy Maddox, b. Jan. 2, 1928, m. William Andrew Fowler.

MADDOX, William W., b. Feb. 14, 1833, S.C., d. Jan. 5, 1890, Lamar Co., Ala. son of Wiley & Miss (Pollard) Maddox - m. Mary Elizabeth Newell, b. Sept. 14, 1833, Elmore Co., Ala., d. Aug. 11, 1915, Lamar Co., Ala. - her mother a native of Ireland. Wm. W. Maddox came to Lamar Co. with his parents from his native state of South Carolina. After becoming a man he established his farm near Vernon, entering the land from the government. During the Civil War he enlisted in Co. I, 26th. Ala. Volunteer Inf. and participated in the Battle of Gettysburg and other major engagements and was wounded twice. Children: 1. James C. Maddox, d. 1920. 2. Nancy C. Maddox, d. 1910, Lamar Co., Ala., m. Samuel C. Harrison. 3. William I. Maddox, d. Feb. 1908, Lamar Co., Ala. 4. Pinkney L. Maddox. 5. Rachel E. Maddox, m. James William Collins. 6. Dr. Stephen E. Maddox. 7. Mary J. Maddox, m. William J. Jones. 8. Julia Ann Maddox, m. John T. Woods. 9. Judge John Thomas Maddox, b. May 2, 1877, Lamar Co., Ala., m. May 29, 1921, Gaila Frances Seay, dau. of Dr. Mark & Frances (Jones) Seay. 10. Bettie Maddox, m. David R. Robertson.

MADISON, George, m. Miss Pendley. Children: 1. W. T. Madison, b. Oct. 16, 1871, Walker Co., Ala. d. Sept. 2, 1949, m. Catherine Clemmons. b. Mar. 6, 1872, Tenn. 2. Susia Madison. 3. Jane Madison. 4. Cennie Madison. 5. Sally Madison. 6. George Madison. 7. John Madison. 8. Jake Madison. 9. Ben Madison. 10. Frances Madison.

MADISON, Henry Hughes, b. Feb. 27, 1905, Fayette Co., Ala. - son of Wm. Thomas & Catherine Madison - m. Aug. 23, 1925, Villa Elizabeth Nichols, b. Mar. 12, 1908, Fayette Co., Ala. - dau. of Wm. Jackson & Coleda Bell Nichols. They were married at Bankston, Fayette Co., Ala. by Mr. Jeff Whitley, J. P. H. H. Madison is a farmer. Children: 1. Nocal Elizabeth Madison, b. Jan. 14, 1927, Fayette Co., Ala., m. Nov. 5, 1945, Erbie Lee Boyd, b. Oct. 12, 1920, Lamar Co., Ala. 2. Norma Cain Madison, b. Nov. 18, 1928, Fayette Co., m. Jan. 19, 1948, Wyman Arion Nix, b. Aug. 29, 1927, Walker Co., Ala. 3. Macon Hughes Madison, b. July 3, 1931, m. Aug. 11, 1954, Ella Frances Bostic, b. June 10, 1929, Marion Co., Ala. 4. Henry Lynn Madison, b. Jan. 13, 1934, Fayette Co., m. Mar. 4, 1956, Mary Ann Fowler. 5. Nathan Eugene Madison, b. June 2, 1940. 6. Noble Elouise Madison, b. July 3, 1943.

MADISON, Vester, b. Feb. 10, 1916, Fayette, Ala. - son of W. T. & Catherine (Clemmons) Madison - m. Mar. 31, 1934, Thelma Aldridge, b. Dec. 28, 1919, Carbon Hill, Ala. - dau. of D. E. & Essis Lee (Hawkins) Aldridge. Children: 1. Marion Bradford Madison, b. July 30, 1935, Fayette, Ala., d. Oct. 15, 1935. 2. Calvin Madison, b. April 25, 1937, Fayette, Ala. 3. Curtis Madison, b. Mar. 3, 1940, Fayette. 4. J. T. Madison, b. April 27, 1942. 5. Martha Madison, b. Dec. 30, 1943. 6. Dale Madison, b. June 24, 1952, Fayette.

MADISON, W. T., b. Oct. 16, 1871, Walker Co., Ala. d. Sept. 2, 1949, - son of George & Miss (Pendley) Madison - m. Catherine Clemmons, b. Mar. 6, 1872, Tenn. - dau. of Jim & Lou Mandie Madison. Children: 1. J. H. Madison, b. Dec. 27, 1893. 2. Mary Frances Madison, b. Aug. 2, 1895. 3. W. N. Madison, b. Nov. 3, 1896. 4. G. W. Madison, b. Jan. 7, 1898. 5. James F. Madison, b. Feb. 16, 1899. 6. Susie Madison, b. Dec. 25, 1900. 7. Fred Madison, b. Apr. 17, 1902. 8. Rilla Madison, b. Jan. 17, 1904. 9. Henry Madison, b. Feb. 27, 1905. 10. Lester Madison, b. Jan. 2, 1909. 11. Chester Madison, b. July 17, 1911. 12. Vester Madison, b. Feb. 10, 1916.

MARTIN, John Drew, m. Leora Humber, b. July 2, 1884, d. Nov. 11, 1952 - dau. of Robert Hayes Humber. Children: 1. Edith Martin, m. Mr. Crawford. 2. Cleston Martin. 3. Rubene Martin, m. Miss Coker.

MARTIN, Wm. Roy, m. Frankie Nuckols. Children: 1. John Arthur Martin, m. Pat. (One child: Frances "Fran" Martin.

MATHES, Alexander, I, b. Mar. 12, 1740, Augusta, Va., d. 1806, Washington Co. Tenn. - son of George Mathes (the immigrant from Ireland.) m. Mar. 21, 1769, Ann Leith, b. Mar. 18, 1749. Alexander Mathes, I, joined the ever moving advance of pioneers, starting about 1780 from Va. they walked through Virginia and Maryland with pack-horses. Alexander was a surveyor and civil Engineer and brought with him his surveyor's instruments. He located land on the Homine branch of the Little Limestone, in what was then the State of North Carolina, now Washington Co., Tenn. The Mathes bought 950 acres of land. There, Salem, a Presbyterian church was founded by Daok in 1780's and Martin Academy, now known as Washington College, near Jonesboro, Tenn. was also founded. Part of this land was given by Alexander Mathes. He was a farmer and a surveyor. Children: 1. Jennie Mathes, b. Jan. 1, 1770, Va. m. John Houston. 2. Miriam Mathes, b. O$_{ct}$. 28, 1771, Va., m. Thomas Alexander Telford. 3. Dr. Allen Mathes, b. Oct. 19, 1773, Va. 4. Alexander Mathes, II, b. Oct. 5, 1775, Va., d. Feb. 12, 1865, Tenn., m. Isabella Ord. 5. George Leith Mathes, b. Sept. 24, 1779, Va. 6. Grace Mathes, b. Jan. 19, 1782, Va. 7. Jeremiah Mathes, b. Jan. 29, 1784, Tenn.

MATHES, Alexander, II, b. Oct. 5, 1775, Shenandoah, Va., d. 1806, Tenn. - son of Alexander, I and Ann (Leith) Mathes - m. July 16, 1799, Isabella Ord, b. April 6, 1776, d. Nov. 23, 1839, dau. of Robert & Ann (Leith) Mathes (Both from Ireland.) Alexander Mathes, II, went to Washington Co., Tenn (then N. C.) with his father, in Oct. 1782; was on the road when Cornwallis surrendered his army in Virginia. He was a farmer and brick mason; was a strict Presbyterian; was a very large man, weighing nearly 300 pounds. He is buried in the churchyard at the Old Salem Church. Children: 1. Alexander Mathes, III, b. Aug. 28, 1800, (All children born Washington Co., Tenn.) d. Feb. 14, 1884. 2. Allen Harvey Mathes, b. Jan. 18, 1802, d. Jan. 27, 1859. 3. Ann Leith Mathes, b. Dec. 23, 1804, d. Nov. 1843. 4. Lucinda Doak Mathes, b. Mar. 15, 1806, d. Feb. 13, 1875. 5. Jane Roe Mathes, b. June 12, 1808, d. Aug. 1, 1867 Texas. 6. Rachel Mathes, b. April 10, 1811, d. Oct. 9, 1856, Mo. 7. Ebenezer Smith Mathes, b. Oct. 3, 1813, d. Oct. 8, 1883. 8. Margaret Mathes, b. July 2, 1816, d. in youth.

Alexander Mathes, II, married second - Isabella McChesney, third - Mary Brannon.

MATHES, Ebenezer Smith, b. Oct. 3, 1813, Washington Co., Tenn., d. Oct. 8, 1883, - son of Alexander, II & Isabella (Ord) Mathes - m. Jan. 10, 1838, 1st. Euphrasis Adelaide McKee, b. 1814, d. Jan. 4, 1857. He was a farmer and a mill owner. Children: (1st. wife - all born Tenn.) 1. Seraphine Mathes, d. at age of 3 yrs. 2. John Woodville Mathes, b. Apr. 1884, d. June 23, 1884, Tenn. 3. McFarland Melancthan Mathes, b. Apr. 29, 1850, d. Nov. 13, 1897. 4. Alexander Perry Mathes, b. May 12, 1854, d. Jan. 15, 1919.

E. S. Mathes second marriage - Mary Ann Jordan, d. 1886. Children: (2nd. wife.) 1. Charles Mathes, b. May 7, 1859, d. June 10, 1859. 2. Joseph Rolla Mathes, b. 1862, d. 1883. 3. Mary Adelaide Mathes, b. 1864, d. Oct. 2, 1919. 4. Mollie Wilza Mathes, b. Apr. 14, 1866, d. June 8, 1880. 5. D. E. Mathes, b. Aug. 21, 1867, d. Aug. 26, 1868.

MATHES, (MATTHEWS), George, b. Ireland, m. wife unknown. His will dated Nov. 5, 1771, Va. George Matthews, the remote ancestor, the first of whom there is any authenic information came to America abt. 1720, in company with Samuel Doak, Sr. the latter having lived in County Antrim, North Ireland. It is believed that George Mathews lived in the same vicinity. George Mathews was among the vast throng of Scoth-Irish Presbyterians who sought relief from persecution in the New World. In the advance a guard of pioneers who subdued the forest built up the waste places. He came to Chester Co., Pa. and about 1740 immigrated to Chennondoah Valley and settled in Augusta Co., Va. Children: 1. Alexander Mathes, b. Mar. 12, 1740, Augusta, Va., d. 1806, Wash. Co., Tenn. 2. George Mathes. 3. Jeremiah Mathes. 4. Allen Mathes. 5. A Daughter who m. John Nelson. 6. And eight other sons names unknown.

MATHES, John Woodville, b. Apr. 1844, Tenn., d. June 23, 1884 - son of Ebenezer Smith & Euphrasie A. (McKee)Mathes - m. June 15, 1866, Eliza Jane Cassandra Jordan, b. Jan. 22, 1838, d. Mar. 10, 1885. John Woodville Mathes served in the United States Army in the Civil War. He lived in Greenville, Tenn. and was a lawyer and in the lumber business. Children: 1. Effie Dean Mathes b. Oct. 20, 1867, Tenn. (All children b. Tenn.) m. Daniel David Arnold. 2. Samuel Rhea Mathes, b. Mar. 25, 1870. 3. Frank Smith Mathes, b. Mar. 22, 1872, d. 1889. (Had been married 3 months when he died.) 4. Edgar Neill Mathes, b. Jan. 10, 1875. 5. Harry Woodville Mathes, b. Nov. 1, 1877, d. Sept. 6, 1911, Memphis, Tenn. 6. John Elmer Mathes, b. Aug. 2, 1879, d. Oct. 29, 1879. 7. Charles Earl Mathes, b. Aug. 2, 1879 (Twin to John Elmer.)

MATHES, Samuel Rhea, b. Mar. 23, 1870 - son of John Woodville & Eliza J. C. (Jordon) Mathes - m. Nov. 28, 1896, Kathleen Hozier. Children: 1. Rosalie Mathes, b. Nov. 19, 1898, m. Dr. Claude Clinton Cannon. 2. Hazel Marguerite Mathes, b. Jan. 7, 1902. 3. Roberta Ollie Mathes, b. Sept. 7, 1905. 4. Samuel Rhea Mathes, Jr., b. Mar. 25, 1908. 5. Eleanor Jane Mathes, b. Sept. 17, 1913.

MATTHEWS, Green, m. Artie Byrd. Children: 1. Jerome Matthews, b. Aug. 8, 1856, d. Mar. 13, 1930, m. 1st. - Sally Richards, b. June 15, 1855, d. June 24, 1894, 2nd. - Josephine Dobb. 2. Lee Matthews, m. Ella Dodson.

MATTHEWS, Herbert Weldon, b. Mar. 30, 1917 - son of Mercer & Earline (McConnell) Matthews - m. Mrs. Justine (Sawyer) Lowery. Children: 1. Daniel McConnell Matthews, b. 1958, d. 1958.

MATTHEWS, Ira Vandiver, b. 1920, m. Wynelle Mitchell - dau. of Harve Mitchell. Ira is the son of Mercer & Earline Matthews and is a Major in the U. S. Air Force. Children: 1. Margaret Mitchell Matthews. 2. Elizabeth Matthews.

MATTHEWS, Jerome, b. Aug. 8, 1856, d. Mar. 13, 1930 - son of Green & Artie Matthews - m. Sally Richards, b. June 15, 1855, d. June 24, 1894. Children: 1. Lillian Matthews, b. Jan. 26, 1880, d. April 22, 1943, m. Dec. 24, 1897, Ira Elam Sherer, b. April 6, 1876, d. Dec. 24, 1952. 2. Laurah Matthews, m. Richard Harkins. 3. Villa Matthews, b. Nov. 20, 1883, d. Oct. 17, 1957, Fay. Co., m. April 15, 1903, Thomas Oscar McConnell, b. June 20, 1881, Fayette, d. June 29, 1955. 4. Mercer Matthews, b. April 6, 1889, d. Feb. 21, 1928, m. June 12, 1916, Earline McConnell, b. Mar. 10, 1891. 5. Artie Matthews, b. Aug. 15, 1891, m. Olen Newman. 6. Samuel Matthews.

MATTHEWS, Lee - son of Green & Artie Matthews, m. Ella Dodson. Children: 1. Lester Matthews. 2. Purvy Matthews, m. Lillian Harris. 3. Sammie Matthews. 4. R. H. "Romie" Matthews. 5. Oliver Matthews. 6. Walter Matthews. 7. Lena

Matthews, m. George Duckworth. 8. Hester Matthews, m. Alfred McCaleb. 9. Dora Matthews, m. Wiley C. McCaleb, Sr.

MATTHEWS, Mercer, b. April 6, 1889, d. Feb. 21, 1928, Fayette Co. - son of Jerome & Sally (Richards) Matthews - m. June 12, 1916, Earline McConnell, b. Mar. 10, 1891, Fayette Co. - dau. of D. O. & Alice (Smith) McConnell. Children: 1. Herbert Weldon Matthews, b. Mar. 30, 1917, m. Mrs. Justine (Sawyer) Lowery. 2. Ira Vandiver Matthews, b. 1920, m. Wynelle Mitchell. 3. Martha Ann Matthews, m. James Morris Roberts. 4. Mary Alice Matthews, b. Sept. 10, 1926, m. April 1947, James Hill Maddox.

MAY, William Edward, m. July 14, 1950, Ella Katheryn Sparks, b. June 4, 1931, Fayette, Ala. - dau. of Whitt & Vera Sparks. Children: 1. Jayre Dianne May, b. Jan. 3, 1952, Harlingen, Texas.

MAY, Willis, m. Alice Dodson, - dau. of John Wm. & Cornelia Dodson. Children: 1. **Willis** May, Jr. 2. Georgia May, m. Joe Edd McConnell. 3. Mary Douglas May. 4. Merle May.

MAYFIELD, Dickson, b. May 23, 1873, d. July 1906, m. Oct. 1896, Hester Carter. They were married at Moore's Bridge in Tuscaloosa Co., Ala. Children: 1. Dixon Carter Mayfield, b. 1899. 2. Mark Hannah Mayfield, b. 1902. 3. James Mayfield, b. Mar. 2, 1904. 4. Henry Jones Mayfield, b. Mar. 21, 1906.

MAYFIELD, James Jefferson, b. Mar. 22, 1861, Moore's Bridge, Tusca. Co., Ala. d. Jan. 1, 1927, m. June 30, 1897, Susan Fitts (Martin). James Jefferson Mayfield, Jr. was the author of Alabama - Code of Laws - 1907 and 1924. Also wrote a number of legal publications that are still used. Children: 1. James Jefferson Mayfield, III. 2. Sara Martin Mayfield.

MAYFIELD, Capt. James Jefferson, Sr., b. May 1, 1834, Sipsey Turnpike, Tusca. Co., Ala. d. Mar. 24, 1901, Tusca. Co., Ala. - son of Obediah & Harriett (Mills) South Mayfield, - m. 1859, Amanda Caroline South, b. Mar. 13, 1839, Davis Creek, Fayette Co., Ala., d. Jan. 28, 1921, Bessemer, Ala. - dau. of J. R. & Elizabeth (Finch) South. They were married in Fayette Co., Ala. He was a teacher, farmer and was a Captain in the Confederate Army. He is buried at Moore's Bridge, Ala. and she is buried in the Evergreen Cemetery at Tusca. Ala. Children: (All born in Tusca. Co.) 1. James Jefferson Mayfield, Jr., b. Mar. 22, 1861, d. Jan. 1, 1927, m. June 30, 1897, Susan Fitts (Martin) 2. John O. Mayfield, b. Aug. 1863, d. Feb. 1864. 3. Lucian Martin Mayfield, b. Mar. 1865, d. July 1866. 4. Surry Foster Mayfield, M. D., b. Nov. 19, 1867, d. Nov. 14, 1958. (He practiced medicine in Tusca. Co. and was the County Health Doctor. Also farmed and operated a drug store. Died at ninety yrs. of age.) 5. Peabody Pegues Mayfield, b. Jan. 2, 1870, d. Mar. 5, 1930, Newtonville, Ala., m. Jan. 3, 1897, Willmetta Jones, b. April 27, 1877, Newtonville, Ala. 6. Dickson Mayfield, b. May 23, 1873, d. July 1906, m. Oct. 1896 Hester Carter. 7. Burwell Lewis Mayfield, b. Jan. 9, 1876, Tusca. Co., Ala. m. Dec. 16, 1903, Velma Sudduth. (Child: Burwell Lewis Mayfield, Jr. b. Aug. 22, 1905.) 8. Ada Mayfield, b. Mar. 12, 1877, d. Jan. 19, 1879. 9. Lyda Mayfield, b. Nov. 6, 1879, m. Nov. 1900, Thomas T. Huey, b. June 6, 1869, Bessemer, Ala. (Mayor of Bessemer - Studied Law after marriage.)

MAYFIELD, Obediah, b. 1798, Chester, S.C., d. 1839, Pickens Co., Ala., m. Harriett Mills, b. Feb. 1804, Ga., d. Mar. 1878, Tusca. Co., Ala. Children:

1. Capt. James Jefferson Mayfield, b. May 1, 1834, Tusca. Co., Ala., d. Mar. 24, 1901, m. 1859, Amanda Caroline South, b. Mar. 13, 1839, Fayette Co., Ala. d. June 28, 1921.

MAYFIELD, Peabody Burdette, M.D., b. Mar. 30, 1900, Newtonville, Ala. - son of P.P. & Willmetta (Jones) Mayfield - m. Aug. 20, 1937, Connie Maude Campbell, b. Mar. 28, 1905, Pyriton, Clay Co., Ala. Dr. P. B. Mayfield was a Psychiatrist at Bryces State Hospital from 1930 to 1943 and is now engaged in private practice in Tuscaloosa, Ala. Children: 1. Camella Caroline Mayfield, b. Aug. 21, 1942, Tusca., Ala.

MAYFIELD, Peabody Pegues. b. Jan. 2, 1870, Moores Bridge, Tusca. Co., Ala., d. Mar. 5, 1930, - son of Capt. J. J. & Amanda Caroline (South) Mayfield - m. Jan. 3, 1897, Willmetta Jones, b. April 27, 1877, Newtonville, Ala. - dau. of Dr. V. W. & Elizabeth (Wommack) Jones. P. P. Mayfield was a teacher and a farmer. "Miss Willie" was postmistress of the Newtonville post office from 1890 to 1906 when the post office was located in her home. Her doctor father's office still stands in the yard of her home, with many of the old relics still intact. Children: 1. Peabody Burdette Mayfield, b. Mar. 30, 1900, (All children born Newtonville.) m. Aug. 20, 1927, Connie Maude Campbell, b. Mar. 28, 1905, Pyritan, Clay Co., Ala. 2. James Wilburn Mayfield, b. July 8, 1902, m. June 15, 1938, Audra Mae Oswalt, b. July 1915, Concord, Fay. Co., Ala. (He is a teacher.) 3. Amanda Mabel Mayfield, b. Sept. 18, 1906. 4. Ruth Elizabeth Mayfield, b. Oct. 29, 1909, m. June 9, 1940, Joseph James Gibson, b. May 31, 1911, Newtonville, Ala.

MEADOWS, Joseph R., m. Rebekah Parkham. Children: 1. Mary Elizabeth Meadows, b. Mar. 9, 1838, d. Jan. 3, 1904, m. W. D. Trantham, b. April 1, 1847.

MELTON, Willis, m. Florence Hasseltine "Tiny" South, b. April 25, 1853, Ala. dau. of James Ransom South. Children: 1. Lena Melton, m. Horace Bobo. 2. Edgar Melton. 3. Clara Melton, m. Tol Ward.

MILES, Landon, b. Feb. 1, 1782, d. Oct. 10, 1858, Cross Anchor, S.C., m. Mar. 12, 1801, Sarah Martin, b. May 23, 1781, d. Oct. 27, 1848, Cross Anchor, S.C. Children: 1. James Aquilla Miles, m. Pricilla Wells. 2. Silas Miles, m. Miss Walker. 3. Daniel Miles, m. Nancy Stroud. 4. Dr. Francis Asbury Miles, m. Elizabeth Heywood. (They are buried in Greenville, S.C.) 5. Wiley M. Miles, b. May 7, 1811, Spartanburg, S.C., m. 1st. - Rebecca Bobo, 2nd. - Mary Elizabeth Floyd Yancy (widow). The name of the second wife of Landon Miles is unknown.

MILES, Thomas, m. 1780? Sarah Farrow, b. Dec. 29, 1752, Va. Children: 1. Landon Miles. b. Feb. 1, 1782, d. 1858, m. Mar. 12, 1801, Sarah Martin. 2. Isaac Miles, b. 1776, (Signed affidavit for Uncle Landon Farrow family Jan. 12, 1846 in Spartanburg Dist. S.C.) 3. Mary Miles, died young. 4. Sarah Miles, m. William Martindale. 5. Nancy Miles, m. James Rainwater. 6. Wm. H. Miles, b. 1794, m. Peggy Rally. 7. Aria Miles, m. Mr. Phillips. 8. Thomas Miles, m. Miss McPherson. 9. Silas Miles.

Sarah Farrow Miles, with her family, left Virginia and settled in Spartanburg Dist., S. C. around the year 1765. Thomas Miles was a Revolutionary War Soldier, a Capt. in Col. Roebuck's Regt. The following is an old record from Stub Intries to Indents for Revolutionary War Claims. " X Part II, S.C. 1786 - No. 3626, Issued to Thomas Miles (.5 .8½ Sterling, duty in Roebuck's

Regt. Lib X - per audited. Interest 0.13" Landon Miles held the military title of Captain and William H. Miles held the military title of Major. Thomas and Sarah Farrow Miles are buried near Cross Anchor, S. C.

MILES, Wilbur Fisk, b. Aug. 9, 1841, Spartanburg Dist. S. C., d. Mar. 6, 1912, m. 1864, Lavenia Angeline Moore, b. Dec. 5, 1841, Fayette Co., Ala., d. Sept. 14, 1909. Both are buried at Mt. Vernon Cem. in Fayette County. Children: 1. James Oliver Miles, d. in infancy. 2. Wiley Owen Miles, d. in infancy. 3. Annie Belle Miles, b. Dec. 19, 1866, d. Sept. 1958, m. George W. Hawkins. (Moved to Texas.) 4. John Frank Miles, b. June 19, 1868, d. 1958. 5. Rebecca Miles, b. July 29, 1870, d. Aug. 10, 1898, Itasca, Texas, m. R. A. Burrow. 6. Ida Jane Miles, d. in infancy. 7. Lucy Eudora Miles, b. Oct. 18, 1874, m. Alfred Cook (Died shortly after.) 2nd. William Cochran. (Lived in Calif. and died in Clinton, Okla.) 8. Musa Ida Miles (Twin) b. June 28, 1878, m. June 20, 1909, James V. Tarwater. 9. Mertie Sherman Miles, (Twin), b. June 28, 1878, d. in Rice, Texas, m. Viola Allen. 10. Olin Tierce Miles, b. May 24, 1881, d. Nov. 2, 1941, m. Ellis Weeks.

Wilbur F. Miles was a farmer. He served as Justice of the Peace for 18 years without defeat. He served as Post Master at a rural post office for 6 years. His family came to Fayette County in 1847 from Spartanburg Dist., S. C. During the Civil War he served as a Confederate soldier, enlisting on May 1, 1862 as 3rd Sergeant at Fayette, Ala. in Co. H. 41st Ala. Inf. Regt. Wounded at Chickamauga. Out with wounds - re-enlisted with Stewart's Batallion as 2nd. Sergeant, Co. F., on Mar. 1, 1864. Served to 1865 and discharged. He served under Capt. Holland M. Bell with Co. H. 41st Ala. Inf. Regt. Before the marriage of Wilbur Fisk Miles and Angeline Moore he presented her with a box of snuff as a gift. It was well received - the Moore family liked snuff. As long as there was a baby in the family, Wilbur Miles tied a diaper around his leg every night when he went to bed. If it was needed in the night he had it ready and warm. The Miles Family was very musical. It was said that Olin was too small to hold the accordian, so he laid it in the floor to play it.

MILES, Wiley M., b. May 7, 1811, Spartanburg Dist. S.C., d. Nov. 5, 1879, m. Dec. 24, 1833, Rebecca Bobo, b. Sept. 16, 1813, Spartanburg Dist., S.C., d. April 6, 1859. Wiley M. Miles was a Methodist Minister. With their six children, the Wiley Miles family came to Fayette County, Ala. prior to Feb. 18, 1847. They settled near the present Mt. Vernon Community. The Rev. Wiley M. Miles gave lands for Mt. Vernon Church Camp Grounds and Cemetery. They had four sons in the Confederate Army. Both are buried at Mt. Vernon Cemetery Fayette County, Ala. Children: 1. Melissa C. Miles, b. Oct. 4, 1834, S.C., m. Thomas Holland. 2. William L. Miles, b. Jan. 29, 1836, S.C., d. July 15, 1900, m. 1st. - Mary Foster, 2nd. - Mary Willis. (William L. Miles was a Methodist Minister and also a confederate soldier. He enlisted on May 29, 1863, at Tuscaloosa, Ala. with Co. G. 41st. Ala. Inf. Regt.) 3. James Daniel Miles, b. Oct. 1, 1837, S. C. (Only member of the family who was red-headed. He served in the Confederate Army enlisting April 14, 1862, at Fayette, Ala. He died while in service prior to July 1, 1863, at Richmond, Va.) 4. Josephine Miles, b. June 4, 1839, S. C., d. July 26, 1863, m. Benjamin F. McClure. 5. Wilbur Fisk Miles, b. Aug. 9, 1841, S.C., d. Mar. 6, 1912, m. Lavenia Angeline Moore. (Confederate record given under W.F.Miles.) 6. Landon Miles, b. Oct. 22, 1845, S.C., d. Oct. 20, 1930, m. 1st. - Elizer Cargile, b. Mar. 5, 1846, d. Jan. 6, 1905, 2nd. - Lou Rena ___. (Landon was a Confederate soldier,

1st. Corporal in Co. A. 9th Ala. Cavalry Regt. Enlisted Aug. 1863, Fayette, Ala. Captures -- Held prisoner -- Paroled south of Selma, Ala.) 7. Francis Asbury Miles, b. Feb. 18, 1847, Ala., m. Dec. 11, 1866, Eveline Ellis. (He d. June 18, 1917.) 8. Julia Ann Miles, b. July 16, 1852, Ala., d. 1897, m. Aug. 3, 1872, George Cargile. 9. Dora Miles, b. June 6, 1854, Ala., d. April 12, 1901, m. Oct. 14, 1872, Rhuebin Cargile.

Wiley M. Miles second marriage - 1862 or 1863, Mary Elizabeth Floyd Yancy (a widow.) Children: (2nd. wife.) 1. Wiley B. Miles, b. July 2, 1864, Ala. 2. Nancy Jane Miles, b. Jan. 2, 1866, d. 1948, m. William J. Smith. 3. Callie Lucinda Miles, b. May 20, 1868, d. Feb. 26, 1932, m. Oct. 20, 1887, William J. Abbott. The second wife of Rev. Wiley M. Miles, Mary Elizabeth Floyd Yancy Miles is buried at Mt. Vernon Cem., by her husband, though there is no marker to her grave.

MILLIGAN, E. Hillard, b. Mar. 1, 1927, Walker Co., Ala. - son of J. R. Milligan - m. May 10, 1947, Norma Louise Thomas, b. Sept. 21, 1930, Jasper, Ala. - dau. of Albert Crutcher Thomas. They were married in Aberdeen, Miss. Hillard Milligan was in the United States Navy from July 24, 1944 to June 5, 1946 and again from Aug. 10, 1950 to April 17, 1953. He was assigned to USS Leyte. Children: 1. Linda Cheryl Milligan, b. Mar. 26, 1952, Fayette, Ala.

MICHAEL, Isaac, b. July 4, 1862, Athens?, Ga.. d. Feb. 24, 1938, Fayette Co., Ala. - son of Benjamin Michael - m. 1887, Margaret Frances Finch, b. Dec. 3, 1866, Fayette Co., Ala., d. May 13, 1908, Fayette Co. - dau. of Masterson Finch. Children: 1. Bertha Michael, b. Oct. 1, 1887, New Chapel, Fayette Co., Ala., m. Oct. 30, 1906, Walter Dale Blackburn. 2. Isaac Nathan Michael, b. Mar. 23, 1889, Franklin Co., Ala., m. Essie White, b. Davis Creek, Ala. 3. Lorenzo Michael, b. June 4, 1891, New Chapel, Ala., m. Jan. 11, 1911, Dora Ann South, b. Jan. 19, 1890, Davis Creek, Ala. 4. Lafayette Michael, b. Sept. 28, 1895, New Chapel, Ala., m. 1st. - Ruby Odom, 2nd. - Minnie Odom. 5.Aaron Roosevelt Michael, b. May 27, 1901, New Chapel, Ala., m. Charlcie Dodson, b. Mt. Vernon, Ala. 6. Benjamin Dewey Michael, b. Dec. 27, 1907, Davis Creek, Ala., m. Ida Hubbert, b. Hubbertville, Ala.

MICHAEL, Lorenzo, b. June 4, 1891, New Chapel, Fayette Co., Ala. - son of Isaac Michael - m. Jan. 11, 1911, Dora Ann South, b. Jan. 19, 1890, Davis Creek, Ala. - dau. of Levi Woodruff South. They were married at the home of Jim Blackburns by George White. Lorenzo Michael is a farmer. Children: 1. South Michael, b. Sept. 18, 1924, Bankston, Ala., d. Sept. 18, 1924, Bankston, Ala.

MINTER, Abner Hill, b. betw. 1780 and 1790, Chatham Co., N.C., m. July 6, 1809, at Chatham Co., N.C., Charity Chapman. He was the son of Joseph & Fanny (Hill) Minter. Abner Hill Minter, moved to Jasper Co., Ga. and removed to Alabama in later years. There is some indication that he marries a second time. He came to Ga. from N.C. and moved from Jasper Co., to Upson Co., Ga. and is found in the census of 1840 (Upson) as being between 50 and 60 yrs. of age at that time. Children: 1. John Minter, b. abt. 1810, m. 1st. - Patience Chapman, 2nd. - Martha Story. 2. Chapman Minter. 3. Lydia Minter. 4. Polly Minter. 5. Charity Minter. 6. Elizabeth "Betsy" Minter, b. abt. 1822, Jasper or Upson Co., Ga., m. Feb. 2, 1836, Jackson Fallin, b. abt. 1815, Jasper or Upson Co., Ga. 7. Nancy Kirkland Minter, m. James Richard Donnon (Putnon Co., Ga.)

MINTER, John, - son of Joseph & Mary Minter - m. Elizabeth Michaux Morgan - dau. of Anthony & Olave Judith (Michaux) Morgan. John Minter operated a fishery. His Will was signed June 14, 1797 in Chatham Co., N. C. Children: 1. Phillip Minter, d. by May 1796. 2. John Minter. 3. Joseph Minter, d. Feb. 1823, m. Frances "Fanny" Hill. 4. Morgan Minter. 5. Agnes Minter. 6. Judith Morgan. 7. Elizabeth Minter, m. Mr. Burns. 8. Jane Minter, m. Mr. Riddle. (Agnes m. Mr. Evans, and Judith m. Mr. Womack.)

MINTER, Joseph, b. Chatham Co., N. C., d. Feb. 1823 - son of John & Elizabeth M. (Morgan) Minter, - m. Frances "Fanny" Hill. Joseph Minter's home was his father's home before him. Joseph owned a shad (Herring fish) factory on a river near his home. His Will was proven May 1823, in Chatham Co., N.C. Children: (Some say 11 in all.) 1. Abner Hill Minter, b. betw. 1780 & 1790, m. July 6, 1809, Charity Chapman. 2. John Minter. 3. Mary Minter. 4. Thomas Minter. 5. Fanny Minter. 6. Hannah Minter.

MINTER, Joseph, m. Mary ___. Joseph's Will was proven June 27, 1774 in Leeds Parish, Fauquier Co., Va. Children: 1. Jacob Minter. 2. John Minter, m. Elizabeth Michaux Morgan, (his will signed June 1797.) 3. Joseph Minter.

MITCHELL, Lewis Vernie, b. Nov. 1, 1926, South Haven, Mich. - son of Lewis L. & Edith (Wheeler) Mitchell, m. Aug. 1, 1947, Ila Mae Fleming, b. Sept. 26, 1927, South Haven, Mich. - dau. of Clinton L. & Frances M. (Benedict) Fleming. Editor and Publisher of "Fayette County Times" May, 1958 to Jan. 1960. Children: 1. Michele Lynn Mitchell, b. Mar. 27, 1949, South Haven, Mich. 2. Robert Lewis Mitchell, b. Sept. 20, 1951, South Haven, Mich. 3. William Clinton Mitchell, b. Oct. 19, 1955, Portland, Ind. Mr. & Mrs. Mitchell moved to Tuscaloosa, Ala. on Labor Day, 1957 and resided there until May 5, 1958, when they came to Fayette, Ala. and bought "The Fayette County Times", the county newspaper.

MITCHELL, Raymond Nelson, m. Mar. 8, 1941, Brownie Lollar, b. July 5, 1916, Lamar Co., Ala. - dau. of L. B. & Lodessa Lollar. R. N. Nelson is from Aberdeen, Maryland and their present residence is Calif. They were married at the First Methodist Church, Fayette, Ala., by Rev. W. F. Price. Mr. Nelson is affiliated with the Travelers Insurance Co. and the U. S. Fidelity & Gurantee Co. Mrs. Nelson is a school teacher. Children: 1. Raymond Nelson Mitchell, Jr., b. Nov. 17, 1943, St. Louis, Mo. 2. Sandra Mitchell, b. Nov. 8, 1946, San Francisco, Calif.

MONTGOMERY, Brady, b. Aug. 11, 1897, Tusca. Co., Ala., m. Jan. 18, 1922, Cora Addie "Mae" Patterson, b. July 6, 1897, Fayette Co., Ala. - dau. of Barney Patterson. They were married in Tuscaloosa Co., Ala. by Rev. Luke Hallman. Children: 1. Opal Mae Montgomery, b. Oct. 9, 1922, Samantha, Ala., m. May 5, 1947, Wilton Stanley Clements, b. Jan., Lexington, Ala. 2. Jean Brady Montgomery, b. Samantha, Tusca. Co., Ala., m. 1st. - David Brown, 2nd. - Vernon Bolton. 3. Betty Jo Montgomery, b. May 30, 1932, Samantha, Ala., m. Aug. 15, 1950, George W. Drummond, b. Jan. 18, 1928, Tusca. Co., Ala.

MOORE, Carson Hunter, b. July 20, 1824, or 1826, Morgan Co., Ala., d. abt. Sept. 17, 1862 - son of Wm. & Elizabeth (Patterson) Moore, m. Sarah Elizabeth Davis, b. April 26, 1828, Ala. - dau. of Mathew, II, & Jane (Lindsey) Davis. Carson Hunter Moore was killed in the Battle of South Mountain, Md.

during the Civil War. He served in the Confederate States Army. Children: 1. Violet Virginia Moore, b. Oct. 8, 1847, d. May 11, 1906, m. John W. Brock, b. Oct. 17, 1845, d. Jan. 10, 1929. 2. John O. Moore. 3. Thomas Moore. 4. Martha Moore. 5. Aurelia Moore. 6. William G. Moore. 7. Asula H. Moore.

MOORE, David, b. Mar. 28, 1835, Athens?, Ga., d. Dec. 19, 1924, Fayette Co., Ala., m. Mary E. Brown, b. Nov. 17, 1837, Athens?, Ga., d. 1925, Fayette Co., Ala. - dau. of Jesse & Miss (Powell) Brown. David Moore served during the Civil War in Co., C. 26th Ala., Inf. Children: 1. Eliza Jane Moore, b. Jan. 13 or 15, 1855. 2. Thomas Jefferson Moore, b. Dec. 9, 1856, d. Feb. 20, 1935 m. S. J. Huggins, b. July 25, 1854, d. Oct. 24, 1922. 3. Mary Anna Moore, b. Sept. 21, 1858. 4. James David Moore, b. April 4, 1860, Fayette Co., Ala., d. Jan. 30, 1932, m. Frances "Fanny" Estes, b. Jan. 23, 1866, d. Mar. 9, 1949. 5. Nancy Catherine Moore, b. Aug. 8, 1862, d. Feb. 4, 1888, m. D. Franklin Plyler. 6. Amandy Eliza Moore, b. Dec. 8, 1866. 7. Martha E. Moore b. Nov. 29, 1868, m. Lige Williams. 8. Sarah Alma Moore, b. July 19, 1870. 9. Joseoh Jackson Moore, b. Jan. 8, 1873, d. 1934, m. Gedora McDonald. 10. Nellie Frances Moore, b. Oct. 23, 1876, d. July 20, 1909. 11. George Washington Moore, b. Dec. 19, 1878, d. Jan. 9, 1935, m. Delia Wycoff, b. June 23, 1886.

MOORE, James H., b. July 18, 1824, d. Mar. 21, 1894, Fayette Co., Ala., m. Leona Estelle Hubbard, b. Oct. 18, 1829, Elyton, Ala., d. Nov. 18, 1872, Fay. Co., Ala. C.S.A. Service - Co. A. 26 Ala. Inf. - Resigned July 1862 - Became Captain of a Cavalry Co. 56 Ala. (Mounted) - Willis Brewer pp 631, 668. Children: 1. Zora I. Moore, m. L. L. "Lon" Cockren. (L. L. Cochren was of Ft. Bend Co., Richmond, Texas.

MOORE, John William, m. Nancy ? Duncan?. They came from Georgia in ox wagons to Alabama and settled just west of Belk, Ala. in 1858. Children: 1. David W. Moore b. Mar. 28, 1835, Gwinnette Co., Ga., m. Mary Elizabeth Brown, b. Nov. 17, 1837. 2. Robert Moore, m. Polly Duncan. 3. William M. "Billy" Moore m. Liza Otts. 4. Gilbert B. Moore, m. Sara Lou Payne. 5. Michael "Mike" Moore, m. ___. 6. Frank Moore. 7. Wash Moore. 8. Jack Moore. 9. Amanda "Mandy" Moore, m. Brit Belk. 10. Sarah Moore. m. Dick Dyer. 11. Sally Elizabeth Moore, m. Dave Taylor.

MOORE Louis Poe, b. Mar. 29, 1924, Montgomery, Ala., - son of J. M. & Stella (Poe) Moore - m. Jan. 29, 1949, Retta Jane Arthur, b. Aug. 20, 1922, Fayette, Ala. - dau. of G.C. & Bessie (Richards) Arthur. Louis Moore is Circuit Solicitor in Fayette County (1959). He is a lawyer and his father served as Probate Judge of Fayette Co. He was serving as Judge at the time of his death in 1942. Children: 1. Jane Arthur Moore (Twin), b. Oct. 24, 1950, Fayette, Ala. 2. Retta Arthur Moore, b. Oct. 24, 1950, Fayette, Ala. (Twin).

MOORE, William, b. Aug. 3, 1777, N. C., d. 1873 at age of 96, m. May 13, 1799 Elizabeth Patterson, b. Aug. 5, 1781, N.C., d. prior to 1860. She was the grand daughter of William & Elizabeth (Peeples) Patterson of Ireland. Wm. & Eliz. are both buried at Mt. Vernon Cem. toward what was then the Cochran farm. The markers have been misplaced. Near them are buried infants of their grand-daughters; Jane Morton, Pearl Bobo and Angeline Miles. William Moore was a farmer and for many years a hatter. William and Elizabeth (Patterson) Moore were born in N.C. but moved to Tenn. where their oldest children were born. They are thought to have moved to Madison County, Ala. in the early

1800's. In 1826 they were living in Morgan County, Ala. In 1830 they were in Fayette Co., Ala. It is believed they came into Morgan Co. with the Patterson and Kirkland families. From there the families came on to Fayette Co. (Information is from marriage records.) Children: 1. Frances P. Moore, b. 1799, Tenn. m. Frank Henry. 2. Rebecca Gullick Moore, b. May 30, 1801, Tenn. m. Jonas Whitley. 3. Polly Craig Moore, b. July 10, 1803. 4. John Patterson Moore, b. July 6, 1805, Tenn. d. Dec. 12, 1843, Fayette Co., Ala., m. Oct. 19, 1826, Morgan Co., Ala. to Elizabeth Kirkland. (There were eight children. The following were minors in 1850: Franklin, Melton, Rebecca and Thomas.) 5. Elizabeth "Betsy" McCain Moore, b. Jan. 17, 1808, Tenn., d. Dec. 24, 1836, m. Oct. 10, 1824, Morgan Co., Ala., to Goings S. Johnson. (The family Bible lists the death of Rebecca Euline Johnson - Jan. 29, 1844. She is thought to have been a child of Elizabeth and Goings S. Johnson.) 6. Harriette Holland Moore b Feb 19, 1810, Tenn , d. Oct. 3, 1816, age 6. 7. William Owen Moore, b. May 11, 1812, Tenn., d. in late 1870's in Texas., m. Sept. 12, 1833, in Fay. Co., Ala. to Mary Ann D. Kirkland. 8. Robert N. Moore, b. June 5, 1814, d. Sept. 12, 1842, (The 1840 Census lists a wife and five children.) 9. Carson Hunter Moore, b. July 20, 1824 or 1826, Morgan Co., Ala., m. 1846 in Fayette Co., Ala. Sarah Elizabeth Davis, b. April 26, 1828, Ala., d. abt. 1862. He was a Confederate Soldier serving with Co. A. 26th Ala. Inf. Regt. He was killed at South Mountain, Md. around Sept. 17, 1862. At this point in the Civil War the campaign plans of Gen. Lee were lost, due to the carelessness of one of his Generals, D. R. Hill. Two Yankee soldiers found the plans wrapped around three cigars. They were turned over to the Northern Gen. McClellan, who at that time was being severely ciritcized for moving so cautiously and slowly. His troups broke through the southern lines at So. Mtn., Md. and the drawn battle of Sharpsburg or Antietam followed. Carson Hunter was killed at this time. He left a wife and seven children who were cared for by his brother William Owens Moore. Draft laws to the effect that a man with eight or ten dependents would be exempt was ignored. Children at the time of the final settlement of the estate in 1868 were: Violet, John O., Thomas, Martha, Aurelia, William O., And Asula H. Moore.)

The above information is from the family Bible, family recollections, court records, article in American Heritage, and from the book "Cities and Camps of the Confederate States" by Fitzgerald Ross; also evidence of Gen. McClellan before Congress. Members of the Moore family were said by Harriet Josephine Moore Humber to be buried near the entrance of the Fayette City Cemetery. Many of the older markers are gone. The family Bible lists the death of Frances Marion Moore, July 19, 1828, thought to have been a child of John P. and Elizabeth Kirkland Moore.)

MOORE, William Owens, b. May 11, 1816, Tenn. (or 1812), d. date unknown (late 1870's) m. Sept. 12, 1833, Mary Ann D. Kirkland, b. 1816, Tenn. d, late 1870's William Owens Moore was a farmer and a Methodist Preacher, also he was a Civil War Soldier. At the age of 47 he enlisted with Co. B. 7th Regt. Ala. Cavalry June 20, 1863, at Greene Co., Ala. He was paroled May 17, 1865 at office of Provost Marshall, Hd. Quarters 16th Army Corps Co. I. - same Regt. Children 1. Robert Franklin Moore, b. May 12, 1835, (All children born Fayette Co.) .. abt. 1858, Lucie Thomas, dau .of Dr. Wm. Thomas. (They removed to Texas in late 1870's and died in Vise Co., Texas. He was a Confederate Soldier .. enlisted April 14, 1862, Co. H. 41st. Ala. Inf. Regt.) 2. Elizabeth Jane Moore, b. Jan. 19, 1837, d, 1921, m. Oct. 10, 1867, Dr. William A. Morton. (In late 1870's they went to Texas with other members of the family, then on to Los Angeles, Calif. where they died.) 3. John A. Moore, b. Dec. 19, 1838, d. 1860. (He was a Methodist Minister - never married.) 4. Levina Angeline Moore, b. Dec. 3, 1841, d, Sept. 14, 1909, m. 1864, Wilbur Fisk Miles. (See Miles family.) 5. Oliver Carson Moore, b. Jan. 9, 1843, d. prior to April 11, 1863. (A Confederate Soldier, died in Virginia prior to April 11, 1863, at which time death claim was filed by his father. He served with Co. 26th Ala. Regt.) 6. Narcissa Pearline Moore, b. Jan. 2, 1845, d, Jan. 7, 1929, buried at Mt. Vernon Cem., m. abt. 1867, James Bobo. (James Bobo was a Confederate Soldier. He enlisted Sept. 1, 1861. When discharged April 9, 1865, he was serving with Co. E. 56th Ala. Inf. Regt. He was wounded at Gettysburg.) 7. Rebecca M. Moore, b. Jan. 2, 1847, m. William Foster. (Moved to Texas with family in late 1870's. Thought to have died in Wise Co., Texas.) 8. William B. Moore, b. June 10, 1849, d. 1869, age 11. 9. Margarette Ann Moore, b. Jan. 16, 1852, d. 1930, in Miss., m. Jan. 9, 1871, Leander May. (Marriage ceremony performed by Rev. Wiley M. Miles.) 10. Amanda O. Moore, b. Mar. 29, 1854, d. 1938, Wise Co., Texas, m. D. Bobo - son of Spencer Bobo. (With family moved to Texas in late 1870's.) 11. Harriet Josephine Moore, b. June 14, 1856, d. Dec. 27, 1938, buried in Fayette City Cem., m. Dec. 16, 1873, Lewis Porter Humber. (Harriet Josephine Moore was named for the Empress, wife of Emperor Napoleon Bonepart of France. She was the youngest child of the William Owens Moore family. She always said that her father cared for 21 children and they lived in his home during the Civil War. Some of his own were still children. He cared for the seven of his brother, Carson Hunter Moore, who was killed in the service, perhaps some children were of his son Robert Franklin Moore and the slave children. -- On waking in the morning the first sounds Aung Jo heard were the slaves kneading dough and preparing to bake bread for breakfast. Chief among the slaves was a woman called Esther. The family Bible lists her with the family records. In the late 1870's William Owen and Mary Ann D. Kirkland Moore moved to Texas, going in covered wagons. Along with them went their son, Robert Franklin Moore, and family and their daughters and families; Dr. W. A. & Elizabeth Morton; Doc and Amanda O. Bobo; and William and Rebecca Foster. They settled in Wise Co., which is northwest of Ft. Worth.

MORGAN, Anthony, still living in 1772, m. Olave Judith Michaux. Anthony Morgan appears in the Taxables of Surry Co., N. C. in 1772, listing (2). He and Olave Judith were the parents of Elizabeth Michaux Morgan, m. John Minter, Will signed 1797.

MORTON, Thomas Benton, b. May 3, 1851, d. May 9, 1917, m. Eudocia Jane McCaleb, b. Jan. 15, 1855, d. Sept. 1, 1923. Thomas B. Morton served Fayette County as Probate Judge. Both are buried in the City Cemetery in Fayette. Children: 1. Mattie Elizabeth Morton, b. 1872, d. 1951, m. Samuel Davis Wade, b. Sept. 13, 1861, d. Nov. 4, 1915. 2. Wilma Morton, b. 1872, Fayette, d. 1925, buried Fayette Cem., m. Edward Penn Goodwin, b. 1869, Fayette, Ala. d. 1934, buried Fayette Cem. - son of Thos. E. & Lucinda Jane (Lindsey) Goodwin. 3. Mary Idelia Morton, b. Mar. 9, 1877, d. Dec. 18, 1941, buried Fay. Cem., m. Francis Marion Jeffries, b. Mar. 25, 1876, d. June 18, 1939, Fayette. 4. Laura Morton, m. Christopher Columbus Word. 5. Elsie Morton m. Harry Adam. 6. Ruby Morton, m. Thomas Collins. 7. John Morton, m. Minnie ___. 8. Alfred Morton, m. Mary Posey. 9. Ned Morton, m. Ruth ___. 10. Claude Morton, m. Emily McCoy. 11. Thomas Benton Morton, Jr., b. 1893, d. 1933, Buried at Fayette City Cem.

MOSLEY, James Burean, b. Dec. 13, 1919, Fayette Co., - son of R. L. & Delia J. (Waldrop) Mosley - m. June 10, 1951, Celia Katherine Pyron, b. Nov. 28, 1924. Children: 1. Malinda Jane Mosley, b. Jan. 7, 1953, Fayette Co. 2. James Allen Mosley, b. Feb. 28, 1954, Fayette Co. 3. Roxanne Mosley, b. Jan. 18, 1960, Birmingham, Ala.

MOSLEY, Reuben Leon, b. Oct. 15, 1884, Fayette Co., m. Sept. 5, 1915, Delia Jane Waldrop, b. Aug. 10, 1894, Lamar Co., Ala. - dau. of Starling V. & Roxanne (Godfrey) Waldrop. Children: 1. Reuben Leon Mosley, b. Mar. 23, 1917, Fayette Co., m. Sept. 15, 1940, Willie Frank Boone, b. Nov. 23, 1918, Berry, Ala. 2. James Buren Mosley, b. Dec. 13, 1919, Fayette Co., m. June 10, 1951, Celia Katherine Pyron, b. Nov. 28, 1924.

MOSLEY, Reuben Leon, Jr., b. Mar. 23, 1917, Fayette, Co., - son of R. L. & Delia J. (Waldrop) Mosley, m. Sept. 15, 1940, Willia Frank Boone, b. Nov. 23, 1918, Berry, Ala. Children: 1. James Wyatt Mosley, b. July 2, 1941, Fayette County, Ala.

MOSS, James, b. Va., d. Spartanburg, S.C., m. Emily Harrison, b. Va. - dau. of Col. Samuel Harrison. Children: 1. Nancy Moss, b. Aug. 12, 1806, Spartanburg, S.C., m. 1823, Garland Foster, b. April 4, 1798, Spartanburg, S.C., d. May 24, 1858, Spartanburg. 2. Richard Moss, m. Aseneth Wood. 3. James Moss, m. Lucy -. 4. Oliver Moss, m. Mary Snoddy. 5. Fannie Moss, m. Spartan Goodlett. 6. Harriett Moss, m. Frank Montgomery. 7. Caroline Moss, m. John Dobbins. 8. Juliett Moss, m. Frank Montgomery. 9. John Ephriam Moss. 10. Sarah Moss.

MURRAY, James, b. Feb. 7, 1775, or 1795, d. June 26, 1825, Fayette Co., Ala. m. June 26, 1817, Polly Ivy, b. Mar. 17, 1800, d. April 12, 1877. Children: 1. Martha Ann Murray, b. June 22, 1824, d. June 1, 1890, m. Thomas Posey McConnell.

MUSGROVE, Babe, m. Exa Bagwell, - Babe is son of John W. Musgrove. Children: 1. Cecil Musgrove. 2. Purnie Musgrove. 3. Musa Musgrove. 4. Bill Musgrove. 5. Belton Musgrove. 6. Lucille Musgrove.

MUSGROVE, Clarence, b. April 21, 1911, Fayette Co., - son of Fant & Ida (Dickinson) Musgrove - m. Mar. 13, 1935, Mary Wilkes, b. April 26, 1917, Fayette Co. - dau. of Chas. & Birdie (White) Wilkes. Children: 1. William Clarence "Bill" Musgrove, b. Oct. 2, 1936, Fayette Co., Ala., m. Aug. 12, 1956, Amelia Brown, b. Fayette, Ala. 2. Bob Musgrove, b. Fayette Co., Ala.

MUSGROVE, Claude, b. Fayette Co., m. Florence Dickinson, b. July 25, 1896, Fayette Co. - dau. of J. F. & M. E. (Dickinson) Dickinson. Children: 1. Fred Musgrove, b. April 25, 1917, Fayette Co., d. Aug. 13, 1937.

MUSGROVE, David, b. 1861, d. 1942 - son of William Musgrove, m. 1885, Drucilla Jones, b. 1868, d. 1919, dau. of H. Russell Jones. Children: 1. Clyde Musgrove. 2. Jim Musgrove, m. Vista Gibson. 3. Claude Musgrove, m. Florence Dickinson, b. July 25, 1896, Fayette Co. 4. Infant Daughter, b. Oct. 15, 1900, d. Oct. 19, 1900. 5. Villa Musgrove.

MUSGROVE, Fant S., b. Jan. 4, 1870, Fayette Co., d. Aug. 22, 1953, Fayette ,

m. Jan. 7, 1906, Ida Ann Dickinson, b. Dec. 15, 1885, Fayette Co., d. May 29, 1941, Fayette, Ala. - dau. of J.F. & M.E. Dickinson. Children: 1. Clarence Musgrove, b. April 21, 1911, Fayette Co., m. Mar. 13, 1935, Mary Wilkes, b. April 26, 1917, Fayette Co. 2. Mildred Musgrove, b. July 2, 1917, Fayette Co., m. Sept. 26, 1940, Hugh H. Corbett. b, Fayette Co., Ala.

MUSGROVE, Jim, - son of David Musgrove, m. Vista Gibson. Children: 1. Annie Lou Musgrove, m. Doyce Garner. (Children: Carolyn and Hoyt Garner.) 2. "Rob" Robert Musgrove, m. Lillian Harkins. (Son: born 1959)

MUSGROVE, John William, b. 1833, d. 1902, - son of W_m. & Betty Musgrove, m. Ann Elizabeth McCollum, b. 1835, d. 1899. Children: 1. Babe Musgrove, m. Exa Bagwell. 2. Walter Bruce Musgrove, b. Jan. 3, 1873, d. July 3, 1944, m. Sept. 9, 1908, Florence Dodson. 3. Lucius Roscoe Musgrove, b. Oct. 28, 1878, m. Annette Corbett, b. July 24, 1888.

MUSGROVE, John William, b. April 3, 1864, d. Feb. 19, 1917, m. Margaret Rebecca __. Children: 1. Walter Mucgrove, m. Ela __. (Child: Frances Rebecca Musgrove.) 2. Autie Musgrove, m. E. C. Goodson. 3. William Brackinridge Musgrove, b. 1904, d. 1949, m. Blanche Mitchell.

MUSGROVE, Lucious Roscoe, b. Oct. 28, 1878, - son of John Wm. Musgrove - m. Annette Corbett, b. July 24, 1888. Children: 1. William Banks Musgrove, b. Aug. 5, 1909, m. Gladys Thomas. (Children: Hugh L. Musgrove, b. Sept. 9, 1930, m. Margaret Bellows; and Joe Bailey Musgrove, and William Richard Musgrove.) 2. Robert Lee Musgrove, b. June 6, 1914, m. Vera Marie McGhee. (Children: Betty Jo and Johnny Lee Musgrove.) 3. Irene Musgrove, m. Richard Roden Adams. 4. Austella Musgrove, m. John David McDonald.

MUSGROVE, Walter Bruce, Jr., b. April 3, 1912, Fayette Co., - son of W.B. & Florence (Dodson) Musgrove - m. Jan. 21, 1933, Lula Annette McConnell, b. Mar. 21, 1917, Fayette Co. - dau. of Thos. O. & Villa (Mathews) McConnell. Children: 1. Ina Loudelle Musgrove, b. Aug. 10, 1936, m. Johnny Clive Williams, b. April 20, 1933. 2. Lauranne Musgrove, b. Dec. 24, 1937, m. Billy O. Watkins, b. Fayette Co., Ala.

MUSGROVE, Walter Bruce, b. Jan. 3, 1873, d. July 3, 1944, - son of John Wm. Musgrove, m. Sept. 9, 1908, Florence Dodson. Children: 1. Walter Bruce Musgrove, Jr., b. April 3, 1912, Fayette Co., m. Jan. 21, 1933, Lula Annette McConnell, b. Fayette Co., Ala.

MUSGROVE, William "Billy", m. Betty Thompson. Children: 1. Sarah Musgrove, m. Mr. Anthony. 2. John William Musgrove, b. 1833, d. 1902, m. Ann Elizabeth McCollum, b. 1835, d. 1899. 3. Felix Musgrove, m. Vivian Corbett. (Children: Lowery and Felix Musgrove, Jr.) 4. David Musgrove. b. 1861, d. 1942, m. Drucilla Jones, b. 1868, d. 1919. 5. Sally Musgrove, b. 1847, d. 1950 6. Fant Musgrove, b. 1870, d. Aug. 22, 1952, m. Ida Dickinson. 7. John William Musgrove, m. Margaret Rebecca __.

NALLS, Martin, b. July 11, 1796, d. Nov. 1, 1824, m. name unknown. Children: 1. Mariah Nalls, b. Nov. 1, 1824, d. Nov. 22, 1900, m. Jacob Shepherd, b. Nov. 5, 1812, d. Mar. 26, 1877.

NALLS, Nathan, m. Elizabeth Clarke. Nathan Nalls came from N. C. with one slave and settled in the southern part of Fayette County, then Tuscaloosa Co. in 1818. Children: 1. Jim Nalls. 2. Bradley Nalls. 3. Marie Nalls. 4. Wiley Nalls. 5. Franklin Nalls. 6. Elizabeth Nalls. 7. Czarina Nalls, b. July 4, 1847, m. Nov. 7, 1866, George W. Gravlee, b. April 30, 1844. 8. Silas Nalls, m. Emily Richards. 9. Maria Nalls, m. Mat Loftis. 10. Sara Nalls, m. Jim Wilson. 11. Malissa Nalls, m. Elias Wilson.

NELSON, Andrew, b. 1762, York Co., Pa., d. Nov. 1, 1850, Winston Co., Ala., m. wife unknown. Andrew Nelson moved to Virginia and while residing in Augusta, Va. volunteered on June 15, 1779 and served as a Pvt. in Capt. John Cunningham's Co. of the Va. Troops until Sept. 15, 1779. On May 11, 1780, he again enlisted with the Virginia Troops and served in Capt. John McKitterick's Co. He was out against the Indians in northwestern Virginia until Aug. 15, 1780. From Dec. 15, 1780 until May 1, 1781 he served in Capt. Jas. Tate's Co. under Col. Campbell. He marched to North Carolina and was in the Battle of Guilford. In 1832, Andrew Nelson was residing in Morgan Co., Ala. In 1840 he was living in Walker Co., Ala. He died on Nov. 1, 1850 while living with his son-in-law, George Ellis near Houston, Winston, Co., Ala. and is buried in Winston Co. in a small graveyard on the east side of Sipsey River, between Double Springs and Addison. Children: 1. Peggy Nelson, m. George Ellis, lived in Winston Co., Ala., later moved to Lawerence Co., Ala. 2. L. S. Nelson, b. Dec. 15, 1797, d. Nov. 2, 1874, m. wife unknown. He is buried in Fike's Graveyard, Walker Co., Ala.?

NELSON, John N., b. June 22, 1818, Morgan Co., Ala., d. May 20, 1896 - son of L. S. Nelson - m. Catherine _, b. Dec. 24, 1827, d. Nov. 11, 1891. John N. Nelson was a Capt. in the Civil War. Children: 1. Sarah Jane Nelson, b. July 1, 1854, d. Mar. 27, 1945, Walker Co., Ala., m. Reuben Monroe Swindle, b. Jan. 12, 1849, d. Feb. 15, 1900, Walker Co., Ala. 2. Lilley Nelson, m. Commodore Woods. 3. Berthina Nelson, m. Jim Odom. 4. Lindy Nelson, m. Ben Fike. 5. Sam Nelson, m. Mary Rutledge.

NELSON, L. S., b. Dec. 15, 1797, d. Nov. 2, 1874 - son of Andrew Nelson - m. wife unknown. L. S. Nelson came to Walker Co., Ala. in 1830's. Children: 1. John N. Nelson, b. Jan. 22, 1818, Morgan Co., Ala., d. May 20, 1926, Walker Co., Ala., m. Catherine __, b. Dec. 24, 1827, d. Nov. 11, 1891. 2. Andrew Jackson Nelson, b. Aug. 3, 1820, Morgan Co., Ala., d. April 6, 1915, Buried at Fikes' Graveyard, Walker Co., Ala., m. Sarah __, b. Feb. 15, 1826, d. Mar. 23, 1900.

NEWBY, James M., b. Mar. 28, 1831, Va., d. April 2, 1908, - son of Mathew Newby - m. Sally A. Barksdale, b. Jan. 12, 1835, d. April 18, 1910. James M. Newby was a Clerk and Justice of the Peace. Children: 1. Luke Pryor Newby, b. Mar. 14, 1853, Limestone Co., Ala., d. Dec. 13, 1936, m. Mary Eliza Johnston, b. Aug. 18, 1860, d. Nov. 21, 1933. 2. Oscar B. Newby, b. Dec. 20, 1855, Limestone Co., Ala., d. July 25, 1928, Athens, Ala., m. Anna Thomas, b. Feb. 27, 1862, d. Oct. 31, 1944, Athens, Ala. 3. Worley M. Newby, b. Nov. 29, 1856, Limestone Co., Ala., d. Dec. 1, 1942, Athens, Ala., m. Mollie Allison, b. Mar. 26, 1870, d. Aug. 28, 1949, Athens, Ala.

NEWBY, Luke Pryor, b. Mar. 14, 1853, Limestone Co., Ala., d. Dec. 13, 1936 - son of James M. Newby - m. Mary Eliza Johnston, b. Aug. 18, 1860, Limestone

Co., Ala., d. Nov. 21, 1933, - dau. of Lem Johnston. Both are buried in the Johnston Family Cemetery. L. P. Newby was a farmer. Children: l. Katie Pearl Newby, b. Nov. 30, 1883, Limestone Co., Ala., m. Jan. 6, 1901, Oscar LaFayette Thomas, b. Aug. 16, 1874, Limestone Co., d. June 7, 1936. 2. Rowe Newby, b. Nov. 18, 1888, Limestone Co., d. July 15, 1936. 3. Herbert Jackson Newby, b. June 23, 1893, Limestone,Co., m. Nov. 25, 1919, Oma Sanderson, b. Dec. 15, 1893, Madison Co., Ala.

NEWBY, Matthew, b. July 18, 1793, Va., d. Jan. 6, 1853 - m. Ann Brooks, b. May 10, 1789, Va., d. Aug. 6, 1856. Matthew Newby was a farmer and settled in Limestone Co., Ala. around 1835. Children: 1. George Newby, b. 1827, Va. 2. Patrick Newby, b. 1829 (Teacher.) 3. James M. Newby, b. Mar. 28, 1831, Va., d. April 2, 1908, m. Sally A. Barksdale, b. Jan. 12, 1835, d. April 18, 1910. 4. Susan Newby, m. Jim Barksdale. 5. Joseph Newby, b. 1836, Ala. 6. Isabelle Newby, b. 1837, Ala. 6. Isabelle Newby. b. 1837, Ala. 7. Benjamin Newby, b. 1839, Ala.

NEWELL, Herbert Moses, b. June 9, 1898, Geneva Co., Ala., d. April 21, 1940, Clanton, Ala. - son of W. M. & Mamie W (McCartha) Newell - m. Dec. 3, 1919, Mabel Fallin, b. May 25, 1902, Birmingham, Jefferson Co., Ala. - dau. of G.W. and Mary E. (Comer) Fallin. Herbert enlisted in the United States Army on July 14, 1915, and was honorably discharged because of disability on July 7, 1916 as a Private. They were married in Wetumpka, Ala. and moved to Clanton, Ala. about 1932, making that their home until he died in 1940. He was a metalsmith and a salesman. Children: 1. Doris Wanda Newell, b. Aug. 11, 1921, Montgomery, Ala., m. July 23, 1944, Isaac Clarence Wagner, Jr., b. Sept. 19, 1920, Monterey, Va. - son of Dr. I.C.Wagner. (They were married in Orlando, Fla. and he is a Major in the United States Air Force. They have two children: 1. Brenda Dent Wagner, b. Aug. 8, 1942, in Florence, S.C. - her father, N.H.Dent was killed in World War II in Italy; and 2. John Garland "Chris" Wagner, b. Feb. 16, 1952, Roanoke, Va.) 2. Edith Clare Newell, b. Dec. 13, 1923, Evergreen, Conecuh Co., Ala., m. June 1, 1946, Thomas Stuart Woodson, b. Jan. 28, 1922, Chattanooga, Tenn. (They were married in Montgomery, Ala. by Rev. J. C. Vickers and Stuart is an electrical engineer with T.V.A. in Knoxville, Tenn. He is the son of Ryland Duke Woodson. They have two children: 1. Robert Stuart Woodson, b. Feb. 21, 1948, Knoxville, Tenn. and 2. Thomas Warren Woodson, b. Sept. 11, 1949, Englewood, Los Angeles Co., Calif.) 3. Herbert Moses Newell, Jr., b. June 20, 1925, Evergreen, Conecuh Co., Ala. m. May 28, 1949, Freida Jeanie Patterson, b. July 17, 1924, Fayette, Ala. 4. Emily Juanite Newell, b. Mar. 6, 1927, Andalusia, Ala., m. Feb. 25, 1945, Roy Lawrence Hayes, b. Nov. 7, 1920, Thorsby, Ala. He is the son of Lawrence & Lilla (Maddox) Hayes. They were married in Clanton, Ala. by Rev. O. C. Loyd. Roy is co-owner with his brother of the Wetumpka Jewelry Co., Wetumpka, Ala. They have three children: 1. Linda Juanita Hayes, b. May 10, 1946, Birmingham, Ala. 2. Roy Larry Hayes, b. July 18, 1949, Birmingham, Ala. and 3. Bruce Herbert Hayes, b. June 2, 1951, Birmingham, Ala.)

NEWELL, Herbert Moses, Jr., b. June 20, 1925, Evergreen, Conecuh Co., Ala. - son of H.M.,Sr. & Mabel (Fallin) Newell - m. May 28, 1949, Freida Jeanie Patterson, b. July 17, 1924, Fayette, Ala. - dau. of V. S., Sr. & Lucy (Bobo) Patterson. Herbert enlisted in the United States Navy on December 7, 1942, at Montgomery, Ala. and was sworn in on Dec. 8, 1942 at the Naval Station in Birmingham, Ala. He served during World War II in the Pacific Theatre of War, and was honorably discharged on June 17, 1946 at Memphis, Tenn. as a Metal-smith 2C. They were married in Fayette, Ala. by Rev. A. M. Nix and Herbert was ordained as a Deacon of the Missionary Baptist Church on Sept. 10, 1952. Children: 1. Herbert Moses Newell, III - "Herbie" - b. April 16, 1956, Fayette, Alabama.

NEWELL, W. J. (William) b. abt. 1822, N. C., d. date unknown - betw. 1850 & 1860, m. bef. 1850, Calli Donia Alexander, b. abt. 1830, Coffee or Dale Co., Ala., d. Mar. 1912, age 83. - dau. of Asa & Rebekah (Ledbetter) Alexander. William Newell was a supply merchant and one of the pioneer settlers of Geneva County, Ala. Children: 1. Mary C. Newell, b. 1849, Ala., m. Marshall Fisher. 2. William Malone Newell, b. Aug. 3, 1856, Ala., d. May 19, 1932, Geneva Co., Ala., m. Nov. 16, 1884, Mamie Warren McCartha, b. Sept. 25, 1865 S. C., d. Feb. 21, 1950, Geneva Co., Ala. 3. Possibly a son named James Redin Newell.

NEWELL, William Malone, b. Aug. 3, 1856, Ala., d. May 19, 1932 - son of W. J. & Callie Donia (Alexander) Newell - m. Nov. 16, 1884, Mamie Warren McCartha, b. Sept. 26, 1865, Abbeville, S. C., d. Feb. 21, 1950, Geneva Co., Ala. - dau. of Clarence L. & Susan Jane (Farrow) McCartha. "Willie" was a farmer. Children: 1. Callie Linden Newell, b. Nov. 23, 1885, Geneva Co., Ala. (All children born Geneva Co., Ala.), m. Colvin Gilmore. 2. Bennie M. Newell, b. Nov. 3, 1887, d. Mar. 15, 1891 - 3yrs. 4 mos. 12 das. 3. Willie Jake Newell, b. Dec. 19, 1888, m. Nov. 2, 1910, Lillie McDougal, b. Mar. 9, 1888, Geneva Co., Ala. 4. Mamie Lucille Newell, b. Dec. 16, 1890, d. Dec. 19, 1954, m. Sept. 9, 1907, Alva McDougal, b. Dec. 19, 1878, Geneva Co., Ala. 5. John Thomas Newell, b. July 25, 1893, d. Jan. 11, 1933, m. Sept. 6, 1919, Minnie Alford, b. Feb. 14, 1895, Samson, Geneva Co., Ala. 6. Herbert Moses Newell, b. June 9, 1898, d. April 21, 1940, Clanton, Ala., m. Dec. 3, 1919, Mabel Fallin, b. May 25, 1902, Birmingham, Ala. 7. Sadie Chicora Newell, b. Aug. 5, 1904, d. Mar. 4, 1913, - 8 yrs. 6 mos. 29 das.

NEWMAN, David Andrew, b. Oct. 11, 1875, Fayette Co., d. May 20, 1942, Fayette Co. - son of Wm. Perry & Julia Ann (Yarbrough) Newman - m. Oct. 11, 1908, Frances Biddie Newman, b. Dec. 5, 1887, Fayette Co., Ala. - dau. of Geo. Wash. & Cenie Paralee (Foster) Newman. Children: 1. Archie Lee Newman, b. May 23, 1912, d. Mar. 4, 1926. 2. Julia Lois Newman, b. Aug. 19, 1915, m. Nov. 2, 1940, Comer T. Bobo. 3. Galen William Newman, b. Dec. 27, 1920. 4. Bernice Mildred Newman, b. Feb. 1, 1924, m. Charles T. Geer.

NEWMAN, George Washington, b. April 12, 1847, Tippah Co., Miss., m. Ceanie Paralee Foster, b. Sept. 12, 1857, Pickens Co., Ala. Children: 1. Frances Biddie Newman, b. Dec. 5, 1887, Fayette Co., Ala., m. Oct. 11, 1908, David Andrew Newman.

NEWMAN, Olen, m. Artie Matthews, dau. of Jerome & Sally Matthews. Children: 1. Beatrice Newman. 2. Christine Newman. 3. Robert Newman. 4. Olen Newman, Jr.

NEWTON, Phillip, m. Rachel Deavours, dau. of Abraham Deavours. Children: 1. Artie Newton. 2. Rilla Newton. 3. Sis Newton. 4. Sally Newton. 5. Davis Newton. 6. Bud Newton. 7. Dr. Kib. Newton.

NEWTON, Robert Bernice, b. May 21, 1888, Fayette Co., d. Oct. 11, 1955, Faye. Ala., m. Winnie Kate Whitley, b. 1893, Fayette Co., Ala. - dau. of James Lee Whitley. Children: 1. Doris Newton, b. Fayette Co., m. Mr. Merritt. 2. Robert Newton, b. Aug. 24, 1916, Fayette Co., d. May 24, 1935, Fayette. 3. John H. Newton, b. Dec. 11, 1919, Fayette Co., d. July 9, 1941, Fayette. 4. Betty Jo Newton, b. July 27, 1926, Fayette Co., m. Newburn Fowler.

NEWTON, W. Claude, m. Lou Ella White, - dau. of S. L. White. Children: 1. Lewallen Newton, m. Lerla Dean Rudisill. (Children: Barbara, Cliff, Joe, Robert, Bill and Bob Newton.)

NEWTON, William Taylor, b. Fayette Co. m. Valutia Jane Whitley, b. Fayette Co. Children: 1. Emma Newton, m. James Van Diver Tarwater. 2. Sally Newton, m. W. L. Stephens. 3. A Son, burned to death. 4. Earl Newton. 5. Maude Newton. 6. Carl Newton. 7. Dr. Eugene Newton (Dentist) m. Miss Otts. 8. Lillian Newton, m. John Gilliam.

NICHOLS, Andrew Curtis, b. Sept. 15, 1879 - son of Wm. F. Nichols, m. Oct. 25, 1899, Elizabeth Ellen Shirley, b. April 3, 1881 - dau. of Josiah S. Shirley. Rev. A. C. Nichols is a Baptist Minister. He was for many years affiliated with the old Robertson Store in Fayette as bookkeeper. Children: 1. Mamie Beuma Nichols, b. July 23, 1900, Fayette Co., Ala. (All Children born Fayette Co.) m. May 18, 1924, Worth Burness Clearman. 2. Ethel Othelia Nichols, b. Dec. 7, 1902, m. Aug. 28, 1929, David Thomas Poynor. 3. William Curtis Nichols, b. Nov. 12, 1907, m. May 30, 1927, Eva Adell Hargett. 4. Miriam Nichols, b. Aug. 21, 1909. 5. Edna Elise Nichols, b. June 24, 1914, m. June 24, 1933, James Andrew Faulkner.

NICHOLS, James T., b. July 25, 1817, d. Nov. 8, 1891, m. May 24, 1838, 1st. - Jane Strong, b. Feb. 14, 1813, d. April 9, 1864 - dau. of Elijah Strong. Children: (1st. wife.) 1. Isham Nichols, b. Nov. 30, 1845. 2. Maranda Nichols, b. June 26, 1848. 3. Sarah Elizabeth Nichols, b. May 7, 1852. 4. Elijah Strong Nichols, b. Feb. 21, 1860, d. Dec. 3, 1925, Fayette Co., Ala., m. Margaret Isabell Montgomery, b. May 10, 1852, d. Mar. 26, 1924, Fayette Co.
    James T. Nichols, second marriage - Elizabeth (Lowery) Nelson, b. Dec. 6, 1834, d. June 28, 1904. Children: (2nd. wife.) 1. James T. Nichols, b. Aug. 14, 1868. 2. William J. Nichols, b. May 16, 1870, m. Mar. 7, 1894, Coleda B. Stough, b. 1876, d. 1946, Fayette Co., Ala.

NICHOLS, Shelby T., b. Feb. 17, 1886, Chickasaw Co., Miss., - son of Sidney & Kizzie M. (Freeman) Nichols - m. Nannie Westbrook, b. Feb. 12, 1891, d. 1958. Children: 1. William H. Nichols, b. Oct. 21, 1910. 2. Floyd Nichols, b. April 25, 1913. 3. James Sidney Nichols, b. Sept. 3, 1915, d. Dec. 7, 1943. 4. Walter Lee Nichols, b. Feb. 11, 1917. 5. Randolph E. Nichols, b. Dec. 14, 1919. 6. Margaret Nichols, b. Oct. 8, 1921. 7. Mary Nichols, b. Sept. 29, 1923. 8. Jack Nichols, b. May 30, 1925. 9. Florence Nichols, b. June 23, 1930.

NICHOLS, William Curtis, b. Nov. 12, 1907, Fayette Co., Ala., m. May 30, 1927, Eva Adell Hargett, b. Russellville, Ala. Wm. Curtis is the son of A. C. Nichols. Children: 1. William Curtis Nichols, Jr., b. April 16, 1929, Fayette, Ala., m. May 29, 1954, Alice Louise Mancill. 2. Eva Jeneil Nichols, b. Aug. 15, 1931, Fayette, Ala., m. Mar. 12, 1950, Thomas Wilburn "Hoss" McCaleb.

NICHOLS, Rev. William Curtis, b. April 16, 1929, Fayette, Ala. - son of Wm. Curtis, Sr. & Eva (Hargett) Nichols - m. May 29, 1954, Alice Louise Mancill. Rev. William C. "Bill" Nichols finished Fayette County High School in 1950 and received his A. B. Degree at the University of Alabama on Aug. 21, 1953. He entered the Baptist Seminary in New Orleans, La. in Sept. 1953. In Sept. 1955 he entered the Baptist Theological Seminary in Louisville, Ky. On Nov. 29, 1955, the First Baptist Church of Tuscaloosa, Ala. ordained him as a Baptist Minister. He received his B. D. Degree from the Seminary in Louisville, Ky. on May 25, 1956. In Sept. 1957 he entered the Teachers College Columbia, New York, N. Y. and received his Master of Theology Degree on May 19, 1959. Wm. C. Nichols and Alice Mancill were married in Tuscaloosa, Ala. at the First Baptist Church. Alice's father, Dr. Mancill is a professor at the University of Alabama. Children: 1. Alice Camille Nichols, b. May 2, 1955, New Orleans, La. 2. William Mancill Nichols, b. Oct. 16, 1958, Brooklyn, N. Y.

NICHOLS, William Franklin, b. Oct. 27, 1852, Fayette Co., d. Mar. 4, 1912, Fayette Co. - son of Wm. L. & Elizabeth (Strong) Nichols - m. 1874, Louise Walker Joiner, b. Feb. 2, 1853, Russellville, Ala., d. Mar. 4, 1931, Fayette Co., Ala. - dau. of David & Rachael Joiner. Children: (All born in Fayette Co.) Three died in infancy. 1. Walter Nichols, b. July 4, 1875. 2. Andrew Curtis Nichols, b. Sept. 15, 1879, m. Oct. 25, 1899, Ellen Elizabeth Shirley, b. Fayette Co., Ala. 3. Delia Nichols, b. Sept. 7, 1881, d. July 11, 1901, m. Dec. 25, 1899, Berryman Beverly Shirley. 4. Leether Jane Nichols, b. Dec. 24, 1883, m. Dec. 27, 1900, Jeffie Garrett Lawrence, b. Oct. 29, 1879, Fayette Co., d. Feb. 6, 1942. 5. Rachael Elizabeth Nichols, b. Sept. 28, 1885, m. Aug. 10, 1902, Walter Felix Berry. 6. William Elbert Nichols, b. Sept. 22, 1887, m. Dec. 25, 1905, Mollie Fowler. 7. Viola Nichols, b. 1891, m. Jan. 1913, Agnew Lane Fowler. 8. Nora Frances Nichols, b. May, 1894, d. 1913, m. 1909, Charlie Butler. 9. Cora Moiselle Nichols, b. Dec. 20, 1896, m. Mar. 19, 1913, Marlin Markham.

NICHOLS, William L., b. 1819, d. Sept. 1853, Fayette Co., m. Elizabeth Strong, d. 1860, Fayette Co., Ala. Children: 1. William Franklin Nichols, b. Oct. 27, 1852, d. Mar. 4, 1912, Fayette Co., m. 1874, Louise Walker Joiner, b. Feb. 2, 1853, d. Mar. 4, 1931, Fayette Co., Ala.

NICHOLS, William Sidney, m. Kizzie Mahala Freeman - dau. of Wm. & Delila (Walters) Freeman. Children: 1. Shelby T. Nichols, b. Feb. 17, 1886, Chickasaw, Co., Miss., m. Nannie Westbrook, b. Feb. 2, 1891, d. 1958. 2. Earl Nichols. 3. Pearl Nichols. 4. Pinkie Nichols. 5. Vera Nichols, m. Marshall Coleman.

NIX, Rev. A. M. b. Aug. 10, 1893, Marion Co., Ala., m. Dec. 7, 1911, T. Viola Strickland, b. July 14, 1889, d. Aug. 21, 1959, 3:15 P.M. Bro. Nix was Pastor of the Fayette First Baptist Church for eighteen years; Pastor of Bethel Baptist Church, near Bluff, since 1927. They made their home in Fay. County in 1941. Children: 1. Viola Nix, b. Sept. 28, 1912, Miss., m. Max Knight. 2. Pauline Nix, b. April 18, 1915, Miss., m. E. E. Anderson. 3. A. M. Nix, Jr., b. June 14, 1918, Tenn., m. Nell Mobley. 4. Guy Martin Nix, b. Aug. 16, 1920, Tenn. 5. Maxine Nix, b. Mar. 27, 1925, Miss., m. Larry A. Brock, b. Fayette Co., Ala.

NIX, James Vincent, b. Nov. 12, 1871, d. Feb. 12, 1950, m. Lona Murphee, b. Oct. 31, 1871, d. Sept. 20, 1957. Children: 1. A. M. Nix, b. Aug. 10, 1893, Marion Co., Ala., m. Dec. 7, 1911, T. Viola Strickland, b. July 14, 1889, d. Aug. 21, 1959. 2. Alvie Nix, b. Mar. 17, 1896, m. __Clark. 3. Annie Nix, b. Oct. 9, 1900, m. Mr. Hughes. 4. Evie Nix, b. June 9, 1903, m. __Davis. 5. James Vincent Nix, Jr., b. Oct. 10, 1906. 6. Lois Nix, b. June 7, 1910, m.__ Berry.

NOLEN, Jack Merrill, b. Feb. 20, 1925, Ashland, Ala., m. Aug. 31, 1949, Dennie Jones Cannon, b. Jan. 29, 1929, Berry, Ala. - dau. of Theron & Mary (Jones) Cannon. Children: 1. Theron Wayne Nolen, b. Dec. 4, 1954, Fayette, Ala. 2. Mary Kathleen Nolen, b. Feb. 27, 1956, Berry, Ala.

NOLES, William Samuel, b. S.C., m. Emma Robertson. Children: 1. Mary Noles, b. Jan. 9, 1847, d. Aug. 27, 1880, Walker Co., Ala., m. John Leonard (or Lanier) Wright, b. Oct. 4, 1847, Walker Co., Ala., d. Aug. 3, 1924, Walker Co.

NORTHAM, William Thomas, b. Jan. 9, 1900, Taylor, Texas, m. May 17, 1931, Dessie Waldrop, b. Oct. 4, 1904, Lamar Co., Ala. Wm. T.'s parents - Benjamin Alexander Northam, b. May 1, 1864, m. 1886, Martha (Kirkley), b. Feb. 26, 1862, Fayette Co., Ala. Grandparents - Ben Northam, b. ?1834 (abt.), Tenn. or N. C. & Nancy Davis b. Mar. 24, 1834, Tenn; and Jim Davis Kirkley, b. 1839, Marion Co., Ala. & "Tinny" (Smith) b. 1840. Great Grandparents - Lampley Northam, b. 1822, Ala., m. 1846, Elma Dodson (dau. Of Tom Dodson) b. 1823, Tenn; Dan Davis, b. 1815, Tenn. m. 1839 __ (her mother was Annie Hawkins); Clarence Kirkley, b. 1800, Fayette Co., Ala., m. 1822 and d. 1839; and Tom Smith, b. 1819, Cullman, Ala., m. 1839 Miss (Hawkins).
    Dessie's parents - Samuel M. Waldrop, b. July 19, 1879, Lamar Co., Ala. m. 1923, Mattie Collins, b. 1884, Lamar Co., Ala. Grandparents - Rev. Silas Waldrop, b. 1847, m. 1867 Miss Yarbrough; and Robert Collins, Jr., b. 1852, m. 1871, Maelene Rainwater, b. 1854. Great grandparents - James Waldrop, d. 1849; and Robert Collins, b. 1820, Ala., m. 1840, d. 1849, Ala. Children: (Wm. Thos. Northam's) 1. Nellie Mae Northam, b. June 18, 1939, Fayette, Ala.

NUCKOLS, Augustus Melville, b. Oct. 26, 1823, Barren Co., Ky, d. Dec. 13, 1896, Fayette, Ala. - son of Pouncey & Mary (Jemison) Nuckols - m. Jan. 7, 1855, Lizzie Ann Hubbard, b. April 1, 1837, Pickens Co., Ala., d. May 16, 1903, Fayette, Ala. - dau. of Rev. Vincent & Mrs. Elizabeth (Murray) Hamm, Hubbard. They were married at Fayette Courthouse, Ala., by Rev. Matthas Davis, a Methodist Minister. J. W. McConnell and A. B. Stewart were the witnesses to the wedding. The granddaughter of Lizzie Ann (Hubbard) Nuckols, Frankie Nuckols Martin had the Vose square piano on which Mrs. Nuckols gave music lessons. The piano arrived by boat in Tuscaloosa and was hauled by ox cart to Pickensville, Ala. before her marriage. The piano was made by Vose & Sons in 1851. A. M. Nuckols was appointed orderly Sgt. Aug. 1863, in Co. F. 41 Ala. Inf. He is shown on the muster roll dated April 17, 1862, Tusca., Ala. After the was he was a teacher and the Superintendent of Education. The old Nuckols home, 260 acres, deed from N. W. Harkins, was the property presently occupied by John D. Parks' summer cottage about 3 miles out of Fayette on the Vernon Road. For that reason the hill descending into the Appling - Renfroe Valley is called Nuckols Hill. A. M. Nuckols died on Sunday morning at 6 A.M., Dec. 13, 1896 and she died on Saturday morning, May 16, 1903 at 8 A.M. Both are buried in the Fayette City Cemetery.

Children: 1. Walter Melville Nuckols, b. Feb. 14, 1856, Probably Pickens Co., Ala., d. Jan. 18, 1895, Fayette, Ala., m. Jan. 6, 1892, Vannie Norris. 2. Frank Arthur Nuckols, b. Mar. 27, 1858, Northport, Ala., d. June 6, 1927, Fayette, Ala., m. Oct. 1904, Mary Ann Smith, b. Dec. 27, 1878, Carroll Co., Miss., d. Dec. 25, 1934, Fayette, Ala. 3. Vincent Hubbard Nuckols, b. Sept. 3, 1860, Fayette Co., Ala., d. April 10, 1900, Fayette, Ala. 4. May Hester Nuckols, b. May 19, 1866, Fayette Co., Ala., d. June 4, 1948, Birmingham, Ala. m. Mar. 5, 1888, Andrew Lawrence White, b. Huntsville, Ala., d. Fayette, Ala. (A. L. White was a Capt. in the C.S.A.) 5. Mary Estelle "Lee" Nuckols, b. Feb. 7, 1869, Fayette Co., Ala., d. June 20, 1943, Fayette, Ala., m. April 8, 1896, Walter DeForest Putnam, b. July 25, 1869, Warren, Ill., d. buried Veteran's Cem., Miss. (They were married in Las Vegas, Nev. Walter D. Putnam was a veteran of the Spanish American War. He served as Pvt. - Co., M. He died Feb. 20, 1938 in the V.A. Hospital in Biloxi, Miss. and is buried in the V.A. Facility Cemetery.) 6. Lizzie Grace Nuckols, b. June 2, 1872, Fayette Co., Ala., d. May 22, 1896, Fayette, Ala. 7. Paul Nuckols, b. June 13, 1875, Fay. Co., d. Dec. 7, 1953, Fayette, Ala., m. Dec. 7, 1903, Dorothy Murphy, b. Gainesville, Ga., d. Dec. 7, 1957, Fayette, Ala. 8. Fritz Nuckols, b. July 24, 1880, Fayette Co., Ala., d. Nov. 1, 1958, Spartanburg, S.C. m. Doris ___.

NUCKOLS, Frank Arthur, b. Mar. 27, 1858, Northport, Ala., d. June 6, 1927 - son of Augustus Melville & Lizzie Ann (Hubbard) Nuckols - m. Oct. 23, 1904, Mary Ann Smith, b. Dec. 27, 1878, Carroll Co., Miss., d. Dec. 25, 1934, Fay. Ala. - dau. of Joseph Patrick & Hassie Kirk (Mothershed) Smith. They were married in West Miss. by Rev. Laird, a Presbyterian Minister. Witness to the wedding was W. W. Caine. Frank Arthur Nuckols was a merchant and a teacher. Mary Ann Nuckols was talented in millinery and sewing. They are buried in the Fayette City Cemetery. Children: 1. Mary Elizabeth Nuckols, b. Jan. 16, 1906, "Old Town", Fayette, Ala., d. Sept. 4, 1910, Fayette, Ala. 2. Frankie Augusta Nuckols, b. Jan. 7, 1908, "Old Town", Fayette, Ala., m. Aug. 1, 1931, William Roy Martin, b. May 29, 1903, Millerville, Clay Co., Ala. 3. Isabel Nuckols, b. Mar. 1, 1910, Fayette, Ala., m. Mar. 27, 1928, Wightman Morrow Cannon. b. Oct. 1, 1900, Fayette, Ala., d. Oct. 3, 1951, Fayette, Ala. 4. Ann Jemison Nuckols, b. Spring of 1916, Fayette, Ala., d. (Lived one week and died, 1916.)

NUCKOLS, Pouncey, d. after 1840, probably 1843, - son of ?Pouncey, Sr. & Susan (Knight) Nuckols - m. 1819, Mary M. Jemison, b. 1800, Ky., d. after 1850, Tusca. or Pickens Co., Ala. Susan Knight was from Hanover Co., Va. They were married at Barren Co., Ky. Children: 1. William G. Nuckols, b. 1821, Ky., m. Sept. 29, 1861 at residence of Jas. H. Freeman, 1st. - Julia Ann ___, b. N. C., 2nd. - Matilda E. Baker. 2. Augustine Melville Nuckols, b. Oct. 26, 1823, Barren Co., Ky., d. Dec. 13, 1896, Fayette, Ala., m. Jan. 7, 1855, Lizzie Ann Hubbard, b. April 1, 1837, Pickensville, Ala., d. May 16, 1903, Fayette, Ala. 3. Virgil Poet "Doc" Nuckols, b. 1828, Ala., m. Carrie Deal. 4. Simminimus Nuckols, b. 1830, Ky., d. in Texas, m. 1849 or 1850, Joseph M. Jemison, b. 1822, Ga. 5. Robert Rhodes Nuckols, b. 1836, Ala., d. Aug. 10, 1908, Va., m. Feb. 12, 1867, Susan Ann Swift, b. Dec. 5, 1842, d. Nov. 19, 1904, Louisa Co., Va. (Robert Rhodes Nuckols, well known newspaper editor, who worked with the following Virginia Newspapers: "Whig", "State" and "Richmond Journal". He stayed in Virginia when his regiment disbanded there. He was in Federal Prison when the war ended. An original Muster Roll dated Sept. 17, 1861 shows Robert Rhodes Nuckols, Private, enlisted from Pickens Co., in

Co. B. 2 Ala. Volunteers, under Capt. Thomas C. Lanier. The 2 Ala. Inf. was mustered out in the spring of 1862. A muster-in roll of Co. B. 42 Ala. Inf. dated at Columbus, Miss, May 16, 1862, shows this man, private, enlisted at Ft. Pillow, Tenn., Mar. 17, 1862.) 6. Helena Jemison Nuckols, b. 1840, Tusca. Ala., m. Oct. 4, 1860, John W. Wiggins. (They were married by Rev. Jesse G. Nash.)

NUCKOLS, Virgil Poet "Doc", b. 1828, Ala., d. Will dated Feb. 19, 1903, and proven Jan. 3, 1907 - son of Pouncey & Mary (Jemison) Nuckols - m. A. Carrie Deal. Children: 1. Pouncey Nuckols,(Lives in Texas.) 2. Robert Nuckols. 3. William Virgil Nuckols, (Dr. E. H. Tubbs, Cordova, Ala., married one of these daughters. William Virgil had a daughter, Maude, who married Dr. ___ Taylor of Tuscaloosa, Ala. and had daughters, Sarah Maude and Mary, Mrs. Earle Johnson.) 4. J. Mack Nuckols, (Mack Nuckols' son Poet Virgil, has a daughter, Mrs. Sam Williams, 3415 - 7 Street, Tuscaloosa, Ala.) 5. Mary Nuckols, m. W. R. Whetstone, (They live in Texas.) 6. Annie H. Nuckols, m. Larkin Butler. 7. Charlie B. Nuckols, died 1944 and buried Quinton, Ala.

OLIVE, Aaron Barney, son of Cecil & Miss (Fulmer) Olive - m. June 1, 1957, Carol Hughes Howton, b. July 26, 1939, Fayette Co., Ala. - dau. of L. T. & Jessie (Freeman) Hughes. A. B. Olive is presently serving in the U. S. Navy and is stationed in Puerto Rico. Children: 1. Sandra Renee Olive, b. Feb. 3, 1959.

ORD, Robert, b. bef. 1750, Ireland, m. Ann Leith, b. Ireland. Robert Ord and Ann Leith were married in Ireland. He served in the American Revolutionary War; belonged to a company of volunteers called "Virginia Blues", enlisting Aug. 28, 1777. He fell in the battle of Guilford Court House, fought by Gen. Green and Lord Cornwallis. In Safell's Records of Revolutionary War, p. 265 the name of Robert Ord is given in a list of Rev. Soldiers of Va. under date of Nov. 30, 1778, in Co. No. 10, Samuel Booker Capt. Lawrence Butler, Lieut. Daniel Morgan's 11th and 15th Va. Regts. Ind. Following is from War Dept., Washington, D. C. No. 1838801: "The records of this office show that one Robert Ord served in the Rev. War as a Private in a detachment under the command of _t. Gibbs, 15th Va. Reg. of Foot, commanded by Maj. Gustavis B. Wallace .. This soldier is shown to have enlisted Aug. 28, 1777, to serve three years and his name last appears on a roll for Nov. 1779 with special remark relative to his service. "The scene of the battle of Guilford Court House is six or seven miles northwest of Greensboro. The graves of the slain were obliterated and no memorial erected until about 1888, when a memorial was erected. The battle was fought Mar. 15, 1781, lasted three hours and 25 minutes. The militia displayed great heroism, repulsed the enemy several times, and after advancing, fell back when compelled in good order. Finally when assailed by British Light Horse were obliged to flee, many were cut down and scattered, but came together again." Following entry is found in Rev. of Augusta Co., Va. Vol. 1, Order bk. No. XVII, p. 264, June 20, 1780 (by Lyman Chalkley): :Ann Ord, soldier's wife, allowed 5 bushels of corn." Isabella Ord, the daughter of Robert and Ann (Leith) Ord, was early left an orphan and was reared by James and Isabella Cunningham. With them she immigrated to Washington Co., Tenn. and married Alexander Mathes, II. Children: 1. Jane Ord, b. 1774. 2. Isabella Ord, b. April 6, 1776, d. Nov. 23, 1839, m. Alexander Mathes, II.

OSWALT, Jacob, b. 1824, m. Joanna Hallman, b. 1830, dau. of Jacob Hallman.

Children: 1. Henry Oswalt, b. 1848, d. 1917, m. Cynthia _. 2. David Alex Oswalt, b. 1852, d. 1925, m. Mary E. _. 3. Zack Oswalt, b. 1854, m. Annie _. 4. Mary Oswalt, b. Sept. 28, 1856, d. Feb. 9, 1927, m. John Poe. 5. Robert Oswalt, b. 1861. 6. Jacob N. Oswalt, b. Mar. 22, 1863, d. May 4, 1939. 7. Jodie Oswalt, b. June 11, 1866, d. Nov. 22, 1934, m. J. N. Black. 8. Ward Oswalt, b. 1866. 9. Joannah Oswalt. 10. Wilbur Collins Oswalt, b. 1873, d. 1937, m. Barbara A. Edmonson. 11. Peninah Oswalt, b. 1873.

OSWALT, Jim, b. Mar. 31, 1868, Ala., d. Jan. 26, 1941, Fayette, Ala., m. H. Addie Doughty, b. June 30, 1871, Fayette Co., d. Mar. 30, 1950, Fayette Co., - dau. of J. F. & Rachel L. A. (Boozer) Doughty. Children: 1. George Roberts Oswalt, b. Mar. 30, 1904, d. May 31, 1941, near Hamilton, Ala., m. Estella Cooper, b. New Mexico. (George was adopted when very young.)

OSWALT, Max Clelion, b. July 12, 1922, Fayette Co., Ala., m. Jan. 14, 1947, Della Jane Cannon, b. Oct. 19, 1923, Fayette, Ala., - dau. of Wm. Louis & Ruby (Jeffries) Cannon. Max C. Oswalt served in the Seabees from Nov. 1942 until Oct. 1945. They were married in Fayette, Ala. by Rev. A. M. Nix. Max is an automobile salesman. Children: 1. Gaines Cannon Oswalt, b. Aug. 11, 1948, Fayette, Ala. 2. Michael Louis Oswalt, b. Jan. 27, 1955, Fayette, Ala.

OWENS, Shade, m. Cerania Slater. Children: 1. William Banister Owens, b. June 10, 1845, Fayette Co., Ala., d. Jan. 19, 1923, m. Mary Catherine Johnson, b. Oct. 15, 1849, Fayette Co., Ala., d. Jan. 3, 1929. 2. John Shade Owens, m. Torie Hendrix. 3. Jim Owens, m. Josephine Merritt. 4. Judie Owens. 5. Martha Owens.

OWENS, William Bannister, b. June 10, 1845, Fayette Co., Ala., d. Jan. 19, 1923, Fayette Co., - son of Shade & Cerania (Slater) Owens - m. Mary Catherine Johnson, b. Oct. 15, 1849, Fayette Co., d. Jan. 3, 1929, Fayette Co. - dau. of Starling & Catherine (Crowe) Johnson. Children: 1. Alice B. Owens, b. June 24, 1870, d. July 25, 1952, m. W. W. Cook, b. Jan. 24, 1868, d. Nov. 29, 1943. 2. B. Donie Owens, b. Feb. 17, 1872, d. 1900, m. W. G. Walden. 3. James Robert Owens (Twin), b. April 2, 1874. 4. Dora Owens, (Twin), b. April 2, 1874, d. Feb. 15, 1876. 5. Osemer Owens, b. Dec. 24, 1876, d. Mar. 12, 1952, m. Thomas H. Foster, b. April 7, 1874, d. July 27, 1945. 6. M. Ozora Owens, b. Feb. 18, 1878, m. 1st. - Rems T. Lindsey, 2nd. - LaFayette Freeman. 7. Shade R. Owens, b. Oct. 23, 1881, m. 1st. - Miss Belk (Dau. of Fred Belk.) 2nd. - Miss Atkins, (dau. of Josh Atkins.) 8. W. W. Owens, b. April 20, 1884, m. 1st. - -Foster, 2nd. - _ Sykes, 3rd. - (Belk) Taylor. 9. Lovie Pearl Owens, b. Sept. 29, 1887, m. Sept. 7, 1905, Lee Allen Plyler, b. Aug. 7, 1886, Fayette Co., Ala. (All the above Owens children born in Fayette Co.)

PACE, Rev. James Osgood Andrews, b. Nov. 15, 1845, Yelo Busha Co., Miss., d. Nov. 1924, Fayette, Ala. - son of Wyatt & Matilda Pace, m. 1886, Josephine Suillen, b. Mar. 5, 1850, Belgreen, Ala., d. Mar. 4, 1906, Jasper, Ala. - dau. of James & Tabitha Suillen. Rev. J. O. A. Pace was ordained as a Baptist Minister in 1872 at Duncan Creek Church, near Russellville, Ala. He preached in Alabama, Mississippi, Tennessee and Texas. He served in the Confederate Army from Oct. 1, 1863 to the close of the War. He served in the Cavalry under Stewart in Co. A. His Captain was Davis Potete. He served under Gen. Joseph E. Wheeler and Gen. Bedford Forest. His son, James Osgood Pace, Jr. was a student minister at Howard Baptist College when he died of typhoid fever.

Children: 1. Addie Pace, b. 1868, Russellville, Franklin Co., Ala., d. Oct. 1890, Franklin, Co., Ala., m. 1889, Robert Lee Reeves, b. 1867, Russellville, Ala., d. 1922, Fayette, Ala. 2. James Osgood Pace,Jr. b. 1870, Russellville, Ala., d. July 20, 1896, Franklin Co., Ala. 3. William Alexander Pace, b. July 13, 1874, Russellville, d. May 1955, Herren, Ill. m. 1902 or 1903, Mamie Young, b. Kendall, Lauderdale Co., Ala. 4. Kate Pace, b. Sept. 16, 1877, Russellville, m. 1900, Benjamin Franklin Hunt, b. June 1877, Wayland Springs, Tenn. 5. Arthur Townsend, b. May 25, 1879, Russellville, d. Mar. 26, 1949, Herrin, Ill, m. 1903, Mollie Kelley, b. Eldridge, Ala., d. 1925, Herrin, Ill. 6. Lizzie Clark Pace, b. July 19, 1884, Russellville, d. Aug. 20, 1896, Franklin Co., Ala. 7. Edna Pace, b. Aug. 19, 1886, Russellville, m. 1910, Dr. James Alexander Branyon, b. Nov. 27, 1868, Belk, Ala., d. Aug. 10, 1942, Fay. Ala. 8. Annie Pace, b. Nov. 5, 1881, Russellville, m. 1908, James P. Wright, b. 1878, Lauderdale Co., Ala., d. Jan. 24, 1958, Florence, Ala. 9. Archie Broadus Pace, b. Feb. 27, 1896, Kendall, Lauderdale Co., Ala., m. 1918, Julia Poindexter, b. 1898, Indianapolis, Ind. Three children died in infancy and are not listed here.

PACE, Wyatt, b. abt. 1815, Carroll Co., Miss., d. 1850, Miss., m. abt. 1844, Matilda Kirk, b. 1815, Ala., d. 1890, Franklin Co., Ala. - dau. of Jessie L. Kirk. After the death of Mr. Pace, Matilda married Mr. McGaha and had two children. Children: (1st. wife) 1. James Osgood Andrews Pace, b. Nov. 15, 1845, Yelo Busha Co., Miss. d. Nov. 14, 1924, Fayette, m. 1866 Josephine Suillen, b. Mar. 5, 1850, Belgreen, Ala., d. Mar. 14, 1906, Jasper, Ala. 2. Octavia Pace, b. Miss, d. Ala., m. Calvin Hovattr, b. Ala., d. Ala. 3. Mary Pace, b. Miss, d. Ala., m. William James, d. Ala. 4. Sallie Pace, b. Miss. m. John Venable. 5. Lewis Pace, b. 1847, Miss, d. Ala., m. Mollie Vincent?. Children of Matilda (Kirk) Pace and Mr. McGaha - 1. Lavina McGaha, b. Ala., d. Ark., m. Clark Fleming, b. Ala., d. Ark. 2. Buck McGaha, b. & d. Ala., m. Jenny --.

PALMER, Artis Kinnie, II, b. Aug. 19, 1915, Fayette, Ala., m. Oct. 9, 1934, Mary Ellis Stoker, b. July 30, 1919, Fayette. A. K., II's parents - Artie Kinnie Palmer, b. Oct. 21, 18__, Fayette, Ala. & Rebecca Exina Stough, b. Aug. 27, 1892. Grandparents - Thomas Alexander & Tissue Elizabeth (Brasher) Palmer; and John N. & Willie Frances (Palmer) Stough. Great grandparents - Levi & Permelia (Williams) Palmer; and Jacob Henderson & Martha Ann (Post) Stough.

Mary Ellis (Stoker) Palmer's parents - James Harvie Stoker, b. May 9, 1883, m. Mar. 10, 1901, Mary A. (Lawrence), b. Oct. 28, 1883, Fayette, Ala. Grandparents - William A. Stoker, b. 1859, m. 1880, Trilla Maran (Davis); and Alexander Lawrence, b. Nov. 1, 1843, Fayette, Ala. & Martha Ann (Adman) b. Sept. 9, 1841, Fayette, Ala. Great grandparents - Martha (Roberts) Stoker; John & Sally Davis; Alexander & __ (Morris) Lawrence; and Nathan & Sally (Taylor) ?Adman. Children: (A. K. Palmer, II's) 1. Jerrie Ellis Palmer, b. Aug. 14, 1939, Fayette, Ala.

PARRISH, Louis M., b. Norfolk, Va., d. April 29, 1923, Fayette, Ala. - son of Capt. William & Sarah Parrish - m. Zada Proost, b. Millport, Ala. - dau. of Wm. Wesley & Caroline (Garrison) Propst. Children: 1. William A. Parrish, m. Eloise Caine. 2. Lewis Hewlett Parrish, m. Little Rock, Ark, Sue Deener. 3. Drewry Propst Parrish, b. Fayette, Ala., d. buried Fayette City Cem., m. in Hollywood, Calif. Jane Winnette.

PARRISH, William Al, b. Millport, Ala., m. Oct. 22, 1927, Eloise Caine, b. Fayette, Ala. Wm. A. is the son of Louis M. & Zoda (Propst) Parrish. Eloise is the dau. of Robert P. & Sallie (Lindsey) Caine. Wm. A. Parrish served in World War I. They have no children.

PARRISH, Capt. William, b. Norfolk, Va., d. buried Norfolk, Va., m. Sarah ___ b. Norfolk, Va. Capt. Wm. Parrish was Captain of the "Merrimac". Children: 1. Louis Mark Parrish. 2. John Parris, b. Norfolk, Va. 3. May Parrish, b. Norfolk, Va., m. John Gibbs. 4. Anna Parrish, b. Norfolk, Va., m. Lewis Drewry, b. Norfolk, Va. 5. William Parriah, Jr., (First Supt. of Southern R.R. System from Columbus, Miss to Birmingham, Ala.)

PASTEUR, James Edward Jackson, b. Mar. 22, 1893, Berry, Fayette Co., Ala. - son of Louis Myer & Melissa Katherine (Hayslette) Pasteur - m. July 21, 1920 Minnie Lee Faulkner, b. April 18, 1896, Lamar Co., Ala. - dau. of Newton Grant & Sarah M. (Draper) Faulkner. Children: 1. James Maurice Pasteur, b. Sept. 23, 1921, Berry, Ala. 2. Vivian L. Pasteur, b. June 16, 1925, Berry, Ala. 3. Clarence Elmo Pasteur, b. Mar. 4, 1927, d. June 16, 1928. (Clarence b. Cordova, Walker Co., Ala.)

PASTEUR, James Maurice, b. Sept. 23, 1921, Berry, Fayette Co., Ala. - son of James Edward & Minnie Lee (Faulkner) Pasteur - m. Dec. 24, 1950, Natalie Snider of Girardean, Mo. Children: 1. Suzette Irene Pasteur, b. July 13, 1951, Ky. 2. Michelle Louise Pasteur, b. Sept. 22, 1953. Ky. 3. Robert Louis Pasteur, b. Oct. 9, 1954, Ky. 4. Stephen Miller Pasteur, b. Nov. 13, 1955, Ky.

PASTEUR, Louis Meyer, b. Sept. 23, 1867, Columbus, Miss, - son of Dr. James Madison Pasteur, first of the family to reside in Fayette Co., Ala. - m. Melissa Katherine Hayslette, b. April 26, 1876, Fayette, Ala. Children: 1. James Edward Jackson Pasteur, b. Mar. 22, 1893, Fayette Co., Ala. 2. Lillie Pasteur, b. June 10, 1896, Fayette Co., Ala.

PATE, Virgil H., m. July 22, 1923, Evie Emmaline Gober, b. Feb. 26, 1904, Franklin Co., Ala. - dau. of W. T. & Nancy L. (Humber) Gober. Children: 1. V. H. Pate, Jr., b. June 8, 1924, Itawamba Co., Miss. 2. Charles E. Pate, b. April 29, 1928, Itawamba, Co., Miss. 3. James H. Pate, b. Jan. 27, 1931, Itawamba Co., Miss.

PATTERSON, Barney, b. Sept. 15, 1875, Fayette Co., Ala., d. Jan. 23, 1940 - son of J. J. & Cenath (Rice) Patterson - m. Sara Louella Taylor, b. Apr. 7, 1881, Fayette Co., Ala., d. Jan. 26, 1931. They lived in Fayette County until all of their children were born and later moved to Mississippi where they lived until their deaths. Both are buried at the Patterson Family Cem. in Fayette Co., Ala. Children: 1. Cora Addie Patterson, b. July 6, 1897, m. Jan. 18, 1922, Brady Montgomery, b. Aug. 11, 1897, Tusca. Co. 2. William Perry Patterson, b. May 3, 1898, m. Mirriam Hollman, b. July 4, _, Fayette Co. 3. Trannie Mae Patterson, b. May 13, 1899, d. Dec. 27, 1957, m. William Bert Taylor, b. Fayette Co. 4. Razy Jane Patterson, b. Sept. 8, 1903, m. Bartie Hollman, b. Fayette Co. 5. Theo Earetane Patterson, b. Dec. 3, 1904, m. Archie Boyd, b. Columbus, Miss. 6. James Ulys Patterson, b. Feb. 11, 1905, m. Cora Mae Kidd, b. Jasper, Walker Co., Ala. 7. Floyd Howard Patterson, b. Sept. 27, 1906, m. Lillie Williamson, b. Fayette Co. 8. Vergie Verilla Patterson, b. Mar. 11, 1908. 9. Infant Daughter, b. & d. 1910. 10. Marvin Sam

Patterson, b. May 10, 1911, m. Ilen Ayres. 11. Woodrow Wilson Patterson, b. Mar. 28, 1914, m. Eloise Guin, b. Tusca. Co., Ala. 12. Mertie Claudine Patterson, b. July 7, 1915, m. Travis Pounder, b. Columbus, Miss. 13. Autie Oleen Patterson, b. Dec. 22, 1916, m. Vollie O'Mary. 14. Coqer Roy Patterson b. Mar. 2, 1918, m. Ezelle Acton, b. Blount Springs, Ala. 15. Troy Leon Patterson, b. Nov. 29, 1920, m. Margaret Duncan. 16. Homer Patterson, b. June 22, 192_, d. Feb. 21, 1945, buried Patterson Family Cem. Killed on Corrigador Island - World War II.

PATTERSON, George Harve, b. Mar. 27, 1877, Fayette Co., Ala. - son of J. J. & Cenath (Rice) Patterson, - m. Elizabeth "Lizzie" Hinton, b. Sept. 18, 1883, Fayette Co., Ala. - dau. of Andrew & Pheobe (Poe) Hinton. George Harve is a farmer and a monument dealer. Children: 1. Verna Clair Patterson, b. Jan. 25, 1902, (All children born Fayette Co.) m. Mar. 6, 1922, Charles William Bobo, b. Jan. 10, 1897, Fayette Co., Ala. 2. Hubert Mitchell Patterson, b. Dec. 29, 1903, m. Mrs Maude (Deason) Collins. 3. Floy Mae Patterson, b. Apr. 25, 1906, m. William David Hunt. 4. Beulah Lee Patterson, b. Dec. 24, 1907, d. May 5, 1908. 5. William Theron Patterson, b. Oct. 16, 1914, m. Ophelia Couch, b. Nov. 27, 1918, Marion Co., Ala. 6. Infant Daughter, b. & d. May 3, 1916. 7. Joe M. Patterson, b. June 1, 1918, m. 1st. - Justine Rainwater, 2nd. - Martha Jane Box, b. Oct. 2, 1924. 8. James Harris Patterson, b. Apr. 16, 1921, m. Nell Matthews.

PATTERSON, James Harris, b. April 16, 1921, - son of G. H. & Lizzie (Hinton) Patterson, - m. Nell Matthews. Children: 1. James Laren Patterson, b. Dec. 18, 1943. 2. George David Patterson, b. Aug. 12, 1947. 3. Rebecca Jane "Becky" Patterson, b. Dec. 9, 1952.

PATTERSON, Joe M., b. June 1, 1918, Fayette Co., Ala. - son of G.H. & Lizzie (Hinton) Patterson, m. Martha Jane Box, b. Oct. 2, 1924. Children: 1. Joe M. Patterson, Jr., b. June 12, 1949. 2. George Mitchell Patterson, b. Jan. 26, 1951. 3. Nancy Clair Patterson, b. June 26, 1954.

PATTERSON, Joseph J., b. Sept. 22, 1842, Fayette Co., Ala., d. May 12, 1918, Fayette Co. - son of Samuel J. & Jalia G. (Richards) Patterson - m. Feb. 15, 1865, Cenath A. Rice, b. June 20, 1846, Fayette Co., Ala., d. June 9, 1917, Fayette Co. - dau. of Jeptha & Palatine (Davis) Rice. J. J. Patterson first entered the service in the Confederate Army as Private on Sept. 17, 1861 at Fayette County, Ala. in the Ala. Regt. Inf. Co. I. and continued until Feb. 1st., 1865 - on furlough at close of war, but captured and appeared on the roll of Prisoners at Tuscaloosa, Ala. on May 22, 1865. He was wounded in Aug. 1861 at Seven Pines, Va. He was ordained to the ministry of the Missionary Baptist Church in 1887. Children: 1. William Castle Patterson, b. May 26, 1866, (All children born Fayette Co.) d. Nov. 11, 1922, m. Feb. 24, 1889, Maranda Jane Doughty, b. June 5, 1869, Fayette Co., Ala., d. May 27, 1954, Prattville, Ala., buried in Patterson Fam. Cem. 2. Angeline Patterson b. July 24, 1867, d. July 24, 1867. 3. Samuel Patterson, b. Jan. 10, 1869, d. 1892. (Died of typhoid fever on the and and hour that had been set for his wedding. He was a school teacher.) 4. Thomas Wilbur Patterson, b. Nov. 22, 1871, d. Sept. 16, 1957, m. Viola Patterson, b. Jan. 18, 1880, Ala. 5. Barney Patterson, b. Sept. 15, 1875, d. Jan. 23, 1940, m. Louella Taylor, b. Apr. 7, 1881, d. Jan. 26, 1931. 6. George Harve Patterson, b. Mar. 27, 1877, m. Elizabeth "Lizzie" Hinton, b. Sept. 18, 1883, Fayette Co. 7. J. Lester Patterson, b. Feb. 23, 1880, m. Mandy Austrilla "Trilly" Hinton. 8. Ida Patterson, b. July 4, 1882, m. Dec. 8, 1901, N. Berkeley Hocutt, b. Mar. 11, 1875, Tusca. Co., d. Mar. 12, 1943. 9. Wiley Patterson, b. Jan. 23, 1884, m. Nancy C. Walters, b. 1888, d. Feb. 1954. 10. Alma Patterson, b. Mar. 29, 1887, m. Dec. 3, 1905, Ausborn A. Poe, b. July 23, 1882, d. Jan. 1951, Fayette Co.

PATTERSON, J. Lester, b. Feb. 22, 1880, Fayette Co., Ala. - son of J.J. & Cenath (Rice) Patterson - m. Mandy Austrilla "Trilly" Hinton, dau. of Andrew & Phoebe (Poe) Hinton. Children: 1. Phebie Lois Patterson, b. Nov. 21, 1901, Fayette Co., d. Jan. 5, 1902. 2. Wilma Patterson, b. Sept. 16, 19__, m. W. F. "Estes" Richards. 3. Infant Son, b. & d. Jan. 20, 1916, Fayette Co., Ala.

PATTERSON, Samuel J., b. Jan. 8, 1804, South Carolina, d. Feb. 20, 1864, Fay. Co., Ala., m. Jalie G. Richards, b. Aug. 1, 1806, Ga., d. Dec. 29, 1887, Fay. Co., Ala. - dau. of James & Lovey(__) Richards. Samuel J. Patterson settled in Fayette County, Ala. on a 640 acre plantation with slaves. He died during the Civil War and The Patterson Family Cemetery was started with his grave. The land was part of the original family plantation. Children: 1. Sallie C. Patterson, b. Oct. 24, 1830, Ala., m. Jim Slaughter. 2. Elizabeth Jane Patterson, b. Dec. 20, 1832, Ala., m. Alexander Downs. 3. George Patterson, b. April 3, 1835, Ala., d. abt. 1892, m. Molly May. 4. Agnes Patterson, b. Dec. 6, 1837, Ala. (Bible record shows that she was an invalid all of her life.) 5. Emily Patterson, b. Mar. 18, 1840, Ala., m. Thomas Davis. 6. Joseph J. Patterson, b. Sept. 22, 1842, Ala., d. May 12, 1918, Fayette Co., m. Feb. 15, 1865, Cenath A. Rice, b. June 20, 1846, Ala., d. June 9, 1917, Fayette Co. 7. Angeline Patterson, b. Mar. 1, 1845, Ala., d. Jan. 1, 1906, Fayette Co., m. William Diongus "Bill" Doughty, b. Sept. 23, 1845, d. Dec. 22, 1905, Fayette Co., Ala. 8. James Patterson, b. Oct. 21, 1848, Ala., d. 1910, m. Sally Miller.

PATTERSON, Thomas Wilbur, b. Nov. 22, 1871, Fayette Co., Ala., d. Sept. 16, Fayette, Ala. - son of J.J. & Cenath (Rice) Patterson - m. Viola Frances Williamson, b. Jan. 18, 1880, Ala. T. W. Patterson was one of the first policemen of the Town of Fayette and served in that position for many years. Children: 1. Samuel Felix Patterson, b. Feb. 22, 1896, (All children born Fayette Co., Ala.) - Felix served in World War I. 2. William Claude Patterson, b. July 11, 1897, m. Ora Hollingsworth. 3. George Patterson, b. Feb. 12, 1899, d. Nov. 7, 1932, Fayette, Ala. 4. Zora Victoria Patterson, b. Sept. 14, 1900, m. Angus Dee Ausborn, b. Jan. 3, 1893, d. June 30, 1955. 5. Essie Evelyn Patterson, b. Nov. 19, 1901. 6. Vister Lydia Patterson, b. Jan. 11, 1909, d. Mar. 21, 1949, Fayette, Ala., m. Elmer S. Alexander, b. Oct. 8, 1905, d. Aug. 25, 1933. 7. Lily Lillian Patterson, b. Oct. 1, 1911, m. 1st. - Ed Gentry, 2nd. - Paul Williams. 8. Thomas Glenn Patterson, b. Dec. 22, 1913, m. Mary Bectom. 9. Malcolm R. Patterson, b. Mar. 30, 1917.

PATTERSON, Victor Samuel, b. Jan. 11, 1895, Fayette Co., Ala. - son of W. C. & Maranda J. (Doughty) Patterson - m. June 24, 1919, Lucy Evelyn Bobo, b. Nov. 5, 1895, Fayette Co., Ala. - dau. of Wm. T. & Lula V. (Dickinson) Bobo. V. S. Patterson was inducted in the United States Army on May 15, 1918, at Fayette, Ala. His unit left the United States for active duty in Germany on July 19, 1918 and returned, after several hard battles, on Mar. 31, 1919. His service number was 2-920-135 and he was honorably discharged at Camp Gordon, Ga. on April 25, 1919 from Military Police Co. #5 as a Private First Class.

They were married at Fayette, Ala. by Rev. L. M. Harris. Victor and Lucy Compounded the formula for Golden Eagle Table Syrup and established the Golden Eagle Syrup business in October, 1928. Children: 1. Victor S. Patterson, Jr., b. April 20, 1920, Fayette, Ala., m. Dec. 22, 1939, Mary Louise Wright, b. Aug. 19, 1921, Corona, Walker Co., Ala. 2. Freida Jean "Jeanie" Patterson, b. July 17, 1924, Fayette, Ala., m. May 28, 1949, Herbert Moses Newell, Jr., b. June 20, 1925, Evergreen, Conecuh Co., Ala.

PATTERSON, Victor S., Jr., b. April 20, 1920, Fayette, Ala. - son of V. S., Sr. & Lucy (Bobo) Patterson - m. Dec. 22, 1939, Mary Louise Wright, b. Aug. 19, 1921, Corona, Walker Co., Ala. - dau. of B. M. & Bessie (Key) Wright. Victor S. Patterson, Jr. enlisted in the United States Navy on Dec. 29, 1941 three weeks after Pearl Harbor and was sworn in at the Naval Station in Birmingham, Ala. He served during World War II in the Atlantic Theatre of War, and was honorably discharged on Sept. 8, 1945, at Boston, Mass. as a Chief Radio Technician. (Radar) They were married at Fayette, Ala. by Rev. Roy Chandler. He is in charge of the Sales Dept. of the Golden Eagle Syrup Co. Children: 1. Richard Stephen "Ricky" Patterson, b. April 6, 1952, Alabama. (Adopted - Nov. 25, 1952)

PATTERSON, Wiley, b. Jan. 23, 1884, Fayette Co., Ala. - son of J.J. & Cenath (Rice) Patterson - m. Nancy C. Walters, b. 1888, d. Feb. 1954. Wiley Patterson is a farmer and moved to Mississippi several years after his children were born. Children: 1. Carie Hasseltine Patterson, b. Aug. 29, 1904, d. Oct. 29, 1904. 2. Clydie Ausborn Patterson, b. Nov. 18, 1905, d. Nov. 25, 1914, Fayette Co. (Wagon run over and killed child when he was 9 years old.) 3. Chester Patterson. 4. Infant Daughter, b. & d. 1929. 5. Audrey Patterson m. Mr. Mordecai. 6. Wiley Patterson, Jr.

PATTERSON, William, b. Ireland, m. Elizabeth Peeples, b. Ireland. He was a farmer and both are of Scotch-Irish descent. Children: 1. William Patterson, b. Nov. 1, 1752, at Farrak County Donegal, Ireland; came to Philadelphia at age of 14; arrived in America in April 1766 and went to work at the counting house of Samuel Jackson. Wm's dau. Elizabeth married Napolean's brother. 2. John ? Patterson. 3. Robert Patterson?.

PATTERSON, William Castle, b. May 26, 1866, Fayette Co., Ala., d. Nov. 11, 1922, Fayette Co. - son of J.J. & Cenath (Rice) Patterson - m. Feb. 24, 1889 Maranda Jane Doughty, b. June 5, 1869, Fayette Co., d. May 27, 1954 - dau. of J. F. & Rachel L. A. (Boozer) Doughty. Wm. C. Patterson was a farmer and a store-clerk. Children: 1. Bertha Adaline Patterson, b. Feb. 12, 1890, Faye. Co., d. Oct. 5, 1946, Fayette, Ala., m. John B. Ford, b. Sept. 9, 1871, Faye. Co., d. May, 1946. (They had one child - a daughter, Johnnie Ford, b. & d. 1930.) 2. Lomus Felix Patterson, b. May 21, 1892, Fayette Co., d. Aug. 30, 1893, Fayette Co., Ala. 3. Victor Samuel Patterson, b. Jan. 11, 1895, Fayette Co., m. June 24, 1919, Lucy Evelyn Bobo, b. Nov. 5, 1895, Fayette Co., Ala.

PATTERSON, William Theron, b. Oct. 16, 1914, Fayette Co., - son of G.H. & Lizzie (Hinton) Patterson - m. Ophelia Couch, b. Nov. 27, 1918, Marion Co., Ala. Children: 1. Charles Arthur Patterson, b. April 28, 1940, Fayette, Ala. 2. Elizabeth Ellen "Betty" Patterson, b. Sept. 25, 1942, Fayette, Ala. 3. Alice Marie Patterson, b. Dec. 12, 1946, Fayette, Ala.

PAYNE, Issac W., b. Jan. 30, 1834, d. Dec. 9, 1927, Fayette Co., m. Elizabeth Hollingsworth, b. Feb. 20, 1844, d. July 11, 1937 - dau. of Jeptha & Martha (Ford) Hollingsworth. Children: 1. Martha Belle Payne, b. Aug. 29, 1869, d. Aug. 6, 1882. 2. Nancy Emily Payne, b. April 27, 1872, d. Jan. 12, 1944. 3. Samuel Jeptha Payne, b. June 16, 1878. 4. James E. Payne, b. June 22, 1882. 5. Mary Exie Payne, b. June 10, 1886.

PETERS, Robert Frierson, b. Oct. 11, 1862, Tusca. Ala., d. Jan. 5, 1941, Fay. Ala. - son of B. F. & Adaline M. (Frierson) Peters - m. June 2, 1891 - 1st. - Annie Lena Jones, b. 1875, Fayette, Ala., d. May 6, 1909, Fayette, - dau. of James B. & Annie (Byars) Jones. Children: Annie Roberta Peters, b. Mar. 22, 1902, Fayette, Ala., d. Nov. 14, 1928, Birmingham, Ala., m. Sept. 9, 1923, Wilton H. Hogan, b. Birmingham, Ala.

Robert F. Peters second marriage - Dec. 16, 1909, Jessie May Richardson, b. Sept. 3, 1890, Birmingham, Ala. - dau. of Hamlet P. & Gertrude (Propst) Richardson. Mr. & Mrs. Peters were married at Fayette, Ala. by Rev. Robert H. Jones. R. F. Peters was an Attorney at Law and Mrs. Peters served the County as Registrar of Circuit Court in Equity from 1935 to 1957. Robert Frierson Peters moved, with his family, to Fayette County about 1864. He was educated in the common schools and by his father. He studied law at the University of Alabama from which he graduated in June 1887 with the degree of Bachelor of Laws and began the practice of his profession in Fayette County and Courts of Alabama where he was actively engaged in the practice of law for over fifty years.

Following is an account of his public life in Fayette Co., Ala.: 1887 - 1892, Clerk Circuit Court,; 1894 - 1898, Mayor of Latona (later Fayette); 1892 - 1899, County Solicitor; 1902 - 1906, Representative State Legislature; 1914 - 1918, Chairman of Fayette County Draft Board - Chairman for Minute Men - Member legal advisory board and fuel committee; 1919 - 1923, Representative State Legislature; 1912 - 1935, Attorney for Fayette County; 1915 - 1935 Register in Chancery (later Circuit Court in Equity.); 1929 - 1931, Editor of "Northwest Alabamian"; 1935 - 1936, County Solicitor; 1935 - 1939, Member of State Democratic Executive Committee; and 1940 - 1941, Attorney for Fayette County. Mr. Peters was also, Royal Arch Mason - Past High Priest and Master of Fayette Lodge; a Charter Member of Fayette Order Eastern Star; Member of Knights of Pythias; and a Member of the Sigma Alpha Epsilon College Fraternity. Children: 1. Mary Marguerite Peters, b. Jan. 4, 1911, Fayette, Ala. m. Henry Grey England, b. Sept. 11, 1905, Oakgrove, Ala.

PETERS, Benjamin Franklin, Rev., b. Sept. 3, 1818, Abbeville Dist., S.C., d. Nov. 3, 1903, Fayette, Ala. - son of Jordan & Elizabeth (Crews) Peters - m. at Tuscaloosa, Ala. - Adaline Matilda Frierson, b. Tusca. Co., Ala., d. Buried at Jasper, Ala. - dau. of Robert & Mary (McCrea) Frierson, Jr. After completing his elementary education at Montgomery, Ala, where his parents lived, Mr. Peters attended school at the University of Alabama, 1836 - 1838. Contemplating the profession of law as his life-work, he entered the University of Virginia in 1838. After graduating in law he practiced in Richmond, Va. for a few years. Convinced of his call to the ministry, he entered Union Theological Seminary, New York, in the autumn of 1844, was graduated in June 1847 and was licensed by the Presbytery of East Hanover in Oct. 1847. The first two years of his ministry were spent in Virginia. He was especially zealous in his advocacy of missionary work and started for northwest Louisiana, and there as a pioneer in a country where organized Presbyterianism was non-existant, he labored for eight long years. He preached all over the parishes

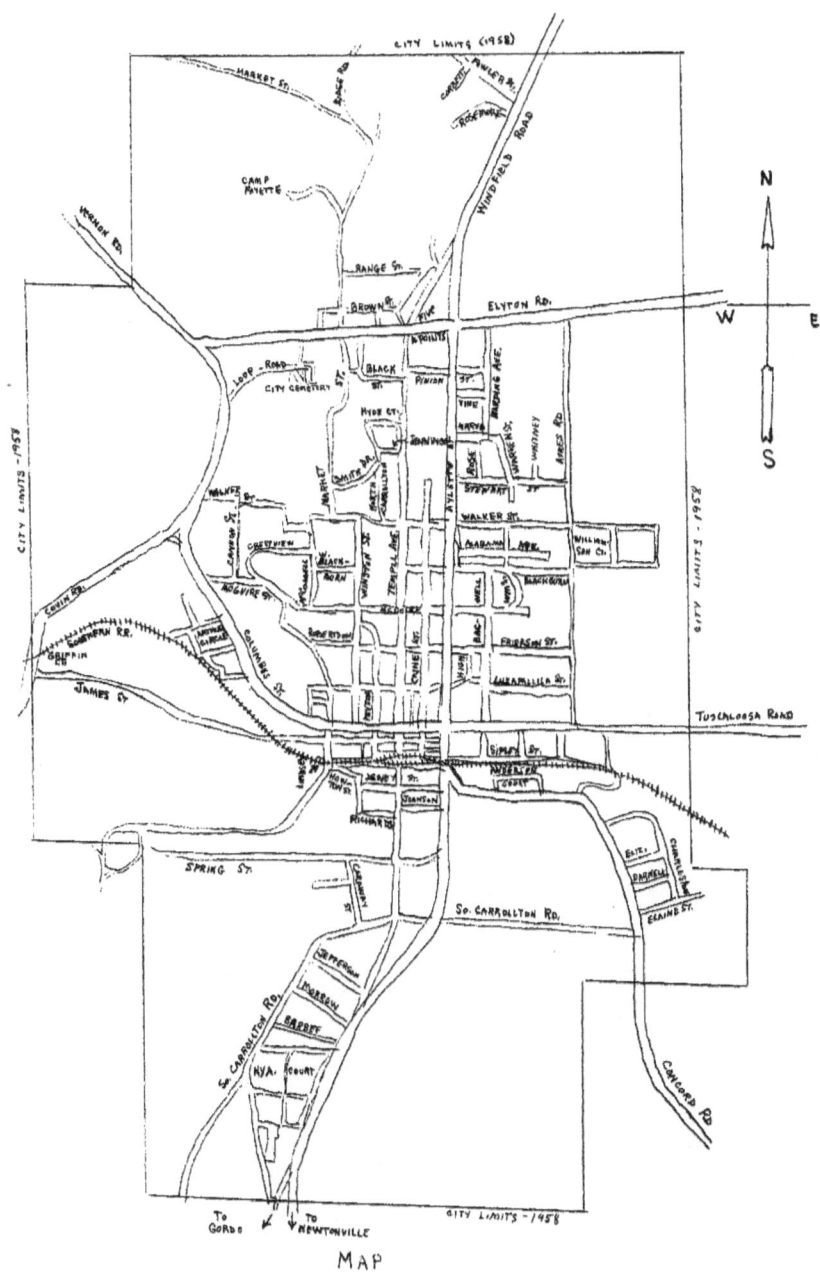

MAP

CITY OF FAYETTE ALABAMA - 1958

of; Claiborne, Webster, Bossier, Caddo and DeSoto, organizing churches. While laboring in Louisiana, he rode two hundred miles, many of them through the roadless region of the Mississippi swamps, on horseback, to the Synod of Mississippi, in sessions at Jackson, Miss. to obtain authority for the organization of a Presbytery in that remote region. He was successful and the Red River Presbytery was brought into existence. With the coming of the civil strife, he returned to Alabama and made Livingston his home for four years, preaching and doing missionary work in the Tuscaloosa Presbytery, especially in Fayette County. Following the conflict, like too many ministers in the impoverished southland, he combined teaching with preaching and taught in Tuscaloosa, Fayette, Lamar and Walker Counties, preaching wherever he went to teach. He was named a member of the Board of Trustees of the University of Alabama in 1866 and 1868. In 1888 his old love for La. returned and for several years he served as Pastor of the Presbyterian Church at Plaquemine, in La. Presbytery. In 1892, he returned to Miss. and although having passed the three score years and ten, he assumed full charge of a group of churches in the Tombigbee Presbytery. He served his presbytery many times as moderator and commissioner to the Assembly. He was chosen to address the Tombeckbee Presbytery on the occasion of the two hundred and fiftieth anniversary of the Westminister Assembly. Children: 1. Robert Frierson Peters, b. Oct. 11, 1862, Tusca. Co., d. Jan. 5, 1941, Fay. Ala., m. 2nd. - Jessie May Richardson, b. Sept. 3, 1890, Birmingham, Ala. 2. Thomas Marion Peters, b. Fayette, Ala., d. Oct. 15, 1927, Fayette, m. Jan. 31, 1893, Ida Guin, b. 1872, d. Dec. 8, 1951, Fayette, Ala. 3. Mary Elizabeth Peters, b. July 15, 1865, Fayette, d. Jan. 4, 1928, Meridan, Miss., m. (Mark) Lemuel Porter, b. Feb. 1, 1850, Houston, Miss., d. Dec. 30, 1926, Meridan, Miss.

PETERS, Jordan, b. native of Greenwood, S.C., d. buried Lowndes Co., Ala., m. Elizabeth Crews. Mr. Peters moved to Montgomery, Ala. in the early part of the 1800's. Children: 1. Benjamin Franklin Peters, b. Sept. 3, 1818, Abbeville, Dist. S.C., d. Nov. 3, 1903, Fayette, m. Adaline M. Frierson, b. Tusca. Co., Ala. 2. Francis Marion Peters, m. Susan Rhodes. 3. Mary Elizabeth Peters.

PETERS, Thomas Marion, M.D., b. Fayette, d. Oct. 15, 1927, Fayette - son of Rev. B.F. & Adaline (Frierson) Peters - m. Jan. 31, 1893, Ida Guin, b. 1872, Fayette Co., d. Dec. 8, 1951 - dau. of Perry C. & Mary Ann (Brock) (Nickols) Guin. Dr. & Mrs. Peters were married at Fayette, Ala. by Rev. B. F. Peters. Dr. Peters was a native of Fayette Co., Ala. He was graduated at Mobile Medical College in Mar. 1890 with honors, both in medicine and pharmacy, and immediately began the practice of medicine and surgery in Fayette and surrounding counties. In later years, he came to be known as one of the outstanding physicians in this section of Ala., especially in the field of diagnostics. He was a member of the County and State Medical Associations and served as County Health Officer. In addition to his professional duties and responsibilities in connection with the drug business which he operated for a number of years, Dr. Peters, served the city of Fayette in the capacity of Mayor for two terms during which time many civic improvements were made. Children: 1. Thomas Marion Peters, II, b. Nov. 12, 1893, Fayette Co., Ala., d. Aug. 7, 1958, Fayette, Ala., m. Aug. 1, 1926, Matsie McKell, b. Nov. 28, 1903, Starksville, Miss.

PETERS, Thomas Marion, II, b. Nov. 12, 1893, Fayette Co., Ala., d. Aug. 7, 1958, Fayette - son of Dr. Thos. M. & Ida (Guin) Peters - m. Aug. 1, 1926, Matsie McKell, b. Nov. 28, 1903, Starksville, Miss. - dau. of Thurston W. & Jane (Cross) McKell. Children: 1. Thomas Marion Peters, III, b. Nov. 21, 1931, Starksville, Miss., m. Vilma Whitley, b. July 1, 1935, Fayette Co.

PETERS, Thomas Marion, III, b. Nov. 21, 1931, Starksville, Miss. - son of T.M., II & Matsie (McKell) Peters - m. Dec. 18, 1954, Wilma Lee Whitley, b. July 1, 1935, Fayette Co. - dau. of George F. "Billy" & Eardile __ Whitley. Children: 1. Marion Duane Peters, b. April 10, 1957, Fayette, Ala.

PLYLER, D. Franklin, b. Mar. 9, 1853, N. C., d. May 17, 1934, Fayette Co., - son of Felton & Nancy (Belk) Plyler - m. Nancy C. Moore, b. Aug. 8, 1862, d. Feb. 4, 1888 - dau. of David & Mary E. (Metcalf or Brown) Moore. D. F. Plyler came to Fayette County with his family at the age of 8 years. Children: 1. Ella Plyler, b. Dec. 16, 1879, d. July 19, 1954, m. Miles Abernathy. 2. James Wesley Plyler, b. Jan. 18, 1881, d. Sept. 9, 1919, m. Mary Yerby. 3. Dave Plyler, m. Cora Branyon. 4. Ollie Plyler, m. 1st. - Delta Holliman, 2nd. - Myrtle Ross. 5. Lee Allen Plyler, b. Aug. 7, 1886, Fayette Co., m. Sept. 7, 1905, Lovie Pearl Owens, b. Sept. 29, 1887, Fayette Co., Ala.

PLYLER, Felton, b. N. C. - son of Frederick & Elizabeth Plyler - m. Nancy Belk, b. Dec. 6, 1822, N. C., d. Sept. 30, 1906. Felton Plyler served in Co. D. 8th Cav. Regt. Co. A. 9th Ala. Cav. and 26th Ala. Regt. under Col. Poe's Co. After he left the army in the north, his family never heard from him again and his wife, Nancy was a pensioner from Fayette Co., Ala. in 1899. Children: 1. D. Franklin Plyler, b. Mar. 9, 1853, N. C., d. May 17, 1934, Fayette Co., m. Nancy C. Moore, b. Aug. 8, 1862, d. Feb. 4, 1888, Fayette Co. 2. Mary Jane Plyler, b. June 20, 1845, d. Feb. 14, 1913, m. George W. Shepherd, b. Nov. 23, 1844, d. Nov. 4, 1909. 3. Marvie Plyler, m. Berry Taylor. 4. Marthy Plyler, m. John Taylor. 5. J. Fred Plyler, b. 1857, N. C. d. Texas. 6. Ella Plyler, b. 1859, N. C., m. J. Q. Bradley. 7. Monroe Plyler. 8. Henry A. Plyler, b. June 25, 1860, Ala., d. Oct. 3, 1865, Ala.

PLYLER, Lee Allen, b. Aug. 7, 1886, Fayette Co., Ala. - son of D. F. & Nancy C. (Moore) Plyler - m. Sept. 7, 1905, Lovie Pearl Owens, b. Sept. 29, 1887 Fayette Co. - dau. of N. B. & Mary K. (Johnson) Owens. They were married at Fayette, Ala. by Rev. George Freeman. He is a farmer. Children: 1. Bessie Mae Plyler, b. Oct. 21, 1907, (All children born Fayette, Co.) m. Carl Johnson. 2. Infant Daughter, b. & d. 1910. 3. Willina Plyler, b. June 7, 1911, m. Robert Posey. 4. Cecil E. Plyler, b. Aug. 14, 1915, d. Oct. 23, 1917. 5. O'Neal Plyler, b. Dec. 11, 1918, m. Feb. 19, 1946, Lancy R. Kelley, b. Oct. 6, 1920, Fayette Co. 6. Lee Allen Plyler, Jr., b. Dec. 27, 1920, m. Ruby Sularian. 7. Vaudine Plyler, b. July 18, 1924, m. Orville Plyman.

PLYLER, O'Neal, b. Dec. 11, 1918, Fayette Co., Ala. - son of L. A. & Lovie (Owens) Plyler, Sr. - m. Feb. 19, 1946, Lancy R. Kelley, b. Oct. 6, 1920, Fayette Co., Ala. - dau. of H. D. & Retta (Johnson) Kelley. They were married in Belk, Ala. by Rev. S. E. Walker. She was married before and the 1st. child listed is by her first marriage. Children: 1. Winston E. Miolen Plyler, b. May 8, 1942. 2. Eindle Sue Plyler, b. April 1, 1947.

POE, Ausborn A., b. July 23, 1882, Fayette Co., Ala., d. Jan. 1951, m. Dec.

3, 1905, Alma Patterson, b. Mar. 29, 1887, Fayette Co., Ala. - dau. of J. J. & Cenath (Rice) Patterson. Children: 1. Floyd Ausborn Poe, b. Nov. 7, 1907, Fayette Co., Ala., m. Elise Fowler. 2. Marvin Loyd Poe, b. April 13, 1911, Fayette Co., m. Evelyn Suggs. 3. Victor Winford "Dick" Poe, b. May 11, 1914 Fayette Co., m. Lona Duke. (Served in World War II.) 4. William Ellis Poe, b. Feb. 10, 1921, Fayette Co., m. Mar. 22, 1947, Marjorie Dare Thomas, b. Birmingham, Ala. ("Bill" was ordained as a Missionary Baptist Minister from the Fayette Baptist Church.)

POE, George Royal, m. Oct. 8, 1948, Laura Augusta Bobo, b. Nov. 12, 1921, Fayette Co., - dau. of Troy L. & Alice (Meadders) Bobo. Children: 1. Myra Ann Poe, b. July 8, 1951. 2. Suzanne Poe, b. Feb. 27, 1956, d. Feb. 28, 1956.

POE, Victor Winford "Dick", b. May 11, 1914, Fayette Co., Ala. - son of A. A. & Alma (Patterson) Poe - m. Lona Duke. V. W. "Dick" Poe served in World War II. Children: 1. Victor Duke Poe, b. & d. 1945, Fayette, Ala. 2. Michael "Mike" Poe, b. July 26, 1953, Miss. (adopted July 27, 1953.)

POE, William Ellis, b. Feb. 10, 1921, Fayette Co., Ala. - son of A. A. & Alma (Patterson) Poe - m. Mar. 22, 1947, Marjorie Dare Thomas. W. E. "Bill" Poe served in World War II. He is an ordained Missionary Baptist Minister; was ordained at Fayette First Baptist Church in Fayette, Ala. Children: 1. Linda Laural Poe, b. Oct. 9, 1951, Fayette, Ala. 2. William Randal Poe, b. Sept. 22, 1955, Fayette, Ala.

POLLARD, Carey Norman, b. Aug. 6, 1927, Fayette, Ala. - son of Carey N. & Maggie (Shirley) Pollard - m. Aug. 3, 1945, Betty Ann Cannon, b. Sept. 5, 1927, Fayette, Ala. - dau. of Wm. Louis & Ruby (Jeffries) Cannon. Carey Norman Pollard served in the United States Navy from April 10, 1945 to June 13, 1946. They were married in Fayette, Ala. by Rev. A. M. Nix. Children: 1. Karen Ann Pollard, b. Jan. 5, 1950, Fayette, Ala. 2. Jeffrey Norman Pollard b. Aug. 9, 1951, Fayette, Ala.

POLSUM, Tom, b. April 15, 1877, Carzell Co., Texas, d. Sept. 24, 1955, Grandview, Texas, m. Bessie Dickinson, b. April 25, 1875, Fayette Co., Ala. - dau. of Peyton I. Dickinson. Children: 1. Eva Polsum, b. Texas. 2. J. E. Polsum, b. Texas. 3. A Son, b. Texas. 4. A Daughter, b. Texas.

PORTER, George Washington, b. Nov. 7, 1866, Fayette Co., Ala., d. Mar. 10, 1914, Fayette Co., m. Frances A. Prater, b. Feb. 6, 1864, Fayette Co., d. Feb. 28, 1955, Fayette Co., Ala. Children: 1. Jessie Valentine Porter, b. Mar. 8, 1889, Fayette Co., (All children b. Fayette Co.) d. June 23, 1941. 2. Lenie Mae Porter, b. Aug. 25, 1890. 3. John Houston Porter, b. Mar. 23, 1892, d. Feb. 28, 1921. 4. Mackey Porter, b. May 22, 1895, d. Dec. 26, 1900. 5. George Eulice Porter, b. June 23, 1898. 6. Fletcher Porter, b. Feb. 15, 1900. 7. Jeannette Porter, b. Nov. 11, 1902, d. Aug. 1941. 8. Cornelious Porter, b. April 1, 1904. 9. Hester Porter, b. July 4, 1906, d. April 1907. 10. Wm. Elmer Porter, b. Sept. 12, 1909.

PORTER, Jack, b. Fayette Co., m. Louise Hinton, b. Jan. 5, 1925, Fayette Co. - dau. of T. Burt & Lizzie (Doughty) Hinton. Children: 1. Larry Porter, b. Sept. 2, 1946, Fayette, Ala. Jack is the son of Denver & Carrie Porter, b. Fayette, Co., Ala.

PORTER, James Billy, b. Dec. 9, 1923, Fayette Co., Ala. - son of Denver & Carrie Porter - m. Oct. 8, 1943, Dorothy Darnell, b. Jan. 25, 1925, Columbia, Colbert Co., Tenn. - dau. of John & Lillian Darnell. Children: 1. Beverly Joy Porter, b. April 9, 1946, Fayette Co. 2. James Michael Porter, b. Sept. 18, 1947, Fayette Co., Ala.

POYNOR, David Thomas, m. Aug. 28, 1929, Ethel Othelia Nichols, b. Dec. 7, 1902, Fayette Co. - dau. of A. C. Nichols. Children: 1. Mary Ellen Poynor b. Oct. 24, 1931. 2. Othelia Thomas Poynor, b. May 9, 1937, m. Joe Meherg. 3. David Thomas Poynor, b. Oct. 10, 1938.

PRATER, Harlan Irby, Jr., b. Oct. 25, 1910, Millport, Ala., m. Sept. 29, 1933, Bernice Melda Arthur, b. April 21, 1912, Belk, Ala. - dau. of Grover C. & Bessie (Richards) Arthur. Children: 1. Harlan Irby Prater, III, b. Jan. 28, 1935, Birmingham, Ala., m. Sept. 6, 1959, Joyce Ann Ruffin. 2. Jerry Arthur Prater (Twin), b. May 9, 1938, Birmingham, Ala. 3. Amelia Jane Prater, (Twin) b. May 9, 1938, Birmingham, Ala.

PREWITT, A. M., b. abt. 1815, Ala., m. Temperance Strong, b. 1820, Ala. - dau. of Wm. M. Strong. Children: 1. John Prewitt, b. 1839, Ala. 2. James Prewitt, b. 1841, Ala. 3. Thomas Prewitt, b. 1843, Ala. 4. Susan Prewitt, b. 1845, Ala. 5. Clina Prewitt, b. 1848, Ala.

PRICE, Dr. Wm. F., D.D., b. Sept. 17, 1870, Valley Head, Ala., d. Aug. 11, 1959, Fayette, Ala., m. June 1, 1907, Ida Bell. He was pastor for the First Methodist Church in Fayette and retired and made their home in Fayette. Children: 1. Evelyn Price. 2. Ida Bell Price.

PRICE, William McPhearson, m. Mar. 18, 1901, Pearl Milam, b. Feb. 7, 1873, Cartersville, Ga., d. Oct. 28, 1958, Fayette, Ala. One of Fayette's beloved characters, Mrs. Price came to Fayette from Stuttgart, Ark. in 1933, after her husband's death, to make her home with her twin sister, Mrs. J. H. Yuckley, who had moved to Fayette in 1912 with her husband and who opened a drug store, known as the Palace Drug Store. Mrs. Price gave her untiring services in helping her sister nurse Capt. Yuckley during his illness and later helped care for their aged mother who lived in Fayette for many years. Mrs. Yuckley died June 17, 1948, leaving Mrs. Price alone. Mrs. Price carried on the household duties, with the aid of Annie Matthews, the cook, just as her sister had always done. "Miss Pearl's" interest in all people helped to make her life a very full and busy one. She was very active in Church affairs until blindness hampered her activities. All who knew "Miss Pearl" loved her.

PROPST, Charlie Dale, b. Sept. 22, 1902, Fayette, Ala. - son of Dan F., Sr. & Susie Emily (Hyde) Propst - m. Sept. 11, 1928, Sophia Russell "Tommie" Parker, b. Sept. 4, 1909, Chickasaw, Ala., - dau. of Ellis Jackson & Margarett (Lang) Parker. Children: 1. Margaret Emily Propst, b. Mar. 25, 1930, Fay. Ala., m. Aug. 7, 1953, Richard D. Reynolds. 2. Charlie Daniel Propst, b. Nov. 17, 1939, Fayette, Ala.

PROPST, Daniel, b. Feb. 8, 1813, Lincoln Co., N.C., d. Aug. 16, 1895, Millport, Ala. - son of Michael & Elizabeth (Faggett) Propst - m. Annie Shelton, b. Mar. 17, 1816, Lincoln Co., N.C., d. Aug. 30, 1908, Millport, Ala. Children: 1. Cynthia Louisa Propst, m. Merril Gentry. 2. Bell Elizabeth Propst, b. Jan. 29, 1849, d. May 10, 1928, Fayette, Ala., m. Robert E. Sanders, b.

July 12, 1851, d. Oct. 31, 1890, Fayette, Ala. 3. Wm. Wesley Propst, b. 1838 d. 1923, Fayette, m. Sarah Caroline Garrison, b. 1843, d. 1933, Fayette. 4. Henry Belton Propst, b. May 13, 1854, d. Aug. 3, 1931, Fayette, m. Oct. 15, 1889, Carrie Cannon, b. April 22, 1870, Fayette, Ala., d. Aug. 22, 1938. 5. Mary R. Propst, b. Mar. 20, 1851, d. Feb. 21, 1927. 6. Daniel Freeman Propst, b. Mar. 2, 1859, d. June 24, 1926, Fayette, m. Susie Hyde, b. Dec. 17, 1874, d. May 2, 1926, Fayette, Ala. 7. John Nelson Propst, b. April 8, 1836, d. Jan. 18, 1916, m. Alice M. Schoolar, b. Aug. 4, 1851, d. Nov. 27, 1925. 8. Toby Propst, b. Sept. 11, 1861, d. Aug. 1, 1863, Fayette, Ala. 9. Thomas M. Propst, b. Aug. 26, 1855, d. June 18, 1878.

PROPST, Daniel Freeman, Jr., b. Aug. 17, 1899, d. Nov. 20, 1937, Fayette, Ala. - son of Daniel F., Sr. & Susie Emily (Hyde) Propst - m. Aug. 20, 1926, Alice Putnam, b. Dec. 3, 1905, Fayette, Ala. - dau. of Walter DeForest & Mary Estelle (Nuckols) Putnam. Children: 1. Lenora Sue Propst, b. Dec. 5, 1929, Fayette, Ala., m. April 19, 1954, Nathan Paul McCully. 2. Mina Louise Propst, b. July 28, 1932, Fayette, Ala., m. June 3, 1955, Terry Allen Kirkley.

PROPST, Daniel Freeman, b. Mar. 2, 1859, d. June 4, 1926, Fayette, - son of Daniel & Annie (Shelton) Propst - m. Susie Emily Hyde, b. Dec. 17, 1874, Fay. d. May 2, 1926, Fayette - dau. of James H. & Francis (Willingham) Hyde. Children: 1. Daniel Freeman Propst, Jr., b. Aug. 17. 1899, Fayette, d. Nov. 20, 1937, Fayette, m. Aug. 20, 1926, Alice Putnam. 2. Charlie Dale Propst, b. Sept. 22, 1902, Fayette, m. Sept. 11, 1928, Sophie Russell Parker. 3. Francis Louise Propst, b. July 14, 1905, Fayette, d. July 5, 1950, m. June 5, _ Novin H. Eubank. 4. Annie Sue Propst, b. Jan. 2, 1910, Fayette, m. June 26, 1929, John F. Wakefield.

PROPST, Henry Belton, b. May 13, 1854, Pickens Co., Ala., d. Aug. 2, 1931, Fayette, Ala. - son of Daniel & Annie (Shelton) Propst - m. Oct. 16, 1889, Carrie Waters Cannon, b. April 22, 1870, Fayette, d. Aug. 22, 1938, Fayette, dau. of Thomas Sidney & Mary Elon (Morrow) Cannon. H. B. Propst was once mayor of Fayette, Ala. He and his brother, Daniel F. Propst donated grounds on which the First Methodist Church of Fayette now stands. They were among the oldest merchants in Fayette. Children: 1. Sara Nell Propst, b. Feb. 5, 1899, Fayette, m. Wallace Porter Lawrence, b. June 11, 1895, Frankfort, Ky., d. Oct. 6, 1952, Fayette. 2. Thomas Cannon Propst, b. Aug. 30, 1890, Fayette, Ala. 3. Henry Raeburn Propst, b. Nov. 26, 1896, Fayette, d. Oct. 29, 1938.

PROPST, Jacob Wilson, b. Oct. 21, 1852, Pickens Co., Ala., d. Nov. 7, 1907, son of Wilson & Rebecca White (Shelton) Propst - m. Oct. 19, 1871, Leona Cornelia Coons, b. June 4, 1853, Pickens Co., Ala., d. Dec. 21, 1941 - dau. of James M. & Martha (Harrington) Coons. Both are buried in Birmingham, Ala. Children: 1. Gertrude Propst, b. Nov. 20, 1872, d. Oct. 2, 1949, Palmetto Pickens Co., Ala., m. Oct. 20, 1889, Hamlet Preston Richardson, b. Sept. 23, 1858 (both b. Pickens Co., Ala.), d. April 12, 1926, Palmetto, Pickens Co., Ala. 2. Florence Rebecca Propst, b. July 29, 1874, Lamar Co., Ala., m. June 6, 1894, Daniel Edward Duggar, b. April 30, 1864, Brooks Co., Ga. 3. Robert W. Propst, b. Lamar Co., Ala., m. Lucille Hill. 4. Lelia Estell Propst. 5. James Grunter Propst.

PROPST, Michael, m. Elizabeth Faggett, - dau. of Jacob Faggett. Children: 1. Wilson Propst, b. June 12, 1815, N.C. (Came to Ala. in 1845.) m. Feb. 14,

1839, Rebecca (Shelton) White, b. Dec. 28, 1809, Lincoln Co., N.C., d. Oct. 27, 1852, buried at Unity Grove, Pickens Co., Ala. 2. Daniel Propst, b. Feb. 8, 1813, N. C., d. Aug. 16, 1895, buried Lamar Co., m. Annie Shelton, b. Mar. 7, 1816, Lincoln Co., N.C., d. Aug. 30, 1908, buried Lamar Co. 3. Nelson Propst, b. N. C., d. in infancy. 4. John Propst, b. N.C. 5. Michael Propst, b. N.C. 6. Wiley Propst, b. N.C., m. Mary Ellis. 7. Sarah Propst, b. N.C. 8. Jacob Propst. 9. Reinhilt Propst, d. in infancy.

PROPST, William Wesley, b. 1838, d. 1923, Fayette - son of Daniel & Annie (Shelton) Propst - m. Sarah Caroline Garrison, b. 1843, d. 1933, Fayette, Ala. Children: 1. Zada Propst, m. Louis M. Parrish. 2. Daisy Pearl Propst, m. Charlie Banks Hyde. 3. Kitty Propst, m. John A. Cobb. 4. Lula Propst, m. Raymond Page. 5. Bill Propst, m. Lula Drake. 6. Cleon Propst, b. 1868, d. 1932, m. 1st. - Mrs. Fannie Appling, d. 1930.

PROPST, Wilson, b. June 12, 1815, Lincoln Co., N. C., - son of Michael & Elizabeth (Faggett) Propst - m. Feb. 14, 1839, Rebecca (Shelton) White, b. Dec. 28, 1809, Lincoln Co., N.C., d. Oct. 27, 1852, Pickens Co., Ala. - dau. of Nelson & Frances (Sadler) Shelton. Rebecca was the widow of a Mr. White. Wilson and Rebecca were married at Lincoln Co., N. C. Rebecca's mother's Will is recorded in Will Book 1, Page 260, Lincoln Co., N.C. Children: 1. Jacob Wilson Propst, b. Oct. 21, 1852, Pickens Co., Ala., d. Nov. 7, 1907, m. Leona Coons, b. June 4, 1853, Lamar Co., Ala., d. Dec. 21, 1941. Both are buried Elmwood Cem., Birmingham, Ala. 2. Julia Elizabeth Propst, b. April 29, 1846, d. July 12, 1935, Fayette, m. 1st. - Dr. Frank Shelton, 2nd. - James E. Bell, b. Aug. 23, 1842, d. Nov. 2, 1916, Fayette, Ala. 3. Daniel Edney Propst. 4. Allen Hamby Propst, b. Feb. 14, 1842, Pickens Co., Ala., d. Dec. 31, 1896, Columbus, Miss., m. Jan. 9, 1872, Martha A. Russell, b. May 7, 1849, Gordo, Ala., d. Jan. 29, 1913, Columbus, Miss. 5. Minerva Propst. 6. Wincie Lucinda F. Propst, m. __Brent. 7. Martin A. Propst, son of Wilson by 2nd. wife.

PRYOR, Joseph, b. Dec. 1, 1767, S. C., d. abt. 1851, m. Sarah __, b. Nov. 25, 1776. Joseph Pryor was a farmer and a Minister of the Gospel. His second wife was Catherine Hughs, born in Ga. Children: (By first marriage.) 1. Mary Pryor, b. May 25, 1793, m. Nov. 9, 1823, John Bryant. 2. John Pryor, b. Nov. 25, 1795. 3. Rachel Pryor, b. Dec. 27, 1797, Tenn., m. Thomas Alexander, b. 1787, Ky. 4. Mourning Pryor, b. Sept. 14, 1800, m. Eli Langford. 5. Elizabeth Pryor, b. July 14, 1803, Tenn., m. Zachriah S. Simpson, b. 1793, S. C. 6. Nancy Pryor, b. Dec. 7, 1805, Tenn., m. Sept. 12, 1824, Manning Clements (Baptist Minister), b. 1801, S. C. 7. Hannah Pryor, b. Sept. 25, 1808, m. Tobias Watson. 8. Samuel O. Pryor, b. Jan. 28, 1811, m. Oct. 9, 1828, Unity Fox. 9. Sarah Pryor, b. Aug. 5, 1813, Tenn., m. Dec. 29, 1830, James L. Clements, b. 1807, Tenn. 10. Margaret Pryor, b. Feb. 10, 1816, Tenn., m. Joseph F. Doughty, b. 1811, S. C. 11. Rebecca Pryor, b. April 29, 1819, d. Feb. 10, 1862, m. Jan. 16, 1834, Mordecai Fulton "Dick" Doughty, b. Sept. 16, 1813, d. Mar. 28, 1871.

PULLIAM, Arch, b. Oct. 10, _Ky., m. Dec. 22, 1941, Laura Mae Jones, b. Oct. 26, _, Fayette Co., Ala. - dau. of Theron & Mary (Jones) Cannon. Children: 1. Mary Wakefield Pulliam, b. April 27, 1944, Birmingham, Ala. 2. Melbourne Cannon Pulliam, b. Feb. 15, 1947, Birmingham, Ala. 3. Elizabeth Jones Pulliam, b. Oct. 24, 1956, Birmingham, Ala.

PUTNAM, Walter DeForest, b. July 24, 1869, Warren, Ill., d. Feb. 20, 1938, Biloxi, Miss., m. April 8, 1896, Mary Estelle Nuckols, b. Feb. 7, 1869, d. June 20, 1943, Fayette, Ala. Even though not a native of Fayette, W. D. Putnam came to Fayette just prior to the Spanish American War (1890's). His original home was Chicago, Ill. and being one of the first "Yankees" to move to Fayette he had many obstacles to overcome. He married Mary Estelle Nuckols, (better known as Lee). Her father fought in the Civil War under Gen. Lee and wanted her called Lee. They were married in Las Vegas, New Mexico. Upon coming to Fayette, Walter DeForest Putnam bought a small store from his brother-in-law, and it was called, or known as the Notion Store, probably the first real notion store in Fayette. During this time he played baseball on the Fayette Team with Joe Caine, Ernest Young, Sam Sanders and many others and anytime the team would say, "Let's play ball!", he would lock the store and off the team would go to Berry, Vernon, or Bankston, anyplace the game might be played. The mode of travel was via the Southern Railroad, that operated between Greenville, Miss. and Birmingham, Ala. Many happy hours were spent with the neighbors, listening to the graphaphones, with the "morning-glory-horn" and the little round cylinder records. He brought first Steamer Car to Fayette and after the first few time it was steamed up, it exploded and severely burned Putnam, so he put it in the "Car Shed" and never used it again. Children: 1. Mina Lee Putnam, b. Sept. 3, 1897, Fayette, m. Oct. 14, 1919, Thomas Winfield Glenn, b. Aug. 17, 1894, Fayette, Ala., d. June 26, 1946, Pensacola, Fla. 2. Elsie Putnam, b. July 20, 1899, d. within a week. 3. Paul DeForest Putnam, b. Oct. 18, 1900, Fayette, m. Lois. 4. Alice Elizabeth Putnam, b. Dec. 3, 1905, Fayette, m. Dan F. Propst, Jr. 5. Walter Harrison Putnam, b. Nov. 12, 1908, Fayette, Ala.

RAINWATER, Miles, b. S. C., m. Sallie Hutchinson, b. N. C. Children: 1. Sally or Sarah Rainwater, b. May 22, 1808, S. C., d. Jan. 19, 1881, Fayette Co., Ala., m. Levingston Bobo, b. Feb. 26, 1806, S. C., d. April 27, 1883, Fayette Co., Ala. 2. Miles Rainwater, b. Mar. 7, 1809 or 1810, d. May 30, 1886, Fayette Co., m. Sarah Edwards. 3. Mary "Polly" Rainwater, b. 1818, S. C., m. Spencer Bobo, b. 1808, S. C. 4. Amanda Jane Rainwater, b. July 14, 1826, S. C., d. May 25, 1896, Fayette Co., m. Mar. 20, 1845, William Wilburn Waldrop, b. Dec. 15, 1822, d. Sept. 15, 1905, Fayette Co. 5. Silas M. Rainwater, b. July 25, 1825, S. C., d. Nov. 2, 1902, Fayette Co., m. Mary Jane Hindman, b. June 1, 1835, d. Aug. 27, 1905, Fayette Co. 6. ? Vashti ? Rainwater.

RAINWATER, Miles, II, b. 1857, Covin, Fayette Co., Ala., d. July 21, 1911, Fayette Co., Ala., m. Sarah Frances "Fannie" Allen, b. Sept. 3, 1863, Lamar Co., Ala., d. 1943, Fayette Co. Children: 1. Winnie Eppie Rainwater. 2. Almus Rainwater. 3. Autie Rainwater. 4. Ellie Rainwater. 5. Rev. O. Clinton Rainwater. 6. Lando Rainwater. 7. Roscoe Rainwater.

RAINWATER, Silas M., b. Luly 25, 1825, S. C., d. Nov. 2, 1902, m. Mary Jane Hindman, b. June 1, 1835, d. Aug. 27, 1905. Both are buried at the Wesley Chapel Methodist Church Cemetery, Fayette Co., Ala. Children: 1. Miles Rainwater, b. 1857, Covin, Fayette Co., Ala., d. July 21, 1911, Fayette Co., m. Sarah Frances Allen, b. Sept. 3, 1863, Kennedy, Ala., d. 1943, Fayette Co.

RAY, Samuel B., m. abt. 1853, in Fayette Co., Nancy Lansdale, b. 1827, Montgomery Co., Ala., d. 1917, Miss. - dau. of Isaac & Sarah (Gentry)(McCool)

Lansdale. They were early settlers of Fayette County. Children: (Had a large family, including -) 1. Galloway D. Ray. 2. Samantha Ray. 3. Alcy Ray. 4. Van Ray.

REED, Thomas, m. Minervia (Jones) Whitney - dau. of Dr. G. G. Jones. Children: 1. Reuben Reed. 2. Polk Reed. 3. Dallas Reed. 4. Pierce Reed.

REESE, John, b. 1806, d. 1903, Fayette Co., m. Ruth Woods, d. 1891, Fayette Co. Children: 1. Katherine Reese, m. Thomas Roberts.

REESE, Terrell M., b. May 6, 1827, Marion Co., Ala., d. Feb. 8, 1907, m. Rhoda Frances Dodson, b. Dec. 22, 1839, d. June 19, 1876. Mr. T. M. Reese was appointed postmaster of Wayside, Ala. on Sept. 16, 1878 and served until the office was dincontinued in 1905. He was a Methodist and was welknown for his profession of surveying land. Children: (1st. wife, above) 1. Alice Reese, m. Mr. Hamilton. 2. Amanda Reese, m. Mr. Tucker. 3. Breal Reese. 4. Devinie Reese, b. Jan. 24, 1873, d. Mar. 3, 1943, m. Robert J. McCluskey.
    Terrell M. Reese married second - Feb. 18, 1877, Margaret Agnes Harris, b. April 26, 1843, Marion Co., Ala., d. Jan. 13, 1917. She was a teacher at Mont Calm, Fayette Co., Ala. in 1873. Children: (2nd. wife) 1. Lovey Reese, b. & d. Aug. 3, 1883, (Twin). 2. Lucy Reese (Twin), b. Aug. 3, 1883, d. Feb. 13, 1913, m. George W. Couch. 3. Albert Reese. 4. Mary Reese, m. Mr. Adkinson. 5. Jennie Lee Reese, m. R. E. Moore, Sr.

RENFROE, Absalom Jackson, b. Aug. 10, 1830, N. C., d. April 18, 1909, buried Fayette City Cem. - son of Thomas Renfroe - m. Sarah E. Freeman, b. Dec. 19, 1838, Fayette Co., d. 1915, buried Fayette City Cem. - dau. of Boswell Freeman. A. J. Renfroe came to Fayette County at the approximate age of sixteen years, in 1854. He taught school in Mobile and served in the War Between the States. In 1867 he moved to the farm, now known as the Renfroe Farm and lived there until he sold it to his son William Renfroe. After moving to Fayette Court House, he operated a general store for many years. He and his family were active members of the Methodist Church. Dates taken from tombstones. Children: 1. Dora Dean Renfroe, buried at Fayette, m. Dean Collins. 2. Hester Renfroe, b. Jan. 29, 1863, d. May 16, 1890, m. H. F. Yarbrough. 3. James William Renfroe, b. Dec. 12, 1864, Fayette Co., Ala., d. July 9, 1914, Fayette, m. Sept. 18, 1888, Cora L. Barton, b. Dec. 26, 1869, Tusca. Co., d. Oct. 28, 1948, Fayette. 4. John Thomas Renfroe, b. Jan. 4, 1866, Fayette Co. d. Mar. 1956, buried Mt. Vernon Cem., m. Lula Humber. 5. Theo Renfroe, b. Mar. 10, 1867, Fayette Co., d. May 15, 1890, buried Fayette. 6. Icy Belle Renfroe, b. April 18, 1869, Fayette Co., d. May 26, 1890, Fayette. 7. Annie Renfroe, b. Fayette Co., d. Texas, m. Mr. Pinion. 8. Henry Shelton Renfroe, b. Fayette Co., d. 1941, Fayette, m. Eula Stephens, b. Fayette Co., d. 1958, Renfroe Cem. 9. Louise Renfroe, b. April 1875, Fayette Co., d. Nov. 28, 1958, Washington, D. C., m. Cecil A. Beasley, b. Lamar Co., Ala. 10. Robert Lee Renfroe, b. Sept. 22, 1879, Fayette, Ala., d. Mar. 11, 1945, Fayette, m. Dec. 22, 1903, Susie Caraway, b. May 28, 1885, Fayette Co., Ala.

RENFROE, James William, b. Dec. 14, 1864, Fayette Co., d. July 9, 1914, buried in Fayette City Cem. - son of A. J. & Sarah (Freeman) Renfroe - m. Sept. 18, 1888, Cora L. Barton, b. Dec. 26, 1869, Tusca. Co., Ala., d. Oct. 28, 1948, buried Fayette City Cem. - dau. of Cloud Thrasher & M. Virginia (Jeffers)

Barton. Mr. & Mrs. Renfroe were married in Columbus, Miss. by Rev. B. F. Phillips. Mr. Renfroe was a farmer and a railroad man. These records are from the Family Bible owned by Mrs. Sara R. Smith. Children: 1. Johnnie B. Renfroe, b. June 30, 1890, d. Nov. 17, 1956, buried Renfroe Cem., m. Mar. 29, 1908, James Edward Ramsey, b. Jan. 16, _, d. Oct. 16, 1954, Renfroe Cem. 2. Dora Dean Renfroe, b. July 6, 1892, m. April 14, 1912, Horace I. Burson, b. Nov. 24, 1886, Calhoun Co., Miss, c. Jan. 21, 1952, buried Renfroe Cem. 3. Sam James Renfroe, b. Aug. 1, 1894, m. Dec. 19, 1918, Naomi Gilbreath, b. Jan. 5, 1897, Albertville, Ala. (He served in World War I.) 4. William Murray Renfroe, b. Dec. 29, 1896, d. April 3, 1949, buried Renfroe Cem., m. Docia Sanders, b. May 7, 1904, Fayette Co. (He served in World War I.) 5. Lucille Renfroe, b. Oct. 1, 1908, d. Nov. 6, 1928, Fayette. 6. Sara Helen Renfroe, b. Jan. 4, 1911, m. Dec. 22, 1935, Linwood Stewart Smith, b. Jan. 1, 1909, Anson, Texas.

RENFROE, John, b. Jan. 4, 1866, d. Mar. 3, 1956, m. Lula Humber, b. Mar. 13, 1876. Children: 1. Archie Renfroe, m. Laddie Edwards. 2. Roy Renfroe, b. Nov. 3, 1895, Fayette Co., Ala., m. Myra Pauline Bobo, b. Oct. 5, 1906, Fay. Co. 3. Clarence Renfroe, m. Gladys __. 4. Charley Renfroe, m. Effie Miles. 5. Thomas Renfroe, m. 1st. - Kate Horton, 2nd. - Wacile Mayes. 6. Louise Renfroe, m. Alex Williams.

RENFROE, Robert Ralph, b. Fayette Co., m. Mary Ellen Hinton, b. Nov. 1, 1923, Fayette Co., - dau. of T. B. & Lizzie (Doughty) Hinton. Children: 1. Mary Elizabeth "Libbey" Renfroe, b. Aug. 29, 1946, Fayette, Ala. 2. Robert Ralph Renfroe, Jr., b. Sept. 8, 1956, Fayette, Ala.

RENFROE, Roy Segal, b. Nov. 3, 1895, Fayette Co., Ala., m. Mar. 3, 1923, Myra Pauline Bobo, b. Oct. 5, 1906, Fayette Co. - dau. of Luther S. & Dena Irene (Ward) Bobo. They were married by the Justice of Peace in Columbus, Miss. Roy is a carpenter, and a farmer. Children: 1. Dorothy Virginia Renfroe, b. Sept. 13, 1924, Fayette, Ala., m. Mar. 2, 1946, John Thomas Lawrence, b. Oct. 3, 1925, Fayette Co. 2. Mary Josephine Renfroe, b. Oct. 27, 1928, Fayette Co., d. Dec. 11, 1933, Fayette Co. 3. Betty Sue Renfroe, b. Mar. 30, 1931, Fayette Co., m. Aug. 1949, Thurman I. Griffin, b. Oct. 6, 1925, Fayette Co. 4. Malinda Jane Renfroe, b. Nov. 6, 1937, Pickwick Dam, Tenn., m. Sept. 30, 1957, Richard T. Williams, b. Dec. 25, 1931, Washington, D. C.

REYNOLDS, Richard Davis, b. Feb. 9, 1930, Clanton, Ala. - son of Omon LaFayette & Willie (Higgins) Reynolds, m. Aug. 7, 1953, Margaret Emily Propst, b. Mar. 25, 1930, Fayette, Ala. - dau. of Charlie Dale & Sophia Russell (Parker) Propst. Children: 1. Margret Emily Reynolds, b. June 18, 1954, Camp Stewart, Ga. 2. Richard David Reynolds, b. Sept. 7, 1957, Fayette, Ala.

RICE, Jeptha, b. June 20, 1804, S. C., d. Oct. 15, 1874, Fayette Co., Ala.- son of Otheniel & Sarah __ Rice - m. July 29, 1826, Pallatiah "Palli" Davis, b. Oct. 9, 1809, Ga., d. April 22, 1887, Fayette Co., Ala. - dau. of Nathaniel Davis. Children: Arthur Rice, b. Oct. 10, 1827, Ala. 2. Elender "Nellie" Rice, b. Feb. 2, 1829, Ala., m. Ezekiel Slaughter. 3. Angeline Rice, b. June 15, 1830, died young. 4. Luther M. Rice, b. Nov. 9, 1831, Ala., d. Oct. 8, 1893, m. Catherine Cannon. 5. Malissa Rice, b. Mar. 7, 1833, Ala., m. 2nd. - James Slaughter. 6. Richard Rice, b. Jan. 14, 1835, Ala., d. young.

7. Jeptha Rice, Jr., b. Mar. 23, 1836, Ala., d. young. 8. Valucia Rice, b. Feb. 17, 1838, Ala., m. J. H. Willingham. 9. Minervy Rice, b. Feb. 17, 1840, Ala., m. James Smith. 10. Pallitiah Rice, Jr., b. June 13, 1842, m. 1st. - Joseph or Robert Doughty, 2nd. - Dr. Boteler (Dentist). 11. Adaline Rice, b. July 22, 1844, Ala., m. John S. Woodard. (Had s sets of twins.) 12. Cenath A. Rice, b. July 2, 1846, Ala., d. June 9, 1917, Fayette Co., m. Feb. 15, 1865, Joseph J. Patterson, b. Sept. 22, 1842, Ala., d. May 12, 1918, Fay. Co. 13. Aurilla Rice, b. Sept. 12, 1848, Ala., m. May 26, 1867, George S. Womack, b. 1838, Ala. 14. William Castle Rice, b. May 13, 1850, Ala., d. May 27, 1907, Fayette Co., m. Oct. 15, 1872, Helon E. Downs, b. 1856, Ala., d. 1945. 15. Hasseltine "Hassie" Rice, b. Sept. 29, 1852, Ala., d. Nov. 29, 1934, Fayette Co., m. Dec. 3, 1871, George Angus Doughty, b. Oct. 19, 1849, Ala., d. Aug. 3, 1920, Fayette Co.

RICE, Othenile or Otheniel, b. abt. 1770 to 1775, N. C. or S. C., d. Feb. 29, 1853, Fayette or Tuscaloosa Co., Ala., m. Sarah __, b. abt. 1775, N. C. d. Oct. 6, 1852, Fayette Co., Ala. They came to this section of Alabama when young and settled while the Indians were still living here. They settled and reared a large family. Children: (Known) 1. James Rice, b. Sept. 20, 1799, Anderson Dist. S.C., d. Jan. 8, 1881, Tusca. Co., Ala., m. May 28, 1826, Mariah T. Files, b. Oct. 29, 1805, d. Sept. 5, 1869, Tusca. Co. Ala. (Dau. of Manly Files.) 2. Jeptha Rice, b. June 20, 1804, S. C., d. Oct. 15, 1874, Fayette Co., Ala., m. July 29, 1826, Palliatiah "Palli" Davis, b. Oct. 9, 1809, Ga., d. April 22, 1887, Fayette Co. 3. Sally or Sarah Rice, b. Jan. 7, 1807, S. C., d. Nov. 13, 1871, Fayette Co., m. Nov. 25, 1824, Green Mercer Richards, b. Sept. 7, 1798, Ga., d. Oct. 7, 1878, Lamar Co.

RICE, Washington Castle, b. May 13, 1850, Tusca. Co., Ala., d. May 27, 1907, m. Oct. 15, 1872, Tusca. Co., Helon E. Downs, b. 1856, Tusca. Co., d. 1945, Northport, Ala. He was the son of Jeptha Rice. She was the dau. of T. Alex. Downs. Both are buried at the Patterson Family Cemetery, Fayette Co., Ala. Children: 1. Barti Rice. 2. Ida Rice, m. John B. Ford. 3. Glenn Rice, m. Sally Robertson.

RICHARDS, Basil Manly, killed from ambush during Civil War. Buried at New Lexington, Ala., m. Susan Appling, b. Nov. 16, 1847, Fayette Co., dau. of Samuel Appling. Children: 1. Joe W. Richards, buried in Jefferson Co., Ala. m. Emma White. 2. Basil Manly Richards, b. New Lexington, Ala., m. Nannie Day, buried at Oakman, Ala. 3. Infant Son, b. & d. New Lexington, Ala.

RICHARDS, Green Mercer, b. Sept. 7, 1798, Ga., d. Oct. 7, 1878 - son of James & Love __ Richards - m. Nov. 25, 1824, Sarah Rice, b. Jan. 7, 1807, S. C., d. Nov. 13, 1871 - dau. of Otheniel & Sarah Rice. The Richards and Rice families were among the first settlers of Fayette County, Ala. Children: 1. James Otheniel Richards, b. Aug. 28, 1825, d. Mar. 30, 1906, m. Jan. 20, 1848, Villa Willingham. 2. Jefferson Adams Richards, b. July 17, 1827, d. Nov. 23, 1875, m. July 1, 1855, Martha Welsh. 3. Emily Elisabeth Richards, b. June 3, 1830, d. Jan. 10, 1903, m. Oct. 23, 1856, Silas Nall, d. Mar. 12, 1868. 4. William Green Richards, b. May 22, 1832, d. Dec. 25, 18__, m. Dec. 21, 1854 Margaret Davis?. 5. Lewis Crawford Richards, b. Sept. 23, 1837, d. killed in Battle at Franklin, Tenn. on Nov. 30, 1864. 6. Sarah Frances Richards, b. May 8, 1840, d. Feb. 21, 1917, m. Feb. 12, 1865, Enoch M. VanDiver, d. Aug. 14, 1922, Fayette, Ala.

RICHARDS, James, b. abt. 1776, Va., d. after 1850, m. Love "Lovey" __, b. abt. 1781, Ga., d. after 1850. They were members of the Concord Baptist Church in 1842. Lovey Richards was a member of the Bethel Baptist Church in Tusca. Co., in 1824. Children: 1. Green M. Richards, b. Sept. 17, 1798, d. Oct. 7, 1878, Lamar Co., Ala., m. Nov. 25, 1824, Sarah "Sally" Rice, b. Jan. 1, 1807, d. Nov. 13, 1871, Fayette Co., Ala. 2. Jalie G. Richards, b. Aug. 1, 1806, Ga., d. Dec. 29, 1887, Fayette Co., Ala., m. Samuel J. Patterson, b. Jan. 8, 1804, S. C., d. Feb. 20, 1864, Fayette Co., Ala. (There were other children, possibly - Martin Richards, b. 1800, Ga., m. Amelia__, b. 1815, Ga. and possible others.)

RICHARDS, Jefferson Adams, b. July 2, or 7, 1827, d. Nov. 23, 1875, - son of Green M. & Sarah (Rice) Richards - m. July 14, 1855, Martha Jane Welch, b. Jan. 15, 1837, d. Sept. 11, 1917, - dau. of John S. & Elizabeth (Baker) Welch. Children: 1. Monta Montgrelia Richards. b. Sept. 13, 1859, Fayette Co., Ala., d. Mar. 17, 1889, m. Benajmine David Williams, b. Aug. 12, 1855, d. Aug. 1, 1930. 2. Holly Hamton Richard, b. Jan. 15, 1868, d. Dec. 12, 1953, m. Miss Taylor. 3. Horace Grafton Richards, b. April 4, 1856, d. July 22, 1936, m. Dec. 24, 1875, Sara Frances Yarbrough, b. April 1, 1859, d. Jan. 27, 1913. 4. John Emma Richards, b. Sept. 17, 1862, Fayette Co., d. Nov. 1938, m. Albert Estes. 5. Frances Isabelle "Iddie" Richards, b. Aug. 7, 1875, d. Jan. 28, 1943, m. Mr. Bickart. 6. Jefferson Adams Richard, Jr. b. Dec. 16, 1864, Fayette Co., Ala., d. July 6, 1949, m. 1st. - Sept. 1, 1887, Retta Jane Taylor, b. Mar. 13, 1871, 2nd. - Frances Jane Young, b. Feb. 17, 1880, Fayette Co. 7. Bedford Forest Richards, b. Aug. 3, 1870, d. July 6, 1892. 8. Silas Mercer "Buddy" Richards, b. Oct. 19, 1857, d. Oct. 24, 1871. (Birthdate on Buddy could be 12 instead of 19.)

RICHARDS, Jefferson Adam, Jr., b. Dec. 16, 1864, Fayette Co., Ala., d. July 6, 1949, Fayette - son of J. A., Sr. & Martha Jane (Welch) Richards - m. Sept. 1, 1887, Retta Jane Taylor, b. Mar. 13, 1871, Fayette Co., Ala., d. June 30, 1903. Children: (All born Belk, Ala. - 1st. marriage) 1. James Carlise Richards, b. Oct. 13, 1888, d. Aug. 30, 1890. 2. Albert Jefferson Richards, b. Sept. 21, 1893, d. Feb. 13, 1902. 3. Dicie Isabella Richards, b. July 19, 1896, d. Feb. 18, 1935, m. Henry K. Donaldson. 4. Bessie Jane Richards, b. Feb. 26, 1891, d. Oct. 16, 1957, m. June 8, 1910, Grover Cleveland Arthur, b. Dec. 13, 1886, d. June 8, 1947. 5. Mattie Eunice Richards, b. Nov. 23, 1898, m. May 3, 1929, Fred Martin Houser, b. Sept. 19, 1896, Richland Co., Ill. 6. Annie Lucille Richards, b. July 23, 1901, m. 1920, Roland Chappell Cobb, b. Vernon, Ala.

Jefferson Adam Richards, Jr., married second - **Frances Jane Young**, b. Feb. 17, 1880, Fayette Co., Ala. Children: (2nd. marriage) 1. Gladys Jefferson "Jeff" Richards, b. June 1, 1913, Belk, Ala., m. Feb. 27, 1942, Dr. John Banks Robertson, b. April 11, 1907, Lamar Co., Ala. 2. Julia Kathleen "Temp" Richards, b. Oct. 14, 1915, Fayette, Ala., m. Dec. 16, 1935, Donald Roy "Don" Hutson, b. Jan. 31, 1913, Pine Bluff, Ark.

RICHARDS, Joe W., m. Emma White, dau. of S. L. White. Children: 1. Virginia Richards, m. Harry J. Sartmyer. (One Child - Sue Patrick, m. James Seay.) 2. Susanette Richards, m. Claud C. Harris.

RICHARDS, W. J. "Estes", m. Wilma Patterson, b. Sept., Fayette Co., - dau. of Lester Patterson. Children: 1. William F. "Bill" Richards, b. Fayette,

m. Billie Jean Sutton. 2. Lloyd Richards, b. Fayette, Ala., m. Betty Sanford. 3. Shirley T. Richards, b. Sept. 10, 1935, Fayette, Ala., m. Aug. 20, 1950, William Clyde Stokes.

RICHARDSON, Hamlet Preston, b. Sept. 23, 1858, Pickens Co., Ala., d. April 12, 1926, Pickens Co., Ala. - son of Wm. Pinckney & Emily (Foster) Richardson - m. Oct. 20, 1889, Gertrude Propst, b. Nov. 20, 1872, Pickens Co., Ala. d. Oct. 2, 1949, Pickens Co., Ala. - dau. of Jacob Wilson & Leona (Coons) Propst. Mr. & Mrs. Richardson were married at Millport, Ala. Both are buried at Unity Grove, at Palmetto, Pickens Co., Ala. Children: 1. Jessie May Richardson, b. Sept. 3, 1890, Birmingham, Ala., m. Dec. 16, 1909, Robert Frierson Peters, b. Oct. 11, 1862, Tusca. Co., Ala., d. Jan. 5, 1941, Fayette, Ala. 2. James Grady Richardson, b. Feb. 1, 1892, m. Oct. 5, 1956, Lucy Lowe. 3. Bera Emily Richardson, b. Nov. 21, 1893, Honey Grove, Texas, m. Tom Slaughter Dorroh, b. Pickens Co., Ala. 4. Ben Foster Richardson, b. May 13, 1896, Pickens Co., Ala. (Palmetto), d. May 16, 1923, Pickens Co., m. Dec. 7, 1921, Lucile Warne, b. McConnellsville, Ohio. 5. Jacob Richardson, b. May 3, 1900, d. April 3, 1902. 6. O. P. Richardson, b. June 18, 1903, Pickens Co., m. Dorothy Blaylock. 7. Julia Bell Richardson, b. Jan. 1, 1906, Palmetto, m. July 12, 1928, William Lamar Irwin, b. Mar. 8, 1906, Birmingham, Ala. 8. Robert Ed Richardson, b. April 2, 1908, d. May 3, 1954, Pickens Co., m. Aug. 22, 1936, Leona Warmuskerkin, b. Detroit, Mich. 9. Henry Propst Richardson, b. Dec. 12, 1912, m. Nov. 23, 1954, Julia Frances Ancaroni, b. July 3, 1923.

RICHARDSON, Moses, b. June 7, 1780, probably Amelia Co., Va., d. Jan. 25, 1851, - son of John Richardson - m. Elizabeth Chapman, b. Dec. 23, 1790, Philadelphia, Pa., d. Nov. 15, 1856, - dau. of John & Mary (Dodson) Chapman. Both are buried at Mt. Zion Church, Spartanburg, S. C. His will is recorded in Spartanburg Co., S. C. in Book D., Page 199. Children: 1. Wm. Pinckney Richardson, b. Jan. 16, 1818, Spartanburg Co., S. C., d. Dec. 26, 1860, Pickens Co., Ala., m. Emily Foster, b. June 1, 1826, Spartanburg Co., S.C., d. July 15, 1894, Pickens Co., Ala. 2. James Thompson Richardson, b. Jan. 5, 1811, m. Missouri Hawkins. 3. John Jefferson Richardson, b. April 20, 1812, m. Harriet Copeland. 4. Thomas Wilds Richardson, b. Jan. 5, 1814, d. June 1, 1830. 5. Elias Benson Richardson, b. Jan. 22, 1816, d. Feb. 6, 1877, m. Elizabeth Wingo (Dau. of Ramson Wingo) 6. Mary Dodson "Polly" Richardson, m. L. D. Hawkins. 7. Matthew B. or P. Richardson, b. Aug. 12, 1825, m. Fannie Ramsey. 8. Oliver Preston Richardson, b. Sept. 4, 1828, m. 1st. - Hester Foster Wingo (dau. of Paschial Wingo), 2nd. - Mrs. Neilson. 9. Lucy Richardson, b. Nov. 17, 1817, d. Aug. 2, 1881.

RICHARDSON, William Pinckney, b. Jan. 16, 1818, Spartanburg Co., S.C., d. Dec. 26, 1880, Lamar Co., Ala. - son of Moses & Elizabeth (Chapman) Richardson - m. Oct. 15, 1850, Emily Foster, b. June 1, 1826, Spartanburg, S. C., d. July 15, 1894, Pickens Co., Ala. - dau. of Garland & Nancy (Moss) Foster. Children: 1. Hamlet Preston Richardson, b. Sept. 23, 1858, Pickens Co., Ala., d. April 12, 1926, Pickens Co., m. Oct. 20, 1889, Gertrude Propst, b. Nov. 20, 1872, Pickens Co., Ala., d. Oct. 2, 1949, Pickens Co., Ala. 2. Rollin O. Richardson, b. Oct. 11, 1854, d. Feb. 3, 1938, Pickens Co., Ala. 3. Willie Richardson, b. Dec. 16, 1860, d. Sept. 13, 1943, Pickens Co., Ala., m. Mar. 5, 1905, M. G. Gunter. 4. Mary F. Richardson, b. April 6, 1852, d. Sept. 28, 1939, m. Feb. 29, ___, David E. Fulmer.

RIDGEWAY, Wilburn A. - son of John Ridgeway - m. Nov. 16, 1944, Laura Mozele Long, b. Jan. 16, 1925, Davis Creek, Ala. - dau. of James F. Long. Children: 1. John Fulton Ridgeway, b. Oct. 8, 1946, Vernon, Ala. 2. James Jerome Ridgeway, b. Oct. 16, 1948. 3. Mary Louise Ridgeway, b. Sept. 12, 1952.

RILEY, David Richmond, b. Mar. 17, 1873, Fayette Co., Ala., d. May 19, 1933, Fayette Co., m. Jan. 6, 1895, Harriett Catherine Gipson, b. July 4, 1871, Fayette Co., Ala., d. Dec. 12, 1941. They were married by Rev. J. P. Dickinson. Both are buried at Musgrove Chapel Church Cem., Fayette Co. Children: (All born in Fayette, Co.) 1. Ellie Riley, b. Feb. 16, 1896, m. July 15, 1937, Birmingham, Ala. Walter C. Curl, b. Feb. 25, 1874, Jefferson Co., d. June 26, 1954. 2. John Thomas Riley, b. June 6, 1898, m. May 17, 1914, by Rev. J. A. Trimm, Ida White, b. June 30, 1905, Fayette Co. 3. Mod D. Riley, b. July 2, 1900, m. Heidleberg, Annie McClellan, b. Miss. 4. Annie Riley, b. Oct. 21, 1902, m. John Reese, d. Dec. 14, 1958. 5. William Morris Riley, bm Jan. 10, 1905, m. Aug. 9, 1932, Ruth Mildred Collins, b. June 11, 1900, Fayette Co., Ala. 6. Helen Riley, b. Aug. 13, 1907, m. Aug. 3, 1931, by Judge Alex J. Smith, Thomas Martin Webster, b. May 29, 1903, Fayette Co., d. Jan. 3, 1957. 7. Robert Lee Riley, b. Nov. 11, 1909. 8. Alfred L. Riley, b. June 18, 1912, m. Mary Belle Roberts, b. Jan. 9, 1909, Fayette, Ala.

RILEY, Martin, m. Wanaka South, b. Oct. 19, 1922, Berry, Ala. - dau. of Carlos South. Children: 1. David Riley (Twin), b. 1955. 2. Donald Riley (Twin) b. 1955.

RILEY, William Morris, b. Jan. 10, 1905, Fayette Co., Ala. - son of David R. & Harriett (Gipson) Riley - m. Aug. 9, 1932, Ruth Mildred Collins, b. June 11, 1900, Fayette, Ala. - dau. of John Newton & Allia (Buckner) Collins. They were married at Prattville, Ala., by Rev. M. L. Harris. William Riley is Assistant Cashier at the Citizen's Bank of Fayette. Mrs. Ruth Riley is Clerk in the Probate Judges Office and has held that position in the county since 1922. Childrer: 1. James William Riley, b. Mar. 13, 1934, Fayette.

ROBERTS, __, m. Frances Willingham - dau. of William Willingham. Children: 1. Caleb B. Roberts. 2. Rebecca Roberts, m. _Jennings. 3. Bradford Smith Roberts. 4. Nancy Roberts, m. __Chambless.

ROBERTS, Howard, m. Nancy Walker. Nancy's mother was a Tate before marriage. Her family is from Walker County, Ala. Children: 1. Humphrey Roberts, m. Sallie M. Shirley, b. Dec. 25, 1868. 2. Alice Roberts, m. Jim Jones. 3. George Roberts, m. Lou McCalough. 4. Climmie "Cissie" Roberts, m. Abner Reeves. 5. Lizzie Roberts, m. Brad Jones. 6. Victoria Roberts, m. (From Texas.) 7. Howard "Bud" Roberts.

ROBERTS, Humphrey, b. July 17, 1859, d. May 31, 1931, m. Sallie M. Shirley, b. Dec. 25, 1868, d. Sept. 21, 1946, - dau. of Wm. B. & Sara (Hendrix) Shirley. Children: 1. William Howard Roberts, m. Sudie Thompson. 2. Virgie Roberts, m. Joe McConnell. 3. Esther Roberts, m. Kilby White, b. Feb. 12, 1887, d. Sept. 16, 1940. 4. Maudie Roberts. 5. Boss Roberts, m. Lula Farquhar. 6. Isadore Roberts, m. Blanche Thompson. 7. Ruth Roberts, m. Victor Davis. 8. Sallie Roberts, m. Bruce Smith.

ROBERTS, Isadore, m. Blanche Alice Thompson, dau. of Frank A. Thompson. Children: 1. William I. Roberts, m. Katherine Smith. 2. Bobby Gaines Roberts, m. Hazel Moss, d. Dec. 1959.

ROBERTS, James Morris, m. Martha Ann Matthews, b. Mar. - dau. of Mercer & Earline Matthews. Children: 1. Alice Ann Roberts, b. Feb. 26, 1958, d. Feb. 27, 1958. (He is the son of Wm. Howard Roberts.)

ROBERTS, Joe, m. Grace Jones, b. 1916, Fayette, Ala. - dau. of S. E. & Maude (McConnell) Jones. Children: 1. Danny Roberts. 2. Katherine Roberts. 3. Edith Roberts. 4. Alice Roberts.

ROBERTS, Joe Murphy, b. April 4, 1910, m. Nov. 1933, Sally Elizabeth McConnell, b. May 5, 1914, Fayette Co., Ala. - dau. of Thos. O. & Villa (Matthews) McConnell. Children: 1. Patricia Nell Roberts, b. May 13, 1935, m. Dec. 28, 1953, Max C. Brasher. 2. Thomas William Roberts, b. Feb. 26, 1946. 3. Joe McConnell Roberts, b. Dec. 4, 1947. 4. Richard Allen Roberts, b. Oct. 14, 1950.

ROBERTS, John, b. S. C., d. 1860, Fayette Co., Ala. - son of Thomas Roberts and grandson of John Roberts - m. Sytha Chandler, b. Mar. 18, 1809, S. C., d. Jan. 6, 1896, Fayette, Ao., Ala. Children: Thomas Roberts, m. Katherine Reese.

ROBERTS, Thomas, b. 1836, Fayette Co., d. 1893 - son of John & Sytha (Chandler) Roberts - m. Katherine Reese, b. 1837, d. 1912, Fayette Co. - dau. of John & Ruth (Woods) Reese. Children: 1. Arvezenia Roberts, b. Aug. 27, 18__, m. James Andrew Strider Bynum, b. Feb. 20, 1866, d. Feb. 15, 1940, Fayette.

ROBERTS, William Howard, b. Nov. 3, 1886, d. Nov. 15, 1951, m. Sudie B. Thompson, b. Sept. 26, 1886, d. Dec. 30, 1944, - dau. of Frank A. Thompson. Children: 1. William Howard Roberts, Jr., m. Dicie Lee Rasberry. 2. Mary Louise Roberts, m. L. E. Pitts. 3. Milton H. Roberts, m. Margie Butler. 4. Morris Roberts, m. Martha Matthews. 5. Roy F. Roberts, m. Carolyn Warn.

ROBERTSON, b. N. C., d. 1860, Winston Co., Ala. - son of Elisha Robertson - m. Adeline Snell, b. April 22, 1822, d. June 8, 1895, Lamar Co., Ala. (or d Jan.) Children: 1. John Robertson, b. 1854, d. July 13, 1919, Maud, Okla. m. Mary Catherine Brown, b. May 15, 18__, Lamar Co., Ala., d. Oct. 3, 1904, Lamar Co. 2. Riel or Riley (W. R.) Robertson, b. April 26, 1844. 3. Elias or Elijah Robertson. 4. George Robertson. 5. Mary Robertson, b. 1851, d. 1929.

ROBERTSON, David Fenton, b. Dec. 17, 1853, d. Dec. 3, 1922, m. Earline Clements. Children: 1. Lavina Robertson, m. Mr. Phillips.

ROBERTSON, Elisha, b. 1774, m. wife unknown. Children: 1. David Robertson, b. N. C., d. 1860, Winston Co., Ala., m. Adeline Snell, b. April 22, 1822, d. June 8, 1895, Lamar Co., Ala.

ROBERTSON, Felix McConnell, b. July 19, 1857, d. Sept. 23, 1926, m. Lucy Belle Wilson, b. Feb. 25, 1862, d. July 20, 1945. Children: 1. Tecumseh Robertson, b. Nov. 3, 1878, d. April 27, 1880. 2. David Fletcher Robertson,

d. about 1950.

ROBERTSON, John, b. 1854, d. July 13, 1919, Maud, Okla. - son of David & Adeline (Snell) Robertson - m. Mary Catherine Brown, b. May 15, Lamar Co. d. Oct. 3, 1904, Lamar Co. - dau. of Rice & Mary A. (Hankins) Brown. Children: 1. Malinda Alice Robertson, b. Dec. 15, 1888, Lamar Co., Ala., m. May 29, 1904, John Samuel Yerby, b. May 24, 1882, Lamar Co., Ala., d. Feb. 19, 1950, Fayette, Ala. 2. Jessie Robertson. 3. Jacob Robertson. 4. Morgan Robertson. 5. Tom Robertson. 6. Lafayette Robertson. 7. Irvin Robertson. 8. Mary Jane Robertson. 9. Sarah Adeline Robertson.

ROBERTSON, Dr. John Banks, b. April 11, 1907, Lamar Co., Ala., m. Feb. 27, 1942, Gladys Jefferson "Jeff" Richards, b. June 1, 1913, Belk, Ala. - dau. of J. A., Jr. & Frances (Young) Richards. Dr. J. B. Robertson, M. D. came to Fayette in 1936 as surgeon for the McNease and Robertson Hospital, which opened in 1937. Dr. & Mrs. Robertson were married in Fayette, by Dr. W. F. "Pete" Price. Children: 1. John Banks Robertson, b. Sept. 27, 1943, Fayette, Ala. 2. Elizabeth Richards Robertson, b. May 19, 1947, Fayette, Ala.

ROBERTSON, John Crichton, b. July 7, 1822, Alyth Scotland (July 9, Tombstone), d. June 9, 1877, m. Sept. 10, 1846, Mary Fletcher Alley, b. Sept. 7, 1831, d. July 13, 1915. Mr. Robertson came to the United States about 1845 and landed at Mobile, Ala. He traveled north and stopped for the night in Fayette Court House, Ala. and on the following day decided to stay for awhile. A few months later, he met Miss Mary Fletcher Alley and he decided to make Fayette County, Ala. his permanent home. Children: (All born in Fayette Co., Ala.) 1. James Nichols Robertson, b. & d. June 30, 1847. 2. Margaret Susan Robertson, b. Aug. 9, 1848, d. Feb. 15, 1932, m. 1875, J. B. Sanford. 3. John C. Robertson, Jr., b. Feb. 3, 1850, d. May 22, 1889, m. Viola Towns. 4. Helen Mar Robertson, b. Dec. 31, 1851, d. Mar. 23, 1923, Colo., m. Nov. 1878, M. M. Hawkins. 5. David Fenton Robertson, b. Dec. 17, 1853, d. Dec. 3, 1922, m. Earline Clements of Columbus, Miss. 6. Felix McConnell Robertson, b. July 19, 1857, d. Sept. 23, 1926, m. Lucy Belle Wilson of Fayette, b. Feb. 26, 1862, d. July 20, 1945. 7. Georgia Estelle Robertson, b. Feb. 10, 1861, d. Oct. 3, 1864. 8. Walter Scott Robertson, b. Nov. 21, 1862, d. April 9, 1901, m. Oct. 17, 1900, Lou Renfroe. 9. Blanche Annie Robertson, b. June 14, 1865, d. June 24, 1865. 10. William Murray Robertson, M. D., b. Oct. 3, 1866, d. June 6, 1933, St. Louis, Mo. 11. Fannie May Robertson, b. June 3, 1871 (Or 1870), d. June 13, 1871 (or 1870). 12. Thomas Henry Robertson, b. Mar. 28, 1871, d. Nov. 14, 1936, m. April 26, 1899, Martha Brockway Sprott of Livingston, Ala., b. Oct. 1, 1872, d. Dec. 22, 1947. 13. Mary Elizabeth "Miss Bessie" Robertson, b. April 29, 1873, d. Feb. 8, 1950. 14. Robert Cleburne Robertson, b. April 24, 1875, d. Dec. 24, 1919, m. Nov. 20, 1899, Maude Moore.

ROBERTSON, John Crichton, III, m. Feb. 14, 1946, Liz Nuckols. Children: 1. John Crichton Robertson, IV. 2. Robert Henry Robertson.

ROBERTSON, Joseph Ramsey, b. Mar. 1, 1859, Fayette, Ala., d. Sept. 28, 1952, Fayette, Ala. - son of Robert & Margaret (Stewart) Robertson - m. Dec. 23, 1877, Malinda Katherine McConnell, b. Aug. 6, 1859, Fayette Co., d. Jan. 6, 1929, Fayette, Ala. - dau. of Thomas Posey & Martha Ann (Murray) McConnell. They were married at the home of Thomas Posey McConnell by Rev. J. N. Glover. He was a merchant. He died at the age of 93 and both are buried in the City

Cemetery, Fayette. Children: (All born in Fayette, Ala.) 1. Robert Bruce Robertson, b. July 3, 1879, d. July 1, 1955, Louisville, Ky., d. Oct. 19, 1903, m Pauline Jones, b. Sept. 13, 1885, Birmingham, Ala., d. Dec. 20, 1947, Birmingham, Ala. 2. Annie Leila Robertson, b. May 12, 1883, m. Jan. 18, 1916, Joseph Ezra Caine, b. Sept. 20, 1884, Fayette, Ala., d. Oct. 15, 1955, Fayette, Ala. 3. Sallie McConnell Robertson, b. Sept. 28, 1885, m. Oct. 25, 1916, Stephen H. Frazier, b. Jan. 15, 1887, Pulaski, Tenn. 4. Lucy Aline Robertson, b. Oct. 9, 1890, m. June 20, 1920, Thomas Levi Lindsey, b. Faye. Ala. 5. Joseph Posey Robertson, b. Feb. 20, 1895, m. April 24, 1920, Dorothy Dean Osborne, b. Jan. 11, 1899, Sunbury, Pa.

ROBERTSON, Robert, b. 1812, Perthshire, Scotland, d. 1887, Fayette, Ala., m. Margaret Stewart, b. Perth Scotland, d. Fayette, Ala. Robert Robertson was a merchant. They were married in Scotland. Children: 1. John S. Robertson, b. Perth Scotland, m. Mrs. Sallie Sherrod, both buried in Columbus, Miss. 2. Elizabeth Ramsey Robertson, b. Perth Scotland, m. John B. Burris, both buried in Birmingham, Ala. 3. Robert Jackson Robertson, b. Fayette Court House, Ala., m. Mollie Enis, b. Fayette Co., Ala. 4. James Robertson, b. Fayette Court House, Ala., d. at 16 yrs. at Fayette, Ala. 5. Joseph Ramsey Robertson, b. 1859, Fayette Court House, d. Sept. 28, 1952, Fayette, Ala., m. Malinda McConnell, b. 1859, Fayette Co., Ala. 6. Emily Robertson, b. Fayette Court House, Ala., d. Aliceville, Ala., m. Elijah Brown Kirksay, both are buried in Columbus, Miss. 7. Mary Robertson, b. Ontario, Canada, d. buried in Canada. 8. Annie Mary Robertson, buried in Fayette, Ala.

ROBERTSON, Robert Bruce, b. July 3, 1879, Fayette, Ala., d. July 13, 1955, Louisville, Ky., m. Oct. 19, 1903, Pauline Jones, b. Sept. 13, 1885, Birmingham, Ala., d. Dec. 20, 1947, Louisville, Ky. (Or B'ham, Ala.?) He was the son of Joe R. Robertson. She was the dau. of Dr. & Mrs. C. C. Jones. R. B. Robertson was a chief clerk of the L. & N. Railroad. They were married at East Lake, Ala., by Dr. C. C. Jones. Children: (Born Birmingham, Ala.) 1. Robert Bruce Robertson, Jr., b. July 19, 19__, m. Audrey Johnson, b. Columbus, Ga. 2. Jackson Ramsey Robertson, b. Feb. 7, 1916, Birmingham, Ala., m. Jeannette Seigler, b. Monroe, La.

ROBERTSON, Thomas Henry, b. Mar. 28, 1871, Fayette, Ala., d. Nov. 14, 1936, Birmingham, Ala. - son of John C. Robertson - m. April 26, 1899, Martha Brockway Sprott, b. Oct. 1, 1872, Livingston, Ala., d. Dec. 22, 1947, Fayette, Ala. - dau. of S. H. Sprott. They were married at Livingston, Ala. He was a merchant. Children: 1. Thomas Henry Robertson, Jr., b. Oct. 5, 1900, d. Nov. 24, 1955, m. Aug. 18, 1931, Evelyn Walker. 2. Augusta Robertson, m. Mr. Cotton. 3. John Crichton Robertson, III, m. Feb. 14, 1946, Liz Nuckols. 4. Samuel Sprott, b. May 6, 1913, d. Jan. 12, 1914. 5. Mary Fletcher Robertson, m. Harry M. England of New Orleans, La.

ROBERTSON, Thomas Henry, Jr., b. Oct. 5, 1900, d. Nov. 24, 1955, - son of T. H. Robertson - m. Aug. 18, 1931, Evelyn Walker - dau. of Edgar Walker. They were married at Fayette, Ala. by Dr. W. R. Seymour. He was a merchant and President of the Citizen's Bank at the time of his death. Children: 1. Thomas Henry "Tim" Robertson, III, b. June 21, 1935, Jasper, Ala., d. Dec. 2, 1948, Birmingham, Ala. - buried at Fayette. 2. William Crichton Robertson, b. Nov. 26, 1939, Fayette, Ala.

ROBINSON, Phillip Noble, m. Aug. 12, 1928, Ruth Gertrude Barnett, b. Sept. 9, 1909, Fayette Co., Ala. - Children: (Born Fayette, Ala.) 1. Phillip Issac Robinson, b. May 15, 1929, d. June 27, 1931.

ROSE, Edward, b. Sept. 27, 1855, Green Co., Ala., d. May 17, 1954, - son of Thomas Archibald & Sarah E. (Jordan) Rose - m. Emily Augusta Going, b. July 1855, Pickens Co., Ala., d. Feb. 1943. Children: 1. Ernestine Rose, m. William Scott Morrow. 2. Thomas Alfred Rose, b. May 23, 1888, Fayette Co., Ala., m. April 18, 1923, Nellie Clare Arnold, b. Oct. 8, 1890, Limestone Co. Tenn. 3. William Henry Rose. 4. James Edward Rose, b. May 11, 1894, Fayette Co., Ala., d. Sept. 4, 1925, m. Lida Hood.

ROSE, Thomas Alfred, b. May 23, 1888, Fayette Co., Ala. - son of Edward Rose - m. April 18, 1923, Nellie Clare Arnold, b. Oct. 8, 1890, Limestone Co., Tenn. dau. of D. D. Arnold. Children: (Born Fayette, Ala.) 1. Emily Dean Rose, b. June 9, 1924, m. Ray Delaney. 2. Thomas Alfred Rose, Jr., b. June 19, 1927, Fayette, m. Dorothy Lillian Houstin.

ROSE, Thomas Alfred, Jr., b. June 19, 1927, Fayette, Ala., m. June 26, 1948, Dorothy Lillian Houstin, b. July 18, 1927. Children: 1. Angela Suzann Rose, b. April 25, 1949. 2. Thomas Alfred Rose, III, b. Nov. 28, 1954. 3. Anthony Carl Rose, b. April 3, 1956.

ROSE, Thomas Archibald, b. 1828, d. 1908, m. Sarah Elizabeth Jordan, b. 1834, d. 1908. Came to Alabama from South Carolina. Children: 1. Neb Rose, 2. Edward Rose, b. Sept. 27, 1855, d. May 17, 1954, m. Emily Augusta Going. 3. Thomas Rose. 4. Laura Rose. 5. Charley Rose.

ROSEMORE, Fredric Michael, b. June 5, 1923, Kings County, New York, m. Jan. 26, 1946 at Birmingham, Ala., Marion Louise Goldstein, b. Aug. 17, 1926, Jefferson Co., Birmingham, Ala. Dr. Rosemore is an Optometrist and came to Fayette in the late 1940's and established his practice.
    F. M. Rosemore's parents - Sidney H. Rosemore, b. New York, m. Minerva Landau, b. New York. Grandparents - Abraham M. Rosemore, m. Fredia Smith - both came from Portugal. Grandfather Landau m. Gennie Zitmore and they came from France.
    Marion Goldstein Rosemore's parents - Charles Goldstein, b. Memphis, Tenn., m. Dora Solin, b. Milwaukee, Wis. Grandparents - Morris & Lena Solin. Children: (Fred & Marion's) 1. Andrew Stuart Rosemore, b. Nov. 16, 1946, Memphis, Tenn. 2. Lance Bruce Rosemore, b. Nov. 5, 1948, Birmingham, Ala. 3. Martha Gale Rosemore, b. May 10, 1951, Fayette, Ala. 4. Susan Lynn Rosemore, Dec. 5, 1952, Fayette, Ala. 5. Margaret Ann Rosemore, b. Oct. 31, 1957, Fay.

ROWLAND, John Denzil, b. Dec. 31, 1913, Lamar Co., Ala. - son of Zeb & Dora (Waldrop) Rowland - m. Mar. 3, 1937, Pauline Tarwater, b. Sept. 2, 1914, Fayette, Ala. - dau. of J. T. & Heartha Tarwater. Children: 1. John Denzil Rowland, Jr., b. Feb. 10, 1939, Fayette, Ala. 2. Susan Coatney Rowland, b. Sept. 28, 1943, Fayette, Ala.

ROWLAND, Wiley Miller, b. Sept. 3, 1844, Murray Co., Ga., d. May 22, 1920, Fayette Co., Ala., m. Sept. 28, 1865, Priscilla Caroline Shackleford, b. Jan. 3, 1845, Elbert Co., Ga., d. Aug. 29, 1921, Fayette Co., Ala. Wiley Miller Rowland was a Veteran of the Civil War. He served with the 50th Ala. Regt.

Children: (All born Lamar Co., Ala.) 1. William Henry Rowland, b. Oct. 28, 1867, d. July 23, 1945. 2. Emma Elizabeth Rowland, b. Oct. 14, 1869, d. Aug. 21, 1950. 3. James Harland Rowland, b. Aug. 22, 1871, d. Dec. 8, 1929. 4. Leila Rowland, b. Mar. 26, 1873, d. Feb. 12, 1908. 5. Ella Frances Rowland, b. July 6, 1875, d. Oct. 8, 1946. 6. Annie Deman Rowland, b. Oct. 20, 1876, d. Feb. 17, 1942. 7. Choice Wiley Rowland, b. April 14, 1878, (M. D.) 8. Mintie Priscilla Rowland, b. June 15, 1879, d. Jan. 31, 1948. 9. DuDonnie Rowland, b. Feb. 18, 1881, d. Dec. 30, 1955. 10. Dixie Rowland, b. June 29, 1882. 11. Alice Mellie Rowland, b. Dec. 2, 1883. 12. Charles Edgar Rowland, b. June 11, 1886. 13. Walter Bailey Rowland, b. Sept. 20, 1887, d. Oct. 17, 1912. 14. Zeb A. Rowland, b. Feb. 10, 1889.

ROWLAND, Zeb A., b. Feb. 10, 1889, Lamar Co., Ala. - son of Wiley Miller Rowland - m. July 23, 1911, Madorah Elizabeth Waldrop, b. Nov. 28, 1892, Lamar Co., Ala. - dau. of Starling V. & Roxanne (Godfrey) Waldrop. Children: (All born Lamar Co., Ala.) 1. Bernice Rowland, b. June 28, 1912, m. Oct. 10, 1930, Arthur Curtis Branyon, b. April 15, 1910, Jefferson Co., Ala. 2. John Denzil Rowland, b. Dec. 31, 1913, m. Mar. 3, 1937, Pauline Tarwater, b. Sept. 2, 1914, Fayette Co., Ala. 3. Dorothy Ann Rowland, b. Mar. 6, 1919, m. Feb. 12, 1943, Woodfin Kirk Grove, b. Oct. 23, 1918, Jefferson Co., Ala. 4. Ruth Rowland, b. June 24, 1921, m. Feb. 25, 1956, Roy Franklin Thomas, b. Mar. 21, 1916.

RUTLAND, Dr. Richard O., m. Nancy Babb. Dr. Rutland and his family came to Fayette in July 1954. He is affiliated with the McNease Clinic. Children: 1. Richard "Ricky" Rutland. 2. Cynthia "Cindy" Rutland. 3. Melissa Rutland, b. 1957, Fayette, Ala.

RUTLEDGE, __, m. wife unknown. Children: 1. Jack Rutledge. 2. William Rutledge, m. Nancy Lawrence. 3. Edward Rutledge, b. 1798, Ky., m. Ky., Elizabeth Logan, b. 1811, Cumberland Co., Ky.

RUTLEDGE, Edward, b. 1798, Ky., m. Elizabeth Logan, b. 1811, Cumberland Co. Ky. Edward Rutledge came to Walker Co., Ala. in 1835. He is a descendant of Edward Rutledge, a signor of the Declaration of Independence (born 1749 - d. 1800). Edward came from Kentucky with his wife, one child, two brothers, Jack and William on pack horses. Children: 1. James Rutledge, b. Nov. 4, 1832, d. May 25, 1918, m. Elizabeth A. Sides, b. Oct. 8, 1839, d. Nov. 11, 1905. 2. Alfred King Rutledge, m. Eliza Sides. 3. David Rutledge, b. July 14, 1839, m. Minerva Jeffries. 4. Joseph Rutledge. 5. Julia Rutledge, m. Samuel O'Rear. 6. Polly Ann Rutledge, m. Vincent Ivey. 7. Ollie Rutledge, m. William "Wid" Swindle. 8. Elizabeth Rutledge, m. Mr. Bolton.

RUTLEDGE, James, b. Nov. 4, 1832, Cumberland Co., Ky, d. May 25, 1918, Walker Co., Ala., m. April 4, 1855, Elizabeth A. Sides, b. Oct. 8, 1839, Walker Co., Ala., d. Nov. 11, 1905, Walker Co., Ala. James Rutledge came with his parents to Alabama when two years of age. On Feb.1, 1862, he enlisted at Jasper as Private in Co. E. 28th Ala. Inf. and served in the C.S.A. during the Civil War. Elizabeth was born at Pleasant Grove in Walker Co., Ala. James served as County Commissioner for four years in Walker Co. Both are buried at the Sides Graveyard in Walker Co., Ala. Children: (All born in Walker Co., Ala.) 1. Lou J. Rutledge, b. May 6, 1856. 2. William Taylor Rutledge, b. June 30, 1857, m. Mary Key - dau. of Thos. Key. 3. Andrew A.

Rutledge, b. Nov. 28, 1859, m. Minerva Key - dau. of John & Charity Key,-b. Mar. 22, 1861, Walker Co., Ala. 4. Mary Ann Rutledge, b. Dec. 21, 1861, d. Oct. 30, 1946, Walker Co., Ala., m. Jan. 12, 1882, Robert Powers Key - son of John & Charity Key - b. Sept. 26, 1859, d. Dec. 28, 1949, Walker Co., Ala. 5. Martha Frances Rutledge, b. Oct. 1, 1864, m. 1st. - Doran Kilgore, 2nd. - William Root. 6. Sarah Rutledge, b. Dec. 26, 1866, m. James Mulligan. 7. King D. Rutledge, b. Aug. 15, 1868. 8. James M. Rutledge, b. Aug. 4, 1869, m. 1st. - Maggie Wright, 2nd. - Fannie Pearson. 9. John R. Rutledge, b. May 7, 1871, m. Mary Nix. 10. Charles Rutledge, b. Jan. 14, 1874, m. Alice Wade. 11. George Houston Rutledge, b. Sept. 8, 1876, m. Dec. 23, 1896, Mollie Crump. 12. Annie Rutledge, b. Mar. 2, 1879, m. James A. Ward. 13. Etta Rutledge, b. June 29, 1884, d. in youth.

SANDERS, Samuel Jesse, Jr., b. Oct. 4, 1908, Fayette, Ala. - son of S. J. Sanders, Sr. - m. Feb. 10, 1946, Gwendolyn Stewart, b. May 27, 1918, Fayette Co., Ala. - dau. of J. Clyde Stewart. They were married at Fayette, Ala.. Sam J. is a local bread distributor for Hardin Bakeries. Gwen is a teacher in the local high school. No Children.

SANDERS, Samuel Jesse, b. April 28, 1886, Fayette, Ala., d. Oct. 9, 1948, Fayette, - son of Robert F. & Bell (Propst) Sanders - m. Aug. 1, 1907, Loudell Smith, b. Dec. 19, 1886, Fayette, Ala. - dau. of Wm. F. & Etta (Neal) Smith. S. J. Sanders served as Postmaster of Fayette from 1930 to 1945. They were married at Fayette, Ala. by Rev. J. E. Morris. Children: (All born Fayette, Ala.) 1. Samuel Jesse Sanders, Jr., b. Oct. 4, 1908, m. Feb. 10, 1946, Gwendolyn Stewart, b. May 27, 1918, Fayette Co. 2. William Edward Sanders, b. June 3, 1911, m. June 11, 1949, Gladys Barber, b. Aug. 27, 1911, Haleyville, Ala. 3. Robert Phillips Sanders, b. Sept. 12, 1925.

SANDERS, Robert Edward, b. July 12, 1851, Gainesville, Ala., d. Oct. 31, 1890, m. Bell Propst, b. Jan. 29, 1849, d. May 10, 1923, - dau. of Daniel Propst. R. E. Sanders was a carpenter. He was killed in a train accident and both he and his wife are buried in the Fayette City Cemetery. Children: (Born Fayette, Ala.) 1. Samuel J. Sanders, b. April 28, 1886, d. Oct. 9, 1948, Fayette, m. Aug. 1, 1907, Loudell Smith, b. Dec. 19, 1886, Fayette. 2. Annie Sanders, b. Oct. 6, 1888, m. William Hammond Humber.

SANDERS, William E., b. June 3, 1911, Fayette, Ala. - son of S. J. & Loudell (Smith) Sanders - m. June 11, 1949, Gladys Barber, b. Aug. 27, 1911, Haleyville, Ala. - dau. of J. N. Barber. They were married at Fayette, Ala. by Rev. Paul Clem. Bill operates an Insurance Agency "The Sanders Agensy" selling general insurance. His military service during World War II was from Nov. 25, 1940 until Dec. 24, 1945 - Master Sgt. in Finance Dept. - 31st Dixie Division - Served twenty-one months in South Pacific. Children: (Gladys' dau. by previous marriage.) 1. Barbare Sue Heath, b. May 15, 1938, Haleyville, Ala., m. June 25, 1959, Joe Allen Davis.

SANFORD, John, m. Martha Hallman, b. 1854, - dau. of Henry J. & Sarah (Langford) Hallman. Children: 1. Dolphus Sanford, b. Aug. 7, 1886, d. Nov. 27, 1906, m. Oct. 23, 1905, Ancey Watson. 2. John Henry Sanford. 3. Lovie Sanford. 4. Nunnally Sanford.

SANFORD, John Burford, b. Feb. 19, 1844, d. Oct. 29, 1898, m. Margaret Susan

Robertson, b. Aug. 9, 1848. Children: 1. Samuel F. Sanford, b. Aug. 16, 1871, d. Sept. 19, 1920. 2. John Thomas Sanford. 3. Mary Jane Sanford, b. Nov. 16, 1876, d. Sept. 23, 1947, Tusca., Ala., m. Augustus Gaines Williams, b. Dec. 25, 1874, Macon, Miss., d. Feb. 17, 1957, Tusca. Ala.

SAVAGE, Arthur, b. Dec. 18, 1873, Fayette Co., Ala., d. Dec. 11, 1919, Fayette Co., Ala. - son of Dudley Thomas & Rizpah Zolicopher (Stillman) Savage - m. Dec. 23, 1899, Mary Charlotte Rogers, b. Aug. 13, 1882, Sciota, Ohio, d. Feb. 22, 1942, Birmingham, Ala. - dau. of James W. & Valeria J. (Lindsey) Rogers. She was adopted and married as Mollie Stillman. They were married at South McAlester, Okla. (then Indian Territory) by I. J. Fannin. Arthur Savage was a farmer, engineer and post master at Hico, Fayette Co., Ala. He is buried in the Savage Family Cemetery in Fayette County, Ala. She is buried in Elmwood Cem., Birmingham, Ala. Children: 1. Myrtle Mae Savage, b. Nov. 17, 1900, Fayette Co., Ala., m. Oct. 19, 1940, by Reb. Peter Marshall, Washington, D. C., William Lawrence Rhoades, b. Feb. 14, 1893, Newark, N. J., d. May 4, 1957, New Jersey. 2. Ruth Savage, b. Dec. 11, 1902, Birmingham, Ala. m. June 15, 1922 in Birmingham, Ala. by Rev. Theo Harris, Joseph Eggleston Johnston, III, b. Nov. 28, 1898, Miss. 3. Thomas Earl Savage, b. June 21, 1905, Hico, Fayette, Ala., d. May 28, 1955, Birmingham, Ala., m. July 2, 1927, at Shelby Co., Ala., Mona Faye Cagle, b. Mar. 11, 1908, Saragossa, Ala. 4. Hattie Mildred Savage, b. Mar. 17, 1908, Birmingham, Ala., d. May 14, 1909, buried Fayette Co., Ala. 5. James Arthur Savage, b. July 27, 1915, Birmingham, Ala., d. Mar. 10, 1917, buried Fayette Co., Ala.

SAVAGE, Dudley Thomas, b. Sept. 4, 1844, Fayette Co., Ala., d. Mar. 21, 1907, - son of John & Mary "Polly" (Strong) Savage - m. Feb. 27, 1871, Rizpah "Rizzie" Zolicopher Stillman, b. July 24, 1848, Vernon, Ala. (then Fayette Co.), d. Dec. 17, or 18, 1932 or 1933, - dau. of Samuel & Nancy Rogers (Hames) Stillman. They were married at Vernon, Ala. by Rev. Elijah Howell. Dudley Thomas was a farmer. He is buried at the Savage Family Cemetery at Hico, Fayette Co., Ala. She is buried at the Macedonia Cemetery, Fayette Co., Ala. The Stillman Family (George) settled in Mass. in 1683, moved to Wethersfield, Conn. in 1703. The family has been traced back 700 years. They are connected in this country with the Wolcotts, Nash, Dickinson, and Russell families. All prominent in early Puritan New England. Thomas Nash was a member of Rev. ' n Robinson's congregation - members left England because of persecution lived in Liedes, Holland ten years before coming to the New World. Hartford, Conn. was named for the home, in England, of Rev. Samuel Russell, religious leader of the colony. Children: (Dudley T. Savage's) 1. Auston Savage, b. Nov. 6, 1872, (All born Fayette, Co.) d. Oct. 12, 1874, Fayette Co. 2. Arthur Savage, b. Dec. 18, 1873, d. Dec. 11, 1919, Fayette Co., m. Dec. 23 1899, Mary Charlotte Rogers, (Mollie Stillman - adopted b. Aug. 13, 1882, Sciota Co., Ohio. 3. Talullah "Lula" Savage, b. Mar. 30, 1875, d. Sept. 19, 1941, Fayette Co., m. George Oscar South, b. Fayette Co., d. Jan. 1, 1951, Fayette Co. 4. Bertha Savage, b. June 10, 1878, d. July 8, 1885, Fayette Co. 5. Edward Savage, b. Sept. 27, 1880, m. Feb. 7, 1904, Vera Alice Yerby. 6. Kate Stillman Savage, b. Dec. 13, 1881, m. Feb. 5, 1902, Alby Wayne Cannon, b. Jan. 21, 1872, Tusca. Co., Ala., d. Feb. 1938, Fayette Co., Ala. 7. Frank Savage, b. Oct. 10, 1884, d. buried Tusca., Ala., m. June 23, 1909, Eula Black. 8. Eunice Savage, b. Feb. 28, 1891, d. Oct. 11, 1944, m. Jan. 13, 1912, John Amos Roberts.

SAVAGE, Edward, b. Sept. 27, 1880, Fayette Co., Ala., m. Vera Alice Yerby, b. May 21, 1883, Fayette Co., Ala. - dau. of W. Inge Yerby. They were married Feb. 7, 1904, by Rev. Frank Wilson at Fayette, Ala. Edward is a farmer. She died Oct. 2, 1955, buried Birmingham, Ala. Children: 1. Louvenia Genera Savage, b. Nov. 12, 1905, Fayette, d. May 10, 1914, Fayette. 2. Rubilea Savage, b. Mar. 17, 1908, Birmingham, Ala., m. Patrick J. Omallev. 3. Thomas Edward Savage, b. Dec. 17, 1910, Birmingham, Ala., m. Feb. 7, 1937, Edna Williamson, b. Fayette. (Children: Thomas Norris Savage.) 4. Amy Rose Savage, b. Feb. 3, 1913, Birmingham, Ala., m. Sept. 11, 1932, Frank M. Paffe, (Children: 1 son, 1 dau.) 5. Rissie Geneva Savage, b. Oct. 23, 1915, Tusca. Ala., m. June 13, 1936, Ercel Brown. (Have 1 son.) 6. William Everett Savage, b. April 11, 1920, Fayette, Ala., m. Dec. 19, 1943, Kathleen Williamson, b. Fayette Co., Ala. (Children: 1. Emlyn Savage. 2. Edward Savage.) 7. Vera Nell Savage, b. Aug. 29, 1922, Fayette Co., Ala., m. July 11, 1947, A. Randolph Mitchell. (Have 1 son and 1 dau.)

SAVAGE, James, m. Augusta Smith. Children: 1. Addie Savage. 2. Charlotte Savage. 3. Vergie Savage, m. 1st. - Mr. Thomason, 2nd. - Mr. Jones. 4. Wm. Savage. 5. Nettie Lou Savage. 6. Mary Savage, died young.

SAVAGE, John, b. Dec. 20, 1803, Union Co., S. C., d. July 22, 1884, Fayette Co., Ala. - son of James Savage - m. Dec. 27, 1828 or 1829, Mary Strong, b. April 1, 1809, Ga., d. Feb. 3, 1884, Fayette Co.- dau. of Elijah & Polly Strong. John Savage was a farmer, and a cotton and woolen mill owner. Both are buried in the Savage Family Cemetery, Hico, Fayette Co., Ala. Children: (All born Hico, Fayette Co., Ala.) 1. Emily Savage, b. Sept. 23, 1830, d. Feb. 1, 1916. 2. Jasper Savage, b. Sept. 9, 1832, d. Storm blew church over and killed him in Miss. (Children: T. Newton and Houston Savage.) 3. Susan Margaret Savage, b. Oct. 6, 1835, d. Sept. 7, 1910, Fayette Co., m. Francis Marion Caine, b. Dec. 10, 1833, d. May 26, 1902 or 1903. 4. Temple Franklin Savage, b. Nov. 26, 1837, m. Nancy _. (Children: John; James, William and Howard Savage.) 5. John Harry Savage, b. April 9, 1840, d. June 10, 1841, Fayette Co. 6. Charlotte Jane "Lottie" Savage, b. June 6 or 8, 1842 or 1841, d. Jan. 8, 1920, Fayette Co., m. Mod D. Wilkes, b. Dec. 13, 1836, d. July 1, 1920. 7. Dudley Thomas Savage, b. Sept. 4, 1844, d. Mar. 21, 1907, Fayette Co., m. Feb. 27, 1871, Rizpah Zolicopher Stillman, b. July 24, 1848, Vernon, Ala., d. Dec. 17, or 18, 1932, or 1933. (Vernon was not in existence in 1848 as that was then Fayette Co., but that is the vicinity of her birth.) 8. Boswell Zachery Taylor Savage, b. Nov. 12, 1847, d. June 1, 1910, Fayette, Co., m. 1st. - Nannie Venoy Doughty, b. 1840, Fayette Co., d. 1904, 2nd. - Effie _ (2nd. wife - 1 child - Charles Savage.)

SAVAGE, Thomas Earl, b. June 21, Fayette Co., d. April 28, 1955, Birmingham, Ala. - son of Arthur & Mary C. (Rogers) Savage - m. July 2, 1927. Mona Faye Cagle, b. Mar. 11, 1908, Saragossa, Ala. Children: 1. Mona Fay Savage, b. April 1, 1932, Birmingham, Ala. - m. Aug. 22, 1951, William Joseph Bennett. (Children: Teresa Karen Bennett, b. Nov. 16, 1953.) 2. Carol Sue Savage, b. Oct. 25, 1933, m. Mar. 2, 1957, Paul R. White. (Child: Jeffrey Paul White, b. May 25, 1958.)

SAVAGE, Victor, b. 1866, Ala., m. Julia Shirley. He was the son of Zach Savage. Children: 1. Cole Savage. 2. Pearl Savage. 3. Zach Savage. 4. Dean Savage. 5. Clarence Savage. 6. Nancy Savage. 7. Victor Savage, Jr.

8. Bess Savage. 9. Troy Savage. 10. Fred Savage. 11. Columbus Savage.

SAVAGE, (Boswell) Zachery Taylor "Zach", b. Nov. 12, 1847, Ala., d. June 1, 1910 - son of John Savage - m. Nancy Venoy Doughty, b. Nov. 22, 1840, Ala., d. April 21, 1904, - Dau. of Mordecai F. Doughty. Children: (All b. Ala.) 1. Victor Savage, b. 1866, m. Julia Shirley. 2. Manny or Zach Savage, Jr., b. 1874. 3. Burton "Bert" Savage, b. 1868. 4. John Savage, b. 1876. 5. Jennie Savage, b. 1872. 6. Jessie Savage, b. 1870.

SAWYER, Arthur, - son of Wm. Bedford Sawyer - m. Myrtie Whitley. Children: 1. H. B. Sawyer, m. Betty Guttery. (Children: William Arthur and Edwin Earl Sawyer.) 2. Lula Mae Sawyer, m. Johnny Davis. (One child: Nancy Davis.) 3. Arthur Sawyer, Jr., m. Ruth Rutledge. (Had two children.)

SAWYER, Dock, son of James H. Sawyer - m. Lillie McCaleb. Children: 1. Jalia Sawyer. 2. Ruby Sawyer. 3. Susie Sawyer. 4. Vaudine Sawyer. 5. Annie Sawyer. 6. Louise Sawyer. 7. Willard Sawyer. 8. Milford Sawyer. 9. James Sawyer.

SAWYER, Edgar, son of Wm. Bedford Sawyer, m. Julia Brown. Children: 1. Louis Sawyer, m. Alcie Aldridge. (One child: Virginia Sawyer, m. Francis Jangerson, Jr.) 2. Gaytheal Sawyer. 3. Thurman Sawyer. 4. Kermit "Dick" Sawyer (Twin). 5. Cladius Sawyer (Twin, m. Frances Dunn. (One child; Hilda Sawyer.)

SAWYER, Henry, son of James H. Sawyer - m. Mary Panter. Children: 1. Eva Sawyer. 2. Pearl Sawyer. 3. Trilla Sawyer. 4. Fenton Sawyer. 5. Robert Sawyer. 6. Travis Sawyer. 7. George Sawyer.

SAWYER, James Hillard, m. Huldah Brasher. James Hillard Sawyer came to Fayette County, legend says, from South Carolina, probably in the late 1850's. He was called "Jim" and served in the Confederate Army, enlisting in May 1862, at Fayette Court House. He served as a Private in Co. A. 26th. (O'-Neal's) Ala. Regt., and was wounded at Malvern Hill, Va. He was discharged in 1865 and filed for a pension April 18, 1898. He died about 1902 and is buried at Enis Graveyard, in Beat No. 3, Fayette Co. His wife died several years earlier and is buried at his side. Children: 1. William Bedford Sawyer, b. Aug. 23, 1860, m. Margarett Hendon. 2. Etta Sawyer, m. Bill Blackwell. 3. Emma Sawyer, m. George Feltman. 4. John Sawyer, m. Orlena Panter. 5. Henry Sawyer, m. Mary Panter. 6. Ella "Shug" Sawyer, m. Frank Brown. 7. Della "Babe" Sawyer, m. Charlie Cook. 8. Ada Sawyer, m. Spencer Cook. 9. Dock Sawyer, m. Lillie McCaleb.

SAWYER, John - son of James H. Sawyer - m. Orlena Panter. Children: 1. Zema Sawyer. 2. Neva Sawyer. 3. Ollie Sawyer. 4. China Sawyer. 5. Clercie Sawyer. 6. Edna Sawyer. 7. Verris Sawyer. 8. Austin Sawyer.

SAWYER, William Bedford, - son of James Hillard & Huldah (Brasher) Sawyer - m. Margarett Hendon - dau. of Andrew J. & Caroline (Harris) Hendon. Children: 1. Edgar Sawyer, m. Julia Brown. 2. Edwin Harris "Toad" Sawyer. 3. Arthur Sawyer, m. Myrtie Whitley. 4. Flossia Sawyer, m. Jackson Tucker. 5. Marvin Sawyer, died at 2 yrs. of age. 6. May Sawyer, m. Charlie Lowery. 7. Carrie Lillie Sawyer, m. Charles Spurgeon Deavours.

SCOTT, B. F., b. Walker Co., Ala., m. May 19, 1898, Susan Aline Hassell, b. Mar. 4, 1875, Fayette Co., - dau. of Geo. T. & Susan Richards Hassell. B. F. Scott was a salesman and both are buried in Birmingham, Ala. Children: 1. Irene Scott. 2. Forrest Lee Scott. 3. Aline Scott.

SCROGGINS, Thomas Coy, m. Nina Oleta McCool, b. June 15, 1918, Fayette, Ala. - dau. of Thos. A. McCool. Children: 1. Lucy Anne Scroggins.

SHAFER, Arthur Estell, b. Jan. 2, 1901, m. July 12, 1923, Kate Christine South, b. Jan. 12, 1905, Fayette, Ala. - dau. of George Oscar "Babe" South. Children: 1. James Oscar Shafer, b. Oct. 23, 1924, Fayette. 2. Norma Kate Shafer, b. Jan. 22, 1932, Jackson, Miss., m. Jeff Gregory. 3. Arthur Jack Shafer, b. Mar. 4, 1933, Jackson, Miss.

SHARP, J. Holley, b. Sept. 11, 1892, Fayette, Ala., d. Dec. 1955, m. Emma Blanche Arnold, b. Sept. 4, 1900, Rome, Ga. - dau. of Daniel David & Effie Dean (Mathes) Arnold. Children: (All born Fayette.) 1. Betty Joyce Sharp, b. Sept. 30, 1928, m. Howard N. Lawrence. 2. James Holley "Jimmy" Sharp, Jr., b. Feb. 5, 1930, m. Harriette Marie Roeha. 3. William Jackson "Billy Jack" Sharp, b. Jan. 2, 1935.

SHAW, Aubrey I., b. Eupora, Miss., m. Ruby Lee Woods, b. April 30 1923, Fayette Co., Ala. - dau. of Wilmot & Hassie (Ballinger) Woods. Children: 1. James Aubry Shaw, b. Mar. 28, 1945, Fayette, Ala.

SHELTON, Andrew Bascom, - son of Samuel Ton Shelton - m. Robert Delona Ellis. Andrew Bascom and Juny Octavis Shelton moved to Fayette Co., Ala. in Dec., 1905 from Pickens Co., Ala. They were the sons of Samuel Ton & Margaret Sherrill (Brotherton) Shelton. Children: (A.B.Shelton's) 1. Lewis Leondus Shelton, b. April 25, 1886, d. Aug. 13, 1952, Fayette Co., m. Nov. 10, 1907, Lenie Mae Porter, b. Aug. 25, 1890, Fayette Co. 2. Juny Gross "Doc" Shelton, b. July 1, 1890, d. Nov. 24, 1935, m. Ruby Harris from Tallassee, Ala. (No children born to this couple.)

SHELTON, Andrew Washington "Buddy", b. June 26, 1929, Fayette Co., m. May 1, 1948, Thomasine "Tommy" Hinton, b. Feb. 6, 1931, Fayette Co., dau. of T. B. & Lizzie (Doughty) Hinton. Children: 1. Andrew "Andy" Shelton, b. Jan. 16, 1949, Fayette. 2. Jerri Shelton, b. Aug. 3, 1950, Fayette, Ala.

SHELTON, Billy Joe, b. Aug. 21, 1922, Fayette Co. - son of Lon Shelton - m. Nov. 3, 1946, Bobbie Lee Wright, b. Feb. 3, 1929, Parrish, Ala. - dau. of B. M. & Bessie (Key) Wright. Children: 1. Jo Anna "JoJo" Shelton, b. April 15, 1949, Fayette. 2. James David "Dude" Shelton, b. April 10, 1952, Calif.

SHELTON, Juny Octavis, b. June 3, 1856, d. April 8, 1941 - son of Samuel T. Shelton - m. Mar. 7, 1875, Minerva Angling Ellis, b. Oct. 29, 1856. Children: 1. Estelle Shelton, b. Nov. 29, 1875, Lamar Co., Ala., d. Dec. 5, 1895, m. Johnnie Mikial Gentry, b. July 11, 1869. 2. Lillian Leone Shelton, b. Mar. 1, 1882, Lamar Co., Ala., m. 1st. - Earl Carpenter, 2nd. - Edgar Morton. 3. Mollie Ton Shelton, b. Aug. 13, 1884, Lamar Co., m. Nov. 25, 1903, Lee Collier Wilson. 4. Anna Beatrice Shelton, b. Nov. 10, 1890, Lamar Co., Ala. 5. Joe Octavis Shelton, Jr., b. July 18, 1897, d. Nov. 26, 1950, m. 1st. - Peggy Hodges, 2nd. - Ruth Tollie.

SHELTON, Lewis Lenodous, b. April 25, 1886, d. Aug. 13, 1952 - son of Andrew G. Shelton - m. Nov. 10, 1907, Lenie Mae Porter, b. Aug. 25, 1890, Fayette Co. - dau. of Geo. W. Porter. Children: 1. Ruby Estell Shelton, b. April 20, 1909, (All born Fayette Co.) m. April 30, 1928, Marx C. "Bennie" Hammond. 2. Alice Beatrice Shelton, b. Aug. 25, 1911, d. June 14, 1952, m. Mar. 5, 1935, Thomas T. Mansfield. 3. Clarice Pearl Shelton, b. July 19, 1913, m. Earnest J. Carroll. 4. Louis Leondous "Bo" Shelton, b. Aug. 16, 1915. 5. Jennie Bob Shelton, b. Jan. 2, 1918, m. Ras Blankenship. 6. Billy Joe Shelton, b. Aug. 21, 1922, m. Bobbie L. Wright. 7. James Alexander Shelton, b. Aug. 26, 1924, m. Mar. 11, 1950, Mary Nell Walton. 8. Willie Faye Shelton, b. Dec. 6, 1926, m. Nov. 1, 1949, Hershel Gartman. 9. Andrew Washington "Buddy" Shelton, b. June 26, 1929, m. May 1, 1948, Tommy Hinton. 10. Bettie Sue Shelton, b. Jan. 23, 1932, m. Oct. 15, 1948, Talmage Lankford.

SHEPHERD, Garland George, b. Lamar Co., d. Oct. 11, 1944, Fayette, m. Jan. 12, 1927, Roxie Lee Hassell, b. Dec. 8, 1886, Fayette Co. - dau. of Geo. T. & Susan Richards Hassell. Garland G. Shepherd was a Service Station Operator. He is buried in Fayette, Ala. Children: 1. George Hassell Shepherd, b. Dec. 11, 1927, Birmingham, Ala., m. Dec. 7, 1957, Margaret Anne Brown, b. Aug. 29, 1930, Birmingham, Ala.

SHEPHERD, George Hassell, b. Dec. 11, 1927, Birmingham, Ala. - son of G.G. & Roxie (Hassell) Shepherd - m. Dec. 7, 1957, Margaret Anne Brown, b. Aug. 29, 1930, Birmingham, Ala. - dau. of Osa Alex. & Ruth (Mitchell) Brown. They were married at Atlanta, Ga. by Thomas J. Holmes. Geo. Hassell Shepherd is Buyer and Traffic Mamager of Celanese Corp. of America.

SHEPHERD, Jacob, b. Nov. 5, 1812, d. Mar. 26, 1877, m. Mariah Nalls, b. Nov. 1, 1824, d. Nov. 22, 1900. Children: 1. Penniah Shepherd, b. Aug. 22, 1849, Fayette Co., d. Jan. 9, 1934, m. Joseph James Gibson, Sr., b. 1849, d. 1934, Fayette Co., Ala. 2. Jim Shepherd, m. 1st. - Elvie Yerby, 2nd. - Miss Berry. (Children by 2nd. wife - Mack Berry and Virgie Berry Shepherd.) 3. Lou Shepherd, m. Jack Cates. 4. Mart Shepherd, m. Mollie Henry. 5. Etta Shepherd, m. Bud Yerby. (Children: Ernest, Vertur, and another who married Mute Baker.) 6. Mack Shepherd, m. Nettie Shelton, (Children: Annie Lou Shepherd Davis, Gordo, Ala.) 7. Czarine Marissa Shepherd, b. Nov. 18, 1852, d. Mar. 1, 1927, Fayette Co., m. Feb. 24, 1874, J. A. Sudduth. 8. Kittie Shepherd, m. John Sullivan. (Children: Buren Sullivan who had a daughter, Betty Jon Sullivan.)

SHEPHERD, Joe H., m. Lula Cannon, dau. of M. F. Cannon. Children: 1. Nina Mae Shepherd, m. Joe R. Johnston. 2. Evelyn Shepherd, m. Crawford Owen. (Child: Crawford Owen, Jr.) 3. Joe H. Shepherd, Jr., m. Dorothy Dugin, (Ch: Joe Neville; Alston and Louise Shepherd.)

SHEPHERD, Mart - son of Jacob S. & Maria (Nalls) Shepherd, m. Mollie Henry. Children: 1. Bertie Shepherd. 2. Emma Shepherd. 3. Joe Shepherd. 4. Sallie Shepherd, m. Dr. Claude Bell. 5. Floyd Shepherd, m. Tiny Freeman. 6. Jake Shepherd. 7. Maude Shepherd, m. Carl Carter. (Dau. Carleton Carter.)

SHEPHERD, Moses C., b. Walker Co., Ala., d. Nov. 18, 1958, Oakman, Ala., m. April 6, 1902, Martha Alabama Hassell, b. Dec. 30, 1882, Fayette Co. - dau. of Geo. T. & Susan Richards Hassell. Children: 1. Loris Shepherd, buried in Walker Co., Ala. 2. Wilson Shepherd.

SHERER, Ira Elam, b. April 6, 1876, Fayette Co., Ala., d. Dec. 24, 1952, Fayette Co., - son of Jonathan D. & Mary (Eason) Sherer - m. Dec. 24, 1897, Lillian Matthews, b. Jan. 26, 1880, Fayette Co., d. April 22, 1943, Fayette Co. - dau. of Jerome & Sallie (Richards) Matthews. Children: (All born in Fayette Co.) 1. Alma Sherer, b. Sept. 6, 1901, m. Jan. 1, 1927, Terrell F. Cannon, b. Jan. 20, 1900, Fayette Co. 2. Mercer Harrison Sherer, b. Aug. 26, 1903, m. Sept. 1927, Jeannette Rickles, b. Altoona, Etawah Co., Ala. 3. Anna Lucille Sherer, b. July 10, 1907, m. Claude S. Campbell, b. Fayette Co. 4. Mary Lee Sherer, b. Sept. 30, 1905, d. Nov. 30, 1914, Fayette Co. 5. Sarah Irene Sherer, b. Aug. 20, 1919, Fayette Co., m. May 1938, Truman C. Herren, b. Fayette Co. 6. Edith Sue Sherer, b. Mar. 31, 1926, m. Thomas Loyd White, b. Fayette, Ala. And three other un-named children who died at birth.

SHERER, Jonathan D., b. Chester Co., S. C. - son of Thomas & Jane Kirkpatrick Sherer - m. in Ga., Mary B. Eason, b. Ga. - dau. of Harrison Eason. Both are buried at the New River Baptist Church in Fayette Co. He was a teacher and a farmer. Children: (All born Fayette Co.) 1. Ira Elam Sherer, b. April 6, 1876, d. Dec. 24, 1952, m. Dec. 24, 1897, Lillian Matthews, b. Jan. 26, 1880, d. April 22, 1943, Fayette Co. (He was a farmer.) 2. Moses E. Sherer, m. June 1912, Eunice Matson, b. Talladega, Ala. (Doctor.) 3. Arie Sherer, d. Oct. 1957, buried Elmwood, Birmingham, Ala., m. Albert Sidney Scott, b. Walker Co., Ala., d. Dec. 1957. (Both were teachers.) 4. Joseph Sherer, d. 1900. (Law Student.) 5. John Sherer, d. Fayette, m. Lucy Jackson, b. Gainesville, Ala. (Lawyer.) 6. Morgan Sherer, d. Texas, m. June 1920, Neta Carpenter, b. Kansas. (Farmer.) 7. Harrison Sherer, d. San Benito, Texas, m. Edith Stobart. (He was a farmer, she was an artist.) 8. Gilder Sherer, (Twin) died as infant. 9. Thenumunda Bethulia Sherer (Twin) died as infant. And three other un-named children who died at birth.

SHERER, Thomas, b. Nov. 20, 1808, d. Sept. 15, 1888, Jasper, Ala., m. July 21, 1836, Jane Kirkpatrick, b. Aug. 12, 1811, Chester Co., S.C., d. Sept. 25, 1886, Jasper, Ala. Children: 1. Jonathan D. Sherer, b. Chester Co., S. C., d. buried at New River Baptist Church Cem, Fayette Co., m. Mary B. Eason. (Buried with J.D.) Four other brothers settled in Walker Co., coming there from South Carolina via Georgia.

SHIRLEY, Beverly V., b. Feb. 14, 1820, Ga., d. 1877, m. June 2, 1839, Malinda Jones, b. Jan. 20, 1818, d. June 1854. Rev. B. V. Shirley was the son of Berryman & Susannah Shirley. She was the dau. of Wm. & Barbara (Coffee) Jones, who lived in Rayburn Co., Ga. The Shirleys came to Walker Co., Ala. first and later, after the Civil War moved to Fayette Co. Children: 1. Martha A. Shirley, b. Mar. 17, 1840. 2. William B. Shirley, b. April 9, 1841, m. Sara Hendrix. 3. Frances Shirley, b. Feb. 16, 1843, d. Mar. 21, 1909, m. George Deavours. 4. Leonard C. Shirley, b. Nov. 26, 1844, m. Martelia Ford. 5. Cosby L. Shirley, b. Jan. 20, 1847, moved to Texas, m. Mary Wilbanks. 6, Josiah Starnes Shirley, b. Feb. 1, 1849, d. Jan. 9, 1936, m. Martha Minerva Hollingsworth, b. Dec. 29, 1848, d. Mar. 14, 1917. 7. Elizabeth Shirley, b. June 15, 1851, m. Mr. Barnett and moved to Texas.
 Rev. B. V. Shirley married second - Verta Nix, d. 1873. Children: (2nd. wife.) 1. Sarah Melissa Shirley, b. Dec. 5, 1856, d. Mar. 12, 1939, m. John Ford. 2. Young Jackson Shirley, b. Mar. 4, 1858. (Mr. Leonard C. Shirley visited in Ga. in 1884 and got this family record at that time.)

SHIRLEY, Berryman, b. Mar. 18, 1795, d. Mar. 3, 1875, m. Susanah __, b. Apr. 8, 1792, d. July 17, 1877. Children: 1. Beverly V. Shirley, b. Feb. 14, 1820, Ga., d. 1877, m. June 2, 1839, Malinda Jones, b. Jan. 20, 1818, d. June 1854.

SHIRLEY, Fenton J., b. Fayette Co., m. Maggie Lou Aycock, b. Lamar Co., Ala. Children: 1. James Hilburn Shirley, b. April 13, 1916, Fayette Co., m. A- della Woods, b. Fayette Co. 2. George Young Shirley, b. Mar. 12, 1921, Fayette Co., m. Betty Jean Valco, b. July 10, 1926, Jefferson Co., Ala.

SHIRLEY, George Young, b. Mar. 12, 1921, Fayette Co., Ala. - son of Fenton J. & Maggie (Aycock) Shirley - m. Betty Jean Valco, b. July 1, 1926, Jefferson Co., Ala. George Young is the City Clerk for The City of Fayette, Ala.

SHIRLEY, James Hilbern, b. April 13, 1916, Fayette Co., Ala. - son of F. J. & Maggie (Aycock) Shirley - m. Adella Woods, b. Sept. 7, 1928, Fayette Co. - dau. of Wilmot & Hassie (Ballinger) Woods. Children: 1. Ronald J. Shirley.

SHIRLEY, Josiah Starnes, b. Feb. 1, 1849, d. Jan. 9, 1936 - son of B. V. & Malinda (Jones) Shirley - m. Martha Minerva Hollingsworth, b. Dec. 29, 1848, d. Mar. 14, 1917. Rev. Josiah Starnes Shirley was a Baptist Minister. Children: 1. Vesta Melinda Shirley, b. Nov. 20, 1871, m. Nov. 20, 1890, Luther Allen Connell, d. May, 1939, Fayette, Co. 2. Martha Ida Shirley, b. 1873, d. infancy, 1873. 3. Annie Delitha Shirley, b. Nov. 2, 1875, m. Dec. 22, 1900, William Lemul Meherg. 4. Berryman Beverly Shirley, b. Aug. 28, 1878, d. Aug., 1947, m. 1st. - Dec. 25, 1899, Delia Nichols, b. Sept. 7, 1881, d. July 11, 1901, 2nd. Jan. 1903, Della Ford. 5. Elizabeth Ellen Shirley, b. April 3, 1881, m. Oct. 23, 1899, Andrew Curtis Nichols, b. Sept. 15, 1879. 6. Sarah Frances Shirley, b. Sept. 26, 1883, m. Sept. 26, 1908, John Newton Ford, d. Aug. 15, 1949. 7. Jonah Josiah Shirley, b. Aug. 13, 1886, d. Feb. 23, 1957, m. 1904, Alice Dill, b. Aug. 1, __. 8. Ethel Shirley, b. July 21, 1889, d. May 23, 1924, m. Dec. 25, 1910, William Arthur Mc- Guff. 9. Rosa Ella Shirley, b. Sept. 1893, d. Oct. 1894.

SHIRLEY __ Parents given names not known. Children: 1. Will Jones Shirley b. May 16, 1850. 2. Jasper N. Shirley, b. April 22, 1852. 3. Mar Bashaba Shirley, b. May 28, 1854. 4. Levy Berry Shirley, b. April 21, 1856. 5. Moses Lafayette Shirley, b. June 21, 1860. 6. Lewis Neal Shirley, b. June 17, 1864.

SHIRLEY, Leonard C., b. Nov. 26, 1844, Ga., d. April 10, 1895 or 1896 -(son-in-law)son of Uriah Barnett) - m. Jan. 19, 1871, Martelia Ford, b. Sept. 30, 1852, Faye. Co., d. Jan. 2, 1926. He served in the last eighteen months of the Civil War and later became a licensed Baptist Minister. Children: 1. Della Vir- ginia Shirley, b. Oct. 27, 1876, Fayette Co., m. Morgan Issac Barnett.

SHIRLEY, William B., b. April 9, 1841, d. Jan. 18, 1900 - son of Rev. B. V. Shirley - m. Sara Hendrix. Children: 1. Sallie Shirley, b. Dec. 25, 1868, d. Sept. 21, 1946, m. Humphrey Roberts, b. July 17, 1859, d. May 31, 1931. 2. Belle Shirley, died at 18 yrs. 3. Beverly Shirley, died in early twenties. 4. Mattie Shirley, b. Mar. 25, 1874, d. Sept. 25, 1896, m. William Watkins, b. Aug. 30, 1876, d. July 17, 1900.

SHIRLEY, Young Jackson, b. Mar. 4, 1858 - son of Beverly V. Shirley, m. Mattie Oswalt. Children: 1. Hester Shirley, b. Dec. 30, 1886, d. Nov. 4, 1954, Fayette, Ala., m. John Garrison, b. Aug. 9, 1889, d. Oct. 17, 1955, Fayette, Ala. 2. Fenton Shirley, b. 1888, d. 1949, Fayette, Ala., m. Maggie Aycock. 3. Fannie Shirley, m. Marion Williamson. 4. Alice Shirley, m. Leonard Harbin. 5. Virgie Shirley, m. Thomas Patton. 6. Felix Shirley, m. Inez Reaves. 7. Maggie Shirley, m. Carey Norman Pollard, b. July 13, 1888, d. Sept. 29, 1927, Fayette, Ala.

SIDES, Henry, b. 1734, North Carolina, d. Walker Co., Ala., m. wife unknown. Henry Sides was of a Holland-Dutch family that immigrated to America shortly before the Revolutionary War. A family tradition states that Henry Sides served with distinction during that war. About 1818, while Alabama was still a territory, Henry Sides, then of advanced age, came to Walker County, Ala. with several married sons and their families. He was a farmer and is buried at the Sides Graveyard in Walker Co., Ala. Children: 1. Henry Sides, Jr., b. Jan. 9, 1779, d. Jan. 15, 1867, m. Susan __. 2. William Sides, b. 1795, N. C., d. Dec. 2, 1868, Walker Co., Ala., m. Cerupta Dill, b. 1801, (Feb. 1795,) N. C. 3. Levi Sides, Judge of County Court. 4. John Sides. 5. Moses Sides.

SIDES, William, b. 1795, N. C., d.(Dec.)or Feb. 2, 1868, Walker Co., Ala., m. Cerupta Dill, b. 1801, N. C. (Feb. 1795), d. Walker Co., Ala. He was the son of Henry Sides. William Sides was the first clerk of Pleasant Grove Baptist Church in Walker Co., Ala., founded in 1842 - first Baptist Church in Walker Co. Children: 1. Elizabeth A. Sides, b. Oct. 8, 1839, Walker Co., Ala., d. Nov. 11, 1905, Walker Co., Ala., m. April 4, 1855, James Rutledge, b. Nov. 4, 1832, Walker Co., d. May 25, 1918, Walker Co. 2. Cole Sides, m. Miss Whatley. 3. William F. Sides, m. 1st. - Miss DeWeese, 2nd. - Mrs. Martha (Kitchens) Stagg. 4. Andy Allen Sides, b. July 17, 1827, m. Mary Malone Staggs. 5. Francis Sides, killed in Battle of Shiloh in Civil War. 6. George Franklin Sides, b. April 30, 1830, d. April 16, 1863, m. Elizabeth Cooner. 7. Frank Sides, m. Frances Kitchens. 8. John B. Sides, m. Peninnah Elizabeth Sartain.

SISSON, Terry B., b. Oct. 13, 1905, Marion Co., Ala., m. July 31, 1932, Audrey E. Carter, b. Nov. 26, 1915, Marion Co., Ala. Terry's parents - Julius B. & Fannie E. (Johnson) Sisson. Grandparents - James & Mary I. (Quaitebaum) Sisson; and John H. & Elizabeth A. (Davis) Johnson. Audrey's parents - Marion F. Carter, b. May 9 __, m. Feb. 14, 1914, Mary Mae Sanderson, b. Dec. 13, __, Marion Co., Ala. Grandparents - Jim & Jean Carter; and George Sanderson. Terry's Children: 1. Patsie Sisson (Twin), b. Dec. 12, 1937, Marion Co., Ala., m. 1959, Troy L. Higginbottom. 2. Charles Sisson (Twin), b. Dec. 12, 1937, Marion Co., Ala.

SMITH, George Washington, b. Mar. 6, 1818, d. Nov. 1, 1864, Mt. Vernon, Ala. m. Elizabeth (Mary Ann) Collins, b. ? 1822, S.C., d. ? 1881, Mt. Vernon, Ala. Children: 1. Hiram Spencer Smith, b. Sept. 25, 1857, Fayette Co., d. Dec. 24, 1930, Fayette Co., m. Dec. 1877, Samantha Cornelia Norris, b. Sept. 18, 1858, Tusca. Co., d. Mar. 24, 1927, Fayette Co. 2. Mary Caroline Smith, b. Sept. 6, 1848, Fayette Co., d. Nov. 3, 1921, Fayette Co., m. William Benton Harkins, b. Sept. 19, 1840, Fayette Co., d. April 4, 1921, Fayette Co. 3. Biddie Abigail Smith, b. April 25, 1860, Fayette Co., d. May or June 25, 1938, Fayette Co., m. Jan. 10, 1878, Joel Wilson Raspberry, b. April 12,

1859, Fayette Co., d. Sept. 10, 1935, Fayette Co. (or Oct.) 4. ? Ben Jack Smith, m. Sarah Dunn.

SMITH, Guthrie J., b. Aug. 25, 1912, Fayette Co., Ala. - son of P. B. & Jennie (Wilson) Smith - m. June 12, 1937, Robbie Lee Lollar, b. Aug. 14, 1914, Lamar Co., Ala. - dau. of Lee B. & Lodessa (Brown) Lollar. Mayor and Mrs. Guthrie J. Smith left Fayette on September 4, 1957 for France as guests of the French Government, to attend the celebration marking the 200th Anniversary of the birth of the Marquis de LaFayette, invitation of the France-American LaFayette Bi-Centinnial Committee. Mayor and Mrs. Smith boarded a plane Tuesday morning in Birmingham, Ala. to fly to Washington, D. C. where they joined twenty other Mayors of towns and cities named for LaFayette. They flew directly to Vichey, France. This was the beginning of a full week of "Red Carpet" treatment in France, including visits to twelve French Cities and Towns with banquets, receptions and varied entertainment. The Premier of France flew to the Castle of LaFayette's birthplace to welcome the group to France. The tour ended in Paris with a personal welcome by the President of France at his home. On Sept. 26, 1957, Mayor and Mrs. Smith arrive home from the twenty-one day vacation to France, England, Switzerland and Holland. Children: 1. Nancy Lee Smith, b. Oct. 9, 1943, Fayette, Ala. 2. Robert Guthrie Smith, b. Sept. 1, 1946, Fayette, Ala.

SMITH, Hiram Spencer, b. Sept. 25, 1857, Fayette Co., d. Dec. 24, 1930, Fay. Co. - son of Geo. Wash. & Elizabeth (Collins) Smith - m. Dec. 1877, Cornelia Samantha Norris, b. Sept. 18, 1858, Tusca. Co., Ala., d. Mar. 24, 1927, Fay. Co. - dau. of Tommy & Harriet (Willingham) Norris. Pioneer family in Mt. Vernon Community. Children: 1. John Alexander Smith, m. Maude White. 2. Thomas W. Smith, m. Sadie Bell. 3. Henry Leech Smith, m. Elsie Gary. 4. Charles Linton Smith, m. Ruth Berry. 5. Garland S. Smith, m. Adine Young. 6. Lillie Bell Smith, b. Sept. 3, 1878, d. Sept. -, m. J. V. Hubbert, b. 1872, d. 1940, Fayette Co. 7. Mary Claudia Smith, b. Oct. 19, 1885, m. Winston C. McClure. 8. Samantha Smith, m. Ruford O. Buckner. 9. Lucy Smith, m. 1st. - Harry O. Unger, 2nd. - Ernest K. Dodson. 10. Musa Smith, m. Martin J. Chewning. 11. Gertrude Smith, m. Charles E. Williams.

SMITH, J. Alex, m. Maude White - dau. of S. L. White. Children: 1. J. Alex Smith, Jr., m. Evelyn Dodds. (Children: Teresa Smith; and Twins - Lynn Smith, and Stephen Smith.)

SMITH, Jasper Ned, b. Nov. 9, 1826, S. C., d. buried Bethlehem Meth. Ch. Cem., m. Jan. 8, 1852, Louisa Amanda Hyde, b. Jan. 9, 1832, S. C., d. buried Cleveland Church of Christ Cem., Fayette Co. Mr. & Mrs. Smith came to Fayette Co. Ala. and settled on North River about the year 1854 or 1856. Mr. Smith operated a Tanning Yard and a farm. Dates from Bible owned by Mrs. J. D. Smith. Children: 1. William F. Smith, b. Sept. 26, 1852, d. buried in Fayette, m. Etta Neal, buried in Fayette, Ala. 2. Martin Luther Smith, b. Feb. 26, 1854. 3. Columbus S. Smith, b. Mar. 11, 1856, d. buried at Berry, Ala. 4. John Dyer Smith, b. Oct. 25, 1858, d. May 30, 1942, buried Hopewell Cem., m. Mar. 28, 1901, Minnie E. Stewart, b. Sept. 13, 1869, Fayette Co. 5. James N. Smith, b. Jan. 20, 1861. 6. Sealy Etta Smith, b. Mar. 1, 1863, d. buried in Carrollton, Ga., m. Cliff Jordan, buried in Carrollton, Ga. 7. E. Leuvina Smith, b. Feb. 3, 1866, d. buried Bethlehem Meth. Ch. Cem., m. Jess Smith, d. buried Bethlehem Cem. 8. Charles N. Smith, b. Feb. 14, 1871, Fayette Co.,

d. buried at Fayette., m. Tulliah Blackburn, d. buried in Fayette. 9. Walter S. Smith, b. Mar. 22, 1873, Fayette Co., d. buried Bethlehem, m. Lou Eva Thompson, b. Fayette Co., Ala.

SMITH, John Dyer, b. Oct. 25, 1858, d. May 30, 1942, buried Hopewell Cem. - son of Jasper Ned & Louisa (Hyde) Smith, m. Mar. 28, 1901, Minnie Estell Stewart, b. Sept. 13, 1869, Fayette Co. - dau. of Ruben & Susan (VanHoose) Stewart. Mr. & Mrs. Smith were married at the home of R. B. Stewart in Fayette, Ala. by William Musgrove. Mr. Smith was a farmer. These records are from the Family Bible owned by Mrs. J. D. Smith. Children: 1. John Rayburn Smith, b. Feb. 11, 1903, Fayette, Ala. 2. Orrin VanHoose Smith, b. June 7, 1905, Fayette Co. 3. Linwood Stewart Smith, b. Jan. 1, 1909, Anson, Texas, m. Dec. 22, 1935, Sara Helen Renfroe, b. Jan. 4, 1911, Fayette, Ala. 4. Ruby Genevieve Smith, b. April 4, 1916, Fayette Co., Ala., m. May 27, 1940, William L. Weems, b. July 28, 1903, Cobb Co., Ga.

SMITH, Julius Crittenden, b. Feb. 20, 1856, d. Aug. 27, 1925 - son of Capt. Richard Allen Smith - m. Feb. 25, 1900, Sarah Eleanor Thompson, b. Mar. 27, 1873, d. Sept. 21, 1927. Children: 1. Mary Elizabeth "Mamie" Smith, b. Nov. 7, 1901, m. Sept. 28, 1921, Dalton Barnes. (Children: John Frank; William Allen; and Joseph Edward Barnes.)

SMITH, Linwood Stewart, b. Jan. 1, 1909, Anson, Texas, - son of John Dyer & Minnie (Stewart) Smith - m. Dec. 22, 1935, Sara Helen Renfroe, b. Jan. 4, 1911, Fayette, Ala. - dau. of James Wm. & Cora (Barton) Renfroe. Mr. & Mrs. Smith were married in Fayette, Ala. by Rev. N. H. Abernathy. They are the owners and operators of the Linwood S. Smith Store and Sawmill on the Winfield Highway. They also operate a farm. Children: 1. Marilyn Stewart Smith, b. June 9, 1937, Fayette, Ala., m. Oct. 18, 1957, Edward Barry McEachern, b. Dec. 14, 1935, Pelham, N. Y. 2. Ned Allen Smith, b. Jan. 12, 1940, Fayette, Ala. 3. Joe Lynn Smith, b. Aug. 6, 1946, Fayette, Ala.

SMITH, Preston B., b. 1878, Fayette Co., Ala., d. Sept. 1952, Fayette - son of J. R. & Anne Smith - m. 1896, Jennie Wilson, b. Feb. 8, 1876, Fayette Co. - dau. of Rev. Frank & Sara Wilson. The Smiths were married by her father, Rev. Frank Wilson, at Fayette, Ala. Children: 1. Fletcher F. Smith, b. Oct. 14, 1898, Fayette Co. (All children born Fayette Co.) 2. Curruth R. Smith, b. Aug. 1900, m. Cecile Aikin, b. Miss. 3. Robert L. Smith, b. Aug. 26, 1902, m. Lyda (Hood) Rose, b. Pickens Co., Ala. 4. Claude W. Smith, b. 1904, m. Lillian Brock. 5. Minnie Mae Smith, b. 1906, m. Robert W. Mason, b. Birmingham, Ala. 6. Guthrie J. Smith, b. Aug. 25, 1912, m. June 12, 1937, Robbie Lee Lollar, b. Aug. 14, 1914, Lamar Co., Ala.

SMITH, Capt. Richard Allen, b. Jan. 30, 1819, d. Mar. 5, 1902, m. Oct. 28, 1839, Elizabeth Ann Wiers, b. Feb. 13, 1820, d. April 6, 1900. Capt. Richard Allen Smith served in Co. B. 5th Ala. Regt. C.S.A. He commanded "Smith Co." 5th Battalion, Ala. Inf., also Co. B. 58th Reg. Ala. Inf. C.S.A. Children: 1. Nathaniel T. Smith. 2. James D. Smith, m. Armanda Norman. 3. William Allen Smith, b. Nov. 9, 1854, d. Jan. 11, 1867. 4. Julius Critterden Smith, b. Feb. 20, 1856, d. Aug. 27, 1925, m. Feb. 25, 1900, Sarah Eleanor Thompson, b. Mar. 27, 1873, d. Sept. 21, 1927. 5. Oscar Smith, b. Oct. 20, 1858, d. Oct. 11, 1878. 6. Doctor Wesley Smith, b. Aug. 11, 1840, d. Nov. 10, 1881. 7. Mary Elizabeth Smith, b. May 14, 1881. 8. Richard J.

Smith, m. Lily Abernathy, b. 1841, d. 1914.

SMITH, Richard J., b. 1840, Fayette Co., Ala., d. 1922, Fayette Co., Ala. - son of Richard & Elizabeth Ann (Wiers) Smith - m. Lilly Abernathy, b. 1841, S. C., d. 1914, Fayette Co. Children: 1. W. T. Smith. 2. John Smith. 3. Oscar Smith. 4. Alice Elizabeth Smith. 5. Eva Smith. 6. Olivia Smith, m. George Howton.

SMITH, Robert Lee, b. July 21, 1874, Covin, Ala., d. Jan. 22, 1900 - son of Russell & Ann Smith - m. Dec. 29, 1895, Ella Francis Branyon, b. Nov. 16, 1880, Belk, Ala., d. Feb. 25, 1957. Robert Lee Smith was a farmer. They were married at Belk, Ala. Children: 1. Vera Smith (Twin), b. June 18, 1898, Fayette Co., m. Oct. 21, 1926, Whitt Sparks, b. Feb. 6, 1886, d. Oct. 1, 1948, Fayette, Ala. 2. Era Helen Smith (Twin), b. June 18, 1898, Fayette Co., m. April 11, 1925, Uridisa Jess Hankins, b. Mar. 21, 1894, Fayette Co., d. Jan. 24, 1959, Fayette, Ala.

SMITH, Sarepta, b. Mar. 28, 1841, Jackson Co., Ga., d. Nov. 10, 1923, Kennedy, Ala., m. Martha Ann Yarbrough, b. May 21, 1831, Spartanburg, S. C., d. Mar. 27, 1911, Kennedy, Ala. - dau. of Stephen & Susan Yarbrough. Sarepta Smith came from Georgia to Fayette Co., Ala. in the early 1850's. At the outbreak of the Civil War, he volunteered and served with distinction with Lee's Army in some of the greatest battles of the war. Among these battles were the second battle of Manasses, Gettysburg, and the battles around Richmond. He was captured in the Penisula Campaigns and placed in prison in New York City. He later served for some time in the Indian Wars of North and South Dakota. Children: 1. Alpha Susan Smith, b. Jan. 27, 1869, Kennedy, Ala., d. Mar. 22, 1952, Fayette, Ala., m. Oct. 6, 1889, John Simpson Branyon, b. Jan. 14, 1861, Fayette Co., d. Nov. 21, 1936, Fayette Co. 2. Mary Hulda Smith, b. Sept. 7, 1871, Kennedy, Ala., m. W. M. Sudduth.

SMITH, Tom L., b. Feb. 5, 1879, d. Nov. 1, 1954, Tusca., Ala., m. Sarah Elizabeth Guin, b. Nov. 16, 1887, Tusca. Co., Ala. Tom L. Smith's parents - John Luther & Mary Jane (Carroll) Smith. Grandparents - Johnathan & Hanna (North) Smith; and Monroe & Nancy (Bennett) Carroll. Sarah Elizabeth's parents - Robert & Jennie (Lynn) Guin. Grandparents - Holten (son of Acey Guin) & Sally (Clanton) Guin. Children: (Tom L. Smith's) 1. Ledger Smith, b. May 9, 1911, Pickens Co., Ala., m. 1934, Pezzie C. Stripling, b. April 26, 1907, Pickens Co., Ala. (Child: Thomas Murl Smith, b. Dec. 30, 1937, Pickens Co. - Pezzie Stripling Smith's parents - Wm. E. Stripling, b. Nov. 1, 1860, & Biddie A. (Brazeal), b. Oct. 27, 1863, Tusca. Co. Grandparents - Tom Newt & Nellie (Sullivan) Stripling; and Harvie & Elizabeth (Pennington) Brazeal.

SMITH, Travis Auldon, b. May 13, 1911, Fayette Co. - son of Howell Smith - m. Feb. 27, 1947, Sarah Willene Humber, b. Aug. 16, 1913, Fayette Co., - dau. of Thos. Bailey Humber. They were married at Fayette, Ala. by Rev. Leroy Lowery. He is a farmer. Children: 1. Howell Thomas Smith, b. Jan. 26, 1948 Belle Glade, Fla. 2. Sarah Frances Smith, b. Mar. 4, 1951, Fayette Co. 3. Rachel Pauline Smith, b. Oct. 27, 1956, Fayette Co., Ala.

SMITH, William Franklin, b. Sept. 26, 1852, Ga., d. Dec. 27, 1936, Fayette, Ala. - son of Jasper N. & Amanda (Hyde) Smith - m. Etta Neal, b. July 4, 1859 Fayette, Ala., d. Sept. 8, 1934, Fayette, Ala., - dau. of George & Elizabeth

Neal. They were married in Fayette, Ala. Both are buried in the Fayette City Cemetery. Children: 1. Velma Smith, b. (All born Fayette, Ala.) d. Fay. m. William Arlington Dodson, b. Fayette, Ala. d, Fayette. 2. Neva Smith, b. April 30, 1884, d. May 7, 1918, Fayette, m. E. E. Thomason. 3. Loudell Smith, b. Dec. 18, 1886, m. Aug. 1, 1907, Samuel Jesse Sanders, b. April 28, 1886, Fayette, d. Oct. 9, 1948, Fayette, Ala. 4. Willetta Smith, b. May 9, 1896, d. July 12, 1937, Fayette, m. Thomas J. Temple, b. July 25, 1896, Miss. d. Feb. 6, 1940, Fayette, Ala.

SMITH, William Russell, b. Mar. 27, 1815, Russellville, Ky., d. Feb. 26, 1896, m. 1843, Tusca. Co., Ala., Jane Binion, died 1844, - dau. of J. H. & Elizabeth (Strong) Binion. Children: (1st. marriage.) 1. Sidney Smith, b. 1843.

Wm. Russell Smith second marriage - 1847, Fayette Co., to Mary Jane Murray, died 1853 - dau. of James & Mary (Moore) Murray. Children: (2nd. marriage.) 1. Lucy Smith, b. 1848, Fayette Co. 2. Sophia Ann Smith, b. 1850, Fayette. 3. William Russell Smith, b. 1853, Fayette, Ala.

Wm. Russell Smith third marriage - 1855, Washington, D. C. to Wilhelmine M. Easby. Children: (3rd. marriage.) 1. Mary Agnes Easby Smith, b. 1855, Washington, D. C. 2. William E. Smith, b. 1856. 3. Wilhelmine Smith, b. 1858. 4. Elizabeth Smith, b. 1865, Huntsville, Ala. 5. Paula Louise Smith, b. 1867, Tusca. Co., Ala. 6. James S. Easby Smith, b. 1870, Tusca. Co. Ala. 7. Ann Agatha Smith, b. 1873, Tuscaloosa, Ala. 8. Rose Mary Smith, 1. 1876, Tuscaloosa, Ala.

In 1844, William Russell Smith was Brigadier General of Militia of Fayette County, a lawyer, and in 1850 was Circuit Judge of Fayette County. During the Civil War he served as Col. with the 26th Ala., Inf. Regt. from Fayette Co. He was a professor at the University of Ala. and served as the fourth president of that institution, retiring in 1870 after having served one year.

SOUTH, Carlos, b. Jan. 24, 1899, Berry, Ala., d. May 7, 1955, Berry - son of Lafayette South - m. Helen _. Children: 1. Wanaka South, m. 1st. - Aster Williamson.

SOUTH, Charles Manley, b. Sept. 8, 1877, d. May 27, 1932, Fayette Co., - son of Levi Woodruff South - m. Aug. 6, 1899, Pearl Sarah Maddox, b. June 1, 1889 Davis Creek, Ala., d. Dec. 13, 1924, Fayette Co. - dau. of Sam Maddox. Children: (All born Davis Creek, Fayette Co., Ala.) 1. Condro Chester South, b. Sept. 1, 1900, m. Mar. 7, 1928, Georgia Lou Traweek (Kelley), b. Aug. 27, 1900. 2. Cora Mattie South, b. Nov. 16, 1903, m. Dec. 30, 1921, Floyd Chester Cannon, b. Oct. 25, 1895. 3. Theron Abbie South, b. Mar. 17, 1905, m. Dec. 24, 1929, Meryl Elizabeth Freeman, b. Jan. 9, 1910. 4. Richmond Pearson South, b. Nov. 1, 1906, m. Oct. 14, 1928, Irene Kizzire, b. April 20, 1909, Davis Creek, Ala. 5. Flora Kathleen South, b. Nov. 25, 1908, m. 1921, Richard Hobson Carr, b. April 5, __, d. Moundville, Ala. 6. Martha Beatrice South, b. April 11, 1917, m. May 3, 1943, 1st - Early Sexton, 2nd. Pool Woodson. 7. Charles Braxter South, b. Nov. 9, 1921, d. Dec. 7, 1941, Pearl Harbor. 8. Clinton South, died in infancy.

SOUTH, General Wheeler, b. May 16, 1880, Davis Creek, Ala., d. Nov. 9, 1950, Fayette Co. - son of Levi Woodruff South - m. Jan. 24, 1904, Mary Maranda "Molly" Kyser, b. Nov. 7, 1885 - dau. of John Kyser. Children: (Born Davis Creek, Fayette Co., Ala.) 1. Cullen Samuel South, b. Feb. 7, 1905, m. Mary

Hagler. 2. Mabel South, b. April 13, 1909, d. Mar. 21, 1950, Fayette, Ala. m. G. Marvin Fowler. 3. Thelma Christine South, b. Dec. 24, 1918, m. A. D. Brittian.

SOUTH, **George Oscar "Babe"**, b. Dec. 25, 1869, Tusca. Co., Ala., d. Jan. 1, 1952, Fayette Co., - son of Levi Woodruff South - m. Feb. 7, 1897, Lula Savage, b Mar. 30, 1875, Fayette Co., Ala., d. Sept. 19, 1941, Fayette Co. - dau. of Thomas Savage. He was a farmer. Both are buried at Mt. Pleasant Cemetery. Children: 1. Eva Mae South, b. Aug. 26, 1898, (All born Fayette Co.) 2. Kate Christine South, b. Jan. 21, 1905, m. Arthur Estelle Shafer, b. Jan. 2, 1901. 3. Cecil Hobson South, b. 1900, Fayette Co., d. May 7, 1918, Fayette Co. 4. Woodruff Thomas "Buster" South, b. Aug. 27, 1906, Fay. Co., m. Oct. 4, 1940, Chloe Spann, b. Mar. 17, 1910, Glen Allen, Ala.

SOUTH, **Huel**, b. Oct. 25, 1866, Tusca. Co., d. April 13, 1941, Fayette Co., - son of Levi Woodruff South - m. Dec. 15, 1897, Madora M. Griffin, b. Sept. 7, 1873, Fayette Co., d. Nov. 28, 1957, Fayette, Ala. - dau. of Thos. J. Griffin. They were married at the home of Tom Griffin. Huel was a farmer. Both are buried at Mt. Pleasant Cem. Fayette Co., Ala. Children: (Born Fayette Co.) 1. Lucy Bell South, b. Sept. 9, 1897, m. May 5, 1923, Archie Leroy "Boot" Brown, b. Aug. 9, 1900. 2. Carl Belton South, b. April 29, 1903, m. April 25, 1925, Gertrude Davis, b. Feb. 5, 1904. 3. Infant Thomas Levi South, b. 1899?, buried in South Family Cemetery.

SOUTH, **James Ransom**, b. July 16, 1911, S. C., d. June 10, 1860, Fayette Co. - son of Francis South - m. Oct. 2, 1831, Elizabeth Finch, b. Feb. 25, 1813, Ga., d. Aug. 22, 1892, Fayette Co., Ala. - dau. of Margaret Finch. They were married in Tuscaloosa Co., Ala. and he was a farmer. Both are buried in the South Family Cemetery, in Fayette Co., Ala. Children: (All born Ala.) 1. Newton M. South, b. Jan. 3, 1832, d. Jan. 26, 1855, Fayette Co. 2. James M. South, d. in Confederate Army in La. 3. Levi Woodruff South, b. May 8, 1836, Tusca. Co., Ala., d. July 13, 1918, Fayette Co., m. June 20, 1865, 1st, - Lucy Jane Hassell, b. July 26, 1845, Tusca. Co., d. Feb. 23, 1886, Fayette Co., 2nd. - Mary Jane Logan Henderson, b. Oct. 30, 1854, Berea, Ala., d. Dec. 17, 1944, Fayette Co. 4. Amanda Caroline South, b. 1841, m. James Jefferson Mayfield. 5. Margaret South, d. Fayette Co., Ala., m. James A. "Babe" Lindsey, b. Jan. 12, 1843, d. July 26, 1884, Fayette Co. 6. Joshua D. South, d. July 7, 1862. 7. Reuben D. South, b. Aug. 14, 1847, d. Feb. 11, 1893, Fayette Co., m. 1st. - Nancy Adeline Hassell, 2nd. - Nancy Gammon. 8. Jerusha Frances South, d. Okla., m. Walker Winn. 9. Florence Hasseltine "Tiny" South, b. April 25, 1853, Ala., d. Okla., m. Willis Melton.

SOUTH, **Jasper R.**, b. S. C., d. June 1860, Fayette Co., m. Elizabeth Finch, b. S. C., d. Mar, 1894, Fayette Co., Ala. Children: 1. Amanda Caroline South, b. Mar. 13, 1839, Davis Creek, Fayette Co., Ala., d. Jan. 28, 1921, Tusca. Co., Ala., m. 1859, Capt. James Jefferson Mayfield, b. May 1, 1834, Tusca. Co., Ala., d. Mar. 24, 1901.

SOUTH, **Levi Woodruff**, b. May 8, 1836, Tusca. Co., Ala., d. July 13, 1918, Fay. Co. - son of James Ransom South - m. June 20, 1865, Lucy Jane Hassell, b. July 26, 1845, Tusca. Co., Ala., d. Feb. 23, or 24, 1886, Fayette Co. - dau. of Geo. Washington Hassell. Levi Woodruff South entered Confederate service Sept. 1861 as a private in Bunks Co. Sharpshooters and continued until Sept. 1862. Reenlisted in Sept. 1862 at Mobile, Ala. in 43 Miss. Regt. Inf. Co.

K. and continued until captured at Vicksburg, Miss. and paroled and exchanged. Pvt. 1864, Fayette, Ala. in 10th Ala. Regt. Cal. Co. K. and continued until May 1865 and discharged. He served in the 10th Ala. Cal. with James Hugh Willingham as a Lt., who was to be his son-in-law thirty years later. Levi W. South was a farmer. Children: (Born in Fayette Co. at Davis Creek.) 1. Huel South, b. Oct. 25, 1866, Tusca. Co., Ala., d. April 13, 1941, Faye. Co., m. Dec. 15, 1897, Madora "Dora" Griffin, b. Sept. 7, 1873, Fayette Co. d. Nov. 30, 1957, Fayette Co. 2. Samuel Lafayette South, b. Oct. 30, 1867, Tusca. Co., d. Oct. 15, 1945, Fayette, m. Jan. 1892, Mattie Pinion, b. Nov. 27, Berry, Ala., d. Jan. 9, 1947, Fayette. Both are buried at Pleasant Hill Cem. 3. George Oscar "Babe" South, b. Dec. 25, 1869, Tusca. Co., d. Jan. 1, 1952, Fayette, Ala., m. Feb. 7, 1897, Lula Savage, b. Mar. 30, 1875, Fayette Co., d. Sept. 19, 1941, Fayette Co. Both are buried at Mt. Pleasant Cem. - his bro. Huel and wife are buried there also. 4. Sarah Elizabeth "Lizzie" South, b. Sept. 17, 1871, Fayette Co., d. Nov. 22, 1903, Fayette Co., m. Jan. 31, 1893, James Roscoe Yerby, b. Hico Beat, Fayette Co., d. Fayette Co. Both are buried at Pilgrim's Rest. 5. Mary Lela South, b. April 11, 1874, d. Aug. 17, 1943, Bankston, Ala., m. Nov. 1, 1896, James Hugh Willingham, b. Sept. 16, 1841, d. Oct. 3, 1917, Bankston, Ala. 6. Charles Manly South, b. Sept. 8, 1877, d. May 27, 1932, Fayette Co., m. Aug. 6, 1899, Pearl Sarah Maddox, b. June 1, 1889, Fayette Co., d. Dec. 13, 1924, Fayette Co., m. 2nd. Virgie Lee Trimm. (Buried at Mt. Pleasant.) 7. General Wheeler South, b. May 16, 1880, d. Nov. 9, 1950, Fayette Co., m. Jan. 24, 1904, Mary Maranda "Mollie" Kyser, b. Nov. 7, 1885, Tusca. Co., Ala. 8. Lucy Jane "Minnie" South, b. Feb. 23, 1886, m. Sept. 16, 1906, William Andrew West, b. June 12, 1881, Fayette Co., d. Oct. 19, 1950, Fayette Co.

Levi Woodruff South second marriage - Dec. 19, 1886, Mary Jane Logan, b. Oct. 30, 1854, d. Dec. 17, 1944, Fayette Co. - dau. of Alexander Logan. Children: (2nd. marriage.) 1. Nancy Josephine South, b. Nov. 29, 1887, m. April 6, 1911, Walter William Maddox, b. Feb. 14, 1889, Tusca. Co. Ala. 2. Dora Ann South, b. Jan. 19, 1890, Davis Creek, Ala., m. Jan. 11, 1911, Lorenzo Michael, b. June 4, 1894, Davis Creek, Ala. 3. Maude Lenora "Daisy" South, b. April 4, 1892, Davis Creek, Ala., m. Oct. 17, 1915, William Leech Jones, b. Dec. 15, 1891, Fayette Co., d. May 25, 1929, Fayette Co. 4. Maggie Beulah South, b. Dec. 29, 1894, Davis Creek, Ala., m. Nov. 16, 1910, James Fulton Long, b. Feb. 18, 1890, Ochlochnee, Ga. 5. Ala Gertrude South, b. Dec. 11, 1900, Davis Creek, Ala., m. Mar. 27, 1923, Paul Mall Golson, b. July 5, 1901, Clanton, Ala. - son of Geo. Wm. Jasper Golson.

SOUTH, Martin Ausburn, b. May 6, 1906, Fayette Co. - son of Martin D. South - m. 1934, Mary Lou Oswalt. Children: 1. Mart Jimmy South, b. Nov. 21, 1936, Fayette Co., Ala.

SOUTH, Martin D., b. Dec. 12, 1878, Fayette Co., d. Mar. 7, 1957, Fayette, Ala., m. Dec. 29, 1901, Nina Louise Hyde, b. Feb. 19, 1879, Fayette Co. He was the son of Reubin D. South. They were married at Fayette, Ala. by Rev. George White. Children: (All born Fayette Co.) 1. Martin Ausburn South, b. May 6, 1906, m. Mary Lou Oswalt. 2. Susie Temperance South, b. Oct. 11, 1908, m. Sept. 25, 1927, Freeland E. Logan, b. Jan. 15, 1909, Fayette Co., m. 2nd. - Joseph Quinton Harris, b. Feb. 19, 1909, Fayette Co. 3. Lena Christine South, b. Jan. 27, 1911, m. Jan. 15, 1934? Jessie Leonard Cotton, b. Mar. 16, 1912, Fayette Co. 4. John Ruben South, b. May 29, 1914, d. July 22, 1943. 5. Sarah Addine South, b. Aug. 20, 1916, m. Nov. 27, 1952, William M. Avant.

SOUTH, Reuben D. - son of James Ransom South - m. Nancy Adeline Hassell, b. 1851, d. Mar. 5, 1888 - dau. of Geo. Wash. Hassell. Children: 1. Martin D. South, b. Dec. 12, 1878, d. Mar. 7, 1957, Fayette Co., m. Mina Louise Hyde. 2. Maude South, m. Mr. Johnson. 3. Nick South, He served in Co. C. 9th Regulars Massacre - Battle of Ballinger in 1900, Niger Island. Killed in Spanish War. 4. Stella South. 5. Cullen Grace South, m. Ozzie Smith, b. Berry, Ala. 6. Dell South, d. Okla. m. George Johnson.

SOUTH, Samuel Lafayette, b. Oct. 30, 1867, Tusca. Co., Ala., d. Oct. 1945, Berry, Ala. - son of Levi Woodruff South - m. Jan. 3, 1892, Mattie Pinion, b. Nov. 27, 1870 or 1873, d. Jan. 9, 1947, Berry, Ala. - dau. of Ab. W. Pinion. Children: 1. Carlos South, b. Jan. 24, 1899, Berry, Ala., d. May 7, 1955, Fayette, Ala., m. Helen. 2. Durward South, m. Mary Schmidt. 3. Howard South m. Evelyn ___.

SOUTH, Woodruff Thomas "Buster" b. Aug. 27, 1906, Fayette Co., Ala., - son of George Oscar "Babe" South - m. Oct. 4, 1940, Chloe Spann, b. Mar. 17, 1910 Glen Allen, Fayette Co. - dau. of J. Benjamin Spann. Woodruff T. South entered military service Aug. 20, 1942 at Ft. McClellan, Ala. His serial No. 34338544. Training Stations: Ft. McClellan, Ala.,; Ft. Eustis, Va.; Ft. Knox, Ky; Camp Campbell, Ky; Camp Chaffee, Ark.; and Ft. Sill, Okla. Left for overseas Feb. 5, 1945, - Theatre, European - Engagements, Central Europe (Germany, France, Belgium.) Returned to United States Oct. 12, 1945 and discharged at Ft. McPherson, Ga. Oct. 18, 1945 as Sergeant. Served thirty-eight months. Decorations received: European-African-Middle Eastern Theatre Medal with 1 Bronze Star; and Good Conduct Medal. No living children.

SPARKS, Robert Samuel, b. Dec. 24, 1928, Fayette, Ala. - son of Whitt & Vera Sparks - m. May 2, 1948, Ruth S. Busch, b. Jan. 13, 1929. Children: 1. Elizabeth Ann Sparks, b. Oct. 11, 1950, Santa Rosa, Texas. 2. Karen Lee Sparks, b. Jan. 24, 1952, Santa Rosa, Texas. 3. Samuel Robert Sparks, Jr., b. June 18, 1954, Santa Rosa, Texas. 4. John Andrew Sparks, b. Jan. 10, 1956, Santa Rosa, Texas.

SPARKS, Whitt, b. Feb. 6, 1886, d. Oct. 1, 1948, m. Oct. 21, 1926, Vera Smith, b. June 18, 1898, Fayette Co. - dau. of Robert Lee & Ella Francis Smith. They were married in Jasper, Ala. by Rev. Pete Price. Children: 1. Samuel Robert Sparks, b. Dec. 24, 1928, Haleyville, Ala., m. 1948. 2. Ella Katheryn Sparks, b. June 4, 1931, Fayette, Ala., m. July 14, 1950.

SPRADLEY, Mannon Thomas, b. Feb. 3, 1929, m. Eva Gober, b. May 25, 1907, Tishimingo Co., Miss. - dau. of W. T. & Nancy L. (Humber) Gober. Children: 1. Jerome Thomas Spradley, b. Dec. 15, 1929.

STACKS, Samuel Hudson, b. 1828, Fayette Co., Ala., d. 1907, m. Susan Hand. Served in Co. K. 30th Ala. Regt. C.S.A. Wounded at the Battle of New Hope Church, Ga. He lost a leg as a result of the wound. Children: 1. Ella C. Stacks, b. May 3, 1862, Fayette Co., Ala., d. Aug. 22, 1901, Fayette Co., m. Dec. 29, 1881, James Wm. Riley Jones, b. Dec. 23, 1861, Fayette Co., d. Mar. 31, 1931, Fayette Co., Ala.

STAMPS, John, b. Mar. 17, 1831, d. April 29, 1887, Fayette Co., m. Sara Derry, b. Nov. 20, 1844, d. April 6, 1931, Fayette Co. - dau. of John & Eliza

(Moore) Berry. Children: 1. Francis Missouri Stamps, b. Nov. 27, ___ Fay. Co., d. July 1957, Fayette Co., m. Euell Cummings Farquhar, b. Aug. 22, 1867, Fayette Co., d. Aug. 19, 1936, Fayette Co. 2. Lum Stamps. 3. Jim Stamps. 4. Lizzie Stamps. 5. Callie Stamps.

STARKEY, Edward, b. June 30, 1929, Tish. Co., Miss., m. Oct. 10, 1953, Mary Yvonne Deaton, b. May 24, 1935, Tish. Co., Miss. They were married at Tishimingo Co., Miss. by Rev. George N. Gober. Children: 1. Daniel Edward Starkey, b. Aug. 12, 1955, Kokura, Japan. 2. Carol Lynne Starkey, b. May 24, 1958, Lawton, Okla.

STEPHENS, Marshall Allen, b. May 30, 1907, Calhoun Co., Ala. - son of Wm. Thos. & Cora Lee (Scott) Stephens - m. Willie Dean Freeman, b. June 20, 1907, - dau. of W. Leander & Dona (Sykes) Freeman. Children: 1. Lloyd Marshall Stephens, b. May 18, 1930, Fayette Co., m. Dec. 27, 1952, Valorice Hallman, b. Feb. 2, 1935, Fayette Co. (Children: Danny Marshall Stephens, b. June 27, 1955; and Karen Denise Stephens, b. Dec. 19, 1957.) 2. Allen McCoy Stephens, b. Mar. 10, 1928, Fayette Co., d. Jan. 9, 1929, Fayette Co. 3. William Ted Stephens, b. Oct. 30, 1933, Fayette Co., m. July 2, 1951, Betty Barton, b. June 7, 1935, (Children: Frances Cheryl Stephens, b. Oct. 20, 1952; Sabrina Jo Stephens, b. Aug. 26, 1955; and William Ted Stephens, Jr., b. Mar. 14, 1957.)

STEWART, Charles, m. Johanna Kirk. Children: 1. Charles Stewart, m. Elizabeth Clemmons. 2. George Stewart, m. Rebecca Utley.

STEWART, Charles - son of Charles & Johanna (Kirk) Stewart - m. Elizabeth Clemmons. Children: 1. Johanna Stewart, b. Jan. 31, 1777, m. Walter Harkins, b. Ireland.

STEWART, Charles C., b. Nov. 3, 1822, Fayette Co., d. Sept. 16, 1878, buried at Stewart Cem. - son of Reuben & Elizabeth (McConnell) Stewart - m. 1847, Louisa Jones, b. April 22, 1832, Tusca. Co., d. May 20, 1906, buried Stewart Cem. - dau. of Fletcher & Sarah (Pearson) Jones. Children: 1. America Stewart, b. Mar. 6, 1849, Fayette Co., m. Clem K. Northcut. 2. John McConnell Stewart, b. Nov. 24, 1854, Fayette Co., Ala., d. Dec. 27, 1878, m. Dec. 25, 1879, Mary Reeves.

STEWART, George, - son of Charles & Johanna (Kirk) Stewart - m. Rebecca Utley - dau. of John & Mary (Cook) Utley. Children: 1. John Stewart, b. May 14, 1793, d. Sept. 20, 1866, m. Annie ___, b. Sept. 23, 1805, d. July 25, 1872. 2. Edith Stewart, m. William Wommack.

STEWART, Jack, m. wife unknown. Children: 1. Mary Jane Stewart, d. Fayette Co., Ala., m. Martin Dyer, b. Oct. 16, 1854, d. Aug. 8, 1944. 2. John Stewart. 3. Tom Stewart. 4. George Stewart. 5. Jim Stewart. 6. Lizzie Stewart. 7. Fannie Stewart.

STEWART, John, b. May 14, 1793, d. Sept. 20, 1866, - son of George & Rebecca (Utley) Stewart - m. Annie ___, b. Sept. 23, 1805, d. July 25, 1872. Children: 1. Nancy Adeline Stewart, b. April 16, 1828, Fayette Co., d. Oct. 25, 1873, Fayette Co., m. Ezekiel Asbury South, b. Mar. 1, 1818, d. June 22, 1891, Fayette Co. 2. Rebecca Utley Stewart, b. Nov. 26, 1829, Fayette Co., m. James Franklin Holliman, b. Jan. 28, 1839.

STEWART, John McConnell, b. Nov. 24, 1854, Fayette Co., d. Dec. 27, 1898, - son of Charles C. & Louisa (Jones) Stewart - m. Dec. 25, 1879, Mary Pamela Reeves, b. Jan. 30, 1859, Fayette Co., Ala., d. April 6, 1939, - dau. of A. J. & Martha (Shirey) Reeves. Both are buried at Stewart Family Cemetery. Children: 1. Mabel Clements Stewart, b. Aug. 11, 1881, Fayette Co., m. Dec. 29, 1910, John D. Hassell. 2. Rosalea Stewart, b. July 21, 1886, Fayette Co. m. June 28, 1909, Albert Brewer. 3. Charles A. Stewart, b. April 30, 1889, Fayette Co., m. Laura Thacker. 4. Vera Stewart, b. July 21, 1891, Fayette Co., m. John Walch. 5. John Clyde Stewart, b. Feb. 3, 1894, Fayette Co., m. Alta Roberts. 6. Arthur R. Stewart, b. Jan. 19, 1897, Fayette Co., d. May 6, 1918.

STEWART, Reuben, b. 1779, Wake Co., N. C. - son of Charles & Elizabeth (Clement) Stewart - m. Elizabeth McConnell, b. 1782. Both are buried at the Stewart Family Cemetery. Children: 1. Anne Stewart, b. Sept. 25, 1806, Cumberland, N.C., m. John Stewart. 2. Mary "Polly" Stewart, b. June 10, 1808, m. Nimrod Dodson. 3. Betsy Stewart, b. April 29, 1810, m. George Hubbert. 4. Nancy Stewart, b. Aug. 15, 1812, m. Spice ? Hamm. 5. Sally Stewart, b. Jan. 15, 1815, m. Mark Russell. 6. Frances Stewart, b. Mar. 8, 1817, m. William Hamm. 7. Joseph Stewart, b. Sept. 8, 1820, m. Sarah Hamm. 8. Charles C. Stewart, b. Nov. 3, 1822, m. Louisa Jones. 9. William Stewart, b. Sept. 8, 1826, m. Alabama _? 10. John McConnell Stewart, b. April 2, 1831, unmarried. John McConnell Stewart, enlisted in the Confederate Army Aug. 1, 1862 and died of typhoid fever at Selma General Hospital, Oct. 29, 1864. He served during the was, made a good record and was promoted to First Lt. Reuben Stewart, the son of Wm. Stewart served during the whole duration of the War and returned with the rank of Lt. John M. Stewart, a grandson of George Stewart, lost a leg at Chickamauga, returned home and was elected County Treasurer of Fayette County, Ala. for two terms. He made his home at Fayette.

STEWART, Rubin J., b. May 26, 1831, Fayette Co., Ala., d. Jan. 28, 1917, - son of Wm. & Polly (Hogan) Stewart - m. Nov. 22, 1866, Susan P. Van Hoose, b. Sept. 3, 1841, Fayette Co., d. May 29, 1930 - dau. of Asa & Nancy (Thornton) Van Hoose. Both are buried at Hopewell Cemetery. Rubin J. Stewart served in the Civil War and was wounded. He farmed. Dates from Bible owned by Mrs. J. D. Smith. Children: (All born Fayette Co.) 1. Murray VanHoose Stewart, b. Sept. 17, 1867, Fayette Co., d. buried Hopewell, m. Mary Barnes, b. Fayette Co., d. buried Hopewell. 2. Minnie E. Stewart, b. Sept. 13, 1869, m. Mar. 28, 1901, John Dyer Smith, b. Oct. 25, 1858, d. May 30, 1942, buried Hopewell. 3. Kirk Leslie Stewart, b. Nov. 5, 1873, d. buried Columbus, Miss. m. Bessie Morman, d. buried Columbus, Miss. 4. Lucy Stewart, b. Sept. 22, 1880.

STILLMAN, Thomas, m. Mary Ward. Thomas Stillman's parents came to the U. S. from England. His mother's maiden name was Love. They had a child to die and was buried at sea while coming over. Children: 1. Martha Ann Stillman, b. Oct. 10, 1835, m. Mr. Williams. (Children: Mattie Williams, m. Mr. Wells, and had one dau. Ruby; Mary Williams, m. James Polk "Jake" Taylor and had - Floyd Taylor, killed as young man while working; Jim Taylor; Grover Taylor, m. Ola Benton; Manie Taylor, m. Maud Benton; Jesse Taylor never married, fought in Mexican "Uprising and was killed in his late "Teens".) 2. Joseph William Stillman, b. Sept. 22, 1836, m. Sallie Weaver. 3. Sarah Hasseltine

Stillman, b. Dec. 7, 1837, m. 1st. - Mr. Crowe, 2nd. - Rev. David Andrews, b. June 15, 1801, d. Dec. 2, 1887, Fayette Co. 4. Benjamin Manly Stillman, b. April 22, 1839, m. America Smith. (On April 23, 1883, B. M. Stillman of Fayette Co. filed an application for the relief of maimed soldiers. He certified that he had been a member of Co. A1. 26th Ala. Inf. Regt., C.S.A. and that during the Seven Days Battle in Virginia on June 30, 1862, he lost his left arm. He produced affidavits to verify his statements and his application was granted.) 5. Mary Elizabeth Stillman, b. May 2, 1840. 6. George Thomas Stillman, b. Aug. 14, 1841, m. Liza Killian. (Children: Twins, Maude m. Mr. Thompson; Claud; Minnie, m. A Pulliam; and Toy Stillman, m. a Stallings.) 7. Susan Judson Stillman, b. Mar. 12, 1843. 8. John Bunyan Stillman b. May 3, 1845. (On Jan. 20, 1894, J. B. Stillman of Fayette Co. applied for a pension for his Confederate military service. He stated that he enlisted Sept. 1, 1863, at Fayette Court House as a Priv. in Co. I. 56th Ala. Cav. C.S.A. and served until the close of the war in 1865. His service has been verified by the Office of the U. S. Adjutant General, Washington, D. S.) 9. Mary Jane Stillman, b. June 9, 1846, m. Silas Waldrop, (Child: Ellora Waldrop, m. Tolliver Shelton and had T. Willie; Linnie Lee and Tolliver Shelton, Jr.) 10. Selena Leona Stillman, b. May 3, 1848, d. May __, 1871, m. George Washington Freeman, b. Nov. 23, 1845, d. Jan. 6, 1920.

STOKER, Henry Earsery, b. Jan. 3, 1887, Walker Co., Ala., d. April 25, 1903, m. Vera Medallion Stough, b. Sept. 4, 1885, Fayette Co. Henry E. Stoker's parents - Jim L. Stoker, b. Aug. 14, 1861, Tusca. Co., m. Rebecca Maddox, b. Mar. 20, 1865. Grandparents - Jim Lesley Stoker (son of John L. Stoker and grandson of Bazarr Stoker) and Martha Sexton; and George & Louise (Sexton) Maddox. Vera M. (Stough) Stoker's parents - John Henderson Stough & Willie Frances Parmer. Grandparents - Jacob Henderson Stough, Jr. & Martha Ann (Poast); and Jessie & Zeru (Lawrence) Parmer. Great grandparents - Jacob Henderson Stough; Ned Poast; Bob & Virgie (Cooper) Parmer; Phillip & Susie (Thompson) Lawrence. Children: (Henry E. Stoker's) 1. James Festus Stoker, b. April 7, 1908, Bankston, Ala. m. May 10, 1936, Lillie Irene McGehee, b. Mar. 26, 1910, Sayre, Ala. (Lillie was the dau. of John Wesley & Lula Agnes (Lee) McGehee. James and Lillie had; Sudie Stoker, b. Mar. 30, 1936, Bankston, Ala.)

STOKES, William Clyde, m. Aug. 20, 1950, Shirley T. Richards, b. Sept. 10, 1935, Fayette, - dau. of W. F. & Wilma (Patterson) Richards. Children: 1. Richard Clyde Stokes, b. Aug. 7, 1955, Fayette, Ala. 2. William Thomas Stokes, b. May 11, 1957, Enterprise, Ala.

STRONG, Elijah, b. June 20, 1785, Va., d. Fayette Co., Ala., m. Oct. 30, 1806, Polly Matthews, b. 1791, Ga., d. Fayette Co. Elijah was the son of Johnson & Mary Ann Strong. He and Polly were married in Clarke Co., Ga. by R. Whigney. He was a farmer and both are buried in Fayette Co. Children: 1. Elizabeth "Betsey" Strong, b. April 14, 1808, Clarke Co., Ga., d. young. 2. Mary Strong, b. April 1, 1809, Clarke Co., Ga., d. Feb. 3, 1884, Fayette Co., m. Dec. 27, 1828 or 1829, John Savage, b. Dec. 20, 1803, Union Co., S. C., d. July 22, 1884, Fayette Co. 3. William McCaley Strong, b. Jan. 12, 1811, Ga. 4. Jane Strong, b. Feb. 14, 1813, Ga., d. Nov. 8, 1891, or April 9, 1864, Fayette Co., m. May 24, 1838, James Thomas Nichols, b. July 25, 1817, d. Nov. 8, 1891, or April 9, 1864, Fayette Co. 5. Susannah Strong, b. Feb. 12, 1814. 6. Elizabeth "Betsey" Strong (No. 2), b. Feb.

12, 1817, Ga., m. James Traweek. 7. Frances Polly Strong, b. July 30, 1819, Fayette Co., Ala., m. Samuel Elijah Crowley. 8. Johnson Sherwood Strong, b. June 4, 1823, Fayette Co., Ala. 9. Caroline Temperance Strong, b. May 12, 1826, ? Abram Prewitt?

STRONG, Jacob J., died before 1851 - son of Wm. M. Strong - m. Elizabeth __, died before 1851. Children: 1. William W. Strong. 2. Travis G. Strong. 3. John H. Strong. 4. Susan D. Strong, m. L. W. Christian. 5. Maranda J. Strong, m. E. W. Jennings.

STRONG, Johnson, b. Oct. 28, 1758, Hanover Co., Va., d. between May 1, 1844 and May 1, 1846, Fayette Co. - son of William Strong - m. abt. 1777, Mary Ann __, b. Mar. 21, 1747, d. July 14, 1823. Johnson Strong was a soldier of the American Revolution. He enlisted about June 1, 1776, Hanover Co., Va. His Captain was Charles Dabney. He was discharged a few days before Christmas 1776 - Volunteered 1777 to labor in Public Iron Works in Buckingham Co., Va. - worked under Thomas Balantine and John Rively. Remainded in public service until latter part of 1779, when he again volunteered in 1781 in Buckingham Co. under the command of Capt. William Cannon. In Battle of Guilford, N. C. Discharged at Dan River, N. C. April 1, 1781 - He enrolled Jan. 9, 1834 for a pension. He lived in the states of Virginia, Georgia, Missouri, and Alabama. Children: 1. Elizabeth "Betsy" Strong, b. Mar. 22, 1778, Hanover Co., Va., m. Isaac Brewer. 2. Frances Strong, b. Jan. 29, 1780, Va., d. Aug. 6, __, m. Samuel Crowley ? 3. William M. Strong, b. Aug. 15, 1781, Va., d. 1840, to 1850, Fayette Co., Ala. 4. Patsy Strong, b. April 13, 1783, Va., m. Mr. Binion. 5. Elijah Strong, b. June 20, 1785, Fayette Co., m. in Clark Co., Ga., Polly Matthews.

STRONG, R. Jeff, b. April 6, 1843, Franklin Co., Ala., d. Aug. 22, 1921, m. Oct. 19, 1868, Martha J. Nichols, b. Nov. 25, 1850, d. Mar. 8, 1918. Married at the home of James Roberts. Children: 1. Pennina Strong. 2. Levie Strong. 3. Carrie Strong, b. April 21, 1876, d. Sept. 19, 1896, m. Dec. 27, 1893, M. H. Roberts, son of Pervie Roberts.

STRONG, William, b. 1730, d. Mar. 1816, m. 1755, Frances Johnson, d. 1827. The Strongs were early settlers of Virginia. John Strong appears in St. Peter's Parish, New Kent County, Nov. 13, 1698 when his son John was baptized. This is the church where years later, Martha Dandridge Curtis Washington worshipped. The Dandridge home was here and she and George Washington were married here. John Strong's sons William and George were also baptised here. William moved to Hanover Co., Va. before 1759 and worshipped at St. Pauls Parish where the minister was Rev. Patrick Henry, uncle of the patriot Patrick Henry. William and Frances (Johnson) Strong were of Virginia. The family moved to Clarke Co., Ga. from Hancock, County, Va. where the father, William became an extensive land and slave owner. Four of their sons served in the American Revolution. Children: 1. Sherwood Strong, b. 1756, d. 1816 to 1828, m. Mary Tibbs. He served in the American Revolution. 2. Johnson Strong, b. Oct. 28, 1758, d. abt. 1849, Fayette Co., Ala., m. abt. 1777, Mary Ann __. Served in American Revolution. 3. William Strong, b. May 1, 1762, d. Aug. 11, 1810, m. Margaret "Peggy" Stokes. served in American Revolution. 4. John Strong, d. abt. 1832. served in American Revolution. 5. Sally Strong (Twin) b. 1760, d. 1816, m. Joshua Flippin. 6. Elizabeth Strong (Twin), b. 1760, d. aft. 1827, m. Mr. Price. 7. Isham Strong, b.

April 22, 1764, d. Jan. 5, 1799. 8. Susannah May Strong, b. 1766, d. Mar. 1817, m. Mr. Moss. 9. Elijah Strong, b. 1768, d. Oct. 5, 1795. 10. Jane Strong, b. 1770, d. aft. 1827, m. 1st. - Mr. Bridgewater, 2nd. - Mr. Stokes.

STRONG, William Elbert, b. Jan. 26, 1845 or 1844, Franklin Co., Ala., d. April 9, 1918, m. Jan. 9, 1868, Amelia Rebecca Pryor, b. Feb. 27, 1844, d. Jan. 9, 1917. Children: 1. John R. Strong, b. Jan. 15, 1869. 2. Willie L. Strong, b. Mar. 19, 1871. 3. Martha Odelle "Della" Strong, b. Oct. 18, 1872. 4. Lula Bell Strong, b. Oct. 13, 1876, m. 1896, James Holland "Holly" Bobo. 5. Arrie Beatrice Strong, b. Nov. 4, 1880, m. Mr. South.

STRONG, William M., b. Aug. 8, 1781, d. between 1843 - 1847, Fayette Co., son of Johnson Strong - m. wife unknown. Children: 1. Mary Tarver Strong. 2. Green H. Strong, b. 1808, Ga. 3. Benjamin W. Strong. 4. Susan Ann Strong, b. July 31, 1817, d. Aug. 20, 1900, Fayette Co., m. Thomas Lyon Willingham, b. April 23, 1807, d. Nov. 8, 1888, Fayette Co. Both are buried at Pleasant Hill Cem. 5. Temperance P. Strong, b. 1820, Ala., m. Abram M. Prewitt, b. 1815, Ala. 6. William C. Strong. 7. Jacob J. Strong, d. bef. 1851, m. Elizabeth _, d. bef. 1851. 8. Elisabeth Strong, m. Thomas Lee.

STUBB, Robert Sherwood, II, b. Nov. 11, 1922, m. June 20, 1943, Laura Ann Cobb, b. June 23, 1923, Vernon, Ala. - dau. of R. C. & Lucille (Richards) Cobb. Children: 1. Robert Sherwood Stubb, III, b. Aug. 7, 1947, Fayette, Ala. 2. Annie Lucille Stubb, b. Feb. 8, 1951, Va.

SUDDUTH, Jarrette Anthony, b. Oct. 24, 1852, son of James S. & Helen (Bell) Sudduth - m. Feb. 24, 1874, Czarina Marassa Shepherd, b. Nov. 18, 1852, d. May 11, 1909 - dau. of Jacob S. & Maria (Nalls)Shepherd-Children: 1. Alma Penina Sudduth, b. Aug. 13, 1875. 2. Lola Ethel Sudduth, b. April 20, 1877, d. Sept. 4, 1958. 3. Robert Lee Sudduth, b. Mar. 1, 1879. 4. Solon Bluch Sudduth, b. Aug. 7, 1881, d. June 13, 1928. 5. Irvin Wilder Sudduth (Twin), b. Oct. 6, 1883, d. May, 1934. 6. Earl Wilbur Sudduth (Twin), b. Oct. 6, 1883. 7. Virgie Valeria Sudduth, b. April 24, 1886, d. Sept. 14, 1956. 8. Mary Susie Sudduth, b. Aug. 1, 1888. 9. Henry Lavaughn Sudduth, b. Oct. 4, 1890. 10. Lillian Sudduth, b. Oct. 15, 1892. 11. Marie Sudduth, b. Dec. 26, 1894, d. July 30, 1900. 12. Jarrette Anthony Sudduth, Jr., b. Sept. 25, 1896.

SUDDUTH, James Smart, b. Nov. 14, 1825, d. Jan. 13, 1888, m. Nov. 20, 1851, Helen Bell, b. Oct. 6, 1832, d. Oct. 23, 1900 - dau. of A. F. & Elizabeth (Middleton) Bell. James S. Sudduth had a brother Jarrette Sudduth, m. Miss Henderson. The brother was born in Ireland and was robbed and murdered in 1836. Children: 1. Jarrette Anthony Sudduth, b. Oct. 24, 1852, d. May 11, 1909, m. Feb. 24, 1874, Czarina Marassa Shepherd, b. Nov. 18, 1852. 2. James Thomas Sudduth, b. Aug. 22, 1855, d. Oct. 31, 1923. 3. John Sudduth, b. May 9, 1858, d, Feb. 28, 1880. 4. Elizabeth Sudduth, b. July 15, 1860, m. Jan. 25, 1881, W. S. Bobo. 5. Holland Sudduth, b. Aug. 27, 1862, d. Oct. 1893, m. Oct. 28, 1886, Lula Barton. 6. Sidney Sudduth, b. Nov. 27, 1865, d. Oct. 4, 1911, m. Jan. 5, 1888, Marlie Andrews. 7. William Montgomery Sudduth, b. Mar. 28, 1868, m. Dec. 23, 1891, Mary Smith. 8. Jennie Sudduth, b. Sept. 28, 1870, d. Dec. 26, 1902, m. Nov. 8, 1890, John W. Graham. 9. Henry Sudduth, b. Sept. 7, 1873, d. Aug. 22, 1938. (Copied from Bible of Bill Sudduth.)

SULLIVAN, Eugene, m. May 20, 1935, Jewel Chesney Little, b. May 28, 1914, Fayette Co., dau. of James Newton & Annie (Wiggins) Little. Children: 1. Sylvia Jean Sullivan, b. Nov. 5, 1936, Shreveport, La. 2. Jimmy Dan Sullivan, b. April 2, 1938, Shreveport, La. 3. Tommy Little Sullivan, b. Nov. 22, 1946, Oklahoma City, Okla.

SUMMERS, Joseph, d. about 1809, m. Ellenor __. Will signed Feb. 3, 1802. Proved Jan. 16, 1809, Newberry Co., S. C. Children: 1. William Summers, m. Susannah __. 2. John Summers. 3. Jesse Summers. 4. James Summers. 5. Ellinor Summers, m. Mr. Waters. 6. Cassandra Summers, m. Mr. Reggs. 7. Mary Summers, m. Mr. Chapman. 8. Ann Summers, m. Mr. Wells. 9. Darcus Summers.

SUMMERS, William, Sr., d. possibly 1823, Newberry Co., S. C. - son of Joseph & Ellenor Summers - m. Susannah, d. Oct. 7, 1829 or 1839, Newberry Co., S.C. Will signed Aug. 19, 1816. Proved Nov. 24, 1823. Children: 1. Joseph Summers. 2. William Summers, Jr. 3. Alse Summers, m. Robert Worthington. 4. Eleanor Summers, m. Henry Cooper. 5. Hezekiah Summers. 6. Tabitha Summers, m. Thomas Worthington. 7. Samuel Summers. 8. Elijah T. Summers. 9. Mary Summers, m. Robert Pitts. 10. Joseph W. Summers.?

SWANN, Sir Francis, b. ? England - son of William Swann. Sir Francis Swann of Denton Court, Kent, England was knighted in 1608. "Visitation of Kent", 1619, Vol. 42 - Harleian Cosiety Publications.

SWANN, Col. Thomas, b. May 1616, d. Sept. 16, 1680 - son of William and Judith (__) Swann - m. Dec. 29, 1668, 5th wife - Mary Mansfield. Burgess of James City County in 1645 and 1649 - He was Lt. Col. of Va. Militia in the Indian Wars abt. 1652. He was sheriff and justice of Surry Co., Va. in 1653, burgess from Surry Co. 1657 - 1658 and a member of the Council of 1660 which asserted principles of liberty not exceeded even by those of the Revolution more than a hundred years afterward. He was a member of Gov. Culpepper's Council at the time of his death in 1680. He is buried at Swann's Pt., Va. five miles from Jamestown, Va. Children: 1. Mary Swann, b. Oct. 5, 1669, m. Richard Bland. 2. Thomas Swann, b. Dec. 14, 1670, m. Elizabeth Thompson. 3. Frances Swann, b. Dec. 14, 1670, d. Apr. 14, 1676, Swann's Pt., Va.

SWANN, Major Thomas, b. Dec. 14, 1670, d. 1705, m. Elizabeth Thompson. Children: 1. Thomas Thompson Swann, m. Elizabeth Reynolds. 2. John Swann. Went to S.C. 3. Samuel Swann, went to S.C.

SWANN, Thomas Thompson, son of Maj. Thomas & Elizabeth (Thompson) Swann - m. Elizabeth Reynolds. Thomas Thompson Swann was sheriff of Nausemond Co., in 1740. Children: 1. Thomas Thompson Swann, m. Jannett Carson Blakeley. 2. Caleb Swann. 3. Samuel Swann. 4. John Swann.

SWANN, Thompson, d. 1778, Powhatan Co., Va.? Will there in 1778 - son of Thomas & Elizabeth (Thompson) Swann - m. Jannett Carson Blakeley - dau. of Wm. & Catherine (Kaiydee) Blakeley. She came with her children to Maury Co. Tenn. Mar. 6, 1806. Thompson Swann was clerk of Cumberland Co., Va. 1754 - 1781. Children: 1. Thomas Thompson Swann, m. Elizabeth (a cousin) Thompson??? 2. John Swann, m. Polly Farrar. 3. Samuel Swann, m. Nancy Taylor.

4. Willis Swann. 5. Elizabeth Swann, m. William McLaurine. 6. Mary Blakeley Swann, m. Maj. Thomas Hubbard. 7. Janett C. Swann, m. David Owen. 8. Catherine Swann, m. Col. William May.

SWANN, William, b. 1586, England, d. Feb. 1638, Surrey Co., Va. - son of Sir Francis Swann - m. Judith __, b. Feb. 5, 1589, d. Mar. 16, 1636, Swann's Pt., Va. William Swann, son of Sir Francis Swann, emigrated from England sometime after 1616 and was granted 1,200 acres of land for influencing twenty-four settlers to come to Virginia. William Swann was a pioneer when he crossed the James River and settled at Swann's Point, five miles from Jamestown. This was prior to 1636, the earliest reference to his settlement there. Several generations of Swanns were born, lived and died at Swann's Point. As late as 1879, the gravestone of Thomas Swann was in evidence bearing the date of death, 1680. This stone was located near the water on the bank of James River. William Swann was among those first Englishmen who established permanently in America. He was collector of Royal Customs, one of the highest offices in the Colony at that time; he was also land register in Va. Children: 1. Thomas Swann, b. May 1616, d. Sept. 16, 1680, buried at his father's feet - m. Jan. 13, 1639, 1st. - Margaret Debton, d. April 5. 1646, Swann's Pt., 2nd. - Sarah Codd, d. Jan. 13, 1654, Swann's Pt., (M. Jan. 18, 1649.) 3rd. July 30, 1655 - Sarah Chandler, d. Nov. 10, 1662, Swann's Pt. 4th. - Mrs. Ann Brown (widow of Henry Brown.) She is buried at "Four Mile Tree". m. 5th - Dec. 29, 1668 - Mary Mansfield (Manefield)

SWANSON, Charles J., b. Jan. 13, 1883, Hamburg, N. Y., d. July 14, 1958, Fayette Co., Ala. - son of Eric & Carolyn Swanson - m. June 4, 1913, Maude Ben Appling, b. Dec. 5, 1889, Mt. Vernon, Fayette Co. - dau. of Jesse & Melissa Appling. They were married at Covin, Ala. by Bro. Wm. Mansfield. Charles J. Swanson was a lumber man. Children: 1. Charles J. Swanson, b. July 5, 1918, Tusca. Co. Ala. 2. Carol Swanson, b. Nov. 13, 1921, Mt. Vernon, m. Aug. 1946, Jack B. Jones, b. May 9, 1919, Birmingham, Ala. 3. Jesse Appling Swanson, b. Sept. 28, 1924, Gadsden, Ala., m. Sept. 27, 1947, Evelyn White, b. Aug. 31, 1929, Kirkland, Fayette Co.

SWANSON, Jesse Appling, b. Sept. 28, 1924, Gadsden, Ala. -son of Chas. & Maude Swanson - m. Sept. 27, 1947, Evelyn White, b. Aug. 31, 1929, Fayette Co., - dau. of Alton & Annie Mae White. They were married at Mt. Vernon, Fayette Co., Ala. by Rev. M. O. Bridges. Jesse is affiliated with the State Highway Dept. Children: 1. Jesse Wayne Swanson, b. Mar. 5, 1949, Fayette, Ala. 2. Mark White Swanson, b. Feb. 2, 1959, Fayette, Ala.

SWINDLE, Dan, b. 1815, S.C., d. Fayette Co., Ala. - m. Caroline Robertson, b. Northport, Ala. He was a school teacher. Children: 1. Reuben Monroe Swindle, b. Jan. 12, 1847, Walker Co., Ala., d. Feb. 15, 1900, Walker Co., m. Sarah Jane Nelson, b. July 1, 1854, d. Mar. 27, 1945, Walker Co., Ala. 2. Dennis Swindle, m. Amanda Myers. 3. Bayliss (or Bailey) Swindle, m. Susan Raburn. 4. William "Wid" Swindle. 5. Crane Swindle. 6. Perry Swindle. 7. Elizabeth Swindle. 8. Minerva Swindle. 9. Haley Swindle.

SWINDLE, Reuben Monroe, b. Jan. 12, 1849, d. Feb. 15, 1900, Walker Co., Ala. - son of Dan & Caroline (Robertson) Swindle - m. Sarah Jane Nelson, b. July 1, 1854, d. Mar. 27, 1945, Walker Co., Ala. - dau. of John N. & Catherine Nelson. Both are buried at Pleasant Hill Cem., Walker Co., Ala. Children:

1. Dan Swindle, b. Jan. 1877, Walker Co., m. Leona Mayfield. 2. Roxy Swindle, b. Nov. 3, 1877, Walker Co., m. Londus Washington Wright, b. July 7, 1870, Walker Co., d. Aug. 29, 1944, Walker Co. 3. Verge Swindle, b. Jan. 1879, Walker Co., m. Pearl Willard. 4. Ida Swindle, m. Jim Bell. 5. Ada Swindle, m. 1st. - Joe Terrell, 2nd. - J. W. Donaldson. 6. Abe Swindle, m. Della Hall. 7. John Swindle, b. Nov. 3, 1891. 8. Ben Swindle, b. April 12, 1893, m. Ada ___. 9. Mary Swindle, b. June ___, m. Joe White.

TABER, Francis Marion, m. Snow White - dau. of S. L. White. Children: 1. Mary Virginia Taber, m. M. C. Fowler. (Children: Thomas; Daniel; Ralph; and Carolyn Fowler.) 2. William Allen Taber, m. Joan Smith. (Children: Claire; Kitty and Allen Taber.)

TARWATER, Dr. James Sidney, b. Aug. 13, 1898, Corona, Walker Co., Ala. - son of J. V. & Emma Lee (Newton) Tarwater, m. 1926, Eloise Jenkins, b. Oneonta, Ala. - dau. of Thomas Jenkins. Dr. Tarwater is a Medical Doctor and a Psychiatrist and is the Supt. of the Alabama State Hospitals. Children: 1. Thomas Sidney Tarwater, b. Feb. 2, 1938, Tuscaloosa, Ala.

TARWATER, James Van Diver, b. May 10, 1866, Moscow, Lamar Co., Ala., d. June 5, 1957, age 91 at the home of his son, Dr. J. S. Tarwater, Tuscaloosa, Ala. - son of B. W. & Susan (Miller) Tarwater - m. 1st. - 1896 or 1897 - Emma Lee Newton, b. Sept. 22, 1872, Fayette Co., d. Sept. 1, 1904 - dau. of Wm. T. & Velutia J. (Whitley) Newton. Children: 1. James Sidney Tarwater, b. Aug. 13, 1898, Corona, Ala., m. Eloise Jenkins. 2. Lewis Alexander Tarwater, b. Oct. 29, 1902, Ala., d. Nov. 10, 1903, Fayette.

James Van Diver Tarwater married second - June 20, 1909, Musa Ida Miles, b. June 28, 1878, Fayette Co. - dau. of Wilbur Fisk & L. Angeline (Moore) Miles. In 1883, at the age of 17, James V. Tarwater with his family moved from Lamar Co., Ala. to the town of Fayette, where he engaged in farming until 1891. From 1891 to 1931 he was engaged in the coal mining business in Walker and Marion Counties. He was Supt. of Corona Coal & Iron Co. and Gen. Supt. of the Gas Light, Coal Co. In Marion Co., at Brilliant, Ala. he was Assistant Supt of the Brilliant Coal Co. At the same time he continued to operate a farm located in Fayette County, Ala. Children: (2nd. marriage.) 1. Ida Marguerite Tarwater, b. April 19, 1910, Corona, Ala., m. Jan. 10. 1942, Artemes Killian Callahan, b. May 18, 1904, Tuscaloosa Co., Ala. 2. Lucy Irick Tarwater, b. April 16, 1912, Corona, Ala., m. May 1, 1937, John Parker Crutcher, Jr.

TAYLOR, Emitte, b. Dec. 25, 1909, Fayette Co., m. Oct. 28, 1935, Eula Jane McCraw, b. June 8, 1908, Fayette, Ala. Emitte Taylor's parents - Roland Shores Taylor, b. Oct. 25, 1857, Miss., m. Nov. 28, 1901, Sarah Alice Moore, b. July 19, 1873, Fayette Co. Grandparents - Tom Moore, m. Anne Reese, b. 1852, Fayette Co.; and Charles A. Taylor, b. 1838, & Sarah A. ___, b. Nov. 12, 1840. Eula Jane (McCraw) Taylor's parents - Vester McCraw, b. April 4, 1877, d. June 2, 1946, m. Nannie Miles, b. 1869, d. 1933. Grandparents - Landon Miles, b. Oct. 22, 1845, m. Liza Cargile, b. Mar. 5, 1846; and E. J. McCraw, b. June 16, 1852, m. J. F. ___, b. April 12, 18__. Children: (E. Taylors') 1. Evelyn Taylor, b. Aug. 3, 1942, Fayette Co., Ala.

TAYLOR, Jesse J., b. 1895, Fayette Co., m. Mamie Moore, b. 1900, Fayette Co. Children: 1. Wynelle Taylor, b. 1918, Fayette Co., m. Morris Hightower, Jr.

b. Winfield, Ala. (Children: Larry; Gloria and Martha Hightower.) 2. Mozell Agnes Taylor, b. Nov. 16, 1920, Fayette Co., d. Oct. 4, 1921. 3. Jeannette Taylor, b. Jan. 3, 1923, Fayette Co., Ala., m. W. Edward Brophy, b. Hattiesburg, Miss. (Children: Brenda Jeanette and Rebecca Lynn Brophy.)

TAYLOR, Moody, m. Elizabeth Henry, b. 1906, - dau. of Jim R. & Mary E. (McConnell) Henry. Children: 1. J. M. Henry, b. 1929.

THOMAS, Albert Crutcher, b. Feb. 24, 1905, Limestone Co., Ala. - son of Oscar LaFayette Thomas - m. Sept. 30, 1925, Merle Aline McLemore, b. Jan. 12, 1906, Limestone Co., Ala. - dau. of Early B. McLemore. Mr. & Mrs. Thomas were married in Athens, Ala. by Rev. R. T. Tyler. Mr. Thomas is an Automobile Dealer in Fayette. Children: 1. Doris Glynn Thomas, b. July 21, 1926, Jasper, Ala., m. Sept. 28, 1946, William Berry Jeffries, b. Jan. 19, 1917, Fayette, Ala. 2. Oscar Lloyd Thomas, b. Sept. 13, 1928, Jasper, Ala. m. Dec. 24, 1955, Lynda Byrd, b. Jan. 30, 1933, Ark. 3. Norma Louise Thomas b. Sept. 21, 1930, Jasper, Ala., m. May 10, 1947, Hillard Milligan, b. Mar. 1, 1927, Walker Co., Ala. 4. Carroll Morris Thomas, b. May 19, 1932, Jasper, Ala., m. Nov. 21, 1951, Milner Jane Young, b. Dec. 1, 1933, Fayette, Ala. 5. Anna Faye Thomas, b. Feb. 25, 1937, Fayette, Ala.

THOMAS, Carroll Morris, b. May 19, 1932, Jasper, Ala. -son of A. C. Thomas - m. Nov. 21, 1951, Milner Jane Young, b. Dec. 1, 1933, Fayette, Ala. - dau. of Maury Young. They were married in Aberdeen, Miss. by Rev. J. D. O'Donnell. Children: 1. Michael Stephen Thomas, b. Aug. 18, 1952, Fayette. 2. Carroll Morris Thomas, Jr., b. Nov. 28, 1955, Fayette, Ala.

THOMAS, Dr. John P., m. Evaline Porter. Pioneers in Mt. Vernon Community - Physician and Local Elder. Children: 1. Martha S. Thomas, b. Oct. 15, 1848, Blountsville, Ala., d. Aug. 16, 1922, m. Reuben J. Brock. 2. O. S. Thomas, A Minister - went to Texas. 3. O. P. Thomas, Minister - went to Texas.

THOMAS, Oscar LaFayette, b. Aug. 16, 1874, Limestone Co., Ala., d. June 7, 1936, Limestone Co., Ala. - son of R. L. Thomas - m. Jan. 6, 1901, Katie Pearl Newby, b. Nov. 30, 1883, Limestone Co. - dau. of Luke Pryor Newby. Oscar L. Thomas was a farmer and a merchant of Limestone Co., Ala. Children: (All born Limestone Co., Ala.) 1. Albert Crutcher Thomas, b. Feb. 24, 1905, m. Sept. 30, 1925, Merle Aline McLemore, b. Limestone Co. 2. Aline Thomas, b. Sept. 24, 1905, m. Mar. 7, 1931, Rion Hayes, b. Aug. 17, 1910, Athens, Ala., d. Nov. 30, 1951. 3. Ruby Prudence Thomas, b. June 22, 1911, m. Jan. 18, 1931, Edwin Dunnivant, b. April 24, 1903, Limestone Co. 4. Georgia Irene Thomas, b. April 11, 1909, m. July 14, 1928, Clifford Hastings, b. May 20, 1909, Limestone Co. 5. Lois Halbrook Thomas, b. Dec. 26, 1913, m. 1955, Lawrence Wehner, b. 1910. 6. Marvin Duane Thomas, b. Mar. 21, 1916, m. Feb. 10, 1932, Catherine Russell, b. Mar. 16, 1914, Limestone Co. 7. Douglas Newby Thomas, b. Jan. 24, 1924, m. Nov. 21, 1945, James B. Ligon, b. Nov. 24, 1923.

THOMAS, Richard Larkin, b. Feb. 3, 1839, Va., d. Dec. 27, 1913, Limestone Co., Ala. - son of William D. Thomas - m. Martha Pricilla Inman, b. Jan. 28, 1849, Va., d. Feb. 5, 1914, Limestone Co., Ala. Richard Larkin Thomas was 2nd. Sgt. under Gen. Joe Wheeler. His occupation was farming and both he and his wife are buried in the Martin Cem., Limestone Co., Ala. Children:

(All born Limestone Co., Ala.) 1. Sallie D. Thomas, b. Mar. 11, 1869, d. Mar. 16, 1929, m. William E. Davis, b. Aug. 25, 1860, d. Mar. 3, 1908. 2. William Albert Thomas, b. Aug. 25, 1870, d. Dec. 19, 1940, m. 1914, Myrtle C. Merriman, b. April 30, 1885. 3. John Larkin Thomas, b. Aug. 8, 1872, d. Oct. 23, 1930, m. Belle Thomas, b. Apr. 5, 1888, Limestone Co., d. Jan. 2, 1957. 4. Oscar LaFayette Thomas, b. Aug. 16, 1874, d. June 7, 1936, m. Jan. 6, 1901, Katie Pearl Newby, b. Nov. 30, 1883, Limestone Co. 5. Richard Lindsay Thomas, b. Sept. 9, 1876, d. Dec. 12, 1955, Athens, Ala., m. 1904, Cleavy Johnson, b. Nov. 27, 1884, d. June 23, 1954, Athens, Ala. 6. Sam W. Thomas, b. 1879, d. Aug. 12, 1902. 7. Paul L. Thomas, b. July 1, 1885, d. April 15, 1914, Athens, Ala. 8. James Price Thomas, b. Aug. 1, 1881, m. Feb. 22, 1903, Sallie Pepper, b. May 23, 1881, Limestone Co. 9. Fred Inman Thomas, b. July 4, 1888, d. Nov. 22, 1944, m. Jan. 2, 1910, Mattie Kent, b. 1890. 10. Mary P. Thomas, b. Mar. 2, 1894, d. April 10, 1950, m. Lucious P. Cary, b. Mar. 8, 1887.

THOMAS, Roy Franklin, b. Mar. 21, 1916, m. Feb. 25, 1956, Ruth Rowland, b. June 24, 1921, Lamar Co., Ala. - dau. of Zeb A. & Dora (Waldrop) Rowland. Children: 1. Elizabeth Anne Thomas, b. June 10, 1957, Aiken, S. C.

THOMAS, William D., b. 1780, Va., m. Sarah __, b. 1790, Va. William D. Thomas was a farmer and came to Limestone Co. in 1843 from Virginia and settled 8½ miles east of Athens, Ala. Children: (All born Va.) 1. Mary Thomas, b. 1815. 2. Henry Thomas, b. 1826. 3. Silas Thomas, b. 1830. 4. Martha Thomas, b. 1832. 5. H. Paul Thomas, b. Sept. 24, 1831, d. Dec. 29, 1908, m. Martha E. __, b. Nov. 10, 1842, d. June 11, 1893. 6. Lindsay Thomas, b. 1815. Was a flag bearer in the Civil War and was killed in Battle of Chickamauga and is buried there. (birth could be 1835.) 7. Richard Larkin Thomas, b. Feb. 3, 1839, m. Martha Pricilla Inman, b. Jan. 28, 1849, d. Feb. 5, 1914.

THOMLEY, Thomas, b. Sept. 12, 1924, Birmingham, Ala. - son of Jim Thomley - m. Nov. 25, 1944, Mary Anita Galloway, b. Dec. 3, 1924, Fayette Co. - dau. of Jesse Galloway. Tommy and Anita were married in Mobile, Ala. Children: 1. Thomas Wayne Thomley, b. Aug. 15, 1945, Mobile, Ala.

THOMPSON, C. K. b. Nov. 25, 1850, d. April 15, 1892, - son of Geo. W. Thompson - m. Lonna Lindsey. Children: 1. Ella Thompson, m. Chellsea South, (Supt of Education 1890.) 2. William Murry Thompson, m. Nanny Sparks. 3. Case Thompson, m. Othea Horten. 4. George Thomas Thompson, m. Maye Berry. 5. Robert L. Thompson. 6. Mary Emma Thompson. 7. William Arp Thompson, m. Kattie Smith. (Children: Ormon Pearson Thompson, m. Bessie Willis; Rev. John Thompson, m. Lillian Hocutt; and Roy Neal Thompson, m. Valerie Hubbert.)

THOMPSON, George Lee, Jr., b. Nov. 17, 1908, Fayette Co. -son of Geo. Lee Thompson, Sr., m. Dec. 17, 1945, Gladys Dillon, b. Sept. 25, 1921. Children; 1. Margaret Ann Thompson, b. April 2, 1946, Mobile, Ala. 2. Doris Edna Thompson, b. Oct. 8, 1947, Mobile, Ala.

THOMPSON, George Lee, b. May 10, 1874, Fayette Co., d. Sept. 3, 1951, Fayette Co. - son of Geo. W. Thompson - m. Olive Edna Carson, b. Sept. 3, 1878, Gilberstown, Ky., d. Jan. 3, 1951, Fayette Co. Children: (All born Fayette Co.)

1. George Lee Thompson, b. Nov. 17, 1908, m. Dec. 17, 1945, Gladys Dillon, b. Sept. 25, 1921. 2. Amos Carson Thompson, b. April 13, 1910, m. in Mobile, Ala. Helion Holiaway. (Children: Alford Carson; Charlie Amos; Brenda; and Sandy Thompson.) 3. Lula Edith Thompson, b. Oct. 31, 1911, m. Hellis R. Yamm, (Children: Carolyn, b. Sept. 4, 1946, Birmingham, Ala. and Robert Yamm.) 4. John Edd Thompson, b. June 13, 1913, m. 1941 in Hartford, Ky., Bennie Dunn. (Children: John Edd Thompson, Jr., b. June 1942, Mobile,; Wm. Lee Thompson, b. Nov. 17, 1946, Mobile, Ala. and Bennie Jean Thompson.) 5. Thomas Joseph Thompson, b. Jan. 17, 1915, m. Ruby __. (Child: Thomas Joseph Thompson, Jr., b. Aug. 1942.) 6. Charlie S. Thompson, b. July 28, 1917, m. in S. C., Catherine Carter. (Children: Charlie S. Thompson, Jr. b. Jan. 8, 1947, Birmingham and Debbie Sue Thompson, b. Fayette, Ala.) 7. Olive Virginia Thompson, b. May 28, 1919, m. Carl Hanna. (Children: Carl Hanna, Jr., b. Birmingham, Ala. and Barbara Jean Hanna b. Birmingham, Ala.)

THOMPSON, George Washington, b. Nov. 26, 1829, Fayette Co., d. Aug. 13, 1895 Fayette Co., m. Dec. 30, 1849, Eliza L. Powell, b. May 23, 1832, d. Feb. 22, 1902, Fayette Co. George Washington Thompson was a Confederate Soldier and is buried at the Bethlehem Cem. Fayette Co. Children: 1. C. K. Thompson, b. Nov. 25, 1850, d. April 15, 1892, m. Lonna Lindsey. 2. Frank A. Thompson, b. Sept. 12, 1852, d. Aug. 4, 1917, m. Mary Gaines, b. May 22, 1858, d. Jan. 21, 1929. 3. Lula E. Thompson, b. Sept. 10, 1859, d. Mar. 14, 1892, m. William Appline. 4. George Lee Thompson, b. May 10, 1874, Fayette Co., d. Sept. 3, 1951, Fayette Co., m. Olive Edna Carson, b. Sept. 3, 1878, Gilberstown, Ky, d. Jan. 3, 1951, Fayette Co., Ala.

THOMPSON, Frank A., b. Sept. 12, 1852, d. Aug. 4, 1917 - son of Geo. W. Thompson - m. Mary Gaines, b. May 22, 1858, d. Jan. 21, 1929. Children: 1. Lou Eva Thompson, m. Walter S. Smith. (Children: Bruce Smith, m. Sallie Roberts.) 2. Josie Thompson, m. Lee Newton. 3. Sudie V. Thompson, b. Sept. 26, 1886, d. Dec. 30, 1944, m. W. H. Roberts, b. Nov. 3, 1886, d. Nov. 3, 1886, d. Nov. 15, 1951. 4. George Emma Thompson, m. L. B. Thomas. 5. Blanche Thompson, m. Isadore Roberts. 6. Mary Lee Thompson.

THOMPSON, Wm., d. abt. 1686, Nansemond Co., Va. (Will), m. Janet __.

THOMPSON, William Ernest, b. April 15, 1935, Fayette Co., m. Dec. 23, 1954 Jimmie Lou Ballinger, b. Dec. 31, 1931, Fayette Co., Ala. - dau. of J. H. & Artie (White) Ballinger. Children: 1. William Jimmy Thompson, b. July 10, 1956, Pensacola, Fla. Ernest is son of Ormon P. & Bessie (Willis) Thompson.

THOMSON, Richard Randolph, b. Jan. 9, 1928, Brownville, Ala. -son of Wm. Joshua & Attie Bell (Kimbrell) Thomson - m. Dec. 5, 1953, Kathleen Sherer Cannon, b. Oct. 23, 1927, Fayette Co. - dau. of Terrell F. & Alma (Sherer) Cannon. They were married at the Presbyterian Manse in Columbus, Miss. by Dr. Horace Villee. Children: 1. Richard Randolph Thomson, Jr., b. July 25, 1954, Fayette, Ala. 2. Thomas Mark Thomson, b. Nov. 14, 1957, Fayette.

THORNTON, David, b. 1783, d. 1867, Fayette Co., Ala. - m. Bathsheba White. Children: 1. Elizabeth Stallworth Thornton, m. 1833, Mathew Hubbert, b. 1810, Tenn. d. 1887, San Luis, Calif. 2. Beersheba Thornton, m. abt. 1833, Benjamin Hubbert, b. 1811, Tenn.

TIDWELL, __, m. Matilda Lansdale, b. 1823, Montgomery Co., Ala., d. bet. 1860 - 1870, Miss.- dau. of Isaac & Sarah (Gentry-McCool) Lansdale. Early settlers of Fayette Co. Children: 1. Sarah Tidwell. 2. Mary Tidwell. 3. Isaac Tidwell. 4. James Tidwell. 5. Austin Tidwell.

TILGHMAN (Tillman), Christopher, b. abt. 1600, Selling, Faversham Hundred, Kent Co., England, m. Ruth Devonshire. Arived in Virginia May 9, 1635. Buried at James City, Va. Christopher was son of Christopher & Anna (Sanders) Tilghman (Tillman). Children: 1. Roger Tilghman, b. 1650. 2. Gideon Tilghman. 3. John Tilghman.

TILLMAN, Frederick, b. Sept. 11, 1775, Edgefield Dist., S.C., d. Mar. 7, 1810 - son of George & Frances (Mitchell) Tillman - m. 1790, Annsybil Miller, d. Mar. 6, 1830. Frederick Tillman served in Capt. John Ryan's Co. of S. C. Rangers in the American Revolution. (Records, D.A.R. and War Dept.) Children: 1. Stephen Tillman, b. 1795. 2. Frances Ann Tillman, b. 1797. 3. Jacob Tillman, b. Aug. 10, 1798. 4. George Washington Tillman, b. 1799. 5. Annsybil Tillman, b. 1800, m. Eli Morgan. 6. John Miller Tillman, b. Mar. 5, 1801. 7. Benjamin Ryan Tillman, b. Mar. 5, 1803.

TILLMAN, George, b. Jan. 10, 1683, Charles City, Va., d. May 4, 1756, Lawrenceville, Va. - son of Roger & Susannah (Parham or Parram) Tillman - m. Jan. 10, 1701, Mary House. (George Tillman's Will is on file in Brunswick Co., Va. Page 183, Book 3.) Children: 1. Roger Tillman, b. Dec. 2, 1701. 2. George Tillman, b. 1705. 3. Tabitha Tillman, b. Sept. 14, 1720, m. Jonathan Butler. 4. William Tillman, b. May 21, 1723. 5. Elizabeth Tillman, b, 1724, m. James Butler. 6. Mary Tillman, b. 1726, m. John Avery. 7. Sarah Tillman, m. 1st. - James Hunt, 2nd. - Anthony Lumpkin.

TILLMAN, George Stephen, b. Jan. 21, 1725, Prince George Co., Va., d. 1781 at the siege of "96" S. C. - Capt. under Col. Wm. Washington - son of Roger & Mary (Goodrich) Tillman - m. 1752, Frances Mitchell, b. May 7, 1726, d. Sept. 5, 1812. Children: 1. Lewis Tillman, b. Mar. 12, 1753. 2. Littlebury Tillman, b. 1759 - Rev. War. - Capt. John Ryan's Co. of S.C. Ranger. 3. Frederick Tillman, b. Sept. 11, 1755. Rev. War. - Capt. John Ryan's Co. of S.C. Rangers. 4. Stephen Tillman, b. June 5, 1764, Rev. War - Capt. John Ryan's Co. of S.C. Rangers. 5. Jacob Tillman, b. 1765, d. April 13, 1789.

TILLMAN, Jacob, b. Aug. 10, 1798, Edgefield Dist., S.C., d. Oct. 9, 1837, buried at Augusta Co., Ala. - son of Frederick & Annsybil (Miller) Tillman - m. Aug. 5, 1819, Mary Mosley. Children: 1. Frederick James Tillman, b. 1821, d. Oct. 5, 1846. 2. John Miller Tillman, b. Dec. 28, 1822. 3. Mary Ann Sybil Tillman, b. Aug. 30, 1824. 4. George Clement Tillman, b. July 21, 1825. 5. Stephen Decatur Tillman, b. Feb. 17, 1827. 6. Frances Mary Ann Tillman, b. 1830, d. 1839. 7. Sarah Elizabeth Tillman, b. 1832. 8. Martha L. Tillman, b. 1833. 9. Elizabeth Hughes Tillman, b. 1825, d. 1855.

TILLMAN, John Miller, b. Dec. 28, 1822, Edgefield Dist. S.C., d. Dec. 3, 1884, Selma, Ala. - son of Jacob & Mary (Mosley) Tillman, m. 1848, Elizabeth Plummer, b. 1827, d. Feb. 14, 1898. John Miller Tillman served in Co. A. 1st. Ala., Inf. in the Mexican War. Children: 1. John Plummer Tillman, b. Jan. 24, 1849, Perryville, Ala, d. Mar. 24, 1923, Birmingham, Ala. 2.

Mary Martha Tillman, b. Dec. 21, 1850, Perry Co., Ala., d. buried Selma, Ala. m. May 20, 1869, Bishop Stewart Melvin. 3. Frank Dennis Tillman, b. 1860, d. 1898, m. Margaret Wilson. 4. Clem Tillman, b. Fe. 11, 1851. 5. Frances Huntington Tillman, b. Feb. 11, 1851, Perry Co., Ala., d. 1921, Mobile, Ala. m. Enos Edward England, b. Mobile, Ala., d. 1902.

TILLMAN, Roger, b. 1650, Accomac Co., Va. -son of Christopher & Ruth (Devonshire) Tilghman - m. Susannah Parham or Parram, b. 1648, d. Mar. 2, 1817, buried at Prince George Co., Va. Roger Tillman changed the spelling of the Family Name. Children: 1. John Tillman, b. 1682. 2. George Tillman, b. Jan. 10, 1683. 3. Jane Tillman, m. Nicholas Robinson. 4. Christine Tillman, m. Robert Abernathy.

TILLMAN, Roger, b. Dec. 2, 1701, Prince George Co., Va., d. Feb. 5, 1761, buried at Brunswick Co., Va - son of George & Mary (House) Tillman - m. 1723, Mary Goodrich. Children: 1. George Stephen Tillman, b. Jan. 21, 1725. 2. Elizabeth Tillman, b. Nov. 15, 1726. 3. Richard Tillman, b. 1727. 4. Roger Tillman, b. 1728. 5. John Tillman, b. 1730. 6. Davis Tillman, b. 1731. 7. Frederick Tillman, b. 1732.

TRANTHAM, W. D., b. Apr. 1, 1847, Scotland, d. buried Columbia, Tenn., m. Mary Elizabeth Meadows, b. Mar. 9, 1838, d. Jan. 3, 1904, Columbia, Tenn., buried in Akin Academy Cemetery, - dau. of Joseph R. & Rebekah (Parkham) Meadows. W. D. Trantham fought in the Civil War and was killed in the Battle of Murfreesboro. He is buried in the Cem. at Columbis with many other Confederate Soldiers. Children: 1. Sallie Elizabeth Trantham, b. Mar. 22, 1856, d. Jan. 3, 1938, m. Pickney Jasper Puckett. 2. Mittie Smith Trantham, b. Aug. 6, 1859, d. Sept. 17, 1894, m. 1881, Dr. Joseph Ephriam White, b. Nov. 5, 1856, d. Jan. 31, 1890.

TRAWEEK, Armond Morris "Poolie", m. Margaret Yerby, b. Oct. 6, 1917, Fayette Co. - dau. of Wm. & Cora (Dickinson) Yerby. Children: 1. Bonnie Sharon Traweek, b. April 26, 1944, Fayette Co. 2. Mary Camille Traweek, b. Sept. 27, 1948, Fayette Co., Ala.

TRAWEEK, George Elton, b. Aug. 15, 1910, Berry, Ala. - son of Will & Pearl Traweek - m. July 12, 1941, Dorothy Claire Galloway, b. Dec. 6, 1921, Corona, Ala. - dau. of Jesse & Maye Galloway. George Elton and Dorothy were married in Fayette, Ala. by Rev. A. M. Nix. Children: 1. George Elton Traweek, Jr., b. April 12, 1942, Fayette, Ala.

TUCKER, Jackson, m. Flossia Sawyer, - dau. of William Bedford Sawyer. Children: 1. Myrtle Tucker, m. Roy Aldridge. (Child: Mary Helen Aldridge.) 2. Horace Tucker, m. Mattie Lou Waldrop. (Children: Reba and Sandra Carol Tucker.) 3. Lois Tucker, m. Ray Bobo. (Children: Foy Rabon; Anita Jane; and Bessie Mae Bobo, m. Charles Bagwell, Jr. - have one child - Charlene.)

TUCKER, Paul M., b. May 5, 1922, Fayette Co., m. Mrs. Aline (Fowler) Williams, b. May 15, 1925, Fayette Co. - dau. of F. M. & Exie (Hollingsworth) Fowler. They own and operate Tucker Hardward Co. Children: 1. Donna Tucker, b. Dec. 18, 1957, Jasper, Ala.

TUCKER, William Cox, b. Oct. 29, 1916, Birmingham, Ala. - son of John Samuel Tucker, M. D. - m. April 11, 1943, Frances Hugh Hay, b. April 25, 1921, Bankston, Ala. - dau. of William Harris & Lillian(Willingham) Hay. They were married at the First Baptist Church in Fayette, Ala. by Rev. A. M. Nix. Dr. W. C. Tucker is a surgeon. William Cox Tucker entered active service in July 1943 as Staff Surgeon, U. S. Naval Hospital, Norman, Okla., then to Dallas, Texas recruiting office. In Sept. 1943, he was attached to a transport ship, General A. E. Anderson, as ship surgeon. He served in this capacity for three and one-half years, seeing service in the Atlantic, Pacific and Indian Oceans. The General A. E. Anderson brought home the first released prisoners from Japan, the surviving men of the Bataan Death March. Wm. Cox Tucker was released from active duty and stationed at the U. S. Naval Hospital in New Orleans, La. from which he was discharged in 1946, with rank of Lt. Sr. Gr. Children: 1. Frances Suzanne Tucker, b. Oct. 6, 1945, Birmingham, Ala. 2. William Cox Tucker, Jr., b. Oct. 1, 1947, Birmingham, Ala. 3. John Alexander Tucker, b. Nov. 5, 1951, Birmingham, Ala.

UNGER, Harry O., Jr., b. June 6, 1925, Fayette Co. - son of Harry O. & Lucy (Smith) Unger - m. Inez White, b. Aug. 25, 1924, Fayette Co. - dau. of Kilby & Esther (Roberts) White. Harry Unger, Jr. was ordained as a Deacon of the Missionary Baptist Church in 1952. Children: 1. Harry O. Unger, III, b. Jan. 11, 1951, Fayette, Ala. 2. Nancy Unger, b. Oct. 21, 1953, Fayette, Ala. 3. Lynn Unger, b. Mar. 14, 1957, Fayette, Ala.

UNGER, Harry O., d. 1925, m. Lucy Smith. Children: 1. Virginia Unger. 2. Harry O. Unger, Jr., b. June 6, 1925, Fayette Co., m. Inez White.

UTLEY, John, m. Mary Cook. John was the son of William & Elizabeth (Turner) Utley and Mary was the dau. of Arthur Cook. Children: 1. Rebecca Utley, m. George Stewart.

VEAZEY, John Madison, b. April 25, 1877, Fredonia, Ala., d. Feb. 23, 1920 - son of Charlie Veazey - m. Dec. 11, 1898, Elizabeth Lou Jordon, b. Sept. 12, 1881, Welch, Ala., d. Dec. 21, 1941 - dau. of Willis & Harriet (Arnett) Jordon. Married at Welch, Ala. He was a farmer. Both are buried at West Point Ga. Children: 1. Eugene Zachery Veazey, b. Aug. 29, 1899, Welch, Ala., d. Mar. 14, 1925, Five Points, Ala. 2. William Charles Veazey, b. Sept. 18, 1901, Fredonia, Ala., m. Oct. 14, 1951. 3. Ida Harriet Veazey, b. Aug. 27, 1903, Welch, Ala., d. Feb. 25, 1920, Five Points, Ala. 4. Jessie Lucile Veazey, b. Feb. 22, 1905, Welch, Ala. 5. Henry Jefferson Veazey, b. Nov. 10, 1910, Welch, Ala. 6. Lou Exa Veazey, b. Mar. 2, 1913, Welch, Ala., m. May 17, 1941. 7. Margaret Irene Veazey, b. Feb. 5, 1915, Welch, Ala., m. Aug. 17, 1939. 8. John Thomas Veazey, b. Nov. 11, 1917, Five Points, Ala. m. June 10, 1938, Madalyn Eloise West.

VEAZEY, John Thomas, b. Nov. 11, 1917, Five Points, Ala. - son of John M. & Elizabeth (Jordon) Veazey - m. June 10, 1938, Madelyn Eloise West, b. Feb. 5, 1921, Fairfax, Ala. - dau. of Miles B. & Marie (Kent) West. The Veazey's were married at Fairfax, Ala. by Rev. C. M. Goforth. They came to Fayette in 1949 when they bought the Griffin Mortuary. Tom is a mortician. Children: 1. Eloise Marie Veazey, b. Feb. 28, 1945, Fairfax, Ala. (Chambers Co.) 2. Linda Annette Veazey, b. Aug. 30, 1948, Nashville, Tenn.

WAGES, George W., b. Blue Mountain, Miss - son of G. W. Wages - m. Mar. 14,

1942, Maxine Ayres, b. Fayette, Ala. - dau. of Ottis & Gertrude Ayres. Children: 1. George W. Wages, III, b. June 10, 1943, Fayette, Ala. 2. Gregory Wages, b. Oct. 12, 1948, Fayette, Ala.

WAKEFIELD, John Francis, b. Aug. 1 __, Carbon Hill, Ala. - son of George & Fannie (Sides) Wakefield - m. June 26, 1929, Annie Sue Propst, b. Jan. 7, 1910, Fayette, Ala. - dau. of Daniel F. & Susie Emily (Hyde) Propst. Children: 1. Sue Francis Wakefield, b. Oct. 6, __. 2. George Wakefield, b. Sept. 17, __.

WALDEN, Jonathan, b. 1800, N. C., m. Sarah __, b. 1803, N. C. Children: 1. Reuben Walden, b. 1829, N. C. 2. Calvin Walden, b. 1831, N. C. 3. Nancy Walden, b. 1833, N. C. 4. Dennis Walden, b. 1836, N. C. 5. Thomas Walden, b. 1839, N. C. 6. John E. Walden, b. 1841, N. C. 7. Foster Walden, b. 1846, N. C.

WALDROP, Coleman Layton, b. Sept. 10, 1874, d. 1957, m. Dec. 29, 1898, 1st. - Mary Virginia Ray, b. Mar. 23, 1880, d. Mar. 14, 1912. Children: (1st. wife.) 1. Amos Murrie Waldrop, b. Oct. 3, 1899, m. Vilma Lewis. 2. Mary Lucille Waldrop, b. Oct. 10, 1902, m. Clarence Edgil. 3. Eunice Virginia Waldrop, b. Dec. 24, 1905, m. Balcus Smith. 4. Miles Ormond Waldrop, b. May 14, 1910, m. Zoe Forister.
Cole Layton Waldrop married second - Aug. 8, 1912, Ethel Annijane Collins. Children: (2nd. wife.) 1. Elwood Layton Waldrop, b. Feb. 9, 1916, m. Imogene Perry. 2. Kelcy Lee Waldrop, b. Sept. 29, 1918, m. Neoma Couch. 3. Mildred Leona Waldrop, b. May 8, 1923, m. James Nipper.

WALDROP, Mack, m. Mertie Teleliah Williamson - dau. of Pink Williamson. Children: 1. Floy Mae Waldrop, m. Locke Collins. 2. Annie Lee Waldrop, m. Sam Andrew Thornton. 3. Brazie Bell Waldrop, m. Willie Holcomb. 4. James Curtis Waldrop, m. Ruth Wiggin. 5. William Clyde Waldrop, m. Christine Andrews. 6. Mertie Lois Waldrop, m. DeLoem Williams. 7. Cecil Mack Waldrop, m. Ozell Van Zant. 8. Hazel Edna Waldrop, m. W. Olive. 9. Louise Elaine Waldrop. 10. Raymond Chester Waldrop, b. Sept. 7, 1919, Fayette Co. d. Oct. 23, 1956, Fayette Co., m. Hazel McConnell.

WALDROP, Milton Miles, b. 1876 - son of S. M. Waldrop - m. Lelea Alice Laster - dau. of Kayle & Mandie (Laid) Laster of Carroll Co., Ga. Children: 1. Eddie Mae Waldrop, m. Hollis Newman. 2. Jonas Waldrop, m. Earline Taylor. 3. Shelton Waldrop, m. Elsie Newman. 4. Noah Waldrop. 5. Mattie Lou Waldrop, m. Esker Hindman. 6. Kelly Ray Waldrop, m. Ardel Morrison. 7. Thomas Waldrop, m. Betty Stokes. 8. Arline Waldrop, m. Graham Brock. 9. Lester Waldrop, m. 1st. - Martha Miner, 2nd. - Gwen Henderson.

WALDROP, Silas Calvin, b. Sept. 19, 1925, - son of Robert Belton Waldrop - m. Dec. 21, 1944, Lula Irene Bobo, b. Sept. 11, 1925, Fayette Co. - dau. of Frank M. & Eula M. (South) Bobo. They were married in Fayette, Ala. by Rev. A. M. Nix. Children: 1. Robert Miles Waldrop, b. Dec. 14, 1947, Fayette. 2. Silas Calvin Waldrop, b. May 27, 1949, Fayette. 3. Shirley Jo Waldrop, b. Mar. 27, 1951, Fayette, Ala.

WALDROP, Silas M., b. May 20, 1848, d. Jan. 9, 1927 - son of James Waldrop - m. Oct. 19, 1871, 1st. - Nancy Yarbrough, b. July 24, 1843, d. June 4, 1882. Children: 1. Dela Etter Waldrop, b. Mar. 22, 1873. 2. Coleman Layton Waldrop, b. Sept. 10, 1874, d. 1957, m. 1st. - Dec. 29, 1898, Virginia Ray, b. Mar. 23, 1880, d. Mar. 14, 1912, m. 2nd. - Aug. 8, 1912, Ethel A. Collins, b. Sept. 11, 1886.

3. Milton Miles Waldrop, b. May 15, 1876, m. Lelea Alice Laster. 4. Sara Bertha Waldrop, b. July 6, 1879, m. Nov. 17, 1901, William Bailey Holliman, d. Aug. 14, 1950. 5. Samuel Murphy Waldrop, b. July 6, 1879, d. Aug. 12, 1955, m. Dec. 22, 1901, Mattie Collins, dau. of Robert Collins.
Silas M. Waldrop m. 2nd. - Dec. 21, 1882, Mary G. Stillman.

WALDROP, Starling Van Buren, b. Mar. 3, 1860, Lamar Co., Ala., d. Aug. 1, 1944, Sulligent, Ala. - son fo Wm. Wilburn & Amanda Jane (Rainwater) Waldrop - m. Dec. 5, 1886, Roxanne Godfrey, b. Aug. 11, 1868, Lamar Co., d. Nov. 14, 1927, Sulligent, Ala. - dau. of Thomas Jefferson & Lucy Adaline (Shackelford) Godfrey. Both of their father served in the Confederate States Army during the Civil War. They are buried in the Wesley Chapel Cemetery, in Fayette Co., Ala. Children: 1. William Carey Waldrop, b. Nov. 11, 1887, (All children b. Lamar Co., Ala.), d. April 29, 1941, m. Dec. 8, 1912. 2. Virgie Lou Waldrop, b. Feb. 3, 1889. 3. Thomas Madison Waldrop, b. Jan. 21, 1891, d. Mar. 23, 1913. 4. Madorah Elizabeth Waldrop, b. Nov. 28, 1892, m. July 23, 1911, Zeb Rowland. 5. Delia Jane Waldrop, b. Aug. 10, 1894, m Sept. 5, 1915, R. L. Mosley. 6. Sam Ray Waldrop, b. Aug. 30, 1896, d. Feb. 10, 1931. 7. Noah Miles Waldrop, b. Feb. 28, 1898, d. Sept. 4, 1899. 8. Herman Bryan Waldrop, b. Jan. 15, 1900, d. Dec. 13, 1939. 9. Lucy Irene Waldrop, b. Sept. 28, 1902, m. Sept. 3, 1924, Gaston Golson. 10. Chester Starling Waldrop, b. Jan. 27, 1904, m. Nov. 9, 1932. 11. Annie Grace Waldrop, b. April 2, 1906, m. June 20, 1925. 12. Arvel Gray Waldrop, b. Aug. 17, 1908, m. Aug. 9, 1936. 13. Len G. Waldrop, b. Oct. 19, 1910, d. Nov. 3, 1912. 14. Barney Lorene Waldrop, b. Dec. 21, 1912, d. April 23, 1914.

WALDROP, William Wilburn, b. Dec. 15, 1823, Spartanburg, S. C., d. Sept. 15, 1904, Fayette Co., Ala., m. Mar. 20, 1845, Jane Amanda Rainwater, b. 1828, Spartanburg, S. C., d. May 20, 1895, Fayette Co. Wm. Wilburn Waldrop was a veteran of the Civil Was having served with the 50th Ala. Cavalry. Children: (All born Lamar Co.) 1. Silas Murphy Waldrop, d. Jan. 8, 1927. 2. Mary Jane Waldrop, d. Nov. 28, 1930. 3. Sarah Waldrop, d. Sept. 13, 1855. 4. Miles Calvin Waldrop, d. Dec. 12, 1928. 5. Lucretia Mariah Waldrop, d. July 4, 1934. 6. William Samuel Waldrop, d. 1893. 7. Elizabeth Waldrop. 8. Starling Van Buren Waldrop, b. Mar. 3, 1860, d. Aug. 1, 1944, m. Dec. 5, 1886, Roxanne Godfrey. 9. Nancy Catherine Waldrop, d. Nov. 8, 1957.

WALKER, Edgar, b. Aug. 28, 1879, Fayette Co., Ala., d. Mar. 18, 1953, Fayette, - son of P. M. Walker - m. Dec. 2, 1903, Sallie White, b. Aug. 28, 1882 Fayette Co., d. Feb. 1, 1943, Fayette, Ala. - dau. of S. L. White. They were married at Fayette, Ala. Edgar Walker was a merchant and a building contractor. Children: 1. Evelyn Walker, b. Fayette, Ala., m. Aug. 18, 1931, Thomas H. Robertson, Jr., b. Oct. 5, 1900, Fayette, Ala. , d. Nov. 24, 1955, Fayette, Ala. 2. Edwyna Walker, b. Fayette, Ala., m. Aug. 17, 1935, James A. Branyon, II, b. Fayette, Ala.

WALKER, Guy, m. Mary Frances McCool, b. Dec. 23, 1909, Fayette Co., Ala. Children: 1. Billy Walker, b. Aug. 14, 193_, Fayette, Ala., m. Nancy __. (Child: Billy, Jr., b. 1958.) 2. Tommy Walker, b. Nov. 1940, Fayette.

WALKER, Pickney Monroe, b. Aug. 12, 1848, d. Jan. 2, 1918, Fayette, Ala. - son of Samuel T. Walker - m. Nov. 7, 1876, Martha Jane Yerby, b. Mar. 7, 1851, Fayette Co., d. Sept. 4, 1934, Fayette, - dau. of Francis M. Yerby. They were married in Fayette County, Ala. P. M. Walker was a farmer and a merchant. Children: 1. Carles Tildon Walker, b. Fayette Co., d. 1950, Birmingham, Ala., m. 1922, Ellis Woods, of Tenn. 2. Ulyss Edgar Walker, b. Aug. 28, 1879, Fayette Co., d. Mar. 18, 1953, Fayette, Ala., m. Dec. 2, 1903, Sallie White, b. Aug. 28, 1882, Fayette Co., d. Feb. 1, 1943, Fayette. 3. Almer Walker, b. Sept. 13, 1881, Fayette Co., d. July 22, 1889, Fayette.

WALKER, Samuel Taylor, b. Union Co., N. C. d. Fayette Co., Ala. - m. Nov. 5, 1843, Elizabeth Scrivner, b. Oct. 18, 1821, d. Nov. 25, 1879, Fayette Co. Children: 1. Samantha Ann Walker, b. Sept. 10, 1844, d. July 25, 1881, m. Jan. 1, 1871, F. M. Laboon. 2. Andrew L. Walker, m. Georgia Horn (Lived in Kennedy, Ala.) 3. Pickney Monroe Walker, b. Aug. 12, 1848, d. Jan. 2, 1918, m. Nov. 7, 1876, Martha Jane Yerby, b. Mar. 7, 1851, d. Sept. 4, 1934. 4. Kerloine Walker, b. Aug. 25, 1851, d. Sept. 15, 1921, m. John J. Hollins. 5. Martha Jane Walker, m. John T. Holliman. 6. Green Walker, b. 1856, d. 1917, m. Fannie Ashcraft.

WALLS, John, b. 1822 ? Tenn., m. Mary___, b. 1829, Tenn.? He was killed during the Civil War. Children: 1. A Daughter, m. Mr. Langford. 2. John Walls, m. Ella Robinson. 3. E. Sue Walls, b. 1847, Ala., d. June 1882, m. Feb. 7, 1878, Anderson Burchfield Comer, b. Oct. 15, 1848, d. April 13, 1911. 4. Sarah C. Walls ??, b. 1848, Ala.

WARD, John W., b. Nov. 17, 1839, Fayette Co., Ala., d. Nov. 1906, Fayette Co., m. Emily Ham, b. Jan. 13, 1847, Fayette Co., d. 1915, Fayette Co. This family lived on Sugar Creek, near Siloam Church, where their ten children were born. They were devout Primitive Baptists. Children: (All born Fayette Co.) 1. Columbus Ward, d. Midland, Texas, m. Emma Whitley, b. Marion Co., Ala., d. Texas. Columbus Ward and wife moved to Texas when young. They had four children. He was murdered on the street by an unknown man in Midland, Texas. His widow remained in Texas and reared her children there. It was believed that the murderer took him for someone else. 2. Ralston Ward, d. Winfield, Ala., m. Mollie Musgrove, b. Fayette Co., d. Winfield, Ala. 3. Delia Ward, d. Fayette Co., m. Bura D. Kirkland, b. & d. Fayette Co., Ala. 4. Lee (female) Ward, b. Sept. 21, 1875, d. July 3, 1900, Fayette Co., m. Willia White, b. & d. Fayette Co. 5. Lula Martilia Ward, b. Mar. 26, 1873, d. 1956, Fayette Co. 6. Louranie Ward, m. Woodville A. Couch, b. Fayette Co., d. Oklahoma. 7. Walter W. Ward, d. Okla., m. Nellie Frye, b. Texas, d. Okla. 8. Cora Jane Ward, d. Vernon, Ala., m. Dr. John M. Roberts, b. Bluff, Fayette Co. 9. Jala Ward, b. 1923, Fayette Co., m. Pervy Lucas, b. Fayette Co., d. 1923, Fayette Co. This couple and their only child was killed by a train at a railroad crossing and all three are buried at Old Union Church, north of Bluff, Ala. 10. Dena Irene Ward, b. Mar. 1, 1889, d. May 8, 1952, Fayette Co., m. Luther Spencer Bobo, b. Mar. 8, 1878, Fayette.

WATERS, ___. Children:1. Col. Philemon Waters. 2. Rosanna Waters, b. 1734 to 1739, Prince William Co., Va., m. 1751, John Thomas Farrow, b. 1727, Prince William Co., Va., d. 1776.

WATKINS, Burl Malcom, b. Feb. 26, 1852, south of Berry in Tusca. Co., d.

Mar. 20, 1931, Fayette Co., Ala., m. Dec. 7, 1876, Wincey Catherine Watkins, b. Jan. 14, 1863, Tusca. Co., d. Mar. 2, 1947, Fayette Co. She was thirteen years old at the time of their marriage. They were first cousins and he was a farmer. Children: 1. Wincey Ernestine "Tiny" Watkins, b. Dec. 7, 1878, m. Aug. 15, 1895, Walker Jenkins. 2. Burl Bascom Watkins, b. June 22, 1880, d. June 18, 1954, m. Dec. 21, 1894, Plina Jenkins. 3. Robert Malcom "Bob" Watkins, b. April 19, 1882, d. Nov. 18, 1948, Fayette Co., Ala., m. Mar. 19, 1904, Roma Atchley. 4. Virgil Roscoe Watkins, b. Jan. 20, 1884, m. Jan. 1, 1907, Lula Platt. 5. Belton Oscar Watkins, b. Feb. 20, 1887, m. Nov. 1, 1908, Ella Morrison. 6. Dora Idella Watkins, b. Nov. 1, 1889, d. June 2, 1927, m. Aug. 10, 1905, Curtis Esco Jenkins, b. Mar. 15, 1885, Fayette Co., d. Aug. 6, 1905. 7. Lester Young Watkins, b. Nov. 1, 1891. 8. Eddie Watkins, b. Jan. 26, 1893, d. Nov. 11, 1897. 9. Luna Hester Watkins, b. Feb. 24, 1894, m. July 18, 1911, Sam Anthony. 10. Lillybell Watkins, b. June 11, 1895, d. Dec. 23, 1895. 11. Amanda Emeline "Emma" Watkins, b. Dec. 12, 1896, Fayette Co., m. Dec. 13, 1915, Albert Lee Anthony. 12. Lilla Watkins, b. Jan. 18, 1899, d. June 23, 1899.

WELBURN, William Harris, b. Atlanta, Ga. (where Peachtree St. now is located.) - son of Wm. Wood Welburn - m. Mary Angeline Looney, b. Tenn. - dau. of Bill Looney. He was a railroad man. Both are buried at Jasper, Ala. Children: 1. George J. Welburn, b. Mar. 10, 1869, d. Aug. 9, 1927, Bankston, Ala., m. Fannie Davis, b. Mar. 8, 1874, Bankston, Ala., d. Mar. 23, 1953, Bankston, Ala. 2. James Anderson Welburn, m. Hollie _. 3. Lucy Ellen Welburn, m. Aug. 16, 1891, Benjamin McFarland Long Hay. 4. Hattie Bell Welburn, b. 1890, Walker Co., Ala., m. Mr. Butler. 5. Viola Welburn, b. Calera, Ala., m. Lewis Sylvester Harbin. 6. Mary Lee Welburn, m. Sam Brain. 7. Della Welburn, m. M. Varner. 8. William Wood Welburn, b. Blount Co., Ala., m. Minnie _. 9. Nettie Welburn, m. Jed Root. 10. Nora Welburn, b. Bankston, Ala.

WELCH, John S., b. 1800, S. C., d. Oct. 26, 1893, m. June 21, 1828, Elizabeth Baker, b. 1805, S. C., d. Sept. 27, 1858. Came to Alabama by 1844. Early settlers of Fayette Co., Ala. Children: 1. Francis M. Welch, b. Aug. 16, 1831, S. C. 2. Robert J. Welch, b. Sept. 4, 1833, S.C., d. July 27, 1848. 3. Martha Jane Welch, b. Jan. 15, 1836, S.C., d. Sept. 11, 1917, m. July 14, 1855, Jefferson Adam Richards, b. July 2, 1827, Fayette Co., d. Nov. 23, 1875. 4. Rev. John Anderson Welch, b. Jan. 3, 1838, S.C., m. Dicey Melissa Pryor. 5. Allsey T. Welch, b. Dec. 17, 1839, S.C. 6. Clary Ann Welch, b. July 27, 1842, Ga. 7. James T. Welch, b. Aug. 29, 1845, Ala. 8. George Washington Welch, b. Jan. 11, 1847, Ala. 9. A. B. Welch, b. July 29, 1849, Ala.

John S. Welch married second - Miss White. Children: (2nd. wife) 1. Miley Dianer Welch, b. Mar. 15, 1861, Ala. 2. Mallicia C. Welch, b. Sept. 11, 1863, Ala. 3. William R. Smith Welch, b. Aug. 15, 1865, Ala.

WEEMS, William L., b. July 28, 1903, Cobb Co., Ga., m. May 27, 1940, Ruby Genevieve Smith, b. April 4, 1916, Fayette Co. Children: 1. Barbara Jean Weems.

WEST, Lee, b. 1871, Ala., d. 1934, New Mexico, m. Quillie Doughty, b. 1872, Fayette Co., d. Dec. 22, 1957, New Mexico, - dau. of J. F. & Rachel L. A. (Boozer) Doughty. Shortly after they married they moved west to Texas and later to New Mexico where they made their home. Children: 1. Jessie Hubert West, m. Pearl Sawyer. 2. Joseph Floyd West, m. Maranda Green. 3. Charles Patrick West. 4. Dovie Lee West, m. Walter Quillin. 5. Curtis Larenzo West, m. Lucille _. 6. James Roy West, b. abt. 1895, m. Dorothy Gould. 7. Nora Lee West, m. Burton Thomas. 8. Flora Mae West, m. Chester Horton. 9. Benjamin Ira West. 10. Walter Clyde West, m. Ruby _. 11. William Lester West, m. Catherine _. 12. Rhoda Hester West, m. Kenneth Coen. 13. Earl West, m. Ruth _. 14. Lucille West, m. Berm Ephram.

WEST, Miles Berry, b. Nov. 25, 1896, Calhoun Ga. - son of James F. & Amanda (Reeves) West, m. April 16, 1920, Marie Kent, b. May 23, 1905, Tallassee, Ala. - dau. of Wm. T. & Myrtis (Land) Kent. Miles Berry West is an electrical engineer. He and Marie Kent were married in LaGrange, Ga. Children: 1. Madelyn Eloise West, b. Feb. 5, 1921, Fairfax, Ala., m. John Thomas Veazey. 2. Miles Berry West, II, b. Oct. 30, 1923, Fairfax, Ala. 3. Robert Lee West, II, b. April 20, 1925, Fairfax, Ala., d. April 1945, buried in West Point, Ga. Killed in Service of World War II.

WEST, William Andrew, b. June 21, 1881, Fayette Co., d. Oct. 19, 1950, - son of Lee West - m. Sept. 16, 1906, Lucy Jane "Minnie" South, b. Feb. 23, 1886, Davis Creek, Ala. - dau. of Levi Woodruff South. They were married at Mt. Pleasant, Fayette Co., Ala. by Rev. Simpson. He was in the lumber business. Children: 1. Virginia South West, b. Aug. 22, 1920, Fayette Co., Ala. 2. Infant Son West, b. & d. Aug. 7, 1913, Fayette Co., Ala.

WHEELER, Theodore Tandy, b. 1864, Greenville Co., S.C., d. 1957, Fayette, Ala., m. Feb. 20, 1908, Sarah Leona Atkins, b. Lamar Co., Ala. T. T. Wheeler was a merchant in Fayette, Ala. from 1913, to 1930. They came to Fayette from Lamar Co., in 1913. Children: 1. Willinel Wheeler, b. Aug. 29, 1910, Lamar Co., Ala., m. Francis Marion Davis, b. Feb. 27, 1906, Williamson Co., Tenn.

WHITE, Andrew Lawrence, b. May 18, 1843, Huntsville, Ala., d. Mar. 14, 1906, Fayette, Ala. - son of Thomas W. & Susan (Bradley) White - m. Mar. 5, 1888, May Hester Nuckols, d. June 4, 1948, buried Elmwood Cem., Birmingham, Ala. - dau. of Augustus M. & Mary (Jemison) Nuckols. (See Owens Ala. IV.) Andrew Lawrence "Sandy" White married prior to above marriage and had the following children: 1. Lawrence White. 2. Thomas White. 3. A married daughter. 4. Ella (Mrs. Walter Lee Gresham). and 5. Sara White. Mrs. Chadwick's "Huntsville Diary" in the Alabama Historical Journal, Summer, 1947 tells of his C.S.A. exploits and Owens Vol. IV, his lineage. He worked as a U. S. Deputy Collector for government stills. He rode horseback and trained hunting dogs as hobbies. Children: (By M. H. Nuckols.) 1. Arthur Nuckols White, b. Feb. 5, 1889, m. Minnie __. 2. Augustine Melville White, b. Sept. 21, 1891, m. 1st. - Sarah _. 3. Grace White, m. J. K. Chambless. 4. Susan Bradley White, m. Harold O. Smith. 5. Adaline Bradley White, b. Nov. 15, 1894, d. Nov. 4, 1895, Fayette Co., Ala.

WHITE, Duncan Eve, b. Mar. 17, 1882, Water Valley, Tenn. d. July 28, 1954, Fayette Co., Ala. - son of Dr. Joseph Ephriam & Mittie (Smith) White - m. 2nd. - Oct. 26, 1928, Sula (Hallman) Morris, b. Feb. 3, 1903, Berry, Ala. - dau. of David M. & Julia Ella (Bennett) Hallman. Mr. & Mrs. White were married in Pulaski, Tenn. At the time of their marriage both were living in Birmingham, Ala. but moved shortly thereafter to Fayette, Ala. which remained their residence, except for about six months in 1940 when they resided in Hattisburg, Miss. Mr. White was a Missionary Baptist Minister and a carpenter by trade. He was also a member of the Masonic Order. He is buried in Elmwood Cem., Birmingham, Ala. Mr. White was first married to Maggie Ann Dallas Rogers and had the following children by that marriage: 1. Mary Thelma White, b. Feb. 23, 1905, m. Mar. 19, 1932, Henry Jefferson Hart, b. Aug. 8, 1902. 2. Ima Ruth White, b. Jan. 2, 1907, m. Nov. 22, 1936, Charles Frederick Weathers, b. July 31, 1901. 3. Maggie Macie White, b. Nov. 8, 1908, m. Sept. 25, 1926, Walter Spears McCombs, b. Jan. 5, 1890. 4. Joe Duncan Rogers White, b. April 1, 1910, m. May 5, 1932, Edith Pauline Horton, b. Feb. 13, 1914. 5. Bessie Lucille White, b. Nov. 4, 1911, m. Nov. 2, 1934, James Chappell Gardiner, b. Sept. 2, 1907. 6. Jessie Woodrow White, b. May 22, 1914, m. Aug. 20, 1933, Clarence Stuart Gates, b. Nov. 16, 1908 7. Earnest Morrison White, b. Sept. 1, 1921, d. Nov. 9, 1958. Earnest Morrison White enlisted in the U. S. Air Force, Oct. 28, 1942, and entered training as a pilot. Later he changed to navigation. On Feb. 12, 1944, he was commissioned 2nd. Lt. He was then assigned overseas with the 532 Bombardment Squadron (H), 381 Bombardment Group (H). He completed 32 missions over enemy territory in the European Theatre of War during World War II. He was commissioned 1st. Lt. in Dec. 1944 and returned home from overseas on June 6, 1945. He was commissioned Capt. in 1950, and was sent overseas again on April 13, 1953, where he served until he returned home April 11, 1956. He was killed in an automobile accident on Nov. 9, 1958, at Del Rio, Texas. At the time of his death he was assigned to Headquarters Strategic Reconnaissance Wing at Laughlin A.F.B. in Texas. He received the following medals: Air Force Medal with 5 Oak Leaves, European Theatre of War with 4 stars of Battles; Pacifia Theatre; American Defense; German Occupation; Victory Medal and Service Medal.

Sula (Hallman) Morris White had one child by her first marriage to Frank Morris: Ella Catherine Morris White, b. April 2, 1927. Duncan Eve and Sula (Hallman) Morris White had one child: Mittie Irene White, b. April 7, 1931.

WHITE, Rev. Ephriam W., b. Sept. 7, 1836, probably Calhoun Co., Ga., d. Dickson, Tenn., m. Jan. 27, 1856, Rachel C. Brittian, b. near Tenn & Ga. Line, d. Hillsboro, Tenn. Children: 1. Dr. Joseph Ephriam White, b. Nov. 5, 1856, d. Jan. 31, 1890, m. 1881, Mittie Smith Trantham, b. Aug. 6, 1859, d. Sept. 17, 1894. 2. Alex White. 3. Callie White, m. Albert Freeman. 4. Mollie White, m. Mr. Hicks. After the death of Rachel, Rev. Ephriam W. White married again. He and his second wife had two children - 1. Charlie White. 2. Pearl White.

WHITE, George Harrison, b. Jan. 28, 1855, Fayette Co., d. Mar. 26, 1920, Fayette Co., Ala., m. June 1874, Amanda Saphronia Farquhar, b. July 1855, Fayette Co., d. Mar. 9, 1941, Fayette Co. - dau. of James & Bashey (McGuire) Farquhar. Children: 1. Naomi Ethel White, b. Mar. 9, 1875, Fayette Co., m. Jesse Jackson Cotton, b. April 3, 1879, Fayette Co. 2. Isaac Wesley White, m. Cornelia Farquhar. 3. Mary Jane White, m. James Wright. 4. Mary Magdaline White, m. McColough - Williams. 5. William Thomas White, m. Laura Blankenship. 6. Anne Laura White, m. Julius Moore. 7. Rufus Rowland White, m. Elizabeth Jones. 8. James Monroe White, m. Mattie Blankenship. 9. Winnie Josephine White, m. _ Porter. 10. Benjamin Bankston White, m. Rosa Ehl. 11. Ella Virginia White, m. John Blankenship.

WHITE, Henry, m. Jennie Doughty, b. abt. 1867, Fayette Co., - dau. of J. F.

& Rachel L. A. (Boozer) Doughty. Children: 1. Clester White, m. Roscoe Williamson. 2. Sally White, m. Bascum Cannon. 3. Flinton White, d. Jan. 1958, m. Jewel Rice. 4. Jessie White (female) m. Jesse Williamson (Male). 5. Lilla White, d. in early life.

WHITE, James W., b. April 23, 1826, Fayette Co., d. Feb. 12, 1891, Fayette Co., m. 1853, Winnie O. Lawrence, b. Sept. 7, 1835, Fayette Co., d. Dec. 4, 1888, Fayette Co. - dau. of George & Sarah (Green) Lawrence. Children: 1. George Harrison White, b. Jan. 28, 1855, Fayette Co., d. Mar. 26, 1920, Fayette Co., m. June 1874, Amanda Saphronia Farquhar, b. July 1855, Fayette Co., d. Mar. 9, 1941, Fayette, Co., Ala.

WHITE, Dr. Joseph Ephriam, b. Nov. 5, 1856, Hillsboro, Tenn., d. Jan. 31, 1890, Nechesville, Texas - son of Rev. Ephriam W. & Rachel (Britton) White, - m. 1881, Mittie Smith Trantham, b. Aug. 6, 1859, Columbia, Tenn. d. Sept. 17, 1894, Sante Fe, Tenn. buried at Goshen Cem., Columbia, Tenn. - dau. of W. D. & Mary Eliz. (Meadows) Trantham. Dr. Joseph Ephriam White was a member of the Masonic Order. Children: 1. Duncan Eve White, b. Mar. 17, 1882, d. July 28, 1954, m. Oct. 26, 1928 at Pulaski, Tenn. Sula Hallman, b. Feb. 3, 1903. 2. Edgar Eugene White, b. Mar. 28, 1884, d. Sept. 3, 1945, m. July 4, 1905 at Tullahoma, Tenn. Lillie Estelle Fite, b. May 20, 1888. 3. Asa Ephriam White, b. April 30, 1886, d. abt. 1888. 4. Bessie Brittian White, b. Aug. 22, 1888, m. Oct. 5, 1906, Edgar Eugene Mann, b. Dec. 23, 1885.

WHITE, J. Winston, b. April 25, 1885, Fayette Co., Ala., d. Oct. 4, 1951, m. Lucy Ann Ballinger, b. Dec. 29, 1888, Fayette Co. - dau. of J. W. & Sally (Bobo) Ballinger. Children: 1. Ralston White, m. Jalia May. 2. Thurston White, m. Grace Thompson. 3. Clara White, m. Edward Black. 4. Jimmie Lee White, m. Opal __.

WHITE, Kilby, b. Feb. 12, 1887, Fayette Co., d. Sept. 16, 1940, - son of Thos. Garrett & Olivia (Byrd) White - m. Nancy Esther Roberts, - dau. of Humphrey & Sallie (Shirley) Roberts. Children: 1. Inez White, m. Harry O. Unger, Jr. 2. Kathryn White, m. John Paul Jones. 3. Betty White, m. Garland Barnes, b. Berry, Ala.

WHITE, Meadie, m. Clara Traweek. Children: 1. Lott White, m. Susie Thompson. 2. Allison Olinthis White, m. Savilla Graves.

WHITE, Starling Lumpkin, b. June 21, 1852, near Rome, Ga., d. April 13, 1939, Fayette Co., Ala. - son of Thomas J. White - m. Mar. 5, 1876, Mary Virginia Jones, b. Feb. 7, 1857, Fayette Co., d. Sept. 28, 1953, Fayette Co. - dau. of H. Russell Jones. Children: 1. Emma White, m. Joe W. Richards. 2. Sallie White, m. Edgar Walker. 3. Etta White, m. Alfred Walker Baker. 4. Maude White, m. J. Alexander Smith. 5. Lou Ella White, m. W. Claude Newton. 6. Snow White, m. Francis Marion Taber. 7. Blanche White, m. Henry Leslie Longcrier. 8. Irene White, m. James Delmar Wright.

WHITE, Thomas Garrett, b. Feb. 28, 1857, d. Aug. 13, 1919, son of Thos. Jefferson & Martha (Sanders) White - m. Olivia Byrd, b. Nov. 15, 1856, d. Mar. 12, 1925 - dau. of Wm. M. Byrd, b. Dec. 23, 1809, and A. B. __, b. June 17, 1813. Children: 1. Birdie White, m. Charley Wilkes. 2. Kilby White, b. Feb. 12, 1887, d. Sept. 16, 1940, m. Nancy Esther Roberts. 3. Corena White, m. Fent Berry.

WHITE, Thomas Jefferson, b. Aug. 29, 1820, Ga., d. Mar. 17, 1865, m. July 24, 1845, Martha C. Sanders, b. June 24, 1828, Ga., d. Sept. 6, 1884 - dau. of Minyard & Flora Sanders. They were married in Georgia. T. J. White is buried in Memorial Cemetery in Richmond, Va. Martha S. White is buried at Hopewell Cemetery, Fayette Co., Ala. Children: 1. Donald Webster White, b. July 1, 1846, Ga., d. Texas. 2. James Minyard White, b. Mar. 15, 1848, Ga. 3. Flora Elizabeth White, b. Mar. 4, 1850, d. May 10, 1923, Fayette Co. m. Elija Jones, d. buried Hopewell, Fayette Co. 4. Starling Lumpkin White, b. June 21, 1852, near Rome, Ga., d. April 13, 1939, Fayette Co., m. Mar. 5, 1876, Mary Virginia Jones, b. Feb. 7, 1857, Fayette Co., d. Sept. 28, 1953, Fayette Co. 5. John Jefferson White, b. June 2, 1855, Ga., d. Texas. 6. Thomas Garrett White, b. Feb. 28, 1857, d. Aug. 13, 1919, Fayette Co., m. Olivia Byrd, b. Nov. 15, 1856, d. Mar. 12, 1925, Fayette Co. 7. Allen White, b. Sept. 28, 1859, d. Texas. 8. Benjamin White, b. Jan. 3, 1862, d. Texas. 9. Jeffie White, b. Feb. 16, 1865, d. Texas.

WHITE, Thornton, b. Oct. 19, 1891, Fayette Co., m. Carrie Ballinger, b. Oct. 7, 1899, Fayette Co., - dau. of J. W. & Sally (Bobo) Ballinger. Children: 1. Franklin White, m. Charlene Cargile. 2. Freddie White, m. Lonell Sims. 3. Nora White, m. 1st. - Ernest Francis, 2nd. - Charley Miller.

WHITLEY, James Lee, b. May 10, 1866, Fayette Co., Ala., d. May 29, 1952, Fayette Co., m. Feb. 10 or 18, 1887, Naomi Fane Farquhar, b. May 9, 1869, Fayette Co., Ala., d. Oct. 25, 1940, Fayette Co. Children: 1. Winnie Kate Whitley, b. 1893, Fayette Co., m. Robert Bernice Newton, b. May 21, 1888, d. Oct. 11, 1955. 2. Fletcher Hargrove Whitley. 3. Howard Grady Whitley. 4. Patrick Henry Whitley. 5. Joseph Marion Whitley (Twin). 6. Mirra Jane Whitley (Twin). 7. James Lee Whitley, Jr.

WHITLEY, Jonas, b. June 19, 1800, N. C., d. Aug. 3, 1872, m. Rebecca Gullick Moore, b. May 30, 1801, Tenn. d. Fayette Co., Ala. Jonas Whitley was a cooper (made cedar buckets, etc.) Both are buried in the Whitson Family Cem. Children: 1. William T. Whitley. 2. Willis Harvey Whitley, b. Oct. 20, 1822, Fayette Court House, Ala., d. Mar. 5, 1885, Fayette Co.. m. Mar. 10, 1853, Elizabeth Jane Davis, b. April 13 or 17, 1829 or 1827, Fayette Co., d. Aug. 8, 1895, Fayette Co. 3. John Whitley. 4. Elizabeth F. Whitley, m. John C. Davis. 5. Mary S. Whitley, b. May 23, 1831, Fayette Co., d. June 24, 1889, Itawamba Co., Miss., m. June 19, 1850, Richard B. Dickinson, b. Feb. 4, 1827, Ala., d. Mar. 1905, Itawamba Co., Miss. 6. Nancy Whitley, m. J. G. Farquhar. 7. T. U. "Schully" Whitley, m. R. A. Crowley.

WHITLEY, Willis Harvey, b. Oct. 20, 1822, Fayette Co., d. Mar. 15, 1885, Fayette Co. - son of Jonas & Rebecca (Moore) Whitley - m. Mar. 10, 18__, Elizabeth Jane Davis, b. April 13, 1829, Fayette Co., d. Aug. 8, 1895, - dau. of John Hawkins Davis. Children: 1. Mary Isabella "Ib" Whitley, b. Fayette, Ala., m. Dec. 13, 1866, James F. Gibson. 2. John Whitley, d. abt. 17 yrs. old - sawmill and gin accident. 3. Jefferson Whitley, b. Jan. 12, 1852, d. Jan. 1934, m. Dec. 7, 1871, Cornelia Stough. 4. James Lee Whitley, b. May 10, 1866, d. May 29, 1952, Fayette, Ala., m. Naomi Jane Farquhar. 5. George Whitley, m. Miss Whitson. 6. Frank Harvey Whitley, m. Lucy Hocutt. 7. Posey Whitley, Invalid from birth. 8. Josephine Whitley, m. Thomas McCracken. 9. Valutia Jane "Jennie" Whitley, m. Wm. Taylor Newton.

WHITNEY, __, m. Minervia Jones. Children: 1. Marion Whitney. 2. Taney Whitney. 3. Susanna Whitney.

WHITSON, W. G. - son of Thos. J. Whitson - m. Manda S. Traweek, b. Aug. 4, 1833, or 1834?, d. Mar. 26, 1910 - granddaughter of __Strong. Children: 1. Tom Whitson. 2. Fent Whitson. 3. Martelia Whiston, b. Nov. 3, 1871, d. Feb. 8, 1958, Bankston, Ala., m. J. Reuben Poe, b. April 4, 1871, d. Dec. 11,1946, Bankston, Ala. W. G. Whitson's father, Thos. J. Whitson entered government land in 1830. Prominent member of Methodist Chudrh and had much to do with the establishment of that church in Walker Co. On Dec. 17, 1826, he was ordained a deacon at Tuscaloosa and on Dec. 23, 1835, at the same place he was ordained an elder. He was a local Methodist preacher prior to 1837.

WILKES, Mod, m. Lottie Savage. Children: 1. Virgie Wilkes, m. Mr. Thomas. 2. John Wilkes, died as a young man. 3. Charley Wilkes, m. Birdie White. 4. Clyde Wilkes, m. Miss Dodson.

WILKINS, John, m. Judith __. Children: 1. Catherine Wilkins, m. Mar. 29, 1757, John Colson Baines, Sr., died before July 19, 1772, Chowan Co., N.C. 2. Charles Wilkins. 3. John Wilkins, Jr., m. July 10, 1767, Mrs. Rachel Hassell. 4. Rebecca Wilkins, m. Oct. 10, 1752, Jno. Cleland. 5. Deborah Wilkins, m. __ Taylor. 6. Elizabeth Wilkins.

WILLIAMS, B. Aug. 12, 1853, d. Aug. 1, 1930, m. Monte Mongrelia Richards, b. Sept. 13, 1859, d. Mar. 17, 1889 - dau. of J.A., Sr. & Martha (Welch) Richards. Children: 1. Mackey David Williams, b. July 31, 1888, m. Lillie Price. 2. Mercer S. Williams, b. Dec. 6, 1880, d. Oct. 17, 1912, m. Leona Carr. 3. Evie Williams, b. Jan. 30, 1883, m. John G. Belk.
  B. D. Williams second marriage - Missouri Wiggins, d. June 8, 1926. Children: (2nd. wife) 1. Elbert Curtis Williams, b. Nov. 12, 1893, m. Alma Parker. 2. Lela Angeline Williams, b. Aug. 10, 1895, d. Mar. 8, 1832, m. P. Freeman. 3. Zebedee Williams, b. Oct. 10, 1896, m. Effie Watson. 4. Ebedee Williams, b. Nov. 23, 1898, d. Jan. 25, 1900. 5. Mattie Lee Williams, b. July 31, 1900, m. Aug. 3, 1919, Bedford William Oswalt, b. Feb. 14, 1893.

WILLIAMS, John, Will drawn Mar. 13, 1745. Children: 1. Sarah Williams, m. James Castellaw, d. abt. 1745.

WILLIAMS, Johnny Clive, b. April 20, 1933, - son of Alex & Louise (Renfroe) Williams - m. Ina Loudelle Musgrove, b. Aug. 10, 1936, - dau. of Wm. Bruce & Lula (McConnell) Musgrove. Children: 1. Johnny Clive Williams, Jr., b. Aug. 7, 1957, Fayette, Ala. 2. Daniel Musgrove Williams, b. Sept. 12, 1959.

WILLIAMS, Richard, b. Dec. 25, 1931, m. Malinda Jane Renfroe, b. Nov. 6, 1937, Pickwick Dam, Tenn. - dau. of Roy S. Renfroe. Children: 1. Stephanie Ann Williams, b. Nov. 30, 1958, Washington, D. C.

WILLIAMSON, Pink, m. Laura Boozer, b. 1838, S. C. - dau. of Andrew Boozer. Children: 1. Billy Tierce (by Laura's 1st. husband, who died just before the child was born.) m. Mattie__. 2. Infant Daughter. 3. Infant Son. 4. Adolphus George Washington Williamson. 5. Sarah Lou Elle Williamson. 6. Mertie Telellah Williamson, m. Mack Waldrop.

WILLINGHAM, Beverly, b. 1785, Ga., d. after 1856, Fayette Co., Ala. - son of William Willingham - m. Abigail __, b. 1790 - 1800. Lived in Tuscaloosa Co. from 1828 to 1847, then moved to Fayette Co., Ala. Children: 1. Thomas Lyon Willingham, b. April 23, 1807, Ga., d. Nov. 8, 1888, m. Susan Ann Strong b. July 31, 1817, Ga., d. Aug. 20, 1900. Both are buried at the Pleasant Hill Cemetery.

WILLINGHAM, C. B., b. 1814, Ga. - son of Reubin Willingham, m. Mary __, b. 1817, Ala. Children: 1. Reubin Willingham, b. 1839, Ala. 2. Edward Willingham, b. 1840, Ala. 3. Martha Willingham, b. 1843, Ala. 4. Nancy Willingham, b. 1845, Ala. 5. William Willingham, b. 1847, Ala. 6. Franklin Willingham, b. 1848, Ala.

WILLINGHAM, George Beverly, buried in Frankston, Texas - m. Margaret __. Children: 1. Robert Beverly Willingham, b. Texas.

WILLINGHAM, Isaac - son of Thomas Willingham, m. Sarah __. Isaac Willingham lived in Bristol Parrish, Prince George Co., Va. from 1731 to 1734, then Isle of Wight Co., Va. and in 1736 moved to Berkley Co., S.C. Two years later land in St. James Grantee Parrish, S.C. Children: 1. William Willingham, b. 1740, St. John's Parrish, Berkley Co., S.C., d. by 1797, Columbia Co., Ga., m. Nancy __. 2. Isaac Willingham, Jr., b. St. John's Parrish, Berkley Co., S.C. 3. James Willingham, b. St. John's Parrish, S. C. 4. Henry Willingham, b. June 16, 1731, Bristol Parrish, Prince George Co., Va., m. Mary __.

WILLINGHAM, Isaac, b. 1800 or 1797, Ga., m. Laura __. Children: 1. Ann Willingham. 2. John Willingham. 3. Elijah Willingham. 4. Louisa Willingham. 5. Isaac Willingham. 6. Thomas Willingham. 7. Rebecca Willingham, b. Oct. 8, 1825, d. Jan. 30, 1860, m. Oct. 17, 1844, Samuel Appling, b. Oct. 24, 1823, d. April 16, 1901.

WILLINGHAM, James Hugh, b. Sept. 16, 1841, Bankston, Ala., d. Oct. 3, 1917, Bankston, Ala. - son of Thomas Lyon Willingham - m. Oct. 5, 1873, Lucy Ann York, b. Sept. 15, 1855, Fayette Co., d. May 1, 1894, Bankston, Ala. - dau. of Jim York. James Hugh Willingham, at the age of twenty, enlisted in Columbus, Miss. in Sept. 1861 as a private in Co. G. 8th Confederate Cavalry (furnishing his own horse - which was probably required for cavalry service.) He was paroled in the fall of 1862. He returned to Co. G. 8th Confederate Cav. In Mar. 1863, he swapped places with a man in Co. B. 5th Ala. Cav., giving him $50.00 to make the change. He was captured at Danville, Ky. -- was paroled at Perryville, Ky. Oct. 20, 1863. He reenlisted as a private in Dec. 1864, in Fayette Co., Ala. in Co. b. 5th Ala. Regt. of Cav. and continued until Jan. 1865 when five companies of the 5th Ala. Cav. and Maj. Woodard's Batallion were combined constituting the 10th Ala. Cav. He reenlisted at Tuscumbia, Ala. as 3rd Lt. in Co. A. 10th Ala. Cav. This group was disbanded and he was paroled at Decatur, Ala. in April 1865. He received a wound in the right cheek and suffered a severe case of measles. He fought in the Battle of Shiloh under Capt. Ed Moore. Capt. W. F. Flood of Columbus, Miss. was one of his commanding officers. He and Lucy Ann York were married at the York home near the Cleveland Church, north of Bankston and he was a farmer, a merchant and at one time the postmaster of Bankston. Children: (1st. marriage) 1. Carrie Lee Willingham, b. July 15, 1875, d. July 12, 1954, Bankston, Ala., m. 1895, Henry George May, b. June --, Birmingham, Ala. 2. Maude Terry Willingham, b. Mar. 4, 1877, Bankston, Ala., d. Nov. 5, 1957, Bankston, m. Aug. 16, 1923, Benton C. Cook, b. Mar. 14, 1875, Hopkinsville, Ky, d. Oct. 27, 1948, Bankston. 3. James Thomas Willingham, b. Oct. 13, 1881, Bankston, d. Oct. 22, 1938, Bankston.

James Hugh Willingham married second - Nov. 1, 1896, Mary Lela South, b. April 11, 1874, Davis Creek, Fayette Co., Ala., d. Aug. 17, 1943, Bankston, Ala. - dau. of Levi Woodruff South. Children: (2nd. marriage) 1. Lillian Beatrice Willingham, b. Nov. 11, 1901, Bankston, Ala., m. 1st. - July 2, 1920, William Harris Hay, b. 1899, Jasper, Ala., d. Mar. 20, 1959, Jasper, Ala., 2nd. - James Taylor Hurst, b. June 13, 1880, Morton, Miss.

WILLINGHAM, John - son of William & Nancy Willingham, m. Nancy __, b. 1788, N.C. Children: 1. Arabella Willingham, m. 1831, John Caraway. 2. Mary Willingham, m. 1828, Calvin Poe. 3. Roann Willingham, m. Dec. 3, 1838, George A. Robertson. 4. Eliza T. Willingham, m. 1839, John J. Richards. 5. Susan F. Willingham, m. Nov. 20, 1848, Columbus W. Slaughter. 6. Elizabeth Willingham, m. Daniel Cook. 7. Bradford Willingham, m. Dec. 14, 1838, Lucy Poe. 8. Nancy Willingham, m. 1836, Robert Freeman.

WILLINGHAM, John Thomas, b. Aug. 9, 1855, d. Feb. 12, 1910, Bankston, Ala. - son of Thomas Lyon Willingham - m. M. F. "Queen" Johns, b. Feb. 6, 1860, d. Aug. 13, 1946, Bankston, Ala. - dau. of B. Johns. Children: 1. Susie Willingham, b. Oct. 11, 1882, d. 1952, Bankston, m. T. A. Echols. 2. Thomas Albert "Burt" Willingham, m. Maude Thompson. 3. Annie Willingham, m. Earl Clifford White. 4. William Rufus Willingham, buried in Dallas, Texas, m. 1st. - Mary Hay. 5. Banks Willingham, b. Nov. 3, 1894, d. Mar. 14, 1913, Bankston. 6. May Willingham, m. J. Quince Bailey, buried Birmingham, Ala. 7. Earl Willingham, b. Aug. 2, 1887, d. Mar. 2, 1913, Bankston. 8. Harry Lee Willingham, m. 1st. - Daisy Rice. 9. Gus Willingham, b. Aug. 23, 1901, d. Feb. 26, 1922, Bankston, Ala.

WILLINGHAM, Reubin, b. Mar. 14, 1793, m. Martha Willingham, b. Sept. 10, 1794 - dau. of William Willingham. Children: 1. Louisa Willingham, b. Apr. 28, 1815. 2. Caleb B. Willingham, b. Sept. 13, 1816, Ga. 3. Nancy B. Willingham, b. April 27, 1823, d. May 16, 1900, Fayette Co., m. Richard Davis, b. Oct. 14, 1812, d. June 19, 1874, Fayette Co.

WILLINGHAM, Thomas - son of John Willingham, m. Elizabeth__. John Willingham, Jr., Thomas Willingham and Edward Willingham were brothers. John Willingham must have come to the United States in the mid or latter 1600's. From 1704 onward are recorded three young Willingham "brothers" all living together in Prince George County, Va. They owned about 400 acres of land. These are thought to be the only Willinghams in America at that time. Children: 1. Issac Willingham, b. Bristol Parrish, Va., m. Sarah __.

WILLINGHAM, Thomas, - son of William Willingham - m. 1807, wife unknown. Children: 1. A Daughter, m. Willis Davis. 2. Elihu Willingham, b. Mar. 12, 1814, d. Jan. 19, 1877, Fayette Co., m. Elizabeth W. _, b. Aug. 23, 1814, d. June 5, 1905. 3. Eli Willingham. 4. William Willingham.

WILLINGHAM, Thomas Lyon, b. April 23, 1807, Ga., d. Nov. 8, 1888, Fayette Co., Ala. - son of Beverly Willingham - m. Susan Ann Strong, b. July 31, 1817 Ga., d. Aug. 20, 1900, Fayette Co. - dau. of William M. Strong. Children:

1. William Rufus Willingham, b. May 30, 1835, Tusca. Co., Ala., d. Feb. 16, 1886, Fayette Co., m. Oct. 25, 1870, Angelyn Jackson, b. Oct. 25, 1870, Berry, Ala., d. Fayette Co. William R. Willingham - A muster roll dated at Camp Holt, 12, June 1862, for Co. I. 38th Ala. Inf. Regt. shows this man as 5th Sgt. Was a prisoner at Selma, Ala. and wrote his mother April 23, 1865, apparently staying in the home of a Mrs. M. (W?) T. Hill. 2. George Beverly Willingham, buried in Frankston, Texas, m. Margaret ___. 3. E. Anderson Willingham, b. 1839, buried Foreman, Ark., m. Frances ___. 4. Benjamin Marshall Willingham, b. 1845, d. during Civil War in Service. 5. James Hugh Willingham, b. Sept. 16, 1841, Fayette Co., d. Oct. 30, 1917, Bankston, m. Oct. 5, 1873, 1st. - Lucy Ann York, b. Sept. 15, 1855, Fayette Co., d. May 1, 1894, Bankston, Ala., m. 2nd. - Nov. 1, 1896, Mary Lela South, b. April 11, 1874, Davis Creek, Ala., d. Aug. 17, 1943, Bankston, Ala. 6. Susan Temperance Willingham, b. Mar. 20, 1853, d. Nov. 25, 1883, Fayette Co., m. John Thomas Hyde, b. Oct. 28, 1846, d. May 6, 1936, Fayette Co. 7. Mary Willingham, d. in infancy. 8. Sarah Frances Willingham, b. Jan. 2, 1848, d. Dec. 6, Fayette Ala., m. James H. Hyde, b. Feb. 24, 1843, d. Jan. 10, 1923, Fayette, Ala. 9. John Thomas Willingham, b. Aug. 9, 1855, d. Feb. 12, 1910, Bankston, m. M. F. "Queen" Johns, b. Feb. 6, 1860, d. Aug. 13, 1946, Bankston. 10. Bulah Ellen Willingham, b. Aug. 14, 1861, Bankston, d. Nov. 17, 1897, Fayette Co.

WILLINGHAM, William, b. 1740, St. Johns Parrish, Berkley Co., S.C., d. Will dated Oct. 25, 1797, Columbia Co., Ga. - son of Isaac Willingham - m. Nancy-. William Willingham, age 35, b. S. C., dated July 6, 1775. In Capt. Woodword's Co., Col. Thompson's Regt. - 1775 - 1778, S.C. Children: 1. Elijah Willingham. 2. Thomas Willingham, m. 1807, Absolom or Judah Trantham of Oglethorpe Co., Ga. 3. Frances Willingham, m. Mr. Roberts. 4. Elizabeth Willingham, m. Mr. Davis. 5. Beverly Willingham, b. 1785, Ga., d. Will dated 1856, m. Abigail ___. 6. George Willingham. 7. John Willingham, b. 1788, N.C., m. Nancy. 8. William Willingham, m. Ann Samuel. 9 Nancey Willingham, b. 1788, N.C. 10. Caleb Willingham, m. between 1808 - 1810, Ga. - Elizabeth Glass. 11. Palcy Willingham. 12. Judea Willingham, m. ___Gaither. 13. Isaac Willingham, b. 1800, m. Rebecca (or Laura or Maude.) 14. Martha Willingham, b. Sept. 10, 1794, d. Nov. 2, 1849, m. 1st. - Reubin Willingham, b. Mar. 14, 1793, 2nd. - June 29, 1852, Troy Griffin, b. July 8, 1801.

WILLINGHAM, William Rufus, b. May 30, 1835, New Lexington, Ala., d. Feb. 16, 1886, Fayette Co. - son of Thomas Lyon Willingham - m. Angelyn Jackson, b. 1852, d. 1933, Fayette Co. - dau. of Jess Jackson. William Rufus Willingham - Confederate Soldier - a muster roll dated at Camp Holt, June 12, 1862, for Co. F. 38th Ala., Inf. Regt. shows him as 5th Sgt. He enlisted in Fayette Co. June 12, 1862 and was 29 yrs. old. Both are buried at the Pleasant Hill Cemetery, near Berry, Ala. Children: 1. Ella Willingham, m. 1st. - Mr. Lambert, 2nd. - Mr. Collins. 2. Walter L. Willingham, b. Aug. 9, 1871, d. April 29, 1911, Fayette Co. 3. Thomas Willingham.

WILSON, Mitt, m. Oct. 29, 1921, Edwyna Freeman, b. May 18, 1904, d. Nov. 10, 1941 - dau of Wm. L. & Mary Ella (Lindsey) Freeman. Children: 1. Jewel Dean Wilson, b. Oct. 11, 1922, m. ___ Lowe. (Child: James Maxwell Lowe, b. Apr. 27, 1943.) 2. Pauline Wilson, b. Sept. 22, 1924, m. L. C. Patrick. (Children: Carl and Donald Patrick.) 3. Opal Wilson, b. Nov. 30, 1926, m. Jack Nelson. (Children: Dennis and Virginia Nelson.) 4. Freeman Wilson, b. Feb. 22, 1937.

WINN, Walker, m. Jerusha Frances. Children: 1. Gertrude Winn. 2. Velma Winn. 3. Annie Winn, m. Arch Gibson. 4. Earl Winn. 5. Minnie Winn, b. Sept. 7, 1872, d. Sept. 7, 1872.

WISE, Albert Lamar, b. Jan. 27, 1927, Tenn. - adopted son of Mrs. Lou Annie (Cardin) Wise Bobo - m. Dec. 29, 1945, Mary Louise Bobo, b. Dec. 17, 1928, Fayette Co. - dau. of F. M. & Eula (South) Bobo. Albert served in the U. S. Navy during World War II. Children: 1. Barbara Ann Wise, b. April 6, 1947, Fayette Co. 2. Albert Lamar Wise, Jr., b. Jan. 2, 1949, Fayette Co. 3. Bobby Wise, b. May 3, 1951, Bessemer, Ala. 4. Peggy Wise, b. June 5, 1953, Bessemer, Ala. 5. Billie Jo Wise, b. Dec. 29, 1954, Bessemer, Ala. 6. Infant, b. & d. Mar. 24, 1958, Bessemer, Ala. 7. Infant Theresa Wise, b. & d. June 21, 1959, Pensacola, Fla.

WOMMACK, William, b. April 12, 1781, d. Mar. 11, 1860, m. Edith Stewart, b. 1798, Cumberland Co., N. C. Children: 1. Anna R. Wommack, b. Oct. 23, 1823, Tusca. Co., Ala., d. 1862. 2. Rebecca Utley Wommack, b. Sept. 26, 1825, Tusca. Co., d. Jan. 1888. 3. Manervia Wommack, b. 1827, Tusca. Co. 4. William John Wommack, b. Mar. 1835, Tusca. d. Sept. 1864. 5. George S. Wommack, b. 1838, Tusca. Co., m. May 26, 1867, Aurilla Rice, b. Sept. 12, 1848. 6. Sarah Helen Wommack, b. 1839, Tusca. Co., Ala. 7. Elizabeth Jane Sophia Wommack, b. Aug. 14, 1841, Tusca. Co., d. Oct. 13, 1860.

WOOD, Edward Thomas, b. July 20, 1817, Walker Co., Ala., d. April 29, 1884 or 1887 - son of John Wood - m. Minerva Woods, dau. of Samuel & Lucy Woods. Children: 1. Charity Elizabeth Wood, b. Dec. 31, 1839, d. Mar. 9, 1890, Walker Co., m. John Key, b. Mar. 13, 1836, Walker Co., d. May 29, 1900, Walker Co., Ala. 2. Lon Wood, m. Whitly Courington. 3. Curle Wood. 4. Prudy Wood, m. James Davis. 5. Commodore Wood, m. Zellie Nelson. 6. Edward Wood. 7. C. A. "Dock" Wood, m. 1st. - Dau. of Thos. Key, 2nd. - Emily Sides, dau. of Wm. Sides. 8. Irene Wood, m. William Odom. 9. Phoebe Wood, m. Sherman Cranford.

WOOD, John, m. wife unknown. Children: 1. Edward Thomas Wood, b. July 20, 1817, Walker Co., d. April 29, 1884, Walker Co., Ala., m. Minerva Woods. 2. James Wood, m. Allie Woods, sister of Minerva's.

WOODS, James David, b. July 8, 1925, d. Oct. 12, 1957, Vernon, Ala. - son of Wilmot & Hassie (Ballinger) Woods.- m. 1950, Theresa Ray Reaves, b. Lamar Co. Ala. James David Woods was a teacher in the Lamar County Schools at the time of his death. Children: 1. David Ray Woods, b. Dec. 24, 1950, Fayette Co., Ala. (James David Woods was born Fayette Co., Ala.)

WOODS, Oscar, b. Fayette Co., Ala. - son of Clinton & Alice (Bobo) Woods - m. Eula Fowler. Children: 1. Opal Woods, 2. Avie Woods. 3. Bernice Woods. 4. Martha Dean Woods. 5. Jerry Woods.

WOODS, Samuel, b. 1794, N. C., m. Lucy ___, b. 1795, Ga. Children: 1. Minerva Woods, m. Edward Thomas Wood, b. July 20, 1817, Walker Co., Ala., d. April 29, 1884, Walker Co., Ala. 2. Lucy Allen Woods, m. John Martin Key. 3. Nancy Woods, m. William Courington. 4. David Woods, m. Betty Staggs. 5. John Hop Woods, m. Lucinda Wilson. 6. Allie Woods, m. James Wood, brother to Edward Thomas Wood.

WOODS, William Clinton, b. 1872, Fayette Co., Ala., d. June 1935, Ark., m. July 26, 1891, Alice Bobo, b. 1875, Fayette Co., d. April 19, 1918, Ark. - dau. of Miles & Lucy A. (Allen) Bobo. They moved to Arkansas in later life and died there. Children: (All born in Fayette Co., Ala.) 1. Wilmot Woods, m. Hassie Ballinger. 2. Oscar Woods, m. Eula Fowler, 3. Sally Lee Woods, m. Virgil Wright. 4. Leevie Woods, b. abt. 1900, d. abt. 1901. 5. Kelso Woods, m. Ruby Stewart. 6. Clifton Woods, m. Cecilla Stewart. 7. Lilly Bee Woods, m. George Barnett. 8. Esther Woods, m. Wilmot Parr. 9. Etta Woods, m. Ira Foster. 10. Garland Woods, m. Lou__. 11. Joseph Woods, m. Mary __.

WOODS, Wilmot, b. Feb. 27, 1892, Fayette Co. - son of W. Clinton & Alice (Bobo) Woods - m. Dec. 30, 1920, Hassie Ballinger, b. Mar. 19, 1893, Fayette Co., - dau. of D. J. & Della (Bobo) Ballinger. Children: 1. William Carey Woods, b. Oct. 16, 1921, Fayette Co., m. Wanda Carol Smith. 2. Ruby Lee Woods, b. April 30, 1923, Fayette Co., m. Aubrey I. Shaw. 3. James David Woods, b. July 8, 1925, Fayette, Ala., d. Oct. 12, 1951, Vernon, Ala., m. 1950, Theresa Ray Reaves. 4. Alice Adelle Woods, b. Sept. 7, 1928, Fayette Co., m. James H. Shirley, b. Fayette Co. 5. Jasper Nell Woods, b. Sept. 22, 1931, Fayette Co., m. Aubrey Oliver "Duke" Howell. 6. Audie Bell Woods, b. Jan. 23, 1934, Fayette Co., m. June 1954, John William Godfrey, Jr.

WOOTTEN, Lt. Thomas, b. 1730, d. 1791, m. Sarah Rabun. Lt. Thomas Wooten was Lt. of Militia of Wilkes Co., Ga. under Col. Elijah Clark. He was granted 200 acres of land for his services. He and his wife came from Bertie Co. N.C. with seven sons and a daughter, ages 1 to 18 years and they brought 8 slaves to Wilkes Co., Ga. with them. Children: 1. Richard B. Wootten, b. 1760, d. 1798, m. Lucretia Cade. 2. Faitha Wootten, b. May 8, 1767, d. Oct. 2, 1807, m. Mar. 1784, Asa Alexander. 3. Pheriba Wootten, m. Cullen Alford. 4. Mary Wootten, m. James Cade. 5. Thomas Wootten, Jr., b. 1778, d. 1848, m. Millie Smith. 6. Lemeul Wootten, m. Nancy Smith. 7. James B. Wootten, b. 1785, d. 1822, m. Pollie Smith. 8. Daniel Wootten. 9. Robert Wootten. 10. John Wootten.

WORTHINGTON, John, d. abt. 1827, Newberry, S.C. - Will signed Aug. 15, 1825, Proved Mar. 17, 1827, Newberry, S.C., m. Elizabeth "Betsy" Davis. Children: 1. Polly Worthington, m. Mr. Hunter. 2. Margaret Worthington, m. Mr. Spearman. 3. Betsy Worthington, m. Mr. Chapman. 4. Sarah Worthington. 5. Fanny Worthington, m. Isaac Herbert. 6. Thomas Worthington, m. Tabitha Summers. 7. Chesley Worthington. 8. John Worthington. 9. Samuel Worthington. 10. Rhoda Worthingtin, m. Mr. Spearman. 11. Reubin Worthington.

WORTHINGTON, Robert, d. before Nov. 1, 1735, Orange Co., Va. Will signed Oct. 2, 1735. Proved Nov. 1, 1735, Orange Co., Va., m. Mary __. Children: 1. Jacob Worthington. 2. Martha Worthington. 3. Mary Worthington. 4. Samuel Worthington, d. Abbeville, S.C. 5. Esther Worthington. 6. Robert Worthington.

WORTHINGTON, Samuel, d. aft. April 20, 1781, Abbeville, S.C. Will signed April 20, 1781, Abbeville, S. C. - son of Robert Worthington, - m. wife unknown. Children: 1. Mary Worthington. 2. Martha Worthington. 3. Robert Worthington. 4. John Worthington, m. Elizabeth Davis. 5. Rachel Worthington. 6. Sarah Worthington. 7. Elijah Worthington.

WORTHINGTON, Thomas, d. abt. Nov. 1829, Newberry, S. C. - son of John & Betsy (Davis) Worthington - m. Tabitha Summers, d. Newberry, S. C., dau. of Wm. & Susannah Summers, Sr. Isaac Herbert applied as administrator of Estate on Nov. 21, 1829. Isaac Herbert became guardian for the following children of Thomas. Children: 1. John R. Worthington. 2. Amelia A. "Emily" Worthington, b. April 2, 1821, Abbeville Co., S. C., d. June 10, 1890, m. Jeremiah McCartha, b. Jan. 2, 1814, Lexington Co., S. C., d. Nov. 18, 1885. 3. Marcus Worthington. 4. Harriett B. Worthington, d. 1838.

WRIGHT, Andrew Jackson "Drew", b. May 23, 1862, Pea Ridge, Fayette Co., Ala., d. Aug. 14, 1920, buried Fayette, Ala. - son of James & Nancy (Kimbrell) Wright - m. Sept. 26, 1886, Savannah Rosaline Hamner, b. Wolf Creek, Ala., d. May 15, 1947, buried at Fayette, - dau. of Clemial Anders & Jane Elizabeth Hamner. A. J. Wright's father was killed in Malvern, Va. during the Civil War, leaving his mother a widow a few weeks before A. J. was born. His father, James Wright was a Fife player and a Cannon took his life. A. J. Wright and Savannah Rosaline Hamner were married at the home of her parents by the Rev. J. P. Harbin. Mr. "Drew" taught school and farmed until he received an appointment as Post Master at Corona, in Walker Co. He also operated a grocery business there. He bought the Morton Farm consisting of between three and four hundred acres of land, north of Fayette and moved his family there in 1907. He also, owned another farm, several houses, was once the owner of the Telephone Co. and he and Dr. Blackburn opened the first automobile agency in Fayette, selling Buicks and Fords. He also operated saw mills and gins over the county. He always said that Fayette would grow north of the town, and one of the last things he did before his death was to go to Montgomery, Ala. and give about a mile of valuable land through this property for highway right-of-way. The Fayette Air-port and the Drive-In Theatre are now on part of the original Wright property. The family was Methodist and he was at one time on the State Republican Executive Committee. Children: 1. Infant Wright. 2. Moody Wright, b. Mar. 4, 1900, d. Sept. 10, 1924 - killed in Auto wreck in Ellsworth, Kansas. 3. Belva Wright, d. Elinor Calif., m. Ervin Randall. 4. James Delmar Wright, m. Irene White. 5. C. Andrew Wright, m. 1931, Marie Smith. Owns hardware business in Birmingham, Ala. 6. Wilmer Wright, m. 1st. - Miley Baskett, 2nd. - Lynn H. Vann. (Children: Mrs. Elizabeth Baskett Johnson and Mrs. Claude Vines.) 7. Ruth Wright, m. Johnnie W. Hester. (Child: Mrs. Herbert Rufus Manning, Jr.) 8. Pauline Wright, m. Ora L. Hood. (Child: Mrs. Charles H. Ellis.) 9. Katherine Wright, m. James C. Guyton. (Children: James Clement and Moody Guyton.)

WRIGHT, Buren Millard, b. Sept. 18, 1894, Walker Co., Ala. - son of L. W. & Roxy Wright - m. Mar. 24, 1918, Bessie Key, b. May 6, 1900, Townley, Ala. - dau. of Robert P. & Mary Ann (Rutledge) Key. They were married at Townley, Ala. by Rev. Turner. B. M. Wright has been affiliated with the Insurance business since the 1930's and came to Fayette in 1937 with the Short Insurance Co. He is presently working with the Jasper office of the Union Life Insurance Co. (originally the Short Co.) He served in the U. S. Army in World War I. Children: 1. Mary Louise Wright, b. Aug. 19, 1921, Corona, Walker Co., m. Dec. 22, 1939, Victor S. Patterson, Jr., b. April 20, 1920, Fayette Co., Ala. 2. Bobbie Lee Wright, b. Feb. 3, 1929, Parrish, Walker Co. Ala., m. Nov. 3, 1946, Billy Joe Shelton, b. Aug. 21, 1922, Fayette Co., Ala.

WRIGHT, Charles Tulion, b. Dec. 24, 1929, m. July 22, 1950, Gladys Ruth Humber, b. Mar. 6, 1933, Tishimingo Co., Miss. - dau. of Charles Claude Humber. Children: 1. Donnie Hal Wright, b. April 26, 1951. 2. Mark Anthony Wright, b. June 2, 1958.

WRIGHT, Jessie Willard, b. Aug. 25, 1916, Fayette, Ala. - son of James Wm. & Maude (Sanford) Wright - m. Mar. 4, 1937, Mary Julia Dunavat, b. Dec. 16, 1921, Fayette, Ala. - dau. of Sidney & Sara Frances (Foster) Dunavant. Jessie Willard Wright's grandparents - Roof & Ima (Sterling) Sanford. Mary Julia Dunavat Wright's grandparents - Andrew & Julia (Howton) Dunavat; and Franklin Marion & Mary Frances (Williams) Foster. Great grandparents - Samuel & Mary Lizzie Beth (Dyer) Dunavant; Math or Matt & Miranda Jane (Nichols) Howton; Riley Foster; and Lewis Williams. Jessie W. Wright's Children: 1. Desiree Wright, b. Dec. 9, 1937, Fayette, Ala.

WRIGHT, John Leonard or Lanier, b. Oct. 4, 1841, Holley Grove, Walker Co., Ala., d. Aug. 3, 1924, Walker Co., Ala. - son of Smiley Wright - m. Mary Jane Noles, b. Jan. 9, 1847, d. Aug. 27, 1880, Walker Co., Ala. - dau. of Wm. Samuel Noles. During the Civil War, John L. Wright served as Sgt. in Co. G. 56 Ala. Cavalry. Both are buried at the Pleasant Hill Cemetery, Walker Co. Ala. Children: 1. Londus Washington Wright, b. July 7, 1870, Walker Co., d. Aug. 29, 1944, Walker Co., m. Roxy Swindle, b. Nov. 3, 1877, Walker Co. 2. Martha Jane Wright, m. Henry Townley. 3. Adolphus Wright, m. Menta Kuton. J. L. Wright married second - Mattie Fikes. Children (2nd. marriage) 1. Carmie Wright, m. Mattie McCluskey. 2. Hillary Wright, m. Celia Brown. 3. Elbert Wright, m. Velta Romine. 4. Ethel Wright, m. Pete McCluskey.

WRIGHT, Londus Washington, b. July 7, 1870, Walker Co., Ala., d. Aug. 29, 1944, Walker Co. - son of John L. & Mary Jane (Noles) Wright - m. Roxy Swindle, b. Nov. 3, 1877, Walker Co., Ala. - dau. of Reuben M. & S. J. Swindle. They were married in Walker Co. and he was a life-time farmer. He is buried at the Pleasant Hill Cem. in Walker Co., Ala. Children: 1. Buran Millard Wright, b. Sept. 18, 1894, (All born Walker Co.), m. Mar. 29, 1918, Bessie Key, b. May 6, 1900, Walker Co. 2. Floyd Wright, b. April 3, 1897, m. Mary Anderson. 3. Verda Wright, b. Mar. 15, 1902, m. Mac Montgomery. 4. Alice Wright, b. Mar. 7, 1900, d. Nov. 8, 1955, buried Jasper, Ala., m. Elias Bell, d. May 30, 1949, buried Jasper, Ala. 5. Lynn Wright, b. Dec. 1904, m. 1st. - Vera Lathan, 2nd. - Addie _. 6. Estell Wright, b. Aug. 18, 1911, m. John Bergen. 7. Bamber Wright, b. Oct. 5, 1908, m. 1st. - Zola Morgan, 2nd. - Mary Alice Waite. 8. Clara Wright, b. April 14, 1906, m. Davis Thrasher. 9. Katie Wright, b. Aug. 5, 1913, m. Gene Sides. 10. James E. Wright, b. April 16, 1918, m. Charlye Shaw. 11. L. W. "Larry" Wright, Jr., m. Clara Crump.

WRIGHT, Simon Tankersley, Jr., - son of S. T., Sr. & Alice L. (McConnell) Wright - m. Sara Kate Branyon, b. Jan. 13, 1926. Children: 1. Susan Wright, b. May 1, 1949, Fayette, Ala. 2. Simon T. Wright, III, b. May 1, 1953, Fayette, Ala.

WRIGHT, Simon Tankersley, b. June 29, 1874, d. July 11, 1952, Fayette, Ala. m. Alice Lucretie "Brownie" McConnell, b. Jan. 9, 1899, Fayette Co., Ala. - dau. of D. O. & Alice (Smith) McConnell. Children: 1. Simon Tankersley Wright, Jr., m. Sara Kate Branyon, b. Jan. 13, 1926, Fayette, Ala. 2. Sarah Alice Wright, b. 1926, m. Sept. 1946, Earl Beck, Jr. (Children: Rolla Earl,

III; Sarah Wright Beck; and Murray McConnell Beck.)

WRIGHT, Smiley, m. Talitha Birdwell, b. June 18, 1821, d. Aug. 1, 1905 - dau. of John & Mary (Allen) Birdwell. Children: 1. Mary Wright, b. 1840, Ala. 2. John Leonard or Lanier Wright, b. Oct. 4, 1841, Walker Co., Ala., d. Aug. 3, 1924, Walker Co., m. Mary Jane Noles, b. Jan. 9, 1847, d. Aug. 27, 1880, Walker Co. 3. Mant Wright, m. Marion Manasco. 4. Caroline Wright, b. Sept. 3, 1847, d. Mar. 28, 1918, m. John Fike, b. Aug. 5, 1849, d. July 14, 1917.

WYCOFF, Samuel W., b. May 4, 1863, Guernsey Co., Ohio, d. June 1, 1948, Belk, Ala. - son of Samuel & Nancy Wycoff - m. Martha Ellen Griffin, b. Nov. 12, 1866, Pirce City, Mo., d. April 8, 1948, Belk, Ala. - dau. of Martin & Sarah Griffin. The Wycoff family migrated from Ohio to Illinois when Samuel W. Wycoff was about six years of age, where he grew up in and around Jefferson Co., Ill. The Griffin family migrated from Missouri to Jefferson Co., Ill, when Martha Ellen Griffin was very small. Samuel and Martha Ellen migrated from Illinois to Fayette, Ala. in February 1898, moving to the old George Coggin house in Old Town, said to be the first house built in Fayette. Samuel and Martha E. Wycoff were members of the Primitive Baptist Church at Harmony, near Belk, Ala. In the earlier days they were members of Hopewell Church, north of Fayette. He was for many years, a member of the local school board. .. Originally the name was spelled Wijkhof. The founder of the family came to New Amsterdam, now New York City, from Amsterdam Holland about 1731 at the age of 12 years as a cabin boy on a ship. Later he became a farm superintendent for the Dutch Governor, living and working where the Bowery section of New York now is. After some time he became a local judge, probably about the same as what is known as a justice of the peace. In the Dutch dialect, he was known as "Wijk Hof" or Village Judge. When the British took over it was required that each family take a family name. He took the name he was usually referred to, "Wijkhof", his given names being Pieter Clausen. One of his grandsons moved to Chester, Pa., near Philadelphia, then one of the sons of this grandson migrated west, to eastern Ohio where the grandfather of Samuel W. Wycoff, Elijah Wycoff was born.
    Children: (Samuel & Martha Ellen's) 1. Nora Ellen Wycoff, b. 1884, Ill. m. Lee Wallace of Belk, Ala. 2. Delia Wycoff, b. June 1886, Ill., m. George Washington Moore, of Belk, Ala. 3. Fred L. Wycoff, b. Sept. 6, 1892, Ill., m. Lola Pollard, presently lives in Anniston, Ala. 4. John W. Wycoff, b. 1894, Ill, b. 1949, Birmingham, Ala., m. Martha Pittman. 5. Grace Wycoff, b. Dec. 5, 1896, m. Arlie Taylor of Winfield, Ala. 6. Thomas Wycoff, b. May 1899, Fayette Co., Ala., m. Altha Guin. 7. Jesse Lee Wycoff, b. May 1902, Fayette Co., Ala., m. Elizabeth Burton. 8. Frank E. Wycoff, b. May 1907, Fayette Co., Ala., m. 1st. - Daisy ___., 2nd. - Frances ___.

YARBROUGH, Ambrose, b. 1710, Yorkshire, England, d. 1789, Union Co., S.C., m. Mary Mason, b. Va. Ambrose Yarbrough and his friend Francis Spencer Bobo came from England together, and settled in Amelia Co., Va. They married cousins (Masons) and migrated south to Union County, S. C. and settled on the Tyger River near each other. The Yarbroughs lived in England from 854 to coronation of George VI. Lord Abingham was seated as head of the family at the coronation. His seat at the coronation was No. 9, so there are only eight titles older than the Yarbrough. Children: 1. Ann or Annie Yarbrough, m. Mr. Pinnell. 2. Jeremiah Yarbrough, m. Temp Richards. 3. Humphrey Yarbrough, m. Mary Blackstock. 4. Mary Yarbrough, m. Stephen Blackstock. 5.

John Yarbrough.

YARBROUGH, Ambrose, b. Oct. 4, 1800, S. C., d. Aug. 17, 1870, Fayette Co., m. Lucinda Bobo, b. Aug. 20, 1802, S. C. He was a blacksmith. Children: 1. Rebekah Yarbrough, b. 1831, S. C. 2. Buley Yarbrough, b. 1834, S. C. 3. DeCalb Yarbrough, b. 1834, S.C. 4. Sarah A. Yarbrough, b. 1840, S. C. 5. Victory Yarbrough, b. 1843, S. C. 6. John T. Yarbrough, b. 1844, S. C.

YARBROUGH, Humphrey, b. Va. or S.C. - son of Ambrose (immigrant from England) & Mary (Mason) Yarbrough - m. Mary Blackstock, b. possibly, S.C. Several of their children settled in Fayette County, Ala. Children: 1. Ambrose Yarbrough, b. Oct. 4, 1800, S.C., d. Aug. 17, 1870, Fayette Co., m. Loucinda Bobo, b. Aug. 20, 1802, S.C. 2. Willis Yarbrough, b. 1817, S. C., m. Sallie Harrison, b. 1817, S.C. 3. Stephen Yarbrough, b. 1808, S. C., m. Susan Layton, b. June 11, 1811, S. C., d. Mar. 7, 1901, Fayette Co., Ala. 4. Hiram Yarbrough, m. Sallie Bobo. 5. John Yarbrough, m. Sallie Miles. 6. Lewis Yarbrough. 7. Sara Frances Yarbrough, m. Edd Bobo. 8. Nancy Yarbrough, b. Nov. 6, 1805, S. C., d. Feb. 7, 1884, Fayette Co., Ala., m. Lewis Bobo, b. Nov. 8, 1804, S. C., d. Jan. 8, 1892, Fayette Co., Ala.

YARBROUGH, Stephen, b. 1808, S. C. - son of Humphrey & Mary (Blackstock) Yarbrough - m. Susan Layton, b. June 11, 1811, S. C., d. Mar. 7, 1901, - dau. of James & Mary (Williamson) Layton. They came to Fayette County as some of the early settlers. Children: 1. Sara Yarbrough, b. 1834, m. Humphries Young. 2. Martha Ann Yarbrough, b. May 21, 1831, S. C., d. Mar. 27, 1911, m. 1st. - Wm. Givan, d. at war, 2nd. - Sarepta Smith, b. Mar. 28, 1841, Ga. d. Nov. 10, 1923, Fayette Co. 3. Turntine "Bud" Yarbrough, b. 1833, m. Caroline Smith. 4. Jeremiah Yarbrough, b. 1836, m. Elizabeth Bobo. 5. Julia Ann Yarbrough, b. 1838, d. Nov. 12, 1904, m. 1st. - Ben Collins, d. in war, 2nd. - William Newman, b. Aug. 31, 1831, d. July 15, 1906. 6. William Yarbrough, b. 1840, d. at war. 7. James P. Yarbrough, b. 1842, d. at war. 8. Nancy Yarbrough, b. 1843, m. Silas Waldrop. 9. Stephen Yarbrough, Jr., b. June 5, 1845, d. Aug. 2, 1912, m. Victoria Bobo, b. Jan. 1, 1841, d. June 31, 1912. 10. Hiram Yarbrough, b. 1849, m. Martha Ann Dennis. 11. Mary Yarbrough, m. Oat Huggins.

YERBY, Amon, b. 1789, (1784) N. C., d. July 1861, near Millport, Ala., m. Rachael __, b. 1798 (1804, N.C.) They came to Alabama from N. C. about 1820. Children: 1. Jemimah Yerby, m. Elijah Holliman. (Had two dau., Frances and another who lived out west and a son, Bud Holliman, who lived in Ala.) 2. Tabitha Octavie Yerby, m. 1st. - Walker Albritton, 2nd. - Daniel G. Kirkland. (Had several children, one son named John lived and died in Fayette Co., Ala.) 3. Sarah Yerby, m. Edward L. Younghance. 4. Mary Virginia Yerby, m. H. Russell Jones. 5. Lucy Yerby, b. 1832, Ala., m. Stephen A. Rogers. (Had - Leroy; Louis; and Baby daughter Rogers.) 6. Martha Yerby, b. 1834, Ala., m. A. J. "Jack" Jones. (Had - Frank; Leander; Geneva and an Infant child when they left for Texas.) 7. John R. Yerby, m. Mattie Van Hoose. 8. A. F. "Alexander" Yerby, served in war, later lived in Ala. and Miss. A. F. was b. 1843,?, Ala. 9. Jasper N. Yerby, b. 1830, Ala., died in Was in 1865, m. Dec. 26, 1851, Rutha Harkins. 10. William J. Yerby, was a war prisoner, d. in War in 1865, m. Mariah Rice. (Had three children: Tolbert; Lizzie; and Louisa Yerby.) 11. James Franklin Yerby, b. 1819, N. C., d. 1899, m. Sarah Ann Dodson, d. 1889.

YERBY, Francis M., b. July 13, 1829, Fayette Co., d. Aug. 10, 1887, Fayette Co. - son of Hogan Yerby - m. Feb. 15, 1850, Lydia Ann Walden, b. Jan. 11, 1833, Fayette Co., d. Jan. 7, 1891, Fayette Co., - dau. of John Walden. Francis M. Yerby was a farmer. Both are buried at Pilgrim's Rest Cemetery in Fayette Co., Ala. Children: (All born Fayette Co.) 1. Martha Jane Yerby, b. Mar. 7, 1851, d. Sept. 4, 1934, Fayette, Ala., m. Nov. 7, 1876, Pickney Monroe Walker, c. Aug. 12, 1848, Fayette Co., d. Jan. 2, 1918, Fayette, Ala. 2. Adda Yerby, m. Nov. 7, 1876? J. Henry Davis. 3. Hallie Yerby, m. Feb. 5, 1878, Huey F. Gilbreath. 4. Nora E. Yerby, d. buried Birmingham, Ala., m. Feb. 21, 1883, Willis N. Caraway. 5. Monica Yerby, m. Mar. 30, 1882, 1st. - **George** Richardson, 2nd. - Frank Wilson. (Both are buried at Pilgrim's Rest Cem.) 6. J. Newton "Bud" Yerby, m. Feb. 13, 1879, M. Etta Shepherd. 7. Minnie Yerby, m. Dec. 24, 1890, R. B. Turner. 8. Ressie Yerby, m. Feb. 1, 1898, D. Will Stokes. 9. Reppie Yerby, m. Dec. 16, 1896, Fent C. Guin. 10. Elizabeth Yerby, m. April 20, 18__, T. W. Hamner.

YERBY, Hogan, b. Jan. 18, 1803, N. C., d. Nov. 14, 1895, Fayette Co., m. Sarah "Sallie" George. Children: 1. Francis M. Yerby, b. July 13, 1829, Fayette Co., Ala., d. Aug. 10, 1887, Fayette Co., m. Feb. 15, 1850, Lydia Ann Walden, b. Jan. 11, 1833, Fayette Co., d. Jan. 7, 1891, Fayette Co. 2. John T. Yerby, m. Adeline Lindsey. 3. Everette Yerby, murdered 1867, m. 1867, Amjemariah Shepherd. 4. Luallen Yerby, killed in War, m. Sarah Dodson. 5. Issac S. Yerby, m. Dec. 18, 1873, Mahala Walden. 6. W. Inge Yerby, m. Fannie Caraway. 7. James C. Yerby, m. Feb. 1, 1871, Margie Bell. 8. J. Newton Yerby, died in war. 9. Margarette Yerby, m. Dec. 31, 1882, Frank M. Laboon. 10. Sarepta Yerby, m. Tom Ray.

YERBY, Issac "Ike", b. Fayette Co., Ala. - son of Hogan Yerby - m. Dec. 18, 1873, Mahala Walden, b. Fayette Co., Ala. They were married at the Walden home by Minister J. E. Bell. Children: 1. Sallie Yerby, m. Dec. 24, 1890, 1st. - R. B. Conner, 2nd. - Clinton White.

YERBY, James C., b. May 18, 1839, Fayette Co., Ala., d. Nov. 25, 1912 - son of Hogan Yerby - m. Feb. 1, 1871, Margie Z. Bell, b. Aug. 15, 1851, Northport, Ala., d. Mar. 31, 1908 - dau. of A. F. Bell. James C. Yerby was a Confederate Volunteer in Co., A. 26th. Ala. Inf. They were married at the home of A. F. Bell by Minister J. O. Jones. Margie Z. Bell came to Fayette County with her parents, A. F. & Elizabeth Bell, in 1853. Children: 1. Posie L. Yerby, m. June 10, 1896, Leona Guin, died in Okla. 2. Effie Yerby. 3. Tosie Yerby, m. W. Wiley Lowery, both died in Okla. 4. Ulyesses Yerby. 5. Thurston Yerby. 6. Lula Lee Yerby, m. H. Lonnie Ward, both died in Okla. 7. Tirzah Yerby, m. James Hallbrook.

YERBY, James Franklin, b. 1819, N. C., d. 1899, m. Sarah Ann Dodson, d. 1889. Children: 1. Joel Yerby, b. 1845, d. 1914, Okla., m. Molly Jones. (Had a son, Houston Yerby and two daughters.) 2. Willis Yerby, m. in Texas. 3. John William Yerby, b. Sept. 27, 1850, m. 1888, Mary Taggart. (Went to Texas. Had eight daughters and one son who lived in various parts of Texas.) 4. Mattie Yerby, b. 1857, Ala., d. 1940, m. B. F. Pounds. (Moved to Texas. Had eight children living in Texas and Okla.) 5. Frank M. Yerby, b. 1862, m. __. (Lived in Texas with five daughters and one son.) 6. Fannie Yerby, b. 1864, m. Pomp Martin. (Had son: Jim Alex Barton Martin, lived in Texas.) 7. T. L. Yerby, b. 1866, moved to Texas.

YERBY, Jasper N., b. 1832, Lamar Co., Ala. (then Fayette Co.) died 1865 in war – Battle of Gettysburg, m. Dec. 26, 1851, Rutha Hankins, b. 1835, d. 1917, Lamar Co. - dau. of Richard Hankins. Children: 1. James Alexander Yerby, Lamar Co. 2. Richard Newton Yerby, b. July 24, 1854, Lamar Co. (Fay. Co. then.) d, June 30, 1942, m. Sarah Ann McCraw. 3. Rachael Ann Yerby, lived in Okla. 4. Jasper Elizabeth Yerby, died in Lamar Co., Ala. 5. Tabitha Yerby.

YERBY, James Roscoe, b. Hico, Fayette Co., Ala., d. Nov. 22, 1903, Fayette Co., m. Jan. 31, 1893, Sarah Elizabeth South, b. Sept. 17, 1871, Tusca. Co. - dau. of Levi Woodruff South. Both are buried at Pilgrim's Rest Cem. Children: 1. Fletcher Yerby, m. Dollie Watson. 2. Leech Yerby, m. 1st. - Pearl Watson, 2nd. - Robbie __. 3. George Yerby. 4. Charles Raymond Yerby, m. Miss Monique.

YERBY, John Samuel, b. May 24, 1882, Lamar Co., Ala., d. Feb. 19, 1950, Fayette Co. - son of Richard N. & Sarah A. (McCraw) Yerby - m. May 29, 1904 Malinda Alice Robertson, b. Dec. 15, 1888, Lamar Co., Ala. - dau. of John & Mary C. (Brown) Robertson. Children: 1. Annie Odell Yerby, b. June 23, 1914, Lamar Co., Ala., m. June 23, 1934, James Milton Dyer, b. Jan. 28, 1912, Fayette Co., Ala. 2. Bradley B. Yerby. 3. Lewis O. Yerby. 4. Leon M. Yerby. 5. Lona Ree Yerby, m. Lawrence Howell. (Children: "Chuck" and John.)

YERBY, John T., b. Fayette Co. - son of Hogan Yerby - m. Adeline Lindsey. Children: 1. Phalitia Yerby, m. July 31, 1879, Charles Edmonds. 2. L. S. "Babe" Yerby, m. Oct. 7, 1885, Alice Collins. 3. Lou Etta Yerby, m. B. L. Rogers. 4. Roscoe Yerby, m. Jan. 31, 1893, Lizzie South. 5. Mack Yerby, m. Nov. 29, 1895, Felicia Horne. 6. Curtis Yerby, drowned at 17 yrs. of age.

YERBY, Luallen, b. Fayette Co., - son of Hogan Yerby - m. Sarah Dodson, b. Fayette Co., d. Texas. Children: 1. Alice Yerby. 2. James T. Yerby, m. April 2, 1884, Maggie Horne.

YERBY, Richard Newton, b. July 24, 1854, Lamar (then Fayette) Co., d. June 30, 1942, Lamar Co. - son of Jasper N. & Rutha (Hankins) Yerby - m. Jan. 10, 1878, Sarah Ann McCraw, b. Jan. 6, 1860, Walker Co., Ala., d. April 28, 1935, Lamar Co. - dau. of Madison & Mary (Perkins) McCraw. Children: 1. John Samuel Yerby, b. May 24, 1882, Lamar Co., d. Feb. 19, 1950, Fayette, Ala., m. May 29, 1904, Malinda Alice Robertson, b. Dec. 15, 1888, Lamar Co., Ala. 2. Jasper N. Yerby. 3. Roland Yerby. 4. Thomas Yerby. 5. Harvey Yerby. 6. Rosetta Yerby. 7. Elizabeth Yerby. 8. Lettie Yerby.

YERBY, W. Inge, b. Fayette Co., Ala. - son of Hogan Yerby - m. Fannie Caraway. Children: 1. Everette "Evy" Yerby, b. Fayette Co., m. July 14, 1889, Alice V. Parker, b. Fayette Co. 2. Aggie A. Yerby, b. Fayette Co., m. Aug. 12, 1891, J. Henry Wilson, b. Lamar Co. 3. Ethel Yerby, m. Jan. 20, 1895, Sid Wilson, b. Lamar Co. 4. Murray N. Yerby, m. Aug. 25, 1903, Mary West. 5. Hiliary Yerby, m. Lula Belle. 6. Ada Yerby, m. Will Taylor. 7. Winton Yerby. 8. Vera Yerby, m. Ed Savage.

YERBY, William, b. Dec. 9, 1874, d. Mar. 6, 1940, m. Cora Dickinson, b. Apr. 15, 1880, Fayette Co. Children: 1. William Edward Yerby, b. Feb. 8, 1913, m. Merle Hocutt. 2. Margaret Yerby, b. Oct. 6, 1917, Fayette Co., m. A. M. Traweek.

YERBY, William Edward, b. Feb. 8, 1913, Fayette Co., Ala. - son of Wm. & Cora (Dickinson) Yerby - m. Merle Ruth Hocutt, b. Fayette Co., Ala. Children: 1. Robert Gaines "Bobby" Yerby, b. May 4, 1945, Fayette Co., Ala. 2. Carl Ed Yerby, b. June 23, 1951, Fayette Co., Ala.

YORK, __. Children: 1. Jim York. 2. Catherine York, d. June 5, 1899, m. Tom J. Davis. 3. Adeline York, m. Mr. Dagwell.

YOUNG, Alexander, b. abt. 1800, d. 1888, buried Corinth Cem., m. Easter Ferguson, d. buried Corinth Cem. Children: 1. Arthur T. Young, b. Nov. 17, 1827, d. April 23, 1878, m. Margaret Ann Given, b. Mar. 11, 1828, d. 1907, Hamilton, Miss. 2. James Paul Young, b. Nov. 13, 1829, d. Mar. 8, 1908, Lamar Co., m. April 30, 1854, Martha Talitha Box, b. Dec. 4, 1835, d. July 7, 1897, Lamar Co. 3. Samuel Young, b. __, 23, 1832, d. Feb. 19, 1884, m. Martha A. Jernigan, b. Mar. 1847, d. Jan. 9, 1888. 4. John A. J. Young, b. April 10, 1834, d. Mar. 15, 1917, Fayette, Ala., m. Dec. 22, 1859, Mary C. Dowdle, b. Aug. 3, 1836, d. April 21, 1912, Fayette, Ala. 5. Robert Young, killed in Battle of Gettysburg, during Civil War. 6. Rufus W. Young, b. Nov. 27, 1845, d. April 7, 1919, m. Laura Box, b. 1846, d. 1927.

YOUNG, Henry M., b. Jan. 9, 1866, Fayette, Ala., d. Sept. 23, 1933, m. Feb. 1894, Ada Estes, b. Oct. 25, 1871, Fayette Co., d. Mar. 16, 1935. Children: 1. Icie Mae Young, b. Feb. 3, 1900, Lamar Co., m. May 14, 1921, John L. Collins.

YOUNG, Humphries, m. Sara Yarbrough, b. abt. 1834 - dau. of Stephen & Sarah (Layton) Yarbrough. Children: 1. John William Young, b. May 12, 1859, Fayette Co., Ala., d. Texas. 2. Mary Elizabeth Young, b. April 6, 1863, m. Riley Taylor. 3. Henry M. Young, b. Jan. 18, 1866, d. Sept. 23, 1933, m. Ada Estes. 4. Susan Paralee Young, b. Feb. 24, 1868, m. John Wallace. 5. Hiram A. Young, b. Feb. 17, 1870, d. Texas. 6. Florida Bell Young, b. Jan. 26, 1872, d. July 1954, m. John W. Wiggins. 7. Humphrus Oscar Young, b. Feb. 25, 1873, m. Levy Gilliam, b. Fayette Co. 8. Viney Ellen Young, b. April 2, 1876, m. Willie Bobo. 9. Frances Jane Young, b. Feb. 17, 1880, m. Jefferson Adam Richards, Jr., b. Dec. 16, 1864, Fayette, Ala. d. 1949. (All these children born Fayette Co.)

YOUNG, James D., M. D., b. Aug. 4, 1868, Lamar Co., Ala., d. April 20, 1954, Fayette, Ala. - son of John A. & Mary C. (Dowdle) Young, - m. Feb. 28, 1897, Effie Humber, b. July 18, 1879, Fayette Co. - dau. of Lewis Porter & Harriett Josephine (Moore) Humber. Dr. J. D. Young practiced medicine in Fayette Co. for over forty years. He was a member of the Masonic Lodge; Order of the Eastern Star; Woodmen of the World; First Methodist Church ans was active in the Fayette County Medical Society. Children: (All born Fayette, Ala.) 1. Milner Young, b. July 6, 1898, m. Oct. 19, 1918, W. Emmett King. 2. James Dorsey Young (Jr.) b. Aug. 14, 1902, m. Oct. 9, 1927, Anna Lee Chambers, b. Mar. 31, 1903, Jacksonville, Ala. 3. W. M. Maury Young, b. June 26, 1907, d. Sept. 5, 1936, m. Mar. 6, 1932, Roberta Culpepper, b. Meridan, Miss. 4. Jewell Adele Young, b. Aug. 17, 1915, m. May 15, 1939, Joe Oliver Campbell, b. Jan. 31, 1915, Fayette, Ala. 5. John Tinsley Young, b. Oct. 6, 1917, m. Mar. 12, 1939, Jewel Banks Brown, b. May 26, 1940, Fayette, Ala.

YOUNG, James Dorsey, b. Aug. 14, 1902, Fayette, Ala. - son of Dr. James D.

& Effie (Humber) Young - m. Oct. 9, 1927, Anna Lee Chambers, b. Mar. 31, 1903, Jacksonville, Ala. - dau. of Oscar Lee, d. 1953, & Lula (McRight) Chambers. They were married in Winfield, Ala. Dorsey was a druggist and operated the Temple Garden Drug Store for many years. Mr. Chambers was a teacher. Children: (All born Fayette, Ala.) 1. James Dorsey Young, II, b. Feb. 19, 1929, m. Nov. 18, 1950, Heraldine "Deanie" Pitts, b. Oct. 9, 1930. 2. Peggy Lou Young, b. Oct. 7, 1932, d. Mar. 19, 1934, Fayette, Ala. 3. Harriett Josephine Young, b. Jan. 28, 1938, m. Philip Loke Hamby, b. Dec. 16, 1935, Birmingham, Ala.

YOUNG, James Dorsey, II, b. Feb. 19, 1929, Fayette, Ala., - son of James Dorsey & Anna Lee (Chambers) Young - m. Nov. 18, 1950, Heraldine "Deanie" Pitts, b. Oct. 9, 1930, Birmingham, Ala. - dau. of H. E. Pitts. Children: 1. James Dorsey Young, III, b. Sept. 3, 1954. 2. Jann Ellen Young, b. Oct. 15, 1957.

YOUNG, John A. J., b. April 10, 1834, d. Mar. 15, 1917, - son of Alexander & Easter (Ferguson) Young - m. Dec. 22, 1859, Mary C. Dowdle, b. Aug. 3, 1836, d. April 21, 1912. Children: 1. Fannie C. Young, b. Oct. 2, 1860, d. Nov. 19, 1878. 2. John A. J. Young, II, b. Sept. 20, 1862, d. June 1, 1923, m. Annie Ferguson. 3. James D. Young, M.D., b. Aug. 4, 1868, Lamar Co., d. April 20, 1954, m. Feb. 28, 1897, Effie Humber, b. July 18, 1879, Fayette, Ala. 4. Ellen H. Young, b. Nov. 8, 1870, d. April 21, 1895, Fay. 5. Joseph W. Young, b. Feb. 19, 1897, d. Iowa. 6. Rev. Luther W. Young, b. Nov. 8, 1875. 7. Wm. M. Young, b. Aug. 28, 1865, d. Mar. 29, 1889. 8. Effie Neeland Young, b. June 20, 1878, d. Oct. 5, 1905.

YOUNG, John Tinsley "Scotty", b. Oct. 6, 1917, Fayette, Ala. - son of Dr. James Dorsey Young - m. Mar. 12, 1939, Jewell Banks Brown, b. May 26, 1919, Lamar Co., Ala. - dau. of Felix Austin Brown. J. T. Young is a merchant. Children: 1. Johnny Banks Young, b. Oct. 12, 1941, Fayette, Ala. 2. Wm. Maury Young, II, b. Oct. 23, 1943, Fayette, Ala.

YOUNGHANCE, Edward L., m. Sarah Yerby, - dau. of Amon Yerby. Children: 1. Cornelius Younghance. 2. John Wofford Younghance. 3. James Younghance. 4. Josie Younghance.

BIBLIOGRAPHY

"A History of Methodism in Alabama" - by the Rev. Anson West, D. D.

Fayette County Manuscript - by Mr. M. L. Coons, former Mayor of Fayette.

"History of Walker County Alabama" - by John Martin Dombhart.

"History of Alabama and Dictionary of Alabama Biography"- by Thomas M. Owen.

"History of Alabama and Her People" - The American Historical Society.

"The Fayette Banner"

"The Northwest Alabamian"

Fayette County Court House Records.

City of Fayette Records.

Fayette County High School Records.

Berry High School Records.

Hubbertville High School Records.

Fayette County Baptist Associational Minutes.

"The Alabama Historical Quarterly" - Winter Issue, 1942.

The National Dept. of History & Archives, Washington, D. C.

Original Church Records of: Fayette Baptist Church; ElBethel Baptist Church
        Concord Baptist Church and Mt. Lebanon Baptist Church.

Records of Mrs. Roy Martin.

Records of Herbert and Jeanie Newell.

Personal Interviews and personal records & papers of countless Fayette People.

The Numerous Families who contributed Personal Data.

INDEX

This index is complete and covers the entire book with the exception of 1830 - 1840 Federal Census for Fayette County and for the Faculty of The Fayette Grammar School; and Faculty and graduating class for Berry High School; Fayette County High School; and Hubbertville High School.

The Census is listed with beginning page (the census itself is listed alphabetically). The schools are listed with the years listed on the pages they appear on (the graduating classes are in alphabetical order and the faculty for each year is listed with these classes).

All other data is completely indexed.

A. & M. Laundry & Dry Cleaners, 43
A. & P. Tea Co. - The Great Atlantic & Pacific Tea Co., 43
Abbott, 152, 185, 196, 235, 242, 307, 333
Abele, 196, 197, 235, 236, 253
Aberdeen, 105
Abernathy, 176, 181, 188, 197, 208, 229, 265, 290, 322, 357, 385, 402
Able, 108
Ables, 109, 167, 169
Abney, 185
Acton, 351
Adam, 337
Adams, 30, 46, 67, 76, 108, 161, 188, 191, 236, 339
Adair, 315
Adcox, 109, 110
Adkins, 106
Adkinson, 363
Adman, 349
Agee, 43, 188
Agerton, 155, 156
Agnew, 21
Aikin, 384
Akin or Akins, 76, 95, 156, 157, 160, 162, 163, 164, 165, 166, 167, 168
Alabama Christian College, 14, 105
Alabama Extension Service, 64
Alabama Mills, Inc., 59
Alabama Power Co., 15, 31, 63
Alabama Telephone Co., 63
Alabama Trust & Saving Co., 15
Albritton, 421
Alawine, 159
Aldridge, 27, 107, 109, 171, 175, 179, 183, 281, 284, 327, 377, 402
Alexander, 12, 106, 108, 109, 125, 147, 172, 175, 192, 194, 197, 198, 199, 207, 212, 235, 311, 342, 352, 361, 417

Alford, 343, 417
Allen, 125, 172, 199, 203, 204, 211, 214, 215, 216, 218, 224, 225, 249, 298, 307, 321, 326, 332, 362, 417, 420.
Alldridge, 76, 197
Alley, 22, 179, 181, 200, 314, 370
Allison, 340
Almon, 73
Alpha Delta RHO Chapter of Alabama, 183
Alsop, 105
Alta Baptist Church, 164
American Legion, 183, 184
Amerson, 76, 110, 111
Amoco Service Center, 53
Ancaroni, 367
Anders, 100, 232
Anderson, 26, 43, 57, 67, 73, 120, 140, 145, 163, 175, 185, 191, 194, 200, 202, 230, 246, 266, 280, 321, 344, 419
Anderson Hardware Co., 43
Anderson Service Co., 43
Andrews, 153, 166, 167, 392, 394, 404
Anglin, 293
Anhalt, 24, 47, 188, 191
Anstead, 296
Anthony, 98, 140, 173, 175, 200, 219, 238, 250, 266, 316, 339, 407
Antioch Post Office, 39
Antioch Baptist Church, 152
Aplin, 200, 221
Apling, 322
Appline, 201, 400
Appling, 6, 31, 98, 180, 200, 201, 207, 271, 282, 298, 314, 361, 365, 396, 413
Arbor Springs Baptist Church, 157
Armbrester, 108
Armentrout, 201

427

Armistead, 185
Armstrong, 172
Arnaz, 321
Arnett, 403
Arnold, 20, 64, 99, 159, 165, 182, 201, 206, 218, 247, 256, 259, 267, 268, 313, 329, 372, 378
Arrington, 253
Arthur, 45, 58, 185, 187, 188, 192, 201, 202, 335, 359, 366
Arthur Lumber Co., 58
Arthur Motor Co., Inc., 45
Ary, 145, 147, 182, 286
Asbury Post Office, 39
Ashcraft, 5, 40, 65, 68, 74, 76, 147, 167, 183, 197, 406
Ashcraft Corner Baptist Church, 157
Asher, 249, 250
Assembly of God Church, 152
Astin, 250
Aston, 202, 250, 288, 300
Atchley, 407
Atkins, 20, 110, 161, 162, 165, 184, 202, 316, 348, 408.
Atlantic Oil Co., Inc. 43
Atley, 227
Ausbon, 106, 110
Ausborn, 352
Austin, 198
Awtrey, 13, 98 (or Autrey)
Autry, 242
Avant, 202, 388
Avery, 401
Aycock, 201, 381, 382
Ayers, 224
Aylin, 65, 184
Ayres, 19, 39, 43, 98, 100, 117, 163, 184, 187, 190, 191, 194, 202, 206, 252, 313, 351, 404
Ayres - Wade H. Associates, 43
Ayres & Wages Blacksmith Shop, 43

Babb, 320, 373
Baggett, 279
Bagwell, 13, 14, 15, 20, 59, 77, 108, 202, 230, 338, 339, 402, 424
Bagwell Real Estate Rentals, 43
Bailey, 105, 111, 167, 173, 174, 189, 191, 195, 203, 213, 237, 414
Baines, 172, 203, 282, 412
Baird, 99, 109, 193
Baker, 16, 68, 71, 76, 98, 109, 154, 156, 157, 158, 161, 164, 165, 166, 168, 169, 172, 173, 181, 201, 203, 207, 266, 271, 282, 283, 284, 346, 366, 379, 407, 410
Balch, 104, 120, 188
Baldwin, 169, 272, 292
Ballinger, 116, 125, 147, 155, 203, 204, 216, 228, 272, 289, 294, 295, 296, 378, 381, 400, 410, 411, 416, 417.
Bank of Berry, 16
Bankhead, 22, 69, 73
Bankhead Broadcasting Co., 101
Banks, 12, 62, 231
Bankston, - Town of, 12
Bankston Baptist Church, 158
Bankston Church of Christ, 173
Bankston School, 105, 106
Bannister, 45
Barbee, 230, 232
Barber, 65, 374
Barbour, 51, 204, 205, 306, 307
Barfield, 106, 107
Barker, 256
Barkley, 148
Barksdale, 340, 341
Barlow, 108
Barnard, 78, 104, 190, 194, 205, 206, 227
Barnes, 14, 15, 16, 44, 47, 60, 107, 108, 109, 110, 147, 171, 175, 179, 181, 184, 189, 191, 192, 206, 217, 225, 226, 280, 285, 300, 384, 391, 410
Barnes Insurance Agency, 44
Barnett, 45, 117, 181, 182, 185, 191, 201, 202, 206, 207, 261, 273, 372, 380, 381, 417
Barnett's Drug Store, 45
Barrett, 251
Barson, 191
Barton, 170, 171, 172, 212, 250, 326, 363, 364, 384, 390, 394
Basket, 20, 37, 61, 418
Bateman, 255,
Bates, 268
Batson, 158, 166, 207, 231
Bealle, 251
Bean, 239
Beard, 41, 77, 96, 156
Beasley, 26, 62, 73, 207, 302, 315, 363
Beauert, 303, 304
Beck, 158, 419, 420

Beckham, 304
Bectom, 352
Bedenbough, 162
Beive, 293
Belisle, 272
Belk, 13, 77, 106, 158, 197, 202,
  207, 208, 263, 264, 286, 325,
  335, 348, 357, 412
Belk, - Town of, 13
Belk Missionary Baptist Church,
  158
Belk School, 115
Bell, 18, 22, 26, 42, 70, 71, 74,
  77, 95, 99, 119, 159, 160, 161,
  165, 167, 168, 187, 192, 202,
  205, 208, 209, 218, 225, 244, 306,
  308, 312, 359, 361, 379, 383, 394,
  397, 419, 422
Belle, 423
Bellows, 339
Belve, 295
Benedict, 334
Bennett, 180, 190, 209, 210, 223,
  277, 278, 376, 385, 408
Bentley, 108, 161, 162
Benton, 191, 200, 391
Benton - Fowler Lumber Co., 61
Berea Church of Christ, 173
Bergen, 419
Berlene, 107
Bernard, 168
Berry, 13, 14, 16, 25, 26, 44, 49,
  53, 72, 73, 77, 97, 98, 99, 104,
  106, 107, 108, 109, 111, 116, 118,
  160, 163, 164, 165, 166, 167, 170,
  171, 172, 179, 183, 184, 188, 189,
  191, 192, 193, 198, 210, 211, 217,
  221, 222, 225, 236, 247, 257, 268,
  269, 271, 299, 300, 301, 318, 319,
  326, 344, 345, 379, 383, 389, 390,
  399, 410
Berry Dry Cleaners, 44
Berry, Town of -, 14, 35
Berry Baptist Church, 158
Berry Church of Christ, 173
Berry Methodist Church, 178
Berry Nazarene Church, 182
Berry Schools, 106 thru 115, (Elementary Faculty; High School Faculty; & each graduating Class - Class listed alphabetically - for each year from 1923.)
  Class of 1922 - 1923, 106

Class of 1923 - 1924, 106
Class of 1924 - 1925, 106
Class of 1925 - 1926, 107
Class of 1926 - 1927, 107
Class of 1927 - 1928, 107
Class of 1928 - 1929, 107
Class of 1929 - 1930, 107
Class of 1930 - 1931, 107
Class of 1931 - 1932, 108
Class of 1932 - 1933, 108
Class of 1933 - 1934, 108
Class of 1934 - 1935, 108
Class of 1935 - 1936, 108
Class of 1936 - 1937, 108
Class of 1937 - 1938, 109
Class of 1938 - 1939, 109
Class of 1939 - 1940, 109
Class of 1940 - 1941, 109
Class of 1941 - 1942, 110
Class of 1942 - 1943, 110
Class of 1943 - 1944, 110
Class of 1944 - 1945, 111
Class of 1945 - 1946, 111
Class of 1946 - 1947, 111
Class of 1947 - 1948, 111
Class of 1948 - 1949, 112
Class of 1949 - 1950, 112
Class of 1950 - 1951, 112
Class of 1951 - 1952, 113
Class of 1952 - 1953, 113
Class of 1953 - 1954, 113
Class of 1954 - 1955, 113
Class of 1955 - 1956, 114
Class of 1956 - 1957, 114
Class of 1957 - 1958, 114
Class of 1958 - 1959, 115
Berryhill, 187, 197
Bertram, 211, 239, 256
Best, 110, 163
Bethabara Baptist Church, 158
Bethabra Baptist Church, 158
Bethany Baptist Church, 158
Bethel Baptist Church, 159
Bethel Church, 32, 33
Bethlehem Baptist Church, 159
Bethlehem Methodist Church, 29, 150, 179
Bethlehem School, 115
Bevan, 44, 158, 159, 163
Bevan Tin Shop, 44
Bevill, 308
Bickart, 366
Bidwell, 242

Big Pond Post Office, 39
Bingham, 7
Binion, 386, 393
Birchfield, (See Burchfield), 227, 239
Birdsay, 256
Birdwell, 211, 212, 420
Bishop, 202
Black, 19, 39, 41, 44, 45, 46, 70, 75, 77, 78, 98, 102, 117, 147, 155, 157, 158, 164, 166, 167, 174, 175, 176, 188, 189, 191, 194, 212, 252, 278, 286, 296, 301, 348, 375, 410
Black's Wrecking Co., 44
Blackburn, 19, 20, 21, 26, 39, 41, 75, 77, 107, 108, 110, 181, 212, 213, 275, 282, 233, 384
Blackstock, 420, 421
Blackwelder, 162
Blackwell, 213, 377
Blacke, 255
Blake, 260
Blakeley, 213, 291, 395
Blakeney, 30, 156, 158, 167, 222
Blakney, 160, 197, 200, 310
Bland, 169, 395
Blankenship, 155, 156, 157, 162, 164, 165, 182, 379, 409
Blankship, 77
Blanton, 110, 111, 308
Blaylock, 367
Bluff Community, 16
Bluff Springs School, 115
Blythe, 274
Bobo, 16, 17, 32, 41, 44, 46, 47, 48, 49, 57, 66, 72, 77, 78, 94, 107, 148, 155, 157, 158, 159, 160, 163, 164, 167, 174, 184, 185, 187, 189, 191, 193, 194, 195, 199, 200, 201, 203, 204, 207, 213, 214, 215, 216, 217, 219, 223, 224, 226, 227, 231, 233, 249, 254, 259, 264, 266, 275, 276, 281, 282, 284, 286, 289, 290, 295, 298, 299, 311, 316, 326, 331, 332, 335, 337, 341, 342, 351, 352, 353, 358, 362, 364, 394, 402, 404, 406, 410, 411, 416, 417, 420, 421, 424
Bobo Grocery, 44
Bobo Gulf Service Station, 44
Bobo's Paint & Body Shop, 44
Bobo Plumbing, 44
Bogard, 25, 26, 59, 161, 192

Boland, 219, 320
Boling, 168, 192
Bolton, 107, 170, 172, 334, 373
Bonepart, 337
Bonner, 108, 109, 110, 111, 120
Boone, 15, 65, 106, 108, 109, 189, 191, 338
Booth, 44
Booth Jewelry Co., 44
Boozer, 219, 220, 251, 252, 281, 348, 353, 407, 410, 412
Boss, 78
Bostick, 327
Boteler, 365
Bounds, 101
Bowen, 97, 109, 111, 317
Bowles, 110, 111, 163, 353
Box, 281, 351, 424
Boyd, 74, 108, 158, 203, 220, 261, 327, 350
Boyles, 47, 184
Bozeman, 45
Bradley, 63, 73, 357, 408
Brady, 107, 109, 262
Bragg, 20, 183, 220, 259, 260
Brain, 407
Brand, 158, 162, 169
Brandon, 258
Brannon, 205, 206, 328
Brannenbery, 174
Branyon, 20, 22, 26, 49, 67, 74, 97, 116, 121, 148, 158, 166, 167, 168, 183, 184, 187, 188, 189, 191, 192, 193, 200, 210, 220, 221, 222, 223, 273, 274, 326, 349, 357, 373, 385, 405, 419
Brasfield, 110
Brasher, 74, 78, 96, 98, 223, 224, 318, 349, 369, 377
Brazeal, 324, 325, 385
Brazelton, 254
Brazil, 158, 213
Brennen Diamond Wells, 4
Brent, 159, 225, 361
Brents, 30
Brewer, 174, 192, 212, 391, 393
Bridgers, 273
Bridges, 147, 182
Bridgewater, 394
Bright, 308
Britling, 67
Brittian, 387, 409, 410
Britton, 410

Brock, 17, 40, 72, 74, 78, 95, 115, 170, 171, 172, 189, 190, 199, 217, 224, 225, 226, 234, 287, 316, 322, 335, 344, 356, 384, 398, 404
Brockman, 22
Brockton Post Office, 40
Brodie, 181
Brogan, 245
Brooks, 250, 302, 303, 305, 320, 341
Brophy, 398
Brotherton, 41, 53, 63, 78, 96, 185, 187, 193, 225, 285, 312, 378
Brotherton Cafe, 53
Brown, 5, 20, 40. 44. 48, 61, 67, 107, 109, 119, 120, 152, 157, 159, 164, 165, 172, 175, 176, 179, 188, 191, 194, 197, 219, 224, 225, 226, 254, 258, 279, 302, 304, 311, 312, 316, 334, 335, 338, 357, 369, 370, 376, 377, 379, 383, 387, 396, 419, 423, 424, 425
Brown's Cafe, 53
Brown Machine Shop, 44
Brownlow, 174
Bruister, 247
Bruner, 110, 218
Bryant, 191, 214, 226, 361
Buckley, 175
Buckner, 125, 211, 215, 216, 226, 227, 238, 239, 368, 383
Buck Snort Post Office, 40
Buford, 243
Burch, 227, 268, 269
Burchfield, 109, 227, 239
Burge, 120
Burgess, 291
Burks, 158, 166
Burleson, 105, 106, 107, 115, 176, 221, 231
Burnett, 125
Burnette, 171
Burney, 324
Burns, 212, 227, 334
Burpo, 176
Burris, 18, 70, 371
Burrough, 73
Burrow, 72, 280, 332
Burson, 191, 364
Burt, 61, 188, 194, 205, 227, 274
Burton, 308, 420
Bus Station Cafe, 44
Busby, 307

Busch, 389
Business & Professional Women's Club, 184
Business, - Private, 43 (Firms)
Butler, 44, 47, 48, 180, 184, 193, 267, 271, 280, 297, 323, 344, 347, 369, 401, 407
Butler Grain Co., 44
Butler Tractor & Implement Co., 44
Buttahatchee, 153
Byars, 44, 152, 214, 294, 302, 303, 354
Byars Service Station, 44
Byler, 12, 35, 36
Bynum, 44, 212, 227, 228, 288, 369
Bynum Garage, 44, 296
Bynum Tractor Sales, 44
Byrd, 224, 225, 297, 329, 398, 410, 411
Byrnes, 256

C. & L. Poultry, 44
Cabral, 231
Caddell, 202, 251
Cade, 417
Cagle, 375, 376
Cahoon, 120
Caine, 18, 19, 20, 38, 39, 62, 63, 72, 119, 161, 188, 192, 193, 228, 229, 255, 264, 270, 315, 349, 350, 362, 371, 376
Caines Ridge Baptist Church, 159
Caldiron, 251
Caldwell, 288
Callahan, 229, 397
Callan, 285
Calloway, 271
Caloway, 151
Calvary Baptist Church, 159
Calvert, 274
Cameron, 111, 187, 229, 300
Cameron Tile Co., 44
Camp, 229, 319
Camp Meetings, 150, 177
Campbell, 39, 44, 51, 67, 78, 109, 110, 111, 125, 163, 187, 191, 194, 217, 229, 285, 291, 304, 331, 380, 424.
Campbell Jewelry Co., 44
Cane Post Office, 40
Cannon, 14, 16, 17, 20, 21, 22, 24, 25, 26, 44, 45, 63, 67, 74, 106, 107, 108, 109, 110, 111, 119, 125, 148, 159, 173, 175, 176, 178, 179,

185, 186, 189, 191, 193, 194, 200,
207, 213, 218, 230, 231, 232, 233,
237, 239, 250, 260, 263, 285, 299,
301, 304, 314, 326, 329, 345, 346,
348, 358, 360, 361, 364, 375, 379,
380, 386, 400, 410
Cannon Drug Store, 44, 233
Canterberry, 52, 160, 171
Canterbury, 219
Cantrell, 46, 140, 294, 303
Caple, 160
Caples, 79, 170
Cappieman, 219
Caraway, 6, 38, 47, 98, 119, 121,
188, 191, 193, 218, 270, 293, 318,
363, 414, 422, 423
Cardin, 219, 416
Cardinal Motel, 45
Carey, 399
Cargile, 27, 30, 46, 71, 104, 109,
110, 111, 125, 147, 160, 166, 169,
181, 184, 191, 218, 233, 234, 235,
238, 262, 263, 267, 298, 332, 333,
397, 411
Carina, 314
Carlyle, 212
Carmack, 46, 95, 163
Carpenter, 16, 22, 152, 191, 272,
378, 380
Carr, 243, 386, 412
Carroll, 325, 379, 385
Carson, 176, 306, 399, 400
Carter, 67, 98, 108, 161, 185, 187,
330, 379, 382, 400
Caryea, 273
Cason, 317
Castellaw, 198, 199, 235, 412
Cast, 172
Castleberry, 96, 98, 289
Cates, 159, 193, 379
Catherine's Beauty Bar, 45
Catholic Mission, 172
Cathrum, 315
Cauley, 265
Cauthen, 324
Cave Springs Post Office, 40
Cawthorn, 172
Census Fayette Co. - 1830 & 1840
(Alphabetical Index to census.)
7, 8, 9, 10, 11
Center School (Guin Pike), 116
Center School (Hubbertville Rd.),
116

Central Drug Store, 43, 45
Chadderdon, 297
Chaffin, 78, 125
Chamber of Commerce, 184
Chambers, 121, 187, 235, 424, 425
Chambless, 48, 72, 78, 120, 167, 184,
193, 309, 368
Chambliss, 155, 281, 408
Chandler, 20, 26, 39, 106, 107, 120,
125, 162, 183, 184, 188, 196, 210,
221, 228, 235, 236, 307, 369, 396
Chaney, 309, 310
Channell, 263
Chapel Hill Baptist Church, 159
Chapman, 110, 236, 262, 298, 333, 334,
367, 395, 417
Chappell or Chapeil, 75, 309, 310
Chappel, 172
Cheatem, 175
Cheatom, 174
Cheatman, __
Charles Baskerville Masonic Lodge #
281, - 189, 190, 191, 192
Charlton, 203
Chatam, 326
Cheek, 245
Chef Cafe, 45
Chef's Amoco Service Station, 45
Cherry, 306
Chewning, 383
Childers, 199
Childrels or Chilfrels, 242, 243
Childress, 184, 226, 242
Childreth, 71
Chilson, 300
Chilton, 307
Chism, 15, 109, 110, 111, 115, 159,
164, 165, 168, 179, 236, 248
Christian, 15, 45, 78, 107, 108, 110,
111, 195, 205, 293, 294, 298, 393
Christine's Beauty Bar, 45
Christopher, 106, 176
Citizen's Bank of Fayette, 62
City Curb Market, 45
City Meat Market, 25, 26
Civitan Club, 184
Clanton, 385
Clardy, 106, 107, 203, 204
Clark, 66, 158, 162, 163, 164, 165,
169, 175, 181, 195, 207, 240, 271,
295, 345
Clarke, 273, 274, 340
Claunch, 293

Clayton, 42, 251, 268
Clear Creek Baptist Association, 153
Clear Creek Post Office, 42
Clearman, 228, 236, 286, 287, 343
Cleland, 412
Clem, 181
Clement, 391
Clements, 14, 105, 107, 108, 154, 155, 156, 158, 159, 160, 164, 165, 166, 167, 168, 314, 334, 361, 369, 370
Clemmons, 237, 327, 390
Cleveland, 186
Cleveland Church of Christ, 173
Clifton, 191, 264
Cline, 39, 67, 178, 237, 285
Coats, 159
Cobb, 45, 54, 66, 70, 71, 74, 166, 184, 185, 225, 237, 305, 361, 366, 394
Cobb Motor Co., 45
Coca Cola Bottling Plant, 59
Cochran, 6, 79, 332
Cochrane, 208
Cockrell, 318
Cockren, 335
Codd, 396
Coen, 408
Coffee, 305, 380
Coggin, 18, 19, 22, 71, 73, 116, 121, 139, 187, 190
Coggins, 183, 186, 187, 190, 230, 237
Colburn, 104, 125, 147, 163, 184, 188, 189, 195, 203, 237
Cole, 12, 42, 106, 107, 108, 109, 110, 145, 168, 177, 182, 230, 231, 269, 307
Coleman, 13, 73, 74, 159, 171, 344
Coker, 327
Colley, 268
Collier, 22, 65, 118, 176, 191, 271
Collins, 6, 7, 13, 15, 30, 47, 58, 71, 79, 104, 106, 108, 116, 121, 156, 157, 159, 164, 167, 168, 175, 184, 186, 190, 191, 194, 195, 210, 211, 214, 222, 227, 231, 233, 234, 237, 238, 239, 252, 256, 280, 286, 296, 327, 337, 345, 351, 363, 368, 382, 383, 404, 405, 415, 421, 423, 424

Collin's School, 116
Colow, 162
Colston, 165, 167, 168, 169
Colwel, 278
Comer, 227, 239, 240, 256, 257, 341, 406
Compton, 303
Conaway, 159, 301
Concord Baptist Church, 159
Concord Primitive Baptist Church, 170
Concord School, 117
Condre, 283
Connell, 45, 120, 158, 159, 165, 167, 168, 169, 205, 221, 223, 240, 281, 312, 324, 381
Conner, 422
Cook, 18, 19, 75, 79, 95, 96, 125, 171, 181, 184, 187, 223, 240, 260, 273, 332, 348, 377, 390, 403, 414
Cooley, 189
Cooner, 382
Coons, 20, 60, 64, 97, 99, 194, 240, 241, 261, 281, 360, 361, 367
Cooper, 39, 46, 71, 184, 189, 241, 348, 392, 395
Cooper T. V. Service, 46
Copeland, 248, 367
Corbett, 40, 71, 160, 162, 184, 191, 224, 241, 250, 339
Cordova Post Office, 40
Corina, 316
Corley, 321
Cornelius, 106, 107, 108, 110, 179
Cornett, 253
Cornwell. 274
Corradine, 172
Corry, 106
Corwin, 100
Cotney, 185
Cotton, 98, 106, 116, 145, 182, 191, 241, 244, 313, 371, 388, 409
Couch, 22, 32, 46, 79, 116, 188, 191, 241, 243, 250, 310, 323, 351, 353, 363, 404, 406
Couch Feed & Hatchery, 46
Counts, 219
County Building & Supply Co., 31, 46
Courington, 109, 110, 308, 416
Courington, R. L. - Sawmill, 59
Covin, 16, 109, 167
Covin Baptist Church, 160, 167
Covin Community, 16
Covin Methodist Church, 180

Covin Post Office, 40
Cowan, 120
Coward, 20, 193
Cowart, 107, 242, 285, 324, 325
Cowden, 292
Cowdon, 6
Cox, 62, 63, 155, 156, 157, 158, 161, 164, 166, 185, 191, 294
Craddock, 152, 174, 175
Cranford, 230, 278, 301, 416
Cravey, 193
Crawford, 327
Crawley, 46, 65
Crawley Grocery, 46
Credit Bureau of Fayette, 46
Crew, 108
Crews, 212, 354, 356
Croley, 242,
Crosby, 270
Crosley, 218
Cross, 148, 175, 357
Crossville Post Office, 40
Crow, 75, 166, 197
Crowder, 173, 174
Crowe, 159, 163, 164, 194, 230, 242, 263, 264, 265, 266, 281, 301, 307, 348, 392
Crowell, 107, 108, 110, 111
Crowley, 13, 98, 106, 195, 204, 286, 393, 411
Crownover, 109, 110, 111
Crumley, 227
Crump, 120, 178, 282, 302, 374, 419
Crutcher, 194, 242, 243, 397
Culpepper, 424
Culver, 320
Cummin, 325
Cunningham, 156, 158, 160, 165, 172, 279
Curl, 95, 181, 368
Curry, 292
Curtis, 158, 193

Daughters of the American Revolution, 185 (D.A.R.)
D. & H. Auto Parts, 46
Daffin, 193
Dailey, 79, 271
Dairies, 60
Dan River Mills, Inc. 59
Daniel, 20, 67, 79, 121, 179, 223, 243, 244, 299, 300
Daniels, 96, 183, 184

Daniel's Chapel Methodist Church, 180
Darden, 186
Darnell, 182, 244, 359
Darwin, 291
Dasher, 105
David, 109
Davidson, 174, 192, 220, 221, 223, 247, 250, 285
Davies, 256
Davis, 46, 64, 67, 70, 74, 75, 79, 80, 97, 107, 108, 109, 110, 111, 120, 147, 148, 150, 155, 156, 157, 159, 162, 163, 166, 168, 160, 171, 172, 176, 182, 185, 186, 193, 209, 222, 223, 224, 231, 232, 235, 237, 244, 245, 246, 247, 248, 249, 262, 263, 277, 283, 284, 285, 292, 308, 324, 334, 336, 345, 349, 351, 352, 364, 365, 368, 374, 377, 379, 382, 387, 399, 407, 408, 411, 414, 415, 416, 417, 418, 422, 424
Davis Creek Post Office, 41
Davis Publishing Co., 46
Davison, 246, 250
Dawson, 157, 198
Day, 365
Day's Gap, 13
Deal, 46, 346, 347
Dean, 109, 171, 270
Dearing, 108, 158
Deering, 167
Deason, 105, 147, 283, 351
Deaton, 246, 289, 295, 318, 390
Deavours, 13, 75, 107, 108, 109, 110, 111, 157, 174, 247, 248, 250, 255, 275, 285, 299, 319, 342, 377, 380
Debton, 396
DeBrus, 207
Deener, 349
Deep South Dairy, 60
Delaney, 247, 372
Dendy, 106
Denison, 256
Dennis, 41, 98, 269, 421
Densler, 185
Dent, 185, 341
Denton, 185
DeRamus, 253, 297
Devonshire, 401, 402
DeWeese, 382
DeWitt's Cafe, 53
DeWoody, 291
Diaz, 176

Dickert, 240
Dickey, 147
Dickerson, 172
Dickinson, 19, 41, 75, 94, 156, 157, 159, 160, 161, 162, 163, 165, 166, 177, 179, 180, 186, 191, 193, 200, 214, 216, 218, 236, 241, 245, 246, 248, 249, 250, 276, 278, 283, 324, 325, 338, 339, 352, 358, 375, 402, 411, 423, 424.
Dickson, 20, 185, 186, 190, 201
Dill, 212, 381, 382
Dillard, 125
Dillion or Dillon, 399, 400
Dixon, 174
Dobb, 176, 329
Dobbins, 338
Dobbs, 15, 16, 20, 46, 52, 67, 74, 79, 105, 107, 108, 109, 110, 111, 120, 155, 157, 158, 167, 168, 173, 174, 175, 176, 184, 188, 223, 227, 247, 250, 262, 319,
Dobbs Brothers Wood Dealer, 46, 61
Dobbs Furniture Co., 46
Doby, 118
Dockery, 188
Dodd, 163, 165, 166, 187, 261, 273
Dodds, 18, 20, 21, 22, 55, 59, 79, 97, 98, 181, 383
Dodson, 20, 32, 39, 40, 50, 56, 80, 95, 104, 116, 148, 161, 165, 172, 184, 188, 196, 215, 224, 232, 235, 236, 241, 250, 276, 287, 302, 304, 322, 329, 330, 333, 339, 345, 363, 367, 383, 386, 391, 412, 421, 422, 423
Donald, 65
Donaldson, 192, 366, 397
Donnon, 333
Dorough, 108
Dorris, 170, 171
Dorroh, 293, 367
Doss, 314
Double Branches Baptist Church, 160
Double Springs Primitive Baptist Church, 170
Doughty, 107, 108, 155, 188, 191, 219, 238, 247, 250, 251, 252, 270, 286, 348, 352, 353, 358, 361, 364, 365, 376, 377, 378, 407, 409, 410
Douglas, 228
Douglass, 273
Dove, 314

Dowdle, 424, 425
Dowling, 277
Downing, 64, 244
Downs, 6, 99, 252, 352, 365
Doyle, 218
Dozier, 27, 281
Drake, 235, 260, 361
Draper, 181, 260, 350
Drewry, 350
Druid Butane Gas Co., 46
Drummond, 334
DuBose, 118, 184
Duckett, 116
Duckworth, 216, 220, 223, 225, 226, 330
Due, 297
Dudley, 189, 235, 256, 311
Duffee, 275
Dugin, 379
Duggar, 360
Duke, 358
Duncan, 19, 46, 99, 170, 173, 175, 335, 351
Dunagan, 323
Dunavat, 419
Duncan Beauty Shop, 46
Dunkin, 279
Dunnam, 260
Dunn, 52, 105, 106, 107, 110, 173, 174, 175, 191, 225, 265, 275, 377, 383, 400
Dunnivant, 398
Durham, 196, 197, 235, 253, 326
Durrett, 98, 283
Durrough, 109
Dyer, 39, 98, 115, 117, 158, 159, 160, 162, 164, 165, 166, 167, 168, 169, 170, 223, 253, 254, 257, 270, 335, 390, 419, 423
Dykes, 152
Dyle, 209
Dyson, 272

Eads, 284
Early Homes In Fayette, 22
Early Business Houses in Fayette, 22
Earnest, 80, 96, 107, 108, 125, 172
Earp, 70
Easby, 386
Easley, 266
Eason, 80, 231, 233, 380
Eastern Star Chapter, 186
Echols, 254, 414

Edge, 109
Edgil, 404
Edfeld?, --
Edmond, 202
Edmonds, 290, 423
Edmonson, 182, 224
Edmons, 71, 98
Edmonson, 109, 110, 111, 348
Edney, 19, 95
Education, 103
Edwards, 80, 217, 227, 242, 248, 249, 254, 263, 278, 279, 286, 290, 362, 364
Efird, 270
Eggar, 171
Egger, 171
Eggerton, 214
Ehl, 140, 174, 409
Ekes, 39
Ekwursel, 20
El Bethel Baptist Church, 160
Eldridge, Town of - 35
Elliott, 254, 270, 271
Ellis, 46, 80, 95, 98, 109, 110, 158, 174, 175, 176, 182, 191, 222, 240, 264, 265, 300, 333, 340, 361, 378, 418
Ellison, 109, 262
Elmore, 46, 47, 213, 254
Emmaus, Primitive Baptist Church, 170
England, 232, 254, 255, 270, 354, 371, 402
English, 256
Enis, 19, 20, 72, 80, 98, 186, 187, 190, 191, 247, 255, 300, 319, 371
Enlow, 255, 256, 295
Enslen, 47, 189
Ephram, 408
Epsilon Chapter of Alpha Delta Kappa, 183
Erickson, 253
Ervin, 189
Esary, 110, 167, 194, 195, 203
Esco, 226, 227
Estes, 39, 158, 174, 175, 220, 250, 311, 335, 366, 424
Eubank, 109, 256, 360
Evans, 106, 107, 108, 109, 110, 111, 201, 211, 256, 275, 334
Everett, 107, 111, 145, 203, 269
Evie, 220
Exchange Club, 188

Ezzell, 105, 319
Ezelle, 317

Fabric, The - Shop, 47
Faggett, 359, 360, 361
Fair, The - Store, 47
Fair, 277
Fairview Farm & Seed Co., 47
Fallin, 239, 256, 257, 317, 333, 341, 342
Falls, 107, 281
Fanning, 269, 270
Farmer, 254
Farmer's Marketing & Exchange Assoc. 47
Farquhar, 33, 35, 96, 98, 166, 180, 253, 254, 257, 268, 304, 307, 309, 368, 390, 409, 410, 411
Farr, 227
Farrar, 395
Ferris, 106
Farriss, 175
Farrow, 229, 257, 258, 259, 260, 319, 320, 331, 332, 342, 406
Faucett, 277
Faulkner, 100, 216, 260, 343, 350
Fayco Metal Culvert Co., 47
Fayette, 26
Fayette Auto Parts, 47
Fayette Banner, 24, 25, 26
Fayette Bonded Warehouse, 47
Fayette Cattle Sale Barn, 46
Fayette Chain Saw Co., 47
Fayette Church of Christ, 174
Fayette, City of 17
Fayette Coca Cola Bottling Plant, 59
Fayette Concrete Pipe Co., Inc., 47, 59
Fayette County Bank, 26
Fayette County Census of 1830 & 1840 (An alphabetical index of the census.) 7, 8, 9, 10, 11
Fayette County Circuit Court, 69
Fayette County Clerk of Circuit Court, 71
Fayette County Clerk of Commissioners Court, 71
Fayette County Clerks of County Courts, 71
Fayette County Court Judges, 71
Fayette County Court Houses, 68
Fayette County Dept. of Pensions & Security (Welfare Dept.), 64

Fayette County Farm Agent, 64
Fayette County Health Dept., 64
Fayette County High School, (Begins
  125 - High School Faculty & each
  Graduating Class listed alphabeti-
  cally - for each year from -)
  Class of 1915 - 1916, 126
  Class of 1916 - 1917, 126
  Class of 1917 - 1918, 126
  Class of 1918 - 1919, 126
  Class of 1919 - 1920, 126
  Class of 1920 - 1921, 126
  Class of 1921 - 1922, 126
  Class of 1922 - 1923, 127
  Class of 1923 - 1924, 127
  Class of 1924 - 1925, 127
  Class of 1925 - 1926, 127
  Class of 1926 - 1927, 128
  Class of 1927 - 1928, 128
  Class of 1928 - 1929, 128
  Class of 1929 - 1930, 128
  Class of 1930 - 1931, 129
  Class of 1931 - 1932, 129
  Class of 1932 - 1933, 129
  Class of 1933 - 1934, 129
  Class of 1934 - 1935, 130
  Class of 1935 - 1936, 130
  Class of 1936 - 1937, 130
  Class of 1937 - 1938, 130
  Class of 1938 - 1939, 131
  Class of 1939 - 1940, 131
  Class of 1940 - 1941, 131
  Class of 1941 - 1942, 132
  Class of 1942 - 1943, 132
  Class of 1943 - 1944, 133
  Class of 1944 - 1945, 133
  Class of 1945 - 1946, 133
  Class of 1946 - 1947, 134
  Class of 1947 - 1948, 134
  Class of 1948 - 1949, 134
  Class of 1949 - 1950, 135
  Class of 1950 - 1951, 135
  Class of 1951 - 1952, 136
  Class of 1952 - 1953, 136
  Class of 1953 - 1954, 136
  Class of 1954 - 1955, 137
  Class of 1955 - 1956, 137
  Class of 1956 - 1957, 137
  Class of 1957 - 1958, 138
  Class of 1958 - 1959, 138
  Class of 1959 - 1960, 139
Fayette County Junior High Schools,
  124

Bankston, 125
Belk, 125
Bobo, 125
Kirkland, 125
Mt. Vernon, 125
Stough, 125
Wayside, 125
Fayette County Home Demonstration A-
  gent, 65
Fayette County Hospital, 65
Fayette County Judges of Probate Court,
  71
Fayette County Missionary Baptist
  Association, 152, 153
Fayette County Pensioners - War of 1812
  75
Fayette County Precints, 73
Fayette County Sheriffs, 72
Fayette County Supt. of Education, 103
Fayette County Tax Assessors, 71
Fayette County Tax Collectors, 72
Fayette County In Tombigbee-Warrior
  Conservation District, 65
Fayette County Training School, 139
Fayette Court House, 37
Fayette First Baptist Church, 160
Fayette Presbyterian Church, 182
Fayette 5¢ & 10¢ Store, 47
Fayette Garden Club, 188
Fayette Grain & Feed Co., 47
Fayette Grammar School, 118
  (Faculty listed each year - where
  available since 1890's.)
  1890's through 1913, 120
  1915 through 1933, 121
  1934 through 1944, 122
  1945 through 1953, 123
  1954 through 1960, 124
Fayette Hotel, 50
Fayette Ice & Coal Co., 47
Fayette Insurance Agency, 48
Fayette Insurance Firms, 47
Fayette Junior Chamber of Commerce,
  189
Fayette Male & Female Institute, 117
  (Honor Rool listing students - 1888)
Fayette Manufacturing Co., 59
Fayette Mattress Co., 48
Fayette Memorial Co., 48
Fayette Mill, Gin & Ice Co., 59
Fayette Motor Co., Inc., 47, 48
Fayette Processing Plant, 48
Fayette Progress Club, 192

Fayette Pure Milk Co., 60
Fayette Radiator Service, 48
Fayette Recapping Co., 48
Fayette Shoe Shop, 48
Fayette Stock Yard, Inc., 48
Fayette Swimming Pool, 66
Fayette Telephone Co., 26
Fayette Used Parts, 48
Fayette Water Works, 66
Fayetteville, 37
Feltman, 219, 260, 377
Fern, 302
Ferguson, 14, 154, 157, 164, 165, 166, 167, 168, 244, 252, 308, 322, 325, 424, 425
Fielder, 212
Fields, 167
Fikes, 175, 419
Fike, 176, 340, 420
Files, 74, 110, 158, 193, 308, 365
Finch, 260, 330, 387
Finly, 184
First National Bank, 62
First Methodist Church, 180
Fisher, 193, 290, 342
Fite, 173, 410
Flat Top School, 139
Flatwoods Baptist Church, 162
Fleming, 18, 253, 334, 349
Flemming, 151
Flint, 251
Flippin, 393
Floyd, 111, 191, 241
Flynn's Store, 48
Folsom, 202
Fondren, 96
Fondrens, 178
Ford, 34, 35, 64, 99, 107, 188, 206, 260, 261, 288, 353, 354, 365, 380, 381
Foreman, 254
Forister, 404
Forsyth, 191, 194, 207, 261, 269, 270
Fortenberry, 13, 98
Foster, 152, 157, 159, 162, 163, 185, 186, 199, 216, 236, 261, 262, 264, 290, 304, 307, 332, 337, 338, 342, 348, 367, 417, 419
Fowler, 13, 20, 38, 48, 57, 67, 72, 80, 107, 108, 109, 116, 125, 147, 162, 164, 165, 168, 169, 174, 175, 182, 184, 185, 189, 190, 191, 194, 211, 217, 223, 247, 262, 273, 274, 286, 288, 313, 314, 318, 326, 327, 343, 344, 358, 387, 397, 402, 416, 417
Fowler Oil Co., 48
Fox, 165, 166, 251, 316, 361
Frances, 416
Francis, 109, 194, 247, 411
Franklin, 245, 249
Franks, 27, 184, 321
Frazier, 185, 193, 262, 371
Frederick, 65, 66, 67
Freeman, 12, 15, 20, 42, 49, 51, 80, 95, 110, 155, 156, 157, 166, 173, 177, 178, 191, 207, 217, 242, 252, 256, 263, 264, 265, 266, 268, 271, 276, 278, 290, 293, 301, 316, 317, 343, 344, 347, 348, 363, 379, 386, 390, 392, 409, 412, 414, 415
Freeman Barber Shop, 49
Freeman Cafe, 53
Freeman Motor Co., 49
Freewill Baptist Church, - Belk, 152
Freewill Baptist Church, - Fayette, 152
French, 279
Friendship Baptist Church (Fayette Co.) 162, 167
Friendship Baptist Church (Tusca. Co.) 162
Friendship Primitive Baptist Church, 170
Frierson, 266, 267, 354, 356
Fritz, 317
Frost, 14, 182
Frosty-Land Drive-In Cafe, 49
Frye, 406
Fulford, 201, 267
Fullerton, 80, 98, 261
Fulmer, 46, 110, 111, 180, 181, 347, 367
Fuqua, 173

Gables, 266
Gaddy, 191
Gage, 223
Gailmard, 287
Gaines, 274, 400
Gaither, 415
Galilee Post Office, 41
Galloway, 39, 48, 109, 182, 184, 191, 201, 267, 268, 281, 399, 402
Gammon, 387

Gams, 12
Ganaway, 240
Gant, 109, 110, 175
Gardiner, 409
Gardner, 33, 67, 81, 96, 110, 155, 156, 159, 163, 166, 168, 191, 194, 211, 227, 268, 269
Garett, 201
Garman, 244
Garner, 230, 278, 287, 339
Garofalo, 269
Garriod, 106, 109, 201
Garrison, 46, 49, 81, 107, 148, 155, 183, 184, 191, 223, 224, 298, 349, 360, 361, 382
Garrison Appliance & Furniture Co., 49
Garrison, Herman T., Store, 49
Gartman, 379
Gary, 168, 269, 270, 383
Gas Board of City of Fayette, 66
Gaston, 272
Gater, 276
Gates, 409
Gathings, 243
Gay, 58, 110, 184, 230
Gayle, 254, 255
Gee, 326
Geer, 147, 175, 195, 342
Gentry, 18, 41, 118, 226, 229, 240, 255, 270, 275, 312, 323, 324, 325, 352, 359, 362, 378, 401
George, 251, 422
Georgia Pacific Railway Co., 37
Gibbs, 350
Gibson, 39, 49, 106, 107, 108, 110, 115, 122, 139, 148, 171, 172, 179, 183, 184, 186, 193, 252, 261, 270, 271, 281, 299, 300, 331, 338, 339, 379, 411, 416
Gibson Dairy Bar, 49
Gibson Self Service Laundry, 49
Gideon, 161
Gilbert, 206
Gilbreath, 364, 422
Gilchrist, 227
Gilliam, 107, 108, 109, 110, 185, 230, 343, 424,
Gilliland, 188
Gillion, 108
Gilmore, 342
Gilpin, 155, 156, 157, 159, 160, 162, 165, 227, 288

Gilreath, 13, 216
Gilstrap, 27
Gipson, 368
Givan, 421
Given, 424
Gladden, 98, 156, 271
Glass, 415
Glen Allen, - City of, 27
Glen, 292
Glenn, 18, 19, 119, 271, 362
Glover, 169
Gober, 271, 272, 295, 350, 389
Godfrey, 167, 272, 338, 373, 405, 417
Going, 98, 110, 372
Golden Eagle Table Syrup Mfgrs., 60
Golden, 279
Goldstein, 372
Golson, 184, 194, 272, 388, 405
Goode, 81
Goodin, 167
Goodlet, 338
Goodrich, 401, 402
Goodson, 53, 339
Goodwater Baptist Church, 162
Goodwin, 18, 19, 20, 26, 49, 52, 62, 69, 70, 71, 72, 81, 119, 155, 156, 161, 162, 186, 190, 192, 194, 272, 273, 296, 299, 315, 337
Goodwin, Joe - Service Station, 49
Goolsby, 81
Goosby, 200
Gordon, 49, 163, 194, 240, 241
Gordon, R. C. Accounting Office, 49
Gore, 151, 245, 281
Goree, 158, 167
Gosa, 81, 263
Gossett, 173
Gould, 408
Gourley, 240, 241
Grace, 148
Grace Arbor Baptist Church, 162
Grace Baptist Church, 162
Graham, 18, 25, 26, 119, 147, 161, 162, 186, 187, 188, 190, 191, 241, 273, 306, 394
Grammar, 167
Graves, 236, 280, 292, 410
Gravin, 199
Gravlee, 49, 67, 110, 111, 120, 147, 148, 154, 155, 156, 157, 158, 159, 161, 162, 164, 165, 166, 168, 193, 221, 273, 274, 275, 340
Gravlees, 30, 49

Graves, 209
Gray, 42, 46, 67, 96, 111, 173, 174, 176, 189, 191, 219, 250, 269, 275, 286, 287, 297, 312, 323, 324, 326
Green, 108, 148, 165, 169, 217, 225, 273, 313, 316, 408, 410
Greene, 172, 216
Greenhill, 192
Greer, 99, 228
Gregg, 107, 108
Gregory, 209, 244, 245, 251, 378
Gresham, 408
Grey, 275, 289, 313,
Grider, 193
Gried, 198
Griffin, 15, 16, 42, 53, 67, 75, 96, 106, 107, 108, 109, 110, 155, 158, 160, 163, 164, 165, 166, 168, 170, 171, 188, 191, 194, 195, 213, 215, 229, 247, 251, 275, 276, 286, 301, 314, 315, 364, 387, 388, 415, 420
Griggs, 272
Grimsley, 15, 20, 43, 60, 61, 63, 161, 181, 185, 187, 192, 193, 250, 276
Grizzell, 189, 313
Grocholski, 49, 219, 276
Grocholski Upholstery Shop, 49
Gross, 225
Grove, 276, 367, 373
Guance, 173
Guennette, 255
Guerney, 265, 276, 277
Guest, 267
Guin, 16, 40, 67, 224, 310, 324, 351, 356, 357, 385, 420, 422
Gulf Oil Corp., 49
Gullate, 109
Gullatte, 109
Gullett, 20, 22, 24, 49, 53, 55, 119, 186, 245, 277, 282, 287
Gullette, 109,
Gullett's, 49
Gullote, 109
Gumbud Baptist Church, 163
Gumbud Community, 27
Gunter, 100, 184, 240, 281, 312, 367
Guriev, 98, 116, 224
Guthree, 171
Guthrie, 181, 308
Gutman, 211
Guttery, 377
Guyton, 171, 281, 418

Guy, 207
Guynes, 325
Gwynn, 218
Gwyn, 215, 218

Habco Southern Textile Co., 61
Hackett, 324
Hackworth, 174, 175
Hadlock, 321
Hagler, 387
Halbert, 171
Hale, 189
Haley Creek School, 139
Haley, 176, 319
Hall, 15, 58, 106, 107, 108, 109, 165, 169, 181, 184, 185, 187, 188, 190, 191, 205, 210, 229, 269, 277, 282, 283, 300, 397
Hallbrook, 422
Hallman, 48, 66, 158, 159, 163, 164, 167, 168, 169, 191, 194, 210, 252, 277, 278, 279, 311, 325, 347, 374, 390, 408, 410
Hallmark, 281
Ham, 125, 148, 216, 406
Hamby, 24, 39, 74, 279, 325, 425
Hames, 375
Hamil, 40
Hamilton, 82, 159, 184, 194, 262, 308, 363
Hamm, 22, 208, 291, 345, 391
Hammock, 13, 81, 95, 110
Hammon, 105, 293, 294, 295
Hammond, 269, 379
Hammonds, 163, 184
Hammons, 159, 165
Hamner, 18, 20, 26, 46, 54, 94, 108, 116, 184, 191, 193, 247, 271, 279, 318, 418, 422
Hamrick, 233, 236
Hams, 32
Hancock, 19, 262
Hand, 303, 389
Handley, 107, 109, 110, 191, 263
Haney, 165, 169, 170, 173, 174, 175, 176, 197, 284
Hankins, 12, 39, 71, 108, 181, 193, 224, 225, 226, 233, 234, 279, 280, 316, 370, 385, 423
Hanlin, 105
Hanna, 400
Hansboro, 325
Harbin, 16, 69, 81, 96, 98, 106, 110,

115, 145, 148, 152, 155, 159, 161, 280, 382, 407
Hardeman, 174
Hardwick, 271, 280
Hargett, 343, 344
Harkins, 19, 22, 24, 30, 32, 38, 61, 69, 81, 104, 118, 181, 183, 184, 188, 192, 224, 234, 237, 239, 240, 267, 280, 281, 329, 339, 382, 390, 421
Harkins Lumber, Co., 61
Harkness, 82, 281
Harmony Grove Baptist Church, 163
Harmony Primitive Baptist Church, 170
Harper, 40, 71, 175, 239
Harrington, 240, 241, 281, 312, 360
Harris, 16, 18, 19, 22, 30, 33, 74, 82, 147, 148, 181, 184, 186, 188, 193, 194, 195, 214, 225, 226, 229, 263, 277, 281, 282, 285, 316, 363, 366, 377, 378, 388
Harrison, 258, 261, 327, 338, 421
Hart, 255, 409
Harton, 72, 117, 152, 161, 218, 222
Harvey, 14, 71, 178, 182, 231, 232, 233
Harvey's Cross Roads Post Office, 42
Hasmer, 157
Hassel, 160
Hassell, 26, 30, 82, 155, 157, 201, 203, 212, 213, 236, 239, 248, 249, 277, 282, 283, 284, 325, 378, 379, 387, 389, 412
Hastings, 398
Haston, 193
Hathaway, 204
Haughton, 20, 43, 50, 201, 285
Haughton Realty Co., 50
Haupt, 184
Hawk, 105
Hawkins, 197, 225, 229, 244, 245, 246, 284, 289, 311, 327, 332, 345, 367, 370
Hay, 121, 163, 187, 284, 297, 403, 407, 414
Hayes, 152, 159, 162, 163, 164, 165, 214, 233, 237, 244, 264, 284, 285, 292, 341, 398
Hayne, 48
Haynes, 320
Hayslette, 350

Head, 105, 158
Heard, 208
Hearn, 151, 231
Heflin, 181
Hellers, 243
Helms, 65
Henderson, 82, 155, 157, 192, 193, 224, 225, 243, 269, 285, 315, 317, 318, 387, 394, 404
Hendon, 96, 111, 163, 175, 247, 285, 377
Hendrix, 164, 219, 260, 348, 368, 380, 381
Henley, 264, 265
Henry, 6, 72, 109, 117, 147, 178, 191, 206, 213, 257, 285, 307, 322, 336, 379, 398
Heralds, 30
Herbert, 417, 418
Herndon, 259
Herren, 47, 50, 125, 140, 175, 183, 189, 315, 380
Herren, E. C., Insurance Agency, 50
Herren, Hoyt - Antique Shop, 50
Herrig, 307
Herring, 235, 236
Herron, 175, 176
Hester, 65, 418
Hewlett, 291
Heywood, 331
Hickman, 65
Hickory Grove Baptist Church, 163
Hicks, 109, 409
Hico Post Office, 41
Higgenbottom, 292, 382
Higgins, 232, 285, 364
High, 278
Hightower, 397, 398
Hilbish, 109
Hill, 57, 98, 100, 281, 333, 334, 360
Hillhouse, 193, 290
Hill Post Office, 41
Hindman, 45, 212, 286, 295, 262, 404
Hinds, 174
Hinson, 192
Hinton, 95, 249, 251, 252, 286, 351, 352, 353, 358, 364, 378, 379
Hiten, 148
Hixson, 201
Hoagland, 285
Hobbs, 82
Hocutt, 67, 82, 95, 107, 108, 109, 110, 111, 165, 191, 252, 286, 287,

441

296, 298, 311, 314, 352, 399, 411, 423, 424
Hodge, 273
Hodges, 24, 32, 50, 74, 187, 188, 191, 321, 378
Hodges Dept. Store, 50
Hodo, 67, 188, 225, 287
Hoffman, 277, 287
Hogan, 354, 391
Hogue, --
Holbrooks, 175, 176, 319
Holcomb, 404
Holcombe, 172
Holder, 20, 50, 65, 106, 188, 192, 194
Holiday, 166
Holiman, 197
Holladay, 184, 185, 188, 191, 192, 193, 287
Holland, 245, 332
Hollaway, 307, 400
Holley, 162,
Hollenbach, 204
Hollida, 210
Holliday, 105, 163, 191
Holliman, 16, 41, 49, 82, 94, 99, 125, 140, 191, 264, 266, 287, 288, 357, 390, 405, 406, 421,
Hollins, 406
Hollingshead, 56, 67, 188, 193, 250
Hollingsworth, 12, 50, 75, 82, 83, 99, 107, 140, 148, 173, 174, 175, 176, 191, 223, 262, 288, 310, 352, 354, 380, 381, 402
Hollis, 50, 73, 74, 117, 147, 152, 191, 278
Hollis Radio & T. V. Service, 50
Hollman, 157, 230, 350
Hollomon, 75
Holloway, 212
Holly, 172
Holmes, 243, 297
Holt, 108, 285
Homes, 82, 201
Honeycutt, 16, 33, 111, 173, 174
Hood, 191, 372, 384, 418
Hook, 188
Hooker, 185, 288, 321
Hoover, 246, 264, 289
Hope, 326
Hopewell Baptist Church, 163
Hopewell Primitive Baptist Church, 29, 149

Hopewell School, 139
Hopkins, 39, 176
Hopper, 200
Horn Church, 30
Horn, 109, 146, 406
Hornbuckle, 254
Horne, 423
Horten, 399
Horton, 158, 159, 160, 162, 163, 164, 166, 167, 168, 169, 174, 207, 364, 408, 409
Hosmer, 157, 158, 165, 166, 167, 168
Hotel Fayette, 50
Houlditch, 162, 163, 289, 311
House, 401, 402
Houser, 366
Housh, 175, 194, 208
Housh's Chapel Church of Christ, 174
Houston, 61, 192, 209, 247, 277, 291, 328
Houstin, 372
Hovatter, 349
Howard, 96, 107, 191, 223
Howard Baptist Church, 163
Howard Church of Christ, 175
Howard Mines Community, 27
Howell, 50, 57, 116, 159, 165, 166, 176, 184, 188, 191, 222, 231, 233, 289, 417, 423
Howell's Flower Shop, 50
Howton, 18, 19, 24, 30, 39, 69, 98, 115, 193, 217, 230, 264, 265, 266, 280, 289, 290, 347, 385, 419
Hozier, 329
Hub, The - 50
Hubbard, 22, 38, 72, 185, 249, 250, 291, 335, 345, 346, 396
Hubbert, 20, 46, 140, 164, 174, 175, 176, 191, 213, 223, 292, 315, 318, 333, 383, 391, 399, 400
Hubbertville Church of Christ, 175
Hubbertville Community, 28
Hubbertville High School, 140 (Elementary Faculty; High School Faculty & each graduating Class - Classes listed alphabetically - for each year from 1936.)
Class of 1935 - 1936, 140
Class of 1936 - 1937, 140
Class of 1937 - 1938, 140
Class of 1938 - 1939, 140
Class of 1939 - 1940, 141
Class of 1940 - 1941, 141

Class of 1941 - 1942, 141
Class of 1942 - 1943, 141
Class of 1943 - 1944, 141
Class of 1944 - 1945, 141
Class of 1945 - 1946, 142
Class of 1946 - 1947, 142
Class of 1947 - 1948, 142
Class of 1948 - 1949, 142
Class of 1949 - 1950, 143
Class of 1950 - 1951, 143
Class of 1951 - 1952, 143
Class of 1952 - 1953, 143
Class of 1953 - 1954, 144
Class of 1954 - 1955, 144
Class of 1955 - 1956, 144
Class of 1956 - 1957, 144
Class of 1957 - 1958, 144
Class of 1958 - 1959, 145
Huckabee, 154, 161, 165, 166
Huddleson, 172
Hudson, 16, 83, 106, 107, 109, 189, 191, 242, 291
Huey, 116, 139, 330
Huffman, 60, 66, 292
Huffstutler, 120, 190
Hugent Community, 29
Hugent Post Office, 41
Hughes, 227, 261, 265, 293, 304, 325, 345
Hughs, 361
Huggins, 158, 335, 421
Hull, 207
Humber, 18, 19, 20, 21, 39, 57, 65, 120, 186, 187, 188, 190, 204, 212, 227, 228, 229, 233, 246, 255, 271, 272, 273, 280, 287, 289, 293, 294, 295, 296, 308, 318, 327, 337, 350, 363, 364, 374, 385, 389, 418, 419, 424, 425
Humphrey, 109, 185
Hunnicutt, 109
Hunt, 253, 297, 316, 326, 349, 351, 401
Hunter, 171, 417
Hurst, 187, 191, 193, 297, 414
Hurt, 254
Hutcheson, 140
Hutchinson, 215, 217, 362
Hutson, 297, 298, 366
Hutto, 200, 234, 298
Hutton, 83
Hyatte, 158
Hyche, 212

Hyde, 18, 19, 20, 22, 72, 96, 98, 121, 173, 174, 186, 192, 193, 218, 256, 298, 299, 319, 359, 360, 361, 383, 384, 385, 388, 389, 404, 415
Hyder, 44, 175, 194, 246

Ideal Market & Grocery, 50
I. G. A. Store, 50
Independence Construction Co., 50
Industries, 58
Ingram, 18, 19, 163
Inman, 26, 308, 398, 399
Inzer, 246
Ireland, 183
Irwin, 198, 367
Isbell, 20, 191, 211, 286
Ivey, 248, 249, 373
Ivy, 323, 338

Jackson, 36, 50, 175, 237, 248, 253, 296, 298, 299, 380, 415
Jacksons, 178
Jake's Place, 50
James, 24, 73, 110, 111, 178, 261, 304, 349
Jangerson, 377
Jarrett, 186, 294
Jaques, 318
Jeffers, 363
Jeffries, 14, 18, 20, 26, 47, 48, 53, 67, 171, 176, 184, 185, 202, 206, 211, 229, 233, 243, 255, 272, 299, 300, 301, 307, 337, 348, 358, 373, 398
Jemison, 345, 346, 347, 408
Jenkins, 6, 46, 64, 94, 106, 109, 152, 397, 407
Jennings, 95, 185, 186, 193, 368, 393
Jernigan, 174, 185, 424
Jinkins, 83, 97
Jitney Jungle Grocery Co., 16, 51
Joe's Record Bar, 51
Johns, 13, 15, 106, 107, 414, 415
Johnson, 15, 15, 41, 42, 63, 84, 96, 97, 98, 105, 106, 107, 108, 110, 111, 147, 152, 158, 159, 164, 165, 166, 167, 168, 171, 173, 175, 182, 188, 191, 197, 225, 242, 248, 262, 264, 282, 283, 284, 292, 301, 306, 311, 316, 319, 320, 336, 347, 348, 357, 371, 382, 389, 393, 399, 418
Johnston, 191, 194, 280, 340, 341, 375, 379

Joiner, 301, 344
Jones, 5, 15, 16, 18, 22, 25, 26, 38, 39, 41, 42, 47, 50, 53, 54, 57, 71, 72, 73, 83, 94, 98, 104, 105, 106, 107, 108, 109, 115, 116, 148, 156, 159, 160, 161, 164, 166, 170, 172, 173, 175, 178, 179, 180, 181, 184, 187, 189, 190, 191, 193, 194, 219, 227, 229, 231, 232, 234, 238, 245, 256, 257, 260, 261, 267, 270, 273, 283, 288, 290, 299, 300, 301, 302, 303, 304, 305, 306, 313, 315, 322, 323, 327, 330, 331, 338, 339, 354, 361, 363, 368, 369, 371, 376, 380, 381, 388, 389, 390, 391, 396, 409, 410, 411, 412, 421, 422
Jordan, 188, 306, 328, 329, 372, 383
Jordon, 72, 105, 190, 201, 204, 403
Joyce, 235
Julia Shelton Chapter Eastern Star, 186
Julion, 84
Julian, 178, 190

Kaiydee (or Kaidyee), 213, 306, 395
Karrah, 15, 191
Karrh, 58, 108
Karulak, 276
Kasten, 314
Keenum, 155, 156
Keenun, 240
Keith, 210
Keller, 95, 109
Kelley, 84, 98, 120, 155, 190, 191, 223, 230, 248, 306, 307, 349, 357, 386
Kelly, 20, 175, 207, 325
Kemmerer, 196, 197
Kemp, 18, 19, 51, 65, 84, 109, 111, 180, 197, 205, 242, 252, 307, 320
Kemp & Barbour General Mdse., 51
Kennedy, 74
Kennon, 150
Kent, 399, 403, 408
Kenum, 253
Kerr, 109, 235, 307
Ketchell, 299
Key, 72, 107, 108, 109, 145, 176, 307, 308, 353, 373, 374, 378, 416, 418, 419
Kidd, 99, 107, 161, 231, 350
Kilgore, 109, 158, 164, 288, 308, 374

Kilgore & Wheat, 51
Killian, 392
Killingsworth, 51, 85, 94, 107, 175, 176, 184, 191, 281, 288, 323
Killingsworth Gin, 51
Kilpatrick, 251
Kimbrell, 20, 38, 48, 59, 73, 84, 106, 107, 108, 109, 111, 158, 164, 169, 172, 184, 188, 191, 195, 251, 292, 400, 418
Kimborough, 303
Kimbrough, 231
King, 47, 157, 161, 191, 261, 308, 309, 316, 424
Kinney, 161
Kirk, 117, 125, 158, 165, 169, 244, 290, 291, 309, 349, 390
Kirkland, 14, 16, 74, 75, 156, 174, 215, 288, 295, 309, 310, 311, 336, 406, 421
Kirkley, 174, 185, 216, 289, 311, 345, 360
Kirkpatrick, 117, 212, 380
Kirkley, 167
Kirksey, 371
Kirzire, 267, 268
Kitchesn, 109, 159, 162, 164, 165, 166, 172, 229, 382
Kizziah, 96, 159, 167, 168
Kizzire, 84, 95, 96, 99, 159, 165, 191, 232, 267, 269, 271, 278, 286, 311, 386
Knight, 116, 152, 344, 346
Knox, 320
Koon, 120
Koster, 159
Kuton, 419
Kuykendall, 73, 104, 140, 191, 287, 311
Kyle, 262
Kyser, 165, 386, 388
Kyzer, 210

Laboon, 406, 422
Lackey, 192
Ladies Aid Society, 153
La Fayette, 3
La Grone, 107, 108, 109, 110
Laid, 404
Lair, 198, 311
Lambert, 311, 312, 415
Lampkin, 274
Lankford, 180

Land, 408
Landau, 372
Landrum, 259
Lane, 85, 95, 97, 98, 255, 266
Laney, 223
Lang, 359
Langford, 277, 278, 279, 311, 361, 374, 406
Langston, 65, 85, 163, 184, 225, 226, 279, 280, 312
Lankford, 379
Lansdale, 226, 275, 312, 362, 363, 401
Larimore, 319
Larwood, 152
Lassiter, 203, 286
Laster, 404, 405
Latham, 158, 169, 175, 191, 257
Lathan, 419
Latona, 68
Lavender, 152
Lawless, 161
Lawley, 66, 72, 194, 225, 312
Lawrence, 29, 51, 53, 61, 71, 72, 74, 109, 163, 166, 175, 187, 188, 191, 194, 241, 250, 251, 269, 279, 280, 302, 303, 306, 313, 314, 316, 344, 349, 360, 364, 373, 378, 392, 410
Lawrence, J. G. & Sons, 51
Lawrence & Jones Garage, 51
Lawrence Lumber, Co., 61
Lawrence Mill Community, 29
Layton, 314, 421
Leatherwood, 148
Lea, 205
Lebanon Baptist Church, 163
Lebrons, 108
Le Blanc, 26
Ledbetter, 176, 197, 198, 342
Ledsinger, 229
Lee, 108, 149, 176, 314, 319, 392, 394
Legg, 22, 74, 178, 189, 190
Legg Community, 31
Leith, 73, 205, 328, 347
Lellie, 253
Lemond, 191
Lemonds, 180
Lenderman, 18
Leonard, 6, 38, 42
Lester, 219, 278, 291
Lett, 111

Levert, 151, 176
Lewellen, 269
Lewis, 85, 95, 106, 164, 173, 192, 404
Leyden, 221
Liberty Baptist Church, 163
Liberty National Life Insurance Co., 51
Library, 101
Light, 321
Ligon, 302, 398
Lindsey, 5, 18, 19, 20, 38, 62, 66, 69, 70, 98, 155, 156, 188, 189, 195, 200, 207, 208, 228, 231, 244, 245, 246, 263, 264, 266, 272, 273, 275, 300, 309, 314, 315, 334, 337, 348, 350, 371, 375, 387, 399, 400, 415, 422, 423
Lint, 107
Lipscomb, 109
Lions Club, Berry, 189
Lions Club, Fayette, 189
Little Hope Baptist Church, 170
Little, 107, 116, 147, 163, 248, 292, 296, 315, 395
Livingston, 66, 148, 195, 315
Lockart, 163, 164, 165, 167, 169
Loden, 241
Loftis, 39, 51, 52, 67, 185, 191, 199, 217, 263, 340
Loftis Cafe, 52
Loftis Electric Shop, 51
Loftis Sewing Center, 52
Logan, 14, 27, 41, 65, 75, 105, 173, 206, 224, 251, 308, 315, 316, 373, 388
Lokey, 157
Lollar, 45, 48, 108, 109, 110, 120, 122, 167, 184, 192, 193, 224, 225, 303, 308, 316, 334, 383, 384
Lollar Motor Co., 45
Long, 39, 58, 85, 194, 236, 265, 284, 288, 294, 314, 316, 317, 368, 388
Longcrier, 317, 410
Longmire, 172
Looney, 317, 407
Loper, 61
Loper Lumber, Co., 61
Love, 85, 198, 257, 317, 391
Lorey, 32
Lotske, 252
Lott, 206, 235
Lowe, 367, 415
Lowery, 26, 52, 108, 120, 152, 155,

174, 182, 222, 223, 256, 257, 279,
  317, 318, 329, 330, 343, 377, 422
Lowrey, 189, 191
Lowry, 108, 318
Lowrey Trucking Service, 52
Loyd, 176
Lucas, 32, 104, 207, 287, 324, 406
Lucille's Beauty Shop, 52
Lukes, 197
Lumpkin, 401
Lunsford, 189
Luttrell, 246, 318
Lyles, 165
Lynn, 252, 385
Lyon, 271
Lytal, 248

M. & M. Chevrolet Co., 46, 52
Mace, 18, 19, 26, 58
Macedonia Baptist Church, 163
Macedonia Primitive Baptist Church, 170
Machine Post Office, 30
Mack, 236
Madden, 57, 120
Maddox, 52, 53, 97, 191, 193, 208, 215, 262, 280, 302, 305, 326, 327, 330, 386, 388, 392
Maddox Motors, Inc. 52
Maddox Service Station, 52
Madison, 106, 145, 176, 189, 197, 220, 237, 327
Malloy, 41, 74
Malone, 170
Manaxco, 85, 95, 280, 309, 420
Mancill, 343, 344
Mangum, 321
Mann, 174, 175, 410
Manning, 148, 418
Mansfield, 181, 228, 262, 379, 395, 396
Maps, 1, 23, 355
Marchbanks, 73, 74, 280
Maries, 172
Markham, 284, 344
Marle, 121
Marler, 159
Marshall, --
Mars Hill School, 145
Martin, 71, 73, 85, 106, 140, 161, 184, 185, 190, 191, 222, 224, 264, 291, 295, 308, 327, 330, 331, 345, 346, 422

Martindale, 331
Mason, 18, 40, 214, 217, 384, 420, 421
Mat, 75
Mather, 172
Mathes, 200, 201, 230, 231, 267, 328, 329, 347, 378
Mathews, 147, 198, 339
Mathis, 152, 194
Matthews, 60, 65, 180, 194, 232, 244, 280, 281, 315, 322, 323, 326, 328, 329, 330, 342, 351, 369, 380, 392, 393
Matson, 380
Maurin, 308
Maxwell, 183, 194, 304
May, 71, 75, 106, 111, 120, 125, 155, 183, 187, 250, 310, 315, 323, 330, 337, 352, 396, 410, 413
Mayes, 364
Mays, 158, 162, 190
Mayfield, 107, 147, 148, 155, 156, 157, 162, 193, 270, 330, 331, 387, 397
Maze, 171
Mazingo, 311
Mead, 230
Meaders, 85
Meadders, 216, 218, 358
Meadows, 99, 155, 239, 330, 402, 410
Meadow Branch Baptist Church, 164
Medders, 307
Meeks, 70, 72, 293, 294
Mehard, 155
Meharg, 156
Meherg, 66, 268, 359, 381
Meigs, 167
Mell, 12
Mellen, 19
Melton, 85, 98, 117, 155, 156, 157, 159, 161, 162, 215, 331, 387
Melvin, 402
Meroney, 64
Merrell, 207
Merriman, 399
Merritt, 109, 183, 343, 348
Metcalf, 161, 357
Methodists, 150, 176
Michael, 260, 292, 333, 388
Michaux, 334, 337
Micheal, 12, 48, 173
Middleton, 74, 104, 208, 209, 246, 394
Milam, 323, 359

Miles, 19, 22, 70, 73, 86, 95, 98, 118, 181, 193, 196, 207, 208, 209, 217, 229, 234, 243, 257, 258, 259, 262, 322, 331, 332, 333, 335, 337, 364, 397, 421
Milford, 160, 161
Military Springs Post Office, 40
Miller, 40, 94, 106, 107, 109, 110, 181, 190, 215, 352, 397, 401, 411
Milligan, 333, 398
Milliner, 108
Mills, 86, 96, 158, 166, 170, 171, 224, 330
Milner, 73
Milstead, 307, 308
Mil Stewart, 307
Miner, 404
Minter, 256, 257, 333, 334
Miss - Ala Stages Bus Line, 15
Mitchell, 13, 72, 97, 101, 108, 163, 182, 193, 195, 199, 201, 238, 241, 293, 314, 316, 321, 329, 330, 334, 339, 376, 379, 401
Mitchum, 117
Mizell, 189
Mobley, 175, 294, 344
Modern Retreading Co., 52
Moiler, 307
Moncrief, 163
Monique, 423
Monroe, 32, 71, 120, 148, 154, 155, 187, 188, 192, 209, 270
Mont Calm Post Office, 32, 41, 251
Mont Calm School, 145
Montgomery, 86, 97, 157, 265, 268, 269, 334, 338, 343, 350, 419
Moon, 171, 248
Moore, 5, 6, 7, 19, 21, 30, 31, 34, 38, 45, 52, 67, 70, 71, 73, 74, 86, 95, 96, 97, 98, 106, 107, 108, 109, 110, 120, 125, 147, 149, 158, 164, 170, 171, 180, 184, 185, 186, 188, 189, 190, 191, 192, 193, 194, 197, 201, 207, 211, 215, 216, 217, 224, 226, 228, 236, 241, 244, 246, 247, 249, 250, 262, 264, 265, 267, 275, 282, 283, 284, 286, 291, 295, 296, 298, 309, 313, 321, 332, 334, 335, 336, 337, 357, 363, 370, 386, 390, 397, 409, 411, 420, 424
Moore's Flowers, 52
Moorefield, 225
Moorman, 73

Mordecai, 353
Morgan, 100, 110, 119, 161, 184, 185, 191, 207, 258, 264, 334, 337, 401, 419
Morman, 391
Morris, 74, 100, 116, 125, 181, 187, 230, 277, 288, 291, 349, 408
Morrison, 404, 407
Morrow, 71, 72, 74, 97, 156, 230, 231, 233, 244, 309, 360, 372
Morton, 18, 19, 38, 70, 71, 73, 106, 120, 290, 202, 233, 243, 272, 273, 299, 300, 335, 336, 337, 378
Moseley, 185
Mosley, 67, 71, 116, 147, 185, 186, 193, 194, 279, 338, 401, 405
Moss, 65, 125, 202, 261, 262, 316, 338, 367, 369, 394
Moss, McCormick Mining Co., 3, 27
Mothershead, 306
Mothershed, 20, 52, 67, 191, 192, 346
Motte, 273
Mottey, 109
Mouchette, 107
Mountain Home Baptist Church, 164
Mozingo, 86
Mt. Carmel Primitive Baptist Church, 171
Mt. Joy Baptist Church, 164
Mt. Joy Church, 32
Mt. Lebanon Missionary Baptist Church, 164
Mt. Olive Baptist Church, 165, 169
Mt. Olive Church of Christ, 175
Mt. Pisgah Baptist Church, 165
Mt. Pleasant Baptist Church, 165
Mt. Vernon Community, 30
Mt. Vernon Methodist Church, 181
Mt. Vernon School, 147
Mueller, 247
Mullally, 191
Mulligan, 374
Mullins, 275
Murchison, 267
Murphee, 345
Murphy, 176, 186, 260, 274, 346
Murrah, 151
Murray, 6, 7, 161, 179, 291, 292, 322, 323, 338, 345, 370, 386
Murry, 150, 151, 291
Musgrave, 41, 42
Musgrove, 68, 73, 74, 86, 116, 179, 180, 189, 191, 241, 249, 250, 281,

303, 316, 323, 338, 339, 406, 412
Musgroves, 32
Musgrove Chapel Methodist Church, 182
Myers, 52, 191, 308, 396

McAdams, 152, 193, 240
McArthur, 67, 173, 175
McBrayer, 317
McBurney, 65
McCabe, 203
McCain, 107, 109
McCaleb, 28, 42, 46, 48, 52, 68, 71, 87, 107, 108, 116, 118, 121, 140, 145, 173, 174, 175, 176, 193, 223, 229, 247, 248, 272, 288, 299, 315, 318, 319, 330, 337, 343, 377
McCaleb's Mill End Shop, 52
McCalough, 368
McCane, 7, 26
McCartha, 219, 260, 320, 341, 342, 418
McCarthy, 315
McCarty, 227, 313
McCarver, 86, 116, 125, 215, 216, 218
McCauley, 266
McCay, 19
McChesney, 328
McChristian, 294
McClain, 307
McClean, 241
McClellan, 268
McClendon, 54, 188, 226, 227, 238
McCleskey, 174, 185, 288, 320, 321, 322
McClung, 71, 297
McClure, 7, 12, 26, 30, 181, 184, 200, 201, 322, 332, 383
McCluskey, 52, 71, 86, 121, 173, 176, 184, 190, 223, 363, 419
McCluskey Shoe Shop, 52
McCollough, 86, 97
McCollum, 72, 74, 158, 161, 169, 170, 173, 223, 252, 318, 319, 339
McColough, 409
McCombs, 409
McConnell, 67, 68, 69, 70, 71, 72, 74, 75, 118, 165, 179, 180, 190, 191, 192, 194, 224, 228, 242, 262, 285, 303, 304, 315, 322, 323, 326, 329, 330, 338, 339, 368, 369, 370, 371, 390, 391, 398, 404, 412, 419

McConnell Chapel Church, 182
McCool, 20, 50, 58, 97, 121, 148, 162, 170, 171, 172, 187, 191, 194, 226, 242, 248, 275, 278, 279, 301, 312, 323, 324, 325, 362, 378, 401, 405
McCord, 161, 166, 167
McCown, 241
McCoy, 46, 337
McCracken, 15, 34, 52, 106, 108, 109, 110, 111, 189, 411
McCracken Heating & Roofing Co., Inc., 52
McCraw, 150, 152, 194, 311, 325, 397, 423
McCray, 267
McCrea, 267, 354
McCullough, 164
McCully, 325, 360
McCulough, 302
McCutheon, 44, 191, 268
McDaniel, 281
McDonald, 87, 105, 109, 125, 174, 175, 194, 202, 214, 223, 258, 280, 300, 308, 318, 319, 326, 335, 339
McDonaldson, 196, 253, 297
McDougal, 342
McDowell, 18
McEachin, 21
McEachern, 384
McFarland, 87, 275, 276, 314
McGaha, 163, 169, 310, 349
McGahey, 191
McGauhey, 40
McGaw, 222, 326
McGee, 125, 224, 260, 282, 325
McGehee, 392
McGhee, 339
McGill, 255
McGinnis, 156
McGough, 71, 171, 187, 188, 191, 193, 326
McGowan, 171
McGowen, 278
McGraw, 111
McGriff, 276
McGuff, 381
McGuinnes, 98
McGuire, 118, 159, 195, 257, 269, 409
McHam, 229
McJunkin, 258
McKay, 22
McKee, 328, 329
McKell, 356, 357

448

McKinney, 72
McLaughlin, 249
McLaurine, 213, 396
McLean, 205
McLemore, 301, 398
McLeod, 106
McMillian, 237
McNat, 107
McNease, 65, 66, 67, 188, 191
McNease & Robertson Clinic and Hospital, 66
McNees, 107
McNeil, 19, 26, 73, 292
McNeill, 199
McPherson, 331
McReynolds, 216, 326
McRight, 212, 235, 425
McSwain, 320
McWhorter, 43
McWright, 182

Nabors, 109, 247
Nall, 365
Nalls, 30, 273, 274, 339, 340, 379, 394
Napoleon, 337
Nash, 164, 255, 375
Nation, 227
National Farm Loan Assn., 53
Naugher, 18, 20, 21, 125, 323
Nazarene Church of Berry, 182
Neal, 71, 95, 109, 110, 151, 275, 374, 383, 385, 386
Neeley, 236
Neil, 198
Neilson, 367
Nelmus, 98
Nelson, 98, 105. 106, 108, 110, 111, 155, 156, 171, 173, 183, 194, 197, 216, 263, 264, 265, 266, 308, 311, 326, 329, 340, 343, 396, 415, 416
Ne Smith, 73
Neville, 191
New Hope Baptist Church (Fayette Co.) 165
New Hope Baptist Church (Tusca. Co.) 165
New Prospect Primitive Baptist Church, 171
New River Post Office, 42
New River Baptist Association, 153
New River Baptist Church, 165
New River Church of Christ, 175

Newby, 340, 341, 398, 399
Newell, 46, 59, 60, 147, 163, 184, 186, 189, 193, 194, 195, 198, 256, 320, 326, 341, 342, 353
Newman, 13, 20, 61, 87, 148, 181, 185, 186, 193, 194, 195, 207, 214, 215, 226, 270, 286, 315, 329, 342, 404, 421
Newman Lumber Co., 61
Newspapers of Fayette County, 100
Newton, 5, 13, 16, 18, 35, 65, 68, 72, 107, 108, 118, 119, 125, 148, 155, 156, 157, 166, 167, 183, 185, 186, 187, 189, 190, 191, 193, 210, 247, 273, 306, 342, 343, 397, 400, 410, 411
Newton Lumber Co., 61
Newtonville Community, 30, 34
Newtonville Post Office, 42
Newtonville School, 147
Nichols, 20, 53, 54, 56, 70, 71, 72, 155, 156, 157, 158, 164, 166, 167, 168, 173, 174, 175, 176, 191, 194, 217, 224, 236, 264, 266, 271, 281, 301, 313, 327, 343, 344, 356, 359, 381, 392, 393, 419
Nichol's Studio, 53
Nicholas, 6
Niles, 324
Nipper, 404
Nix, 155, 159, 161, 162, 167, 168, 169, 225, 262, 301, 327, 344, 345, 374, 380
Noe, 239
Nolen, 53, 171, 184, 191, 232, 345
Nolan, 195, 326
Noland, 293, 294, 295
Noles, 345, 419, 420
Norman, 98, 245, 384
Norris, 38, 147, 156, 170, 171, 172, 189, 239, 251, 267, 275, 286, 313, 315, 346, 382, 383
North, 385
North Highland Baptist Church, 165
North River Baptist Association, 153
North River Primitive Baptist Church, 171
Northam, 311, 345
Northcut, 390
Northcutt, 87
Norton, 203, 224, 254, 255
Novis, 229
Noyle, 271

Nuckols, 19, 21, 22, 24, 26, 47, 95, 104, 120, 147, 156, 157, 162, 185, 193, 209, 233, 291, 327, 345, 346, 347, 360, 362, 370, 371, 408
Nunn, 106, 145
Nunnally, 271

Oak Grove Methodist Church, 32, 33
Oak Grove Baptist Church, 165
Oak Ridge Baptist Church, 165
Oakes, 280
Oakley, 317
Odear, 260
O'dell, 194
Oden, 108, 152
Odom, 13, 186, 193, 333, 340, 416
Old Boxes Church, 32
Old Hickory School, 148
Oldfield, 290
Oline, 108
Olive, 16, 22, 75, 98, 107, 109, 155, 156, 157, 161, 162, 166, 168, 178, 191, 230, 252, 293, 347, 404
Oliver, 21, 324
Omalley, 376
O'Mary, 280, 326, 351
O'Rear, 373
Ord, 185, 186, 328, 347
Orr, 203
Osborn, 107, 110, 181, 243
Osborne, 180, 371
Oswalt, 20, 53, 72, 117, 148, 184, 189, 191, 194, 195, 206, 218, 233, 238, 251, 252, 278, 281, 331, 347, 348, 382, 388, 412
Oswalt Dry Cleaners, 53
Otts, 39, 171, 286, 287, 335, 343
Owens, 39, 96, 186, 189, 264, 301, 348, 357
Owen, 87, 185, 186, 379, 396
Owing, 98

Pace, 95, 120, 193, 219, 221, 222, 309, 348, 349,
Paden, 245
Padgett, 237
Paffe, 376
Page, 22, 253, 302, 361
Palace Beauty & Gift Shop, 53
Palmer, 98, 155, 156, 169, 182, 349
Palmer's Plumbing & Heating, 53
Pan Am Cafe, 53
Pan Am Service Station, 53

Pane, 87
Panter, 108, 176, 377
Papazan, 87, 278
Pardington, 255
Parham, 401, 402
Parker, 74, 191, 194, 223, 264, 265, 303, 305, 306, 359, 360, 364, 412, 423
Parkham, 241, 331, 402
Parks, 12, 13, 61, 107, 192, 345
Parks Lumber Co., 61
Parmer, 392
Parr, 417
Parram, 401, 402
Parris, 96
Paris, 171
Parrish, 67, 158, 191, 229, 306, 349, 350, 361
Pasteur, 260, 350
Pastuer, 163
Pate, 165, 166, 271, 306, 307, 315, 350
Patrick, 415
Patterson, 15, 20, 53, 60, 71, 73, 87, 94, 117, 123, 139, 140, 148, 156, 157, 158, 159, 160, 162, 163, 166, 168, 183, 184, 186, 187, 191, 193, 194, 198, 218, 225, 251, 252, 265, 287, 311, 334, 335, 336, 341, 350, 351, 352, 353, 358, 365, 366, 392, 418
Patterson Shoe Shop, 53
Patton, 106, 107, 110, 172, 382
Pavlac, 276
Payne, 175, 288, 335, 354
Payton, 281
Pea Ridge Church of Christ, 176
Pearce, 110, 306, 307
Pearson, 226, 261, 374, 390
Peden, 233
Peeples, 271, 335, 353
Pendley, 16, 88, 106, 109, 110, 172, 327
Penn, 317
Pennington, 40, 158, 159, 165, 167, 171, 385
Pepper, 399
Perkins, 73, 87, 152, 181, 188, 220, 222, 279, 294, 296, 325, 423
Perry, 53, 54, 87, 111, 147, 173, 175, 188, 191, 194, 195, 208, 211, 215, 254, 288, 319, 323, 326, 404
Persinger, 179

Peters, 18, 19, 20, 25, 26, 67, 70, 74, 98, 100, 104, 118, 165, 169, 182, 184, 186, 187, 189, 190, 192, 255, 265, 267, 282, 303, 354, 356, 357, 367
Peterson, 106, 107, 147, 148, 193, 253, 273
Pettis, 64, 188, 193
Petty, 281
Peyton, 65, 70, 71, 184
Phagan, 115
Philadelphia Baptist Church, 166
Phillips Drug Co., 233
Phillips, 18, 19, 21, 22, 42, 73, 88, 105, 106, 147, 168, 191, 271, 285, 317, 331, 369
Phipps, 203, 237
Pickel (Pickle), 88, 98, 288
Pierce, 100, 211
Pike, 211
Pilgrim's Rest Baptist Church, 166
Pine Grove, 32
Pinion, 88, 98, 108, 173, 363, 388, 389
Pinkerton, 31, 72, 152, 215, 226, 227
Pinnell, 420
Piper, 58
Pipkin, 152
Pirtie, 187
Pisgah Baptist Church, 166
Pitts, 64, 67, 158, 181, 191, 241, 280, 369, 395, 425,
Pittman, 420
Place, 272
Platt, 407
Pleasant Grove Baptist Church, 166
Pleasants, 294
Pleasant Hill Baptist Church, 166, 182
Pleasant Hill Primitive Baptist Church, 171
Pleasant Ridge Baptist Church, 167
Pless, 109
Plott, 109
Plummer, 255, 401
Plunk, 105
Plyer, 287
Plylar, 174
Plyler, 175, 197, 287, 307, 325, 335, 348, 357
Plyman, 357
Poast, 392
Poe, 30, 46, 47, 48, 54, 66, 72, 88, 94, 108, 109, 110, 152, 155, 156, 159, 161, 162, 172, 189, 191, 194, 195, 213, 218, 219, 278, 310, 335, 348, 351, 352, 357, 358, 412, 414
Poe's Construction Co., 54
Poindexter, 349
Pollard, 20, 184, 233, 291, 326, 358, 382, 420
Polsom, 249, 358
Polous, 257
Ponder, 182
Pool, 271
Poole, 307
Poore, 148
Pope, 48, 193, 287
Poplar Springs Primitive Baptist Church, 171
Popwell, 14
Porter, 69, 94, 158, 179, 187, 191, 194, 207, 213, 244, 263, 286, 356, 358, 359, 378, 379, 409
Portwood, 171
Posey, 174, 175, 337, 357
Posnick, 187
Post, 349
Pounder, 351
Pounds, 174, 175, 422
Powell, 5, 6, 30, 35, 149, 185, 197, 203, 229, 282, 335, 400
Powers, 33
Poynor, 343, 359
Prater, 95, 106, 184, 193, 201, 216, 358, 359
Pratt, 315
Prentice, 65
Presbyterians, 151
Presbyterian Church of Fayette, 182
Preston, 19, 303
Prewitt, 359, 393, 394
Price, 18, 88, 94, 148, 173, 181, 192, 262, 300, 311, 359, 393, 412
Primitive Baptist Church, 170
Prisson, 165
Pritchett, 173, 188, 195, 243
Private Businesses, 43
Progress Club, 192
Prophecy of God Church, 33
Propst, 18, 19, 20, 21, 24, 25, 26, 119, 167, 184, 186, 187, 188, 190, 191, 193, 201, 208, 233, 240, 241, 256, 270, 279, 296, 298, 299, 311, 314, 325, 349, 350, 354, 359, 360, 361, 362, 364, 367, 374, 404

Pruett, 170
Pruitt, 100
Providence Primitive Baptist Church, 171
Pryor, 98, 251, 252, 361, 394, 407
Public School No. - Union Church, 148
Public Services, 63
Puckett, 120, 402
Pugh, 244
Pulliam, 179, 232, 361, 392
Pulpwood, 61
Purcell, --
Putman, 24, 25, 26
Putnam, 54, 58, 192, 193, 271, 311, 325, 346, 360, 362
Pyron, 338

Quality Store, 54
Qualtebaum, 382
Quillin, 408
Quinn, 66

Rabun, 417
Raburn, 172, 396
Radio Station W.W.W.F., 50, 101
Railroad, Georgia Pacific, 17, 18, 37,
Railroad, Mobile & Gulf, 37
Rainey, 109, 162, 164, 166, 167, 169, 288
Rainwater, 105, 199, 215, 216, 217, 289, 331, 345, 351, 362, 405
Raley, 234, 235
Ralls, 181
Rally, 331
Rambsey, 324
Ramsey, 364, 367
Randall, 418
Randolph, 42, 171, 172, 173, 174, 175, 176, 191, 268, 273
Raney, 155, 156, 157, 166
Raper, 184
Rasberry, 226
Raspberry, 225, 286, 369, 382
Rawls, 306
Ray, 18, 73, 88, 95, 98, 99, 106, 108, 109, 110, 197, 246, 265, 285, 293, 306, 312, 324, 325, 362, 404, 405, 422
Rayfield, 263
Raynes, 109
Reaves, 104, 121, 190, 382, 416, 417

Rechtman, 191
Rector, 119, 280
Redden, 40, 184, 191
Reed, 75, 110, 148, 187, 305, 319, 363
Reeks, 290
Reese, 33, 43, 68, 89, 95, 116, 147, 148, 189, 190, 208, 227, 228, 284, 322, 325, 363, 368, 369, 397
Reeves, 62, 89, 94, 105, 155, 156, 158, 160, 161, 162, 165, 167, 169, 284, 313, 349, 368, 390, 391, 408
Reggs, 395
Rehobeth Baptist Church, 167
Reid, 178
Reisweig, 173
Religion, 149
Renfro, 52, 119, 186, 187, 189, 190, 191, 314
Renfroe, 18, 19, 31, 46, 54, 139, 188, 193, 194, 216, 219, 275, 286, 298, 314, 363, 364, 370, 384, 412
Renfroe Construction Co., 54
Representatives from District representing Fayette County, 74
Reynolds, 71, 73, 74, 99, 170, 171, 265, 297, 324, 359, 364, 395
Rhoades, 375
Rhodes, 356
Rice, 163, 168, 180, 215, 227, 230, 232, 246, 250, 252, 260, 262, 275, 285, 287, 292, 350, 351, 352, 353, 358, 364, 365, 366, 410, 414, 416, 421
Rich, 14, 198
Richards, 6, 14, 17, 20, 22, 41, 54, 58, 60, 63, 73, 164, 191, 201, 218, 237, 247, 280, 283, 297, 320, 330, 335, 340, 351, 352, 359, 365, 366, 367, 370, 380, 392, 394, 407, 410, 412, 414, 420, 424
Richards Theatre, 45, 54
Richardson, 40, 89, 96, 97, 108, 223, 236, 255, 261, 354, 356, 360, 367, 422
Richmond & Danville Extension Co., 17, 37
Rickles, 380
Rickman, 215
Riddle, 334
Ridgeway, 316, 368
Riley, 62, 71, 94, 199, 239, 368
Ritch, 290
Rivers, 253

Robbies Children's Wear, 54
Roberson, 232
Roberts, 54, 63, 73, 89, 95, 99, 111, 158, 159, 171, 172, 179, 180, 181, 184, 188, 189, 191, 193, 194, 199, 224, 227, 228, 234, 239, 241, 270, 271, 274, 275, 284, 304, 322, 323, 330, 349, 363, 368, 369, 375, 381, 391, 393, 400, 403, 406, 410, 415,
Roberts Motor Co., 54
Roberts - Nichols Hardware Co., 54
Robertson, 17, 18, 19, 20, 21, 22, 24, 25, 26, 50, 55, 60, 62, 65, 66, 67, 68, 115, 116, 119, 120, 152, 157, 167, 168, 172, 182, 184, 186, 187, 188, 191, 192, 193, 199, 200, 207, 215, 216, 224, 226, 228, 229, 240, 243, 253, 262, 279, 281, 291, 314, 315, 323, 327, 345, 365, 366, 369, 370, 371, 375, 396, 405, 414, 423
Robertson, T. H. & Sons, General Merchandise, 55
Robinson, 89, 96, 109, 158, 166, 181, 207, 250, 372, 402, 406
Robson, 172
Roby, 170
Rockford, 281
Rochelle, 258
Rocky Mount Baptist Church, 160, 167
Rodgers, 207, 271
Rodgerson, 255
Roe, 116
Roebuck, 258, 259
Roeha, 378
Rogers, 120, 161, 167, 178, 216, 235, 236, 375, 376, 421, 423
Romaine, 419
Root, 374, 407
Roper, 109
Rosalind City Community, 31, 32
Rose, 19, 20, 24, 26, 38, 49, 50, 55, 119, 182, 185, 186, 195, 201, 247, 372, 384
Rose Market, 55
Rosemore, 55, 184, 191, 372
Ross, 357
Rother, 205
Roundtree, 242
Rourke, 255
Rowland, 110, 192, 193, 199, 221, 222, 224, 276, 372, 373, 399, 405

Roy, 15, 180
Roycroft, 94, 180, 282, 283
Ruching, 309
Rudicell, 67, 343
Ruffin, 359
Rushing, 159
Russell, 32, 70, 89, 147, 192, 211, 361, 375, 391, 398
Rutland, 67, 188, 189, 373
Rutledge, 107, 108, 171, 307, 308, 340, 373, 374, 377, 382, 418
Ryan, 199

Sadler, 361
Salem Baptist Church, 167
Salem Nazerene Church, 182
Salem Primitive Baptist Church, 171
Salter, 174, 186, 187
Samples, 179
Samuel, 415
Sanders, 13, 20, 26, 38, 43, 45, 47, 55, 97, 119, 171, 181, 184, 186, 187, 188, 190, 194, 207, 223, 242, 273, 296, 302, 325, 359, 362, 364, 374, 383, 401, 410, 411
Sanders, - The Agency, 55
Sanderson, 235, 341, 382
Sands, 13
Sandsprings Baptist Church, 162, 167
Sanford, 19, 22, 74, 96, 109, 118, 120, 125, 174, 191, 194, 205, 266, 269, 278, 367, 370, 374, 375, 419
Sardis Community, 32
Sardis Post Office, 33
Sartain, 382
Sartmeyer, 366
Satterwhite, 307
Saunders, 290
Savage, 64, 74, 89, 96, 188, 190, 228, 230, 252, 375, 376, 377, 387, 388, 392, 412, 423
Savages, 30, 41
Sawyer, 96, 98, 107, 109, 110, 151, 174, 224, 240, 247, 260, 285, 317, 329, 330, 377, 402, 408
Sawyers, 175, 182
Sayers, 213
Sayres, 189
Scharnagle, 306
Scheaffer, 151
Schmidt, 389
Schoolar, 360
Schroeder, 214

Schultz, 152
Scofield, 106
Scoggins, 226, 317
Scott, 43, 105, 163, 181, 187, 188, 218, 274, 282, 378, 380, 390
Scotty's Cafe, 44, 56
Scrivner, 15, 63, 108, 109, 110, 179, 406
Scroggins, 325, 378
Seaborn, 191
Sease, 219
Seay, 14, 15, 74, 178, 179, 207, 327, 366
Secor, 298
Seigler, 371
Selective Service System, 67
Self, 240
Sellman, 90, 156
Sellers, 283
Selman, 155, 157, 167
Senators Representing Fayette County, 73
Senn, 219
Sewing Basket, 56
Sexton, 56, 172, 280, 386, 392
Sexton's Beauty & Barber Shop, 56
Seymore, 160, 162, 164
Seymour, 299
Shackleford, 156, 282, 372, 405
Shady Grove Baptist Church, 168
Shady Grove Nazerine Church, 182
Shafer, 378, 387
Shanks, 151
Shannon, 63, 308
Sharkey, 285
Sharp, 42, 172, 194, 201, 378
Sharpe, 185, 186, 313
Shaw, 255, 378, 417, 419
Sheffield Post Office, 42
Shelton, 19, 21, 22, 46, 58, 95, 118, 186, 195, 208, 223, 225, 228, 264, 265, 270, 286, 298, 299, 359, 360, 361, 378, 379, 418
Shepherd, 14, 15, 16, 26, 42, 56, 90, 95, 105, 106, 107, 109, 110, 111, 168, 173, 179, 185, 186, 189, 191, 192, 193, 206, 209, 229, 231, 270, 271, 276, 282, 339, 357, 379, 380, 394, 422
Shepherd Baptist Church, 168
Shepherd's Style Shop, 56
Sheppard, 225

Sherer, 89, 121, 232, 329, 380, 400
Sherrer, 191
Sherrod, 193, 276, 371
Shiltman, 90
Snip, 71
Shipman, 47, 184
Shipp, 74
Shirey, 391
Shirley, 110, 154, 155, 156, 157, 160, 162, 163, 165, 166, 168, 169, 178, 191, 194, 202, 206, 219, 222, 261, 275, 288, 305, 313, 322, 343, 344, 358, 368, 376, 377, 380, 381, 382, 410, 417
Shook, 107, 152, 187, 191
Shumaker, 324
Shumake, 321
Sibley, 243
Sides, 212, 308, 373, 382, 404, 416, 419
Sieverman, 186
Siloam Baptist Church, 168
Silvertown Baptist Church, 168
Simmons, 166
Simms, 207
Simpson, 74, 105, 106, 108, 109, 110, 116, 145, 181, 182, 247, 261, 292, 361
Sims, 62, 110, 174, 189, 194, 287, 411
Sinclair Refining Co., 56
Sinclair Service Station, 56
Sipsey River Navigation Co., 34
Sipsey Valley Oil & Fertilizer Co., 59
Sipsey Valley Baptist Church, 168
Sisson, 382
Sizemore, 89, 116, 148, 294
Skelton, 42, 110, 163, 164, 165
Skipper, 90, 282, 284
Skinner, 109, 111
Slater, 348
Slaughter, 353, 364, 414
Slosser, 180
Smelser, 175
Smith, 7, 12, 13, 18, 19, 20, 25, 26, 29, 30, 38, 39, 41, 45, 47, 48, 56, 57, 59, 61, 63, 65, 66, 71, 75, 91, 95, 96, 98, 99, 100, 104, 105, 106, 108, 109, 110, 115, 116, 119, 120, 125, 147, 148, 158, 159, 165, 166, 168, 170, 171, 173, 174, 176, 179, 180, 181, 185, 187, 188, 189, 190, 191, 192, 194, 195, 196, 197, 198, 199, 202, 205, 207, 208, 210, 213,

219, 220, 222, 224, 230, 231, 244,
250, 252, 253, 254, 262, 263, 264,
265, 266, 272, 274, 276, 280, 284,
285, 286, 288, 289, 290, 296, 298,
304, 306, 316, 317, 321, 322, 323,
325, 326, 330, 333, 345, 346, 364,
365, 369, 372, 374, 376, 382, 383,
384, 385, 386, 389, 391, 392, 394,
397, 399, 400, 403, 404, 407, 408,
410, 417, 418, 419, 421
Smith, Bruce - Store, 56
Smith Chicken Farm, 56
Smith - Linwood S. General Store, 56,
Smitherman, 203
Smyley, 64
Smyrna Primitive Baptist Church, 172
Snell, 369, 370
Snider, 350
Snoddy, 185, 338
Snodgrass, 296
Snow, 105, 303, 307, 308
Solin, 372
Sorrels, 171
South, 15, 69, 90, 96, 104, 109,
123, 155, 156, 193, 195, 202, 214,
217, 219, 226, 241, 260, 262, 275,
279, 282, 284, 294, 295, 299, 305,
311, 315, 316, 326, 330, 331, 333,
368, 375, 378, 386, 387, 388, 389,
390, 394, 399, 404, 408, 414, 415,
416, 423
Southern Lumber Co., 61
Southern Railway Co., 26, 37
Southern United Life Insurance Co., 57
Southside Baptist Church, 168
Sowell, 73
Spain, 68
Soann, 122, 158, 160, 165, 387, 389
Sparks, 90, 109, 330, 385, 389, 399
Spaulding, 204
Spear, 271
Spearman, 417
Speed, 286
Spence, 65, 158
Spencer, 159, 164, 165, 167, 212, 213
Spiller, 90, 95, 167, 173, 254
Spradley, 271, 389
Sprewell, 171
Spring Hill School, 148

Springer, 191
Sprinkle, 201
Sprinkles, 46
Sprott, 242, 255, 370, 371
Spruill, 99
Squires, 176
Srygley, 174
Stacks, 229, 257, 303, 304, 305, 389
Staggs, 212, 302, 416
Stagg, 382
Sts. James & John Catholic Mission, 172
Stallworth, 26
Stallings, 392
Stamps, 211, 254, 257, 389, 390
Standard Oil Co. Bulk Plant, 57
Standard Furniture Co., 57
Stanley, 14, 90, 97, 116, 147, 156, 193, 201, 241, 246, 284
Stansberry, 175
Starkey, 246, 390
Stars & Bars U. D. C. Chapter, 193
State Farm Insurance Agency, 44
Steele, 314
Steeley, 106
Stephens, 18, 96, 186, 198, 266, 343, 363, 390
Stephenson, 42
Sterling, 419
Sterman, 57, 187, 188, 190, 191
Sterman's Store, 57
Stevenson, 152
Stewart, 6, 26, 27, 31, 32, 91, 98,
108, 110, 111, 116, 123, 148, 155,
156, 159, 161, 162, 173, 175, 183,
186, 188, 192, 193, 213, 217, 223,
224, 253, 254, 259, 274, 292, 294,
370, 371, 374, 383, 384, 390, 391,
403, 416, 417
Stewart Community, 31
Stiff, 108
Stillman, 96, 98, 263, 265, 266, 375, 376, 391, 392, 405
Stinson, 170, 313
Stith, 213
Stobart, 380
Stocks, 91, 271
Stoddard, 75
Stoker, 191, 220, 349, 392
Stokes, 53, 165, 166, 173, 195, 367, 392, 393, 394, 404, 422
Stolley, 255
Stone, 121, 162

Story, 189, 333
Stough, 32, 33, 125, 148, 152, 175, 183, 191, 302, 343, 349, 392, 411
Stough Community, 31, 32, 33
Stovall, 65, 184, 194, 305
Straugher, 207
Strawn, 159, 165
Stribbling, 171
Strickland, 107, 108, 110, 159, 160, 170, 293, 344, 345
Stricklin, 248
Striegel, 290
Stripland, 223
Stripling, 157, 385
Strong, 12, 42, 91, 214, 217, 242, 269, 275, 299, 343, 344, 359, 375, 376, 386, 392, 393, 394, 412, 413, 414
Strother, 191
Stroud, 331
Stubb, 394
Stubblefield, 206
Stubbs, 237
Stucki, 288
Studdard (or Studard), 15, 65, 96, 106, 107, 109, 110, 148, 175, 187, 291
Studdard's Cross Roads, 169
Sudduth, 19, 24, 30, 73, 155, 186, 208, 218, 224, 236, 298, 324, 330, 379, 385, 394
Suggs, 104, 252, 265, 278, 358
Suillen, 348, 349
Suiarian, 357
Sullivan, 41, 42, 265, 315, 325, 379, 385, 395
Summers, 71, 72, 320, 395, 417, 418
Summerall, 250
Summerford, 235
Sumrall, 191, 231
Sutherland, 191
Sutherlin, 206
Sutton, 367
Swan, 213
Swann, 290, 291, 395, 396
Swanson, 200, 303, 396
Sweat, 164
Sweedenburg, 159, 167, 168
Swift, 346
Swinwood, 106, 299
Swindle, 279, 308, 340, 373, 396, 397, 419
Sykes, 26, 264, 266, 348, 390

Sylvan, 198
Taber, 397, 410
Tabernacle Church, 178
Taggart, 107, 422
Tailor, 170
Taliferro, 236
Tallula Post Office, 40
Tanksley, 171
Tanner Brothers Wholesale Produce Co. 57
Tanzy, 218
Tarwater, 5, 6, 18, 95, 148, 187, 190, 193, 194, 229, 243, 332, 343, 372, 373, 397
Tate, 31, 117, 368
Tatum, 167, 323, 324
Taylor, 12, 13, 20, 41, 60, 65, 74, 75, 91, 92, 95, 96, 108, 109, 110, 148, 155, 156, 159, 165, 168, 169, 171, 172, 173, 175, 176, 180, 187, 188, 189, 190, 191, 192, 193, 194, 201, 207, 225, 226, 230, 236, 237, 242, 251, 256, 266, 267, 280, 285, 313, 335, 347, 348, 349, 350, 351, 357, 366, 391, 395, 397, 398, 404, 412, 420, 423, 424
Teal, 253
Tearce, 107
Telford, 328
Temple, 386
Temple Garden Drug Store, 44
Terrell, 397
Terrill, 218
Terry, 43, 62, 95, 105, 108, 119, 156, 161, 168, 183, 192, 311
Terry Drug Store, 57
Thacker, 171, 391
Thaxton, 258
Thomas, 45, 46, 95, 100, 109, 110, 147, 156, 178, 179, 193, 224, 242, 249, 258, 287, 292, 300, 301, 333, 336, 339, 340, 341, 358, 373, 398, 399, 400, 408, 412
Thomason, 47, 63, 376, 386
Thomason, E. E. - Insurance Agency, 47, 57
Thomley, 268, 399
Thompson, 65, 71, 72, 74, 110, 115, 158, 160, 163, 165, 166, 170, 171, 173, 179, 180, 184, 187, 192, 193, 201, 203, 210, 212, 215, 218, 229, 232, 245, 250, 253, 256, 261, 271,

301, 339, 368, 369, 384, 392, 395,
  399, 400, 410, 414
Thomson, 57, 184, 189, 232, 400
Thomson Implement Co., Inc., 57
Thornburgh, 257
Thorne, 120
Thornton, 5, 16, 20, 25, 26, 71, 72,
  100, 108, 109, 110, 111, 173, 181,
  189, 191, 245, 292, 391, 400, 404
Thrasher, 419
Threat, 98
Threet, 263
Tibbs, 393
Tidwell, 92, 109, 110, 171, 240,
  281, 312, 401
Tierce, 179, 181, 219, 412
Tigett, 159, 187, 229
Tilghman, 401, 402
Tiller, 109
Tilley, 164, 165
Tillman, 254, 255, 401, 402
Timbs, 315
Timmons, 119, 181
Tims, 324
Tim's Modern Cleaners, 57
Tipper, 281
Tipton, 26, 174, 176
Tirey, 110
Tittle, 110
Tobin, 303
Todd, 191
Tolbert, 192
Tolle, 175
Tollie, 378
Tomlin, 105, 116
Torbert, 277
Townes, 277
Townley, 419
Towns, 370
Townsend, 12, 92, 98, 155, 156, 157,
  158, 162, 163, 164, 166, 167, 168,
  169, 281, 306
Townson, 166
Trabue, 306
Trammell, 107, 193
Trantham, 331, 402, 409, 410, 415
Trapp, 240
Trappe, 213
Travis, 314
Traweek, 13, 106, 107, 108, 109,
  110, 111, 159, 186, 268, 386, 393,
  402, 410, 412, 423
Trawick, 246

Treadaway, 72, 104, 106, 326
Treadway, 38, 186, 210
Trim, 162, 166, 167, 168, 169
Trimm, 286, 287, 368
Tripp, 254
Tubbs, 236, 347
Trull, 310, 311
Truman, 304
Tucker, 57, 92, 107, 108, 125, 163,
  169, 174, 175, 176, 184, 192, 194,
  240, 262, 281, 284, 363, 377, 402,
  403
Tucker Hardware Co., 57
Tunnell, 197
Turnbow, 159
Turner, 26, 106, 107, 110, 116, 120,
  125, 186, 191, 206, 261, 282, 403,
  422
Tutwiler, 324, 325
Tyner, 92, 95, 98, 108

U. D. C. Chapter No. 1672 - 192
Underwood, 105
Unger, 163, 189, 383, 403, 410
Union Baptist Church, (Fayette Co.,)
  169
Union Baptist Church, (Marion Co.)
  169
Union Grove Baptist Church, 169
Union Primitive Baptist Church, 172
Union Underwear Co., 59
Unity Baptist Church, 169
Usury, 120
Utley, 390, 403

V. F. W. Post 5406 - 194
V.F.W. Ladies Auxilliary, 195
Vail, 39, 171
Valco, 381
Vance, 303, 305
Vanderbilt, 175
Van Diver, 18, 20, 97, 98, 104, 120,
  139, 187, 192, 231, 282, 365
Vandiver, 39, 171, 189
Van Hoose, 37, 38, 70, 71, 73, 384,
  391, 421
Vann, 418
Vansant, 98
Vanshan, 172
Van Zant, 404
Varner, 407
Varnon, 99, 224
Vardaman, 253

Vasser, 273
Vaudeville Theatre, 58
Vaughn, 63, 158, 160, 166, 320
Vaught, 211
Veazey, 67, 184, 188, 192, 403, 408
Veazey's Mortuary, 67
Venable, 349
Vernon, 39, 40
Veterans of Foreign Wars, 184
Vice, 189
Vick, 58, 97, 98, 104, 106, 107, 108, 111, 148, 184, 192, 268, 269
Vickery, 216, 284
Vick Brothers Store, 58
Vick Implement Co., 58
Vick Oil Company, 58
Vincent, 349
Vines, 418
Vogue Beauty Shop, 58
Voyles, 308

Wade, 173, 175, 176, 215, 316, 337, 374
Waid, 181
Waite, 419
Wages, 43, 158, 202, 403, 404
Wagner, 173, 341
Waggoner, 173
Wakefield, 97, 205, 206, 360, 404
Walborn, 110
Walch, --
Walden, 72, 279, 348, 404, 422
Waldon, 12, 263, 286
Waldrop, 95, 121, 145, 148, 156, 164, 165, 167, 168, 193, 194, 214, 221, 238, 265, 266, 272, 276, 286, 288, 323, 338, 345, 362, 372, 373, 392, 399, 402, 404, 405, 412, 421
Walker, 13, 15, 20, 26, 65, 109, 120, 152, 158, 159, 161, 162, 164, 165, 166, 167, 168, 169, 189, 193, 205, 206, 209, 213, 218, 220, 221, 222, 256, 258, 261, 273, 279, 280, 302, 323, 325, 331, 368, 371, 405, 406, 410, 422
Wallace, 26, 56, 148, 152, 174, 208, 302, 306, 325, 420, 424
Walls, 239, 240, 256, 406
Wally, 206
Walters, 6, 75, 99, 159, 162, 165, 188, 189, 193, 218, 263, 265, 292, 344, 352, 353
Walton, 38, 45, 64, 109, 110, 174, 184, 194, 314, 379
Ward, 42, 75, 92, 99, 110, 115, 152, 188, 215, 216, 231, 240, 243, 258, 263, 295, 310, 323, 324, 331, 364, 374, 406, 422
Ware, 220, 222
Warmack, 188
Warmuskerkin, 367
Warn, 369
Warne, 367
Warner, 285
Warren, 97, 152, 212, 280, 292
Washam, 242
Washburn, 238, 239
Waters, 230, 257, 259, 260, 395, 406
Watkins, 65, 67, 71, 92, 110, 111, 125, 147, 184, 192, 200, 220, 229, 252, 284, 294, 296, 339, 381, 406, 407
Watley, 236
Watson, 94, 108, 165, 167, 171, 227, 229, 238, 286, 287, 361, 374, 412, 423
Watts, 139, 159, 161, 167, 256
Wayside Community, 33
Wayside Methodist Church, 33
Wayside Post Office, 43
Wayside School, 33
Weatherly, 13
Weathers, 12, 13, 94, 160, 163, 164, 165, 166, 168, 173, 409
Weaver, 152, 248, 249, 278, 391
Webb, 280, 301
Webster (or Websters), 32, 122, 125, 183, 184, 192, 257, 368
Weeks, 97, 213, 332
Weems, 58, 188, 384, 407
Weems, Fruniture Co., 58
Wehner, 398
Weir, 151
Welborn, 192, 244
Welburn, 30, 182, 284, 317, 407
Welch, 98, 116, 120, 204, 215, 322, 323, 365, 366, 407, 412
Weldon, 106, 207
Wellburn, 110
Wells, 193, 243, 331, 391, 395
Welsh, 365
Wesley Chapel Methodist Church, 182
West, 16, 107, 171, 178, 251, 252, 254, 259, 260, 293, 388, 403, 407, 408, 423
Westbrook, 108, 343, 344
Western Auto Associate Store, 58

Western Newspaper Union, 25
Westmoreland, 176
Wharton, 274
Whatley, 382
Wheat, 192
Wheeler, 32, 98, 173, 174, 175, 176, 238, 239, 245, 277, 334, 408
Whetstone, 347
Whisenant, 92
Whiserhunt, 292
White, 13, 41, 45, 92, 93, 95, 96, 99, 106, 109, 110, 116, 125, 145, 147, 155, 156, 157, 159, 161, 163, 164, 165, 166, 168, 176, 179, 187, 189, 193, 203, 204, 205, 212, 216, 223, 226, 233, 241, 248, 249, 251, 257, 265, 271, 273, 277, 288, 302, 303, 304, 313, 317, 324, 333, 338, 343, 346, 361 365, 366, 368, 376, 380, 383, 396, 397, 400, 402, 403, 405, 406, 407, 408, 409, 410, 411, 412, 414, 418, 422
Whitehead, 183, 194, 280
White's Chapel Church of Christ, 176
Whitley, 96, 110, 187, 190, 191, 192, 244, 246, 248, 249, 281, 305, 336, 343, 357, 377, 397, 406, 411
Whitney, 24, 193, 302, 306, 363, 412
Whitson, 108, 109, 111, 168, 174, 177, 182, 411, 412
Whittimore Brothers Corp., 61
Whorton, 205, 206
Wiers, 384, 385
Wiggins, 51, 184, 194, 217, 227, 292, 315, 347, 395, 404, 412, 424
Wilbanks, 380
Wiley, 67, 99, 253
Wilkerson, 168, 184, 220, 222, 238
Wilkes, 93, 118, 152, 161, 338, 339, 376, 410, 412
Wilkins, 203, 412
Willard, 397
Willcutt, 93, 174, 175, 176
Williams, 13, 18, 19, 38, 62, 70, 71, 74, 96, 107, 109, 125, 152, 171, 176, 181, 192, 195, 198, 204, 205, 206, 207, 218, 228, 235, 262, 302, 335, 339, 347, 349, 352, 364, 366, 375, 383, 391, 404, 412, 419
Williams Motor Co., 58
Williamson, 13, 50, 58, 108, 109, 110, 111, 163, 187, 193, 194, 198, 205, 219, 227, 230, 243, 250, 263, 266, 314, 350, 351, 352, 376, 382, 386, 404, 410, 412, 421
Williamson Jewelry Co., 58
Willingham, 12, 13, 15, 41, 42, 61, 75, 93, 108, 109, 110, 155, 156, 157, 193, 200, 237, 246, 254, 260, 262, 276, 284, 297, 298, 299, 311, 312, 360, 365, 368, 383, 388, 394, 403, 413, 414, 415
Willis, 116, 154, 155, 157, 159, 164, 165, 167, 203, 204, 227, 257, 332, 399, 400
Wilson, 13, 20, 22, 71, 73, 74, 93, 97, 100, 152, 154, 156, 157, 160, 164, 166, 167, 168, 179, 180, 181, 192, 193, 198, 218, 223, 226, 230, 266, 290, 291, 293, 295, 301, 307, 318, 340, 369, 370, 378, 383, 384, 402, 415, 416, 422, 423
Wimberley, 93, 99, 139, 170, 171, 172, 196, 244, 245, 302 (or Winberly)
Windham, 14, 22, 32, 106
Windle, 158
Winfield, Baptist Church, 169
Wingo, 261, 367
Winn, 271, 282, 324, 387, 416
Winnette, 349
Winter, 159
Winters, 252, 307
Wise, 214, 219, 416
Witherspoon, 267
Wofford, 245, 314
Wolcotts, 375
Wolf, 75
Wolfe, 167, 284
Womack, 334, 365
Wommack, 208, 206, 331, 390, 416
Wood, 42, 74, 161, 307, 308, 323, 338, 416
Woodard, 20, 47, 58, 184, 192, 365
Woodard, - Gus Grocery Store, 58
Woodmen of The World, 195
Woods, 12, 13, 15, 93, 108, 173, 174, 175, 194, 203, 215, 217, 223, 228, 245, 272, 275, 280, 281, 289, 292, 307, 308, 327, 340, 363, 369, 378, 381, 406, 416, 417
Woodson, 256, 341, 386
Woodward, 93
Wool Factory, 62
Woolbright, 212
Wooten, 197, 198, 199

Wootten, 417
Word, 337
Worford, 72, 395
Worthington, 320, 417, 418
Wright, 41, 58, 63, 74, 98, 108,
    110, 121, 148, 168, 179, 187, 188,
    191, 193, 194, 195, 197, 212, 273,
    274, 292, 293, 300, 301, 308, 322,
    345, 349, 353, 374, 378, 379, 397,
    409, 410, 417, 418, 419, 420
Wright's T. V. Shop, 58
W. W. W. F. Radio Station, 101
Wycoff, 335, 420
Wyers, (Or Wayers) 92, 96, 175, 176
Wynn, 293, 295

Yamm, 400
Yancy, 331, 333
Yarbrough, 106, 107, 108, 214, 215,
    217, 314, 342, 345, 363, 366, 385,
    404, 420, 421, 424
Yeager, 186
Yellow Creek Baptist Association,
    153
Yellow Front Store, 16, 24, 58
Yerby, 19, 22, 30, 39, 42, 93, 94,
    95, 97, 99, 106, 108, 109, 110,
    116, 152, 161, 162, 183, 184, 194,
    208, 249, 253, 254, 279, 283, 286,
    303, 309, 325, 357, 370, 375, 376,
    379, 388, 402, 406, 421, 422, 423,
    424, 425
Yielding, 301
York, 42, 246, 301, 413, 415, 424
Young, 25, 26, 39, 47, 51, 56, 58,
    66, 94, 187, 190, 192, 201, 218,
    226, 229, 231, 235, 238, 261, 291,
    297, 308, 349, 362, 366, 370, 383,
    398, 421, 424, 425
Young's Drug Sundries, 58
Younghance, 229, 421, 425
Yuckley, 20, 192, 359

Zeanah, 110, 179
Ziegler, 119, 120
Zinniż, 38
Zion, 177
Zion Methodist Church, 182
Zitmore, 372

www.ingramcontent.com/pod-product-compliance
Lightning Source LLC
Chambersburg PA
CBHW030424020526
44112CB00044B/108